RODALE'S
ULTIMATE ENCYCLOPEDIA of
ORGANIC GARDENING

The Indispensable Green Resource *for* Every Gardener

NEWLY REVISED AND UPDATED

EDITED BY **FERN MARSHALL BRADLEY,**
BARBARA W. ELLIS, AND **ELLEN PHILLIPS**

WITH DEBORAH L. MARTIN

RODALE.

RODALE *wellness*

Live happy. Be healthy. Get inspired.

Sign up today to get exclusive access to our authors, exclusive bonuses,
and the most authoritative, useful, and cutting-edge information on health,
wellness, fitness, and living your life to the fullest.

Visit us online at RodaleWellness.com
Join us at RodaleWellness.com/Join

First published in hardcover by Rodale Inc. in 1959.

First published in paperback by Rodale Inc. in 2009.

Printed in the United States of America

Rodale Inc. makes every effort to use acid-free ♾, recycled paper ♻.

Illustrations by Michael Gellatly

Photographs pages 1, 41, 182, 325, 333, 363, 390, 500, 611, 632 istockphoto; 206, 234, 315, 405, 520, 577 Rodale Images;
101, 174, 380 Robert Cardillo; 280 Mitch Mandel/Rodale Images

Book design by Christina Gaugler

Library of Congress Cataloging-in-Publication Data is on file with the publisher.

ISBN 978-1-63565-098-3 paperback

Distributed to the trade by Macmillan

3rd Printing   paperback

Follow us @RodaleBooks on 🐦 📘 📌 📷

We inspire health, healing, happiness, and love in the world.
Starting with you.

To Robert Rodale, whose ideas and spirit live on in all of our gardens, and to the organic gardeners and farmers who share his vision and continue his work.

Contents

G

H

I

J–K

L

M

Introduction

Well-worn copies of *The Encyclopedia of Organic Gardening*, edited by J. I. Rodale, are part of gardening book collections in libraries, homes, and garden sheds across North America. In the decades since this remarkable book was published in 1959, organic gardening has changed from a fringe movement to mainstream. True to the vision of J. I. and Robert Rodale, organic gardening is now widely recognized as the safest, most economical, and most practical method for home gardeners.

In 1989, Rodale's garden book editors launched a project to rejuvenate the encyclopedia, with the goal of creating a resource that would reflect gardeners' wishes to use organic methods and to learn about breakthroughs in organic pest control. This new encyclopedia would include not only raising food crops but also maintaining perennials, annuals, trees, shrubs, and lawns without chemicals.

To achieve that vision, ideas and input were sought from many gardeners, writers, and editors. Robert Rodale also lent his unique insights, one of his last contributions to a Rodale gardening book before his death. Then a broad range of garden experts and writers was enlisted to draft entries in their areas of interest. A team of editors carefully blended and refined their work to create *Rodale's All-New Encyclopedia of Organic Gardening*.

In 2007, Rodale realized that it was time to update this vital reference book yet again, and engaged three members of the 1992 edition's editorial team—Barbara W. Ellis, Ellen Phillips, and Fern Marshall Bradley. These editors (dedicated organic gardeners all) reread and discussed the entire book, painstakingly choosing outdated entries to remove, adding new entries, and updating plant and organic pest control information throughout. And in light of the vital issues faced by gardeners in an era of climate change and declining natural resources, they added an all-new section on gardening sustainably.

Now a decade later, this essential gardening guide has been updated once more. Information included in the previous edition's "green gardening" section is now expanded into new entries on topics such as Green Roofs, Invasive Plants, Pollinators, Rain Barrels, and Water Conservation, reflecting issues and interests that have become mainstream, along with organic practices and growing concern for the environment. Plant names have been updated to include the most current determinations made by botanists while also retaining the names most widely used by growers and retail nurseries. Since the previous editions, some popular landscape plants have fallen out of favor as their aggressive habits or other undesirable features have come to light. Many of these remain in this encyclopedia, because they continue to be widely available, but with caveats about their use and suggestions for less troublesome alternatives.

Trends in garden design change as prevailing tastes shift from naturalistic to formal or from modern to traditional. Plants go in and out of fashion, as well. New cultivars are introduced and—if they are good—become widely grown. Historians and fans of beloved heirlooms continue to perpetuate and preserve the plants grown decades, or even centuries, ago. New products for controlling pests or extending the season or cultivating the soil become available. Yet much of the fundamental practice of gardening remains as it was in 1959 when J. I. Rodale published the first edition of this encyclopedia. Plants still need light and water and nutrients. Gardeners still place seeds into the soil and anticipate the moment when those seeds will reward their efforts with beautiful flowers, luscious fruits, crisp vegetables, or welcoming shade. From compost-making to watering, the basics of organic gardening are evergreen and worth incorporating in your own garden practices. The goal with this revised edition, as for all previous editions, was a comprehensive, easy-to-use book that provides practical information on the entire realm of organic gardening.

How to Use This Book

This book is organized to reflect the way you garden. We've grouped information into useful, complete entries that will provide all you need to know about a particular topic, rather than spreading out facts in thousands of short entries. For example, the instructions you need to plan, plant, and care for a vegetable garden are in one entry: Vegetable Gardening. The Compost entry tells you everything you need to know to make and use compost (and compost tea). Entries on Annuals, Perennials, and Trees describe how to get started, how to use these plants in your landscape, and how to keep them flourishing. Each of these entries includes lists of specific plants for particular environmental conditions and uses.

Individual food crops and ornamentals entries provide additional specialized information. For example, the Tomato entry offers lots of tips for growing the biggest, best, earliest tomatoes. Dozens of special entries—including Cut Flower Gardening, Edible Landscaping, Habitat Gardening, Rock Gardens, Weather and Weather Lore, and Wildlife Gardening—will stimulate your gardening imagination and curiosity.

How to Find It

Scan the table of contents to get a general picture of the encyclopedia's range and focus. Under each letter is a list of the entries that begin with that letter. It's fun and informative to flip to interesting entries that catch your eye. We've included illustrations as well as lots of tips and unusual topics that we hope will liven up your browsing sessions.

If you want information on a particular subject, such as how to control Japanese beetles, turn to the back pages to a vital, if often unappreciated part of a book: the index. Flip to the Japanese beetle listing in the index, find the subentry for "control of," and you'll be referred directly to page 455, where you'll find a description of the beetles and the damage they cause and a list of the best organic control methods. You'll find the index is an important tool in getting the most from your encyclopedia.

There are other special features to help you find the information you need. Throughout the book, you'll see cross-references to other entries that contain information related to the subject you're reading about. You can also flip to the Quick Reference Guide on page 678 for a mini-index of major gardening topics, such as Landscaping or Perennials. For each topic, you'll find a list of all entries in the book that include information on that topic.

The "Key Words" heading in entries is your cue to look for essential gardening terms that will aid in your understanding. More terms are included in the book's glossary, which begins on page 669.

Plant Names

All plants have a botanical name and a common name. Scientists create botanical names, usually derived from Latin words, to help categorize plants. Common names are the ones we use in casual speech or writing about plants.

This book lists food plants—fruits, herbs, nuts, and vegetables—by common name, so you can look up the Apple, Peach, Pepper, or Tomato entries and find just what you're looking for. However, ornamental plant entries are organized by botanical names. This eliminates possible confusion when plants have multiple common names. For example, if you turn to the Heuchera entry, you'll learn that these beautiful spring- and summer-blooming perennials have several common names, including heuchera, coralbells, and alumroot. For more information on how plants are named, see the Botanical Nomenclature entry.

If you're not familiar with the botanical names of ornamentals, look in the index for the common name of the plant that interests you. The index listing will refer you to the correct botanical name. We've also included cross-reference entries with common names of highly popular ornamentals, such as maples and marigolds, right in the body of the encyclopedia. For example, if you turn to "Maple" on page 366, you'll find the instructions to "see *Acer*"; *Acer* is the botanical name for maples.

The Heart of the Matter

Of the 314 entries in this book, 28 form the core of the encyclopedia. Together, they are a handbook of organic gardening basics. When you read an entry about a specific plant, you may need to refer to core entries, where we've compiled lots of basic information that applies to specific plants. Core entries fall into four categories:

Gardening techniques: Garden Design, Landscaping, Planting, Propagation, Pruning and Training, Seed Starting and Seed Saving

Organic garden management: Animal Pests, Beneficial Insects, Compost, Cover Crops, Fertilizers, Mulch, Pests, Plant Diseases and Disorders, Pollinators, Soil, Water Conservation, Watering, Weeds

Food crops: Brambles, Edible Landscaping, Fruit Trees, Herbs, Nut Trees, Vegetable Gardening

Ornamental plants: Annuals, Biennials, Bulbs, Groundcovers, Perennials, Shrubs, Trees

You may find it valuable to read most of these entries soon after getting this book. If you're an experienced gardener, it will be an interesting refresher course. If you're a beginner, the core entries are a great first step to a lifelong enjoyment of your organic garden.

—*The Editors of Rodale Garden Books*

A

ACER

Maple. Deciduous trees with single or multiple trunks.

Description: *Acer floridanum*, Florida maple, southern sugar maple, is a small (to 25 feet in the landscape) tree with a single-trunked, rounded habit. This native of the southeastern United States deserves to be used more widely there for its reliable fall color and heat tolerance. Zones 7–9.

A. buergerianum, trident maple, can have single or multiple trunks supporting an oval or rounded crown. It normally attains a height of 20 to 25 feet in the landscape but can grow twice as tall. Like many maples, it has three-lobed leaves borne in pairs; the lobes all point in the same direction, away from the base of the leaf. Red or orange fall color may develop in some years. The bark of trident maple is gray and brown, sometimes with orange tones, becoming scaly with age. Zones 6–7.

A. ginnala, Amur maple, grows 15 to 20 feet tall in the landscape. While most maples' flowers are neither fragrant nor showy, Amur maple bears highly fragrant blooms in early spring. The three-lobed leaves have an extended center lobe and may turn scarlet in fall. An introduction from Asia, Amur maple is listed as weedy or invasive in some states but its use is not restricted. Zones 3–7.

A. japonicum, full-moon maple, is another small (20 to 30 feet) Asian maple with considerable landscape value. Full-moon maple's leaves are palmately compound and nearly circular in outline. Flowers are purplish or red. Fall color is crimson and/or yellow in most years and appears more reliably in northern areas. Zones 5–8.

A. negundo, box elder, is a northern American native often disdained for its weediness and soft wood, yet it grows in poor soil and difficult sites where many other trees can't. It has multiple stems, a rounded crown, and a mature height of 50 to 70 feet. Yellow-green flowers appear in early spring before its compound leaves unfold; fall color is a soft yellow. Abundant winged fruits can be messy and lead to numerous seedlings. Zones 2–9.

A. palmatum, Japanese maple, normally grows

15 to 20 feet tall; its branches may spread as wide as the tree is tall, creating a layered appearance unlike the more upright form of other maples. The many cultivars offer countless options of twig and leaf color, gnarled or mounded habits, plus lacy threadleaf forms. Protect from direct wind in the North and direct sun in the South. Zones 5–8.

A. pensylvanicum is known as moosewood or striped maple. The green chalk-striped bark of this 15- to 20-foot northeastern woodland native has considerable landscape interest. Look for yellow fall color. Striped maple performs best in cool climates under partial shade. Zones 3–6.

A. platanoides, Norway maple, is a widely planted street tree with a round, dense crown and tolerance for difficult urban conditions, such as air pollution and poor soil. It grows 40 to 50 feet tall and holds its broadly palmate leaves late into fall. Norway maples cast deep shade, making it difficult to grow turfgrass beneath them. This maple's abundant, shade-tolerant seedlings allow it to colonize native woodlands, earning it classification as invasive in parts of the Northeast and central United States. Zones 4–6.

A. rubrum, red or swamp maple, is a North American native that reaches heights of 40 to 60 feet. Pyramidal in youth, red maple sprawls and arches with age. The smooth gray trunk and branches are distinctive, particularly when trees are grouped. Red flowers open before the leaves and are a softly colorful sign of spring. Fall color is bright red and/or orange. Hardiness and heat tolerance vary within the species; choose a cultivar suited to your location. Zones 3–8.

A. saccharinum, silver maple, is touted for its fast growth, but it's also weedy and weak wooded and may be prone to breakage. Growing 50 to 70 feet high, silver maple is upright, with spreading branches and a rounded crown; its leaves are deeply lobed and silvery beneath. The pale pink flowers appear before the leaves in spring. Look for yellows or reds in fall foliage and a gray, furrowed trunk. Zones 3–8.

A. saccharum, sugar, rock, or hard maple, gets its names from the maple sugar derived from its rising spring sap and from the durability of its wood. It has a single trunk and a rounded crown, gray-black furrowed bark, and a mature height of 50 to 70 feet. Sugar maple's fall color is legendary; in good years the leaves turn gold, orange, and scarlet. Zones 3–7.

How to grow: With the exception of large maples, like red, sugar, silver, and Norway, used as shade trees, most maples benefit from light shade. Generous mulch and a shaded root zone are also advantages. Most maples require acid soils that are evenly moist but well drained, although red maple and box elder occur naturally on swampy sites. Grown in their preferred conditions, maples are relatively problem-free trees. Scorched leaf margins may occur on trees suffering from drought or reflected heat from pavement or cars. Red and silver maples growing in high-pH soil may develop yellowed foliage caused by manganese deficiency. Box elders attract box elder bugs, which like to overwinter indoors. In fall, groups of these black-and-orange insects move into buildings and become household pests.

Landscape uses: Japanese, full-moon, and Amur maples make fine focal points in small-scale settings; larger areas might call for trident maple or sugar maple. Red, striped, and sugar maples are good choices for naturalizing; Norway maple, although tough, is overplanted. Use box elders to supply shade on difficult sites.

ACHILLEA

Yarrow. Summer- and sometimes fall-blooming perennials; herbs; dried flowers.

Description: Yarrow bears profuse 2- to 6-inch flattopped heads of tiny flowers in shades of white, yellow, gold, pink, salmon, rust-orange, purple, and red on 2- to 5-foot stems. Soft, finely cut, aromatic foliage is green or gray.

Achillea 'Moonshine' bears 3-inch soft yellow clusters on 1- to 2-foot stems atop striking, gray-green, dense leaves. Zones 3–8.

A. 'Coronation Gold' holds its stately 3- to 4-inch golden blooms on stems 3 feet or taller over silvery green, loosely ferny foliage. Zones 3–8.

A. millefolium, common yarrow, produces small white flower clusters rising 1 to 2 feet above mats of ferny green leaves and is the parent of many colorful cultivars and hybrids. Zones 3–8.

How to grow: Plant or divide yarrows in spring or fall. Divide every 2 to 3 years to keep plants vigorous and less likely to lean over when in bloom. Plant in full sun in average, well-drained soil. Generally tough and adaptable, yarrows tolerate poor soil and drought well. In very humid regions, yarrows with gray or silvery leaves may succumb to leaf diseases within a year or two, so grow green-leaved yarrows in those areas. You may want to stake the taller cultivars, especially if you grow them in fertile garden soil.

Landscape uses: The flat flower heads of yarrows provide a pleasing contrast to mounded or upright, spiky plants in a border. Try them alone in a hot, dry area. Fresh or dried, yarrows are wonderful as cut flowers. For long-lasting dried flowers, cut the heads before they shed pollen and hang them upside down in a warm, well-ventilated, sunless room to dry.

AGERATUM

Ageratum, flossflower. All-season annuals.

Description: Ageratums bear clouds of small, fuzzy, blue, pink, or white flowers on 1-foot mounds of rather large, rough, dark green leaves. Dwarf varieties grow to only 6 inches.

How to grow: Start from seed 8 weeks before the last spring frost or buy transplants. After all danger of frost is past, set out transplants in full sun or partial shade and average soil. Space dwarf cultivars about 6 inches apart; taller ones need 10 inches.

Landscape uses: Ageratums look best massed in beds and borders or as an edging for taller plants. The blue cultivars combine beautifully with yellow marigolds.

AJUGA

Ajuga, bugleweed. Perennial groundcovers.

Description: *Ajuga reptans*, ajuga or common bugleweed, forms attractive dark green rosettes 2 to 3 inches wide and spreads by runners 3 to 10 inches long. Cultivars may have bronze, purple, or variegated foliage. Sturdy blue, white, or pink flower spikes bloom in May and June, reaching 4 to 6 inches tall. Zones 4–8.

How to grow: In spring, set young plants 6 to 12 inches apart in moist, well-drained soil in full sun or partial shade. Ajugas will tolerate heavy shade but not heat or drought. Fertilize lightly—overfeeding encourages diseases.

Landscape uses: Use this groundcover to provide carpets of spring color. It is attractive planted under trees or along borders. Don't plant ajuga next to your lawn unless you use a sturdy edging; ajuga readily spreads into and overtakes turfgrass.

ALCEA

Hollyhock. Summer-blooming biennials.

Description: *Alcea rosea*, hollyhock, is an old-fashioned favorite that bears its 3- to 5-inch rounded blooms in two forms: saucerlike singles with a central, knobby yellow column, or double puffs strongly reminiscent of tissue-paper flowers. Colors include shades of white, pink, red (sometimes so dark it appears almost black), and yellow. The blooms decorate much of the 2- to 9-foot, upright, leafy stems that rise above large masses of rounded or scalloped, rough leaves. Zones 3–8.

How to grow: Set out larger, nursery-grown plants in spring for summer bloom or smaller ones in fall for bloom next year. You can also start them from seed. Sow in midwinter for possible bloom the same year, or start them after the hottest part of summer for planting out in fall. Most hollyhocks self-sow readily if you let a few flowers mature and produce seeds. They prefer full sun to light shade in average to rich, well-drained, moist soil. Water during dry spells, and stake the taller cultivars.

Hose off spider mites and handpick Japanese beetles, which eat both flowers and leaves. Aptly named rust disease shows up as reddish spots on the leaves and stems and can quickly disfigure or destroy a planting. Removing infected leaves and all dead leaves may help, or grow plants in out-of-the-way spots where the damage is less noticeable.

Landscape uses: Hollyhocks look their best in informal areas such as cottage gardens, along fences and foundations of farm buildings, and on the edges of fields. Try a small group at the rear of a border.

ALL-AMERICA SELECTIONS

Since 1932, the nonprofit organization All-America Selections (AAS) has tested and evaluated vegetables and flowers to select superior cultivars that will perform well in home gardens. AAS tests new cultivars each year at more than 30 flower and 20 vegetable test gardens at universities, botanical gardens, and other horticultural facilities throughout the United States and Canada.

Each year's new entries are grown next to past winners and standard cultivars. Those that earn the judges' approval display the All-America Selections Winner symbol on seed packets, plant labels, and in garden catalogs, alerting home gardeners to plants that are practically guaranteed to perform well in their gardens.

The AAS judges look for flowers with attractive, long-lasting blossoms. They also consider uniformity, fragrance, and resistance to disease, insects, and weather stress. Vegetables are evaluated for yield, flavor, texture, pest resistance, space efficiency, nutritional value, and novelty effect.

Gold Medal winners are flowers and vegetables that represent a breeding breakthrough, such as 'Sugar Snap' pea, the first edible-podded shell pea, and 'Profusion White' zinnia, a long-blooming, mildew-resistant cultivar that doesn't need deadheading to continue blooming. A second tier of awards recognizes outstanding flowers and vegetables as AAS Flower, Bedding Plant, or Vegetable Award Winners.

In addition to the AAS test gardens, there are more than 200 AAS display gardens in North America. These gardens showcase past, present, and future AAS winners in a landscape setting. Visiting a display garden near you is a great way to see these plants in a garden setting and to get ideas for using them in your garden and landscape.

The American Rose Society (ARS) publishes the *Handbook for Selecting Roses*, updated every year, with a listing of rose cultivars rated for quality. The ARS awards the American Garden Rose Selections designation to rose introductions recognized for their desirable qualities.

The All-American Daylily Selections Council (AADSC) is a nonprofit organization that evaluates daylily cultivars at test sites across North America. Since 1985, its experts have evaluated nearly 6,000 cultivars. Winners of the All-American Daylilies designation have performed excellently across at least five hardiness zones.

For more information on AAS, ARS, or AADSC, call or write to the organizations or visit their Web sites (see Resources on page 673).

ALLIUM

Allium, ornamental onion. Spring- and summer-blooming perennial bulbs.

Description: Don't let the "onion" in "ornamental onion" keep you from growing these showy cousins of garlic and leeks. Their beautiful flowers more than make up for the oniony aroma they give off when bruised or cut. All bear spherical or nearly round heads of loosely to densely packed starry flowers on wiry to thick, stiffly upright stems. The grassy or straplike leaves are of little interest. In fact, the foliage on most ornamental onions starts dying back before, during, or soon after bloom and can detract from the display.

A. aflatunense, Persian onion, bears 4-inch-wide, tightly packed, lilac globes on 2½- to 3-foot stems in mid-spring. Zones 4–8.

Chives in the Flower Bed

Two alliums normally confined to the herb garden make great choices for borders. Clumps of common chives (*Allium schoenoprasum*) add grasslike foliage and bright cotton balls of light violet flowers in Zones 3–9. Try garlic chives (*A. tuberosum*) in a sunny or partly shady border in Zones 4–8. Lovely 2- to 3-inch heads of white, rose-scented flowers bloom on 2-foot stems above handsome, dark green, narrow, strappy leaves in dense clumps. Cut flowerstalks before garlic chives produce seed or the plants will self-sow and become weedy.

A. caeruleum, blue globe onion, azure-flowered garlic, produces 2-inch, medium blue balls on stems that rise up to 2½ feet above grassy leaves in late spring; it multiplies quickly. Zones 2–7.

A. christophii, star of Persia, bears spidery lilac flowers in spectacular globes to 1 foot wide on 1- to 2-foot stiff stems in late spring to early summer. Dried seed heads are also showy. Zones 4–8.

A. giganteum, giant onion, lifts its 4- to 6-inch crowded spheres of bright lilac flowers 3 to 4 feet or more above large, rather broad and flat leaves in late spring. Zones 4–8.

A. moly, lily leek or golden garlic, bears its sunny yellow blooms in 2- to 3-inch clusters on slightly curving, 10-inch stems in late spring. Zones 3–9.

A. oreophilum, pink lily leek, bears loose, 2-inch clusters of rose-red blooms on 6- to 8-inch stems in late spring. Zones 4–9.

A. sphaerocephalon, drumstick chives, round-headed leek, blooms in midsummer with tiny, purple-red flowers in 2-inch oval heads on stems up to 2 feet tall above grassy foliage. Zones 4–9.

How to grow: Alliums are easy to grow in full sun or very light shade. Site them in average, well-drained soil that you can allow to become completely dry when the alliums are dormant in summer. Plant them with their tops at a depth roughly three times their width. Don't try to grow alliums in heavy clay soil. Give Persian onions, stars of Persia, and giant onions a few inches of loose winter mulch.

Landscape uses: Plant alliums in borders, cottage gardens, and among rocks. Grow them with low- or open-growing annuals and perennials, which will disguise the unsightly leaves as they die down. Combine star of Persia with tall bearded irises and old-fashioned roses for a spectacular show. Small masses of giant onion blooming among green clouds of asparagus foliage make an unforgettable and unusual picture. All alliums last a long time as cut flowers; many also dry well in silica gel. Harvest the seed heads for arrangements before they become completely dry and brown.

AMARYLLIS

See *Hippeastrum*

ANEMONE

Anemone, windflower, pasqueflower.
Spring-blooming and late-summer- to fall-blooming tubers and perennials.

Description: *Anemone blanda*, Grecian windflower, produces cheerful daisylike flowers to 2 inches wide in shades of white, pink, red-violet, and blue on 3- to 6-inch plants with ferny leaves. Once established, they multiply to form low-spreading carpets. They die back completely several weeks after blooming stops in spring. Zones 4–8.

A. ×*hybrida*, Japanese anemone, also sold as *A. hupehensis* var. *japonica*, blooms in late summer and fall with 2- to 3-inch single, semidouble, or double blooms in white or shades of pink. The flowers appear on leafless stems 2 to 5 feet above mounded, cut leaves. Zones 4 (with protection) and 5–8.

A. tomentosa 'Robustissima' is another Japanese anemone, also sold as *A. vitifolia*, grapeleaf anemone. Plants bear silvery pink flowers 2 feet above the foliage and are hardier than hybrids. Zones 3–8.

How to grow: In mid-fall, before planting the barklike, dead-looking tubers of Grecian windflowers, soak them in warm water overnight to plump them up. Place the tubers on their sides about 2 inches deep and no more than 4 inches apart. Choose a site where the foliage of other plants will hide the yellowing leaves in summer. Grecian windflowers thrive in sun to part shade with average, well-drained soil containing some organic matter. Water in spring if the weather is dry. Mulch with compost or leaf mold to hold moisture in the soil and encourage self-sown seedlings to grow and produce colonies.

Divide or plant the creeping underground stems of Japanese anemones in spring. Give them partial shade, or full sun if the soil is quite moist. They thrive in deep, fertile, moist but well-drained soils enriched with plenty of organic matter. Poorly drained sites, which promote rot, can be fatal in winter. Water during drought. Keep plants out of strong wind, or be prepared to stake them. Cover with several inches of oak leaves or other light mulch for the first winter after planting in northern zones.

Landscape uses: Grow Grecian windflowers in masses in the light shade of tall trees or with other woodland plants and bulbs. Also try them toward the front of borders (sow sweet alyssum on top of them to hide the dying leaves) or among rocks or paving stones. Japanese anemones are glorious in borders and woodland plantings, where they will form colonies of long-stemmed flowers to cut.

ANIMAL PESTS

Four-footed creatures can cause much more damage than insect pests in many suburban and rural gardens. They may ruin your garden or landscape overnight, eating anything from apples to zinnias. Most animal pests feed at night, making it tricky to figure out who the culprits are.

Follow these guidelines for coping with animal pests.

Identify the pests. Ask your neighbors what kinds of wildlife are common garden marauders in your neighborhood. Sit quietly looking out a window toward your garden at dawn or dusk, when animals tend to become active. Check for droppings or tracks around your garden, and consult a wildlife guide to identify them.

Assess the damage. If it's only cosmetic, you may decide your plants can tolerate it. If the damage threatens harvest or plant health, control is necessary. If damage to ornamental plants is limited to one plant type, consider removing it and replacing it with plants that are less appealing to animal pests.

Take action. A combination of several tactics to deter animal pests often gives the best results. For a vegetable or kitchen garden, a sturdy fence may be the only effective choice. Barriers, like nylon netting, can work well to protect individual plants. Homemade or commercial repellents give inconsistent results, so experiment with them to find what works in your gardens. Scare tactics such as scarecrows and models of predator animals may frighten pest animals and birds. In extreme cases, you may choose to kill the pests by flooding their underground tunnels or by trapping or shooting. It's up to the individual to decide if the damage is severe enough to warrant these methods. If you decide to shoot or trap any animals, check first with your state Department of Environmental Resources to learn about regulations and required permits.

Deer

Deer have a taste for a wide range of garden and landscape plants. A few deer are a gentle nuisance; in areas with high deer pressure, they can be the worst garden pest you'll ever encounter. Deer are nocturnal but may be active at any time. Where deer have grown accustomed to humans, you may spot them browsing in your garden even in the middle of the afternoon.

Barriers: If deer are damaging a few select trees or shrubs, enclose individual plants with cages made from galvanized hardware cloth, placed so tender branch tips and buds are shielded from browsing.

Fences: Fencing is the most reliable way to keep deer out of a large garden or an entire home landscape, but it can be quite costly, especially if you have it professionally installed. Consider these effective options for deer fencing.

- Conventional wire-mesh fences should be 8 feet high for best protection. A second, inner fence of about 3 feet high and placed 3 to 4 feet from the outer fence will increase effectiveness because double obstacles confuse deer and impede their ability to jump the taller barrier.

🌿 Slanted fences constructed with electrified wire are an excellent deer barrier. Installing this type of fence is a job for a professional.

🌿 Deer are not likely to jump a high, solid fence, such as one made of stone or wood.

🌿 Polypropylene (plastic) mesh deer fencing is costly but easier to install on your own than an electric fence.

🌿 For small gardens, up to 40 by 60 feet, a low enclosure made of snow fencing or woven-wire fencing may be effective, because deer tend to avoid jumping into a confined space.

For more about deer fencing, see the Fencing entry.

Repellents: For minor deer-damage problems, repellents may give temporary protection until the deer grow accustomed to the repellent and resume browsing. When food is scarce, deer may even learn to use the odor of repellents to guide them to choice food sources. Periodically changing from one type of repellent to another can increase your chances for success. You can make your own or buy a commercial repellent. Keep in mind that scent-based repellents may keep you out of the garden, too!

🌿 Hang bars of highly fragrant soap from strings in trees and shrubs. Or nail each bar to a 4-foot stake and drive the stakes at 15-foot intervals along the perimeter of the area.

🌿 Try using human hair. Ask your hairdresser to save hair for you to collect each week. Put a handful of hair in a net or mesh bag (you can use squares of cheesecloth to make bags) and hang bags 3 feet above the ground and 3 feet apart. Pet hair collected from your dog's or cat's brush also may be used this way.

🌿 Farmers and foresters repel deer by spraying trees or crops with an egg-water mixture. Mix 5 eggs with 5 quarts of water for enough solution to treat ¼ acre. Spray plants thoroughly. You may need to repeat the application after a rain.

🌿 Commercial repellents are available at garden centers. Read labels to see if a product contains only organic ingredients and to find out if it is safe for use on food crops. You may have to experiment to find one that offers good control. Watch for new products coming on the market, too.

🌿 Experiment with homemade repellents by mixing bloodmeal, bonemeal, hot sauce, or garlic oil with water. There are many recipes for concocting repellents, and results are variable. Taste repellents, such as hot sauce, require that deer take at least one bite of your plants. Saturate rags or string with odor-repellent mixtures, and place them around areas that need protection.

🌿 Gardeners who have canine companions that regularly patrol their yards report that they have few deer problems, even in the absence of a fence or repellents. It seems that the scent of the dogs is enough to discourage deer from spending much time in the area.

"Deer-proof" plants: If fencing your yard is beyond your budget, and repellents aren't doing the trick, try renovating your landscape with plants that deer don't like to eat. Over time, remove plants that routinely suffer deer damage. Replace them with shrubs, vines, and perennials with a reputation for being deer-proof. What deer will and won't eat tends to vary widely from one region to the next and depending on how hungry the deer are. Ask your Cooperative Extension Service for a list of plants that gardeners have found to be locally deer-proof, and consult the Resources on page 673 for books on the topic.

Ground Squirrels and Chipmunks

Ground squirrels and chipmunks are burrowing rodents that eat seeds, nuts, fruits, roots, bulbs, and other foods. They are similar, and both are closely related to squirrels. They tunnel in soil and uproot newly planted bulbs, plants, and seeds. Ground squirrel burrows run horizontally; chipmunk burrows run almost vertically.

Traps: Bait live traps with peanut butter, oats, or nut meats. Check traps daily.

Habitat modification: Ground squirrels and chipmunks prefer to scout for enemies from the protection of their burrow entrance. A tall groundcover that blocks the view at ground level may deter their attacks on your garden.

Other methods: Place screen or hardware cloth over plants, or lay wire poultry netting atop the soil over bulbs and seeds. Try spraying repellents on newly planted beds of bulbs and seeds.

Mice and Voles

Mice and voles look alike and cause similar damage, but they are only distantly related. Both are active year-round. They eat almost any green vegetation, including tubers and bulbs, and tend to cause the most harm in winter and early spring when natural foods are scarce. When unable to find other foods, mice and voles will eat the bark and roots of fruit trees. They can do severe damage to young apple trees.

Barriers: Sink cylinders of hardware cloth, heavy plastic, or sheet metal several inches into the soil around the bases of trees. You may be able to protect bulbs and vegetable beds by mixing a product containing slate particles into the soil, or plant bulbs within a loose "basket" of poultry netting.

Traps and baits: Some orchardists place snap traps baited with peanut butter, nut meats, or rolled oats along mouse runways to catch and kill them. A bait of vitamin D is available. It causes a calcium imbalance in the animals, and they will die several days after eating the bait.

Other methods: Repellents such as those described for deer may control damage. You can also modify habitat to discourage mice and voles by removing vegetative cover around tree and shrub trunks. Keep mulch a few inches away from tree trunks to avoid providing hiding places where mice and voles can nest and feed.

Moles

In some ways, moles are a gardener's allies. They aerate soil and eat insects, including beetle grubs and other plant pests. However, they also eat earthworms. Their tunnels may uproot desirable plants in the garden and create tripping hazards in your lawn. Mice and other small animals may use the tunnels and eat the plants that moles have left behind.

Traps: Harpoon traps placed along main runs will kill the moles as they travel through their tunnels.

Barriers: To prevent moles from invading an area, dig a trench about 6 inches wide and 2 feet deep. Fill it with stones, coarse gravel, or dry, compacted material such as crushed shells. Cover the barrier material with a thin layer of soil.

Habitat modification: In lawns, insects such

as soil-dwelling Japanese beetle grubs may be the moles' main food source. If you're patient, you can solve your mole (and your grub) problem by applying milky disease spores, a biological control agent that infects grubs, to your lawn. This is more effective in the South than in the North, because the disease may not overwinter well in cold conditions. However, if you have healthy organic soil, the moles may stick around to feed on earthworms once the grubs are gone.

Other methods: You can flood mole tunnels and kill the moles with a shovel as they come to the surface to escape the water. Repellents such as those used to control deer may be effective. Unfortunately, repellents often merely divert the moles to an area that is unprotected by repellents.

Pocket Gophers

These thick-bodied rodents tunnel through soil, eating bulbs, tubers, roots, seeds, and woody plants. Fan- or crescent-shaped mounds of soil at tunnel entrances are signs of pocket gopher activity.

Fences and barriers: Exclude gophers from your yard with an underground fence. Bury a strip of $\frac{1}{4}$- to $\frac{1}{2}$-inch mesh hardware cloth so that it extends 2 feet below and at least 2 feet above the soil surface around your garden or around individual trees.

Flooding: You can kill pocket gophers as you would moles, by flooding them out of their tunnels. Bear in mind that this method may require a substantial amount of water—running a hose for 15 minutes or longer—to drive the rodents into the open.

Rabbits

Rabbits can damage vegetables, flowers, and trees at any time of year in any setting. They also eat spring tulip shoots, tree bark, and buds and stems of woody plants.

Fences: The best way to keep rabbits out of a garden is to erect a chicken-wire fence. Be sure the mesh is 1 inch or smaller so that young rabbits can't get through. You'll find instructions for constructing a chicken-wire fence in the Fencing entry.

Barriers: Erect cylinders made of $\frac{1}{4}$-inch hardware cloth around young trees or valuable plants. The cages should be $1\frac{1}{2}$ to 2 feet high, or higher if you live in an area with deep snowfall, and should be sunk 2 to 3 inches below the soil surface. Leave a gap of 1 to 2 inches between the mesh barrier and the trunk it protects to keep rabbits from nibbling the bark through holes in the mesh. Commercial tree guards are also available.

Other methods: Repellents such as those used for deer may be effective. Commercial inflatable snakes and owl replicas may discourage rabbits from frequenting your garden.

Raccoons

Raccoons prefer a meal of fresh crayfish but will settle for a nighttime feast in your sweet corn patch. Signs that they have dined include broken stalks, shredded husks, scattered kernels, and gnawed cob ends—raccoons tend to be destructive in their quest for tasty treats and enjoy (and destroy) fresh tomatoes, grapes, and other garden delicacies besides sweet corn.

Fences and habitat modification: A fence made of electrified netting attached to fiberglass posts will keep out raccoons, rabbits, and woodchucks. Or if you have a conventional fence, add a single strand of electric wire or polytape around the outside to prevent raccoons from climbing the fence. Try lighting the garden at night or planting

Look, Don't Touch

While we may wish that solving animal pest problems were as easy as posting a "Look, Don't Touch" sign, we should heed the warning ourselves when dealing with animal pests. Wild animals are unpredictable, so keep your distance. They may bite or scratch and, in doing so, can transmit serious diseases such as rabies. Any warm-blooded animal can carry rabies, a virus that affects the nervous system. Rabies is a threat in varying degrees throughout the United States and Canada. Among common garden animal pests, raccoons and skunks are most likely to be infected. It's best never to try to move close to or touch wild animals in your garden. And if you're planning to catch animal pests in live traps, be sure you've planned a safe way to transport and release the animals before you set out the baited traps.

squash among the corn—the vines may provide some deterrence to raccoons moving among the corn. Motion-activated lights or water sprayers may also discourage raccoons and other nocturnal garden raiders.

Barriers: Protect small plantings of sweet corn by wrapping ears at top and bottom with strong tape. Loop the tape around the tip, then around the stalk, then around the base of each ear. This prevents raccoons from pulling the ears off the plants. Or try covering each ear with a paper bag secured with a rubber band.

Woodchucks

Woodchucks, or groundhogs, are found in the Northeast, the Mid-Atlantic, parts of the Midwest, and most of southern Canada. You are most likely to see woodchucks in the early morning or late afternoon, munching on a variety of green vegetation. Woodchucks hibernate during winter. They're most likely to be a pest when they emerge in early spring, eating young plants in your gardens. Like winter-weary gardeners, woodchucks love tender lettuces and newly sprouted peas.

Fences: A 2- to 3-foot-high chicken-wire fence that extends below the soil surface will keep out woodchucks. See instructions for constructing one in the Fencing entry.

Barriers: Some gardeners protect their young plants from woodchucks by covering them with plastic or floating row covers. Make sure to tuck in the edges to discourage critters from slipping underneath the cover to feast.

Other Animal Pests

The following animals cause only minor damage to gardens or are pests only in certain regions.

Armadillos: These animals spend most of the day in burrows, coming out at dusk to begin the night's work of digging for food and building burrows. Their diet includes insects, worms, slugs, crayfish, carrion, and eggs. They will sometimes root for food in gardens or lawns. Armadillos cannot tolerate cold weather, which limits their range to the southern United States.

A garden fence is the best protection against armadillos. You also can trap them.

Prairie dogs: Prairie dogs can be garden pests in the western United States. They will eat most green plants. If they are a problem in your landscape,

Scare Tactics

Many gardeners report success in using commercial or homemade devices to frighten birds away from their crops.

Fake enemies. You can scare birds by fooling them into thinking their enemies are present. Try placing inflatable, solid, or silhouetted likenesses of snakes, hawks, or owls strategically around your garden to discourage both birds and small mammals. They'll be most effective if you occasionally reposition them so that they appear to move about the garden. Hang "scare-eye" and hawklike balloons and kites that mimic bird predators in large plantings. Use four to eight balloons per acre in orchards or small fruit or sweet corn plantings.

Weird noises. Unusual noises can also frighten birds. A humming line works well in a strawberry patch or vegetable garden. The line, made of very thin nylon, vibrates in even the slightest breeze. The movement creates humming noises inaudible to us but readily heard and avoided by birds. Leaving a radio on at night in the garden can deter some pests but may bother neighbors more. A word to the wise: Commercially available ultrasonic devices that purport to scare animal and bird pests are unreliable.

Flashes of light. Try fastening aluminum pie plates or unwanted CDs to stakes with strings in and around your garden. Blinking lights may work, too.

Sticky surfaces. Another tactic that may annoy or scare birds is to coat surfaces near the garden where they might roost with Bird Tanglefoot.

And don't forget two tried-and-true methods: making a scarecrow and keeping a domestic dog on your property.

---

control them with the same tactics described for ground squirrels and pocket gophers.

Skunks: Skunks eat a wide range of foods. They will dig characteristic cone-shaped holes in your lawn while foraging for grubs and may eat garden plants, including ripening tomatoes and melons. Skunks can be a real problem when startled by pets or unwary gardeners.

Keep skunks out of the garden by fencing it. Treating your lawn with milky disease spores to kill grubs may eventually make your landscape less inviting to skunks.

Squirrels: Squirrels eat forest seeds, berries, bark, buds, flowers, and fungi. Around homes, they may feed on grain, especially field corn. Damage is usually not serious enough to cause concern. Try using repellents such as those suggested for deer control to protect small areas.

Bird Pests

To the gardener, birds are both friends and foes. While they eat insect pests, many birds also consume entire fruits or vegetables or will pick at your produce, leaving damage that invites disease and spoils your harvest.

Some of the birds likely to raid your vegetable gardens are blue jays and blackbirds such as crows, starlings, and grackles. If you grow berries or tree fruit, you may find yourself playing host to beautiful but hungry songbirds such as cedar waxwings and orioles. You'll have to decide which you enjoy more—eating the fruit or bird-watching!

In general, birds feed most heavily in the morning and again in late afternoon. Schedule your control tactics to coincide with feeding times. Many birds have a decided preference for certain crops. Damage may be seasonal, depending on harvest time of their favorite foods.

You can control bird damage through habitat management or by blocking their access or scaring them away from your garden (see "Scare Tactics"). For any method, it is important to identify the bird. A control effective for one species may not work for another. Also, you don't want to mistakenly scare or repel beneficial birds.

Try these steps to change the garden environment to discourage pesky birds.

- Eliminate standing water. Birds need a source of drinking water, and a source near your garden makes it more attractive.

- Plant alternate food sources to distract birds from your crop. Many fruit-loving species prefer mulberries (*Morus* spp.) and will flock to those fruits. Provide winged guests a mulberry tree to distract them from raspberries or blueberries meant for human consumption.

- In orchards, prune to open the canopy, since birds prefer sheltered areas.

- In orchards, allow a cover crop to grow about 9 inches tall. The growth will be too high for birds who watch for enemies on the ground while foraging.

- Remove garden trash and cover possible perches to discourage smaller flocking birds like sparrows and finches that often post a guard.

You can also take steps to prevent birds from reaching your crops. The most effective way is to cover bushes and trees with lightweight plastic netting, and to cover crop rows with floating row covers (see the Row Covers entry). Use supporting stakes to keep netting from resting on fruit bushes and secure it at ground level. Clever birds will perch on the netting and snatch berries through the mesh if they can reach them.

ANNUALS

When gardeners think of annuals, they think of color, and lots of it. Annuals are garden favorites because of their continuous season-long bloom. Their colors run the spectrum from cool to hot, subtle to shocking. The plants are as varied in form, texture, and size as they are in color. Gardeners favor annuals for their versatility, too. They may be showstoppers that make an eye-catching focal point in the garden, or they may fill supporting roles, adding accent colors or a backdrop of greenery.

In the strictest sense, an annual is a plant that completes its life cycle in one year—it germinates, grows, flowers, sets seed, and dies in one growing season. Gardeners don't stick to the strict botanical definition of the term, however, and use the term *annual* to describe any plant that will bloom well in the same year it is planted and then die after exposure to end-of-season frosts or freezes. Within the realm of annuals, there are plants that can tolerate cold temperatures, ones that can't stand a whisper of frost, and others that are actually shrubs or perennials. Many popular plants we grow as annuals are really tender perennials, including wax or semperflorens begonias (*Begonia ×semperflorens-cultorum*), impatiens (*Impatiens walleriana*), lantana (*Lantana camara*), and zonal geraniums (*Pelargonium ×hortorum*). We treat them as annuals because they're not hardy in most climates and are killed by winter's cold and replaced each season.

Annuals have as many uses as there are places to use them. They are excellent for providing garden color from early summer until frost. They fill in gaps between newly planted perennials. They are popular cut flowers. Annuals can make even the shadiest areas of the late-summer garden brighter. And since you replace them every year, you can create new designs with different color schemes as often as you want.

There are hundreds of great annuals for home gardens, more than could possibly be described on these pages. Since matching plant to site is one of the most important considerations in choosing which annuals to grow, start by consulting the lists of annuals for different kinds of sites (shade, wet soil, etc.) throughout this entry. Then, to learn more about specific plants on those lists, refer to the Quick Reference Guide on page 678 to see which specific annuals are described elsewhere in this book. Also check the Recommended Reading on page 675 for titles of some excellent books that offer more complete information on annuals.

Landscaping with Annuals

Annuals are beautiful additions to the home landscape. You can use them alone or in combination with other kinds of plants. Bedding out is the traditional way of using annuals. English gardeners of the Victorian era created extensive, colorful displays, usually with intricate patterns of closely spaced, often very low-growing annuals set against emerald lawns, called bedding schemes. That's why annuals are often called bedding plants.

When designing with annuals, remember that a little color goes a long way. Bright oranges, pinks, and reds may clash. Choose annuals with care, and make sure you create a pleasing color combination. See the Garden Design entry for ideas on how to visualize your garden and create a design. Here are some of the best ways to landscape with annuals.

Annual Plantings

You can follow the lead of Victorian gardeners and create formal or informal designs with annuals in island beds or in borders. Fences, hedges, and brick or stone walls all make attractive backdrops for annual gardens. Arrange annuals in drifts for maximum color impact from their flowers. Don't forget to include some plants that have spectacular foliage, such as coleus and cannas (*Canna ×generalis*).

An annual garden is a great opportunity to try out a color scheme—hot colors with brilliant oranges and fiery reds and yellows, for example, or a design with all soft pastels. This can help you determine within a single season if you like the resulting display. In addition to the generic seed packets of mixed-color annuals offered at most nurseries, catalog and Internet seed specialists offer many popular annuals in packets of individual colors. These allow you to buy and grow only white zinnias, spider flower, and marigolds, for example.

Annuals are ideal for outlining or edging garden spaces. Compact growers like wax begonias, creeping zinnia (*Sanvitalia procumbens*), and edging lobelia (*Lobelia erinus*) make fine edgings for garden beds.

Annuals are popular for cutting because they flower enthusiastically throughout the growing

KEY WORDS *Annuals*

Hardy annual. An annual plant that tolerates frost and self-sows. Seeds winter over outside and germinate the following year. Examples: globe candytuft (*Iberis umbellata*), spider flower (*Cleome hassleriana*).

Half-hardy annual. An annual plant that can withstand light frost. Seeds can be planted early. Plants can be set out in fall and will bloom the following year. Often called a winter annual. Examples: pansies (*Viola ×wittrockiana*), sweet peas (*Lathyrus odoratus*).

Tender annual. Also called a warm-weather annual, these are annual plants from tropical or subtropical regions, easily killed by light frost. The seeds need warm soil to germinate. Most annuals are in this category. Examples: marigolds (*Tagetes* spp.), petunias (*Petunia* spp.), zinnias (*Zinnia* spp.).

Tender perennial. A plant that survives more than one season in tropical or subtropical regions, but that is easily killed by light frost. Examples: coleus (*Plectranthus scutellarioides*), Persian shield (*Strobilanthes dyerianus*).

---

season. Grow them in a special cutting garden or mix with other flowers. See the Cut Flower Gardening entry.

Perennial and Mixed Plantings

Annuals are a wonderful choice for adding color to a perennial garden, and they're especially valuable for summer color after popular perennials like peonies have finished blooming for the season. Some gardeners leave unplanted spaces in their perennial gardens specifically for filling with annuals along with tender perennials like cannas and dahlias. You can also sprinkle seed of annuals such as larkspur (*Consolida ajacis*) or spider flower between clumps of perennials. Or consider planting tall annuals such as common sunflower (*Helianthus annuus*) or Mexican sunflower (*Tithonia rotundifolia*) to create vertical accents along the back of a border or between shrubs.

Annuals also are valuable for helping a new perennial garden look its best while it is getting established. Since many perennials are slow-growing by nature, the average perennial garden takes up to 3 years to look its best. Annuals are perfect for carrying the garden through the first few seasons. Fill in the gaps between those slowpoke plants with the tall spikes of snapdragon (*Antirrhinum majus*), flowering tobacco (*Nicotiana alata*), and blue cupflower (*Nierembergia hippomanica* var. *caerulea*). You may need to stake or prune overly enthusiastic annuals midseason to keep them from overwhelming their more subdued perennial neighbors.

Other annuals that are perfect for mixed plantings are annual ornamental grasses, including big quaking grass (*Briza maxima*), purple fountain grass (*Pennisetum setaceum* 'Rubrum'), hare's-tail grass (*Lagurus ovatus*), and Job's tears (*Coix lacryma-jobi*). They add elegance to the garden, with clean, simple lines and soft textures. Annual grasses are wonderful to combine with bold-textured plants like 'Autumn Joy' sedum (*Hylotelephium* 'Herbstfreude') and coneflowers (*Rudbeckia* spp.). Annual grasses are especially valuable for cutting and drying.

Shade Gardens

Shade-tolerant annuals can play an important role in brightening up shade in woodland gardens, where blossoms are hard to come by after spring wildflowers fade. You can fill a shaded spot entirely with annuals—impatiens and wax begonias are two popular choices—but they're even more effective when combined with shade-loving perennials. A moist, shaded spot that glows with multicolored impatiens set off by ferns and hostas is a welcome summer sight. See the opposite page for a list of plants that will perk up shady areas.

If your shaded site is created by shallow-rooted trees like maples, which can make it practically impossible to dig or plant a garden, don't despair. Instead, fill large tubs or containers with potting soil and plant them with impatiens, begonias, sapphire flowers (*Browallia* spp.), coleus, and other shade-loving annuals. Use caladiums, begonias, or wishbone flowers (*Torenia fournieri*) in pots around a shaded patio or deck. Caladiums are also nice under trees to perk up beds of pachysandra and other groundcovers. Add spring color to shaded sites with pansies. Begonias or impatiens make a colorful edging for a shaded patio or walk. Sapphire flowers are great for a formal border in dappled shade at the edge of a lawn.

Trellises and Posts

Annual vines make fast-growing screens, providing privacy and shade. Use them to create garden rooms or to hide unattractive views or utility areas such as garden workstations or compost bins. These vines don't need a formal trellis or extensive training. You can cover a pillar or lamppost with chicken wire for quick and easy support. Store the wire at the end of the season. Or they can easily climb strings suspended from an overhead pole or wire. Branches made into a tepee frame make a unique trellis, too. Garden centers even sell collapsible trellises that can be moved from place to place for a temporary screen. Annual vines also are excellent choices for training up shrubs, and they let you add summer flowers to an otherwise humdrum all-green hedge.

A fence festooned with bright blue morning glories is a beautiful sight. But if you think about it, what would the morning glory be without its bright green, heart-shaped foliage, especially in the afternoon when the flowers fade? Don't ignore foliage effects when you select annual vines. Cardinal climber (*Ipomoea* ×*multifida*) has lacy finger-like foliage, while the round foliage of nasturtiums (*Tropaeolum* spp.) is attractive and edible, too.

Many vines combine flowers, foliage, and showy fruits. Bottle gourds (*Lagenaria* spp.) are very decorative. Their huge yellow flowers are edible, and the hard-shelled fruits have many craft uses. Scarlet runner beans (*Phaseolus coccineus*) combine handsome foliage, pretty flowers, and edible beans. Whatever your gardening style may be, annual vines deserve a place scrambling up a trellis, post, or pillar.

See "Annual Vines" for a list of plants to try.

Containers

Many annuals are perfect container plants. Their fast growth, easy culture, and low cost make them irresistible for pots, window boxes, and planters. Best of all, you can create decorative container gardens quickly—especially if you start with large-size annuals—and move them around the garden to mix and match your display.

Select as large a container as you can comfort-

Annuals for Shade

If trees, walls, or buildings on your property dictate that shaded beds and borders are your lot in life, you can still enjoy colorful gardens. Count on cheerful annuals to perk things up. The jewel-like hues of impatiens or coleus will brighten even the darkest areas under trees. It's surprising how many annuals do tolerate shade. Plants in this list will grow in partial shade. An asterisk (*) indicates a plant that will tolerate full shade.

Anchusa capensis (summer forget-me-not)

Begonia ×semperflorens-cultorum (wax begonia)

Browallia spp. (sapphire flowers)

Caladium ×hortulanum (caladium)

Catharanthus roseus (Madagascar periwinkle)

Colocasia esculenta (elephant's ear)

Hypoestes phyllostachya (polka-dot plant)

Impatiens walleriana (impatiens)*

Lobelia erinus (lobelia)

Mimulus ×hybridus (monkey flower)

Myosotis sylvatica (woodland forget-me-not)

Nemophila menziesii (baby blue eyes)

Nicotiana alata (flowering tobacco)

Nierembergia hippomanica var. *caerulea* (blue cupflower)

Omphalodes linifolia (navelwort)

Perilla frutescens (perilla, beefsteak plant)

Plectranthus scutellarioides (coleus)*

Salvia splendens (scarlet sage)

Thunbergia alata (black-eyed Susan vine)

Torenia fournieri (wishbone flower)*

Viola tricolor (Johnny-jump-ups)

Viola ×wittrockiana (pansy)

---

ably manage. Small containers dry out far too quickly and create extra work. Choose a light soil mix that drains well but holds moisture. There are two schools of thought when it comes to planting. Some gardeners are careful not to overplant. Annuals grow fast and will quickly fill a container. Other gardeners pack containers with lots of plants because they like the immediate look of abundance. Crowded plants won't bloom as well as plants that are given more space, and they will require more watering. Fertilize containers regularly with a balanced organic fertilizer. (See the Fertilizers entry for choices.)

You can start container gardening in early spring with pansies. Summer and fall bring endless choices for sun or shade. Fill containers with a single species, all red zonal geraniums, for example, or create gardens with several different annuals. One good way to compose an attractive arrangement is to include four kinds of plants: flags, fillers, accents, and trailers. Flags are tall plants that give the composition height, such as ornamental grasses and cannas. Fillers bring handsome fine-textured foliage and/or small flowers to the mix, and include curry plant (*Helichrysum italicum* ssp. *serotinum*), polka-dot plant, and even bushy, small-leaved forms of basil.

Annuals with Striking Foliage

These annuals all have outstanding foliage that is interesting in its own right. Some, like wax begonias, zonal geraniums, and morning glories, also produce cheerful flowers. Use foliage annuals to complement floral displays or as accents on their own.

Alternanthera ficoidea (copperleaf)

Amaranthus tricolor (Joseph's-coat)

Atriplex hortensis (orach, mountain spinach)

Bassia scoparia f. *trichophylla* (summer cypress, burningbush)

Begonia ×semperflorens-cultorum (wax begonia)

Beta vulgaris (Swiss chard)

Brassica oleracea (ornamental kale)

Caladium ×hortulanum (caladium)

Canna ×generalis (canna)

Euphorbia marginata (snow-on-the-mountain)

Foeniculum vulgare 'Rubrum' (bronze fennel)

Hibiscus acetosella (African rosemallow)

Hypoestes phyllostachya (polka-dot plant)

Ipomoea batatas (ornamental sweet potato)

Iresine spp. (bloodleafs)

Ocimum basilicum (basil)

Pelargonium ×hortorum (zonal geranium)

Perilla frutescens (perilla, beefsteak plant)

Plectranthus scutellarioides (coleus)

Ricinus communis (castor bean)

Senecio cineraria (dusty miller)

Strobilanthes dyerianus (Persian shield)

Tradescantia pallida 'Purpurea' (purple heart)

Zea mays 'Variegata' (ornamental corn)

Accent plants feature bold, eye-catching foliage or flowers and include ornamental peppers (*Capsicum* spp.), dwarf dahlias, or zonal geraniums. Finally, trailers spill over the edge of the pot to add a charming frame with either pretty leaves or bright flowers. Trailers include bacopa (*Sutera cordata*), edging lobelia, and petunias.

For fall containers, ornamental kales and cabbages, zonal geraniums, and snapdragons remain attractive until hard frost. Tender perennials such as coleus, begonias, and lantanas may be pruned and brought indoors for winter.

Hanging baskets were made for annuals. They signal the arrival of summer. Use seasonal displays of fuchsias, ivy geraniums (*Pelargonium peltatum*), trailing lantana (*Lantana montevidensis*), and trailing petunias to highlight a porch, breezeway, or gazebo. Grow plants singly or in combination to create eye-catching displays. Vines are especially nice in hanging baskets and are easily controlled. Choose a medium-weight potting soil that holds moisture. Remember to water often. In midsummer, baskets may need watering two or three times a day. Fertilize regularly with a balanced organic fertilizer. See the Container Gardening entry for more information on growing annuals in containers.

Choosing What to Buy

With so many different species and cultivars on the market, you'd think it would be impossible to decide which plants to buy. It's easier to narrow your choices if you keep a checklist of what you're looking for and stick to it.

First, choose plants that match your garden design. If you need a tall plant with pastel flowers, don't be swayed by a flat of endearing French marigolds. Adopt a simple rule: Don't buy plants unless you have a place for them. This will save you money and frustration, and your garden will benefit from your restraint.

Next, when it comes to which cultivar to buy, look at the mature size, rate of growth, how long it takes to bloom, and special considerations (for example, you may not like heavily veined petals). Most annuals are easy to grow from seed, and there are good reasons to raise your own seedlings. For one thing, you'll have many more cultivars to choose from if you buy seed instead of plants, because mail-order catalogs and Internet suppliers offer more choices than garden centers do. And when you grow your own seedlings, you can do so organically, which most commercial producers of annual bedding plants don't.

Growing Your Own Annuals

It's better to start most annual seeds in pots or flats indoors rather than sowing them directly into the garden. Indoor planting gives you more predictable

Annual Vines

Whether they are trained onto a trellis, over a fence, up a pole, or through the branches of a sedate green hedge, the following vines add interest and appeal to gardens. All of these grow best in full sun.

Cardiospermum halicacabum (balloon vine, love-in-a-puff)

Cobaea scandens (cup-and-saucer vine)

Cucurbita pepo (miniature pumpkin)

Ipomoea alba (moonflower)

Ipomoea quamoclit (cypress vine, star glory)

Ipomoea tricolor (morning glory)

Lablab purpureus (hyacinth bean)

Lathyrus odoratus (sweet pea)

Mandevilla ×amabilis 'Alice DuPont' (mandevilla)

Maurandya scandens (chickabiddy, creeping gloxinia)

Phaseolus coccineus (scarlet runner bean)

Rhodochiton atrosanguineus (purple bell vine)

Solanum jasminoides (potato vine, jasmine nightshade)

Thunbergia alata (black-eyed Susan vine)

Tropaeolum majus (nasturtium)

Tropaeolum peregrinum (canary vine)

Annuals for Dry Sites

Unlike most annuals, these plants are adapted to dry soils. Grow them in areas you don't want to water often or in beds where the soil stays very dry.

Amaranthus tricolor (Joseph's coat)

Arctotis stoechadifolia (African daisy)

Bassia scoparia f. *trichophylla* (summer cypress, burningbush)

Centaurea cyanus (cornflower, bachelor's button)

Convolvulus tricolor (dwarf morning glory)

Coreopsis tinctoria (calliopsis)

Dimorphotheca sinuata (Cape marigold)

Dorotheanthus bellidiformis (Livingstone daisy)

Eschscholzia californica (California poppy)

Euphorbia marginata (snow-on-the-mountain)

Eustoma exaltatum ssp. *russellianum* (showy prairie gentian, lisianthus)

Felicia spp. (blue marguerites)

Gazania spp. (treasure flowers)

Gomphrena globosa (globe amaranth)

Limonium spp. (statices, sea lavenders)

Lobularia maritima (sweet alyssum)

Mirabilis jalapa (four-o'clock)

Pennisetum setaceum (fountain grass)

Portulaca grandiflora (moss rose)

Salvia spp. (sages)

Sanvitalia procumbens (creeping zinnia)

Senecio cineraria (dusty miller)

Thymophylla tenuiloba (Dahlberg daisy)

Tithonia rotundifolia (Mexican sunflower)

Verbena ×*hybrida* (garden verbena)

---

results. Out in the garden, wind, rain, insects, slugs, compacted soil, and other hazards often combine to reduce seed germination and seedling survival below acceptable levels. There is one advantage to direct-seeding, though. With so many gardening chores, you may welcome the opportunity to get things into the ground and be more or less done with them.

When you're deciding whether to sow annual seeds indoors or out, remember that direct-seeding in the garden works best with larger seeds that are less likely to be washed away or buried too deeply. Also, certain plants like poppies, morning glories, and sweet peas don't like to be disturbed and should always be sown directly where they are to grow. For seed-starting basics, along with information on sowing seed outdoors in the garden, see the Seed Starting and Seed Saving entry.

Self-sowing annuals: Some annuals such as portulaca, spider flower, and sapphire flower may self-sow in the garden after the first year you plant them. Their seeds survive winter and germinate in spring when the soil warms up. If seedlings grow in the right place, you have it made. But more than likely you'll have to transplant these volunteer plants to spots where you want them to grow.

Saving seeds: Certain annuals such as cosmos, sweet peas, and ornamental grasses produce seeds that you can collect and sow the next year. However, most annuals are hybrids, and their seeds may produce plants that are less vigorous—and often less attractive—than their parents.

New plants from cuttings: You can grow many annuals easily from cuttings. A cutting is a portion of the stem that is cut off and rooted to form a new plant. Take cuttings from tender perennials that are grown as annuals. Coleus, begonias, geraniums, fuschias, and impatiens are some common annuals that root easily. Cuttings are a great way to save a favorite color of coleus or rejuvenate an old geranium that has gotten too big for its container. Taking cuttings also saves you money—because they're a virtually free source of new plants for next year's gardens. See the Cuttings entry for directions on taking and rooting cuttings.

Planting Annuals

The first warm days of spring draw droves of gardeners to the nurseries. It's tempting to buy annuals early and get them into the ground. While early shopping may be advisable to ensure the best selection, don't be too hasty. Know the last spring frost date for your area, and don't plant tender annuals out in the garden until after this date. When buying annuals, be aware that plants raised and kept in greenhouses will need to be hardened off before they can be safely planted in the garden unless the weather has already warmed up and temperatures are reliably above the point of frosts and freezes. See the Transplanting entry for directions for hardening off seedlings.

Planting is easy in well-prepared soil. Most annuals perform best in loamy soil that's well

Annuals for Damp Sites

If you're trying to garden in a low area where soil conditions tend to be boggy, don't despair. You can grow some of the most beautiful annuals on a damp site. One of the most striking annuals of all— the towering castor bean—doesn't mind having its roots in a damp location. All the annuals in this list tolerate moist soil. An asterisk (*) indicates a plant that thrives in very moist soil.

Caladium ×hortulanum (caladium)

Catharanthus roseus (Madagascar periwinkle)

Cleome hassleriana (spider flower, cleome)

Exacum affine (Persian violet)

Hibiscus spp. (mallows)

Impatiens walleriana (impatiens)

Limnanthes douglasii (meadowfoam)*

Mimulus ×hybridus (monkey flower)*

Myosotis sylvatica (woodland forget-me-not)*

Ricinus communis (castor bean)

Plectranthus scuttellarioides (coleus)*

Torenia fournieri (wishbone flower)

Viola ×wittrockiana (pansy)

drained and moisture retentive, with plenty of organic matter. See the Soil entry for more information on preparing a bed for annuals.

With cell packs, push out the plant from below into your waiting hand. The roots will usually be

SMART SHOPPING
Annuals

A smart shopper never leaves home without a list—choose the annuals you want to grow and know how many you need before you get to the garden center. Then, before you buy, check the plants carefully, keeping these guidelines in mind:

- Make sure the plants are well rooted. Gently tug on the stem; a plant with damaged or rotten roots will feel loose.

- Choose lush but compact plants.

- Avoid leggy and overgrown plants. The crown (top of the plant) should be no more than three times the size of the container.

- Never buy wilted plants. Underwatering weakens plants and slows establishment.

- Check for insects on the tops and undersides of leaves and along stems.

- Avoid plants with yellow or brown foliage. They have either dried out or have disease problems.

- Don't buy big plants. They are expensive, and smaller plants will quickly catch up once they are planted.

- Buying seeds is easier, since seed quality is usually the same for all companies, but keep these hints in mind.

- Compare costs of seeds from different companies and check seed counts per package.

- Buy seeds by named variety or cultivar so you'll get exactly what you want.

- Check the date on the back of the package. Make sure you buy fresh seeds.

- Mail ordering requires trust, so start small. Order from a few companies, and see which seeds give the best results.

- Be wary of deals and bargains that seem too good to be true.

tightly packed in the ball of soil. You can pop them in the ground as is, and studies have shown that they'll probably do just fine. If roots are very tightly packed, though, don't be afraid to break them up a bit—make shallow cuts along the outside of the rootball with a sharp knife, or loosen the roots with your fingers. This encourages roots to grow out into the surrounding soil and prevents the plants from becoming stunted.

Fast-growing annuals quickly recover from the shock of transplanting.

Remove the rims and bottoms of biodegradable (such as peat, coir, or compressed paper) pots before planting. If there are not too many roots sticking through, remove the whole pot. This allows maximum contact between the garden soil and the potting soil. Slice the outside of peat pellets in at least three places to cut the net that encircles them.

Remove plants from nursery containers one at a time so the rootballs won't dry out from exposure. If the soil in the flats is dry, water the plants before planting. Be careful not to plant too deeply—set out plants at the same depth as they were growing in the flat or pot. Firmly pack the soil around the stem. Water thoroughly and deeply as soon as planting is done. Avoid planting during the heat of the day, or plants may wilt and die before you get water to them.

If you're planting a formal design, you'll want the annuals spaced evenly in your bed or border. Use a yardstick or make a spacing guide by marking a board at 2-inch intervals. Common spacing for most annuals is 10 to 12 inches apart.

Informal designs do not require such careful attention to placement, and spacing can be estimated using the length of your trowel as a guide.

Maintaining Annuals

If you've prepared the soil well before planting, maintenance chores are straightforward. Keep the soil evenly moist throughout the growing season. An inch of water per week is suitable for most garden plants, though some annuals will thrive in drier soils.

Weeding is important in any garden. Turning the soil for planting is likely to uncover weed seeds that will sprout amid your annuals. Regular hand-weeding will ensure that annuals aren't competing with weeds for light, moisture, and fertilizer. Frequent cultivation helps control seedling weeds and breaks up the soil surface, allowing water to penetrate. Put down a light mulch that allows good water infiltration to help conserve water and keep down weeds. Shredded leaves, buckwheat hulls, cocoa shells, and bark mulch are good choices.

Many annual hybrids have been selected for compact growth, reducing the need for pinching/pruning and staking. However, some older cultivars and annuals grown for cut flower production may need staking. Tall plants such as snapdragons and spider flower may need staking, especially in areas with strong winds or frequent thunderstorms. Many annuals benefit from thinning or disbudding. This will increase flower size and stem strength. Removing spent flowers (known as deadheading) keeps annuals in perpetual bloom. If you want to save seed, stop deadheading in late summer to allow ample seed set. Remove yellowing foliage during the growing season to keep down disease. If plants get too dense, remove a few of the inner stems to increase air circulation and light penetration.

Coping with Problems

Like any plants in the garden, annuals can fall prey to pest and disease problems. The best way to avoid problems is with good cultural practices, good maintenance, and early detection. Healthy plants develop fewer problems. Here are a few simple tips.

- Water early in the day to allow plants to dry before evening. This helps prevent leaf spot and other fungal and bacterial problems.
- Don't overwater. Waterlogged soil is an invitation to root-rot organisms.
- Remove old flowers and yellowing foliage to destroy hiding places for pests.
- Remove plants that develop viral infections and dispose of them.
- Never put diseased plants in the compost.
- Early detection of insects means easy control.

Many insects that attack annuals can be controlled by treating the plants with a spray of water from a hose. Treat severe infestations with an appropriate organic spray or dust, following label recommendations. For more on natural pest and disease control, see the Pests and Plant Diseases and Disorders entries.

ANTIRRHINUM

Snapdragon. Summer- and fall-blooming annuals.

Description: Snapdragon flowers may be white, shades of red, yellow, orange, pink, or purple, or bicolored or tricolored. Most snapdragons bear the characteristic "dragon mouth" flowers that earn them their common name, but there are also single, open (penstemon-flowered) and double (azalea-flowered) cultivars. Upright cultivars grow 1 to 3 feet tall, with long flower spikes atop stiff stems bearing small leaves. Dwarf cultivars grow 4 to 12 inches tall with almost equal spread.

How to grow: Sow seeds of tall cultivars indoors 8 to 10 weeks before the last spring frost for bloom beginning in midsummer, or in late spring for plants to winter over in Zones 7 and warmer for bloom late next spring. You also can buy transplants for setting out after hard spring frosts are past. Pinch plants when they are 3 to 4 inches tall for more bloom spikes. Stake them as they grow or pile up to 4 inches of soil around the base of the plants. After bloom, cut plants back halfway, and feed them for a second bloom. Sow seeds of dwarf cultivars indoors a month before the last frost, or sow directly outdoors after the danger of hard frost is past. When sowing snapdragons, press the seeds onto the soil surface and do not cover them, since they need light to germinate.

Snapdragons provide color all season and beyond the first light frosts in fall. They do best in a sunny spot with light, sandy, humus-rich soil with a neutral pH. Rust, a fungal disease, can cause brown spots on leaves, flowers, and stems, followed by wilting and death of the plant. Grow only rust-resistant cultivars.

Landscape uses: Grow the tall cultivars in a cutting garden for superb cut flowers, but don't overlook their use as vertical accents in beds and borders. Dwarf forms make colorful groundcovers and fill gaps left by withering bulb foliage.

APPLE

Malus pumila and other spp.
Rosaceae

The simple pleasure of biting into a freshly picked, homegrown apple is within easy reach for most gardeners. Growing your own apples organically takes a bit of planning and perseverance, but it is worth the modest effort involved. Apple trees come in a range of sizes to suit any yard and make good landscape trees.

Selecting trees: Since apple trees take 3 or more years after planting to bear fruit, it pays to select trees carefully. Here are some factors to consider as you choose from the many tempting cultivars offered by nurseries.

- Apples are subject to many serious diseases such as apple scab. Choose resistant cultivars; new ones are released every year. 'Enterprise' and 'Liberty' are immune to apple scab and resistant to cedar-apple rust, powdery mildew, and fire blight.

- Select trees that fit within your space and keep fruit within your reach. Apple trees can be very large or quite compact, depending on whether they're standard, semidwarf, or dwarf. Standard trees can reach heights of 30 feet and take from 4 to 8 years to bear first fruit. Most home gardeners prefer dwarf and semidwarf trees, which are grafted on a rootstock that keeps them small. These trees grow 6 to 20 feet tall (depending on the rootstock used) and produce full-size apples in just a few years. See "A Range of Rootstocks" on page 26 for more information on advantages and disadvantages of various rootstocks. The final height of your tree will also depend on which cultivar you select, because some cultivars naturally are more compact than others. Growing conditions and pruning and training techniques affect mature height, too. The cultivars 'Haralson' and 'Honeygold' have a strong, horizontal branching habit, making them easy for beginners to prune.

- Apple trees bear fruit on short twigs called spurs, but some cultivars also are available as nonspur types that produce fruit directly along their branches. Spur-bearing cultivars produce more heavily in a single season than nonspur trees do, but nonspur trees may have a longer productive life.

- Most cultivars need to be pollinated by a second compatible apple or crabapple that blooms at the same time. To ensure that you'll get a crop of fruit from your tree, you'll need a pollinizer tree within 40 to 50 feet. Some cultivars, such as 'Mutsu' and 'Jonagold', produce almost no pollen and cannot serve as pollinizers. If you have space for only one tree, you can improve fruit set by grafting a branch of a suitable pollinizer onto the tree or by placing a bucket of blooming branches from a pollinizer under your tree when it is in bloom. Some nurseries sell "combination" trees that have multiple cultivars grafted onto one rootstock and, as a result, are self-fruitful.

- Consider your climate, because some cultivars and rootstocks are hardier than others. Your tree will produce more fruit and live longer if it is suited to your area. Find out which cultivars are common in local orchards—especially those that are growing fruit organically or using least-toxic methods. University apple-breeding programs are good sources of new cultivars that have been developed for particular climates and to withstand common pests and diseases.

- Grow what you like and what you will use. Taste-test a variety of apples from local farmers' markets and orchards before you decide what to grow. The range of aroma, taste, flesh texture, shape, color, and size of apples is far greater than a trip to your local supermarket would ever begin to suggest. Some apples keep longer in storage than others, an important consideration if you hope to enjoy your harvest for months rather than weeks. And certain cultivars are preferred for cider making, while others are considered best for baking. Think about how you will use the apples you grow and choose cultivars to match.

Planting: Buy dormant 1-year-old unbranched grafted trees, sometimes called whips. Plant apples in the early spring in most areas, or in late fall in the Deep South. Space standard trees 20 to 30 feet apart, semidwarfs 15 to 20 feet, and dwarfs 10 to 15 feet. Start training immediately.

The Fruit Trees entry covers many important aspects of growing apples; refer to it for instructions on planting, pruning, and care.

Fertilizing: Healthy apples grow 8 to 12 inches

A Range of Rootstocks

All apple trees you buy from catalogs or nurseries are made by grafting small pieces of the cultivar onto rootstocks.

There are many fine apple rootstocks available. Shop around until you find a nursery that offers cultivars you want grafted onto the rootstock that best suits your growing conditions.

Different rootstocks have a greater or lesser dwarfing effect. Some don't have strong roots and need staking, while others are very strongly rooted. An interstem is a cultivar grafted between the rootstock and fruiting cultivar. Using an interstem can be the most successful way to achieve a dwarfing effect. The following list gives soil, disease, and size information for some common apple rootstocks.

- **Seedling:** Strong roots, full size, but slower to produce fruit

- **M.27:** Good for containers, needs staking; makes a bush 15 percent of full size

- **M.9:** Does well in moist, well-drained soil or even clay, and poorly in light, dry soil, needs staking, susceptible to fire blight, resistant to collar rot; 25 to 35 percent of full size

- **M.26:** Likes well-drained, slightly dry soil, needs staking; 30 to 40 percent of full size

- **Mark:** Doesn't usually need staking, resistant to collar rot and fire blight, very cold-hardy; 30 to 40 percent of full size

- **M.7:** Does well in deep, somewhat wet soil, susceptible to root rot and crown gall; 40 to 60 percent of full size

- **MM.106:** Does well in well-drained soil, susceptible to collar rot and winter damage; 45 to 65 percent of full size

- **MM.111:** Tolerates a wide range of soils, drought resistant, resistant to fire blight and collar rot; 65 to 85 percent of full size

- **Interstem M.9/MM.106:** Strong, well-anchored tree, resistant to collar rot; about 50 percent of full size

- **Interstem M.9/MM.111:** Tolerates extremes in soil drainage, needs staking the first few years; about 35 percent of full size

- **Bud 9:** Resists collar rot, strong rooting; about 30 percent of full size

per year. Have the soil tested if growth is less. Low levels of potassium, calcium, or boron may cause reduced growth and poor-quality fruit.

Apples thrive with a yearly mulch of 2 inches of compost. Growing a cover crop, such as buckwheat or fava beans, under your trees provides weed control, encourages beneficial insects, and helps improve soil structure.

Apples benefit from foliar feeding. Spray seaweed extract when the buds show color, after the petals fall, and again when young fruits reach ½- to 1-inch diameter to improve yields. If soil testing shows calcium is low, spray four more times at 2-week intervals. Gypsum spread on the soil also raises calcium levels.

Pruning: Begin training your trees to a central leader shape immediately after planting. Prune trees yearly, generally in late winter or early spring. Illustrated instructions for the central leader system are on page 226.

Thinning: Once your tree starts bearing, you need to remove excess fruit if you want large and flavorful apples. Thinning also helps prevent trees from bearing fruit every other year. Remove the smaller apples in each cluster before they reach 1 inch in diameter. Leave one fruit per spur on dwarfed trees, two per spur on larger trees. After thinning, remaining fruits should be at least 6 inches apart.

Problems: Insects and diseases can be a major frustration for organic apple growers, but choosing resistant cultivars and using pheromone-baited insect traps makes it easier to grow apples organically.

Common apple pests include apple maggots, codling moths, green fruitworms, leafhoppers, mites, and plum curculios. Small discolored spots and pits on the skin are a sign of apple maggots; in severe infestations, whole fruits are misshapen and gnarled. When codling moth larvae tunnel into fruits, they often leave large, obvious entrance scars. For descriptions and control methods, see page 231.

Aphids, scale, and tarnished plant bugs can cause problems; see page 454 for controls.

Fall webworms and tent caterpillars spin webs in branches and munch on leaves. Remove and destroy webs as soon as you see them. Spray Btk (*Bacillus thuringiensis* var. *kurstaki*) where caterpillars are feeding.

Leaf rollers pull leaves together and spin small webs. They feed on buds, leaves, and developing fruit. Native beneficial insects such as parasitic wasps help control them. Spray dormant oil just before bud break to kill eggs. Monitor with pheromone traps, and spray with Btk or neem before they spin webs; handpick after webs appear.

To help prevent disease problems, burn all prunings as well as fallen leaves and fruit, or put them in sealed containers for disposal with household trash. Here are some common diseases to watch for.

1. Apple scab infects apple trees in many parts of North America. This fungal disease shows up on leaves as olive green spots with rough, feathery edges. The leaf spots later become raised and look velvety. Raised, dark green areas appear on developing apples; the areas turn black as the misshapen fruits mature. Plant resistant cultivars to avoid it. In fall, rake up and dispose of fallen leaves, apples, and prunings where the disease overwinters. Or you can scatter ground limestone on fallen leaves after harvest and then apply a layer of compost. Scab likes damp weather. At the pink bud stage, spray trees with liquid sulfur mixed with spreader sticker as soon as the buds show green, and if the weather is wet, repeat sprays every week until petals fall.

2. Black rot causes small brown spots on fruit, which may expand in zones of brown and black. Black dots appear on the spots, and apples shrivel and mummify. It also causes cankers on twigs. Remove and destroy cankers and mummified fruit. Spray with sulfur to control.

3. Cedar-apple rust causes bright orange spots on leaves and fruit. Fruits may drop prematurely. Eastern red cedar (*Juniperus virginiana*) and other junipers are alternate hosts for the rust fungi; remove any of these trees growing within 300 yards. Also remove susceptible flowering crabapples and hawthorns. Plant resistant cultivars. Spray with sulfur at the

pink bud stage and again 10 days later. Spray again 10 days after petal fall.

4. Powdery mildew covers leaves and shoot tips with a white to pearly gray velvety layer. It kills buds at the shoot tips, causing deformed trees. Plant resistant cultivars. Prune out infected shoots during dry conditions. Spray as for apple scab. Moisture stress increases trees' susceptibility to powdery mildew; keep trees adequately watered throughout the growing season.

5. Bitter pit, small pockets of brownish, corky tissue just under the skin that often only appear after harvest, is due to calcium deficiency. If bitter pit has been a past problem, spray leaves with seaweed extract to help correct it. Or spray foliar calcium in a seaweed base at full bloom and again when petals fall. High nitrogen levels increase the problem.

6. Collar rot is encouraged by winter injury. The cankers form near the soil line and can girdle and kill trees. Choose resistant rootstocks and plant in well-drained soil.

Harvesting: Apples ripen from midsummer through late fall. Early apples tend to ripen unevenly over several weeks. Late apples can all ripen the same day. If you have room for a few trees, you can select cultivars that ripen at different times and pick apples all season.

Taste apples to decide when they are ready to pick. Skin color and the first fallen apple may be good clues, but flavor is the most reliable indicator of ripeness. If they taste starchy, they are still immature. Some apples are ideal picked early. Others improve as they linger on the branch. You may have to experiment to find when each cultivar tastes best.

Lift each fruit in the palm of your hand and twist the stem. If ripe, it will part easily from the twig without tearing. Handle apples with care so they don't get bruised.

Storage: Apples vary greatly in their keeping quality. In general, late apples are better keepers than summer apples. Store apples in a humid refrigerator at temperatures just above 32°F. If you have several trees full of fruit, you might want to invest in an apples-only refrigerator. Remember to check regularly for that one bad apple that really will spoil the barrel.

APRICOT

Prunus armeniaca
Rosaceae

Growing apricots can be challenging, but the sweet, aromatic fruit makes it well worth your effort.

The Fruit Trees entry covers many important aspects of growing apricots and other tree fruits; refer to it for additional information on planting, pruning, and care.

Selecting trees: Most apricots are self-fruitful, but many will bear more fruit when cross-pollinated by a second variety. They are quite winter hardy but tend to break into flower rapidly in spring; frosts often damage the flowers, which will reduce the harvest. Choose varieties carefully, because many don't do well in high-humidity areas; also, the fruit of many cultivars can suffer heat damage in areas that have extremely hot summers.

Late-blooming, disease-resistant cultivars include 'Jerseycot', 'Harcot', and others starting with *Har-*, including 'Harglow'; and 'Puget Gold', 'Sungold', and others ending with *-gold*. Consult your local Cooperative Extension Service for recommended cultivars for your climate.

Planting: Space 20 to 25 feet apart, or a little closer for better pollination.

Pruning: Train apricot trees to an open center shape as shown on page 227. Where diseases are a problem, limit pruning cuts, and slow growth by spreading young limbs.

Thinning: If your tree avoids losing its blooms to late frost, it may set too many fruit, and you'll need to hand-thin in spring or early summer. Remove blossoms or pea-size fruits so the remaining fruit will be 4 to 6 inches apart. Thinning in humid climates also helps prevent disease problems.

Harvesting: Apricots bear fruit 4 to 5 years after planting. Harvest when the skin turns a beautiful orange and the fruit is soft. They dry well in a food dehydrator.

Problems: Apricots suffer from many of the same problems as peaches; see the Peach entry for more information.

AQUILEGIA

Columbine. Spring- and early-summer-blooming perennials.

Description: Unique, elaborate flowers resemble a star within a star. Each flower has five spurs, either long and delicate or short and knobby, curving behind the outer star. Flowers in shades of white, yellow, pink, red, blue, purple, and bicolors are borne above mounded, fanlike, green or blue-green foliage.

Aquilegia canadensis, wild columbine, bears 1- to 1½-inch graceful, hanging, red and yellow flowers on 1- to 2-foot plants. A hummingbird favorite. Self-sows. Zones 3–8.

A. ×hybrida, hybrid columbine, a diverse group that includes many named cultivars and series, most featuring spurred or doubled flowers in a wide range of colors on 1- to 3-foot plants. Zones 3–9.

A. vulgaris, European columbine, has 1-inch, knobby-spurred blooms in shades of pink, blue, and purple on 1- to 3-foot plants. Zones 3–9.

How to grow: Columbines grow best in partial shade and average to rich, well-drained, moisture-retentive soil. They all reseed prolifically. Two or three species or cultivars grown together will hybridize and produce seedlings with many shape and color variations, so keep them apart if you wish to preserve your favorites. Small plants, including self-sown seedlings, transplant well in spring or fall. Mature plants are difficult to transplant. You can try to divide your favorites in late summer, taking care not to disturb the fleshy roots too much, but expect mixed results. Leaf miners often make disfiguring tunnels in the foliage. Cut off and discard infested leaves; new leaves will replace them.

Landscape uses: Mass columbines in borders, woodlands, informal beds, or cottage gardens. Use wild columbine in shady wildflower gardens. Allow self-sown seedlings to fill gaps and cracks in rock gardens and walls.

ARBORVITAE

See *Thuja*

ARTEMISIA

Artemisia, mugwort, sagebrush, wormwood. Shrubby, sometimes woody perennials and annuals used primarily for their foliage.

Description: Rarely grown for their flowers, artemisias make up for their scarcity of showy blooms by producing striking gray to almost silver (or, in the case of *Artemisia lactiflora*, green), usually aromatic foliage.

Artemisia annua, sweet Annie, sweet sagewort, is an annual that is popular in dried flower crafting. Its camphor-scented, fernlike green foliage often is used to form the base of dried arrangements or wreaths. The feathery plants can reach 6½ feet in height and produce clusters of tiny green-gold flowers.

A. lactiflora, white mugwort, flaunts its large but lacy green leaves and summer-blooming 1- to 2-foot-long, creamy flower clusters 6 feet above its quieter cousins. Zones 4–9.

A. ludoviciana, white sage, grows 2 to 4 feet tall and spreads rapidly, bearing coarsely toothed, 4-inch elongated silvery leaves. 'Valerie Finnis' and fine-textured 'Silver King' are reliable garden choices from this species. Zones 3–9.

A. 'Powis Castle', 'Powis Castle' wormwood, grows 2 to 3 feet tall but spreads its branches of very fine gray foliage 3 to 4 feet for a shrubby effect. Zones 6–9.

A. schmidtiana, silver mound artemisia, resembles a 1- to 2-foot-high and -wide rounded pile of silver feathers. 'Ever Goldy' is a gold-leafed selection; 'Nana' is more compact than the species. Zones 3–7.

How to grow: Set out white sage and white mugwort plants or divisions in spring or fall. It's better to start with small plants of 'Powis Castle' and silver mound artemisia in spring, rooting cuttings in summer for overwintering to provide insurance for next year. The gray-foliaged artemisias luxuriate in sunny, very well-drained (or even dry) sites with average to poor soil. Their foliage will turn greenish and/or the plants will flop open in shade, rich soil, and high humidity. Control the tendency of white sage cultivars to spread rampantly by dividing often and by cutting back hard in late spring. White mugwort tolerates some shade and requires evenly moist and fertile soil. It often needs a sturdy support. Sweet Annie is usually grown from seed in the cutting garden.

Landscape uses: Artemisias provide some of the best silver-grays for sunny borders, beds, and large difficult areas, such as near heat-reflecting driveways and swimming pools. Their gray tones can separate and make peace between bold colors in a border or liven up sometimes-monotonous all-pastel combinations. Edge a formal bed with silver mound artemisia or group it in irregular masses in the front of a border. Let 'Powis Castle' cozy up to a rock or hide dying bulb foliage. Giant white mugwort commands a spot at the back of a border. Its gentle foliage and flower colors tone down the bright golds and yellows of tall daisy family members.

ARTICHOKE

Cynara scolymus
Asteraceae

Artichokes are perennials grown for their edible flower buds. They're easy-to-grow favorites in mild, humid areas along the West Coast, but they'll also grow anywhere across the country in Zone 7 or warmer. All it takes is 100 frost-free days, the proper site, and some winter protection or indoor winter storage. In Zone 6 or colder, try early-maturing varieties bred to be grown as an annual crop.

Planting: The large, thistlelike plants can produce well for 3 to 7 years, so give them plenty of room in a sunny area. In hot areas, provide some

Annual Artichokes

By choosing a variety that's been developed for early maturity and starting seeds indoors, you can grow artichokes as an annual crop in areas colder than Zone 7. 'Imperial Star' and 'Colorado Star', a purple artichoke, both have been bred for annual production. Start seeds indoors about 2 months before your last spring frost, keeping the seedlings between 60° and 70°F. Move the plants to a cold frame 2 weeks before the last frost date to provide a chilling session (temperatures below 50°F, but above freezing), which helps induce flower bud formation. Then plant them into a prepared bed in your vegetable garden. Whenever a spell of cool weather is predicted, cover the plants with cloches or row covers to protect them from the cold. Each plant should produce up to eight flower buds.

afternoon shade; hot spells can stunt and toughen the delicious buds.

Many gardeners plant dormant root divisions from nurseries. In short-season areas, seed-grown artichokes are better because they mature earlier. Before sowing, refrigerate seeds in damp peat moss for 2 weeks to promote germination. Plant them ½ inch deep in 4-inch pots, 6 to 8 weeks before the last frost. Place in a warm, south-facing window and keep the soil moist.

Prepare your artichoke bed several weeks before planting (hint—you can put them in your orna-mental perennial garden if you wish—their silvery leaves are quite attractive). Incorporate compost to promote fast growth and tender buds. When the earth warms, dig 6-inch-deep trenches and line with compost. Plant roots 4 inches deep and seedlings at the level at which they grew in the pot. Space 4 to 6 feet apart in rows 7 feet apart. Protect from late frosts.

Growing guidelines: As the weather warms, mulch to keep soil moist, cool, and weed-free. Water frequently when temperatures exceed 75°F; feed monthly with compost tea (see the Compost entry for compost tea brewing instructions).

In Zones 7–8, you may want to try overwintering the plants in the ground. After the first killing frost, strip off the dead foliage. Pile leaves over the plants and cover them with upside-down boxes; top with a thick layer of soil and mulch for insulation. In spring, when the ground has fully thawed, uncover promptly to prevent plants from sprouting too soon.

In most areas, it is best to dig up the roots in fall, brush off the soil, and cut stems 2 to 3 inches above the crown. Store roots in mesh bags in a cool but frost-free place; replant in spring.

Renew plants every 3 years by cutting rooted suckers (offshoots) from parent plants. Replant the suckers in a new bed and water them immediately to get them off to a good start.

Problems: Watch for aphids, caterpillars, slugs, and snails. For more information about aphids and caterpillars, see page 454. See the Slugs and Snails entry for control methods for these pests. To prevent disease, plant in well-drained soil and practice good garden sanitation.

Harvesting: Cut buds before the petals open, with 3 inches of stem. Use quickly for best flavor; buds will keep in refrigeration for up to a month.

ASARUM

Wild ginger. Spring-blooming deciduous or evergreen perennial groundcovers.

Description: Subtle, ½-inch urn-shaped blooms in purplish green and maroon hug the ground and hide beneath spreading mounds or mats of rounded, kidney-shaped leaves.

Asarum canadense, Canadian wild ginger, is a native species that bears dull green, fuzzy, 4-inch-wide deciduous leaves in 10-inch-tall mounds. Zones 3–8.

A. europaeum, European wild ginger, produces 6-inch mounds of dark green, smooth, shiny foliage that is evergreen where winters are mild. Zones 4–8.

Note that edible ginger is a different species: *Zingiber officinale*. It is hardy only to Zone 8 but can be grown in containers.

How to grow: Shallowly cover the creeping rhizomes of potted plants or divisions in spring or early fall. Plant in shade or morning sun in humus-rich, well-drained, acidic (pH 5.5 to 6.5) soil. Water in dry spells.

Landscape uses: Grow in masses between taller perennials and shrubs. Wild gingers are beautiful among large rocks or at the base of a tree.

ASCLEPIAS

Butterfly weed. Summer-blooming perennial.

Description: *Asclepias tuberosa*, butterfly weed, bears ¼-inch, starry, bright orange flowers in dense flattopped clusters 6 inches or wider over 2- to 3-foot erect mounds of 2- to 6-inch dark green elongate leaves. Cultivars are available in shades from red to yellow ('Hello Yellow'), and there is also an excellent seed-grown strain, 'Gay Butterflies', in mixed colors. Zones 3–9.

How to grow: Set out container-grown plants during the growing season or bareroot plants in spring. When dividing clumps in spring, take care not to break the long, brittle older roots. Butterfly weed grows lustily in full sun in average, well-drained soil. It tolerates hot, dry sites.

Landscape uses: Mass in borders and cottage gardens; naturalize in a meadow. With age, single clumps make imposing specimens. Perfect for butterfly gardens, as the blooms attract butterflies and bees, and the foliage forms a natural nursery for caterpillars of monarchs and other gorgeous butterflies.

ASIAN VEGETABLES

As influences of cuisines from around the world continue to shape the tastes of palates across North America, gardeners are increasingly interested in growing vegetables such as edamame, daikon, and bitter melon that were hard to find outside of specialty markets not too long ago. Asian vegetables are not just delicious; many, like yard-long (asparagus) beans and winged beans, are fun to grow and share, too.

Some of the vegetables that feature in Asian-style dishes, including Asian melons, eggplant, cucumbers, and tomatoes, are simply cultivars of familiar veggies and are grown like other cultivars of their species. You can find growing instructions for them in the basic vegetable entries throughout this encyclopedia.

To enjoy growing some of the more unusual Asian vegetables in your garden, refer to the chart (opposite). Most of the major garden seed suppliers offer a selection of Asian vegetable seeds.

Asian Vegetables at a Glance

This chart includes 12 great Asian vegetables that will grow well in North American gardens. For general cultural information for some of these crops, you can also refer to the Bean, Cabbage, Cucumber, Melon, Radish, and Spinach entries as appropriate.

PLANT NAME	DESCRIPTION	CULTURAL REQUIREMENTS	COMMENTS
Bitter melon (*Momordica charantia*), Cucurbitaceae; also called bitter cucumber, balsam melon, balsam pear.	Vigorous cucumber-like vines produce green, white, or orange fruits that resemble wrinkled, bumpy, or warty cucumbers.	Plants need warm weather, full sun, and plenty of moisture. Soak seed for 24 hours before planting indoors to transplant later, or direct-seed outdoors when the soil is warm. Plants need the same care as cucumbers, and they respond well to trellising.	Depending on the cultivar, bitter melons range from quite bitter to mild. All types are used extensively in stir-fries and other Asian dishes.
Bok choy (*Brassica rapa* var. *chinensis*), Brassicaceae; also called bok choi and pak choi.	Attractive cabbage relatives with long, thick white stems and dark green leaves. Leaves and stems are used fresh and cooked.	Sow seed in early spring or fall; grow like cabbage. Space plants 8–12 in. apart in the row and 12 in. between rows. Harvest entire small heads or larger individual leaves.	Young bok choy is delicious in salads, sautéed, or stir-fried. Chopped bok choy leaves are excellent additions to Chinese dishes.
Chinese okra (*Luffa acutangula* and *L. aegyptiaca*), Cucurbitaceae; also known as loofah (luffa) and sponge gourd.	Young fruit, leaves, blossoms, and seeds have culinary value. Mature fruits are dried and skinned to make sponges.	Start seed indoors and transplant outdoors when frost danger has passed. Grow as you would other gourds. Harvest fruit when 6 in. long for eating. For sponges, allow to mature and dry on vines.	Immature fruits ("okra") are sweet. Use like zucchini. Can also be sliced and fried like okra, which, along with the young fruits' appearance, gives the plant its name. Loofah sponges are valued for bathing and general cleaning.
Daikon (*Raphanus sativus* var. *longipinnatus*), Brassicaceae; also called Chinese radish.	Distinctively torpedo-shaped radishes in white and a wide variety of colors. Larger cultivars can reach 2 ft. long and 3 in. wide. The flesh has a crisp texture and flavor.	Sow seed in deep, rich soil and cultivate like a common radish. Space according to cultivar. Read catalog or seed packet for best season to plant. Stores well.	Root adds mildly spicy flavor to salads, Chinese sauces, and stir-fried seafood. Traditionally diced and made into a sweet pickle in Korea. Steam peppery leaves or add to clear soup.

(continued on page 34)

Asian Vegetables at a Glance *(cont.)*

PLANT NAME	DESCRIPTION	CULTURAL REQUIREMENTS	COMMENTS
Edamame (*Glycine max*), Fabaceae; also called green soybean.	Bushy plants bear short, hairy green pods. Harvested and eaten when both pods and beans are still bright green but pods have filled out.	Sow seed 1–2 in. deep in warm soil and full sun; cultivate like a bush bean. Space 6–8 in. apart.	Traditionally boiled and served salted in the pod as an appetizer; split the pods and eat the beans, discarding the pods. Beans can also be shelled and steamed or boiled. Good protein source.
Long bean (*Vigna unguiculata* ssp. *sesquipedalis*), Fabaceae; also called yard-long and asparagus bean.	Pods can reach 38 in. long and are stringless and tender. Red or green pods are borne on 8–10 ft. vines.	Sow seed 1–2 in. deep and 4–6 in. apart after soil has warmed. Provide strong, tall trellises or tepees. Heat and drought tolerant.	Luscious flavor is more like an asparagus-bean cross than pure green bean. Best sautéed or stir-fried rather than boiled or steamed.
Mizuna (*Brassica juncea* var. *japonica*), Brassicaceae; known as Japanese greens or Japanese mustard.	Attractive, compact green plant matures in 35 days, tolerates heat, and is easy to grow. Serrated leaves are used fresh and cooked.	Sow seed in early spring; grow like spinach. Space plants 6 in. apart in the row and 8–10 in. between rows. Make successive plantings. Harvest leaves or entire plant.	Blend with lettuce and crisp vegetables for an unusual, nutritious salad. Stir-fry with Asian vegetables. Add to cream and clear soups for flavor and texture.
Napa cabbage (*Brassica rapa* var. *pekinensis*), Brassicaceae; also known as michihli, tientsin, and Chinese celery cabbage.	Compact, delicately flavored cabbage. Savoyed green leaves on light green stalks reach 13–16 in.	Grow like other cool-weather cabbage. Excellent fall crop. Space 1–1½ ft. between plants in the row with 1½ ft. between rows. Keep well watered. Matures in 75 days.	Use in coleslaw or stir-fry for a crisp texture. Traditionally pickled, as in kimchi. Will store 2–3 months in a cool environment.
Oriental mustards (*Brassica juncea*, *B. rapa* var. *japonica*), Brassicaceae	Attractive red or green loose-leaf or heading mustards. Loose-leaf types mature in 45 days; heading mustards need 60–75 days. Plants tolerate heat and light frost, and they're easy to grow.	Direct-seed in early spring or fall. Space plants 6 in. apart in the row, thinning to 10 in.; use thinnings in salads and stir-fries. Leave 10–12 in. between rows.	Mustards are great for spicing up salads and stir-fries. Greens can also be sautéed, steamed, boiled, and added to soups and fried rice dishes. Heading types are excellent pickled.

PLANT NAME	DESCRIPTION	CULTURAL REQUIREMENTS	COMMENTS
Shungiku (*Glebionis coronaria*), Asteraceae; also known as edible chrysanthemum, and *tongho* in Chinese.	Beautiful yellow single chrysanthemum flowers are edible, but the plant is grown primarily for the edible leaves.	Self-sowing annual. Sow seed in mid-spring; cover lightly with soil. Thin as needed, enjoying thinnings in dishes. Harvest individual leaves or entire plants as needed.	Enjoy leaves and flowers raw in salads, or stir-fry leaves with other Asian vegetables.
Winged bean (*Psophocarpus tetragonolobus*), Fabaceae	Vining plants produce bean pods with 4 winged edges.	Soak seed for 24 hours before planting. Plant outdoors after frost danger has passed and grow as you would other beans. Grow Thai winged bean in the South, Hunan winged bean in the North.	Cook leaves like spinach. Winged pods are delicious fresh or cooked and are high in protein. Sauté pods and roots alone or stir-fry with other Asian vegetables; also good in soup. Roots have a nutty flavor.
Winter melon (*Benincasa hispida*), Cucurbitaceae; also known as wax gourd, Chinese preserving melon, and white gourd.	The oblong melons are 10–12 in. long and weigh 10–15 lbs.	Start seed indoors and transplant outdoors when frost danger has passed. Grow as you would any vining melon.	Traditionally, the waxy rind is carved, and the melon hollowed out, then filled with vegetables, meat, and broth. It is steamed before serving.

ASPARAGUS

Asparagus officinalis

Asparagaceae

Asparagus is a perennial vegetable grown for its delicious young shoots. Rich in B vitamins, vitamin C, calcium, and iron, asparagus is one of the first crops to be harvested in the spring. Fresh-picked spears from the garden are far more tender and tasty than store-bought ones.

Asparagus thrives in any area having winter ground freezes or dry seasons. The mild, wet regions of Florida and the Gulf Coast are about the only places where it's difficult to grow.

Planting: Select and prepare your asparagus bed with care; this crop will occupy and make good use of the same spot for 20 years or more. It can tolerate some shade, but full sun produces more vigorous plants and helps minimize the risk of disease. Asparagus does best in lighter soils that warm up quickly in spring and drain well; standing water will quickly rot the roots. Prepare a planting bed about 4 feet wide by removing all perennial weeds and roots and digging in plenty of aged manure or compost.

Asparagus plants are monoecious—each individual plant is either male or female. Some varieties of asparagus, such as 'Jersey Knight' and 'Jersey Giant', produce all male or primarily male plants, so they're more productive—male plants yield more harvestable shoots because they don't have to invest energy in producing seeds. Choose an all-male variety if high yield is your primary goal. If you like to experiment, you may also want to grow an heirloom variety or a purple-stalked variety like 'Purple Passion'. With an all-male variety, 25 plants are usually adequate for a household of four; plant double that amount for standard varieties. (Ardent asparagus lovers recommend tripling these quantities.)

Planting asparagus. Asparagus crowns push toward the surface over time, so they're planted in trenches several inches deep. To start with, cover the crowns with only 2 to 3 inches of soil.

Starting asparagus from 1-year-old crowns gives you a year's head start over seed-grown plants. Two-year-old crowns are not usually a bargain. They tend to suffer more from transplant shock and won't produce any faster than 1-year-old crowns. Buy crowns from a reputable nursery that sells fresh, firm, disease-free roots. Plant them immediately if possible; otherwise, wrap them in slightly damp sphagnum moss until you are ready to plant.

To plant asparagus crowns, dig trenches 12 inches wide and 6 inches deep (8 inches in sandy soil) down the center of the prepared bed. Soak the crowns in compost tea for 20 minutes before planting. See the Compost entry for instructions for making compost tea. Place the crowns in the trenches 1½ to 2 feet apart; top them with 2 to 3 inches of soil. Two weeks later, add another inch or two of soil. Continue adding soil periodically until the soil is slightly mounded above surface level to allow for settling.

Growing guidelines: Apply mulch to smother weeds, which compete with the young spears and

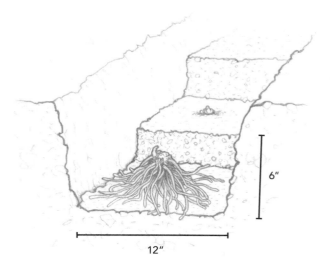

Planting asparagus. Asparagus crowns push toward the surface over time, so they're planted in trenches several inches deep. To start with, cover the crowns with only 2–3 inches of soil.

reduce yields. Carefully remove any weeds that do appear. Water regularly during the first 2 years after planting. As asparagus matures, it crowds out most weeds and sends long, fleshy roots deep into the earth, so watering is less critical. Fertilize in spring and fall with liquid fertilizer (such as compost tea) or by side-dressing with compost or a balanced organic fertilizer.

Leave winter-killed foliage, along with straw or other light mulch, on the bed to provide winter protection. Remove and destroy the fernlike foliage before new growth appears in spring; it can harbor diseases and pest eggs.

If you want to grow white asparagus, which has a slightly milder flavor than green asparagus, blanch the spears by heaping up soil or mulch over the bed before they emerge.

Problems: Healthy asparagus foliage is neces-

Starting Asparagus from Seed

It takes patience to start your asparagus patch from seed, but there are advantages to gain from the extra wait. Seed-grown plants don't suffer from transplant trauma like nursery-grown roots, and you can buy a whole packet of seed for the same price you'll pay for one asparagus crown. Most seed-grown asparagus plants eventually outproduce those started from roots. Growing from seed also allows you to selectively discard female plants and plant an all-male bed, no matter what variety you choose to grow.

In the North, start seedlings indoors in late February or early March. Sow single seeds in peat pots, place the pots in a sunny window, and use bottom heat to maintain the temperature of the mix in the pots at 77°F. When the seeds sprout, lower the temperature to 60° to 70°F. Once the danger of frost is past, plant the seedlings (which should be about 1 foot tall) 2 to 3 inches deep in a nursery bed.

When tiny flowers appear, observe them with a magnifying glass. Female flowers have well-developed, three-lobed pistils; male blossoms are larger and longer than female flowers. Weed out all female plants. The following spring, transplant the males to their permanent bed.

sary for good root and spear production. Asparagus beetles, which chew on spears in spring and attack summer foliage, are the most prevalent problem. The ¼-inch-long, metallic blue-black pests have three white or yellow spots on their backs. They lay dark eggs along the leaves, which hatch into light gray or brown sluglike larvae with black heads and feet. Control by handpicking; spray seriously infested plants with insecticidal soap. These methods also control the 12-spotted asparagus beetle, which is reddish brown with six black spots on each wing cover. Asparagus miner is another foliage-feeding pest; it makes zigzag tunnels on the stalks. Destroy any infested ferns.

Avoid asparagus rust, which produces reddish brown spots on the stems and leaves, by planting resistant cultivars. Minimize damage from fusarium wilt, which causes spears, leaves, and stems to be small with large lesions at or below the soil line,

by purchasing disease-free roots and using good garden sanitation. Crown rot causes spears to turn brown near the soil line. Prevent crown rot by planting in raised beds, maintaining good drainage, and keeping soil pH above 6.0.

If your asparagus bed does become infected by disease organisms, your best option is to start a new bed in a distant part of the garden, using newly purchased or grown plants.

If young spears turn brown and become soft or withered, they may have been injured by frost. Cover spears with mulch or newspaper when freezing nights are predicted.

Harvesting: Don't harvest any spears during the first 2 years that plants are in the permanent bed. They need to put all their energy into establishing deep roots. During the third season, pick the spears over a 4-week period, and by the fourth year, extend your harvest to 8 weeks. In early spring, harvest spears every third day or so; as the weather warms, you might have to pick twice a day to keep up with production. Cut asparagus spears with a sharp knife or snap off the spears at, or right below, ground level with your fingers.

ASTER

Aster, Michaelmas daisy. Late summer- and fall-blooming perennials.

Description: Most asters bear clouds of daisylike, ½- to 3-inch-wide flowers in shades of white, pink, red-violet, blue, purple, and lavender. The bushy, mounded to upright plants have uninteresting elongated leaves.

Aster ×frikartii, Frikart's aster, produces 2- to 3-inch yellow-centered blue daisies on 2- to 3-foot open, airy mounds beginning in midsummer. 'Mönch' is an outstanding cultivar with deep blue flowers. Zones 5–9.

A. novae-angliae (reclassified as *Symphyotrichum novae-angliae*), New England aster, sports smaller (to 1½ inches) but more numerous violet blooms in late summer. Flowers are borne in dense clusters atop upright, arching stems from 3 to 6 feet tall. Cultivars offer nearly the entire color range found among asters. 'Andenken an Alma Pötschke' (salmon to cerise flowers) and 'Purple Dome' are two popular cultivars. Zones 3–9.

A. novi-belgii (reclassified as *Symphyotrichum novi-belgii*), New York aster, Michaelmas daisy, blooms in late summer with flowers usually 1 inch across on plants ranging from foot-tall mounds to impressive 6-foot giants. Colors among the many cultivars are similar to those of New England asters. Zones 3–9.

Many of the plants once included in the genus *Aster* have been reclassified into new genera, the

Try Tatarian Aster

Need something impressive for your fall garden? Tatarian aster, *Aster tataricus* (sometimes sold as Tartarian aster), bears pyramidal, 1- to 2-foot clusters of small lavender flowers atop upright plants reaching 8 feet tall. Give it plenty of room, though, because the lowest leaves may grow 1½ feet long, and it spreads fast in sunny spots with warm, light soil (especially in the South), quickly filling large areas. Divide every other year or let it romp. Zones 3–8.

most common of these being *Eurybia* (primarily woodland species), and *Symphotrichum* (the Michaelmas daisies). Popular species and cultivars likely still will be found under the name of *Aster*, but seek help from growers' Web sites or nursery staff if you can't find your favorites.

How to grow: Set out new plants or divisions in early spring, or in fall after bloom, in a sunny, well-drained but evenly moist spot with average fertility. Most asters resent drought and will show their displeasure by dropping their lower leaves prematurely, by not reaching their full height, and by blooming over a briefer season. On the other hand, avoid soggy soil, especially for Frikart's aster, or it won't survive winter. Pinch back all but the dwarf forms in early summer so they'll branch out and produce more blooms, though they'll flower slightly later than if left unpinched. If not pruned, the taller asters tend to fall over as they bloom, so stake them or allow them to arch over and through other plants. Less-fertile soil promotes slightly shorter, sturdier growth, as does dividing clumps every 2 to 3 years. To minimize powdery mildew problems, grow asters in a sunny, open site with good air circulation and even soil moisture. Cultivars of New England asters (*Symphyotrichum*) tend to be mildew resistant.

Landscape uses: Mass asters in the front and middle of mixed borders, or devote an entire bed to early, midseason, and late-blooming cultivars. Their billowy habit and masses of flowers are mainstays of the autumn garden. Their cool flower colors contrast beautifully with the warm yellows, golds, and reds of chrysanthemums, goldenrods, late-season annuals, and fall foliage. New England asters bring rich color to moist meadows and other naturalized sites. Asters and ornamental grasses are an excellent combination. Or for a cool, sophisticated look, combine Frikart's asters with silver-leaved artemisias and pink- to rust-flowered 'Autumn Joy' sedum (*Hylotelephium* 'Herbstfreude').

ASTILBE

Astilbe, false spirea. Summer-blooming perennials.

Description: Astilbes have tiny, fuzzy flowers in many shades of white, pink, and red. Flowers are borne in open or dense plumes above clumps of shiny, attractive, often red-tinged fernlike foliage.

Astilbe ×*arendsii*, Arendsii hybrid astilbes, include the entire color range on plants growing from 1½ to 4 feet tall. Choice cultivars include white 'Bridal Veil', dark cherry-red 'Fanal', and lilac-purple 'Amethyst'. Zones 3–8.

A. chinensis, Chinese astilbe, is 1 to 3 feet tall. *A. chinensis* var. *pumila* bears deep pink flowers on stiffly upright stems to 1 foot tall above low, tight foliage. *A. chinensis* var. *taquetii*, the giant of the group, bears foot-long, narrow plumes that rise to

4 feet above large, imposing foliage. Its best-known cultivar, 'Superba', bears clear pink flowers. Zones 3–8.

Astilbe 'Sprite', a hybrid of *A. simplicifolia* with soft pink flowers above low-growing, glossy green foliage, was named the Perennial Plant of the Year for 1994 by the Perennial Plant Association. Zones 3–8.

How to grow: Plant or divide astilbes during spring or fall, barely covering the new pink shoots. Astilbes grow best in partial shade (except in areas with cool summers, where they take full sun) in moist, slightly acid, humus-rich soil. Provide extra water in drier soils to prevent leaf scorch. Chinese astilbe tolerates drier soils better than most. Scatter a little organic fertilizer around the crowns in spring to help them increase steadily. Handpick or trap slugs and snails, which abound in the moist conditions astilbes prefer.

Landscape uses: Grow astilbes in large drifts in semishady borders, woodlands, low spots, and along streams. Astilbes look magnificent at the base of a wall or among large rocks. Smaller types, especially *A. chinensis* var. *pumila* and its cultivars, are ideal for the front of borders, in rock gardens, or as edgings. Leave spent flower spikes on the plants for winter interest.

AVOCADO

Persea americana
Lauraceae

Avocado trees are attractive, broad-leaved evergreens. The delicious yellow-green flesh of the fruits is rich in healthy fats, fiber, and B vitamins. They are easy to grow outdoors in Zones 9–11, including where they are grown commercially—California, Florida, and Texas. Avocado trees also make attractive houseplants but are unlikely to bear fruit indoors.

Selecting trees: Mature avocado trees reach 15 to 45 feet tall and spread as wide as they are high, so give them plenty of space. The fruits of Mexican types have dark, rough skins; the plants are hardy to about 22°F. Guatemalan × West Indian hybrids' fruits have smooth, green skins and the plants are less hardy. Not all avocado cultivars are self-fertile; check pollination requirements before you plant. If your neighbors also grow avocados, chances are their trees will pollinate yours.

Planting: Purchase a grafted tree of a named cultivar and plant it slightly higher than it was growing in the original container. If space is an issue or if you will be growing your avocado in a container, select a dwarf cultivar. Choose a location with full sun and very well-drained soil with a pH of 5.5 to 6.5. If you have poor drainage, plant your tree in a large raised bed or mound. Avoid windy locations, as the trees are prone to breakage.

Care: Water young trees weekly, mature trees every other week, or often enough to prevent wilting. If your water contains a lot of salts, flood the tree every fourth watering to flush out built-up salts and lessen possible root damage. Apply a thick layer of organic mulch out to the drip line to conserve water and protect roots. Keep the mulch 1 foot away from the trunk.

Avocados don't require much fertilizer. If a young tree is not growing vigorously, an application of compost in early spring to midsummer can provide a needed boost. If new leaves yellow, have the soil tested and amend as indicated; spray with foliar fertilizer such as compost tea or liquid seaweed for quicker results. See the Compost entry for compost tea brewing instructions.

Pruning: Avocados need very little pruning. Pinch back upright shoots to control the height. Other than that, limit pruning to damaged branches, as heavy pruning will reduce yields and expose the trunk to sunburn damage.

Problems: The most common avocado problem is root rot. Symptoms include no new growth, very small fruit, and leaf yellowing and wilting. In advanced cases, a tree may die or survive in poor health for many years. Prevent root rot by providing good drainage and not overwatering.

Avocados are sometimes attacked by fungal diseases such as anthracnose, scab, and powdery mildew that thrive in high humidity. Control fungal diseases by spacing trees widely and trimming back surrounding trees to increase sunlight.

Insects do very little damage to avocado trees unless the tree is weakened by disease.

Some cultivars naturally tend to bear fruit lightly, then heavily, in alternate years.

Harvesting: Grafted avocados start to bear in about 3 years. Season of ripening varies depending on cultivar and location. Avocados stay hard on the tree and soften only after they are picked. They are ready to harvest when they reach full size and the skin starts to change color. Pick one and let it sit indoors for a day or two. If the stem end doesn't shrivel or turn dark, you can pick others the same size. You don't need to pick them all at once, but don't leave them on the tree too long or they'll begin to lose flavor.

Harvest avocados by cutting the fruit from the tree, leaving a small piece of stem attached. Handle carefully to avoid bruising. Avocados are ready to eat when they yield slightly when squeezed.

AZALEA

See *Rhododendron*

B

BABY'S BREATH

See *Gypsophila*

BALLOON FLOWER

See *Platycodon*

BAMBOO

For many people, the word *bamboo* conjures up images of dense thickets of rampant, aggressively spreading canes. While this is true of many types of bamboo, some species are not invasive. Evergreen members of the grass family, bamboos range from petite miniatures to massive giants. There are more than 100 species of bamboo, found from the tropics to mountaintops. While most bamboos are tropical or subtropical, there are hardy bamboos that can survive temperatures of −0° to −20°F.

There are two main types of bamboos: running and clumping. Running types send out far-reaching rhizomes and can colonize large areas. Control running bamboos with 3- to 4-foot-deep barriers of sheet metal or concrete, or routinely cut off new shoots at ground level. Clumping types form tight clusters that slowly increase in diameter.

As they grow, bamboos store food and energy in roots and rhizomes. At the start of the growth cycle, the canes grow out of the ground rapidly to their maximum height. The leaves and canes produce food, which is stored in the rhizomes for the next growth cycle. Young bamboos usually are slow to establish, while older plants have more stored food and therefore grow more quickly.

Plant or divide bamboos in spring. Most enjoy full sun or partial shade. Bamboos tolerate a range of soil conditions as long as adequate moisture is present, but most fare poorly in boggy or mucky soils. They are seldom bothered by pests. A carefully chosen bamboo is a beautiful addition to any garden. Low-growing types, such as pygmy bamboo (*Pleioblastus* spp.), are ideal as groundcovers or for erosion control. Small clumping bamboos,

Five Beautiful Bamboos

Here are five reliable and attractive bamboos to consider for use in home landscapes.

Bambusa multiplex **'Alphonse Karr' (hedge bamboo):** Up to 20 feet tall; good for containers; clump-forming habit. Zones 8–10.

Fargesia dracocephala **'Rufa':** 8 feet tall; vigorous, cold-hardy, and wind-tolerant; clump-forming habit. Zones 5–9.

Phyllostachys nigra **(black bamboo):** Up to 30 feet tall; jet black canes with green foliage and a running growth habit. Zones 7–10.*

Pleioblastus viridistriatus **(dwarf greenstripe bamboo):** 3 to 4 feet tall; variegated foliage, running growth habit. Zones 5–10.*

Yushania boliana, **also sold as** *Borinda boliana:* Up to 30 feet tall; heat-tolerant, noninvasive timber bamboo; clump-forming habit. Zones 7–10.

*Consult local ordinances before planting uncontained running bamboo species in your landscape; some municipalities restrict bamboo plantings in the wake of conflicts resulting from rampant bamboos that have outgrown their legal boundaries.

for example some of the species and cultivars of *Fargesia*, can serve as delicate accents; taller species, such as clumping *Yushania boliana*, make

good screens or windbreaks. Some, like black bamboo (*Phyllostachys nigra*), make excellent specimens for large tubs, both indoors and outdoors, where their running habit can be contained.

Because it grows rapidly, a bamboo makes a good candidate for creating a carbon sink—a planting that stores carbon and is intended to help counteract the increase in CO_2 in the atmosphere. See the Carbon Sinks entry for details on this practice.

BAPTISIA

Baptisia, false indigo, wild indigo. Late-spring-blooming perennials.

Description: *Baptisia australis*, blue false indigo, bears 1-inch pealike purple-blue flowers in loose, 1-foot spikes. The 3- to 4-foot, dense, bushy plants bear handsome 3-inch, cloverlike, gray-green leaves. Handsome black 2- to 3-inch seedpods dry well and rattle when ripe. Zones 3–9.

How to grow: Set out small plants or divisions in spring. These long-lived plants won't need division for many years. Move self-sown seedlings when small. Grow in sunny, well-drained, average soil; allow plenty of room. Partial shade and rich soil promote weaker stems that need staking. Baptisias are drought tolerant and pest resistant.

Landscape uses: Feature single specimens in a border, or mass several baptisias as a foliage background for other plants. Allow plants to naturalize in a meadow.

BARBERRY

See *Berberis*

BASIL

Ocimum basilicum
Labiatae

Description: Sweet basil is a bushy annual, 1 to 2 feet high, with glossy opposite leaves and spikes of white flowers. Basil leaves are used in cooking, imparting their anise (licorice) flavor to dishes. Many cultivars are available with different nuances of flavor, size, and appearance, including selections with cinnamon, clove, lemon, and lime overtones, as well as purple-leaved types such as 'Dark Opal' and 'Red Rubin'. One of the most popular herbs in the garden, basil adds fine flavor to tomato dishes, salads, and pesto.

How to grow: Plant seed outdoors when frosts are over and the ground is warm, start indoors in individual pots, or buy plants in late spring to early summer. If you start seeds indoors, a heat mat or other method of warming the soil is helpful in encouraging the seeds of this warmth-loving herb to germinate. Plant in full sun, in well-drained soil enriched with compost or aged manure. Space large-leaved cultivars, sometimes called lettuce-leaf basils, 1½ feet apart and small-leaved types such as 'Spicy Globe' 1 foot apart. Basil needs ample water. Mulch to retain moisture after the soil has warmed. Pinch plants frequently to encourage bushy growth, and pinch off flower heads regularly so plants put their energy into foliage production.

Grow a few basil plants in containers so you can bring them indoors before fall frost. Or make a second sowing outdoors in June to have small plants to pot up and bring indoors for winter. As frost nears, you can also cut off some end shoots of the plants in the garden and root them in water, to be potted later.

Basil can be subject to various fungal diseases, including fusarium wilt, gray mold, and black spot, as well as damping-off in seedlings. Avoid these problems by waiting to plant outside until the soil has warmed and by not overcrowding plants. (If fungal disease strikes, refer to the Plant Diseases and Disorders entry for organic controls.) Japanese beetles may skeletonize plant leaves; control pests by handpicking.

Harvesting: Begin using the leaves as soon as the plant is large enough to spare some. Collect from the tops of the branches, cutting off several inches. Handle basil delicately so as not to bruise and blacken the leaves.

You can air-dry basil in small, loose bunches, but freezing is the best way to preserve its flavor. To freeze basil, puree washed leaves in a blender or food processor, adding water as needed to make a thick but pourable puree. Pour the puree into ice-cube trays and freeze, then pop them out and store them in labeled freezer bags to use as needed in sauces, soups, and pesto. Pesto (a creamy mixture of pureed basil, garlic, grated cheese, and olive oil) will keep for a long time in the refrigerator with a layer of olive oil on top.

Uses: This widely used herb enhances the flavor of tomatoes, peppers, and eggplant. It is great in spaghetti sauce, pizza sauce, and ratatouille. It's also excellent for fish or meat dishes, combining well with lemon thyme, parsley, chives, or garlic. Try it in stir-fries or in vegetable casserole dishes. Fresh basil leaves are delicious in salads. Try lemon- and lime-scented cultivars in fresh fruit salads and compotes. Basil is also a staple ingredient in Thai and Vietnamese cuisine; cultivars such as 'Siam Queen' give the most authentic flavor to these dishes. Basil vinegars are good for salad dressings; those made with purple basils are colorful as well as tasty.

BATS

Once feared because of their nocturnal, swooping, hunting habits, bats are helpful allies in combating garden and agricultural pests without toxic pesticides. One bat can catch a thousand insects in a single night. If you put up a bat house and attract a colony to your yard, they'll consume literally millions of pests with no further input from you. What a deal!

In the past, bats were the victims of a lot of bad press. They supposedly tangled in women's hair, sucked blood, and spread rabies. The truth is that bats have no interest in human hair, male or female. North American bats eat insects and sometimes fruit, but no blood. As for rabies, scientists once blamed bats for much of the spread of the disease but have since decided that was an overreaction. Only about 1 percent of bats get the disease themselves, and far fewer pass it on to humans. In 30 years of record keeping, only 12 to 15 cases of human rabies have been traced to bats. Most of these incidents were avoidable: The victim was not attacked by a swooping bat but instead picked up a diseased bat flapping around on the ground. (A grounded bat is a sick bat.) To avoid a bite, don't handle bats barehanded. If you must move them, use a shovel.

Of the nearly 1,000 bat species worldwide, 46 species are native to North America. The little brown bat, a common US species, eats moths, caddis flies, midges, beetles, and mosquitoes. Other bats are important plant pollinators, including such southwestern species as the long-nosed bat and Mexican long-tongued bat.

The best way to attract bats is to put up a bat house, a wooden box like a flattened birdhouse with an entrance slot in the bottom. You can buy

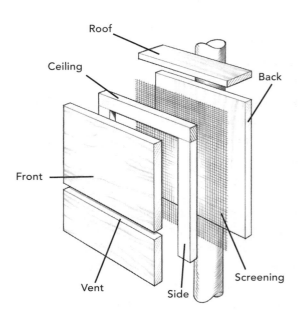

Bat house. From the outside, bat houses look like long, flat birdhouses without the round entrance holes. But instead of using a door in front, bats fly in through the bottom. They cling to the partitions inside to roost.

bat houses from stores, catalogs, and Web sites that sell outdoor bird supplies.

If you're handy, it's easy to make your own. Make the entrance slot of your homemade bat house ¾ inch wide. Scribe grooves in the inside back wall about ¹⁄₁₆ inch deep and ½ inch apart so the bats can hang on, or attach plastic mesh screening to the inside back wall. Fasten the house 15 to 20 feet above the ground on the east or southeast side of a building or the trunk of a shade tree. Then be patient. If there are many roosts available in the neighborhood, bats may take several years to move into yours.

To learn more about bats and bat houses, check out batcon.org, the Web site of Bat Conservation International.

BEAN

Phaseolus spp. and other genera
Fabaceae

Dried or fresh, shelled or whole, beans are a favorite crop for home vegetable gardens. They are easy to grow, and the range of plant sizes means there is room for beans in just about any garden. Among the hundreds of varieties available, there are types that thrive in every region of the country.

Types: All beans belong to the legume family. Snap and lima beans belong to the genus *Phaseolus*, while mung, adzuki, garbanzo, fava, and others belong to different genera. In general, there are two main bean types: shell beans, grown for their protein-rich seeds, which are eaten both fresh and dried; and snap beans, cultivated mainly for their pods.

The two groups are further divided according to growth habit. Bush types are generally self-supporting. Pole beans have twining vines that require support from stakes, strings, wires, or trellises. Runner beans are similar to pole beans, although runners need cooler growing conditions. Half-runners, popular in the South, have a growth habit somewhere in between pole and bush beans.

Adzuki beans, which come from Japan, are extra rich in protein. The small plants produce long, thin pods that are eaten like snap beans. When mature at 90 days, each pot contains 7 to 10 small, nutty-tasting, maroon-colored beans that are tasty fresh or dried.

Black beans, also called black turtle beans, have jet black seeds and need approximately 3 months of warm, frost-free days to mature. The dried beans are popular for soups and stews. Most are sprawling, half-runner-type plants; 'Midnight' black turtle bean is an improved selection with an upright growth habit.

Black-eyed peas, also called cowpeas or southern peas, are cultivated like beans. They need long summers with temperatures averaging between 60° and 70°F. Use fresh pods like snap beans, shell and cook the pods and seeds together, or use them like other dried beans.

Fava beans, also known as broad, horse, or cattle beans, are one of the world's oldest cultivated foods. They are second only to soybeans as a source of vegetable protein, but they're much more common as a garden crop in Europe than in the United States. You won't find a wide range of varieties in most seed catalogs, unless you choose a seed company that specializes in Italian vegetables. Unlike other beans, favas thrive in cold, damp weather. They take about 75 days to mature. Fava beans need to be cooked and shucked from their shells and the individual seed skins peeled off before eating.

Garbanzo beans, also called chickpeas, produce bushy plants that need 65 to 100 warm days. When dried, the nutty-tasting beans are good baked or cooked and chilled for use in salads.

Great Northern white beans are most popular dried and eaten in baked dishes. In short-season areas, you can harvest and eat them as fresh shell beans in only 65 days. Bush-type Great Northerns are extremely productive.

Horticultural beans are also known as shell, wren's egg, bird's egg, speckled cranberry, or October beans. Both pole and bush types produce a big harvest in a small space and mature in 65 to 70 days. Use the very young, colorful, mottled pods like snap beans, or dry the mature, nutty, red-speckled seeds.

Kidney beans require 100 days to mature but are easy to grow. Use these red, hearty-tasting dried seeds in chili, soups, stews, and salads.

Lima beans, including types called butter beans or butter peas, are highly sensitive to cool weather; plant them well after the first frost. Bush types take 60 to 75 days to mature. Pole types require 90 to 130 days, but the vines grow quickly and up to 12 feet long. Limas are usually green, but there are some speckled types. Use either fresh or dried in soups, stews, and casseroles.

Mung beans need 90 frost-free days to produce long, thin, hairy, and edible pods on bushy 3-foot plants. Eat the small yellow seeds fresh, dried, or as bean sprouts.

Pinto beans need 90 to 100 days to mature. These large, strong plants take up a lot of space if not trained on poles or trellises. Use fresh like a snap bean, or dry the seeds.

Scarlet runner beans produce beautiful climbing vines with scarlet flowers. The beans mature in about 70 days. Cook the green, rough-looking pods when they are very young; use the black-and-red-speckled seeds fresh or dried.

Snap beans are also known as green beans. While many growers still refer to snap beans as string beans, a stringless cultivar was developed in the 1890s, and few cultivars today must be stripped of their strings before you eat them. Most cultivars mature in 45 to 60 days. This group also includes the flavorful haricots verts, also called filet beans, and the mild wax or yellow beans. For something unusual, try the yard-long asparagus bean, popular in Asian cuisines. Its rampant vines can produce 3-foot-long pods, though they taste best when 12 to 15 inches long. Once the pods have passed their tender stage, you can shell them, too.

Soldier beans, whose vinelike plants need plenty of room to sprawl, are best suited to cool, dry climates. The white, oval-shaped beans mature in around 85 days. Try the dried seeds in baked dishes.

Garden cultivars of soybeans, also called edamame, are ready to harvest when the pods are plump and green. Boil or steam the pods, then shell and eat the seeds. Or you can let the pods mature and harvest as dry beans. Try 'Tohya', 'Butterbean', and other varieties. The bush-type plants need a 3-month growing season but are tolerant of cool weather. Seek early cultivars such as 'Envy' for areas with a short growing season.

Planting: In general, beans are very sensitive to frost. (The exception is favas, which require a long, cool growing season; sow them at the same time you plant peas.) Most beans grow best in air temperatures of 70° to 80°F, and soil temperature should be at least 60°F. Soggy, cold soil will cause the seeds to rot. Beans need a sunny, well-drained area rich in organic matter. Lighten heavy soils with extra compost to help seedlings emerge.

Plan on roughly 10 to 15 bush bean plants or three to five hills of pole beans per person. A 100-foot row produces about 50 quarts of beans. Beans are self-pollinating, so you can grow cultivars side by side with little danger of cross-pollination. If you plan to save seed from your plants, though, separate cultivars by at least 50 feet.

Bean seeds usually show about 70 percent germination, and the seeds can remain viable for 3 years. Don't soak or presprout seeds before sowing. If you plant in an area where beans haven't grown before, help ensure that your bean crop will fix nitrogen in the soil by dusting the seeds with a bacterial inoculant powder for beans and peas (inoculants are available from garden centers and seed suppliers).

Plant your first crop of beans a week or two after the date of the last expected frost. Sow the seeds 1 inch deep in heavy soil and 1½ inches deep in light soil. Firm the earth over them to ensure soil contact.

Plant most bush cultivars 3 to 6 inches apart in rows 2 to 2½ feet apart. They produce the bulk of their crop over a 2-week period. For a continuous harvest, make plantings at 2-week intervals until about 2 months before the first killing frost is expected.

Bush beans usually don't need any support unless planted in a windy area. In that case, prop them up with brushy twigs or a strong cord around stakes set at the row ends or in each corner of the bed.

Pole beans are more sensitive to cold than bush beans. They also take longer to mature (10 to 11 weeks), but they produce about three times the yield of bush beans in the same garden space and keep on bearing until the first frost. In the North, plant pole beans at the beginning of the season—usually in May. If your area has longer seasons, you may be able to harvest two crops. To calculate if two crops are possible, note the number of days to maturity for a cultivar, and count back from the average first fall frost date, adding a week or so to be on the safe side.

Plant pole beans in single rows 3 to 4 feet apart or double rows spaced 1 foot apart. Sow seeds 2 inches deep and 10 inches apart. Provide a trellis or other vertical support at planting or as soon as the first two leaves of the seedlings open. Planting pole beans around a tepee support is a fun project to try if you're gardening with children, but it will be more difficult to harvest the beans than from a simple vertical trellis.

Growing guidelines: Bush beans germinate in about 7 days, pole beans in about 14. It's important to maintain even soil moisture during this period and also when the plants are about to blos-

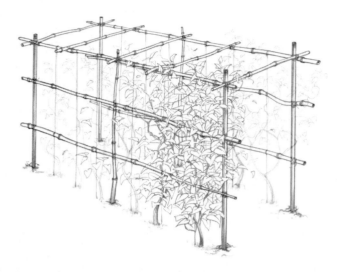

Bean trellis. Growing pole and runner beans on a trellis produces a clean, high-yielding crop in a small space. Use sturdy wooden or metal stakes for the uprights and bamboo poles for the crosspieces.

som. If the soil dries out at these times, your harvest may be drastically reduced. Water deeply at least once a week when there is no rain, being careful not to hose off any of the blossoms on bush beans when you water. Apply several inches of mulch (after the seedlings emerge) to conserve moisture, reduce weeds, and keep the soil cool during hot spells (high heat can cause blossoms to drop off).

Beans generally don't need extra nitrogen for good growth because the beneficial bacteria that live in nodules on bean roots help to provide nitrogen for the plants. To speed up growth, give beans—particularly long-bearing pole beans or heavy-feeding limas—a midseason side-dressing of compost or kelp extract solution.

Problems: Soybeans, adzuki, and mung beans are fairly resistant to pests. Insect pests that attack other beans include aphids, cabbage loopers, corn earworms, European corn borers, Japanese beetles, and—the most destructive of all—Mexican bean beetles. You'll find more information on these pests in the chart on page 454.

Leaf miners are tiny yellowish fly larvae that tunnel inside leaves and damage stems below the soil. To reduce leaf miner problems, pick off and destroy affected leaves.

Striped cucumber beetles are ¼-inch-long yellowish orange bugs with black heads and three black stripes down their backs. These pests can spread bacterial blight and cucumber mosaic. Apply a thick layer of mulch to discourage them from laying their orange eggs in the soil near the plants. Cover plants with row covers to prevent beetles from feeding; handpick adults from plants that aren't covered. Plant later in the season to help avoid infestations of this pest.

Spider mites are tiny red or yellow creatures that generally live on the undersides of leaves; their feeding causes yellow stippling on leaf surfaces. Discourage spider mites with garlic or soap sprays. Using a strong blast of water from the hose will wash mites off plants, but avoid this method at blossom time or you may knock the blossoms off.

To minimize disease problems, buy disease-free seeds and disease-resistant cultivars, rotate bean crops every 1 or 2 years, and space plants far enough apart to provide airflow. Don't harvest or cultivate beans when the foliage is wet, or you may spread disease spores. Here are some common diseases to watch for.

- Anthracnose causes black, egg-shaped, sunken cankers on pods, stems, and seeds and black marks on leaf veins.

- Bacterial blight starts with large, brown blotches on the leaves; the foliage may fall off and the plant will die.

- Mosaic symptoms include yellow leaves and stunted growth. Control aphids and cucumber beetles, which spread the virus.

- Rust causes reddish brown spots on leaves, stems, and pods.

- Downy mildew causes fuzzy white patches on pods, especially of lima beans.

If disease strikes, destroy infested plants immediately, don't touch other plants with unwashed hands or clippers, and don't sow beans in that area again for 3 to 5 years.

Harvesting: Pick green beans when they are pencil size, tender, and before the seeds inside form bumps on the pod. Harvest regularly and thoroughly to encourage production; if you allow pods to ripen fully, the plants will stop producing and die. Pulling directly on the pods may uproot the plants. Instead, pinch off bush beans using your thumbnail and fingers; use scissors on pole and runner beans. Cut off and discard any overly mature beans you missed in previous pickings. Serve, freeze, can, or pickle the beans the day you harvest them to preserve their fresh, delicious, homegrown flavor.

Pick shell beans for fresh eating when the pods are plump but still tender. The more you pick, the more the vines will produce. Consume or preserve them as soon as possible. Unshelled, both they and green beans will keep for up to a week in the refrigerator.

To dry beans, leave the pods on the plants until they are brown and the seeds rattle inside them. Seeds should be so hard you can barely dent them with your teeth. If the pods have yellowed and a rainy spell is forecast, cut the plants off near the ground and hang them upside down indoors to dry. Put the shelled beans in airtight, lidded containers. Add a packet of dry milk to absorb moisture, and store the beans in a cool, dry place. They will keep for 10 to 12 months.

BEE BALM

See *Monarda*

BEES

See Beneficial Insects

BEET

Beta vulgaris
Chenopodiaceae

Beets are a high-yield addition to any vegetable garden. They thrive in almost every climate and in all but the heaviest soils. You can bake, boil, steam, or pickle beets for use in soups, salads, and side dishes. Try growing a patch specifically for harvesting the delectable greens, which contain vitamins A and C and more iron and minerals than spinach, a close cousin. While beets with deep red—and messy to prepare—roots are best known, cultivars with roots that are golden, white, or red-and-white striped are readily available and offer the same nutritional and culinary benefits.

Planting: Beets can grow in semishade but prefer full sun. They like deep, loose, well-drained, root- and rock-free soil. Like all root crops, beets benefit from hilled-up rows or beds. Dig in plenty of mature compost to lighten heavy soil.

Beets are most productive at temperatures of 60° to 65°F. Where summers are hot, plant them as a spring or fall crop, and as a winter crop in the Deep South. Sow this hardy vegetable directly in the garden a full month before the last expected frost or as soon as you can work the soil. When planting in summer or fall during hot and dry weather, soak seeds for 12 hours to promote germination.

Sow seeds ½ inch deep and 2 to 4 inches apart with 12 to 18 inches between rows. Except for a few monogerm (single-seeded) types, each beet seed is actually a small fruit containing up to eight true seeds. Thin the resulting clusters of seedlings to one per cluster. Transplant thinnings or enjoy the tiny, tender leaves in salads or as cooked greens. If you're growing beets for greens only, then you don't need to thin. Plant successive crops every 2 weeks until the weather begins to turn hot.

Growing guidelines: Early weeding is critical to success with any root crop, but beet roots bruise easily, so carefully hand-pull weeds that sprout near your young beet plants.

Once the roots reach 1 inch in diameter, harvest every other one, water well, and mulch to keep down weeds and conserve moisture. Be sure to provide about 1 inch of water a week. Otherwise, plants bolt (go to seed), and the roots will crack or become stringy and tough. Quick growth is the secret for tender roots, so water with compost tea or liquid seaweed extract every 2 weeks. See the Compost entry for instructions for making compost tea. Side-dress with compost at least once halfway through the growing period.

Problems: Beets that are thinned promptly and weeded and watered regularly usually are insect- and disease-free. The most common pests are leaf miners and flea beetles, but they seldom cause serious damage to beet roots. If you are growing beets for their foliage, controlling these pests may be more of a priority. Leaf miners are tiny black flies whose larvae tunnel within the beet leaves; control them by removing affected leaves. For more information on flea beetles, see page 455.

Boron deficiency can cause brown hearts, black spots in the roots, or poor growth. If you've had problems with these symptoms, apply a foliar spray of liquid seaweed extract every 2 weeks and enrich your garden with compost and green manures to increase the supply of boron in the soil.

Harvesting: You can snip off up to a third of a plant's greens without harming the roots. To harvest the roots, hand-pull carefully to avoid bruising them. Beet roots are best when 1½ to 3 inches in diameter; they'll start to deteriorate if you leave them in the ground for more than 10 days after they reach their full size. After pulling the roots, shake off the soil, and twist off—don't cut off—the tops, leaving an inch or so of stems to prevent the roots from bleeding. To store beets for up to 6 months, layer undamaged roots between sand, peat, or sawdust in boxes; store in a cool place. You can also can or freeze beet roots or leaves.

BEGONIA

Begonia. Tender perennials grown as summer- and fall-blooming annuals or houseplants; one hardy perennial species.

Description: The genus *Begonia* contains over 1,500 species and hundreds of thousands of cultivars, grown for their beautiful flowers, as is the case with tuberous and wax begonias, or attractive leaves, as with rex and cane begonias. Begonias generally fall into one of four major groups— fibrous-rooted, tuberous-rooted, rhizomatous, and cane-stemmed—each with different habits and needs.

Begonia ×*semperflorens-cultorum*, wax begonia, is

a tender perennial commonly grown as a reliable annual. Flowering begins when plants are small and continues until frost. Wax begonias bloom in shades of white, pink, and red, plus blended and edged combinations, on plants that can reach more than 15 inches by autumn. The male flowers normally have four petals (two rounded and two narrow) with showy yellow stamens in the center; the females have two to five smaller rounded petals around a tight, curly yellow knob. Female blooms occur in pairs, one on either side of each male flower. The shiny, thick, 1½- to 4-inch leaves may be green, reddish to bronze, or speckled with yellow, and appear waxy, giving these plants their common name. Perennial in Zone 10; elsewhere, grow as an annual or container plant and bring indoors when frost threatens.

Another popular type of begonia is the cane-stemmed group, including the angel-wing begonias. This group gets its name from its fleshy, jointed stems that visually resemble bamboo canes. Representing several species and cultivars, these houseplants produce plain green or mottled leaves and clusters of brightly colored flowers. Upright cultivars can grow several feet tall; plants with drooping branches are ideal for hanging baskets.

The showy plants called hybrid tuberous begonias (*B.* ×*tuberhybrida*) produce lavish, roselike blossoms. Single or double male flowers can grow to 6 inches or more across, blooming in bright and pastel shades of white, pink, red, yellow, salmon, and combinations. The upright plants grow to about 2 feet tall. Perennial in Zone 10; in colder climates, bring indoors when frost threatens or treat as annuals.

Rex begonias' (*B. rex-cultorum*) popularity as houseplants makes them the most widely grown rhizomatous begonias. They produce large green or reddish leaves, often attractively patterned with

Hardy Begonias

Most people think of begonias as bedding, hanging-basket, or indoor plants, but there is also a handsome perennial begonia that can take the cold. Winter hardy to Zone 6 (Zone 5 with protection), hardy begonia (*Begonia grandis*) bears large, open sprays of pink or white blooms from late summer into early fall on 1- to 2½-foot arching clumps of striking, angel-wing-type leaves. It thrives in partial shade (out of hot afternoon sun) and fertile, moist but well-drained soil with plenty of organic matter. Plant or divide in spring when it emerges, typically later than most plants. It looks stunning in a bed of ajuga or in woodland plantings with hostas and ferns.

silver or black markings; their flowers typically are small and unremarkable.

How to grow: Buy plants or start wax begonias from seed, allowing 4 months from sowing to setting out transplants after the frost date. Take cuttings of particularly nice plants toward the end of summer to grow as houseplants through winter; root cuttings from them in early spring for planting out after frost. Set wax begonias out after the last frost in partial to dense shade; they'll grow in full sun in cool-summer areas if kept evenly moist. Plant in average, moist but well-drained soil; water during drought.

Start tuberous begonias indoors, planting them about 8 to 10 weeks before your frost-free date in a loose growing medium. Barely cover tubers with the concave side up (it should have little pink buds coming out of the center) and moisten lightly. Give lots of water and light after the shoots emerge. Move tubers to individual 4- or 5-inch pots when shoots are 1 to 3 inches tall. After all danger of frost is past, plant in partial shade in fertile, moist, but well-drained soil with plenty of organic matter. Water liberally in warm weather; douse every 3 weeks or so with compost tea or fish emulsion. (See the Compost entry for instructions for making compost tea.) Stake plants to prevent them from falling under the weight of the flowers.

For container-grown tuberous begonias, choose larger pots (8 inches is a good size) and fill with a loose, rich potting mix. Care for them as you would plants in the ground. For hanging baskets, plant no more than three tubers in a 12-inch basket, and water frequently. To promote branching, pinch plants when they are about 6 inches tall.

When the leaves turn yellow and wither in fall, lift plants out of the ground with soil still attached. After a week or so, cut the stems to within a few inches of the tuber. Once the stem stub dries completely, shake the soil off the tubers and store in dry peat or sharp sand (aka builders' sand) at 45° to 55°F. Leave pot-grown plants in their soil and bring indoors during winter, or store as you would those grown in the ground. Start them again next spring, replacing the soil for those in pots.

Angel-wing and rex begonias need plenty of bright but indirect light. Grow them indoors in a rich, well-drained potting mix. In summer, they appreciate some extra humidity, along with evenly moist soil and a dose of fish emulsion every 2 weeks. In winter, water more sparingly and do not feed.

Indoors, begonias usually are pest-free. In the garden, slugs may be a problem; see the Slugs and Snails entry for details on controlling these pests. Stem rot threatens tuberous begonias in poorly drained soil; mildew may whiten the leaves where air circulation is poor. Flower buds may drop in humid weather or if the soil is too dry.

Landscape uses: Outdoors, grow begonias anywhere you want some color in shady beds and borders, or use them in containers or hanging baskets, alone or with other decorative container plants, for portable color.

BELLFLOWER

See *Campanula*

BENEFICIAL ANIMALS

See Bats; Birds; Pests; Toads

BENEFICIAL INSECTS

Insect allies far outnumber the insect pests in organically managed yards and gardens. Bees, flies, and many moths help gardeners by pollinating flowers; predatory insects eat pest insects; parasitic insects lay their eggs inside pests, and the larvae that hatch then weaken or kill the pests; dung beetles, flies, and many others break down decaying material, which helps build good soil.

Bees and Wasps

Honeybees play a key role in agriculture because of their importance in pollinating crops, but other wild bees and wasps also are important pollinators and natural pest-control agents.

Bees: All bees gather and feed on nectar and pollen, which distinguishes them from wasps and hornets. As they forage for food, bees transfer stray grains of pollen from flower to flower and pollinate the blooms. There are some 20,000 species of bees worldwide. Of the nearly 5,000 species in North America, several hundred are vital as pollinators of cultivated crops. Many others are crucial to wild plants.

Pesticide use, loss of habitat, and pest problems such as mites have vastly reduced wild and domestic bee populations. For more than a decade, beekeepers and farmers have struggled with hive losses attributed to a phenomenon known as colony collapse disorder (CCD). While CCD continues to decimate honeybee populations in the United States, its cause remains unclear. In hives affected by CCD, worker bees suddenly die out, leaving behind the queen bee, the nurse bees, and the unborn brood (which in turn die without the support of the worker bees). Researchers studying CCD continue to explore several possible causes, including diseases or parasites, the damaging effects of chemical pesticides on bees' nervous systems or immune systems, hive disruption resulting from climate change, bees' exposure to nectar and pollen from genetically modified plants, and lack of diversity in bees' food sources. No single factor has yet been identified as the cause of CCD, which has leveled off but still threatens honeybees and the farmers who rely upon them.

The good news is that native bees ranging from bumblebees to tiny "sweat bees" remain hard at work pollinating crops and gardens. Make your garden welcoming to all kinds of bees by including plants that bloom from late winter and early spring to well into fall. Leave some bare ground available for the bees to tunnel in to make nests, and provide a shallow water source where they can drink. Avoid using any broad-spectrum pesticides, even organic ones, around flowers where bees are actively gathering nectar.

Parasitic wasps: Most species belong to one of three main families: chalcids, braconids, and ichneumonids. They range from pencil-point-size trichogramma wasps to huge black ichneumon wasps. Parasitic wasps inject their eggs inside host insects; the larvae grow by absorbing nourishment through their skins.

Yellow jackets: Most people fear yellow jackets and hornets, but these insects are excellent pest predators. They dive into foliage and carry off flies, caterpillars, and other larvae to feed to their brood. Don't destroy the gray paper nests of these insects unless they are in a place frequented by people or pets, or if a family member is allergic to insect stings.

Beetles

While some beetle species, such as Japanese beetles and Colorado potato beetles, are notorious garden pests, others are among the best pest fighters around.

Lady beetles: This family of small to medium, shiny, hard, hemispherical beetles includes more than 3,000 species that feed on small, soft pests such as aphids, mealybugs, and spider mites. (Not all species are beneficial—for example, Mexican bean beetles also are lady beetles.) Both adults and larvae eat pests. Most larvae have tapering bodies with several short, branching spines on each segment; they resemble miniature alligators. Convergent lady beetles (*Hippodamia convergens*) are collected from their mass overwintering sites and sold to gardeners, but they usually fly away after release unless confined in a greenhouse.

Ground beetles: These swift-footed, medium to large, blue-black beetles hide under stones or boards during the day. By night they prey on cab-bage root maggots, cutworms, snail and slug eggs, and other pests; some climb trees to capture armyworms or tent caterpillars. Large ground beetle populations build up in orchards with undisturbed groundcovers and under stone pathways and mulched areas in gardens.

Rove beetles: These small to medium, elongated insects with short, stubby top wings look like earwigs without pincers. Many species are decomposers of manure and plant material; others are important predators of pests such as root maggots that spend part of their life cycle in the soil.

Other beetles: Other beneficial beetles include hister beetles, tiger beetles, and fireflies (really beetles). Both larvae and adults of these beetles eat insect larvae, slugs, and snails.

Flies

Beneficial species of flies are pollinators or insect predators or parasites.

Tachinid flies: These large, bristly, dark gray flies place their eggs or larvae on cutworms, caterpillars, corn borers, stinkbugs, and other pests. Tachinid flies are important natural suppressors of tent caterpillar or armyworm outbreaks.

Syrphid flies: These black-and-yellow or black-and-white striped flies (also called flower flies or hoverflies) are often mistaken for bees or yellow jackets. They lay their eggs in aphid colonies; the larvae feed on the aphids. Don't mistake the larvae—unattractive gray or translucent slug-like maggots—for small slugs.

Aphid midges: Aphid midge larvae are tiny orange maggots that are voracious aphid predators. The aphid midge is available from commercial insectaries and can be very effective if released in a home greenhouse.

Other Beneficials

Dragonflies: Often called darning needles, dragonflies and their smaller cousins, damselflies, scoop up mosquitoes, gnats, and midges, cramming their mouths with prey as they dart in zigzag patterns around marshes and ponds.

Lacewings: The brown or green, alligator-like larvae of several species of native lacewings prey upon a variety of small pest insects, including aphids, scale insects, small caterpillars, and thrips. Adult lacewings are delicate, ½- to 1-inch green or brown insects with large, transparent wings marked with a characteristic fine network of veins. They lay pale green oval eggs, each at the tip of a long, fine stalk, along the midrib of lettuce leaves or other garden plants.

True bugs: True bug is the scientifically correct common name for a group of insects. This group includes several pest species, but there are also many predatory bugs that attack soft-bodied insects such as aphids, beetle larvae, small caterpillars, pear psylla, and thrips. Assassin bugs, ambush bugs, damsel bugs, minute pirate bugs, and spined solider bugs are valuable wild predators in organic farms and gardens.

Spiders and mites: Although mites and spiders are arachnids, not insects, they are often grouped with insects because all belong to the larger classification of arthropods. Predatory mites are extremely small. The native species found in trees, shrubs, and surface litter are invaluable predators. Phytoseiid mites control many kinds of plant-feeding mites, such as spider mites, rust mites, and cyclamen mites. Some also prey on thrips and other small pests. Many types of soil-dwelling mites eat nematodes, insect eggs, fungus gnat larvae, or decaying organic matter.

It's unfortunate that so many people fear spiders, because they are some of the best pest predators around. We are most familiar with spiders that spin webs, but there are many other kinds. Some spin thick silk funnels; some hide in burrows and snatch insects that wander too close, while others leap on their prey using a silk thread as a dragline. Mulching vegetable gardens with straw offers the dual benefits of confusing/impeding some common pests and providing habitat for spiders that prey on pest insects.

Encouraging Beneficials

The best way to protect beneficial insects is to avoid using toxic sprays or dusts in the garden. Even organically acceptable sprays such as insecticidal soap and neem can kill beneficial species, so use them only when absolutely necessary to preserve a crop and then only on the plants being affected. Be careful when you handpick or spray pest insects, or you may end up killing beneficial insects by mistake. While many beneficials are too small to be seen with the unaided eye, it's easy to learn to identify the larger common beneficials such as lacewings, tachinid flies, and lady beetles.

You can make your yard and garden a haven for beneficials by taking simple steps to provide them with food, water, and shelter, as shown in the illustration on the opposite page.

Food sources: A flowerbed or border of companion plants rich in pollen and nectar, such as catnip, dill, and yarrow, is a food source for the adult stages of many beneficials, including native bees, lacewings, and parasitic wasps.

Water: Many types of beneficial insects are too small to be able to drink water safely from a stream, water garden, or even a regular birdbath. To provide a safe water supply for these delicate insects, fill a shallow birdbath or large bowl with stones.

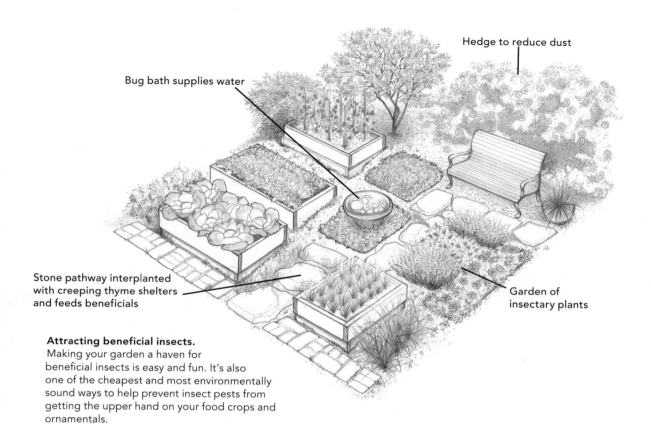

Hedge to reduce dust

Bug bath supplies water

Stone pathway interplanted
with creeping thyme shelters
and feeds beneficials

Garden of
insectary plants

Attracting beneficial insects.
Making your garden a haven for
beneficial insects is easy and fun. It's also
one of the cheapest and most environmentally
sound ways to help prevent insect pests from
getting the upper hand on your food crops and
ornamentals.

Then add just enough water to create shallow stretches of water with plenty of exposed landing sites where the insects can alight and drink without drowning. You'll need to check this bug bath daily, as the water may evaporate quickly on sunny days.

Shelter: Leave some weeds here and there among your vegetable plants to provide alternate food sources and shelter for beneficial species. Plant a hedge or build a windbreak fence to reduce dust, because beneficial insects dehydrate easily in dusty conditions. And set up some permanent pathways and mulched areas around your yard and garden. These protected areas offer safe places for beneficials to hide during the daytime (for species that are active at night), during bad weather, or when you're actively cultivating the soil.

To learn more about encouraging beneficial insects in your yard, visit the Web sites of organizations such as the Xerces Society; see Resources on page 673.

Buying Beneficial Insects

Many garden supply and specialty companies offer beneficial insects for sale to farmers, nursery owners, and gardeners. You can buy everything from aphid midges to lady beetles and lacewings to predatory mites.

Buying and releasing beneficial insects on a

Pollinator Gardens

Even if your yard seems too small or too urban to provide much wildlife habitat, you can encourage a crucial wildlife population: native pollinators. With honeybees at risk from disease, parasites, and threats like colony collapse disorder, our native bees are more crucial than ever to our food supply and to all plants that need insect pollination in order to reproduce.

Here's how to attract and nurture pollinators wherever you live.

Offer a flower buffet. Bees need nectar for energy and protein-rich pollen to raise their young. Plant a variety of flower types and colors. Favorite colors of pollinators include blue, purple, violet, white, and yellow. Plant annuals and perennials—some bee families prefer one over the other. Include native wildflowers, because they may be more attractive to pollinators than exotics. Observe your flowers, and plant more of whatever the bees seem to like best.

Keep it simple. Choose basic forms of flowers—those called "single" rather than the fluffy, petal-packed double forms. Garden show-offs with ruffly, double petals such as marigolds and double hollyhocks are a bust for bees—some have no pollen or nectar; others are too dense for bees to penetrate.

Try for continuous three-season bloom. Different bees have different life cycles—and need food at different times of year. Spring bulbs aren't very attractive to bees, so for spring, include some fruit trees or flowering shrubs. Borage and calendulas are good spring choices, too. For fall, consider sedums, stonecrops, asters, and goldenrods.

Plant clumps. Research suggests that bees stay longer in gardens of at least 3 to 4 feet in diameter. Plant large clumps of each flower type—finicky bees may ignore small displays, even if they're bursting with pollen and nectar.

Add water. A birdbath or drip irrigation line provides thirsty bees with clean water—and keeps them in your garden instead of scouting elsewhere for water.

Leave some ground bare. Most native bees are solitary creatures that live alone in the ground rather than building a hive. Each female digs her own nest tunnel, creates cells for raising offspring, and then stocks it with pollen and nectar. She needs bare ground that's well drained and sunny. To encourage native bees, leave small areas here and there around your yard clear of heavy mulch—some bees prefer steep, south-facing slopes, while others call flat ground home. Or create nesting areas with wood blocks or tubes for the native bees who naturally nest in abandoned beetle tunnels.

large scale, such as a commercial farm field, or in a confined place, such as a greenhouse, can be a very effective pest-control tactic. However, in a typical home garden it's rarely worthwhile. Chances are that most of the insects you release will disperse well beyond the boundaries of your yard. While that may be helpful for your neighborhood in general, it won't produce any noticeable improvement in the specific pest problem that you hoped the good bugs would control in your garden. Overall, it's more effective to invest money in plants that attract beneficial insects to your yard than it is to buy and release beneficial insects.

If you decide to experiment with ordering beneficial insects, make sure you identify the target pest, because most predators or parasites only attack a particular species or group of pests. Find out as much as you can by reading or talking to suppliers before buying beneficials.

Get a good look at the beneficials before releasing them so that you'll be able to recognize them in the garden. You don't want to mistake them for pests later on. A magnifying glass is useful for seeing tiny parasitic wasps and predatory mites. Release some of the insects directly on or near the infested plants; distribute the remainder as evenly as possible throughout the surrounding area.

BERBERIS

Barberry. Thorny evergreen or deciduous shrubs.

Description: *Berberis julianae*, wintergreen barberry, grows from 3 to 6 feet and has shiny, evergreen, oblong leaves that may turn rich red during a cold winter. Zones 6–8.

B. thunbergii, Japanese barberry, is a popular, but invasive, deciduous shrub that is best avoided because seedlings (sown by songbirds) crowd out native plants in wild areas. Zones 4–8.

Both barberry species produce small yellow flowers in spring and berries in summer and fall.

How to grow: Barberries need full sun and tolerate a wide range of soil conditions. In the North, plant wintergreen barberry in a spot protected from winter winds; in the South, site it out of summer wind and plant in fall or winter.

Landscape uses: Use wintergreen barberry in hedges, shrub borders, or as foundation shrubs. Resistance to deer browsing has earned Japanese barberry widespread use in North American landscapes, from which it subsequently escaped to compete with native plants that lack such protection. This aggressive nonnative also provides excellent habitat for black-legged (aka deer) ticks (*Ixodes scapularis*) that carry Lyme disease. While it is still widely available, Japanese barberry should not be purchased or planted, and established plants should be removed.

BETULA

Birch. Single- or multiple-trunked deciduous trees.

Description: Birches offer year-round landscape interest with their peeling bark, graceful branches, and magnificent fall color.

Betula lenta, sweet birch, is a handsome native with red-brown, cherrylike bark and a pyramidal habit in youth. Like other birches, it bears drooping flower spikes called catkins in spring; these are interesting but not showy. The leaves stay freshly green and unmarred through summer, turning yellow in fall. Crushed or scratched twigs yield a rich, root beer aroma. Where it grows wild, sweet birch has been a source of the oil for making homemade root beer. Zones 4–6.

B. nigra, river birch, is a native tree found growing along riverbanks and rich bottomlands in much of the eastern United States. Pyramidal in youth, this multitrunked tree reaches heights of 30 to 40 feet in the landscape; the occasional old-timer approaches 100 feet. River birch features shredding, papery bark in shades of cream and pale salmon, and clear yellow autumn leaf color in most years. 'Cully', sold as Heritage, has creamy white inner bark that compares with the white bark of popular but insect-prone *B. papyrifera*. Zones 4–8.

B. papyrifera, paper or canoe birch, is a native of the northern evergreen forests and performs best in cooler climates. Known for its white bark with dramatic black markings, this tree develops a rounded outline with age. Most paper birches hold their lower branches; be sure to allow space for the tree's mature spread in your landscape plans. The yellow fall color combines well with its bark and with the reds and oranges of other trees. Plan on a mature height of 50 to 70 feet. Zones 4–8.

B. pendula, European white birch, is similar in many ways to paper birch. Its branches have a drooping habit, and its bark splits into black fissures toward the base. Zones 3–6.

B. populifolia, gray birch, is a workhorse among birches. Thriving in almost any soil, this handsome tree has grayish white bark with black markings and a multitrunked habit. A good birch for minimal-maintenance situations. Zones 4–6.

How to grow: Most birches require light shade. Give them evenly moist, humus–rich soil, a shaded root zone, and plenty of mulch. River birch tolerates some standing water. Planted out of their element, birches soon begin to decline and, if they haven't already, attract insects such as the bronze birch borer and the birch leaf miner. Stressed trees most often feature D-shaped holes left in the bark by borers and brown paperlike leaves caused by leaf miners; reduce the risk of both problems by selecting an appropriate planting site. Gray and river birches, especially Herit-

age, show resistance to these devastating insects.

Landscape uses: Sweet or paper birch are good choices for naturalizing in the shade of taller trees. Use gray or river birch in clumps or masses.

BIENNIALS

Botanically speaking, biennials are plants that complete their life cycle in 2 years, germinating the first year then flowering and producing seeds in the second. During the first growing season, true biennials germinate and produce a mound of foliage, called a rosette, which is a circular cluster of leaves usually borne at or just above the ground. They winter over in rosette form. In the second season, they send up a flower stalk. After blooming, biennials produce seeds and die at the end of the season.

True biennials, such as Canterbury bells (*Campanula medium*), standing cypress (*Ipomopsis rubra*), Miss Willmott's ghost (*Eryngium giganteum*), and sweet William (*Dianthus barbatus*), are winter hardy in most regions and usually have fleshy taproots. While some may hold on and bloom for a third or even a fourth season, they produce the best bloom during the second season from seed.

Plants don't always follow our clear-cut definitions, though. In reality, gardeners grow some plants as biennials whether they're true biennials or not. These include short-lived perennials that can winter over with some protection—such as pansies and English daisies (*Bellis perennis*). These plants bloom best when planted in late summer or fall, mulched or otherwise protected over winter, then pulled up and replaced after they bloom the following spring or summer. (Check with your local Cooperative Extension office or local gardeners to determine how to grow biennials in your area,

Biennials for Sun and Shade

As these lists show, there are more biennials than you think—including such beloved favorites as hollyhocks, Canterbury bells, sweet Williams, forget-me-nots, evening primroses, and foxgloves. Some are best suited for sun, some prefer shade, and a few thrive in both conditions. Perennials grown as biennials are also included here.

Biennials for Sunny Sites

Alcea rosea (hollyhock)

Campanula medium (Canterbury bells)

Cynoglossum amabile (Chinese forget-me-not)

Dianthus armeria (Deptford pink)

Dianthus barbatus (sweet William)

Eryngium giganteum (Miss Willmott's ghost)

Glaucium flavum (yellow horned poppy)

Ipomopsis rubra (standing cypress)

Lavatera arborea (tree mallow)

Lunaria annua (honesty, money plant)

Malva sylvestris (high mallow)

Matthiola incana (stock)

Myosotis spp. (forget-me-nots)

Oenothera spp. (evening primroses)

Onopordum acanthium (cotton thistle)

Silene armeria (sweet William catchfly)

Verbascum spp. (mulleins)

Biennials for Shady Sites

Campanula medium (Canterbury bells)

Digitalis purpurea (foxglove)

Lunaria annua (honesty, money plant)

Myosotis spp. (forget-me-nots)

Phacelia bipinnatifida (fernleaf phacelia)

---

since the best schedule varies depending on your climate and hardiness zone.)

To make matters more confusing, some biennials can be grown as annuals. For example, if sown indoors in midwinter, 'Foxy' hybrid foxglove (*Digitalis purpurea* 'Foxy') will bloom its first year from seed.

Many true biennials, along with plants grown as biennials, readily self-sow their seed. Miss Willmott's ghost, honesty or money plant (*Lunaria annua*), foxglove (*Digitalis purpurea*), woodland forget-me-not (*Myosotis sylvatica*), and hollyhock (*Alcea rosea*) all are reliable self-sowers. Thus, if you plant seed of these biennials 2 years in a row, you'll have plants in bloom every year from then on—providing the same effect in the garden as perennials do. Just remember to allow some flowers to mature each year and set seed for next year's plants.

In the following discussion, the term *biennial* is used to refer to any plants grown as biennials, not just to true biennials.

Biennials in the Landscape

Biennials are attractive in flowerbeds and borders throughout the landscape, and large-size plants such as hollyhocks (*A. rosea*) can even be used as stand-alone specimen plants or for adding color to a shrub border. For best results, interplant them with annuals the first year while the rosettes of foliage are still small. The second season, add more annuals around the plants to fill the spaces the biennials will leave in the garden after they have finished blooming.

Keep in mind that if you buy plants the first year, you will have bloom the first season. If you are starting your own seeds, plan ahead, since it will take two seasons to get the floral display you want. The flowers of most biennials last several weeks before fading. Some, including honesty and mulleins (*Verbascum* spp.), have attractive seed heads that you can use in dried arrangements.

Buying and Starting Plants

Popular biennials like pansies and hollyhocks are sold by nurseries along with annual bedding plants in spring. They have been grown for the first season by the nursery and are offered at a stage where they will bloom in the current season. Plant and maintain them as you would annuals.

Purchase only healthy, bright green, well-rooted plants. Avoid overgrown, leggy, or wilted plants—their performance will be disappointing. Some biennials, including pansies and foxglove, are offered for fall planting. Plant them in early fall to allow ample time for the roots to get established. Mulch the rosettes after hard frost. This protects the crown and prevents repeated freezing and thawing of the soil that can cause roots to heave out of the ground.

Many choice biennials are not offered by nurseries as plants. If you want them, you'll have to grow them from seed. You'll find the broadest range of biennials offered by Internet and catalog seed retailers.

Biennials can be difficult to transplant successfully (many have taproots). To minimize transplanting problems, sow seeds indoors in individual pots, peat pots, or cell packs. Use a sterile commercial soil mix or a compost-based potting mix. Start seeds of true biennials in early summer so seedlings will be ready to plant out in fall. Sow seeds of pansies, English daisies, and other perennials treated as biennials in August. Protect the young plants with mulch or keep them in a cold frame until early spring.

You can also direct-seed biennials into well-prepared outdoor beds. Keep the seedbed evenly moist but not wet. Take care to protect the seeds from disturbance until they germinate and become well established. Sow seed thickly, then use small scissors to clip off unwanted seedlings. When seedlings are established, mulch the beds to conserve water.

Planting and Maintenance

Most biennials prefer loamy soil with ample organic matter and pH between 6.0 and 7.5. If you're already growing a wide variety of flowers, you'll probably have no trouble with most biennials. For best results, plant biennials in a bed with soil that has been turned to at least a shovel's depth. Thoroughly incorporate organic matter such as compost, along with any necessary soil amendments and fertilizers. (Have your soil tested if you are unsure about its fertility.)

Set purchased plants with their crowns at or just below the soil surface. If you're transplanting biennials from peat pots, remove all or a portion of the pots. Handle biennial transplants carefully, since many have taproots. Take care not to damage the taproot when planting.

Keep plants well watered until they're established. An inch of water per week is adequate for plants that are growing in well-prepared soil. Most are fine without supplemental fertilizer: Compost or other organic matter added to the soil at planting time should suffice. Weed the beds regularly so that your biennials won't have to compete for light, water, and nutrients. Once plants are established, mulch them to conserve soil moisture and control weeds.

Pinching the plants may help control the height and spread of some biennials, but it is generally unnecessary. Removing spent (faded) flowers prolongs the blooming season. You may have to stake certain tall plants such as standing cypress, stocks, and mallows, especially in areas with high winds.

As a rule, biennials are fairly pest-free. Good cultural practices are the best prevention for both insects and diseases. If serious problems do flare up, spray with an appropriate organic control. Plants with viral diseases should be destroyed. For more on pest and disease control, see the Pests and Plant Diseases and Disorders entries.

BIOLOGICAL CONTROL

See Beneficial Insects; Pests

BIOTECHNOLOGY

Some organizations, scientists, and politicians claim that no matter what challenges we face from climate change, resource depletion, and rising population, technology will provide solutions. One form of technology that many see as a possible solution is genetic engineering.

It began in 1971 with a microscopic bacterium that was genetically altered to devour oil spills. In the wake of that first genetically engineered organism, a powerful, profit-driven industry, including many of the same companies that produce chemical pesticides, developed around this new science. In 2013, genetically engineered crops covered approximately half of all cropland in the United States—including more than 90 percent of all the soybeans and more than 80 percent of all cotton and corn. Above 90 percent of sugar beets grown are genetically engineered, representing about half of the sugar sold in the States. As a result, more than 75 percent of processed food products in American grocery stores contain genetically modified ingredients.

While its advocates hail genetic engineering for its potential to increase crop productivity and reduce the need for pesticides, others have serious concerns about genetically engineered plants. Here are some of the reasons why scientists, farmers, gardeners, and consumers in the organic community continue to question the safety of introducing GMOs into the environment and into our food system.

Superbugs. Most of the 60-plus genetically engineered plants currently cleared for use fall into two basic categories: plants engineered to include their own pesticide, a toxin produced by the Bt (*Bacillus thuringiensis*) bacterium; and plants engineered to survive exposure to weed killers, including the so-called Roundup Ready soybeans and cotton.

Bt is a natural and highly effective pesticide that has long been used by organic growers to control caterpillars and other pests, without harm to wildlife or humans. Organic farmers and gardeners use it sparingly. Now it is introduced into each cell of a genetically engineered plant, from the roots to the pollen to the chaff plowed under after harvest. Since the Bt is ubiquitous, it is inevitable that insects will develop resistance to it. With Bt constantly present in millions of acres of crops, Bt-resistant insect strains will evolve in as little as 3 to 5 years, the biotech industry's own scientists acknowledge.

Current directives that require farmers to interplant these Bt-carrying crops with nonmodified varieties are expected to merely delay the inevitable. And when the inevitable happens, organic growers will lose a powerful pest control and conventional growers will return to using chemical pesticides.

Superweeds. Some herbicide-tolerant crops (such as canola oilseed, or rape) are cross-pollinating with wild cousins and could create herbicide-resistant weeds. The new, stronger weeds will defeat the purpose of engineering the plants and may coax farmers into using more powerful poisons to kill weeds. (It is the same process that produced insect resistance to many pesticides used in large-scale farming, leading to use of more toxic pesticides at higher application rates.)

Harm to wildlife. Even the pollen produced by genetically engineered plants like the Bt-carrying ones described earlier contains the pesticide. Scientists in the United States and Europe have evidence that this pollen travels beyond the primary crops and infects other insects, including nonpest species. Because Bt affects all caterpillars, pollen from Bt-modified crops may be contributing to the decline of monarch butterflies and other desirable species. Some research indicates that honeybees may be harmed by feeding on proteins found in genetically engineered canola flowers.

Variety, Hybrid, or GMO—What's the Difference?

New varieties of plants pop up all the time in nature. Wind and animals help plants cross-pollinate. Once these natural processes create a variety—a naturally occurring modification—it tends to stay around; the seedlings turn out just like the parent.

When humans deliberately cross closely related members of a species to produce slight variations in the offspring, the process is called hybridization, and the products are called hybrid cultivars. (The word *cultivar* is an abbreviated form of "cultivated variety.") To produce more of a hybrid cultivar, you must isolate the two specific parents so you get genes only from those specific sources. (That's why seeds collected from hybrid plants rarely produce seedlings that share the desirable characteristics of the parent.) Most of us have enjoyed improved plants, both varieties and hybrids, in the form of more interesting hostas, sweeter raspberries, or bigger Gerbera daisies.

More recently, scientists learned how to determine which genes control every characteristic of every living organism—and they have developed techniques that allow them to take genes from one animal, plant, bacterium, or virus and transfer the genes into another organism. The results of this kind of process are called genetically engineered plants or genetically modified organisms (GMOs). Genetic engineering has unprecedented power to "engineer" the nature of any living organism.

Harm to soil. Microbiologists at New York University have found that the Bt toxin in residues of genetically altered corn and rice crops persists in soils for up to 8 months and depresses microbial activity. Another study showed that a genetically engineered soil microbe killed wheat plants when it was added to their soil.

Hidden allergens. DNA directs the production of proteins. Proteins are common causes of human allergies. When DNA from one organism is spliced into another, can it turn a nonallergenic food into one that will cause an allergic reaction in some people? A biotech seed company tried to change the protein content of soybeans by adding a gene from the Brazil nut. When researchers tested the modified soybean on people with sensitivity to Brazil nuts (but no sensitivity to soybeans), they found it triggered an allergic reaction. (Based on those findings, the company shelved development of the altered soybean.)

Religious and moral considerations. People who choose not to eat animals for religious or moral reasons face an almost impossible task with many genetically engineered foods. If genes from flounder are spliced into tomatoes, or genes from chickens are added to potatoes, are the resulting organisms really still purely vegetables? Without mandatory labeling, how can people who object to eating any trace of meat know what they are getting?

Indentured farmers. Who owns the food industry? The corporations committed to genetic engineering research—many of the same companies that produce chemical pesticides—are rapidly buying up seed companies and gaining control of entire food-production systems and educational-research facilities. Farmers who use this patented technology, meanwhile, are forbidden to save their own seed (it's patented). Instead they must buy it from the company each growing season, leading them into a costly cycle of corporate dependency.

Pollen drift. Organic farmers could lose their certification and face financial ruin if their fields are contaminated by wind-borne pollen from nearby genetically modified crops. Even nonorganic farmers are at risk for problems. In Canada, Monsanto accused a canola grower of patent infringement after the company allegedly found genetically engineered Roundup Ready canola plants in his fields. The farmer claimed he had never planted Monsanto seeds. After mediation efforts failed, he filed a $10 million lawsuit against Monsanto, claiming libel, trespass, and contamination of his fields.

What You Can Do

Perhaps you cannot control what neighboring farmers are growing, or what foods line the grocery shelves, but you can control (to some extent) your own choices about what you grow and what you eat.

Grow your own. Grow your own food if you can, using seeds or plants from trusted sources. Organic gardeners and farmers, and several seed-exchange organizations, are dependable sources.

Save seeds from your garden. Keep records. If you are using hybrid vegetable or fruit cultivars, they may not come out the same as last year's crop; learn which varieties do reproduce faithfully.

Buy local. Buy food from local farmers at a farmers' market, food co-op, or grocery stores that offer local produce. Let the sellers know why you are choosing them.

Minimize processed foods. When you shop at the grocery store, buy foods that are as close to their natural form as possible and preferably organic. The more processed the foods, the greater likelihood they contain genetically modified products.

Ask questions. If you are gardening near a farm, ask the farmers whether they plant any genetically modified seed. Your neighbors should understand your interest in knowing. (Your questions may even cause them to think about the concerns.) Be tactful, however: Farmers' decisions are usually made with survival in mind; it has always been a hard business and farmers don't need lectures. It may take larger changes in the food system to allow farmers to change their choices.

Garden smart. If you know your neighbors use genetically modified seed, reconsider your own practices in order to protect wildlife. Perhaps you shouldn't plant a butterfly garden near a GMO-seeded cornfield.

Try a little activism. Become active in the politics of food. Whether you are inclined to join organizations (many regional and national choices) or operate independently (writing to your congressperson, for example), the debate has room for your voice.

BIRCH

See *Betula*

BIRDS

Birds are most gardeners' favorite visitors, with their cheerful songs, sprightly manners, and colorful plumage. Birds are also among nature's most efficient insect predators, making them valuable garden allies. In an afternoon, one diminutive house wren can snatch up more than 500 insect eggs, beetles, and grubs. Given a nest of tent caterpillars, a Baltimore oriole will wolf down as many as 17 of the pests per minute. More than 60 percent of the chickadee's winter diet is aphid eggs. And the swallow lives up to its name by consuming massive quantities of flying insects—by one count, more than 1,000 leafhoppers in 12 hours.

Unless your property is completely bare, at least some birds will visit with no special encouragement from you. Far more birds, however, will come to your yard and garden if you take steps to provide their four basic requirements: food, water, cover, and a safe place in which to raise a family. Robins, nuthatches, hummingbirds, titmice, bluebirds, mockingbirds, cardinals, and various sparrows are among the most common garden visitors.

Food and Feeding

Food is the easiest of the four basic requirements to supply. If your landscape is mostly lawn and hard surfaces, you can use feeders as the main food supply while you add plantings of seed-producing annuals and perennials, grasses, and fruiting trees and shrubs. And if your yard is already a good natural habitat, where plants are the primary food source (as they should be), feeders can still provide extra nourishment during winter, early spring, drought, and at other times when the natural food supply is low. Also, carefully placed feeders allow you and your family to watch and photograph birds.

Some birds, including juncos, mourning doves, and towhees, feed on the ground, while others, including finches, grosbeaks, nuthatches, titmice, and chickadees, eat their meals higher up. To attract as many different birds as possible, use a variety of feeders—tube feeders for sunflower seed and Nyjer (also called niger or thistle seed), platform feeders, hopper feeders, shelf and hanging types, and (in cool weather) suet cakes in special suet cage feeders. No matter what the style, the feeder should shield its contents from rain and snow, and it should be easy to fill and clean. It should hold enough birdseed that you don't have to refill it every day, but not so much that the food spoils before birds eat it all.

Place feeders at varying heights, near the protective cover of a tree or shrub if possible. You can spread them around the yard or group them in one or more "feeding stations" where they're easy to see from the kitchen, deck, or wherever you and your family enjoy bird-watching. Remember to site them where they're easy to get to—a feeder at a far end of the yard means a long trek out to fill it, and you'll be less likely to keep up with it, especially in bad weather, when birds may need it most.

Best birdseed: You can attract virtually all common seed-eating birds with just two kinds of birdseed: black oil sunflower seed (the smallest of the sunflower types and a favorite of many birds) and white proso millet (the food of choice among ground-feeding species). Some birds have special favorites: goldfinches, pine siskins, and purple finches love Nyjer; tufted titmice and chickadees enjoy peanut kernels. Woodpeckers, chickadees, titmice, and nuthatches love suet blocks. To attract the greatest possible diversity of birds, use black sunflower seed in your tube feeders, and a mix that includes black sunflower and millet in tray, platform, hopper, and ground feeders. Round out the menu with such nourishing but more species-specific seeds as red proso millet, black- and gray-striped sunflower seeds, peanut kernels, Nyjer (in special tube feeders with tiny openings), and milo and cracked corn for ground feeders.

High-quality birdseed and seed mixes are available from wild bird specialty stores and mail-order and catalog wild bird specialty suppliers. Locally, check out pet stores, nature centers, farm stores, garden stores, and hardware stores to find a reliable source of seeds and other foods to fill your feeders.

Creating a bird garden. Diversity is the key to attracting birds to your yard. Include various types of seed and feeders; a rich array of plants, birdhouses, and nest sites; and make sure water is available year-round.

Suet: In cold weather, birds need lots of calories to maintain their body heat. Woodpeckers especially appreciate suet. You can buy suet cakes that are shaped to fit suet cages, are tidy and convenient to use, and are rendered so they hold up better if the weather warms. Or you can buy raw suet from the butcher at your grocery store (it's usually available at the meat counter in winter). Hang the fat in a plastic mesh bag (such as an onion bag) or wire holder (to keep large birds from stealing the entire chunk), or dip pinecones in melted suet and hang the cones from branches.

Special feeding: Birdfeeders will attract the most customers in winter and early spring, when natural food supplies are low. But summer feeding is also rewarding. Fruits such as oranges, apples, and bananas attract many species, including orioles, robins, tanagers, and mockingbirds. Simply cut the fruit in half and stick it on tree branches, or on one of the special fruit feeders available from wild bird suppliers.

Use your vegetable garden as a source of food for birds. Grow a few rows of sunflowers, wheat, sorghum, and/or millet just for them. In fall, let late-maturing vegetables and flowers (coneflowers are special favorites) go to seed. And don't till under cover crops such as buckwheat and rye until spring.

Hummingbirds: Hummingbirds are popular summer visitors in almost all parts of the country and year-round residents in parts of the Southwest and California. You can easily attract them to your garden with feeders that dispense a sugar-water ("nectar") solution. Sugar water, however, provides only a quick energy boost and no real sustenance, so it's best to hang hummingbird feeders near natural nectar sources, such as columbines, honeysuckles, and tube-shaped flowers. You can buy sugar-water nectar for hummingbird feed-

ers, or make your own by mixing ¼ cup of sugar in 2 cups of water. Boil the water first, then add the sugar and let the solution cool before pouring it into the feeder.

To keep mold from developing, clean nectar feeders every 3 to 4 days in very hot water (you can add white vinegar in a 1-to-10 ratio of vinegar to water to disinfect them, then rinse well in hot water), using a bottle brush to clean the feeding ports. Because you'll be cleaning the feeders often, choose disk-shaped feeders with flat feeding ports; they're the easiest style to clean. When the feeders are dry, refill them with fresh sugar solution. Don't use honey or brown sugar to make the nectar—it can foster a fungal growth on the hummingbirds' beaks. And rather than adding red food coloring to the solution, choose a feeder with red feeding ports to attract the hummers and grow some tempting red flowers in your garden.

Squelching squirrels and bigger birds: Hungry squirrels and chipmunks can be a problem at feeders. They can get into even hard-to-reach feeders and, once there, quickly empty them. Keep them away from pole-mounted stations by attaching a metal collar on the pole just beneath the feeder. You can also buy domed plastic squirrel guards from stores, catalogs, and Web sites that sell wild bird supplies, and attach them over or underneath hanging or pole-mounted feeders.

But the best defense against aggressive squirrels is to buy the right kind of birdfeeder. A good choice is a metal hopper feeder with perches that drop down under a squirrel's weight, causing a metal barrier to close tightly over the feeding ports. These heavy-duty feeders are nearly indestructible and usually do the trick. Other options are the popular battery-operated hanging feeders that send squirrels flying when they land on a perch.

Bird-Attracting Basics

Try these techniques to make your yard more inviting to birds.

- Offer a variety of seed in different styles of feeders placed at varying levels to cater to the needs of different species.

- When adding plants, choose species that are native to your region so birds will find familiar fruits, seeds, and nesting sites.

- Mix short trees and shrubs with tall trees, and include some evergreens like junipers (eastern red cedar) for food and shelter.

- Combine open spaces with dense plantings.

- Grow grasses, vines, and flowers for seeds and nectar.

- Put birdbaths in the open, so birds will have a clear view when drinking, but near cover, to provide a fast escape.

- Buy a heated birdbath or add a heating coil in winter to keep the water surface open for thirsty birds.

If large or aggressive birds such as grackles and pigeons dominate your feeders and frighten away small birds, distract them with other snacks. Toss some cracked corn and milo or stale bread on the ground several yards from the stations to draw the bigger birds away. (But clean it up nightly so you don't also attract rats or other unwelcome hungry visitors.) Another effective solution is to simply add more feeders to reduce the competition. Large birds tend to avoid tube feeders, preferring tray and platform feeders. By providing both types, you'll make sure the smaller birds get their share.

Water All Year

Providing water is likely to attract an even wider range of birds than putting out birdfeeders will. A clean, accessible, reliable water source can help birds survive in winter when natural water sources are frozen, and it's also helpful during droughts or in arid regions such as the Southwest.

Set a birdbath in the open and at least 3 feet off the ground. Choose a spot near shrubs or overhanging branches to provide an escape route from cats, hawks, and other predators. The water in the bath should be no deeper than 2 inches. Putting a few rocks or pebbles in the birdbath will help birds get their footing. Birds (including hummingbirds) are particularly attracted to the sound of moving water, and many birdbaths now come with a drip hose attachment or built-in recirculating fountain feature. (Some of the fountains are even solar powered.) You can buy a separate drip hose attachment for your current birdbath, or simply hang a leaky can or jug, filled with water daily, from a branch over the bath.

In winter, birds need shallow, open water. Commercial immersion water heaters will keep the water in birdbaths thawed in winter, or buy one of the many birdbath models with a heating element built in. They are available from stores, Web sites, and catalogs that sell wild bird supplies. You can try to keep water from freezing by pouring warm water into the baths as needed, but on very cold days, the water can refreeze in less than an hour, so a heating element or heated birdbath is a better option.

Cover and Nest Sites

Cover is any form of shelter from enemies and the elements. Different bird species favor different kinds of cover. Mourning doves, for example, prefer evergreen groves, while many songbirds prefer the refuge of densely twiggy shrubs. Likewise, most species require a particular kind of nest site in which to raise a family. Some birds, including red-winged blackbirds, nest in high grass; others, such as cardinals, nest in dense foliage; and still others, such as woodpeckers, owls, and bluebirds, are cavity nesters, raising their young in nests built in holes in tree trunks.

You can add more nest sites and attract many types of birds to your yard with birdhouses. Different species have different housing requirements, but there are ready-made birdhouses and build-your-own plans for accommodating everything from bluebirds to barn owls. Whichever birdhouse you choose, make sure that it is weather resistant, that its roof is pitched to shed rain, and that there are holes in the bottom for drainage and in the walls or back for ventilation. Whether you build or buy, avoid models with a perch beneath the entry hole—birds don't need it, but it makes it easier for squirrels, raccoons, and other predators to raid the nests within. A hinged or removable top or front makes cleaning easier. Position birdhouses with their entrance holes facing away from prevailing winds, and clean out the boxes after every nesting season.

Landscaping for Birds

Feeders, birdbaths, and birdhouses play important roles in attracting avian friends. But trees, shrubs, and other vegetation can do the whole job naturally. Plants provide food, cover, and nest sites, and because they trap dew and rain and control runoff, they help provide water, too.

When adding plants to your landscape, choose as many native, food-bearing species as possible, with enough variety to assure birds a steady diet of fruit, buds, and seeds throughout the year. Mix plantings of deciduous and evergreen species to maintain leafy cover in all seasons. Species that are native to your region are generally best, because the local birds evolved with them and will turn to them first for food and cover. Combine as many types of vegetation as possible: tall trees, shorter trees, shrubs, grasses, flowers, and groundcovers. The greater the plant diversity, the greater the variety of birds you will attract. See "Trees and Shrubs for Birds" for some top choices.

Hummingbirds have their own landscape favorites. Preferred trees and shrubs include tulip tree (*Liriodendron tulipifera*), mimosa (*Albizia julibrissin*), cotoneasters (*Cotoneaster* spp.), flowering quinces (*Chaenomeles* spp.), and rose of Sharon (*Hibiscus syriacus*). A trumpet vine (*Campsis radicans*) is a gorgeous sight in bloom, with its large, showy orange-red flowers, and it is a hummingbird favorite, as are honeysuckles (*Lonicera* spp.), nasturtium (*Tropaeolum majus*), and morning glory (*Ipomoea tricolor*). Favored perennials include columbines (*Aquilegia* spp.), common foxglove (*Digitalis purpurea*), fuchsias (*Fuchsia* spp.), cardinal flower (*Lobelia cardinalis*), penstemons (*Penstemon* spp.), torch lilies (*Kniphofia* spp.), sages (*Salvia* spp.), delphiniums (*Delphinium* spp.), and bee balm (*Monarda didyma*).

Of course, there is a flip side to landscaping for the birds, especially if you grow berries for your family. Bird netting may be a necessity if you don't want to share your cherries and blueberries with your feathered friends. Fortunately, netting and other simple techniques—such as growing

Trees and Shrubs for Birds

To attract birds to your landscape, look at plants from a bird's point of view. Do they provide food and shelter? Nest sites? Try to plant a variety to provide birds with protective cover and a varied diet throughout the year. The following trees and shrubs are excellent food sources—producing berries, nuts, or seeds that birds will flock to. Evergreen species provide food but are also especially important for winter cover. These species will grow in most regions of the country.

Deciduous Shrubs

Cornus sericea (red-osier dogwood)

Ilex verticillata (winterberry)

Morella spp. (formerly *Myrica* spp.; bayberries)

Prunus pumila (sand cherry)

Pyracantha spp. (firethorns)

Rubus spp. (raspberries and blackberries)

Sambucus nigra ssp. *canadensis* (American elderberry)

Vaccinium spp. (blueberries)

Viburnum spp. (viburnums)

Evergreen Shrubs

Cotoneaster spp. (cotoneasters)

Ilex spp. (hollies)

Mahonia aquifolium (aka *Berberis aquifolium*; holly-leaved barberry)

Taxus cuspidata (Japanese yew)

Deciduous Trees

Amelanchier spp. (serviceberries)

Carya spp. (hickories)

Celtis spp. (hackberries)

Cornus florida (flowering dogwood)

Crataegus spp. (hawthorns)

Diospyros virginiana (American persimmon)

Fagus grandifolia (American beech)

Fraxinus americana (white ash)

Prunus spp. (cherries)

Malus spp. (crabapples)

Morus spp. (mulberries)

Sorbus spp. (mountain ashes)

Quercus spp. (oaks)

Evergreen Trees

Ilex opaca (American holly)

Juniperus spp. (junipers)

Picea spp. (spruces)

Pinus spp. (pines)

Pseudotsuga menziesii (Douglas fir)

Tsuga canadensis (Canada hemlock)

yellow-fruiting rather than red cherries—will prevent or minimize damage. (For more on controlling birds, see the Animal Pests entry.) But most seed- and fruit-eating birds favor wild food sources and are drawn to gardens only for their relative abundance of insects.

BLACKBERRY

See Brambles

BLANKET FLOWER

See *Gaillardia*

BLEEDING HEART

See *Dicentra*

BLUEBELLS

See *Mertensia*

BLUEBERRY

Vaccinium spp.

Ericaceae

Blueberries are among North America's few cultivated native fruits. They are one of the most popular fruits for home gardeners for their ornamental value, pest resistance, and delicious berries. Some gardeners think they're hard to grow because they require acid soil, but that requirement is actually quite easy to meet.

Types of Blueberries

In northern zones, gardeners choose highbush blueberries (*Vaccinium corymbosum*) and lowbush blueberries (*V. angustifolium*) and hybrids and cultivars of the two species for their productivity and their hardiness. Southern gardeners usually raise cultivars of rabbiteye blueberry (*V. virgatum*,

V. ashei). All these species and their cultivars bear delicious fruit on plants with beautiful white, urn-shaped flowers and bright fall foliage color.

Lowbush blueberries: Although the fruit of the lowbush blueberry is small, many people consider its flavor superior to that of other blueberries. These extremely hardy plants are good choices for the North. Lowbush plants spread by layering and will quickly grow into a matted low hedge. Native lowbush blueberries are the most hardy, especially with snow to protect them in northern locations. Zones 2–6.

Highbush blueberries: Highbush are the most popular home-garden blueberries. Most modern varieties grow about 6 feet tall at maturity, and each bush may yield 5 to 20 pounds of large berries in mid- to late summer. Crosses between highbush and lowbush species have resulted in half-high selections such as 'Northland' and 'Northblue'. These large-fruiting, productive plants grow $1\frac{1}{2}$ to 3 feet tall, a size that is easy to cover with bird-proof netting or with burlap (for winter protection). Dwarf selections of *V. corymbosum* also are available. Popular varieties include self-fruitful 'Sunshine Blue', which reaches 3 to 4 feet tall, and Peach Sorbet (aka 'ZF06-043'), a productive $1\frac{1}{2}$- to 2-foot-tall bush with colorful foliage. Highbush blueberries vary in hardiness, but many cultivars grow well in the North if you plant them in a sheltered spot. Some growers raise them in large pots and store them in an unheated greenhouse or cold frame for winter. Good varieties for the North include 'Bluecrop', 'Patriot', and 'Jersey'. Gardeners in the South and Pacific Northwest should choose varieties with a low chilling requirement, such as 'Misty' and 'Sunshine Blue'. Zones 3–8.

Rabbiteye blueberries: Rabbiteyes are ideal for warmer climates. They'll tolerate drier soils than highbush plants can, although they will benefit from irrigation during dry spells. The plants grow rapidly and often reach full production in 4 to 5 years. Most modern varieties grow up to 10 feet tall and may yield up to 20 pounds of fruit per bush; some are hybrids between rabbiteye and highbush blueberries. Rabbiteyes and their hybrids are not reliably hardy north of Zone 7. They do not grow well in areas that are completely frost-free, however, because they need a chilling period of a few weeks to break dormancy and set fruit. Zones 7–9.

Planting

Blueberries are particular about their growing conditions, so be sure to choose a suitable spot. They need a moist but well-drained, loose, loamy, or sandy soil with a pH somewhere in the range of 4.0 to 5.5 (the specific range depends on which type you want to grow). Test your soil before planting. If you need to reduce the pH, you can do so by working in lots of composted pine needles or oak leaves, or compost made from pine, oak, or hemlock bark. (You want the soil around the plants' roots to be about a 50–50 mix of your soil and compost.) If you can't get a supply of the proper compost, you can add moist sphagnum peat moss to the planting bed in its place. All of these acidic organic materials will help lower pH.

Adding elemental sulfur is another acceptable method (1 to 7 pounds per 100 square feet of garden space, depending on your soil test results), but bear in mind that the sulfur will harm the mycorrhizae that associate with blueberry roots to aid their growth (for more about mycorrhizae, see the Soil entry). Avoid using the commonly prescribed aluminum sulfate, a chemical source of sulfur that is toxic to many soil organisms and changes the flavor of the fruit. For more information on adjusting soil pH, see the pH entry. Building up the soil with organic matter and other amendments *before* you plant is much easier and helps blueberries establish more readily.

Because most blueberries are not self-fertile, you must plant at least two different cultivars to get fruit, and three are even more effective for good cross-pollination. Plant different cultivars near each other, as the blossoms are not especially fragrant and do not attract bees as readily as many other flowers. If you have a large plot set aside for blueberries, try interplanting the cultivars. Keep good records of your plantings, so that if you lose a cultivar you'll be able to replace it with a kind that's different from the surviving plants. Blueberries grow slowly and don't reach full production until they're 6 to 8 years old, so get a head start with 2- or 3-year-old plants.

After enriching the soil and making sure it's acidic enough for blueberries, cultivate it thoroughly to allow the roots to penetrate easily. Blueberries are shallow rooted, so all the nutrients and moisture the plants need must be available in the top few inches of soil.

In spring or fall, set highbush and rabbiteye blueberries 5 feet apart in rows spaced 7 to 9 feet apart. Set lowbush plants 1 foot apart in rows 3 feet or more apart. Water your plants with a liquid organic fertilizer such as compost tea or fish emulsion directly after planting and once a week for the next 3 to 4 weeks. See the Compost entry for instructions for making compost tea.

Maintenance

Keep plants weed-free, but avoid cultivating or hoeing around them; it's easy to damage the shallow roots. Maintain a thick layer of organic mulch around the plants, and hand-pull any weeds that emerge. Pine needles, oak leaves, or shavings/sawdust from oak, pine, or hemlock are great mulches that help to maintain soil acidity. Even with a mulch, though, blueberries can dry out quickly, so water often during dry periods.

Blueberries don't need heavy fertilizing, but nitrogen is important for healthy plants. Those lacking nitrogen have stunted growth and yellow leaves that later become a reddish color. Each spring, apply fish meal or soybean meal under the mulch around each plant. Use ¼ to 2 cups per plant, depending on the size of the plant and how well it is growing.

Pruning

Like most bush fruits, blueberries benefit from pruning as they become older. Yearly pruning helps to encourage large fruits and maintain productivity. Proper pruning also lets sunshine into the bushes, which aids in ripening the berries. Late winter is the ideal time for pruning.

In general, both highbush and rabbiteye plants respond to the same type of pruning. For the first 3 to 4 years, prune only to make sure each bush is growing in a strong upright shape. If the fruit buds are too numerous, remove some of them to get fewer but larger berries. (You can distinguish fruit buds on the dormant plants because they are fatter than leaf buds.)

After 4 years, when the plants are producing well, cut out a few of the thick older canes each year, as shown at right. Thin out branches that are crowding each other and the twiggy ends of canes if they seem too thick. Cut back any plants that are growing too high to harvest conveniently.

For highbush blueberries in Zones 3–4, a different type of pruning is recommended because

Pruning blueberries. For established rabbiteye blueberries and most highbush blueberries, annual pruning involves cutting out a few older canes and thinning crowded branches and twiggy branch tips.

they grow more slowly and don't get as tall. Severe pruning would be likely to reduce production drastically for many years. Instead, it's usually only necessary to thin out the twiggy ends of the branches and cut out any wood that is broken or winter damaged. When the bush is about 20 years old, it is beneficial to remove some of the older wood and gradually renew the plant.

Lowbush plants naturally form low, open-growing shrubs. Prune to remove injured branches and thin out the older canes. Cut up to half of the older canes at ground level each year, and harvest berries from the uncut stems. The next year, remove the stems you left the previous year, and harvest fruit from the new stems.

Problems

Although commercial growers encounter a variety of insects, home gardeners rarely have any problems. The blueberry maggot and cherry fruitworm are the most troublesome insects that are likely to appear. The larvae tunnel in the fruit, making it unsuitable for consumption. Reduce the chances of damage by cleaning up all the old fruit in a planting before winter. If there is a serious infestation, cover the bushes with screening in spring to prevent egg laying.

Diseases are seldom a concern in the North but tend to be more common in the South. Botrytis tip blight kills new growth, and stem canker causes cracks in the canes. Cut away any growth that shows signs of abnormal appearance. Mummy berry makes the fruit rot and fall off. To prevent it, plant resistant cultivars, keep the berries picked, and clean up any dropped fruit.

Viral diseases, such as stunt, are difficult to control and invariably result in the gradual deterioration of the plant. Buy from a reputable nursery to get disease-free plants.

Birds are particularly fond of blueberries. To prevent damage, cover the bushes with tightly woven netting before the berries begin to ripen. Secure the netting at ground level to keep clever birds from sneaking underneath it—robins are especially adept at this—and support the netting on tall stakes that hold it 6 inches or more away from blueberry bushes to prevent birds from perching on the net and feasting on berries through the openings.

Harvesting

Blueberries ripen over a long season, and you don't need to pick them daily, as you do with strawberries. Different cultivars ripen to various shades of blue, so be careful not to pick them too early if you want the best flavor; taste them to determine when they're at their peak. Don't pull berries from the stem; instead, gently twist them off with your fingertips. If the berries don't come off with slight pressure, they're not ready for harvest. Blueberries keep for several days after picking if you keep them cool and dry. They are also ideal for freezing.

BOG GARDENS

See Water Gardens

BONSAI

The goal of the traditional Asian art of bonsai (pronounced BONE-sigh) is to replicate the look of an old tree shaped by time and weather, but dwarfed and grown in a pot. Traditional bonsai trees are not houseplants. They need protection during temperate zone winters but are kept outside during the growing season and only brought indoors occasionally for display. Tropical trees like small-leaved figs (*Ficus* spp.) can be used to create bonsai suitable for growing indoors, however.

Bonsai (which means "tree in a pot" in Japanese) can be created from evergreens and deciduous trees, or from almost any plant with a solid, woody trunk and stout limbs. Bonsai fruit trees—often quince, plum, or crabapple—may bear small fruit. The best plants for bonsai have tapering trunks with interesting shapes, bends, or twists. Scars, gnarls, and stumps give the tree an aged look.

There are five basic bonsai training styles: formal upright, informal upright, broom-shaped, windswept, and cascade. The formal and informal upright styles are for conical, tightly branched trees. The branches of a broom-shaped tree are more spreading, so that the tree resembles an upside-down broom. Windswept tree trunks grow nearly horizontally. Cascading trees fall away over the pot rim, as trees growing on cliffs or rock outcroppings often do.

Bonsai artists develop the styles through a combination of pruning, pinching, and wiring. The trunk is the primary focus of a bonsai tree, and asymmetrical patterns in the branches complement the trunk. Experienced bonsai artists sometimes scar or strip the tree's bark as well.

The container for a bonsai tree is like the frame of a picture: It should enhance the effect without distracting the viewer from the main attraction. In general, earth-tone containers flatter evergreens, while glazed pots complement deciduous or flowering trees.

If you're intrigued by the art of bonsai and want to learn how to create your own, there are many books on the subject, both for traditional bonsai and indoor, or houseplant bonsai, as well as a wealth of information on the Internet (see Recommended Reading on page 675).

BOTANICAL NOMENCLATURE

Rose, Iris, Daisy, Fern—there are many wonderful plant names that are also used as names for people. The crossover of human and plant names is fun. However, sorting out confusing and overlapping common plant names isn't fun for puzzled gardeners trying to use the Internet to figure out the identity of a particular plant, to decide what to order from a garden catalog, or to find the plants they want at a nursery. Some plants have several common names. For example, the popular shade-tolerant annual many gardeners call impatiens is also known as patient Lucy, Zanzibar balsam, patience plant, busy Lizzy, sultana, and sultan snapweed.

Fortunately, gardeners can keep the names and the plants straight by learning about and using botanical nomenclature. Botanists developed this systematic way of naming plants so they could precisely classify every plant they study. This system gives a plant a two-part name, which identifies the plant and classifies it in relation to other plants. The two parts of the name are the genus name and the species name. A species is a group of individual plants that share common attributes and are able to breed together. A genus is a group of one or more species with closely similar flowers, fruits, and other characteristics.

Genus and species names are analogous to people's first names and surnames. The genus name is like a surname: It indicates a group of plants that have some shared characteristics, just as a surname links a group of related human beings. Genus names are often derived from Greek or Latin words, or from the names of people. For example, *Allium* (the genus of onions and their kin) is the Latin word for garlic, and *Nicotiana* (the genus of tobacco) was named for Jean Nicot, who introduced tobacco to Europeans. It's usually easy to see the shared traits of plants in a genus. Gardeners often refer to plants by using the generic name (the name of the genus) as a common name. When gardeners talk about irises, dahlias, and anemones, they use the genus names *Iris*, *Dahlia*, and *Anemone* as common names.

The species name is like a person's first name. By itself, a species name won't help you identify a particular plant. For example, many plants bear the species name *odorata* because they are fragrant, so the name *odorata* alone doesn't refer to any one kind of plant. It takes both names, the genus and the species, to identify a plant as, for example, white pine (*Pinus alba*) and white oak (*Quercus alba*). Together, the two parts identify a particular species of plant and distinguish it from all other species of plants.

In nature, most members of a species look pretty much the same, aside from differences due to age or growing conditions. Minor but consistent variations that occur within a species in nature are called subspecies (ssp.), varieties (var.), or forms (f.). For example, doublefile viburnum is *Viburnum plicatum* f. *tomentosum*. It bears flat, showy flowers in rows on top of the branches, unlike the species, Japanese snowball viburnum (*Viburnum plicatum*), which bears snowball-like flowers.

Among cultivated plants, however, there can be wide variation within a species. Gardeners have always singled out and propagated individual plants with noteworthy form, color, fragrance, or flavor. Any cultivated plant with select features that are passed along when the plant is reproduced by seed or by asexual propagation is called a cultivar, short for *cultivated variety*. To be proper, cultivar names should follow the species name, as in *Salvia officinalis* 'Tricolor'. (In addition, botanical varieties can also have cultivars—for example, *Viburnum plicatum*

f. *tomentosum* 'Mariesii' is a large-flowered form of doublefile viburnum.) For convenience, though, most gardeners refer to vegetables, fruits, and annual flowers by the cultivar name first and then the common name, as in 'Silver Queen' sweet corn.

Botanical names and groupings sometimes change, as botanists correct past errors or achieve new understanding. Usually a specialist will grow, observe, and study all the plants in a genus for many years before publishing a revised classification. (Botanists also are using gene mapping to study the relationships among plants.) Several more years may pass before a revised botanical name or grouping is widely adopted.

BOXWOOD

See *Buxus*

BRAMBLES

Rubus spp.

Rosaceae

Raspberries and blackberries are among the most delicious and desirable fruits you can grow in a home garden. The fruits of brambles (thorny members of the genus *Rubus*) are frequently treated as gourmet fruit not because they are hard to grow, but because they don't ship well.

Selecting Brambles

Brambles can produce fruit for 10 to 25 years. It's important to choose cultivars that have the characteristics you want and suit your climate, but for some types of brambles, you'll have a very wide range of cultivar choices. It's a good idea to visit a local raspberry and blackberry grower and ask which varieties grow well locally. To find a grower in your area, check the list of member growers at the Web site of the North American Raspberry & Blackberry Association (NARBA). The North American Fruit Explorers' Web site is also a great source of information about brambles and other fruits. (See Resources on page 673 for Web site addresses.) Be sure to ask about hardiness and disease resistance. If you have space to grow more than one variety, try to choose varieties with different ripening seasons to extend your harvest.

Raspberries: There are two types of raspberries: summer bearing and fall bearing. In some areas of the country, their bearing season may overlap, so you can harvest raspberries from early summer until frost. Red and yellow cultivars are summer or fall bearers. All black and purple raspberries are summer bearers.

Red and yellow raspberries are the easiest raspberries to grow. Their fruit is sweet and fragrant. Yellow raspberries are mutations, or sports, of reds and tend to be very sweet. The color is less attractive to birds, too.

Black raspberries are not as winter hardy as red ones but tend to tolerate more summer heat. They also are more prone to viral and fungal diseases and have stiffer thorns. The berries are seedy but have very intense flavor. They are good eaten fresh or in preserves.

Purple raspberries are hybrids resulting from crosses between reds and blacks. The canes are generally more winter hardy than the black parent's canes. They tend to be very spiny and productive with large, intensely flavored berries.

Blackberries: In general, blackberries are less winter hardy than most raspberries. In northern areas, the roots may survive without protection, but the overwintering canes are often killed above

the snow line. But because blackberries tend to be extremely vigorous, even a very short portion of surviving cane will often produce a surprising amount of fruit.

Blackberries can be divided into three general groups: erect, semierect, and trailing.

The erect type has strong, upright canes that are usually thorny and don't require support. They tend to be more winter hardy than the other types and produce large, sweet berries.

Semierect blackberries are thornless and more vigorous and productive than the erect type. Most of them grow better if supported. The fruit is tart and large and has a solid core. The plants bloom and mature later than the erect type.

Trailing blackberries, or dewberries, are the least winter hardy. They need support, are early ripening, and have large, wine-colored to black fruit of distinctly good flavor.

Hybrids: Raspberry-blackberry hybrids combine the characteristics of their parents. Most of them are very winter tender. Some are thornless. The fruit resembles blackberries.

Planting and Care

Brambles prefer deep, sandy-loam soil, but they will grow in almost any soil with adequate drainage and a pH range of 6.0 to 7.0, preferably near 6.5. Choose a site with good air circulation, avoiding low-lying areas and frost pockets. Full sun is preferred. In southern areas, partial midday shade will prevent sun-scalded fruit. In exposed locations, give your berries a windbreak.

Soil Preparation

Brambles thrive in soils with high organic content. Incorporate plenty of organic matter as you prepare the site for planting. Have the soil tested, and amend it if necessary. If you have perennial weeds, eradicate them before planting brambles because the young plants do not compete well with weeds. Grow a cover crop (which will also help improve soil organic matter content), cultivate repeatedly, or use a thick, organic mulch to smother out the weeds.

Planting

Plant brambles in very early spring. The exception is plants produced by tissue culture, which have young, tender leaves. Plant them after all chance of frost has passed, or provide frost protection. Set bareroot plants 1 to 2 inches deeper than they were in the nursery. Dig a large enough hole so the roots will fit without bending. Don't let roots dry out while planting. Cut the canes back to about 6 inches tall—if you leave too much topgrowth in place, it will be harder for the plants to become established quickly.

Plant Spacing

Row spacing should be wide enough to allow sunlight and air to reach all plants and to allow you to walk or mow between the rows without damaging yourself or the plants. For home gardeners, this means at least 5 feet between rows for raspberries and 7 feet for blackberries.

Some types of brambles produce suckers. Red and yellow raspberries spread 12 to 15 inches a year, so plant 1 to 2 feet apart, depending on how soon you want a solid hedgerow. Black raspberries and most purples don't sucker but form clusters of canes from their crowns. Plant them 2½ to 3 feet apart. Blackberries sucker vigorously; space them 5 to 6 feet apart in rows.

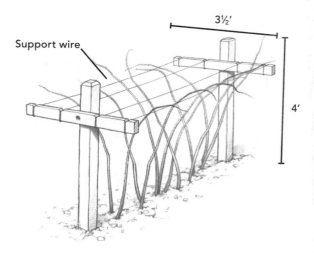

T-trellis. This trellis can be used with a single set of wires for fall-bearing raspberries or a double set of support wires for summer-bearing raspberries.

Trellising

Although many brambles can be grown without a support system, all are best grown on a trellis. Trellising reduces disease problems, saves space, and speeds pruning and picking.

T-trellis: Summer-bearing raspberries do well on a T-trellis like the one illustrated above. Construct it as follows:

1. Set a sturdy 4- by 4-inch post at each end of the row and about every 20 feet in between. Posts should be set at least 2 feet deep and extend 4 to 6 feet aboveground.

2. Add a notched 2- by 4-inch cross arm to each post to hold wires. Each cross arm should have four notches. The height of the cross arms will depend on how vigorous your brambles are. Try putting them about 3 feet high, and move them if necessary.

3. Cut two lengths of 12- or 14-gauge wire or synthetic baling twine a little longer than the

trellis, and fasten the ends to either side of the end post cross arms.

4. After pruning, put the wires in the outer notches, and arrange the canes outside the wire. Tie each cane individually to the wire. Or use a set of two wires on each side of the cross arm, and sandwich the canes between them. After harvest, move the wires to the inside notch to keep the new canes upright.

Hedgerow trellis: All types of bramble fruit do well when supported by a hedgerow-type trellising system. To construct it:

1. Set a sturdy 4- by 4-inch post at each end of the row and about every 20 feet in between.

2. Hammer upward-slanting nails into both sides of each post 3 feet and 4 feet above the ground.

3. Cut four lengths of wire slightly longer than the trellis and twist the ends of the wires into a loop to fit over the end nail.

4. After pruning, lift the wires onto the nails to hold the canes upright between them. (Future pruning is easier if you can remove the wires, so don't staple them to the posts—just rest them on the nails.) Tuck new canes between the wires. A variation of this trellis uses 1-foot cross arms to hold the wires farther apart.

Pruning

For pruning purposes, let's divide the brambles into four categories: fall-bearing raspberries, summer-bearing raspberries, black and purple raspberries, and blackberries. The plants produce two kinds of canes: primocanes and floricanes. Primocanes are new shoots that arise from the main plant or new suckers that rise from roots away from the main plant. In their second year of growth, these canes are then called floricanes. Most brambles bear fruit only on floricanes.

Since each site and cultivar is different, as you prune, you will want to adjust cane densities to fit your needs.

Fall-bearing raspberries: Fall-bearing raspberries are the exception: They bear fruit on their primocanes. Because of this, pruning fall-bearing raspberries is easy because you don't have to decide which canes to save. Mow or cut off these brambles as close to ground level as possible after leaf drop in fall. The most common problem is not cutting the canes low enough to the ground. If stubs are left, some of the buds on them will sprout in spring and grow into weak, unproductive branches.

Summer-bearing raspberries: Summer-bearing raspberries and erect blackberries bear fruit on second-year canes called floricanes. Prune bearing canes off at ground level immediately after the harvest has finished. To avoid spreading diseases, do this when the canes and leaves are dry.

Dormant-prune every year in very early spring before growth starts. Drop any trellis wires out of the way. If you didn't remove the spent floricanes after harvest, cut them off at ground level now. Cut off any spindly canes, and thin the remaining ones to leave two to four of the largest, straightest canes per foot of row. Cut off any suckers that are sprouting outside the row as well. Cut the remaining canes back to 4 to 5 feet and reinstall the trellis wires, or tie the canes to your support system. Pruning summer bearers is illustrated on the opposite page.

Black and purple raspberries: These brambles bear fruit on second-year canes, with most of their fruit on side shoots. During summer, cut the tip off each cane when it's about 2½ to 4 feet high.

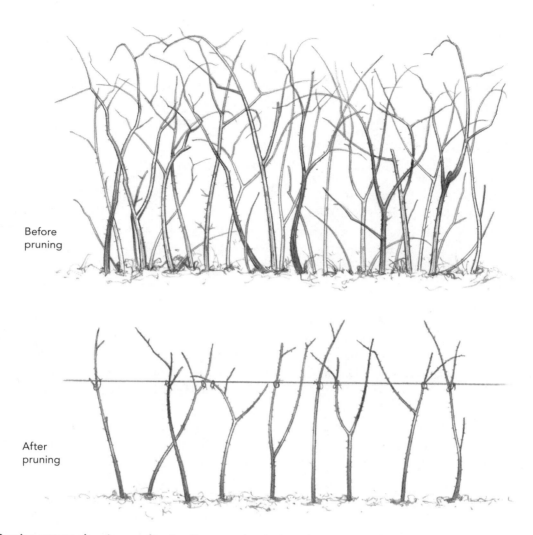

Before
pruning

After
pruning

Pruning summer-bearing raspberries. Prune raspberries in early spring. Remove all spent floricanes and thin remaining canes to two to four per foot of row.

This will force it to develop sturdy side branches the first year. After harvest, cut the spent floricanes back to the ground.

Dormant-prune every year as for summer-bearing reds, thinning the remaining canes to leave six to nine of the largest, straightest ones per hill. Prune back the side branches to 8 to 12 inches, and remove any spindly ones.

Blackberries: Trailing and semierect black-berries are usually left to grow on the ground along the row during the first season. Blackberries bear fruit on second-year canes. Prune spent flori-canes off at ground level immediately after the harvest has finished.

In very early spring, select the thickest six to nine canes per hill, cut them back to about 7 feet, space them along the trellis, and tie them. Shorten side branches to 10 to 15 inches; remove spindly ones.

Harvesting

Brambles ripen in early summer. Red raspberries tend to ripen first, followed by black raspberries, and even later by blackberries. Berries do not keep ripening after harvesting. For best flavor and ease of picking, wait until they are fully ripe. Some raspberries offer a slight resistance to picking even when fully ripe. Let your taste tell you when to pick. Red raspberries vary in color at maturity from light to dark red. Some purple ones change from red to purple to almost black, with sugar levels increasing as the color darkens. Raspberries slip off the stem when picked, leaving a hollow inside the fruit.

Blackberries, although they also vary in color, are typically shiny black when not quite ripe and dull black when fully ripe. They come off the canes more easily when fully ripe.

Pick your berries as early in the morning as possible, when they are cool. If the berries are wet, let them dry before picking. Handle them gently and place, don't drop, them into a shallow container. Refrigerate immediately.

It's easier to pick berries with both hands free. Tie two long strips of sturdy cloth like apron ties to a large tin can or small bucket. Tie your picking can around your waist, or hang it around your neck. Put your berry basket in the bottom if you like. Carry an extra basket to put overripe or moldy berries in as you pick; removing these berries will help prevent rot problems from occurring later.

Problems

While there are many insects and diseases that can attack brambles, there are few bothersome pests in any given area. See the Pests entry for more information on control methods.

Insects

Certain common garden pests attack brambles. Aphids can spread viruses. Japanese beetles feed on leaves and ripe fruit. Tarnished plant bugs feed on buds, blossoms, and berries; stink bugs feed on ripening fruit. See pages 454 to 456 for descriptions and controls. Keep surrounding areas weed-free to limit tarnished plant bugs.

Picnic or sap beetles sometimes damage ripening fruit. These small black beetles are attracted to any overripe or fermenting fruit. To control them, pick all berries promptly. Trap the beetles with the rind of a muskmelon or watermelon; dump the pests into soapy water to dispatch them.

If leaves turn pale and speckled, you may have a spider mite problem. Hot, dry climates and seasons encourage them. See page 231 for controls.

The small green larvae of the raspberry sawfly feed on young leaves, often leaving only the leaf skeleton. Handpick the larvae or spray with insecticidal soap.

Tiny, light yellow worms feeding on the fruit are eastern raspberry fruitworm larvae. They overwinter in the ground; adult beetles emerge in spring. The larvae feed on leaves, flower buds, and berry cores. Berries may drop before they ripen. Remove and destroy infested fruits. Cultivate in late summer to reduce overwintering insects. The following season, spray spinosad when blossom buds appear and again just before they open.

Cane borers cause shoot tips or whole canes to wilt and die during the growing season. They puncture two parallel rings of holes around the cane. To control them, cut off wilted canes about 6 inches below the holes or swelling and destroy. They overwinter inside canes, so collect and burn or discard all prunings.

Crown borers feed on the base, roots, and sometimes shoots of plants, causing whole shoots to wilt and die. Cut wilted shoots back to below ground level and destroy. Squash rust-colored egg masses you see on the leaves in late summer.

Sometimes leaves will develop many small punctures, or even large tears, but no obvious insect culprit is seen. The problem may be the wind. Windblown leaves can be rapidly shredded by thorns on the canes. Trellises and windbreaks reduce damage.

Diseases

The following diseases can affect brambles.

- Raspberry mosaic, blackberry sterility, and leaf curl are major bramble viruses. Mosaic stunts plants and causes yellow-blotched, puckered leaves. Sterility results in vigorously growing plants that produce only nubbins—tiny, crumbly, malformed berries—or no berries at all. Leaf curl causes dark green, tightly curled, and malformed leaves. Viruses can drastically reduce yields. There is no cure. Infected plants should be dug up and disposed of immediately.

- Plant virus-resistant cultivars and purchase plants only from nurseries that market virus-free tissue culture or certified bareroot plants. Remove all wild brambles within 500 to 1,000 feet, especially upwind, and keep aphids off your brambles because they spread viruses.

Plant black raspberries away from red and yellow ones, because black raspberries are more susceptible to viruses.

- Anthracnose causes leaves and canes to develop round sunken purple spots that enlarge to oval shapes with gray centers and raised borders. It also causes black, sunken spots on fruit.

- Cane blight causes shoot tips to wilt and die in midsummer. Canes are often purple or brown. Summer tipping black raspberries gives the disease organism a natural opening; be sure to do it on a dry day.

- Orange rust attacks black raspberries and some blackberries. In spring, the undersides of the leaves are covered with bright, orange fungal growth. Dig up and burn infested plants.

- Verticillium wilt causes canes to turn bluish black from the soil line upward, and leaves to yellow and drop. The fungus also attacks vegetables like tomatoes and peppers. Avoid planting brambles where verticillium-susceptible crops have been grown previously.

- Phytophthora root rot causes stunted plants, yellow leaves, or scorched leaf margins. Avoid it by providing good drainage.

- Fruit rots are caused by various fungi. Wet weather during maturity can cause severe problems. Pick the berries as soon as they are ripe, and remove any moldy ones immediately.

- Powdery mildew shows up as a white powder on the lower sides of leaves and can spread to shoot tips. Fruit may be stunted. Potassium bicarbonate sprays can help control it. Powdery mildew often affects plants that are moisture stressed; provide supplemental water during dry periods but avoid wetting canes and foliage when watering.

🌿 Crown gall causes lumpy, corky swellings on the roots and bases of canes. Avoid wounding when cultivating, or use mulch instead.

Fungi need warm temperatures and humid conditions to thrive. Anything you do to keep the aboveground parts of the plants dry will be to your advantage. Select a planting site with good air circulation and drainage. Avoid overhead watering. Keep rows narrow, and thin canes to recommended densities. Avoid excessive nitrogen. Trellis canes for best air circulation. Remove spent canes right after harvest. Collect and destroy all prunings. If fungal diseases were a problem in previous years, apply lime-sulfur spray in spring when the first leaves are ¼ to ½ inch long.

BROCCOLI

Brassica oleracea, Italica Group
Brassicaceae

Broccoli is a great choice for a home garden. Freshly cut broccoli heads are rich in vitamins and minerals. They're delicious raw in salads or lightly steamed, and they freeze well. If you choose a variety such as 'De Cicco' or 'Waltham' that produces plentiful side shoots, you can enjoy several cuttings from each plant in your garden. Broccoli raab and Chinese broccoli are fast-growing, cool-loving broccoli relatives that produce small, tender flowering shoots that you can eat—buds, stems, leaves, and all.

Planting: Broccoli prefers full sun, but partial shade can prevent plants from bolting (going to seed) in areas with warm spells. Provide a rich, well-drained soil, with plenty of compost.

Cool days and nights are essential once the flower heads start to form. Select a cultivar that will mature before the weather in your area turns hot. Gardeners in most temperate areas can harvest both spring and fall crops. Choose a fast-maturing variety like 'Packman' for a spring crop. In areas without ground freezes, try growing a third crop by planting a slow-maturing variety such as 'Marathon' in winter.

If you're starting your own seedlings, sow your spring crop indoors 7 to 9 weeks before the last expected frost. Seeds should germinate in 4 to 5 days. After the seeds germinate, place pots in a sunny area or under lights and maintain the temperature at 60° to 65°F; keep the soil moist but not wet. Whether you grow your own or buy from a local grower, to avoid premature heading, make sure seedlings are the proper size before transplanting them into the garden—about 6 inches tall, with two to four true leaves. Before transplanting, harden them off for at least a week, as described in the Transplanting entry. Set the young plants 1 to 2 inches deeper in the garden than they grew in the pots or flats. Space them 1 to 2 feet apart in rows 2 to 3 feet apart. Closer spacing will produce smaller heads. Firm the soil and water well.

Protecting young broccoli plants from temperature extremes is critical for a successful crop. A prolonged period of nights around 30°F and days in the 50° to 60°F range can produce tiny, immature heads called buttons. To prevent this, protect plants with cloches or row covers during cool weather. Unexpected warm spells can cause the heads to "rice," or open too soon.

For fall crops, you can start seedlings indoors or sow seeds directly in the ground in July or August. In mild-winter climates, plant in the late fall for a spring harvest.

Growing guidelines: The trick to producing

good broccoli is to keep it growing steadily. Two to 3 weeks after transplanting, water with compost tea or side-dress with bloodmeal or fish emulsion, and water deeply. See the Compost entry for instructions for making compost tea. Repeat monthly until a week before harvesting the flower head. This regimen also encourages large and tender side shoots, which you can harvest until hot weather or a heavy ground freeze ends the broccoli season.

Cultivate around young plants to get rid of weeds and keep the soil loose. When daytime temperatures exceed 75°F, put down a thick layer of organic mulch to cool the soil and conserve moisture. Broccoli needs 1 to 1½ inches of water a week. A lack of water will result in tough stems, so water plants deeply during dry spells. Fall crops need steady (but slightly less) water.

Problems: Of all cabbage-family plants, broccoli is often the least affected by pests, and fall crops tend to have fewer problems than spring ones. Possible pests include aphids, cabbage loopers, imported cabbageworms, cabbage maggots, cutworms, and flea beetles. See the chart on page 454 for more information on controlling these insects.

Other pests include slugs, mites, and harlequin bugs. Slugs chew holes in plant leaves; see the Slugs and Snails entry for controls. Mites are tiny red or black pests; their feeding causes yellow stippling on the leaves. Knock them off the plant with a strong blast of water, or spray with insecticidal soap. Control harlequin bugs—black insects with red markings— by handpicking or applying soap spray.

Diseases are seldom a problem. Black leg produces dark spots on leaves and stems. Symptoms of black rot include yellowing leaves and dark, foul-smelling veins. Prevent these diseases with good cultivation and crop rotation. In case of clubroot, which shows up as weak, yellowed plants with deformed roots, destroy the infected plants. Plant your next crop in another part of the garden; before planting, apply lime to boost soil pH to about 7.0.

Leaf spot shows up as enlarging, water-soaked spots that turn brown or purplish gray. Fusarium wilt, also known as yellows, causes lower leaves to turn yellow and drop off and makes broccoli heads stunted and bitter. Destroy plants afflicted with leaf spot or fusarium wilt to prevent these diseases from spreading.

Harvesting: Harvest before the florets start to open and turn yellow. Cut just below the point where the stems begin to separate. Once you've harvested the main head, tender side shoots will form in the leaf axils all along the lower stalk. Keep cutting, and broccoli will keep producing until the weather turns too hot or too cold. Can, freeze, or pickle broccoli, or keep it refrigerated for up to 2 weeks. Green cabbage loopers and imported cabbageworms often go unnoticed on harvested heads and can end up in your cooked broccoli. To prevent this, drive them out by soaking and swishing the heads in cool salt water with a little vinegar added for 15 minutes before cooking.

BRUSSELS SPROUTS

Brassica oleracea, Gemmifera Group
Brassicaceae

Brussels sprout plants take up a fair amount of space, but the reward is a bountiful harvest of tasty sprouts. The sprouts, which look like mini cabbages, form along the 2- to 3-foot stems under umbrella-like foliage, and need up to 100 days to mature.

Planting: The hardiest cabbage-family crop, Brussels sprouts survive freezing temperatures better than hot spells. Time your plantings so that overnight fall frosts will bring out the sprouts' sweetness. You'll find that you'll plant this crop quite late, after you've set out warm-season crops like peppers and squash. To determine the timing of planting, count back the number of days to maturity from your first fall frost—that's the date to set transplants in the garden. In mild-winter areas, time the crop for a winter-to-spring harvest.

To start your Brussels sprout plants from seeds (indoors or out), sow seeds ½ inch deep. When seedlings are 5 to 7 inches tall, space or thin them to 2 feet apart. Set transplants deeper than they grew originally, with the lowest leaves just above the soil. Firm the ground around the plants and water well.

Growing guidelines: Mulch to retain soil moisture, and hand-pull any weeds to avoid damaging the shallow roots of the sprout plants. Foliar feed lightly once or twice a month with compost tea or seaweed extract. See the Compost entry for instructions for making compost tea. Stake in areas with strong winds. The leaves will turn yellow as sprouts mature; remove these leaves as they fade to give sprouts room to develop.

Problems: See the Cabbage entry for insect and disease control information.

Harvesting: Small sprouts (about 1-inch diameter) are the most tender. Harvest them as they mature from the bottom of the stalk upward. Remove sprouts by twisting them from the stem. Pinching off the plant tops forces sprouts to mature faster. Just before a severe freeze, uproot the plants, remove any remaining leaves, and hang the stalks with sprouts intact upside down in a cool place for a few more weeks of harvesting.

BUDDING

All plants have buds: small undeveloped shoots awaiting a signal to grow into new stems and leaves. The propagation technique called budding involves cutting a bud from one plant and inserting it in the stem of another plant, called the rootstock. Budding is a type of grafting, a propagation method in which a piece of plant stem is wedded to another plant.

Many plants can be either grafted or budded. Budding is a common practice for fruit trees and roses. In ideal conditions, a budded plant can grow 2 to 6 feet in its first season.

When you graft a bud onto another plant, the cambium, or inner growing tissue of the plant, produces a special thin wall of cells called callus. These callus cells eventually develop into new cambium cells (cells that transport water and nutrients). These cells form a continuous path from the rootstock to the grafted bud, so that water and nutrients can pass between the plant and the bud. Good contact between the bud and rootstock is essential for this growth and merger of cambium and bud to occur.

Nursery growers and gardeners bud plants in order to change plant characteristics or improve plant performance. For example, a desirable but tall-growing apple cultivar might be budded onto a dwarfing rootstock. Rootstocks can also lend vigor, hardiness, and insect or disease resistance. For successful budding, the bud plant and the rootstock must be compatible; that is, it must be possible to join the two pieces and grow the new plant to maturity.

In general, closely related plants are compatible. Roses, for example, are budded onto other roses, apple cultivars onto other apples. Rootstocks for budding are usually ½ inch or a little

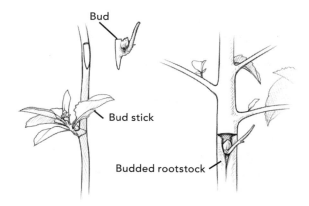

Bud

Bud stick

Budded rootstock

T-budding. This technique involves cutting a single bud from a plant and inserting it in a T-shaped cut near the stem base of the rootstock plant. Be careful to insert the bud right side up, or the two parts will not unite.

larger in diameter. See the Grafting entry for more information on choosing and planting rootstocks.

A thin, sharp knife is essential for budding. For a few bud grafts, a sharp pocketknife or razor blade is sufficient. If you plan to do many bud grafts, consider investing in a good-quality budding knife, which curves upward at the tip. Look for this special type of knife in plant supply catalogs. You'll also need some type of wrapping material, such as electrical tape, to cover the union.

Season: Budding is usually done in late summer (August or September). For successful budding, the bark must slip, or lift easily; this occurs when the cambium layer is active. When buds are inserted toward the end of the growing season, the union heals in a few weeks. The buds remain dormant until the following spring. If buds do start to grow early, they may be winter-killed.

Getting started: Use only healthy and vigorous plants for budding. In dry weather, water the rootstock plant thoroughly a few days before budding. Collect bud sticks—pieces of stem from which you'll cut buds—in the morning of the day

you plan to graft. Prepare them from the midsections of ¼-inch-diameter branches with buds from the current season's growth. Avoid immature branch tips and the dormant buds at the branch base. Cut the leaf blades off the stem, leaving ½ inch of the petiole (the stalk that joins the leaf to the stem). This piece of petiole will serve as a handle, making it easier to hold the bud after you cut it out of the stem. Keep the bud sticks moist by putting them in a plastic bag lined with wet paper towel or damp peat moss. Remove the lower leaves from the rootstock.

Method: The illustration at left shows the steps of this common budding technique.

1. Make a shallow 1- to 1½-inch vertical cut in the bark low down on the rootstock. At the top of this cut, make a horizontal cut about 1 inch long to form the top of the T.

2. Prepare the bud. Be sure to select a leaf bud, which is usually narrow and pointed, and not a plump, round flower bud. Make a shallow horizontal cut above a suitable bud. Place the knife blade ¾ inch below the bud, and make a shallow upward cut that meets the first cut.

3. Slide the bud piece off the stem. Dip the severed bud in water and keep it moist until you are ready to insert it into the graft.

4. Use the tip of your knife to pry open the two flaps of bark. Gently slide the bud under the bark flaps. Wrap the union with masking tape or electrical tape, but don't cover the bud itself.

Aftercare: Check the buds 3 to 4 weeks after grafting, and cut the wrapping material. If the buds you inserted look dry and brown instead of green and vigorous, try rebudding on another part of the stem. Keep the soil around the budded rootstock free of weeds, and protect the stem from animals. In spring, remove the top of the rootstock plant by making a clean, sloping cut just above the successful bud. Stake the developing shoot to encourage straight growth. Remove any suckers that grow from the rootstock.

BUDDLEJA

Butterfly bush. Deciduous summer-blooming shrubs.

Description: *Buddleja alternifolia*, fountain buddleja, produces arching branches and grows 12 feet tall. Plants bear alternate, silvery gray leaves and lavender flowers in the leaf axils of last year's growth. Zones 5–9.

   B. davidii, orange-eye butterfly bush, although popular, can be invasive. Its tendency to spread aggressively by self-sown seedlings to wild areas has led some states to declare this Chinese native a noxious weed. Butterflies flock to butterfly bush flowers for their nectar, but the plants do not support butterfly larvae (caterpillars). Plants bear white, red, pink, or purple flowers on the current season's growth. 'Black Knight' produces dark purple flowers. 'Lochinch' bears 1-foot panicles of lavender-blue flowers with orange centers. Zones 6–8.

   How to grow: Butterfly bushes require full sun and fertile, loamy soil. Prune fountain buddleja immediately after flowering; either remove one-third of the plants' oldest branches or cut it to the ground. If you grow orange-eye butterfly bush, cut plants to the ground in winter.

   Landscape uses: Use fountain buddleja in mass plantings, in perennial borders, or in butterfly gardens.

BULBS

In spring, winter-weary gardeners start scanning the landscape for the welcome evidence of the changing seasons—clusters of crocuses, oceans of daffodils, kaleidoscopes of tulips. Beyond the familiar favorites of spring are a host of other blossoms that arise from bulbs. Dahlias, lilies, gladiolus, and many other familiar flowers are classified as bulbs. Bulbs are a diverse group of perennial plants, including true bulbs, corms, rhizomes, and tuberous roots—all structures that store nutrients to support growth and bloom.

Bulbs through the Year

We tend to think of bulbs as spring flowers, but that's because few other flowers are competing with spring bulbs for our attention. Bulbs can contribute to the garden's beauty in every season. Here are some of the best bulbs for each season, with tips on how to use them. You can also find more about these bulbs in many of the individual plant entries throughout this encyclopedia. For a list of individual bulbs covered in the book, consult the Quick Reference Guide on page 678.

Bulbs in Winter

If you live in Zones 7–9, you can enjoy the late-winter bloom from bulbs planted in the garden. For gardeners in Zones 6 and north, plant these lovely small bulbs for early-spring bloom. These bulbs are also suitable for planting or naturalizing in lawn grass, as their foliage will mature before the grass needs cutting.

   Snowdrops (*Galanthus nivalis*) have bell-like green-and-white flowers and will form colonies in woodland sites. Use them in rock gardens, in pockets of soil between tree roots, or in groups at the front of the border.

For a bright yellow carpet of buttercup-like, quarter-size flowers, plant winter aconites (*Eranthis hyemalis*). These are sometimes hard to establish, but after several years, they'll self-sow and spread nicely. Other golden additions for the cold months are very-early-blooming daffodils, such as 'February Gold' (*Narcissus* 'February Gold'), or miniature irises such as reticulated iris (*Iris reticulata*) and Danford iris (*I. danfordiae*).

The Bulbs of Spring

Spring is that magical season when our gardens come alive. Among the first bulbs to bloom is glory-of-the-snow (*Chionodoxa luciliae*) in lovely soft blue or pink. These often bloom with the last of winter bulbs and the darker blue or white Siberian squill (*Scilla siberica*). Of course, crocuses, daffodils, hyacinths, and tulips are mainstays of the spring garden. By choosing carefully among the many daffodil and tulip cultivars available (there are early, midseason, and late bloomers), you can plan for blooms all spring in a variety of shapes and colors.

Use anemones to create a spring carpet under larger bulbs. Grecian windflowers (*Anemone blanda*) are available in pink, blue, and white. They have large daisy flowers and ferny foliage through May.

Plant grape hyacinths (*Muscari* spp.) as edgings, in borders, under trees and shrubs, and as accents. Grape hyacinths have a long bloom season and are very easy to grow. *Muscari armeniacum*, a deep blue, is the most common and least expensive. 'Blue Spike' is a showy double cultivar. The early dwarf tulips flower in mid-spring, too, so they're a natural combination with grape hyacinths.

Native trout lilies or dogtooth violets (*Erythronium* spp.) are perfect for woodland gardens. They have white, yellow, or purplish pink lily flowers; some species have beautifully mottled foliage.

Fritillaries (*Fritillaria* spp.) like a rich, well-drained woodland location. Try 8- to 10-inch-tall checkered lily (*F. meleagris*) or the stately crown imperial (*F. imperialis*), which has yellow or orange-red flowers atop sturdy 3- to 4-foot-tall stems.

Clumps of summer snowflakes (*Leucojum aestivum*) are attractive in perennial gardens. They have glossy daffodil-like foliage and pendulous, white-and-green, bell-shaped flowers.

Nodding star-of-Bethlehem (*Ornithogalum nutans*) with its silver-green flower spikes is very attractive. You can naturalize *O. umbellatum*, star-of-Bethlehem, in lawn grass, but keep it out of the garden and wildflower plantings—it is very invasive. Regular mowing will keep it in check.

Most alliums (also called ornamental onions) make their appearance in early spring and bloom through June. This diverse and decorative genus ranges from the giant onion (*Allium giganteum*), with 4- to 6-inch globes of pinkish purple flowers borne on 3- to 4-foot stems, to the lily leek (*A. moly*), bearing small clusters of bright yellow flowers on 14-inch stems.

Foxtail lily (*Eremurus stenophyllus*) is one of the tallest bulbs, reaching 2½ to 6 feet. It has bottle-brush-shaped flower spikes in white, pink, or yellow. Like the alliums, bloom continues into early summer. Foxtail lilies need very well-drained soil. They make wonderful specimens and accents.

Summer-Blooming Bulbs

Lilies, which are hardy bulbs, are among the stars of the summer border. Many tender bulbs also shine at this time of year, including tuberous begonias, cannas, caladiums, dahlias, and gladiolus. These bulbs are usually planted as annuals in Zones 3–7, but they may be stored indoors over winter and replanted the following spring. Many will perennialize in Zones 7–9.

Calla lily (*Zantedeschia aethiopica*) looks best grown in clumps that maximize its decorative foliage and white, pink, yellow, or orange flowers. Callas also can tolerate wet soil; try growing them at the edge of a pond or in a container in the water. Callas are hardy in Zones 7–9 but need winter protection in Zone 7.

Crocosmia (*Crocosmia* ×*crocosmiiflora*) is an orange- to red-flowered gladiolus-like plant that is hardy in Zones 6–9. Its 2- to 3-foot-tall sprays of fiery flowers are effective in clumps in the border or naturalized in a well-drained wildflower meadow.

Fall-Flowering Bulbs

Dahlias, caladiums, some species of lilies, and other summer bulbs extend their summer show into fall. But certain bulbs flower only in fall.

Autumn crocus, also called meadow saffron (*Colchicum autumnale*), is a crocus look-alike hardy in Zones 5–9. Plants produce large clusters of purple, pink, or white flowers in September and October. Large, glossy leaves appear in spring.

There are also true crocuses that bloom in fall, including *Crocus speciosus*, showy crocus, with lavender-blue flowers, hardy in Zones 5–9, and *C. sativus*, saffron crocus, with purple flowers and edible stamens, hardy in Zones 6–9. Other fall-flowering species and cultivars are available with lilac blue, white, or purple flowers. Plant these hardy bulbs in August and September for bloom in October and November.

Spider lilies (*Lycoris* spp.) are a group of hardy bulbs that emerge and bloom in a day or two, earning the name magic lilies. Red spider lily (*L. radiata*) has clusters of bright red flowers with prominent stamens that give them a spidery look. It usually blooms in September and is hardy in Zones 7–10. Magic lily (*L. squamigera*) bears showy pink trumpet-shaped flowers on 2-foot stems. It is hardy in Zones 6–10 and blooms in July through August.

Hardy cyclamen (*Cyclamen hederifolium*) is a beautiful small plant for massing in dry shade (the prevailing condition under trees and shrubs). Its heart-shaped, silver-dollar-size, mottled foliage is as lovely as the uniquely shaped pink flowers it bears in September and October. Plants are hardy in Zones 5–9. Wild collection of hardy cyclamen puts native populations at risk; confirm that plants are nursery propagated before you buy.

Growing Hardy Bulbs

Hardy bulbs such as daffodils, tulips, crocuses, and lilies can stay in the ground year after year like perennials. Their care requirements are different from those of tender bulbs like dahlias, which must be dug every winter or treated as annuals north of Zone 9. (For information on growing these bulbs, see "Growing Tender Bulbs" on page 93.)

Planting Hardy Bulbs

Planting hardy bulbs is easy when you do it right. Here are steps to foolproof planting.

Selecting a site: Almost all bulbs are sun lovers and grow best in full sun. However, this is only true when they're actively growing. By the time spring-blooming bulbs go dormant, they can tolerate full shade. That's why spring bulbs like daffodils

KEY WORDS *Bulbs*

True bulbs. True bulbs, like onions, have layers of food-storing scales surrounding the central leaves and flowering stem. Often, the bulbs are covered with a papery skin, called the tunic. Daffodils, tulips, lilies, and hyacinths all are true bulbs.

Corms. A corm is a rounded, swollen stem covered with a papery tunic. Unlike true bulbs, corms are solid, with a bud on top that produces leaves and flowers. Crocuses and gladioli are corms.

Tubers. Like Irish potatoes, tubers are fleshy underground stems that have eyes or buds from which leaves and flowers grow. Some tubers, such as caladiums and tuberous begonias, are cormlike. But unlike corms, which sprout roots only from the bottom, tubers also sprout roots from the sides and top. Other tubers, such as anemones, are woody.

Tuberous roots. Tuberous roots are swollen, fleshy roots. They have a pointed bud on top and roots that sprout from the bottom. Dahlias have tuberous roots.

Rhizomes. Rhizomes masquerade as roots, but they are actually thick, horizontal stems. Roots grow from the bottom of the rhizome; leaves and flowers sprout from the top. Callas, cannas, and bearded irises have rhizomes.

Perennialize. To come up year after year.

Naturalize. To spread naturally in the landscape like a wildflower. Daffodils are perhaps the best-known bulbs for naturalizing because they'll spread as readily as wildflowers. Many of the small bulbs, including winter aconites, snowdrops, crocuses, and miniature irises, also naturalize well.

Little bulbs. A general term used to refer collectively to the many species of small, hardy bulbs, especially spring-blooming ones. These include crocuses, snowdrops, winter aconites, squills, and grape hyacinths.

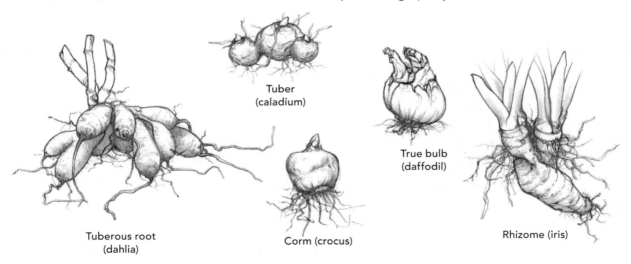

Tuber
(caladium)

True bulb
(daffodil)

Tuberous root
(dahlia)

Corm (crocus)

Rhizome (iris)

and crocuses grow well under deciduous trees and shrubs—their active growing season occurs before the trees leaf out. Some bulbs, like pink daffodils, will have better color if they're grown in partial shade.

Bulbs need loose, humus-rich soil for best performance; they won't bloom well in poor, compacted soils. Most bulbs also need well-drained soil and will appreciate the addition of decomposed organic matter like compost or composted pine bark. If you have poorly drained or compacted soil, try growing bulbs in raised beds, which will enhance drainage and make for easier planting. Bulbs prefer a pH of 6.0 to 7.0 but will tolerate slightly more acidic soils.

Determining planting times: Plant spring-flowering and early-summer-flowering bulbs like crocuses, daffodils, and tulips in fall so they can develop a root system and meet their cold requirements. (Hardy bulbs usually need a certain number of hours of cold temperatures to bloom.) It's best to wait until soil temperatures are below 60°F at 6 inches deep before planting. Follow these rules of thumb: In Zones 2–3, plant bulbs in September; in Zones 4–5, September to early October; in Zones 6–7, October to early November; in Zone 8, November to early December; and in Zone 9, December. In Zone 9, precooling may be necessary; see "Forcing Bulbs" on page 94 for more on this technique.

Soak anemones (*Anemone* spp.) and winter aconite (*Eranthis hyemalis*) tubers overnight in warm water before planting, to bring them out of dormancy. Plant anemones in fall for spring bloom in Zones 4–8 Because it is difficult to tell the top from the bottom of anemone tubers, plant them on edge.

Spacing bulbs: Place bulbs in your flowerbed according to flowerstalk height. For greater impact, plant in clusters of 10 or more rather than singly in rows. Plant large bulbs 5 to 6 inches apart and small bulbs 1 to 3 inches apart. Leave room to interplant with perennials, groundcovers, or annuals.

Planting techniques: The general rule for planting depth is three to four times the widest diameter of the bulb. This depth will help to protect the bulbs against frost, animals, and physical damage from hoeing. Deeper planting will also help bulbs naturalize and perennialize.

The thought of planting a boxful of bulbs can be daunting, but with the right tools and techniques, bulb planting is fairly easy. A heavy-duty tubular bulb planter large enough for daffodil bulbs is the ideal tool for prepared beds. It's a cup-shaped steel cylinder with a foot bar and a long handle. Insert the bulb planter in the soil by stepping on the foot bar. Twist the planter, lift it out, then place a bulb in the bottom of the hole. Fill the hole with dirt from the planter, then repeat with the next bulb.

For planting bulbs in unworked soil, around tree roots, and among groundcovers, you need a stronger tool. Choose a naturalizing tool (a straight steel blade with a forked end, topped by a foot bar and long handle), a crowbar, or a narrow spade with a sharp cutting edge and a foot bar. Push the blade halfway into the soil and pull back, then push down hard so the blade goes completely into the soil. Push forward so the blade lifts up the soil to make a planting slot. Put in a bulb, remove the tool, step down to firm the soil, and repeat with the next bulb.

There's a special trick to planting small bulbs like crocuses and grape hyacinths. Using a narrow trowel, one person can easily plant several hundred small bulbs in an hour, as shown in the illustration on the opposite page. This works both in prepared soil or when planting directly through lawn grass.

Planting small bulbs. To plant small bulbs quickly and efficiently, just stab a bulb trowel into the soil like a dagger and pull it toward you to make a hole for the bulb. Drop in a bulb, pull out the trowel, and step on the spot to close the hole.

Caring for Hardy Bulbs

For the most part, bulbs are undemanding plants. Plantings of daffodils, for example, can thrive and even multiply for years with little, if any, care. But bulbs do benefit from basic routine care, and they'll reward your efforts with more vigorous growth and spectacular bloom displays.

Mulching: Blanket newly planted bulbs with a light, organic mulch like pine needles or straw to aid moisture retention and offer protection from frost heaving. Mulch will help keep down weeds in established plantings during the growing season. It will also help maintain even moisture levels in the soil. Most bulbs can emerge through 2 to 3 inches of light mulch. Keep a layer of light mulch such as pine needles, salt hay, weed-free straw, or ground, composted bark on established plantings. Renew as needed.

Feeding: For many years, bonemeal was considered the best food for bulbs. But bonemeal is not a complete bulb food—it is only a good source of phosphorus and calcium. Start your bulbs off right with a topdressing of a complete organic fertilizer, dried manure, or compost in fall after planting. (Don't put fertilizer in the holes with the bulbs.) This will provide the bulbs with nutrients from the time root growth begins until the foliage matures.

To give your bulbs the complete nutrition they need for top-notch performance, mix 2 pounds of bloodmeal (for nitrogen), 2 pounds of bonemeal (for phosphorus and calcium), and 3 pounds of greensand or wood ashes (for potassium) per 100 square feet of garden bed. If your soil is acid, wood ashes will raise the pH; if it's already near neutral, use greensand. Unfortunately, bonemeal tends to attract rodents and dogs, which may dig up your bulbs to get to it. For established plantings, apply your homemade bulb food as topdressing in early spring when the foliage is just beginning to emerge from the ground, followed by 2 more pounds of dried bloodmeal per 100 square feet in early fall. (If you wait to fertilize until after bloom, it's too late—the foliage will have died by the time the nutrients reach the bulb's roots.)

If you don't want to mix your own bulb food, a simpler alternative is to top-dress with ¼ inch of dried manure (about 2 bushels) per 100 square feet in spring and fall, or 2 bushels of compost in fall and 2 pounds of bloodmeal in spring. Whichever source of nutrients you use, don't scratch the fertilizer into the soil surface—you might damage the bulbs, and rains will wash in the nutrients without further help from you.

Watering: When your bulbs are actively growing, they need about ½ inch of moisture per week, from rainfall or watering or a combination of both. This is particularly important in fall to support good root growth before freezing weather sets in, in spring when active topgrowth starts, and especially in April and May, when the foliage is out and bulbs are manufacturing food for next year's bloom.

Handling bulb foliage: Allow bulb foliage to die naturally rather than mowing or cutting it off. Bulbs need at least 8 weeks of leaf growth after bloom to produce food for the next season's blooms. When the foliage begins to turn yellow or

SMART SHOPPING
Bulbs

Whether you buy bulbs from a garden center, an online retailer, or a specialty grower, bear these tips in mind.

- Buy the biggest bulbs you can afford— you get what you pay for. Look for categories like "exhibition size," "jumbo," "top size," and "double- (or triple-) nosed" for the best bloom. Smaller bulbs, often called "landscape size," are less expensive and good for naturalizing.

- Inspect bulbs as soon as you receive them in the mail or before you buy them at a garden center. Healthy bulbs are sound, solid, and heavy. Lightweight, spongy, soft bulbs won't grow well. If you are in doubt, heft the bulbs in your hand. Healthy bulbs are solid and seem heavy for their size.

- Small nicks and loose skins do not affect the development of the bulb. In fact, loose skins (tunics) make it easier for the bulbs to sprout. However, don't buy bulbs (especially tulips) that completely lack the protective tunic.

- Bulbs should not have mold or show signs of rot. Powdery mildew, a blue-gray fungus, is a sign that the bulbs have become damp. Basal rot is a fungal disease that shows up as brown streaks near the base of the bulb.

- If you receive a delivery of damaged or diseased bulbs, contact the company immediately. A reputable bulb dealer will replace them or give you a refund.

- Plant bulbs as quickly as possible. If you can't plant them at once, store bulbs in a dry place with good ventilation and get them in the ground as soon as you can.

- If you buy species bulbs rather than cultivars, make sure they are nursery propagated, not collected from the wild, a practice that endangers native populations. See the Wildflowers entry for buying tips.

fall over, you can cut it. Don't braid foliage or bind it with rubber bands while waiting for it to ripen. This is not only unsightly, it actually harms the bulbs—it cuts off sunlight and air, hampers flower production, and encourages rot.

Deadheading: After tulip flowers bloom and fade or fall off, remove seed heads to conserve the bulb's resources. Deadhead other bulbs only if they look unsightly; seed formation won't weaken them significantly.

Dividing: Hardy bulbs—especially daffodils—can become overcrowded after many years in the same site. Clumps that cease to bloom or produce few or undersized flowers are probably overcrowded. When this happens, dig and divide the bulbs when their foliage is half yellowed. By then, the bulbs will have ripened but will still be easy to find. Separate the bulbs and replant immediately in well-drained soil, then top-dress with compost. Be sure you set each species at the proper depth and spacing. Transplant bulbs you'd like to move to another site in the same manner.

Propagating hardy bulbs: The easiest way to propagate hardy bulbs—especially the ones that are good for naturalizing, such as daffodils—is to dig them when the foliage yellows, separate the offsets on each bulb, and replant. You can plant them at the same depth and location as the mature bulbs, but they might reach flowering size sooner if you grow them in a nursery bed for two or three seasons first.

Propagate crocuses and other bulbs that arise from corms in much the same way. Dig them and separate the small new corms, called cormels, that form alongside the parent corm.

There are two ways to propagate lilies: Pick the small bulbils that form along the stem above the leaves or the bulblets that form at the base of the stem. Then plant the bulbils or bulblets in a nursery bed, where they'll need to grow for several years to attain blooming size. You can also scale lily bulbs to propagate them. Remove the scales one at a time, and place them in a shallow flat or pot filled with moist vermiculite or peat moss. Bury the scales about halfway, and keep them moist. Small bulblets, which can be transplanted to a nursery bed, will form at the base of each scale.

Coping with pests: Hungry rodents are almost certain to be your bulbs' worst problem. Protect bulbs like crocuses and tulips from voles by adding a handful of fine crushed gravel to each planting hole on top of the bulb. Fine marble chips or crushed road gravel the size of peas (but sharp, rather than round) are best, or you can buy a commercial product specially designed for this purpose.

Some bulbs are naturally rodent-proof. Daffodils are poisonous, so rodents leave them alone. The skunklike odor of fritillaries (*Fritillaria* spp.) bulbs repels hungry voles, mice, and squirrels.

Try interplanting bulbs with a groundcover to deter rodents. If you have a serious rodent problem, protect larger bulbs like tulips and lilies by planting the bulbs in a hardware-cloth cage. When you prepare the planting bed, dig a 12-inch-deep trench around the bed and line it with ½-inch wire mesh.

Growing Tender Bulbs

If hardy bulbs need the same basic care as perennials, tender bulbs need to be treated like annuals. Set them out in late spring when the soil warms, and give them rich soil and lots of food and water. Like annuals, tender bulbs are big feeders. When fall frosts threaten, you can dig your tender bulbs, cure them (air-dry them in cool, dry, well-ventilated conditions), and store them until spring, or consign them to the compost heap with your other annuals.

Forcing Bulbs

There's nothing mysterious about forcing hardy bulbs into bloom out of season. It's all a matter of giving them a compressed life cycle: a cool fall for root growth and a cold winter dormancy, followed by the warmth and water of spring. The trick is in manipulating the seasons to shave off a few weeks and get early bloom. (Some mail-order catalogs offer prechilled bulbs, which have already had their cold treatment and are ready for forcing.)

Gathering Materials

Start in fall with the biggest, fattest, healthiest bulbs you can find. Check bulb catalogs for cultivars that are recommended for forcing. Tulips, daffodils, hyacinths, crocuses, grape hyacinths, snowdrops, miniature irises (*Iris reticulata* and *I. danfordiae*), and glory-of-the-snow all force well.

The best containers for forcing are shallow, wide pots, often called bulb pans, because they won't tip over when the bulbs grow tall and top-heavy. Drainage holes are a must.

To make a good basic potting medium, mix equal parts of potting soil, peat moss, and perlite, and then add one part of coarse sand or fine gravel to each two parts of soil mix. If you want to save the bulbs for next year, add a balanced organic fertilizer when planting.

Planting the Containers

You'll be planting to make a show, so crowd the bulbs into the container, leaving only a little space between. Plant the bulbs shallowly with their noses poking out of the ground to encourage fast growth.

Plant tulip bulbs, which usually have one side less well rounded than the other, in a circle with the flat sides toward the outside of the pot. That way, the first leaf of each bulb will grow from the flat side, and the flower stems will be bunched in the middle. To squeeze more daffodils into a container,

Planting Tender Bulbs

To get your tender bulbs off to a good start, start by selecting a well-drained site in full sun; exceptions are callas (*Zantedeschia* spp.), caladiums, and tuberous begonias, which prefer partial shade.

Plant tender bulbs like cannas, callas, dahlias, and glads after all danger of frost is past in spring. These bulbs are frost tender and won't start growth in the ground until the soil warms above 60°F. Set these bulbs out directly in the garden, or start them indoors and transplant them.

Plant tender bulbs in a well-worked bed enriched with plenty of organic matter. Dahlias, tuberous begonias, cannas, and caladiums all prefer evenly moist soil, so keep them watered and mulch well after planting. Make sure plants are spaced far enough apart to allow good air circulation; tuberous begonias and dahlias may develop powdery mildew if they're planted too close together or in a spot with still air.

plant them in two layers. Place the bottom bulbs on a 2-inch layer of potting mix, cover them to their necks, then set more bulbs between them and cover to the top. Try this with Dutch iris and small spring bulbs, too. Press firmly to settle the bulbs in place and keep them from heaving out.

The Cold Treatment

In addition to the cold period they need to bloom, most spring bulbs need several weeks of darkness and cold temperatures (33° to 50°F) to give them time to grow a healthy set of roots before freezing weather sets in. Tulips need a total of 14 to 20 weeks of cold (including the cool fall period). Daffodils need 16 to 22 weeks. Hyacinths will root at warmer temperatures than others and need 10 to 14 weeks. Crocuses, snowdrops, and other small bulbs need about 12 weeks of cold.

Keep the bulbs moist during this period. You can leave pots outside under a blanket of mulch or in a cold frame until it's time to bring them indoors. Or you can dig a trench and store the pots buried up to their rims in coarse sand. Protect the pots from bulb-hungry rodents.

Bring bulbs indoors when the tips have grown about 1 inch tall. Put them in a cool but bright place at no more than 50° to 55°F. Higher temperatures will rush new growth, making it pale and spindly. Once the flowers start to bloom, move your containers anywhere you want a touch of early spring color. They'll last longer in a cool spot.

After flowering, give the bulbs a dose of organic fertilizer, and water regularly to keep the foliage growing. Plant them outside when the ground thaws. With good care, they'll recover and produce a beautiful show of blooms after 1 to 2 years of growth.

Starting bulbs indoors: Give tuberous begonias and caladiums a head start by potting them up indoors in early spring and transplanting them when the soil warms outside. Start them in flats or pots in a peat-based potting soil. Set the tubers near the top of the pot, barely covering them with soil. Keep the soil mix evenly moist but not wet. Put the flats or pots in a warm, bright place. When the new shoots are several inches tall, pot up the plants or plant them outdoors at the same level as they grew in the pots.

Caring for Tender Bulbs

Tender bulbs need the same basic conditions as other summer flowers: humus-rich soil, ample water, mulch, and periodic fertilization. (The larger dahlia cultivars are heavy feeders and appreciate supplemental feedings to support their lush growth.) However, tender bulbs need special storage and propagation techniques. For more on general care, see the Annuals entry.

Storing tender bulbs: If you live north of

Zone 9, tender bulbs like dahlias, glads, caladiums, and tuberous begonias won't normally survive winter if left outdoors. However, you can dig these bulbs, keep them indoors over winter, and replant them in spring—a worthwhile technique if you grow special cultivars. Lift tender bulbs that you wish to save in fall as the foliage begins to die. Let the bulbs dry in a cool, dry place with plenty of air movement (best under a fan). Then store them at 50° to 60°F in wood shavings, dry peat moss, or another suitable porous, dry material. Check several times during winter and discard any damaged, soft, or rotten bulbs.

Dahlias are hardy in Zones 9–10; elsewhere, dig and store them for winter. Glads are reliably hardy in Zones 9–10 but can be successfully overwintered in protected locations as far north as Zone 6. (If you want to experiment, leave a few bulbs well mulched in a sheltered site and dig the rest.)

Propagating tender bulbs: You can increase your stock of favorite dahlia cultivars in fall when you've dug the tuberous roots and allowed them to dry, or store the clumps whole and divide them in spring. Use a sharp, sterile knife. Make sure that each division has a piece of stem attached; new shoots sprout only from that part of the plant. Discard any thin or immature roots.

Divide tubers like tuberous begonias and caladiums in spring. Cut them into pieces, making sure each piece has an eye or bud. Let the pieces dry for 2 days, then plant them. Gladiolus corms produce small cormels, which you can grow to flowering size in 2 to 3 years. Dig, cure, and store the cormels the same way you treat the mature corms. In spring, plant the cormels in a nursery bed at the same time you put the mature corms out in the garden.

BUTTERFLY BUSH

See *Buddleja*

BUTTERFLY GARDENING

It's easy to fill your garden with a fluttering rainbow. Nearly every locale across the country offers some butterflies that you can attract into your garden by meeting just a few of the beautiful insects' basic needs.

Every butterfly passes through four distinct life stages: egg, caterpillar, chrysalis, and adult. This is called complete metamorphosis. Of course, you can't attract a chrysalis or egg, but you can entice the adults who start the cycle. Adding flowers like zinnias, cosmos, coneflowers, daisies, and other butterfly favorites to your garden is an easy way to attract these nectar seekers.

But in some species, the adult butterfly doesn't eat anything at all. Its only function is to reproduce, mating and laying eggs for the next generation. You can still attract these butterflies—as well as those that drink nectar—by supplying suitable food plants for their caterpillars to munch. In most species, when the female is ready to lay her eggs, she seeks out the host plant species that her caterpillars will need for food.

A caterpillar is an eating machine, but many species will eat only a few types of plants. The caterpillar of the monarch butterfly, for example, eats only milkweeds (*Asclepias* spp.); black swallowtail caterpillars seek out parsley and relatives such as dill and Queen Anne's lace. And as any gardener who's fought off cabbage worms can tell you, the common white cabbage butterflies prefer brassicas (cabbage-family crops) for their host plants.

Supplying food for nectar-seeking adults and host plants for egg laying are the best ways to attract butterflies into your garden. Use low-growing groundcovers such as clovers and grasses to provide sunning spots for adults to warm themselves. Walls, hedgerows, and similar windbreaks create protected spots that butterflies will appreciate.

Adding a source of water is as essential for attracting butterflies as it is for birds. Creating a "mudhole"—a shallow, permanent puddle—offers butterflies both water and minerals from the mud. Or make a butterfly "bath" from the basin of a birdbath (without the stand) or a plate or shallow bowl placed directly on the ground. Fill it with pebbles to give the butterflies good perching spots, then add just enough water to surround the stones

without covering them completely. Butterflies will come flocking!

Planning Your Garden

If you want to add the living color of butterflies to your garden, start by using some of the recommended plants in the lists on page 98. Milkweeds (*Asclepias* spp.) make an unusual addition to the wild garden or middle border, though it's a good idea to contain their vigorous roots in a buried bottomless bucket. The oddly shaped, sweet-smelling flowers will attract a variety of feeding butterflies, and from summer through early fall, monarchs ready to lay eggs will seek out your planting. If you're extra lucky, you may find a delicate monarch chrysalis hanging below

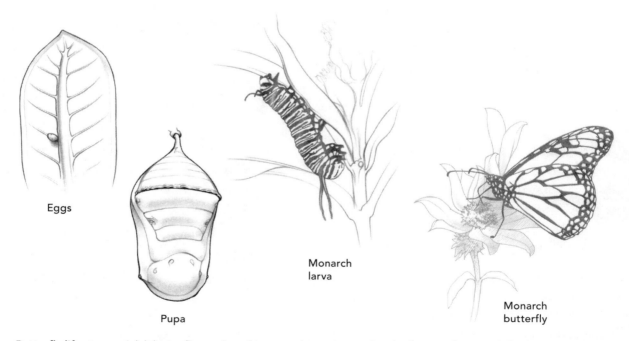

Eggs

Pupa

Monarch larva

Monarch butterfly

Butterfly life stages. Adult butterflies such as this monarch are attracted to the flowers of many wildflowers and garden plants for nectar. Its larvae eat only milkweed leaves. Each species of butterfly has a different caterpillar host plant, and that's where to look to find their eggs, larvae, and pupae.

Plants for Butterflies

Plants may serve as nectar sources for butterflies, as host plants for caterpillars, or as food for both adults and larvae. To increase the number of butterflies flitting about your garden, plant as many host plants and nectar sources in your yard and gardens as you can.

Blend butterfly-attracting weeds such as alfalfa, clovers, Queen Anne's lace, milkweed, and cabbage-family members like field mustard (*Brassica rapa*) into a wildflower patch. And plant some extra parsley just for the larvae of the beautiful swallowtail butterflies. Some plants that butterflies appreciate are garden pests. These include dandelions, nettles, teasel, and thistles. Use common sense when creating your butterfly garden and choose plants that please you and visiting butterflies.

The lists below include butterfly favorites suitable for all parts of the country.

Perennials and Annuals

Ageratum houstonianum (ageratum, flossflower)

Asclepias spp. (milkweeds, butterfly weed)

Aster spp. (asters)

Coreopsis spp. (coreopsis, tickseeds)

Echinacea purpurea (purple coneflower)

Erigeron spp. (fleabanes)

Eupatorium spp. (bonesets)

Eutrochium spp. (joe-pye weeds)

Grindelia spp. (gumweeds)

Helenium autumnale (sneezeweed)

a milkweed leaf like a jade pendant, decorated with shining gold dots. Milkweed's well-behaved relative, butterfly weed (*Asclepias tuberosa*), bears glowing orange, red, or yellow flower clusters and looks equally at home in a sunny wildflower meadow or perennial border. While the showy flowers of aptly named butterfly bushes (*Buddleja alternifolia* and *B. davidii*) attract a wealth of butterflies, they do not provide food for caterpillars of any species and have proven invasive in several states. Many environmentally conscious gardeners avoid buddlejas because they easily escape the bounds of the garden by self-sowing.

If your aim is to attract a particular species, take the time to find out its favorite nectar plants or caterpillar host plant(s). A field guide to butterflies is helpful in planning the butterfly garden. Look for a book with information about the plants that caterpillars eat, the plants from which the adults take nectar, and the drinking, sunning, or other unique habits of the adults. Detailed, full-color illustrations of both the caterpillar and adult stages, and information about the geographical area in which the insects are found, are valuable. Books specifically on butterfly gardening are another excellent reference. Look online or at nature-oriented bookstores for titles to choose. You'll also find extensive online information on butterflies

Helianthus spp. (sunflowers)

Heliotropium arborescens (common heliotrope)

Hemerocallis spp. (daylilies)

Hylotelephium spectabile (showy stonecrop)

Lavandula spp. (lavenders)

Leucanthemum ×*superbum* (Shasta daisy)

Leucanthemum vulgare (oxeye daisy)

Lobularia maritima (sweet alyssum)

Mentha spp. (mints)

Monarda spp. (bee balms)

Phlox spp. (phlox)

Rudbeckia spp. (coneflowers, black-eyed Susans)

Salvia spp. (sages)

Solidago spp. (goldenrods)

Symphyotrichum spp. (asters, Michaelmas daisies)

Tagetes patula (French marigold)

Thymus spp. (thymes)

Verbena spp. (vervains)

Vernonia spp. (ironweeds)

Alcea rosea (hollyhock)

Zinnia spp. (zinnias)

Trees and Shrubs

Lonicera spp. (honeysuckles)

Rhus spp. (sumacs)

Salix spp. (willows)

Syringa vulgaris (common lilac)

Tilia americana (basswood)

Vaccinium spp. (blueberries)

and butterfly gardening. See Resources on page 673.

If your goal is to attract as many butterflies as possible, check a field guide or search online to find out which species are found in your area, then create a checklist. Use your list to develop a custom-tailored butterfly garden of food and host plants. A local natural history museum, college entomology department, or butterfly club can give you more pointers. Entomology departments and agricultural extension services frequently publish articles and brochures on butterfly gardening in their state; you can also find many of these online.

BUXUS

Boxwood. Evergreen shrubs or trees.

Description: *Buxus microphylla*, littleleaf boxwood, is a compact, dense, rounded shrub about 3 feet tall at maturity. Glossy green leaves are arranged in pairs on the angled twigs. Early spring flowers are inconspicuous. Hardiness varies; select cultivars adapted to your location. Most cultivars grow in Zones 6–8.

B. sempervirens, common boxwood, is a shrub or small tree of 6 to 15 feet at maturity. The leaves are dark green above and light green below, turning brown or bronze in winter, and are borne in pairs.

Common boxwood grows best in warm, moist situations. Zones 6–8.

How to grow: Boxwoods are healthiest when protected from direct sun and wind; the drying effects of these elements cause discolored foliage and dieback of late-season growth. Avoid exposed sites and fertilize in spring or in very late fall after plants are dormant. Plant in evenly moist, humus-rich soil and mulch well to keep roots cool. Plan to give winter protection to boxwoods in open areas or at the northern extremes of their hardiness.

Landscape uses: A staple of formal gardens, boxwood's dense compact shape, fine foliage, and slow growth make it useful in landscape situations ranging from small borders to large hedges. Boxwood is a favored plant for topiary, where its slow growth and tolerance of severe pruning allow gardeners to trim it into fantastic shapes. Dwarf boxwoods make excellent edgings for herb gardens. Some people find the odor of boxwood foliage offensive; give it a sniff before you plant to see if you are among them.

CABBAGE

Brassica oleracea, Capitata Group
Brassicaceae

Cabbage thrives in cool weather. In most areas, you can plant an early crop for fresh eating and a late crop—usually the more problem-free and tasty of the two—for use into the winter months. Choose early varieties such as 'Primax' for summer harvest; midseason and late-season cultivars for storage. Mini cabbages such as 'Gonzales', harvested when only 6 inches in diameter, are perfect for small gardens. Loose-leaf versions include Chinese cabbages, like bok choy (see the Asian Vegetables entry), and ornamental cabbages.

Planting: You can buy transplants from a local grower, but cabbage is easy to grow from seed. Plan to set out early types 4 weeks before the last expected frost date. Sow seeds indoors, ¼ inch deep and 2 inches apart, around mid-January or February in the South and in March in the North. Place in a sunny spot or under lights with temperatures between 60° and 70°F, and keep the soil uni-

formly moist. When daytime temperatures reach 50°F and seedlings have three leaves, plant them outdoors.

Plant seedlings in the garden slightly deeper than they grew in flats. Space 6 to 12 inches apart in rows 1 to 2 feet apart. Wide spacing produces bigger heads, but young, small cabbages are tastier. To get both, plant 6 inches apart and harvest every other one before maturity. Stagger plantings at 2-week intervals for a longer harvest.

Start your late crop in midsummer, sowing seeds in flats or directly in the garden. Space these seedlings farther apart than the spring crop, and place them so a tall crop, such as corn or pole beans, provides some afternoon shade.

Growing guidelines: Soil texture is not critical, but early cabbages do best in a sandy loam, while later types prefer a heavier, moisture-retaining soil. Side-dress seedlings with rich compost 3 weeks after planting. Hand-pull weeds to avoid damaging cabbage's shallow roots; mulch to keep the soil moist. Uneven watering can cause a sudden growth spurt that will make the developing head split. If you see a cabbage head starting to crack, twist the plant a half turn and pull up to slightly dislodge the roots and thus slow the plant's growth. Or use a spade to cut the roots in one or two places 6 inches below the stem. This also helps to prevent cabbage from bolting (producing a flowerstalk).

Avoid wetting the foliage during cool weather or periods of high humidity, because constantly wet leaves are prone to disease. Cut back on water as cabbage matures. If leaves start to yellow, provide a midseason nitrogen boost with compost tea. See the Compost entry for instructions for making compost tea. This type of feeding can also encourage a slow-growing crop to mature before hot weather or a winter freeze sets in.

Problems: Major cabbage pests include cabbage maggots, imported cabbageworms, cabbage loopers, and cutworms. You'll find information on controlling them in the table on page 454. The harlequin bug, a small shiny black insect with red markings, causes black spots and wilting leaves; control by handpicking or applying insecticidal soap. Slugs may chew ragged holes in leaves; see the Slugs and Snails entry for controls.

Black leg, a fungal disease, forms dark spots on leaves and stems. Black rot symptoms include black and foul-smelling veins. Clubroot prevents water and nutrient absorption. Fusarium wilt, also known as yellows, produces yellow leaves and stunted heads. Remove and destroy plants affected by these diseases. If clubroot has been a problem in your garden, test soil pH before planting and add ground limestone if needed to raise the pH to at least 6.8

Good growing conditions, crop rotation, and the use of disease-resistant cultivars are the best defenses against cabbage-family crop problems. Also, thoroughly clean up the garden at the end of the season, removing all remaining leaves and roots.

Harvesting: Use a sharp knife to cut heads when they are firm. Leave stalks and roots in place to produce tasty little cabbages; eat them like Brussels sprouts or let them develop into a second crop of small heads. Fresh cabbage has the best flavor, but late-season cultivars keep well in a moist, cool place (32° to 40°F) for as long as 5 to 6 months. Use split heads for making sauerkraut.

CALADIUM

Caladium. Summer or fall tuberous plants grown for foliage.

Description: Selections of *Caladium bicolor*, angel wings or fancy-leaved caladium, light up shady areas with their 6- to 12-inch pointed, heart-shaped leaves marked with white, pink, red, and green. Leaves are borne in 1- to 2-foot, loose, arching bunches. Hooded, off-white flowers are inconspicuous. Hardy only in frost-free soil; treat as annuals or container plants elsewhere. Zone 10.

How to grow: Start caladiums indoors about 4 to 6 weeks before all danger of frost is past. Plant tubers in a loose, fast-draining mix such as peat, sand, perlite, vermiculite, and compost, barely covering the tops. (The end with tiny buds is the top.) Plant the tubers in shallow boxes, flats, or pots. Keep warm (70°F is ideal), and give plenty of water once growth begins. Plant out after the soil is warm, in partial shade with a few hours of morning sun, or under tall trees. Caladiums grow best in fertile, well-drained, moist, humus-rich soil. Apply fish emulsion or compost tea every 3 to 4 weeks to encourage new leaves and bright colors. See the Compost entry for instructions for making compost tea. Handpick or trap slugs and snails. Unless you live in Zone 10 or warmer, dig up caladiums after the first frost, remove the soil after it has dried, and store the tubers almost dry at around 65°F in peat or vermiculite. Start them again in spring.

Landscape uses: Mass caladiums in shady beds and corners, or tuck groups of three to five as accents between larger plants such as ferns, hostas, or shrubs. To brighten shady areas, use cultivars with white-variegated leaves. Show off several caladiums in a large container with elephant's ears (*Colocasia* spp.), begonias or impatiens, and trailing petunias in complementary colors.

CALENDULA

Pot marigold. Spring- and fall-flowering annuals; edible flowers; herbs.

Description: *Calendula officinalis*, pot marigolds, bear single or double, daisylike, 2- to 4-inch flowers in shades of yellow, gold, and orange on 1- to 2-foot-tall open mounds of rough, straplike leaves.

How to grow: Start indoors in late winter or plant seeds directly where they are to bloom. Lightly cover the seeds in a sunny area in well-drained, average soil as soon as frost leaves the ground. Transplant or thin to stand no more than 1 foot apart. Pot marigolds will also self-sow.

Landscape uses: Mass calendulas in mixed annual and perennial plantings or in a cutting garden, or use them to add bright splashes of color to an herb garden. You can also use them to conceal the dying foliage of spring bulbs.

CALIBRACHOA

Calibrachoa, million bells, trailing petunia. Summer-blooming annual or tender perennial.

Description: Closely related to petunias, calibrachoas are 3- to 9-inch-tall plants with trailing stems and a mounding habit. Abundant 1-inch-wide, trumpet-shaped flowers appear continuously from early summer to frost. Blooms come in shades of blue, purple, red, pink, yellow, gold, and white.

How to grow: Give calibrachoas a site in full sun or very light shade with rich, moist, well-drained soil. Plants tolerate dry spells and continue blooming even in hot weather. They produce very little seed, and available cultivars are vegetatively propagated. Start with purchased transplants and set them outside after the last spring frost. Space plants 8 to 10 inches apart.

Landscape uses: Calibrachoas are ideal choices for containers and hanging baskets. They also make an attractive temporary groundcover or edging for the front of a flowerbed.

CAMPANULA

Bellflower, harebell. Late-spring- and summer-blooming perennials or biennials.

Description: All bellflowers produce lovely single blue, purple, or white star- or bell-shaped flowers above deep green, often toothed foliage. There are many species and cultivars to choose from. All are usually longer lived in cooler areas. The following are among the best.

Campanula carpatica, Carpathian harebell or tussock bellflower, bears a profusion of upward-facing, open, 1-inch bells in white and blue shades. These blooms are held individually on threadlike stems, usually 8 inches above tight mounds of shiny green 2-inch leaves; flowers appear in early summer and sporadically throughout the growing season. Zones 3–8.

C. glomerata, clustered bellflower, has dense 4-inch clusters of narrow, pointed purple bells on

Low-Growing Bellflowers

Though tall bellflowers are striking, the shorter species can be stunning in the front of a border, in rock gardens, and as groundcovers. Try earleaf, or fairy thimble, bellflower (*Campanula cochlearifolia*), Dalmatian bellflower (*C. portenschlagiana*), Serbian bellflower (*C. poscharskyana*), and bluebell bellflower (*C. rotundifolia*). These species range from 4 inches to 12 inches tall, with graceful bell- or star-shaped flowers in sky blue, blue-violet, lilac blue, purple, or white.

1- to 2½-foot erect stems above spreading masses of dark green, rough, fuzzy leaves in late spring and early summer. Zones 3–8.

C. persicifolia, peach-leaved bellflower, carries open, 1½-inch, widely spaced white or blue bells on upright stalks to 3 feet above a rosette of slender, 8-inch glossy leaves during summer. Zones 3–7.

C. medium, Canterbury bells, is a biennial usually grown as a hardy annual. It bears loose spikes of showy, 2-inch-long, violet-blue bells on plants 2 to 4 feet tall. Zones 3–8.

How to grow: Plant or divide bellflowers in spring in sunny, average, well-drained soil. Carpathian harebell, especially, needs good drainage. Provide some afternoon shade in warmer zones. Clustered bellflower tolerates wetter sites but not boggy conditions. Remove flowers soon after bloom to encourage rebloom on Carpathian harebell and peach-leaved bellflower. Most come relatively true to type from self-sown seed. Handpick or trap slugs and snails.

Landscape uses: Mass taller bellflowers in borders, cottage gardens, and naturalized areas. The cool blue and white shades of peach-leaved bellflowers contrast nicely with pink and red old-fashioned roses. Carpathian harebells look better in small-scale settings, such as rock gardens, walls, and among cracks in paving stones. Avoid *C. rapunculoides*, the creeping or rover bellflower, an invasive plant that is almost impossible to control once it gains a foothold.

CANDYTUFT

See *Iberis*

CANNA

Canna. Summer- and fall-blooming tender perennials.

Description: *Canna ×generalis*, hybrid cannas, bear 4- to 6-inch irregularly shaped blooms in cream, yellow, pink, red, orange, and combinations. The flower clusters appear above substantial clumps of broad green, cream- or yellow-striped, or rich purple-bronze leaves on upright plants 2 to 8 feet tall. Dig and store rhizomes indoors to overwinter in the North; leave in the ground in Zones 7–10.

How to grow: Start cannas about a month before all danger of frost is past. Plant the rhizomes horizontally with the tips pointing up; cover with about 1 inch of potting mix. When the weather warms, plant out in full sun and fertile, well-drained, moist, humus-rich soil. Mulch with compost, shredded bark, or pine needles when the shoots are about 1 foot tall to control weeds and conserve moisture. Give cannas plenty of water during hot weather and drench liberally with fish emulsion or compost tea during the first 6 to 8 weeks. See the Compost entry for instructions for making compost tea. Handpick Japanese beetles. Remove spent flowers if you can reach them. To overwinter cannas in Zone 6 and colder, dig the clumps after frost blackens the foliage and cut them back to 6-inch stubs. Allow the soil to dry, shake it off, and store the clumps in barely moist peat at 46° to 50°F. In spring, cut the clumps into pieces with one to three eyes (buds) each and start again.

Landscape uses: Cannas add a tropical touch—as well as much-needed height—to any flower border. Grow groups of three plants in a border, repeated along its length, or use as accent plants in clusters of three at intervals along a fence or on each side of a gate or driveway. Cannas look great in or along the edge of water gardens, and they're spectacular container plants, as long as you give them a large container with humus-rich potting soil and plenty of room to spread. For containers, choose cannas with striking foliage, like the yellow-and-green striped 'Striata' (also sold as 'Bengal Tiger' and 'Pretoria') and the red-, orange-, and purple-striped 'Phasion' (sold as Tropicanna). Pair them with trailing plants like nasturtiums, gold moneywort (*Lysimachia nummularia* 'Aurea'), and ornamental sweet potato vines (*Ipomoea batatas* 'Blackie' or 'Margarita'). Dark-leaved canna cultivars like 'Australia' contrast boldly with red, gold, and orange flowers, and all the tall cannas can temporarily screen out an unsightly view.

CARBON SINKS

One proposal for counteracting the rise of atmospheric CO_2 is to plant trees as "carbon sinks."

After all, carbon compounds are a major component of plant cells, so trees represent a huge potential reservoir of stored carbon.

Researchers have discovered other plants that work well as carbon sinks, too, such as switchgrass (*Panicum virgatum*) and other warm-season grasses. These grasses store carbon in their stems and leaves, but the real carbon sink they stimulate is belowground. The roots of these grasses associate with mycorrhizal fungi that produce a substance called *glomalin*—a gluey material that contains lots of carbon. Up to one-third of the carbon in soil is stored in glomalin, which helps bind soil particles together and is the key substance that gives soils good tilth. When organic matter content of the soil is high, glomalin tends to be high, too—so simply by following good organic soil management practices in your garden, you're taking one small step to help fight global climate change.

If you'd like to go beyond that, and you have enough space, consider planting an area of your yard as a carbon sink. Of course, your carbon sink can serve other roles as well. A strategically placed, long-lived shade tree will be a carbon sink that also helps shade your home in the summer. Or a row of evergreens can serve as a windbreak.

If you don't have the right spot for a majestic shade tree, a stand of bamboo can serve as a carbon sink instead. Bamboo is even more efficient at storing carbon than shade trees are, and bamboo can serve as a living "wall" or screen for a garden room. New varieties have colorful canes that provide a great four-season landscape accent. You can even grow types that produce canes sturdy enough to serve as garden stakes. For most gardeners, the key point in success with bamboo is to choose a clumping type rather than a running type that can easily overrun a home landscape. See the Bamboo entry for details on growing bamboo.

CARROT

Daucus carota var. *sativus*
Apiaceae

Orange carrots may be best known, but these sweet, crunchy roots also come in white, yellow, crimson, and even purple. You can grow a rainbow of carrots and taste-test to see which hues are your favorites. More important than color, though, is choosing the right root size and shape to suit your soil. Carrot size and shape varies by type, and there are five major categories. Ball-type, Chantenay, and Danvers carrots have blocky shapes that can produce roots in heavy or shallow soil, while slender Nantes and Imperator carrots need deep, loose soil. All types are available in early and late cultivars; many are disease and crack resistant. Some catalogs don't describe carrots by type but will point out which cultivars do better in heavy or poor soil.

Planting: To produce the best crop possible, deeply cultivate your planting area or build up a raised bed. Loose, rock-free soil is the goal for optimal carrot root development. If you have heavy soil, add plenty of mature compost.

Start sowing this cool-weather crop 3 weeks before the last expected frost; plant again every 2 to 3 weeks after that. Most cultivars take 70 to 80 days to mature, so sow your last planting 2 to 3 months before the first expected fall frost. In Zone 8 and warmer, plant carrots in fall or winter.

Rake the soil free of lumps and stones. Broadcast the tiny seeds, or for easier weeding, plant in rows. Put a pinch of about six seeds to the inch.

They will take 1 to 3 weeks to sprout (they germinate more slowly in cold soil than in warm), so mix in a few quick-growing radish seeds to mark the rows. Cover with ¼ to ½ inch of screened compost, potting mix, or sand—a little more in warm, dry areas—to make it easier for the delicate seedlings to emerge. Water gently to avoid washing seeds away; keep the soil continuously moist for best germination.

Growing guidelines: Thin seedlings to 1 inch apart when the tops are 2 inches high, and be thorough, because crowded carrots will produce crooked roots. Thin again 2 weeks later to 3 to 4 inches apart.

As the seedlings develop, gradually apply mulch to maintain an even moisture level and reduce weed problems. It's best never to let young carrot plants dry out. However, if the soil dries out completely between waterings, gradually remoisten the bed over a period of days; a sudden drenching may cause the roots to split. Carrots' feeder roots are easily damaged, so hand-pull any weeds that push through the mulch, or cut them off just below the soil surface. Cover carrot crowns, which push up through the soil as they mature, with mulch or soil to prevent them from becoming green and bitter.

Problems: The biggest threats to carrots are four-footed critters such as deer, gophers, woodchucks, and rabbits. For controls, see the Animal Pests entry. Otherwise, carrots are fairly problem-free.

Keep a vigilant watch—particularly in the Northwest—for carrot rust flies, which look like small green houseflies with yellow heads and red eyes. Their eggs hatch into whitish larvae that burrow into roots. Infested roots turn dark red and the leaves black. Infestations usually occur in early spring, so one solution is to delay planting until early summer, when damage is less likely. Or cover plants with a floating row cover to keep flies away.

Parsleyworms are green caterpillars with black stripes, white or yellow dots, and little orange horns. They feed on carrot foliage, but they are the larval stage of black swallowtail butterflies, so if you spot them on your carrots, try not to kill them. Instead, transfer them to carrot-family weeds such as Queen Anne's lace, and watch for chrysalises to form, and later, beautiful butterflies!

The larvae of carrot weevils, found from the East Coast to Colorado, tunnel into carrot roots, especially in spring crops. Discourage these grubs by rotating crops.

Nematodes, microscopic wormlike animals, make little knots along roots that result in stunted carrots. Rotate crops and apply plenty of compost, which is rich in predatory microorganisms. (For more controls, see the Plant Diseases and Disorders entry.)

Leaf blight is the most widespread carrot disease. It starts on leaf margins, with white or yellow spots that turn brown and watery. If leaf blight is a problem in your area, plant resistant cultivars.

Hot, humid weather causes a bacterial disease called vegetable soft rot. Prevent it by rotating crops and keeping soil loose. The disease spreads in storage, so don't store bruised carrots.

Carrot yellows disease causes pale leaves and formation of tufts of hairy roots on the developing carrots. The disease is spread by leafhoppers, so the best way to prevent the problem is by covering new plantings with row covers to block leafhoppers.

Harvesting: Carrots become tastier as they grow. You can start harvesting as soon as the carrots are big enough to eat, or leave them all to mature for a single harvest. Dig your winter storage crop before the first frost on a day when the soil is moist but the air is dry. Since spading forks tend to bruise roots, hand-pull them; loosen the soil with a trowel before you pull. Watering the bed before harvesting softens the soil and makes pulling easier.

Carrots are excellent to eat both fresh and cooked. Note that purple-rooted varieties will lose their purple pigment if cooked in water, but they tend to keep it when roasted.

To save harvested carrots for winter use, prepare them by twisting off the tops and removing excess soil, but don't wash them. Layer undamaged roots (so they're not touching) with damp sand or peat in boxes topped with straw. Or store your fall carrot crop right in the garden by mulching the bed with several inches of dry leaves or straw.

CATMINT

See *Nepeta*

CAULIFLOWER

Brassica oleracea, Botrytis Group
Brassicaceae

The sweet and mild flavor of homegrown cauliflower more than justifies the extra care it requires. Cauliflower is not difficult to grow, but it is sensitive to extreme temperatures. Primarily a cool-weather crop, cauliflower won't produce heads in hot, dry weather and is frost tolerant only as a mature fall crop. Most cultivars need about 2 months of cool weather to mature, though some require as little as 48 days and others more than

95 days. To grow cauliflower successfully, the key steps are to choose the right cultivar for your climate, plant at the proper time, and provide a steady supply of moisture.

Planting: Like other cabbage-family members, cauliflower needs soil that is rich in nitrogen and potassium, with enough organic matter to retain moisture. In warm climates, plant in fall or late winter for an early-spring harvest. In colder areas, cauliflower usually performs best as a fall crop.

To avoid disturbing roots at transplanting, start cauliflower seedlings indoors in peat or paper pots. Plant seeds ¼ to ½ inch deep, 4 to 6 weeks before the last average frost. Provide constant moisture for seedlings but avoid waterlogged soil; use bottom heat, if necessary, to keep the soil temperature around 70°F.

Harden off young plants gradually before transplanting them to the garden. Set the seedlings 15 to 24 inches apart. Make a saucerlike depression around each plant to help hold water. Firm the soil, and water seedlings thoroughly. Cover beds with floating row cover to prevent insect pests from damaging tender transplants.

Growing guidelines: Provide at least 1 inch of water a week, soaking the soil to a depth of 6 inches. Cauliflower requires constant moisture to produce large, tender heads; soil that dries out between waterings will cause heads to open up and become "ricey." Use a thick layer of compost or organic mulch to conserve soil moisture, limit weeds, and cool the soil. Be careful not to disturb cauliflower roots when weeding, because damaged roots produce uneven growth. Fertilize young plants monthly with fish emulsion or compost tea. If you want to speed up growth, feed every 2 weeks. See the Compost entry for instructions for making compost tea.

Romanesco

A chartreuse relative of both cauliflower and broccoli, romanesco produces heads of bright green, tightly spiraled, pointed florets that typically have a mild, nutty flavor. Also called broccoflower, romanesco has the same cultural needs in the garden as cauliflower and other cabbage family crops.

When the flower heads (curds) of white-headed cultivars are about the size of an egg, blanch them by shading out the sunlight. Otherwise they'll turn yellowish and become, if not less tasty, certainly less appealing. Prepare plants for blanching on a sunny afternoon when the plants are totally dry, because damp heads are more susceptible to rot. Just bend some of the plants' own leaves over the head and tuck them in on the opposite side, or secure the leaves at the top with soft twine, rubber bands, or plastic tape. Use enough leaves to keep out light and moisture, but allow room for air circulation and for the heads to grow.

Once the blanching process begins, be careful to avoid splashing water on the heads or leaves. Unwrap occasionally to check on growth, to look for pests, or to allow heads to dry out after a rain. In hot weather, heads can be ready to harvest in a matter of days. In cool periods, the maturing process can take as long as 2 weeks. Blanching is not necessary when you're growing varieties that produce purple, lime green, or orange heads, or with self-blanching types, which have leaves that naturally curl over the head.

Problems: Pests—such as aphids and flea

beetles—tend to trouble cauliflower more in spring than in fall. Cabbage maggots, sometimes called root maggots, can also be a serious problem. Caterpillars, such as cabbage loopers and imported cabbageworms, are other common cauliflower pests. For more details on these insects and appropriate controls, see page 454.

In boron-deficient soil, cauliflower heads turn brown and leaf tips die back and become distorted. If this occurs, foliar feed with liquid seaweed extract immediately, and repeat every 2 weeks until the symptoms disappear. For subsequent crops, provide boron by adding compost to the soil, or plant fall cover crops of vetch or clover.

Crop rotation, good garden sanitation, and using resistant cultivars will prevent most cauliflower diseases. These include black leg, black rot, clubroot, and fusarium wilt (yellows). See the Cabbage entry for more information on these problems.

If your cauliflower heads taste bitter, chances are the problem was lack of moisture or another factor that slowed the growth of the plants. For your next crop, be sure to plant in soil with plenty of organic matter, keep the soil surface mulched, and water regularly.

Harvesting: Mature cauliflower heads can range in size from 6 inches to 12 inches across. Harvest when the buds are still tight and unopened. With a sharp knife, cut them off just below the head, along with a few whorls of leaves to protect the curds. Use or preserve right away. Note that cooking will cause the color of orange, green, and purple cauliflower florets to fade.

If you don't have time to harvest your crop before a heavy frost strikes, remember that the heads will still be edible unless they thaw and freeze again. Cut the frozen heads and cook them right away. To store plants for about a month, pull them up by the roots and hang them upside down in a cool place.

CELERY

Apium graveolens var. *dulce*
Apiaceae

Contrary to popular belief, celery is not all that difficult to grow. The main things this crop requires are rich soil, plenty of water, and protection from hot sun and high temperatures. Grow celery as a winter crop in the South, a summer crop in the far North, and a fall crop in most other areas.

Planting: You can buy transplants from nurseries, but cultivar choices expand when you grow celery from seed. You can choose dark green 'Tall Utah 52-70R Improved', experiment with self-blanching types such as 'Golden Boy' and 'Tango', or try red-stalked varieties such as 'Redventure'. For a late-summer crop, sow seeds indoors 10 to 12 weeks before the last average spring frost. Soak the tiny seeds overnight to encourage germination. Fill a container with a mix of two-thirds compost and one-third sand, and plant in rows 1 inch apart. Cover the seeds with a sand layer ⅛ inch deep, then cover the flats with damp sphagnum moss or burlap until seeds sprout.

Place in a bright spot out of direct sun, and keep the temperature at 70° to 75°F during the day and about 60°F at night. Provide plenty of water and good drainage and air circulation. Transplant the seedlings into individual pots when they are about 2 inches tall. At 6 inches, harden off the plants for about 10 days, and then transplant them into the garden in a bed that's high in organic matter (from a cover crop or added compost).

Space the plants 6 to 8 inches apart in rows 2 to 3 feet apart. Set them no deeper than they grew in pots. Water in each seedling with compost tea. See the Compost entry for instructions for making compost tea.

For a fall crop, sow seeds indoors in May or June and follow the same directions, transplanting seedlings in June or July. Provide shade in hot, humid weather.

Growing guidelines: Apply several inches of mulch and provide at least 1 inch of water a week. Gently remove any weeds that might compete for nutrients with celery's shallow roots. Feed every 10 to 14 days with compost tea or a balanced organic fertilizer. If night temperatures are consistently below 55°F, protect plants by covering them with cloches; otherwise, the stalks become weak.

Blanching celery destroys some nutrients but prevents stalks from becoming bitter. It also protects fall crops against heavy frosts. You can grow a self-blanching variety, such as the heirloom 'Golden Self-Blanching', or blanch conventional varieties by one of these methods:

- Gradually heap soil up around the plants as they grow, keeping the leaves exposed.
- Two weeks before harvest, tie the tops together, and mound soil up to the base of the leaves.
- Cover the stalks with large cans (remove both ends first), drain tiles, or sleeves made of paper or other material.
- Line up boards, secured with stakes, along each side of a celery row to shut out the sun.

Water carefully after setting up your blanching system, avoiding wetting the leaves and stalks, or they may rot.

Problems: Celery's main enemies are parsleyworms, carrot rust flies, and nematodes. See the Carrot entry for more information on these pests. Celery leaf tiers are tiny yellow caterpillars marked with one white stripe; control by handpicking. Attacks of tarnished plant bugs show up as black joints or brown, sunken areas; see page 454 for controls.

Common diseases include early and late blight, which both begin as small dots on the leaves, and pink rot, which shows up as water-soaked stem spots and white or pink coloration at stalk bases. Crop rotation is the best way to avoid for disease problems.

Distorted leaves and cracked stems can indicate boron-deficient soil; correct by spraying plants with liquid seaweed extract every 2 weeks until symptoms disappear.

Harvesting: Cut the plant off just below the soil line, or cut single stalks of unblanched celery as needed. To preserve a fall crop before freezing temperatures set in, pull up the plants and place them in deep boxes with moist sand or soil around the roots. Store in a cool place; they will keep for several months.

CELOSIA

Crested cockscomb, plumed cockscomb, celosia. Summer- and fall-blooming annuals; dried flowers.

Description: *Celosia argentea* is often subdivided into groups: Cristata, representing the crested cockscombs whose flowers resemble the undulating combs atop roosters' heads, and Plumosa, which produce feathery plumes of bright flowers. Some sources separate the celosias into two species: *C. argentea*, the plumed varieties, and *C. cristata*, the crested ones. However they are identified botanically, celosias bear blooms in a jewel-toned rainbow of cream, yellow, orange, red, and reddish purple. Crested varieties bear wavy, rounded, velvety flower heads that reach 4 to 12 inches across on thick, 6- to 24-inch-tall stems with long, narrow, green or dark red leaves. Feathery plumed cockscombs share the same color range and plant habits, producing 4- to 12-inch-long flamelike heads.

How to grow: Start seeds about 4 weeks before the last frost, or direct-seed outdoors after the ground warms up. Plants resent root disturbance, so transplant carefully into a sunny, well-drained spot with average to fairly rich soil. They tolerate infertile soil and drought very well, but for the largest flower heads, water regularly, side-dress with a high-phosphorus fertilizer such as bonemeal, and stake the taller cultivars. Wide spacing (8 to 12 inches apart for dwarfs, 1½ feet for tall types) produces larger flower heads.

Landscape uses: Dwarf crested cockscombs lend interest to beds, edgings, and pots. Keep tall, large-headed plants in the cutting garden. Plumed cultivars are excellent for massing in beds and borders. For drying, cut either type when in peak color and hang upside down in a warm, well-ventilated place out of direct sun.

CENTAUREA

Cornflower, bachelor's buttons. Late-spring- to early-summer-blooming annuals and perennials.

Description: *Centaurea cyanus*, cornflower or bachelor's buttons, is a popular summer-blooming annual that bears shaggy, 1½-inch, circular, swollen-based blooms in shades of white, pink, red-violet, blue, and violet. The 1- to 2-foot upright or slightly floppy plants are clad in long, skinny, grayish, fuzzy leaves that become much smaller toward the top.

C. montana, mountain bluet or perennial cornflower, resembles its annual cousin but is a perennial, offering 2- to 2½-inch, open disks of finely cut, fringed petals , almost always in a deep, rich blue, on 1½- to 2-foot open mounds of lance-shaped, gray-green foliage. Zones 3–8.

How to grow: Plant both types in full sun to very light shade in average to less fertile, well-drained soil to keep plants compact.

You can start cornflowers a few weeks ahead of the last hard frost and plant them out as small plants just before the last frost; however, they settle in much better if sown directly after frost leaves the soil in spring or in early fall.

Plant mountain bluets in early spring or early fall. Divide often to keep plants vigorous, or allow the usually abundant self-sown seedlings to replace them. Plants deteriorate soon after bloom, so you may want to cut them back nearly to the ground, leaving a few to produce seeds.

Landscape uses: Grow cornflowers in masses in informal borders, cottage gardens, cutting gardens, or meadow plantings. Site with other plants that can fill the gaps left after bloom. Both naturalize readily; bachelor's buttons are considered weedy to invasive in some parts of the United States. Cornflower blossoms are edible and make a lovely garnish for salads.

CHARD

Beta vulgaris, *Cicla Group*
Amaranthaceae

Grow mild-flavored, prolific Swiss chard for its huge, succulent leaves and celerylike stems (actually leaf petioles). This "leaf beet" prefers consistent cool conditions but withstands cold and heat better than most greens. Varieties vary in stem color, heat and pest tolerance, and flavor. 'Monstruoso', an Italian heirloom, and 'Fordhook Giant' produce broad white stalks that may stand in for celery or bok choy. The multicolored stems of 'Bright Lights' make it a popular choice for container gardening and edible landscaping. Chard selections with gold stems ('Bright Yellow') or red ones ('Rhubarb') are as ornamental as they are nutritious and tasty. Chard leaves' flavor is similar to beet greens or spinach.

Planting: Chard tolerates partial shade and a range of soils. In spring, broadcast seeds directly in the garden 1 to 2 weeks before the last expected frost; rake to cover seeds. You can also plant seeds or buy transplants in late summer for a fall crop.

Growing guidelines: Thin seedlings gradually until plants are 8 to 10 inches apart; use the thinnings in salads or sauté them lightly. When plants are about 6 inches tall, fertilize them with alfalfa meal or fish emulsion. Mulch well in areas with hot summers and keep the soil consistently moist. If your plants eventually bolt (produce flowerstalks) during a hot spell, uproot them, and look forward to your fall crop.

Problems: See the Spinach entry for disease and insect control.

Harvesting: Pick leaves as needed. Baby leaves are very tender, larger leaves are best prepared like spinach; cook the stems as you would asparagus.

CHERRY

Prunus spp.
Rosaceae

Do you crave the flavor of sweet cherries despite their steep price? Do you love homemade cherry pie or the sight of a cherry tree in full bloom? If so, grow your own sweet and tart cherries and enjoy a hearty harvest that is sure to satisfy your cherry craze.

Selecting trees: Tart cherries (*Prunus cerasus*), also called sour or pie cherries, are easy to grow. Use the tangy fruit for baking, or let it overripen on the tree for fresh eating. Sour cherries are self-fertile and will set fruit alone. They grow only 20 feet tall and bear fruit at an earlier age than sweet cherries. Sour cherries are hardy in Zones 4–7.

Sweet cherries (*P. avium*) do best in mild, dry climates, but cultivars have been developed that can grow well in other conditions. Most sweet cherries need a second compatible cultivar for pollination; shop carefully to be sure you get trees that can share pollen. If you have room for only one tree, choose a self-fertile cultivar such as 'Stella' or 'Vandalay'; always look for cultivars that are suitable for your local climate and growing conditions. Sweet cherries can grow into trees 35 feet or taller, but they're available on dwarfing rootstocks that will keep the trees as small as 10 feet. Most cultivars are hardy in Zones 5–7 and also thrive in Zones 8–9 in the Pacific Northwest.

Sweet cherries come in purple, red, and yellow. There are firm-fleshed types and soft-fleshed types. Soft-fleshed types tend to be less prone to cracking.

Duke cherries are hybrids between sweet and tart cherries and tend to be sweet/tart flavored and hardy in Zones 4–9.

So-called bush cherries such as Nanking cherry

(*P. tomentosa*) and sand cherries (*P. pumila* and *P. pumila* ssp. *besseyi*) are relatives that bear small cherrylike fruit on shrubs and small trees. Many of these are better adapted to difficult growing conditions and harsh winters than cherry trees.

Rootstocks: Tart cherries are small trees no matter what rootstock they are grafted on. Standard sweet cherries are grafted on seedling rootstocks such as 'Mazzard' (*P. avium* 'Mazzard') and Mahaleb cherry (*P. mahaleb*). 'Gisela' rootstocks (Gisela 3, Gisela 5, Gisela 6, Gisela 12) are popular for their dwarfing effects; different selections are preferred in various growing regions. 'Mazzard' typically is recommended for heavy soils. Mahaleb rootstocks fare better in light soils and produce small trees that bear within 2 to 4 years of planting. For cherry-growing success, shop for trees from a nursery in your geographic region and on rootstocks that meet the particular growing challenges where you live.

Planting and care: Tart cherries grow well throughout much of the United States. They need about 1,000 chill hours below 45°F in winter. This limits their range to the Carolinas and northward through Zone 4. Although all cherries need well-drained soils, tart cherries tolerate moderately heavy soils better than sweet cherries. Space tart cherries 20 to 25 feet apart, sweet cherries 25 to 30 feet apart. Dwarf trees may be planted more closely.

Sweet cherries are not as winter hardy as tart cherries. Early autumn frosts also can damage sweet cherry trees. Commercially, sweet cherries grow best in the West, where summers are dry.

Cherries bloom early and are susceptible to frost damage. Sweet cherries bloom earlier than sour cherries. For site selection and frost protection ideas, see the Peach entry.

Once the fruit sets, watch soil moisture levels.

Cherry fruit matures early and fast. It is particularly sensitive to moisture availability in the last 2 weeks of ripening. If the soil is too dry, the swelling cherries will shrivel. If it is too wet, they will crack and split. If you live in an area prone to heavy summer rainfall, choose cultivars that resist cracking. Spread a thick organic mulch out to the drip line to help maintain soil moisture at a constant level. Irrigate as necessary to keep the soil evenly moist.

Healthy cherry trees will grow about 1 foot a year. If your tree's progress is slower or the new leaves are yellow, have the soil and/or foliage tested for nutrient deficiencies. See the Soil entry for instructions on taking a soil sample. Mulch each spring with a thin layer of compost out to the drip line. Don't fertilize after midsummer. This could encourage new growth that won't harden before fall frosts.

The Fruit Trees entry covers some important aspects of growing cherries and other tree fruits; refer to it for additional information on planting, pruning, and care.

Pruning: A central leader form is best for dwarf tart cherries. Use a modified central leader form for semidwarf and standard cherry trees. Spreading the branches while they are young will help control height and encourage earlier bearing. After the trees reach bearing age, prune to let light penetrate to the interior of the tree. Prune tart cherries lightly each winter to stimulate new growth and thin tangled branches. Prune sweet cherries less frequently, only every third or fourth year. Cut back heavy tops on overgrown sweet cherry trees to force new fruiting wood to develop on lower branches.

Problems: Fruit cracking and hungry birds are two of the biggest problems when raising cherries. Most insect and disease problems are less severe on tart cherry trees than on sweet. For information on pest control methods, see the Pests entry.

Birds can strip all the cherries from a backyard tree in very little time. Covering trees with netting before the fruit starts to ripen is the most effective way to stop bird damage. You can also try planting a mulberry tree nearby that fruits at the same time as your cherries to lure birds away from the harvest. See the Animal Pests entry for more ways to discourage feathered scavengers from stealing your cherries.

Cherry fruit fly, green fruitworm, peach tree borer, mites, and plum curculio all attack cherries. The chart on page 231 describes and lists controls for all of them. Aphids and scale can also cause problems; page 454 lists descriptions and controls for both. Sawfly larvae (pear slugs) sometimes skeletonize cherry leaves; see the Pear entry for description and controls.

Shothole borers can attack cherries and other fruit trees. They make small holes in the bark of twigs and trunk. The holes are often covered with gum. The larvae are pinkish white and about 1/8 inch long. Prevent the tiny black adults from laying eggs by painting trunk and large branches in spring, summer, and fall with white latex paint diluted 1:1 with water. These pests most often attack wounded or diseased trees, so their appearance may be a sign that your trees are in trouble and you need to consider removing them.

Pear thrips can cause disfigured leaves and blossoms. Naturally occurring predatory mites usually provide control, but if your trees become severely infested, spray with insecticidal soap.

A few serious diseases pose problems for cherry trees. Be on the lookout for these common woes.

🌿 Brown rot and perennial canker attack cherries and other stone fruit; see pages 233 and 234 for descriptions and controls.

🌿 Black knot can infect cherries; see the Plum entry for details.

🌿 Cherry leaf spot appears as small purple spots on upper leaf surfaces. The spots later turn brown, and their centers may fall out. Leaves turn yellow and drop before autumn. Clean up and dispose of fallen leaves each winter. Plant resistant cultivars. If leaf spot is a problem in your area, plan a preventive spray program with lime sulfur or sulfur. Lime sulfur may discolor fruits, so don't use it after young fruits begin to develop.

🌿 Powdery mildew can be a problem on cherries. See the Apple entry for description and control.

🌿 A number of viruses attack cherries. Buy virus-free stock and avoid planting in old cherry orchards or near wild chokecherries (*P. serotina*, *P. virginiana*).

Harvesting: When the fruit begins to drop, it is ready to pick. Tart cherries can be left to sweeten on the tree for a day or two.

To pick cherries, gently pull off clusters, keeping the stems on the fruit. Avoid tearing off the fruit spurs (small woody twigs to which the cherry stems are attached) or future crops may be diminished.

CHRISTMAS TREES

With as little as a 10- by 20-foot plot of land, you can grow eight Christmas trees in your backyard. In 6 to 8 years, you can harvest your own beautiful 6-foot Christmas tree. In addition to the personal pleasure of harvesting your freshly cut tree, you'll be saving the dollars you'd have paid at a tree lot.

A Living Christmas Tree

Decorate a container-grown or balled-and-burlapped evergreen for Christmas, and then plant it outside to enjoy the memories it holds for many years to come. This sounds simple, yet the stress on the plant is so great that many ex-Christmas trees end up in the chipper. Keep in mind that balled-and-burlapped trees can be very heavy, so have a plan of action for moving yours.

A living evergreen tree's chances for a successful transition from your living room to your yard are best if it remains indoors for only a few days. A longer stay will make the tree break dormancy and produce tender new growth. If this happens, keep your tree in a cool, sunlit room through winter, and treat it as a giant houseplant.

To enjoy a living tree for the holidays and beyond, follow this plan of action.

1. Dig a planting hole in late fall before the ground freezes. Fill the hole with loose straw. Save the soil—needed for later planting—in an area where it's protected from freezing.

2. For best selection, choose your tree early. Store it in an unheated garage or outdoors.

3. A few days before Christmas, place the tree indoors, well away from heat sources. Check soil moisture daily.

4. After Christmas, remove the straw from the hole and plant the tree, using the reserved soil. Water thoroughly, and spray the needles with an antidesiccant.

Plus, fresh Christmas trees are recyclable and an eco-friendly alternative to artificial trees.

Choosing the right tree: Think about the kind of Christmas tree you usually buy. Is it fat and full-branched, or tall and spindly with plenty of room for ornaments to hang? Many commercial trees, especially the firs and pines, are carefully clipped for years to achieve the perfect Christmas tree look. Other species, such as balsam fir or eastern red cedar, are enjoyed imperfections and all.

Here are some popular Christmas tree types to get you started.

- Long-needled: Scots pine (*Pinus sylvestris*), eastern white pine (*P. strobus*), red or Norway pine (*P. resinosa*), Austrian pine (*P. nigra*).

- Short-needled: balsam fir (*Abies balsamea*), Douglas fir (*Pseudotsuga menziesii*), southern balsam fir or Fraser fir (*Abies fraseri*), Colorado blue spruce (*Picea pungens*), Norway spruce (*P. abies*).

- Scaled needles: cypresses (*Cupressus* spp.), eastern red cedar (*Juniperus virginiana*).

Some Christmas trees like it hot. But some like it cold, some like it moist, and some like it dry. Ask your local nursery owner or Cooperative Extension office to recommend species that thrive in your area.

Planting and care: Plant your trees in an area of full sun, about 6 feet apart. Start by planting two or three small trees from 1- or 2-gallon pots the first year. Arrange trees in staggered rows for best use of space. Plant another tree or two each year until you've planted eight trees. Once you cut the first tree in 6 to 8 years, remove the stump the following spring and plant a new young tree. Remember, you will harvest them before they reach mature size. Evergreen trees require little or no fertilizer for healthy growth. Mulch with well-rotted manure around the selected tree a year before cutting, for deep green color.

If you want to shear your trees to encourage the classic Christmas tree shape, do so in spring. See the Evergreens entry for instructions on pruning and shearing.

Pine-tip moths and sawflies feed on and distort new growth. Check your trees closely for their caterpillar-like larvae, which may appear from May through September. Snip off damaged branch tips and destroy them. You can spray sawflies with insecticidal soap, or with pyrethrins or neem for severe infestations.

For more information on growing Christmas trees, you can find a grower in your area (search by ZIP code), research types of trees, find a tree-recycling program, and much more by visiting the National Christmas Tree Association's Web site; see Resources on page 673.

CHRYSANTHEMUM

Chrysanthemum, garden mum, daisy.
Summer- and fall-blooming perennials, cut flowers.

Description: *Chrysanthemum* ×*morifolium* (syn. *Dendranthema* ×*grandiflorum*), garden or hardy mums, can bring brilliance to your autumn garden. They fall roughly into two groups: the 1- to 1½-foot mounded cushion mums sold in bloom

seemingly everywhere in fall, plus some 2- to 3-foot upright types; and a huge range of specialist-favored exhibition cultivars. Florist's mums, grown as potted plants, are frequently not hardy, and they need such a long season to flower that even where they'll survive winter, they often won't bloom before the first fall freeze. By far the best choices for most gardeners are those from the first group. Ranging in size from ½ to 4 inches, the mostly double, rounded flowers, in white, yellow, orange, red, rust, lavender, and purple, harmonize beautifully with their dark green, aromatic foliage.

Hundreds of years of selective breeding have resulted in five distinctive chrysanthemum bloom shapes: Button mums have small, tidy petals; daisy mums have daisylike flowers; decorative mums develop 2- to 4-inch-wide double flowers; football mums are oversize, with ruffly petals; and spider mums have long, thin, arching petals. Only decorative, button, and daisy types are reliably hardy in the garden. Zones 4–9.

Several beloved garden flowers have been reclassified and moved from the genus *Chrysanthemum* into other genera. One of the most popular is *Leucanthemum* ×*superbum* (formerly *Chrysanthemum* ×*superbum*), Shasta daisy, perhaps the quintessential daisy, with large, abundant, cheerful blooms. In early summer, plants display single to double, 2- to 4-inch white or cream flowers borne on stiff 1- to 2-foot stems atop elongated, shiny dark green leaves. The cultivar 'Becky' was named Perennial Plant of the Year for 2003 by the Perennial Plant Association. Zones 4–8.

Another popular reclassified plant is *Tanacetum coccineum* (formerly *Chrysanthemum coccineum*), painted daisy, named for its bold flower colors, also known as pyrethrum daisy. However, the better source of the popular botanical insecticide, pyrethrum, is a relative, *Chrysanthemum cinerariifolium*. Among gardeners, painted daisies are beloved for their flowers alone. Plants bear single to double 2- to 4-inch blooms in shades of white, pink, and red in early summer. The weakly upright, 2- to 3-foot flower stems rise above delicate lacy leaves up to 10 inches long. Zones 3–7.

How to grow: Start garden mums with rooted cuttings bought in spring, or divide last year's clumps, replanting only the most vigorous pieces. You also can buy plants in bloom in fall and plant them directly into borders. Plant in full sun in average to slightly rich soil with excellent drainage; water during drought. Add a little extra fertilizer in late spring and midsummer. For dense plants with lots of flowers, pinch out the tips one or two times before July 15 in the North and August 15 in the South. Hose regularly to deter aphids and mites. To avoid nematode problems, don't grow mums in the same place for more than a few years.

Plant or divide Shasta and painted daisies in spring or early fall in a sunny, average to slightly rich, very well-drained soil. Shasta daisies grow easily and quickly from seed, but seed-grown painted daisy plants may produce misshapen flowers. Painted daisies don't ship well, so buy locally grown plants. After the flowers fade, cut plants back and fertilizer lightly to promote rebloom. Painted daisies benefit from support, such as from wire forms or twiggy branches, when in bloom.

Landscape uses: Plant garden mums in borders with other fall-blooming perennials like asters and goldenrods for a stunning autumn show. Their ornamental foliage and bushy habit make mums good foliage plants in a border, too. Mums are bold plants that make an impressive display in a bed by themselves or in containers on a patio or deck.

Grow Shasta daisies in masses throughout sunny borders and in cottage and cutting gardens. Their round flowers contrast nicely with spiky or mounded blooms. Grow painted daisies in informal settings and cottage gardens.

CINQUEFOIL

See *Dasiphora*

CITRUS

Citrus **spp.** and hybrids

Rutaceae

Citrus trees have shiny, evergreen leaves; fragrant flowers; and attractive, often tasty and persistent fruit. In northern climates, you can grow dwarf citrus trees in tubs and bring them indoors during winter. "Indoor-Outdoor Citrus" on page 119 has more information about how to grow citrus trees in containers.

Selecting trees: There are so many types of citrus that you may have trouble deciding which to grow. Edible types include calamondin (×*Citrofortunella mitis*, also called ×*Citrofortunella microcarpa* and *Fortunella japonica*), citrange (×*Citroncirus webberi*), citron (*Citrus medica*), grapefruit (*C.* ×*paradisi*), lemon (*C.* ×*limon*), Key lime (*C. aurantiifolia*), kumquats (*Fortunella* spp.), tangerine or mandarin orange (*Citrus reticulata*), orange (*C.* ×*sinensis*), rangpur lime (*C.* ×*limonia*), pomelo or shaddock (*C. maxima*), sour or Seville orange (*C. aurantium*), tangelo (*C.* ×*tangelo*), and temple orange or tangor (*C.* ×*nobilis*).

Consider the yearly range of temperatures and possible frost when making your selection. Local nurseries usually stock citrus trees that grow well in the area. The fruit of all types is easily damaged by frost, but the leaves and wood of some are more cold resistant than others. In general, limes are the least hardy, oranges slightly hardier, and calamondins and kumquats are the most hardy, withstanding temperatures as low as 12° to 15°F. Hardy orange (*Poncirus trifoliata*) is hardy into sheltered areas of Zone 5. It's a thorny, deciduous tree that serves as an unusual ornamental, but its small yellow-orange fruit is not edible.

A single mature citrus tree yields more than enough fruit for a family. If you plant more than one tree of the same type, select cultivars with different harvest times, or plant different types of citrus so you won't be overwhelmed with one kind of fruit. Almost all citrus are self-pollinating. A few hybrids are not; be sure to check for the kind you want when you buy.

Select sturdy nursery-raised trees. A 1-year-old tree should have a trunk diameter of ¾ inch. A 2-year-old plant should have a diameter of at least 1 inch. Those with fewer fruits and flowers are better because they have put more energy into sturdy top and root growth.

Rootstocks: Most commercially grown citrus fruits are grafted onto rootstocks. Trifoliate orange and sour orange are both good rootstocks where cold-hardiness is important. Sour orange is susceptible to nematode attacks and shouldn't be used where they are a problem. 'Milam' lemon is a nematode-resistant rootstock. If you live in an area where salt accumulation in soil is a problem, choose a salt-tolerant rootstock such as 'Cleopatra' mandarin orange. Your local extension office can tell you what rootstock is best in your region.

Planting: Citrus do best at a pH of 6.0 to 6.5.

They are not fussy about soil but do require good drainage. If drainage is a problem, plant in a raised soil mound about 1½ feet high.

Select a sheltered area with full sun, such as a sheltered, south-facing alcove of a building. Citrus flowers attract bees, so don't plant them in high-traffic areas.

You can plant citrus at any time of year, but it's best to plant container-grown trees in spring. Keep the graft union 6 inches above the soil surface when planting. Full-size trees require at least 25 feet between trees; dwarf trees need less.

Citrus bark is thin and easily sunburned. Wrap the trunk with commercial tree wrap or newspaper for the first year, or paint it with diluted white latex paint.

Care: In dry areas, water newly planted trees at least once a week for the first year. Once established, trees need less-frequent watering, but never wait until leaves wilt to water. Water stress can cause developing fruit to drop; prolonged drought causes leaf drop and may kill the tree. Water slowly and deeply; shallow sprinkling does more harm than good. In drought areas, construct a shallow watering basin that extends from 1 foot away from the trunk to 1 foot beyond the drip line. Or install drip irrigation under a thick layer of mulch to conserve water and protect shallow feeder roots. Keep mulch at least 6 inches away from the trunk.

In citrus-growing areas, soils often lack organic matter and nitrogen. Spread compost, well-rotted manure, or bloodmeal on the soil surface out to the drip line four times a year, beginning in February.

Pruning: Most citrus trees need little pruning beyond removing dead or broken branches. Limit the tree's size by thinning out energetic shoots that outgrow other branches. Thin branches

Indoor-Outdoor Citrus

Where cold winters preclude citrus in the garden, the attractive small trees make fine patio/sunroom plants. Indoors, they need a well-ventilated area with high humidity and at least half a day of full sun. During summer, a sheltered, partially shaded spot outdoors is ideal.

Select a container that is deep and wide enough for the tree you choose. A calamondin will fruit in a 10-inch pot, a 'Meyer' lemon will grow to 6 feet in a 5-gallon pot. If you plan to move them in and out, choose containers you can handle easily. Or mount wooden planters on casters; set other heavy containers on wheeled stands. Citrus need loose, well-drained potting mix and benefit from the addition of bonemeal. The Container Gardening entry gives guidelines for selecting suitable containers, preparing planting mixes, and caring for plants.

Citrus need warm days (70° to 75°F) and cool nights (45° to 55°F) during winter. During summer, they like it as warm as possible. If you move your trees indoors during winter and outdoors during summer, acclimatize them by setting containers in an intermediate area for a few days so they can adjust gradually. Leaf burn may occur with sudden climate changes.

Don't let the potting mix dry out. Water whenever the top ½ inch of potting mix starts to dry out. Water thoroughly until water drains from the bottom, but don't let the plant sit in water. At least once a month, water with liquid fertilizer such as seaweed extract. Mist leaves frequently, and group plants to conserve humidity.

If your citrus flowers indoors, you'll need to pollinate it by hand for a good fruit set. Take a small artist's brush or a cotton swab and transfer pollen from one blossom to another. Giving the plant a slight shaking also transfers pollen.

Container-grown citrus need a light yearly pruning. Thin out entire branches rather than shortening them, or you'll get a flush of new branches sprouting below the cut. When plants become rootbound, repot in fresh potting mix in a larger container. To keep the plant small, prune off circling roots and cut back some of the remainder. Shake out as much of the old potting mix as you can, repot in fresh mix, and cut back topgrowth by about one-fourth.

Many citrus are naturally dwarf and adapt well to container culture. Suitable types and cultivars include calamondin, 'Owari Satsuma' mandarin, 'Improved Meyer' lemon, 'Eureka' lemon, 'Bearss' seedless lime, Key lime, 'Eustis' limequat, 'Washington Navel' orange, 'Nagami' kumquat, 'Moro' blood orange, 'Oroblanco' grapefruit, and rangpur lime.

rather than shortening them. Remove suckers as soon as they emerge from the ground. See the Pruning and Training entry for instructions on correct pruning technique.

You can revitalize an old and unproductive citrus tree by pruning severely in early spring. Wear thick gloves if the tree has thorns. Cut off all branches 2 inches or larger in diameter flush to the trunk, and feed and water heavily for the next year. Very severe pruning may stop fruiting for up to 2 years.

Winter protection: Citrus are usually grown outdoors in climates where frost is rare: Zones 9–10 and the warmer parts of Zone 8. While some types of citrus are more cold-hardy than others, all citrus fruit is vulnerable when frost does occur. In areas where mild frosts are common, don't plant cultivars that bear in winter and early spring. Since succulent new growth is more prone to frost injury, withhold fertilizer and extra water in late summer to limit new growth. When frost does threaten, cover trees with large fabric sheets. Use fans to keep air circulating around the trees. Symptoms of frost damage include yellow wilting leaves or greenish shriveled leaves. Should frost damage appear, wait until spring growth starts to see the true extent of damage. A tree that loses all its leaves can still rejuvenate. If damage is severe, dieback may continue during the growing season.

Harvesting: Citrus trees usually bear in 3 to 4 years. It can be hard to tell when citrus fruit is ready to pick. Color is not a good indicator. Fruit can have ripe coloration several months before being ready to harvest or may remain green and unappealing even when ripe and juicy inside. Use the taste test to determine when fruit is at its peak flavor. Allow fruit to ripen on the tree before picking.

Use pruning shears to cut stems close to the fruit when harvesting. Don't just pull fruit off the tree. Ripe citrus fruit can remain on the tree for up to 3 months. Once harvested, citrus can be stored in the refrigerator for 3 or more weeks.

Problems: Citrus trees in the home garden are relatively untroubled by pests. Much of the damage that does occur is cosmetic and has no effect on the internal fruit quality. In dry climates, pests such as scale, whiteflies, mealybugs, thrips, and mites may cause problems. In humid climates, fungal diseases are more likely to cause problems.

Scale insects appear as small, hard bumps on leaves, twigs, and fruit. Sooty mold may be present. Predatory lady beetles attack scale. Summer oil spray also controls them.

Whiteflies suck leaf sap. Clouds of tiny white flies appear when foliage is disturbed. Fruit is pale and stunted. Leaves are dry and yellowing and may show black sooty mold, which grows on the honeydew excreted by the pests. Ladybugs, lacewings, and parasitic wasps help control whiteflies. Repeated strong water sprays knock whiteflies off trees. For added control, spray with insecticidal soap.

Thrips cause distorted, yellow-streaked new growth in spring. Blossoms turn brown, and developing fruit shows a ring at the blossom end. To reduce chances of thrips infestation, keep citrus adequately watered. Lacewings help control thrips. Neem oil can wipe out thrips if you catch an infestation early on. For severe infestations, apply insecticidal soap.

Mites cause pale leaves, sometimes with yellow spots. Fruit may have dark brown markings, and leaves may drop. Spray leaves with cold water regularly to remove dust, and provide adequate water. Ladybugs, lacewings, and predatory mites attack mites.

Mealybugs are white, cottony or waxy insects that feed on sap. They secrete honeydew, which attracts ants and encourages sooty mold. They are controlled by the mealybug destroyer, a ladybug type of beetle. Horticultural oil sprays also provide control.

Snails may climb trees and feed on leaves. Encircle tree trunks with a copper barrier strip to prevent snail problems.

Root rot can damage citrus trees. Too much fertilizer, cultivation, and gopher gnawing all can encourage the disease. Avoid injuring roots, and ensure good drainage.

Dead bark near the soil line and large amounts of gummy sap indicate foot rot. Keep the tree base dry and remove discolored wood. Foot rot problems can be avoided by providing good drainage at planting.

Viral diseases are a major problem in some areas. Purchase only virus-free trees.

CLEMATIS

Clematis. Perennial or woody vines.

Description: Clematis are mostly twining woody vines, growing 5 to 18 feet long. Most are deciduous with lobed or trifoliate leaves made up of toothed leaflets. Feathery seed heads follow the blooms and linger into early winter. The popular large-flowered hybrids, familiar to many gardeners, have showy 3- to 6-inch flat blooms and come in many shades of blue, purple, red, pink, white, cream, and yellow. Zones 4–9. Species clematis are less widely grown but also desirable. Their delicate blooms, shaped like saucers, stars, or bells, are delightfully different from common garden flowers. Many of them are vigorous enough to use for screening.

Clematis armandii, Armand clematis, is one of the few evergreen clematis with large leaves. It is fast growing (to 10 feet) with fragrant, white, star-shaped blooms in late spring. Zones 7–10. Grow *C. heracleifolia*, a perennial (herbaceous) clematis, with light staking for support. It bears clusters of fragrant, blue, 1-inch flowers in late summer. Zones 3–8. *C. macropetala*, big-petal clematis, is a vigorous vine (to 12 feet), with nodding double blooms of blue, pink, or white in spring. Zones 3–7.

C. terniflora (also known as *C. maximowicziana* and *C. paniculata*), sweet autumn clematis, is a vigorous nonnative invasive vine from Japan (to 7 feet) that is covered with fragrant, white, 1-inch blooms from August through October. Zones 4–9. Native *C. virginiana*, virgin's bower or devil's darning needles or woodbine, is an excellent native substitute. It bears white flowers on vines to 20 feet in late summer and fall. Zones 4–8. *C. montana*, anemone clematis, is also a vigorous vine (to 20 feet), with white or pink 2½-inch open flowers in May and June. Zones 6–8.

C. tangutica, golden clematis, is a strong climber (to 15 feet) with bright yellow, 3- to 4-inch nodding flowers borne in June and July. Zones 2–8. *C. texensis*, scarlet or Texas clematis, is a vigorous vine (to 9 feet) with scarlet 1-inch bell-shaped blooms from midsummer through frost. Zones 4–8.

How to grow: Transplant container-grown clematis plants in spring or fall. Plant in moist, well-drained soil. Give the roots cool conditions, but plant in full sun. (To achieve this seemingly contradictory goal, plant clematis where the roots will be shaded by a nearby shrub, or mulch well.) Research has found that clematis don't need additional lime; ignore advice to the contrary. Plant where a support is available for the vine to twine around—a pillar, tree trunk, or trellis will work well. Clematis stems break easily, so install your trellis or stake before planting.

Clematis wilt is the only serious problem of clematis. When the fungus attacks, the entire plant or afflicted branch will droop and shrivel. Remove all diseased parts, even if it means cutting the plant to the ground. Plants may recover, resprouting from the roots. Good sanitation is important, as the fungal spores can overwinter on dead leaves. Do not add infected material to the compost heap—burn or otherwise destroy it. Do not replant a clematis in a site where wilt has been a problem.

Some clematis bloom on old wood (growth from previous seasons), while others bloom on the current year's growth. For clematis that bloom on old wood, thin or shape them immediately after flowering. Heavily prune clematis that bloom on new wood in late winter or early spring before bud break. (Ask the seller which type of clematis you're buying.) Remove all dead shoots and trim vines back to the first pair of plump buds. Untangle vines growing on walls and tie them to a trellis in a fan pattern.

Landscape uses: Large-flowered clematis are ideal for growing on walls, fences, arbors, and posts, or up through shrubs. Most of the species are very vigorous and create good screens. You can use the herbaceous perennial clematis in a perennial or mixed border.

CLOCHES

See Season Extension

COCKSCOMB

See *Celosia*

COLD FRAMES

Cold frames and hotbeds give gardeners some control over the one thing most beyond their control—the weather. By creating an area of close-to-ideal conditions right where the plants need them, cold frames and hotbeds help gardeners stretch the seasons and make it possible to grow plants accustomed to warmer climates. A cold frame can add a month or more to each end of the growing season, and in warmer climates can enable gardeners to grow plants outdoors through winter.

Gardeners most commonly use cold frames in early spring for starting or hardening off seedlings or transplants destined for the garden. However, there are many other uses for cold frames. A moist, shady frame provides a good start to fall crops in the dry heat of summer; in winter, the same frame offers a spot for cold-treating spring bulbs for forcing. A cold frame also may be useful for rooting cuttings of woody plants or perennials taken any time of year.

Form and Function

A traditional cold frame is a rectangular, boxlike structure, with sides made from boards, plywood, bricks, or concrete blocks, supporting a glass top that might be made of old windows. Other suitable, light-admitting covers for a cold frame include fiberglass, Plexiglas, or heavyweight polyethylene tacked to a frame. Gardeners use blocks, sticks, or a solar-powered vent (available from garden supply companies) to prop the lid open for ventilation.

The lid's size usually determines the dimensions of the cold frame, especially if the lid is a recycled window. Still, it should be larger than 2 by 4 feet to hold enough plants to make it worthwhile, and not much larger than 3 by 6 feet so the plants within are easy to reach. Build the back wall 4 to 6 inches higher than the front so the lid slopes forward to maximize the amount of light that reaches the plants inside and allow snow and water to slide easily off the lid. A white or light-colored frame interior increases the amount of light reflected onto the plants.

Cold frames are essentially passive solar collectors. To get maximum benefit from the heat and light of the sun, a frame's sloping lid should face south—southeastern or southwestern exposures are the next best choices. Ideally, the site should receive full sun from midmorning to midafternoon during winter and early-spring months. Hotbeds need a full-sun exposure as well.

Build a cold frame on a site that is fairly level and well drained. If possible, place the frame with its north side next to a building, fence, or hedge for protection from winter winds. Select a site that is near a water supply and is easy to monitor year-round. Deciduous trees overhead aren't necessarily bad; they'll provide summer shade without blocking winter sun.

Permanent or Portable?

A cold frame may be permanent or portable. Permanent frames are built over foundations that are either dug into the ground or constructed on the surface. Aboveground models provide less frost protection than ones built over a dug foundation, but both provide more reliable protection from the cold than portable frames. Permanent frames generally are sturdier and longer lasting.

Portable frames, which are basically bottomless boxes with clear lids, function in much the same way as permanent frames. These are often available ready-made from Web sites and catalogs that sell greenhouse supplies. Many models are collapsible for storage when not in use. However, their reduced insulating capacity makes them subject to wider temperature fluctuations. In the vegetable garden, portable frames can extend the season for spring or fall crops such as lettuce or spinach, or keep frost off late-ripening crops. In areas with mild winters, use them to grow winter crops of cold-tolerant vegetables. Placed over garden beds, portable frames will provide adequate winter protection for many perennials. In summer, use a portable frame to create a cool, shady spot for seedlings.

Hot or Cold?

Hotbeds and cold frames are structurally identical, except that hotbeds contain a source of artificial heat. Traditionally, rotting manure served as the heat source, but today, electric heating cables typically provide the warmth. Because hotbeds have a steady source of heat, they can be used earlier in the season than most cold frames, and they create ideal conditions for starting most types of seeds.

Make any frame with a dug foundation into a hotbed by adding an electric heating cable. You can also use portable frames, although they don't conserve heat as well as permanent frames, but you need a pit at least 1 foot deep to hold most heating cables. For best control over temperatures within the frame, select a heating cable with a thermostat.

To make a hotbed, spread a 2-inch layer of vermiculite on top of a gravel layer at the bottom of your pit or dug foundation. Spread the cable on the vermiculite, using long loops to evenly distribute

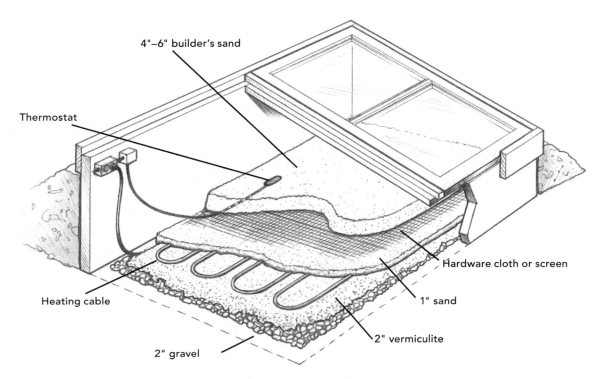

4"–6" builder's sand

Thermostat

Heating cable

2" gravel

2" vermiculite

1" sand

Hardware cloth or screen

A modern hotbed. A heating cable sandwiched between a layer of vermiculite and a layer of sand will transform a cold frame into a hotbed, letting you start seeds outdoors even earlier.

the heat. Don't let the cable wires cross; keep loops at least 8 inches apart and 3 inches away from the frame edges. Cover the cable with 1 inch of sand, followed by a layer of screen or hardware cloth to protect it from digging tools or other sharp objects. Cover the screen with 4 to 6 inches of coarse builder's sand in which to sink pots.

Frame Management

Ensure success by carefully monitoring the conditions inside your hotbeds or cold frames. As with any gardening situation, the plants require proper light, moisture, and temperature levels.

Temperature control: The key to using a cold frame successfully is keeping it cool, not

warm. The temperature inside the cold frame should stay below 75°F for summer plants and below 60°F for plants that normally grow in spring and fall. The way to keep temperatures cool inside a cold frame is to lift the lid to vent the frame.

Venting a cold frame is necessary even in winter, because on a sunny winter day, whatever the outdoor temperature, the temperature in an unvented, insulated frame can rise to 100°F or more. A thermometer, placed in a shaded spot in the frame, is a must for determining when to vent. A good rule of thumb: On sunny days when outdoor temperatures are above 40°F, prop the lid open 6 inches; if outdoor temperatures rise above 50°F, remove the lid. Make sure you close the lid or put it back on the frame in late afternoon to trap heat inside for the cold night to come. Solar-powered automatic openers, triggered by temperature, will vent the frame when you aren't home, but it's best to learn the temperature nuances of your frame as well. A thermometer with a remote sensor gives you the welcome option of monitoring the temperature from indoors on sunny but cold winter days.

In unusually cold weather, or if you have an uninsulated, aboveground frame, bank bags of leaves, bales of hay, or soil around the frame. Stack bricks or plastic gallon jugs filled with water against the inside of the north wall as passive solar collectors; enhance the heat absorption of either with a coat of black paint. Both will absorb heat during the day and release it at night, as will black garbage bags of leaves piled against the outside of the frame. If it's going to be a frigid night, insulate the glass lid before dark by covering it with old blankets, newspapers, bags of leaves, or straw bales. Snow is also a good insulator, but brush heavy snow off the glass so it doesn't break.

Watering: Until you become familiar with the conditions in your frame, check plants frequently to be sure they have enough water. This is especially important in warm weather when plants are actively growing. Check the moisture of the soil at a depth of between 1 and 1½ inches; for most plants, soil should remain constantly moist, but not soggy. Water whenever plants look droopy, but avoid watering on cold, cloudy days. To discourage fungal diseases, water early in the day. Use water that's about the same temperature as the growing medium, because cold water can shock plants and slow their growth. If you have dormant plants in your frame that you plan to store there over winter, water them thoroughly for the last time 2 weeks before the first fall frost is predicted, then check moisture every few weeks.

Containers: Growing plants in containers has several advantages over planting directly in soil in the frame. Plants in containers can easily be added, moved around, or removed without disturbing the frame's other inhabitants. Soil mixes can be customized to suit individual plants, as can watering and fertilizing schedules, so the frame can hold a variety of plants. Also, using individual pots helps control diseases, which can spread quickly in frames. Place pots on the layer of gravel at the frame's bottom, or sink to the rims in 4 to 6 inches of sand over the gravel.

Pests and diseases: Check your frame regularly for evidence of disease or insect infestation. In mild weather, uncontrolled insects, slugs, or other pests can thrive in a cold frame or hotbed. Before placing a pot in the frame, check it for hitchhiking pests.

The warm, moist conditions inside a frame may also encourage plant diseases. Generous spacing and proper ventilation can help prevent disease problems. Remove and discard infested, diseased, or sick-looking leaves and plants as soon as you spot them, because problems spread rapidly.

If serious problems develop, remove all plants and sterilize the inside of the frame. To sterilize, pour boiling water into the gravel and/or sand at the bottom of the frame, or leave the glass lids tightly closed during summer to allow heat to build up inside the frame. If you grow plants directly in soil at the bottom of your frame, it is a good idea to dig it out completely every 2 to 3 years and replace it with fresh soil.

Frame maintenance: The moist, warm environment inside a frame subjects it to rapid deterioration. If paint starts flaking, repaint as soon as the frame is free of plants. Let a newly painted frame air for several weeks before putting plants in it, to avoid exposing plants to potentially harmful

Spring ritual. Harden off seedlings in your cold frame in spring before planting them out in the garden. Use a notched wooden support or install a solar-powered automatic opener to vent the frame on sunny days.

fumes. Recaulk as necessary to maintain airtight conditions. Keep the sash and inside of the frame clean to increase the amount of light available to plants.

Year-Round Uses

The uses you find for your frame depend not only on what your gardening needs are but also on where you live, what exposure you have available, and what type of frame you select. Experiment to find the best ways to use your cold frame and/or hotbed, as well as the best seasonal schedule for your area.

Spring: To harden off seedlings started indoors, move them to a cold frame a week or two before they're scheduled for transplanting. Gradually open the lid for longer periods each day. To keep the seedlings from suffering sunburn, shade them at first by using wood lath or burlap or by painting the glass with a mixture of clay soil and water. Expose them gradually to full sun.

Cold frames are also good places to germinate seeds in early spring—especially those of cold-tolerant vegetables, perennials, and annuals. Sow seeds in flats or pots placed directly in the frame about 2 months before the last spring frost date. For an even earlier start, sow seeds in a hotbed or indoors, and move seedlings to a cold frame after their first transplanting. This frees up space for more tender plants indoors and eliminates the succulent, rank growth of seedlings grown in warm temperatures. Later in the season, sow tender annuals in the frame.

Where the growing season is short, use a cold frame to start long-season plants such as melons that otherwise might not mature, or plant very early spring crops of lettuce or spinach.

Summer: During summer, store the glass cover for your cold frame in a protected place and substitute screens to keep out leaves and debris. In late summer, use a frame shaded with a grid of wood lath over the screens to start fall crops of heat-sensitive vegetables such as lettuce. Raise seedlings in pots or flats, then transplant to the garden when temperatures begin to cool. Summer-sown perennials or biennials can be germinated in pots or flats, held over their first winter under the cold frame, and moved to the garden the following year. Root woody and herbaceous cuttings in a lath-shaded frame. The contained environment provides ideal rooting conditions.

Fall and winter: As the days shorten and temperatures drop, replace the glass lid, and your cold frame becomes an ideal place to sow seeds of hardy annuals, perennials, wildflowers, shrubs, or trees. With seed sown in fall or early winter, the object is not to germinate the seed immediately but to provide a cold treatment so it will germinate the following spring. Sow seed just before the ground freezes so it doesn't germinate before winter arrives.

Fall crops of lettuce and spinach can thrive in cold frames well after the first frost. Fall is also the time to move perennials, herbs, and container-grown plants that might not be quite hardy outdoors under cover for winter protection. Dig semihardy herbs such as lavender and rosemary from your garden and keep them in a cold frame over winter. You can also use your cold frame for giving pots of hardy spring bulbs such as daffodils and crocus a cold treatment before forcing them into bloom. See the Bulbs entry for complete instructions.

COLEUS

See *Plectranthus*

COLLARD

Brassica oleracea, Acephala Group
Brassicaceae

A popular staple of Southern cuisine, collards are quite cold resistant. A touch of frost mellows the flavor of the wavy broad green leaves and, although collards tolerate heat better than many cabbage-family crops, in the South, collards grow best in late fall, winter, and early spring.

Planting: Sow seeds ¼ inch deep in spring, 4 weeks before the last expected frost. Space seedlings 1 foot apart in rows 3 feet apart. For a fall crop, broadcast seed 8 to 10 weeks before the first expected frost; thin to 12 inches apart.

Growing guidelines: Foliar feed with liquid seaweed extract two or three times during the growing season.

Problems: See the Cabbage entry for disease- and insect-control measures.

Harvesting: Start picking outer leaves when plants are 1 foot tall. Frosts improve flavor without harming collards.

COLUMBINE

See *Aquilegia*

COMMUNITY GARDENS

On abandoned lots and at schools, office parks, retirement centers, and churches in thousands of diverse locations across North America, gardeners without land of their own and those who want to beautify their neighborhoods come together to create community gardens. Some are strictly ornamental, but many produce food for the members themselves and for needy people in the community. All bring a variety of benefits to the participants and to the surrounding area. The benefits include:

- Providing fresh, healthful produce for people in areas where it is not often found.

- Creating a quiet green space where residents can relax and find respite from the stress of daily life.

- Bringing together people of different ages, backgrounds, and income levels to work collaboratively for the good of their neighborhood.

- Improving safety—studies in St. Louis, Chicago, and other cities found that people living near community gardens suffer less crime and domestic strife than those who don't.

Many European cities offer residents small plots (called "allotments") in the surrounding area where gardeners can enjoy the experience of sowing and growing. But in the United States and Canada, community gardens are typically organized and led by local volunteers. Often, members have individual plots where they grow food for themselves, but in some gardens the group shares all the labor and the harvest.

In most North American cities, municipal parks departments and/or nonprofit organizations provide support and resources to community garden groups. If you want to start a community garden where you live, get in touch with the American Community Gardening Association (communitygarden.org), a national organization of gardening and open space volunteers and professionals. It offers programs and support for community garden volunteers.

Six Steps to Getting a Community Garden Started

There are many details to work out in launching a community garden, but they can be divided into these broad steps.

1. Get Together

It takes a community to start a community garden. You'll need at least one or two superorganized people to recruit neighbors with a shared passion but varying ages, backgrounds, and skills. At every step, include the people who will benefit from the garden in the planning process.

2. Secure Land

In some cities, online maps like Living Lots NYC identify open spaces. Property-records departments help decipher lot ownership; private owners may lease land. Many locales have agencies that rent out public land for gardens. Terms can vary, so learn local laws and explore options for longevity, including establishing a trust. Get permission and a written lease to use any space. If your garden plan includes physical improvements such as fencing, creating raised beds, or adding soil, try to obtain at least a 3-year lease. Your group needs to be able to use the site long enough to justify its investments.

3. Draw Up Plans

Individual or shared beds? Edibles or botanicals? Structured leadership or consensus? Agree on your purpose, garden design, and shared values. All gardens start with dirt. In cities, where contaminants are prevalent, soil testing and remediation are a must. If you're growing edibles, bring in fresh soil and build raised beds out of wood or concrete blocks. Then set up a composting system to fertilize soil. Mulch is handy for weed-free pathways between beds. Gardens on old tenement lots often have leftover brick for public walkways. In wet climates, opt for gravel or permeable paving. Water is a necessity. Locales like New York City provide hydrant access, but rain barrels help conserve municipal supplies. Shaded seating and communal areas welcome neighbors and give relief to sweaty gardeners. A grill or outdoor kitchen facilitates gatherings; many gardens host workshops and performances. In others, the arts are integrated through sculptures and murals. Invite wildlife in with trees and maybe a landscaped pond with a fountain powered by solar panels. Good fences make good neighbors, and a sign that states the garden's name, hours, contacts, and calendar says, "We're here!" Where theft is prevalent, a lock on the gate is essential. You'll want one on the toolshed, too. Fence-side ornamentals—especially native flowering shrubs that attract pollinators or help feed the residents of your bee boxes—beautify the neighborhood. And since kids are the future of the movement, dedicated children's beds help pass on the skills.

4. Find Funds

Many municipalities have grants programs for gardeners. Banks and other local businesses might also sponsor you. You'll find more options at the American Community Gardening Association (ACGA) Web site. (See Resources on page 673.)

5. Build It Up

Botanical gardens and parks outreach programs often help with soil, seeds, equipment, and building materials as well as guidance on organic growing. Test and remediate soil and create ways to recycle and conserve, including composting and rainwater harvesting.

If your group needs horticultural information or other gardening support, contact the Cooperative Extension Service (there's an office in every county), garden clubs, or garden centers. To learn more about managing a community garden, check the ACGA Web site.

6. Make Friends

Local officials, media, and members of the community can all support and enjoy your efforts.

COMPANION PLANTING

Planting marigolds and herbs among the vegetables in your garden to confuse or repel plant pests is a well-known example of the practice of companion planting. Garden lore contains hundreds of recommended plant combinations, such as nasturtiums planted amid cucumbers to repel cucumber beetles or the traditional "three sisters" practice of growing corn, beans, and squash together to take advantage of complementary growth habits.

Modern research substantiates the effectiveness of some companion plants in repelling pests or attracting pest predators and parasites. However, the mechanisms that cause a plant to repel or attract pests remain largely unverified, and many companion planting practices represent a combination of folklore and fact. Evidence from scientific studies and gardeners' experimentation indicates several possible ways in which companion planting works.

- Masking or hiding a crop from pests
- Producing odors that confuse and deter pests
- Serving as trap crops that draw pest insects away from other plants
- Acting as "nurse plants" that provide breeding grounds for beneficial insects
- Providing food to sustain beneficial insects as they search for pests
- Creating a habitat for beneficial insects

Whatever the cause, it does seem clear that areas planted to a single crop (monoculture) attract more pests than beds of mixed crops or those that are interplanted with herbs and flowers. It's fun to try your own companion planting experiments and see what works in your garden.

Repel with Smell

Research has shown that night-flying moths (the adults that produce destructive larvae such as cutworms and caterpillars) approach flowers by flying upwind. If netting is placed over flowers, the moths will still land and feed, indicating that they react to flower odor. However, moths won't land on colored flowers that lack a noticeable aroma. This explains why strongly scented companion plants such as marigolds may protect plants from pests. If pests can't smell your prize plants, or if the scent isn't right, they may go elsewhere to feed and lay eggs.

Popular plant choices for repellent or masking fragrances include the following:

Marigolds: Plant them as thickly as you can in a vegetable garden, but keep in mind that unscented marigolds won't work for this trick. Make sure you choose strongly scented species and cultivars, such as French marigold (*Tagetes patula*).

Mints: Cabbage pests and aphids dislike peppermint and other members of this fragrant family. Since mints can grow out of control, set potted mints around your garden or plant them in areas where their growth can be controlled.

Rue: Oils from the leaves of rue (*Ruta graveolens*) give some people a poison-ivy-like rash, so use this low-growing plant with care and wear gloves when handling it. However, what annoys people also deters Japanese beetles. Grow rue as a garden border or scatter leaf clippings near beetle-infested crops.

Sweet basil: Interplant *Ocimum basilicum* in vegetable or flower gardens, or chop and scatter the leaves to repel aphids, mosquitoes, and mites. Use pots of basil on patio or picnic tables to discourage flies from joining outdoor activities.

Tansy: Used as a mulch, tansy (*Tanacetum vulgare*) may cause cucumber beetles, Japanese beetles, ants, and squash bugs to go elsewhere for a meal. It attracts imported cabbageworms, however, limiting its appeal as a repellent, and it can be invasive. If you're already growing it in your garden, using it as a mulch around veggies other than cabbage-family crops is a good way to keep its growth in

check while benefiting your crops, but don't plant it just for this purpose.

More Companion Planting Combos

There are many other interplanting options, too. Don't forget that simply interplanting crops from different families helps deter pests. Adding fragrant plants to the mix will up the ante. Try the following combinations in your garden.

- Plant basil and/or onions among your tomatoes to deter tomato hornworms.

- Combine thyme or tomatoes with cabbage plantings to limit flea beetles, cabbage maggots, white cabbage butterflies, and imported cabbageworms.

- Sow catnip by eggplant to discourage flea beetles.

- Set onions in rows with carrots to impede rust flies and some nematodes.

- Grow radishes or nasturtiums with your cucumbers for cucumber beetle control.

- Grow borage with tomatoes, cucumbers, and strawberries to repel pests and attract beneficials.

- Grow cilantro with spinach to repel aphids and attract beneficial tachinid flies.

- Grow summer savory with beans to repel bean beetles.

- Alternate double rows of corn with double rows of snap beans or soybeans to enhance the growth of the corn.

- Interplant peanuts with corn or squash to increase the yields of both crops.

Scientific Support

Research into the facts behind companion planting folklore shows that many practices derive their success from naturally occurring compounds within the plants. As these compounds are isolated and identified, the preferred companion plants of past gardens may become the source of modern-day botanical controls.

Here are some results of scientific studies of companion plants and natural compounds.

- A potato plant grafted onto a tobacco plant root becomes resistant to the destructive Colorado potato beetle.

- A mustard oil extracted from turnip roots effectively deters pea aphids, Mexican bean beetles, and spider mites.

- African marigolds (*Tagetes erecta*) exude a chemical called thiopene from their roots that repels soil nematodes.

- The presence of asparagus roots in the soil leads to a decline in the stubby root nematode population.

- Growing collards as a trap crop effectively protects cabbage from diamond-back moth larvae.

- Boston fern leaves contain a feeding deterrent effective against southern armyworm.

- A chemical found in tomato plant leaves is toxic to some weevil species.

🌿 Plant spinach, lettuce, or Chinese cabbage at the base of trellised peas, where they benefit from the shade and wind protection.

🌿 Grow tomatoes, parsley, or basil with asparagus to help control asparagus beetles.

Nasturtiums also deter whiteflies and squash bugs, but they are more often used as a trap crop for aphids, which prefer nasturtiums to other crops. Planting a ring of them around apple trees limits woolly aphid damage to the trees (although the nasturtiums won't look too great). Zonal geraniums (*Pelargonium* spp.) and petunias work the same way to lure Japanese beetles from roses and grapevines. Petunias will also act as a trap crop for beetles and aphids when planted among cucurbits (cucumbers, pumpkins, and squash).

Support Beneficials

The idea of gardening to attract insects may seem odd, but in the case of beneficial insects, this companion planting technique can really pay off. Beneficial insects are a boon to the garden in two ways: They help control pests, and they assist in crop pollination. Although some beneficials feed on pests, nearly all need host plants to provide food and shelter during some or all of their life cycles.

Many beneficial insects are quite tiny and have

short mouthparts. They can't reach deeply into flowers for food. Plants with numerous, small flowers, containing easy-to-reach pollen and nectar, provide the necessary high-protein and high-sugar meals that support beneficial insect populations.

Help beneficial insects get a jump on early spring aphid activity by planting gazanias, calendulas, or other small-flowered plants that will grow in your area despite early-season cool weather. Beneficial insects need a series of blossoms to sustain them from spring until fall.

Herbs such as fennel, dill, anise, and coriander are carrot-family members that produce broad clusters of small flowers attractive to beneficials. Grow these culinary items near your vegetables to keep parasitic wasps nearby. Composite flowers such as sunflowers, zinnias, and asters also attract beneficials and have a longer season of bloom than carrot-family herbs.

Use this list of plants and the beneficials they attract to lure these useful insects to your garden.

> *Achillea* spp. (yarrows): Bees, parasitic
>   wasps, hoverflies
> *Angelica archangelica* (angelica): Lady
>   beetles, lacewings
> *Chamaemelum nobile* (Roman
>   chamomile): Parasitic wasps,
>   hoverflies
> *Iberis* spp. (candytufts): Syrphid flies
> *Ipomoea purpurea* (morning glory): Lady
>   beetles
> *Nemophila menziesii* (baby blue eyes):
>   Syrphid flies
> *Oenothera biennis* (common evening
>   primrose): Ground beetles
> *Solidago* spp. (goldenrods): Lady
>   beetles, predaceous beetles, parasitic
>   wasps

For more on attracting and encouraging these tiny garden allies, see the Beneficial Insects entry.

COMPOST

Inside a compost pile, billions of bacteria, fungi, and other organisms feed, grow, reproduce, and die, recycling kitchen and garden wastes into an excellent organic fertilizer and soil conditioner. This process of decomposition occurs constantly and gradually in nature. When you build a compost pile, you're simply taking advantage of—and accelerating—nature's process to create an invaluable soil amendment for your garden.

Composting offers benefits to both the environment and your pocketbook. By making compost, you'll reduce or eliminate the need to buy fertilizers. Compost improves soil structure and moisture retention and can actually protect plants from certain diseases. Composting leaves and other yard wastes is the environmentally responsible—and money-saving—alternative to sending them to a landfill or incinerator. Plus, as much as three-quarters of your household waste is compostable, too.

Building a Compost Pile

Your goal in building a compost pile is to provide conditions in which a "microherd" of composting organisms will thrive. Composting organisms' needs are simple: a balanced diet of carbon and nitrogen, moist conditions, and a steady supply of oxygen.

The Basics

To build a compost pile, gather a variety of organic materials—leaves, seed-free pulled weeds, straw, and vegetative kitchen scraps, for example—and heap them together in a pile. Add some rich garden soil or finished compost to "seed" the pile with composting organisms, and moisten everything thoroughly. Then step back and wait: The organisms will go to work digesting the organic materials in the pile. Several months later, you'll have finished compost.

Check your compost pile occasionally to make sure it hasn't dried out or become too wet. If you wish, you can also speed up the composting process by turning and mixing the materials occasionally. Read on to learn more about how and why composting works and how you can get the best results possible from your composting efforts.

Gathering Materials

Begin your search for compost ingredients in your own backyard, kitchen, and neighborhood. You probably won't have to travel far to find a wealth of great composting materials. You'll be looking for

two types: "browns" and "greens." Brown materials are high in carbon, and carbon compounds are what composting organisms "eat" in order to keep functioning and reproducing. Green materials contain relatively high amounts of nitrogen. Microorganisms need nitrogen for reproduction, because nitrogen is a basic building block of their cell structures.

High-carbon, "brown" ingredients are almost always plant materials: straw and dry leaves are two common "browns." Many "greens" (nitrogen sources), such as manure and bloodmeal, come from animals, although fresh plant matter, such as grass clippings, is also nitrogen rich. High-nitrogen materials tend to be moist and often sloppy, but they're not always green in color (manure and coffee grounds are just two examples of "green" compost ingredients that are brown). In general,

KEY WORDS *Composting*

Aerobic. Describes organisms living or occurring only in the presence of oxygen.

Anaerobic. Describes organisms living or occurring when oxygen is absent.

Composting. The art and science of combining organic materials under controlled conditions so that the original raw ingredients are transformed into humus.

C/N ratio. The proportion of bulky, dry, high-carbon materials to dense, moist, high-nitrogen materials. The ideal C/N ratio for stimulating compost organisms is 25–30:1; finished compost's C/N ratio is about 10:1.

Cold, slow, or passive pile. A compost pile that receives little or no turning, allowing some anaerobic decomposition to occur; composting proceeds slowly and at cooler temperatures.

Hot, fast, or active pile. A compost pile that is turned or otherwise aerated frequently, stimulating high temperatures and producing finished compost in a relatively short time.

Sheet composting. Layering undecomposed organic materials over the surface of a garden bed, typically at the end of the growing season, giving them time to decompose before working them into the soil the following spring.

C/N Ratios of Common Compost Ingredients

Use these lists as a guide to choosing composting materials for your pile. Keep in mind that a small amount of a super-carbon-rich material like sawdust (500:1) will change the carbon-nitrogen ratio of your pile just as much as a large amount of straw, which is only 80:1.

HIGH-CARBON MATERIALS	C/N RATIO
Leaves	80:1–40:1
Straw	80:1
Pine needles	110:1–60:1
Paper	170:1
Sawdust	500:1
HIGH-NITROGEN MATERIALS	C/N RATIO
Alfalfa hay	12:1
Table scraps	15:1
Grass clippings	19:1
Manure, rotted	20:1
Timothy hay	25:1
Weeds, freshly pulled	30:1
Fruit wastes	35:1

high-carbon materials are brown or yellow, dry, and bulky. Straw is a classic example, but the output from your home office paper shredder qualifies as compost fodder too!

C/N ratios. The proportion of carbon to nitrogen in a material (or a compost pile overall) is called the C/N ratio. You can use it as a benchmark for mixing composting materials in the right amounts. If the C/N ratio of a compost pile climbs too high (excess carbon), microorganisms will run out of nitrogen and won't be able to reproduce. Their population size will drop quickly, so composting activity will slow down. Conversely, if the C/N ratio dips too low (too little carbon), the

microorganisms won't have a sufficient energy source, so they'll stop working. In this case, the compost pile may start to smell bad as the unused nitrogen in the pile escapes into the air.

The ideal C/N ratio for a compost pile overall is 25–30:1, and if you're good at math, you can do some fancy calculating to figure out an ideal mix. Refer to the chart below for specific C/N ratios of common compost materials. The chart is also useful even if you prefer a less precise approach: Simply aim for a mix of two parts high-carbon materials to one part high-nitrogen materials (you can use a trash can, garden cart, or 5-gallon bucket as your unit of measure).

Most organic materials supply a wide range of other nutrients needed by compost organisms and plants, too, and so the greater the variety of materials you include in your compost pile, the better the end product will be. You can also mix in mineral-rich materials such as rock phosphate or greensand to tailor the nutrients in your compost to match the needs of your soil and plants. See the Fertilizers entry for information on mineral sources you can add to your compost pile.

Compost Bins and Pens

Building a compost pile is as simple as clearing a site and heaping up materials, but many gardeners like to put their compost in some type of enclosure. Compost bins are made of wood, plastic, concrete, bricks, or just about any durable, weatherproof material. Whether permanent or portable, bins can protect compost from the weather, conserve heat during composting, and keep out scavenging animals.

You can also collect composting materials inside a ring of wire fencing or a wood-and-wire frame as shown at right. These structures are useful for piles you want to turn frequently and also for building piles in sequence. To turn the compost, you simply unfasten the enclosure and then reposition it next to the pile of composting materials. Then shovel or fork the materials into the now-empty pen.

It's convenient to set up the frame near, or even right inside, your vegetable garden. When the bin is full, you can move the frame to another convenient location and begin a new pile.

Managing Moisture

All living organisms need water, but too much moisture drives out air, drowns the pile, and washes away nutrients. A successfully functioning

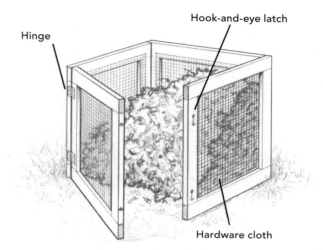

Wood and wire compost bin. Construct a portable bin using four sides made of 3- by 3-foot pieces of ½-inch hardware cloth fastened to two-by-fours. Use hinges and hooks and eyes on one side to make a door.

compost pile is about as damp as a moist sponge. There are several ways to control moisture levels in compost piles.

- Build your pile on a site that is well drained. If necessary, start with a bottom layer of sand or gravel to make sure the pile never sits in a puddle.

- Sprinkle each layer with a watering can or garden hose as you construct the pile. Or, after you build the pile, loop a soaker hose in rings over the pile surface and turn on a slow flow that will gradually moisten the pile. Check the moisture level every few days and, if necessary, add water when you turn your compost.

- Mix very wet, sloppy materials such as fruit wastes with absorbent ingredients such as sawdust or shredded dry leaves.

- If your pile seems too wet, use a garden fork or composting fork to fluff and turn the materials.

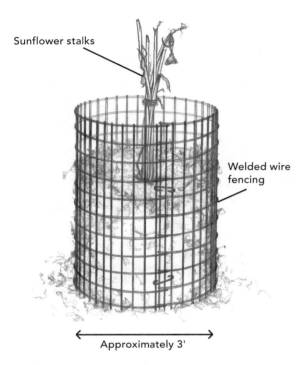

Sunflower stalks

Welded wire fencing

Approximately 3'

Wire compost pen. A 10-foot length of 4-foot-wide welded wire fencing forms a circular compost pen slightly larger than 3 feet in diameter. Fasten the ends of the fencing together with wire or reusable clips. Use a bundle of sunflower stalks to direct moisture to the center of the pile.

🌿 Protect your pile from the weather. Compost in a covered bin, or place a layer of hay or straw over your pile.

🌿 Shape your pile to work with weather conditions. In humid climates, build a pile with a rounded top, which tends to shed excess water. In dry climates, a sunken, or concave, top helps water soak into the pile.

Aerating Your Compost

Supplying enough air to all parts of a compost pile encourages thorough decomposition. Fre-

quent turning is the most straightforward way to do this, but there are other aerating techniques to use in addition to or even in place of turning.

🌿 Build a base of coarse material such as brush or wood chips under your pile to allow air penetration from below.

🌿 Shred leaves, hay, and garden debris before composting. Use materials such as paper and grass clippings sparingly, because they tend to form impermeable mats when wet.

🌿 Insert sticks into the pile when building it, then pull them out later to open air passages. You can also poke holes in the compost with a garden fork or crowbar.

🌿 Bury perforated drainpipe at intervals in a passive compost pile as an excellent way to improve aeration. Sunflower stalks and straw also conduct air into compost; cornstalks don't hollow out as they decay and won't work for this purpose.

🌿 Limit both the height and width of the pile to 5 to 6 feet to avoid compression.

Other Composting Methods

Conventional compost piles aren't the only way to make great compost. You may want to experiment with composting right on top of your garden beds (sheet composting) or making compost in special bins with composting worms added (vermicomposting).

Sheet Composting

Nowhere is it written that gardeners must till, spade, and generally churn up more soil than an army of earthworms to have successful gardens. How do you garden without digging or cultivating? It's easier than you might think. Simply start collecting all manner of organic wastes and spread them evenly over a garden bed, making sure that the base layer is a high-nitrogen material such as kitchen wastes. Moisten the whole thing, and top it with a few inches of a dry material like straw or shredded leaves to keep in the moisture. Earthworms will work their magic on the smorgasbord of organic materials that you've heaped on the soil surface. *Note:* If you have pet dogs, you'll need to put a temporary fence around this bed, too, or they'll probably dig right through the covering layer to search for goodies beneath.

Trash Can Composting

You don't need a lot of space to compost successfully. You can make a simple outdoor composter by cutting out the bottom of a trash can and setting the can firmly into the ground to prevent tipping. Use several such cans for continuous waste composting; simply wait 6 months to a year, depending on your climate, for the finished product. Chopping your wastes first speeds up the process, as does occasional turning or fluffing of the can's contents. Air holes, drilled into the sides and lid, provide aeration to keep the system working and encourage earthworms to inhabit your garbage can composter.

Compost tumblers, also called barrel or drum composters, are available at most garden centers and from mail-order garden suppliers. These devices offer many of the benefits of hot composting while easing the effort of turning. Compost tumblers work quickly; used according to the manufacturer's instructions, they produce finished compost in about 2 weeks. Their capacity tends to be limited, however; once the drum is full, you have to wait until composting is complete before adding new materials. Store kitchen wastes in plastic buckets with tight-fitting lids during this time, using sawdust or similarly absorbent materials to minimize odors. Also, it's important to shred or chop all materials before adding them to the tumbler. The compost won't "cook" unless everything in the tumbler is the right size and is kept moist.

Vermicomposting

Even apartment dwellers can make compost indoors with the help of earthworms. A worm box, with air holes, drainage, and a healthy earthworm population, helps turn food wastes into compost with very little effort on your part. As a rule of thumb, you'll need a container with 1 square foot of surface area for each pound of waste material added per week—a box 3 feet square and 1 foot deep can accommodate most of an average household's food wastes. You can also use a plastic garbage can, modified to allow drainage and aeration, as a worm-powered indoor composter. Read the Earthworms entry to learn more about composting with earthworms.

Making Hot Compost

Hot compost is generally ready to use in less than 8 weeks after you build the pile. Frequent turning is the secret: It keeps the compost well aerated so that decomposer organisms can work efficiently. Keep your compost working properly by monitoring the temperature and turning the pile as soon as the temperature drops. The object is to maintain elevated temperatures until decomposition is complete. A thermometer is helpful but not essential; you can stick your hand down into the pile to see how hot it is. Or insert a metal rod into your compost. If the rod feels hot to the touch after a few minutes in the pile, your compost is heating properly.

Proceed with Caution

Think twice before you add the following materials to a compost pile:

Lime and wood ashes. Adding lime to a compost pile can moderate pH and odors, but it's not always a desirable addition. Lime can trigger the release of nitrogen into the atmosphere in the form of ammonia, particularly from piles that include manure. Instead, moderate pile pH by adding crushed eggshells, bonemeal, or wood ashes, which also provide potash. Like lime, wood ashes are alkaline and will raise the pH of your compost. Use wood ashes in moderation to avoid high pH levels because high pH conditions can inhibit microorganism activity and limit nutrient uptake by some plants.

Neighborhood yard wastes. Leaves and grass clippings from your neighbors' yards are a great source of compost fodder, but not if your neighbors use chemical herbicides and pesticides—their yard wastes may contain harmful chemical residues.

Fats and meat scraps. It's wise to keep fatty kitchen leftovers and meat scraps separate from the kitchen wastes you collect for composting. These materials break down very slowly, and their presence in a compost pile can attract undesirable animals, including rats.

Manure. Manure from cows, horses, chickens, rabbits, and other domestic livestock is fine for composting, as long as you handle it carefully. Manure may contain strains of *E. coli* bacteria that can cause serious—even life-threatening—illness, so always wear gloves when you're working with it, and wash up thoroughly afterward. Make sure that compost made from manure is fully mature before you apply it to your garden.

Temperature and critical mass: Too large a pile interferes with aeration, but a minimum size of 3 feet in each dimension is needed for optimal heating. Given the proper C/N ratio, moisture, and aeration, your compost will heat up even in cold winter weather. A hot pile can reach temperatures of 160°F but will produce satisfactory results if it cooks along at about 120°F. Northern gardeners sometimes insulate their piles with hay bales or leaves to help composting continue throughout winter.

Pros and cons: The main advantage of hot composting is its speed—even in cooler climates you can process six or more batches in a season. Thus, hot composting is a good way to generate a lot of compost quickly. Plus, the high temperatures in a hot compost pile will kill many weed seeds and pathogens. Practice your hot-composting skills, though, before you include diseased plants or seed-bearing weeds on your list of compost ingredients. Weeds such as Canada thistle that sprout readily from small pieces of root also are better left out of the compost bin.

The major disadvantage of hot composting is the labor involved in turning the compost every few days. It is also a less forgiving process than others: If the moisture level or C/N ratio is wrong, you have to make adjustments. Another drawback is that the whole pile must be built at once, so you'll need to stockpile materials until you have enough to build a pile of the minimum size necessary.

Hot composting conserves less nitrogen than cooler methods because fast bacterial growth requires extra nitrogen, some of which inevitably drifts off in the form of ammonia. Finally, studies have shown that compost produced at high temperatures doesn't suppress soilborne diseases as well as cool compost can, since hot composting also kills the beneficial bacteria and fungi that would attack such pathogens once the compost is added to garden soil.

Using Compost

Finished compost is a versatile material that you can apply freely at any time of year without fear of burning plants or polluting water. For most garden applications, use compost that is well finished—aged long enough so that the decomposition process has stabilized. Unfinished compost retards the germination and growth of certain plants, although others, such as corn and squash, seem to thrive on partly finished compost. Try these tips for using compost around your garden and yard.

Vegetables and annuals: Incorporate compost into the top inch or two of all annual beds (including your vegetable garden) before seeding or transplanting. Apply compost during the growing season as a mulch or side-dressing.

Trees and shrubs: If your soil is poor, avoid backfilling the planting hole with compost-enriched soil, since roots will tend to ball up inside the hole instead of branching out in search of nutrients. Instead, top-dress with compost over the entire root zone after planting.

Lawns: Spread compost when establishing new seedlings and rejuvenating your lawn in spring. Add fine compost when you aerate, so it comes in contact with roots.

Potting mixes: Compost provides an excellent medium for starting seeds and growing houseplants. Contrary to popular belief, pasteurization is unnecessary—heating compost actually suppresses disease-fighting microbes, allowing airborne pathogens to populate the growing medium. Simply screen your compost to remove large pieces and mix the fine compost with sand, peat moss, and other amendments to create a custom potting mix. (Use the large pieces you screen out as mulch or to "seed" a new compost pile.)

Compost Tea

Compost tea is an effective, mild, natural fertilizer for seedlings and garden plants, and it can suppress fungal plant diseases. The tea-brewing process extracts, and in some cases grows and multiplies, nutrients and beneficial bacteria and fungi from compost and suspends them in water in a form that makes them quickly available to plants.

When you brew compost tea, be sure to use mature, sweet, earthy-smelling compost. Sour or unpleasant odors indicate anaerobic decomposition and mean that the compost contains few of the beneficial microbes you want in your "tea." The best source of compost for tea making is a mature (3- to 8-month-old) pile. Keep in mind that harmful strains of E. coli can be present in the raw ingredients of a compost pile. Minimize the risk by maintaining a hot pile or allowing the compost to mature fully. And don't apply compost tea to any vegetable within 3 weeks of its planned harvest date.

Municipal Compost

Municipal compost operations range from small, leaf-composting facilities to huge systems capable of turning 800 tons per day of waste into compost. Most facilities use windrows that are either turned every few days with mechanized compost turners or aerated using forced-air methods. A few are fully enclosed, automated "in-vessel" compost systems that take in refuse at one end and sort, grind, mix, moisten, and aerate it on its way to the other end of the process, where it arrives as finished compost.

Whether they are highly sophisticated or very simple, municipal compost programs' primary interest is reducing the volume of materials going to landfills. While they also may produce high-quality compost, this is not their main goal, and savvy gardeners looking to use compost from the local facility would do well to learn what goes into the mix in their municipality and how the materials are handled and turned into compost.

Municipal compost facilities often make their product available to area residents at little or no cost. To locate nearby composting facilities, contact local governing bodies responsible for solid waste management; most states maintain listings of operating or planned compost facilities as well. The quality of compost produced by municipal operations can vary considerably, depending on the nature of the materials composted, the skill of the facility's operators, and how long the product has been allowed to mature. Most states prohibit distribution of compost containing heavy metals or other toxic contaminants to the public.

It's a good idea to test municipal compost for herbicide residues before you apply it to gardens or use it to make a potting mix. Simply sow seeds of sensitive crops such as cucumbers, tomatoes, or peas (make sure the seed is viable) in containers filled with compost. Watch the seedlings for several weeks. If the seedlings germinate poorly or are not properly formed, it's a sign of a problem. You won't know whether the cause is herbicide residue or simply poor-quality compost, but whatever the cause, you won't want to use that compost in your garden.

Making compost tea doesn't require any special equipment. Here's how to do it.

1. Fill a bucket with one part compost to five parts water, stir well, then let the mixture ferment—outdoors (the fragrance is strong!)—for 10 days to 2 weeks. Protect the brewing tea from extreme temperatures—it shouldn't be in danger of freezing or in full sun that will cook all the good organisms in it.

2. After 10 to 14 days, strain the tea into another bucket, allow it to settle, and fill your sprayer with liquid from the top (without stirring up

any of that bottom sediment). Use cheesecloth, burlap, old nylons, or other fabric to strain out the solids, and return these to your compost pile.

3. Spray the tea without further dilution. This fermented recipe is particularly good for suppressing diseases and is a fine general-purpose foliar fertilizer. You can also use it to water seedlings and transplants.

4. Pour any sediment in the bottom of your sprayer back into the compost pile. Get another batch of tea brewing so it's ready in 2 to 3 weeks for a follow-up application. Be sure to wash tea-sprayed produce before you eat it.

CONEFLOWER

See *Echinacea; Rudbeckia*

CONSOLIDA

Larkspur. Spring- and summer-blooming annuals.

Description: Delphinium look-alikes, larkspurs are cool-weather annuals with feathery leaves and showy, spikelike clusters of spurred flowers in shades of rich blue, deep purple, lavender, pink, and white. Standard cultivars are 2 to 4 feet tall; dwarfs reach 1 to 2 feet. Plants bloom all summer in areas with cool summers; in spring and early summer where summers are hot.

How to grow: Since larkspurs resent transplanting, sow seeds outdoors where the plants are to grow in fall for bloom the following year or in spring beginning as soon as the soil can be worked. Sow new seeds every 3 to 4 weeks to extend the bloom season. You can also start seeds indoors in individual pots or purchase transplants and move them with care. Stake tall cultivars. Plants will self-sow, so leave some flowers in the garden to set seeds.

Landscape uses: Use larkspurs to fill in over spring-blooming bulbs and plant them in perennial gardens for added color. Tall cultivars make excellent cut flowers; be sure to include them in the cutting garden.

CONTAINER GARDENING

Pots, tubs, and half barrels overflowing with flowers add appeal to any garden, but container gardens can serve practical purposes, too. Gardening in containers is ideal for those with little or no garden space, and pots that raise plants up off the ground can make gardening accessible to people whose mobility is limited. In addition to growing flowers, gardeners tending a balcony, a small yard, or only a sunny patch on their driveway can produce a wide variety of vegetable crops in containers. Basil, chives, thyme, and other herbs also are quite happy growing in pots, which can be set in a convenient spot right outside the kitchen door.

Container plants add versatility to gardens large and small. They lend instant color, provide a focal point in the garden, or tie in the architecture of the house to the garden. Place them on the ground or raise them on pedestals, mount them on windowsills, or hang them from your porch. A pair of matching containers on either side of the front walk serves as a welcoming decoration, while containers on a deck or patio can add color and ambience to sitting areas. You can use single large containers for outdoor decoration, but also consider arranging groups of pots, both small and large, on stairways, terraces, or anywhere in the garden. Clusters of pots can contain a collection of favorite plants—succulents, such as hen and chicks (*Sempervivum* spp.), or herbs used both for ornament and for cooking, for example—or they may feature annuals, dwarf evergreens, perennials, or any other plants you'd like to try. Containers provide the perfect opportunity to experiment with new or unfamiliar plants, allowing you to "test grow" them for a season before you buy and plant a whole border full. Houseplants summering outdoors in the shade also make handsome additions to container gardens. Window boxes and hanging baskets offer even more ways to add instant color and appeal.

Containers planted with a single species—rosemary (*Rosmarinus officinalis*) or a bold variegated ornamental grass, for example—can be stunning garden accents. Containers planted with a mix of plants are fun to create and offer almost unlimited possibilities of combinations. The best combinations depend on plants that feature handsome foliage and flowers produced over a long bloom season. One easy guideline for choosing the plants to combine in a container is to include "a thriller, a spiller, and a filler." That translates to at least one focal-point plant (the thriller), such as coleus or a geranium with multicolored leaves, for example, combined with several plants that spill over the edge of the pots—such as petunias, bacopa (Sutera cordata), creeping zinnia (*Sanvitalia procumbens*), or ornamental sweet potato (such as Ipomoea batatas 'Blackie'). Finally, add the fillers, which are plants with smaller leaves and flowers that add color and fill in the arrangement all season long. Good fillers include salvias (*Salvia* spp.), verbenas (*Verbena* spp.), ornamental peppers (*Capsicum* spp.), and wax begonias (*Begonia ×semperflorens-cultorum*) as well as foliage plants like parsley or licorice plant (*Helichrysum petiolare*). You may also want to include a plant for height, such as an ornamental grass like purple fountain grass (*Pennisetum setaceum* 'Rubrum'). Add a trellis or pillar to a container and you can use a vine to add height to the composition. You'll need a total of five or six plants for an 18- or 24-inch container, for example.

Choosing Containers

Pots and planters come in a wide range of sizes, shapes, materials, and styles. You can also modify everyday containers such as bowls or barrels to be planters.

Size: When choosing a container, keep in mind that it's easier to grow plants in large containers than small ones. Large containers hold more soil, which stays moist longer and is less subject to rapid temperature fluctuations. Small hanging baskets are especially prone to drying out; during hot summer weather you may have to water them twice a day to keep plants alive.

It's also important to decide what plant you want to grow in each container. Several factors help determine how large and deep the container must be. Consider the size and shape of a plant's root system; whether it is a perennial, annual, or shrub; and how rapidly it grows. Rootbound plants, which have filled up every square inch of the soil available, dry out rapidly and won't grow well. Choose a large pot or tub for a mixed planting, one that will offer enough root space for all the plants you want to grow. Light-colored containers keep the soil cooler than dark containers.

The maximum size (and weight) of a container is limited by how much room you have, what will support it, and whether you plan to move it. If your container garden is located on a balcony or deck, be sure to check how much weight the structure will safely hold.

Drainage: Whatever container you choose, drainage holes are essential. Without drainage, soil will become waterlogged and plants may die. The holes need not be large, but there must be enough so that excess water can drain out. If a container has no holes, try drilling some yourself. A container without holes is best used as a cachepot, or cover, to hide a plain pot. Cachepots (with holes and without them) are useful for managing large plants and heavy pots: Grow your plant in an ordinary nursery pot that fits inside a decorative cachepot so you can move them separately.

Self-watering, double-walled containers, hanging baskets, and window boxes are available. These are useful for dealing with smaller plants that need frequent watering.

Materials: Each type of container has merits and disadvantages.

- Clay or terra-cotta containers are attractive but breakable and are easily damaged by freezing and thawing. In northern areas, most need to be stored in a frost-free location to prevent cracking and are not suitable for hardy perennials or shrubs that will remain outdoors year-round.

- Cast concrete is long lasting and comes in a range of sizes and styles. These can be left outside in all weather. You can even make attractive ones yourself. Plain concrete containers are very heavy, so they are difficult to move and not suitable for using on decks or balconies. Concrete mixed with vermiculite or perlite, or concrete and fiberglass blends, are much lighter.

- Plastic and fiberglass pots and planters are lightweight, relatively inexpensive, and available in many sizes and shapes. Choose sturdy and somewhat flexible containers and avoid thin, stiff ones—they become brittle with cold or age.

- Containers made of polyurethane foam weigh up to 90 percent less than terra-cotta or concrete containers, yet they look remarkably like their much-heavier cousins. Polyurethane foam containers resist chipping and cracking and can insulate roots against both hot and cold temperatures, making them a good choice for holding plants that will stay outside year-round.

- Wood is natural looking and protects roots from rapid temperature swings. If you're reasonably handy, you can build wooden planters yourself. Choose a naturally rot-resistant wood such as cedar or locust, or use pine treated with a nontoxic preservative. (Don't use creosote, which is toxic to plants.) Molded wood-fiber containers are sturdy and inexpensive.

- Metals are strong, but they conduct heat, exposing roots to rapid temperature fluctuations. Exposure to moisture and fertilizers can cause corrosion and deterioration of metal containers. Some metals may leach compounds that make them undesirable for growing edible plants. If you crave the look of metal for your container garden, consider using metal containers as cachepots over more utilitarian containers.

Preparing Your Containers

Since containers are heavy once they are filled with moist soil, decide where they will be located and move them into position before filling and planting. If watering during the day poses a problem, look for sites that receive morning sun and are shaded during the hottest part of the day, even if you are growing plants for full sun. Afternoon shade will reduce the amount of moisture plants need.

While your containers must have drainage holes, the traditional practice of covering the holes with pot shards or gravel before you add potting mix is unnecessary. The covering doesn't improve drainage, and pot shards may actually block the holes. Instead, prevent soil from washing out by placing a layer of paper towel or newspaper over the holes before adding mix. If your container is too deep, you can put a layer of gravel or Styrofoam in the bottom to reduce the amount of potting soil required.

Plain garden soil is too dense for container plantings. For containers up to 1 gallon in size, use a houseplant soil mixture; see the Houseplants entry for a recipe. For larger containers, use a relatively coarse soilless planting mixture to maintain the needed water and air balance. Buy a commercial container planting mix or make your own from equal parts of compost, pulverized pine or fir bark, and perlite or vermiculite. For each cubic foot of mix add 4 ounces of dolomitic limestone, 1 pound of rock phosphate or colloidal phosphate, 4 ounces of greensand, 1 pound of granite dust, and 2 ounces of bloodmeal.

Many of the components of potting soil are lightweight, dust-producing materials that can irritate your eyes, skin, and lungs. Vermiculite can contain low levels of asbestos; compost and peat moss may contain mold spores. When you work with potting soil and other soil, observe the following precautions.

🌿 Work outdoors or in a well-ventilated garage or garden shed.

🌿 Wear a dust mask.

🌿 Dampen individual ingredients before mixing them together to minimize the amount of dust in the air.

🌿 When you're finished, wash your hands thoroughly. If you've been working with vermiculite, be aware that the dust can cling to your clothing. Remove and wash dusty clothing as soon as possible to avoid dispersing asbestos inside your house.

You may want to mix in one of the special superabsorbent polymers—synthetic substances that hold large amounts of water available for plants. They improve water availability without making the soil soggy. While these products are not naturally occurring substances, they appear to be inert and to have no toxic breakdown products.

Premoisten soil either by watering it before you fill containers or by flooding the containers with water several times and stirring. Be sure the soil is uniformly moist before planting. Peat moss, in particular, is difficult to moisten thoroughly once it's in a container. Dampen your mix before filling your pots and before putting in plants. Keep peat-based mixes evenly moist after planting, as they are difficult to rewet if they dry out completely.

Plant in containers as you would in the garden. If you are planting a mixed container, ignore spacing requirements and plant densely; you will need to prune plants once they fill in. For trees and shrubs, trim off any circling roots and cover the rootball to the same level as it was set at the nursery. Firm the planter mixture gently and settle by watering thoroughly. Don't fill pots level to the top with soil mixture—leave space for watering.

Selecting Plants

Almost any vegetable, flower, herb, shrub, or small tree can grow successfully in a container. Dwarf and compact cultivars are best, especially for smaller pots. Select plants to suit the climate and the amount of sun or shade the container will receive. If you are growing fragrant plants, such as heliotrope (*Heliotropium arborescens*), place containers in a site protected from breezes, which will disperse the perfume.

Use your imagination, and combine upright and trailing plants, edibles, and flowers for pleasing and colorful effects. Container gardens can be enjoyed for one season and discarded, or designed to last for years. When designing permanent containers, remember that the plants will be less hardy than usual because their roots are more exposed to fluctuating air temperature. Nonhardy plants will need to have winter protection or be moved to a sheltered space. Consider how heavy the container will be and how you will move it before choosing a plant that must be moved indoors for the winter.

Here are suggestions to get you started.

Vegetables and herbs. You can grow vegetables in individual containers—from large pots to 5-gallon buckets or half barrels, the largest of which will accommodate a single tomato plant or two or three smaller vegetables such as broccoli or cabbage. Dwarf or bush forms of larger vegetables such as tomatoes, pumpkins, and winter squash are best suited to container culture. Have fun with theme gardens. Plant a salad garden with colorful lettuces, dwarf tomatoes, chives, and parsley. Or perhaps try a pizza garden, with different types of basil, plus tomatoes and peppers. Or plant a container with edible flowers such as marigolds, pansies (*Viola* ×*wittrockiana*), and nasturtiums (*Tropaeolum majus*).

Annuals. For containers that remain attractive all summer long, choose warm-weather annuals that bloom all summer or have foliage that remains attractive. Geraniums, marigolds, wax begonias, coleus (*Plectranthus scutellarioides*), scarlet sage (*Salvia splendens*), and flowering tobaccos (*Nicotiana*

spp.) all are good choices, but you will find many, many more in garden centers and seed catalogs. Experiment, and if one plant doesn't work out, don't worry about it—just cut it down and try something else. For large containers, dwarf cannas and dwarf dahlias also make satisfying additions.

Perennials and shrubs. Containers planted with hardy perennials and shrubs can be grown and enjoyed from year to year. Hostas and daylilies (*Hemerocallis* spp.) are great container plants, but many other perennials work as well. Try ferns, European wild ginger (*Asarum europaeum*), sedges (*Carex* spp.), lavender, spotted dead nettle (*Lamium maculatum*), sedums, and lungworts (*Pulmonaria* spp.). Ornamental grasses are great in containers, too, as are dwarf conifers and small shrubs.

Caring for Container Plants

Water container plants thoroughly. How often depends on factors such as weather, plant size, and pot size. Don't let soil in containers dry out completely, as it is hard to rewet. To keep large containers attractive, spread a layer of mulch on top of the potting mix, much as you would in the garden. This will also help retain moisture. Leave an inch or so of unmulched space around plant stems.

Container plants need regular feeding. Fertilize them by watering with diluted fish emulsion, seaweed extract, or compost tea. Or foliar feed by spraying the leaves with doubly diluted preparations of these solutions. Start by feeding once every 2 weeks; adjust the frequency depending on plant response.

Since containers are focal points in the garden, you will probably want to give them special attention to keep them looking their best. Remove tattered leaves and deadhead spent flowers. Prune back plants that get leggy or stop blooming. To keep mixed pots attractive, dig out or cut back any plants that don't grow well or that clash. You can add something else or let other plants in the container fill the space. Keep an eye out for pests like aphids and mites; see the Pests entry for control guidelines.

COREOPSIS

Coreopsis, calliopsis, tickseed. Summer-blooming annuals; late-spring- to fall-blooming perennials.

Description: *Coreopsis tinctoria*, annual calliopsis, bears loads of single, 1- to 2-inch, broad-petaled daisies in shades of yellow, gold, red, brown, and combinations. The 1- to 2-foot erect plants are scantily clad in fine, threadlike leaves.

C. *grandiflora*, large-flowered tickseed, bears 2½-inch, deep yellow daisy flowers on 1- to 2-foot perennial plants; leaves may be lance-shaped or lobed. Zones 4–9.

C. *lanceolata*, lanceleaf coreopsis, bears single, semidouble, or double yellow daisies on 1- to 2-foot perennial plants; leaves are lance-shaped. Zones 4–9.

Perennial hybrid coreopsis—from C. *grandiflora* and C. *lanceolata*—bears single to double, 1½- to 3-inch, mostly gold daisies on long, leafless stems above loose sheaves of long, medium green leaves; some have red-ringed centers. Plants grow 10 to 36 inches tall. Zones 4–9.

C. *rosea*, pink tickseed, bears numerous 1-inch, pink daisy flowers on mounded 1- to 2-foot perennial plants with needlelike leaves. Zones 4–8.

C. *verticillata*, threadleaf coreopsis, produces many 1- to 2-inch, starlike blooms in yellow and gold shades atop 1- to 3-foot spreading mounds of delicate, airy foliage. C. *verticillata* 'Moonbeam',

with pale yellow flowers, was named Perennial Plant of the Year for 1992 by the Perennial Plant Association. Zones 3–8.

How to grow: Sow annual calliopsis in spring (in fall in the South) where they are to bloom in a sunny, average to less fertile, well-drained spot. Although their bloom season is short, they tolerate heat and drought very well, and will self-sow freely for the next year or perhaps for a second crop in fall.

Give perennial coreopsis similar conditions, dividing them every few years in spring or fall. Taller hybrids need staking; prompt deadheading will prolong bloom throughout much of the growing season. Cut back threadleaf coreopsis after the main flush of bloom to encourage another heavy bloom in fall. Or let it continue to bloom unchecked, although it will bloom less spectacularly.

Landscape uses: All coreopsis are excellent plants for borders and cottage gardens. Taller coreopsis will also brighten meadow and prairie gardens. Hybrids provide plenty of cut flowers.

CORN

Zea mays
Poaceae

Historically speaking, corn is more American than apple pie: It's been cultivated in North American gardens for more than 4,000 years. Even though it takes a large share of garden space, many gardeners make room for sweet corn because of the unbeatably sweet, distinctively corny flavor of fresh-picked ears.

The sugar in the kernels of ears of open-pollinated sweet corn varieties starts changing to starch almost as soon as you pick the ears. However, plant breeders have developed dozens of new and ever-sweeter cultivars that retain their sugar content for days. If sweetness is your prime goal, choose varieties listed as supersweet (abbreviated as sh2 in seed catalogs), but keep in mind that these may not be as vigorous as other types of sweet corn. If you prefer good old-fashioned corny flavor, pick standard (su) varieties. For a compromise of sweetness and vigor, choose sugary-enhanced varieties (se). Or, if you like to experiment with the latest innovations, try planting a synergistic variety (syn). These varieties produce ears with a combination of sugary-enhanced kernels and supersweet kernels on each ear. Whichever type you decide to grow, it's a good idea to check with other local growers or your Cooperative Extension Service to see what varieties have a good track record in your area.

If you have lots of garden space, you may also want to try growing some popcorn or ornamental corn, which has similar planting and care needs as sweet corn. Don't despair if your small growing space makes corn seem out of the question—dwarf varieties meant for container or raised-bed culture may be found from seed catalogs and online seed vendors. Ornamental corn cultivars—like other tall ornamental grasses—make attractive temporary screens or backdrops for a flowering border. A large container of growing corn provides a dramatic vertical accent on a patio and, if you're willing to hand-pollinate, can yield a few ears for the table as well.

Planting: Corn is very susceptible to frosts. You can lose a crop if you plant too early. Corn doesn't transplant well, either, so if you garden in a short-season area and want to start corn indoors, use biodegradable pots to avoid disturbing the roots at transplanting time. It's better to wait until all danger of frost is past and the soil warms up to the 60°F needed for seed germination. If the weather stays cool, spread black plastic on the planting area to warm the soil more quickly.

If you want corn only for fresh eating, plant a minimum of 10 to 15 plants per person. To extend your harvest, sow an early-maturing type every 2 weeks for 6 weeks, or plant early, midseason, and late types at the same time. To avoid cross-pollination, keep different corn cultivars (especially supersweets) 400 or more yards apart, or plant them so they develop tassels 2 weeks apart.

Site your corn patch in a sunny, wind-protected area. Corn is a nitrogen-hungry crop, so it thrives in a place where soil-enriching crops like beans, hairy vetch, or clover grew the previous season. To prepare the soil to suit corn's needs, add 20 to 30 pounds of compost per 100 square feet before planting.

The best way to promote complete pollination is to plant corn in blocks rather than long individual rows—a block should be at least three rows wide. If you plant only one or two rows, hand-pollinate to improve kernel formation, as described on the next page.

For early plantings, sow seeds only 1 inch deep; in the hot weather of midsummer, plant kernels up to 2 inches deep. The average germination rate for sweet corn is about 75 percent, so plant three seeds together every 7 to 15 inches. They should germinate in 7 to 10 days. Thin to one plant every 15 inches. To avoid disturbing remaining plants, remove unwanted seedlings by cutting them off at soil level.

Growing guidelines: Corn doesn't compete well with weeds, so clear the area thoroughly before planting and cultivate around the young stalks for the first month of growth. After that, corn's shallow roots will spread out as much as 1 foot from the stalk and are easily damaged by cultivation. Instead, apply mulch to prevent weeds from sprouting.

Corn needs about 1 inch of water a week, particularly when the stalks begin to tassel. Water stress during pollination will result in ears with lots of missing kernels, so don't skip watering your corn patch. Apply water at the soil surface by using a soaker hose or drip irrigation. Avoid spraying plants from above, which could wash pollen off the flowering tops.

When the stalks are 6 inches tall, side-dress them with bloodmeal or diluted fish-based fertilizer, and repeat the feeding when they are about knee-high. Don't remove any side shoots or suckers that appear; they won't harm production, and cutting them might damage roots.

Problems: Cutworms sometimes attack corn seedlings, and flea beetles may chew holes in the leaves of young plants. You'll find details on controlling these pests on page 454.

Corn earworms are one of the most common corn pests. They also attack tomatoes and are most prevalent in the southern and central states. Earworm moths lay eggs on corn silks, and the larvae crawl inside the husks to feed at the tips of the developing ears. The yellow-headed worms grow up to about 2 inches long and have yellow, green, or brown stripes on their bodies. To prevent earworm problems, use an eyedropper or spray bottle to apply a mixture of vegetable oil, Bt (*Bacillus thuringiensis*), water, and a few drops of dishwashing liquid to the tip of each ear several days after the silks emerge. Or you can try pinning a clothespin to the tip of each ear once the silks start to turn brown to prevent the worms from crawling through to the ear.

European corn borers are 1-inch-long,

Hand-Pollinating Corn

To produce kernels, wind must deposit pollen from the tassels (corn's male flowers) onto each of the silks (pollen tubes) on the ears. Every unpollinated silk results in an undeveloped kernel. If you're planting only a single or double row of corn plants, you can improve pollination by transferring pollen from tassels to silks yourself. Collect pollen as soon as the silks emerge from the ears and the tassels have a loose, open appearance. Wait for a morning when there's no breeze, and shake the tassels over a dry bucket or other container to release the pollen. Collect pollen from several plants. Immediately transfer the pollen into a small paper bag and sprinkle the powdery material onto the silks of each ear in your corn patch. Repeat once or twice on subsequent days for best results.

beige-colored caterpillars marked with tiny black dots. They feed on foliage, especial near the top of the stalk where the leaves emerge. They also bore into the developing ears. Bt and spinosad are effective controls if applied early, before the borers tunnel into the stalks. Corn borers overwinter as full-grown larvae in weed stems and old cornstalks. Pull up and destroy such winter refuges to break their life cycle.

Cucumber beetle larvae, also known as corn rootworms, feed on corn roots, causing plants to weaken and collapse. Adults are yellow beetles with black stripes or spots. To kill the rootworms, apply *Heterorhabditis* nematodes to the soil (for more information on these nematodes, turn to page 447).

Seed-corn maggots attack kernels planted too deeply in cool soil. These yellowish white maggots are ¼ inch long, with pointed heads. If they attack, wait until warmer weather to plant another crop at a shallower level.

Animal pests can seriously reduce your corn yields. Birds may be a problem at both seeding and harvesting time, while raccoons are fond of the ripening ears. For information on discouraging these creatures, see the Animal Pests entry.

Clean garden practices, crop rotation, and planting resistant hybrids are the best defenses against most common corn diseases, including Stewart's wilt, a bacterial disease that causes wilting and pale streaks on leaves.

Corn smut is a fungal disease that makes pale, shining, swollen galls that burst when mature and release powdery black spores. Cut off and dispose of galls before they open. If necessary, destroy affected plants to keep smut from spreading. It can remain viable in the soil for 5 to 7 years. The immature galls have a texture similar to mushrooms and are prized in Mexican cuisine for their trufflelike flavor.

Harvesting: Three weeks after corn silks appear, start checking ears for peak ripeness. Pull back part of the husk and pierce a kernel with your thumbnail. If a milky liquid spurts out, the ears are at prime ripeness—rush those ears to the table, refrigerator, or freezer. Ears on the same stalk usually ripen a few days apart. A completely dry silk or a yellow or faded-green sheath means the ear is past its prime.

Leave ornamental corn and popcorn on the stalks to dry until the first hard frost. If the weather is cloudy and wet, cut and stack stalks in a cool, dry place until the corn dries.

CORNFLOWER

See *Centaurea*

CORNUS

Dogwood. Single- or multiple-stemmed deciduous spring-flowering trees or shrubs; herbaceous groundcovers.

Description: The many plants in this genus share characteristic foliage and flowers. The simple, ovate leaves come to a point at the end, and paired veins extend lengthwise from the midrib toward the leaf tip. The flowers, noteworthy in many species, feature petal-like bracts that surround the small, true blossoms. Some dogwoods have showy, white or brightly colored bracts, while others bear less-noticeable leaflike bracts.

Cornus canadensis, bunchberry, is native to the woods of North America and grows best in cool regions. Give it shade and acid soil. This herbaceous groundcover grows to 9 inches and has greenish white bracted flowers in spring that resemble those of flowering dogwood. Red berries appear in fall. Zones 2–5.

C. florida, flowering dogwood, grows in the shade of other trees in the forests of the eastern United States. In the landscape, it reaches heights of 20 to 40 feet and has a graceful, layered branching habit. Heart-shaped white or pink bracts surround the true flowers in early spring. Red berries that are favored by many birds and leaf color in shades of burgundy, scarlet, orange, and yellow appear in fall. Choose your dogwood from a nursery offering cultivars for your region because heat, drought, and cold tolerance vary within the species. Zones 5–8.

C. kousa, Kousa dogwood, has a vase-shaped

habit, layered branching, and a maximum height of about 20 feet in the landscape. The flowers appear in late spring and are surrounded by white, pointed bracts. Raspberry-like fruits are green through summer, coloring pink when the leaves turn reddish in fall. Shedding bark reveals patches of tan and cream. Zones 5–7.

C. sericea, red-osier dogwood, is a native North American shrub. Its habit is loose and broadly rounded. The red stem color intensifies during dormancy, becoming strongest in the weeks just prior to bud break. White flowers bloom in flat-topped clusters; white berries contrast nicely with reddish fall foliage. Zones 2–7.

How to grow: Dogwoods usually require partial shade, although some tolerate full sun in cooler climates. Provide evenly moist, humus-rich soil, good drainage, and mulch to shade the roots. (Swamp dwellers like red-osier dogwood tolerate some standing water.) Dogwoods have little tolerance for air pollution, reflected heat, and other urban conditions. Insects and diseases that afflict dogwoods include dogwood borer, anthracnose, and stem canker. To counteract them, provide an appropriate planting site and minimize environmental stresses on the tree; for example, water during dry spells and protect trunks and stems from being damaged by enemies such as lawn mowers.

Although common across the eastern states, flowering dogwoods grown as specimens rarely prosper in full sun in the middle of lawns. Flowering is abundant for a few years, but soon you see dead wood, sucker shoots at the tree's base, and unthrifty growth. If decline doesn't finish off such trees, borers will. However, solitary trees do seem less likely to suffer anthracnose, a fungal disease that causes patches of dead tissue in the leaves, prospers in warm, wet weather, and is transmitted by splashing rain. Full sun and good air circulation around single trees limit anthracnose's spread.

Landscape uses: Plant dogwoods for wildlife food in woodland gardens. Shrubby dogwoods are appropriate for grouping and screening. Use the red- or yellow-twigged shrubs where they can be seen on snowy days. Tree dogwoods make nice focal points but work better (visually and culturally) in groups. Try Kousa dogwood—or new hybrids between Kousa and flowering dogwoods—as a replacement for flowering dogwood, especially in sunny, dry locations.

COSMOS

Cosmos. Midsummer- to fall-blooming annuals.

Description: *Cosmos bipinnatus* bears 2- to 4-inch broad-petaled, daisylike flowers in shades of pink, red, and white, on mounds of light green, feathery foliage up to 5 feet. *C. sulphureus* has 2-inch orange, red, or yellow flowers and fernlike, dark green leaves on plants up to 3 feet.

How to grow: Direct-sow cosmos after danger of spring frost, in full sun in loose, average, well-drained soil. If necessary, transplant only when very small. Cut fading flowers for more blooms. Tall cultivars may need staking.

Landscape uses: Mass the tall cultivars by themselves or at the back of a border; use shorter cultivars in midborder clumps. Cosmos also make excellent cut flowers.

COTONEASTER

Cotoneaster. Deciduous or evergreen spring-blooming shrubs or groundcovers.

Description: *Cotoneaster apiculatus*, cranberry cotoneaster, is a low (to 20 inches), spreading groundcover with round, deep green, glossy leaves. Small pink flowers appear in spring, followed by red cranberry-like fruits. Fall foliage turns reddish before it drops. Zones 5–7.

C. divaricatus, spreading cotoneaster, eventually grows wider than tall, with a mature height of about 5 feet. Its purplish stems bear glossy oval leaves and pale pink spring flowers. Red berries appear in fall, accompanied by red foliage in most situations. Zones 5–8.

C. horizontalis, rockspray cotoneaster, is a spreading, mounding, layered plant with a functional height of 2 to 3 feet and a wider spread. It bears glossy green, rounded foliage that occasionally turns red before falling, revealing a herringbone branching structure. Zones 5–8.

C. multiflorus, many-flowered cotoneaster, is a deciduous shrub that attains a mature height of 8 to 12 feet. The broadly oval foliage is dull rather than glossy, with little fall color. This cotoneaster is known for its abundance of small white flowers in spring. Bright red berries are borne in fall. Zones 4–6.

C. salicifolius, willowleaf cotoneaster, grows to a height of 8 to 12 feet. Its gracefully arching branches bear slender, glossy, leathery leaves that usually persist through winter and may blush to a handsome red if the weather turns unusually cold. Small white flowers, largely hidden by the foliage in spring, are followed by slightly more visible red berries in autumn. Zones 6–8.

Note that in spite of appearances, cotoneaster is pronounced "kuh-tow-nee-AS-ter."

How to grow: Cotoneasters thrive in a variety of soils, and most can tolerate wind exposure. Provide full sun and good drainage. North of Zone 8, plant in spring and fall; in Zone 8, plant in fall or winter. Once established, most cotoneasters will thrive without additional watering.

Fire blight is a major concern and severely limits the use of these plants in the South. This disease causes new shoots to wilt suddenly, turn dark, and die back. It eventually spreads, killing the whole plant. Lush new growth is particularly susceptible, so avoid overfertilizing.

Landscape uses: Because of their spreading habit, cotoneasters are ideal as groundcovers, borders, barriers, screens, and massed plantings. They're also good in mixed borders and foundation plantings. Rockspray cotoneaster makes an effective espalier.

COTTAGE GARDENING

Cottage gardening originated during the Middle Ages, when most people lived in very small houses—cottages—with even smaller plots of land around their homes. Unless you were a lord or a member of the landed gentry, there just wasn't room for separate flowerbeds, herb gardens, vegetable gardens, and the like. Instead, people grew a patchwork of herbs, flowers, vegetables, and fruit trees outside their front door. These cheerful gardens can still be found along the lanes of English villages.

A focus on thrifty gardening was also characteristic of cottage gardens, since people didn't have money to spend on ornamental plants and there weren't any nurseries or garden centers. Seeds, cuttings, and transplants were passed along and cherished, and the hardier the plant, the more popular it was. Thus, plants that self-sowed and were easy to grow became cottage-garden staples.

Even if you don't live in a cottage, you might enjoy a colorful, informal, low-maintenance cottage garden. Today, we tend to think of cottage gardens as flower gardens, perhaps with

Best Cottage-Garden Plants

These cheerful flowers will give your cottage garden a joyful, exuberant look. The annuals self-sow freely, returning to your garden each year. And many of these spreading perennials have adorned cottage gardens for hundreds of years. Cottage-garden plants aren't fussy; most prefer full sun and average soil.

Annuals

Browallia spp. (browallias, sapphire flowers)

Calendula officinalis (calendula, pot marigold)

Centaurea cyanus (cornflower)

Cleome hassleriana (cleome, spider flower)

Consolida ajacis (rocket larkspur)

Cosmos bipinnatus (cosmos)

Ipomoea spp. (morning glories)

Lobularia maritima (sweet alyssum)

Lunaria annua (honesty)

Mirabilis jalapa (four-o'clock)

Myosotis sylvatica (woodland forget-me-not)

Nemophila menziesii (baby-blue-eyes)

Nigella damascena (love-in-a-mist)

Papaver rhoeas (corn poppy, Shirley poppy)

Viola tricolor (Johnny-jump-up)

Perennials

Achillea filipendulina (fernleaf yarrow)

Achillea millefolium (common yarrow)

Achillea ptarmica (sneezewort)

Alchemilla mollis (lady's mantle)

Anchusa azurea (Italian bugloss)

Artemisia ludoviciana 'Silver King' ('Silver King' artemisia)

Coreopsis verticillata (threadleaf coreopsis)

Delphinium spp. (delphiniums)

Digitalis spp. (foxgloves)

Echinacea purpurea (purple coneflower)

Hemerocallis spp. (daylilies)

Iris hybrids (bearded iris)

Lathyrus latifolius (perennial pea)

Lavandula spp. (lavenders)

Leucanthemum ×*superbum* (Shasta daisy)

Lychnis coronaria (rose campion)

Monarda didyma (bee balm, monarda)

Oenothera fruticosa (narrowleaf evening primrose)

Oenothera speciosa (showy evening primrose)

Phlox subulata (moss phlox, moss pink)

Rudbeckia spp. (coneflowers)

Tanacetum parthenium (feverfew)

Viola odorata (sweet violet)

Viola sororia (woolly blue violet)

some ornamental herbs, a flowering shrub or two, and some roses spilling over a wooden fence. (For gardens that combine flowers with vegetables, fruits, and herbs, see the Kitchen Gardens entry.) Site your cottage garden in full sun, on both sides of the path to the front or back door, and enclose the garden with a rustic fence. A decorative gate or arbor at the garden's entrance can add a charming touch. A cottage-style garden would also look lovely surrounding a toolshed or other outbuilding.

Traditionally, the path leading through a cottage garden proceeded in a straight line from the lane to the door—its purpose was functional, not decorative. However, you might prefer to make a meandering path through your garden. Cover the path with bark chips, old paving bricks, or cobblestones. Or create a fragrant path with stepping-stones nestled among low-growing, scented "path herbs" such as Roman chamomile (*Chamaemelum nobile*), woolly thyme (*Thymus pseudolanuginosus*), or Corsican mint (*Mentha requienii*).

The delightful informality of a cottage garden makes it a perfect place for accessories. A swing or bench is at home there, and so is a sundial, beehive, wind chime, gazing ball, or other ornament. Add a birdbath to welcome the many birds and butterflies that will visit your profusion of flowers, or place a rustic birdhouse on a pole. Remember not to overload your cottage garden with ornaments, though—the emphasis should always be on the flowers.

Plants for Cottage Gardens

If you have room, consider a small flowering tree or two along the fence for year-round structure—perhaps a crabapple, dogwood, or dwarf fruit tree. Old-fashioned fragrant flowering shrubs such as lilacs (*Syringa* spp.), sweet mock oranges (*Philadel-phus coronarius*), and shrub roses in the corners add structure and enhance the garden's homey feeling. And don't forget a rose of Sharon (*Hibiscus syriacus*) for the hummingbirds!

Choose flowers that fit the casualness of the cottage-garden style, like self-sowing annuals and spreading perennials. Fragrance and color are the hallmarks of cottage-garden flowers. You can mix ornamental herbs like anise hyssop (*Agastache foeniculum*), rosemary, and lavender with your flowers. Pineapple sage (*Salvia elegans*) and other fruit-scented sages, as well as many other species of ornamental salvia, are tender perennials but are worth growing as annuals north of their hardiness limits because their colorful flower spikes are hummingbird and butterfly magnets. If you have a greenhouse, sunroom, or sunny porch, you can set out pots of these plants in your cottage garden and bring them inside for winter.

To complete the effect, drape climbing roses, 'Gold Flame' honeysuckle (*Lonicera* ×*heckrottii* 'Gold Flame') or Jackman clematis (*Clematis* 'Jackmanii') over a fence or arbor. Use fragrant favorites like violas, pansies, or sweet alyssum as edging plants along the walk.

Caring for Your Cottage Garden

Because part of its charm comes from its informal design, a cottage garden requires less work to maintain than more manicured gardens. But weeding can be a challenge in spring, when you have to decide which are self-sown annual, perennial, and herb seedlings and which are weeds. Thin or transplant flower seedlings as needed.

Add a top-dressing of compost and mulch each year after seedlings are well established. Pick off spent flowers of annuals early in the season to encourage more blooms, but allow flowers to ripen into seed heads or pods in late summer so they can disperse seeds to fill next year's garden.

COVER CROPS

Sown to build the soil, to prevent erosion, to block weeds, or to serve as mulch for other plants, cover crops provide many benefits in the garden. Incorporating cover crops into the soil increases organic matter content, improves tilth, and supports healthy populations of earthworms and other desirable soil organisms. Gardeners who lack access to—or choose to not use—animal manures, or whose supply of compost falls short of their garden's needs, can include cover crops, also called green manures, in their planting plans for garden areas that are replanted annually, such as vegetable or annual flowerbeds.

There are lots of great ways and great reasons to include cover crops in your gardening routine.

- Plant a cover crop such as buckwheat or clover in fall, after finishing the harvest and clearing debris from the beds.

- Sow a fast-growing cover crop such as oats or red clover in spring in areas where you plan to plant warm-weather crops like peppers. Let the cover crop grow for several weeks, then turn it under a few weeks before it's time to plant the peppers.

- Include cover crops in your a crop rotation scheme to disrupt pests and diseases.

- When planning a new garden bed of any kind—for food crops or ornamentals—it's a great idea to plant the area in a cover crop for part or all of a growing season to build the soil.

- Use a cover crop to help bring tough weed problems under control (for more about this use of cover crops, see the Weeds entry).

The chart on the pages 156–157 will help you choose the cover crops that are best suited to your garden. If you select a legume, plan to apply bacterial inoculant so your soil will get maximum benefit from the crop's nitrogen-collecting ability. Different legume crops require different strains of inoculant. Use the specific strain required by the legume you're planting or a product that's a blend of many types of nitrogen-collecting bacteria. You'll find inoculants at well-stocked garden centers, or order them from online garden supply retailers.

Planting Cover Crops

Prepare the bed for planting as you would for any seed-sown crop. Remove all weeds and plant residues and rake the soil free of clumps before sowing. If possible, sow seed when rain is in the forecast. The seedlings will not establish well if the soil surface dries during the germination period. You can sow seed with a manually powered mechanical seeder that consists of a seed reservoir attached to a crank-operated seed broadcaster. For small areas, though, it's easy to broadcast seed by hand. If you're sowing less than 1 pound of seed per 1,000 square feet, mix the seed with fine sand or screened soil before spreading. Cover larger-seeded crops, such as Austrian peas or soybeans, with ¼ to ½ inch of soil; there's no need to cover small-seeded crops.

After seeding, tamp the soil with the back of a hoe or spade to ensure good contact between soil and seed and water thoroughly but gently to avoid washing away the seeds. You can cover the newly seeded area with loose straw or grass clippings to help prevent drying. Keep the seedbed evenly moist until the seeds have germinated. For large plots (1 acre or more), a small seed drill pulled by a farm or garden tractor will plant and cover the seed in one pass.

Planting Living Mulches

Some gardeners sow a crop such as alsike or white clover between rows of young squash or corn plants where it acts as a living mulch—it's a growing crop, but it serves all the functions of a standard mulch while also adding nitrogen to the soil. You can plant living mulches between many vegetable row crops.

This system works well only if you seed the living mulch in a weed-free seedbed. After planting the main crop, keep all areas between the rows and between individual plants clear of weeds for about 1 month. Cultivate lightly just before planting the mulch crop and pick out any exposed weed roots to prevent them from reestablishing. Work carefully to avoid disturbing the root systems of your vegetable plants. The annual cover crop will die down at frost or can be dug in when you prepare the soil for winter cover.

Late-season plantings of broccoli and cauliflower can benefit from undersowing with a winter-hardy cover crop such as hairy vetch. To undersow, let the vegetable crop get established for about 1 month, keeping the area weed-free. When the vegetable plants are 6 to 8 inches tall, broadcast the green manure seed over the entire area, not just between the rows. The vetch will germinate and grow, covering the soil without interfering with the vegetable crop. Harvest the crop in fall, and leave the vetch in place to protect the soil over winter. The following spring, cut off the vetch topgrowth close to the soil surface. The cut stems will die and dry out, forming a weed-suppressing

mat. You can simply push aside the mulch mat as needed to plant transplants.

Oats are also effective as an undersown, or living mulch, crop. Planted anytime from the middle to the end of summer, the crop will suppress weeds but won't set seed itself. The oats will die down during winter, leaving a thick layer of mulch to prevent soil erosion and suppress late-fall and early-spring weeds. Shallowly till or dig in the oats 2 weeks before planting the following spring. Or to conserve time and effort, hand-pull the mulch back in spots and transplant established seedlings into it. It will retard weed growth until it decomposes, by which time the plant's leaves will be shading the area.

Turning Under the Crop

In general, you'll need to cut down or dig in cover crops 3 to 4 weeks before you replant the bed. The old-fashioned way to turn in a cover crop was to use a rotary tiller, but that undoes some of the soil-building benefit that the cover crop supplies. Instead, try one of these options.

- Bury the cover crop under a heavy layer of mulch, such as chopped leaves, to kill it. Then use a hand tool to lightly work the killed tops into the soil.
- Pull up the crop by its roots and lay it on the bed surface as mulch.
- Cut off the crop at ground level as soon as flowers form. Leave the cut material in place.
- If you keep chickens, turn them loose on the plot to turn under the cover crop.

Keep in mind that, in general, it's more work to incorporate a perennial cover crop than an annual one.

Cover Crops for Home Gardens

Cover crops vary in the benefits they provide your garden. For example, nonlegumes such as Sudan grass and winter rye add lots of biomass and improve soil structure because of their extensive root systems, while legumes such as clover add nitrogen that helps break down all that plant matter. Thus, planting a mix of a grass and a legume can be an especially good strategy.

CROP	WHEN TO SOW	RATE PER 100 SQ FT	CULTURAL REQUIREMENTS	COMMENTS
LEGUMES				
Alfalfa (*Medicago sativa*)	Spring	1.5 oz.	Needs good drainage and pH higher than 6.5	Significant nitrogen contribution. Perennial.
Alsike clover (*Trifolium hybridum*)	Spring or late summer	1.5 oz.	Tolerates poor drainage and acid soils.	Low-growing perennial.
Austrian winter pea (*Pisum sativum* var. *arvense*)	Late summer or fall	3–6 oz.	Prefers well-drained soils.	Winter legume for warmer climates. Annual.
Crimson clover (*Trifolium incarnatum*)	Spring or fall	1–1.5 oz.	Likes neutral, well-drained soils.	Tall clover with dense root system. Annual.
Hairy vetch (*Vicia villosa*)	Late summer or fall	1.5 oz.	Tolerates moderate drainage. Winter cover with rye.	Good nitrogen capture; grows well in northern climates. Annual.
Red clover (*Trifolium pratense*)	Spring or late summer	1 oz.	Somewhat tolerant of acidity and poor drainage.	Good phosphorus accumulation; grows quickly for incorporating during same season. Biennial.
Soybean (*Glycine max*)	Spring or summer	6 oz.	Tolerates poor drainage.	Inoculate for nitrogen fixation. Annual.

CROP	WHEN TO SOW	RATE PER 100 SQ FT	CULTURAL REQUIREMENTS	COMMENTS
White (Dutch) clover (*Trifolium repens*)	Spring or late summer	0.5–1 oz.	Tolerates droughty soils.	Good for under-sowing as a living mulch. Perennial.
Yellow sweet clo-ver (*Melilotus officinalis*)	Spring or summer	1–1.5 oz.	Intolerant of acid soils and poor drainage.	Root mass accu-mulates phos-phate from rock powders. Biennial.
NONLEGUMES				
Annual ryegrass (*Lolium multiflorum*)	Spring	1.5–2 oz.	Tolerates a wide range of soils.	Provides fast cover; good for establishing slow-growing crops. Annual.
Buckwheat (*Fagopyrum esculentum*)	Spring or summer	3–5 oz.	Tolerates infertile and acid soils.	Accumulates phosphorus. Annual.
Oat (*Avena sativa*)	Spring or summer	4–6.5 oz.	Prefers well-drained loamy soil. Tolerates some acidity.	Quick-growing summer crop. Quick cover for helping establish clover. Annual.
Rape (*Brassica napus*)	Spring or summer	0.5 oz.	Prefers moder-ately well-drained loam.	Good cover for short growing periods in sum-mer. Annual.
Sudangrass (*Sorghum ×drummondii*)	Spring or summer	1.5–3 oz.	Will tolerate somewhat poorly drained soils.	Produces very large mass of root growth and top-growth in sum-mer. Annual.
Winter rye (*Secale cereale*)	Spring or summer	5–10 oz.	Prefers well-drained soil.	Very winter hardy, grows well in early spring. Annual.

CRABAPPLE

See *Malus*

CROCUS

Crocus. Spring- or fall-blooming corms.

Description: Crocuses bear nearly stemless, 1- to 2-inch-wide starry goblets in white, cream, yellow, gold, and purple, many marked or brushed with a contrasting color. Grassy leaves, usually quite short when in bloom, elongate to 4 to 6 inches. The familiar spring-blooming Dutch hybrid crocuses produce relatively large blooms in white, yellow, and purple shades, plus purple stripes on white, to 6 inches tall. Zones 3–9.

Species crocuses include early spring-blooming *Crocus chrysanthus*, golden crocus, which grows to 6 inches. Zones 4–9. Fall-blooming *C. speciosus*, showy crocus, bears lavender-blue flowers and can reach 6 inches or more. Zones 5–9.

How to grow: Plant crocus corms in fall at a depth two to three times their width in a sunny or partially shaded spot with average, well-drained soil enriched with organic matter. Plant fall-blooming crocuses as soon as they are available in mid- to late summer. Do not remove leaves until they have yellowed, when you can also lift and divide the corms. Rodents may eat the corms unless a resident dog or cat keeps them at bay. Slugs sometimes devour the flowers of fall-blooming species.

Landscape uses: Grow massed in thin grass (do not mow until the foliage has died back after blooming ends), in rock gardens, or in clumps along a path or at a doorstep. In borders, overplant with low-growing annuals like sweet alyssum so you won't disturb them later in the season. Grow fall-blooming species in low groundcovers such as vinca (common periwinkle) to help support the flower stems.

CROP ROTATION

Crop rotation is a systematic approach to deciding which crop to plant where in your vegetable garden from one growing season to the next. Crop rotation is very important to organic farmers, and it can benefit home gardeners, too. The general principles of crop rotation offer guidance for developing a planting plan, but it's up to individual farmers and gardeners to devise a unique crop rotation based on their chosen crops, the space that's available, and the objectives they hope to achieve.

The goals of crop rotation are to help manage soil fertility, to help avoid or reduce problems with soilborne diseases, and to disrupt the lifecycles of (and thus the damage caused by) soil-dwelling insects such as corn rootworms.

Balancing soil fertility: Each crop has unique nutrient requirements and draws specific nutrients from the soil where it grows. Some, like corn and tomatoes, are known as heavy feeders that require substantial amounts of soil nitrogen and phosphorus. If you plant corn in the same spot year after year, the nitrogen and phosphorus in that plot will be depleted more quickly than in other parts of your garden. Changing the location of corn each year allows you to replenish those nutrients in that part of the garden, so it's ready when the next hungry crop comes along.

Other crops also demand lots of nitrogen. These tend to be the green and leafy crops, such as lettuce, cabbage, and broccoli. Fruiting crops, such as tomatoes and melons, require abundant

Rotating Vegetable Families

Susceptibility to pests and diseases runs in plant families. Leave at least 2, and preferably 3 or more, years between the times you plant members of the same crop family in an area of your garden. When planning a rotation scheme, refer to this list of the eight family groups most often planted in vegetable gardens along with suggestions for their order in a successful rotation plan.

FAMILY NAME	COMMON CROPS	ROTATION RELATIONS
Amaryllidaceae Alliums, onions	Onions, garlic, leeks	Rotate with legumes; avoid planting in soil with undecomposed organic matter.
Apiaceae Umbels, carrot family	Carrots, parsnips, parsley, dill, fennel, coriander	Moderate feeders. Precede with any other plant family; condition soil with compost before planting. Follow with legumes or heavy mulch.
Asteraceae Asters, sunflowers	Lettuce, endive, escarole, radicchio, Jerusalem artichoke, sunflowers	Light to moderate feeders but benefit from adequate nitrogen. Easy to rotate with most other crop families.
Brassicaceae Brassicas, cole crops, cabbage family	Broccoli, Brussels sprouts, cabbage, cauliflower, kale, kohlrabi, mustards, radishes, turnips	High level of soil maintenance required for good root health. Heavy feeders. Precede with legumes; follow by first cultivating the soil to expose pests for predation, then spread compost.
Cucurbitaceae Cucurbits, squash family	Cucumbers, gourds, melons, squash, pumpkins, watermelons	For improved pest control, precede with winter rye or wheat; follow with legumes.
Fabaceae Legumes, bean family	Beans, peas, soybeans, clovers, vetches	Beneficial to soil; few pest problems. Rotate alternately with all other garden crops when possible.
Poaceae Grains, grass family	Wheat, oats, rye, corn	Plant before tomato- or squash-family crops to control weeds and improve soil's ability to handle water.
Solanaceae Nightshades, tomato family	Eggplant, peppers, potatoes, tomatillos, tomatoes	Heavy feeders with many fungal enemies. Precede with cereal grain or grass; follow with legumes.

phosphorus. Peas, beans, and other legumes add nitrogen to the soil but also need lots of phosphorus. By comparison, most root vegetables and herbs are light feeders, with relatively modest fertility requirements.

The rule of thumb for balancing soil nutrients through rotation is to avoid planting the same general category of crop (root, legume, leafy, or fruiting) successively in the same place. It's best to follow nitrogen-fixing legumes such as peas or beans with nitrogen-loving leaf crops or nutrient-hungry fruiting crops. Then, follow the heavy feeding crops with light-feeding root crops.

Disease and pest prevention: If you have a large home garden, you may want to base your crop rotation on plant families rather than on nutrient needs. This can help diminish diseases and pests, because closely related crops tend to suffer from the same problems. For example, Colorado potato beetles like to eat potato plants, but they also enjoy feasting on tomato leaves and eggplant foliage. Since these beetles overwinter in the soil, if you plant eggplant in a spot where you grew potatoes the year before, you may have a beetle problem for your eggplants from the day they're planted. Likewise, several serious bacterial and fungal diseases overwinter in plant debris in the soil.

Lengthy rotations are sometimes necessary to control chronic soilborne problems. Bean anthracnose fungus can persist in soil for up to 3 years, so a 4-year rotation is needed to keep the disease at bay. The same holds true for such fungal diseases as fusarium wilt and verticillium wilt. A few problems, such as clubroot, persist in the soil for even longer, so rotation is less useful for controlling them.

Choosing your crop rotation plan: If you have a small garden, you may not be able to set up an effective rotation by crop family. That's also true if you grow only a few kinds of crops. In that case, stick to a basic soil-balancing rotation. But if you have a large plot and grow many different crops, you may enjoy the challenge of setting up a rotation by crop family. Refer to the chart on the previous page to learn which crops belong to the same family.

Keep in mind that cover crops can be included in a rotation plan to discourage specific types of pests and to improve soil. For example, beetle grubs thrive among most vegetables, but not in soil planted in buckwheat or clover. A season of either crop can greatly reduce grub populations and at the same time will increase soil organic matter content.

CUCUMBER

Cucumis sativus
Cucurbitaceae

Cool and juicy cucumbers are popular for both eating fresh and preserving as pickles. These frost-sensitive tropical natives like warm, humid weather and need at least 8 hours of sun a day. But since they require only 55 to 60 days from planting to picking, cucumbers will grow well in most regions as long as they get enough natural rainfall or supplemental water.

Types: Cucumbers range from petite gherkins and blocky picklers to torpedo-like market varieties, small lemon-shaped heirlooms, and long, thin, Asian types; there are also seedless and disease-resistant cultivars. Middle Eastern, or gourmet, cucumbers require no peeling—a nutritious advantage, since most of this vegetable's vitamin A and C content, along with a number of minerals, is in the skin.

Bush cultivars produce compact vines that require less space in the garden. For high yields, try a gynoecious cultivar; instead of the usual male and female flowers, these plants produce only female blooms and, thus, more cucumbers. Cultivars labeled as parthenocarpic are able to set fruits without pollination, making them a good choice for growing under cover.

In seed catalogs, cucumbers are often divided into slicing types, used for salads or cooking, and smaller, fast-growing pickling kinds. Sometimes a cultivar is labeled "dual-purpose," meaning that you can harvest them small for pickling or larger for slicing.

Planting: Cucumber yields are highest in fertile, clay soil with plenty of humus, but they will grow well in most good vegetable garden soils. Good drainage is essential.

The biggest mistake most gardeners make is planting cucumbers too early. It's best to wait until the soil temperature reaches 70°F—at least 1 week after the date of the last frost. Spreading black plastic over the planting area will promote the soil warmth cucumbers need.

When you start seeds indoors, keep the air temperature between 70° and 80°F during the day and no colder than 60°F at night. Use peat pots instead of flats to avoid disturbing the cucumber roots during transplanting. Sow three or four seeds ½ inch deep in each pot, about 2 weeks before the last frost. When two or three true leaves have developed, snip off (don't pull) all but the most vigorous seedling. Harden off the plants before transplanting by putting them outdoors during the day and bringing them in at night.

Plant up to three vines of each variety you want to grow. Rather than planting all your cucumbers at once, plan to stagger plantings a couple of weeks apart to extend the harvest (just make sure the fruits will have time to mature before fall frost).

You can grow cucumbers either in hills or in rows next to a fence or trellis. Make hills 2 feet wide; space hills or rows 4 to 5 feet apart (3 feet apart for bush cultivars). In each hill, place three transplants or sow seven or eight seeds; thin to the best three seedlings when they are a few inches tall by cutting the unwanted ones at ground level. If you're planting in rows, plant seedlings 1 foot apart, or sow seeds 1 inch deep with three to five seeds per foot of row and thin seedlings to 1 foot apart.

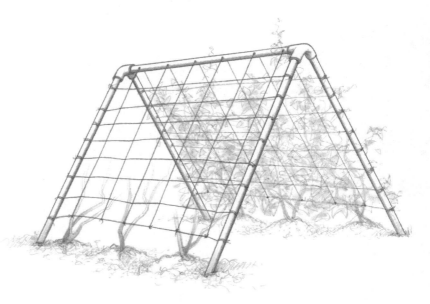

A-frame trellis. Training cucumbers on a stakes-and-string trellis saves garden space, keeps fruits up off the ground, and allows for good air circulation, which helps prevent disease problems.

If you're growing gynoecious cultivars, remember to plant a few of the specially marked male seeds. Mark the male seedlings with a stake or flag to ensure you don't thin them by mistake. Plants from these seeds will bear male flowers, which provide the pollen necessary for fertilization. One or two male plants will provide enough pollen for all the female flowers.

To make good use of garden space, consider interplanting cole crops, such as early cabbage, cauliflower, or broccoli, with your cucumbers; they should be ready to harvest around the time the cucumber seedlings come up. Radishes, bush beans, and lettuce are other good choices for intercropping with cukes. Just plan ahead when planting the early crops so that you leave enough space to plant the cucumber seeds or plants around them.

Growing guidelines: Cucumbers are 95 percent water, so adequate moisture is vital to a good cucumber crop. A thirsty plant simply stops growing, and its fruits are likely to be deformed, bitter, or flavorless. Soak the soil deeply when watering in dry weather. Soaker hoses along rows are good for this purpose. Or punch a few very small holes in a coffee can, plastic jug, or soda bottle, and sink the bottom of the container into the middle of each hill. Keep it filled with water to maintain the even moisture the plants need. Avoid handling or brushing up against foliage when it's wet to prevent the spread of diseases. Weed by hand until the seedlings are 1 foot tall; then side-dress with alfalfa meal or compost, water well, and lay down at least 2 inches of an organic mulch, such as straw, hay, grass clippings, or leaves. In addition to conserving moisture and suppressing weeds, the mulch will help keep fruits clean and healthy.

Male flowers appear first, followed by female blooms about a week later. Bees will spread the pollen from one to the other. If long periods of cloudy, rainy weather keep the bees inactive, you can do the job yourself by carefully picking a male flower and—after removing the petals—brushing its pollen-covered anthers against the stigmas in the center of the female blossoms. (See the Squash entry for an illustration of this technique.) Unpollinated blooms will produce tiny, curled, seedless cucumbers.

Problems: Cucumber beetles are a widespread and potentially serious pest. They not only chew on plants, particularly young seedlings, but also spread diseases such as bacterial wilt and mosaic. Adult cucumber beetles are $\frac{1}{4}$ inch long with black heads and greenish yellow wings; they chew large ragged holes in plant leaves. There are two species: the spotted cucumber beetle and the striped cucumber beetle. As many as three generations of beetles occur in a single growing season. Here's how to battle them.

- Inspect the foliage and insides of flowers daily, particularly in the early morning; handpick and destroy any beetles you find by shaking them into a jar of soapy water.

- Lure striped cucumber beetles away from your cucumbers by planting radishes nearby.

- Plant later in the season after the first round of beetles has finished feeding and laying eggs.

- Cover young plants with a fine netting, such as cheesecloth, or with a floating row cover. Remember that a cover will also keep bees out; if you leave the cover on after flowering begins, you'll have to hand-pollinate the flowers to get a crop.

- Apply a coating of kaolin clay to the foliage, including leaf undersides, twice a week to deter the beetles from feeding. Reapply after heavy rain.

- Drench the soil around your plants with *Heterorhabditis* nematodes to kill cucumber beetle larvae and thus prevent damage by second-generation beetles. For more information on these nematodes, turn to page 447.

🌿 As a last resort, apply pyrethrins to control large infestations quickly.

Squash vine borers are 1-inch-long white caterpillars that burrow into the plants' main stems, leaving sawdustlike droppings at their entry holes and causing the vines to wilt. At the first sign of this pest, cut a slit along the stem of the affected plant, remove and destroy the larvae, and cover the injured area and several close-by vine joints with moist soil. This enables the plant to put out new roots to help it recover. You can also attack the borers by injecting the stems with Btk (*Bacillus thuringiensis* var. *kurstaki*).

Handpick green melon worms that feed on foliage and occasionally munch their way inside a fruit. Handpicking and keeping the garden clean will also help control young pickleworms, pale yellow caterpillars with black spots that turn green- or copper-colored as they grow.

Other cucumber pests include cutworms, aphids, and spider mites. For information on controlling cutworms and aphids, see page 454. Spider mites are tiny creatures that feed on the underside of leaves, causing yellow stippling on leaf surfaces; control by spraying the plants with water to knock off the pests.

Prevent cucumber diseases by planting resistant cultivars and rotating cukes and related vine crops on a 3- to 4-year basis. Minimize the spread of disease spores by keeping cucumbers away from melons, pumpkins, and squash; avoid handling wet vines. Keep the garden clean and free of perennial weeds, particularly ragweed and ground cherry, which can harbor disease. Here are some common diseases to watch for.

🌿 Anthracnose produces hollow, water-soaked spots on the leaves that enlarge and turn brown. It can also blacken and pit the fruits, making them inedible.

🌿 Bacterial wilt, spread by cucumber beetles, starts with a single wilted leaf, followed by the wilting of the entire plant.

🌿 Downy mildew appears in damp weather and results in irregular yellow or purplish spots on the leaves, which soon curl up and die.

🌿 Mosaic, spread by both aphids and cucumber beetles, shows up as rough, yellow-mottled leaves, stunted plants, and whitish fruit.

If these diseases infect your crop, destroy the affected vines or put them in sealed containers for disposal with household trash. Do not put diseased plant material into your compost pile.

Harvesting: Pick cucumbers frequently, before they mature. With some cultivars, especially small pickling types, it may be necessary to harvest daily. If the seeds of even one fruit are allowed to mature, the whole vine will stop producing. Overripe white-spined cucumbers turn creamy white; black-spined ones turn a yellowish orange.

By picking regularly, you can extend the harvest to around 6 weeks. Gently twist or clip off each cucumber, being careful not to break the vines. Cucumbers keep refrigerated for 1 to 2 weeks, but pickling is the best method for long-term storage.

CURRANT

Ribes **spp.**
Grossulariaceae

It's hardly surprising that currants have been cultivated for centuries; these easy-to-grow plants produce generous quantities of tasty fruit with very little maintenance. Currants are deciduous shrubs with an upright or spreading habit, growing 3 to 7 feet high and wide. They bear ¼- to ¾-inch-diameter black, red, pink, green, golden, yellow, or creamy white fruit. The black fruits are the most intensely flavored, while the pale whites have a more delicate flavor.

These cold-hardy plants begin growth in very early spring. They flower and fruit on wood that is 1 or more years old. Each bush can continue to yield over a period of 15 to 20 years. When deciding how many bushes to plant, remember that currants can be prolific producers. Five-year-old black currant bushes often yield 10 pounds or more of fruit per bush; red and white types may yield more than 15 pounds. Currants are mostly self-fertile, but many cultivars benefit from cross-pollination, so it's wise to plant several different cultivars if you have room. Zones 3–5.

Types: Currants encompass several species and hybrids of *Ribes*. Black currants are *R. nigrum* (European black currant), *R. americanum* (American black currant), *R. odoratum* (clove currant), and *R. aureum* var. *villosum* (buffalo currant). Black currants are commercially important for preserves, juices, wine making, and fresh eating. 'Ben Sarek' is a highly productive, disease-resistant dwarf variety. 'Titania' is tall, but resistant to white pine blister rust. Red and white currants were developed from *R. rubrum* (red currant) and *R. petraeum* and their hybrids. Red currants such as 'Jonkheer van Tets' and 'Cascade' are popular for making intensely colored and flavored jellies and juices.

Planting: Choose a protected site with full sun if possible. Currants do well in partial shade, but the fruit will be more tart. Moist but well-drained loamy soil is ideal; clay soils loosened with organic matter are also good. Avoid poorly drained soils and frost pockets.

Plant red, white, and buffalo currants with the topmost root 1 inch below the surface; other black currants should be 3 to 4 inches deeper than they grew in the nursery. Conditions permitting, you can plant currants from November to early March, although early fall planting is best. Black currants need 8 feet all around them. Space bushes of other currants 5 to 6 feet apart in rows at least 6 feet apart. Rows should run north to south when possible, to allow maximum sunlight to reach each plant.

Care: Currants are shallow-rooted plants, so avoid cultivation after planting. Maintain a 2- to 3-inch mulch layer to hold in moisture and smother weeds; hand-pull any weeds that do emerge. Currants benefit from regular applications of high-nitrogen organic fertilizer. Keep the soil evenly moist; water deeply in dry weather.

Pruning: For red and white currants, the usual form is an open, cup-shaped bush on a 6-foot main stem. To maintain this form, cut back leaders by half and laterals to one to three buds at planting and thereafter every fall. Make cuts just above a downward- and outward-facing bud; remove all suckers from the bottom 6 inches of the stem.

Another popular pruning style for currants is vertical cordons (upright, single-stemmed plants spaced 2 feet apart), ideal for small gardens. Establish cordons by training a single vertical stem up a 6-foot stake. At planting, remove all but one of the leaders; cut back the remaining stem by half and its side branches to a few buds. Keep mature cordons at their desired height by summer-pruning the leader to one bud.

Black currants are grown as multistemmed bushes. Cut each cane back to only two buds above the soil at planting time. In the years after planting, prune back leaders to one-half or one-third of their length and laterals to one to three buds. After the second or third year, also cut a few of the oldest stems to the ground each year to encourage vigorous new growth.

Problems: Imported currantworms are green, caterpillar-like larvae that feed on leaf edges. Control by handpicking or spraying plants with a strong stream of water to dislodge the larvae. Gooseberry fruitworm attacks both currants and gooseberries. Larvae burrow into the fruit just before it ripens, eat the pulp, and then spin a silken webbing joining fruits and leaves. Destroy affected fruit and cultivate lightly under bushes to expose the pupae for birds to eat. Currant borers cause stems to wilt suddenly; prune off affected stems below the entrance hole, and burn them or place them in sealed containers for disposal with household trash.

Diseases include American gooseberry mildew, which causes white powdery patches on leaves and shoots. Some varieties are resistant to the disease. To control mildew, prune shoot tips back by a third and spray the plant with sulfur fungicide or a potassium bicarbonate spray. Leaf spot causes brown patches on leaves, with early defoliation. Clean up affected foliage and fallen leaves. If the infection seems severe enough to threaten the plant's health, apply a sulfur- or copper-based spray for control.

Historically, a major concern when growing currants was white pine blister rust. This disease needs both a species of *Ribes* and a white or other five-needled pine to complete its life cycle. While it has little effect on *Ribes* species, it causes fatal cankers on pine trees. In the early 1920s, the federal government established a ban on growing and selling any *Ribes* species. In the 1960s, the federal restrictions were removed as white pines became less important as timber trees. Some states still have restrictions. Contact your Cooperative Extension Service to find out if planting currants is permitted where you live. If you have white pines on your property, site *Ribes* species at least 200 feet away from the trees, or choose rust-resistant cultivars.

Harvesting: Early cultivars are ready for picking in mid-June; later ones, especially some black currants, ripen into September. Pull off entire fruit clusters, rather than the individual fruits. Ripe fruit will stay on the plant for several days. Once picked, though, currants don't keep well, so use them as soon as possible.

Although you can eat the fruit fresh when it's fully ripe, currants most often are used in preserves, jellies, and juices. Fruit from mild, sweet black currants also makes excellent wine. White currants are best eaten fresh or canned whole in light syrup. All currants freeze well.

CUT FLOWER GARDENING

Few things are as satisfying as gathering an armful of the flowers you love in the colors you want. With your own cutting garden, you can grow your favorite flowers and enjoy fresh-cut bouquets all season long.

You may choose to grow flowers for cutting in much the same way as vegetables are traditionally grown for harvest, with all the plants of each species together in rows or raised beds. Or you can mix your cutting flowers in ornamental borders and beds. Each approach has its advantages. If you already grow vegetables, you'll find that adding cut flowers to the vegetable garden makes it glow with vivid colors. You probably never thought a

Best Flowers for Cutting

Most cutting-garden flowers prefer full sun with average soil and moisture. Plant different colors and shapes, so you'll have a variety of flowers to work with. Flower shapes can be grouped by their use in arrangements: linear, for line and height; round, for mass or a focal point; and filler, to unify and add an airy look. Here are some good choices to get you started. Plant names are followed by flower shape and color.

Annuals

Ageratum houstonianum (ageratum, flossflower): Round; blue, lavender, white, or pink

Antirrhinum majus (snapdragon): Linear; white, pink, red, orange, yellow

Calendula officinalis (pot marigold): Round; yellow, orange

Callistephus chinensis (China aster): Round; white, yellow, pink, red, blue

Coreopsis tinctoria (calliopsis): Round; yellow, red

Cosmos spp. (cosmos): Round; white, pink, red, yellow, orange

Limonium sinuatum (statice): Filler; white, pink, purple-blue, yellow

Matthiola incana (stock): Linear; white, pink, rose, lavender

Salvia spp. (salvias, sages): Linear; red, pink, white, blue, violet

Tagetes spp. (marigolds): Round; orange, yellow, red, bronze, white

Zinnia elegans (zinnia): Round; white, pink, red, yellow, orange

vegetable garden could be so pretty! When grown in blocks, cut flowers are as easy to tend as vegetables, too. Another advantage of growing flowers for cutting in blocks or rows in a garden specifically designated for cutting is that you won't deplete the display in other parts of your landscape that you've designed to provide outdoor color. Finally, growing cut flowers in rows makes it easy to compare cultivars planted side by side to see which you like better or which grow better for you.

If you want to grow cut flowers throughout your ornamental gardens, interplant annuals and perennials, including ornamental grasses, with bulbs, roses, and herbs to create spectacular mixed beds and borders. To make sure the flowers you cut won't leave "holes" in your border, grow at least three plants of each perennial intended for cutting and six or seven of each annual. When you design mixed flowerbeds and borders, group the plants of one species or cultivar in masses for the most striking visual effect.

Whether you grow cut flowers in a separate garden or in your regular ornamental beds, you can supplement the materials from your cutting garden with foliage and flowers from the rest of your landscape. Grow roses with other shrubs in a foundation planting, as a border or screen at the edge of the property, or around a deck or patio. Train vines on arbors, trellises, or fences to supply

Perennials

All the perennials listed here are long-blooming, but don't overlook flowers that bloom in a single season—peonies in early summer or sneezeweeds (*Helenium* spp.) from late summer to fall, for example.

Achillea spp. (yarrows): Round; yellow, pink, white

Aster spp. (asters): Round; white, pink, red, lavender, blue

Campanula spp. (bellflowers): Round, linear; white, pink, blue

Chrysanthemum spp. (chrysanthemums): Round; white, pink, red, orange, yellow

Delphinium spp. (delphiniums): linear; white, blue, purple

Dianthus spp. (pinks): Round; white, pink

Echinacea purpurea (purple coneflower): Round; mauve, white

Echinops spp. (globe thistles): Round; blue

Gaillardia spp. (blanketflowers): Round; yellow, red, orange

Gypsophila paniculata (baby's breath): Filler; white

Leucanthemum ×*superbum* (Shasta daisy): Round; white

Liatris spp. (blazing stars): Linear; white, pink, purple, magenta

Penstemon spp. (penstemons, beardtongues): Linear; red, pink, white, purple, blue

Phlox spp. (phlox): Round; white, pink, red, orange, lavender

Rudbeckia spp. (coneflowers): Round; yellow

Salvia spp. (sages): Linear; purple-blue

graceful stems for arrangements. Trees and shrubs provide foliage, flowers, berries, and branches for cutting. You can turn a shady spot into a lovely garden of ferns and hostas that will supply foliage for arrangements.

Making Cut Flower Choices

When you're deciding which plants to include in your garden, remember to grow a variety of plant forms, so you'll always have the right shapes for any arrangement. Satisfying arrangements generally have three primary elements: tall, spiky flowers and foliage for line; large, flat, round flowers and foliage for focal points or mass; and small,

airy flowers and foliage for fillers.

Choose plants that bloom for a long period and hold up well as cut flowers. Many annuals bloom almost nonstop during summer; most perennials flower for a week to well over a month. Make sure you grow flowers that bloom at different seasons to have bouquets indoors throughout the year.

Think first about color when selecting the flowers you'll grow. The most effective arrangements coordinate with the colors in your home—you wouldn't want orange flowers in a pink room, for example. If one color predominates in the house, grow flowers that complement that color.

Height also matters when choosing plants for cutting. For flower arrangements, it is easier to use longer stems. New cultivars of annuals and perennials frequently are shorter, more compact-growing plants. As you choose plants, note the mature blooming height.

Growing fragrant flowers makes both gardening and flower arranging more pleasurable. Scented perennial flowers that are good for cutting include lily of the valley (*Convallaria majalis*), peonies (*Paeonia* spp.), many pinks (*Dianthus* spp.), and garden phlox (*Phlox paniculata*). Annuals such as flowering tobaccos (*Nicotiana* spp.), stocks (*Matthiola* spp.), sweet pea (*Lathyrus odoratus*), and bells of Ireland (*Moluccella laevis*) are also good choices. Don't overlook trees and shrubs such as lilacs, magnolias, and roses.

Most herb foliage, flowers, and seed heads can bring fragrance as well as form to arrangements. For example, try using dill (*Anethum graveolens*), fennel (*Foeniculum vulgare*), lavenders (*Lavandula* spp.), lemon balm (*Melissa officinalis*), lemon verbena (*Aloysia triphylla* or *A. citrodora*), mints (*Mentha* spp.), or rosemary (*Rosmarinus officinalis*).

Among the best hardy bulbs for cutting are daffodils, hyacinths, irises, lilies, tulips, alliums (*Allium* spp.), grape hyacinths (*Muscari* spp.) and montbretias (*Crocosmia* spp.). Tender bulbs that make great cut flowers include dahlias, gladioli, tuberous begonias, African lilies (*Agapanthus* spp.) as well as tuberose (*Polianthes tuberosa*).

Site Selection and Care

To grow cut flowers successfully, choose the planting site carefully and prepare the soil well. Most of the plants you'll want to grow for cutting will thrive in well-drained, humus-rich soil and full sun. Check the cultural requirements of the specific plants you've chosen and group plants with similar needs together.

To produce the best-quality cut flowers and foliage, your plants will need top-notch care. Give them adequate water and fertilizer, be diligent about weeding and deadheading (removal of faded flowers), and provide winter protection and pest control when necessary. Laying an organic mulch, such as compost or shredded leaves, conserves moisture, inhibits weeds, and keeps flowers and leaves clean and mud-free. Commonsense care and careful plant selection will give you a constant supply of beautiful cut flowers all season.

CUTTINGS

Plants have the amazing capacity to regenerate from small pieces of tissue called cuttings. These small portions of stems, leaves, or roots will form new roots and shoots if given the right treatment.

Taking cuttings is the most common way to propagate many types of ornamental plants. Because raising plants from cuttings is an asexual type of reproduction, the new plants will look exactly like the parent.

Materials and Methods

All types of cuttings need a medium to support them while they grow roots and some type of structure to protect them during the rooting period. It's also important to observe good sanitation to minimize disease problems.

Media: The best media for rooting cuttings are moisture retentive but well drained and free of insects, diseases, and weed seeds. Commonly used media are sand, perlite, vermiculite, and peat moss. No one material or combination is ideal for all plants, but an equal mixture of vermiculite and sand or perlite is useful in most situations. Soil is

Foliage for Cutting

Don't overlook foliage when you're cutting flowers for arrangements. Adding beautifully colored, textured, shaped, or variegated foliage can integrate the different shapes and colors of your flowers and give an arrangement added charm and sophistication.

Herbs are a great choice for arrangements. The delightfully aromatic leaves of scented geraniums (*Pelargonium* spp.), artemisias, and lavender cotton (*Santolina chamaecyparissus*) add a special dimension to a vase of flowers. Annuals and tender perennials also are great for adding foliage color to arrangements. Consider planting caladiums (*Caladium* spp.) or coleus (*Plectranthus scuttellarioides*) for showy foliage to include in arrangements as well.

Many perennials produce interesting foliage along with their flowers, including lady's mantle (*Alchemilla mollis*), ligularias (*Ligularia* spp.), and lamb's ears (*Stachys byzantina*).

Shade-loving plants such as ferns, hostas, pachysandra, and bergenias (*Bergenia* spp.) are easy to grow and offer a range of texture and leaf shapes. In addition, some hostas and pachysandras have variegated foliage, which can add color and drama to any arrangement.

Don't neglect your trees and shrubs when scouting for foliage to enhance arrangements. Evergreens such as boxwoods (*Buxus* spp.), false cypresses (*Chamaecyparis* spp.), spruces (*Picea* spp.), yews (*Taxus* spp.), and hemlocks (*Tsuga* spp.) supply attractive foliage all year. Hollies (*Ilex* spp.), Japanese aucuba (*Aucuba japonica*), cherry laurel (*Prunus laurocerasus*), and magnolias are other good choices.

not a good propagation medium, especially in containers. Unlike the other materials, soil is not sterile and can compact severely from frequent waterings. Only very hardy cuttings are planted directly into soil.

Some plants, such as various houseplants, coleus, and willows (*Salix* spp.), will root directly in water. This method is fun to try, but if you want to save the cutting, plant it in potting soil while the roots are still small. Plants may have difficulty adapting to soil if their roots remain in water too long.

Structures: Cuttings need a protected, high-humidity environment while they root. Cuttings don't have roots to take up water, but they still lose moisture through their leaves. Keeping the surrounding air moist minimizes water loss and helps cuttings survive until they can support themselves.

On a small scale, plastic bags are great for protecting cuttings. Support the bag so plastic does not rest on the cuttings and encourage rot. (A wire frame made from a coat hanger works fine for this.) Provide ventilation by occasionally opening the bag for an hour or two. In most cases, you won't have to add water until the cuttings form roots. To harden off rooted cuttings, gradually open the bag for longer periods.

For large numbers of cuttings, a cold frame or greenhouse is more practical (see the Cold Frames

Rooting Hormones

Rooting hormones—synthetic versions of natural plant hormones—can encourage root formation on stem cuttings of difficult plants and increase the number of roots on others. Commercial rooting hormones are usually available at garden centers in powder form; be aware that some products contain chemical fungicides. Product labels will suggest uses, or experiment with treated and untreated cuttings.

A solution known as willow water can encourage rooting. Cut willow stems into 1-inch pieces and place them in a small container; add about 2 inches of water, cover, and let stand for 24 hours. Remove the stems, insert cuttings, and let them soak overnight before planting.

cent bleach solution (one part bleach to nine parts water). Check plants often during rooting and remove any fallen leaves or dead cuttings. Don't overwater; do provide adequate ventilation.

Softwood Stem Cuttings

Take softwood cuttings from succulent spring growth of woody plants such as azaleas and magnolias. Treat stem cuttings of herbaceous plants like softwood cuttings, including annuals or tender perennials such as coleus, geraniums, and impatiens. Because these cuttings are from young tissue, they form roots easily but need high humidity to prevent wilting.

Season: Take softwood cuttings from April

and Greenhouse Gardening entries). You can set pots of cuttings on the soil or plant directly in the soil inside a cold frame. Close the frame and cover the glass with shading material, such as cheesecloth or wooden laths (like snow fencing or lattice); gradually remove the shading when roots form. Ventilate and harden off by gradually opening the cold frame for longer periods.

Sanitation: Since crushed plant tissue is an invitation to rot, use a clean, sharp tool (such as a knife or scissor-type pruning shears) to collect and prepare cuttings. Never propagate from diseased or insect-infested plants. Plant cuttings in fresh, sterile propagation mix that is stored in closed containers. Pots and propagation areas should be scrubbed clean and, if possible, sanitized by rinsing with a 10 per-

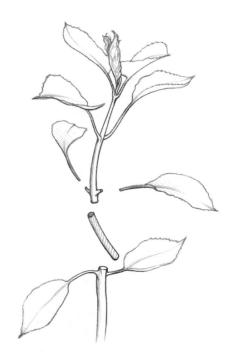

Softwood and herbaceous cuttings. Take these cuttings from stems that snap when bent. Remove the cutting just below a node; discard the stem piece left on the parent down to the uppermost node.

through June, when new leaves are fully expanded but stems are still soft. Take houseplant cuttings any time; take tender perennial cuttings for over-wintering in late summer.

Getting started: Water the parent plant a day or two before taking cuttings. Fill a container with moist propagation mix.

Method: Collect cuttings in the morning or on cloudy, cool days, and keep them moist until planting. Cuttings should be 3 to 6 inches long; they usually include a terminal bud. Remove leaves from the lower half of the stem, and apply rooting hormone if desired. Insert the cutting to about one-third of its length, firm the medium with your fingers, and water to settle the cutting. Enclose the container in plastic, or place it under a mist system in a cold frame or greenhouse.

Aftercare: Ventilate plants; water as needed to keep the medium moist but not wet. Softwood and herbaceous cuttings root quickly, often in 2 to 4 weeks. When roots appear, harden off the cuttings and transplant to a pot or into the garden.

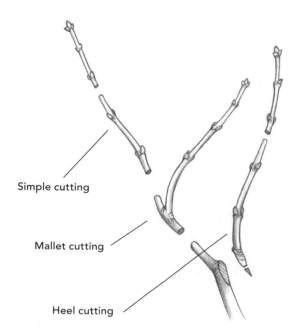

Simple cutting

Mallet cutting

Heel cutting

Hardwood cuttings. Take simple cuttings from the midsections of branches. For difficult-to-root plants, take a heel or mallet cutting, each with a bit of older wood at the base.

Hardwood Stem Cuttings

Take hardwood cuttings from woody plants during their dormant period. Hardwood cuttings don't require high-humidity conditions. This method is effective for some types of woody plants and vines, including grapes, currants, willows, and some roses.

Season: Take cuttings after leaf fall and before new growth begins in spring. Mid-autumn is often the best time to collect and plant cuttings, so they can form roots before the buds begin to grow.

Getting started: For potted cuttings, fill the container with moist propagation mix. If you are planting cuttings outdoors or into a cold frame, prepare a deep, well-drained nursery bed.

Method: Collect 4- to 8-inch cuttings from vigorous, 1-year-old wood, a few inches below the terminal bud. Make a sloping cut at the top, slightly above a bud, and a straight cut at the base, slightly below a bud. Stick cuttings 2 to 4 inches apart in the medium, with the top bud about 1 inch above the surface. Be sure the cuttings point upward: Double-check that you've stuck the ends with straight cuts into the medium. Plant fall cuttings soon after they are taken, or store them upside down in moist peat moss or perlite and plant right side up in spring. Cover fall-planted cuttings with 6 to 8 inches of mulch to prevent frost heaving; remove mulch in spring. Plant late-winter cuttings directly into pots or soil.

Aftercare: Keep cuttings moist. They usually root rapidly in spring, but it is best to leave them at least until fall. Transplant rooted cuttings to the garden or into pots.

Evergreen Cuttings

Broad-leaved and needled evergreens are often propagated by stem cuttings. Try this method on plants such as arborvitaes (*Thuja* spp.), hollies (*Ilex* spp.), and boxwoods (*Buxus* spp.).

Season: Collect broad-leaved cuttings in late summer. Take needled cuttings in fall or winter; yew and juniper cuttings should have had some frost.

Getting started: Fill a container with moist propagation mix, or prepare a well-drained bed in the base of a cold frame.

Method: Collect 4- to 6-inch tip cuttings in the proper season. Some cuttings benefit from a piece of older wood—a heel—left at the base of the stem. To take a heel, pull sharply downward on the base of a side shoot as you remove it from the parent plant; trim the excess with a knife.

Wounding is another way to encourage the rooting of difficult plants. Create a wound by cutting a shallow sliver on the side of the cutting near the base. This process stimulates cell division and enhances water uptake but also increases the chance of disease problems.

Before planting, remove lower leaves and side shoots. To save space with large broad-leaved cuttings, cut each remaining leaf in half. Apply rooting hormone if desired. Plant cuttings to about one-third of their length, firm the soil, and water to settle the cuttings. Place potted cuttings indoors in a plastic bag or in a greenhouse; alternately, set pots in a cold frame, or plant directly into the frame.

Aftercare: Ventilate and water if necessary. Once roots appear, gradually harden off the cuttings. The new plants are best left in place until autumn and then planted in the garden or in a pot.

Broad-leaved evergreen cuttings. To save space in flats, you can remove up to half of the leaves from a cutting, and for broad-leaved cuttings, cut off half of each remaining leaf. Some broad-leaved evergreen cuttings benefit from wounding: Use a sharp knife to make a shallow 1-inch cut, or wound, at the stem base.

Root Cuttings

The easiest way to reproduce some perennials, including bear's breeches (*Acanthus* spp.) and globe thistles (*Echinops* spp.), is to dig and root the roots.

Season: Dig roots in late winter or early spring. Collect pencil-thick roots from larger perennials; thinner ones from plants such as drumstick primroses (*Primula denticulata*). Collect roots from bleeding hearts (*Dicentra* spp.) and Oriental poppies (*Papaver orientale*) in midsummer.

Getting started: Fill a pot with moist propagation medium.

Method: Remove soil from around the base of large perennials and cut off several pencil-thick roots. For smaller plants, dig the entire clump, wash off the soil, and clip off roots. Place cuttings immediately in a plastic bag. Cut roots into 2- to 3-inch-long sections. Since cuttings must be planted "right side up," make a straight cut at the top of the root, nearest the plant, and slanted cuts away from the plant. Stick the cuttings in the propagation medium with the tips just under the surface. Or lay them horizontally, just under the soil surface.

Aftercare: Water thoroughly to settle the cuttings, then keep them moist, but not wet. Wait until you see roots emerging from the bottom of the pot before moving them to larger pots or the garden, since root cuttings frequently produce topgrowth before they have adequately rooted.

Leaf Cuttings

Some plants with thick or fleshy leaves can produce roots and shoots directly from leaf pieces. This is a popular method for houseplants such as African violets, many fancy-leaved begonias, and snake plants (*Sansevieria* spp.).

Season: Take cuttings any time of the year. Use healthy, young, but fully expanded leaves.

Getting started: Thoroughly water the parent plant a day or so before collecting cuttings. Fill a container with moist propagation medium.

Method: Cut snake plant and streptocarpus leaves into 2-inch-long pieces. Plant the pieces right side up, about 1 inch deep. Peperomias and African violets are reproduced by leaf petiole (the stem that supports the leaf) cuttings. Detach a leaf along with 1½ to 2 inches of its petiole. Plant vertically or at a slight angle, so the petiole is buried up to the leaf blade. After planting, water the cuttings to settle them in the soil. Begonias can be

---

Propagation Pointers

Try these tips for best success with cuttings.

- Plant large numbers of cuttings in wooden or plastic flats; use pots for small quantities.

- Cuttings are usually 4 to 6 inches long, but they can be shorter if the stock plant is small; get at least two nodes (leaf-stem joints). Nonflowering shoots are best. Remove flowers and flower buds from unrooted cuttings.

- Soil warmth encourages root formation. Place containers of cuttings on a propagation mat, a board over a radiator, or the top of your refrigerator.

- Don't tug on cuttings—check the bottom of the container to see if roots are visible.

- Be adventurous! Try different techniques on a range of plants to see what works for you. Label your experiments and record results for future reference.

---

propagated with whole leaves: Make three or four cuts across the veins of fancy-leaved types, then pin them to the soil surface with pieces of wire.

Aftercare: If excessive condensation occurs, ventilate the cuttings. When new leaves appear, usually in 6 to 8 weeks, gradually harden them off. Sever plantlets from the parent leaf if it has not already withered away; transfer rooted plants to pots.

D

DAFFODIL

See *Narcissus*

DAHLIA

Dahlia. Summer- and fall-blooming tender perennials.

Description: Dahlia flowers range in size from 1 inch to well over 1 foot wide and are available in all colors except blue and green, in solids and mixes, often brushed or speckled. They also come in many forms, so check the bloom type when you order plants online or through catalogs so you won't be surprised at bloom time. Single flowers have one row of petals around a yellow center. Semidoubles have a few rows of petals around the center. The anemone form resembles a single but also has a tuft of petals around the center; collarettes have a collar of petals instead of a tuft. Cactus dahlias are double flowers with tubular, almost pointy petals. Formal decoratives are double flowers with broad petals in a neat pattern, while informal decoratives are doubles that look less neat and often have twisted petals. Ball dahlias have double, ball-shaped flowers with cupped petals turned toward the center; pompons are like balls, but are less than 2 inches wide.

Most dahlias grow 2 to 6 feet tall and may spread almost as wide, bearing thick bamboolike stems and lush green or dark purple-red foliage resembling giant celery leaves. (The famous cultivar 'Bishop of Llandaff' bears scarlet semidouble blooms above foliage so dark it's almost black.) The leaves may be only 3 to 4 inches long, or they may exceed 1½ feet. Dahlias are hardy in Zones 8–11 if soil is well drained and not allowed to freeze; otherwise, lift them for winter.

How to grow: You can start dahlias indoors, treating them like caladiums (see the Caladium entry), or plant them directly into the open ground after it has warmed up. Either way, plant them outdoors after all danger of frost is past, in full sun and deep, fertile, moist but well-drained soil enriched with plenty of organic matter. Whether plants are already in leaf or not yet growing, set the roots horizontally 3 to 6 inches below the soil surface. If already started, carefully break off the lowest leaves to encourage additional roots to form. Don't cover unsprouted tuberous roots completely at planting time—gradually fill in the holes as the plants grow.

After setting out each plant, immediately drive a sturdy stake 6 inches from the growing point, especially for tall cultivars. Don't wait until the plants are up and growing, or you may damage the tuberous roots. Mulch thickly with pine needles, straw, or compost after plants are at least 6 inches tall and the soil is warm. Water often, and fertilize liberally throughout summer with fish emulsion, liquid seaweed, compost tea, bonemeal, or other fertilizers not excessively high in nitrogen. See the Compost entry for instructions for making compost tea.

When plants are about 6 to 10 inches tall, pinch out the center to promote branching and more flowers. You can pinch them again after they put out another 6 inches of growth. Tie the shoots to the stake as they grow long enough. When the flower buds reach the size of a pea, remove the side buds to allow the center one to grow as large as possible for its type, or leave the side buds on for more but smaller flowers.

Handpick slugs and snails when the plants are small, and apply soap sprays to control spider mites in summer. Corn stem borers may attack dahlias, so be on the lookout for wilting shoots and cut them back until you find the borer. Cucumber beetles and grasshoppers relish the flowers; handpick these pests daily. For more cucumber beetle control options, see the Cucumber entry. To help keep viruses from spreading, immediately destroy

Dahlias from Seed

Some dahlias grow and bloom heavily the first year from seed. They bear semidouble to double, 2- to 3-inch flowers in white, pink, red, yellow, and orange on plants about 1 foot tall, often with dark reddish leaves. Sow indoors in late winter for summer bloom, or sow directly in the garden after the last frost for later bloom. Although not as glorious as most of their taller relatives, these dahlias are much easier to grow. Give them the same soil conditions you would any dahlia. Grow as annuals and reseed next year, or store tuberous roots of your favorites for next season. All do well in borders, beds, and pots.

any stunted plants or those with yellow-streaked, twisted leaves.

After frost blackens the plants, cut them back to a few inches above ground level, lift the clumps from the ground, and store them on their sides while waiting for the soil on the tubers to dry. Label them with their cultivar names, using an indelible pen or attachable tag. Store as entire clumps with the soil remaining on them, or remove the soil and store the root clumps in barely moist peat or vermiculite in a cool (45° to 50°F) spot, sprinkling a little water on the peat or vermiculite to plump up withered tuberous roots. To multiply your collection, cut up the clumps in spring, making sure each piece has a small pinkish "eye" attached to it.

Landscape uses: Many of the shorter and

medium-height dahlias make excellent additions to the late-summer and fall border. Taller dahlias can temporarily screen out an unpleasant view. They're also colorful in front of a tall hedge (leave a few feet between the hedge and the dahlias). Add dahlias to your cut flower garden for beautiful late-season bouquets.

DAISY

See Chrysanthemum

DASIPHORA

Cinquefoil. Spring- and summer-blooming deciduous shrubs.

Description: *Dasiphora fruticosa* (aka *Potentilla fruticosa*), shrubby cinquefoil, is an exceptionally hardy shrub. It has a low, twiggy, rounded form, growing to 2 to 4 feet tall and wide. The compound leaves are a soft gray-green. Lemon yellow, 1-inch flowers cover the plant in late spring, followed by sporadic bloom through summer and into fall. Zones 2–7.

How to grow: Cinquefoil does best with full sun in well-drained soil. Once established, it needs little supplemental watering. Prune in late winter before growth begins.

Landscape uses: Because of its compact size, cinquefoil makes a good foundation plant. It is also effective as a specimen, in mixed borders, or in a massed planting.

DAYLILY

See *Hemerocallis*

DELPHINIUM

Delphinium, larkspur. Summer- and repeat-blooming perennials.

Description: *Delphinium elatum* hybrids, hybrid delphiniums, bear 2- to 3-inch single, starlike or semidouble, rounded flowers, in white, pink, lavender, blue, purple, and combinations on dense spikes that rise 4 to 6 feet above maplelike leaves on long stems. Zones 3–7.

D. ×*belladonna*, belladonna delphiniums, have 1½- to 2-inch single blooms in white and blue, borne loosely on numerous spikes above smaller, deeply lobed leaves; plants grow 3 to 4 feet. Zones 3–7.

How to grow: Set out plants or rooted cuttings in spring; sow seeds indoors in winter for summer bloom or in midsummer for bloom next year. Plant in a sunny site in fertile, humus-rich, moist but well-drained soil. Delphiniums prefer regions with cool summers; if you have hot summers, try them in a partly shady, moist area. While good air circulation is desirable, avoid sites where winds will batter the tall flowerstalks.

Feed and water hybrid delphinium cultivars regularly. They'll also need staking to support their towering flower spikes. Deadhead, water, and fertilize all cultivars immediately after flowering to promote rebloom. Wide spacing increases air circulation, reducing disease problems. Hose off spider mites regularly if they appear. Divide and replant overgrown clumps in spring.

Landscape uses: Use tall cultivars as exclamation points alone or in groups at the back of borders and against buildings, fences, walls, and hedges—anywhere you'd like a strong vertical accent. Mass shorter cultivars in borders or a cutting garden. Delphiniums are ideal for cottage gardens.

DIANTHUS

Pinks, carnations. Spring- and summer-blooming perennials.

Description: Cheerful pinks offer a variety of single to double flowers in shades of white, pink, and red. The petals are fringed and often banded with color. Flowers may be richly clove scented and are borne on thin stems above tufted or mat-like grassy leaves.

Dianthus ×*allwoodii*, Allwood pinks, produce mostly double 1- to 2-inch blooms in summer, 12 to 15 inches above attractive gray-green mounds of foliage. Zones 4–8.

D. deltoides, maiden pinks, bear masses of ¾-inch flowers 6 to 12 inches above spreading mats of leaves for several weeks in summer. Zones 3–9.

D. gratianopolitanus, cheddar pinks, bear ½- to ¾-inch flowers up to 1 foot above small mounds of narrow, gray-green leaves in spring and sporadically through the season. Zones 3–9.

D. caryophyllus, florist's carnations, need greenhouse conditions and are not suitable for the garden.

How to grow: Plant or divide in spring or fall in a sunny spot with average to low fertility and well-drained, slightly alkaline soil. Although maiden pinks tolerate very light shade, anything less than full sun usually results in weak, floppy stems and dead central leaves. Maiden and cheddar pinks will rebloom if promptly deadheaded. To avoid crown rot disease, don't plant pinks in poorly drained soil.

Landscape uses: Perfect for edgings and in rock and cottage gardens, pinks are also delightful in groups in the front of borders or filling gaps in stone paths. Grow maiden pinks as a groundcover; try the tiny ones in shallow pots. Cheddar pinks make great groundcovers, too. Allwood pinks make good cut flowers.

DIASCIA

Diascia, twinspur. Summer- to fall-blooming annual or tender perennial.

Description: Charming relatives of snapdragons, diascias bear heart-shaped leaves and loose racemes of ¾-inch flowers in shades of pink. Each flower has two spurs in the back and five rounded lobes in front. The low-growing, 1-foot-tall plants have sprawling stems that spread to 2 feet.

How to grow: Diascias need full sun to light shade and rich, well-drained, evenly moist soil. Start seeds indoors 8 to 10 weeks before the last spring frost, sow seeds outdoors 2 weeks before the last frost, or purchase started plants. Pinch plants when they are 3 inches tall to encourage branching, and cut them back to 3 inches after the first flush of bloom to encourage repeat flowering. They may stop blooming during hot summer weather. Take cuttings in late summer or dig plants for overwintering indoors.

Landscape uses: Use diascias to add color to beds, borders, and rock gardens. They're also a great choice for containers.

DICENTRA

Bleeding heart. Spring- and recurrent-blooming perennials; wildflowers.

Description: Bleeding hearts bear clusters or sprays of heart-shaped flowers above mounded leaves.

Dicentra eximia, fringed bleeding heart, blooms in late spring and sporadically through the season, with clusters of narrow, ¾-inch pink flowers on 1- to 1½-foot slender stems. Its blue-green leaves are delicate and ferny, often with a grayish sheen. Zones 3–9.

D. spectabilis, old-fashioned bleeding heart, now listed by some sources as *Lamprocapnos spectabilis*, blooms in spring. It bears 1½-inch pink-and-white flowers that dangle in rows from gracefully curving stems up to 2 feet long, above a 2- to 3-foot mass of blue-green leaves. Some cultivars bear pure white flowers, and one, 'Gold Heart', has chartreuse-gold foliage and deep pink flowers. Zones 2–9.

How to grow: Set out bleeding hearts in early spring. Plant either pot-grown specimens or divisions, but handle them with care, since bleeding hearts have brittle roots that are easily damaged and generally resent disturbance. Grow them in partial shade and well-drained, humus-rich soil. Most reseed prolifically where conditions suit them. Water all bleeding hearts during drought. Old-fashioned bleeding heart tolerates full sun if given plenty of moisture during active growth. It dies back to the ground in summer or even sooner in hot, sunny spots (though in cool, shaded areas, the foliage may remain until early fall); remove the leaves when they start to turn brown and unsightly. Divide overgrown clumps when plants go dormant.

Landscape uses: Grow fringed bleeding hearts in woodland plantings, shady rock gardens and walls, and even in the shade of larger plants in sunny borders. Old-fashioned bleeding hearts are one of the best plants for spring borders and combine well with tulips. Grow old-fashioned bleeding hearts with hostas, ferns, and astilbes to fill in blank spots when the foliage dies in summer, or overplant carefully with annuals.

DIGITALIS

Foxglove. Summer-blooming perennials and late-spring- to early-summer-blooming biennials.

Description: *Digitalis purpurea*, common foxglove, is a biennial that carries long spikes of 2- to 3-inch, tubular, open-faced bells in shades of white, pink, and red-violet (usually spotted inside), on 4- to 5-foot upright, leafy plants. In the first year, young plants form a tight rosette of oblong leaves to 1 foot or more; the next spring and early summer, the bloom spikes emerge, set with progressively smaller leaves stopping just below the flowers. Zones 4–8.

Perennial *D. grandiflora* (also sold as *D. ambigua*), yellow foxglove, is similar to common foxglove, bearing spikes of 2-inch yellow flowers marked with brown inside on 2- to 3½-foot open clumps of dark green, narrower, more pointed leaves. Zones 3–8.

D. ×*mertonensis*, strawberry foxglove, is a short-lived perennial that produces spikes of 2½-inch rosy pink blooms patterned with coppery lines on 3- to 4-foot oval-leaved plants. Zones 3–8.

How to grow: For biennial foxgloves, set out nursery-grown plants in late summer, or start from seeds sown in midsummer. Outdoors, sow in a protected spot away from strong sun and wind, scattering the seed into lightly raked open ground. Or start in flats, lightly pressing the fine seed into the growing medium. Foxgloves grow best in partial shade and average to fertile, moist but well-drained, humus-rich soil. They tolerate full sun farther north if kept moist. Water if the soil is dry, especially in spring. Keep stakes handy, particularly if the plants are growing in windy areas. After the ground freezes, place pine needles, straw, or other light mulch under the leafy crowns to help prevent root damage in winter.

After bloom, cut the flower stems off to encourage possible bloom the next year, or remove the entire plant. If you allow some plants to go to seed, foxgloves will self-sow readily and form impressive stands where conditions suit them.

Grow perennial foxgloves in similar conditions, dividing every 2 to 3 years in spring to keep them vigorous.

Landscape uses: The dramatic vertical spires of foxgloves add height and contrast to more rounded and spreading shapes in a border or cottage garden. Allow them to naturalize in lightly shady, moist woodland settings. Plant in the cutting garden for stunning cut flowers.

DIVISION

Division is a quick and reliable way to propagate many types of multistemmed plants with almost guaranteed success. Dividing—separating a plant into several smaller new plants—works well for increasing groundcovers, clump-forming perennials, bulbs, and tubers. You can divide ornamental grasses and suckering shrubs, as well as houseplants and herbs. Division is also an effective way to rejuvenate overcrowded clumps of perennials and other plants.

Season: The best time to divide garden plants is when they are dormant. In general, divide spring- and summer-blooming plants in fall, and fall-blooming plants in spring. If possible, divide houseplants in spring as new growth starts. Divide plants with tubers and tuberous roots, such as dahlias and tuberous begonias, before planting in spring.

Getting started: The key to division is starting with a vigorous parent plant. If the soil is dry, water the plant thoroughly the day before. Whenever possible, wait for cool, cloudy weather (or at least evening) to reduce moisture loss from the plant during the process.

Method: To divide a hardy plant, lift it from the soil with a fork or spade. Separate small clumps

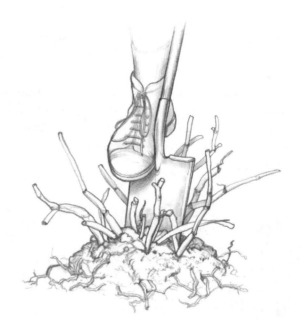

Dividing herbaceous plants. Use a sharp spade to divide perennials or tough clumps of ornamental grasses. Try not to chop at the roots; make single, clean cuts whenever possible.

by pulling off the vigorous young plantlets; cut larger clumps apart with a knife or pry them apart with back-to-back forks. To divide heavy clumps such as ornamental grasses, cut them apart while they are still in the hole, then pull up the clump in pieces. Cut apart iris rhizomes with a knife. Discard the woody growth at the center of divided clumps. When dividing plants, make sure that each piece you remove has its own root system. Otherwise, new divisions won't grow.

Lift clumps of hardy bulbs after the foliage yellows and dies down. Separate the bulbs and replant them at the proper depth and spacing. Divide tubers and tuberous roots in early spring. Cut dahlia crowns apart with a knife: Make sure each swollen root has at least one bud, located on the stems where the roots join the crown. Cut begonia and caladium tubers into two or three sections, each with a visible bud or sprout. Expose the cut areas to air for a day or two before planting.

Aftercare: Replant divisions as quickly as possible, to the same depth as the original plant, and water them thoroughly. Mulch fall divisions well to protect the developing roots from frost heaving.

DOGWOOD

See *Cornus*

DOUBLE-DIGGING

See Soil

DRIP IRRIGATION

If you're not using drip irrigation in your garden, now's the time to start. Drip irrigation is a highly efficient way to water, saving time and helping to conserve precious supplies of clean water. Studies show that well-designed drip systems use at least 30 percent, and in some cases 50 percent, less water than other methods of watering such as sprinkling.

A drip irrigation system delivers water directly to the root zone of a plant, where it seeps slowly into the soil one drop at a time. Almost no water is lost through surface runoff or evaporation, and soil particles have plenty of opportunity to absorb and hold water for plants. It also means very few nutrients leach down beyond the reach of plant roots. Furthermore, since drip irrigation delivers water directly to the plants you want to grow, less is

wasted on weeds. The soil surface between the plants also remains drier, which discourages weed seeds from sprouting.

For busy gardeners, the main benefit of drip irrigation is the savings of both time and effort. Drip systems eliminate the need to drag around hoses and sprinklers. For systems that use a timer, gardeners need only spend a few seconds to turn the system on; the timer automatically turns it off.

Plants watered with drip systems grow more quickly and are more productive, because they have all the water they need and their growth isn't slowed by water stress. (This is especially true when drip irrigation is used in conjunction with mulch.) Also, plants watered by drip irrigation don't end up with wet foliage from a sprinkler spray, and that can help prevent some foliage diseases such as powdery mildew.

As wonderful as it is, drip irrigation won't meet every watering need in your yard and garden. For smart tips on hand watering or using sprinklers, see the Watering entry.

Start with Soaker Hoses

The easiest way to experiment with drip irrigation is to buy a couple of soaker hoses. These hoses (some made from recycled tires) ooze water over their entire length. You simply position a soaker on the soil surface next to the plants you want to water, and then connect the open end of the hose to your garden hose and turn on the water supply. You can move the hose from one bed to another in your garden, or buy several and leave them in place. Soaker hoses can be used for short runs (100 to 200 feet) over flat surfaces. A soaker hose delivers water less precisely than a drip irrigation system but is still significantly more efficient than a sprinkler.

Drip Irrigation Systems

Soaker hoses are great for row crops such as carrots and beans, but for watering trees and shrubs or a series of containers, drip irrigation offers a more sophisticated and targeted way to water. Drip irrigation systems move water at low pressure through a series of tubes and other hardware and deliver it to precise locations and specific plants of the gardener's choosing. Although each system is different, water generally flows out of your faucet through a timer (which is optional), a filter, a pressure regulator, and into a series of hoses or pipes that carry water to emitters, which are small devices that release water drop by drop to the plants. Some systems use drip tape—flattened plastic hoses with holes at regular intervals. A complex system may contain two or more individual lines as well as valves that allow for watering specific parts of the garden.

Designing a System

The first step in designing a drip irrigation system is deciding what you want the system to water. Is it only for your vegetable garden, or will you use drip irrigation for your entire landscape? Topography is also a consideration: If your garden is hilly, you'll probably need to use emitters that compensate for pressure changes in the line.

Keep in mind that plants can become "addicted" to drip irrigation, because roots will concentrate in the area where the water is available. When designing a drip system to carry water along the rows of a vegetable garden or to the roots of a prized rhododendron, it's important that the water be spread uniformly throughout the irrigated area so root growth will be uniform. For example, if you are irrigating larger plants such as trees and shrubs, place emitters on two or more sides of each plant to encourage roots to grow out in all directions rather than clustering on one side. For the same reason, it's best to use your system to provide a long, slow watering. If you turn it on for frequent, short waterings, water won't have a chance to spread far in the soil, and consequently the roots will form a tight, ball-like mass around the emitters.

You can design your own system, but most companies that sell drip irrigation equipment will design systems for you if provided with a scale drawing of your garden, information on what you're growing, your soil type, and garden topography. Their design will come complete with a list of parts and spacing for emitters. Whatever method you choose, start by making a fairly accurate drawing of your garden to determine how many feet of tubing you'll need.

If you're designing your own system, consider asking a few gardening friends to adopt drip irrigation, too. That way you can split the cost of the system components, which have a lower base cost when you buy large quantities such as 500-foot-long rolls of drip tape or sets of 100 emitters.

Kits for beginners. A low-risk way to get started with drip irrigation is to buy a starter kit. Most companies that sell drip irrigation systems also offer kits for both small and large gardens, which come with the essential components necessary to set up the system. Keep in mind that kits often don't include parts such as pressure regulators, timers, backflow preventers, and line filters. Be sure to buy a kit that can be expanded, so you can add to your system over time.

E

EARTHWORMS

The pale red garden earthworm is often called "nature's plow." That's because an earthworm pushes through soft earth with the point of its head. If the soil is hard, the worm eats its way through, forming interconnected burrows, some several feet deep. Burrows loosen the soil, admitting air and water and helping roots grow. A single acre of cultivated land may be home to as many as 500,000 earthworms, each making the soil a better place for plants.

Earthworms in your garden: When you add nitrogen-rich compost to your soil, you help worms thrive. However, adding synthetic nitrogen fertilizers may repel earthworms. Worms are very sensitive to physical and chemical changes and will flee the salty conditions that result from an application of chemical fertilizer.

As an earthworm feeds, organic matter passes through its body and is excreted as granular dark castings. You may see these small casting piles in your garden. An earthworm produces its weight in castings daily. Worm castings are a wonderful fertilizer, rich in nutrients otherwise unavailable to plants.

In cold weather, a soil search will turn up mature and young earthworms as well as eggs. By late spring, most worms are mature. As temperatures rise, activity slows; many lay eggs and then die. By midsummer, most worms are very young or protected by egg capsules. As the weather cools, young worms emerge. With wet weather, they grow active, making new burrows and eating extra food, resulting in more worm castings. Egg laying occurs again. Activity continues as long as soil stays damp.

After a heavy rain, earthworms often appear aboveground. They haven't drowned. Fresh water doesn't disturb earthworms—they need ongoing skin moisture to breathe—but stagnant or contaminated water forces them from their burrows.

Earthworms can survive in soil that freezes gradually, but sudden freezing can kill them. Protect earthworms against sudden freezes with mulch or a cover crop, both of which also provide worms with food.

Earthworm Bins

You can raise earthworms yourself—a process called vermiculture or earthworm composting— using purchased red worms, *Eisenia fetida*, also called red wigglers or manure worms. These are the kind of worms often sold for fishing. You can buy them from a bait store or order them from a compost/garden supply company. Kept in a cool place, such as a basement, a worm bin provides a composting system for kitchen scraps and a source of rich, fertile worm castings for the garden. For more information on vermiculture, see Resources on page 673.

Commercial bin systems. Commercially available bins are typically made from durable black plastic, with stacked trays that fit on top of a base. The trays have mesh bottoms for drainage, and the base catches "worm tea" and dispenses it from a spigot so you can use it to water your plants. A lid keeps light out and worms from escaping. You fill the lowest tray with a moist filler material (usually a soaked coir fiber brick and/or shredded paper, with a little compost or garden soil mixed in to provide beneficial organisms). The filler should be uniformly damp but not wet, just like any working compost pile. Once you add the worms, you can begin adding kitchen scraps every day or so as the worms consume them, transforming them and the filler into nutrient-rich castings. As with any compost pile, keep meat, fats, and dairy products out of the pile. Coffee grounds and filters, tea bags, oatmeal, bread, and fruit and veggie scraps are excellent worm compostables.

As each tray fills with castings, you can repeat the process in the tray above. Worms will migrate through the mesh to the new source of food, and you can then spread the contents of the lower tray on your garden or greenhouse beds or use it to enrich potting soil. Put the newly emptied tray at the top of the bin, and the cycle can go on indefinitely. Another advantage of commercial multitray bins is that they're portable, so you can set one up outdoors in a shaded area during the growing season, then move it to the greenhouse, sunroom, or basement when cold weather arrives and continue composting.

Homemade bins. Commercial bins work beautifully but can be pricey. If you don't want to pay big bucks for a worm bin, you can make your own from a plastic storage bin, such as one that is 3 feet by 2 feet by 1½ feet deep, or from a modified garbage can, washtub, or wooden box. Use an awl to punch small holes in the sides of plastic washtubs or garbage cans for aeration. To keep conditions moist but well drained, make a drainage area in the bottom of the bin; use a rigid divider to separate it from the worms' living quarters. A loose cover keeps flies and light out and worms and moisture in.

Just as with commercial bins, it's best to fill the bin with soaked coir and newspaper. (You can buy compressed coir bricks from garden supply stores, catalogs, and Web sites and from sources of worm-composting supplies.) Garden soil may also be added. Make sure the mix is as damp as a wrung-out sponge rather than wet. Then introduce the purchased earthworms to their new home. Use your purchased worms for composting only—most commercially available worms are species that live only in manure or very rich soil and will not survive in average garden soil. One exception is the enriched soil in a greenhouse bed—if the greenhouse stays above freezing, worms will do very well there. Likewise, don't collect earthworms from your garden to add to your worm compost bin—those "outdoor" worms, *Lumbricus terrestris*, sometimes called nightcrawlers, prefer cool soil to cozy compost, and will spend their time trying to escape your bin.

Feed your worms well-chopped vegetable matter mixed with a bit of water. Soft foods are best for the first few days; if food doesn't disappear in 24 hours, reduce the amount. For faster composting, run the food through a blender, since worms don't have teeth to tear off large chunks. The population should double in about a month; after 60 days, your bin should be full of rich compost.

To harvest the compost, but save your earthworms for another session, place the compost outdoors on a sheet of heavy plastic or fabric, and let it sit for about an hour. The worms will cluster together to stay cool and moist. Dig in and find the cluster. Return the worms to the bin with fresh bedding. Let the compost air-dry for a day or two, then use it around your garden. Vermicompost is great for nourishing houseplants—sprinkle it on top of the soil in a pot and scratch it gently into the surface. Add it to potting mix for houseplants or outdoor containers, or use it instead of soil to cover newly planted seeds in the garden.

ECHINACEA

Coneflower, purple coneflower. Summer-blooming perennials; wildflowers; medicinal herbs.

Description: *Echinacea purpurea*, purple coneflower, bears 3- to 6-inch daisies with prominent spiky orange centers. Flowers are borne in shades of rose, purple, mauve, and white on 2- to 4-foot upright plants with rough, dark green foliage. An explosion of exciting hybrids has introduced plants with orange, gold, and even green flowers, as well as semidouble and double forms. The cultivar 'Magnus', which holds its petals out in typical daisy form rather than drooping downward, was chosen as a Perennial Plant of the Year by the Perennial Plant Association. 'White Swan' has pure white, reflexed petals surrounding the golden-orange central cone. Zones 3–8.

How to grow: Plant or divide in spring or early fall in full sun and average, well-drained soil. Once established, water only during severe drought. Pick off Japanese beetles.

Landscape uses: Mass in wildflower meadows or grow along a sunny wall or fence. Coneflowers combine well with larkspurs, yarrows, and phlox. They also are attractive in perennial borders, and look great with ornamental grasses and other daisy flowers, including black-eyed Susans and Shasta and oxeye daisies. The hedgehoglike centers persist through fall and winter atop sturdy stems and are popular with finches and other seed-eating birds.

ECO-SMART GARDENING

Call it "eco-friendly," "earth-friendly," or just "green," eco-smart gardening simply means making choices that take into account the effects of your actions on the environment beyond your immediate surroundings. Eco-smart gardeners acknowledge that everything we do—in our gardens, our homes, our communities—has an impact on everything else. Every choice we make to use resources wisely, whether it's water, soil, organic matter (yard waste), paper goods, energy, even money, is part of our total impact on the environment around us. While you may choose to apply this philosophy to other areas of your life, the garden is a perfect place to begin making environmentally friendly choices.

For example, by growing some of your own food, you can reduce the fuel you use to drive to the grocery and use less of the packaging that comes with many supermarket products. If you choose and plant shrubs, trees, and groundcovers that help shelter and support wildlife, you'll find that they'll accomplish other useful purposes as well, such as keeping your home cooler in the summer and providing privacy as more homes and people crowd around you. Your garden may include plantings designed to divert rainwater into the soil instead of into the polluting pathway of stormwater drainage systems. Maybe you'll even decide to plant a stand of fast-growing trees or bamboo to offset some of the carbon you produce in your day-to-day living. (See the Rain Gardens and Carbon Sinks entries.)

Starting a backyard vegetable garden, choosing plants for a perennial garden, or planting a small grouping of trees and shrubs may not seem related to global climate change or environmental issues such as disappearing rain forests. But many scientists believe that home landscapes can be part of the solution to these complex problems. For example, many gardeners who continue to use chemical pesticides do so because they think that the small amount they buy and use doesn't have any significant impact. But overall, US gardeners spend more than $11 billion in just one year on pesticides. And acre for acre, home gardeners apply more pesticides to their lawns and gardens than US farmers do on their fields. If every US gardener decided to go organic, what an amazing difference that could make! And if every gardener decided to launch a green gardening effort as well, the impact could have exciting and world-changing potential.

Buy Thoughtfully

Part of being an eco-smart gardener involves reducing the number of things that you buy—

making compost instead of buying soil amendments, swapping plants with fellow gardeners, or sharing large power tools among neighbors. When you do need to buy a new tool, supplies, or plants for your garden, it's not always easy to figure out which item is the "greenest." Some things to consider are the transportation miles (i.e., fossil fuels expended) to transport the items to your local garden center, the packaging, and the materials used to manufacture the item. For example, if you have a choice between locally produced compost and bagged peat moss as a soil amendment, the compost is almost always the greener choice.

Gardening gloves: Made in the United States or made in China? Potted plants: in a plastic pot or in a pot made of materials that will biodegrade in the soil or a compost pile? Wood timbers for raised beds: naturally rot-resistant or treated with a preservative? Made from local wood or from wood shipped from a thousand miles away? The range of locally made materials is increasing as our consciousness increases. Sadly, the item produced far away may still carry the lower price tag.

When it comes to being "green," the gardening industry (whether garden centers, greenhouses, or nurseries) has many environmentally harmful practices, among them the use and marketing of synthetic fertilizers and pesticides. But looking beyond going organic to going green in your garden, take some time to figure out how you can avoid other harmful practices. Buying plants and other supplies packaged in plastics (and then discarding the packaging) is a big one. Plastics account for up to 25 percent of the contents of landfills, and plastics are a petroleum product, too! Fortunately, alternatives are appearing. Some plant producers now offer bedding plants and landscape plants in biodegradable containers made from materials such as dried manure, rice straw, and coir. Biodegradable plastics are becoming better and more available, and they're made from materials such as corn and bamboo rather than petroleum. You may even be able to find grain-based decorative containers that are ultimately biodegradable (they last about 5 years, and then you can dispose of them in your compost pile).

Lastly, sometimes buying green means buying the best quality you can afford instead of the cheapest you can find, because quality lasts longer. That includes garden tools, watering supplies, plant containers, birdbaths, fencing, and all the stuff that will end up in a landfill if it breaks or wears out. A long-lasting item is often (but not always) the more expensive one. One way to find out which gardening items provide lasting service is to ask longtime gardeners what's lasted for them. If you make the right choices, you may even be able to pass on your fine pruners and beloved shovel to the next generation of gardeners in your family or at your community garden.

EDIBLE LANDSCAPING

Edible landscapes do double duty—they produce food and make our yards attractive at the same time. The goal of edible landscaping is to incorporate as many edible plants as possible into a landscape that still follows the general guidelines of garden design. To get started, all you really need is the ability to look at your current landscape with new eyes. Instead of a conventional ornamental small flowering tree, could you plant one that also bears fruit? When filling ornamental container plantings for your deck or patio, could you choose herbs, attractive veggies, or container fruit trees instead of the usual annual flowers? Once you start looking, the options are almost endless.

The concept of edible landscaping has its roots in ancient Egyptian pleasure gardens, which included fish ponds, flowers, grape arbors, and fruit trees. But by the Renaissance, gardeners had begun to exclude edible plants from their formal ornamental gardens. They planted separate herb gardens, vegetable gardens, and orchards. Flower gardens, luxuries only possible for the wealthy, became status symbols, and food crops were banished to small backyard plots and "truck gardens." Edible landscaping didn't make a comeback until the 1980s, when gardeners who recognized that many edible plants are also beautiful reintroduced them to the general landscape.

Creating an Edible Landscape

Bringing vegetables and fruit trees out of hiding and into the overall landscape makes gardening even more rewarding. Even if you don't have the luxury of designing an edible landscape from scratch, there are lots of ways to add edibles within an existing landscape. There's no need to redesign and uproot your whole yard overnight, instead, you can gradually transform your existing plantings to create an edible landscape. In all but the most rigorously planned edible landscapes, many, but not all, of the plantings are fruit trees, berry bushes, vegetables, and other food-producing plants.

Start by including some edibles with your annual flowers. Forget the traditional practice of planting vegetables in rows—they'll grow just as well interplanted among ornamentals and herbs. Use the same design rules you would with flowers alone. Try accenting a flowerbed with deep green rosettes of arugula, small mounds of 'Spicy Globe' basil, speckled romaine or crinkly red-leaf lettuce, and the upright, blue-green leaves of onion sets.

Plant perennial herbs and vegetables in your existing ornamental borders—make room by relocating or replacing existing plants. For example, lavender, chives, variegated lemon thyme, and rosemary will add four-season interest to a border. There are strawberries that thrive in sun and shade, creating a lush groundcover in garden beds. Artichokes are perennial in Zones 9–10; their silvery, spiky foliage makes an interesting foil for other plants.

Don't forget trees. If you've been thinking about planting an ornamental flowering tree, consider a crabapple known for its delicious fruit, such as 'Centennial', rather than one grown simply for its blooms. A dwarf flowering peach or a pluot (a hybrid cross between a plum and an apricot), or a dwarf fruiting sweet cherry such as 'Lapins' or 'Compact Stella', is a great alternative to a flowering cherry. The fruiting trees' flowers are just as gorgeous as those of the purely ornamental tree, *and* they produce abundant harvests of delicious fruit. Be sure to choose disease-resistant cultivars that have been bred to thrive in your climate and conditions.

If you need to remove an existing tree or shrub that has died or outgrown its site, consider a fruit or nut tree as a replacement. A nut tree (pecan, hickory, English walnut, Chinese chestnut, piñon pine—whatever is suitable for your climate) can replace a large shade tree. Consider replacing an existing hedge with shrubby hazelnuts (filberts) or rugosa roses with their showy, vitamin-C-rich hips. Depending on where you garden, citrus trees such as lemon or grapefruit, or native fruits like pawpaws and serviceberries, can be good replacements for medium-size trees.

Conditions that might otherwise prove challenging can become opportunities for the edible landscaper. Acidic soil? Consider blueberries, which provide three-season beauty as well as delicious fruit, with a groundcover planting of cranberries. Wet soil? Elderberries will thrive. A parched, sunny site? The pads and fruits (tunas) of prickly pears are important edible crops in dryland areas.

There are several other special ways to incorporate edibles into your existing landscape.

- Convert areas of lawn into new garden beds and include edibles in the design.

- Replace grass with food-producing groundcovers in some areas. Alpine strawberries produce fruit all summer and tolerate light shade, while violet flowers are edible as well as ornamental. In sunny areas, herbs such as chamomile, creeping thymes, and lemon thyme can replace grass on paths around stepping-stones.

- Make use of existing walls and fences, or add new ones. Train dwarf fruit trees against them, or use them to support raspberries, blackberries, or vegetables. You'll find directions for training dwarf fruit trees to a fence or trellis in the Fruit Trees entry.

- Plant a fruiting hedge. Besides rugosa roses, you can grow beach plums, shrubby serviceberries, fruiting viburnums like highbush cranberry, blueberries, and many others as hedge plants.

- Build an arbor or trellis. Grapes are traditional, but hardy kiwi also can be a good choice for a large arbor. Vegetables like cucumbers, melons, and beans work well, too, but may need special support for the heavy fruits.

- Add containers to your landscape. Many dwarf fruit trees can be grown in large tubs. Dwarf citrus and figs will grow even in northern climates if the trees are moved to a cool, sunny, indoor location during the winter. Strawberry jars are good for strawberries or herbs. For more suggestions, see "Colorful and Tasty, Too" on page 189.

🌿 Don't forget the tender food plants. If you have a greenhouse, sunroom, or other appropriate bright space to overwinter tropical and semitropical plants, you can grow even more edibles at home. Coffee, tea, cinnamon, cardamom, ginger, citrus, figs, pomegranates, vanilla—there are many plants that will flourish outside during the growing season, then overwinter happily indoors until warm weather rolls around again.

Selecting Plants

Food-producing plants can fill roles in every part of your landscape. Fruit and nut trees come in a wide range of sizes and shapes, provide shade, and may provide spring blooms and/or fall color. Berry-producing shrubs, such as blueberries and wild plums, also provide flowers and fall color. Some blueberry bushes even have attractive red branches in the winter.

The flowers of certain annual and perennial flowers, such as nasturtiums and chives, are edible, as well as their leaves and even nasturtium buds (when pickled, they're a great substitute for capers). Many herbs and vegetables have interesting foliage, and some have showy flowers or brightly colored fruit. Fruiting vines such as grapes, melons, and climbing beans will cover fences and trellises. Some edibles, such as creeping thymes and alpine strawberries, make good groundcovers.

Your personal taste and how much space you have available will determine what you plant. Consider these factors as you select plants.

🌿 What foods do you like and use most? You're defeating the purpose of an edible landscape if you plant crops you won't want to eat.

🌿 How big is each plant and how much will it produce? Hardy kiwi vines are vigorous and can produce hundreds of fruits. Will you be able to use them?

🌿 Do you have a location suitable for growing edibles? Many fruit and vegetable crops will thrive only when they receive at least 6 hours of direct daily sun. Your choice will be limited if you have a shady yard, but you can expand your options by growing edibles in containers on a sunny deck or patio.

🌿 What fresh foods can you buy locally, and which are expensive or difficult to find? You may decide to plant raspberry canes and forgo zucchini plants. Good raspberries command high prices at the grocery store, while zucchini in season is cheap (or available free from friends).

A Gallery of Edibles

Almost all food-producing plants have ornamental value. The following listings are only a small sampling of the many excellent edible landscape plants available. To see which of the following plants are covered in other entries in this encyclopedia, refer to the Quick Reference Guide on page 678.

Trees: In warm climates, citrus (orange, lemon, lime, grapefruit) are versatile trees. They are large enough to provide good shade, cooling the house or an area of the garden during the heat of the day. They retain their shiny deep green leaves through the winter, and they have fruit in various stages of development and ripeness on their branches year-round. When in flower, their fragrance perfumes the air. The flowers of the orange tree are extremely sweet and can be used to flavor honey, sugar, and tea or serve as a beautiful garnish.

In the East, if your flowering dogwood (*Cornus florida*) trees are in decline, replace them with Kousa dogwood (*C. kousa*). It blooms in June (later

Colorful and Tasty, Too

Once you begin working with edible landscaping designs, you'll discover there are nearly limitless possibilities for attractive combinations of food-producing and ornamental plants. Get started with ideas from the combinations listed below, suitable for container plantings or for garden beds.

- Curly parsley and yellow pansies (*Viola* spp.)
- Red-leaf lettuce with dwarf yellow marigolds (*Tagetes erecta*)
- Red chard and New Zealand spinach (*Tetragonia tetragonioides*)
- 'Spicy Globe' basil with 'Atlas' carrots and dwarf orange marigolds (*Tagetes erecta*)
- Dwarf curly kale with dusty miller and nemesia (*Nemesia* spp.)
- Sorrel with curly parsley, trailing lobelia (*Lobelia erinus*), and alpine strawberries
- Eggplant and ageratum
- Yellow zucchini and coreopsis (*Coreopsis* spp.)
- 'Royal Burgundy' bush beans with 'Royal Carpet' alyssum (*Lobularia maritima* 'Royal Carpet') and oregano
- 'Bright Lights' or other colorful mix of Swiss chard with French marigolds (*Tagetes patula*) and purple-leaf basil such as 'Dark Opal' or 'Red Rubin'

than the flowering dogwood), the flowers are longer lasting, and it has brilliant fall foliage. The edible fruit resembles a pale strawberry. It is tartly sweet, with a pearlike, mealy texture, and is favored by birds and wildlife. Another dogwood with edible fruit is Cornelian cherry (*C. mas*), a shrub or small tree that has clusters of small yellow flowers followed by tart, cherrylike fruits traditionally used in preserves. For container culture or in mild-winter areas, figs make intriguing accent plants with handsome leathery leaves. Dwarf fruit trees work well in small areas and are attractive when trained into espaliers against a fence or wall.

Shrubs: A blueberry bush can be a good foundation plant but must have acid soil to thrive. Where soil pH makes blueberries difficult, choose cultivars developed for containers. Bush cherries, wild plums, gooseberries, currants, hazelnuts, and highbush cranberries (*Viburnum opulus* var. *americanum*, formerly *V. trilobum*) make good hedges. Tightly planted raspberries or blackberries create a living fence. Some shrub-type roses, such as rugosa roses, produce large, bright orange or red, edible rose hips with 60 times the vitamin C of an orange. The hips can be used to make tea, jam, or jelly.

Ornamentals: Some plants normally grown as ornamentals have edible parts. Leaves and seeds of Joseph's coat (*Amaranthus tricolor*), leaves and flowers of anise hyssop (*Agastache foeniculum*), seeds of love-in-a-mist (*Nigella damascena*), and leaves and flowers of nasturtiums and violets are edible.

Edibles with showy flowers and foliage: Edibles can have colorful and attractive flowers too. Here's a sampling to consider: amaranth, artichoke, cardoon, chives, dill, Jerusalem artichoke, nasturtiums, okra, rosemary, and salsify.

The foliage of edibles comes in many interesting colors and forms. Various cultivars of artichoke, cabbage, cardoon, kale, lavender, leeks,

Unusual Fruits

As you choose fruit-bearing plants for your property, don't forget to look past the usual apples and peaches. Many lesser-grown plants produce flavorful fruits and make attractive additions to the landscape. Here you'll find descriptions of several uncommon plants and their fruits, as well as notes on their culture. Some of these, such as medlar and pomegranate, have rich histories as edibles but are not widely grown in home gardens because of very specific cultural requirements. Others are more recently recognized for their edible qualities but have yet to be widely adopted. While plant breeders have improved many of these fruiting crops, cultivar availability tends to vary by region and changes as interest in a particular fruit increases or wanes. Seek out a specialty grower to have access to the greatest variety of improved selections and to find the cultivars that are best for your growing conditions.

Banana (*Musa acuminata, M. balbisiana, M. ×paradisiaca*)

Fruit: Besides the familiar, large, yellow banana (primarily 'Cavendish') of our markets, there are cultivars with red fruits and cultivars with small, finger-size fruits. As with other fruits, cultivars vary in flavor and sweetness. Bananas ripen without regard to season.

Plant type: A treelike, perennial herb with velvety leaves 4 to 8 feet long and 1 foot or more across. Depending on culti-

var, height varies from 8 to 25 feet. Suckers grow up from around the base of the stem, enlarging and eventually replacing stems that fruit, then die.

Culture: Plant in full sun but sheltered from strong winds, in rich, well-drained soil. Depending on the vigor of the cultivar, set plants 10 to 15 feet apart. No pollination is needed for fruiting. Prune off some suckers from the base of the plant so that only one or two will be fruiting at a time. Zone 10.

Cultivars: 'Dwarf Cavendish', 'Dwarf Orinoco', 'Dwarf Red', 'Lady Finger', 'Manzano'

Cornelian Cherry Dogwood (*Cornus mas*)

Fruit: Fruits are usually oval, fire-engine red, with a single stone. Some cultivars have barrel- or pear-shaped fruits; color may vary from yellow through dark purple. Flavor is tart, with varying degrees of sweetness, depending on the cultivar and how long fruit is left hanging. Fruits ripen from summer through autumn, depending on the cultivar. Attractive to wildlife.

Plant type: A long-lived, oval-headed tree or large shrub, growing up to 25 feet tall. The bark is attractive, flaking off in muted shades of tan and gray. Masses of yellow flowers appear on leafless branches in very early spring, but they rarely are damaged by frost. Leaves turn mahogany red in autumn.

Culture: Cornelian cherry tolerates a wide range of soils. Though it will grow in partial shade, full sun is needed for best fruiting. The flowers are self-fertile, but cross-pollination may further increase yield. The plant rarely needs pruning, only enough to shape it and keep it in bounds, if necessary. Zones 4–8.

Cultivars: Many cultivars have been selected for their ornamental rather than edible qualities. 'Elegant', 'Pioneer', and 'Redstone' produce abundant red fruits; yellow-fruited 'Flava' bears sweeter fruit than most seedling plants.

Cranberry (*Vaccinium macrocarpon*)

Fruit: The ½- to ¾-inch, tart red berries ripen in autumn. Fruits usually are eaten cooked.

Plant type: Evergreen vine with long, thin stems rising about 1 foot off the ground. The vines creep along the ground and root to form a solid mat of plants. Leaves are small, leathery, and glossy, dark green.

Culture: Cranberries need a sunny site with soil that is very acidic (pH 4.0 to 5.0) and high in organic matter. Commercially, cranberries are grown in sunny bogs that are flooded in winter. While a bog for cranberries is unnecessary, the plants demand consistent moisture during the growing season and cold winters. No cross-pollination needed. Zones 3–8.

Cultivars: Seek "no-bog" cultivars suitable for your local conditions. When searching for plants, don't confuse cranberry with highbush cranberry (*Viburnum opulus* var. *americanum*), an entirely different plant.

Feijoa (*Acca sellowiana*, formerly *Feijoa sellowiana*), also known as pineapple guava

Fruit: Fruits are torpedo-shaped or round, 1 to 3 inches long, and have a green skin and yellowish, jellylike interior. The sweet-tart flavor is reminiscent of pineapple, strawberry, and mint. Ripens in autumn.

Plant type: Evergreen tree or small shrub about 10 feet high and wide. Leaves are glossy green above with silvery undersides. Edible flowers appear on new growth. Petals are white, tinged with purple.

Culture: Tolerates part shade, but does best in full sun in a variety of soil types. Thrives in dry climates. Some cultivars require cross-pollination; others are self-fruitful. Prune lightly each year to prevent overcrowding of branches. Harvest fruits as they drop to the ground. Zones 8–10, but fruit flavor is best in cooler summer climates.

Cultivars: Most breeding and cultivar selection takes place in New Zealand.

Goji Berry (*Lycium barbarum*)

Fruit: Oblong bright red berries about the size and shape of a grape tomato begin ripening in early summer and continue throughout the growing season. The fruits are used fresh, dried, or in juice.

(continued)

Unusual Fruits *(cont.)*

Plant type: Somewhat rambling deciduous shrub that reaches 10 to 12 feet tall and spreads about 4 feet wide. The long canelike stems are best supported on a fence or trellis and pruned to maintain the desired height.

Culture: Goji berry may be grown in a 5-gallon or larger container. A Chinese native related to tomatoes and peppers, goji berry grows best in well-drained soil of slightly acidic to near-neutral pH. Plants are self-pollinating. Zones 3–7.

Cultivars: As this fruit's reputation as a nutrient-dense superfood grows, more cultivars will likely become available.

Highbush Cranberry (*Viburnum opulus* var. *americanum*, formerly *V. trilobum*), also known as American cranberrybush

Fruit: Showy red fruits are 1/3 inch across and borne in clusters that are ready for harvest in autumn. The tart berries make excellent preserves and jellies. Except for having a single, hard seed, the fruit resembles that of the true cranberry. Attractive to wildlife.

Plant type: Deciduous, round-topped bush 8 to 12 feet high. Bushes are covered in spring with large clusters of white flowers. The large, three-lobed leaves turn red in August; fruits decorate plants through winter if not harvested.

Culture: Moist, well-drained soils in full sun or partial shade. Keep plants productive by removing one or two of the oldest stems each year and thinning new stems. Zones 2–7.

Cultivars: Selections have been made primarily for ornamental and landscape qualities such as fall color and compact growth. 'Phillips' and 'Wentworth' are noted for improved fruit production.

Jostaberry (*Ribes ×nidigrolaria*)

Fruit: The 5/8-inch black fruits of this hybrid have a flavor somewhat reminiscent of its parents: black currant and two gooseberry species. Jostaberries are borne in clusters of three to five berries on wood at least 1 year old. Fruit ripens in summer. Attractive to wildlife.

Plant type: Shrub that produces vigorous upright branches up to 6 feet tall. The glossy dark green leaves are deciduous, although they hang on to the plant late into fall. Stems are thornless, unlike jostaberry's gooseberry parents.

Culture: Jostaberries prefer well-drained, moderately fertile soil. Mulch to keep roots cool. Plant in a sheltered site to protect early-spring blooms from frost. Keep plants productive by removing one or two of the oldest stems each year. Zones 4–7.

Cultivars: Cultivars vary in availability; some require cross-pollination.

Jujube (*Ziziphus jujuba*), also known as Chinese date

Fruit: Fruits range from cherry- to plum-size. Just-ripe fruit has mahogany skin and white flesh that is crisp and sweet like an apple. Left to ripen longer, the fruit dries and wrinkles, and the flesh becomes beige and concentrated in flavor. Fruits ripen in late summer and autumn.

Plant type: Small, deciduous tree with small, glossy leaves and a naturally drooping habit. Young trees and some clones have spines. Trees sometimes send up many suckers. Masses of fragrant yellow flowers are present for an extended period.

Culture: Thrives in the sunniest and warmest possible locations. Not finicky as to soil. Avoid cultivating ground around trees because this increases tendency of plants to sucker. Blossoms late enough to escape spring frosts, but yield in some areas increases with cross-pollination. Zones 6–10.

Cultivars: 'Lang' and 'Li' are most available in the United States.

Lingonberry (*Vaccinium vitis-idaea*)

Fruit: Slightly smaller than, but otherwise similar to, cranberries in appearance and flavor. An early crop ripens in summer, but the main crop ripens in autumn.

Plant type: Sprawling, evergreen shrub with leathery, oval leaves. The plant grows from a few inches to 1 foot in height. Spreads by underground rhizomes. Blooms in spring and again in summer.

Culture: Grows best in full sun or partial shade and in acidic soil (pH 4.0 to 5.0). Set plants 1 foot apart in all directions to even-tually form a solid mat of plants. Apply an organic mulch after planting. Cross-pollination increases yields. Zones 1–6.

Cultivars: 'Ida', 'Red Pearl', 'Regal'.

Medlar (*Crataegus germanica*, also called *Mespilus germanica*)

Fruit: Fruit resembles a small, russeted apple. It ripens in late autumn but must be allowed to soften indoors. Ripe fruit has a baked-apple texture and a brisk, winelike flavor—much like old-fashioned applesauce with cinnamon.

Plant type: Small, deciduous tree. Flowers appear in late spring, after shoots have grown a few inches, and are white or slightly pink.

Culture: Grows best in a sunny location in any soil that is well drained and reasonably fertile. Plants are self-fertile. The tree needs little pruning beyond shaping when young. On older trees, prune out diseased or interfering wood. Zones 5–8.

Cultivars: 'Breda Giant', 'Marion'; few cultivars typically are available.

Mulberry (*Morus alba, M. nigra, M. rubra*)

Fruit: Fruits are shaped like blackberries but may be white, lavender, dark red, or black. Flavor may be sweet or a pleasant balance of acidity and sweetness. Ripening begins midsummer and continues for a few weeks or more, depending on the cultivar. Attractive to wildlife.

(continued)

Unusual Fruits *(cont.)*

Plant type: Deciduous 20- to 40-foot tree. Leaves are 2 to 5 inches long and may be pointed or divided into two or more lobes, even on the same tree. Male and female flowers may be borne on the same or separate trees.

Culture: Needs full sun, but not finicky as to soil. Don't plant near walkways or driveways, where stains from fallen fruits would be tracked indoors or splatter on cars. Most cultivars are self-fertile. No pruning is needed once young trees have been trained to a sturdy framework. Birds compete avidly for the fruit. Zones 5–10, depending on the cultivar.

Cultivars: Choose selections noted for high-quality fruits; beware male cultivars that produce no berries but abundant, allergy-inducing pollen.

Pawpaw (*Asimina triloba*), also called Hoosier banana, Michigan banana

Fruit: Pawpaw is the largest fruit native to North America. Greenish yellow skin becomes deeper yellow as the oblong fruit ripens. Flesh inside is creamy white and custardy, tasting like banana with hints of vanilla, pineapple, and mango. Embedded in the soft pulp is a row of large brown seeds. Fruit ripens in late summer and autumn.

Plant type: Small, pyramidal, deciduous tree with long, drooping leaves. Trees produce suckers and gradually form groves if suckers are not removed. Flowers are lurid purple, though not prominent, and appear late enough in spring to escape frosts. Leaves turn an attractive yellow in autumn.

Culture: Full sun or partial shade in any well-drained soil. Young trees benefit from shade. Trees do not need pruning, although mowing or cutting off suckers is necessary to contain the trees' tendency to spread. Zones 5–9.

Cultivars: Selections of pawpaw vary in availability, although new ones arise occasionally from university breeding programs and backyard pawpaw enthusiasts. 'Sunflower' and 'Overleese' are among the oldest and best-known cultivars; Shenandoah grafted pawpaw produces fruits of up to 1 pound each. Most cultivars ('Sunflower' is an exception) need cross-pollination.

Pomegranate (*Punica granatum*)

Fruit: Fruit is round and the size of a large apple. Inside the hard shell are hundreds of seeds, each surrounded by a sweetish-tart juice sac. Fruit color ranges from off-white to purplish or crimson. Fruit ripens in late summer.

Plant type: Deciduous or semideciduous small tree or shrub, 15 to 20 feet tall. Flowers are brilliant orange-red and are borne periodically from spring through summer toward the ends of branchlets.

Culture: Plant tolerates a wide range of

soil conditions. Train to a single or multiple stem, then prune every winter by thinning out crowded areas and removing interfering branches and some of the suckers. Zones 8–10, but yields best-quality fruits in dry, hot climates.

Cultivars: 'Foothill Early', 'Granada', 'Paper Shell', 'Ruby Red', 'Smith' (sold as Angel Red), 'Sweet Spanish', 'Wonderful'.

Prickly Pear (*Opuntia ficus-indica, O. tuna*, other species)

Fruit: Fruits, called tunas, are 1 to 3 inches across, pear- or fig-shaped, and yellowish green to dark purple in color. Except in some cultivars, the skin is covered with spines that must be rubbed off. Pulp is sweet, seedy, and red.

Plant type: Plants grow 3 to 15 feet tall. Cacti with flat pads covered with thorns, except for certain thornless cultivars. Pads are also edible once thorns have been rubbed or burned off, and play a significant role in southwestern Native cuisine. Flowers are very showy, orange or yellow.

Culture: Plant in full sun in well-drained soil or sand. Zones 5–10, depending on species.

Cultivars: Botanist Luther Burbank developed a spineless prickly pear, intended for cattle forage, that is popular for making nopales, a Mexican dish using cactus pads. White-fruited cultivars may be found as well as seedless and low-thorn selections.

Rose Hips (mostly *Rosa rugosa*, but other *Rosa* species also)

Fruit: Brilliant scarlet red, orange, or yellow, urn-shaped fruit good for jelly or for drying for use in herbal teas. Ripe flavor is good raw, but fruits are very seedy. The fruits (hips) ripen in late summer. The most renowned rose hip producer is *R. rugosa*, commonly known as the rugosa or Japanese rose.

Plant type: Deciduous shrub 4 to 8 feet tall with prickly stems and wrinkled leaves. Blooms heavily in spring and sporadically until frost. Flowers are 2 inches across, with single, semidouble, or double white, rose, purple, or pink petals, depending on the cultivar.

Culture: Tolerates almost any soil, even salty beach sand near the ocean. Full sun preferred. For maximum flowering and fruiting, prune away very old wood at or near ground level each winter. Self-fertile. Zones 2–7.

Serviceberry (*Amelanchier* spp.), also known as Juneberry and saskatoon

Fruit: Fruits are the size of blueberries and are dark blue, purple, or, in the case of a few cultivars, white. Flavor is sweet and juicy, with a hint of almond from the seeds. Fruits ripen in June or July, but the harvest season is very short for an individual plant. Attractive to wildlife.

(continued)

Unusual Fruits *(cont.)*

Plant type: Serviceberries with tasty fruits are represented by plants ranging in size from low-growing, spreading shrubs to small trees. In early spring, the plants are covered with white blossoms. Autumn color can be spectacular, as the leaves turn shades of purple, orange, and yellow.

Culture: Grows in sun or partial shade in a wide range of soil types. Tree species need little pruning. Bushy species should be pruned each winter, cutting away at their bases any shoots more than 4 years old, and thinning out the previous season's shoots so only a half dozen of the most vigorous ones remain. Birds are very fond of serviceberries. Zones 3–8.

Cultivars: *Amelanchier* selections tend to focus on the ornamental aspects of these large shrubs and small trees, but all bear edible fruit in early to mid-summer. *Amelanchier alnifolia* is a popular species for fruit production.

---

marjoram, onion, rosemary, and sage feature shades of gray and blue. (Sage foliage can also be variegated yellow and green; purple and green; and pink, white, purple, and green.) Beets, purple basil, red cabbage, red chard, purple ornamental kale, red lettuces, and purple mustard feature pink and red shades. Carrots, endive, white ornamental kale, variegated lemon balm, nasturtiums, and thyme feature light green, yellow, and white foliage. Fennel offers feathery, coppery bronze foliage. Asparagus has attractive green fernlike foliage.

Many hot peppers have it all: variegated white and green, or white, purple, and green foliage; attractive starlike white or purple flowers; and decorative fruits in green, white, yellow, cream, orange, red, and purple, often all on the same plant.

Vines: Peas look lovely trained on a fence and can be followed by cucumbers or squash as the season progresses. Hardy kiwi is a vigorous climber. Scarlet runner beans have bright red-orange flowers and are pretty planted with white-flowering cultivars of beans. Yard-long beans and asparagus beans produce fascinating fruit, often red or purple, an instant conversation piece. Indeterminate tomatoes can be trained on a trellis or arbor; let the side shoots grow in for maximum coverage. Cherry tomatoes work nicely in hanging baskets, and their colorful fruits add bright accents of red, orange, or yellow against the dark green leaves.

Groundcovers: Strawberries produce delicious fruit and attractive foliage; some species, such as alpine and Peruvian strawberries, will grow in shade. Violets produce edible ornamental flowers. Many herbs, including creeping thymes, Corsican mint, and pennyroyal, are low growing and vigorous and can be used as groundcovers.

Fragrant edibles: Certain fragrances, like the scent of marigold and zonal geranium (*Pelargonium*) foliage, may be attractive to some people and annoying to others. The most fragrant edibles include basil, chamomile, chives, fennel, mint, oregano, parsley, sage, strawberry, thyme, and fruit-scented sages like pineapple sage. Creeping varieties of thyme and oregano are low growing and work well planted between stepping-stones, where they will release their fragrances when brushed or lightly stepped on.

EGGPLANT

Solanum melongena
Solanaceae

A classic eggplant is deep purple and pear-shaped, but when you grow your own, you can try a cornucopia of colors and shapes, from elongated lavender and white Asian varieties to snow white selections and round violet-blushed Italian types. For successful growth and productivity, eggplants need steadily warm growing conditions for at least 3 months. Eggplants growing in cold soil or exposed to chilly weather typically grow poorly and produce fewer fruits and are more prone to insect and disease problems.

Planting: Give eggplants a head start on the growing season by starting them indoors 6 to 9 weeks before the average last frost date. Soak seeds overnight to encourage germination; sow them ¼ inch deep in a loose, fine medium, such as vermiculite. Use bottom heat to maintain a soil temperature of 80° to 90°F for the 8 to 10 days required for sprouting. Transplant seedlings to individual pots once they reach 3 inches. When outside nighttime air temperatures are above 50°F, gradually expose them to the outdoors to harden them off. Keep transplanting your seedlings into larger pots as you wait for both outdoor air and soil to warm up to at least 70°F.

Try growing eggplants in raised beds, which heat up more quickly in spring. Plants given plenty of room are healthier and more productive, so space them 2½ to 3 feet apart in all directions. Water well, pour 1 to 2 cups of compost tea around each plant, and firm the soil gently. See the Compost entry for instructions for making compost tea.

Eggplants are also good for container growing, with one plant per 5-gallon pot. Look for new introductions specifically developed for container culture.

Growing guidelines: Mulch immediately after transplanting, and gently hand-pull any invading weeds. Interplant an early crop, such as lettuce, between the eggplant transplants. When the eggplants bloom, apply more liquid fertilizer and repeat monthly. For best production, plants need 1 to 1½ inches of water a week.

Problems: Flea beetles, which chew many tiny holes in leaves, are eggplant's worst pest. To avoid this problem, keep plants indoors until early summer, or cover outdoor plants with floating row cover or dust the foliage with kaolin clay (reapply it after rain). If plants become severely infested, spraying *Beauveria bassiana* or spinosad may knock back the population of flea beetles and save your plants.

Handpick and destroy yellow-and-black-striped Colorado potato beetles and the yellow masses of eggs they lay on leaf undersides. Handpicking is also effective for tomato hornworms, 4-inch green caterpillars with white stripes. Don't destroy those covered with tiny white cocoons; these contain the parasitic offspring of the beneficial braconid wasp. Tiny spider mites cause yellow-stippled leaves; control these pests by knocking them off the plant with a spray of water. For details on controlling aphids and cutworms, see page 454.

The most common eggplant disease is verticillium wilt. Avoid it by planting resistant cultivars and by rotating crops.

Harvesting: Pick eggplant when the skin takes on a high gloss. To test, press the skin. If the indentation doesn't spring back, that fruit is ready for harvest. To harvest, cut the stem with a knife or pruning shears. Eggplants will keep for 2 weeks if refrigerated. If you cut open an eggplant fruit and find that the seeds inside have turned brown, the fruit is past prime quality and the flavor may be bitter. The best way to avoid this is by picking fruits on the young side, when they are one-third to two-thirds of their fully mature size.

ELDERBERRY

Sambucus spp.
Adoxaceae

Although they're not widely cultivated in North America, elderberries are worth trying for their beautiful—and edible—flowers and the unique flavor of the fruit: a medley of grape, raspberry, and blackberry. Just be sure you have plenty of room for these large, spreading plants; they're not for small gardens!

Types: *Sambucus nigra*, European or black elderberry, reaches 10 to 30 feet tall. It bears large clusters of yellowish white flowers in June, followed by shiny black berries in September. Most commercially available cultivars of this species have been selected for their ornamental qualities; for fruit production, choose American elderberry. Zones 5–8.

S. nigra ssp. *canadensis*, American elderberry, grows 6 to 12 feet tall. Native throughout most of the United States and Canada, it produces similar clusters of flowers in late June and, later, purple-black berries. Cultivars have been selected for larger fruits, improved flavor, and earlier ripening. Northern gardeners often raise elderberries as substitutes for grapes where the latter are not hardy or fail to ripen before frost. Zones 3–9.

Planting: Elderberries like a sunny location with lots of room to spread. They thrive in deep, moist soil well supplied with organic matter. Set young plants 5 feet apart in rows at least 8 feet apart, and keep them 10 feet from other plantings. Elderberry flowers are self-pollinating, but the plants are more productive if two or more cultivars are planted near each other.

Care: Use a thick layer of organic mulch to conserve moisture. If plants aren't growing well, apply an organic plant food containing nitrogen under the mulch; otherwise, fertilization usually isn't needed. Water in dry seasons.

Pruning: Prune away dead canes in spring, and cut out all the old canes whenever bushes become crowded. Vigorous elderberries produce an abundance of suckers, so keep plants in neat rows by frequent clipping or mowing. Dig and transplant suckers if you want new plants.

Problems: Elderberries are remarkably free from disease and insect pests, but birds love the fruit, and it is not easy to cover the tall bushes with netting at harvesttime. If birds aren't too numerous and you have the space, plant extra bushes. When berries are abundant, birds tend to tire of them after a few days and leave the ones that ripen later. Or pick berries a day or two before they are ripe and set them in a warm room, where they'll continue to ripen.

Winter damage can be a problem some years. The plant's roots are very hardy, but extreme cold sometimes injures the canes. Fortunately, the fruit forms on new growth, so even when damage is severe, it seldom affects the crop. Since blooms don't appear until summer, late spring frosts never hurt them. If, however, you live where fall frosts come early, plant early-ripening cultivars for the best results.

Harvesting: The clusters of tiny white flowers in summer are good for tea and other treats. Pick them as soon as they open, and dip them in a batter and fry them. To make a tasty "tea," add a few flower clusters to a gallon glass jar filled with water and a bit of lemon juice and sugar. Set it in the sun for a day, then strain out the flowers.

Soon after blooming, green fruits form and ripen to a rich dark purple-black color. Pick the whole fruit cluster and strip off the berries later when you're ready to use them. Most people do not eat elderberries out of the hand (the raw berries, and other plant parts, are somewhat toxic) but instead make them into tarts, pies, and other desserts or process them into jelly, juice, or wine. They're a great substitute for blueberries in many recipes.

ELM

See *Ulmus*

ENDIVE

Cichorium endivia

Asteraceae

The loose, lacy-edged leaves of curly endive are slightly bitter, as are the broad leaves of its close relative, escarole. Both crops have the same growing requirements, and although you can plant them as spring crops, they are ideal for fall harvesting: Frost improves the plants' flavor and makes them less bitter.

Planting: Both curly endive and escarole prefer humus-rich soil in full sun.

For an early-summer harvest, sow seeds indoors in flats 2 months before the last frost date; thin to 6 inches apart. Four weeks after sowing, plant the 4- to 5-inch seedlings 1 foot apart, slightly deeper in the soil than they were in flats. Provide shade if the weather turns hot.

For fall crops, seed in July, about 90 days before the date of the first frost; stagger plantings every

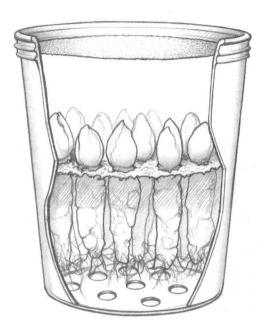

Belgian endive. Enjoy a special addition to salads by growing Belgian endive in containers indoors during the winter.

2 weeks to extend the harvest. Water the ground thoroughly before sowing three seeds per inch; cover the seeds with ⅓ inch of sand, soil, or compost. Thin the seedlings to at least 1 foot apart in all directions. Overlapping leaves can cause the plants to rot.

Growing guidelines: Water regularly, because leaves will be tough and bitter if the soil dries out. Endive needs about 1 inch of water per week. Wet plants tend to rot, though, so soak the soil, not the foliage.

Blanching keeps light out of the plant's interior and turns the heart a creamy yellow color. To blanch endive during the last 2 to 3 weeks of growth, tie the leaf tops together with rubber bands or twine, or cover the plant with an overturned clay pot. Make sure the leaves are dry when

Forcing Belgian Endive

Belgian endive (*Cichorium intybus*) is a different species from curly endive and escarole. Under normal growing conditions, Belgian endive produces bitter greens, but when grown indoors out of season, it makes a delicious winter salad crop.

Start by sowing seeds outdoors in late spring in a bed with deep, loose soil. Dig up the roots in fall, and cut off the tops 2 inches above the crown. Trim the roots and set them upright in boxes, deep pots, or a plastic 5-gallon bucket. Fill the containers with potting mix to the tops of the roots; add 6 to 8 inches of sand on top of that. Set the pots in a spot where the temperature stays between 60° and 70°F, and keep the sand moist. Harvest the heads when their tips peek up through the sand.

you do this, or the head may rot. Blanching produces a milder, less bitter flavor, but it also reduces endive's vitamin content.

Problems: Endive is usually problem-free. To avoid rot while plants are being blanched, untie plants after a rainstorm, and let the leaves dry before retying. For details on controlling the few aphids or cutworms that may attack, see the chart on page 454.

Harvesting: Harvest individual leaves or an entire plant when needed. Cut the plants with a knife at ground level. If you leave undamaged roots and 1 inch of stem, new growth may occur in warm weather.

EPIMEDIUM

Epimedium, bishop's hat. Deciduous, evergreen, or semievergreen perennial groundcovers.

Description: *Epimedium grandiflorum*, long-spurred epimedium, fairy wings, grows 1 foot tall. Leaves are divided into leathery, heart-shaped leaflets to 3 inches long. New leaves are tinged with pink, maturing to green, then turning bronze in autumn. In spring, plants bear loose sprays of small, spurred flowers in white, pink, or violet. Zones 3–8.

How to grow: Epimediums thrive in humus-rich, well-drained soil in shade; they will also do well in sun with evenly moist soil. Mulch plants with leaf mold to retain moisture. Divide after flowering, setting plants 8 to 10 inches apart. Cut off old leaves in late winter before flowering. Plants are evergreen in the South with protection, deciduous or semievergreen in the North.

Landscape use: Epimediums are grown primarily for their striking foliage. Use them in the shade garden, including in dry shade, under trees, and among shrubs.

EROSION

See Soil

ESPALIER

See Pruning and Training

EUCALYPTUS

Eucalyptus, gum tree. Evergreen or deciduous flowering trees or shrubs.

Description: *Eucalyptus cinerea*, silver-dollar tree, argyle apple, grows 20 to 30 feet in the landscape with an open, irregular form. The aromatic juvenile foliage is round, silvery gray-green, and arranged in pairs on the branch. Reddish brown fibrous bark is typical of the group of eucalyptus Australians call stringybarks. Zones 8–10.

E. gunnii, cider gum, has a mature height of 15 to 40 feet. Cider gum has shedding, green-and-white mottled bark and yellow fall flowers. The evergreen leaves are opposite, round, and blue-green when young, maturing to a darker green, lance shape. Zones 8–10.

How to grow: Native to Australia, eucalyptus trees are invasive in some parts of California and in Hawaii. They produce a chemical that inhibits the growth of plants around them. In addition, their bark litter is extremely flammable, making them poor landscape choices in fire-prone areas. Eucalyptus are grown primarily on the West Coast of the United States where conditions are similar to those of their native habitat. The Southeast's warm autumns cause late-season growth, which leads to cold injury. In cold-winter regions, fast-growing eucalyptus may be grown as annual shrubs. If you do grow eucalyptus, give them full sun and dry, extremely well-drained soil. High fertility and excess moisture cause root rot and rank topgrowth. Provide support, such as stakes, when necessary. Bees make excellent honey from the flowers of most eucalyptus.

Landscape uses: Eucalyptus trees are used on dry, infertile sites where screening or bank stabilization might be necessary, but native trees are better choices. Some gardeners grow eucalyptus strictly for the juvenile foliage, which is used in floral arrangements, or as houseplants. In this case, the plants are cut back close to the ground each year (a practice called coppicing) to prevent the development of adult foliage.

EUONYMUS

Euonymus, spindle tree. Evergreen or deciduous shrubs or small trees; evergreen groundcovers or vines.

Description: *Euonymus alatus*, burning bush or winged spindle tree, is a popular 12- to 15-foot, deciduous shrub grown for its scarlet fall foliage. It invades wild areas, forming dense thickets, because birds carry its seeds from bushes planted in backyards and public landscapes. Whenever possible, avoid making new plantings of burning bush. Consider native alternatives such as spicebush (*Lindera benzoin*), strawberry bush (*Euonymus americanus*), maple-leaf viburnum (*Viburnum acerifolium*), wild hydrangea (*Hydrangea arborescens*), or red chokeberry (*Aronia arbutifolia*). Zones 4–8.

E. bungeanus, winterberry euonymus, is a tree-form euonymus that grows to a mature height of about 18 feet. As the tree ages, interesting striations appear on its trunk. This tree has yellow fall color and pink fruits, which open to expose bright, red-orange seed coats that persist into the winter. Zones 4–7.

E. fortunei, wintercreeper, is an evergreen species with countless cultivars that have green or variegated leaves and range from groundcovers to vines to tall shrubs. It, too, is an aggressive invasive that is best avoided because it spreads rapidly, can climb and weaken trees, and can outcompete native species. It is prone to serious infestation by scale insects. Zones 4–9.

E. japonicus, Japanese euonymus, is an evergreen shrub that grows to a mature height of 6 to 12 feet with an upright form. The dark green, serrated, leathery leaves often display dramatic variegated patterns. Zones 8–9.

How to grow: Site deciduous species in full sun to promote robust growth and fully developed fall color. Plant evergreen euonymus in a spot protected from sun and wind. North of Zone 8, plant in fall or spring; in Zones 8–9, plant in fall or winter. Euonymus thrives in humus-rich soil with even moisture and good drainage. The deciduous species appear to be less susceptible to scale than the evergreens, but they do sometimes get it—usually on the branches rather than the leaves. Control scale with oil sprays. Deer with few other food sources will eat deciduous euonymous; where deer are a problem, choose another shrub.

Landscape uses: Although they are still widely sold, burning bush and wintercreeper both are invasive exotics that should not be planted because of the ease with which these species crowd out native plants. Whenever possible, choose native alternatives.

EVENING PRIMROSE

See *Oenothera*

EVERGREENS

Gardeners know that there's far more to evergreens than just Christmas trees. All plants that retain their green color throughout the year can properly be called evergreens, from trees and woody shrubs to perennials, so there is a broad range of shapes and sizes to choose from. Woody evergreens are divided into two groups according to the general shape of their leaves. Narrow-leaved or needle-leaved evergreens include plants such as junipers (*Juniperus* spp.), pines (*Pinus* spp.), spruces (*Picea* spp.), and yews (*Taxus* spp.).

Broadleaved evergreens, which usually have showy flowers or fruit, have leaves in a variety of shapes and sizes that usually are somewhat thickened or leathery. In general, broadleaved evergreens are not as cold-hardy as needle-leaved evergreens, but some types, such as evergreen azaleas and rhododendrons (*Rhododendron* spp.) and hollies (*Ilex* spp.) are widely adaptable. Tender evergreens, such as gardenias (*Gardenia* spp.), are landscape plants only in the warmest regions of the country; elsewhere they may be grown in containers or treated as annuals. Some species—sweet bay magnolia (*Magnolia virginiana*), for example—are evergreen in warm climates, semievergreen in moderate climates, and deciduous in the coldest part of their range.

There are evergreens suitable for growing throughout the United States. For the best choices for your garden, consult your local Cooperative Extension office or a botanical garden or nursery in your area. You'll also find more information on specific evergreens throughout this book. For listings of specific evergreens, check the Quick Reference Guide on page 678.

Landscaping with Evergreens

Low maintenance and moderate water use are two important advantages of evergreens, and there are many reasons to incorporate them into your landscape plan. Evergreens add color and form to the winter landscape in areas where deciduous plants predominate. Use them to screen unattractive views year-round and to create secluded, private

KEY WORDS *Evergreens*

Evergreen. A plant that retains its leaves year-round.

Deciduous. A plant that drops its leaves in fall.

Semievergreen. A plant that keeps some of its leaves year-round. Many semievergreen plants, including many perennials, are evergreen in mild climates and semievergreen to deciduous in colder regions.

Candles. New shoots that grow from the branch tips of needle-leaved evergreens in a flush of spring growth.

---

sitting areas. In summer, depend on them to provide a backdrop for deciduous shrubs and flowering perennials.

To reduce the lawn area in your yard, replace lawn grass with low-growing evergreens such as creeping juniper (*Juniperus horizontalis*), bearberry cotoneaster (*Cotoneaster dammeri*), bearberry (*Arctostaphylos uva-ursi*), or dwarf, spreading forms of Japanese holly (*Ilex crenata*). Evergreen perennials such as moss phlox (*Phlox subulata*), sedums (*Sedum* spp.), and hens and chicks (*Sempervivum* spp., *Jovibarba* spp.) also make excellent evergreen lawn substitutes.

Since popular evergreens like pines and junipers require at least 8 hours of sun per day to perform well, when choosing shrubs or groundcovers, be sure to use shade-tolerant species on sites that are in partial shade. Evergreens that thrive in partial to full shade include rhododendrons and azaleas, American holly (*Ilex opaca*), and hemlocks (*Tsuga* spp.).

Evergreens are always a popular choice for foundation plantings. To avoid a spotty appearance, select species with similar form for a foundation planting or an evergreen shrub border. For example, try grouping spreading junipers with cotoneasters, dwarf forms of false cypress (*Chamaecyparis* spp.), Japanese pieris or lily-of-the-valley bush (*Pieris japonica*), yews (*Taxus* spp.), and hollies. Evergreens are most attractive when they are left to retain their natural shape and allowed to blend together. Shearing them into regimented gumdrop-shaped mounds not only prevents this, it also increases maintenance for the life of the plant, since you'll have to shear them at least annually to maintain the shape.

Whether you are planning a foundation planting or a shrub border, or just selecting evergreens to accent your landscape, be sure to learn the mature height and spread of the plants you are considering. In most cases, named cultivars are the best choice, since they have been selected for outstanding characteristics like dwarf size, unusual form, outstanding foliage or flower color, and reliable hardiness or performance. It pays to shop for just the right evergreens instead of picking up inexpensive, unnamed plants at big box stores. For example, American arborvitaes (*Thuja occidentalis*) look very cute and well-behaved growing in nursery pots, but plant one under a window, and you are going to be forever hacking that plant back, since the species matures at 30 to 60 feet. At a better

Which Is Which?

Sorting out the needle-leaved evergreens takes close-up detective work. Here are some clues to help you identify them,

- Arborvitaes (*Thuja* spp.) and false cypresses (*Chamaecyparis* spp.): Scalelike needles in fan-shaped sprays; soft to the touch.

- Firs (*Abies* spp.): Needles are flat, soft, two-sided, 1 to 2½ inches long.

- Hemlocks (*Tsuga* spp.): Needles are flat, ¼ to 1 inch long, with two white-band markings on the underside.

- Junipers (*Juniperus* spp.): Sharp awl-shaped needles, as well as fans of scale-like needles; both types harsh to the touch.

- Pines (*Pinus* spp.): Needles are thin, 2 to 5 inches long, in bundles of two, three, or five.

- Spruces (*Picea* spp.): Needles are thin, ½ to 1¼ inches long, with four sides and sharp points. Feel the edges by rolling needles between thumb and finger.

- Yews (*Taxus* spp.): Needles are flat, lustrous, dark green, ½ to 1½ inches long. Young twigs have green bark.

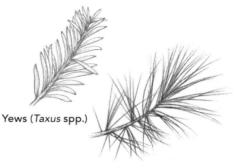

Yews (*Taxus* spp.)

Pines (*Pinus* spp.)

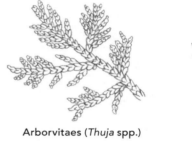

Arborvitaes (*Thuja* spp.)

Spruces (*Picea* spp.)

Hemlocks (*Tsuga* spp.)

Firs (*Abies* spp.)

Junipers (*Juniperus* spp.)

nursery, you may pay a little more, but you can find a cultivar that is exactly the size you need, so you'll save time and money in the long run. It's also important to be patient. Give your new small plants time to mature and fill the space you have planned.

Consider using evergreens to create a backdrop to provide contrast and to showcase other flowering shrubs and perennials. Plant a living privacy fence to screen the deck, pool, or lawn. For an accent plant, choose a weeping white pine such as *Pinus strobus* 'Pendula' or a blue Atlas cedar such as *Cedrus atlantica*, Glauca Group. Evergreens can even help save money on fuel bills, too: Plant them as a hedge to break the force of winter winds or to shade an area from hot summer sun.

Planting and Care

Most evergreens like rich, humusy, moist but well-drained soil. Cypress (*Cupressus* spp.), junipers, and pines tolerate dry soil once their roots are established. Some evergreens, such as lily-of-the-valley bush, heaths and heathers (*Erica* spp. and *Calluna* spp.), laurels (*Kalmia* spp.), and azaleas and rhododendrons, prefer acid soil. See the pH entry for information on how to alter soil pH in the planting area for these plants.

Carry an evergreen by its rootball or container, never by the trunk or branches. For planting and staking instructions, see the Planting entry. If your evergreens develop pest or disease problems, consult the Pests and Plant Diseases and Disorders entries.

Pruning

Evergreens that are the proper size for their location need very little pruning. Their natural growth habit is interesting and attractive. To remove unhealthy or errant growth, use a thinning cut, pruning off branches nearly flush against the branch from which they originate. For information on how to make pruning cuts correctly, see the Pruning and Training entry.

Unlike broadleaved evergreens, needle-leaved evergreens aren't quick to resprout after pruning. Take care to prune them properly. Follow these steps when pruning evergreens.

- Thin evergreens by removing branches any time of the year. Cut stray branches far enough to the inside of the plant to hide the stub. Branches cut back beyond the green needles generally will not sprout new growth.

- Don't cut the central leader at the top of the tree—an evergreen without its central leader will have a drastically different shape.

- Prune arborvitaes, hemlocks, junipers, and yews throughout the growing season.

- Cut back firs, pines, and spruces only in spring when "candles" of new growth appear at the tips of the branches. To encourage denseness or shape the tree, cut off about half or two-thirds of the candle.

- Trim your evergreens gradually. If you cut off more than a third of the total green on the plant, it may die.

F

FENCING

No matter how fond of animals you may be, there is nothing heartwarming about the sight of some furry creature munching away on your garden's bounty. Repellents, traps, and scare devices can help discourage, or fend off, hungry wildlife. But in many cases, especially in rural areas, a fence may be the only effective way to keep marauding mammals away from your landscape plantings and food crops.

The size and type of fence to use depends largely on the kind of animal you're trying to stave off. A simple 2-foot-high chicken-wire fence will discourage rabbits, but a more formidable barrier is necessary to deal with such garden burglars as deer, raccoons, skunks, or woodchucks.

Cost and appearance are also important considerations. A solid or picket-style wooden fence is attractive but expensive and difficult to install. Wooden fences tend to shade the perimeter of the garden and require regular maintenance. Wire fencing and electric fencing are less costly but are by no means inexpensive, particularly in the case of a large area.

You may be able to forgo fencing off your entire garden or orchard by erecting barriers around only those beds or crops most vulnerable to animal pests. A fenced plot for corn and melons is a good idea where raccoons are a problem. You'll find more information about making barriers for individual plants, as well as suggestions for using traps and repellants, in the Animal Pests entry.

Chicken-Wire Garden Fence

A simple 3-foot-high chicken-wire fence and a subterranean chicken-wire barrier can protect your garden from nearly all small and medium-size animals, including the burrowing types.

Chicken wire comes in a variety of widths and mesh sizes and is sold in 50-foot rolls. The 1-inch mesh is best for excluding animal pests.

Building the fence: The first step in building a fence is to decide where you want it to run. Mark the corners with small stakes and measure the perimeter. You will need two lengths of 1-inch mesh chicken wire, one 3 feet wide for the fence itself, and another 1 foot (or more) wide to line an underground trench. Or purchase one length wide enough to do both.

You also need one 5-foot post for each corner, additional posts for long sections, and one post for each side of the gate(s). Steel T-posts are inexpensive, can be driven into the ground with a hammer or sledge, and come with clips for attaching the fencing. Rot-resistant wooden posts such as locust provide excellent support, but you'll need a posthole digger to set them. Also, nailing or stapling fencing to dense wood can be difficult.

Stretch string between the small stakes to mark the fencing line. Dig a trench 6 inches deep and at least 6 inches wide along the outside of the string. Set the posts 2 feet deep along the marked fence line.

Line the trench with the 1-foot-wide chicken wire bent into the shape of an L, so that the wire covers the bottom of the trench as well as the side nearest the fence, as shown. Be sure the wire extends an inch or so above ground level and is securely attached to the posts.

Stretch the 3-foot-wide chicken wire between the posts and attach it to them. The fencing should overlap the chicken wire lining the trench by 2 or 3 inches. Use wire to fasten the two layers together. (If you use a single, wider length of chicken wire, you save this last step.) Then refill the trench with soil.

Altering the design: If woodchucks are a serious problem, make the wire-lined trench a foot or more deep and up to 3 feet wide. If you're trying to keep gophers out, dig the trench 2 feet deep and 6 inches wide, line it with ¼-inch mesh hardware cloth, and/or fill it with coarse gravel.

Raccoons are good climbers. To foil them, extend the top part of the fence to at least 4 feet, and don't attach the topmost 1 foot of fencing to the posts. When the burglars clamber up, the loose

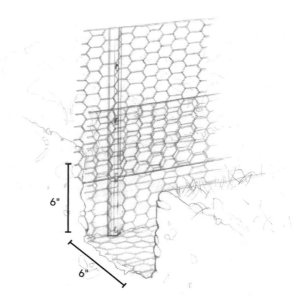

Chicken-wire fence. A chicken-wire fence supplemented with a 6-inch trench lined with additional chicken wire provides protection against animals that try to burrow underneath fences to raid a garden.

section will flop backward and keep the raccoons from climbing over the top.

If pests continue to raid your garden despite the chicken-wire barrier, you can add a single-strand electric fence, as shown on the next page.

Most garden supply stores sell easy-to-install electric fence kits, with solar-powered or conventional plug-in battery-powered chargers, 100 feet of wire, and plastic posts. You'll find a wealth of options on the Internet for purchasing individual components designed with the home gardener in mind.

Deer Fencing

Fencing deer out of a garden requires a more sophisticated approach. A six-strand high-voltage electric fence, with the wires spaced 10 inches apart and the bottom one 8 inches off the ground, is an effective deterrent. But it is an impractical choice for many small-scale growers because of the high cost and complex installation.

Another alternative is to build a fence that is simply too high for a deer to jump over. The absolute minimum height for a jump-proof nonelectric deer fence is 8 feet. Standard woven-wire farm fencing comes 4 feet tall, so it's a common practice to stack one course on top of another to create an 8-foot fence. This method is neither inexpensive nor easy. Yet another option is weather-resistant polypropylene mesh fencing, which is sold as deer fencing and is available in kits for home garden use. Polypropylene mesh is available in several strengths: Use the highest strength if deer are a problem in your area.

Yet another option is to erect two fences, 3 or 4 feet high and spaced 3 feet apart, of welded-wire

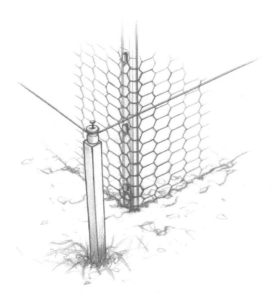

Animal-proof fence. Adding a low, single-strand electric fence 6 inches outside a nonelectric fence should keep out virtually any animal pest except deer. Set up the electric fence with the wire 4 to 6 inches above ground level.

or snow fencing. Deer seldom jump a fence when they can see another fence or obstacle just on the other side. If you already have a fence around your garden and deer become a problem, add a 3-foot nonelectric or a 2-foot single-strand electric fence 3 feet outside the existing one.

FERNS

Ferns are the quintessential shade plants. Their graceful, arching fronds conjure up images of shaded retreats and cool walks by wooded streams. Ferns will grow in the deepest, darkest woodland. They will grow in moist soil and even standing water. However, not all ferns are limited to the shade. Marsh fern, cinnamon fern, and bracken fern grow in full sun. (See "Ferns for Special Uses" on page 210 for more on this.) But most ferns prefer moist soil and partial shade.

Ferns in the Landscape

Use large ferns as foundation plantings along with or instead of shrubs. Plant them along fences or walls to break up the flat expanse, or place them to hide the "bare ankles" of sparse shrubs or perennials. Large hostas and ferns will add interest to a shaded spot. Mass plantings of ostrich fern (*Matteuccia struthiopteris*) and osmundas (*Osmunda* spp.) are very effective for filling bare spaces or adding depth in the shade of tall trees. They also form a perfect backdrop for annuals and perennials.

Use medium-size ferns such as New York fern (*Thelypteris noveboracensis*), lady fern (*Athyrium filix-femina*), and maidenhair fern (*Adiantum pedatum*) in combination with spring wildflowers. Their unfurling fronds are a beautiful complement to spring beauty (*Claytonia virginica*), wild blue phlox

(*Phlox divaricata*), and others. Fronds will fill in the blank spots left when wildflowers and spring bulbs go dormant.

Try ferns along the border of a shaded walk to define the path, or ferns with creeping rhizomes on a slope to hold the soil. Mix textures and add evergreen ferns such as wood ferns (*Dryopteris* spp.) and Christmas ferns (*Polystichum acrostichoides*) for late-season and winter interest.

Crown-forming ferns like interrupted fern (*Osmunda claytoniana*) and cinnamon fern (*O. cinnamomea*) have a graceful vase shape and make excellent accents alone or in small groupings. They grow slowly, so they won't take over the garden like some running ferns such as eastern hay-scented fern (*Dennstaedtia punctilobula*). Plant rampant growers where they can spread to form groundcovers and fill in under shrubs. For low, wet areas, chain ferns (*Woodwardia* spp.), osmundas, and marsh fern (*Thelypteris palustris*) are stunning. Combine them with the spiky foliage of yellow flags (*Iris pseudacorus*) and arrowheads (*Sagittaria* spp.).

Since foliage is the fern's major attraction, consider the color and texture of the fronds. The most colorful garden fern is the Japanese painted fern, *Athyrium niponicum*. Its hybrids and cultivars, including the many cultivars of *A. n.* 'Pictum', may have fronds that are gray, blue-gray, gray-green, gray-white, or seemingly variegated with colorful burgundy midribs. (In fact, 'Pictum' is considered so outstanding that it was named Perennial Plant of the Year for 2004 by the Perennial Plant Association.) All of these but the gray-green cultivars look great with blue hostas and heucheras with garnet or purple foliage or gray leaves with garnet veining (*Heuchera* 'Palace Purple' is a well-known purple-leaved cultivar). The explosion in heuchera breeding has also produced cultivars with gray-green foliage, some with garnet veining, that combine beautifully with the gray-green cultivars of Japanese painted fern; add green or green and white hostas for textural contrast.

Japanese painted ferns aren't the only ones that offer color and shine to the shade garden. Chartreuse-colored interrupted fern and maidenhair fern combine well with dark ferns and other foliage. The coppery new fronds of autumn fern (*Dryopteris erythrosora*) and its orange-red cultivar 'Brilliance' add warmth to shady sites and look lovely with chartreuse-leaved hostas, heucheras, and Allegheny foamflowers, as well as heuchera cultivars with coppery foliage. The shiny fronds of ferns such as autumn fern, deer fern (*Blechnum spicant*), and hart's-tongue fern (*Asplenium scolopendrium*) glisten in filtered sunlight.

Preparing the Soil

Ferns generally require rich, moist soil with extra organic matter. Some require a drier, less-fertile soil. If ferns haven't done well for you in the past, have your soil tested by your local extension service or a soil-testing lab to determine soil fertility and pH. Some ferns are extremely fussy about pH. For more on soils, soil testing, and pH, see the Soil and pH entries.

For large and medium-size ferns, dig the planting area deeply (at the very least, turn the soil to a spade's depth). Plant smaller ferns such as Japanese painted fern as you would any perennial. Sprinkle on organic fertilizer, if needed, when you add soil amendments. For more on organic fertilizers, see the Fertilizers entry.

Buying and Planting Ferns

Garden centers offer a few ferns, but you can find more through nursery catalogs and Web sites that

Ferns for Special Uses

Not all ferns are made for the shade—some can take full sun and dry soil. And many ferns are evergreen, enhancing the garden all year. These ferns are all hardy to at least Zone 6; many are hardy to Zone 4, and some to Zone 3.

Ferns for Sunny Sites

Unlike most ferns, deer fern (*Blechnum spicant*), eastern hay-scented fern (*Dennstaedtia punctilobula*), fragrant wood fern (*Dryopteris fragrans*), and sword ferns (*Polystichum* spp.) can stand at least a half day of sun. For full sun and moist soil, choose water clover (*Marsilea quadrifolia*), sensitive fern (*Onoclea sensibilis*), marsh fern (*Thelypteris palustris*), and chain ferns (*Woodwardia* spp.). Ferns that thrive in full sun and dry soil include lip ferns (*Cheilanthes* spp.), parsley fern (*Cryptogramma crispa*), polypody ferns (*Polypodium* spp.), bracken (*Pteridium aquilinum*), and rusty woodsia (*Woodsia ilvensis*). You can grow interrupted fern (*Osmunda claytoniana*) in either full sun and moist soil or shade and dry soil.

Evergreen Ferns

Evergreen ferns add color and structure to the garden all year. The best evergreen choices include spleenworts (*Asplenium* spp.), grape ferns (*Botrychium* spp.), parsley fern (*Cryptogramma crispa*), wood ferns (*Dryopteris* spp.), hart's-tongue fern (*Asplenium scolopendrium*), polypody ferns (*Polypodium* spp.), sword ferns (*Polystichum* spp.), and chain ferns (*Woodwardia* spp.).

---

specialize in perennials, shade plants, or ferns. No matter where you buy, make sure plants are nursery propagated, not collected from the wild. Large plants at low prices usually mean wild-collected plants. Don't be afraid to ask for the vendor's sources.

Plant ferns in fall or early spring. Garden-center plants will be potted, but mail-order plants are likely to arrive bareroot. Remove potted plants from their containers, cutting the plastic if necessary. Very carefully score the rootball with a sharp knife. Make three to five shallow cuts lengthwise down the rootball. This breaks up the solid mass of fibrous roots that often forms along the container wall. Plant the fern at the same level at which it was growing in the pot. Planting too deeply will kill plants with single crowns.

Set bareroot plants with creeping rhizomes (underground stems that produce both roots and fronds) ½ to 1 inch below the surface. Large rhizomes can be planted deeper. Set single-crowned ferns like osmundas and ostrich ferns with the crown above soil level. Place the upper part of the rhizome above the soil surface, with the crown 3 to 5 inches above the soil, depending on the plant's size. Finally, don't plant too thickly, since most ferns spread rapidly.

Continuing Care

Ferns are a carefree group of plants. Mulch with shredded leaves or bark to help control weeds and conserve moisture. Ferns never need staking, pinching, or pruning. You may have to remove an occasional damaged frond, but that—and watering during dry periods while the plants are getting established—about sums up the care requirements for ferns during the growing season.

Each spring, remove last fall's leaves from the fern bed, shred them, and return them to the bed. Clear the bed early to avoid damage to emerging fiddleheads. Don't rake the beds, or you may damage crowns and growing tips. You won't need fertilizer if you leave the mulch to rot into the soil.

FERTILIZERS

For organic gardeners, creating a living soil, rich in humus and nutrients, is the key to growing great fruits and vegetables, abundant flowers, and long-lived ornamental trees and shrubs. The overall fertility and viability of the soil, rather than the application of fertilizers as quick fixes, is at the very heart of organic gardening.

But, like all gardeners, organic gardeners have to start somewhere. Your soil may be deficient in certain nutrients, it may not have excellent soil structure, or its pH may be too high or too low. Unless you've lucked into the perfect soil, you'll have to work to make it ideal for gardening. And even if your soil is rich and fabulous, hungry annual vegetables and flowers need supplemental feeding to produce and look their best. To learn about soil building, turn to the Soil, Organic Matter, and Compost entries. To learn how to use organic fertilizers to feed your plants during the soil-building years, read on here.

Chemical versus Organic

Many organic materials serve as both fertilizers and soil conditioners—they feed both soils and plants. This is one of the most important differences between a chemical approach and an organic approach toward soil care and fertilizing. Soluble chemical fertilizers contain mineral salts that plant roots can absorb quickly. However, these salts do not provide a food source for soil microorganisms and earthworms and will even repel earthworms because they acidify the soil. Over time, soils treated only with synthetic chemical fertilizers lose organic matter and the all-important living organisms that help to build healthy soil. As soil structure declines and water-holding capacity diminishes, more and more of the chemical fertilizer applied will leach through the soil. In turn, it will take ever-increasing amounts of chemicals to stimulate plant growth. When you use organic fertilizers, you avoid throwing your soil into this kind of crisis condition.

The manufacturing process of most chemical fertilizers depends on nonrenewable resources, such as coal and natural gas. Others are made by treating rock minerals with acids to make them more soluble. Fortunately, organic fertilizer products made from natural plant and animal materials or from mined rock minerals are gaining widespread acceptance among gardeners and are much more available than they were even 10 years ago. However, the national standards that define and distinguish organic fertilizers from chemical fertilizers are complicated, so it can be hard to be sure that a commercial fertilizer product labeled "organic" truly contains only safe, natural ingredients. When considering options for your garden, look for label terms like "natural organic," "slow release," and "low analysis." Be wary of products claiming to be organic that have an NPK (nitrogen-phosphorus-potassium) ratio that adds up to more than 15. By reading labels and shopping at businesses that offer organic products, you'll find plenty of products

KEY WORDS *Fertilizers*

Fertilizers. Materials that feed growing plants.

Soil conditioners. Materials added to feed and enrich the soil.

NPK ratio. The three numbers on a fertilizer label that identify the percentage of three major plant nutrients—nitrogen (N), phosphorus (P), and potassium (K)—in that fertilizer.

Top-dress. To apply fertilizer evenly over a field or bed of growing plants.

Side-dress. To apply fertilizer alongside plants growing in rows.

Broadcast. To spread fertilizer evenly across an area, by hand or with a spreading tool.

Foliar feed. To supply nutrients by spraying liquid fertilizer directly on plant foliage.

Leaching. The downward movement or runoff of nutrients dissolved in the soil solution.

---

formulated to provide appropriate amounts of the nutrients your plants need while supporting and improving the health of the soil in your garden.

Using Organic Fertilizers

If you're a gardener who's making the switch from chemical to organic fertilizers, you may be afraid that using organic materials will be more complicated and less convenient than using pre-mixed chemical fertilizers. Not so! Organic fertilizer blends can be just as convenient and effective as blended synthetic fertilizers. You don't need to custom feed your plants organically unless it's an activity you enjoy. While some longtime organic gardeners will spread a little bloodmeal around their tomatoes at planting, and then some bonemeal just when the blossoms are about to pop, most gardeners will be satisfied to make one or two applications of general-purpose organic fertilizer throughout the garden during the growing season.

Convenient products like dehydrated organic cow-manure pellets and liquid seaweed make it easy to fertilize houseplants and containers, too. (Don't use fish emulsion indoors, though, because of its strong odor. Save it for your outdoor containers and garden plants.)

If you want to try a plant-specific approach to fertilizing, you can use a variety of specialty organic fertilizers that are available from Internet garden supply companies or at most well-stocked garden centers and home stores. You can find everything from organic tomato and rose fertilizer mixes to organic fertilizer mixes especially created for transplants, lawns, heavy bloom production, even containers.

You can also make custom mixes to address your plants' specific needs. For example, you can use bat and bird guano, composted chicken manure, bloodmeal, chicken-feather meal, or fish meal as nitrogen sources. Bonemeal is a good source of phosphorus, and kelp or greensand are organic sources of potassium. The chart on common organic fertilizers on pages 214 to 216 lists average nutrient analysis and suggested application rates for the most commonly available organic fertilizers.

Dry Organic Fertilizers

Dry organic fertilizers can consist of a single material, such as rock phosphate or kelp (a type of nutrient-rich seaweed), or they can be a blend of many ingredients. Almost all organic fertilizers provide a broad array of nutrients, but blends are specially formulated to provide balanced amounts of nitrogen, potassium, and phosphorus, as well as micronutrients. There are many commercial blends, but you can make your own general-purpose fertilizer by mixing individual amendments.

Applying dry fertilizers: The most common way to apply dry fertilizer is to broadcast it and then hoe or rake it into the top 4 to 6 inches of soil. You can add small amounts to planting holes or rows as you plant seeds or transplants. Unlike dry synthetic fertilizers, most organic fertilizers are nonburning and will not harm delicate seedling roots.

During the growing season, boost plant growth by side-dressing dry fertilizers in crop rows or around the drip line of trees or shrubs. It's best to work side-dressings into the top inch of the soil.

Liquid Organic Fertilizers

Use liquid fertilizers to give your plants a light nutrient boost or snack every month or even every 2 weeks during the growing season. Simply mix the foliar spray in the tank of a backpack sprayer, and spray all your plants at the same time.

Plants can absorb liquid fertilizers through both their roots and through leaf pores. Foliar feeding can supply nutrients when they are lacking or unavailable in the soil, or when roots are stressed. It is especially effective for giving fast-growing plants like vegetables an extra boost during the growing season. Some foliar fertilizers,

Mix and Match

If you want to mix your own general-purpose organic fertilizer, try combining individual amendments in the amounts shown here. Just pick one ingredient from each of the three groups below. Because these amendments may vary in the amount of nutrients they contain, this method won't give you a mixture with a precise NPK ratio. The ratio will be approximately between 1-2-1 and 4-6-3, with additional insoluble phosphorus and potash. The blend will provide a balanced supply of nutrients that will be steadily available to plants and will encourage soil microorganisms to thrive.

Nitrogen (N)

2 parts bloodmeal

3 parts fish meal

Phosphorus (P)

3 parts bonemeal

6 parts rock phosphate or colloidal phosphate

Potassium (K)

1 part kelp meal

6 parts greensand

such as liquid seaweed (kelp), are rich in micronutrients and growth hormones. These foliar sprays appear to act as catalysts, increasing nutrient uptake by plants. Compost tea and seaweed

(continued on page 217)

Common Organic Fertilizers for Home Gardens

Use this table to select the appropriate fertilizers and application rates for your garden. The table lists the NPK ratio, where relevant, as well as the content of other significant nutrients. It also lists the primary benefit of each fertilizer: Some supply particular nutrients, some help balance soil minerals, and others primarily enrich the soil with organic matter.

Use suggested application rates based on your soil's fertility. If your soil fertility is low, you'll need to add more of an amendment than you would for medium or adequate fertility. Determine soil fertility with an assessment of your soil by a soil-testing laboratory, as well as your personal observations and the specific requirements of the crops you are growing.

ORGANIC AMENDMENT	PRIMARY BENEFIT	AVERAGE NPK RATIO OR MINERAL ANALYSIS	AVERAGE APPLICATION RATE PER 1,000 SQ FT	COMMENTS
Alfalfa meal	Organic matter	5-1-2	Low: 50 lb. Med: 35 lb. Adq: 25 lb.	Contains triaconatol, a natural fatty-acid growth stimulant, plus trace minerals.
Bloodmeal	Nitrogen	11-0-0	Low: 30 lb. Med. 20 lb. Adq: 10 lb.	—
Bonemeal (steamed)	Phosphate	1-11-0 20% total phosphate 24% calcium	Low: 30 lb. Med: 20 lb. Adq: 10 lb.	Higher grades contain as much as 6-12-0.
Coffee grounds	Nitrogen	2-0.3-0.2	Incorporate in compost	Acid forming: needs limestone supplement.
Colloidal phosphate	Phosphate	0-2-0 18 to 20% total phosphate 23% calcium	Low: 60 lb. Med: 25 lb. Adq: 10 lb.	—
Compost (dry commercial)	Organic matter	1-1-1	Low: 200 lb. Med: 100 lb. Adq: 50 lb.	—
Compost (homemade)	Organic matter	0.5-0.5-0.5 to 4-4-4 25% organic matter	Low: 2,000 lb. Med: 1,000 lb. Adq: 400 lb.	—
Compost (mushroom)	Organic matter	Variable	Low: 350 lb. Med: 250 lb. Adq: 50 lb.	Ask supplier whether the material contains pesticide residues.

ORGANIC AMENDMENT	PRIMARY BENEFIT	AVERAGE NPK RATIO OR MINERAL ANALYSIS	AVERAGE APPLICATION RATE PER 1,000 SQ FT	COMMENTS
Cottonseed meal	Nitrogen	6-2-1	Low: 35 lb. Med: 25 lb. Adq: 10 lb.	May contain GMOs or pesticide residues.
Eggshells	Calcium	1.2-0.4-0.1	Low: 100 lb. Med: 50 lb. Adq: 25 lb.	Contains calcium plus trace minerals.
Epsom salts	Balancer, magnesium	10% magnesium 13% sulfur	Low: 5 lb. Med: 3 lb. Adq: 1 lb.	—
Fish emulsion	Nitrogen	4-1-1 5% sulfur	Low: 2 oz. Med: 1 oz. Adq: 1 oz.	—
Fish meal	Nitrogen	5-3-3	Low: 30 lb. Med: 20 lb. Adq: 10 lb.	—
Granite meal	Potash	1%–4% total potash	Low: 100 lb. Med: 50 lb. Adq: 25 lb.	Contains 67% silicas and 19 trace minerals.
Grass clippings (green)	Organic matter	0.5-0.2-0.5	Low: 500 lb. Med: 300 lb. Adq: 200 lb.	—
Greensand	Potash	7% total potash plus 32 trace minerals	Low: 100 lb. Med: 50 lb. Adq: 25 lb.	—
Gypsum	Balancer, calcium	22% calcium 17% sulfur	Low: 40 lb. Med: 20 lb. Adq: 5 lb.	Do not apply if pH is below 5.8.
Kelp meal	Potash, trace minerals	1.0-0.5-2.5	Low: 20 lb. Med: 10 lb. Adq: 5 lb.	Contains a broad array of vitamins, minerals, and soil-conditioning elements.
Limestone, dolomitic	Balancer, calcium, magnesium	51% calcium carbonate 40% magnesium carbonate	Low: 100 lb. Med: 50 lb. Adq: 25 lb.	—
Limestone, calcitic	Balancer, calcium	65%–80% calcium carbonate 3%–15% magnesium carbonate	Low: 100 lb. Med: 50 lb. Adq: 25 lb.	—

(continued)

Common Organic Fertilizers for Home Gardens *(cont.)*

ORGANIC AMENDMENT	PRIMARY BENEFIT	AVERAGE NPK RATIO OR MINERAL ANALYSIS	AVERAGE APPLICATION RATE PER 1,000 SQ FT	COMMENTS
Oak leaves	Organic matter	0.8-0.4-0.1	Low: 250 lb. Med: 150 lb. Adq: 100 lb.	—
Peat moss	Organic matter	pH range 3.0–4.5	As needed	Use around acid-loving plants.
Rock phosphate	Phosphate	0-3-0 32% total phosphate 32% calcium	Low: 60 lb. Med: 25 lb. Adq: 10 lb.	Contains 11 trace minerals.
Sawdust	Organic matter	0.2-0-0.2	Low: 250 lb. Med: 150 lb. Adq: 100 lb.	Be sure sawdust is well rotted before incorporating.
Soybean meal	Nitrogen	7.0-0.5-2.3	Low: 50 lb. Med: 25 lb. Adq: 10 lb.	May contain GMOs.
Sul-Po-Mag	Potash, magnesium	0-0-22 11% magnesium 22% sulfur	Low: 10 lb. Med: 7 lb. Adq: 5 lb.	Do not use with dolomitic limestone; substitute greensand or other potassium source.
Wheat straw	Organic matter	0.7-0.2-1.2	Low: 250 lb. Med: 150 lb. Adq: 100 lb.	—
Wood ashes (leached)	Potash	0-1.2-2	Low: 20 lb. Med: 10 lb. Adq: 5 lb.	—
Wood ashes (unleached)	Potash	0-1.5-8	Low: 10 lb. Med: 5 lb. Adq: 3 lb.	—
Worm castings	Organic matter	0.5-0.5-0.3	Low: 250 lb. Med: 100 lb. Adq: 50 lb.	Contains 50% organic matter plus 11 trace minerals.

Source: *Reprinted with permission from Necessary Trading Company.*

FIG 217

extract are two common examples of organic foliar fertilizers. See the Compost entry for instructions for making compost tea. Avoid using compost tea made from manure-based composts for foliar feeding of edible crops.

Applying liquid fertilizers: With flowering and fruiting plants, foliar sprays are most useful during critical periods (such as after transplanting or during fruit set) or periods of drought or extreme temperatures. For leaf crops, some suppliers recommend biweekly spraying.

When using liquid fertilizers, always follow label instructions for proper dilution and application methods. You can use a surfactant, such as coconut oil or a mild soap (¼ teaspoon per gallon of spray), to ensure better coverage of the leaves. Otherwise, the spray may bead up on the foliage and you won't get maximum benefit. Measure the surfactant carefully; if you use too much, it may damage plants. A slightly acid spray mixture is most effective, so check your spray's pH. Use small amounts of vinegar to lower pH and baking soda to raise it. Aim for a pH of 6.0 to 6.5.

Any sprayer or mister will work, from hand-trigger units to knapsack sprayers. Set your sprayer to emit as fine a spray as possible. Never use a sprayer that has been used to apply herbicides.

The best times to spray are early morning and early evening, when the liquids will be absorbed most quickly and won't burn foliage. Choose a day when no rain is forecast and temperatures aren't extreme.

Spray until the liquid drips off the leaves. Concentrate the spray on leaf undersides, where leaf pores are more likely to be open. You can also water in liquid fertilizers around the root zone. A drip irrigation system can carry liquid fertilizers to your plants. Kelp is a better product for this use, as fish emulsion can clog the irrigation emitters.

Using Growth Enhancers

Growth enhancers are materials that help plants absorb nutrients more effectively from the soil. The most common growth enhancer is kelp (a type of seaweed), which has been used by farmers for centuries.

Kelp is sold as a dried meal or as an extract of the meal in liquid or powdered form. It is totally safe and provides some 60 trace elements that plants need in very small quantities. It also contains growth-promoting hormones and enzymes. These compounds are still not fully understood but are involved in improving a plant's growing conditions.

Applying growth enhancers: Follow the directions for spraying liquid fertilizers when applying growth enhancers as a foliar spray.

You can also apply kelp extract or meal directly to the soil; soil application will stimulate soil bacteria. This in turn increases fertility through humus formation, aeration, and moisture retention.

Apply 1 to 2 pounds of kelp meal per 100 square feet of garden each spring. Apply kelp extract once a month during the growing season.

If fresh seaweed is available, rinse it to remove the sea salt and spread it over the soil surface in your garden as a mulch, or compost it. Seaweed decays readily because it contains little cellulose.

FIG

Ficus carica
Moraceae

If you'd like to try growing an unusual fruit crop that's delicious and nearly trouble-free, consider figs. These trees will grow well unprotected in Zones 8–10, and also in colder areas if you choose hardier cultivars and give plants proper winter protection.

The Fruit Trees entry covers many aspects of growing tree fruits; refer to it for more information on planting and pruning.

Selecting trees: More than 200 fig cultivars are grown in North America, with a broad range of fruit shapes and colors. It's important to select a cultivar adapted to your climate, such as 'Brown Turkey', 'Chicago', or 'Celeste' for colder areas. Look for self-pollinating cultivars, as some figs are pollinated by tiny, specialized flies native to the Mediterranean and won't set fruit without them. (Reputable US nurseries sell only self-pollinating figs.)

Planting and care: Plant as you would any young tree. Figs need a sunny spot that's protected from winter winds. Mulch trees well with compost, and apply foliar sprays of seaweed extract at least once a month during the growing season.

Container culture: Because figs are tricky to grow in the ground where temperatures drop below 10°F, if you live north of Zone 7 it makes sense to grow your figs in containers. Use a large container (such as a half barrel), preferably plastic to control the weight. Use regular organic potting soil and plant figs at the same depth they grew at the nursery, top-dressing the container with compost. Water when the soil is dry an inch below the surface; if you let containers dry out completely, the figs may lose their leaves. (Leaves will regrow, but it stresses the plant and lessens fruit production.) Set pots in a sunny part of the patio, deck, or yard. You can use foliar sprays or water with liquid seaweed (kelp) or compost or manure tea monthly to give plants a boost.

Pruning and propagation: Use a shovel to disconnect suckers that sprout from the roots throughout the growing season; replant or share them with friends. Figs don't require formal train-

ing; just thin or head back as needed to control size. You can propagate figs by taking cuttings, but the easiest way is to bend a low-growing branch down and secure it to the ground or the soil in a container with a U-shaped wire; cover lightly with soil (and a rock if it resists staying buried) and check for rooting. Once the stem has rooted, sever it from the mother plant with pruning shears and it's good to go.

Winter care: If temperatures drop to 10°F or colder in your area, and you're growing cold-hardy figs outdoors in the ground, you can protect them with a cylindrical cage of hardware cloth filled with straw for insulation (don't cover it with plastic, which can overheat).

Or you can trench the figs each fall and unearth them every spring. To trench plants, prune them back to about 6 feet in late fall and head back any spreading branches. Tie branches with rope or twine to make a tight cylinder. Dig a 2-foot-deep trench as long as the tree is tall, starting at the rootball of the tree. Place boards on the bottom and sides of the trench. Dig out soil from the roots opposite the trench until the tree is free enough for you to tip it into the trench. Wrap the tree in heavy plastic, bend it into the trench (this will take some effort), and fill around it with straw or dried leaves. Put a board over the tree and shovel soil over the board. Resurrect trees in spring after danger of hard frost is past.

Never try to grow figs in the ground north of Zone 6 (even there, plant the very most cold-tolerant cultivars). Instead, grow your figs in containers and bring them indoors for winter. Keep them in an unheated garage, shed, or other protected area where temperatures don't dip below 20 degrees. The figs will drop their leaves and go dormant, but you should still water them when the soil dries. Figs will stay green all winter in a greenhouse and may even bear fruit in the warm, sunny greenhouse climate. Make sure you water them regularly, and watch the undersides of leaves for greenhouse pests like aphids. In either case, bring plants back outdoors when the weather warms and the last frost date is past.

Problems: Generally, figs do not suffer from insect or disease problems in North America. Keep birds away with netting; spread wood ashes around the base of trees to keep ants from climbing up to fruits. Keep plants well watered to avoid leaf drop, especially when they're growing in containers.

Harvesting: In warm climates, you can harvest figs twice—in June and again in late summer. In colder areas, expect one harvest in late summer or fall. Make sure you know the color of your fig's fruit when it's ripe. Some figs turn brown when ripe, while others are gold or even green. Check trees daily for ripe fruit in season. Ripe fruits are soft to the touch; skin may begin to split. Figs will keep up to 1 week in the refrigerator, but they spoil easily. Cook figs by simmering them with a dash of lemon and honey for about 20 minutes, mashing them as they cook. Then puree in a food processor, blender, or food mill. The puree freezes well and makes an excellent cookie filling, sauce for ice cream or poached pears, or spread for toast. You can also dry figs in a food dehydrator for nutritious snacks.

FORCING

For centuries, gardeners have used a variety of techniques to force flowers to open, vegetables to sprout, and fruits to ripen out of season. On the long, dark days of late winter, nothing lifts the spirits as much as the sight of a few branches of golden forsythia or coral-colored flowering quinces (*Chaenomeles* spp.), or a pot of fragrant

purple hyacinths. And if you use row covers or have a home greenhouse, you can extend the harvest period for many fruits and vegetables beyond the usual growing season.

Branches of spring-flowering trees are easy to force for indoor display. You can force almost any spring-blooming tree or shrub from mid-January or early February on. Earlier than this, most forcing fails because buds have not had sufficient chilling to break their natural winter dormancy.

Experiment with a variety of things from your garden, cutting heavily budded branches on a mild day. Select stems of medium thickness or better, since these contain large quantities of stored sugars needed to nourish flower buds. Use a sharp knife or pruning shears to cut the branches; slice diagonally just above a bud. Cut branches at least 2 to 3 feet long; shorter branches are less effective in arrangements. Keep plant health and form in mind as you harvest branches for forcing: Cut as carefully as you would when pruning. To ensure a steady supply of flowers, cut fresh branches every week or so.

After you bring the branches indoors, strip flower buds and small twigs from the bottom few inches of the stems. Slit up the stem ends a few inches or crush slightly with a hammer to encourage water absorption. Some may bloom faster if you submerge them completely in a tepid water bath for a few hours before making your arrangement. Recut stems and change the water in the containers every few days.

Besides forsythias, pussy willows, and fruit trees such as apples, cherries, plums, and almonds, some proven favorites for forcing are flowering quinces (*Chaenomeles* spp.), lilacs (*Syringa* spp.), witch hazels (*Hamamelis* spp.), hawthorns (*Crataegus* spp.), mock oranges (*Philadelphus* spp.), spireas (*Spiraea* spp.), wisterias (*Wisteria* spp.), spicebush (*Lindera benzoin*), alders (*Alnus* spp.), and horse chestnut (*Aesculus hippocastanum*). Most of these will burst into bloom within 2 to 6 weeks of cutting if forced at temperatures between 60° and 70°F. The closer it is to the plant's natural blooming period when you cut the branches, the less time it will take for them to open. You can control blooming time to some extent by moving branches to a cooler room to hold them back or placing them in a warm, sunny window to push them ahead.

When arranging forced branches in containers, keep in mind the beauty of stems as well as flowers. Don't crowd them together so tightly that the intersecting tracery of the branches is obscured.

For more information on forcing, see the Bulbs, Cold Frames, Endive, and Greenhouse Gardening entries.

FORSYTHIA

Forsythia. Deciduous spring-flowering shrubs.

Description: *Forsythia ×intermedia*, border forsythia, grows to 8 feet. It produces bright yellow flowers in early to mid-spring, followed by 3- to 5-inch medium green leaves on arching branches. Often it has good yellow-purple fall foliage color. Zones 4–8.

F. viridissima 'Bronxensis', Bronx green-stem forsythia, is a low (10- to 12-inch) groundcover with bright green foliage and primrose-yellow early spring blooms. Zones 5–8.

How to grow: Forsythias grow best in full sun. Provide water in summer to help them get established. Prune after blooming to encourage vigorous growth. Every year, remove about a third of the stems at ground level.

Landscape uses: Use for spring color in a massed planting or as a hedge.

FOXGLOVE

See Digitalis

FRUIT TREES

Fruit trees bloom abundantly in spring, and they're trimmed with colorful fruit in summer and fall. That makes them a great choice for any home landscape, both for their ornamental value and for the succulent edible treats you'll harvest. The flavor of tree-ripened apples, peaches, and other fruits is unmatched. And if you check on the prices of organic fruit in your area, you'll find that growing your own can be a real money saver, too. However, to reap good quality fruit, you must make a commitment to pruning, monitoring, and maintaining your trees.

Selecting Fruit Trees

Before you buy, determine which fruit trees can survive and bear fruit in your climate. You'll find specific information on climate requirements in the individual fruit tree entries throughout this book (for a list of the fruits covered, refer to the Quick Reference Guide on page 678). In general, northern gardeners should choose cultivars that will survive winter cold, blossom late enough to escape late-spring frosts, yet still set and mature fruit before the end of the growing season. Southern gardeners need cultivars that have minimal chilling requirements and that also will tolerate intense summer heat and humidity. For all organic gardeners, choosing cultivars that are disease resistant is especially important. Check with local organic fruit growers or with your local extension office to see which cultivars have a good track record in your area.

Temperature: Many types of fruit trees need a

KEY WORDS *Fruit Trees*

Standard. A full-size fruit tree, usually maturing to at least 20 feet in height, depending on species.

Dwarf and semidwarf. Fruit trees grafted on size-controlling rootstocks. Dwarf trees often mature to 8 to 10 feet in height. Semidwarf trees may reach 12 to 18 feet.

Genetic dwarf. A fruit tree that stays quite small without a dwarfing rootstock.

Rootstock. A cultivar onto which a fruiting cultivar is grafted. Rootstocks are selected for strong, healthy roots, for tolerance of difficult soil conditions, and/or for dwarfing effect.

Whip. A young tree, often the first-year growth from a graft or bud.

Scaffolds. The main structural branches on a fruit tree.

Pome fruit. Fruit that has a core containing many seeds, such as apples and pears.

Stone fruit. Fruit with a single hard pit, such as cherries, plums, and peaches.

Low chill. Requiring fewer hours of cool temperatures to break dormancy.

High chill. Requiring more hours of cool temperatures to break dormancy.

Self-fruitful. A tree that produces pollen that can pollinate its own flowers.

Compatible cultivars. Cultivars that bloom at approximately the same time and can successfully cross-pollinate.

Crotch. The angle of emergence of a branch from the trunk.

Suckers. Shoots that sprout out of or near the base of a tree.

Watersprouts. Upright shoots that sprout from the trunk and main limbs of a tree.

---

dormant period during which temperatures are below 45°F (tropical fruits are an exception). Without this winter chilling, the trees will not fruit properly. Breeders have developed low-chill cultivars, which flower and fruit with as little as half the usual cold requirement. This allows farmers and gardeners as far south as Texas, northern Florida, and parts of California to grow fruits such as apples, peaches, and pears. Extra-hardy, high-chill cultivars for the far North require longer cold periods and flower a week later than most.

If winter temperatures in your area drop below −25°F, stick with the hardiest apple and pear cultivars; between −20° and 0°F, you can try most apples and pears, sour cherries, European plums, and apricots; if minimum temperatures stay above −5°F, you can consider sweet cherries, Japanese plum, nectarines, and peaches. If minimum temperatures in your area are above 45°F, be sure to choose low-chill cultivars.

Spring frosts: Freezing temperatures can kill fruit blossoms. If you live in an area with unpredictable spring weather and occasional late frosts, look for late-blooming or frost-tolerant cultivars, especially for apricots and plums.

Humidity: In humid regions, select disease-resistant cultivars whenever possible. Diseases that can seriously affect fruits, such as apple scab and brown rot, are more troublesome in humid conditions.

Usefulness: If you are fond of baking, top your backyard fruit tree list with sour cherries and cooking apples, which make excellent pies. For canning, look for suitable cultivars of peaches, nectarines, and pears. For jellies, try apricot, plum, and quince. If you're interested in fruit for fresh eating, think about how long the fruit will last in storage. Some apples stay good for months if kept cold, but soft fruits must be eaten within about 1 week or they will spoil.

Choosing a Tree Type

Fruit trees come in shapes and sizes for every yard. Most home gardeners prefer dwarf or semidwarf trees, which fruit at a younger age and are easier to tend.

Standards: Standard apple and pear trees can reach 30 feet or taller, becoming small shade trees that can be underplanted with flowers or groundcovers. They are long lived and hardy but require more space. It can be a challenge to harvest fruit from these trees, too. Standard stone fruit trees can grow quite large as well, but it's possible to limit their size by training (directing the trees to a particular form), pruning, and limiting fertilizer.

Grafted semidwarfs: Apples grafted on size-controlling rootstocks grow well. However, stone fruit trees grafted onto dwarfing rootstocks often are more difficult to grow well. For more information on the effects of rootstocks on grafted fruit trees, see the Grafting entry.

Genetic dwarfs: Genetic dwarf or miniature trees are naturally compact trees grafted on a standard-size root system. They reach about 7 feet and bear one-fifth as much normal-size fruit as a standard tree. Genetic dwarfs tend to be shorter

lived and less winter hardy than standard trees. Northern gardeners may do best growing these dwarf trees in planters and moving them to a protected area, such as an unheated storage room, where temperatures remain between 30° and 45°F in winter. Genetic dwarfs are ideal for the Pacific Northwest or the southern United States. In fact, in those areas they may be preferable to standard trees because they need less winter cold to flower.

Pollination requirements are another important factor to consider when selecting trees. Most apples, pears, sweet cherries, and Japanese plums are not self-fruitful. You must plant a second compatible cultivar nearby to ensure good pollination and fruit set. Peaches, nectarines, tart cherries, and some European plums are self-fruitful. Some cultivars of apples, pears, sweet cherries, and European plums are somewhat self-fruitful but set better crops when cross-pollinated. Refer to individual fruit tree entries for details about pollination requirements. If you lack enough space to plant two fruit trees in your garden, consider coordinating with a neighbor to plant compatible cultivars so you each can enjoy a bountiful harvest.

Planting Fruit Trees

Plant fruit trees in a small traditional orchard, or intersperse them in borders, mixed beds, or a vegetable garden. You can even put a dwarf apple at the end of a foundation planting. Some will grow in lawns, but most perform better in a prepared bed where they are spared competition from turf grass or other groundcovers.

Site Selection

Be certain the site you choose has the right growing conditions for fruit trees.

Sunlight: Even 1 or 2 hours of daily shade may make fruit smaller and less colorful. Envision the mature size of trees and shrubs close to your planned site. If their shadow will encroach on your fruit trees in years to come, you may want to select a different site. Sour cherries tolerate a bit of shade better than other tree fruits do.

Shaded soil in early spring can be beneficial because cool soil can delay flowering, perhaps until after late killing frosts.

Soil: Fruit trees need well-drained soil. Sandy soils can be too dry to produce a good crop of fruit. Wet, clayey soil encourages various root rots. See "Soil Preparation" to learn how to cope with less-than-ideal soil.

Wind: Blustery winds in open areas or on hill-tops can make training difficult, knock fruit off trees early, or topple trees. Staking will help trees resist the force of prevailing winds. Where wind is a problem, you can slow it by erecting a hedge or fence. However, don't box the tree in and stifle the breeze. Air circulation is helpful for reducing diseases.

Slope: Plant near the top of a gentle slope if possible. Planting on a north-facing slope or about 15 feet from the north side of a building helps slow flowering in spring and protects blossoms from late frosts. Planting on a south-facing slope can hasten flowering and lead to frost damage. Sheltered alcoves on the south side of a house protect tender trees. Avoid planting in a frost pocket, which is an area at the bottom of a slope where cold air collects, as shown at right. Trees planted in frost pockets have a higher risk of spring frost damage to flowers and young fruit.

Tree Spacing

The amount of room your trees will need depends on their mature height and width, how they are trained, soil fertility, and tree vigor. Give every tree plenty of space to grow without impinging on neighboring plants or spreading into shady areas. Small trees, such as dwarf peaches and nectarines, require only 12 feet between trees, while standard apple trees need 20 to 30 feet between trees.

Soil Preparation

To make the effort and expense of planting fruit trees worthwhile and to maximize yield and fruit quality, it pays to prepare the soil properly. Plan ahead, and take these steps in the season preceding the year you plan to plant.

✿ Test the soil and follow recommendations to correct deficiencies. Keep in mind that fruit trees prefer soil high in calcium, magnesium, and potassium, with balanced levels of nitrogen, phosphorus, and micronutrients. Excessive nitrogen can lead to lush growth that is more susceptible to certain insect and disease problems.

Frost pockets. Cold air collects in a frost pocket at the bottom of a slope. Frost pockets can also occur midslope at a point where buildings, small rises, or trees stop the cold air flow on their uphill side.

SMART SHOPPING

Fruit Trees

If you can't find the kind of fruit trees you want locally, turn to the Internet or to mail-order catalogs to locate nurseries that specialize in fruit trees, ideally located in a climate similar to your own.

Most of the information you need to make the proper selection, such as chilling requirements and insect and disease resistance, should be listed on the nursery's Web site or in its catalog. However, you may have to call the nursery to find out what rootstock is used and make your own decision about its compatibility and potential in your area. Also, if the nursery doesn't list pollination requirements, ask whether a particular cultivar is self-fruitful. If it's not, ask for names of compatible cultivars.

If you do decide to buy trees at a local garden center, be wary of trees offered in containers. These trees may have been shipped to the garden center bareroot, had their roots trimmed to fit a container, and been potted up just for the sake of appearance. This treatment will not help the tree grow any better, and the stress to the roots may actually set the tree back.

After planting, you can sow annual green manures such as buckwheat beneath the trees. These crops will smother weeds and provide shelter for beneficial insects that help control pest insects. Annual cover crops die with frost and decompose to humus over winter.

🌿 Raise soil organic matter content by adding compost or planting a green manure crop.

🌿 Clear out all roots of perennial weeds. To reduce the number of annual weed seeds, lightly cultivate the top 6 inches of soil several times and, if possible, plant a cover crop the season before you plant.

🌿 Amend clayey or sandy soils throughout the area where the roots will extend. A good rule of thumb is to amend the area out to where you estimate the branch tips of the full-grown tree will reach. Add up to 50 percent organic matter, preferably leaf mold and compost. Make a raised growing bed if necessary to improve

drainage. Break up any subsoil hardpan and add drainage tiles to eliminate standing water.

Planting Instructions

Plant fruit trees while dormant in early spring, or in fall where winters are quite mild. Fall planting gives roots a head start, because they continue to grow until the soil freezes. However, fall planting is risky in areas where the soil freezes, because the low temperatures may kill the newly grown roots.

Most nurseries stock bareroot fruit trees. Plant the young trees as you would any bareroot tree. See the Planting entry for full instructions. Set a tree growing on standard roots at the same depth or slightly deeper than it grew at the nursery. If the tree is budded or grafted, set the bud union—the crooked area where the scion and rootstock join—2 inches above soil level. Scions can rot if trees are set too deeply, and the trees can lose rootstock effects.

You may be able to speed a young tree's establishment by dipping the roots in powdered bonemeal before you plant. Also apply compost tea at planting. See the Compost entry for instructions for making compost tea.

Aftercare

Follow-up care each year is critical to your ultimate goal in planting fruit trees: a harvest of plentiful yields of healthy fruit.

Training and Pruning

To grow top-quality fruit, and to have easy access for harvesting, you need to establish a sturdy and efficient branching framework. The three main methods for training fruit trees are open center, modified central leader, and central leader. All three systems encourage the growth of branches with wide crotches that are less likely to split when burdened with a heavy fruit load. Which method you use depends on the type of fruit tree and whether it's a dwarf, semi-dwarf, or standard tree. Ask a knowledgeable local nursery owner or your Cooperative Extension agent which method is best for the trees you plan to grow.

It's important to establish the main branches while the tree is young. You'll then maintain tree shape of your bearing trees each year with touch-up pruning. Central leader trees produce more fruiting spurs, important for spur-type apple and pear cultivars. For nectarines, peaches, and Japanese plums, use open center training to maximize air circulation and sunlight penetration among the branches, which will help reduce disease. For instructions on how to make cuts correctly as you train and prune your trees, see the Pruning and Training entry.

Spread young branches so they will develop broad crotch angles. Use clothespins to hold branches out from the trunk, or insert notched boards in the crotch angle. Branches that aren't spread will be weaker and more likely to break.

In certain circumstances, it's best not to train. Some fruit trees, including apricots and pears, are particularly susceptible to disease, which can invade through pruning cuts or attack young growth that arises near the cuts. If disease is a problem in your area, you may want to limit pruning to general maintenance or renewal of fruiting wood. In the far North, keep training to a minimum, since new growth is more susceptible to winter injury. However, leave some young suckers on main scaffolds to act as renewal wood in case main branches are injured by cold.

Central leader training: Follow these instructions and refer to the illustration on page 226 when training a young fruit tree to a central leader form.

1. Head back a 1-year-old whip to 2½ feet at planting.

2. In mid-June, select four branches that emerge in different directions and are spaced several inches apart along the trunk as scaffolds. The strongest-growing, uppermost shoot will be the central leader, which becomes the trunk. Pinch off all other shoots.

3. For the following few years, repeat this process by heading back the central leader in early spring about 2 feet above the previous

set of scaffolds. Then in June, select an additional layer of scaffolds. Choose branches that are at least 1½ feet above the last set of scaffolds. Scaffolds should spiral up the trunk so each branch will be in full sun.

Modified central leader pruning is similar to central leader, but once you've trained four or five main scaffold branches, you'll cut the central leader off just above the highest scaffold branch to open the center of the plant to sunlight.

Open center training: Follow these instructions and refer to the illustration on the opposite page when training a young fruit tree to an open center form.

1. Head back a 1-year-old whip to between 2 and 2½ feet.

2. At the beginning of June, choose three scaffolds that emerge in different directions and are separated along the trunk by about 4 inches. Cut off all others.

3. In the third and fourth years, thin as lightly as you can to avoid delaying fruiting.

4. Once peach, nectarine, and Japanese plum trees begin to bear, they fruit only on year-old branches. To ensure plenty of fruiting wood, cut the scaffolds back to the same height every year, encouraging the growth of 1 to 1½ feet of new fruiting wood. Thin overly crowded or short and weak fruiting spurs.

General pruning tips: Whether you train your trees to a specific form or not, it's a good idea to prune off shoots that emerge low on the trunk and any branches that cross and rub. Where one limb grows above and shades another, or when two branches of equal length and diameter arise at one fork, select one branch to keep and prune off the other. During summer, remove suckers that sprout

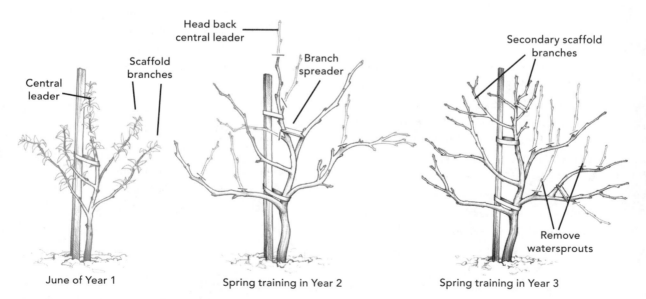

June of Year 1

Central leader

Scaffold branches

Head back central leader

Branch spreader

Spring training in Year 2

Secondary scaffold branches

Remove watersprouts

Spring training in Year 3

Central leader training. This style of training produces a tree with a strong central trunk with scaffold limbs branching off in a spiral pattern. It works well for apples and pears.

near the tree base, waterspouts that shoot out from the trunk or main limbs, and any dead or diseased wood.

When to prune varies with the tree type. You can prune apples and pears in early spring before the trees break dormancy. For stone fruits that are susceptible to cankers caused by disease organisms, wait until bud break, when they are less likely to be infected. Prune away dead and diseased branches on all kinds of fruit trees as the growing season continues. Stop pruning by the end of August in areas where winter injury is a concern. Late pruning can stimulate a flush of new growth that could be damaged when cold weather sets in.

Fertilizing

Even with thorough advance soil preparation, your fruit trees will benefit from fertilization. Nutrient consumption varies with tree type and age, soil, and growing conditions. For instance, you may have to fertilize a fruit tree growing in your lawn more frequently than if the soil around the tree is cleared and mulched (unless you fertilize your lawn regularly, in which case your trees may receive too much fertilizer). Don't simply fertilize on a set schedule. Overfertilizing can encourage soft new growth that is susceptible to disease attack and winter injury.

Monitor tree growth to determine when trees need fertilizing. Nonbearing apple trees should grow 1½ to 2 feet per year; those producing fruit average 8 to 12 inches. Mature peach trees should grow 1 to 1½ feet each year. If your tree seems to be lagging, have the nutrient levels in the leaves analyzed. Call your local extension office for information about leaf analysis.

Fertilize only in spring. Spread materials on the soil surface in a circle around the trunk out

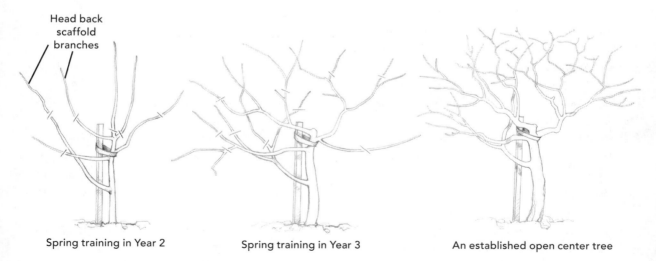

Head back scaffold branches

Spring training in Year 2   Spring training in Year 3   An established open center tree

Open center training. Trees trained to an open center have a vase- or bowl-like form that lets lots of light and air reach the center of the tree. Use an open center form for nectarines, peaches, and Japanese plums.

to the edge of the leafy canopy. If the tree is growing in the lawn, make holes with a crowbar around the perimeter of the branches and drop fertilizer below the grass roots. Avoid high-nitrogen fertilizers. The best fertilizer for fruit trees is compost because it has a good balance of nutrients. Foliar seaweed sprays improve tree health, increase yields, and increase bud frost resistance. Spray trees when buds start to show color, when petals drop, and when fruit is ½ to 1 inch.

Mulching

Mulched trees will have access to more water and nutrients, especially if you use soil-enriching mulch such as compost or shredded leaves. Mulch will also keep down weeds that compete with trees for water and nutrients. It prevents excessive evaporation of soil moisture, a necessity around young or weak trees, in dry climates, and in sandy soils. In areas with fluctuating winter temperatures, mulch will eliminate damage from frost heaving. Mulch can keep the soil cooler in spring and delay flowering of early-spring bloomers such as apricots or peaches, hopefully beyond the threat of frost.

The drawback of mulching is that it can make heavy soils too wet and can harbor pests, especially mice and voles.

When mulch is needed, apply a 3- to 6-inch layer of organic mulch in an area from 1 to 2 feet away from the trunk out to just beyond the branch tips. Fluff the mulch with a spading fork occasionally so it doesn't compact. Check the soil moisture level occasionally. If the soil is staying overly wet, rake the mulch back to prevent root rot. Push the mulch out from under the tree boughs during leaf fall so that you can rake up the fallen leaves afterward (this helps prevent disease problems). Afterward, respread the mulch.

Watering

Ideally, the soil around fruit trees should be evenly moist, neither dry nor waterlogged. Moisture is especially important to young trees and trees bearing ripening crops. Thoroughly soak the root system of newly planted trees, and repeat whenever the soil becomes dry for the next few months.

After the tree is growing well, your watering schedule will depend on the weather and climate. If the weather has been dry, even during a mid-winter warm spell, stick your little finger down in the soil around the drip line. If you do not feel moisture below the surface, water the tree thoroughly. If you have several fruit trees, a drip irrigation system is ideal (see the Drip Irrigation entry). In cold climates, stop watering by early fall to harden the plant for winter.

Winter Protection

Protect your trees against winter sunscald, frost heaving, and pest damage, all of which can injure or kill fruit trees. Sunscald occurs when sun-warmed wood is killed by nighttime cold. The damaged area becomes dry, sunken, and attractive to borers and diseases. Prevent sunscald by wrapping the trunk with a white plastic tree guard or painting it up to the first scaffold branch with white latex paint diluted 1:1 with water.

To minimize frost heaving—shifting of soil when it freezes and thaws—apply mulch only after the soil freezes. This is especially important for young trees that can suffer extensive root damage due to frost heaving.

Flower and Fruit Care

Once your trees reach maturity, there are some extra activities involved in their seasonal care. Some trees may require hand-pollinating, others may need young fruit thinned, and all will have to be harvested.

Hand-pollinating: Early-flowering fruit trees can suffer partial to full crop loss if the weather is not mild when the tree is in bloom. If temperatures aren't high enough for insect activity, flowers won't be pollinated and fruit won't develop. If there's a cold spell when your trees are blooming, you can save your crop by hand-pollinating. Simply collect pollen from one tree by rubbing flowers gently with an artist's brush or cotton swab, then brush the pollen onto the flowers of a compatible cultivar.

Be sure nights are frost-free if you plan to hand-pollinate. If you expect a late frost, you can cover small trees with plastic or spray them with a frost-protecting product. As a last resort, try sprinkling water on trees all night. Use care, as the weight of ice that forms on the trees can break branches.

Thinning: Because fruit trees tend to be over-burdened by young fruit, it's important to thin out the excess on all trees except those with cherry-size fruit. Without your intervention, the weight of the fruit may actually break limbs. The stress from the excessive fruit load may also reduce the number of flower buds the tree produces the next year. Disease problems such as brown rot can spread quickly among crowded fruits, ruining the crop before it ripens. In addition

Restoring Old Trees

Without regular care, a fruit tree gradually may become overgrown, minimally productive, and home for hordes of pests and diseases. Should you save the old tree or start over with a new one? If the tree has a lovely shape, a vital position in your landscape, or sentimental value, it may be worth keeping. Here's how to restore it.

- If the tree is suffering from diseases such as scab, black knot, or fire blight, begin a spray program to help lessen damage.

- Remove dead and diseased branches.

- Check for trunk or root rot and, in warm climates, nematodes.

- Prune back any neighboring trees and shrubs that shade the fruit tree.

- Take a leaf analysis for nutrient levels, and correct soil nutrient deficiencies. Use a foliar seaweed spray to restore tree vigor while the soil comes back into balance.

- When the tree is reasonably healthy, you can begin to prune it into a productive shape. Gradually thin out unproductive branches to open the canopy to sunlight. To minimize water-sprout and sucker regeneration, take off no more than one-quarter to one-third of the new wood on the tree or on a particular branch during any one year.

to avoiding problems, thinning lets you channel all the tree's resources into fewer but bigger and more beautiful fruit.

Thin when the fruit is young, the smaller the better. First clip or twist off all insect-damaged or deformed fruits. Then remove the smaller fruits. Leave only the biggest and best.

If you can't reach the upper limbs of large trees, tap the limbs with a padded pole to shake loose some of the extras. On small apple, nectarine, and peach trees with big fruit, thin fruit to 6 to 8 inches apart. Plums and apricots can be more closely spaced, about 3 to 5 inches apart.

Even after thinning, fruit may become heavy enough to tear a branch. For extra support, prop branches up with a forked stick. On central leader trees, you can secure branches to the central leader with a rope or with a chain covered with garden hose.

Harvesting: Since color is a key indicator of ripeness for most tree fruits, be aware of the ripe color of your trees' fruits. Most fruit is ready to harvest when the green undercolor changes to yellow or the fruit softens and drops. Grasp the fruit in the palm of your hand and twist it off the stem carefully so you don't damage the branch. Handle the ripe fruit gently so it does not bruise.

Pests and Diseases

Growing fruit trees using only organic pest control methods requires patience and vigilance. Fruit is so succulent and tasty that it attracts a wide range of pests, from mites to deer. Watch diligently for pests, and control them before they damage the tree or the fruit.

Insects and diseases: Take as many preventive steps as possible to avoid insect and disease problems on your fruit trees. Your best first choice is to plant insect- and disease-resistant cultivars. Pick up and destroy infested or diseased fruit that falls prematurely. Prune out diseased or pest-infested wood.

Learn to identify common pests, and know their life cycles. When pest problems arise, select the most environmentally gentle method of control, such as encouraging or releasing predatory insects. Move on to the use of *Bacillus subtilis*, horticultural oil, soap sprays, and Bt (*Bacillus thuringiensis*), depending on the pest you need to control. Reserve botanical insecticides such as neem as a last resort. While they break down rapidly in the environment and are generally less toxic than synthetic chemical pesticides, they should still be used with caution. The Pests entry offers details on control methods.

Animal pests: Deer will eat young shoots, twigs, and fruit. Raccoons will harvest ripe peaches the night before you plan to pick them yourself. Rodents and rabbits will chew on bark during winter. Birds are especially troublesome pests of cherries and plums. For control suggestions, see the Animal Pests entry.

Propagating Fruit Trees

Most fruit trees consist of a preferred fruit-producing cultivar grafted onto the rootstock of a different cultivar. Dwarfing rootstocks are successful for apples and sometimes for stone fruits.

Home gardeners can try their hand at budding or grafting fruit trees. For information on these techniques, see the Budding, Grafting, and Propagation entries. You'll find recommendations for propagating specific fruits in the individual fruit tree entries.

Fruit Tree Insects and Diseases

Pest control is serious business when it comes to fruits. Here you'll find descriptions of the most persistent tree fruit pests and diseases, the damage they cause, and organic methods you can apply to minimize damage.

PROBLEM	HOSTS	DAMAGE	CONTROL
INSECTS			
Apple maggot (*Rhagoletis pomonella*) Adults: ¼-inch black flies with yellow legs. Larvae: white maggots.	Apple, blueberry, plum; related flies attack cherry, peach, and walnut. Found in eastern and northwestern United States and Canada.	Larvae tunnel through fruit, which drops early; early cultivars usually most damaged.	Collect and destroy fallen fruit daily; hang baited red sticky ball traps (1–6 per tree), remove traps when fruit colors; cover young fruits with nylon barriers; plant white clover to attract predators.
Codling moth (*Cydia pomonella*) Adults: gray-brown moths, ¾-inch wingspan. Larvae: pink or white caterpillars, brown heads. Eggs: white eggs laid on leaves, twigs, fruit.	Apple, pear. Found throughout North America.	Larvae burrow into fruit. Entry holes are surrounded by dead tissue and sawdust-like material. Fruit interior is dark and rotted. Young fruit may drop.	Sow cover crop to support predators and parasites. Put out 1 codling moth trap per dwarf tree. Cover young fruits with nylon barriers. Spray Bt (*Bacillus thuringiensis*), starting 15 days after petal fall; repeat 5 and 10 days later.
Green fruitworm (*Lithophane antennata*) Adults: fuzzy-looking gray or purple moths, 1½-inch wingspan. Larvae: light green, with lengthwise stripe on sides, 1 inch. Eggs: tiny, pale gray, sand-dollar-shaped, laid singly on branches.	Apple, apricot, cherry, peach, pear, plum, quince. Found in northern states and southern Canada.	Larvae chew leaves, flower buds, and green fruits. May cause premature fruit drop. Developed fruits show healed-over brown depressions or holes.	Monitor with pheromone traps. Spray Bt (*Bacillus thuringiensis*) when larvae are feeding. Spray neem for severe infestations. Plant wild carrot and dill to encourage parasitic wasps. These controls are also effective for leaf-rolling pests.
European red mite (*Panonychus ulmi*), **other mites** Adults: pale brown or reddish, spider-shaped insects, visible with hand lens. Eggs: tiny, reddish, laid in groups around bases of buds and fruit spurs.	Apple, apricot, cherry, peach, pear, plum, quince. Found in most fruit-growing areas of North America.	Heavy infestations cause off-color, bronzed foliage, reduced tree growth, and fewer flower buds the next season.	Plant groundcovers to encourage mite predators. If you've had past mite problems, spray dormant oil anytime after buds break until green leaf tips reach ½ inch. Check leaves with hand lens; spray insecticidal soap or horticultural oil if more than 10 mites per leaf.

(continued)

Fruit Tree Insects and Diseases (cont.)

PROBLEM	HOSTS	DAMAGE	CONTROL
Peach tree borers (*Synanthedon exitiosa* and *S. pictipes*) Adults: steel blue, clear-winged moth with yellow or orange markings, 1-inch wingspan. Larvae: white with brown head, 1 inch. Eggs: tiny, brown or gray, laid in bark crevices.	Apricot, cherry, peach, plum. Found throughout North America.	Borers enter bark on lower trunk and injured limbs. Masses of gummy sawdust appear around entrance holes. Branches or whole trees may be stunted and die.	Keep trees healthy and avoid injuring the trunk. If gum appears on trunk (a sign of borer activity), probe holes with wire to kill borers. To kill young larvae before they enter the tree, spray weekly with Bt (*Bacillus thuringiensis*) from late July until the end of August.
Plum curculio (*Conotrachelus nenuphar*) Adults: gray or brown 1/3-inch beetles with a prominent snout (weevils). Larvae: 1/2-inch grayish white grubs. Eggs: tiny, white, laid under skin of fruit.	Apple, blueberry, cherry, peach, pear, plum, quince. Found throughout eastern North America.	Small semicircular scars left on green fruit. Larvae burrow and feed on interior of fruit. Fruits drop prematurely.	Collect fallen fruit. Monitor with light green sticky ball traps hung in trees. Knock weevils out of tree onto sheet and destroy. To deter curculios from laying eggs, spray trees with kaolin clay at petal fall and repeat weekly for up to 8 weeks.
DISEASES			
Bacterial leaf spot (*Xanthomonas arboricola* pv. *pruni*) Overwinters in small cankers in twigs.	Apricot, peach, plum. Common east of the Rocky Mountains.	Many small, dark spots on leaves; centers dry and drop out, leaving shot holes. Small, sunken dark spots or cracks on fruit.	Plant resistant varieties when possible. Fertilize trees as needed to maintain vigorous growth, and prune to improve air circulation. Sprays are not effective against this disease in home orchards.
Brown rot (*Monilinia fructicola, M. laxa*) Overwinters in dried fruit on tree or ground.	Apricot, peach, plum. Found throughout the United States and Canada.	Flowers and new growth wilt and decay. Developing or mature fruit show soft, brown spots that enlarge rapidly and may grow gray mold.	Prune yearly while dormant and also thin branches in midsummer to improve air circulation. Remove and destroy dried fruit, cultivate soil before bloom. Cut out infected twigs. Apply *Bacillus subtilis* and/or compost tea to help prevent infection. Spray sulfur during bloom and before harvest if weather is humid.

PROBLEM	HOSTS	DAMAGE	CONTROL
Canker, perennial (*Leucocytospora cincta, L. leucostoma*) Overwinters in cankers and dead wood.	Apricot, cherry, peach, plum. Found in all areas except the western United States.	Sunken, oozing cankers on trunk or twigs. May cause wilting or death of branches or trees.	Avoid mechanical injury. Cut out cankers and dead wood and destroy them. Paint the south side of trunks and large lower branches to prevent winter injury. Apply mulch around trees to reduce water stress.
Fire blight (*Erwinia amylovora*) Overwinters in cankers.	Apple, pear, quince. Found throughout North America.	Young tender shoots die back suddenly. Leaves turn brown or singed looking and remain on the twig. Bark may become water soaked and ooze.	Select resistant cultivars. Cut off blighted twigs at least 8 inches below the infected tissue on a dry day. Sanitize pruning tools between cuts. Limit high-nitrogen fertilizers.

FUCHSIA

Fuchsia. All-season tender perennials grown as annuals or houseplants.

Description: *Fuchsia ×hybrida*, hybrid fuchsia, bears distinctive 1- to 3-inch bell- or teardrop-shaped flowers in shades or combinations of white, pink, red, and purple. Blooms seem to dance upon upright or hanging stems ranging from 1 to 5 feet and bearing ¾- to 3-inch green or reddish purple leaves.

How to grow: Plant in the ground or in large pots in partial shade (morning sun is best) and fertile, moist but well-drained, humus–rich soil. Give plants as much root space as possible. Fuchsias dislike hot summers. Water and fertilize often in summer. Before frost, take the plant inside, reduce watering, and allow leaves to drop. Water very lightly until spring, then cut stems back to a few inches. Repot if rootbound, and resume watering.

Landscape uses: Use in hanging baskets, window boxes, or containers. Grow as standards in large pots, trained to a single "trunk." In Zones 9 and warmer, heat-tolerant fuchsias such as 'Gartenmeister Bonstedt', an upright, shrubby cultivar, can be grown outdoors all year. Fuchsias are hummingbird favorites, so add them to a deck or patio to attract these flying jewels to your yard.

G

GAILLARDIA

Blanketflower. Summer- to fall-blooming annuals and perennials.

Description: Blanketflowers bear 2-to 4-inch single or double daisies in shades of red, yellow, and orange (often red tipped with yellow). The long, curved or leaning stems grow to 3 feet above loose mounds of hairy, gray-green leaves to 1 foot long. *Gaillardia pulchella*, annual blanketflower, usually grows a bit more upright and is smaller in all its parts than G. ×*grandiflora*, perennial blanketflower, hardy in Zones 4–9.

How to grow: Start annual blanketflowers from seed about 3 weeks before the last frost, or direct-sow into a sunny spot with average to less fertile, well-drained soil. They take heat and drought very well. Deadhead to promote more blooms. Give perennials the same conditions, making certain the soil drains well in winter. Plant or divide every few years in spring.

Landscape uses: Mass in perennial borders and cutting gardens, or naturalize in dry, sunny spots. Try dwarf perennial cultivars such as 'Goblin' as edgings; they look at home among rocks or in containers. Blanketflowers are salt tolerant, so they make colorful additions to seaside gardens.

GARDEN DESIGN

When it comes to garden design, the first rule is that there's no single correct approach. Some gardeners thoroughly plan out their gardens on paper before they plant, while others seemingly tuck plants in at random yet still produce a gorgeous display. Still others start with a plan created by professionals, or one from a book or magazine, then add their own touches. Whether a design is backed up by paper plans or just a knack for putting the right plant in the right place, basic aesthetic principles are the foundation of the best and most satisfying gardens. Whether you want to design a flower garden or plant a shrub border, these sound design principles will help you make decisions as you plan.

Design Styles

There are two general types of garden design styles—formal and informal. Formal gardens exhibit classical symmetry. Flowerbeds, terraces, pools, and other features are generally rectangular and walks are straight. Or beds and other features are round or oval with walks that curve around them.

Informal gardens can work well in either small or large spaces. The outlines of beds sweep along the land's features. Lawns, terraces, walkways, and other features are irregularly shaped, with one gentle arc leading to another. Natural-looking woodland wildflower gardens or free-form island beds of perennials are both examples of informal style. If the lay of your land is irregular, it will lend itself to an informal design.

Basic Design Principles

Regardless of style, all well-designed gardens make use of three essential principles—balance, proportion, and repetition—to blend the various parts of the garden into a harmonious whole.

Balance: When elements on two sides of a central point are similar in size or visual weight, they are balanced. Balanced design gives the viewer a peaceful, restful feeling; unbalanced, lopsided, design is unsettling. Balance doesn't necessarily mean symmetry; you don't need mirror-image plantings to accomplish it. Symmetrical balance—with matching plants on either side of a walkway, for example—is a hallmark of formal gardens, while asymmetrical balance is characteristic of informal gardens. In an informal design, several good-size clumps of a perennial might balance one large shrub, for example.

Proportion: Garden features (plants, flowerbeds, terraces, etc.) are in proportion when their scale is in pleasing relationship to their surroundings. For example, a large clump of 9-foot-tall giant reed planted in a bed with low-growing, 2- to 3-foot perennials creates a picture that is out of proportion. Similarly, a huge shed would be out of proportion in a small yard.

Repetition: Repeating an element—color, texture, shape, or even building materials like landscape timbers or brick—throughout a garden adds unity and harmony to a design, so the parts of the garden fit together more compellingly. For example, repeating the color red at intervals in a flowerbed leads the eye through the design and creates a feeling of wholeness and rhythm. You can repeat the same plant or use different species with similarly colored blooms to achieve the same effect.

Plants and Design

The color, height, form, and texture of plants play a vital role in any garden. All plants change from season to season and year to year. They may grow taller than planned, spread too vigorously, or not bloom when expected. Balancing and working with these changes is what makes gardening an art. Even the most carefully designed gardens are never static; their owners adjust and develop the design over time.

Color: In a garden, color can be used in many ways. One gardener may prefer bright reds and yellows, another soft pinks, blues, and lavenders. Color can influence the mood of a garden. Hot colors—vibrant reds, oranges, and yellows—are cheerful and bright. Cool colors—greens, blues, and purples—are more serene.

Color can influence perceived perspective. Hot or warm colors appear to bring an object or scene closer. Cool colors tend to recede or push the object farther away, so they're a good choice for making a small garden seem larger. Use them in large clumps to catch the eye, and remember they can be easily overwhelmed by warm colors.

Use balance, proportion, and repetition to design your color scheme. Strive for balanced distribution of color. A large planting of one color can overwhelm a design. Repeating a color at intervals can unify the design. Use clumps of a single plant or several different species with the same flower color.

Height: Plant height should also be balanced and in proportion. In a planting in front of a fence or other backdrop, plant the tallest plants in the back, the shortest in front. If the garden is a free-form shape, put the tallest plants at the widest parts of the border. In island beds, which can be viewed from all sides, plant the tallest plants in the center, with shorter plants around the edges.

Form: This term refers to shape—round, vertical, creeping, or weeping, for example. It's used to describe the entire plant or just the flowers. For example, delphiniums are vertical plants with spike-shaped bloom stalks; marigolds are mound-shaped with round blooms. Intersperse different plant forms throughout a design for balance and interest. Form can be used like color, although it's more subtle. Repeating a form at intervals strengthens unity and harmony. You needn't repeat the same plant to achieve this effect; several different plants that have similar forms will do.

Texture: Plant leaves can look coarse, crinkled, glossy, fuzzy, or smooth. Flowers can be feathery and delicate or waxy and bold. Using plants with a variety of textures—and repeating interesting textures at intervals—adds interest and appeal. Like form, texture is a subtle characteristic.

Formal design. Formal gardens can be unfussy and simple, making them a good choice for a small yard. That doesn't mean they have to be boring, though. Here, straight paths, clipped edging plants, and a central garden ornament create a formal atmosphere. A tidy mix of flowers and other plants in the beds complements the layout of the garden.

Planning Considerations

Before you start buying and planting plants, take time to decide what role you want the garden to play in your overall landscape. Flower or shrub borders can be used to edge walkways or terraces, to define a work or play area, embellish a fence, or provide privacy. See the Landscaping entry for details on how to make a plan for your property.

Site characteristics: Learning everything you can about the site you've chosen is an essential step for designing a garden that will grow and thrive. Take time to learn about the soil: Is it sandy or clayey? Well drained or boggy? Is it rich in organic matter or does it need improvement? Is the site in full sun, dappled shade, or deep shade? Once you know what conditions exist, you can look for plants that will thrive there naturally. Matching plants to the site is more practical than trying to modify the site to match the requirements of the plants. Why? Plants matched to their site will perform well from the start; routine gardening practices such as soil improvement and mulching will only improve their performance.

Size: Several factors play a role in determining the best size for your garden. Available space may be the main consideration, but keep in mind what landscape purpose the garden is to serve. For example, if you need a shrub border to screen an unattractive view or create a private patio space, determine the size by walking around your yard and studying where the largest plants need to be planted to accomplish your purpose. (If your yard is really small, don't forget to include vines, which can be trellised to create a privacy screen without taking up much space. See the Trellising entry for options.) Smaller shrubs and perennials that connect these larger plants into a continuous border can be filled in later, as time and budget permit. The beauty of having an overall plan is that you'll be able to work gradually toward your goal.

For a flower garden that blooms all season, you'll need enough space to accommodate a variety of plants that will provide an extended bloom period. About 125 square feet will give you enough room to mass flowers for a succession of color. For a formal garden, a 5- by 25-foot rectangle, two 5- by 12½-foot beds, or a 12-foot-diameter circle all provide about 125 square feet. In an informal garden, make free-form shapes, or plan several related beds divided by paths. In general, don't plan gardens that are less than 4 feet or 5 feet wide if you want a lush effect. Don't plan them any wider if you want to be able to tend the plants without stepping into the bed or if you want an access path on either side.

Time and money: These last considerations are critical: How much time and money do you

Informal design. Informal gardens feature gentle curves and free-form shapes that flow together. Garden ornaments and special plants are often placed along pathways so they are hidden at one moment and revealed the next. Plants are asymmetrically balanced—with three small plants balancing a single large one, for example—to create a pleasing and restful design.

want to spend? You can plan for features that reduce maintenance, but any garden will require basic care—especially in the early stages. Consider how much time you want to devote to such tasks as weeding, staking, watering, and pruning. Look for tough, low-maintenance plants if you want to keep these chores to a minimum.

Plants and supplies also cost money; decide how much you want to spend before you start to dig. (See the Nursery Bed entry for a practical way to minimize your plant investment.) If you're not realistic about what size garden you can control, it will end up controlling you, and you'll be forever playing catch-up with weeds and a wealth of other problems. Once you have at least a general garden plan, you can plant each area as time and budget permit. Plan your garden so you'll have time to enjoy it.

Creating a Design

Designing the garden and selecting the plants in it may seem overwhelming, since there are so many plants to choose from—species of perennials, annuals, bulbs, herbs, flowering shrubs, and more, not to mention all the cultivars available! But don't let yourself drift away in a sea of plant names. Chances are, your growing conditions are right for only a fraction of what's available. Let your moisture, soil, and light conditions limit the plants you choose. If you have a garden bed that gets full sun and tends toward dry soil, don't plant shade- and moisture-loving perennials like hostas and ferns. Instead, put in plants that thrive in full sun, like daylilies and ornamental grasses. And don't forget to choose only plants that are hardy in your area.

Once you've narrowed your choices to plants that do well in your area and conditions, the key to successful design is to choose plants that look good both in and out of bloom. Pay special attention to what the foliage of perennials and shrubs will look like when the plants are out of bloom.

If you intend to create your garden without using a paper plan, it's a good idea to jot down the specifics of your growing conditions on a small piece of paper—a 3- by 5-inch card is perfect—or store the details on a smartphone. Keep this list with you and refer to it while at garden centers or plant sales, so you aren't smitten by every pretty bloom you see and end up with a car full of plants that won't grow well on your site. Remember, too, the basic principles of design—color, height, form, and texture—and try to select plants that will be attractive together as well as grow well together. And even if you don't draw out a formal design plan, as described in the next section, understanding the steps that go into one or making a plant list to guide your purchases will help you select plants that will work well together.

Creating a Plan

To make a plant list and develop the design you'll need regular and colored pencils or crayons, a tablet of paper (for plant lists), graph paper, tracing paper, and a soft eraser. Use graph paper with a scale of ½ inch equals 1 foot. Tape two sheets together, if necessary. You can also make plant lists on a smartphone, tablet, or computer and, if you like, download a garden design app or invest in design software and use it to create your plan.

To get an idea of how many plants you'll need, consider the approximate size at maturity of the types of plants you want. Perennial plants generally need 2 to 4 square feet at maturity; that means you can fit from 30 to 60 of them in a 125-square-foot garden. Shrubs and small trees may need from 9 to 25 or more square feet.

Making a plant list: Selecting the plants for

PLANT NAME & BLOOM SEASON	LESS THAN 1'	1' TO 3'	MORE THAN 3'	YELLOW	RED/PINK	BLUE/ LAVENDER	WHITE	ATTRACTIVE FOLIAGE
EARLY SUMMER								
1 *Phlox divaricata* (wild blue phlox)	✓					✓		
2 *Paeonia* (peonies) (pink)		✓			✓			
3 *Chionanthus virginicus* (white fringe tree)			✓				✓	
MIDSUMMER								
4 *Leucanthemum × superbum* 'Snow Lady' (Shasta daisies)		✓					✓	
5 *Coreopsis verticil- lata* 'Moonbeam' (coreopsis)		✓		✓				
6 *Echinacea purpurea* (purple coneflowers)			✓		✓			
LATE SUMMER/FALL								
7 *Sedum* 'Autumn Joy' (Autumn Joy sedum)		✓			✓			
8 *Panicum virgatum* (switchgrass)			✓					✓
9 *Anemone × hybrida* (Japanese anemones)		✓			✓			

Creating a plant list. A chartlike plant list helps ensure that you pick plants with a range of heights, bloom colors, and bloom times. Start with plant names along one side. Sort plants according to bloom season, then indicate height and bloom color. Number the list and use the numbers when you draw your design.

any garden is a challenge. There are literally thousands to choose from and a confusing array of flower colors, sizes, shapes, and textures. Start with a list of favorite plants, either on paper or on computer, then add ones you've admired in other gardens, nurseries, photographs, books, magazines, and nursery catalogs. Leave plenty of space between plant names for notes. Jot down plant descriptions, growing tips, bloom time, height, color, hardiness, and culture.

Keep an eye out for perennials with good foliage and a long season of bloom. Trees and shrubs with winter interest—like evergreens or ones with ornamental bark or branching habits—are also invaluable, as are shrubs and other plants that bloom when few other plants in the garden are in flower. Don't worry about making your list too long.

Periodically review your list and cross off plants that won't grow well in the site and don't fit your needs. If you have only shade to offer, cross off plants that need full sun. Do you want only easy-care plants? Eliminate those that need staking or deadheading to look their best. Do you want to save on water bills? Cross off any that may need supplemental watering.

Charting selections: Next, make a chart to help identify plants that will add the most to your design. On a clean sheet of paper or using spreadsheet software, make a column on the left labeled "Plant Name & Bloom Season." Draw lines across the page at intervals to indicate sections for each season of bloom. If you have a large garden, you can use a separate sheet for each bloom season. Write down the bloom seasons you want in the first column—early, mid-, and late summer, for example. Leave enough space under each season to list plant names.

Divide the right side of the chart into several columns for plant heights and colors. You'll need three or four columns to indicate various heights and as many columns for flower colors. Add an extra column to indicate plants with attractive foliage or winter interest. See page 239 for a sample chart.

Starting with the first plant on your list, enter it under the appropriate bloom season on your chart. Then indicate height and color with a check mark in the appropriate columns. Repeat this process for each plant on your list. When you finish, look the chart over to make sure you have a fairly equal representation of check marks under each column. Will some flowers of each color be blooming in each season? Are there a variety of heights? Add and subtract plants until you have a balance in all

the categories and a manageable number of plants to grow. Last, number the plants on your list. Use these numbers to fill in the spaces as you draw your garden design.

Drawing Your Design

If you're working on paper instead of using an app or software program, draw an outline of your garden to scale on graph paper. Use tracing paper over the graph paper so you can start over easily if you need to. Begin drawing shapes on the tracing paper to indicate where each plant will grow. (Try to draw them to scale, based on the sizes you determined.) Instead of drawing neat circles or blocks, use oval or oblong shapes placed in horizontal drifts that will flow into one another.

Arrange plants, especially perennials and small shrubs, in clumps of several plants. Because of the basic design principles of balance and repetition, you'll want to repeat clumps of at least some species. So, as a general rule, you'll probably want half as many plants on your list as you can fit in your border. In our example, that would mean 15 to 30 plants on the list.

Beginning with the first plant on your list, study its "profile" and decide where you want to plant it. Transfer its name or number to the corresponding shape—or shapes if you want to repeat it in more than one spot—on your diagram. Do this with all the plants on your list.

As you work, you'll have to decide how many of each plant you want to grow. You may wish to follow the "rule of three" for perennials that are relatively small at maturity. Three plants will make an attractive clump when mature. For large plants, such as peonies, you may want only one plant; for others, two.

Place the tallest plants in the back of your diagram. It's a good idea to mix up heights somewhat to create interest. Let some tall plants extend forward into the middle group, and some medium-size ones up front. Try to mix shapes and textures throughout, planting glossy, dark-green-leaved plants next to ones with gray-green, fern-like foliage, for example.

Also consider color combinations as you work, and avoid large masses of single colors. To visualize how your garden will look at each season, put a sheet of tracing paper over your completed design. Check your plant list to find out which plants bloom in early summer, for example. Trace the plants blooming at that time on your tracing paper. Then color them the appropriate color. Do the same for the other seasons of bloom, using a separate sheet of tracing paper for each.

Strive for a balanced composition in every season, with the color evenly distributed throughout the border during each bloom period. Are all the reds or yellows off to one side so that the design looks lopsided? Are the color combinations pleasing to you? Are major color combinations repeated at rhythmic intervals to tie the border together? Would it help to add more plants of a particular color?

As you grapple with these problems and refine your design, be sure to make changes on both tracing paper and master diagram. Expect to redo your design several times before you feel you have it right. Think of it this way: Each sheet of crumpled paper—virtual or literal—brings you closer to your goal of creating a beautiful garden, tailor-made by and for you.

Growing with Your Design

Keep in mind that one of the most compelling and challenging aspects of gardening is that a garden and its design are ever-changing. Whether you use a detailed plant list and paper chart or design by tucking in perennials and shrubs guided only by gut instinct, you'll have plants that thrive and eventually grow too large plus others that don't grow at all. You'll also have combinations that don't work and ones that are stunning and worth repeating. See the Division entry for information on dividing overgrown plants and filling in holes left by plants that have died.

Throughout the season, plus from year to year, take time to examine your garden carefully. Notes about when there isn't enough in bloom, combinations that don't work, or flowers and foliage in a friend's garden that would be stunning in yours can be invaluable. Jot down notes on a calendar or anywhere that will remind you during the proper season to look for plants to add that will enhance your design. Growing with your design and changing it is part of gardening, so if you don't like something you see, remember a spade is the perfect tool for editing your beds and borders. Use it to separate colors that clash by moving one of the offenders or to make room for a choice addition you can't be without.

GARDENIA

Gardenia, cape jasmine. Evergreen spring-flowering shrubs.

Description: *Gardenia jasminoides*, common gardenia or cape jasmine, grows 3 to 5 feet tall with a spreading habit. Thick, dark green, 2- to 4-inch leaves have a shiny surface. Creamy white, waxy, 2- to 3½-inch-wide, sometimes double, intensely fragrant flowers appear in late spring and early summer. Zones 8–10.

How to grow: Provide moist, well-drained, humus-rich soil and light shade. Plant in fall or winter. Water to establish, and when needed in dry weather. Scale, whitefly, mealybugs, and nematodes can limit use of gardenias in parts of the South.

Landscape uses: Use gardenias around foundations and patios and in borders where you will enjoy their stunning fragrance. They also can be grown as houseplants in cold-winter regions, where they make handsome patio plants through the summer months.

GARDENING SAFELY

When you're gardening, a few commonsense precautions can mean the difference between enjoyment and injury. Gardening can be tough on skin, muscles, and joints, but if you follow good practices and procure the right tools and equipment, you'll be able to garden safely now and for years to come.

Stretching: The first thing to remember is that gardening is exercise, just like running or aerobics. To prevent muscle strain, it helps to do a few simple stretching exercises after your gardening session. (You don't need to "warm up" with stretches before you start gardening, though.)

If you already incorporate stretches into your exercise routine, simply do them after gardening, too. If stretching isn't part of your routine, ask for a demonstration at your local gym or health center.

Good gardening posture: Think about it—a lot of gardening activities almost require you to stand on your head! Weeding and planting are two examples of gardening tasks that you do with your hands and face close to the ground. If you do these activities standing up and bent double, you can put a tremendous strain on your back. And unless you come from a culture that habitually relaxes by squatting on heels instead of sitting in a chair, squatting down will feel uncom-

fortable and put undue stress on your knees.

Instead, bring yourself closer to ground level in a comfortable manner. The best choice is kneeling, and it's helpful to cushion your knees with a waterproof kneeling pad or individual kneepads. Kneepads, which strap on over your jeans, are less cushioned than a kneeling pad but offer the advantage of mobility—they move with you as you work your way down the bed or row. Some kneelers are designed with side supports so you can use them with the cushion on the ground as a kneeling pad, or flip the whole device with the other end up to convert it to a handy garden seat.

If you have knee troubles or reduced mobility, here are three other options.

- A convertible kneeler—just use the seat at all times.
- A sturdy plastic bucket with a handle and a padded lid. You can carry seed packets and supplies in the bucket, then sit on it while you do your gardening chores.
- A mobile gardening "chair," or tractor scoot, which is basically a tractor seat on wheels. The seat is broad and comfy, and you can scoot along the row or bed as you work.

Tools: Choose tools that work for you. Using a poorly designed tool can make gardening twice the work it should be. If you have carpal tunnel syndrome, arthritis, or limited strength, choosing the right tools is essential. Ergonomic tools have been designed for comfort and ease of use. These tools do their job with much less effort on your part.

Whether you choose an ergonomic tool or a standard design, make sure you "try" before you buy. Practice making the motions you'd normally do with the tool while you're still in the store. If it's a trowel, a pair of pruners, or a hand fork, make sure the grip is comfortable. If it's a long-handled tool, think about whether it's too short or long for you to use easily. Check the weight and balance. Better to look a little silly in the store than risk blisters or worse in the garden!

One last thing about tools, and that's basic tool safety. A sharp tool like a pair of pruners can actually be dangerous if the blades are dull, since you have to exert tremendous pressure to get them to work, and the dull blades can slip under the force, cutting you instead of the branch you're pruning. Of course, they can also be dangerous when they're sharp! And remember that any tool is a hazard if you leave it out in the garden where someone can trip on it, or worse, step on the blade and hit themselves on the head with the handle. Always put your tools away after you've finished with them. As for power tools like chain saws, use them responsibly if you want to stay out of the emergency room.

For more on choosing, using, and maintaining tools, see the Tools and Equipment entry.

Protective wear: Thorns. Brambles. Stickers. Sharp sticks and stones. Sunburn. Poison ivy, oak, and sumac. Mosquitoes. Ticks. Gardeners face a whole range of minor but miserable hazards. Fortunately, it's easy to avoid injury and discomfort if you take a few simple precautions.

First, wear protective clothing. Jeans or other long pants, sturdy shoes or boots, a long-sleeved shirt, and a hat to protect your head, face, and neck from UV damage are basic gardening wear. If it's hot out, choose a lightweight shirt and a straw or cotton hat with good ventilation. Remember that even a hat won't provide complete protection, so use sunscreen and don't forget your UV-blocking sunglasses.

Gloves are the gardener's ally, protecting hands from cuts, scrapes, and rash-inducing plants like poison ivy. Choose specially coated "rose gloves" or "thorn-proof gloves" if you know you'll be working around plants with thorns or spines.

Those long pants and sleeves are a good defense against both poison plants and ticks. But you still need to take a commonsense approach: Check both your clothing and your skin for ticks when you come in after a gardening session, and wash your hands with a poison-ivy oil remover such as Tecnu before you rub your eyes or touch bare skin.

Preventing heatstroke and dehydration: Overheating is a danger whenever you exercise in hot, humid weather, and hot weather makes dehydration an issue as well. Using good sense is the best prevention for both hazards. Take a chilled bottle of water to the garden with you, and remember to pause and drink frequently. You can also hold the cold bottle against your neck and forehead to cool off fast, or pour some of the chilled water onto a bandanna and tie it around your neck.

When it's hot out, do your gardening early in the day and in the evening, when the temperatures start to drop. Avoid the peak heat hours of 11:00 a.m. to 3:00 p.m. Wear a hat to keep the sun off your head, and make yourself take breaks.

First aid: Carrying a few sizes and shapes of adhesive bandages and some analgesic/antiseptic swabs or pads in your pocket is always a smart idea. After all, gardening is a contact sport! With just these items on hand, you can immediately clean and bind up minor cuts, punctures, and scrapes.

What about bites and stings? Unless you happen on a nest of yellow jackets or ants, it's extremely unlikely that you'll be bitten or stung by an insect or spider. Ant bites are aggravating, but unless you live in areas with fire ants (in which case you already know to watch out for nests), they're more of an aggravation than anything else.

A bee or wasp sting hurts. Pull or scrape out the stinger if it's a bee sting, and whether it's a bee or wasp sting, put a paste of baking soda and water on the site of the sting.

If you're seriously allergic to bee and/or wasp stings, take every precaution and always carry a bee sting kit, which usually contains an antihistamine pill and an adrenaline or epinephrine injection to counter the allergic reaction. Talk to your doctor and make sure you know how to use the kit before you end up in a situation where you need it.

GARLIC

Allium sativum
Amaryllidaceae

Garlic should be a staple of every organic garden. Garlic cloves are great for seasoning all kinds of foods or for roasting and eating whole. The robustly flavored young greens are a wonderful chivelike garnish for many dishes, or they may be made into a delicious garlic-greens pesto. You may decide to devote part of your garlic patch solely to greens production! An added benefit of garlic growing is that homemade garlic oil spray is an effective deterrent for many garden pests. For a recipe, see page 451.

Types: There are two types of garlic, softneck (*Allium sativum* var. *sativum*) and hardneck (*A. sativum* var. *ophioscorodon*). Hardneck garlic is also known as seedstem (or top-setting or bolting) garlic because in late spring, just before the bulbs expand, they will produce a flower stem (which should be removed for best yields—it's edible, too). Hardneck garlic yields larger cloves and usually tastes better but is more difficult to prevent from sprouting in long-term storage. Softneck garlic has

a longer shelf life, is a little easier to grow (especially in warmer regions), and may have slightly higher yields than hardneck garlic. Softneck bulbs have an inner row of frustrating hard-to-work-with small cloves on the inside of each head; hardneck bulbs don't. Almost all garlic sold in supermarkets is softneck.

Elephant garlic (*A. ampeloprasum*) produces huge bulbs weighing up to 1 pound apiece. The plants are large overall, growing as tall as 4 feet. You can use the cloves as you would regular garlic in cooking, but elephant garlic has a much milder flavor.

Planting: For a satisfying harvest, order garlic bulbs from a garlic grower rather than planting garlic cloves purchased from the supermarket. When you buy direct from a grower, you'll know that the bulbs haven't been treated with an anti-sprouting chemical, and you can choose varieties that will grow well in your area.

Garlic grows best in deep, rich soil and full sun. Plant garlic in fall, on or around Columbus Day in most of the country, and a little later in the Deep South. The bulbs should have a little root growth before winter, so that they won't be heaved out of the ground by frost. Spring-planted garlic rarely provides satisfactory bulb yields but will produce good greens.

Separate a bulb into individual cloves, keeping the papery skin covering each clove intact. Select large cloves for planting, and plant only healthy cloves. If you've ordered from a reputable supplier, this should not be a concern, but check cloves carefully for streaks or signs of decay if you're planting cloves you've saved from a previous crop. To prepare the cloves for planting, fill a quart jar with water and add 1 tablespoon of baking soda and 1 tablespoon of liquid seaweed. Soak the garlic cloves in this solution for 2 hours prior to planting to help prevent fungal disease and encourage vigorous growth.

Plant in a weed-free, prepared bed, in rows 1 foot apart. Plant the presoaked cloves in 3-inch-deep furrows, placing each with its flattened root end down and the pointy end up. Space the cloves 4 to 6 inches apart (space elephant garlic 8 inches apart). Cover loosely with soil, then mulch lightly or interplant with a cover crop that will winter-kill in your area. You can expect to harvest 5 to 10 pounds of bulbs per 20 feet of row.

Growing guidelines: In spring, encourage vigorous leaf growth by applying foliar seaweed or fish emulsion spray every 2 weeks. Watering is important during the bulb-forming stage; provide extra water if conditions are dry in early summer. Weeds are probably garlic's biggest enemy, so weed beds regularly.

Problems: To prevent disease problems, avoid excess standing moisture in your garlic bed. Viruses, sometimes a problem, usually do nothing worse than diminish yield. See the Onion entry for information on controlling insect pests.

Harvesting: Check plants frequently once the leaves begin to turn brown. Bulbs should be at full size, with wrappers formed around each bulb. If you harvest the bulbs too early, they won't reach their full size. Dig them too late, and the outer wrapper will be more likely to tear, resulting in lower quality and poor keeping ability. Cure garlic in a hot, dry, dark, and airy place for a few weeks. Trim roots and neck, then store in cool, dry, dark conditions. Softneck varieties are best for making garlic braids.

GAYFEATHER

See *Liatris*

GERANIUM

Geranium, cranesbill. Spring- and summer-blooming perennials.

Description: Don't confuse these perennials with the popular annual geraniums, which are in the genus *Pelargonium*. Perennial geraniums bear many ¾- to 2-inch rounded flowers in shades of white, pink, magenta, blue, and violet. Plants form 6- to 36-inch spreading, mounded, or slightly upright plants with scalloped to deeply cut 1- to 8-inch leaves, often with striking red, burgundy, or orange fall color. The patented violet-blue hybrid geranium Rozanne (aka 'Gerwat', hardy in Zones 5–8) was named Perennial Plant of the Year for 2008. Zones 3–8. Hardiness zone range depends on the individual species or cultivar, so check before you buy.

Geranium ×*cantabrigiense*, Cambridge geranium, forms an attractive groundcover with trailing stems and scalloped leaves. Plants reach 6 to 8 inches tall and 8 to 12 inches wide, with white, pale pink, red-violet, or raspberry-red flowers. 'Biokovo', the 2015 Perennial Plant of the Year, grows 6 to 10 inches tall and bears white flowers with pale pink centers. Zones 4–8.

G. cinereum, grayleaf cranesbill, is a low, spreading plant that's well suited for rock gardens and other well-drained, sunny sites. Plants reach 6 to 12 inches tall and 12 inches wide with incised leaves and inch-wide pink flowers with prominent veins. Zones 4 (with protection) and 5–7.

G. ×*oxonianum* has produced some of the most famous geranium cultivars, including the pink-flowered 'A.T. Johnson', 'Claridge Druce' with lilac-pink blooms, and 'Wargrave Pink'. Floriferous plants have deeply cut leaves and reach 15 to 18 inches tall and 12 to 24 inches wide. Zones 4–8.

G. sanguineum, bloody cranesbill, is a hardy, shade-tolerant species. It reaches 8 to 12 inches tall and 12 to 24 inches wide, with attractive palmate leaves and inch-wide bright pink flowers. 'Album' has white flowers; 'Shepherd's Warning' has deep rose-pink flowers and reaches just 6 inches tall. The variety *striatum* has pale pink, rose-veined flowers. Zones 3–8.

How to grow: Plant or divide in spring or fall. Grow in a sunny spot with average, well-drained but moisture-retentive soil. Give partial shade in hotter, drier areas. Excess fertility leads to floppy growth. Generally easy to grow and trouble-free.

Landscape uses: Mass geraniums in borders, informal gardens, and lightly shaded woodlands, or as a colorful groundcover. Use them to soften upright plantings of Siberian iris, ferns, ornamental grasses, and other spiky perennials. Use dwarf species in rock gardens and other sunny, well-drained sites.

GINGER

Zingiber officinale
Zingiberaceae

Ginger is an herbaceous perennial that produces glossy, bamboolike foliage on 36-inch stems that arise from the familiar knobby rhizomes sold in grocery produce sections. In its native tropics, ginger develops a tall flowerstalk topped by a conical spike of yellow flowers that protrude from yellow-green bracts, but ginger plants rarely bloom when grown in containers. Beyond the areas where it is hardy, ginger can be grown in containers as an annual crop. Cuttings from the lush foliage lend fresh flavor to tea or soup stock, and simply rustling the leaves as you pass by releases a heavenly scent. While most American grocers sell only cured ginger—harvested from such steamy parts of the globe as China, India, and Nepal—a growing number of specialty growers harvest crisp, succulent baby rhizomes for sale in late autumn. Zones 9–12.

Planting: Buy a piece of ginger the size of your thumb with several bumpy nodules at the tips—these are the buds. Opt for plump chunks, not those withering in their own skin. Skin on the delicate buds should be thinner and lighter colored; forgo pieces with darkened buds. Like potatoes, conventional ginger is irradiated and chemically treated to stop it from sprouting at the supermarket. That means it won't sprout in your home, either. Be sure you buy organic, untreated rhizomes for your planting stock.

Growing guidelines: Begin by presprouting your ginger. This requires a bit of patience, as ginger takes its time getting started. Create a terrarium using a takeout container with a clear lid. Choose one just a few inches deeper than the diameter of your rhizome and punch drainage holes in the bottom. Put an inch or two of potting soil below the rhizome and cover it lightly with just ½ inch of potting mix. Water well. Replace the lid, but don't seal it tightly. Maintain the soil at 70°F and moist to the touch, watering only when the soil dries. A sprout will emerge in 6 to 8 weeks.

Ginger is a heavy feeder and an even heavier drinker that needs a lot of room to grow. Given the space, a chunk the size of your thumb will easily grow to fill a 2-gallon pot over the course of about 6 months. Choose a pretty container with good drainage holes and a deep saucer. Use well-draining, fertile soil with plenty of coir. Gently place your presprouted rhizome on top of 4 inches of potting mix and bury all but the sprout tip. Place it in a warm, sunny window or in a sunny, sheltered spot outdoors where temperatures range from 60° to 90°F.

Like Irish potatoes, ginger rhizomes will burst through the soil and turn green in the sun. Commercial growers boost yields by watering regularly and hilling the rhizomes once a month. To achieve the same result at home, water weekly with organic plant food, and once a month sprinkle several inches of rich compost into your pot, protecting the rhizome itself from sun exposure.

Harvesting: Hold the greens at their base, where they emerge from the soil and lift the entire rhizome (this is a good project to do outdoors, over an old newspaper or drop cloth). Snap off a chunk of the rhizome, then place the rest of the plant back in its pot, sprinkle on more potting soil or compost, water heavily, and treat it gently for a few days. Like any fragile transplant, protect it from glaring sunlight and wild temperature swings while it recovers.

Uses: Baby ginger has a mild flavor and, unlike its cured counterpart, it's juicy with more snap and less string. Best of all, the skin is so thin and pretty, there's no need to peel. Steep slices in hot water with lemon and honey for a soothing tisane or toss chunks in the juicer with apples, carrots, or kale. Sauté with veggies. Feeling adventuresome? Create an infusion with your favorite libation, steep in simple syrup, or candy it by simmering in sugar syrup.

GLADIOLUS

Gladiolus, glads. Summer- and fall-blooming corms.

Description: *Gladiolus ×gandavensis*, hybrid gladioli or glads, bear 2- to 5-inch triangular blooms, many with ruffled edges, in an enormous range of colors (except true blue) in solid shades and combinations. The blooms are arranged neatly and closely up one side of stiffly upright stems from 1½ to 5 feet tall that rise out of a fan of swordlike leaves. Many are hardy in Zones 7–10.

How to grow: Because an individual plant's flowers last in good condition for about 10 days, begin planting the corms after the last severe frost and continue at 10-day to 2-week intervals until midsummer for a longer bloom season. Full sun encourages strong growth and vigorous corm production for next year, but the plants also tolerate light shade. Depending on the height of the cultivar, cover with 3 to 6 inches of fertile, well-drained, moist soil. Add organic matter like compost if your soil is heavy. Plant closely (3 to 6 inches apart) to save space and to make staking easier. Mulch with pine needles, straw, or other light material when the leaves are about 6 inches tall. Water well during dry spells. Give plants an application of fish emulsion or compost tea as the fans begin to elongate in the center and as the flower spike becomes visible within the leaves. See the Compost entry for instructions for making compost tea.

Most glads grow tall and may blow over in storms or even fall under their own weight when in bloom, so stake them individually if you grow only a few. If you're growing clumps of glads, provide a corset of stakes and twine running in all directions between them. Or grow them in rows with two parallel strings on either side tied firmly to strong stakes.

Thrips cause streaky leaves and deformed flowers; control them in spring before planting by soaking the corms in very hot water (hotter than you can bear but not boiling). To help control fusarium wilt and viruses, immediately lift and destroy any plant that turns yellowish and looks stunted. In fall, or after the foliage is quite yellow, dig up the corms and store in a dry place until the soil clinging to them is dry. Shake off the soil, cut the foliage off at 1 to 2 inches above the corm, and break off the shriveled dead corm under the new one(s). Store the new corms dry and cool (around 45°F) in plastic mesh bags.

Landscape uses: Grow a few small clusters massed between other border plants that can disguise the fading foliage, or remove glads after they bloom. Smaller-flowered species glads such as *Gladiolus tristis*, ever-flowering gladiolus, and *G. communis*, corn flag, often look better in perennial borders than traditional garden gladiolus. All glads make excellent cut flowers, so grow bunches of them in a cutting garden where you can attend to their special needs.

GOLDENROD

See *Solidago*

GOOSEBERRY

Ribes spp.

Grossulariaceae

Gooseberries come in a kaleidoscope of colors—golden yellow, green, orange, pink, red, purple, and almost black—with a corresponding diversity of flavors. They are wonderful for preserves and refreshing summer wines; some are at their best eaten fresh at full ripeness.

Gooseberries are deciduous shrubs that grow 3 to 6 feet high and wide. The arched branches are usually armed with long, sharp spines. They fruit on wood a year or more old; each plant can produce for more than 30 years. Five-year-old bushes yield 6 to 9 pounds of fruit on early cultivars and 12 pounds or more on later ones. Gooseberries perform best in northern climates, where cool moist summers favor slow ripening that brings out the fruit's subtle flavor. Zones 3–6.

Types: Gooseberries belong to two species of *Ribes*: *R. uva-crispa* (from Europe) and *R. hirtellum* (from America). European dessert gooseberries rival the finest grapes and other fruits in flavor and appearance. They are, however, often less heat tolerant and more mildew susceptible than small-fruited American types. 'Invicta' is a popular European variety that is mildew resistant. 'Poorman' is a mildew-resistant hybrid. 'Hinnonmäki Röd' is a high-yielding red-fruited cultivar that is mildew resistant. 'Captivator' is a semithornless hybrid.

Jostaberries are a hybrid of gooseberry and black currant (*R. nigrum*). The black fruits are ½ inch and larger, and the bushes resist many pest and disease problems.

Planting: Gooseberries require similar planting, pruning, and nutritional treatments as their close relatives, red and white currants, which also belong to the genus *Ribes*. See the Currant entry for details. For gooseberries, be sure to choose a protected, sunny site; gooseberries also do well in partial or dappled shade. Jostaberries are grown like red currants, but leave 8 feet all around at planting.

Care: Maintain a 2- to 3-inch mulch layer to conserve water and reduce weeds. Keep the soil evenly moist. Gooseberries need lots of potassium and magnesium and low amounts of nitrogen. Leaf margin scorching and weak wood are symptoms of potassium deficiency. If your soil is deficient in potassium, fertilize with granite dust. For a magnesium deficiency, apply dolomitic limestone or Epsom salts.

Thinning is only necessary if you want large fruits or if a plant has set an exceptionally heavy crop; if necessary, remove every other fruit in late

May. Never let the ground dry out once fruit starts to ripen, as a heavy rain or watering might cause the berries to burst.

Pruning: Summer prune gooseberries starting in July. Cut back laterals of the new season's growth to three to five leaves, leaving leaders unpruned. Always prune just above an upward- and outward-facing bud. In fall, cut out any crossing, broken, or unproductive canes.

Problems: The federal ban on planting any species of *Ribes* (because of its role in the disease cycle of white pine blister rust) was lifted in the 1960s, leaving a patchwork of state regulations. Contact your county's extension office for information on your locality's status. See the Currant entry for more information on common problems.

Harvesting: Gooseberries ripen over a 2- to 3-week period, so bushes must be picked over several times. Be sure to wear gloves to protect your hands from spines as you pull off the fruit. Pick early cultivars when fruit is not yet ripe (in early June) for culinary use or processing. Late cultivars ripen in mid-July through early August. Dessert berries keep for up to 2 weeks after harvesting, refrigerated in a sealed container. All kinds freeze well.

GOURD

Cucurbita spp. and others
Cucurbitaceae

For a crop that's both fun and practical, try growing gourds. Many species' sturdy, colorful fruits can be transformed into a variety of unique and useful items, including bottles, bowls, spoons, musical instruments, birdhouses, and sponges.

Gourd enthusiasts commonly divide gourds into hard- and thin-shelled types. Hard-shelled fruits are produced by white-flowered bottle gourds (*Lagenaria siceraria*); these are the gourds to use for crafts such as birdhouses. Yellow-flowered gourds (*Cucurbita pepo* var. *texana* and others) produce colorful, decorative, thin-shelled gourds that are more closely related to pumpkins.

Planting: Grow this crop in hills or on fences or trellises. Provide a deeply worked, well-drained soil to which you've added one heaping shovelful of compost per plant.

Large gourds can take up to 140 days to mature; start long-season types indoors several weeks before the last frost. Soak seeds overnight to promote germination. Grow the seeds in peat pots to avoid disturbing the sensitive roots at transplanting time. Plant the seedlings outdoors after the last frost date.

Sow shorter-season gourds directly after the last frost, following the seed-packet directions for each specific cultivar. Place about five seeds each in hills spaced 5 feet apart; thin to one strong seedling. Or plant in a row along a fence or trellis, thinning the plants to 2 to 3 feet apart.

Growing guidelines: Gourds will flatten on the side in contact with the ground as they mature. Flat-bottomed gourds make good containers, but slow-maturing gourds that rest on soil for a long time can rot. Avoid this problem by growing them on a trellis or by spreading several inches of mulch around plants before the stems begin to sprawl. Besides protecting the developing gourds, the mulch also conserves soil moisture and helps keep weeds down. Side-dress in midsummer with compost, and keep the soil evenly moist.

Problems: See the Squash entry for insect and disease control.

Harvesting: Let gourds ripen on the vines until the stems are brown, but be aware that frost will soften and ruin the fruits of some types of gourds. Always handle gourds carefully, because

Gourds for the Birds

Looking for a great garden project? Try growing your own birdhouses! Bottle gourds (*Lagenaria siceraria*) can be ideal homes for a variety of birds, including purple martins, swallows, chickadees, and wrens.

Planting and growing requirements for bottle gourds are the same as for other gourds. Bottle gourds can tolerate light frosts, so let them ripen on the vines; mature bottle gourds have hard, light brown shells. Bring them indoors and allow them to cure for several months in a cool, dry place until you hear the seeds rattle inside as you shake the gourd.

Drill a 1- to 2½-inch hole in the side of each gourd; make the smaller-size hole for small birds like wrens, the larger-size hole for large birds like martins. Drill a few small holes in the bottom of the gourd for drainage. Drill two more holes in the top, and thread a piece of waterproof cord or wire through these holes to hang the house. You may want to paint, varnish, or shellac the gourd house before you hang it, although it should last about 2 years if untreated.

they bruise easily. Harvest by using a sharp knife to cut through the stem 2 to 3 inches away from the gourd. Dry off any moisture.

Gourds are dry when the seeds rattle around inside. Some, like sponge gourds (*Luffa aegyptiaca*), may dry sufficiently on the vine; others you'll need to harvest and dry indoors. To reduce the chances of spoilage, wipe gourds with a mild vinegar solution.

Place hard-shelled types on a rack with good air circulation. Smaller gourds can dry in less than a month, but large types may take up to 6 months. Use a knife to scrape off any mold that appears. To prepare gourds for display, remove the thin outer shells with steel wool.

To dry thin-shelled gourds, place them on trays in an airy place or hang them in mesh bags. You can wax, paint, varnish, or shellac thin-shelled types, but don't cut or carve them until the protective coating is completely dry.

Grow sponge gourds, or loofahs (luffas), for their spongelike, fibrous interiors. Pick them young and green for a soft sponge; fruits with yellow or brown skins produce hard, scratchy sponges. Soak the gourd in water for several days, then peel off the skin. Cut off one end and shake out the seeds; your sponge is now ready for use.

For more on growing and preserving gourds, visit the American Gourd Society's Web site (see Resources on page 673).

GRAFTING

Many gardeners who routinely propagate plants in other ways view grafting—attaching a piece of living plant onto another plant—as an almost mystical technique, beyond the ability of the average green thumb. Grafting does require some advance planning and the proper tools, but with a little practice, you can learn to graft.

Grafting is commonly used to propagate woody plants that produce few or no seeds. It is also useful for propagating named plant cultivars that do not pass along their desirable characteristics in their seeds.

Grafting can help you get the most from limited

garden space. For example, if you want to grow fruit trees that need cross-pollination, graft a branch or two of the needed pollinator onto the desired plant. You can also, within limits, graft several fruit cultivars onto one rootstock; the resulting plant will yield different fruits on a single trunk. Grafting produces large plants quickly and can encourage early bearing on fruit trees. In general, grafting is suitable for propagating many types of ornamental trees, roses, and fruit trees, plus some conifers.

Grafting Basics

Before you grab a knife and head for your favorite tree, it's helpful to understand how grafting works. When you graft, your aim is to join the cambium—the actively growing tissue that produces cells that conduct water and nutrients—of two plant stems. The stem of the parent is the rootstock; the stem you are joining to it is called the scion.

When you cut and join the scion and rootstock, the cambium of each part produces wound tissue called callus. Eventually the two areas of callus meet, and the cells intermingle. Some of the callus develops into cambium cells, which form a bridge between the cambium of the scion and that of the rootstock. Once there is a continuous connection between the two cambium layers, the graft is successful and the parts can continue to grow normally.

The key to success with grafting is practice. Collect prunings from less-desirable plants, bring the pieces indoors, and practice the appropriate cuts before attempting to graft a valuable specimen. Make clean, flat grafting cuts so there is maximum contact between scion and rootstock; also, make your cuts quickly, and don't allow the surfaces to dry out.

Try to choose a scion and rootstock that have the same diameter so there is maximum cambial contact. If the rootstock is larger than the scion, matching the cambium layers on one side of the union is sufficient. Wrap the joint firmly to press the cuts together and to protect the finished graft from being knocked out of alignment. Besides adding support, wrapping and waxing a graft protects the union from drying.

Scions: Scions are 1-year-old stem pieces, generally 3 to 6 inches long with a diameter of $\frac{1}{8}$ to $\frac{1}{4}$ inch. Be sure scions have leaf buds, which are usually narrow and pointed; avoid plump, round flower buds. Scions should be dormant when grafted because actively growing leaves will draw moisture out of the scion and inhibit the healing process. Collect scion material in early or late winter, a few weeks or months before you plan to graft. Don't use frozen wood or wood that shows signs of winter damage. For evergreens, collect scions from the previous year's shoots. The stem should be mostly green, with a bit of brown bark at the base. For deciduous plants, take scion material from the middle portions of suitable stems, because branch tips are low in stored nutrients and the buds near the base of the stem may be slow to produce new shoots.

Cut the stems you collect into 6- to 12-inch pieces, bundle them together, and store in a plastic bag containing damp peat moss. If you will be grafting in a few weeks, store the bag in your refrigerator (about 40°F). To store for longer periods, keep the stem pieces at temperatures closer to 33°F. Before grafting, remove the pieces from storage and soak them in water until you are ready to prepare the scions.

Rootstocks: In most cases, you can grow your own rootstocks, although some types (such as dwarfing stocks) are not readily available. The

KEY WORDS *Grafting*

Grafting. The process of joining a stem piece to another plant in such a way that the parts are united by living tissue and continue to grow.

Rootstock. The plant that supplies the root system for the grafted plant.

Scion. The stem piece joined to the rootstock graft.

Cambium. A thin layer of actively growing tissue between the bark and the wood.

Callus. A mass of plant cells that have not yet developed a specific function; produced in a wounded area.

Compatible. A given scion and rootstock are compatible when they can be successfully grafted and grown to maturity.

---

rootstock can be a seedling, a cutting, or a mature tree. Seedling rootstocks are easy and inexpensive to produce. They often have deeper root systems than cuttings and are less likely to have virus problems. Because seeds are genetically variable, though, they may not all produce the same effect on the grafted plant. If you want a rootstock for a specific trait, such as disease resistance, cuttings provide more uniform results. The process known as topworking, which uses mature trees for rootstocks, is most commonly practiced in orchards. Topworking involves cutting back the limbs of an undesirable tree and grafting on scions of a more useful cultivar.

A rootstock can influence a scion in many ways. Apple scions, for example, are grafted onto a range of rootstocks, producing dwarf, semidwarf, or full-size versions of the scion cultivar. Some plants, such as hybrid tea roses, may produce weak root systems if you grow them from cuttings; graft them onto rootstocks of other rose types to get more vigorous plants.

Besides regulating the size of the grafted plant, rootstocks also can provide pest resistance or tolerance to less-than-ideal soil conditions. Species and cultivars that are adaptable to a wide range of conditions often make good rootstocks. *Rhododendron* 'Cunningham's White', for example, can tolerate a pH up to 7.0, so other normally acid-loving rhododendron cultivars are often grafted onto that rootstock. These new plants can adapt to a wider range of soil pH. Some rootstocks extend the range of a given plant by providing a hardier root system.

Two-year-old seedlings or 2- to 3-year-old cuttings make the best rootstocks. Outdoors, graft onto rootstocks planted in a nursery bed or directly in the garden. In autumn, about 18 months before you want to do spring grafting, plant the rootstocks in your chosen site. For a single garden specimen, follow normal transplanting procedures. If you confine your grafting projects to a specific area, prepare a deep, well-drained, fertile nursery bed. Plant rootstocks 1 to 3 feet apart in rows, with 2 to 3 feet between the rows.

For indoor grafting, grow the rootstocks in pots, or transplant 1-year-old seedlings into pots the autumn before grafting, and store them in a cold frame. Bring them into the greenhouse 4 to 6 weeks before you plan to graft. Make sure all rootstock plants are clearly labeled, so you'll know exactly what they are when you need them.

Materials: The most important grafting tool is a razor-sharp knife. A penknife will serve for grafting, but for best results, a special grafting knife is a good investment. Grafting knives have strong, straight steel blades that can be sharpened to a fine edge. They are often available through plant and seed catalogs. You'll also need a sharp pair of pruning shears to collect scion material and to cut back rootstock tops. Scissor-type shears make clean cuts without crushing delicate plant tissues.

Grafting ties provide support for the union, hold in the moisture to provide humidity, and protect the wounds from disease organisms. Cut rubber bands, waxed string, masking tape, and electrical tape are all suitable for grafting. Apply the wrapping material in a single layer, to about 1 inch on each side of the union. When using tape, overlap the edges slightly as you cover the stem. Check wrapped grafts after a month or two, and carefully cut the tie if necessary. If an uncut tie does not break down on its own, it may girdle and kill the rapidly growing stem of an otherwise successful graft.

Grafting waxes serve a purpose similar to that of ties; the two are often used together. Waxes are important for protecting exposed cuts, such as the upper tips of scions and the surfaces of cleft grafts. Commercial grafting wax is sometimes available in garden centers or through plant supply catalogs. Instead of wax, you can apply a commercial tree paint. This material is applied in a liquid form that eventually solidifies. If it rains within 24 hours of use, make another application. With either type of covering, check the treated area 2 to 3 days after grafting, and apply more wax or paint if any cracks have appeared.

Graft failure: You can minimize the chances of graft failure by making the right cuts, providing the proper callusing conditions, and protecting the fin-

ished grafts. But in some cases, these precautions aren't enough to ensure success. If either the stock or scion is infected with a plant virus, the union may not heal properly. Compatibility between the stock and scion also is important for creating and keeping a successful graft. To be compatible, the two parts must be from closely related plants. You can generally graft one cultivar onto another of the same species with a high success rate; this is usually also true of different species within a genus, such as tomato (*Solanum lycopersicum*) on potato (*S. tuberosum*). In certain cases, you can graft plants from different genera, such as pears (*Pyrus* spp.) on quinces (*Cydonia* spp.). It's uncommon to get successful grafts between plants in different families. Sometimes incompatibility causes immediate graft failure; in other cases, it becomes visible only after several years of growth. Symptoms of incompatibility include slow healing of the graft union, lack of vigor, early fall color, or branch dieback; a clean break at the graft union is an obvious sign. There isn't much you can do if these problems occur. Fortunately, delayed incompatibility is uncommon.

Planting and maintenance: Placement of the graft union relative to the soil surface is important. In general, if you choose a rootstock for a particular trait, such as dwarfing effect, set the union above soil level. If you don't, the scion may begin to produce its own roots, and after the scion roots become established, the rootstock will lose its influence on the scion.

In other cases, the purpose of the rootstock is to provide roots for scions that are slow to form their own. Hybrid lilacs (*Syringa* spp.), for example, are sometimes grafted onto privet (*Ligustrum* spp.) seedlings. Once the parts unite, the rootstock supports the plant until the scion produces its own roots. In this case, plant the graft union slightly below the soil surface. When buying a grafted plant, you may want to ask the salesperson for planting advice.

Another special maintenance aspect of grafted plants is the removal of shoots and suckers growing from the rootstock. Vigorous rootstocks may produce many suckers, which can shade out and kill a weaker scion. Check your grafted plants several times a season and remove any suckers. Scions sometimes grow up to several feet during the first season. Stake these shoots or head them back; otherwise, they are prone to breakage.

Whip-and-Tongue Graft

Whip-and-tongue grafting is used for many types of ornamental and fruit trees. It is best for small plant material, from ⅛ to ¼ inch in diameter. The major advantage of this method is the high level of cambium contact; one disadvantage is the degree of advance planning involved. Before grafting, rootstocks should be allowed to establish themselves for at least a year after you plant them. Once grafted, it will take 3 to 4 years to produce a garden-size tree.

Season: Whip-and-tongue grafting is done outdoors in early spring, before bud break. If possible, choose a warm day; it's hard to make a good grafting cut when your fingers are numb!

Getting started: Remove your stem pieces from storage and let them soak in water until you are ready to make your cuts.

Method: First, prepare the scion. If possible, choose a stem that is the same diameter as the rootstock stem. Cut a 4- to 5-inch section, with at least two to three leaf buds, from the scion stem. Make the top cut just above a bud, and the bottom cut about 1 inch below a bud. To make the tongue, position the knife blade across the angled cut, about a third of the way from the point of the cut; make a downward cut about ½ inch into the stem.

Next, prepare the rootstock. With pruning shears, cut the rootstock stem to about 4 inches above the ground. Use the knife to make a sloping cut similar to that on the scion, putting the blade above a bud and cutting upward. Also make a ½-inch-deep vertical cut downward into the stem, a third of the way down from the point of the cut.

To join the two pieces, align the cuts and push the tongue of the rootstock into that of the scion. The illustration below illustrates this technique. If the two stems are the same diameter, you will get good cambium contact all around; otherwise, match the cambium layers on one side of the union. To secure and protect the graft, carefully wrap the area with a grafting tie such as electrical tape. Cover the

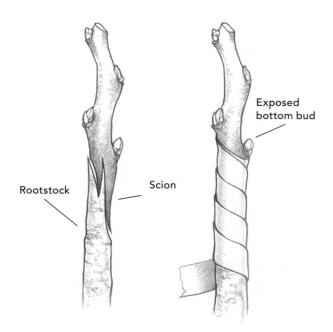

Joining a whip-and-tongue graft. Prepare the rootstock and scion with equal, sloping cuts. Make vertical cuts into the stems to create the "tongues." Carefully push the two pieces together so the tongues interlock, then wrap the joint.

wrapped area and the cut top of the scion with commercial grafting wax or wound paint.

Aftercare: Check the graft in a few days; if any cracks have appeared in the wax or paint coating, make another application. The scion should begin to grow in 3 to 4 weeks. If the tie does not disintegrate on its own, carefully cut and remove it about a month after grafting. Stake the graft if necessary, and remove shoots and suckers from the rootstock.

Side Veneer Graft

Use side veneer grafts on Japanese maples and evergreens, especially dwarf conifers that are very slow growing or difficult to root. This technique is carried out indoors, on potted 1- or 2-year-old seedlings generally ¼ to ½ inch in diameter. A greenhouse or a temperature-controlled propagation mat or a board resting on a radiator is very helpful. Soil warmth promotes root growth and callus formation, but warm air encourages vigorous shoot growth that may inhibit healing.

Season: Late winter is the best time to do side veneer grafts.

Getting started: In December and January, gather and store scion material. When you are ready to graft in February, remove the material from storage and soak the pieces in water until you need them. If possible, the scions should be 4 to 6 inches long, but they can be shorter if you are working with dwarf conifers. In January, about 6 weeks before grafting, bring the potted rootstock into the greenhouse.

Method: Prepare the rootstock by stripping the leaves off of a few inches of stem near the base of the plant. Use a sharp knife to make a shallow downward cut 1 to 1½ inches long, starting about 3 inches above the soil surface. Make another short downward cut inward from the other side of the rootstock to meet the first cut; remove the chip of wood. To prepare the scion, select a piece with a stem diameter equal to or smaller than the rootstock. Use a knife to cut the base of the scion, with a long sloping cut on one side and a short inward and downward cut on the other. Join the scion and rootstock, as shown in the illustration below, by fitting the base of the scion into the notch on the rootstock stem, so that the long cuts are next to each other. Match the cambium layers on one or both sides, and then wrap the graft.

Aftercare: High humidity is helpful for callus formation, so you may want to mist the grafted plant frequently. Keep soil on the dry side; water lightly but frequently. The graft will take 6 to 8 weeks to unite; if necessary, cut the tie about 2 months after grafting. Harden off the plant by gradually exposing it to cooler

Scion ——   —— Rootstock

Making a side veneer graft. Prepare the scion and rootstock by making a cut near the base of the stem, and another short slice inward to meet the base of the first cut. To join the two pieces, fit the base of the scion into the notch on the rootstock stem. Then wrap the graft with tape, waxed string, or rubber ties.

temperatures and lower humidity. Cut back the top of the rootstock in stages, removing about half when the graft has been hardened off and the rest a month or so later.

Cleft Graft

Try cleft grafting on more mature rootstocks, at least 1 inch in diameter. This method is often used in topworking fruit trees, resulting in a newly productive tree in as little as 3 years.

Season: Use cleft grafting in spring, when the buds on the rootstock plant start to swell.

Getting started: Remove previously collected scions from storage, and soak them in water until you need them. Prepare the rootstock by cutting the end of a stem or branch cleanly with a sharp saw.

Method: To prepare the rootstock, use a sharp knife to split the stem, as shown in the illustration below. Tap a large knife (not your grafting knife) into the wood with a mallet to make a 2-inch cleft.

Then pull out the knife, and use the mallet to tap in a wooden wedge or the pointed end of a screwdriver to hold the cleft open. Next, cut two scions from stem pieces about ¼ inch in diameter, each about 4 inches long, with two or three buds. Use your knife to make two long sloping cuts on each scion, one on each side of the stem. Angle the cuts so one side of the scion is slightly thicker than the other. The bottom bud should be on the wider side, just above the cuts forming the wedge. Insert the scions into the cleft on the rootstock. Make sure the wider side of the scion is toward the outside. Match the cambium layers by settling the scion slightly within the edge of the rootstock bark. Carefully remove the wedge or screwdriver from the cleft. Cleft grafts usually don't need tying or wrapping, because the pressure of the split stock should hold the scions firmly, but be sure to wax or paint the cut surfaces.

Aftercare: Check the graft a few days later; rewax if necessary. If both scions grow, cut the weaker one back by half the first season, and remove it completely the next year; in the meantime, the weaker scion will produce tissue that helps heal the cleft. Remove shoots and suckers from the rootstock. If a scion makes excessively vigorous growth, either brace it or prune it back to avoid breakage.

Preparing a cleft graft. Preparing a cleft graft involves cutting an opening in the horizontal surface of the rootstock stem and inserting the scions into the cleft. A wooden wedge helps to hold the cleft open.

Labels: Scions, Wooden wedge, Rootstock

GRAINS

Raising grains such as wheat, spelt, oats, rice, buckwheat, barley, millet, and rye in your backyard doesn't require any special machinery, and you may be surprised at how little space it takes to grow a substantial supply of home-grown grains.

A typical family uses about a bushel of wheat (60 pounds) a year, plus about ¼ to ½ bushel of other grains. Given reasonably good conditions, you should be able to grow a bushel of wheat in a 20- by 50-foot plot (1,000 square feet).

Planting and Growing

Grains are easy to plant: Simply work the soil into a good seedbed and broadcast the seed by hand or with a crank-type seeder. Rake the soil lightly to work the seed into the top 2 inches of ground. Spread a 2- to 4-inch layer of loose straw mulch after seeding to help conserve moisture and control weeds.

You can purchase small amounts of common grain seed at most farm stores. Some general garden seed catalogs carry a few types, too.

Wheat: Wheat (*Triticum* spp.) is the most widely consumed grain in North America. It makes excellent bread and pasta, and has tasty whole or cracked kernels. Wheat sprouts also are very tasty.

Wheat prefers a nearly neutral soil (about 6.4 pH) and does best with a cool, moist growing season followed by warm, dry weather for ripening.

Winter wheat is planted in fall, stays green until early winter, then goes dormant until spring. The onset of warm weather causes rapid new growth, and seed heads develop within 2 months. Winter wheat ripens about the first week of June in the South, later in the North.

Spring wheat is planted at the beginning of the growing season and ripens in mid- to late summer. It tolerates drier conditions than winter wheat but doesn't yield as well.

Hard red winter and hard red spring wheat are used for bread baking. Soft red winter and white wheat are used primarily for pastry flour. Durum wheat is used for making pastas. Regardless of their commercial use, all the wheats make good bread. There are many cultivars; choose those commonly grown in your area.

Plant spring wheat at about the same time as the average last killing frost. Plant winter wheat at about the time of the average first fall frost. If Hessian fly, a common wheat pest, is a problem in your area, be sure to plant after the "fly date." Check with your local extension office for this date. Use about 4 pounds of seed per 1,000 square feet.

Spelt: Spelt (*Triticum spelta*), also called spelt wheat, is an ancient grain grown for its nutty-tasting, highly nutritious seeds that are easily digested. Spelt is used to make pasta, breads, and flour, and the seeds also are sold for sprouting. Many individuals who are allergic to wheat can tolerate spelt, and spelt contains a different form of gluten than wheat does. If you have a wheat or gluten allergy, check with your doctor before trying spelt products.

Spelt grows successfully in poorer soils than wheat, including heavy clay, and tolerates dryer conditions as well. Grow it as you would winter wheat, planting in fall and harvesting in spring.

Rye: Rye (*Secale cereale*) adds a rich flavor to bread or rolls. Cracked rye can also be used in other baked goods or served as a cooked grain. Rye sprouts are sweet and crunchy.

Rye grows better than wheat in cold, wet climates. It also grows in poor soils that won't support wheat, but yields about 30 percent less.

Plant rye in the same manner and at the same rate as winter wheat any time from late summer to late fall. Rye ripens 7 to 10 days before winter wheat.

Oats: Oats (*Avena sativa*) are highest of all cereal grains in protein and lowest in carbohydrates. Oats make tasty table fare, but most cultivars have a

Supergrains

Amaranth and quinoa are both grown extensively in other parts of the world for their seeds and edible leaves. Both types of seed contain about 16 percent protein and are high in fiber and in amino acids often absent in cereal grains.

Amaranth: Grain amaranth (*Amaranthus* spp.) is a relative of the familiar ornamental amaranth. Amaranth seed is white to yellow, round, and very small. It makes a tasty porridge and can be toasted to make a crunchy topping. The flour must be mixed with other flour for baking.

Grain amaranth matures in about 120 days. Start the plants indoors, or direct-seed in rows and thin to 1 to 3 inches apart. Seed is ready to harvest when it starts to dry. Cut the whole seed heads and hang them in clusters or in a cloth sack to dry.

Thresh by beating the bag; sift chaff from seed with a fine screen.

Quinoa: Pronounced "keen-wah," quinoa (*Chenopodium quinoa*) seed is the staple grain of the Andean highlands. It is a close relative of the potherb known as good King Henry (*C. bonus-henricus*). Quinoa seed is tiny and, when cooked, has a delicate flavor and a fluffy texture. It can be used like rice—just be sure to rinse the raw seed first or it will be bitter. Quinoa flour gives a moist texture to baked goods when mixed with other flours.

Quinoa is adapted to high mountainous areas, and most cultivars will not make seed in areas where temperatures reach 95°F. Plant seed ½ to 1 inch deep in cool soil; the crop is easy to grow. Its culture and appearance is similar to amaranth.

---

tough hull that's hard to remove. Hull-less, or naked, oats (*Avena nuda*) are virtually hull-free, making them easier to process.

Oats need lots of moisture and favor a cool climate and fertile, well-drained soil. In the South, plant oats in fall for harvest the following summer. But in general, it's best to plant oats in very early spring. Plant about 2 to 3 pounds of seed per 1,000 square feet.

Corn: As home gardeners, we think of corn (*Zea mays*) as sweet corn, but fresh ground cornmeal is wonderfully fragrant and tasty, too. Choose a dent or flint type for cornmeal, and a flour type for a finer meal, rather than a sweet-corn cultivar. Indian corn and field corn are familiar dry-corn types.

Grow dry corn as you would sweet corn; see the Corn entry for details. Remember to separate dry- and sweet-corn cultivars, so they won't cross-pollinate. Dry corn is normally left on the plant until after frost, but it can be picked after the husks begin to dry. Bring husked ears under cover to finish drying.

Barley: Barley (*Hordeum vulgare*) is a delicious, nutty-tasting cereal grain, especially good in casseroles, soups, and pilaf. The grain has an outer hull that should be removed. Pearl barley has been milled to remove the tough husks. Barley flour is low in gluten and is mixed with other flours for making bread.

Plant 4 pounds of seed per 1,000 square feet.

Spring-sown barley matures in about 70 days, while fall-planted barley ripens about 60 days after growth resumes in spring.

Rice: Although rice (*Oryza sativa*) is typically considered a warm-climate crop, there are early-maturing cultivars that will grow in most parts of North America. Rice is often grown in flooded fields, but it will also thrive under the same conditions as corn. Wild rice (*Zizania aquatica*) is native to North America and grows in ponds and slow-moving water.

Soak seed for 24 hours and plant in flats of moist, mucky soil about a month before your last frost. Prepare raised beds with plenty of organic matter and cover with a thick organic mulch. Transplant on 9-inch centers, pushing the mulch aside. Water rice once or twice a week so that it gets about 1 to 1½ inches from rain and irrigation combined. When rice flowers, make sure it gets plenty of water; cut back once the grain starts to harden. Rice is hard to hull.

Millet: Millet is a catchall name for at least five different genera and assorted species of cereal grains native to Asia and Africa, where the hulled grain is a staple food in many countries. We are most familiar with it as the shiny, little, round, yellow or orange brown seeds in birdseed mixes. It is higher in essential amino acids than other cereal grains and has a subtle, nutlike flavor when baked or cooked. To bring out its full taste, roast the grain in a pan with a little oil before using.

Millet will tolerate poor soils. The plants mature very quickly—some in just 30 days. You can sow millet almost any time from spring through late summer. Plant about 1 pound of seed per 1,000 square feet.

Buckwheat: Buckwheat (*Fagopyrum esculentum*) isn't a cereal grain. It belongs to the family Polygonaceae, as do rhubarb and garden sorrel. It is commonly grown as a green manure crop and as a bee forage plant. The amino acid composition of the seed surpasses that of all other cereal grains, and the flour's earthy flavor makes it a welcome addition to treats such as flapjacks and breads. The seed matures in just 70 to 80 days; it makes a good second crop in a two-crop rotation.

You can plant buckwheat almost any time from spring to late summer, in almost any type of soil. Generally, late-June or July plantings yield the most seed. Sow about 2½ pounds per 1,000 square feet. Buckwheat seeds ripen at varying rates, so watch the crop carefully and harvest when most of the seed is ripe.

Harvesting and Using

Harvest cereal grains about 7 to 10 days before they're fully mature and dry. The grain heads should still be greenish or just turning yellow, the stalks mottled with green. Pinch a kernel with your thumb and index finger. It should be soft enough to be dented by your thumbnail but not so soft that it squashes.

Cut the stalks just above ground level, and gather and tie them into bunches. (The traditional tool for cutting grains is a scythe.) Stack or hang the bunches in the field or under cover to dry. The grain will cure in 10 to 14 days. When you bite a kernel between your teeth, it should be hard and crunchy.

Threshing: To thresh, put a bundle or two on a sheet spread over a hard surface, such as a patio or floor. Beat the seed heads with a length of rubber hose or an old mop handle to knock the seeds from the stalks.

Winnowing: Next, clean the grain of chaff and hulls. Pour the grain slowly from one bucket to another in front of a fan. The breeze should be strong enough to blow the chaff away, but not so strong that it takes the kernels with it. Repeat until clean.

Storing: Keep small quantities of cereal grains in a refrigerator or freezer. You can also store thoroughly dry grain in a cool, dark place in sealed jars to protect it from insects.

Hulling: Hulling grain with tough hulls is one of the biggest stumbling blocks for home gardeners. You can hull small quantities by roasting the grain in an oven at 180°F for 60 to 90 minutes and then running the kernels lightly though a blender and picking out the cracked hulls. For larger quantities, use a grain grinder.

Milling: Grains can be cracked or ground into flour in a good household blender. Grind ¼ cup at a time, taking care not to let the motor labor too much. If you make a lot of flour, you may want to buy a hand-cranked or electric flour mill. Grind only as much as you will use in a few weeks, and store prepared grains in the refrigerator or freezer; they go rancid rapidly.

GRAPES

Vitis spp.
Vitaceae

Grapes make a wonderful treat straight from the vine or preserved as jelly, juice, or wine. They thrive in full sun and need good drainage and protection from late frosts.

Selecting Grapes

There are four main types of grapes grown in North America: European, or wine grapes (*Vitis vinifera*); American, such as 'Concord' (*V. labrusca*); hybrids between European and American; and muscadine (*V. rotundifolia*).

Early settlers to North America found native grapes growing rampantly. Many good fresh eating and juice grapes have been selected from the native species, including 'Concord' and 'Niagara'. American grapes have a strong grape or "foxy" flavor and slipskins, which means that the berries can easily be squeezed out of the skins.

Vinifera (European) grapes produce most of the world's table grapes, wine, and raisins. They are not as hardy as their American cousins, are much more susceptible to diseases, and require more work to harvest a satisfactory crop.

Plant breeders have crossed and recrossed vinifera and American species and created grapes to satisfy almost every taste and use. Many of them are as hardy as their American parent, to about −10°F, and have good disease resistance.

If you grow seedless cultivars, you probably won't get grapes as large as those on bunches for sale at the market. Commercial growers dip or spray clusters with synthetic growth regulators so they'll produce big berries.

If you live in the far South, you may only be able to grow muscadine grapes. They make good jelly and juice and a distinctive, sweet wine.

Rootstocks: American and hybrid grape cultivars can be grown on their own roots. Vinifera grape roots are very susceptible to phylloxera, a sucking insect native to the eastern and southern United States and now spread throughout the world. Choose vines grafted on American rootstocks. Certain American rootstock cultivars are also resistant to nematodes and the virus diseases they transmit.

Planting and Care

Begin preparing your site a year before you plant your vines. Eliminate perennial weeds from your planting site; see the Weeds entry for methods.

Have the soil tested. Prepare the site thoroughly prior to planting, adding lots of organic matter and any amendments needed to correct deficiencies. Grapes do best at pH 5.0 to 6.0. Nitrogen, potassium, and magnesium deficiencies are the most common nutritional problems of grapes; in the West, excess iron and boron in soils can cause toxicity symptoms.

Plant dormant, 1-year-old vines in spring before their buds begin to swell and open. Soak roots for 1 to 2 hours before planting, in a pail of water with a handful of bonemeal.

Prune each vine back to leave two leaf buds before planting; also cut back long roots so they'll fit easily into the hole without bending. Leave 1 to 2 inches of trunk above ground and make a shallow basin around the vine to hold water. If you are planting grafted vines, be sure to keep the graft union above ground level.

Pruning and Training

There are many ways to train grapes. Three of the most common methods for home gardeners are cane pruning, spur pruning, and head training. If you are new to grapes, don't let talk about training and pruning scare you. Grapevines are very forgiving. You can train cane- and spur-pruned vines on an existing fence or wall. If you're planning to plant several vines, you'll probably need to build a trellis; see the illustration on page 263 for details.

The training method you select depends on where you live and what cultivars you grow. Cane pruning is a good choice for cultivars in which the first few buds on a cane are not fruitful, such as 'Thompson Seedless', and for people who want a heavy crop, because cane pruning results in long vines with many buds.

Head-trained plants stand alone like little trees.

They need sturdy, individual stakes until the trunks get strong enough to support the vine. Head-trained vines are simple to prune, but fruit and foliage bunch around the head, which can create a favorable environment for pests and diseases, especially in humid climates. Head training is primarily used for wine grapes in dry areas.

Early Training

No matter what training method you plan to use, all vines are treated the same until the second winter after planting.

First growing season: During their first summer, the vines need to grow a strong root system. Use drip irrigation or a soaker hose if needed to keep the soil damp but not soggy. From mid-August on, water only if the leaves wilt so the vines will harden off for winter. Mulch or cultivate to control weeds.

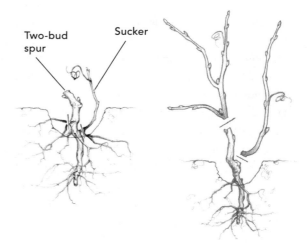

Two-bud spur   Sucker

Early pruning. Prune newly purchased vines back to two buds before planting. The first winter, select the strongest, straightest shoot and cut it back to two buds. Prune off all other shoots. The vine will look very much like the little vine you purchased the previous spring.

You can let the vines sprawl on the ground the first year, or tie them loosely to a small stake to keep them out of harm's way.

First winter: Any time from midwinter on, select the strongest, straightest shoot and prune off all the others. Cut the chosen shoot back to two live buds. The result will look very much like the little vine you planted the previous spring. But remember, the first season is for growing roots. Go ahead and cut off all that top growth; you'll have a better plant in the long run. If cold injury is a problem in your area, wait until the buds start to swell so you can see which ones are alive. You may want to select two shoots rather than one as insurance against injury.

Second growing season: If you haven't done so already, place a stake in the ground as close as possible to the vine. When new shoots are 6 to 12 inches long, select the sturdiest, most upright shoot and tie it loosely to the stake. Break off the remaining shoots with your fingers. If you are developing two trunks, save one shoot on each. As the shoot grows tie it to the stake at 12-inch intervals to form a straight trunk.

If you're growing grapes on a trellis, mark the stake at a point about 6 inches below the first permanent trellis wire. This will be the height of the vine head—the top of the trunk. Side arms will grow out from here, and the lateral shoots will grow up to the higher trellis wire. For vines growing against a fence or wall, you can choose to make the vine head at about 3 feet, or let the trunk grow taller and allow the vines to cascade down from the side branches.

When the shoot reaches the desired height, break off the small shoots that are growing above each leaf near the base of your trunk-to-be, but don't remove the leaves. Let the side shoots grow on the five leaf nodes just below the vine head; cut the tip off the

main shoot when it grows a few inches or so above the vine head. Prune off any suckers below the soil line as close to the trunk as possible.

If your vine doesn't reach the desired height by the end of the second season, it probably hadn't developed enough roots to produce the size plant you wanted. Cut the vine back to two buds, and let it try again the next summer.

Second-Winter Pruning

Any time from midwinter on, remove any shoots from the trunk or roots.

Cane- or spur-pruned vines: Select two sturdy, pencil-size canes near the mark you made to show the top of your trunk. Tie them to the training wire. Buds should be spaced about every 4 to 5 inches along the canes; rub off any extras. Shorten the canes so each has 10 buds.

Head-trained vines: Select five pencil-size canes just below the mark on the stake and prune them back, leaving two buds on each. Cut off the main shoot just above the head.

Third Growing Season

Now that your vine has a strong root system, it shouldn't need water very often unless your soil is very sandy. Tie up or pinch back shoots in danger of breaking. Clip off all or most of the flower clusters this year.

Third-Winter Pruning

Continue to prune off any shoots or suckers on the trunks or roots.

Cane-pruned vines: Select a pencil-size shoot from near the base of each of the previous season's canes or from the top of the trunk. Cut off and remove all other growth from the previous season. Cut the new canes back to 10 buds, and tie them securely to the wire.

Spur-pruned vines: Cut each upright shoot along the horizontal arms back to two buds. Leave a two-bud spur every 4 to 5 inches; remove any extras.

Head-trained vines: Cut each of the five canes back to two-bud spurs.

Training Bearing Vines

In the fourth growing season, vines are ready to bear a normal crop. For large table grapes, give vines 1 inch of water per week. For small, highly flavored wine grapes, don't water unless the vine is wilted.

Fourth winter: In the fourth and subsequent winters, you may want to add a few new spurs and keep a few more buds on each cane for the next season. The vigor of a vine will tell you how many buds and spurs it can support. If your vine has many spindly shoots and little fruit, try leaving fewer total buds the next winter. If it has long, thick shoots and few clusters, leave more buds the next winter. For cane-pruned vines, select new canes as for third-winter pruning.

Spur-pruned and head-trained vines need different treatment. Select a pencil-size shoot from near the base of each spur, and cut it back to two buds. You will need to develop replacement spurs every few years because the original ones become unwieldy. Select shoots on the main arm or base of the spur, cut them back to two buds, and remove the old spurs.

Subsequent growing seasons: During spring through mid-July, position shoots so light penetrates through the foliage. On short-trunk, trellised vines, tuck the shoots behind the catch wires above the training wire. If shoots reach the top of the trellis and hang down, they will shade the fruit and the canes where next year's flower buds are forming. Prune off the tips if they get too long. Especially on head-trained vines, pick off leaves and small shoots near fruit clusters to let in light. This is important because it promotes ripening and discourages pests. You may want to remove or thin clusters to increase berry size or improve quality. If you have too heavy a crop, the fruit may be slow to ripen as well.

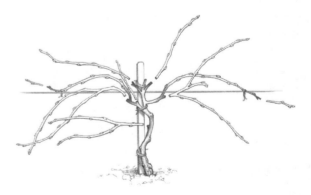

Cane pruning. During the second winter of growth, tie two canes near the top of the trunk to the training wire. Rub off buds to leave buds spaced 4 to 5 inches apart. Shorten the canes to 10 buds. The third winter, select a pencil-size shoot from near the base of each of the previous season's canes or from the top of the trunk.

Winter Protection

There are grape cultivars that will tolerate severe winter cold. You can grow cultivars beyond their normal northern limit by training trunks only 1 foot high and covering vines with mulch during winter, or by bending whole vines over and burying or mulching them for winter.

Once grape buds begin to swell in spring, they become more frost tender. All species are susceptible to frost damage at temperatures below 31°F. See the Fruit Trees entry for more information on site selection and frost protection. Autumn frosts seldom cause damage because the high sugar content of the berries keeps them from freezing and the outer canopy protects both the foliage and fruit beneath it. If you live in an area with short seasons, plant an early-ripening cultivar.

Fertilization

On most sites, careful soil preparation before planting eliminates the need for heavy fertilization. Mulch lightly with compost in late winter each year. Overfertilizing can cause vines to grow rampantly and produce little fruit. When in doubt, don't fertilize. Compost tea and dilute seaweed extract sprays are good general foliar fertilizers. See the Compost entry for instructions for making compost tea. If you suspect you have a specific nutrient problem, have a leaf analysis done; see page 552 in the Soil entry for information on this procedure.

Harvesting

Grapevines bear by their third or fourth growing season. Harvest when the fruit tastes ripe. Support the cluster with one hand and cut its stem with pruning shears. Handle clusters gently, and lay them in a basket or flat. Harvest large quantities in the morning, small amounts any time of day. Move picked fruit to a cool, protected place as soon as possible.

Problems

Insects: Grape berry moths lay eggs on flower clusters. The greenish or purplish larvae spin silver webs and feed on buds and flowers. Control grape berry moth with mating-disruption pheromone dispensers.

Many caterpillars can feed on grape leaves. Control by spraying Bt (*Bacillus thuringiensis*). Japanese beetles are fond of grape leaves. A few won't hurt the vines, but complete defoliation will. See the chart on page 454 for control methods.

Diseases: Prevention and good housekeeping are the best ways to avoid disease problems. Mulch or cultivation will help prevent fungal spores from splashing up from the soil and infecting new growth. Keep the area under vines weed-free to increase air movement and reduce disease problems. Fungal diseases thrive in dark, humid environments, so arrange shoots in the leaf canopy so some light falls on all foliage. Cut off leaves shading fruit clusters. Remove infected plant parts and dispose of them.

Sprays of *Bacillus subtilis* or sulfur help prevent disease. If you've had past problems with fungal diseases, you may want to consider a regular preventive spray program. Coat all parts of the vines, including the undersides of leaves, before symptoms appear. Consult with your local extension service concerning timing of sprays.

Common grape diseases include the following:

🌿 Black rot causes rusty brown leaf spots, which develop small, black, spore-producing dots in

Trellising Grapes

While a trellis requires some effort to build and maintain, it's the best way to manage your vines. Each vine you grow will need about 8 feet of trellis. To construct a trellis, set 8-foot posts 24 feet apart and 2 feet into the ground (one post set every third vine). If you have soft ground, consider installing guy wires from the end posts to keep them from being pulled over. Secure the guy wires with a block of concrete set into the ground or with an earth screw.

Stretch 9- or 10-gauge galvanized wire between the end posts, 2½ feet above ground level, and clamp it securely. Then staple it to the other posts. Add another trellis wire at the top of the posts, and one or two additional wires between them.

Hammer large nails between each pair of trellis wires. These nails will support catch wires, used to lift the vines up to the perma-nent trellis wires during the season. To make catch wires, cut two pieces of lighter-gauge wire that are as long as the full trellis. Connect short pieces of chain over the end post nails, and let the wire rest on all the other nails.

Grape shoots will climb permanent trellis wires on their own, or they can be tucked through by hand during the season. Movable catch wires go around the trellis like a giant rubber band and keep shoots pointing up. Drop the catch wires to the nails below the vine heads when you prune each winter. Once growth starts and shoots are about 2 inches long, raise the catch wire to the nails above the vine head; as you lift it, the wire will pick up any shoots that are straying from the trellis. Raise the wire to the next set of nails as the shoots grow, or use a second catch wire.

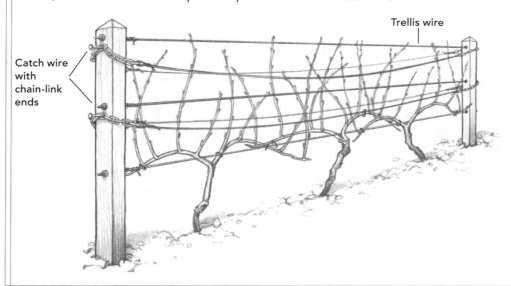

Trellis wire

Catch wire with chain-link ends

moist weather. It turns green berries into hard, black "mummies."

🌿 Botrytis bunch rot can cause leaf spots but primarily attacks the flower or fruit clusters. Infected berries turn brown and soft, and whole areas of the cluster become covered with powdery brown mold.

🌿 Downy mildew first shows up as lighter blotches on leaves, which are covered with a fine white powder on the undersides. Young shoots and fruit clusters may be covered with white powder in severe cases. If infection occurs early in the season, fruit clusters may ripen unevenly.

🌿 Powdery mildew appears first as a gray moldy-looking material on canes, then on the leaves, and finally on the berries, which split or stop developing.

🌿 Crown gall and cane dieback can be problems. Avoid damaging bark when cultivating, and sanitize pruning shears between vines. Winter injury can make vines more prone to problems.

🌿 Viruses can cause ring-shaped spots or mottling on leaves, and other symptoms. To prevent virus problems, buy only certified virus-free vines. Dig up and burn or destroy any vines that become infected.

GRAYWATER

Graywater is the water from showers, tubs, sinks, dishwashers, and washing machines—all household water except the water in your toilets. Chronic water shortages in some areas have increased people's interest in recycling graywater in the garden.

Since it's "used" water, graywater is usually not pure. It might contain soap, detergent, cooking oil,

food particles, chemicals from cosmetics and perfumes, dyes, hair and skin, and even fecal matter. It's important to know how to use it as safely as possible.

Graywater is safe to use in gardens as long as you strictly follow these guidelines.

🌿 Use the least contaminated water first, choosing in this order (best to worst): shower and bath, bathroom sink, utility sink, clothes washer, kitchen sink, and dishwasher water. (The last two often contain high amounts of grease and food pieces. If you use kitchen water, keep the grease and solid particles to a minimum.)

🌿 Use fresh water for food crops whenever possible, and apply the graywater to flower gardens or landscape plants. If you must use graywater for food crops, apply it to the soil around corn, tomatoes, and other aboveground plants. Do not use it on seedlings, leafy vegetables, or root crops.

🌿 Because wastewater is alkaline, avoid using it on acid-loving plants such as hollies, rhododendrons, and blueberries.

🌿 Do not use water used to wash diapers or water containing bleach, chlorine, boron, or detergents with softeners (sodium-based compounds). High-phosphate detergents are a problem because they contain high amounts of sodium. (Sodium salts damage soil structure as well as plants and can raise soil pH too high, so that plants cannot grow.)

🌿 Test soil pH in spring and fall. If the sodium salts are raising the pH too high, you'll be advised to spread calcium sulfate or another sulfur product in order to lower the pH.

🌿 Keep adding organic matter, especially compost, to your soil. The biological activity of the soil organisms will help to diffuse any soil contaminants quickly.

🌿 Alternate graywater with fresh water to cleanse the soil of sodium salts from soaps and detergents.

🌿 Do not use household water in the garden if the water has been treated with sodium-based softeners.

🌿 Find out if your municipality imposes any restrictions on the collection and use of graywater. Storage is typically the part of the process most subject to regulation—you're less likely to run afoul of local ordinances if you're simply diverting household graywater and applying it right away.

🌿 Find out if your local government has any programs that support graywater use. In areas where water shortages are a common concern, various agencies may offer guidance on setting up a diversion system, tips for using graywater safely and effectively in your garden, or even subsidized equipment and installation assistance.

How to Capture Graywater

If you're just planning to use graywater during short-term droughts, collect and haul the water in buckets and containers. You can also set up a siphon or pump with a hose directed through the bathroom window to move water directly from a bathtub to a garden, or remove the trap under a sink and catch the water in a bucket as it drains. Enterprising country people have long figured out many ingenious ways to get water outside when the well was running low. (One routine involved dumping water from the tub out the bathroom window to the handy garden cart below.) Using graywater is a water-wise choice, but once you've been through the routine you'll never again take rain for granted.

If you want to use graywater on a regular basis,

you may need to hire a plumber to direct your water directly from the house to an outside area.

Once you've moved graywater to the garden, be sure to use it up quickly. Storing graywater creates opportunities for bacteria and other pathogens to build up, creating potential health hazards. Apply the water directly to the soil, not onto the plants themselves. Pour the graywater on flat garden areas; avoid steep slopes where runoff could be a problem. Be sure to avoid water runoff into streams. Ideally, pour the water through mulch—another way to filter the impurities. Don't concentrate graywater in any one location, but rotate the areas where you use it. One recommendation is to limit graywater use to a half gallon of water per week per square foot of garden. (For a 10- by 10-foot garden, that's 50 gallons per week.)

GREENHOUSE GARDENING

Greenhouse gardening is a great way to extend the pleasure of gardening year-round. Depending on the type of greenhouse you choose, it's possible to enjoy colorful and exotic flowers like orchids, cultivate gourmet vegetables such as European seedless cucumbers, or start seedlings for the outside garden. A greenhouse can even add warmth, humidity, and oxygenated air to your home in the winter.

A greenhouse may be attached to your home or freestanding. Your choice will depend on many factors, including your house design, budget, and gardening needs. Because a greenhouse is an investment, and the type you need will depend on your climate and what you want to grow in it, it's important to do your homework up front. (For example, the type of wall and roof material you choose will depend on your climate as well as your budget.) Talk to other greenhouse owners and comparison shop before choosing a style and model to buy.

If you're not sure how much use you'll actually make of your greenhouse or feel tentative about getting started, a good way to get your feet wet is with a temporary or "pop-up" greenhouse. Many kits are available in a range of styles and sizes. They're made of lightweight frames that snap together and UV-protected poly coverings, and they are designed to put up and take down fast. Another option is to start with a cold frame and work your way up from there as you gain confidence. (See the Cold Frames entry for more on those.)

Many types of greenhouses are available as kits of modular prefabricated sections for both free-standing and attached structures. You can find these through greenhouse and garden supply catalogs and Web sites as well as through advertisements in the back of most gardening magazines.

Some people prefer to build their greenhouse from scratch. Check your library or bookstore for useful references about designing and building a freestanding or attached, energy-conserving greenhouse; see Resources on page 673.

Tending a Greenhouse

Greenhouse gardening is similar in many ways to gardening outside. The plants still need adequate nutrients and water, plus protection from insect pests and diseases. You still must tie, prune, and tend to them.

But the greenhouse environment is very different from that of a backyard garden. The very things that make greenhouse growing more controlled and convenient also make it more demanding. In a greenhouse, you control temperature, humidity, soil aeration, soil moisture and drainage, fertility levels, and light. This degree of environmental control gives you a tremendous amount of latitude as well as some new responsibilities.

Temperature: Heaters, vents, and fans are your allies in temperature control. Even in a well-designed, solar-efficient greenhouse, outside conditions are sometimes so cold and cloudy that auxiliary heat is needed to keep plants growing at an optimum rate.

Vents and fans help to cool the greenhouse. On a sunny day, even at −20°F, greenhouse air can heat up well beyond desirable levels. If the greenhouse is attached, you can move this hot air into your home. But in a freestanding unit, hot air must have a way to exit, and cool air a way to enter. Passive vents allow for this sort of movement, as do thermostatically controlled exhaust fans and intake vents. Manually operated vents are relatively inexpensive, but you'll need to check them at least twice a day and open or close them as necessary. Automatic ventilation systems are more costly, but they save time and reduce the chances of excessive cooling or heating.

Adjust air temperature in the greenhouse according to the level of light. In general, summer crops grow best at temperatures of about 75° to 85°F in the daytime and 60° to 75°F at night. On cloudy days, these temperature ranges should be somewhat lower, since the plant is not manufacturing as many sugars as usual.

Winter air temperatures can go as low as 45°F at night without damaging most leafy green crops and shouldn't go much above 65° to 70°F during the day. Spring seedlings vary in their temperature preferences. Cool-weather crops, such as broccoli and lettuce, grow most vigorously at 50°F nights and 60° to 65°F days, while warm-weather plants such as tomatoes and squash require nights at a minimum of 55°F and days of at least 65°F but no higher than 80°F.

Ornamentals typically need night temperatures no lower than 55°F, and tender tropicals can require night temperatures of 60°F or even higher.

Investigate the temperature requirements of the plants you plan to grow before installing your greenhouse and heating system so you can match the heater to your plants' needs. You can find a wide range of heater types and sizes, from free-standing propane heaters to powerful wall-mounted electric heaters. As with the greenhouses themselves, all greenhouse equipment is available through greenhouse and garden supply catalogs and Web sites.

Air circulation: Air circulation is extremely important to plant health. Good air circulation strengthens the woody tissue in stems and decreases the opportunities for fungi to attack your plants. Dense plant growth can interfere with air circulation and contribute to excessive relative humidity. Leave adequate space between plants and prune so that leaves from adjacent plants don't touch each other.

Plants use carbon dioxide from the air to manufacture sugars. In a closed greenhouse, carbon dioxide can be so depleted that plant growth is slowed. Remember to ventilate to change the air supply at least once each morning, even if you have to add extra heat.

Besides vents and fans, one low-tech way to increase air movement is by installing screened windows and doors in your greenhouse. By opening a window on one end and the door panel on the other, you'll have cross-ventilation. Positioning windows at the top and bottom of the greenhouse walls allows warm air to rise and escape from the upper windows and cooler air to enter through the lower ones.

Humidity: Greenhouses that feel like rain forests don't produce sturdy, healthy plants. Relative humidity should be close to 70 to 85 percent during high-growth periods. At levels of 90 to 95 percent, plant growth is weak, early bolting occurs, and fungal diseases become a real problem. Decrease humidity levels by venting or exhausting humid air and watering only when necessary. Growers in arid climates can increase humidity levels in the greenhouse by spraying water on the floor.

Light: Light levels in a greenhouse are partially determined by the design. When planning a greenhouse, check shade patterns from roof overhangs at the summer solstice in June and modify the plan if the shade is too great.

Fluorescent lights are very useful when you're growing spring seedlings, particularly in cloudy regions. They can give a boost to midwinter greens and the last of the fall-fruiting crops. Ornamentals will also be healthier and more attractive with supplemental lighting. Shop-light setups suspended over raised benches are easy to install. You can choose fluorescent bulbs designed for plant growth, bulbs that mimic sunlight, or simply pair cool and warm bulbs in your fixtures. For intense light in a smaller area, another option is a compact fluorescent setup.

For plants like sun-loving orchids and tomatoes that require the equivalent of direct sunlight, you can set up HID (high-intensity discharge) lighting systems with special bulbs. These systems are costly, though, and tend to give off a great deal of heat, so they're typically used by specialists and professionals rather than people with home greenhouses. Most plants will do fine with natural light and supplemental fluorescent lighting.

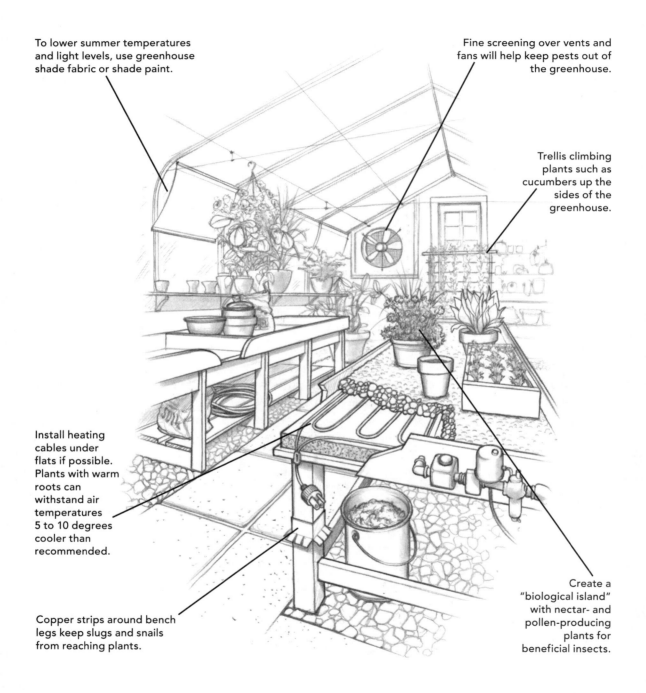

To lower summer temperatures and light levels, use greenhouse shade fabric or shade paint.

Fine screening over vents and fans will help keep pests out of the greenhouse.

Trellis climbing plants such as cucumbers up the sides of the greenhouse.

Install heating cables under flats if possible. Plants with warm roots can withstand air temperatures 5 to 10 degrees cooler than recommended.

Copper strips around bench legs keep slugs and snails from reaching plants.

Create a "biological island" with nectar- and pollen-producing plants for beneficial insects.

Organic greenhouse gardening. In a home greenhouse, you can grow vegetables, herbs, and flowers, propagate new plants, and overwinter tender ones. It's an ideal setting for organic methods, such as releasing insect predators and parasites to control pests.

Whatever system you choose, adding a timer will give you control over the amount of light your plants receive without having to worry about turning the lights on and off manually. Timers can also control automated watering and mist systems, fans, heaters, and other equipment.

Don't forget that plants can receive too much light as well as too little, especially in summer. Special greenhouse shade fabric panels are available in many sizes, as well as lengths you can order or cut to fit. You can choose from screening fabrics that will provide light shade to heavy shade, or protect plants from both too much light and heat buildup. Typically, you attach them over the greenhouse roof, though in areas of intense light you can choose a size that will cover the upper part of the walls.

Another option is to use shading paint developed for greenhouses. You can find paint that dries white but becomes transparent in rainy weather to let in more light. Make sure you choose a paint specially developed for greenhouses so you can wash it off before winter.

Soils and fertility: Commercial growers sometimes amend the soils under their greenhouses and plant right in them. Home greenhouse growers usually find it easier to use benches with individual pots set on them or growing beds filled with a soil mix.

Soil mixes for containers, benches, and beds should be lighter and more fertile than most garden soils. Good soil mixes drain fast, hold moisture well, contain balanced and slow-release organic nutrients, and have a slightly acid pH. For more on soil mixes, see the Houseplants entry.

If you buy a potting mix, make sure you choose one that's organic. There are many options available in garden centers and from garden supply catalogs and Web sites. If you choose to make your own potting soil, a basic recipe is two parts soil, two parts finished compost, one part peat moss, and one part vermiculite or perlite. If the soil is clayey, add sand; if it's too sandy, use vermiculite instead of perlite and increase the proportion of peat moss. Test the pH and adjust it if necessary.

Add compost and other amendments such as vermiculite each spring and fall. Good midseason fertilizers include compost tea and side-dressings, earthworm castings, liquid fish emulsion, and seaweed. Foliar feed plants by spraying leaves with dilute compost tea, nettle tea, or liquid seaweed for extra nutrients and some disease resistance. Fertilize less in winter, when cool soil temperatures inhibit microbial activity. See the Compost entry for instructions for making compost tea.

Pests and Diseases

Good plant health, through good nutrition and environmental control, is the first line of defense against both pests and diseases. But even in the best circumstances, some pests may bother your plants.

Aphids, mites, and whiteflies are the most common serious insect problems in a greenhouse. Use mechanical controls such as vacuuming, squashing, and washing at the first sign of trouble. Yellow sticky traps are effective against whiteflies. If pest populations continue to grow, soap or pepper sprays or appropriate botanical controls such as neem may be useful.

Biological control with predatory insects such as green lacewings and ladybugs, and parasites such as *Encarsia formosa*, are extremely effective. To meet the needs of these insect allies, set up a small "biological island" in a warm, bright spot with pots of parsley-family members (Apiaceae), such as chervil and dill, and small-flowered ornamentals, such as scented geraniums, lobelias, and salvias. Kept in

Good Greenhouse Crops

Many great garden vegetables also adapt well to greenhouse culture. The healthiest, highest-yielding greenhouse plants are grown close to their natural season. With artificial lights and a good heater, you can get tomatoes in December, of course, but the plants will be more prone to insect and disease problems and won't yield as well as they do in May or October.

Succession planting makes sense for all quickly maturing green crops. For example, you'll have tender young lettuce all through spring if you plant a few seeds each week rather than a season's supply all at once. If you want to harvest cold-resistant leafy greens through the winter months, plant them by October.

CROP	WHEN TO PLANT
Beet greens, chard, Asian greens, lettuce, mustard, other leaf crops	Mid-February to May; August to mid-October
Herbs	Mid-February to mid-October
Tomatoes, peppers, and eggplants	Mid-February to March
Squash-family crops, including cucumbers	March to late April

bloom for the entire greenhouse season, these plants provide nectar and pollen for the beneficial insects.

Tempting as it is to bring outdoor peppers, eggplants, and herbs into the greenhouse at summer's end, you'll be running the risk of importing pests with them. It's far better to start plants or buy transplants expressly for the greenhouse. If you decide to take the risk of bringing plants in, quarantine the plants inside sacks made of tightly woven translucent material for at least 7 to 10 days. Aphids and damage from such pests as mites and thrips will be easier to see after this time. If problems appear, it's generally best to throw the plant out.

Fungal diseases are usually the greatest disease problems in a greenhouse. Providing adequate ventilation and spacing between plants and monitoring humidity levels are the best ways to prevent fungal problems. Preventive sprays can also help minimize disease incidence. Fermented nettle tea and dilute compost tea, sprayed on leaves at weekly intervals from the seedling stage onward, inhibit many diseases while also providing trace elements. Sanitation is important, too; isolate or dispose of sick plants, and clean up spilled soil and dropped leaves in the aisles and under benches.

Using a Greenhouse

For many gardeners, the prospect of growing vegetables year-round is a powerful incentive for building a greenhouse. Tomatoes, cucumbers, and lettuce are some of the most popular greenhouse crops. If your plants don't produce fruit, keep in mind that the protected greenhouse environment excludes natural pollinators like insects and wind. You may have to gently shake the plants (like tomatoes) or hand-pollinate them (in the case of normally insect-pollinated plants like cucumbers and squash) to get fruit. See "Good Greenhouse Crops" on the opposite page to learn more about growing vegetables indoors.

Growing flowers is perhaps the most common use of a greenhouse. You can encourage potted plants such as orchids to bloom for enjoyment in the greenhouse or your home. If you like flower arranging, try raising plants such as sweet peas for a constant supply of fresh cut flowers. A greenhouse is also an ideal place to force potted bulbs and to overwinter frost-tender potted plants. (Be sure, though, to inspect any outside plant for insects and diseases before bringing it indoors.) For more information on forcing bulbs, see the Bulbs entry.

Besides protecting established plants, a greenhouse can provide the perfect environment for many propagation techniques. Growing your own vegetable and flower transplants from seed can save money while allowing you to grow less-common cultivars, and you'll know that they were raised without chemical pesticides and fertilizers. Herbaceous cuttings root quickly in the warm, moist conditions. And you can bring potted plants indoors in late winter to get them ready for grafting. See the Budding and Grafting entries for more details.

GREEN MANURE

See Cover Crops

GREEN ROOFS

Also called living roofs, green roofs are not merely rooftops that are green colored but those that are covered with living plants. Besides using space efficiently—especially in cities that are running out of plantable soil—green roofs help the environment and save money in the long run (although a green roof costs more to install than a traditional roof). Green roofs can save up to half of a building's air-conditioning costs, and if many green-roofed buildings are clustered together, they can have a cooling effect on an entire neighborhood. Because a green roof prevents heat loss through the roof, it can reduce heating costs by 25 percent.

Once relatively rare, the environmental benefits of green roofs have made them a viable option for new construction worldwide. From private homes to municipal buildings and from hotels and convention centers to manufacturing facilities, any structure with a flat or gently sloping roof may be designed to include a covering of living plants. Green roofs can be found on top of Chicago and Atlanta's city halls and on the Vancouver Convention Centre in British Columbia. New York City has acres of green rooftops. Ford Motor Company's plant in Dearborn, Michigan, has a 10-acre roof covered with vegetation. In Germany, about 12 percent of flat-roofed buildings are now planted.

A properly constructed green roof will last longer than a conventional roof. Green roofs filter out air pollution and benefit birds, especially in urban areas. They help sequester carbon, and they capture and recycle rainwater that would otherwise be lost as runoff.

Building a green roof is a sophisticated project. You can't just climb up on top of your house, dump some soil there, and plant petunias. You'll need to consult a knowledgeable builder—and if you own an older house or building, you may learn that it's not able to bear the weight of a roof planting.

If your house is a good candidate for a green roof, you'll first have to choose between installing an intensive green roof or an extensive one. The intensive roof is the heaviest: It comprises 2 to 4 feet of soil as the medium for growing a complete garden including trees. Extensive green roofs, in contrast, use only 2 to 6 inches of growing mix (not topsoil). The advantage is that they're much lighter; the disadvantage is that plant choices are more limited. This type of project will become easier as gardeners, engineers, and scientists collaborate to find even more ways to grow the rooftops green.

GROUNDCOVERS

Groundcovers are the original landscape problem solvers. Where lawn grass won't grow easily or well, groundcovers come into their own. You can use plants like Japanese pachysandra (*Pachysandra terminalis*) or epimediums (*Epimedium* spp.) to cover bare spots in the dense shade and dry soil under trees. Choose tough, deep-rooted groundcover perennials like daylilies (*Hemerocallis* spp.) or St. John's worts (*Hypericum* spp.) to stabilize slopes. Low-growing shrubs like creeping juniper (*Juniperus horizontalis*) and bearberry cotoneaster (*Cotoneaster dammeri*) are good along stairways, paths, and plantings of larger shrubs. Cover wet, boggy sites with plants like Chinese astilbe (*Astilbe chinensis*) or sweet flags (*Acorus* spp.) instead of mowing a quagmire.

For weed control and reduced yard mainte-nance, groundcovers can't be beat. But they're also excellent for covering up plants that are past their peak. For example, groundcovering perennials like hostas will mask dying daffodil foliage so it can ripen in peace without becoming an eyesore. You can also use groundcovers like creeping mazus (*Mazus reptans*) or bugleweeds (*Ajuga* spp.) under spring bulbs, ferns, and perennials. Their leaves will set off the taller and more colorful plants, plus the groundcovers will help keep the soil covered and eliminate the need to mulch.

Shrubs or herbaceous perennials that look attractive all season, grow vigorously, and spread quickly to carpet the ground make the best groundcovers. It's also important to look for low-maintenance plants that will thrive in the conditions your site has to offer. Although groundcovers typically are under about 18 inches tall, don't let plant height limit you too much. While ground-huggers under 2 or 3 inches are important along a stepping-stone pathway, taller plants—from 2 to 3 feet—make great groundcovers in a wide range of situations. Even taller plants used en masse are a perfect choice for covering a large area: Look for suckering shrubs or shrubs that have spreading branches and are wider than they are tall at maturity.

Keep in mind that some plants spread too vigorously to be good groundcovers. While plants like English ivy (*Hedera helix*), vinca or periwinkles (*Vinca* spp.), and wintercreeper (*Euonymus fortunei*) grow on nearly any site, in most situations, it's best to avoid planting these and the other invasive groundcovers listed on the opposite page. Once established, they can become garden bullies that quickly spread beyond the bounds of your site and may infiltrate wild areas and crowd out native plants.

Invasive Groundcovers

It's best to seek out alternatives to these widely sold, but invasive, groundcovers. Also check with your local extension office or your state's Department of Natural Resources for plants that are problematic or even legally restricted in your area.

Aegopodium podagraria (bishop's goutweed)

Duchesnea indica (mock strawberry)

Euonymus fortunei (wintercreeper)

Euphorbia cyparissias (cypress spurge)

Hedera spp. (ivies)

Houttuynia cordata (chameleon plant)

Lysimachia nummularia (creeping Jenny)

Phalaris arundinacea (variegated ribbon grass)

Securigera varia (crown vetch)

Vinca spp. (vinca, periwinkles)

How to Use Groundcovers

Why use groundcovers when you can just grow grass? For adaptability, resilience, and uniformity, lawn grasses are tough to beat. They withstand heavy foot traffic, rough play, and all the abuse a family can muster. However, it requires a lot of time and effort to keep lawn grasses healthy and attractive. They aren't a good choice for sites under trees and shrubs or those with wet soil. A lawn also requires regular mowing, which releases greenhouse gases, and needs much more water than groundcovers or many other types of plant-

ings. Reducing your lawn to the smallest size you need for outdoor activities and replacing it with groundcovers and other plants will save time, work, and resources. It also will create a more dynamic landscape.

Underplanting trees and shrubs is another good way to use groundcovers. Replace lawn with groundcovers under a group of trees and shrubs to create an island of handsome vegetation. Not only will underplanting help unify your landscape design, it also helps protect the trunks of trees and shrubs from banging and scraping by lawn mowers. Underplanting eliminates the need to spend precious gardening time hand-trimming around each trunk. A mixed planting of hostas, with their beautiful leaf patterns and colors, looks wonderful under trees. So do ferns, astilbes (*Astilbe* spp.), and many native wildflowers. Or try blue-green lilyturf (*Liriope* spp.) for a cool contrast to the lighter lawn grass.

You can grow groundcovers instead of lawn grass where you want to limit water use. As everyone who's spent their evenings or weekends holding a hose knows, lawns are thirsty. Xeriscaping, a landscape philosophy based on water conservation and minimizing damage to the landscape, uses extensive plantings of tough, drought-resistant groundcovers. These adaptable plants reduce environmental impact, save water, and cut maintenance time. For more on water-wise gardening techniques, see the Watering and Xeriscaping entries.

Groundcovers can perk up the landscape in the off-season. Think about fall and winter in your garden. Many groundcovers take on beautiful hues as cool weather returns. Some, like lilyturf and bearberry (*Arctostaphylos uva-ursi*), display colorful fruits. Seed heads of ornamental grasses are loveliest late in the season. Evergreen foliage shines against light snowfalls.

Don't forget to go beyond problem solving when you're using groundcovers—after all, you have to look at them, too. A yard full of pachysandra may get the ground covered, but it's not nearly as appealing as a combination of groundcover plants. Think about mixing shapes, textures, and colors in exciting combinations. Feathery ferns with white-variegated hostas and low, glossy-leaved European wild ginger (*Asarum europaeum*) will make a shady site much more interesting than any one of the three alone. A mix of ajugas (*Ajuga* spp.)—perhaps 'Pink Beauty' (a pink-flowered, green-leaved cultivar) with the bronze-leaved 'Bronze Beauty' and the large-leaved, blue-flowered 'Catlin's Giant'—will add more sparkle to a sunny spot than a single culti-

var. Finally, there are a great many groundcovers that feature showy flowers, including daylilies, Chinese astilbe (*Astilbe chinensis*), hardy geraniums (*Geranium* spp.), thymes (*Thymus* spp.), and plumbago (*Ceratostigma plumbaginoides*).

Don't be afraid to try something new if a combination falls flat. If a plant doesn't work where you've put it, just move it: Your best design tool is your shovel.

Choosing the Best Groundcovers

The cardinal rule in gardening is to match the plant to the site. To get the best performance from

Groundcovers for Dry Shade

Dry shade—the kind usually found under shade trees and shrubs—is one of the most difficult conditions gardeners face. Other places where dry shade is often a problem are under eaves and on shaded slopes, where rainwater tends to run off. Plenty of plants grow in damp shade or in dry, sunny sites, but what usually grows under water-hogging trees and shrubs are bare spots. Fortunately, groundcovers can come to the rescue and create lush plantings to replace the eyesores.

Here is a list of good perennial groundcovers for dry shade. Plant heights range from creeping to 1½ feet.

Carex pensylvanica (Pennsylvania sedge)

Ceratostigma plumbaginoides (plumbago)

Convallaria majalis (lily of the valley)

Dryopteris filix-mas (male fern)

Epimedium spp. (epimediums)

Helleborus ×hybridus (hybrid hellebores)

Liriope spp. (lilyturfs)

Mahonia repens (creeping mahonia)

Ophiopogon spp. (mondo grasses)

Pachysandra procumbens (Allegheny spurge)

Pachysandra terminalis (Japanese pachysandra)

Polygonatum spp. (Solomon's seals)

Sedum ternatum (woodland stonecrop)

Waldsteinia fragarioides (barren strawberry)

Groundcovers for Wet Sites

Trying to grow a lawn on a boggy site is an effort doomed to failure. Rather than living with a muddy weed patch, landscape the area with some of these attractive perennial groundcovers that grow in wet soil. You can create a beautiful wetland garden by mixing drifts of plants with different foliage and a wide range of flowering times. Plant heights range from creeping to 3 feet, so match the plant to the scale of your site.

Acorus gramineus (sweet flag)

Alchemilla mollis (lady's mantle)

Anemone canadensis (meadow anemone)

Astilbe chinensis (Chinese astilbe)

Brunnera macrophylla (Siberian bugloss)

Carex spp. (sedges)

Coreopsis rosea (pink tickseed)

Equisetum spp. (horsetails)

Galium odoratum (sweet woodruff)

Hosta spp. (hostas)

Primula spp. (primroses)

Rodgersia pinnata (featherleaf rodgersia)

Thelypteris palustris (marsh fern)

loving, deep-rooted yarrows (*Achillea* spp.) to stop erosion on a dry, sunny bank.

Don't forget maintenance. Plant vigorous growers like sedums or pachysandra where you need dense cover to control weeds, not in a small space where they would quickly get out of control. For a small space that's not weed prone, choose airy plants like foamflowers (*Tiarella* spp.) or Roman chamomile (*Chamaemelum nobile*) that won't be in a hurry to overgrow the site. In both cases, a well-chosen groundcover will reduce your yard work, while a badly chosen groundcover will pitch you into a losing battle.

When you're looking for a good groundcover, let your needs limit your choices. Focus on the plants that suit your garden and your design. First, define your needs by asking yourself a few key questions.

- Is your site shaded, partially shaded, or in full sun?
- Is your site moist or dry?
- Do you need a ground-hugging plant for the site, or would a taller plant look better?
- Do you want bold or fine texture?
- How important are flowers? Flower color?
- Can you use variegated foliage to brighten things up?
- Should the plant be evergreen or deciduous?

Read more about how to choose plants in the Garden Design entry.

Planting and Maintenance

When you're trying to plant and establish a new groundcover, removing existing weeds and preparing

a groundcover, you must give it the growing conditions it needs. Plant shade-loving, shallow-rooted Bethlehem sage (*Pulmonaria saccharata*) to cover a bare area in the shade of a maple tree, and sun-

Groundcovers for Slopes

If you've ever tried to mow grass on a slope—sliding down after the mower, struggling to push it back up, or hauling it up and down on a rope—you know why a carefree planting of groundcovers is a better idea. Good groundcovers for slopes should transplant readily, provide cover quickly, and send down deep roots to keep the soil from eroding. Choose plants that can take the full sun and drought conditions of most slopes. Here's a selection of the best perennial groundcovers for sunny slopes. They range in height from ground-huggers to 3-foot shrubs, so match the groundcover to the scale of your slope. For slopes in shade, use the list on page 276.

Achillea spp. (yarrows)

Arctostaphylos uva-ursi (bearberry)

Cerastium tomentosum (snow-in-summer)

Comptonia peregrina (sweet fern)

Cotoneaster spp. (cotoneasters)

Delosperma spp. (hardy ice plants)

Forsythia 'Arnold Dwarf" (dwarf forsythia)

Hemerocallis spp. (daylilies)

Hypericum spp. (St. John's worts)

Juniperus cultivars (creeping junipers)

Pteridium aquilinum (bracken)

Rudbeckia fulgida var. *sullivantii* 'Goldsturm' ('Goldsturm' black-eyed Susan)

Sedum spp. (sedums, stonecrops)

---

the soil properly at planting time are essential, especially on difficult sites. See the Soil entry for soil preparation options and the Weeds entry for strategies to eliminate weedy competition for your new groundcovers.

Space plants according to their growth rate and size at maturity. Check labels for recommendations. In general, space perennials, ornamental grasses, and other herbaceous plants 1 to 3 feet apart, depending on the mature size of the plant. Plant junipers and other large woody plants at least 3 feet apart.

Arrange the plants within the bed according to your design. Dig a hole for each plant large enough to accommodate the loosened rootball. If you're using container-grown plants, be sure to set them at the same depth they were growing in

the container. Soak the roots of bareroot plants for several hours before planting, then remove them from the water one at a time when planting, and spread the roots evenly over a dome of soil in the bottom of the planting hole. Check the level of the crown to make sure it's at the right planting depth. Water each plant in as you plant it. (For more how-to-plant techniques, see the Planting entry.)

Mulch the site after planting to control weeds and reduce moisture loss. Water newly set plants thoroughly, and keep the planting evenly moist until plants are well established, which will take an entire growing season for woody plants. Pull weeds early to avoid competition.

Groundcovers as a group are tough, trouble-free plants. But some pest and disease problems are inevitable in any garden situation. Prevention is the best control. Keep plants healthy, well watered, and mulched. Remove weeds that can harbor pests. If problems arise, consult the Pests entry.

Growing Your Own Groundcovers

Groundcovers are a diverse group of plants, but most are easy to propagate. Propagation techniques vary according to whether you're dealing with a shrubby, vining, or perennial groundcover. While many groundcovers can be grown from seed started indoors or direct-seeded outdoors, you'll get quicker results from fast-growing groundcovers if you take cuttings or divide them.

Take cuttings from perennial groundcovers like spotted dead nettle (*Lamium maculatum*), plumbago (*Ceratostigma plumbaginoides*), pachysandra, and sedum in early to midsummer. You can divide groundcovers in spring or fall. If the plant is a vine, like clematis, or a creeper, like ajuga, creeping phlox (*Phlox stolonifera*), or foamflowers (*Tiarella* spp.), sever rooted plantlets from the parent stem. Lift clumps of perennials like astilbe, bergenias, blue fescue (*Festuca glauca*), dwarf crested iris (*Iris cristata*), daylily, and hosta, and separate the crowns.

A slow but easy method of propagating woody groundcovers like cotoneasters and junipers is layering—encouraging branches to root where they touch the ground. For more on propagation techniques, see the Cuttings, Division, Layering, and Seed Starting and Seed Saving entries.

GYPSOPHILA

Baby's breath. Summer-blooming annuals and perennials.

Description: Most kinds of baby's breath resemble earthbound clouds when in bloom, with hundreds of tiny, five-petaled, single or double flowers in white or pink shades. The open, multibranched plants bear narrow, gray-green leaves 1 to 4 inches long. *Gypsophila elegans*, annual baby's breath, blooms for a short season and rarely exceeds 2 feet. *G. paniculata*, perennial baby's breath, blooms over a longer season and can grow to 3 feet tall and wide. Zones 3–9.

How to grow: Both kinds of baby's breath need a sunny site with average to less-fertile soil that is neutral or slightly alkaline and moderately moist but well drained. Sow annual baby's breath once the weather is warm directly where it is to grow. Make several sowings 2 weeks apart for a longer bloom season. Plant perennial baby's breath in spring and divide only if necessary; the long, fleshy roots resent disturbance. Double cultivars like 'Bristol Fairy' are sometimes propagated by grafting, so plant the graft union below the surface of the soil to encourage new roots to form. Perennial baby's breath tolerates heat quite well. Cut it back immediately after bloom to encourage fresh growth and possible rebloom. Stake tall cultivars.

Landscape uses: Both annual and perennial baby's breath are beautiful in borders, cottage gardens, and other informal plantings. Fill the gaps they leave after bloom with asters and other fall-blooming plants. Grow baby's breath in a cutting garden for bouquets; blooms can be used either fresh or dried. To dry them, gather some stems in full bloom and hang them upside down to dry.

H

HABITAT GARDENING

In the United States, widespread, ill-planned development is the greatest cause of species endangerment and extinction, destroying vital habitat for plants ranging from cacti and orchids to wildflowers and native trees and shrubs. Habitat destruction also threatens insects, birds, amphibians, and many other kinds of wildlife. Worldwide, up to 600,000 species have become extinct in just the past 50 years. Some projections warn that if this rate of habitat destruction continues, we could lose half of the earth's species by 2050.

The most threatened habitat in the world is tropical forestland, which makes up only 6 percent of the earth's land surface but is home to an estimated 50 to 90 percent of all species. Even though tropical forests may be a long distance from your garden, you can notice one effect of their destruction in your own yard—fewer migratory songbirds. Many songbird species are in decline due to

loss of their winter habitat in Central America and South America. Global loss is local loss, and in the long run, what we do locally has global impact as well.

The common theme of natural habitats in most regions is biodiversity. If you want to replicate natural landscapes and help with habitat, create a landscape that combines different kinds of plants that grow compatibly together and benefit birds, butterflies, and other animals. Most natural habitats include groups of trees and shrubs surrounded by perennials, including grasses and groundcovers. A successful habitat garden provides homes for creatures ranging from tiny parasitic wasps and fast-flying hummingbirds to toads, squirrels, and perhaps even a red fox.

Here's how to get started.

- Analyze your site to decide if it's most suited for a woodland, prairie, wetland, oceanside, or desert plant and animal community.

- Choose native trees and shrubs, or other site-appropriate species that benefit wildlife. Plants with berries are often the best choices. Include both evergreen and deciduous plants.

- Cluster the trees and shrubs in islands or wide borders and hedgerows around your property. Start with just one plant cluster, and work over time to create an entire landscape of naturalized plant groups.

- Cover the areas around the tree and shrub clusters with perennials and grasses. Choose plants that spread (without becoming weedy). Use annuals to fill in while the groundcovers are spreading. Remember diversity—plant a variety of species.

- Encourage pollinators and other beneficial insects by choosing many kinds of flowers to provide pollen and nectar. Select flowers that bloom at different times from spring through fall, as well as some that offer generous seed heads toward autumn.

- Provide water in as many ways as possible—birdbaths, fountains, streams, water gardens, and dishes of water or shallow pools at the soil level. All creatures need water, and birds are drawn to the sounds of water splashing or dripping. Be sure you arrange to keep the water available in the heat of summer and all through the winter as well, since your habitat will be a year-round home for many species.

- Allow plants to grow naturally. While it's appropriate to prune out the occasional diseased or rubbing branches, a natural landscape is not the place for sheared shrubs. Contrary to classic pruning advice, a few crowding, overlapping, and touching branches on trees and shrubs is natural and desirable. The goal is to provide shelter and safety for many creatures.

- Tolerate the litter. In nature, leaves, fruit, and needles fall, cover the ground, and eventually decompose, adding organic matter and nutrients to the soil. Let that happen. (The exception here is diseased or pest-infested litter, which you should destroy rather than leave in place.)

- Allow some logs to lie and snags (dead trees) to stand. Dying or dead trees or shrubs provide food and homes for many kinds of creatures and are part of a natural system. Where you can tolerate an untidy look, leave them in place—a pileated woodpecker showing up for an appetizer may be your reward!

- Make a brush pile. Perhaps the back of your property is suitable for brush piles. Especially if they are built upon large logs or rocks (so small animals or ground birds can scurry under), brush piles provide dining, safety, or places to raise a family.

- Consider the animals you do not welcome. That could mean deer—if so, avoid plants they prefer and choose those they rarely eat. If you are worried about rats, be sure your birdfeeders have catch trays so seed will be less likely to drop on the ground. Embracing diversity doesn't mean you give up all control over the territory; you just have to be smarter than a rat! You may need repellants, barriers, or fences, for specific reasons. True ecological balance is difficult to achieve, especially because your little habitat lies within an imbalanced world. But in most cases, naturalized landscapes present few problems with pests of any kind.

For more information about and plant choices for habitat gardens, see the Birds, Water Gardens, and Wildlife Gardening entries.

Wildlife Corridors

When large tracts of natural habitat are broken up by development, roads, or even farms, it creates big problems for many species of wildlife.

Too small for comfort. Many wild creatures, such as the lovely wood thrush, can thrive only deep within large tracts of woodland. When those interior areas are reduced, populations of these woodland species decline.

Too much edge. Some predatory species that are not so desirable—crows, for example—thrive when there's lots of edge. (Edge is the boundary between two types of habitat, for example, woodland and open areas such as the cut-grass borders along a roadway.) As buildings, roads, and parking lots break up woods or meadows, the more vulnerable many species become to predators. (The inci-

dence of roadkills increases, too.)

Not enough connections. When appropriate habitat occurs only in isolated "islands," migratory mammals or birds may not be able to migrate successfully. This can lead to inbreeding and an imbalance in predator/prey relationships. Both situations produce weaker populations or eventual death.

Openings for invasive species. The more the plant life or soil of a natural area is disturbed (by digging, brush mowing, bulldozing, etc.), the more likely aggressive plant species are to invade. Purple loosestrife and giant hogweed colonize roadside ditches; Japanese honeysuckle and multiflora rose thrive where meadows have been cleared.

What You Can Do

Creating wildlife corridors is one way to counteract habitat loss in your area. These

HAMAMELIS

Witch hazel. Deciduous fall- or winter-flowering shrubs and small trees.

Description: *Hamamelis vernalis*, vernal witch hazel, a native species, grows 6 to 10 feet tall and can spread wider than its height. Fragrant yellow to red flowers appear in late winter to early spring and are showy for almost a month. Golden yellow fall foliage color is very showy. Zones 4–8.

H. virginiana, American witch hazel, another native, grows 15 to 20 feet tall and wide. Its spicy-scented, saffron yellow flowers unfurl as its clear yellow fall foliage is dropping. Zones 3–8.

H. mollis, Chinese witch hazel, reaches 10 to 15 feet tall and wide. It is spectacular in the landscape because its blooms appear in midwinter, often against a backdrop of snow. Zones 5–8.

H. ×intermedia, hybrid witch hazel, is a cross between Chinese and Japanese (*H. japonica*). Its many cultivars are large shrubs or small trees that reach 15 to 20 feet tall and are popular landscape specimens because of their showy and sweet-scented floral displays in mid- to late winter when few other blossoms are to be found. 'Arnold Promise' bears bright yellow flowers; 'Jelena' has orange blossoms; the flowers of 'Diane' are bold red-orange. Zones 5–8.

corridors allow wildlife to move from one large tract of habitat—such as a park, wildlife sanctuary, or undeveloped private land—to another. They include culverts or overpasses when necessary so that animals can cross highways. Habitat biologists recommend that these corridors between major habitats should be at least 1,000 feet wide to accommodate many species. If you're lucky enough to live next to one of these existing wildlife corridors, you can be part of the solution by keeping your yard as natural as possible, preventing cats and dogs from roaming free, removing invasive plant species, and minimizing light pollution.

Even if you don't live next to a large-scale wildlife corridor, you still can work together with your neighbors or local government to provide a smaller-scale sanctuary or corridor, which can provide excellent habitat for wild creatures such as foxes and can encourage migrating songbirds. Imagine if everybody living along your street gave a 20- or 50-foot strip back to nature, and all those strips connected (some with water features, too). That's a neighborhood wildlife corridor!

Another option is to lobby your local government agencies to create a wildlife corridor or park. Start by finding out whether your community has a plan for providing "green space" and what it entails. Then, talk with local leaders and residents to help them understand that "green space" such as athletic fields and biking trails is not the same as wildlife habitat. By spreading the word, you may help convince local officials to set aside some green space as the kind of undeveloped natural area that will help preserve and encourage native plants and wildlife.

All species have dull green, 2- to 6-inch leaves. In autumn, seed capsules can catapult seeds many feet.

How to grow: Grow witch hazels in partial shade, especially in the southern end of their range. Common witch hazel grows best in moist, humus-rich soil, with plenty of mulch. Prune only to remove branches that are dead, dying, crossing, or rubbing.

Landscape uses: Witch hazels make good specimens. American witch hazel is lovely in a native planting. Plant winter-blooming hybrids near an entrance or walkway where you can enjoy their fragrance.

HARDENING OFF

See Transplanting

HEDERA

Ivy. Evergreen woody vines.

Description: *Hedera helix*, English ivy, is a vigorous evergreen vine with shiny three- to five-lobed leaves, 2 to 5 inches long. Although this vine is very well known, it should be planted with caution because it is a nonnative species that can become invasive in some regions. It easily spreads beyond gardens, where it blankets woodlands, outcompetes native wildflowers, and overwhelms trees. Plants spread by stems that twine and attach by rootlets. Zones 5–9; some cultivars are hardy to Zone 4.

H. canariensis, Algerian or Canary ivy, is similar to English ivy but more tolerant of heat. Zones 9–10 and the milder parts of Zone 8. *H. colchica*, Persian ivy, displays large leaves and coarse growth. Zones 6–9. Both of these species show invasive potential in warmer regions.

How to grow: If you choose to grow ivies, plant them on sites where buildings, paved walkways, or other structures will keep them contained. Start with rooted cuttings or transplants in spring or fall. Plants prefer moist, humus-rich, well-drained soils and tolerate acid or alkaline conditions. Give them partial or dense shade—they won't tolerate full sun or hot sites. Ivies are relatively free of pest and disease problems. Prune regularly to keep them from spreading.

Landscape uses: Ivies serve well as groundcovers or climbing vines and are valued as low-maintenance plants. They are especially useful in dense shade, where little else will grow. Site them very carefully and keep them away from sites where they can spread to wooded areas. The vines have holdfasts on aerial rootlets that allow them to cling to brick and masonry walls. However, be aware that rootlets can work their way into cracks in the wall and eventually dislodge pieces of brick or stone. Birds feed on the blue-black berries and contribute to the spread of ivies into woodlands, where they may grow unnoticed and unchecked until they have overtaken an area.

Use small-leaved or variegated ivies to grow over topiary forms, plant them in containers or hanging baskets, or grow them as houseplants.

HEDGES

Plant a hedge for a privacy screen to block out unwelcome views or traffic noise or to add a green background to set off other plantings. Hedges also provide excellent wind protection for house or garden. Thick, tall, or thorny hedges make inexpensive and forbidding barriers to keep out animals—or to keep them in. Many plants make excellent hedges. Even tall or bushy annuals can make a temporary hedge; plant herbs such as lavender for an attractive low hedge.

A formal hedge is an elegant, carefully trimmed row of trees or shrubs. It requires frequent pruning to keep plants straight and level. The best plants for formal hedges are fine leaved and slow growing—and tough enough to take frequent shearing. An informal hedge requires only selective pruning and has a more natural look. A wide variety of plants with attractive flowers or berries can be used.

Shaping a hedge. Prune a hedge so that its base is wider than the top. This allows light to reach all parts of the plants and keeps your hedge growing vigorously.

Hedge Plants

Most hedges are shrub or tree species; this list is a mix of common and uncommon hedge plants. An asterisk (*) indicates a plant that will work well for a formal hedge.

Evergreen Trees

Chamaecyparis lawsoniana (Lawson cypress)

Juniperus spp. (junipers)

Prunus laurocerasus (cherry laurel)*

Tsuga canadensis (Canada hemlock)*

Deciduous Trees

Carpinus betulus (European hornbeam)*

Crataegus spp. (hawthorns)*

Fagus spp. (beeches)

Evergreen Shrubs

Berberis aquifolium (formerly *Mahonia* spp.) and other species (holly-leaved barberry)

Buxus spp. (boxwoods)*

Cotoneaster spp. (cotoneasters)*

Ilex crenata (Japanese holly)*

Ligustrum spp. (privets)*

Taxus spp. (yews)*

Deciduous Shrubs

Chaenomeles speciosa (Japanese quince)

Diervilla lonicera (bush honeysuckle)

Forsythia ×intermedia (forsythia)

Ligustrum spp. (privets)*

Philadelphus spp. (mock oranges)

Rosa spp. (shrub roses)

Viburnum spp. (viburnums)

Planting and Pruning

It's best to plant young plants when starting a hedge. Full-grown specimens are more apt to die from transplanting stress in the early years, and finding an exact replacement can be difficult. It's easier to fill a gap in an informal hedge.

For an open, airy hedge of flowering shrubs, allow plenty of room for growth when planting. For a dense, wall-like hedge, space the plants more closely. You may find it easier to dig a trench rather than separate holes. To ensure your hedge will be straight, tie a string between stakes at each end to mark the trench before digging. See the Planting entry for details on preparing planting holes and setting plants.

Broad-leaved plants used as a formal hedge need early training to force dense growth. For a thick, uniform hedge, reduce new shoots on the top and sides by one-third or more each year until the hedge is the desired size. Cutting a formal hedge properly is a challenge. Stand back, walk around, and recut until you get it straight—just like a haircut. Shear often during the growing season to keep it neat.

Needled evergreens require a different technique. Avoid cutting off the tops of evergreens until they reach the desired height. Shear sides once a year, but never into the bare wood. See the Evergreens entry for more pruning tips.

Prune informal hedges according to when they bloom. Do any needed pruning soon after flowering. Use thinning cuts to prune selected branches back to the next limb. Heading cuts that nip the branch back to a bud encourage dense, twiggy growth on the outside. To keep informal hedges vigorous, cut two or three of the oldest branches to the ground each year.

For fast, dense growth, prune in spring. This is also a good time for any severe shearing or pruning that's needed. For more about when and how to prune, see the Shrubs and the Pruning and Training entries.

HEIRLOOM PLANTS

Heirloom plants are most often thought of as old-time varieties of vegetables that come true from seed. That means that they're open-pollinated, so (assuming you don't plant other cultivars that could cross-pollinate nearby) you can save seed from your plants every year for the following year's garden. In addition to wonderful heirloom vegetables, most cottage-garden flowers and herbs fall in this category, too. Of course, many plants have been lovingly passed down through the generations as cuttings, and even the hybrids that replaced most open-pollinated plants in commerce now boast some old "heirloom" cultivars of their own. But usually, "open-pollinated" continues to be the hallmark of herbaceous heirloom plants.

Some famous heirlooms have been sold and passed down in families or communities for hundreds of years; others date just to the early 1900s. What they all have in common is that backyard gardeners have prized them for their beauty, flavor, fragrance, or productivity. Because home gardeners thought highly enough of these plants to save seed from them year after year, we can still enjoy them today.

Characteristics: Heirloom fruits and vegetables are often not suited to large-scale production. Many types don't ripen all at once so they aren't easily harvested mechanically. They often don't keep well during shipping and storage and many of them don't have a consistent appearance. They may even look a little odd, like some of the warty-skinned melons or striped green tomatoes.

But heirlooms are often ideal for home gardeners. Many heirloom crops have a more pleasing flavor and texture than their hybrid replacements, and many spread their harvest over a longer period so families can enjoy picking just what they need for each day's meals rather than having to harvest a bumper crop all at once. If grown for years in one locality, the heirlooms have adapted to the climate and soil conditions of that area and may outproduce modern cultivars. Others may be less productive than today's hybrids but offer greater disease and insect resistance, which is invaluable to organic gardeners. (On the other hand, some heirlooms are less resistant than hybrids bred specifically to resist particular diseases.) Heirloom plants also add interest to garden and table, with a wide range of shapes, colors, and flavors unavailable in modern cultivars.

Heirloom plants are a tangible connection with the past. Like fine old furniture and antique china, the garden plants of earlier generations draw us closer to those who have grown them before us. Some heirloom cultivars have fascinating histories. 'Mostoller Wild Goose' bean, said to have been collected from the craw of a goose shot in 1864 in Somerset County, Pennsylvania, was once grown by Cornplanter Indians. 'Hopi Pale Grey' squash is a Pueblo Indian legacy that was almost lost to cul-

N

tivation and remains one of the most sought-after winter squashes. 'Anasazi' corn, found in a Utah cave, is thought to be more than 800 years old. And many gardeners have heard the story of 'Radiator Charley's Mortgage Lifter' tomato, a huge, meaty cultivar that helped its discoverer, an unemployed mechanic, pay off his mortgage during the Depression.

Cultivars like these are eagerly sought by both gardeners and collectors, who maintain them for their historic value just as archivists maintain old papers and books. See the list at right for other well-known examples.

Genetic diversity: As fewer seed companies remain in existence and those that survive offer a dwindling number of cultivars, there's an even more vital reason for growing old cultivars: These open-pollinated heirloom plants represent a vast and diverse pool of genetic characteristics—one that will be lost forever if these plants are allowed to become extinct. Even cultivars that seem inferior to us today may carry a gene that will prove invaluable in the future. One may contain a valuable but yet undiscovered substance that could be used in medicine. Another could have the disease resistance vital to future generations of gardeners and plant breeders.

The federal government maintains the Plant and Animal Genetic Resources Preservation Unit in Fort Collins, Colorado, as part of its commitment to maintaining genetic diversity, but the task of preserving seed is so vast that the government probably cannot do a complete job on its own. Heirloom gardeners recognize the importance of maintaining genetic diversity, and many feel a real sense of urgency and importance about their own preservation work. Thanks to them, to seed companies that remain committed to offering open-pollinated heirlooms to the public, and to organizations like Seed Savers Exchange that are

Famous Heirlooms

Here is a sampling of the best-known heirloom cultivars. This selection just skims the surface to whet your appetite.

Beans: 'Cherokee Trail of Tears', 'Dragon Tongue', 'Hutterite Soup', 'Jacob's Cattle', 'Mayflower', 'Old Homestead'

Corn: 'Black Aztec', 'Country Gentleman', 'Golden Bantam', 'Stowell's Evergreen'

Cucumbers: 'Boston Pickling', 'Chinese Yellow', 'Lemon', 'White Wonder'

Lettuce: 'Amish Deer Tongue', 'Black-Seeded Simpson', 'Merveille des Quatre Saisons', 'Parris Island Cos', 'Tom Thumb'

Squash: 'Rouge Vif d'Etampes', 'Turk's Cap', 'White Scallop', 'Winter Luxury Pie Pumpkin'

Tomatoes: 'Amish Paste', 'Bloody Butcher', 'Brandywine', 'Cherokee Purple', 'German Lunchbox', 'Green Zebra', 'Mule Team', 'Persimmon'

Watermelons: 'Charleston Gray', 'Dixie Queen', 'Georgia Rattlesnake', 'Moon and Stars', 'Stone Mountain'

dedicated to maintaining diversity in the garden, the future of heirloom plants looks bright.

Getting started: If you'd like to start growing heirloom plants in your garden, try ordering seed from small specialty seed suppliers that carry old cultivars. Also, you can contact nonprofit organizations that work with individuals to preserve heirloom plants, such as the Seed Savers Exchange. Some gardening magazines also have a seed swap column. See Resources on page 673 for contact information for seed exchanges. For directions on how to save seeds from your garden, see the Seed Starting and Seed Saving entry.

HELIANTHUS

Sunflower. Summer- to fall-blooming annuals and perennials.

Description: *Helianthus annuus*, common sunflower, is an annual that lights up gardens with single or double daisies in shades of cream, yellow, orange, and red-brown on plants 2 to 10 feet tall or taller. For more details, see the Sunflower entry.

H. ×multiflorus, many-flowered sunflower, is a perennial that bears 3- to 5-inch golden blooms on upright, bushy plants to 5 feet. Blooms appear from late summer to fall. Zones 4–8.

How to grow: Start annual sunflowers indoors a few weeks before the last frost, or sow directly in full sun and average to rich, moist but well-drained soil. Water and fertilize regularly. Provide similar growing conditions for perennials; plant in spring. Divide overgrown clumps in fall every 3 or 4 years. Sunflowers are usually drought tolerant once established.

Landscape uses: Grow in borders for summer and fall color, in informal and meadow gardens, and in cutting gardens.

HELLEBORUS

Hellebore. Winter- to early-spring-blooming perennials.

Description: Hellebores bear 2- to 3-inch, shallow bowl-shaped flowers and 1-foot palm-shaped evergreen leaves. *Helleborus foetidus*, green-flowered or stinking hellebore, bears striking clusters of char-

treuse flowers held well above blue-gray or dark forest green leaves. 'Wester Flisk' is an outstanding cultivar. Zones 5 (with protection) and 6–9.

H. niger, Christmas rose, bears white flowers in winter or early spring among 1-foot mounds of foliage; 'Potter's Wheel' and 'Nell Lewis' are outstanding cultivars; 'Blackthorn Strain' is a selection of the hybrid *H. ×sternii*. Zones 3–8.

H. orientalis, Lenten rose (more often *orientalis* hybrids, *H. ×hybridus*), blooms in early spring, with white, green, pink, yellow, purple, maroon, or almost black flowers among handsome, 1½-foot shiny green leaves. Flowers are often speckled with a contrasting color, and some cultivars, such as 'Party Dress', have double flowers. Many outstanding cultivars and strains are available. The hybrid Lenten rose (*H. ×hybridus*) was named Perennial Plant of the Year for 2005 by the Perennial Plant Association. Zones 4–9.

How to grow: Set out pot-grown or small plants in the spring or fall. Divide these slow-to-establish but long-lived plants in spring, but only when you want new plants. They thrive in partial to full shade and well-drained, moisture-retentive, humus-rich soil. Keep out of drying winter winds. Established hellebores can self-sow profusely; transplant seedlings to their permanent positions in spring. (Note that a seedling may take 2 to 5 years to reach flowering size, so be patient. These long-lived plants are worth the wait.)

Landscape uses: Allow to naturalize in woodland plantings and among shrubs. Feature with early snowdrops and crocuses. A perfect complement to other shade plants such as hostas, ferns, wild gingers (*Asarum* spp.), bleeding hearts (*Dicentra* spp.), heucheras, and astilbes, hellebores are deer resistant. Contact with hellebores' foliage can cause skin irritation. Wear gloves and long sleeves when working with hellebores, and avoid planting them where you are likely to brush against the plants. All parts of hellebore plants are poisonous.

HEMEROCALLIS

Daylily. Mostly summer-blooming perennials; some bloom in spring and fall.

Description: Daylilies (*Hemerocallis* spp.) bear 2- to 8-inch-wide trumpet-shaped flowers in tones of almost every floral color except pure white and blue. Individual blooms last for only 1 day, though plants produce many buds, which provides a long display period. Flowers are borne on 1- to 6-foot (but usually $2\frac{1}{2}$- to $3\frac{1}{2}$-foot) top-branched, strong stems above fountainlike clumps of strap-shaped, roughly 2-foot-long, medium green leaves. Famous cultivars include the classic tall, fragrant, yellow 'Hyperion', compact, gold-flowering 'Stella de Oro', and reblooming, lemon-yellow 'Happy Returns'. Zones 3–9.

How to grow: Plant or divide daylilies any time from spring to fall, though early spring and early fall are best. Divide 4- to 6-year-old clumps by lifting the entire clump from the ground and inserting two digging forks back-to-back, pulling them apart to split the tight root mass. Replant as single, double, or triple "fans." (A fan is a division of a daylily plant, consisting of fleshy roots, a crown, and leaves.) Daylilies grow in sun or partial shade. Plant in average to fertile, well-drained, moisture-retentive soil (though plants will tolerate drought). Routinely deadhead spent blooms, which otherwise collect on the stalks and spoil the display. Watch for thrips, which brown and disfigure the buds; control them with soap spray or by removing infested flowers.

Landscape uses: Grow as specimens or groups in borders, or showcase daylilies in beds of their own. Many tougher, older cultivars make excellent groundcovers and bank plantings to control erosion and weeds. They also look beautiful planted along a fence or stone wall. Try showy rebloomers (like the 'Returns' series) as specimen plants in half-barrel containers.

HEMLOCK

See *Tsuga*

HERBS

Every gardener should grow at least a few herbs, even if only in pots on a sunny porch. Herbs contribute to our cuisine and our well-being; serve as decorative additions in gardens, bouquets, and wreaths; and fascinate us with their rich history and lore.

The word *herb* means different things to botanists and gardeners. For the botanist, an herb is basically any seed-bearing plant that isn't woody; it's where our word *herbaceous* comes from, as in herbaceous perennial. But for herb gardeners, what distinguishes an herb from other plants is its usefulness. As *Merriam-Webster's* dictionary puts it, an herb in this sense is "a plant or plant part valued for its medicinal, savory, or aromatic qualities."

Above all, whether used for flavorings, fragrances, medicines, crafts, dyes, or teas, herbs are truly useful plants. They're also among the most familiar garden plants, because they have been part of daily life since the dawn of human history, long before humans began intentionally planting gardens. From the beginning, people recognized certain plants' abilities to heal and to promote health. From there, it was a short step to using those plants for flavoring food and scenting the dwelling place.

Gardening with Herbs

There are nearly as many ways to incorporate herbs into your garden as there are herbs to choose from. A traditional herb garden is delightful, but herbs add interest to flower gardens, too. You can mix herbs into plantings of perennials or annuals, for example. One advantage of growing herbs apart from ornamentals, though, is that you won't spoil the flower garden display when you harvest your herbs.

Herb growing can be as simple or as complicated as you choose to make it. Most herbs are easy to grow—they demand little (typically full sun and good drainage) and give a lot. You can grow herbs successfully in anything from a simple arrangement of pots to a stylized formal garden. Only a few types of herbs are prima donnas that demand coddling. Also, some that are not hardy in the North must be brought indoors for winter or treated as annuals and replaced each year.

Vegetable Gardens

If your goal is to grow herbs in quantity, it makes sense to plant them in rows or beds in your vegetable garden for ease of care and harvest. Plants such as oregano, savory, santolina, thyme, culinary sage, and lavender do best in full sun in well-drained soils to which lime and grit have been added. Place them on specially prepared ridges or in raised beds. Angelica can be settled into a wettish spot. Dill, cilantro (coriander), parsley, chives, garlic chives, French tarragon, mints, and basils will thrive in a sunny site in well-drained soil containing lots of organic matter.

Herbs are often used as companion plants in the vegetable garden. According to folklore, in some cases backed by scientific studies, certain herbs can either aid or hinder vegetable growth. Herbs also help deter pests. And of course, they add beauty to your vegetable beds. See the sidebar on the opposite page and the Companion Planting entry for more details.

Herbs and Flowers

Many herbs are suitable for a mixed border or bed—a flower garden that combines perennials, annuals, and shrubs. You may already have some herbs in your garden, although you may think of them as flowers or foliage plants. In fact, roses such as the apothecary's rose (*Rosa gallica* var. *officinalis*) and damask rose (*R.* ×*damascena*) have been grown for centuries for their medicinal and fragrant qualities.

English lavender cultivars such as 'Hidcote' or 'Munstead' are always welcome among the flowers in beds or borders. Pure blue, silky flowers on delicate wiry stems make blue flax (*Linum perenne*) a favorite in flowerbeds. Feverfew (*Tanacetum parthenium*) is another herb often used in mixed borders. Its lacy, bright green foliage sets off small, pure white single or double daisies. Catmints (*Nepeta* spp.), with sprays of blue-lavender flowers, pungent, gray-green leaves, and a tufted habit, are lovely with lilies and roses.

Many gray-leaved herbs, such as the artemisias (*Artemisia* spp.), lamb's ears (*Stachys byzantina*), and Russian sage (*Perovskia atriplicifolia*), with its silvery foliage and misty blue flowers, are useful for separating and blending colors in the garden. Even a culinary workhorse like dill can be used to fine effect in the mixed border. Its delicate, chartreuse flowers and lacy foliage add an airiness to any planting.

Herbs in Containers

Herbs and containers are a happy combination, especially for a gardener short on space, time, or stamina. Maintenance chores—except for watering—are eliminated or much reduced. Even if your garden has

Herbs for a Mixed Border

Many herbs will thrive in a sunny mixed bed or border with average to rich, well-drained soil. These herbs are showy enough to hold their own in any garden. Plants are perennials unless otherwise noted.

***Achillea* spp. (yarrows):** Yellow, white, red, or pink flowers; used medicinally and dried for herbal crafts

***Calendula officinalis* (pot marigold):** Annual with bright orange or yellow daisy-like flowers; used medicinally and in cooking

***Digitalis purpurea* (common foxglove):** Biennial with tube-shaped pinkish purple or white flowers; formerly used medicinally (do not try this today!)

***Echinacea purpurea* (purple coneflower):** Rosy purple daisies with high, bristly centers; roots used medicinally

***Lavandula angustifolia* (lavender):** Lavender or purple flowers; flowers and foliage used for fragrance and herbal crafts

***Linum usitatissimum* (common flax):** Blue flowers; used medicinally

***Monarda didyma* (bee balm):** Shaggy rose or pink blossoms; dried blossoms and foliage used for tea, fragrance, and herbal crafts

***Tropaeolum majus* (garden nasturtium):** Annual with abundant flowers in shades of orange, yellow, and red; used in cooking and as a companion plant

plenty of space, a potted collection adds interest to a sunny porch, patio, or deck. Keep that "sunny" aspect in mind when planning your container herb garden—most herbs need full sun and good drainage whether they're grown in pots or in the ground. (Mints are an exception, fond as they are of moist soil.) In fact, one great reason to grow herbs in containers is if much of your yard is in shade but your patio, deck, or dooryard is sunny.

An assortment of terra-cotta pots brimming with herbs used for cooking makes a charming—and useful—addition to a kitchen doorstep. Or try a sampler of mints in a wooden half barrel—the notorious perennial spreaders stay in control, will come back year after year, and are handy when you're ready to brew a pot of tea. Hanging baskets of nasturtiums will add delightful color to your collection of container herbs, and the leaves, flow-

ers, and spicy buds are all edible. For information on potting soil mixes for container plants, see the Container Gardening and Houseplants entries.

Some tender herbs are often grown—or at least overwintered—in containers because they aren't hardy and won't survive northern winters. These include rosemary (*Rosmarinus officinalis*), sweet bay (*Laurus nobilis*), myrtle (*Myrtus communis*), pineapple sage (*Salvia elegans*), and lemon verbena (*Aloysia triphylla*). See page 296 for directions on keeping these tender herbs from year to year.

Formal Herb Gardens

Most gardeners would probably include an exquisitely groomed formal herb garden on their wish list. But if you have the impulse to make a formal herb garden, bear in mind that they're not for everyone. These carefully planned gardens with

Herbs for Shady Gardens

Although most herbs require a sunny site, there are some herbs that will grow in shade. Provide these shade-loving herbs with loose, rich soil and plenty of moisture. This list includes herbs grown for fragrance, culinary uses, and teas. Many are American natives that were used medicinally. Grow them from seed or buy plants from nurseries that propagate their own stock, rather than gathering them from the wild.

***Actaea racemosa* (black snakeroot):** Spikes of small white flowers; roots used medicinally

***Anthriscus cerefolium* (chervil):** White-flowered annual; culinary herb

***Asarum canadense* (Canadian wild ginger):** Attractive groundcover; used medicinally

***Caulophyllum thalictroides* (blue cohosh):** Blue berries (poisonous); roots used medicinally

***Coptis trifolia* (three-leaf goldthread):** Small shiny-leaved plant with threadlike yellow creeping roots used medicinally and for dye

***Galium odoratum* (sweet woodruff):** Low-growing plant with white flowers; excellent groundcover; dried foliage and flowers used for fragrance

***Gaultheria procumbens* (wintergreen):** Creeping evergreen with tasty leaves and berries; used medicinally and for teas

***Hamamelis virginiana* (American witch hazel):** Shrub with autumn flowers with petals like small yellow ribbons; used medicinally

***Hydrastis canadensis* (goldenseal):** Thick yellow root used medicinally and for dye

***Melissa officinalis* (lemon balm):** White-flowered mint-family member; used for fragrance and teas

***Mentha* spp. (mints):** Rampant-growing herbs with pungent foliage used medicinally and for fragrance and teas

***Myrrhis odorata* (sweet cicely):** Ferny, fragrant foliage; smells of licorice; culinary herb

***Polygonatum* spp. (Solomon's seals):** Dangling bell-like flowers; roots used medicinally

***Sanguinaria canadensis* (bloodroot):** White flowers in early spring; used medicinally

***Viola odorata* (sweet violet):** Violet, white, purple, rose, or blue flowers in spring; will spread; used for fragrance

---

their neatly trimmed, geometric arrangements require intensive management to keep them looking their best.

Knot gardens, in which miniature hedges in different colors and textures create the look of intertwining strands, are a classic feature of formal herb gardens. Dwarf boxwoods (*Buxus* spp.), lavender (*Lavandula* spp.), lavender cotton (*Santolina rosmarinifolia* and *S. chamaecyparissus*), and germander (*Teucrium chamaedrys*) are popular knot-garden plants. You can also mix textures and colors of mulches—brown cocoa shells, white marble chips, gray-blue crushed granite, and so on—to elaborate the knot garden. However, while knot gardens can be an intriguing challenge to plan and plant, even a modest version requires constant maintenance. Everything must be kept under control—constant trimming and shaping are essential, and all the plants must be in top-notch health if the knot pattern is to remain attractive.

If you're ambitious enough to try a knot garden, keep it small, so that replacements and maintenance aren't overwhelming. You'll need to replace individual specimens in the clipped hedges that don't make it through winter. Replacements can be hard to find in the same size as the plants that remain intact. If you have space, keep a few extra plants growing in a nursery bed or other out-of-the-way spot for just such emergencies.

Another type of formal herb garden consists of a pattern of squares or diamonds with contrasting borders. You can grow a different herb in each square, or grow alternating squares of the same herb—the key is to grow just one herb in each square—to make a pattern. The squares are tied together with either edgings of knot-garden plants forming a low, meticulously groomed hedge around each square, or by narrow pavings of bricks between the squares with wider brick paths typically dividing the garden into quadrants. Like a knot garden, a garden of this type requires a great deal of grooming and attention to detail.

Informal Herb Gardens

Perhaps one of the easiest and most rewarding ways to use herbs in the landscape is in an informal herb garden. An informal garden can be a free-form island bed, with the tallest herb plants in the center and the shortest around the edges. Or it could be more like a perennial border, set against a background such as a wall, hedge, fence, or building and defined with either straight or curved lines.

So many flowering plants have been used as herbs that even the most rigid purist—one who plants a garden of only traditional herbs—could enjoy plenty of color and texture. Such a garden also would have an abundance of fragrances, plus an added bonus of plenty of herbs to use in wreaths, potpourris, or other projects.

An informal garden of ornamental herbs could feature billows of poppies, yarrows, and lavenders (one herb nursery offers 46 species and cultivars!). Masses of painted daisies (*Tanacetum coccineum*), catmints (*Nepeta* spp.), artemisias, and flax (*Linum* spp.) might be backed by white spikes of Culver's root (*Veronicastrum virginicum*), tall foxgloves (*Digitalis* spp.), or Canadian burnet (*Sanguisorba canadensis*). For further textural interest, try the elegant leaves and umbels of angelica (*Angelica archangelica*), the shaggy blossoms of bee balm (*Monarda didyma*), and the fragrant, frothy plumes of white mugwort (*Artemisia lactiflora*), one of the few artemisias with green leaves.

Gray-leaved plants provide good contrast but use caution when choosing artemisia cultivars unless you will confine them with a physical barrier. Many, such as 'Silver King', are determined spreaders and quite aggressive. By comparison, 'Powis Castle' is a large, attractive silver-leaved artemisia that grows well without becoming rampant. 'Powis Castle' is not reliably hardy north of Zone 6, but cuttings root easily during summer and can be kept in pots indoors during winter.

Yarrows (*Achillea* spp.) have been used medicinally for ages and fit well in any herb garden. Cultivars now offer wonderful colors—shades of rose, buff, apricot, and crimson, as well as their usual yellows, white, and pink. Still pretty in the garden are the well-known selections 'Coronation Gold', in deep yellow, and the pale lemon 'Moonshine'. The flowers of 'Coronation Gold' dry particularly well for winter bouquets.

Include hyssop (*Hyssopus officinalis*) and anise hyssop (*Agastache foeniculum*) in an informal garden, too. Although members of the mint family, they spread by means of seeds instead of stolons. The ordinary hyssop is a bushy, 2-foot plant whose flowers come in blue, pink, or white. Anise hyssop is taller and produces dense spikes of bluish lavender flowers in August when perennial flowers are scarce.

Culinary sage and other salvias, rue, and orris (*Iris germanica*) are other good choices for an informal garden.

Use low-growing or mat-forming herbs to front the tall and midsized plants. Try clove pinks (*Dianthus caryophyllus*), chives, santolinas (both green and gray), and thymes.

Growing Herbs

Herbs are generally undemanding plants. Given adequate light and good soil, they will produce well and suffer from few problems. Some herbs are perennials; others are annuals. Keep in mind that tender perennial herbs will behave like annuals in the northern states unless you grow them in containers and bring them indoors for winter.

Annual Herbs

Common annual herbs are basil, chervil, cilantro (coriander), dill, summer savory, and parsley, which is actually a biennial that is grown as an annual. More-exotic annuals include Jerusalem oak goosefoot (*Dysphania botrys*, also called feather-geranium), safflower (*Carthamus tinctorius*), sweet Annie (*Artemisia annua*), and sweet-scented marigold (*Tagetes lucida*), a tender perennial that can substitute for French tarragon. Sweet marjoram (*Origanum majorana*) is not hardy north of Zone 6, but it lives through winter in the South.

Plant seeds for chervil, cilantro (coriander), and dill outdoors where they are to grow, in spring or fall. These herbs are extremely difficult to transplant successfully. If you want a head start on outdoor planting, sow them in peat pots for minimum root disturbance at planting time. Sow sweet Annie and Jerusalem oak goosefoot outdoors in autumn.

Herb seedlings are often tiny and slower-growing than weeds, so it makes sense to start them indoors if you can. Start basil, marigolds, marjoram, and summer savory indoors in flats or pots, and move them to the garden when no more cold weather is expected. Parsley takes so long to come up that you might be better off starting it

Herb wheel garden. Planting herbs in a wagon wheel frame creates a garden that's as attractive as it is productive. Plant each wedge-shaped section with a single type of herb, repeating sections for herbs you like best. If you like, choose a theme such as pizza, salsa, or salad herbs, or herbs for dips.

indoors, too. Outdoors, you will be down on your knees every day trying to sort out the baby parsley plants from the weeds, which germinate quickly and will always have a head start.

Some annual herbs, such as dill, self-sow so generously there is little need to plant them year after year if the plot where they are growing is kept weeded. If you allow a parsley plant to remain in the garden the second year and set seed, it, too, will self-sow. This makes for convenience and good strong plants as well, because self-sown plants are almost always sturdier than those started indoors under lights. For more information on starting herb seeds, see the Seed Starting and Seed Saving entry.

Perennial Herbs

Perennial herbs can be grown from seed, but they take longer to germinate than the annuals. It's better to start out by buying young plants of perennial herbs such as mints, sages, and thymes. If you're growing named cultivars that may not come true from seed, it makes even more sense to buy plants. Once you've gotten started, increase your supply by dividing plants such as mint or by taking cuttings, which works well for rosemary and myrtle. For more on propagating herbs, see the Division and Cuttings entries.

Many perennial herbs need no help once they're established in your garden. Sweet woodruff (*Galium odoratum*) will supply you with bushels of foliage for potpourri while it covers the ground. Chamomile, chives, feverfew, garlic chives, lemon balm, and winter savory will self-sow seemingly eternally.

Horehound, oregano, and thyme usually sow some seedlings, but fennel and lovage seem to stay in one place without multiplying. Some of the catmints (*Nepeta* spp.) self-sow; others don't.

You may prefer to propagate certain perennial herbs by means of cuttings because they are espe-cially beautiful, fragrant, or flavorful forms or cultivars. (Plants propagated from seed don't always resemble their parents, whereas those from cuttings do.) If you have a fine lavender such as 'Hidcote' and you would like to have more without paying for more plants from the nursery, take 3- to 4-inch cuttings of the semihard tips and gently remove the lower leaves, Press the cuttings into a mixture of damp peat and sand in a light but not sunny spot, cover with a cloche or jar, and start yourself some new plants. You can also do this with thymes, taking cuttings from a silvery or variegated plant or any one that you especially like. Lemon verbena is sterile and must be propagated this way. Luckily, it roots readily.

French tarragon (*Artemisia dracunculus* var. *sativa*) must also be purchased as a plant, since it never sets viable seed. The so-called Russian tarragon offered as seed has no culinary value. When French tarragon is grown in sun or part sun and in light, well-watered but well-drained soil, it usually thrives and spreads enough to divide one plant into many each spring. It is hardy at least through Zone 5. However, if you do not succeed with it, due to severe cold or to high summer temperatures in your area, try the annual marigold from Mexico and South America called sweet-scented marigold (*Tagetes lucida*). It makes an excellent substitute.

General Care

Like nearly all plants, herbs require well-drained soil. While most do best in full sun, they will accept as little as 6 hours of sunlight a day. Incorporate compost or other organic matter into the soil, and cultivate carefully to keep out weeds. Mulch everything except the Mediterranean plants (marjoram, oregano, rosemary, sage, winter savory, and thyme) with a fine, thick material such as straw that neither acidifies the soil nor keeps out the rain.

Avoid pine bark (chipped or shredded) and peat. Mediterranean plants prefer being weeded to being mulched, since they are used to growing on rocky hills with no accumulation of vegetable matter around their woody stems. In the colder areas of the country, protect your plantings of catmint, horehound, lavender, rue, thyme, winter savory, and sage with evergreen boughs in winter.

Gardeners who grow their plants out in the sun and wind will have little trouble with disease or insect damage. Basil is sometimes subject to attack by chewing insects, but if you follow good cultural practices and grow enough plants, the damage can be ignored. You'll rarely have the need to take measures to control insect pests on herbs, but if you do, opt for handpicking pests or knocking them from plants with a strong spray of water. It's best to avoid applying even organic insecticides to culinary herbs, since any residues may affect flavor and fragrance.

Overwintering Tender Perennials

To overwinter frost-tender herbs such as rosemary (*Rosmarinus officinalis*), sweet bay (*Laurus nobilis*), myrtle (*Myrtus communis*), pineapple sage (*Salvia elegans*), scented geraniums (*Pelargonium* spp.), and lemon verbena (*Aloysia triphylla*), you can either grow them permanently in pots or take cuttings of plants at the end of the season, root them, then pot them and hold them over winter indoors until the following spring. This latter method works well for nonwoody herbs like basils and pineapple sage.

Shrubby or woody plants, like sweet bay or rosemary, are best grown in pots so they can be moved indoors when winter cold threatens. In summer, set them in a spot outdoors where they get morning but not afternoon sun. Some gardeners take their tender herbs out of their winter pots and put them into the ground for summer. However, this is an extremely stressful procedure for the plants, because the roots they send out in garden soil have to be chopped back in fall and forced into pots for winter.

During winter months indoors, keep herbs in a cool, sunny window, and make sure they never dry out. Rosemary especially must be watered frequently, although never left to sit in water. Verbenas will shed most or all of their leaves during winter. Water them very sparingly until early spring, when tiny leaf buds begin to appear along their branches.

These plants don't really object to being grown in pots, but they don't tolerate being indoors very well. You may have to help them fight off bugs and diseases during winter months. Potted herbs in the house may become afflicted with scale, aphids, or other pests. (Scented geraniums are the exception; these plants tend to shrug off pests.) Keep a close watch for signs of infestation. See the Houseplants entry for information on controlling these pests. In spring, move the plants outside. Within a few days, their relief will be visible, and they'll start growing happily again.

Before bringing herbs in for winter, turn them out of their pots and put them into larger ones, adding new soil mixed with compost. When, after some years, the pots have reached the limit of what you want to lift, turn out the plants and root-prune them. If the roots form a solid, pot-shaped lump (as they certainly will in the case of rosemary), take a cleaver or large kitchen knife and slice off an inch or two all the way around. Fill in the extra space with fresh soil and compost. Cut back one-quarter to one-third of the topgrowth to balance what you have removed from the bottom.

Harvesting and Storing

Cut and use your herbs all summer while they are at their very best. The flavor of the herb leaves is at its peak just as the plants begin to form flower buds. Cut herbs in midmorning, after the sun has dried the leaves but before it gets too hot. You can cut back as much as three-quarters of a plant without hurting it. (When harvesting parsley, remove the outside leaves so that the central shoot remains.) Remove any damaged or yellow foliage. If the plants are dirty, rinse them quickly in cold water and drain them well.

You will want to preserve some herbs for use during winter months. Drying is an easy way to preserve herbs, although you can also freeze them in plastic bags or preserve them in olive oil.

Air-drying: Dry herbs as quickly as possible in a dark, well-ventilated place. Attics and barns are ideal, but any breezy room that can be kept dark will do. Hang the branches by the stems, or strip off the leaves to dry them on racks through which the air can circulate. Drying on racks is the best way to handle large-leaved herbs such as sweet basil or comfrey. It's also good for drying rose petals or other fragrant flowers for potpourris.

To keep air-dried herbs dust-free and out of the light while drying, you can cover them with brown paper bags. Tie the cut herbs in loose bunches, small enough so that they don't touch the sides of the bag, then tie the bag closed around the ends of the stems. Label each bag.

After a few weeks, test for dryness. When the leaves are completely dry and crisp, rub them off the stems and store them in jars out of the light.

Dehydrating: If you have an electric dehydrator, it's an easy, ideal tool for drying your herbs. Strip off the leaves and place them on the dehydrator trays so they're not touching, and follow your dehydrator's instructions for the appropriate time and setting.

Oven drying: You can also dry herbs on racks made of metal screening in a gas oven that has a pilot light. Turn them twice a day for several days. Or dry in an oven at very low heat—150°F or lower. When herbs are crisp, remove the leaves from the stems and crumble them into jars.

Microwave drying: Microwave-dried herbs retain excellent color and potency. Start by laying the herb foliage in a single layer on a paper towel, either on the oven rack or on the glass insert. Cover the leaves with another paper towel and microwave on high for 1 minute. Then check the herbs, and if they are still soft, keep testing at 20- to 30-second intervals. Microwave ovens differ in power output, so you'll have to experiment. Keep track of your results with each kind of herb.

Microwave drying is a bit easier on plant tissue than oven drying, because the water in the herb leaves absorbs more of the energy than the plant tissue does. The water in the leaves gets hot and evaporates—that's why the paper towels become damp during the drying process—leaving drying plant tissue behind. The plant tissue heats up a little because of the contact with the water, but the water absorbs most of the heat. In a conventional oven, all the plant material gets hot, not just the water.

Using Herbs

If you have only a tub or two in which to grow herbs, you might plant a few culinary herbs or lavender for fragrance. If you have a big garden, you can experiment with medicinal plants as well as with material to dry for teas, colorful, fragrant bouquets, wreaths, and potpourris.

Herbs for Cooking

If you're not accustomed to using herbs in cooking, start out by exercising restraint. If you

Culinary Herbs

There's a wide range of herbs for adding flavor to everything from salad dressing to dessert. This list includes popular herbs for livening up your meals.

Angelica (*Angelica archangelica*): In salads, soups, stews, desserts

Caraway (*Carum carvi*): With vegetables or in soups, stews, or bread

Chervil (*Anthriscus cerefolium*): In soups and stews, or with fish or vegetables

Chives (*Allium schoenoprasum*): In soups, salads, and sandwiches

Coriander (*Coriandrum sativum*): In salads, stew, or relish; popular in Thai and Mexican cooking

Dill (*Anethum graveolens*): With fish or vegetables; in salads or sauces; seed used for pickling

French tarragon (*Artemisia dracunculus* var. *sativa*): In salads or sauces; with meat, fish, or vegetables

Garlic (*Allium sativum*): In all kinds of dishes, except desserts

Garlic chives (*Allium tuberosum*): In soups, salads, and sandwiches

Lovage (*Levisticum officinale*): Used like celery, in soups, stews, salads, or sauces

Mints (*Mentha* spp.): In jellies, sauces, or teas; with meats, fish, or vegetables

Oregano (*Origanum vulgare* subsp. *hirtum*): In sauces, or with cheese, eggs, meats, or vegetables

Parsley (*Petroselinum crispum*): In all kinds of dishes, except desserts

Rosemary (*Rosmarinus officinalis*): With meat or vegetables; in soups or sauces

Sage (*Salvia officinalis*): With eggs, poultry, or vegetables

Savories (*Satureja* spp.): In soups or teas, or with vegetables, especially beans

Sweet basil (*Ocimum basilicum*): With meats or vegetables, in sauces, pesto, and salads

Sweet bay (*Laurus nobilis*): In soups, stews, or sauces

Sweet marjoram (*Origanum majorana*): Used like oregano

Thyme (*Thymus vulgaris*): With meat or vegetables

---

overdo it, you might find you have overwhelmed the original flavor of the meat or vegetable whose flavor you meant to enhance. Remember that ounce for ounce, dried herbs have more potent flavor than fresh ones. Study cookbooks' herb recommendations, and when you've learned the usual combinations (French tarragon with fish or chicken, or basil with tomatoes and eggplant, for instance), experiment on your own. You could invent some new and wonderful dishes. See the list above for ideas to get started.

Herbs for Teas

While you're gathering herbs for the kitchen, include some to use for tea. Herbal teas can be soothing, stimulating, or simply pleasant. Many of them are wonderful aids to digestion or for allaying cold symptoms. Some, such as lemon balm, pineapple sage, and lemon verbena, make refreshing iced teas or additions to iced drinks.

You can make herb tea with dried or fresh leaves, flowers, or other plant parts. To make herb tea, place leaves into an herb ball in an earthenware or china pot or mug. Start with 1 tablespoon of dried herbs or 2 tablespoons of fresh herbs per cup, and adjust the quantity to suit your own taste as you gain experience. Then add boiling water and steep for 5 to 10 minutes before removing the herb ball and serving the tea.

One word of caution: Not all herbs are suitable for making tea. If you're experimenting with making herbal teas, remember that some herbs can make you ill if ingested. Research before you brew. See the list at right of herbs you can safely brew and sip.

Herbs for Fragrance

Flowers release their perfume into the air so freely, you need only walk past them to enjoy the scent of roses, lilacs, honeysuckle, clove pinks, or any other highly fragrant flower. Occasionally, we can detect the scent of lavender or thyme when they are baking in the hot sun. But plants with aromatic leaves do not, as a rule, release the odor of their oils unless you rub a leaf or walk on the plant or brush against the branches while working around them.

The leaves of scented geraniums (*Pelargonium* spp.) (just one example of the many fragrant-foliaged herbs) are wonderful to rub between your fingers.

Tea Herbs

Of all the uses for herbs, the one many people enjoy most is making and drinking herb tea. Historically, herb teas were used as medicines, and many people still brew and drink them today for their medicinal effects. For others, herb tea is simply the beverage of choice. Brew a tasty pot from any of the following herbs. The herb's name is followed by the parts to be used for brewing.

Angelica (*Angelica archangelica*): Leaves

Bee balm (*Monarda didyma*): Leaves

Catnip (*Nepeta cataria*): Leaves and flowers

Chamomile (*Chamaemelum nobile*): Flowers

Costmary (*Tanacetum balsamita*): Leaves

Elderberry (*Sambucus* spp.): Flowers

Lemon balm (*Melissa officinalis*): Leaves

Lemon thyme (*Thymus citriodorus*): Leaves

Lemon verbena (*Aloysia triphylla*): Leaves

Mints (*Mentha* spp.): Leaves

Roses (*Rosa* spp.): Hips and petals

Rosemary (*Rosmarinus officinalis*): Leaves

Sage (*Salvia officinalis*): Leaves

Scented geraniums (*Pelargonium* spp.): Leaves

They come in a wide variety of scents, including lemon rose, lemon, mint, nutmeg, rose, and ginger. Their many different fragrances, and their leaf and flower variations, make them fascinating to collectors and gardeners alike.

Lavender, lemon balm, lemon verbena, scented geraniums, rosemary, and sweet woodruff are among the best-known herbs grown for fragrance.

All can be preserved by air-drying (see page 297 for directions). For more suggestions of herbs to grow for fragrant flowers, foliage, or fruit, see the list below.

Making sachets and potpourri are two good ways to preserve the scent of herbs to add fragrance to linens or to the rooms of your house. Sachets are made with combinations of dried herb leaves and,

Fragrant Herbs

Here are some of the fragrant herbs that can be used, fresh or dried, for herbal crafts such as wreaths, potpourri, sachets, or arrangements. Plant name is followed by common uses.

***Aloysia triphylla* (lemon verbena):** Highly prized for potpourri and tea

***Artemisia abrotanum* (southernwood):** Dried branches traditionally hung in closets to repel moths

***Artemisia annua* (sweet Annie):** Sweetly aromatic flowers and foliage make good filler for herbal wreaths

***Dysphania botrys* (Jerusalem oak goosefoot):** Fluffy gold branches good for herb wreaths

***Galium odoratum* (sweet woodruff):** Leaves especially fragrant when dried; used in potpourri, wreaths, and as a tea

***Lavandula angustifolia* (lavender):** Flowers and foliage used in many herbal crafts

***Melissa officinalis* (lemon balm):** Used in teas, food, potpourri, and commercially in soap and toilet water

***Mentha* spp. (mints):** Fragrant foliage used in teas, potpourris, wreaths, and other herbal crafts; orange mint probably best for fragrance

***Monarda didyma* (bee balm):** Blossoms and foliage used in wreaths, potpourris, and teas

***Pelargonium* spp. (scented geraniums):** Wide variety of its fragrant leaves used in sachets and potpourris; edible flowers

***Rosmarinus officinalis* (rosemary):** Fragrant, needlelike leaves used for tea, cooking, and winter sachets

***Salvia elegans* (pineapple sage):** Wonderfully fragrant leaves and scarlet flowers used in wreaths and other herbal crafts; edible flowers

***Santolina chamaecyparissus* (lavender cotton):** Used in herb wreaths; odor of gray foliage may be too medicinal for sachets or potpourri

***Thymus* spp. (thymes):** Leaves and tops used in sachets and wreaths

Herbs for Repelling Insect Pests

Planting herbs as companion plants in the vegetable and flower garden is a time-honored but not infallible way of helping to deter some pests. See if your most troublesome pests are on this list, and if so, give companion planting with the appropriate herbs a try.

Allium sativum (garlic): Useful against aphids, Japanese beetles

Artemisia spp. (artemisias): Repel flea beetles, cabbage worms, slugs

Coriandrum sativum (coriander): Discourages aphids

Lavandula spp. (lavenders): Repel moths; combine with southernwood, wormwood, and rosemary in a moth-deterring sachet

Mentha spp. (mints): Deter aphids, cabbage pests, flea beetles

Nepeta cataria (catnip): Useful against ants, flea beetles

Ocimum spp. (basils): Deter flies and other insects

Pimpinella anisum (anise): Repels aphids

Rosmarinus spp. (rosemaries): Repel moths; use in sachets

Satureja hortensis (summer savory): Protects beans against Mexican bean beetles

Tanacetum coccineum (painted daisy, pyrethrum): Dried flower heads can be used as insect repellent

Tanacetum parthenium (feverfew): Repels many insects

Tanacetum vulgare (common tansy): Discourages Japanese beetles, ants, flies; can be invasive, so best for a large container

---

frequently, lavender blossoms as well as rose petals, crumbled or ground. You can dry rose petals by spreading them on sheets or screens in a dark, airy place. Petals of apothecary's rose (*Rosa gallica* var. *officinalis*) are the most fragrant.

Potpourri is a mix of flower petals and leaves used whole for decorative effect; it can be made with fresh or dried leaves and petals. Some potpourris include dried orange or lemon peel and spices such as cloves and allspice. Experiment with different combinations and see which ones you prefer. The fragrance is usually set with a fixative, such as orris root. Or simply enjoy the fragrance of your potpourri while it lasts, stirring occasionally to release more scent. When a batch of potpourri

loses its color and freshness, compost it and replace with freshly made mix.

Companion Planting

Many herbs are used as companion plants for vegetables and ornamentals. The herbs may help confuse or ward off harmful insects, or they may even act as trap plants to attract harmful insects, which can then be picked off and destroyed. The numerous, small flowers of herbs such as dill, cilantro, and mints provide nectar to tiny beneficial wasps that help protect the garden from several troublesome pests. Companion herbs may be used to attract bees for pollination or because of a benign effect on neighboring plants. You may want to try planting your basil by your tomatoes; mint by the cabbages; and catnip, which discourages flea beetles, by the eggplant. Or try putting a few garlic plants near roses or anything else victimized by Japanese beetles.

Some plants may be detrimental to another's growth; keep dill away from the carrots, fennel away from beans, and garlic and onions away from all legumes. As you carry out experiments in your garden, keep records for your own benefit and perhaps for that of other gardeners. See the list on page 301 and the Companion Planting entry for more suggestions about helpful and harmful plant companions.

Herbs as Standards

A standard plant is one trained to a single stem, with leaves and branches only at the top. Standard roses, sometimes called tree roses, are used in formal gardens or designs. Herbs are sometimes trained as standards to serve as accents in herb gardens, particularly in formal ones. Standard herbs make charming table decorations, especially at holiday time.

A simple design of a rounded head atop a single stem is a classic. You can also create multilayered standards or train herbs into upright wreath shapes. Here's how to train a basic herb standard.

1. Insert a slim bamboo stake of the height you want your standard to attain, pushing the stake in until it touches the bottom of the pot.

2. Cut back all side branches below the desired height to 1½ inches. Allow leaves that grow from the main stem to remain.

3. Tie the stem to the stake with slender strips of raffia or twist-ties at 2-inch intervals.

4. As new shoots appear at the top, clip the tips to encourage branching and to make a bushy head.

5. When your plant reaches the desired height, pinch off the tip of the top shoot and remove all the lower leaves and branch stems to within 4 to 5 inches of the top. Shape the head with clippers to form a rounded globe.

Best Herbs for Standards

Choose herbs with a sturdy stem that can support the weight of the full, rounded head. Lemon verbena, myrtle, rosemary, scented geraniums, lavender, and sweet bay can be trained into attractive standards. The main stem will thicken with age, but standards should remain tied closely to their stakes to protect them from damage. Running children and animals or high winds can easily tip them over.

Scented geraniums with a compact growth habit and tightly packed leaves make excellent can-

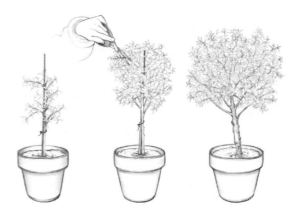

Training an herb standard. Choose a young, straight, single-stemmed plant for making an herb standard. Attach the plant to a stake and pinch new shoots at the tip as they appear. Over time, your herb plant will fill out to the form of a miniature tree.

didates. With the small-leaved types, aim for a tight globe of foliage and pinch off the flowers. The larger-leaved ones are suitable for a less-formal effect; allow them to decorate themselves with flowers if they wish. In fact, they look splendid when blooming.

If you want a scented geranium standard to be 3 feet tall, remove all side shoots from the bottom 2 feet of stem. When the central stem has reached 3 feet, pinch the tip. As the crown burgeons, keep it trimmed to encourage branching.

HEUCHERA

Heuchera, coralbells, alumroot. Spring-to summer-blooming perennials.

Description: *Heuchera micrantha* and its hybrids (chiefly with *H. americana* and *H. villosa*) are noted more for their foliage than their airy sprays of small, unobtrusive flowers. Plants form showy 1- to 2-foot clumps of maplelike leaves in shades of purple, garnet, chartreuse, silver, and peach, and there are many cultivars with foliage that is variegated with contrasting veins. Some choice selections include 'Garnet', with brilliant red-purple autumn color; 'Pewter Veil', with smoky gray and purple leaves; 'Amber Waves', with gold and pink leaves; 'Palace Purple', with purple-brown foliage; 'Peach Melba', with peach-colored leaves; 'Creme Brulee', with burnt orange foliage; and 'Key Lime Pie', with chartreuse foliage. Zones 4–8.

Heuchera sanguinea, coralbells, and hybrid coral bells, *H. ×brizoides*, bear clouds of delicate ½-inch hanging bells in shades of white, pink, red, and green. Flowers are borne on thin, 1½-foot stems above low mounds of rounded to maplelike 2-inch evergreen leaves. Zones 3–8.

How to grow: Plant in spring. Grow in partial shade in moist but very well-drained, humus-rich soil. Plants tolerate full sun in the North if kept moist. Good drainage and loose mulch help reduce freeze-and-thaw winter damage to the fragile roots. Support weak stems with thin, twiggy branches. Divide in spring when the centers die out.

Landscape uses: Mass in open woodlands, in borders, and among rocks. Contrast with hostas, ferns, columbines, iris, bleeding hearts, or wildflowers.

HIPPEASTRUM

Amaryllis. Winter- and spring-blooming bulbs for pots.

Description: *Hippeastrum* hybrids, commonly called amaryllis, bear flamboyant 4- to 12-inch-wide, trumpet-shaped blooms in white, pink, red, and salmon, usually in clusters of four on leafless stems normally rising 1 to 3 feet. Cultivars may have petals that are striped, streaked, or outlined with a second color, and many newer cultivars bear double flowers. Arching fans of broad, straplike leaves appear during or after flowering. Hardy in Zones 8–10, amaryllis plants are usually grown indoors as showstopping container plants.

How to grow: Choose a pot that will allow about 1 inch of growing space between the bulb and the rim. For a suitable soil mix, see the Houseplants entry. Plant with one-third to one-half of the bulb above the soil line. Water slightly until growth starts, then water often. Grow in a warm (65° to 70°F) spot in a sunny window, especially after the leaves develop. Most bloom 4 to 8 weeks after growth begins. Once the flowers open, moving the plant to a cool spot out of direct sun will lengthen the life of the flowers.

When the flowers fade, cut off the flowerstalk close to the bulb. Return the plant to a sunny window and water regularly. You may keep the plant inside all year, feeding every 2 to 3 weeks with liquid seaweed, fish emulsion, or other organic fertilizer. You can put your amaryllis outside after danger of frost is past in a spot with morning sun or under the shade of tall trees, or knock them out of their pots and grow them in the open ground. Gradually reduce water in late summer to encourage dormancy. After a few months' rest, replace the top few inches of soil or repot and begin again.

HOLLY

See *Ilex*

HOLLYHOCK

See *Alcea*

HONEYSUCKLE

See *Lonicera*

HORSERADISH

Armoracia rusticana
Brassicaceae

This pungent root crop makes a wonderful sauce for meat and fish and a great addition to mustards and other condiments, but beware—it's a vigorous perennial that can quickly spread beyond the boundaries of its planting area.

Planting: Horseradish seldom produces seeds, so you'll need to start plants from root cuttings in moist, rich soil. Horseradish roots can grow several feet deep; good soil preparation will encourage thick, straight roots. Plant in early spring by digging a trench and laying the root cuttings in it. Position the large end of each cutting slightly higher than the small end. Cover the roots with 6 to 8 inches of soil; space 1 foot apart in rows 3 to 4 feet apart.

To prevent your horseradish patch from becoming a weedy nuisance, either plant it in an out-of-the-way area, or dig it up completely each year and replant only a few of the roots. Another method is to plant it in a bottomless bucket that you've sunk into the soil.

Growing guidelines: Horseradish plants are usually problem-free. Water when needed, particularly in late summer and fall, when the plants do most of their growing.

Harvesting: Pick a few spring leaves as needed for salads; use a spading fork to dig roots in October or November, after active growth has stopped. The hardy roots will keep in the ground for several months; unharvested pieces will sprout the following spring.

HORTICULTURAL THERAPY

Horticultural therapy involves the cultivation and appreciation of plants and nature to relieve an illness or disability. In a sense, all gardeners practice it when they enjoy working in the garden. People with mild to severe physical, developmental, emotional, and mental disabilities also benefit from the therapeutic effects of plants.

Horticultural therapy is practiced in such diverse settings as rehabilitation and mental health centers, nursing homes, schools, and hospitals.

Many older and disabled people practice horticultural therapy in their homes. Sometimes teachers use horticultural therapy in the classroom.

Horticultural therapists make gardening accessible by creating gardens with wide, wheelchair-friendly paths, raised beds and containers for easier access, and specially adapted tools. They may choose plants based on color, fragrance, and/or texture to enhance the sensory experience of gardening.

Many universities now offer classes and degrees in horticultural therapy. The American Horticultural Therapy Association lists accredited programs on their Web site, so you can find a college or university near you offering a degree or certificate in horticultural therapy. For more information, contact the association or visit their Web site (see Resources on page 673).

HOSTA

Hosta, plantain lily, funkia. Summer- and fall-blooming perennials grown primarily for their foliage.

Description: Hostas display 6- to 48-inch-wide mounds of lancelike to broad, long-stemmed leaves in green, white, yellow, and bluish solid colors and variegations. Distinctive venation patterns on many varieties' leaves create a quilted appearance. Trumpet-shaped white to pale lavender flowers, sometimes fragrant but often not very showy, are borne on stalks above the leaves. Many of the famous hosta cultivars, such as the huge blue-leaved 'Krossa Regal' and massive chartreuse-leaved 'Sum and Substance', are hybrids.

Hosta fortunei, Fortune's hosta, grows into a clump, 1 to 2 feet tall and wide, of 5- to 6-inch oval leaves. Zones 3–8.

H. plantaginea, August lily, holds 6-inch, sweetly fragrant white trumpets 2 feet above bold, 8-inch, light green leaves in 2- to 3-foot-wide clumps in late summer. Zones 3–8.

H. sieboldiana, Siebold's hosta, bears quilted bluish 1-foot leaves in 2- to 3-foot mounds up to 4 feet wide. 'Frances Williams', with huge gray-green leaves with wide yellow margins, is one of the most famous of all hostas. Zones 3–8.

Grow *H. ventricosa*, blue hosta, for its 3-inch hanging blue-violet bells on 3-foot stalks above rich green, 8-inch leaves in 2-foot-wide mounds. Zones 3–9.

H. venusta, miniature hosta, and its hybrids and cultivars produce petite 3- to 6-inch-tall mounds of wavy green to blue-green leaves that are perfect for tucking into a rock garden or at the edge of a shady border. With time, plants spread to no more than 1 food in diameter. 'Blue Mouse Ears' was named 2008 Hosta of the Year by the American Hosta Growers. Zones 3–8.

How to grow: Plant or divide hostas in spring or fall. They prefer partial to deep shade and moist, well-drained soil with some organic matter. Some can take full sun in the North if they are kept moist. Yellow- and blue-leaved cultivars color better if given morning sun. Some older cultivars of Fortune's hosta and blue hosta withstand very dry soil and deep shade. Slugs and snails can chew holes in emerging leaves in spring; otherwise, hostas are quite durable and easy to grow.

Landscape uses: Grow in groups or, in the case of showy cultivars, as specimens. Hostas cover dying bulb foliage, so they're excellent companions for spring-blooming bulbs. They lighten up dark, shady areas under trees or in corners. These shade-garden staples look gorgeous with ferns, wild gingers (*Asarum* spp.), hellebores, heucheras, and other shade plants.

HOUSEPLANTS

Houseplants add beauty to our homes, filter pollutants from the air, and have been shown to promote feelings of calmness. The term *houseplants* encompasses hundreds of species and thousands of cultivars, from exotic orchids and cacti to the familiar and beloved African violet. Succeeding with—and enjoying—houseplants comes down to choosing plants that are suited to the conditions in your home and understanding and providing for their basic needs.

Starting Off Right

When you buy a new plant, it should include a label with information about its light, moisture, soil, and temperature requirements. Check this before you buy the plant—some need high humidity, strong light, or other conditions that may be difficult to provide in a normal household environment. Buy plants from a reputable plant store, houseplant catalog, or Web site.

If you're unsure what a plant is or whether it would thrive in your conditions, ask a store clerk, check out a houseplant book from the library, or do a little online research before you buy. To learn about plants you're considering for your home, look on a houseplant database such as Tropicopia (see Resources on page 673).

Choose plants that look well taken care of and vigorous. Inspect plants closely for signs of insects or disease, making sure to check the undersides of leaves and stems. If you see any insects or signs of insect feeding such as holes, punctures, or deposits of leaking sap, don't buy. Portions of the plant that are wilted or discolored, or leaves that are speckled or have dead areas, also may indicate disease or insect damage. If you see anything suspicious, don't buy the plant. If you do not know what the plant should look like, ask a knowledgeable salesperson.

Light Is the Key

When selecting a plant, be sure its light requirements match your proposed location. A plant that needs direct sun, like a cactus and many herbs and orchids, will slowly die in a dim corner.

Analyzing light levels: The number and position of the windows in a room and the location of a plant determine the amount of light it gets. Light intensity drops off rapidly as you move away from a window. Plants that aren't receiving enough light often become elongated and pale. Or they may just fail to grow at all and drop their lower leaves. (A plant moved from a greenhouse into your home may also drop some leaves at first as it adjusts to the lower light levels.) Too much light, on the other hand, may burn the leaves of low-light plants like African violets and phalaenopsis (moth) orchids.

Most houses have many good locations for plants that need low light, and fewer suitable locations for plants that need moderate to bright light. Place light-loving plants as close to windows as possible; south-facing windows will provide the most light. Remove sheer curtains and keep windows clean to maximize light. Wash plants regularly to remove dust.

Rotate plants that need moderate light between a low- and a high-light location every few days. You should also rotate plants as they come into bloom, moving them to a table or other area where you can enjoy the flowers, then back to a higher-light area when bloom has passed.

Maximizing window space: To give your plants more light, add shelves or plant hangers to windows or provide plant stands to increase the amount of space you have available. If your windowsills are narrow, you can install shelf brackets under the sills and add boards to widen the windowsills. You can also install several shelves across a window and create a curtain of plants. Heavy Plexiglas is good for upper shelves. Use wood screws to mount brackets to wooden window frames. To mount brackets on the wall next to the window, use appropriate wall anchors.

Adding artificial light: Plant stands with attached light fixtures are another option. There are tabletop setups with a single light or two- and three-tiered stands with multiple lights. A three-tiered plant stand is the perfect setup for a large collection of houseplants, giving them the light they need without blocking your windows or taking up table or counter space. You can adjust the height of the lights to suit plants' needs, and use regular fluorescent lights (pairing warm and cool bulbs is best) or special full-spectrum or grow lights. Growing plants together like this also raises the humidity around the plants, especially if you put them on trays filled with pebbles and water. And it makes watering easy since the plants are all in one place.

Summering outdoors: An excellent way to increase the amount of light your plants receive is to use them to decorate your patio or garden in summer. Direct sunlight can easily burn leaves of houseplants accustomed to low light levels. Always place them in the shade at first and gradually move only those that like direct light out into sunnier locations. You may need to water smaller plants daily during hot spells, especially those in clay pots.

Watering

Various factors—including size of containers, season, rate of growth, light, and temperature—will affect how much water each plant requires. Some plants need water only when the soil surface has dried out, while others need to be kept constantly moist. You shouldn't follow a strict schedule year-round, because you may overwater or underwater. Learn each plant's preference, and check each pot before you water.

There are various ways of determining how much moisture is in the soil. Don't wait until the plant wilts to water it. Looking at the surface color of the soil helps, but doesn't tell the whole story. Learn to judge how moist the soil is by hefting the pot. Or push your finger into the soil an inch or so and feel for moistness. Avoid overwatering, which can suffocate the plant's roots; if in doubt, wait.

Always water thoroughly, until water seeps out the bottom of the pot. Use pots with drainage holes and saucers, but never allow plants to sit in water. If the soil becomes very dry, it may shrink away from the pot sides, allowing water to run through rapidly without being absorbed. If this happens, add water slowly until the soil is saturated, or set the pot in a tub of water for a few minutes. Water will also run out rapidly if the plant is rootbound, in which case it needs repotting in fresh potting medium and a larger container.

Feeding

Plants growing in a rich organic potting mix containing organic matter and bonemeal need little additional fertilizer if repotted regularly. During active growth in spring and summer, most plants

Five Causes of Houseplant Failure

Killing a houseplant that was billed as "foolproof" can leave you despairing that your home decor will ever include anything leafy and green that's not made of synthetic fibers. But having a black thumb is not a permanent condition, and keeping houseplants happy and healthy is mostly a matter of avoiding these all-too-common pitfalls.

Wrong plant for your place: Not every species will work in every home. A plant's light, temperature, and moisture needs should be within the range of what you can reasonably provide. Knowledgeable employees at garden centers can help guide you to the right plant for your conditions. If you're buying a plant as a gift or are looking for something that's especially hardy, consider philodendrons. Newer varieties have red, yellow, or orange foliage.

The light's not right: Aloe, cacti, Boston ferns (*Nephrolepis exaltata*), and crown of thorns (*Euphorbia milii*) require a lot of light, so a cubicle or the corner of your living room isn't the right place for them. On the flip side, split-leaf philodendron, aka Swiss cheese plant (*Monstera deliciosa*), begonias, and epiphyllums (such as Christmas cactus) thrive in low-light or filtered-sun environments. Simply moving the plant to another spot in the house could work wonders.

Over- or underwatering: Since succulents and cactus plants prefer dry soil, watering daily will harm them. Once a week is plenty. Another option for the forgetful: the ZZ plant (*Zamioculcas zamiifolia*), which requires water only once every 2 weeks or so. Plants that are blooming require watering more often than when they're in a dormant period. If you know your plants' needs, you can develop a schedule for watering; otherwise check to see if the soil is dry before you water—overwatering kills just as surely as underwatering. When you water plants, avoid wetting the leaves; this promotes fungal growth. If you're truly hopeless about watering, look for helpful reminder apps, soil monitors, or even terra-cotta worms

appreciate regular doses of a liquid organic fertilizer such as fish emulsion (if you can stand the smell—this is a better choice for houseplants summering outdoors) or liquid seaweed. Mix at half the strength recommended on the label, and apply at the recommended frequency or more often as needed. You can also find a selection of organic fertilizers designed for houseplants, including composted manure pellets and guano; use them according to package directions. Fertilize less during winter, when lower temperatures and light levels slow most plants' growth.

Temperature and Humidity

Many popular houseplants are well suited to the warm, dry conditions found in most homes. Others, including many ferns, will only do well if you that make it easier to see when plants are getting thirsty.

Summer exposure: Moving houseplants outdoors for the summer seems logical, but it can cause harm even to plants with high light requirements. After months indoors, exposure to direct sun can burn tender leaf tissues. And overwatering by rainfall can promote rot in the pot. If you want to move your plants to the open air, make the transition gradually, start them in a sheltered spot, and keep tabs on moisture levels. Be on the lookout for pests that may flock to houseplants visiting the outdoors, too. Spider mites, mealybugs, and scale insects prey on houseplants and tend to cluster on undersides of leaves and stems. Check these areas carefully and wipe clustered pests away with a mild soap solution (rinse with clear water afterward) or wash mites away with a spray of water. For persistent or extensive infestations, spray with insecticidal soap or neem oil, according to label directions.

Problems in the pot: Plastic pots tend to retain moisture, so they're best for plants that like a lot of water. Porous clay pots, on the other hand, are the perfect choice for plants that prefer drier conditions, like cacti, orchids, and succulents. Also, consider the size of the pot. Don't choose a pot thinking that the plant will grow into it—extra room in the pot can lead to moisture problems. When you're transplanting, select a pot that's 2 to 4 inches larger in diameter than the current one. Pay attention to what you fill the pot with, too. Dirt from your yard and packaged topsoil will become compacted in a container. Instead, use an indoor potting mix that is loose enough to allow the roots to grow easily, but not so loose that the water just runs right through to the bottom. You can purchase mixes specifically for the type of plant you're growing (ask someone at the garden center if you're not sure what mix to choose), and there are many organic choices available, too. Refresh the potting mix every year or two.

provide extra humidity. Place a large saucer or tray filled with water and pebbles under the pot, but be sure the pot doesn't sit in water. Mist plants often, run an electric humidifier, or group several plants together to increase humidity.

It's important to know what temperature your plants prefer. Some plants require cool winter temperatures either to bloom or to overwinter successfully. South African plants like clivias need a cool, dry rest period to bloom. Overwintering herb plants such as rosemary and sweet bay do best with cool winter temperatures.

Organic Potting Soil

Good soil structure and fertility are maintained outside by the addition of organic matter, and by freezing, thawing, and earthworm activity—conditions

Easy-Care Houseplants

From low-light to outright neglect, these tough-but-attractive houseplants will carry on without complaint. Those with asterisks (*) are first-rate for cleaning indoor air, too!

Aglaonema commutatum (Chinese evergreen)

Aloe vera (aloe; prefers moderate to bright light)

Aspidistra elatior (cast-iron plant)

Beaucarnea recurvata (ponytail palm; prefers bright light)

Chlorophytum comosum (spider plant)*

Cissus rhombifolia (grape ivy)

Crassula ovata or C. argentea (jade plant; prefers filtered sunlight)

Dracaena marginata (dragon tree)

Epipremnum aureum (golden pothos)*

Ferns (various species, including *Nephrolepis exaltata*, Boston fern)*

Hedera helix (English ivy)*

Philodendron spp. (philodendrons)*

Saintpaulia ionantha (African violet)

Sansevieria trifasciata (snake plant)

Spathiphyllum spp. (peace lilies)*

label if it doesn't say "organic," as it may contain synthetic chemical fertilizers and very little organic matter) or blend your own. If you have a lot of plants, you may want to make your own mix, both to save money and to provide a rich organic soil.

To prepare a good potting mix, combine one to two parts commercial organic potting soil or good garden soil; one part builder's sand or perlite; and one part coir fiber or peat moss, compost, or leaf mold. Add 1 tablespoon of bonemeal per quart of mix.

Each of these components provides specific benefits to the plants: Soil contains essential minerals. Sand and perlite assure good drainage, which prevents disease and allows air to reach the roots. Sand will make the mix much heavier. Perlite, an expanded volcanic rock with many tiny air spaces, will make it lighter. Compost or leaf mold (organic matter) makes the mix rich. Both release nutrients slowly, help maintain proper soil pH, improve soil drainage, and hold moisture. Peat moss is acidic and has few nutrients, but greatly increases the water-holding capacity of a mix. Coir fiber, made from coconut hulls, doesn't acidify the soil and isn't endangered, as some sources of peat moss may be, and it also retains moisture, so it's an excellent peat replacement in soil mixes.

For plants that need extra-rich soil, double the amount of compost or leaf mold. If the plant needs acid soil, double the amount of peat moss. For cacti and succulents that like drier conditions, add an extra half to one part coarse sand.

You may want to add other organic amendments such as bloodmeal, guano, pelletized manure, rock phosphate, or greensand. See the Fertilizers entry for the specific nutrient content of each. See the Container Gardening entry for more information about adding soil amendments to potting mixtures and for blending potting mixtures to use in large pots.

that don't occur in the containers of indoor plants. For that reason, a good organic potting mix is important for houseplants. As they grow, your plants should be repotted into fresh soil in larger containers. Use commercial organic potting soil (read the

Repotting

Repotting—moving a plant into a larger pot—keeps the root system in balance with the foliage and adds fresh soil and nutrients. Generally, the best time to do your repotting is in spring, when most plants resume active growth. It's a great outdoor activity for a sunny spring day. Remember not to put your newly repotted plants in full sun right away, though. If you're setting them outside for the growing season, keep them in partial shade for at least a week to give them time to settle in to their new pots before gradually moving them to a sunnier site. If you're returning them to the house, place them where they were previously growing.

Don't overpot. Move a plant to a pot only a few inches larger in diameter—enough to allow about 1 inch (or 2 inches for larger plants) of fresh soil around the rootball in the new container. If you repot in a container that's too big, the extra soil may hold too much moisture, or the plant may not flower.

To determine if it's time to repot, place one hand on the surface of the soil with the stem between your fingers, flip the pot upside down, and tap the bottom of the pot to loosen the rootball. If lots of roots are visible on the rootball and beginning to circle the pot, it's time to repot. For large plants that are harder to remove from their pots, check for roots coming up to the surface—this is also a sign that the plant is due to be repotted. For any size plant, water running rapidly through the rootball can indicate that roots have filled the pot, leaving very little room for water-retaining soil.

To repot, work any encircling roots loose. Place the plant's rootball in the new pot, and fill around it with fresh potting mix. Keep the plant at the same depth in the soil, placing it so that the soil surface is 1 inch below the pot's rim. Don't push the new soil down too firmly, just water thoroughly after repotting to firm it.

Containers

Whatever containers you choose, be sure they have holes in the bottom, and use saucers to catch the excess water. If you use unglazed clay saucers, be sure to use plastic liners to protect furniture and floors. Or set pots and saucers on trivets or trays for protection.

Clay: Clay pots are porous. Air can pass through them to plant roots, and excess moisture can evaporate more easily. They are a good choice for plants that like dry conditions, like cacti and succulents. They are also heavy, which can help prevent top-heavy plants from tipping over but makes larger plants difficult to move. Should a clay pot topple, it is likely to smash into numerous pieces, so if you choose clay, make sure it's stable once you've set it in place.

Plastic: Plastic is lightweight and a good choice for plants that might dry out too easily in clay pots. It also stays clean, while clay pots may become discolored with use. Air can't pass through plastic to roots, but this won't be a problem if you use a good commercial mix or add plenty of sand or perlite to ensure good soil aeration.

Decorative: Many beautiful ceramic and glazed clay containers are available at home and garden centers. Some have holes in the bottom and matching glazed saucers, while others, called cachepots, have solid bottoms. If you choose a cachepot, you'll need to set a second container in which you've planted your houseplant inside the cachepot. The actual plant pot should have drainage holes to allow water to drain out, but of course it can be very plain since it will be concealed inside the ornamental pot. Be sure to allow space below the inner pot for drainage within the cachepot, and don't let water stand in the bottom of the decorative pot.

Special containers: Some plants benefit from special containers, such as orchid pots or glass terrariums. Orchid pots or containers may be clay, wood, or plastic, but usually have many openings to allow air to reach the roots and water to run out quickly. Moisture-loving ferns and other terrarium plants thrive in enclosed terrarium conditions. If you decide to set up a terrarium, make sure you choose plants that will remain in scale with your container. Bulb pots are also different from ordinary pots, usually being taller and thinner. And, of course, bonsai require special shallow trays to keep their roots confined. But for most houseplants, you can select the type and style of container that suits the size and kind of plant you're growing without worrying too much about your choice.

Pests and Diseases

If you grow your plants in a good organic potting mix, give them the correct amount of water and light, and repot regularly, you shouldn't have many insect or disease problems. Inspect any new plants to avoid bringing problems in.

It's a good idea to inspect your plants regularly to catch developing problems early. Isolate suspect plants. Yellowing or discolored leaves may mean disease or incorrect light or watering practices. Overwatering probably kills more houseplants than anything else does. Double-check the plant's requirements, remove damaged areas, and watch for developments.

Yellowing leaves or a general chlorotic (yellowed or pale) color may also indicate that your plant has been in its pot too long and needs to be repotted in fresh organic soil or fed with a good organic fertilizer. But don't overfeed, since that can also lead to poor plant health. Keeping a good balance, both in terms of water and fertilizer, is the key to healthy plants.

Damaged or deformed plants or sticky deposits may indicate insect problems. These pests are common on indoor plants:

Mealybugs: These insects look like tiny tufts of white cotton. They are often found under leaves and in sheltered areas of stems. Both the immature stage and the adults can crawl but often cluster together in one place. Remove each insect with rubbing alcohol on a cotton swab, or spray with insecticidal soap.

Whiteflies: These ubiquitous pests are about $\frac{1}{16}$ inch long. They fly around in a cloud whenever an infested plant is disturbed. Wipe crawling young off of the undersides of leaves, vacuum up the flying white adults, spray with insecticidal soap, or place a yellow sticky trap on a stake in each pot to catch them.

Mites: Mites are tiny pests about the size of a grain of salt. You are likely to notice plant symptoms before you actually see the pests themselves. Leaves attacked by mites are stippled or mottled; flowers may be deformed. Wash plants with a hose or shower to remove pests, mist daily, and spray with insecticidal soap. Spider mites get their name because of the webs they build under plant leaves and on connecting branches where they meet the stem. If you see yellow stippling on leaves, check under them for signs of webbing. Control as you would any mite, but be sure to spray the undersides of the leaves.

Aphids: Aphids are small, translucent, pear-shaped insects. They may be many colors, including white, green, and black. Sticky deposits of plant sap in growing tips may indicate aphid activity. Remove these soft-bodied sucking insects by hand or wash them off with sprayed water. If you see ants on your plants, it may also be a sign of aphid infestation, as ants are aphid "shepherds" who herd the aphids in return for the tasty honeydew they excrete.

Scale: Plants such as citrus and bay trees may also be prone to scale, which you typically see as hard or soft brown or black bumps on stems. Like aphids, they suck plant sap and excrete sticky honeydew, which can then turn black with mold and prevent leaves from photosynthesizing effectively. You can scrape off minor infestations with a fingernail. For more serious problems, apply horticultural oil spray.

Whatever treatment you use for any of these pests, repeat it several times to control later hatchings. Follow label instructions for any pesticides you apply.

HYACINTHUS

Hyacinth. Spring-blooming bulbs

Description: *Hyacinthus orientalis*, garden hyacinth, bears many 1-inch starry flowers in white, pink, red, yellow, blue, and violet. The sweetly fragrant flowers are borne in loose to dense upright clusters about 1 foot above straplike leaves. Nearly all hyacinths offered for sale are hybrid cultivars. Zones 3–8; give winter protection in Zones 3–5.

How to grow: Plant bulbs with the tops about 5 inches belowground in a sunny spot with average, well-drained soil enriched with rotted manure or compost. Fertilize lightly when shoots emerge in spring. After flowering, allow the foliage to yellow before removing it. If rodents dig and eat the bulbs, plant bulbs in wire mesh cages.

Landscape uses: The biggest bulbs produce

the largest, densest spikes for formal beds and forcing in pots. Smaller bulbs produce more graceful stems that are lovely in borders, shrub plantings, and woods. As bulbs grow and reproduce over the years, hyacinths' flower spikes tend to become more open—the individual flowers become less tightly crowded on the upright flower heads. Some gardeners prefer the looser look that comes with age, while others feel it spoils the formal effect hyacinths give in a spring garden.

HYDRANGEA

Hydrangea. Deciduous summer-blooming shrubs or small trees.

Description: *Hydrangea arborescens*, smooth hydrangea or hill-of-snow, a native species, forms a 2- to 5-foot spreading mound. It has large (3- to 6-inch), deep green oval leaves. Dense, flat, or rounded flower clusters grow on the current season's wood. Zones 4–8.

H. macrophylla, bigleaf hydrangea or florist's hydrangea, reaches 3 to 6 feet tall. It bears pink flowers when grown in near-neutral soils and blue in acidic soils. There are two types of cultivars: Hortensia types form round flower clusters; lacecap types have flat clusters of small, fertile flowers surrounded by an outer circle of larger, showier, sterile flowers. Most cultivars bloom on the previous year's wood, but newer introductions bloom on both old and new wood for a summerlong display. Zones 6–8.

H. paniculata, panicle hydrangea, grows in tree or shrub form to a height of 4 to 15 feet. It blooms on the current season's wood, with pyramidal clusters of creamy white, mostly sterile flowers. Zones 4–9.

H. quercifolia, oakleaf hydrangea, reaches 6 feet

tall and has rich, cinnamon brown, layered bark when mature. This native species bears showy 10-inch flower panicles that change from white to pink to brown. Large, lobed leaves turn red to burgundy in fall. Zones 5–8.

How to grow: Hydrangeas prefer evenly moist, humus-rich soil with good drainage. They will grow in partial shade or in full sun, provided they receive adequate soil moisture. Prune big-leaf hydrangea after blooming and the others in winter. Unless you have a tree form, cut older branches to the ground.

Landscape uses: Smooth hydrangea and oak-leaf hydrangea are most at home in a woodland garden; they also look attractive in massed plantings and foundation plantings. Large plants make striking specimens. Bigleaf hydrangea and panicle hydrangea have strong form and color; use them sparingly as specimens.

HYLOTELEPHIUM

Stonecrop. Perennial flowers or groundcovers.

Description: Stonecrops in the genus *Hylotelephium* were formerly classified as *Sedum*, and these fleshy, succulent plants are similar to the closely related sedums. Stonecrops, so called for their native habitats among rocks, are drought-tolerant perennials that produce upright mounds of fleshy green to glaucous foliage. Some species have blue-green, reddish, purple, or variegated foliage; leaves of many species turn red in late fall. Showy pink, red, or purple flowers open from pinkish buds in summer into fall.

Hylotelephium telephium, stonecrop or live-forever, is a fleshy, upright, herbaceous perennial. It and the species *H. spectabile*, showy stonecrop, are the likely parents of popular hybrid stonecrops. Despite the change of genus name, hybrid stonecrops remain favorites in the perennial garden for their ease of care and long season of interest.

H. 'Autumn Joy' (formerly *Sedum* 'Autumn Joy' or 'Herbstfreude') grows upright, producing 2-foot bushy plants. Its 5- to 6-inch flower clusters bear starry blooms that open coral pink in summer, then deepen to copper in fall, while the leaves turn brilliant red.

H. 'Vera Jameson' grows 9 to 12 inches tall, with blue-green leaves and pink flower clusters borne in late summer.

H. erythrostictum 'Frosty Morn', 'Frosty Morn' garden stonecrop, bears foot-tall clumps of blue-green leaves with white edges and is covered with starry light pink or white flowers in late summer and early fall. Zones 3–9.

How to grow: Stonecrops are easy to grow in any well-drained, average to gravelly soil in full sun or light shade (in hot summer conditions). They are tolerant of poor soil and hot, dry weather, but may grow floppy in rich soil or shady locations. Cut back leggy plants in late spring to control height. Propagate them in spring or summer by division or cuttings. Detached leaves may be rooted to make new plants.

Landscape uses: Stonecrops are striking in beds and borders. 'Autumn Joy' is a useful all-season plant; its persistent rusty brown dried flower heads add interest to the winter garden. Feature it with ornamental grasses and other tough perennials like daylilies and *Rudbeckia fulgida* var. *sullivantii* 'Goldsturm'.

I

IBERIS

Candytuft. Spring- and summer-blooming annuals and perennials.

Description: *Iberis umbellata*, globe candytuft, is an annual that produces 1-inch clusters of tiny flowers in shades of white, pink, red-violet, and purple through much of summer on upright plants to 15 inches.

I. sempervirens, perennial candytuft, is actually a low-growing evergreen subshrub that bears abundant white flower clusters on 6- to 12-inch-tall, 12- to 24-inch spreading mounds of narrow, dark green, needlelike leaves. Most cultivars bloom only in spring, though 'Autumn Snow' reblooms in fall. Zones 3–9.

How to grow: Sow the annual type where it is to bloom in a sunny or lightly shaded spot with average, moist but well-drained soil; allow to reseed for bloom next year. Plant or divide perennial candytuft in spring or fall; give it similar conditions. Cut back partway after bloom for compact growth and possible rebloom in fall. Water during

drought. Mulch in summer, and lightly cover with pine needles or straw in winter to prevent sun and wind damage.

Landscape uses: Plant at the front of borders, among rocks, or in cottage gardens. They also look lovely along paths, stone stairs, and walls. Combine them with spring-blooming bulbs and perennials.

ILEX

Holly. Evergreen or deciduous shrubs or trees.

Description: *Ilex ×attenuata*, topal holly, is an evergreen with an upright, narrowly pyramidal form, growing 20 to 30 feet tall. The leaves are small, dark green, and glossy. The fruits, which are red and rounded, appear on the current year's growth. Zones 6–8.

I. cornuta, Chinese holly, is twiggy, dense, and rounded, with flowers blooming on the previous year's growth. Fruits are red and rounded; the evergreen leaves are glossy green and five-spined, with the terminal spine pointing downward. Zones 6–8.

I. crenata, Japanese holly, is a densely layered, compact evergreen with small, notched leaves and black fruit. There are many fine cultivars available; most are much smaller than the species, which grows to 15 feet tall in the landscape. Zones 6–8.

I. ×meserveae, blue holly, bears spiny blue-green leaves, purplish stems, and red berries. The source of many popular cultivars, this evergreen hybrid grows about 7 feet tall. Zones 5–7.

I. opaca, American holly, is pyramidal in youth, open and irregular with age. Growing to heights of 15 to 30 feet in the landscape, this native may reach 50 feet in the wild. The evergreen leaves are spiny, dull dark green above, and yellow green beneath. Dull red berries form on the current year's growth. Zones 5–9.

I. verticillata is the swamp-dwelling native winterberry. It has a twiggy, rounded habit and grows 6 to 10 feet tall. Its oval leaves drop off in autumn, exposing plentiful brilliant red berries that are very effective in massed plantings. Zones 4–9.

I. vomitoria, yaupon, is a Southeastern native with an upright, irregular tree form or mounded shrub form. Yaupon has smooth gray twigs, notched evergreen leaves, and translucent red berries. The shrub form grows 3 feet tall; the tree form grows 15 to 30 feet. Zones 8–10.

How to grow: Hollies are dioecious, meaning that individual plants are either male or female. Therefore, with few exceptions, you must have a male holly of the same species in the vicinity in order to have a nice crop of berries. Purchase hollies from a reliable source to ensure that you get both male and female plants. Hollies need full sun to partial shade and evenly moist, well-drained, humusy soil. Avoid windy sites and (except for winterberry) poor drainage.

Landscape uses: Plant hollies in groups for hedges, barriers, screens, or a mass effect. A single specimen makes a stunning focal point. Hollies are also good in natural landscapes, since their berries provide food for wildlife.

IMPATIENS

Impatiens, patient Lucy, garden balsam.
Annuals and tender perennials used as annuals.

Description: Two species are commonly grown, *Impatiens walleriana*, impatiens, and *I. balsamina*, garden balsam. Both bear 1- to 3-inch flat or roselike flowers in white, pink, rose, red, orange, lavender, purple, or spotted and banded combinations. The succulent-stemmed plants can grow 8 to 36 inches tall.

I. walleriana cultivars cover the entire height range on spreading, green-leaved plants, while annual *I. balsamina* types resemble 2-foot trees with longer green leaves. New Guinea hybrids have large flowers and elongated green or multicolored leaves.

I. capensis, jewelweed, is a weedy annual native that produces bright orange to yellow flowers atop 2- to 5-foot, succulent stems. Jewelweed grows well in moist, shady conditions and self-sows with abandon. Its juicy leaves and stems are a folk remedy for skin irritation caused by poison ivy and insect bites.

How to grow: Sow seeds indoors in early spring for planting after danger of frost is past, or buy transplants, especially of New Guinea hybrids, which are often grown from cuttings. Plant in partial shade and average soil. Water during droughts. New Guinea hybrids will grow in full sun if the soil is kept constantly moist. Root cuttings of your favorites in late summer for overwintering indoors.

Spider mites can cause yellow-stippled leaves, especially in too much sun or very dry weather. Control by spraying plants with a blast of water or by applying soap spray every 3 to 5 days for 2 weeks. A fungal disease, impatiens downy mildew, affected growers in the eastern United States in 2010 and 2011 and caused widespread loss of crops of *I. walleriana* and its hybrids. *I. balsamina*, rose balsam, is also susceptible to this disease, which causes yellowing, wilting foliage, downy growth on leaf undersides, blossom drop, and collapse of plants. There is no cure for infected plants; buy only healthy looking plants and remove and destroy any showing symptoms. Disease spores remain in the soil for several years; avoid planting susceptible impatiens where infected plants have grown. New Guinea impatiens are highly resistant to the fungus.

Landscape uses: Impatiens are superb for beds, in masses among shrubs, as edges for plantings or structures, and in pots. White- or pastel-flowered impatiens will light up the gloomy areas under trees and other shady sites with their bright blooms. In warmer areas, self-sown seeds may naturalize to form a dramatic groundcover. Impatiens, especially the New Guinea hybrids, also make lovely houseplants.

INSECTS

Gardeners tend to ignore most insects—until they find holes in the leaves of their favorite plants or until the mosquitoes start biting. In a rash rush to exterminate the offenders, some may assume that every insect is an enemy, but that's far from true. As much as 90 percent of the insects in your backyard are beneficial ones like soldier bugs, lady beetles, and lacewings that naturally help to keep pests in check. Honeybees and beneficial wasps also are harmed by broad-spectrum control efforts, and crop pollination can suffer as a result. Finally, a great many insects are completely benign—they may live in your garden but do no harm to your plants—and these, too, are harmed by wide-ranging pesticide applications.

In the amazing-but-true category, consider the fact that four out of every five animals on earth are insects. And there are more species of beetles than there are of all other animals, including insects, put together. Estimates of the total number of insect species range from 2 million to 10 million. No one knows how many more species are yet to be discovered, especially in the tropics and other remote regions.

There are good reasons to learn about the behavior and biology of the insects in our gardens. The most important one is that a little knowledge about how insects function can help us prevent pest damage without using invasive and potentially toxic control methods.

Insect Anatomy and Life Cycles

All insects have six legs, and their bodies are divided into three sections: the head, thorax, and the abdomen. They have two antennae that help in sensory perception, and most insects have two pairs of wings located on the thorax. (Flies have only one pair of wings.) Insects breathe through small air tubes located along the length of their bodies called spiracles.

Some insects have strange and complicated life cycles. The best-known example is the transformation of a wormlike caterpillar into a sensationally beautiful butterfly. In general, insects follow one of the two main patterns of development.

KEY WORDS *Insects*

Metamorphosis. A change in form during the development of an insect.

Larva. An immature stage of an insect.

Caterpillar. The larva of a moth or butterfly.

Grub. The larva of a beetle.

Maggot. The larva of a fly.

Pupa. A hardened shell formed by a larva, within which the adult stage develops.

Cocoon. A protective cover for a pupa.

Chrysalis. The pupa of a butterfly.

Nymph. An immature stage of an insect that does not form a pupa.

Parasite. An animal or plant that lives in or on, and draws nourishment from, another organism.

Parasitoid. An insect that parasitizes another insect.

Predator. An animal that attacks and feeds on other animals.

Complete metamorphosis: In this pattern, the immature insect is transformed during a resting stage into an adult that looks like a completely different organism. The adult insect usually inhabits a different environment and eats different food than it did at the immature stage. In some cases, one stage may be a pest, while the other is harmless. For example, parsleyworms, which feed on carrots, dill, and related plants, are the larvae of black swallowtail butterflies.

As the larva grows, it periodically sheds its skin until it reaches its full size. It then forms a pupa and enters a resting stage. When the adult has finished forming inside, it splits open the pupa and emerges and expands its wings. When its outer skeleton has hardened, it flies away to search for food and mates.

Incomplete metamorphosis: Insects that follow this pattern develop from immature to adult in gradual stages without forming a pupa. The insect starts life as an egg, which hatches into a nymph. The nymph sheds its skin several times as it grows, becoming more and more like the adult with each

molt. It gets progressively larger, its body lengthens, and wing pads appear where its wings will grow. The last molt is to the adult stage, with fully formed wings and reproductive organs. The nymph and adult usually have the same type of diet.

Winter Survival

Knowing how and where both pest and beneficial insects spend winter can give you important clues about how to either control or encourage them. Most insects in the temperate zones sense the shortening daylength and cooler temperatures of autumn. Their bodies prepare for winter by building up energy reserves and by undergoing chemical changes so that their blood won't freeze. Many adult insects cannot survive winter, but at least one of their life stages, such as egg, larva, or pupa, can withstand the long cold period in a state of hibernation (called diapause in insects). The overwintering stages of many pests, including armyworms and sawflies, burrow deep into the soil or into litter on the ground. Cultivating the soil in early spring can expose these hidden hibernators to predators such as birds. Other pests, such as leaf rollers and tent caterpillars, pupate or lay eggs in cracks and crevices in tree bark. Scraping egg masses off of bark and spraying trees with dormant oil can help to eliminate these pests.

One good way to encourage beneficial insects, and give benign ones garden space, is to cultivate a hedge or border of companion plants that are rich in pollen and nectar. Plants that belong to either the daisy family, Asteraceae, such as daisies (*Leucanthemum* spp.), yarrows (*Achillea* spp.) or sunflowers (*Helianthemum* spp.), or the mint family, Lamiaceae, including catmints (*Nepeta* spp.) and mints (*Mentha* spp.), are good choices.

Feeding Habits

Insects have a wide variety of feeding habits; some are vegetarians, others are carnivores. Some eat nearly anything, while others can eat only one species of plant. But only a minority of insects feed on our crop or ornamental plants.

Plant eaters: These insects chew or suck on leaves, stems, or roots for food. They are usually pests—aphids, gypsy moth caterpillars, and Colorado potato beetles are some examples. Some are considered beneficial and have been used in biological control programs to combat weeds.

Parasites: Some insects, such as mosquitoes and blackflies, suck blood from birds and mammals; others, like lice and fleas, are skin parasites on animals. Parasitoid insects are generally beneficial from the gardener's standpoint, since they live and grow inside host insects until the hosts eventually die. The adults of many parasitoids feed on pollen and nectar.

Predators: Predators such as lady beetles and ground beetles can eat hundreds of insects during their life cycles. Many predators, such as pirate bugs, are also adapted to survive by sucking plant juices or eating pollen when prey is scarce.

Omnivores: Some insects have evolved the ultimate survival strategy: They eat almost anything. Cockroaches and earwigs are omnivores; they eat many sorts of animal or vegetable material—even soap, glue, and paper bindings.

Scavengers: Dung beetles, carrion beetles, fly larvae, and other insects live on decaying vegetable or animal material, breaking down the dead tissues or organic matter and hastening their decay.

Fungus feeders: The larvae of fungus gnats and some obscure species of lady beetles feed on fungi.

The first step in deciding whether an insect is a pest or a beneficial is to identify it. See Recommended Reading on page 675 for a list of books that will help you identify insects in both groups. For more information on insects that help your garden and how to create habitat for them, refer to the Beneficial Insects entry. For information on preventing and controlling pest insect problems, see the Pests entry.

INVASIVE PLANTS

Deciding to include native wildflowers, shrubs, and vines in your landscape is fun and usually quite easy to do. But what about the flip side of the problem—beating back the invasives?

The problem can seem overwhelming, but many governmental and nonprofit agencies are working hard to combat invasives. Your individual contribution may seem minute, but if every home gardener decided to help fight invasive species, who knows what we could accomplish?

The Alternatives Strategy

What if you're tempted by some attractive, useful plants in a nursery, but you know they're nonnative and on some "invasives" list? Resist temptation, because it is highly likely that noninvasive alternatives exist. Many invasive plant eradication organizations, conservation organizations, or extension services offer lists of alternatives. Here are a few to start with.

Japanese honeysuckle (*Lonicera japonica*) and Oriental bittersweet (*Celastrus orbiculatus*) alternatives: American bittersweet (*Celastrus scandens*), Dutchman's-pipe (*Aristolochia macrophylla*), trumpet honeysuckle (*Lonicera sempervirens*), trumpet vine (*Campsis radicans*)

Bishop's goutweed (*Aegopodium podagraria*) alternatives: Canadian anemone (*Anemone canadensis*), spotted dead nettle (*Lamium maculatum*), sweet woodruff (*Galium odorata*)

Buckthorn (*Rhamnus cathartica*) alternatives: Allegheny serviceberry (*Amelanchier laevis*), hophornbeam (*Ostrya virginiana*), downy serviceberry (*Amelanchier arborea*), American hornbeam (*Carpinus caroliniana*), nannyberry viburnum (*Viburnum lentago*), shadblow serviceberry (*Amelanchier canadensis*), witch hazel (*Hamamelis virginiana*)

Purple loosestrife (*Lythrum salicaria*) alternatives: Bee balm (*Monarda didyma*), blazing star (*Liatris spicata*), spotted joe-pye weed (*Eutrochium maculatum*), purple coneflowers (*Echinacea* spp.)

Tatarian honeysuckle (*Lonicera tatarica*) alternatives: Arrowwood viburnum (*Viburnum dentatum*), highbush cranberry (*Viburnum opulus* var. *americanum*), silky dogwood (*Cornus amomum*), winterberry (*Ilex verticillata*)

Help Stem the Tide

Here are some things you can do to help prevent the spread of invasive plants.

Shun invasives. Learn which plants are known to be invasive in your region and don't buy or plant them or use decorations that contain them—hanging a fall wreath that features Oriental bittersweet, for example, can easily add hundreds of seedlings to your property as birds eat the berries. Ask your local extension service office for a list of plants that are invasive in your area, or consult the lists on the National Invasive Species Information Center Web site (see Resources on page 673).

Set limits. If you are using plants that have aggressively spreading roots, even if they're not listed as invasive, plant them within a barrier or in containers, just in case. Sometimes we've discovered a plant's invasive potential only after the fact. For example, periwinkle (*Vinca* spp.), long considered a benign groundcover, has turned out to be an invasive that can spread across the ground surface in natural woodland areas, outcompeting native wildflowers such as trilliums. And note that root barriers won't do anything to stop invasives such as barberries and bittersweet that spread easily by seed.

Keep an eye on new plantings. When you try a new garden or landscape plant, watch for invasive characteristics. Look for "volunteers"—its seedling offspring—in adjacent lots, fields, or woods. Pay attention to clues that it may be invasive, such as prolific seed production, rapid expansion by rhizomes or runners, or berries that attract birds (who ingest them and transplant them with built-in fertilizer!).

Don't be a carrier. Don't transport invasive plants (or animals), on purpose or by accident. That includes not taking firewood from a campground back home (emerald ash borers travel in it). It also means respecting international or state laws about imported plants, food, or other products,

and not sneaking in that cool plant or driftwood when you come home from vacation.

Remove What You Can

Once you've learned to identify common invasives, remove them where you can. If you see one clump of garlic mustard, a multiflora rose plant, or a Japanese honeysuckle vine at some corner of your property, dig and destroy it. If there are a few purple loosestrife or common reed grass plants in a ditch, uproot them or at least cut off the seed heads and bag them carefully.

If you encounter a thriving stand of garlic mustard or knotweed, digging out all the plants may be more than you can do. Instead, cut them off at the roots as early in the season and as often as possible.

Fighting Back

The specific methods for fighting invasive plants vary depending on the plant's growth habit and how it spreads. Here are some quick tips on fighting a few of the most widespread invasives.

Common reed grass (*Phragmites australis*): Do not dig it, as roots simply break and resprout. Cutting annually in July may slow its spread.

Garlic mustard (*Alliaria petiolata*): This weed can be controlled with great diligence if you pull it out by the roots before it flowers, and then bag or burn all the plant parts. Another option is to repeatedly cut stands of garlic mustard close to ground level to prevent the plants from flowering.

Japanese knotweed, Mexican bamboo (*Polygonum cuspidatum*): Cut at least three times each growing season. In gardens, heavy mulch or dense shade may kill it over time.

Multiflora rose (*Rosa multiflora*): If individual plants pop up on or near your property, stop them by pulling or digging (at least 6 inches down and 6 inches out from the crown) them out. Large infestations are usually beyond control by a single organic gardener.

Russian olive, autumn olive (*Elaeagnus angustifolia, E. umbellata*): Pull seedlings or dig clumps; cut off to a stump and remove or bury the stump. Do not mow or burn.

You will have to pick your battles, since some of the problems are daunting or dangerous to your health (giant hogweed, for example), and you may not have the strength, numbers, or tools for the job. Nothing about the problem of invasive species is easy. But educating yourself and others is a start.

One dilemma that many of us face is the landscape plants already growing in our yards that have turned out to be invasives. You may have a Japanese barberry hedge, a huge swath of vinca, or a beautiful butterfly bush—all of which are invasive in some areas of the country. Should you leave these plants in place or remove them? It's a tough decision, and not all experts agree. However, Botanic Gardens Conservation International, a nonprofit network of botanic gardens working to conserve threatened and endangered plants worldwide, recommends removing them.

Some people and organizations recommend using potent herbicides to kill aggressive invasive plants, arguing that the herbicide is the lesser of two evils. But ask yourself, how do they know this is true? The full extent of the environmental and health problems caused by widespread herbicide use is an ever-unfolding story. As organic gardeners, we should always be suspicious of claims that using synthetic chemicals is the "best way" or the "only way" to combat a problem.

IPOMOEA

Morning glory, moonflower. Warm-weather annual or tender perennial vines.

Description: *Ipomoea alba*, moonflower, is a twining, 8- to 10-foot vine with heart-shaped leaves. The fragrant, white, trumpet-shaped flowers open only at night. *I. nil*, *I. purpurea*, and *I. tricolor*, all called morning glory, are similar. All are twining vines with heart-shaped leaves. The funnel-shaped blue, white, blue-purple, or crimson blooms open in the morning and in the afternoon.

Several species bear small red flowers that are excellent for attracting hummingbirds, including *I. coccinea*, red morning glory, which reaches 12 feet; *I. ×multifida*, cardinal climber, to 6 feet; and *I. quamoclit*, cypress vine or star glory, growing to 20 feet.

Gardeners also grow ornamental forms of sweet potato (*I. batatas*) for their chartreuse, bronze, or purple-black leaves.

All are tender perennial vines grown as warm-weather annuals.

How to grow: Plant morning glory seed outdoors after all danger of frost is past. Nick the hard seed coat for faster germination. Except ornamental sweet potatoes, which are allowed to trail on the ground, all morning glories need a stake or strings to climb on, and supports should be installed from the start. To grow ornamental sweet potatoes, start with purchased transplants. You can harvest tubers and overwinter them to grow plants for next year. See the Sweet Potato entry for details. Give morning glories average, well-drained soil and full sun to partial shade.

Landscape uses: Plant vining morning glories next to fences, porch rails, trellises, and arbors. Use ornamental sweet potatoes as temporary groundcovers, in containers, or as fillers in flowerbeds.

IRIS

Iris, flag. Mostly spring- to early-summer-blooming perennials and bulbs.

Description: Irises offer a huge range of colors and patterns, heights, and bloom times, with variations on a common theme of flower shape and plant form. The basic flower shape consists of three inner (often erect) petals, called standards, surrounded by three other petals (usually arching out and down), called falls. Leaves are almost always flat and long, resembling swords; they grow in rather open to quite dense upright or arching clumps from bulbs or creeping rhizomes. Some have fibrous roots.

By far the most popular group is the large collection of hybrids termed the "bearded" irises, named for the hairy caterpillar-like tuft creeping out of the center of each fall. Flowers range from barely 2 inches wide to 7-inch giants in what is probably the widest color range of any plant group, lacking only pure red. They bloom in early summer, from 2 inches to nearly 5 feet above stiff, swordlike leaves. A number of cultivars rebloom from late summer into fall, to double the show; these reblooming cultivars are worth seeking out. Zones 3–8.

In place of a beard, "beardless" irises flaunt a colorful spot, called a signal, or an intricate pattern of lines. Blooms on *Iris sibirica*, Siberian iris, rarely exceed 3 inches wide and are more open and graceful then most bearded irises; they occur in shades of white, red-violet, blue, and purple (plus a few rare pinks and yellows, such as the yellow-and-white 'Butter and Sugar') on upright, grassy clumps averaging 3 feet tall. They bloom toward the end of the bearded's season. Zones 3–9. *I. ensata* (formerly *I. kaempferi*), Japanese iris, bears 4- to 10-inch, six-petaled flattish or more double flowers in shades of white, pinkish lavender, red-violet, blue, and violet, often exotically edged, lined, and speckled. Most grow to about 2½ to 3 feet and are broader-leaved and less dense than Siberians, blooming a few weeks later. Zones 4–9. Very early-spring-blooming, bulbous *I. reticulata*, reticulated iris, produces narrow-petaled, sweetly scented 3-inch blooms, mostly in blue and purple shades with orange or yellow signals, among sparse, four-sided leaves that may grow to 1½ feet after bloom. Zones 5–9.

How to grow: Most bearded irises are easy to grow, but they do have specialized needs. Plant and divide every 3 to 4 years in summer or early fall, splitting them into individual "fans" with the rhizome attached, or into divisions with a few fans. Trim leaves back before planting to make up for root loss. They grow best in full sun or very light shade and average to rich, well- drained soil. Barely cover the rhizome and point the leafy end in the direction you want it to grow, ideally out from the center of a group of three to five of a kind.

Bearded irises tolerate drought very well when dormant (usually beginning about 6 weeks after bloom), but water them well up to the time dormancy sets in and after division. Fertilize routinely in spring and early fall, keep weeds and other plants away from the rhizomes, mulch loosely the first winter after division, and be ready to stake the tall cultivars when they bloom.

Soft rot attacks during wet seasons in poorly drained soil, entering though wounds in the rhizome made from premature leaf removal or too-close cultivation; it can also be carried on the body of the iris borer. The eggs of this pest hatch in spring, producing 1- to 1½-inch-long, fat, pinkish larvae. The larvae enter a fan at the top and tunnel down toward the rhizome, where they may eventually eat the whole interior without being noticed.

In fall, remove dead, dry leaves, which often carry borer eggs, and destroy badly infested fans in spring. You can also crush borers in the leaves by pinching toward the base of the telltale ragged-edged leaves or by running your thumb between the leaves and squashing any borers you find. They are also vulnerable when you divide the clumps; check every rhizome for this pest. If you find a few borers, try cutting them out, but destroy badly infested rhizomes.

Siberian irises enjoy similar conditions to bearded irises, tolerating wetter soil and requiring less frequent division in spring or fall. Be certain to replant as soon as possible after dividing them. Rot and borers seldom plague them.

Grow Japanese irises in much the same way, providing shade from the hottest sun. Water well before and during bloom. They need acid soil and benefit from a few inches of mulch in summer.

Plant reticulated irises in fall about 3 inches deep and a few inches apart in average to more fertile, very well-drained soil. Grow with annuals and perennials to fill the gaps left by their leaves, which wither by summer.

Landscape uses: Smaller bearded irises are perfect in rock gardens and along paths and beds.

For mid- to late-spring bloom, plant taller ones in a perennial border or in a separate bed to provide optimum conditions. They also look splendid among garden ornaments and along patios. Siberian and Japanese irises are good choices for borders and wet sites, such as along a stream or the edge of a pond, although they prefer slightly drier conditions in winter. Reticulated irises look at home among rocks, naturalized in thin grass, or at the front of borders.

IRRIGATION

See Drip Irrigation; Watering

IVY

See *Hedera*

J-K

JAPANESE GARDENS

Gardens in the Japanese style are the result of a rich, centuries-long tradition of landscape art. Devoted to capturing the essence of nature, the design of a Japanese garden strives toward nature as the ideal. The look and mood convey overriding simplicity and quiet serenity. Japanese gardens are not symmetrical or colorful, as Western gardens tend to be, and they feature relatively few different plants. Evergreens play an essential role in the design, and there is minimal change in the garden from season to season. Some select spring-blooming plants mark the beginning of the growing season, and deciduous shrubs or trees like Japanese maples (*Acer palmatum*) bring foliage color to mark the fall season. Plants are grouped in asymmetrical balance to create harmony but maintain a composition that could exist in nature.

All too often, beginners put together a collection of stone lanterns, bamboo fences, and koi ponds instead of delving deeper into the essence of Japanese garden design. Japanese gardens are pri-

marily intended as quiet, peaceful spaces for meditation and contemplation, and the design strives toward perfect combinations of line, mass, and texture. Ornaments such as lanterns are used very carefully, and are placed only where an architectural accent is necessary to focus the design.

The study of Japanese gardens can take a lifetime, and there are entire books devoted to this topic. See Resources on page 673 for Internet sites that offer a good overview of the philosophy and resources available.

Elements in the Japanese Garden

Because Japanese gardens strive to represent nature in the garden, natural elements are typically miniaturized, stylized, or symbolized to re-create portions of a natural landscape such as rocks, water, and borrowed scenery.

A variety of techniques create the illusion of size and distance in Japanese gardens. Planting large trees in the foreground and progressively

Garden Styles

Since each Japanese garden is designed for its specific site, they are all unique. There are, however, three basic styles of gardens.

Hill-and-pond gardens: Called *chisen kaiyu shiki teien*, this style was originally brought to Japan from China and is designed for walking through. Gardens of this style feature a hill or hills, with a pond at the front of the garden. Depending on the garden, the pond can be real or represented by an expanse of raked gravel. Visitors stroll through the garden to enjoy a series of carefully designed vistas.

Flat gardens: This style of garden, called *hira-niwa*, consists of a flat space and is a garden "picture," designed to be viewed from a single angle, often a platform. Typically used in front of palaces or temples, flat gardens also are used in courtyards. Raked gravel representing the seashore or a lakeshore, often with minimal plantings, is one typical picture, but a flat garden can feature plants, rocks, water, and other elements arranged in a three-dimensional picture. Flat gardens are designed for contemplation.

Tea gardens: Simplicity is the key in a tea garden, called *roji* or *cha-niwa*, whose function is to guide participants along the path that leads to the tearoom. A tea garden features an austere design with a very limited, simple use of plants. It also features a stone basin for handwashing and stone lanterns to light the path at nighttime.

---

smaller ones in the distance is one way to make a garden seem larger than it actually is. Trees are pruned and trained to make them appear larger and older than they really are. Brighter colors and bolder textures in the foreground, with paler and finer ones farther away, also help make the spaces seem larger.

Rocks are a fundamental element in a Japanese garden. They are used more as sculptural elements than rocks in a Western garden would be. Rocks either stand alone or are arranged in groups to serve as accents. There are many rules and guidelines that govern their placement. In general, rugged, irregularly shaped rocks represent cliffs and mountains, while rounded ones symbolize lakeshores and riverbeds.

The pathway through a Japanese garden has symbolic meaning and represents life's journey. Stepping-stones are firmly placed to provide secure footing but are arranged so visitors need to pay close attention to where they are stepping and thus to their surroundings.

Water, either real or represented, is an important part of a Japanese garden. Free-form ponds may have a mixture of stones, plants, or timbers edging them. Water also is commonly represented by stretches of raked gravel or areas covered with rounded river rocks. Japanese gardens frequently feature bridges that span real or represented expanses of water.

While Japanese gardens are typically enclosed to screen out the outside world, fences and other screens are always unobtrusive. If views outside the garden are available, plantings inside it can be used to frame the borrowed scenery, such as a view of a distant mountain.

Plants for a Japanese Garden

You can use all native Japanese plants for your garden or use similar plants that are native to your region. Whenever possible, plant disease-resistant selections, since each plant in the garden is essential to the design and needs to always look its best. Evergreens form the basis of every Japanese garden. Unlike in Western gardens, where evergreens are cultivated so their branches and foliage cover the base of the plant, in Japanese gardens the evergreens are typically pruned to reveal the trunk and framework of branches. Use trees and shrubs that can be pruned and shaped for the site. Evergreen trees to consider include Deodar cedar (*Cedrus deodara*), Japanese black pine (*Pinus thunbergii*), Japanese red pine (*P. densiflora*), Japanese white pine (*P. parviflora*), junipers (*Juniperus* spp.), sawara false cypress (*Chamaecyparis pisifera*), and umbrella pine (*Sciadopitys verticillata*).

Evergreen azaleas (*Rhododendron* spp.) are a good evergreen shrub for a Japanese garden, as are dwarf forms of Hinoki false cypress (*Chamaecyparis obtusa*), camellias (cultivars of *Camellia japonica* and *C. sasanqua*), heavenly bamboo (*Nandina domestica*), Japanese pieris (*Pieris japonica*), Japanese holly (*Ilex crenata*), and junipers (*Juniperus* spp.).

In addition to Japanese maples (*Acer palmatum*), various deciduous trees can be used in a Japanese garden. Consider crabapples (*Malus* spp.), cherries (*Prunus* spp.), Kousa dogwoods (*Cornus kousa*), Chinese redbud (*Cercis chinensis*), and Japanese pagoda tree (*Styphnolobium japonicum*). There's also a place for deciduous shrubs such as azaleas (*Rhododendron* spp.), witch hazels (*Hamamelis* spp.), cotoneasters (*Cotoneaster* spp.), glossy abelia (*Abelia*

×*grandiflora*), and bigleaf hydrangea *(Hydrangea macrophylla)*.

Vines such as clematis (*Clematis* spp.) as well as tree peonies (*Paeonia suffruticosa*) are appropriate, as are carefully placed specimens of perennials such as Japanese iris (*Iris ensata*).

Caring for a Japanese Garden

Because of their simple, elegant design, Japanese gardens are relatively easy to maintain. Raking lawns, sweeping walkways, and trimming perennials, as necessary, are all routine tasks. Gravel "ponds" need to be raked regularly to maintain a pattern. Eliminate any weeds that appear by hand-pulling or by hoeing. (Laying a thick layer of newspaper over the area before you spread the gravel will prevent weeds.)

Since Japanese gardens feature fewer plants than Western-inspired ones, it's important to keep each plant in top form. Watch for insect infestations and deal with them promptly, and prune away any branches that show signs of disease. Plants in the garden also need regular pruning to direct their shape and keep them natural looking, yet elegant.

JASMINUM

Jasmine. Winter- or spring-blooming shrubs or vines.

Description: *Jasminum nudiflorum*, winter jasmine, is a twiggy, 4- to 5-foot-tall shrub. It has green arching stems and opposite leaves, each bearing three 1-inch leaflets. In winter, its fragrant ¾- to 1-inch lemon yellow flowers bloom directly on the stems. Zones 6–9.

J. officinale, common white jasmine, is a deciduous or semievergreen vine that can climb about

10 to 15 feet. Fragrant ¾- to 1-inch white flowers appear in spring, then sporadically until frost. Leaves are opposite and compound, with five to nine ½- to 2½-inch leaflets per leaf giving a lacy texture. Zones 7–9.

How to grow: Both jasmines benefit from full sun. Provide well-drained soil, and water during the first two growing seasons. Once established, the jasmines need little supplemental watering. Overgrown winter jasmines benefit from postbloom rejuvenation pruning; cut them right to the ground.

Landscape uses: Winter jasmine is especially useful for grouping on banks and walls, and as a foundation plant. Common white jasmine is a good vine for posts and arbors. (Be sure to provide attachments for the stems to cling to during the first growing season or two.)

JERUSALEM ARTICHOKE

See Sunchoke

JOSTABERRY

See Gooseberry

JUGLANS

Walnut. Deciduous, nut-bearing trees.

Description: The trees in this genus produce edible nuts; you'll find more information on care and culture in the Nut Trees entry.

Juglans nigra is the native North American black walnut. It has an upright oval form and a trunk that displays an interlacing diamond pattern in its brown-black bark. Normally growing 50 to 75 feet tall, black walnut occasionally reaches more than 100 feet. Its alternate compound leaves consist of 15 to 23 dull green, 2- to 5-inch-long leaflets that show little or no fall color before dropping in autumn. Green husked fruit forms in fall; the walnut and shell are inside. Zones 5–7.

J. regia, Persian or English walnut, shares many characteristics with black walnut, but grows only to 40 to 60 feet in the landscape. The nuts of English walnut are more easily freed from their fleshy outer husks than those of black walnut, and the inner shells are thinner, simplifying removal of the nut meat. English walnuts are widely grown in California for nut production; these are the walnuts most often sold in stores. Hardiness varies by cultivar. Zones 5–8.

How to grow: Provide a site with full sun, good drainage, and deep, rich, moist soil. Black walnut trees can tolerate a range of other soils. Walnuts can retard the growth of plants around them through a chemical competition known as allelopathy. The trees' roots exude a substance called juglone that may be toxic to plants growing nearby, although not all plants are affected by it. Tomatoes are especially susceptible to juglone injury. Many shade-loving perennials are fine under walnuts. As a general rule, maintain a distance equal to at least 1½ times a walnut tree's height between it and susceptible plants.

Landscape uses: Walnuts make a coarse-textured shade tree for large-scale situations. Wood and nut production are also desirable.

JUNIPERUS

Juniper. Needle- or scaly-leaved evergreen trees, shrubs, or groundcovers.

Description: *Juniperus chinensis*, Chinese juniper, can be either a mounded shrub growing 4 to 6 feet tall or an erect, conical tree that can reach a mature height of 50 feet. The blue-green or gray-green evergreen foliage can be scaly or needlelike, often with both forms on the same plant, and rather prickly. Zones 4–8.

J. horizontalis, creeping juniper, is a native shrub with a low, prostrate, horizontally layered form that grows no more than 2 feet tall. Foliage may spread to 4 to 8 feet per plant at maturity. Its blue-gray or green scaly foliage turns a soft plum purple in winter. Zones 2–8.

J. virginiana, eastern red cedar, is a native tree that reaches a mature height of 50 to 100 feet with an upright, pyramidal form. The silvery to deep blue-green foliage droops slightly with age and bears waxy blue-gray berries. Zones 3–8.

How to grow: All junipers require full sun and well-drained soil. Chinese juniper and eastern red cedar benefit from evenly moist soil conditions. Creeping juniper tolerates dry soils, seaside or alkaline conditions, and deicing salts. Prune junipers only to control the size of spreading shrubs; never shear. Phomopsis twig blight can pose problems during a wet spring; prune and destroy diseased twigs. Bagworms can infest junipers at any time; handpick and destroy the larvae. If you are in or near an apple-growing area, be aware that juniper is the alternate host for cedar-apple rust, a disease that overwinters on eastern red cedar and severely injures apple trees.

Landscape uses: Junipers are a good choice for hot, dry, sunny spots that are out of reach of regular watering. There are hundreds of cultivars in many colors, shapes, and sizes. Choose appropriate cultivars for specimens, massed plantings, foundation planting, groundcovers, screens, hedges, and windbreaks.

KALE

Brassica oleracea, Acephala Group
Brassicaceae

Frost sweetens this vitamin- and mineral-packed cooking green's flavor. Kale can thrive in semi-shade and in cloudy climates; hot weather turns it tough and bitter. Some varieties have very curly, frilly leaves; others are smoother. 'Red Russian' has purple stems and relatively tender, frilly blue-green leaves that develop a magenta hue after frost.

Planting: Rich soil promotes faster growth and more tender leaves. Where summers are cool, sow seeds in early spring, 1/2 inch deep in rows 2 1/2 feet apart. For a fall-winter crop, sow seeds or set out transplants at least 6 weeks before the first frost; rake to cover seeds.

Growing guidelines: Thin plants to 2 feet apart. Keep the soil moist. Mulch established plants to control weeds.

Problems: See the Cabbage entry for insect and disease controls.

Harvesting: Harvest outer leaves as needed; use young tender leaves for salads and older leaves for cooking.

KITCHEN GARDENS

Kitchen gardens have been around since people first decided to grow plants for their use rather than simply gathering them from the wild. It's the ultimate in practical gardening—growing fruits, veggies, herbs, and edible flowers right outside the kitchen door. Step outside, harvest the freshest and most flavorful produce, then cook and serve. What could be easier or better than that?

In England and France, where kitchen gardens

are called potagers (poh-tah-JAYS), a lot of planning goes into making sure these humble gardens are as attractive as they are practical. Potagers feature patterned beds and arches where herbs, edible flowers, and fruits mingle with the carefully selected vegetables in a celebration of color, flavor, fragrance, and form.

Whether you design a simple kitchen garden or an elegant potager, here are some basics to get you started.

Choosing Plants

Because space in a dooryard garden is always at a premium, reserve your kitchen garden for delicate crops you want to pick a bit at a time—lettuces and other salad crops, edible-podded peas, scallions, radishes, and cherry tomatoes. Crops that are beautiful as well as edible, such as strawberries and ornamental hot peppers, with their variegated foliage and multicolored fruits, are a natural for a kitchen garden, too. Plant those space-hogging, main-harvest crops such as corn, squash, beans, storage onions, cabbages, and the like in your regular vegetable garden.

Include some perennial crops and containers in your kitchen garden, too. Flank the entrance to the kitchen garden with a pair of rugosa roses with their showy, edible rose hips, or blueberries, which, like rugosas, are ornamental in three seasons and produce a bumper crop of luscious berries. If you have room, grow a grapevine or a pair of hardy kiwi vines on an arbor leading into the kitchen garden. If you have a greenhouse or sunroom, your choices are even greater. You can position matching large containers of figs, pomegranates, or citrus plants at each side of the entrance during the growing season, then move them to the greenhouse or sunroom for winter.

Herbs and edible flowers will also brighten your kitchen garden. (See the list below for some delightful choices.) You could even surround the kitchen garden with a border of daylilies to give it definition. (Both the unopened buds of daylilies, valued in stir-fries, and the open flowers are edible.) Herbs were among the first kitchen-garden plants because of their ornamental value and numerous uses.

Edible Flowers for the Kitchen Garden

Edible flowers are the perfect companion plants for kitchen gardens, adding color and fragrance as well as ornaments for salads, cakes, and cold soups, and garnishes for the plate. Here are some excellent choices for your kitchen garden.

Bee balm, monarda (*Monarda didyma*)

Borage (*Borago officinalis*)

Calendula, pot marigold (*Calendula officinalis*)

Daylilies (*Hemerocallis* spp. and hybrids)

Johnny-jump-ups, violets (*Viola* spp.)

English lavender (*Lavandula angustifolia*)

Marigolds (*Tagetes* spp.)

Nasturtium (*Tropaeolum majus*)

Roses (*Rosa* spp. and hybrids)

Scented geraniums (*Pelargonium* spp.)

Sweet pea (Lathyrus odoratus)

Herbs for the Kitchen Garden

It's a good idea to have a small herb garden easily accessible to the kitchen door so that you can snip a few herbs while cooking—even if it's raining. To grow herbs successfully in a dooryard garden, be sure the soil has good drainage and the area is in sunlight for at least 6 hours per day.

A kitchen garden is the perfect place for thyme, parsley, marjoram, oregano, and cilantro. You might want to include several kinds of basils—sweet, small-leaved, and purple—since they have such different flavors. Rosemary makes a handsome tall shrub for the kitchen garden planted directly in the ground or, in colder areas, in containers. This is the place for French tarragon, too; it's not decorative enough for a flower border. Plan on keeping a rigorously controlled mint plant or two close at hand as well. Plant mint in tubs aboveground or in bottomless sunken buckets to keep it from crowding out other plants.

Chervil, once started, will seed itself under a shrub, sticking to its spot for the rest of your life. Dill will show up dependably every spring if you let a few flower heads set seeds. Consider the variegated sages as well, both for their decorative contributions to the garden's beauty and for their culinary properties.

Chives and garlic chives are two more kitchen-garden favorites. Be sure to cut the dying blossom heads from the latter, though, because it's as ruthless a colonizer as the mints, although it spreads only by seed, not by roots. Its umbels of white starry flowers add beauty in the garden, and the flat leaves add interesting flavor when chopped and sprinkled on salads and soups.

You may decide to make your kitchen garden more ambitious and duplicate a Colonial garden, complete with the medicinal and culinary herbs that early European settlers grew and relied upon. This project would contain different plants than you'd find in a typical kitchen garden. (For example, a Colonial garden wouldn't have included basils, French tarragon, or coriander.) Visiting historical gardens is a good way to get ideas for your own garden.

KIWI

Actinidia spp.
Actinidiaceae

Kiwifruits are a gourmet treat eaten fresh or in preserves, baked goods, and ice cream. They also contain 10 times the vitamin C of oranges. Southern gardeners can grow "fuzzy" kiwifruit (the type sold in grocery stores), and hardy kiwis can be grown throughout most of the United States. Kiwi vines are ornamental and require little care except pruning. Untrained vines grow rampantly and will clamber over anything in their paths, strangling trees or forming a tangled thicket of vines. Trellised, they are beautiful and high yielding.

Selecting vines: The fruits of hardy kiwis are the size of large grapes. They have smooth skin and may be eaten unpeeled, unlike their fuzzy cousins. *Actinidia arguta* survives to −25°F (Zone 4); its vines can reach 40 feet long. *A. kolomikta*, sometimes called 'Arctic Beauty' kiwi, is hardy to −40°F (Zone 3). It leafs out later than *A. arguta* and so is less susceptible to frosts. Male 'Arctic Beauty' plants have lovely pink-and-white variegated foliage.

Chinese kiwis, *A. chinensis*, produce golden-fleshed fruits that are less furry than the kiwifruits found in most supermarkets. The vines are hardy only to 10°F, and their trunks need winter protection.

"Fuzzy" kiwifruit, *A. deliciosa*, is the familiar brown, furry, egg-size fruit with the bright green interior. The cultivar 'Hayward' is most commonly grown for commercial production. Zones 8–9.

Most kiwis produce male and female flowers on separate plants; plant one male for every three or four females to ensure fruit set. A few cultivars such as 'Issai' (*A. arguta*) and 'Blake' (*A. deliciosa*) can produce fruit without another vine. They are also less vigorous and easier to control.

Planting and control: Kiwis do best at a pH of 6.0 to 6.5 and prefer well-drained soil. They like full sun but will tolerate partial shade. *A. kolomikta* prefers shade in hot climates.

Kiwis need support. Grow them on a trellis, arbor, or sturdy fence. A mature, bearing vine is very heavy, so build a strong arbor.

Plant vines in spring. Prune back newly planted vines to four or five buds. When these buds grow, select a sturdy shoot to be the main trunk and snip off the others. Tie it to the support, encouraging it to grow to the top of the arbor. When it does, cut off the tip to stimulate side branches.

Once a month each summer, prune all new growth back to four or five buds. This produces a dense, twiggy vine that bears large clusters of fruit. Prune overgrown vines back severely.

Kiwis tolerate drought but produce better if they get at least 1 inch of water a week. They are heavy feeders; apply 30 pounds of rotted manure or compost to each vine in early spring.

Problems: Kiwi vines suffer from few if any insect or disease problems.

Harvesting: Vines bear in 2 to 3 years. The fruits ripen in late summer. Pick them just before they are fully ripe and allow them to soften at room temperature. It may take some experimentation to get the ripening right, so keep trying.

Kiwis keep in the refrigerator for 2 months if stored before softening.

KOHLRABI

Brassica oleracea, Gongylodes Group
Brassicaceae

Kohlrabi looks like a turnip growing aboveground. It's a cabbage-family member, so it's no surprise that the edible white, green, or purple "bulbs" (which are actually swollen stems) have a cabbage-turnip flavor. Kohlrabi is, however, milder and sweeter than either of those vegetables.

Planting: Kohlrabi grows in loose, average soil. For a spring crop, direct-sow seeds 4 to 6 weeks before the last average frost; plant ¼ inch deep, 10 seeds per foot. Or start seedlings for a fall crop indoors 6 to 8 weeks before the last average frost. When seedlings are around 4 inches tall, thin plants to (or set out transplants at) 5 inches apart in rows 1 foot apart.

Growing guidelines: Keep plants well watered and free of weeds; put down a mulch to help accomplish both tasks. Cultivate carefully to keep from damaging the delicate, shallow roots.

Problems: See the Cabbage entry for insect and disease controls.

Harvesting: Use young leaves in salads and stir-fries. Harvest immature "bulbs" when they are no more than 2 inches in diameter, cutting the stems 1 inch below the swollen stem. Remove the leaf stems and leaves, and use the remaining stem as you would turnips. Substitute shredded kohlrabi for some or all of the cabbage in your favorite slaw recipe. Kohlrabi will keep for several weeks in the refrigerator and for several months in a cold, moist, root cellar.

LAGERSTROEMIA

Lagerstroemia, crape myrtle. Deciduous, summer-flowering trees or shrubs.

Description: *Lagerstroemia indica*, crape myrtle, flowers on new growth in white, pink, or watermelon red. When grown as a tree, it has an upright, narrowly vase-shaped, multitrunked form, and a mature height of about 20 feet. Some cultivars feature dark bark that peels away to expose lighter patches. When grown as a shrub, plants may reach 2 to 12 feet in a season. Northern gardeners grow dwarf forms of crape myrtle as semiwoody perennials that sprout from the roots each year. Fall color varies. Zones 7–9.

 How to grow: Give lagerstroemias full sun and good drainage. Shade promotes powdery mildew, which can be a serious problem. A National Arboretum breeding program produced many mildew-resistant cultivars; look for these selections when buying crape myrtles. Prune in winter to promote vigorous growth for good flowering. Cut shrub forms entirely to the ground level. Shape tree forms by pruning out sucker shoots, watersprouts, and rubbing branches. Prune away spent flowers and seed heads. In Zones 8–9, midsummer deadheading results in a second bloom in fall.

 Landscape uses: Lagerstroemias work beautifully as screens, street trees, or focal points.

LAMIUM

Lamium, dead nettle. Trailing perennial groundcovers.

Description: *Lamium maculatum*, spotted lamium or spotted dead nettle, has 1- to 2-inch-long, heart-shaped, trailing leaves. Cultivars have beautiful white- or silver-variegated foliage. The small, hooded, pink, magenta, or white flowers open in whorls on stalks 6 to 8 inches high. Plants bloom from April through June and again in September. Zones 3–9.

 L. galeobdolon, yellow archangel, is a yellow-flowered species, sometimes listed as *Lamiastrum galeobdolon*, that has a reputation as an aggressive spreader. Selections with clump-forming habits may be somewhat better behaved but still should be used judiciously. Zones 4–8.

How to grow: Spotted lamium prefers partial shade and average, moist soil. It tolerates full sun and even poor soil. Don't fertilize these plants, or they may spread too extensively. Propagate by seeds, cuttings, or root division in spring.

Landscape uses: Spotted lamium is prized for its lengthy flower display and for its interesting silvery foliage. It's an excellent choice for a shady site and looks attractive under trees and shrubs, in rock gardens, with larger perennials, or in drifts. Members of the mint family, lamiums possess the ability to run, especially in moist soil conditions, but they are prized for their ability to tolerate dry shade. Despite their rambling tendencies, most are easily controlled by pulling or mowing should they escape their intended spot in the garden.

LANDSCAPE MAINTENANCE

Mowing, watering, weeding, and other chores are an essential part of keeping your landscape looking its best. Fortunately, there's a rhythm to the work a garden requires, and the more gardening experience you gain, and the more familiar you become with your own landscape, the easier it will be to maintain.

To stay on top of landscape maintenance, get in the habit of walking around your yard every few days and looking carefully at your plants. Keeping on top of chores helps minimize maintenance, since you can often correct problems with a minute or two of timely attention.

Maintenance Calendar

There's a best season to tackle most gardening tasks, which makes it easy to spread maintenance throughout the year. Consult with local experts to determine the best time to tackle gardening chores—gardeners, staff at local botanic gardens, your extension office, and local nurseries are good sources of information. You'll find information on maintenance on the Internet as well, but be sure to look for local, or at least regional, advice, since the best time to prune or plant varies widely from Maine to Florida or Minnesota to California. Make a note of tasks and the ideal times to tackle them, so you can start a calendar for essential maintenance. Here are some tasks to include:

Winter to Early Spring

- Sharpen and recondition garden tools. Sharp blades cut and dig more smoothly than blunt ones do, making gardening tasks easier. Give tools a protective coating of light oil.

- Prune trees and shrubs.

- Order seeds and begin seed-starting activity, so you'll have plants to move to the garden once the weather warms.

- Weed garden beds during warm spells. Many weeds appear in winter and have set seed by the time spring arrives.

- Watch for perennials and other plants that have heaved out of the ground because of cycles of freezing and thawing. Replant and mulch them.

- In the South and West, clean out garden beds and cut back perennials that have been damaged by winter weather.

Spring and Summer

Outdoor activity really heats up from spring through summer. Begin tackling these tasks once the weather has warmed in your region.

- The best season for planting will depend on your spring frost dates, so check before you uncover beds or begin planting. Be sure to test the soil to make sure it's dry enough to work before you dig. It should crumble when you squeeze a handful. Also don't walk on the garden soil, especially when it is wet, because you will compact it.

- In the South and West, by early spring the weather is usually perfect for preparing new garden beds and amending the soil with organic matter.

- Divide summer- and fall-blooming perennials in early spring, but wait until later in the season in the North.

- Keep weeding garden beds to eliminate weeds before they take over.

- Prune spring-blooming shrubs and trees, if necessary, as soon as they have finished flowering. Remove diseased or dead wood anytime.

- Water transplants regularly. In general, flower gardens should receive 1 inch of rain a week, either from rainfall or watering. To prevent disease problems and use water efficiently, water deeply and apply the water directly to the soil or mulch, not on plant foliage.

- In late spring or early summer, side-dress perennials with organic matter or a balanced organic fertilizer.

- Begin installing stakes and supports for perennials, before they grow so large that corralling them is difficult or impossible.

- Fertilize lawn grass with a balanced organic fertilizer or well-rotted compost. Warm-season grass needs feeding in late spring, then again a few weeks later. Feed cool-season grass in mid-spring when it begins to grow.

- Attend to flowers by removing spent blooms and cutting back perennials that benefit from a postflowering haircut.

- Edge lawn to keep grass from invading flowerbeds. Install edging strips to eliminate this chore from your list.

- If you plan to plant new areas in fall, prepare the soil in those areas in late summer.

Fall

- In the South, once searing summer temperatures subside, it's time to cut back flowers and vegetables and replant for the long, cool fall season.

- Prepare soil and beds for spring planting and also catch up on weeding.

- Divide spring- and early-summer-blooming perennials.

- Plant spring-flowering bulbs.

- Feed lawns planted with cool-season grasses like bluegrass with a balanced organic fertilizer or compost.

- Fall is a great time of year to prepare new garden beds, either by digging them or by smothering existing vegetation with layers of newspaper and organic matter. Smothered beds will be ready to plant in spring.

- Collect tools, hoses, stakes, and other gardening equipment and bring it inside for winter storage.

- Mulch gardens once the soil freezes.

Creating a Low-Maintenance Landscape

While many chores are enjoyable, few gardeners want to increase the amount of time they spend working in their gardens, unless that means adding a new flowerbed or vegetable plot. Use these tips to reduce the amount of routine maintenance your garden requires. You'll also find more detailed maintenance information in many other entries in this book (refer to the Quick Reference Guide on page 678 for a list).

Use mulch: Keeping the soil covered with mulch suppresses weeds and reduces the need to water. Apply a generous layer—2 to 4 inches—of shredded leaves, bark, or other organic material around perennials, groundcovers, and annuals, as well as around trees and shrubs. Keep the mulch an inch or two away from plant stems to prevent problems with pests and diseases. See the Mulch entry for more on how it can save time in the garden.

Choose the right tool for the job: A good tool can make a tiresome chore a pleasure. Buy good-quality tools and keep them sharp and well maintained. Sharp blades make landscape maintenance much easier. See the Tools and Equipment entry for more on how to select good-quality tools and the best tools to add to your collection.

Tour your garden regularly: Walk through your garden daily or every few days, if possible, to keep an eye on plants and see what tasks need doing—shrubs that need pruning, perennials that are overgrown, or vines that need trellising, for example. Tend to tasks on the spot, or keep notes about what chores you need to make time for before they get out of hand.

Weed a bit at a time: Keep up with yard maintenance chores like weeding by spending a little bit of time every day. Fifteen minutes a day can take the place of a grueling once-a-week weeding session. If you don't have time to completely weed your garden, walk through and pull off weed flowers to reduce the number of seeds and future weed populations. Or if the soil moisture conditions are just right for pulling a particular weed—dandelions or wild onions, for example—devote yourself exclusively to eliminating that particular weed and ignore the others. See the Weeds entry for more information on controlling weeds.

Reduce the size of your lawn: Replacing lawn grass with groundcovers or other plants cuts the time it takes to mow, plus it reduces time spent watering, trimming, fertilizing, and spraying. You're best off replacing sparse, weedy grass under trees and shrubs with beds of shade-loving groundcovers, perennials, and other plants. Also eliminate awkward spots that are slow or difficult to mow. See the Groundcovers and Lawn entries for more ideas for reducing the time spent on your lawn.

Add organic matter: Soil improvement isn't a once-and-done chore. Every time you replant your vegetable garden or add a new perennial to your flower garden, add organic matter to the soil. If you're not disturbing the soil by planting or tilling a crop under, mulch with organic matter—anything from grass clippings or finished compost to chopped leaves. Earthworms and soil-dwelling insects will gradually carry it down into the soil for you.

Pick your plants carefully: Matching the plants you choose to the soil, sun, and other conditions that exist naturally on your site ensures that your garden will grow well with minimal effort from you. Selecting native plants is a good place to start (see the Native Plants or Wildflowers entries for more information) but you can also find many nonnative species that will thrive.

Avoid invasives: Fast-growing plants that spread widely and invade native habitats, like English ivy (*Hedera helix*), may seem like a good thing at first, but eventually they'll require constant pruning and other maintenance to keep them in check. Avoid growing species that have been deemed invasive in your area.

LANDSCAPING

You don't have to be an artist to create a beautiful and enjoyable outdoor environment around your home. Landscaping is a form of personal expression, an outward extension of the care you put into arranging the inside of your house. A well-designed landscape provides outdoor spaces you and your family can use, whether that means you want shady, secluded areas for sitting or space for touch football. It also looks attractive all year round and ideally requires a minimum of maintenance. There is no "right" landscape; what works for your neighbor may not suit your needs or look good on your site.

Having a beautiful and unique landscape depends on four basic steps: gathering ideas, creating a design, installing plants and structures, and maintaining the landscape. Attractive landscaping will help you enjoy your home and increase its value as well.

Gathering Ideas

Before putting anything on paper, start the design process by looking around for ideas. Great landscaping ideas are all around you. Look at homes in your community and take note of landscapes that catch your eye. See if a garden club in your area sponsors tours of local gardens; these "open gardens" are a great way to get a close view of plants and design ideas that are appropriate for your area. Public parks and botanical gardens can also give you planting ideas.

Consider a design that will encourage birds and local wildlife to share your space by creating a habitat that provides them with food, water, shelter, and a place to raise their young. For more information on attracting native creatures, see the Birds and the Wildlife Gardening entries. Also check out the wide variety of gardening books available on landscape design as well as sites on the Internet devoted to landscaping; see Recommended Reading on page 675. You'll find a wealth of photographs and tips about other people's success stories.

As you develop your ideas, you'll want to decide which of the basic garden design styles—formal or informal—most suits your property and your personality. Formal gardens are symmetrical, with rectangular, round, or oval beds and other features, while informal designs feature free-form shapes. See the Garden Design entry for more on these two styles.

Creating a Design

Creating a design starts with a wish list, based on the ideas you've gathered from books and neighboring properties. This list should include design ideas, garden structures, and specific plants. This is the time for thinking big, so go ahead and put down anything that you'd like to see in your yard—the sky's the limit.

The next step is figuring out what you really need in your landscape, and making a list for that as well. If you have children, a play area may be the most important use of the yard. If you do a lot of entertaining, a shady arbor might be just the place for parties. For a large family, parking may be a major consideration. Besides play areas, entertaining, and parking, think about privacy, security, noise reduction, food production, pets, and flowers.

Pare down the lists: Compare your wish list with your needs list. Some things will probably

Garden Rooms

To create a landscape that's intriguing, intimate, pleasing, and useful, try to visualize it as a series of garden "rooms." Like a room in a house, each outdoor room has walls, a floor, and a ceiling. The walls could be a hedge, a row of trees, a fence, a trellis, or some combination of these elements. The walls don't have to be tall; they just need to mark off the space. The floor might be turf, mulch, groundcovers, crushed stone, stone pavers, or wooden decking; tree branches, an arbor, or even the sky itself may serve as the ceiling.

Think about the types of rooms you would like to use outdoors. A patio or deck for gatherings may be one room, a secluded sitting area another. You may also want a play area for kids or dogs, a utility area for composting, and an area set aside for the vegetable garden. These rooms need doorways, too—don't forget to think about gates or openings in the walls so you can move from one to another.

Breaking a landscape down into rooms makes it easier to identify the elements (plantings, structures, and hardscaping) you need to add or change. For example, if you want to separate the vegetable garden from the rest of your yard, you need to plan some sort of wall, such as a hedge or a wood fence. If you are enclosing the garden to protect it from animals, you might try a woven wire fence planted with attractive vines.

When you view your landscape as a combination of these elements, the whole process of planning a design is much more manageable. If you see a landscape that you particularly like, try to figure out what makes it special. Is there an attractive fence that sets off an area, or has your neighbor come up with a clever way to screen the front yard from the street? You may not want to copy any of these ideas exactly, but they will give you some idea of what is possible for your own home. The unlimited combinations of these elements make it easy to create a landscape that is unique to your property.

---

appear on both lists. The rose hedge on your wish list, for example, may match your need to keep romping pets out of the vegetable garden. Other wants and needs may be totally incompatible. If your yard is a popular place for neighborhood football or volleyball games, a delicate rock garden might be out of the question. Discuss the lists with your family, and decide which elements are acceptable to everyone. Also, don't forget to consider maintenance needs. A lovely perennial border can quickly deteriorate into a tangled mess if you don't have time to take care of it. The list on page 342 offers suggestions on creating a design that will require minimal care.

Determine a style: Your site will determine some of your choices. The style of your home may influence the feel of the design. If you have a brick house, the landscape might include formal brick paths and clipped evergreen hedges. A house with natural wood siding lends itself to wood-chip paths and rail fencing. You'll also need to plan access, such as paths, steps, and ramps.

Take note of wet, shady, and rocky spots, and try to take advantage of them. A wet spot may not be a desirable play area, but it could be a good place for a group of moisture-loving plants. Also, think of the landscape as it changes through the seasons. Evergreens and berried shrubs, along with a bench in a sunny spot, can make your yard a pleasant winter retreat. A little careful planning can give the land-scape four-season appeal. Don't forget details like specimen plants, interesting rocks, or sculpture to give the garden character. Refer to the Quick Reference Guide on page 678 for a list of other entries in this book that offer tips and ideas on landscape elements, theme gardens, and specific plant choices.

Draw a plan: Start the actual design by making a basic plan of your property using a landscaping app or design software or plotting it on paper. Nothing will inspire you to look more closely and

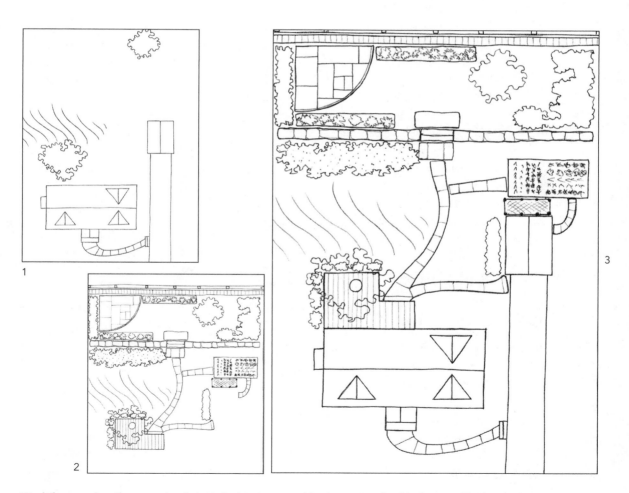

Work from a plan. Start your landscape design process with a basic site plan (1) of your yard. Sketch ideas on an overlay (2) to help visualize the finished result (3).

critically at your landscape. Make as accurate a plan as possible, and include all your garden's features—paths, trees, buildings, fences, and walkways. Draw it to scale, measuring distances with a 100-foot tape measure and transferring this information to graph paper. A scale of ¼ inch = 1 foot is workable; tape sheets together if your property is large. This will make a valuable permanent record you can work from and give you the best idea of where your landscape is heading.

Use sheets of thin tracing paper as overlays to sketch in ideas and see how they fit while you work on the design. That way, you can use your master plan again and again until you decide on the best arrangement of pathways, flowerbeds, and other landscape features. You can then transfer the final design to your master plan.

Whether you design your home landscape yourself or leave it to a professional, make sure that the finished plan fits your needs. Don't add a deck just because all your neighbors have them if what you really want is a dooryard herb garden. And while you don't want to copy your neighbors exactly, try to keep the general theme of the region in your design. A woodland garden in the Southwest would look as out of place as a cactus garden in New England.

Landscape Renovation

If you are starting with an existing landscape rather than a bare lot, you'll no doubt have trees, shrubs, and other plantings to deal with before you start creating a design. Try to identify the plants already growing in your yard, determine when (and if!) they have flowers or other features, and also evaluate how healthy they are. Common garden wisdom states that you should wait a year, watching what comes up and what flowers when, before making changes. That's good advice to follow, if you can

wait that long. However, there may be features you want to change right away—overgrown hedges, dead or dying trees, or unattractive plantings that are located in the wrong place. In this case, eliminate unwanted plants, and transplant ones that can be moved either to a holding bed or to a final location while you create a design. Here are some other suggestions for dealing with existing plantings.

- Cover unattractive shrubs with annual vines for a year while you plan your design.

- Reduce the size of overgrown shrubs like forsythias by renewal pruning (which often entails cutting them to the ground after they bloom in spring). Most evergreens will not tolerate renewal pruning, but many flowering shrubs will.

- Cut down and dig out overgrown shrubs or trees that block windows and walkways. Or thin out the older stems and cut them back hard to encourage more-attractive growth.

- Salvage what you can from weedy, overgrown beds: Dig up remnants of perennials and bulbs you'd like to save for another spot and plant them in a holding bed. Then cut down the remaining growth in the bed and cover everything with a thick layer of newspaper (10 sheets at least) topped with organic mulch. Replant once you have developed a design.

- Replace disease- or insect-prone shrubs and trees with more tolerant selections.

Designing with Nature

One of the best inspirations for landscape design is nature, and gardeners can use natural wild landscapes as inspiration for their designs. This means visiting the woods—or the prairie, or the Alaskan tundra, or whatever natural scene appeals to you most—and bringing back ideas. When you design a natural garden, you're not trying to make an exact copy of a natural scene. Instead, you want to reproduce the feel of a favorite place. Follow these points to successfully translate nature's lessons to your garden.

Understanding your site: Sun, shade, soil, moisture, and exposure will determine the kind of landscape you create and the plants you grow there. Watch the movement of the sun across your yard and check for wet spots after a good rain. It's best to choose plants adapted to the soil, sun, and other conditions that exist naturally. Otherwise, you'll need to amend your soil and make other changes necessary to accommodate the plants you wish to grow.

Organize garden spaces: Next, decide how large an area to develop. Start small! A few choice trees, shrubs, and groundcovers can be the beginning of a woodland garden; a small pond can be a focal point for a future bog garden. Decide where to place the beds and where the paths will go. Keep the paths under 4 feet wide to maintain intimacy. In a prairie or meadow, a 3-foot path allows the plants to brush you as you pass, providing a direct experience of the landscape.

Create the illusion of depth by layering the vegetation away from the path. Place low plants close for easy inspection. Use shrubs to close off views or to fill empty spaces. If your yard is small, borrow views from your neighbors.

Plant placement: Place plants in the garden as they would grow in nature based on what the plants require for best growth. Try to space the plants randomly—after all, plants tend to grow in clumps in nature, not in uniform rows or singly. When grouping, place plants close together at the center of the planting and more loosely at the edges. Add a small clump or single plants in a sep-

arate spot from the main planting to give the look of a chance seedling.

Punctuate low plantings and groundcovers with vase-shaped ferns or upright plants like grasses. Accent straight tree trunks with the arching stems of wildflowers like Solomon's seal (*Polygonatum* spp.). Also combine plants with different textures to make your natural landscape interesting and appealing.

Plant selection: Choose plants to match the conditions of the site and the requirements of your design. If you are using only natives, base your plant selection on the natural site your design is modeled on. (See the Native Plants entry for more on gardening with natives.) In a mixed planting, select harmonious colors, forms, and textures. Foliage is more important than flowers because it is effective all season. Design around desirable plants already on your site.

Look toward maturity: As conditions change in the garden, the composition will also change. Trees will produce more dense shade as they grow; if a tree dies, that will open up a sunny spot. Plants will grow too large and need division. Seedlings will come up at random. Nature is always at work. Enjoy and use the opportunities she provides.

Implementing a Plan

Once you actually have a plan, the next step is to carry it out. The first consideration in installation is often the cost. If you can't or don't want to do everything at once, consider carrying out the plan over several years. It's usually best to start with structures, such as fences and buildings as well as major pathways—the hardscape portion of the landscape. See the Stonescaping entry for information on using stone and pavers to create pathways, terraces, or other structures. Next, add the trees and hedges. Eventually, add smaller shrubs, flowers,

Design for Low Maintenance

Keep these time-saving pointers in mind when designing your landscape.

- On a steep, hard-to-mow slope, build terraces to break the slope into steps or plant the incline with groundcovers.

- Plan on installing brick or stone mowing strips around trees and flowerbeds to keep out grass and make mowing easier.

- Avoid using sharp angles or fussy curves when laying out flowerbeds; mowing around them is more difficult than along straight lines and smooth curves.

- Reduce lawn area and cut down on mowing time by installing decking or low-maintenance groundcovers.

- Minimize obstacles that make you stop and start. Group the obstacles you want to keep—the birdbath, lawn furniture, and the pool, and arrange them so the lawnmower can cut around them easily. Consider keeping the furniture on a patio or deck, putting the birdbath on a mulched surface, or using sawdust or sand under the swing set. If you can mow without stopping, backing, and turning, it's less wear and tear on you and the machine. Less gas, too. One other benefit—there may be no need at all for a weed whacker because you can get at everything with the mower.

- If you want to grow fruit, but don't have time for crops that need extensive pruning or training, try easy-to-grow bush cherries, blueberries, strawberries, or raspberries.

- Minimize fall leaf-raking chores by planting small-leaved trees such as black locust (*Robinia pseudoacacia*).

- Plant slow- and smaller-growing trees and shrubs to reduce pruning chores.

- Plan on informal hedges, which rely on natural shrub shapes; formal hedges require repeated shearing to keep their shape.

- Choose disease- and insect-resistant plants to reduce pest problems.

and groundcovers. This approach makes it fairly easy to install the landscape on your own.

If you do want to carry out the plan all at once, it may be best to hire a professional; this is especially true if the plan includes grading and drainage changes or irrigation and lighting systems. For your protection, get three bids for large projects, and make sure you have signed contracts before work begins. Also, don't forget to check local regulations and acquire necessary permits before starting.

After you have spent all this time developing and installing your landscape, you'll certainly want to take good care of it. In new landscapes, watering is probably the most important task. Regular watering for the first year or two helps plants settle in. After that, water your plants less frequently to encourage strong root systems. For more information on landscape care, see the Landscape Maintenance entry.

LARKSPUR

See *Consolida*

LASAGNA GARDENING

See Raised Bed Gardening

LATHYRUS

Sweet pea. Cool-weather annuals.

Description: Sweet peas (*Lathyrus odoratus* and others) bear short spikes of butterfly-like 1-inch blooms in white, pink, red, orange, cream, or purple, plus bi- and tricolors. The flowers appear on weak 6-foot vines or 15-inch mounds of pealike foliage. Some, but not all, cultivars feature fragrant flowers.

How to grow: Sweet peas grow and bloom best in cool weather. Plant seeds outdoors 2 inches deep in late fall or early spring, in a sunny spot with rich, moist, slightly alkaline soil. Provide support for vining cultivars. Pick flowers often for more bloom. Control aphid infestations with soap spray.

Landscape uses: Vines make temporary screens. Bushy plants brighten edges, beds, pots, and window boxes.

LAVANDULA

Lavender. Evergreen, summer-blooming perennial herbs.

Description: The species most commonly grown for its fragrant oil is common lavender, *Lavandula angustifolia* (also sold as English lavender, and under the botanical names *L. officinalis*, *L. spica*, and *L. vera*). Common lavender bears narrow, grayish to sea green, aromatic leaves on woody stems growing 1 to 3 feet tall. In summer, 2-inch-long spikes of fragrant, lavender-blue flowers appear above the foliage. 'Munstead' and 'Hidcote' are the best-known cultivars. Zones 5–9.

L. ×intermedia, lavandin, grows 18 to 24 inches tall and has a long bloom season. Cultivars in this group, including 'Grosso' (lavandin) and 'Provence', are grown commercially for lavender oil for the perfume industry. Zones 5 (with protection) and 6–9.

L. stoechas, French or Spanish lavender, produces pinecone-shaped pink or purple flower heads topped by a few larger, sterile bracts that give it a "bunny ears" appearance. Plants reach 12 to 36 inches tall. Showy and aromatic, *L. stoechas* is less cold-hardy than common lavender and is often treated as an annual in northern regions. Zones 7–10.

How to grow: Lavender needs a sunny site with good drainage and average soil. It is drought tolerant once established but must have excellent drainage to survive. Take stem cuttings to renew plants that are getting too woody. Prune regularly to promote bushy growth and remove winter damage.

Landscape uses: Plant in containers, borders, or rock gardens. Use low-growing cultivars to outline beds in herb gardens, and taller plants as specimens or as an herbal "hedge." Planting lavender along paths will allow garden visitors to brush against the plants and release their distinctive fragrance.

Harvesting: Dry the flowers for use in crafts such as potpourri, sachets, sleep pillows, and wreaths, or add them to herb teas. (To dry lavender, cut the stems when the flower spikes just begin to color up.) The fresh flowers add a beautiful, flavorful touch to salads, fruit dishes, and iced cakes, especially when used with other edible flowers such as nasturtiums.

LAWNS

Lush green lawns are a standard feature of yards large and small all across North America. Lawns have their good points and their drawbacks, too. A carpet of green grass adds a pleasing, unifying element to a landscape and makes a great place to play or relax. A nice-looking lawn can enhance the value of your home.

On the other hand, lawns are not low maintenance or very friendly to the environment. Taking steps to reduce the amount of lawn in your yard is one of the best ways to become a more "green" gardener. Eliminating lawn saves water, since keeping lawn grasses green requires from two to four times more water than groundcovers or other landscape plants need for good growth. Watering lawns can be a major drain on precious water resources in arid climates. Keeping grass mowed and trimmed uses precious fuel, contributes greenhouse gasses to the atmosphere, and simply takes time. Finally, a well-tended lawn requires fertilizing, pest control, and other time-consuming care.

Reducing Lawn Maintenance

While you probably don't want to eliminate every square inch of lawn, there are steps you can take to reduce the size of your lawn and to cut down on the amount of maintenance it requires. Start by evaluating how much lawn you need and want. Lawn is an ideal surface for play areas for children, adults, and dogs, and it is also a good choice for relaxing, barbecuing, and other activities. Then

Don't Fight the Moss

If you have an area under mature trees where moss seems to be the only thing that will grow, celebrate it instead of fighting it. After all, it's green and lush, and it doesn't need watering, mowing, or trimming. It never needs fertilizer, since it absorbs nutrients directly from the air and rainwater. It's a zero fossil-fuel proposition. If there isn't any moss growing naturally in your yard, you can find specialty companies that sell moss starter kits.

use the tips below to eliminate lawn on sites where it isn't essential and reduce maintenance on sites where you want to keep your lawn.

- Consider the size and shape of your lawn. Rounded shapes with curved edges are most pleasing to look at, and they also can be mowed in a series of continuous loops, making them quickest and easiest to mow.

- Replace lawn under and around trees and shrubs with beds of groundcovers or mulch.

- Use groundcovers, not lawn, in awkward, hard-to-mow corners.

- Cover slopes and other difficult-to-mow sites with groundcovers or shrubs.

- Eliminate lawn on shady sites, where it does not grow well. Replace it with shade-loving groundcovers, perennials, or shrubs.

- Replace aggressive old strains of lawn grass with improved cultivars or mixtures to increase disease resistance and adaptability.

Mowing Gets Reel

Grandpa did it, and during the energy crisis of the 1970s, lots of people tried mowing the old-fashioned way, with a person-powered reel mower. Modern reel mowers are things of precision and beauty, designed to cut smoothly and push easily. A good one may cost as much as a gas- or electric-powered mower but will repay your investment in energy savings and clean air.

Reel mowers are not for every lawn. They work best on relatively flat ground and can be difficult to use on sloped land. Do research and definitely try before you buy to make sure you are up to the physical requirements of pushing a reel mower's whirling cutting blades over the area covered by your lawn. If you can, go for it—it's good for you and for the environment. You'll feel closely in touch with your lawn, and you can even hear the birds. (And it may really give you the incentive to cut back on the lawn!)

🌾 Use edging strips spaced along the lawn to keep grasses from invading mulched areas as well as the flowerbeds.

🌾 Accept clovers as beneficial nitrogen-fixers in your lawn, not weeds.

🌾 During droughts, water modestly once a week. Provide sufficient water to keep your grass alive, but not enough to coax it out of heat-induced dormancy.

Maintaining Lawns

Whether your lawn is large or small, it needs regular care to look its best. The biggest time requirement is weekly mowing during the growing season, but lawn grass also requires regular feeding, edging, and other attention to stay green and healthy.

Mowing: Sharpen your mower blade at the beginning of each season to make sure the grass blades are cut, rather than torn, when you mow. Remove only one-third of the grasses' topgrowth each time you mow to keep grass healthy and vigorous. The best height for mowing depends on the species of grass, but in general, the higher you cut your grass, the deeper its roots will grow, increasing its tolerance of heat and drought. Cut low-growing grasses, such as Bermuda grass and zoysia grass, no shorter than 1 inch; 1½ inches is better. Cut taller grasses, such as bluegrass and tall fescue, no shorter than 2 inches; 2½ to 3 inches is better. Mow high during summer droughts. To cut very tall grass, set your mower blade at its highest setting. In the course of the next two mowings, lower the blade until you are cutting at the usual height.

If you mow regularly, let your grass clippings lie where they fall. They will eventually rot and add organic matter to the soil beneath. Large mats of cut grass sitting on your lawn block sunlight and promote disease. Rake them up and use as mulch in other parts of your yard or add them to the compost pile.

Fertilizing: The first step in growing a well-fed lawn is to use a mulching lawn mower and let nitrogen-rich grass clippings remain where they fall when cut. You'll also want to apply compost or other organic material to feed your grass. (Relying on high-nitrogen chemical fertilizers can lead to problem-prone, shallow-rooted turf that needs mowing more often.)

The most important thing to note is the time of year when the grass begins to grow rapidly. This is the ideal time to apply a good organic fertilizer. In the North, where cool-season grasses have a growth spurt in spring and another in fall, plan to fertilize twice. For warm-season grasses, fertilize in late spring, just as your lawn greens up, and again a few weeks later.

Choose a finely pulverized, weed-free organic fertilizer, such as processed manure or sifted compost, and spread evenly over the lawn just before rain is expected. Mow the grass about a week after you fertilize. For more ideas on what to feed your grass, see the Fertilizers entry. Corn gluten meal is a natural fertilizer that also prevents many types of weed seeds from germinating. To learn more about this double-duty substance, see the Weeds entry.

Dethatching: All lawns have thatch, a layer of clippings and stems that gradually decomposes and feeds the roots. There's no need to remove it if the layer is no thicker than about $\frac{1}{4}$ inch. Thatch problems often start with overuse of synthetic chemical fertilizers, which make grass grow fast and lush. As clippings build up into a thick layer of thatch, grass plants are unable to get enough air for healthy growth. Use a thatch rake to break up thatch in a small lawn; rent a vertical mower to dethatch a larger area.

Aerating: Since lawns often bear heavy foot traffic, the soil below them becomes compacted over time. Grass roots have trouble growing down and out and instead concentrate their growth at the surface. Prevent or fix compacted lawns by aerating every 2 to 3 years. Aerating a turf consists of poking tiny holes through the turf into the soil below. Use a step-on core cultivator for small areas; rent a power aerator machine for larger lawns. Mow the lawn and spread a thin layer of organic fertilizer. Aerate in one direction; repeat crosswise. Water deeply.

KEY WORDS *Lawns*

Cool-season grass. A grass that grows strongly in spring and fall, often remaining green in winter but tending to go dormant when the hot days of summer come. Examples: Kentucky bluegrass, fine fescues.

Warm-season grass. A grass that grows well in summer, even in hot, dry climates, and is usually dormant in winter. Examples: Bermuda grass, centipede grass, zoysia grass.

Stolon. A specialized stem that creeps below the surface of the soil, rooting and sprouting new plants along the way.

Sod. Strips of living grass that have been peeled, roots and all, from the soil.

Plugs. Small pieces of sod used to start a lawn of creeping types of grass such as zoysia grass. Plant plugs in scooped-out holes, 6 to 12 inches apart.

Sprigs. Pieces of rooted grass stem or stolon, extricated from shredded sod. Plant sprigs 6 inches apart to start a lawn of creeping types of grass.

Thatch. A layer of grass clippings and other dead plant parts that accumulates in a lawn.

Repairing Lawns

Ruts left by heavy vehicles or scars created when shrubs or trees are removed call for prompt spot repairs. If damage occurs in winter, prepare the soil and cover it with a mulch until spring.

Loosen the soil in the damaged site, setting aside any grass plants that seem healthy. Keep them damp and shaded as you work. Add a ½-inch layer of compost or other organic matter to condition the soil, along with enough good topsoil to raise the level of the damaged area 1 inch above the surrounding soil level, and fill in any holes or low places. Reseed or replant, matching the primary species in your yard. Water regularly for a month.

Planting New Lawns

Sometimes you will want to plant an area with lawn, such as around a newly laid patio area, or if you're moving into a newly built home that's surrounded by bare earth. To get your lawn off to the right start, choose grasses carefully to match your conditions.

Selecting Lawn Grasses

Build a strong lawn by using grass species adapted to your climate. Hybridizers are constantly introducing new cultivars that exhibit improved disease and pest resistance, as well as improved drought tolerance. These are some of the most widely grown lawn grasses.

- Bermuda grass (*Cynodon dactylon*), which is a fine-textured, drought-resistant grass popular in warmer climates. Becomes buff brown in winter. Numerous runners create a wear-resistant turf. Open-pollinated strains are extremely aggressive; modern hybrids are much easier to keep from invading flowerbeds.

- Buffalo grass (*Bouteloua dactyloides*), a creeping, warm-season grass. Tolerates drought and will grow in alkaline soil. Good wear tolerance. Brown in midsummer and fall.

- Centipede grass (*Eremochloa ophiuroides*), a coarser-leaved, warm-season, creeping grass with good drought tolerance. Plant in low-wear areas.

- Fine fescues (*Festuca* spp.), which is dark green, fine-textured, creeping, cool-season grasses with good shade tolerance, often mixed with Kentucky bluegrass.

- Kentucky bluegrass (*Poa pratensis*), a lush dark green turfgrass with narrow blades that requires substantial sunshine. Favored cool-season lawn grass. May become dormant during summer droughts or during winter freezes. Creeping stolons knit a tough turf.

- Turf-type tall fescue (*Schedonorus arundinaceus*), a coarse, medium green grass good for sun or shade, increasingly popular in the central United States. Updated cultivars remain green most of the year. Drought resistant. Grows in low clumps and doesn't creep, so is often mixed with other grasses.

- Zoysia grasses (*Zoysia* spp.), medium green, creeping, fine-textured grasses for full sun. Green in warm weather, tan in winter.

Seeding and Planting Lawns

All lawn grasses require at least 4 inches of good topsoil in which to stretch their roots. If your new yard has been scraped down to the subsoil, you will have to spread new topsoil. Site preparation is the same whether you plan to begin with seed or sod: Cultivate new or existing topsoil thoroughly, adding a 1-inch layer of compost or other organic

Reducing Power Consumption in the Garden

The lawn mower, the leaf blower, and the weed whacker add up to a noisy, fuel-hungry trio that many gardeners feel are a necessary evil. But have you calculated how much gasoline you use each year to maintain your home landscape? What can you do to reduce the use of power tools in the garden? Try these power-saving tips to use your lawn mower less and dispense with most of the other noisemakers.

Give up some of the lawn. How much lawn do you really need? Could some of it be groundcovers, perennial beds, or islands of mixed plantings (trees/shrubs/ perennials) surrounded by groundcovers or mulch? If the front has to have a manicured lawn, could the backyard have some mown paths, play areas, and the rest be meadow grasses or naturalized woodland plantings? Make a commitment to reduce the size of your lawn every growing season. As your lawn shrinks,

you'll have reduced the amount of fuel you use each time you mow.

Cut the grass taller. It's not just to get you out of the lawn-mowing habit, it's about healthy grass. Especially in the heat of summer, cutting a lawn short over and over stresses the plants. They have to put all that effort (with little water to fuel them) into growing up to reach the sunlight—and then here you come again! Taller lawns also have fewer weeds, since the grass itself denies the sunlight from ground-clinging weeds.

Sharpen the blades. Sharp blades and a tuned-up lawn mower cut more efficiently. Plus, dull blades leave uneven grass and make jagged cuts in the grass blades, permitting diseases to enter the plant tissue.

Stop watering your lawn in summer. That means less mowing because there is less growing. Turfgrass specialists have shown that in the Northeast, for instance,

matter. Rake out all weeds and roots, cultivate again, and rake smooth. Use a roller to evenly compact the site and make it level.

Seeding: Be picky when shopping for grass seed. Improved cultivars of the best lawn grasses cost more than their open-pollinated cousins, but they offer superior performance. Choose named cultivars that have been specially bred for drought tolerance, insect and disease resistance, or other traits. Use a mechanical seeder for even distribution. Roll after seeding and keep the site constantly moist for 2 weeks. Start mowing 3 weeks after seeding.

Laying sod: Sod is the fastest way to an attractive lawn, although the cost is higher than seed. It's ideal for spot repairs, especially in high-traffic areas or on slopes. Plant cool-season species in early spring or from late summer to early fall; plant warm-season grasses in late spring to early summer. Use only fresh, green strips. Keep them shaded and damp until planted. Groundcovers are the best choice for slopes, but if you decide to plant grass on a slope, be sure to work crosswise along the slope. Roll or walk on the strips after planting to push the roots into the soil. After planting, water every 2 to 3 days for 3 weeks.

most lawns can endure 6 weeks with only 1/4 inch of water and survive. Yes, they will turn brown. That's normal summer dormancy for many kinds of grasses. When fall rains arrive, the green returns.

Part with your string trimmer. If you plan your landscape carefully, with all its edges and obstacles, you can dispense with weed whacking altogether. String trimmers (and lawn mowers) are one of the causes of death for trees, anyway. (They don't do much for the furniture legs you bump, either, not to mention the perennials.) So keep the plants mulched, or surrounded by groundcovers, so you don't have to cut anywhere near the trunks.

Make easier edges. Two kinds of edges are sensible, easy to live with, and cut down on mowing time and weed cutting: flat stone edging and V-trenches. Pavers, bricks, or stones laid flat and placed at or just below the soil level allow mower wheels to ride right over them, so there's no tall edge of grass left that requires trimming with a weed whacker. A V-shaped trench with sides 3 to 5 inches deep and the opening 4 to 6 inches wide also serves well as an edging.

Let your shrubs meet. Instead of using a gas- or electric-powered hedge trimmer to carve shrubs into individual meatballs or gumdrops, and maintaining mulch-covered ground between them, let shrubs retain a more natural shape and grow together to cover the soil and eliminate those empty spaces. Not only will you reduce the amount of shearing plants require, once they grow together you won't have to mulch nearly as often. Underplanting with groundcovers also helps fill those empty gaps between shrubs.

Plugs and sprigs: Some types of lawn grasses—including rhizomatous warm-season grasses such as St. Augustine, zoysia, and centipede—are planted using plugs or sprigs, as well as sod. Plugs and sprigs are less expensive than sod, but you have to wait while they grow together to form a dense lawn. To use these, prepare the soil as you would for sod, and be sure to keep the plugs or sprigs moist and cool until they are planted. Plant plugs individually, in rows. Sprigs, which are the runners or stolons of the grass can also be planted in rows or they can be broadcast over the planting area and then individually pressed down into the soil surface. (You can buy sprigs by the bushel or tear up sheets of sod to make your own.) With both plugs and sprigs, it's important to keep the soil evenly moist, but not too wet, until they are established and growing actively. This can take 4 weeks or more.

Coping with Problems

A healthy lawn is naturally more resistant to weed, insect, or disease problems. A tight cover of vigorous grass will outcompete weeds. Loose, well-drained soil helps prevent disease problems. Proper fertilization goes a long way toward preventing lawn problems since it encourages growth of strong, healthy turf. Most updated turfgrass cultivars offer genetically improved resistance to diseases and some insects. If you have lawn areas that are chronically problematic, consider replanting them with an improved cultivar or trying an alternative to lawn grass. See the Groundcovers entry for suggestions of plants that work well as substitutes for lawns.

There are a few simple steps to take if your lawn develops weed or pest problems. Use a small, sharp knife to slice off any established weeds about 1 inch below the soil surface. If more than half of the plants in your lawn are weeds, it is best to renovate the lawn by replanting.

Subterranean insect larvae, such as white grubs, occasionally cause serious damage when they feed on grass roots. Apply milky disease spores for long-term control of these pests. Biological insecticides that utilize parasitic nematodes control numerous insects likely to feed beneath your lawn. For more ideas on reducing pests and diseases, see the Pests and the Plant Diseases and Disorders entries.

LAYERING

Layering is a way of propagating plants by encouraging sections of stems to sprout new roots. The rooted stems are cut from the mother plants and planted. This simple and reliable method produces good-sized new plants in a relatively short time.

Simple Layering

Simple layering involves bending a low-growing branch to the ground and burying several inches of stem. It is used to propagate many types of vines and woody plants, including grapes and magnolias.

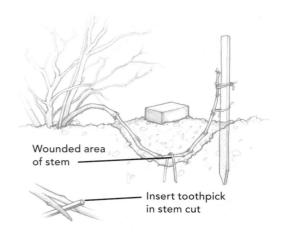

Wounded area of stem

Insert toothpick in stem cut

Simple layering. Pin a wounded stem in a trench and cover it with soil. Stake the exposed tip. A brick laid on the soil over the buried stem helps to retain moisture.

Season: Spring is the best time to start simple layers. Choose flexible, vigorous 1-year-old shoots about as thick as a pencil.

Getting started: Thoroughly water the soil around the plant. The next day, bend a shoot down to the soil. Measure back 9 to 12 inches from the top of the shoot, and mark the spot where that point on the stem touches the ground. Release the shoot, and dig a 4-inch hole at the marked point. Make sure that the side of the hole closest to the parent plant slopes gently to the hole's center. Work in several handfuls of finished compost.

Method: Remove leaves and side shoots along the chosen stem from 6 to 15 inches behind the stem tip. Wound the stem by making a shallow 2-inch-long cut at a point about 9 inches behind the tip. (Far enough away from the parent plant that it can be buried.) Insert a toothpick or small pebble in the cut to keep it open. Dust the cut with rooting hormone. Bend the prepared stem down into the hole, and use a wire pin to keep the wounded area in contact with the soil. Stake the stem tip if it doesn't stay upright by itself. Cover the pinned stem with the soil you removed earlier, and water the area thoroughly.

Aftercare: Keep the layered area moist and weeded. The stem may root by fall; check by uncovering the stem, removing the wire pin, and tugging lightly. If the stem feels firmly anchored, it has rooted. Sever it from the parent plant, but leave it in place until spring. Then pot it up or transplant it. If the stem is not well rooted, replace the soil and wait a year before separating it from the parent plant.

Tip Layering

Shoot tips of certain plants root when they touch the ground. This phenomenon, called tip layering, happens naturally in brambles.

Season: Plant tip layers in late summer, using the ends of the current season's growth. Make sure you use healthy, vigorous canes.

Getting started: Prepare a hole as you would for simple layers; judge the placement of the hole by the tip of the stem.

Method: Bend the stem tip down to the prepared planting hole. Lay the cane against the sloping side and place the tip against the farthest edge of the hole. Replace the soil, and water the area well.

Aftercare: Keep the soil moist to promote rooting. By early autumn, shoots will appear and roots will have formed; cut the original cane where it enters the soil. In mid-autumn or the following spring, carefully dig up the rooted tip, and plant it in its new position.

Air Layering

Air layering is similar to simple layering, but the stem is covered with long-fibered (unmilled)

sphagnum moss rather than soil. You can air-layer upright stems of trees, shrubs, and indoor plants such as philodendrons and weeping figs (*Ficus benjamina*).

Season: Outdoors, start air layers in early fall with young wood, or in spring with the previous season's growth. Indoors, air layers can be done any time, but it's best to start when plants begin growing actively in spring.

Getting started: Soak the sphagnum moss in water for a few hours or overnight. Before using, wring the excess water out of the moss so it is moist but not dripping wet.

Method: Start with a healthy, vigorous stem. Decide where you want the roots of the new plant to be, anywhere from 6 to 18 inches behind the tip. Remove all leaves and side shoots for 3 inches on

Air layering. Wound the stem and tuck a bit of moss into the wound. Wrap the remainder around the stem, and cover with plastic.

either side of that point. Wound the stem by making a shallow 2-inch-long cut into it. Dust the wounded area with rooting hormone and tuck a bit of moss into it. Wrap the ball of moist moss around the wound and tie it with string. Next, cover the moss ball with a piece of clear plastic about 6 inches square. For indoor plants, tie the plastic at both ends with string or twist ties. Use waterproof tape to secure the ends on outdoor air layers; make sure the ends are completely sealed. For outdoor plants, also cover the plastic wrap with foil or black plastic and tie or tape it to the stem; this will keep the layered area from getting too hot in the sun. If the moss looks dry during rooting, open the plastic, moisten the moss, and reseal.

Aftercare: Indoor plants can produce roots in a few months; outdoor plants may take one or two growing seasons. You'll be able to see the roots growing in the moss. Cut off the top of the plant below the new roots and remove the plastic. Soak the rootball for 3 to 4 hours, pot it up, and place it in a sheltered spot for a few days. Let outdoor plants grow in their pots for a few months before planting them out.

LEEK

Allium porrum
Amaryllidaceae

The sweetest and most delicately flavored of all onions, leeks are easy to grow. They are resistant to pests and diseases, and by planting a selection of varieties, you can harvest from late summer throughout winter. For winter harvest in cold-winter regions, be sure to plant one super-hardy variety like the heirloom 'Giant Musselburgh'.

Planting: Sow seeds indoors in flats 2 to 3 months before the last average frost. Keep them at a temperature of 65° to 70°F during the day and 55° to 60°F at night. When seedlings are 3 inches tall, thin to 1 inch apart; at 5 inches tall, thin to 2 inches apart.

Leeks love crumbly, rich loam, but they will do well in any well-prepared soil. When seedlings are about 8 inches tall, transplant to the garden, placing them in 6-inch-deep holes spaced 6 inches apart in rows at least 1½ feet apart. The tips of the plants should be just a few inches above the surface. Water the seedlings, and replace the soil loosely around the plants.

Growing guidelines: Keep the soil evenly moist, and feed with compost tea once a month during the growing season. (For instructions on making compost tea, see the Compost entry.) When leeks are pencil-size, bank soil or mulch around the lower 2 to 3 inches of stem; this will cause the edible part of the stem to elongate and develop a creamy white or pure white color. Many gardeners think that this blanching technique also improves the flavor of leeks.

Problems: See the Onion entry for insect and disease controls.

Harvesting: Leeks take 70 to 110 days to mature; their flavor is best after a light frost. Dig leeks as needed. To protect them from hard freezes, cover them with clear plastic supported by wire hoops or with a thick layer of mulch. Leeks will keep a few weeks if refrigerated; to store them longer, pack them in a box with moist soil and store in a cool, dry place. Use leeks in any recipe that calls for a delicate onion flavor.

LETTUCE

Lactuca sativa
Asteraceae

Lettuce greens are so easy to grow, so nutritious, and so delicious picked fresh from the garden that everyone should grow them. Grow lettuce in the vegetable garden, tuck it into flowerbeds, or cultivate it in containers. With regular watering, shade from hot sun, and succession planting, you can enjoy homegrown lettuce almost year-round in much of the country.

Types: Home gardeners can choose from dozens of different cultivars, each with its own special flavor, appearance, and texture.

Cabbagelike crisphead, or iceberg, lettuce stands up to hot weather and ships well; it is the old standby in stores. It also has the thickest, crunchiest leaves of any lettuce. Iceberg lettuce is the least nutritious type, but like all lettuce, it is a good source of dietary fiber. After years of being dismissed as worthless, iceberg lettuce has undergone a renaissance among chefs, so you're as likely to encounter an iceberg wedge with house-made blue cheese dressing in a restaurant as a salad of spring greens or mesclun mix.

The crunchy, spoon-shaped leaves of romaine, or cos, lettuce are much more nutritious. In addition to being heat tolerant and easy to grow, the big-leaved types also produce crisp, white hearts that can substitute for celery. Romaine is the traditional choice for Caesar salads. Red-leaved and red-speckled romaine lettuces are especially beautiful in salads. Because romaine lettuce is both crunchy and nutritious, it's a great choice for sandwiches.

Butterhead, or Boston, lettuce has soft, tender, rich green outer leaves and white to yellowish hearts. It is also high in nutrition, and its taste and texture are excellent. Many butterheads, particularly the quick-maturing cultivars, require cool weather and an excellent soil to produce well.

Fast-growing, nutritious leaf lettuce tolerates much warmer temperatures than head lettuce.

Most cultivars have loose, open growth habits and leaves that range from smooth to frilly. Harvest the outer leaves of leaf lettuces, and the plants will grow new ones for later picking, or pull entire heads at once.

Lettuces sold as spring mix or mesclun mix are typically blends of several loose-leaf cultivars that are harvested when they're just a few inches tall. You can find many different combinations available from seed companies, or mix your own favorites for a signature blend. Mesclun also typically features a few spicier greens like radicchio and mustard. See the Salad Greens entry for more about mesclun.

Planting: Lettuce needs a humus-rich, moisture-retentive, but well-drained soil with plenty of nitrogen.

Broadcast the seeds and rake lightly to cover them, or sow seeds ¼ inch apart and as thinly as possible in rows 6 inches apart. A small seed packet will plant a 100-foot row and produce some 80 heads, or about 50 pounds of leaf lettuce. Germination rate is over 80 percent.

Although lettuce is primarily considered a cool-season crop, it is possible to extend the harvest with some careful planning. If you're a real lettuce lover, try the following schedule.

1. Start romaine, iceberg, or other head lettuces indoors 4 to 6 weeks before your last frost date, making three small sowings at weekly intervals. Set out the seedlings successively as soon as the ground is workable. At the same time, direct-seed leaf lettuce outdoors at 2-week intervals. If the soil temperature is at least 35°F, germination should take place in 6 to 12 days. If you plan to harvest only outer leaves as the plants grow, or harvest the crop for spring mix or mesclun, you can sow the

entire loose-leaf crop at once. Choose cold-tolerant cultivars for spring planting (you can find them individually or as a "cool-season mix" or "winter mix" of cultivars from many seed companies).

2. As the weather warms, plant heat-resistant cultivars (you can find them individually or as a "warm-season mix" of cultivars from many seed companies). If you place them in shady areas and give them adequate water, they are less likely to bolt and go to seed during hot spells. You can also cover the lettuce bed with floating row cover to shade it, but leave the ends (and, preferably, the sides) open for air circulation. If the earth is very warm, try presprouting the seeds to get better germination. Place the seeds on wet blotting paper or mix them with a little damp peat moss and perlite; store in the refrigerator for 5 days before sowing.

3. In midsummer, switch back to head or romaine types, making successive sowings—again, in shady areas—for a fall harvest that can last until frost. In milder climates, cover immature heads with cloches to prolong the harvest; in cold-winter areas, transplant a few heads into pots and let them continue growing in a greenhouse or sunny window. You can also sow cold-tolerant loose-leaf lettuces as you did in spring, keeping the bed evenly moist and shaded until outdoor temperatures cool down. If you have a cold frame or a greenhouse with an in-ground bed, you can continue sowing lettuce, extending the season even further.

Growing guidelines: When the seedlings have four leaves, thin head or romaine lettuce to 12 to 16 inches apart. Do the same for leaf lettuce unless you plan to harvest entire plants instead of leaves; in that case, 4-inch spacing is adequate. Thin butterheads to 3 to 5 inches apart.

Lettuce is 90 percent water and has very shallow roots, so keep the soil surface moist but not soggy. Make sure the crop gets at least 1 inch of water a week from rain or irrigation; otherwise, leaves can be thin and bitter, and the plants might bolt to seed. To help prevent disease, try to water on sunny mornings, so the leaves can dry by evening. After a good rain or watering, apply a thick layer of mulch to conserve moisture, suffocate weeds around the easily damaged roots, and keep lettuce leaves free of dirt. To promote quick growth, side-dress with compost or fish emulsion once or twice during the growing season.

Just before bolting, lettuce plants start to elongate and form a bitter sap. To keep this from happening, pinch off the top center of the plant. Pull up and discard any plant that goes to seed. If you are a seed saver, wait and save seeds from the last plants to bolt, since quickness to bolt is a bad trait. Seed savers should also be aware that different lettuce cultivars can cross with each other and with wild lettuce, so next year's plants may not come true from your saved seed.

Problems: The most likely pests are aphids, cutworms, and slugs. For details on controlling these pests, see page 454 and the Slugs and Snails entry.

Soggy soil and crowded plants can encourage bottom rot, a disease that turns lettuce plants black and foul-smelling. There are only a few varieties that are resistant to this disease, which has spores that can persist for years in the soil. If you've had problems with bottom rot, choose varieties with an upright form rather than a spreading form, and try planting your lettuce plants on 4-inch-tall ridges of soil. Be careful to avoid wetting the leaves when you water.

Gray mold makes grayish green or dark brown spots on lower leaves and is usually brought on by damp, overcast weather. Injured seedlings are particularly vulnerable. Pull up any infected plant and dispose of it far from the garden.

Harvesting: Pick lettuce in the morning to preserve the crispness it acquires overnight. Watch your crop closely, as mature plants deteriorate quickly. To test the firmness of heading types, press down gently on lettuce hearts with the back of your hand; don't pinch them, as this can bruise the hearts. Use a sharp knife to cut heads below the lowest leaves, or pull plants out by the roots. Harvest leaf types as needed. Lettuce tastes best when eaten fresh but will keep up to 2 weeks when refrigerated.

LIATRIS

Blazing star, gayfeather. Summer-blooming perennials.

Description: Blazing stars bear small, shaggy flowers in white, pink, purple, or magenta along dense spikes from a few inches long to 2 feet or more. Plants have grasslike leaves. *Liatris aspera*, rough blazing star, grows 4 to 6 feet. *L. spicata*, spike blazing star, is the best blazing star for gardens, rarely exceeding 3 feet; its best-known cultivar, 'Kobold', bears dense spikes of mauve flowers that make good cut flowers. Zones 3–8.

How to grow: Plant or divide (infrequently) in spring in a sunny spot with average, moist but well-drained soil. Blazing stars tolerate both drought and excess moisture in summer, but standing water in winter is fatal.

Landscape uses: Feature small groups of the native American perennial in a border or a meadow or prairie garden. It is also fine for the cutting garden. Tone down magenta blazing stars with pale

yellow, medium blue, and cream flowers. They also work well with ornamental grasses.

LIGUSTRUM

Privet, ligustrum. Deciduous or evergreen shrubs or small trees.

Description: Privets were once popular as hedging plants, and they're still found in many backyards. Unfortunately, though, the black berries that these shrubs produce are relished by birds, which spread the plants into wild areas. Many species of privets have been identified as invasive, because once they're established in the wild, privets outcompete native species. Responsible gardeners no longer plant privet.

Species now identified as invasive in at least one state include *Ligustrum amurense*, Amur privet, an upright deciduous shrub reaching 15 feet tall, and *L. obtusifolium*, border privet, a 10- to 12-foot shrub. Both are hardy in Zones 4–7. *L. vulgare*, common privet, *L. sinense*, Chinese privet, and *L. ovalifolium*, California privet, also have been identified as weedy or invasive in some states. Consult your local extension office to learn which species are problematic in your area.

How to grow: Privets are able to grow in a variety of soils, climates, and light levels, but they do require good drainage. One reason Amur and border privets are popular is that they can be planted bareroot, which is cost-effective when many plants are needed, as with a hedge. Shear formal privet hedges during the growing season to keep them tidy. Informal hedges may need occasional rejuvenation pruning; tree forms may need pruning to open or shape them.

Landscape uses: Privets are useful for hedges, but responsible gardeners should consider less-invasive options.

LILAC

See *Syringa*

LILIUM

Lily. Late-spring- to late-summer-blooming perennial bulbs.

Description: Lilies have 3- to 12-inch, usually bowl- or trumpet-shaped flowers in white, pink, red, yellow, orange, lilac, and green, many dotted in maroon or near black. Plants bear a few to two dozen or more blooms on 2- to 7-foot stems with narrow leaves. Most lilies are hardy in Zones 3–8 or 4–8. Give winter protection in the North, especially during the first winter.

There are three major groups of hybrid lilies. By choosing some cultivars from each group, you can have lilies blooming all summer. The early-summer-blooming Asiatics normally grow 2 to 4 feet and bear bowl- or cup-shaped, 3- to 5-inch flowers in nearly the entire color range. The summer-blooming trumpets and Aurelians grow 4 to 7 feet, producing large clusters of trumpet- to bowl-shaped, often fragrant, 4- to 6-inch blooms in all colors but bright red. Last to bloom in late summer are the spicily fragrant 3- to 6-foot Orientals in the white-pink-red range, some with distinct yellow stripes; blooms may be 1 foot wide and almost flat.

Besides the popular hybrid lilies, there are many beautiful species. *Lilium candidum*, Madonna lily, features pure white, lightly fragrant blooms in summer on 2- to 4-foot stalks. *L. regale*, regal lily, bears fragrant white flowers on majestic 4- to 6-foot stalks in summer; flowers have wine red shading on the outside. *L. speciosum*, showy lily, bears 15 to 30 fragrant flowers on 4- to 5-foot stalks in late summer; flowers are white, flushed pink, with pink or red spots. *L. superbum*, Turk's-cap lily, bears 20 to 40 nodding flowers on 4- to 7-foot stalks in late summer; flowers are orange-red and spotted.

How to grow: Lilies thrive in sun or partial shade in deep, fertile, moist but well-drained, humus-rich soil out of strong winds. Lilies never go completely dormant, so plant the fragile bulbs carefully soon after you receive them. Fall planting is best. Prepare the soil to 1½ feet deep and mulch the site heavily to keep the soil unfrozen and ready for planting in very late fall, which is when many dealers ship. Most lilies produce roots along the belowground part of their stems; therefore, plant the bulbs with no less than 6 inches of soil above the top of the bulb. (Madonna lilies are the exception; they need just 1 inch of soil.) Mark the site to avoid injuring emerging shoots in spring.

Mulch with several inches of compost or finely shredded bark to keep the soil cool. Water during dry spells and douse with compost tea or fish emulsion monthly from late spring to early fall. See the Compost entry for instructions for making compost tea. Stake tall lilies and deadhead after bloom. After the tops die, cut the stems to a few inches above the ground.

Aphids spread devastating viral diseases; dig and destroy any plants with yellow-streaked or deformed leaves or dramatically stunted growth. Many gardeners in New England have given up trying to grow lilies because of an invasion of lily leaf beetles, a pest accidentally introduced from Europe. These small red beetles and their sluglike larvae feed on lily leaves, stems, and flowers. Scientists are testing a parasitic wasp as a control measure; handpicking is the only other feasible control.

Deer and woodchucks relish lilies; see the Animal Pests entry for control measures.

Landscape uses: Plant specimens or groups throughout borders and lightly shaded areas such as open woodlands. Some of the larger, more robust lilies grow happily near shrubs if given a few feet of their own space.

LIRIOPE

Liriope, lilyturf. Evergreen perennial ground-covers.

Description: *Liriope muscari*, big blue lilyturf, and *L. spicata*, creeping lilyturf, form dense, dark green mats of tufted, grasslike leaves. Big blue lilyturf is taller, with clumps 1 to 1½ feet wide and leaves ½ inch wide and 2 feet long. The showy, violet-blue blossoms resemble grape hyacinths and bloom from July to September. The flower spikes rise above the leaves. Shiny black berries persist through winter. The narrow leaves of creeping lilyturf measure ¼ inch across and 8 to 12 inches long. Flowers are pale lavender to white, with black berries appearing after the late-summer blossoms have faded. Unlike big blue lilyturf, the leaves of creeping lilyturf turn yellow and are unsightly through winter. Creeping lilyturf also has been designated as invasive in some states: Consult your extension service to see if it is a problem in your area. Both species are hardy in Zones 6–10.

How to grow: Liriopes can grow in deep shade to full sun in rich, acid, well-drained but moist soil. However, they prefer filtered sunlight in protected locations. Plants are tolerant of drought and salt spray. Add leaf mold or other organic matter to your soil if it isn't humus rich. Divide clumps in spring or fall and plant them 1 foot apart. In late fall, mow or clip back plants to encourage new growth.

Landscape uses: Liriopes are excellent groundcovers for difficult locations, including seashore areas. They are also attractive along paths, around the edges of flower gardens, and in rock gardens.

LOBELIA

Lobelia. All-season annual and midsummer- to early-fall-blooming perennials and wildflowers.

Description: *Lobelia erinus*, edging or bedding lobelia, produces intricate blooms in shades of white, red-violet, and blue (many with a striking white "eye"). These annual plants produce spreading clumps to 6 inches or trailing forms that may reach a few feet long by the end of the season. Small leaves often assume rich bronzy purple shades.

Perennial *L. cardinalis*, cardinal flower, bears brilliant red flowers on long spikes above unbranched to more bushy plants reaching 3 to 4 feet. Rich green leaves provide a sharp contrast. Zones 2–9. *L. siphilitica*, great blue lobelia, grows 2 to 3 feet tall with spikes of pure blue flowers. Zones 4–8. Hybrid cardinal flower, *L. ×speciosa*, also grows 2 to 3 feet tall with flowers in shades of red, blue, or purple, sometimes with bronze foliage. Zones 3 (with protection) and 4–9.

How to grow: Start edging lobelia from seed indoors in late winter in the North or sow directly farther south. Provide full sun in cooler areas and part shade in warmer areas to prolong bloom. Grow in average, moist but well-drained soil. A light mulch is also beneficial.

Plant or divide cardinal flowers and great blue lobelia every few years in spring or after bloom. They prefer a partially shaded spot (full sun in the North if soil is constantly moist) in average to rich, moist to wet, humus-rich soil. Water freely in summer if they're in a traditional border setting.

Mulch in summer with bark or chips; replace with straw or hay in winter in the North. Zones 2–5.

Landscape uses: Mass edging lobelia at the front of borders, along paths, and in pots, especially cascading types. Feature a clump of cardinal flower, hybrid cardinal flower, or great blue lobelia in a moist border or naturalize by a stream or pond. Hummingbirds especially love the brilliant red spikes of cardinal flowers—they're must-have plants for the hummingbird garden.

LOBULARIA

Sweet alyssum. Long-season annuals.

Description: *Lobularia maritima*, sweet alyssum, is a creeping annual that bears clusters of fragrant, tiny white, rose, peach, or purple flowers atop spreading, 4-inch cushions of small, narrow leaves.

How to grow: Sow seeds thinly in spring where they are to grow, indoors 8 weeks before frost, or start with transplants. Just press seeds onto the soil surface, since light is necessary for germination. Pick a sunny or lightly shaded spot with well-drained, average soil. Make later sowings or shear plants in midsummer to extend bloom into fall. Plants withstand heat and drought. They also self-sow.

Landscape uses: Edge a path or bed with one or more colors, or use them to fill in between paving stones and along walls. Or use them to soften the edge of a pot or window box. Plant sweet alyssum where you can enjoy its delightful fragrance. Its multiple small flowers and long season of bloom make it an inviting food source for bees and other pollinators and for tiny beneficial insects; tuck a few plants into corners of your vegetable garden to support your local beneficials.

LOCAL FOOD MOVEMENT

Choosing to buy and eat locally produced food is one of the best-publicized suggestions for helping to reduce our carbon footprint. The logic is easy to follow: Buying and eating spinach, lettuce, or tomatoes grown by a local farmer is a green choice because it saves the fossil fuel cost of shipping that produce from across the country (or across the world).

Shopping at a farmers' market or subscribing to a local CSA (community-supported agriculture) farm are great green choices, but the greenest choice of all is to start growing some of your own food. No matter where you live—city, suburbs, or country—your green gardening efforts should start with a vegetable garden or berry patch. Convert some of your lawn to a vegetable garden (which will also cut down on the need to use fossil fuel for mowing). If you don't have a garden space, grow veggies and small fruits in containers on your patio or deck. Urban gardeners may be able to grow food crops on the rooftop or in a community garden. Choose something you love to eat, and get started!

Even if you need only a small garden to feed yourself, you don't have to stop your food gardening efforts there. Call a local food bank in your area and ask if it accepts donations of fresh seasonal produce. Or join with other gardeners to start a local chapter of Plant a Row for the Hungry, a national program of the Garden Writers Association that encourages home gardeners to set aside a row in their gardens and commit to donate the food from that row to a food pantry or other local agencies working to alleviate hunger. It's a satisfying and worthwhile way to combine your green gardening efforts with service to your community.

Go Local and Seasonal

It's relatively easy to add more seasonal foods to your diet by finding out what's in season where you live and including those ingredients in your meals. Visit localharvest.org for a list of foods available near you during any season.

Here are some additional ways to eat more locally and seasonally:

1. **Garden.** Food doesn't get more local or seasonal than when it grows in your backyard. Even growing a small amount of food gets you in touch with the changing seasons. And gardening doesn't have to end when the weather cools. You can grow cool-season crops in many climates by installing simple protection devices, such as hoop tunnels or cold frames.

2. **Shop at the farmers' market, join a CSA, or buy a farm share.** Farmers' markets, community supported agriculture programs, and meat and dairy shares are excellent ways to get to know farmers, connect to where your food comes from, and naturally evolve your diet throughout the seasons.

3. **Visit U-pick farms.** Want buckets of berries or fruit for a fraction of the typical grocery store cost? Visit pickyourown.org to find a nearby U-pick farm where you can harvest fruit yourself and pay by the pound. You'll get to know different fruit seasons well; you may even count down the days to blueberry season.

4. **Forage.** Foraging doesn't have to be scary or overwhelming. From wild berries to fresh dandelion greens, food grows all around us. Find a local foraging class and invest in a field guide to start learning about wild food sources. If you're so inclined, hunting is another way to eat locally.

5. **Learn to cook seasonally.** Fortunately, more restaurants and food companies are dedicated to sourcing foods locally and seasonally. However, most don't. Cooking is the best way to take advantage of the bounty of seasonal food. When you use fresh, seasonal ingredients, you'll be amazed at how delicious homemade meals taste. Different cooking methods are appropriate in different seasons. For instance, raw salads make more sense in summer than winter. Rely more on warming food preparation methods in cold months and cooling methods in warm months.

6. **Learn simple preservation methods.** Seasonal eating doesn't mean only eating what's growing outside at a certain time. People around the world have been using methods to preserve crops for thousands of years. By freezing, dehydrating, and storing crops in proper conditions, you can eat local food for several months after harvest without investing in a root cellar or canning equipment. Many crops, such as nuts, winter squash, beans, onions, garlic, and potatoes, can simply be stored in jars or ventilated boxes in a cold basement or unheated room. Ambitious preservers may want to investigate other methods, including canning, smoking, dry salting, pickling, and fermenting.

You'll find Web sites that can help you eat locally and seasonally in Resources on page 673.

Eating Seasonally

Hand in hand with the idea of eating locally is the practice of eating seasonally. Not so very long ago, this was the norm, before refrigerated trucks stocked our supermarket shelves year-round with fresh produce from across the globe. However, there are many reasons to choose seasonal foods. Eating seasonally helps you eat healthier, more nutritious food and be more in sync with the natural world. Seasonal eating usually is better for the environment than the standard American diet, because foods grown locally require less energy and resources to produce and transport. And eating seasonally helps support the local or regional economy.

Even with all the benefits, adopting a diet that more closely reflects the seasons can be a challenge when imported strawberries and cucumbers tempt us year-round at the grocery store. But you don't need to eschew all of your favorite imported or exotic foods (think coffee, for example). Even a modest transition to more local and seasonal foods can have a positive effect on your health and that of the planet.

Here are some of the advantages of eating seasonally.

- There are health advantages to sourcing food as locally as possible and adapting your diet to reflect local seasons. That's because the foods in season within your own region can help your body adapt to the environment.

- Eating seasonally encourages people to eat a wider variety of nutritious foods. Although there are 80,000 edible plant species, very few are included in the modern, industrialized diet. Globally, only 30 plant species make up 95 percent of the calories people eat. Within those 30 species, we eat far fewer varieties of vegetables and fruits than our ancestors did because our industrial agricultural system relies primarily on fruit and vegetable types that produce large yields and

LONICERA

Honeysuckle. Deciduous, semievergreen, or evergreen shrubs or vines.

Description: Most honeysuckles are deciduous (some are semievergreen or evergreen) shrubs or vines. While they are valued for their sweetly fragrant and showy, trumpet-shaped, 1- to 3-inch flowers, some are invasive plants that spread by twining vines and/or seed (via birds eating the berries, which appear in late summer or fall). The shrubs have loose upright or rounded growth habits. Honeysuckles have opposite, roundish leaves that range in color from dark green through blue-green to apple green.

Lonicera ×*brownii*, Brown's honeysuckle, is a vining honeysuckle that looks and behaves much like its parent, *L. sempervirens*, but it is more cold-tolerant. It has red or orange-red flowers and blooms summer through fall. Zones 3–9.

L. fragrantissima, winter honeysuckle, is a 6- to 10-foot, open, semievergreen shrub that is invasive hold up well during long-distance transport and long-term storage. These are not necessarily the most nutritious types. Moreover, these crops lose nutrition during long-distance transport and storage, even when temperature and humidity are carefully controlled.

- Getting more produce from local sources is an excellent way to eat a more diverse range of nutritious crops because home gardeners and small farmers can select fruit and vegetable types based on optimum nutrient content. Foods grown close to home typically retain the most nutrients because they're handled minimally and eaten quickly after harvest.

- Seasonal produce is nearly always more flavorful than produce that's shipped long distances. Small, local farmers can make flavor a high priority when deciding which vegetable and fruit varieties to grow. And the shorter distance to market translates to more flavor: Anyone who's eaten a store-bought tomato in January and a sun-ripened one in August has tasted the difference.

- Eating seasonally can also be more affordable than relying exclusively on the grocery store. Purchasing the freshest, tastiest, and most nutritious food available is also relatively inexpensive at farm stands and farmers' markets. Farmers' markets sometimes get a bad rap as being elitist and expensive. However, in studies done in four different regions, the produce at farmers' markets was the same price or less expensive than it was in grocery stores.

- When you buy food locally, more of your dollars stay in your community. According to the Farmers' Market Coalition, for every $100 you spend at a farmers' market, $62 remain in your local economy and $99 remain in your state.

in a few states. Plants bear fragrant white blooms before the leaves in very early spring. Zones 5–9.

L. ×*heckrottii*, goldflame honeysuckle, is an outstanding, evergreen or semievergreen vine, reaching 10 to 20 feet long. It has blue-green leaves and bears abundant, slightly fragrant flowers that are magenta with yellow interiors. Plants flower in late spring and summer. Zones 4–9.

L. maackii, Amur honeysuckle, is a large (10 to 15 feet), rangy, upright deciduous shrub that is invasive in many states. In late spring, plants bear fragrant flowers that open white, then turn yellow. Birds spread the plant when they eat its red fall fruit. Zones 3–8.

L. morrowii, Morrow honeysuckle, another widely invasive species, is a 6- to 8-foot, rounded deciduous shrub with bluish green foliage. In late spring, plants bear fragrant flowers that open white and turn yellow. Birds spread the plant when they eat its showy red berries. Zones 5–8.

L. nitida, boxleaf honeysuckle, is a dense shrub to 6 feet with small, shiny, dark green leaves that

A Hazardous Honeysuckle

Japanese honeysuckle (*Lonicera japonica*) is the most invasive of the honeysuckle clan. Plants bear dark green foliage and fragrant blooms from June to September. Flowers open white and turn yellow. This familiar roadside honeysuckle is decorative in bloom, but be warned: It requires vigorous pruning to keep it in bounds. Escaped plants easily cover fields, roadsides, and the edges of woods, smothering local vegetation. This species has been declared an invasive pest in more than 30 states. Instead of adding this potentially troublesome vine to your yard, pick another vining honeysuckle such as trumpet honeysuckle, *L. sempervirens*, a well-behaved native alternative.

are nearly evergreen. The fragrant flowers are inconspicuous and are followed by dark blue fruit. It is useful for hedges. Zones 6–9.

L. pileata, privet honeysuckle, is very similar to boxleaf honeysuckle, but has a prostrate habit and can be used as a groundcover. Zones 6–9.

L. sempervirens, trumpet honeysuckle, is a native, semievergreen to evergreen twining vine that grows to 20 feet long. The showy, scarlet and yellow-orange flower clusters bloom in summer and are followed by bright red berries in fall. Zones 4–9.

L. tatarica, Tatarian honeysuckle, is a large (10 to 12 feet), upright deciduous shrub that is widely invasive. It bears blue-green foliage and red, pink, or white flowers that are not fragrant. Birds spread

the plant by eating the red fall berries. Zones 3–8.

How to grow: Honeysuckles transplant easily. Plant in good, well-drained soil in full or partial sun. They tolerate a range of soil types and pH. Prune after flowering by cutting the oldest wood to the ground and gently shaping the shrub. If plants have become overgrown, cut to the ground and allow them to resprout.

Landscape uses: Use shrub honeysuckles as hedges and screens, or as part of a shrub border. Use the vines to cover banks, fences, walls, or arbors. Remember that they require a support to twine around.

LUPINUS

Lupine. Late-spring- to early-summer-blooming annuals and perennials.

Description: Perennial *Lupinus* 'Russell Hybrids' are the most widely grown lupines, bearing spectacular spikes of pealike flowers in a wide color range to 4 feet above large clumps of palmlike leaves. Zones 3–6. *L. texensis* and *L. subcarnosus*, Texas bluebonnets, are native annuals that produce spikes of blue flowers on plants to about 1 foot.

How to grow: Set out nursery-grown perennials in spring, or start seeds in late winter to plant out after frost. Grow in full sun to partial shade in moist but well-drained, acid, humus-rich soil. Lupines need cool summers and grow poorly in hot, humid summers and dry soil. Direct-sow annuals onto a sunny site with average to less fertile soil.

Landscape uses: Mass hybrids in borders. Annual lupines look best in natural settings such as meadow and prairie gardens.

M

MAGNOLIA

Magnolia. Evergreen or deciduous, single- or multitrunked flowering trees and shrubs.

Description: Few plants rival the dramatic beauty of the American South's magnolias in bloom. Available in a wide variety of sizes, shapes, and flower colors, magnolias have alternate, usually glossy foliage and gray bark; large, softly fuzzy, silver-gray buds form in summer for the following year's bloom.

Magnolia grandiflora, southern magnolia or bull bay, is a native evergreen with leathery and glossy green leaves and waxy white, heavily fragrant flowers. It is pyramidal in form and attains heights of 50 to 75 feet in the landscape, 100 feet in nature. Dwarf cultivars, to 20 feet, also are available. The flowers can be as wide as 15 inches; they bloom abundantly in late spring and sporadically through summer. Conelike seedpods form in summer and fall, splitting open to reveal bright red seeds that fall out and hang from threads. Zones 6–9.

M. ×*soulangeana*, saucer magnolia, is a mul-tistemmed, deciduous tree or shrub that grows to 25 feet. The flowers bloom in shades of pink and magenta in spring before the dark green leaves appear. Zones 5–8.

M. stellata, star magnolia, is a small (6 to 12 feet), deciduous, multistemmed shrub that produces white flowers in early spring before the leaves. The blossoms are composed of several long, strap-shaped petals that give a starlike effect. Leaves are 2 to 4 inches long and dark green above with lighter green undersides. Zones 4–8.

M. virginiana, sweet bay magnolia, is a semievergreen, multistemmed, native tree that has an upright, open, loose habit. The leathery, oblong leaves are dull green with silvery white undersides. Small white flowers are waxy and fragrant, appearing in a flush in late spring, then sporadically through summer. Seedpods resemble those of southern magnolia. Zones 6–9.

How to grow: With the exception of sweet bay, which benefits from the light shade of taller trees, magnolias perform best in full sun. Choose a site with humusy, well-drained soil with even moisture. Pest problems are minimal. Spring frosts frequently ruin the flowers of star and saucer magnolias; avoid giving these early bloomers a southern exposure that encourages premature bud break. Star magnolia is prone to suckering shoots that grow up through the plant and detract from its structure; remove them. Prune immediately after flowering before buds are set for the next year's bloom. Some gardeners object to the deep shade cast by southern magnolia and the difficulty of growing anything amid its shade, surface roots, and slow-to-decompose old leaves.

Landscape uses: Use magnolias in groups, for naturalizing, or as specimens. Star magnolia is especially useful in small-scale situations.

MALUS

Crabapple. Deciduous spring-flowering trees or shrubs.

Description: Hybrid cultivars of crabapples are far more common in gardens than the species. Plants bear pink or white flowers and red or yellow fruit. Hybrids with weeping or upright forms along with standard or dwarf habits are available. Many hybrids feature outstanding disease resistance. This genus also includes apples; you'll find more information on culture, pruning, and pest control in the Apple entry.

Malus floribunda, Japanese flowering crabapple, is a shrub or tree with a broad, arching form and a mature height of about 25 feet. The flowers are deep red in bud, opening rose; the fruits are yellow. Zones 4–7.

M. hupehensis, tea crabapple, is a vase-shaped tree that grows 25 feet tall. Fragrant flowers are pink in bud, opening white, and heavy in alternate years. Fruit is greenish yellow with a reddish blush. Zones 4–7.

M. sargentii, Sargent crabapple, is a shrub or small tree that grows about 6 feet tall. Gnarled with age (and possibly thorny), this plant grows wider than tall and produces pink flower buds that open white. It tends to flower heavily in alternate years. The fruits are red. Zones 4–7.

M. sieboldii, toringo or toringa crabapple, is an arching shrub that grows about 12 feet tall. Flowers are pink in bud, fading to white when open; fruits are red to yellow-brown. Zones 4–7.

How to grow: Give crabapples full sun and well-drained, evenly moist, acid soil. Prune to remove dead wood any time; prune in winter (when you can get a good look at the tree's structure) for watersprouts and crossing or rubbing branches. Do shaping and size-reduction pruning when flowering finishes and before the next year's flower buds are set in June or July.

Fire blight, apple scab, and cedar-apple rust are common crabapple problems. Fire blight, a bacterial disease, spreads to trees when they are in bloom. Infected blossoms shrivel and turn brown; later, young branches turn black and wilt into a characteristic cane-handle shape. Olive green spots on the undersides of leaves are the first signs of apple scab. Spots on upper leaf surfaces and blossoms and corky "scabs" on fruit follow as this fungus progresses. Cedar-apple rust is a fungus that needs both *Malus* and *Juniperus* "cedar" species to complete its life cycle. On crabapples, it causes yellow spots that turn orange on leaves and fruits. All three of these diseases disfigure flowering crabapples, often defoliating trees and causing gradual decline. Avoid disease problems by planting resistant species and cultivars; exclude susceptible *Juniperus* species from *Malus* plantings. Japanese flowering crabapple shows good resistance to apple scab but is moderately susceptible to fire blight. Sargent crabapple resists fire blight and apple scab. Both toringo and tea crabapples are resistant to scab and rust; tea crabapple is somewhat susceptible to fire blight.

Landscape uses: Crabapples are impressive in groups or individually as focal points in the landscape. Few trees rival them for showy spring blossoms. Use crabapples to add flowering interest to a wildlife feeding area; the abundant fruits will attract birds and animals. Some trees produce excellent fruits for jelly making.

MANURE

In the days when most families kept a milk cow or small chicken flock, manure was a standard garden fertilizer. But with the advent of chemical fertilizers, many gardeners stopped using manure. Organic gardeners have rediscovered the benefits of manure as a soil conditioner and compost ingredient.

Most garden centers sell bagged composted manure, and while it costs more, bagged manure saves you the time and effort of locating, hauling, and composting fresh manure.

If you want to try composting fresh manure, seek out local farms—ideally, a local organic farm. While many farmers spread manure on their fields or use it for making their own compost, they may be willing to give—or sell—you some, provided you do the hauling. Other good sources are local stables or feedlots. Urban gardeners can contact the city zoo or visit a fairground or circus after the animals have left town. Don't use manure from dogs or cats—it may carry disease organisms that can be particularly dangerous to children.

Nutrients in Manures

While all animal manures are good sources of organic matter and nutrients, specific sources vary in nutrient content. It's useful to know whether the manure you're using is rich or poor in a particular nutrient such as nitrogen. NPK analysis refers to percentages of nitrogen (N), phosphorus (P), and potassium (K).

KIND OF MANURE	NPK ANALYSIS
Chicken	1.1-0.8-0.5
Cow	0.6-0.2-0.5
Duck	0.6-1.4-0.5
Horse	0.7-0.3-0.6
Pig	0.5-0.3- .5
Rabbit	2.4-1.4-0.6
Sheep	0.7-0.3-0.9
Steer	0.7-0.3-0.4

Using Manure

Don't put raw manure in or on garden soils. Raw manure generally releases highly soluble nitrogen compounds and ammonia, which can burn plant roots and interfere with seed germination. Also, don't incorporate raw manure into unplanted garden beds. Raw manure often is filled with weed seeds, so spreading it on soil can create serious weed problems.

The best way to use manure as a fertilizer is to compost it. Manure is a prime source of nitrogen, potassium, and phosphorus, and is rich in bacteria. Manure is important in a rapid composting method that requires a high-nitrogen, high-bacteria heat-up material. See the Compost entry for directions on making hot compost.

The Manure of Suburbia

If tracking down a source of manure and collecting it seems like more trouble than it's worth, consider substituting fresh grass clippings, the "manure of suburbia," for the rural brown kind. When fresh, grass clippings rival manures in nitrogen content (their nutrient analysis is around 4-1-2). While your lawn will benefit from letting this rich resource return to the soil when you mow, there's no harm in bagging or raking up clippings occasionally to give your compost pile a nitrogen boost. Add fresh grass clippings—from organically tended lawns only, please—to your compost pile in thin layers interspersed with dry, high-carbon materials such as shredded fall leaves, to keep the grass layers from turning into stinky slimy mats. Just like manure, grass clippings can jump-start a compost pile. If you're gathering grass clippings from beyond the borders of your own organic lawn, make sure they are chemical-free. Herbicides have been known to persist through the composting process to cause damage to gardens where the finished compost was applied.

Manure and pesticides: Manure from conventional (nonorganic) farms may contain pesticides or pesticide residues. Some farmers spray manure piles with pesticides to kill fly larvae. Manure may also contain residues from antibiotics or other livestock medications. These chemicals can suppress microbial populations in compost. It's best to ask the farmer whether the manure or the animals that produced it have been treated with medications or pesticides.

Manure and pathogens: All manure contains some bacteria—even manure from animals treated with antibiotics. Most of the bacteria in manure are beneficial, however some of those bacteria may be a form of E. coli or other pathogens that can cause serious illness, or even death. To be safe, always wear gloves when you handle manure, and always wash your hands thoroughly afterward. The best footgear to wear is a pair of rubber boots that you can scrub and hose off afterward. And for safety reasons, don't use manure-based compost for making compost tea.

MAPLE

See *Acer*

MARIGOLD

See *Tagetes*

MASTER GARDENERS

If you like working with plants and people, you can become a Master Gardener. Master Gardeners are trained volunteers who assist the Cooperative Extension System, a program of the US Department of Agriculture's National Institute of Food and Agriculture that works through land-grant colleges and universities and local offices to provide practical, science-based information, including gardening advice, to the public.

As a Master Gardener candidate, you'll receive

in-depth training in horticulture and backyard gardening from university and extension specialists. You'll learn about the basics of vegetable and ornamental gardening, as well as landscaping, plant diseases, and insects. A typical training program involves 30-plus hours of training in horticulture-related topics the first year, with 8 hours of additional update training each year thereafter.

After you complete your training, you will volunteer to serve at your local extension office. The extension staff will help match your talents and interests with the needs of the extension office and the gardening public. You might teach small groups through classes and workshops at libraries, botanical gardens, or fairs and other events. Or you may answer individual gardener's questions by phone while staffing a garden hotline, by mail, by e-mail, or in person. You can also assist in preparing garden-related newsletters or work with special audiences such as physically challenged adults or troubled teens. A typical volunteer workload is 50 hours the first year and 20 hours each subsequent year.

Once you become a Master Gardener, you can receive updates and training through your local extension office, participate in statewide or regional meetings, and even attend a biennial national conference for Master Gardeners.

The Washington State Extension office developed this program in 1972 to help handle the overwhelming number of home gardening questions. Today, Master Gardeners can be found throughout the United States, and a similar program exists in Canada. To become a Master Gardener, contact your local extension office, or visit the Web site of the American Horticultural Society to learn about training opportunities and requirements in your state.

MEADOW GARDENS

If you love wildflowers and enjoy the sights and sounds of birds and butterflies in your garden, a meadow garden may make a handsome addition to your yard. Meadow gardens can be any size you like. They are excellent for preventing erosion on rocky or steep sites but are also effective for any sunny spot. Use them to cover unused portions of your yard or to reduce the size of your lawn. Meadow gardens also bring biodiversity into the backyard landscape, supporting beneficial insects, birds, and other wildlife.

A meadow garden mimics the beauty of a natural meadow or old field, with a progression of flowers that bloom from early summer to frost. While annuals play a role in early years, in established meadows perennials provide the majority of the flowers. (Plantings along roadsides that consist of annuals like cosmos, *Cosmos* spp., are certainly beautiful, but they are not self-perpetuating and must be oversown or replanted annually or every couple of years.)

In addition to flowers like rudbeckias (*Rudbeckia* spp.), goldenrods (*Solidago* spp.) and asters (*Aster* spp.), successful meadows also contain a variety of meadow grasses that help crowd out weeds, protect the soil, and add their own beauty. Most are clumping, warm-season grasses that grow slowly in spring and fall, thrive in the heat of summer, and go dormant in winter. In addition to stabilizing the soil and providing support for the flowers, grasses add color and texture to the meadow, especially when they change color in fall.

While meadow gardens are low-maintenance landscape features, advertising campaigns have portrayed them as requiring no care whatsoever. Some ads indicate that establishing a beautiful meadow requires nothing more than scattering wildflower seeds over an established lawn or weedy field and standing back to watch the flowers appear. In fact, seeds of any kind—even those of tough, hardy wildflowers—need some help to grow into established plants. Typical turfgrasses or established weeds easily overwhelm seedling meadow flowers because their mat-forming roots crowd out other plants. Plus, meadows do require some routine maintenance.

Getting Started

Fortunately, it's easier to create a beautiful, self-perpetuating meadow than a flowerbed. To make your own meadow, just follow the soil preparation, timing, sowing, and watering methods you'd use to establish a new lawn.

Select a site in as much sun as possible for your meadow—full sun is best. Well-drained, average soil is fine for most meadow plants, which grow well in average to even poor soil and actually tend to flop in rich soil. Ordinary soil will give you the best meadow, because meadow plants feed lightly. In general, you don't have to fertilize or improve soil at all, although if your soil is very high in clay or sand, work in compost or other organic matter to improve it before you plant.

You can plant meadows on other types of sites, including wet areas, areas that have been disturbed and are subject to erosion, and steep slopes. In this case, look for seed mixes specially blended for these tough conditions. Meadow and prairie specialists will offer a variety of mixes for special sites, including woodland edges, and some also will custom blend mixes for your specific site.

If you're just starting out, it's best to begin with a small, manageable plot. You can always increase the size of your meadow in future years. If you have a newly graded landscape, starting a meadow

is as easy as sowing a lawn. Simply sow your meadow seed mix on the areas where you want a low-maintenance lawn alternative.

Seed Mixes and Other Options

A meadow garden should be composed of native warm-season grasses and flowering annuals, biennials, and perennials that will spread and self-sow to create a self-maintaining field of flowers and foliage. Unfortunately, many packaged meadow mixes contain no grass seed at all. If grass seed isn't in your mix, purchase it separately. Choose one or more of the grasses listed on the opposite page, or you can find sheep's fescue (*Festuca ovina*) at many farm supply centers, and it works well in meadow gardens in most areas of the country if sown at 1 pound per 1,000 square feet.

Don't let pretty pictures seduce you into buying the wrong seed mix. Read the label, and don't purchase any meadow mix that doesn't list the species in it—all of them. Be sure the mix you buy is formulated for your region of the country; the more local, the better.

You don't have to buy a premixed assortment of wildflower seeds for your meadow. If you prefer, identify which species would be suitable for your site and buy them individually. Again, be sure to include grasses. Mix your choices together before sowing.

Many commercial seed mixes include both annuals and perennials. The annuals will bloom the first year and make a pretty meadow that first growing season, but they rarely reseed as expected. For splashy annual color every year, overseed with annuals each spring. Meanwhile, during that first season, the perennials will be sprouting, putting down sturdy roots, and just getting themselves established. The perennials

Best Plants for Meadow Gardens

These wildflowers and grasses are the most dependable natives for meadows across the country. Look in a wildflower gardening book, check with a wildflower society, or refer to wildflower seed catalogs to find the plants that do best in your area.

Wildflowers for Meadow Gardens

Asclepias tuberosa (butterfly weed)

Baptisia australis (blue false indigo)

Coreopsis lanceolata (lanceleaf coreopsis)

Echinacea purpurea (purple coneflower)

Gaillardia pulchella (blanketflower)

Helenium autumnale (common sneezeweed)

Heliopsis helianthoides (oxeye sunflower)

Lespedeza capitata (round-headed bush clover)

Liatris spicata (spike blazing star)

Lupinus perennis (wild lupine)

Monarda fistulosa (wild bergamot)

Penstemon digitalis (foxglove penstemon)

Ratibida pinnata (prairie coneflower)

Rudbeckia hirta (black-eyed Susan)

Senna hebecarpa (wild senna)

Solidago spp. (goldenrods)

Symphyotrichum novae-angliae (New England aster)

Grasses for Meadow Gardens

Andropogon virginicus (broom sedge)

Bouteloua curtipendula (sideoats grama)

Elymus villosus (silky wild rye)

Festuca spp. (fescues)

Koeleria macrantha (prairie June grass)

Panicum virgatum (switchgrass)

Schizachyrium scoparium (little bluestem)

Sorghastrum nutans (Indian grass)

---

should flower the second season and get even better as the years pass and clumps increase in size. Perennials may even self-sow.

If you're impatient for flowers, consider planting your meadow with plugs or with container-grown or bareroot perennials. If you like, transplants allow you to arrange flowers and grasses in large, naturally shaped drifts for a look that is halfway between a garden and a meadow, where plants pop up at random. Starting with established plants, however small, is more expensive than sowing seed, but your meadow will establish more quickly. You can also grow your own transplants in a nursery bed, where they can receive extra attention, and then move them to the meadow site once they are large enough to be transplanted.

Another option is to grow your meadow from seed and then augment it with container-grown plants. Look for native meadow species at your local garden center or at botanic garden or wildflower plant sales.

Prairie Gardens

Prairies are the rolling grasslands that originally covered much of the Midwest, and today prairie remnants and reconstructions are an important source of garden inspiration. The two general types of prairies are tallgrass prairies, featuring big bluestem (*Andropogon gerardii*), among many other plants, and shortgrass prairies, featuring little bluestem (*Schizachyrium scoparium*).

In the landscape, prairie gardens can be planted on sunny sites and a wide range of soils, just like meadow gardens. They, too, feature flowers as well as grasses and are planted just like meadow gardens, from soil preparation to the sowing of seeds or the planting of small transplants. The plants that predominate in a prairie garden differ somewhat, however. Grasses include bluestems, sideoats grama grass (*Bouteloua curtipendula*), and prairie dropseed (*Sporobolus heterolepis*), among others. The appropriate mix of prairie plants varies according to the soil and moisture conditions on your site. The list below includes some, but far from all, of the native species you could include in a prairie garden. Look for plants native to your area to design an appropriate mix.

Agastache foeniculum (anise hyssop)

Allium cernuum (nodding onion)

Baptisia australis (wild blue indigo)

Dalea candida (white prairie clover)

Echinacea pallida (pale purple coneflower)

Echinacea purpurea (purple coneflower)

Euthamia graminifolia (formerly *Solidago graminifolia*, flat-top goldentop)

Eutrochium maculatum (spotted joe-pye weed)

Filipendula rubra (queen of the prairie)

Geum triflorum (prairie smoke)

Helenium autumnale (sneezeweed)

Lathyrus venosus (showy vetchling)

Lespedeza capitata (round-headed bush clover)

Liatris pycnostachya (prairie blazing star)

Liatris spicata (spike blazing star)

Penstemon albidus (white penstemon)

Penstemon digitalis (foxglove penstemon)

Silphium integrifolium (rosinweed)

Silphium laciniatum (compass plant)

Silphium perfoliatum (cup plant)

Solidago nemoralis (gray goldenrod)

Symphyotrichum laeve (smooth blue aster)

Symphyotrichum oolentangiense (sky-blue aster)

Site Preparation and Sowing

Your greatest adversary in establishing a successful meadow garden will be weeds. The battle begins when you prepare the soil, and continues through planting time and for at least one or two seasons. An established meadow garden, especially one with grasses, should have thick enough foliage to shade out most weeds if you get rid of aggressive species like johnsongrass, thistles, and bindweeds early on.

The fight is most fierce at the start because the newly cleared soil offers an open invitation to airborne seed and because weed seed lying dormant in the soil springs to life when the ground is cleared. Soilborne weeds are particularly troublesome if you till the soil when sowing the meadow mixture, because dormant seed lying too deep to germinate comes to the surface and sprouts. Handle weed control using one of the following methods.

Strip the surface: On a small site, simply strip off lawn grass and/or weeds with a spade, slicing shallowly under the grass to remove the roots. Prepare a seedbed by raking the remaining soil, removing any remaining weed roots in the process, and then sow.

Smother them out: Smother existing vegetation by covering it with black plastic, layers of newspaper (10 sheets thick) or corrugated cardboard topped by grass clippings or mulch, or even pieces of old carpet. If the site is covered with lawn grass, you can smother it in summer for sowing in fall or the following spring. If the site is covered with perennial weeds like thistles or quackgrass, be prepared to keep it smothered for 1 or even 2 years before it is ready to plant. Once plants on the site are dead, rough up the soil surface or till very shallowly (to avoid bringing new weed seeds to the soil surface) and sow.

Outcompete with buckwheat: Some meadow gardeners prepare sites by tilling and planting several successive crops of buckwheat. You'll start this process in spring to prepare for fall planting of your meadow mix. See the Weeds entry for more on this method.

Till them away: You can also eliminate weeds by tilling a site repeatedly. Start preparing the soil in midsummer by tilling the site either by hand or with a power tiller, wait 2 weeks until weed seeds have sprouted, and then till or hoe the soil shallowly to disrupt the weed seedlings. (Shallow disking is essential, because deeper tilling brings up more weed seed.) Repeat the process every 2 weeks until weeds stop resprouting and it is time to sow. Keep in mind that this method will cause major disruption to populations of earthworms and beneficial soil microorganisms. Near the end of the sequence, add some rich (but weed-seed-free) compost or an inoculant to the soil to help reestablish beneficial bacteria and fungi.

Once the soil is tilled and weeded, sow the meadow garden. Do this in either spring or fall, depending on your climate. Where winter temperatures are mild, such as in the South and Mid-Atlantic, fall sowing works best; in northern states and other areas where cold winter weather prevails, spring sowing is better. It is essential to sow the seed thickly to keep out weeds. Sow at a heavy application rate, as much as twice the rate on the package directions. Mix seed with equal portions of clean river sand to facilitate even spreading. Rake over the area two or three times to settle the seeds into the soil. If possible, shake clean straw over the site, as you would over a newly sown lawn.

Caring for a Meadow

Keep your meadow watered throughout the first growing season to help the plants get established. Once the meadow is up and growing, hand-weed as needed.

To keep woody plants from taking over your wildflower meadow and shading out the flowers, mow it back to about 6 inches from the ground each year in late winter. A regular lawn mower won't do the job because it cuts too low—use a scythe or a small tractor. You can also periodically hand-weed to eliminate tree and shrub seedlings and keep most weeds at bay. If desired, sow seeds of annual flowers every year for a good show. This means some yearly soil preparation when sowing.

MELON

Cucumis melo and other genera
Cucurbitaceae

The succulent flavor of vine-ripened melons is worth the special effort it takes to grow them. Homegrown melons outshine those from the grocery store because melons pack up on sugar during their final days of growth—commercial melons just can't compete because they're picked a little green for shipping.

Most melons need nutrient-rich soil, plenty of sunshine, and at least 3 to 4 months of warm weather. Melons can take up lots of space. A single watermelon vine, for example, can sprawl across 100 square feet and produce only two fruits; muskmelons, on the other hand, can provide at least a dozen fruits in a 16-square-foot area. If you have limited space, try bush cultivars, or grow standard types vertically on a strong fence or trellis.

Types: What we call cantaloupes are actually muskmelons. This class of melon has pumpkinlike ribbing and skin covered with a netting of shallow veins. Its fragrant flesh ranges from salmon to green. 'Athena' and 'Pulsar' are popular cultivars for home gardens. True cantaloupes, often called "Charentais" melons, grown mostly in Europe, have orange flesh and rough, scaly skin with dark, distinct veins.

Winter melons (also a type of muskmelon) ripen as the weather starts to turn cool and will keep for fairly long periods if stored properly. This group includes honeydews, Crenshaws, casabas, and Persians. These larger, more oval fruits have waxy skins that can be smooth or wrinkled, with less-fragrant flesh.

Winter melons require a growing season of well over 100 days and are more susceptible to diseases, but they're certainly delicious. Honeydews have smooth, creamy white skins and lime green flesh that takes on a slight golden tinge when mature; some varieties have orange flesh. Crenshaws have salmon pink flesh with a distinctive flavor. The tenderness of their wrinkled yellow-green skins makes them difficult to ship. Casabas have wrinkled, golden skins and white flesh that stays sweet and juicy over a long period. Large, round Persian melons have thick, orange flesh.

Watermelons fall under a different botanical classification, *Citrullus lanatus*, but they thrive under the same cultural conditions that other melons require. Compact cultivars such as 'Sugar Baby' and 'Sorbet' (which is also seedless) are perfect for smaller home gardens. 'Petite Yellow' is one of several small yellow-fleshed cultivars for home gardens.

Planting: Melons need the sunniest spot possible with plenty of air circulation to help them dry out quickly after rain and prevent disease. Melon roots usually extend from 2 to 10 inches into the earth, but some go as deep as 4 to 5 feet. Therefore, the soil must be loose and moisture retentive but well drained. Since melons will be one of the last things you plant in your vegetable garden, you might want to give them an extra boost by working 2 to 3 inches of compost into the planting area.

Vines may not set fruit if they are chilled as seedlings, so don't plant until the soil has warmed to between 70° and 80°F. Get a head start by planting seeds indoors in 4-inch peat pots. Start them just 2 to 4 weeks before transplanting, because seedlings that develop tendrils or more than four leaves may have difficulty later in establishing roots. Sow several seeds ½ inch deep in each pot, and place the pots in a south-facing window or other sunny spot. Provide bottom heat if necessary to bring the soil temperature to 75°F. Thin 2-inch-tall seedlings to the strongest plant by cutting the others off at soil level. A few days before planting, harden off the seedlings by setting them outdoors in a sunny area during the day and bringing them in at night.

You can grow large crops in rows, but most melons seem to do better in hills, mounds of soil raised 3 to 4 inches above the surrounding garden bed. For most cultivars, space hills 4 to 6 feet apart; vigorous growers like watermelons may require 6 to 12 feet between hills, while some bush types need only 2 feet.

When planting directly in the garden, sow six seeds per hill no earlier than 2 weeks after the last frost date. Thin to two or three plants per hill, or in short-season areas, thin to only one plant per hill, so it won't have to compete with the other vines for nutrients.

In colder climates, lay black plastic or black paper mulch a few weeks prior to planting or transplanting to warm up the soil and keep it warm once the plants are in the ground. Anchor the mulch securely to keep it from shifting and covering young plants. You can also use cloches or hot caps, such as plastic jugs with the bottom cut out, to shield seedlings from cold temperatures early in the season.

Growing guidelines: If you're not using plastic or paper mulch, apply several inches of organic mulch just as the vines start to elongate. This covering will suppress weeds and help keep the fruits clean and disease-free. Provide generous amounts of water, particularly right after transplanting and as the fruits develop.

Male flowers appear first, at leaf joints on the main stem and on larger side shoots. Around a week later, fruit-producing female flowers form on secondary side shoots. Despite the many female blossoms, each vine will produce only three or four melons. Most young melons will grow to the size of an egg, then shrivel as they send their nutrients back into the vines. Fertilize with compost tea when the fruits set and again 2 weeks later. See the Compost entry for instructions for making compost tea.

Though melon vines look robust, they are actually quite delicate—always handle them carefully. If they start to sprawl outside the area where you wish them to grow, gently guide them back toward the center of the planted area.

In areas colder than about Zone 7, remove flowers and smaller fruits from the vines after midsummer; these won't have time to mature before frost, and they use up energy that should go into ripening the two or three larger fruits you've left on each vine.

Problems: Striped and spotted cucumber beetles can be serious pests. The beetles, which spread bacterial wilt as they feed, tend to be more destructive to direct-seeded plants than to transplants. They often attack around the time the plants flower. Tents of cheesecloth, mosquito netting, or floating row covers are the best protection from beetles, but you must remove these coverings when female flowers form so that bees can pollinate them. Spraying young plants with kaolin clay may deter beetles from feeding. You can also use a handheld vacuum cleaner to remove beetles from the plants (dump the collected beetles into soapy water to kill them). As a last resort to fight a cucumber beetle infestation, spray a pyrethrin product.

Melon aphids can also be a problem. See page 454 for more information on aphid control measures.

Squash vine borers, which eat their way up the stem of a plant and cause the leaves to wilt, may also attack melons. See the Squash entry for information on this pest.

Resistant cultivars and crop rotation are the best defenses against melon diseases, including downy and powdery mildews. Mildews are common in wet weather. Downy mildew produces yellow spots on leaf surfaces, with purplish areas on the undersides. Powdery mildew causes powdery white areas on leaves and stems. Even a small amount of mildew can affect the sweetness of melons because the fungus will siphon off the vine's sugar to fuel its own growth. Sprays of potassium bicarbonate (or baking soda) can help prevent powdery mildew. Cut off and destroy any affected branches.

Bacterial wilt produces limp leaves and stems that secrete a white sticky substance when cut. Remove and destroy affected plants. Reduce the chances of bacterial wilt by controlling cucumber beetles and aphids.

Harvesting: The stem of a vine-ripened fruit should break cleanly with no pressure at all on the stem; just picking up the fruit should be sufficient; this is called the "slip" stage. You can often judge the ripeness of cantaloupes and muskmelons by scent alone.

Some gardeners determine the ripeness of a watermelon by thumping it, with a resulting ringing sound if it's green and a dull or dead sound if it's ripe. However, a dull or dead sound can also mean that the fruit is overripe. Other growers harvest when the "pig's-tail" tendril where the water-

melon attaches turns brown, but on some cultivars this tail dries up at 7 to 10 days before the fruit is ripe. Instead, look at the bottom surface or "ground spot" on a watermelon. If it has turned from a light straw color to gold, orange, or rich yellow, it's ripe for picking.

Storage time for various melons kept in a cool place can vary from 2 weeks for a cantaloupe to 8 weeks for a casaba.

MERTENSIA

Bluebells. Spring-blooming perennial wildflowers.

Description: *Mertensia virginica*, Virginia bluebells, bear graceful hanging clusters of pink buds that open into sky blue bells. The 1- to 2-foot arching clumps have 8-inch, broad, blue-green leaves. Zones 3–9.

How to grow: Plant container-grown bluebells in early spring or divide the brittle roots in fall. Bluebells prefer sun or partial shade and humus-rich soil with even moisture during growth. They go dormant soon after bloom, and then established plants will tolerate dry soil. Self-sown plants can multiply quickly. If you wish to divide your bluebells, mark their location while they're blooming in the spring, before the plants go dormant, so you can find them in fall.

Landscape uses: Bluebells are at their best with bulbs in borders or woodland settings. Grow with annuals, perennials, ferns, and other plants to disguise dying foliage.

MESCLUN

See Salad Greens

MILKWEED

See *Asclepias*

MILLION BELLS

See *Calibrachoa*

MINT

Mentha spp.

Lamiaceae

Description: Mints are perennial herbs with squared, four-sided stems clad in opposite leaves and topped by spikes of small lipped flowers. All parts of the plants are pungent. Most mints are rampant spreaders, forming a thick mat of spreading stolons (creeping underground stems) just under the surface of the ground. Aboveground, plants produce 2- to 3-foot upright stems. Most are hardy in Zones 3–8, but check the species you want before you buy.

The genus *Mentha* has many species and cultivars. *Mentha* ×*piperita*, peppermint, and *M. spicata*, spearmint, are the most familiar. Herb gardeners may also grow *M. suaveolens*, the furry apple mint; citrusy *M. aquatica*, orange mint; popular chocolate mint, *M.* ×*piperita* f. citrata 'Chocolate'; *M. requienii*, the creeping Corsican mint; and numerous hybrids or variegated forms.

How to grow: All mints prefer a cool, moist spot in partial shade but will also grow in full sun. Mint is extremely variable from seed. Instead, order plants from a reputable source, or visit a nursery to find plants whose flavor and aroma appeal to you. One plant of each cultivar you select will soon provide more than enough mint for home use—the big problem is to keep them from overrunning all neighboring plants. To avoid this, plant mints in bottomless containers that are at least 15 inches deep and sunk in the ground with 1 or 2 inches protruding above the soil surface, or plant above the ground in tubs and barrels.

Harvesting: Snip leaves or sprigs as needed. To harvest in quantity, cut stems to within an inch or so above the ground. You can make several harvests, depending on the length of the season. Hang mint in loose bunches to air-dry, dry individual leaves on a tray in a food dehydrator, or freeze in self-sealing bags.

Uses: Enjoy aromatic mint teas hot or iced. Peppermint tea, a centuries-old remedy, can calm an upset stomach. Add chopped fresh leaves to lamb, rice, salads, or cooked vegetables. Corsican mint is an attractive creeper, good between paving stones or in the rock garden.

MONARDA

Bee balm. Summer-blooming perennials; wildflowers; herbs.

Description: *Monarda didyma*, bee balm, bears shaggy 2- to 3-inch flowers in white, pink, red, and purple. Spreading colonies of 2- to 4-foot upright plants bear 3- to 6-inch fragrant leaves on the square stems characteristic of the mint family. Because mildew can plague this species, choose mildew-resistant cultivars such as the red-flowered 'Jacob Cline' and rose-pink 'Marshall's Delight'. Zones 4–8.

How to grow: Plant or divide in spring or fall in a sunny site with average, well-drained, moisture-retentive soil. Shade produces floppy stems and mildewed leaves. Divide bee balm often to curb its spread and reduce disease problems; cut back nearly to the ground after bloom for a new crop of healthy leaves.

Landscape uses: Group in borders and herb gardens; allow to naturalize in moist meadows. Hummingbirds love them.

MORNING GLORY

See *Ipomoea*

MULCH

The best time-saving measure a gardener can take is applying mulch. This goes for every garden site, from vegetable garden to flowerbed. Mulched gardens are healthier, more weed-free, and more drought resistant than unmulched gardens, so you'll spend less time watering, weeding, and fighting pest problems.

There are two basic kinds of mulch: organic and inorganic. Organic mulches include formerly living material such as chopped leaves, straw, grass clippings, compost, wood chips, shredded bark, sawdust, pine needles, and even paper. Inorganic mulches include gravel, stones, black plastic, and geotextiles (landscape fabrics).

Both types discourage weeds, but organic mulches also improve the soil as they decompose. Inorganic mulches don't break down and enrich the soil, but under certain circumstances they're the mulch of choice. For example, black plastic warms the soil and radiates heat during the night, keeping heat-loving vegetables such as eggplant and tomatoes cozy and vigorous.

Using Organic Mulches

There are two cardinal rules for using organic mulches to combat weeds. First, be sure to lay the mulch down on soil that is already weeded, and second, lay down a thick enough layer to discourage new weeds from coming up through it. It can take a 4- to 6-inch layer of mulch to completely discourage weeds, although a 2- to 3-inch layer is usually enough in shady spots where weeds aren't as troublesome as they are in full sun.

Wood chips and bark mulch: You can purchase bags of decorative wood chips or shredded bark from a local garden center to mulch your flower garden and shrub borders. A more inexpensive source of wood chips might be your tree-care company or the utility company. They may be willing to sell you a quantity of chips at a nominal price—or they may even leave a free pile of chips at your door if you catch them while they're working in your neighborhood. Many community yard waste collection sites offer chipped yard debris or composted grass clippings and fall leaves to residents for free (or for a small fee). Be aware that free chips from tree trimmers may include shredded poison ivy.

Shredded leaves: If you have trees on your property, shredding the fallen leaves creates a nutrient-rich mulch for free. You can use a leaf-shredding machine, but you don't really need a special machine to shred leaves—a lawn mower with a bagger will collect leaves and cut them into the perfect size for mulching.

You can spread a wood chip or shredded leaf mulch anywhere on your property, but it looks especially attractive in flowerbeds and shrub borders. Of course, it's right at home in a woodland or shade garden. Wood chips aren't a great idea for vegetable and annual flowerbeds, however, since you'll be digging these beds every year and the chips will get in the way. They do serve well as a mulch for garden pathways, though.

Grass clippings: Grass clippings are another

readily available mulch, although it's a good idea to return at least some of your grass clippings directly to the lawn as a natural fertilizer (see the Lawns entry). It's fine to collect grass clippings occasionally to use as mulch, and the nitrogen-rich clippings are an especially good choice for mulching vegetable gardens—as long as the lawn hasn't been treated with herbicides or other chemicals. Your vegetables will thank you for the nitrogen boost!

Compost: If you have enough compost, it's fine to use it as a mulch. It will definitely enrich your soil and make your plants happy, but keep in mind that when any kind of mulch is dry, it's not a hospitable place for plant roots. You may want to reserve your compost to spread as a thin layer around plants and top it with another mulch, such as chopped leaves. That way the compost will stay moist and biologically active, which will provide maximum benefit for your plants. Mulching vegetables with compost can help prevent disease problems by preventing soil-borne pathogens from splashing onto plants when it rains.

Pine needles: Pine needles are a trim-looking mulch for garden beds. They allow water to pass through easily, and they break down slowly. Despite what you may have heard, using pine-needle mulch will not make your soil significantly more acid.

Straw and hay: Another great mulch for the vegetable garden is straw, salt hay, or weed-free hay. It looks good and has most of the benefits of the other mulches: retaining soil moisture, keeping down weeds, and adding organic matter to the soil when it breaks down. Straw mulch helps control vegetable garden pests by confusing some—Colorado potato beetles, for example—and by creating inviting habitat for beneficial spiders that prey on pest species. Be sure the hay you use is weed- and seed-free, or you'll just be making trouble for your garden. And don't pull hay or straw up to the stems of vegetables or the trunks of fruit trees or you'll be inviting slug and rodent damage.

Organic Mulching Mechanics

Spreading organic mulch saves labor and nurtures plants by:

- Preventing most weed seeds from germinating; the few weeds that do pop through the mulch will be easy to pull.
- Keeping the soil cool and moist in summer, reducing the need to water.

Double mulch stops weeds. If you know that a garden bed is filled with weed seeds or bits of perennial weed roots, use a double-mulching technique to prevent a weed explosion. Set plants in place, water them well, then spread newspaper and top it with organic mulch.

🌿 Decomposing slowly, releasing nutrients into the soil.

🌿 Encouraging earthworm activity, improving soil tilth and nutrient content.

🌿 Keeping dirt from splashing on flowers and vegetables.

🌿 Preventing alternate freezing and thawing of the soil in winter, which can heave plants from the soil.

Nothing, unfortunately, is perfect. When using organic mulches, keep in mind the following facts.

🌿 As low-nitrogen organic mulches such as wood chips and sawdust decay, nitrogen is temporarily depleted from the soil. Fertilize first with a high-nitrogen product such as bloodmeal or fish meal to boost soil nitrogen levels.

🌿 An organic mulch retains moisture, which can slow soil warming; in spring, pull mulch away from perennials and bulbs for faster growth.

🌿 A wet mulch piled against the stems of flowers and vegetables can cause them to rot; keep mulch about 1 inch away from crowns and stems.

🌿 Mulch piled up against woody stems of shrubs and trees can cause them to rot and encourages rodents, such as voles and mice, to nest in the mulch. Keep deep mulch pulled back about 6 to 12 inches from trunks.

🌿 In damp climates, organic mulches can harbor slugs and snails, which will munch on nearby plants; don't spread mulch near slug-susceptible plants.

🌿 Organic mulches are usually more or less acidic, depending on their content; mix some lime with the mulch beneath plants that prefer neutral or slightly alkaline soil.

Using Plastic Mulch

Mulching a vegetable garden with sheets of black plastic film can do wonders. When it's spread tightly over a smooth soil surface, black plastic will transmit the sun's heat to the soil beneath, effectively creating a microclimate about 3°F warmer than bare soil. Because the plastic film remains warm and dry, it protects the fruits of vining crops such as strawberries, melons, and cucumbers from rotting and keeps them clean. And of course, the mulch prevents weed growth and retains soil moisture.

Infrared transmitting (IRT) plastics cost more than standard black plastic, but they can result in even higher yields. These plastics warm the soil as well as clear plastic does but also control weeds as well as black plastic.

In raised bed gardens, lay down a sheet of plastic over the entire bed. Bury it at the edges or weigh the plastic down with rocks. Then punch holes in it for the plants. A bulb planter makes quick work of hole cutting. Sow seeds or plant transplants in the holes.

Because water can't permeate plastic, the mulch retains soil moisture but it also keeps rainwater from soaking the planting bed. Thus, the ideal watering system for a plastic-covered bed is soaker hoses or drip hoses laid on the soil surface before you put down the plastic (see Drip Irrigation for more details).

Don't use plastic as a mulch under shrubs. Although it keeps out weeds and can be camouflaged with decorative mulch, black plastic

Plastic Imperfection

Although black plastic mulch seems like a great boon to organic gardeners, its use is not problem-free. One issue of concern with black plastic is its manufacture (it's a petroleum product) and its disposal—there are very few places it can be recycled. If you carefully lift black plastic at the end of the growing season and store it in a dry place over winter, you should be able to reuse it for several years, but eventually if will become torn and you'll have to throw it away.

An alternative is a biodegradable plastic mulch (cornstarch based). These materials are designed to break down in place by the end of the growing season, and you can dig any remaining bits into the soil. However, one of the breakdown products of biodegradable plastic mulch is carbon dioxide. Black paper mulch made from recycled paper is also available, but these products are usually treated with a synthetic anti-microbial substance to prevent them from breaking down too quickly.

Unlike black plastic, landscape fabrics let air and water through to the soil beneath while keeping weeds from coming up. But landscape fabrics (geotextiles) have some of the same drawbacks as black plastic. To begin with, they are petroleum products. When exposed to light, they degrade over time, so to make them last longer, you have to cover them with a second mulch (they're ugly, so you'd want to, anyway). However, many gardeners have discovered that shrub roots grow up into the landscape fabric, creating real problems when you eventually want to remove it. And weeds that germinate in the surface mulch send roots down into the fabric, too, tearing it when you pull them out.

destroys the shrubs' long-term health. Because water and air cannot penetrate the plastic, roots grow very close to the soil surface—sometimes right beneath the plastic—seeking moisture and oxygen. The shallow roots suffer from lack of oxygen and moisture and from extremes of heat and cold. Eventually the plants decline and die. Stick to organic mulches such as shredded leaves, bark, wood chips, or compost under your trees and shrubs.

N

NARCISSUS

Daffodil, narcissus, jonquil. Spring-blooming bulbs.

Description: Daffodils, the first showy flowers of the season, bear blooms with a cup- or trumpet-shaped corona surrounded by six outer petals collectively called the perianth. Flowers measure from less than 1 inch to over 6 inches wide. Colors include shades of white, yellow, orange, pink, and red. Daffodils are available in many flower forms and sizes (the American Daffodil Society has established 13 daffodil classes), from the clusters of tiny, fragrant flowers borne by tazetta types to the 4-inch-wide trumpet types, with their large, tubular coronas. Heights vary from species a few inches tall to sturdy hybrids reaching 2 feet. Flowers are borne singly or in clusters, above straplike or, rarely, reedlike leaves. Thousands of cultivars are available, and most are hardy in Zones 3–8.

In addition to the cultivars, four species worth considering include: *Narcissus cyclamineus*, bearing strongly swept-back golden perianths and promi-

nent trumpets and growing to 1 foot, Zones 6–9; *N. jonquilla*, the classic jonquil, with multiple flattish, fragrant golden flowers on 1½-foot stems among rushlike leaves, Zones 4–9; *N. poeticus*, the poet's narcissus, with a rounded white perianth and a fine, fragrant, red-and-green cup, blooming at the end of daffodil season and reaching 1 foot, Zones 4–9; and *N. triandrus*, angel's tears, bearing multiple hanging white blooms on 1-foot stems, Zones 4–9.

How to grow: Plant in early fall (or late summer in the far North) in a spot that receives sun in spring. Set the bulbs at a depth 2 to 3 times their width in average, well-drained soil containing organic matter. (Daffodils tolerate less-fertile soils but will probably not bloom as well.) Add some alfalfa meal, bonemeal, and wood ashes, scratching them in around the bulbs. Water if fall rains are scanty. Cover with a few inches of light mulch in the North after the ground begins to freeze. Remove the mulch in early spring and scatter more fertilizer, again watering if rain falls short. After bloom, deadhead daffodils if they set seed, provide water if necessary, and let the foliage turn yellow before cutting it off near the soil line. Never tie it up in bunches, because sun must reach the leaves for them to manufacture food for next year's flowers.

With good culture, after several years one bulb will multiply into a large, tight mass that will bloom less freely. Dig up the entire clump after the leaves turn yellow but before they disappear and separate out the largest bulbs for replanting immediately, or store them in a shady, well-ventilated spot until fall planting time. Plant the smaller bulbs in a nursery area for growing into blooming-size bulbs or naturalize them. Fertilize each year in fall as you would for newly planted bulbs. Don't plant soft or squishy bulbs, and destroy any with streaked foliage, which indicates viral infection.

To naturalize daffodils, plant them in thin, rough grass that you can leave unmowed until the leaves have yellowed. Then leave them to their own devices, perhaps adding a little fertilizer to boost them along.

Daffodil bulbs are poisonous, so they don't fall prey to animal pests like tulips and other bulbs do. A lucky break for gardeners, and another reason to plant plenty!

Landscape uses: Plant sweeping masses or small groups in thin grass or in woodlands, or grow them in borders and beds, allowing companion plants to partially disguise the foliage as it fades after blooming is finished. Site them close to the house and near windows for easy viewing indoors on cold days; bring some indoors for cut flowers. Many cultivars are excellent for forcing in winter. (See the Bulbs entry for more on forcing.)

NASTURTIUM

See Tropaeolum

NATIVE PLANTS

Any plant that grows naturally in the habitat where it evolved is a native, or indigenous, plant. Most experts subscribe to the view that North American native plants are those species already present on the continent at the time when Europeans first arrived. Plants brought to North America by settlers, immigrants, and plant collectors, either deliberately or accidentally, are called nonnative, introduced, alien, or exotic species. Introduced species that have escaped gardens and now grow in wild areas throughout North America are called naturalized plants. Orange daylilies (*Hemerocallis fulva*), oxeye daisies (*Leucanthemum vulgare*), and Queen Anne's lace (*Daucus carota*) are three examples of nonnative species that have naturalized widely throughout North America.

All plants have a native location—the part of the world where they first occurred. A few species still are found only in their native habitat, but most plants have been transferred and transplanted to a wide variety of countries and continents through the intentional or accidental actions of people. Throughout history, settlers seeking new lands tended to take their food and medicinal plants with them. Plant explorers sought out unique perennials, trees, shrubs, and vines from remote locations and collected their seeds or cuttings to raise in nurseries, hoping to find treasures that would become new landscape favorites.

Many of the results of these horticultural undertakings are positive—imagine how much more limited our diets would be if we grew and ate only the plants native to North America, for example. But some immigrant plants have turned out to be troublemakers—they've not only done well growing in gardens and cultivated landscapes, they've escaped into natural areas and outcompeted the native plants there. Many gardeners have heard of the most notorious exotic invasives, including multiflora rose and Japanese knotweed. Unfortunately, some popular garden plants have turned out to be invasive, too, depending on where you live. Japanese barberry is one example. Long recommended to attract birds, these shrubs have turned out to be a problem because of those bright berries that birds love. The birds eat the berries, fly off to the woods, and defecate, depositing the barberry seeds along with their waste. The seeds sprout, and the bushes crowd out native shrubs and wildflowers.

Figuring out how to combat invasive plants and to conserve native plants is not easy, and the situation has become more complex as the changing climate also causes a shift in the areas in which plants can survive. There are predictions that some native plants, such as sugar maples, will be greatly reduced in their native ranges as weather patterns change. Plant conservation organizations are studying the best ways to respond to these problems.

If nonnative plants cause so many problems, it seems that growing only native plants would be the right thing to do. However, that seemingly simple solution isn't realistic in our modern landscapes. In North American home landscapes and gardens, more than 90 percent of the plants we grow originated in other parts of the world. Of those nonnatives, only a small number are known to be invasive.

In a few cases, native plants have gotten out of control, too, because of human-caused changes in their native environment. For example, the native hay-scented fern now outcompetes other plants in woodland areas in the eastern United States. It turns out that this species used to live compatibly with neighboring plants, but as forest soils have become more acid over time due to acid rain, the hay-scented fern has become dominant because it can thrive in the more acidic conditions.

A balanced approach may be to choose a native plant whenever you can, as long as it is suitable for the site and compatible with the plants around it. Favor wildlife-friendly plants—but not the nonnatives that displace native plants. Identify plant communities such as northeast woodland, prairie, or wetland plants, and group them together. For more information on choosing and using native plants, see the Native Plants entry.

Keep in mind that many experts feel that home gardens and cultivated landscapes will be the only refuge for some native plants as their natural habitats are developed or overrun by invasives. If every home gardener decided to protect just a few of the plants native to their area, what a difference it could make!

The Return of Natives

Why has interest in gardening with native plants grown so much in recent years? One reason is a concern about native plant species becoming rare in the wild. Another is an appreciation that native plants are well suited to the soil, climate, natural rainfall, and other conditions in their native range. Thus, a garden planted with regional natives will use less water and require less maintenance than one planted with species that are not as well suited to the site.

Another reason for the rise in popularity of natives is in reaction to nonnative species such as Japanese knotweed that have turned out to be very aggressive. These species have escaped from gardens and overtaken large areas, and it's difficult to reclaim such an invaded area for any other horticultural purpose. Gardening with native plants avoids the potential risks that nonnatives pose.

Landscaping with Natives

The best way to create a native plant garden is to start with a local or regional focus. After all, although plants native to Florida or Georgia are North American natives, that doesn't mean they will thrive—or even survive—in gardens in Oregon or Alaska, for example.

Start your search for native plants to include in your garden by consulting local nature centers, native plant societies, or native plant nurseries. You can also search on the Internet by plugging "native plants" into your browser. Either add your state to the search parameters or look for national sites that let you select your state for a regionally adapted list.

You may decide to hire a landscape designer or work with a garden consultant to choose plants, but before you do, set your goals for what you want to create. Are you going to include only species native to your county, your state, or your region? You can narrow your focus further by growing only strains, or ecotypes, of plants that evolved in your immediate area. Choosing local ecotypes allows you to grow individual plants that are best adapted to your immediate area. For example, while a particular wildflower may be native over a large area from Minnesota south to Georgia, individual plants grown from seed collected in Georgia may be far more tolerant of heat and humidity than their northern relatives. Or do you want to include any plant that's native to North America in your garden?

You'll also need to decide if you want to grow only native plants, or if you want to include non-natives. Many gardeners wouldn't be happy without a wide range of both natives and nonnative plants, since many beloved garden plants, including hostas, peonies, many roses, and the majority of our favorite fruit and vegetable crops, aren't North American natives.

Cultivated forms of plants present another question. Do you want to grow only native species, including varieties and forms that occur naturally? For example, crested iris (*Iris cristata*) bears bluish lilac flowers; both the species and its white-flowered variant, *I. cristata* f. *alba*, fall into this category. Or do you want to include cultivars (cultivated varieties) of native species? These have been carefully selected for particular characteristics that appeal to gardeners, but they also are less diverse genetically and in appearance than the species. For example, 'Henry's Garnet' Virginia sweetspire (*Itea virginica* 'Henry's Garnet') features larger flowers and richer autumn leaf color than the species. Maturing at 3 to 4 feet, it also is more compact than the species, which ranges from 5 to 10 feet.

There are many ways to incorporate native plants into your landscape. Consider the following ideas.

- Shade gardens are perfect for native woodland wildflowers, ferns, shrubs, and small trees.
- Plant a wildflower meadow on a sunny site using a seed mix of local perennials and grasses. Add container-grown natives purchased at local native plant sales.
- Include native plants in perennial beds and borders. Showcase unusual native perennials like sweet joe-pye weed (*Eutrochium purpureum*) and Culver's root (*Veronicastrum virginicum*) in perennial borders along with familiar native garden plants like phlox (*Phlox* spp.) and bee balm (*Monarda didyma*).
- Re-create a style of landscape that appeals to you and suits your site. For example, if you have a rocky hillside, consider covering it with native

rock garden plants. If you have a sunny site, but love shady woodlands, start by planting native trees, then fill in underneath them with woodland wildflowers.

🌿 Replace lawn areas with native groundcovers such as creeping juniper (*Juniperus horizontalis*) or fragrant sumac (*Rhus aromatica*).

Layer for a Natural Look

You can use native plants to re-create or restore natural landscapes on your property. Start by looking closely at the topography, exposure, and soil on your site. Is the area flat, rolling, or hilly? Does it face east or west? Is it in sun or shade? For how much of the day? What about moisture and soil type? Is it a well-drained, sandy slope or a mucky bottom? Think about how these conditions match those in various parts of your yard.

Next, look at the way the plants are arranged or layered in nearby natural, undeveloped areas. Do tall trees shelter small flowering trees, which in turn rise above a diversity of deciduous and evergreen shrubs, ferns, and wildflowers? Is there mostly a cover of grasses, with an occasional wildflower, shrub, or tree? The way plants grow with others is part of the distinctive look of a native plant community. It's a look you'll want to bring to your own yard, if you want your woods or meadow to look "real."

Now identify the dominant species. If you removed all the oaks, for example, would the woodland be radically altered? If a particular groundcover were gone, would the look of the woods change? These key species will be vital to reproducing the scene in your home landscape. Note other showy or abundant species that will add interest and variety to your design.

Another important consideration is how the plants grow. Some plants grow in masses or drifts; others are sprinkled sparingly across the land. Look at the spacing. Are plants clumped or do they grow singly? Do they cluster at the bases of trees? Make notes, take photographs, or sketch the patterns you see.

As you look, you'll see that repetition of key elements—like the brown tree trunks in a forest—unifies the landscape. When you see the tree trunks, you think, "forest." In a prairie, unity comes from the continuous background of grasses and the virtual absence of trees and shrubs. To make a recognizable natural landscape at home, you have to give it a unified look. But balance unity with diversity. The unexpected in nature is what keeps us excited. Choose a variety of plant forms, textures, and colors to keep your landscape exciting. See the Landscaping entry for more information on creating an effective landscape. See the Invasive Plants entry to learn about native alternatives for common invasive exotics.

NECTARINE

See Peach

NEMATODES

See Pests; Plant Diseases and Disorders; Soil

NEPETA

Catmint. Spring- to summer-blooming perennials.

Description: *Nepeta* ×*faassenii*, blue catmint, produces a profusion of ½-inch blue-violet blooms borne in clusters over 1½- to 2-foot spreading mounds of 1- to 1½-inch fragrant, gray-green, scalloped leaves. Zones 4–8. *N. cataria* is the rather weedy herb, catnip, beloved of felines. Zones 3–7.

How to grow: Plant in spring or fall (or divide in spring) in a sunny spot (partial shade in the South) with average, well-drained soil. Cut back by half and fertilize lightly after flowering for fall rebloom. Buy cutting-grown plants to make sure you get *N. ×faassenii* rather than its less-attractive parent, *N. racemosa*, which can be grown from seed.

Landscape uses: Group near the front of borders; grow as an edging along walks or beds or as a low hedge or among rocks. Combine with roses, pinks, and gray-leaved plants in a cottage garden.

NURSERY BED

A nursery bed is an area designed for nurturing plants that need special care and attention before they are planted in the garden. Creating your own nursery bed is a great way to save money on plants. If you're planning a garden that calls for lots of groundcovers or hostas, for example, buy only a plant or two of the required species or variety. Then systematically propagate those plants for a year or more by division, cuttings, or layering (depending on what works best for the type of plant), until you have a small nursery of plants to transplant to your garden. Here are some other suggestions for using a nursery bed.

- Grow seedling perennials for a few seasons in a protected spot until you have good-sized clumps that are large enough to transplant.
- Direct-sow seeds into a nursery bed, then move plants to the garden once they're established.

- Move excess transplants to a nursery bed until their roots have recovered from dividing or transplanting.
- Care for small, newly purchased perennials. Mail-order plants that arrive in small pots or bareroot specimens may not be ready for the garden proper, so use a nursery bed to grow them on and get them established.
- Coddle divisions that need extra attention. Although clumps of daylilies or hostas can be cut in two and replanted easily, if you want the maximum number of plants, separate out all the fans or plants in a clump, then watch them closely and care for them in a nursery bed until they are well established.
- Nurture cuttings, plants that have been layered, or suckers that have been removed from a parent plant until their roots are established and plants are ready to go into the garden.
- Grow replacement plants. Use your nursery bed as a warehouse for flowers like chrysanthemums or impatiens that can be moved into the garden in full bloom to fill an empty spot. Or use it to grow replacement plants to fill spots in a boxwood hedge, for example.

Creating a Nursery Bed

Select a protected location in partial shade for your nursery bed. An east-facing site is best. Also be sure to select a location with easy access to a hose, since plants in a nursery bed will require frequent watering. Since a nursery bed is a working area of the garden—somewhat like a compost pile—and not a display bed, a spot that's out of the way but easy to get to is ideal.

Prepare the soil for your bed the same way you would for a perennial or vegetable garden. See the

Soil entry for details. Be sure to remove rocks, dirt clods, and twigs, and use screened compost to amend the soil, since fine-textured soil is best for growing small plants. Don't add any more fertilizer than you would in your garden—in fact less is better, since too much fertilizer will encourage weak, rank growth.

Plan on installing posts or framework over your nursery bed to support lightweight screens and/or shade cloth to protect plants. Tiny seedlings and cuttings in a nursery bed need protection from direct sun, hard rain, wind, and pests in order to thrive. Another option is to build a large, open-topped cold frame. Line the bottom with hardware cloth to prevent voles and other pests from entering, then fill the frame with soil. Use the sides of the frame to support screens over the plants (see the Cold Frames entry for more details).

Using a Nursery Bed

Once your nursery bed is ready to accept occupants, you'll no doubt find more than enough plants to fill it. Arrange plants in rows to simplify weeding, mulching, and basic care. Be sure to moisten the soil before moving new, vulnerable plants to the nursery bed, and water each plant as you set it in the ground. Ideally, transplant on a cloudy or rainy day. Protect plants from sun, rain, and wind with screens and/or shade cloth suspended overhead. Sheets of wood or plastic lattice and overturned bushel baskets also work well to protect new nursery bed residents.

Visit your nursery bed daily—especially just after moving in new plants. The objective is to coddle your plants and make the transition as gentle and seamless as possible. Make sure the soil stays evenly moist, and check carefully for pests (see the Pests entry for problems to watch for) and other

problems. Keep the nursery bed well weeded, since weeds can easily outcompete perennials or other plants that are just getting established. Mulch with chopped leaves or another light mulch, but keep it a couple of inches away from the stems of seedlings, cuttings, and other plants.

Once plants have overcome the shock of being moved, they'll put down root growth and send up new topgrowth. See the Transplanting entry for guidelines on the best times to move plants to their permanent locations in the garden.

NUT TREES

Reliably long lived, often simply gargantuan in size, and possessing many unique physical attributes, nut trees are an important part of American culture. Grown since Colonial times, nut trees are truly a multipurpose crop, providing shade, beauty, edible nuts, valuable lumber, and wildlife habitats.

Nuts are excellent sources of the same proteins and fats commonly found in meats. Many nuts contain up to 30 percent protein by weight, while fresh beefsteak contains less than 20 percent. Except for chestnuts, which are nearly 50 percent carbohydrate, most nuts also contain 50 to 70 percent fat. Nearly all of this fat is unsaturated. Nuts are also good sources of certain vitamins and of minerals, mined by the deep root systems of the trees.

Nut trees provide us with some of our finest building materials. Black walnut trees are especially prized for their exceptional, beautifully grained lumber. An ideal single specimen can sell for as much as $30,000. Lumber cut from nut trees is prized by woodworkers and craftspersons for its beauty, strength, and durability.

The natural beauty of nut trees is enhanced by

the abundance of wildlife that makes full use of their generous bounty. Squirrels, partridges, wild turkeys, deer, and other enjoyable creatures enrich our suburbs and small towns with their presence while gleaning American's nut crops. Nut trees are a natural choice for gardeners who want to attract local wildlife.

Although they respond best with ideal growing conditions, many nut trees are wonderfully adaptable to a range of sites. You can plant them on steep slopes to stop soil erosion or in soils too rocky to be plowed. And nut-producing plants come in a range of sizes, from bushy filberts to towering hickories, so there's one to fit in almost every garden.

Selecting Nut Trees

People often ask whether they should plant cultivars or seedling nut trees. Named cultivars are produced vegetatively, usually by grafting or budding, yielding genetically identical clones. The advantage of grafted trees is that you know exactly what you are going to get with respect to hardiness, cracking quality, flavor, size, and other crop characteristics. Seeds, on the other hand, are always somewhat different genetically. This genetic diversity can make a stand of seedlings less susceptible to serious insect or disease problems than a stand of genetically identical cultivars.

Where high-quality nut production is of greatest importance, as with pecan or English walnut trees, stick to named cultivars where available. For trees such as black walnut and butternut, where timber value may be as important as the nut quality, plant a few grafted trees and use high-quality seedlings to fill out the rest of the planting. The resulting forest will be much healthier, and the cost of seedling trees is also a fraction of that of grafted ones.

Planting and Care

These low-maintenance plants can adapt to a range of sites. They generally need very little extra care once established. Keep in mind that many nut trees, including pecans and most black and English walnuts, need cross-pollination; be sure to plant more than one cultivar or seedling of each kind, or make sure a suitable pollen provider is nearby, if your property is too small to accommodate more than one large nut tree.

Planting: Soil requirements vary; "Nut Trees for Home Use" on page 388 tells about the particular cultural conditions each kind of tree prefers. In general, though, nut trees thrive in deep, rich, moist, loam or clay-loam soil. Top-grade soils bring out the best in nut trees; one well-documented study identified an entire grove of black walnuts that had reached an average height of 100 feet in only 26 years!

Planting nuts directly into the ground is a nice idea, but experience has proven that planting high-quality seedlings is far more successful. Squirrels and other rodents have an uncanny ability to sniff out planted nuts. In addition, most reputable nurseries screen their seedlings, discarding weak and unhealthy trees, so you'll get better plants.

Most nut trees have a deep anchoring taproot, making them a bit more difficult to establish than other trees. Whenever possible, start with small, young trees; they will often adjust more quickly and begin growing sooner than larger trees. Make sure you dig the planting hole deep enough to accommodate the taproot.

Aftercare: Water the planted tree thoroughly and top-dress with 6 to 8 inches of compost or mulch to help keep the soil underneath moist. (Keep the mulch away from the trunk, though, to

Nut Trees for Home Use

Besides producing a tasty crop, many nut trees are beautiful, long-lasting landscape specimens. Depending upon how much space you have available, you may want to try planting one or several of the nut trees described below in your home landscape. For information on other popular nut trees, see the *Quercus* (oak), *Pinus* (pine), and *Juglans* (walnut) entries.

Almond (*Prunus dulcis*): Small tree (20 to 30 feet) with beautiful flowers that bloom very early; drought tolerant; needs rich, well-drained soil; Zones 7–9.

Beechnut, American beech (*Fagus grandifolia*): Large tree (50 to 100 feet) with smooth blue-gray bark; slow growing but long-lived; prefers a wooded site with rich, moist, rocky soil; Zones 2–8.

Buartnut (*Juglans ×bixbyi*): Hybrid of butternut (*J. cinerea*) and heartnut (*J. ailantifolia*); medium-size tree (40 to 70 feet) that produces large quantities of attractive nuts; nuts may stain pavement; prefers rich, deep soil; Zones 4–8.

Butternut (*Juglans cinerea*): Graceful tree (40 to 70 feet) but susceptible to disease; nuts will stain pavement; prefers rich, deep soil; Zones 3–7.

Chestnut, Chinese (*Castanea mollissima*): Small tree (10 to 20 feet) that's good for small yards; Chinese-American crosses will be taller; prickly burs surround nuts; needs light, sandy loam soil; Zones 5–8.

Chestnut, European (*Castanea sativa*): Stately, long-lived tree (50 to 90 feet); prickly burs surround nuts; needs rich, loamy soil; Zones 5-8.

Filberts, hazelnuts (*Corylus* spp.): Small tree or multistemmed bush (10 to 40 feet) with crimson foliage in autumn; husks litter the ground; needs rich, light, well-drained soil; Zones 2–8.

Ginkgo (*Ginkgo biloba*): Stately, slow-growing tree (30 to 60 feet) with beautiful foliage; nuts are encased within foul-smelling fruits on female trees; needs rich, moist, heavy soil; Zones 4–8.

Heartnut (*Juglans ailantifolia*): Fast-growing tree (30 to 60 feet) with light-colored bark and lacy foliage; nuts can stain pavement; needs deep, rich soil; Zones 5–8.

Hickory, shagbark and shellbark (*Carya ovata* and *C. laciniosa*): Stately, long-lived tree (60 to 120 feet); husks will litter the ground; prefers rich soil; Zones 3–8.

Pecan (*Carya illinoinensis*): Stately, long-lived tree (70 to 150 feet); husks litter the ground; needs deep, rich, moist soil; Zones 6–9.

avoid rodent damage.) Failure to keep the moisture level high around the newly planted tree can cause the soil in the hole to shrink away from the taproot during hot, dry weather. Insufficient water during the first year is probably the leading cause of death in newly planted nut trees. Water young trees deeply once a week during dry spells until they are established.

Once they have settled in, the trees should grow rapidly, producing crops anywhere from 3 to 7 years after planting, depending on the type of nut and the local climate.

Pruning: Unlike fruit trees, most nut trees don't require special pruning techniques to produce good crops. Prune nut trees as you would any shade tree, removing dead, diseased, or crossing branches regularly. If you've planted grafted trees, be sure to prune off any suckers that may arise from the rootstock. For trees that are eventually intended for timber, keep side limbs pruned off to about 12 to 16 feet up the trunk.

Problems

Although a host of pests and diseases can attack nut trees, none of these are usually lethal. The best pest-control program is to maximize a tree's natural resistance by keeping it healthy. Applying Bt (*Bacillus thuringiensis*) is an effective control for many leaf-eating caterpillars. Resistant cultivars are available for some pests and diseases. Pick up fallen leaves, twigs, husks, and nuts regularly to remove possible overwintering sites for pests and diseases.

Chestnut blight (*Cryphonectria parasitica*) is a serious fungal disease of American chestnut trees (*Castanea dentata*). Since the early 1900s, it has wiped out nearly all American chestnuts. Nut enthusiasts have begun to identify strains that appear to be resistant to the blight, but until effective control measures or proven resistant cultivars are available, crosses between Chinese chestnut (*C. mollissima*) and American chestnut trees may be better choices. Or choose another type of nut.

Harvesting

Most nuts are best gathered as soon as they become ripe. Remove the outer husk as soon as possible to prevent mold or darkening of the nut kernel. Store the husked nuts in their shells in a cool, dry, rodent-free area. Allow the nuts to cure (dry) for 1 to 3 months. After curing, most nuts will keep in the shell for at least a year.

O

OAK

See *Quercus*

OENOTHERA

Evening primrose. Late-spring- to summer-blooming perennials.

Description: *Oenothera speciosa*, showy evening primrose, pink ladies, bears 2-inch, fragrant, cup-like four-petaled flowers in white turning to pink, or uniformly soft pink. Blooms are borne one to a stem on 6- to 15-inch masses of sprawling stems with elongated 3-inch lance-shaped leaves in summer. Zones 5–8.

O. fruticosa, narrowleaf evening primrose, flaunts an abundance of similarly shaped, slightly smaller, bright yellow blooms in small clusters; they open from red-tinged buds in late spring. The 1½- to 2-foot upright reddish stems bear dark green lance-shaped leaves that turn purple in fall. Zones 4–8.

Several species formerly included in the genus *Oenothera* have been reclassified under the generic name *Calylophus*. Most of the renamed plants were those known by the common name sundrops.

How to grow: Plant in spring or fall; divide in early spring or after bloom. Evening primroses thrive in full sun or very light shade in average to less-fertile, moist but well-drained soil, tolerating dry soil quite well. Fertile soil encourages rapid spread, especially with showy evening primrose, which spreads by creeping roots and may become invasive unless curtailed every season by pulling up unwanted plants.

Landscape uses: Evening primroses are well suited to borders if their spreading ways are not a problem. Otherwise enjoy them in low-maintenance masses in hot, dry, infertile areas.

OKRA

Abelmoschus esculentus
Malvaceae

Okra, native to Africa and a beautiful relative of hibiscus, was brought to North America in the 1600s. This tropical plant quickly became popular in the Deep South both as a side dish and as a thickening for gumbo and stews. It can, however, thrive in any climate where corn will grow. Depending on the cultivar, the large-flowered, fast-growing plants reach 2 to 6 feet tall. Varieties with colorful stems and leaves, such as 'Burgundy', make attractive garden borders.

Planting: Okra needs full sun. It will grow in ordinary garden soil but does best in fertile loam, particularly where a nitrogen-fixing crop, such as early peas, grew previously.

In the South, plant the first crop in the early spring and a second crop in June. In short-season areas, start plants indoors 6 weeks before setting them out (3 to 4 weeks after the last frost date). Sow two seeds per peat pot and clip off the weaker seedling.

When seeding okra directly in the ground, wait until after the soil has warmed and the air temperature is at least 60°F. Use fresh seed, and soak it overnight or nick each seed coat with a file to encourage germination. Sow seed ½ inch deep in light soil and 1 inch deep in heavy soil; spacing is 3 inches apart in rows 3 feet apart. Thin seedlings to 18 to 24 inches apart, always leaving the strongest of the young plants.

Growing guidelines: When okra is 4 inches tall, mulch to keep out weeds and conserve moisture. Water during dry spells. Every 3 to 4 weeks, side-dress with compost or feed with compost tea. (See the Compost entry for instructions for making compost tea.) In areas with long, hot summers, cut the plants back almost to ground level in midsummer and fertilize to produce a second crop.

Problems: Okra seldom succumbs to pests or diseases. Handpick any stinkbugs that appear; these light green, shield-shaped bugs cause misshapen pods. To control corn earworms, cabbage loopers, aphids, or flea beetles, see the chart on page 454. Fusarium wilt, a soilborne disease, is sometimes a problem in hot regions. If the disease causes leaves to yellow and wilt, pull and destroy affected plants. Crop rotation is the best preventive measure.

Harvesting: About 50 to 60 days after planting, edible pods will start to appear. They are tough when mature, so harvest daily with a sharp knife when they are no more than finger-size and when stems are still tender and easy to cut. Pick frequently and the plants will keep producing until killed by frost. Be sure to remove and compost any mature pods you might have missed earlier.

Many people find their skins are sensitive to the pods' prickly spines, so wear gloves and long sleeves when harvesting, or plant a spineless variety such as 'Clemson Spineless'.

ONION

Allium cepa and other species
Amaryllidaceae

Dried or fresh, raw or cooked, onions are an indispensable ingredient in many dishes and cooking styles. Onions are easier to grow than you might think, and they're a great plant for tucking into spare corners and along the edges of garden beds.

Types: Onions come in a wide variety of shapes, sizes, and colors. The white, yellow, or red bulbs range in size from small pickling onions to large Spanish cultivars; they can be globe, top, or spindle shaped.

Most onions can be pulled young as green onions called scallions, but there is also a perennial bunching type, *Allium fistulosum*, that produces superior scallions and is practically disease- and insect-proof. Each bulb of the multiplier or potato onion (*A. cepa*, Aggregatum Group) multiplies into a bulb cluster, so with every harvest, you'll have bulbs to replant for a continual supply.

The Egyptian or top onion (*A. ×proliferum*) produces a bulb cluster at the end of a long stem with a second cluster frequently forming on top of the first. It also has an underground bulb, which is often too pungent to eat. Other tasty sources of oniony flavor include chives (*A. schoenoprasum*), garlic chives (*A. tuberosum*), and shallots (*A. cepa*, Aggregatum Group). For information on other onion relatives, see the Garlic and Leek entries.

Planting: You can grow onions from transplants, sets, or seeds. Transplants, which are seedlings started in the current growing season and sold in bunches, are available from nurseries and by mail order. They usually form good bulbs over a short period of time (65 days or less), but they are subject to diseases. Choice of cultivars is somewhat limited.

Sets are immature bulbs grown the previous year and offer the most limited cultivar choices. They are the easiest to plant, the earliest to harvest, and the least susceptible to diseases. They are, however, more prone to bolting (sending up a flowerstalk prematurely) than are seedlings or transplants.

If you plant onion sets, the sets may be identified only as white, red, or yellow, rather than by variety name. Most growers prefer white sets for green onions. When buying sets, look for ½-inch-diameter bulbs, because they're the least likely to bolt.

Growing onions from seed offers the great advantage of a wide choice in cultivars. The challenge with starting from seeds is that your crop will take up to 4 months to mature—gardeners in cold-winter areas will need to start their onion seedlings indoors.

Always check a cultivar's daylength requirement or recommended latitudes before you buy, because daylength affects how and when onions form bulbs. Short-day onions, such as 'Giant Red Hamburger', will form bulbs as soon as days reach 10 to 12 hours long. They're suitable for southern latitudes only. Long-day types, like 'Sweet Sandwich' and 'Southport Red Globe', need 13 to 16 hours of summer daylight in order to form bulbs. They're the type to grow in more northern latitudes.

Onions like cool weather in the early part of their growth, so plant them in spring, except in mild-winter areas, where onions are grown as a fall or winter crop. Generally speaking, onions grow tops in cool weather and form bulbs when the weather warms.

Plant onion seeds 4 to 6 weeks before the last average frost—or even earlier indoors or in a cold frame. When indoor seedlings are 2 to 3 inches tall, harden them off by exposing them to above-freezing night temperatures.

Outdoors, sow seeds thickly in rows about ½ inch deep. You can try mixing in radish seeds both to mark the planted rows and as a trap crop to lure root maggots away from the onions. Thin seedlings to 1 inch apart, and thin again in 4 weeks to 6 inches apart. For transplants or sets, use a dibble to make planting holes 2 inches deep and 4 to 6 inches apart. Use the closer spacing if you plan to harvest some young plants as green onions. For sets, open a furrow 2 inches deep and place the sets stem (pointed) end up 4 to 6 inches apart, and then fill in the furrow. One pound of sets will plant about 50 feet of row.

Growing guidelines: The practices you use will depend on the specific crop you're growing. In general, onions grow best if you keep them well weeded. Use a sharp hoe to cut off intruders; pulling or digging weeds up can damage the onions' shallow roots. Once the soil has warmed, put down a mulch around and between the plants to discourage weeds and to hold moisture in the soil.

Dry conditions cause bulbs to split, so water when necessary to provide at least 1 inch of water each week; keep in mind that transplants require more water than sets do. Onions can't compete well with weeds, so it's important to direct water right to the onion roots. Two good watering methods for achieving this are shown below.

If you've prepared your soil well, no fertilizing should be necessary. Always go easy on nitrogen, which can produce lush tops at the expense of bulbs. New growth from the center will stop when the bulbs start forming.

Egyptian onions, chives, and shallots require slightly different cultivation from regular onions. Here are some guidelines for growing these onion relatives.

- Plant Egyptian onions in fall throughout the country; harvest some in spring as green or bunching onions. In midsummer or fall, miniature bulbs will form at the stem tip, where most onions form flowers. Pick these tiny bulbs when the tops begin to wilt and dry. Use them fresh or store in the freezer.

- Plant chives and garlic chives in early spring in rich soil. They will tolerate partial shade put prefer full sun. Seeds are very slow to germinate, so most growers prefer to plant clump divisions, which can be harvested after 2 months. Space the clumps, each of which should contain about six bulbs, 8 inches apart.

- Cut the grasslike, hollow tops frequently to maintain production. The pom-pom-like lavender flowers are very attractive—and edible—but always remove the spent flowers to reduce the chance of rampant self-seeding. Dig up, divide, and replant every third year. Transplant to containers and move indoors for winter harvests. Chives are almost as good frozen as they are fresh.

- Shallots, a favorite of French chefs, have a blue-green stem that's used when young. In addition, it has a gray, angular, mild-flavored bulb that's related to the multiplying onion and is used like a mild-flavored garlic. Shallots will tolerate all but the most acid soils, but dig the earth deeply because the plants put down 8-inch-long feeder roots. However, they have no lateral roots, so space them just 2 to 3 inches apart.

Propagate shallots by dividing bulb clusters. Each clove, in turn, will produce four to eight new bulbs. In February or March, plant them 1 inch deep, barely covering the tip of the clove. Keep the soil weed-free and slightly moist, but don't fertilize. In early summer, draw the soil away from the

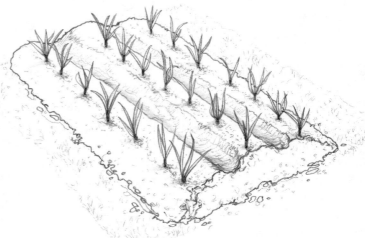

Watering onions. To water onions efficiently, extend soaker hoses along the row close to the plants. Or open a small trench between rows and fill it with water. This keeps the roots supplied while leaving most of the soil surface dry, inhibiting weed seed germination.

bulbs. Harvest shallots as green onions at any time. Cutting the tops off near soil level will produce new tops, and such harvesting actually increases bulb production. Bulbs mature in about 5 months. Pull and store like onions.

Problems: You can generally expect a disease- and insect-free crop. One possible pest is onion maggots: ⅓-inch-long white, legless larvae that travel in line from one bulb to the next and burrow upward to feed on the stems. To reduce the chances of extensive damage, scatter-plant onions throughout the garden. (This interplanting can also benefit other garden plants; many *Allium* species will ward off pests—such as aphids, Japanese beetles, and carrot flies—from roses, lettuce, carrots, beets, parsnips, and members of the cabbage family.) Placing a thin layer of sand around onion bulbs may discourage adult flies from laying their eggs at the bottoms of the plants.

Barely visible onion thrips tend to attack during hot, dry weather in July or August. They produce deformed plants with silvery blotches on the leaves. Thrips overwinter in weeds, so reduce pest populations by keeping the garden clean. Try spreading a reflective mulch, such as aluminum foil, between rows to confuse the thrips. If you catch the problem early, you can spray plants with *Beauveria bassiana* or spinosad to combat thrips. As a last resort apply neem to control a serious infestation.

A disease called smut causes a swelling or hardening of leaves just above the neck, which eventually bursts and spills powdery black spores over the plant. Downy mildew, a purplish mold, shows up in midsummer during warm, humid weather. Onions are also subject to pink root, which causes roots to turn various colors and then shrivel, and neck rot, which causes tissues to form a hard, black crust. All these problems are caused by fungi in the soil and can be avoided by rotating crops and by working humus into the onion bed to provide good drainage.

Harvesting: Once onion tops turn yellow, use the back of a rake to bend them over horizontally. This stops the sap from flowing to the stems and diverts the plant's energy into maturing the bulb. A day or so later, when the tops turn brown, pull or dig the bulbs on a sunny day, and leave them to dry in the sun. Lay the tops of one row over the bulbs of another to help prevent sunscald.

When the outer skins are thoroughly dry, wipe off any soil and remove the tops—unless you intend to braid them. Store in a cool, dry place; hang braided onions or those kept in mesh bags in an airy spot. Such dried bulbs will keep for about 4 months to 1 year.

ORCHIDS

If you can grow houseplants, you can grow orchids. Many orchids are tough, durable plants that will bloom year after year on a windowsill. These sturdy beauties only look fragile and exotic!

Getting Started

Before you buy an orchid, think about where you plan to put it. Different species do best at specific light levels and temperature ranges. You'll get the best bloom if you match plant to place. Some of the best windowsill orchids and their preferred conditions include:

- *Paphiopedilum* spp., exotic-looking orchids that resemble our native ladyslippers, need low to medium light (an east- or west-facing window) and temperatures between 55° and 75°F.

- *Phalaenopsis* spp., moth orchids, need low to medium light and temperatures between 70° and 80°F.

🌿 *Cattleya* spp., the classic corsage orchids, need medium to high light (a south-facing window) and temperatures of 70° to 80°F.

🌿 Equitant *Oncidium* spp., butterfly orchids or miniature oncidiums, need the same conditions as cattleyas. Very compact growers.

There are two other points to consider when buying orchids. First, although orchids bloom for a long time (sometimes months), when they're not in bloom, they're foliage plants. Some paphiopedilums and phalaenopsis have beautifully patterned foliage that makes them attractive even when not in bloom. Second, orchids can take years to reach blooming size. When you buy a plant, specify "blooming size" to make sure it will flower the first year.

Growing Great Orchids

Orchids will not grow in garden soil. Instead, use a mix sold especially for orchids or combine two parts Douglas fir bark to one part perlite. Use fine-grade bark for paphiopedilums, medium grade for the others. Buy bark where you buy your orchids—at greenhouses and well-stocked garden centers or through mail-order catalogs. For best growth and bloom, repot once a year, since fir bark breaks down and orchids need a loose, fast-draining medium.

Thorough watering once a week is enough except for large or very small plants. Household humidity that's comfortable to you (40 to 60 percent) is fine for orchids. (A humidifier will be good for you and your plants!) Or set the pots on pebble-filled trays and add water to the trays to increase the humidity around your plants. Make sure the water doesn't reach the top of the pebbles. In summer, orchids thrive outdoors; hang them in trees or set them in another shady spot.

Feed orchids twice a month with a balanced organic fertilizer, and give a nitrogen supplement such as fish emulsion at each feeding.

Orchids are remarkably problem-free. Use insecticidal soap to control the most common pests: mealybugs, scale, and spider mites. If a plant shows signs of disease, isolate it, remove affected parts with a sharp, flame-sterilized knife, and watch for recurrences.

OREGANO

Origanum spp.
Lamiaceae

Description: There are many species of oregano, including the annual *Origanum majorana*, or sweet marjoram (formerly *Majorana hortensis*). Seeds and plants of *O. vulgare* are often mistakenly sold as the oregano used for cooking. It is good as an ornamental, but unfortunately it has almost no flavor to contribute to food. The plants have erect, hairy, square stems with oval, pointed leaves up to 2 inches long and small, tubular, rose-purple to white flowers borne on 1-inch spikes.

The oregano to buy or grow for kitchen use is Greek oregano, *O. vulgare* ssp. *hirtum*. This small-leaved perennial plant forms low, spreading mounds, with spikes of white flowers rising about 1 foot above the foliage. It is marvelously aromatic. Try two exceptional oreganos for even more amazing flavor: the strain 'Kaliteri' and the cultivar 'Hot & Spicy'. Beautiful golden oregano, *O. vulgare* 'Aureum', adds a bright note to the herb garden or a container with its low form and chartreuse-gold foliage, but it is not as good a culinary oregano as many of the others.

How to grow: Start seeds or buy labeled plants. Site oregano in a raised bed or on a ridge of soil into which you have incorporated some grit or very fine gravel, and lime if your soil tends to be acid. Culinary oregano is not as winter hardy as the purple-flowered *O. vulgare*, which is hardy in Zones 4–9, but it may survive in Zone 5 if grown in full sun with good drainage, and is reliably hardy in Zones 6–9. It often seeds itself, making lots of nice small plants for spring. If you find it hard to overwinter, grow it in pots and bring them indoors to a cool, sunny window until it's warm enough to set out again.

Harvesting: Cut the long stems just as the flower heads are forming; harvest immediately after the dew has dried. Dry oregano to preserve the sweet, sharp aroma and flavor, hanging bunches in a warm, dry, dark place or drying stems on a tray in a food dehydrator, then stripping off the leaves, composting the stems, and storing leaves whole until needed. For best flavor, crumble the dried leaves into a dish as you prepare it. Oregano is one of the few herbs that tastes better dried than fresh.

Uses: The purple-flowered wild oregano, or *O. vulgare*, is useful as dried flower material, as it has good, dark rose-purple flowers that dry well on their wiry stems and look good in wreaths and arrangements. You can also plant masses of it to hold up an eroding sunny bank. Some people claim that oregano tea relieves stomach upsets and indigestion. The white-flowered culinary oregano, used sparingly, will contribute just the flavor needed in Italian, Mexican, or Greek cooking. It's essential in pizza and marinara sauces and complements tomato, pepper, and eggplant dishes, as well as enhancing recipes made with shellfish and eggs. If you'd like to make your own chili powder, combine dried oregano, dried chipotle chiles, cumin seeds, garlic powder, and salt to taste, and pulverize in a blender or coffee grinder until powdered.

ORGANIC GARDENING

Simply stated, organic gardening is a method that uses our understanding of nature as a guide for growing plants without using synthetic chemical pesticides or synthetic fertilizers. But gardening organically is much more than what you don't do. When you garden organically, you think of your plants as part of a whole system within nature that starts in the soil and includes the water supply, people, wildlife, and even insects. An organic gardener strives to work in harmony with natural systems and to minimize and continually replenish any resources the garden consumes.

In a natural system—a meadow or a woodland, for example—there's no need for synthetic pesticides or fertilizers. Some insects eat plants, but natural predators and parasites help keep their numbers in check. Also, nature tolerates some damage. No one worries whether wild plants and fruits have perfect cosmetic quality. Natural ecosystems also make their own fertilizers. Nature's cycle of growth, death, and decay is continuous. As plants and animals die, rodents, insects, earthworms, and microscopic soil creatures consume their bodies, and nutrients are released. These nutrients feed new generations of plants.

Many gardeners choose the organic method because they want to be good stewards of the environment. They are concerned about pollution of air, water, and soil and about protecting the health of their families and communities. They know that synthetic pesticides can destroy wildlife, bees, and other beneficial insects and may have an effect on food quality and safety. Tending an organic garden connects them with the soil and makes them feel close to nature.

Getting Started

Organic gardening begins with attention to the soil. You regularly add organic matter to the soil, using locally available resources wherever possible. And everyone has access to the raw ingredients of organic matter, because your lawn, garden, and kitchen supply them every day. Decaying plant wastes, such as grass clippings, fall leaves, and vegetable scraps from your kitchen, are the building blocks of compost, the ideal organic matter for your garden soil. If you add compost to your soil, you're already well on your way to raising a beautiful, healthy garden organically.

Here are some other basic suggestions to help you get started.

- Read about gardening and growing plants, especially using the organic method. Learning about gardening is an ongoing process gardeners enjoy throughout their lives.

- Learn more about your soil. You may want to have it tested by the extension office in your county or by a private laboratory. Use the results as a guide to bring your soil into balance with a long-term approach—biological changes aren't instant and may take several years! Add lime, compost, or organic fertilizers as needed. Maintain soil balance by growing green manure crops and adding organic matter each season.

- Start a compost pile. Recycling garden wastes and increasing soil organic matter content are two fundamentals of organic gardening. Composting helps you do both. There are many simple designs for compost enclosures, or you can just make a compost heap in a shaded corner of your yard.

- Use a plan and keep records. Find out about the plants you want to grow and which types will grow best in your area. Draw a sketch of your garden and decide what will go where, then revise it as you work. Begin a garden journal for keeping records through the season. Stock up on supplies and tools you may need during the gardening year.

- Prevent pest problems before they happen. Always check plants to be sure they're healthy before you bring them into the garden. Keep plants healthy with timely feeding and watering. Create a diverse ecosystem to encourage beneficial insects. Use row covers to exclude pests; build a fence to exclude animals. Remove diseased and insect-infested plant material from the garden. Handpick insect pests and their eggs. Try biological control techniques. As a last resort, use botanical insecticides.

- Learn to identify weeds, and eliminate them while they're small. Be diligent! A light cultivation several times early in the season may be all you need. Don't let weeds mature and produce seed for the next season.

Backyard Organic and Certified Organic

Organic gardening has deep historical roots, and a relatively recent development in the United States and other countries is the regulation of organic agriculture by the government. In the United States, farmers who want to label their products as "organic" must comply with regulations of the Organic Foods Production Act, which was passed by Congress as part of the 1990 Farm Bill. In response to this legislation, the USDA created the National Organic Program (NOP), which established a certification program designed to assure consumers that foods labeled organic have been grown, processed, or handled in compliance with standards designed to keep the food, as well as agricultural workers and the environment, free of harmful contaminants. The law also covers organic livestock and its meat, eggs, or milk. The program accomplishes this goal by deciding what substances can and cannot be used to feed crops and control pests if the crop is to be designated as organic. For example, to label their products organic, farmers cannot use toxic synthetic pesticides and fertilizers, genetically engineered seeds or other materials, sewage sludge, irradiation, antibiotics, growth hormones, and fresh manure (the manure must be composted or a waiting period must be observed between the application of manure to a field and harvest of any crop that is likely to be eaten raw).

Home gardeners do not need to follow NOP standards, of course, but if you operate a small market garden and earn more than $5,000 from it annually, you must comply with federal standards in order to sell your produce as organic. This entails keeping detailed records of practices and materials, plus on-farm inspections and periodic residue testing. Acceptable practices and materials are set by the US Secretary of Agriculture and the National Organic Standards Board, which consists of organic farmers, organic food handlers and retailers, environmentalists, and consumers. A number of private organizations and some state agriculture departments also operate and enforce their own standards, provided they are consistent with federal guidelines. These organizations also continue to participate in the debate about additional amendments to the national standards for organic food production. For more information about organic certification and NOP standards, see Resources on page 673 or ask your local extension office or state agriculture department for the names and addresses of certification groups active in your area.

A Brief History of Organic Gardening

Organic farming can be traced to several historical philosophies that influenced the way farmers raised crops many years ago. The development of organic gardening closely followed that of organic farming, since the practices that farmers used in their fields were often adopted in the home garden.

Genesis of the Organic Method

In the mid-1800s, dominance over the environment was the conventional agricultural philosophy in many Western countries. Scientists considered soil a sterile medium, useful only for holding plants in place. Crop production was a matter of chemistry.

In the early 1900s, the discovery of manufacturing processes to produce artificial fertilizers, the development of modern pesticides, the improvement of transportation methods, and the demand for farm products helped pave the way for increased crop specialization. Chemical farming became the predominant method in North America and Europe.

Charles Darwin was one of the first scientists to study living organisms in the soil. As a result of reports he wrote on his work in the 1880s, several new philosophies about the relationships between soil and plants evolved. Only a small number of modern farmers and scientists accepted these views, which took a holistic approach. They recognized the importance of returning nutrients to the soil, and the roles of soil animals, humus, and organic matter in crop production.

Biodynamics: In the early 1920s, Rudolf Steiner, an Austrian philosopher and author, founded the biodynamic method of farming. Biodynamic farmers embraced the holistic view of the farm as a living system. Both biodynamic and organic gardening methods avoid using synthetic chemicals and strive to produce vigorous, healthy plants that naturally are less susceptible to pest damage. Both methods recycle nutrients through composting and use raised beds, crop rotation, and companion planting.

What sets biodynamics apart from similar gardening practices is the philosophy behind it. Biodynamic gardeners use secret preparations of plant and animal materials to stimulate crop production and place importance on timing farming practices to coincide with phases of the moon. They attempt to understand the true nature of their crops and livestock: in other words, what each plant and animal really needs to grow to its potential. In biodynamic terms, an ideal farm is a self-supporting system. Livestock feed off the land and supply manure. Composted manures fertilize the soil and provide nutrients for new plant growth, completing the cycle of life. Rather than emphasizing measurable yields, biodynamic supporters seek a healthful product produced with minimal environmental impact.

The biodynamic concept also incorporates the theory of planetary influences on plant growth. Biodynamic gardeners believe these forces manifest themselves in plant characteristics such as vigor and nutrient content. Calendars of cosmic rhythms, such as moon phases and planetary events, guide these gardeners in determining ideal times to complete certain tasks, such as planting and cultivation. Biodynamic farming remains a separate and specialized method, practiced more widely in Europe than in the United States. To learn more about it, see Resources on page 673.

The organic method: Two independent schools of thought developed in the early 1900s that promoted the importance of humus in soil. Eventu-ally, both schools merged to form what we call the organic method. The new farmers regarded the agricultural environment as a living system that required recycling of organic wastes. They believed that the new synthetic fertilizers and pesticides were fatal to the environment. An explosion of publications in the 1940s promoted this new, organic method. Among them was *Organic Farming and Gardening*, founded by J. I. Rodale in 1942.

At that time, Sir Albert Howard introduced a special slow-composting system, the Indore method, and wrote eloquently about the importance of humus, soil microbial life, and soil aeration. Lady Eve Balfour, a leader of the organic movement in Great Britain, echoed Howard's ideas in her book, *The Living Soil* (1943). Soon after, Rachel Carson published the environmental classic, *Silent Spring* (1954), which directly questioned the influence of agricultural chemicals on the environment. These books and others helped carry organic farming concepts to farmers and scientists in North America and Europe.

A small segment of farmers adopted the organic method, and more gardeners became aware of their options. There was no longer only one way to grow crops. For many years, the organic method was considered radical or unusual, embraced by some home gardeners but largely ignored by commercial farmers.

Gradually, as concerns about the environment, food safety, and pesticides in the food chain increased, more large-scale farmers switched to organics. They found that the organic method was a viable way to run a farm, not just a garden. Still, the term *organic* lacked a definition. Attempts to define it often resulted merely in a long list of what organic gardeners didn't do. Everyone knew that organic growers didn't use synthetic pesticides and fertilizers. What exactly did they do?

Organics Come of Age

By 1980, farmers and scientists across the nation were asking questions about organics. The USDA responded by offering this detailed definition of organic farming: "A production system which avoids or largely excludes the use of synthetically compounded fertilizers, pesticides, growth regulators, and livestock feed additives. To the maximum extent feasible, organic farming systems rely upon crop rotations, crop residues, animal manures, legumes, green manures, off-farm organic wastes, mechanical cultivation, mineral-bearing rocks, and aspects of biological pest control to maintain soil productivity and tilth, to supply plant nutrients, and to control insects, weeds, and other pests." This definition officially recorded not only what organic growers don't use but also the special techniques that they do use to raise crops successfully.

Concurrently, J. I. Rodale's son, Robert Rodale, was developing the ideas of a larger

Masters of Their Field

If you want to refine your gardening skill or simply learn more about the origins of organic methods, you may enjoy reading books by or about these great leaders of organic farming and gardening.

Sir Albert Howard (1873–1947). One of the first proponents of a holistic approach to agriculture. Howard believed that soil organic matter, humus, and proper aeration play key roles in soil fertility and plant nutrition because they support soil microbial life. Organic gardeners in the United States largely follow the guidelines and methods established by Howard in the early 1900s and published in his book *An Agricultural Testament* (1940).

Helen (1904–1995) and Scott Nearing (1883–1983). These pioneers of self-subsistent organic farming founded the Social Science Institute, a publishing organization for many of their books and articles that influenced the back-to-the-land movement of the 1960s and 1970s. Their books include *The Maple Sugar Book: Together with Remarks on Pioneering as a Way of Living in the Twentieth Century* (1970) and *Living the Good Life: How to Live Sanely and Simply in a Troubled World* (1970).

J. I. Rodale (1898–1971) and Robert Rodale (1930–1990). The Rodales brought the organic method to popular knowledge and acceptance by American gardeners through the books and magazines published by Rodale Press in Emmaus, Pennsylvania. Both authored numerous books about organic gardening, health, and other topics.

Ruth Stout (1884–1980). Known to gardeners as the woman who originated the year-round, mulched, no-work garden. Her gardening books include *The Ruth Stout No-Work Garden Book* (with Richard Clemence, 1971), *How to Have a Green Thumb without an Aching Back* (1955), *Gardening without Work* (1961), and *I've Always Done It My Way* (1975).

organic philosophy—regeneration. He coined the term *regenerative agriculture*. Rodale felt that regeneration of renewable resources was essential to achieving a sustainable form of agriculture. He also believed that regenerative agriculture could nurture new ideas for general social leadership in addition to solving problems in agriculture and gardening.

An important boost for organic farming came in 1988, when the USDA began a program to fund research and demonstrations on what it named low-input sustainable agriculture (LISA), which has since been renamed the Sustainable Agriculture Research and Education (SARE) program. The goal of the USDA SARE program is to advance environmentally sound, profitable farming systems that are beneficial to the surrounding community. SARE administers a nationwide research and grants program and also develops and distributes information about sustainable agriculture; see Resources on page 673.

Once market gardeners and farmers realized there were alternatives to the conventional method—and as demand for organic produce increased—a new generation of organic farmers and gardeners began to see many exciting improvements and discoveries, a process that continues today.

ORGANIC MATTER

Understanding the importance of organic matter is crucial to success with organic gardening. Organic matter is a term that encompasses a wide variety of living or dead plant and animal material, ranging from kitchen wastes and shredded leaves to well-rotted manure and compost. Here's what adding organic matter to your soil can do.

1. Supply nutrients for plants by providing surfaces where nutrients can be held in reserve in the soil.

2. Facilitate better drainage by loosening soil structure.

3. Store water in the soil.

4. Help increase air drainage.

5. Increase the activity and numbers of soil microorganisms.

6. Encourage earthworms.

You can increase your soil's organic content by mulching with organic materials such as compost or shredded leaves, or by digging or tilling them into the top several inches of the soil. Then, to maintain a healthy, humus-rich soil, make adding organic matter part of your yearly garden activities.

Organic matter does not remain unchanged once you add it to soil because soil microorganisms act to break it down to simpler compounds. That's a good thing, because these compounds are then food for your plants. You can renew soil organic matter by side-dressing crops with compost, mulching during the growing season, and mulching or planting a cover crop during winter.

As a general rule, strive to maintain 5 to 6 percent organic matter in your soil. Don't overdo it! Adding too much fresh organic matter, such as plant stalks, sawdust, and other plant residues and uncomposted manure, can overstimulate soil microorganisms, which then consume so much nitrogen and other plant nutrients that soil fertility temporarily declines.

Keep in mind that in hot, humid climates, organic matter breaks down more quickly than in cool or dry climates. If you want to slow the loss of soil organic matter, cultivate the soil as little as possible, and when you do work the soil, do it gently, by hand, rather than using a rotary tiller.

You can learn more about the importance of organic matter and about materials you can use to increase soil organic matter content by reading the Compost, Cover Crops, Mulch, and Soil entries.

ORNAMENTAL GRASSES

Ornamental grasses are grown for their special decorative value and bring luxurious foliage, showy flowers, or vivid fall color to the landscape. In addition to true annual and perennial grasses, this group also includes sedges, rushes, and other grasslike plants.

Ornamental grasses vary widely in their growth habits. Some, such as prairie dropseed (*Sporobolus heterolepis*) and Oriental fountain grass (*Pennisetum orientale*), form clumps of foliage that grow straight upright or arch gracefully. Others, including reed canary grass (*Phalaris arundinacea* var. *picta*) and blue lyme grass (*Leymus arenarius*) spread rapidly from underground stems called rhizomes or aboveground stems called stolons. Spreading grasses are ideal for naturalizing or erosion control, but they also can be very invasive. Clump-forming grasses like miscanthus (*Miscanthus sinensis*) and fountain grass (*Pennisetum alopecuroides*) also can be invasive due to self-sown seeds. Unless you're willing to cut off their ornamental flower spikes and dispose of them before they set seed, they can become a maintenance nightmare.

Grasses are divided into two main groups: cool-season growers and warm-season growers. Cool-season grasses grow from fall into spring. They tend to be evergreen and are generally more moisture tolerant. Cool-season grasses usually flower in late winter and spring and grow rapidly during these times; they often slow down or even stop growing in summer.

Warm-season grasses are dormant in winter. They begin growth in spring, bloom during summer and fall, and go dormant with the onset of cool temperatures. Warm-season grasses often display brilliant fall colors, including orange, red, and purple. During winter, the dried foliage and seed heads can be quite attractive.

Grasses can add a new dimension to any garden design. The airy foliage and flower heads bend and rustle with the slightest wind, adding the elements of sound and movement to the garden. Try adding grasses to an herbaceous border, as individual specimens or in a mass. In the landscape, use tall grasses as windbreaks or screens to block an unpleasant view. Sedges and golden hakone grasses (*Hakonechloa macra* 'Aureola' and 'All Gold'), with their straplike leaves, make a beautiful contrast to other shade plants such as astilbes, ferns, hostas, and hellebores. Grasses such as fescues (*Festuca* spp.) also make beautiful, low-maintenance groundcovers.

Growing Ornamental Grasses

Grasses can adapt to a variety of soil textures from sand to clay. Most grasses are drought tolerant. A site with moist but well-drained, loamy soil of average fertility will suit most of these plants. At least a half day of full sun is usually ideal, although some grasses, such as most sedges (*Carex* spp.) and hakone grass (*Hakonechloa macra*), grow well with more shade. In general, those with thin, wide leaves accept more shade and are less drought tolerant.

Grasses require very little maintenance. Fertilize only if you have very sandy soil. Pests and diseases are rarely a problem. Most gardeners cut their plants back close to the ground once a year (generally in early spring). If you leave seed heads for winter interest, the grass may self-seed. Cultivate lightly around clumps in spring to uproot unwanted seedlings.

Six Great Grasses

The plants listed below are clump-forming grasses that will not spread widely in the garden. Two popular ornamental grasses, miscanthus and pennisetum (fountain grass), are not on this list. Though both are highly ornamental, they self-sow lavishly, creating a maintenance problem. The plants in this list, by contrast, are both ornamental and well behaved.

Briza media (**common quaking grass**): A cool-season grass that grows 1 to 1½ feet high with an equal spread. Showy flowers appear in spring over tufts of green foliage. Zones 4–9.

Calamagrostis ×acutiflora (**feather reed grass**): A warm-season grass growing 3 to 5 feet high and wide. Flowers, which can reach 6 feet, bloom in summer over arching clumps of medium green foliage that turns orange-brown in fall. Zones 4–9.

Chasmanthium latifolium (**northern sea oats**): This native warm-season grass grows 2 to 3 feet high with an equal spread.

Flowers appear in summer over upright arching clumps of light green foliage that bronzes in winter. Plants can spread by enthusiastically self-sown seed. Zones 4–9.

Helictotrichon sempervirens (**blue oat grass**): A cool-season grass that grows 1½ to 2 feet high and wide. Plants produce flowers in spring but are primarily prized for the 2½-foot-tall clumps of blue foliage. Zones 5–9.

Panicum virgatum (**switchgrass**): A native warm-season grass with pinkish flowers in late summer to fall. Cultivars such as 'Dallas Blues', with blue foliage from 4 to 6 feet tall, are best. May spread some by rhizomes. Zones 5–9.

Sporobolus heterolepis (**prairie dropseed**): A native warm-season grass with arching, threadlike leaves that form 15-inch-tall, 2-foot-wide clumps. Fine-textured, 30-inch panicles of flowers appear above the leaves in late summer, and foliage turns orange, then brown in fall. Zones 3–9.

Routine care is determined largely by whether a plant is a cool-or warm-season grass. The best time to plant, transplant, and divide cool-season grasses is from late winter to early spring or from late summer to fall. Don't disturb them in summer, when they are dormant. For warm-season grasses, plant, dig plants for transplanting, and divide them from late spring through early summer. Avoid disturbing these grasses in late summer to fall when they are blooming.

Grasses are easy to propagate by seed or division. Sow seed of annuals indoors about 4 weeks before the last frost. Transplant (or sow seeds directly) into the garden after danger of frost is past; thin to 6 to 12 inches apart. Seed is also an inexpensive way of increasing many perennial species, although named cultivars featuring variegated foliage or other characteristics generally do not come true from seed.

To propagate cultivars or renew old clumps, divide existing plants. Lift plants from the ground, separate them into smaller clumps, and replant. For large grasses, which can be very heavy and woody, chop the clump into pieces with a sharp spade, then lift them up out of the hole. To learn more about this technique, see the Division entry.

OVERWINTERING

Many plants grown as perennials in warm climates are not hardy enough to withstand the freezing temperatures in northern areas. Northern gardeners can leave these plants outdoors to die at the end of the season or they can overwinter them until the next growing season. Overwintering involves protecting the plant from the cold, either in the garden or in a sheltered place. There are many overwintering techniques, ranging from covering dormant plants with a thick layer of mulch to moving plants to a cold frame, sunny windowsill, or cool basement. What works for one type of plant might be fatal to another. Check individual plant entries for specific overwintering instructions.

An easy way to overwinter some plants is to grow them in containers year-round and use them as houseplants or on the sun porch during winter. Slow-growing woody plants such as lavender, rosemary, and tarragon make the transition from outdoor plant to houseplant and back very successfully and can thrive for many years.

You can hold many types of nonhardy plants, often called tender perennials, indoors over winter. Cutting back, digging up, and potting plants growing in the garden is one option for overwintering, but this may cause transplant shock, especially if the plants are large. An easier way to save tender perennials is to take and root cuttings, and then keep the cuttings indoors over winter. Many summer bedding plants, including impatiens,

begonias, geraniums, and coleus, can be overwintered this way. Rooted cuttings take up less space indoors than entire plants, and there is less chance of inadvertently overwintering diseases or insect pests. Take cuttings from your overwintering plants in late winter to propagate more transplants to move outdoors once the weather warms. To keep them from getting leggy as winter progresses, pinch them or keep them under plant lights. See the Cuttings entry for instructions on how to take cuttings.

The fleshy roots of cannas, dahlias, and even four o'clocks (*Mirabilis jalapa*), along with tender bulbs like caladiums (*Caladium* spp.) and tuberous begonias (*Begonia* spp.), can be dug and stored over winter. See the Canna, Dahlia, Caladium, or Begonia entries for techniques to try.

Geraniums (*Pelargonium* spp.) and other tender plants can be overwintered two ways. Bring them indoors as described above, or force them into dormancy. Forcing dormancy is useful if you're short on space for houseplants or want to save time and effort on winter care. Put the plant, either potted or with newspaper wrapped around its rootball, in a cool (not below 40°F), preferably dark place for winter. Allow the soil to dry somewhat but not completely; check every few weeks and water sparingly if needed. In spring, replant outside after danger of frost is past or place in a warm, well-lit place and resume watering.

Many tender perennials go dormant by themselves but need protection. Cover them with a thick layer of mulch, or dig and move to a cold frame or cool basement. Overwinter container plants outdoors by packing them in the center of large boxes packed full of leaves. Wrap shrubs and vines that need winter protection, or bury them in trenches (see the Fig entry for more information on burying plants).

P

PACHYSANDRA

Pachysandra, spurge. Evergreen perennial groundcovers.

Description: *Pachysandra terminalis*, Japanese pachysandra or Japanese spurge, has oval, glossy, dark green, 1- to 3-inch leaves set in whorls 6 to 8 inches high. Plants have underground creeping stems that spread steadily, producing a thick carpet. In May, white flower clusters appear on stout, fuzzy spikes. Japanese pachysandra has been identified as an invasive species in some areas. Zones 4–9.

  P. procumbens, Allegheny spurge, is native to the eastern United States. Leaves are coarsely toothed at the ends and mottled with purple. Flowers are white and borne near the ground. Plants are evergreen in the South, semievergreen to deciduous in the North, and are a handsome native groundcover. Zones 5–9.

How to grow: Pachysandras prefer partial shade in rich, moist, slightly acid soil. The plants can adjust to deep shade, but the leaves yellow in full sun. In fall, top-dress the soil with dehydrated manure or mulch lightly with compost. Rejuvenate old plantings by mowing in spring. Propagate in spring by division or cuttings. Space plants 6 to 12 inches apart.

Landscape uses: Plant pachysandras under shallow-rooted trees or broad-leaved evergreens. Pachysandras are excellent groundcovers for banks, slopes, or any difficult shaded areas. Keep Japanese pachysandra away from wooded areas or other sites where it may spread beyond the garden, because it can compete with populations of native wildflowers.

PAEONIA

Peony. Spring-blooming perennials.

Description: Cultivars of *Paeonia lactiflora*, common garden or Chinese peony, bear 3- to 8-inch single to double blooms in white, pink, and red shades, many with tufted (and sometimes yellow) centers. Common garden peonies bloom over a 4- to 6-week season above elegant, 4- to 10-inch, glossy, dark green leaves on shrublike plants averaging 3 feet tall and wide. The foliage remains attractive throughout the growing season, often flushing red, purple, or bronze in fall. Two famous fragrant cultivars that have stood the test of time are 'Festiva Maxima', a double white flecked with red, and 'Sarah Bernhardt', a soft pink double. Zones 2–8. *P. officinalis*, common peony, bears 4- to 5-inch satiny, vivid purplish red blooms on 1½- to 2-foot mounds of medium green, matte foliage resembling the common garden peony's. It blooms about a week before the common garden peony. Zones 3–8.

Tree peonies are derived from several species, including *P. suffruticosa* and *P. delavayi*. Unlike herbaceous peonies, tree peonies have woody stems that don't die back to the ground in winter. The single, semidouble, or double flowers may be up to 10 inches across and come in white, pink, red, salmon, deep purple, yellow, and apricot. The sometimes-fragrant blooms appear in mid-spring on sturdy, well-branched, 4- to 6-foot shrubs with divided dark green leaves. The plants are slow growing, but they can live for decades with a little extra care once established. Zones 3–8; provide winter protection in Zones 3–5.

How to grow: Plant peonies during late summer in the North or early fall in the South. If you wish to increase a favorite plant, divide herbaceous peonies at the same time. (Expect at least a year for the plant to settle in before blooming again.) Peonies prefer a sunny spot (partial shade in the South and for pastel cultivars) with fertile, well-drained soil. They can remain in the same spot for many years, so prepare a roomy planting hole with lots of compost.

Improper planting is a common reason for failure to bloom. For herbaceous peonies, make sure the tips of the pointed, pinkish new shoots, called eyes, are just 1 to 2 inches below the surface of the garden bed. Plant tree peonies with the graft union about 6 inches below the soil surface.

Remove foliage of herbaceous peonies when it dies down after frost. Tree peonies benefit from a light yearly pruning to promote bushy growth; also, remove all suckers from the rootstock. Both kinds of peonies benefit from a layer of mulch the first winter or two after planting. In early spring, feed plants with a balanced organic fertilizer; keep soil evenly moist throughout the growing season. Peonies often flop over from the sheer weight of the blooms or from a heavy rain; to prevent this, use a plant hoop to keep the stems upright, pushing it into the ground as growth emerges in spring. Single-flowered peonies are less likely to flop than those with heavier blooms.

Botrytis blight can cause wilted, blackened leaves and make buds shrivel before opening. Remove wilted parts immediately. Cut stems to ground level after frost blackens leaves. Anthracnose appears as sunken lesions with pink blisters on stems. Pruning off infected areas and thinning stems to improve air circulation will help lessen anthracnose problems. Infection by root knot nematodes can cause plants to wilt, become stunted, and have yellowed or bronzed foliage. Roots may be poorly developed and have tiny galls on them. Dig out and destroy severely infected plants.

Landscape uses: Use as specimens or in small groups in borders. Grow peonies alone in beds or in dramatic sweeps along a lawn, foundation, wall, walk, or driveway, or around a focal point such as a fountain or statue. Fragrant cultivars make delightful cut flowers.

PALMS

Palms. Evergreen trees or shrubs.

Description: Approximately 4,000 species of palms are found in the world's tropical and sub-tropical regions; palm fruits, oils, and building materials make the palms an economically important family. Eight or nine genera of palms are native to the United States, where they occur mostly in the southern coastal regions. For palm resources, visit the Web site of Jungle Music Palms & Cycads or the International Palm Society; see Resources on page 673.

Cycas revoluta, Japanese sago palm or simply sago palm, is not a true palm but a similar type of plant known as a cycad that is often included with palms for practical purposes. It consists of a rosette of stiff, coarse, compound leaves that are a dull dark green and 2 to 7 feet long. Japanese sago palm may develop a trunk after many years but will stay within the range of 3 to 5 feet tall. The plant bears a conelike male flower and a female flower that may eventually bear fruit. Zones 8–11.

Rhapidophyllum histrix, needle palm (also called porcupine palm, hedgehog palm, and blue palmetto), forms a low rounded clump with a coarse outline. The 3- to 4-foot-long foliage is blue-green and fanlike, with black needlelike sheaths protruding at the bases of leaves. This palm is hardier than most, tolerating temperatures down to 0°F. Zones 7–11.

Sabal minor, dwarf palmetto, forms a mounding, coarse-textured rosette of stiff, fanlike, compound leaves growing 3 to 8 feet long. Small whitish flowers appear on stalks in summer, followed by black fruits in autumn. Often found growing in the shade of taller trees, dwarf palmetto grows 3 to 5 feet tall. Zones 8–11.

Sabal palmetto, cabbage palmetto (also called Carolina palmetto), is a Southeast coastal native that can survive temperatures of 10° to 20°F in its home habitat. Cabbage palmettos reach 80 to 90 feet tall and bear fan-shaped leaves that are 5 to 6 feet long, 7 to 8 feet wide, and deeply divided. Cabbage palmetto is the state tree of both South Carolina (it is featured prominently on the South Carolina state quarter) and Florida. Zones 8–11.

Serenoa repens, saw palmetto, is similar to dwarf palmetto in many ways. It has olive to blue-green, fan-shaped foliage with coarse serrations along the edges. Large branches (up to 3 feet) of small, fragrant white blossoms appear in summer and are favorites of bees. Berrylike, bluish black fruits provide food for wildlife. Saw palmetto spreads via rhizomes, making it difficult to transplant or remove. Zones 8–11.

Trachycarpus fortunei, windmill palm or Chinese fan palm, has an erect form with a slender trunk and a head of large, fan-shaped leaves of dull dark green. The texture is coarse and bristly from the stiff crown to the fiber-covered trunk. Look for yellow flowers among the foliage and bluish fruits developing afterward. At heights of 15 to 30 feet, windmill palm is a good choice for small spaces, such as courtyards and entryways. It's also more cold-tolerant than most palms, surviving temperatures down to 5°F. Zones 7–11.

Washingtonia filifera, petticoat palm or California fan palm, is a West Coast native that lines streets in southern California and Florida. Petticoat palm, so-named because its persistent foliage hangs down from the crown to form a "petticoat" around the trunk, grows to 50 feet tall in the landscape; fan-shaped gray-green leaves may be 6 feet wide on mature plants. Zones 9–11.

How to grow: Most palms require full sun and fertile, moist, slightly acid soil. Dwarf palmetto is somewhat shade tolerant and often lives beneath a hardwood canopy; cabbage palmetto will also tolerate partial shade. Fertilize lightly in spring and summer. Palms are extremely susceptible to cold injury, so don't do anything (like heavy or late fertilization) that would cause plants to produce tender new growth in fall. Cold injury is most damaging when it affects the palm's crown, from which all new growth arises; plants that suffer damage to leaves may look unhealthy but will survive.

Landscape uses: Use low-growing palms for naturalizing, groundcovers, barriers, massed plantings, or foundation plants. Don't plant sharp-leaved saw palmetto or needle palm in high-traffic or play areas, but consider either for a durable hedge. Use windmill and petticoat palms as focal points. Petticoat palms and cabbage palmettos are good street trees in California and Florida. Beyond the coastlines of the Southeast and Southwest, even hardy palms are limited to container growing in the United States.

PAPAVER

Poppy. Spring- to summer-blooming annuals, biennials, and perennials.

Description: Poppies bear saucer- to bowl-shaped blooms with prominent central knobs. Single, semidouble, and double poppies bloom on long stems above masses of hairy leaves; flower colors include solid shades and combinations of white, pink, red, purple, yellow, and orange. The delightful state flower of California, the annual or tender perennial California poppy, is in an entirely different genus (though also in the poppy family); its botanical name is *Eschscholzia californica*.

Annual *Papaver rhoeas*, corn poppy or Flanders poppy, produces 2-inch red blooms on sparse-leaved plants usually reaching 2 feet.

P. somniferum, breadseed poppy, is an annual that produces the tasty black seeds used to coat bagels and other baked goods. Showy white, purple, or red flowers bloom atop 3- to 4-foot-tall stems; a prominent central capsule in each flower holds the prized seeds that may be harvested once the capsules have dried.

Biennial or short-lived perennial *P. nudicaule*, Iceland or arctic poppy, bears 2- to 6-inch, mostly single, orange, salmon, pink, or white blooms over basal rosettes of gray-green leaves; plants reach 1 to 1½ feet tall. Zones 2–7.

Perennial *P. orientale*, Oriental poppy, offers dazzling 6- to 10-inch-wide red, scarlet, white, pink, or purple flowers (most with striking black blotches inside) on stems from 2½ to 4 feet above dense, leafy masses. Zones 2–7.

How to grow: All poppies are easy to grow and prefer full sun to very light shade and average to rich, moist but well-drained soil. Direct-sow corn poppies and bread poppies in spring; start Iceland poppies in late summer in the North (fall in the South) for bloom the next year. All will self-sow if seed capsules are left to mature in the garden. Plant container-grown Oriental poppies in spring or in summer after the leaves disappear, which is an ideal time to divide them if necessary. Give Oriental poppies plenty of room in the bed or border—mature plants can take up as much as 3 feet of bed space. Provide light, loose mulch in winter.

Landscape uses: Grow in borders and informal gardens, or enjoy a solid bed or mass of bread, corn, or Iceland poppies. Combine Oriental poppies with later-blooming annuals and perennials like asters to fill the large gaps when the poppies go dormant, but leave room for leaves that reemerge in fall. Flowers last a few days in water if cut ends of the stems are seared in a flame.

PARSLEY

Petroselinum crispum
Apiaceae

Description: Parsley is a decorative 8- to 18-inch biennial with much-divided leaves. In its second year, it produces small yellow flowers in flat umbels. To some, the leaves have a bitter taste and smell of camphor; most people, however, enjoy the pleasantly pungent flavor.

There are two distinct kinds of parsley—curly and flat-leaved. Flat-leaved or Italian parsley (*Petroselinum crispum* var. *neapolitanum*) has luxuriant, shiny leaves and contains more vitamin C than the curly kind. It also has superior flavor. Curly parsley (*P. crispum* var. *crispum*) has ruffled leaves; it is popular in cooking and as a garnish. All parsley contains three times as much vitamin C, weight for weight, as oranges. It is also a fine source of vitamin A and iron. Both types will grow in Zones 3–9, though in zones colder than Zone 5, parsley should be treated as an annual.

How to grow: You can plant parsley outdoors in spring, but since it is slow to germinate (4 to 6 weeks), it's better to start seeds indoors. In either case, first soak the seeds in warm water for several hours or overnight.

For a reliable supply, sow new parsley plants each year. Although it's hardy, parsley will flower and die the second year unless you remove the flowerstalks. Parsley plants that do flower in the garden will often self-sow. Pot up small plants in fall for indoor use.

Harvesting: Pick leaves as you need them. Freeze chopped or whole parsley in self-sealing bags to keep more of its fresh flavor, or dry them on screens in a food dehydrator or in an oven or microwave.

Uses: You can use parsley to enhance salads as well as main and side dishes, since its flavor combines well with most other culinary herbs and nearly all foods except sweets. It is traditionally one of the French fines herbes used in soups, omelets, and potato dishes; it's delicious in soups, stews, and pasta sauces; and it is indispensable in Middle Eastern dishes like tabbouleh.

PARSNIP

Pastinaca sativa
Apiaceae

Parsnips are large carrot-shaped roots with a distinctive nutty-sweet taste. They require 100 to 120 days to mature and need a bit of extra soil preparation, but parsnip lovers know they're worth the effort. Prepare parsnips like carrots—steamed or sliced into soups or stews. For an extra-special treat, try roasted parsnips.

Planting: Parsnip's cream-colored root grows 8 to 24 inches long, with 2- to 4-inch-wide shoulders. Take extra care in preparing the planting area. Loosen the soil to a depth of 2 feet; remove rocks or clods. Dig in 2 to 3 inches of compost; avoid high-nitrogen materials that can cause forked roots.

In most areas, sow seed ½ to 1 inch deep in spring or early summer. Your goal is for the crop to mature at about the time of your first fall frost. In the South, plant parsnips in fall for a spring harvest. Use only fresh seeds, and soak them for several hours to encourage germination. Even then, germination will be slow and uneven, so sow the seed thickly and mark the rows with a quick-maturing radish crop. Cover the seed with a light material such as vermiculite or fine, sifted compost and water gently; keep the soil evenly moist.

Growing guidelines: Keep young plants free

of weeds, and use a light mulch to conserve moisture. Parsnips have long roots and tolerate dry conditions, but your crop will be more successful if watered regularly.

Problems: Parsnips are usually problem-free. See the Carrot entry for details on controlling problems that do occur.

Harvesting: Harvest roots after a hard frost for the best flavor. Dig and store like carrots, or mulch with a thick layer of hay and leave in the ground over winter, harvesting as needed. Pull the entire crop in early spring before new growth spoils its flavor.

PEA

Pisum sativum
Fabaceae

The crisp texture and sweet taste of fresh peas embodies spring. Ancient peoples foraged for peas in the wild long before they were domesticated. Romans, however, believed fresh green peas were poisonous and had to be dried before they could be eaten. It wasn't until the time of King Louis XIV of France that a French gardener developed a green-pea hybrid known as petits pois. Fresh peas soon became the rage at the king's court and thereby quickly gained widespread popularity.

Types: Still a garden favorite, peas are one of the first vegetables that you'll plant and harvest in spring. There are extra-early, early, midseason, and late types, taking 7 to 10 weeks to mature. Vining peas need trellises to grow on, while dwarf types need little or no support. Vining peas usually produce a heavier crop than do dwarfs.

Among green—or English—peas, there are wrinkled-seeded types and smooth-seeded types, both of which must be shelled. While wrinkled green peas are sweeter, smooth ones are hardier and better for super-early spring planting and for autumn and winter crops. If you've had problems with pea diseases, look for disease-resistant varieties such as 'Maestro'. If you want to can or freeze peas, choose a variety such as 'Dakota' that has a heavy and concentrated pod-setting period.

Snow peas and snap peas have edible pods. Snow peas produce flat pods that you can eat either raw or cooked. Snap peas are eaten either as young flat pods or after the peas have grown and are fat and juicy in the pods. Snow and snap peas are available in both vining and dwarf versions. New varieties of dwarf snow peas such as 'Golden Sweet' have pods that stay tender longer than traditional snow peas.

Some edible-podded cultivars have strings running down each pod that you must remove before eating; fortunately, "stringless" cultivars such as 'Sugar Sprint' have been developed that eliminate this task. Edible-podded peas are perfect for stir-fries and other Oriental dishes.

Field peas or cowpeas—which include black-eyed peas, crowder peas, and cream peas—are, botanically, beans. These plants thrive in areas with long, hot summers. See the Bean entry for information on cultivating these crops.

Planting: Give early peas a sunny spot protected from high winds. Later crops may appreciate partial shade. You can also plant peas in mid- to late summer for a fall crop. If possible, sow your fall crop in a spot where tall crops such as corn or pole beans will shade the young plants until the weather cools.

Early peas in particular like raised beds or a sandy loam soil that warms up quickly. Heavier soils, on the other hand, can provide cooler conditions for a late pea crop, but you'll need to loosen the ground before planting by working in some organic matter. Being legumes, peas supply their own nitrogen, so go easy on fertilizer. Too much nitrogen produces lush foliage but few peas.

Peas don't transplant well and are very hardy, so there's no reason to start them indoors. Pea plants can survive frosts but won't tolerate temperatures over 75°F. In fact, production slows down drastically at 70°F.

Southern gardeners often sow peas in mid- to late fall so the seeds will lie dormant through winter and sprout as early as possible for spring harvest. On the West Coast and in Gulf states, you can grow peas as a winter crop. Elsewhere, if the spring growing season is relatively long and cool, plant your peas 4 to 6 weeks before the last frost, when the soil is at least 40°F. For a long harvest season, sow early, midseason, and late cultivars at the same time, or make successive sowings of one kind at 10-day to 2-week intervals until the middle of May.

When planting peas in an area where legumes haven't grown before, you can improve your crop's yields by treating the seeds with an inoculant powder of bacteria, called rhizobia. This treatment promotes the formation of root nodules, which contain beneficial bacteria that convert the nitrogen in the air into a form usable by plants. All legumes—peas, beans, clovers, etc.—benefit from inoculation at planting time, and each legume has a particular species of rhizobia that it needs. For home gardeners, combination inoculant products are available that can be used on a variety of legume crops' seeds. To use an inoculant, roll wet seeds in the powder immediately before planting.

Space seeds of bush, or dwarf, peas 1 inch apart in rows 2 feet apart. Bush peas are also good for growing in beds. Sow the seeds of early crops 2 inches deep in light soil or 1 inch deep in heavy soil; make later plantings an inch or two deeper.

Thin to 2 to 3 inches apart. This close spacing will allow bush peas to entwine and prop each other up.

Plant vining types in double rows 6 to 8 inches apart on either side of 5- to 6-feet-tall supports made of wire or string, with 3 feet between each double row. Put trellising or other supports in place at planting time. The simpler the support, the easier it is to remove the vines at the end of the pea season and reuse it.

Generally speaking, 1 pound of seeds will plant a 100-foot row and should produce around 1 bushel of green peas or 2 bushels of edible pods. Another rough guideline is to raise 40 plants per person. Unused seed is good for 3 years.

To make good use of garden space, interplant peas with radishes, spinach, lettuce, or other early greens. Cucumbers and potatoes are good companion plants, but peas don't do well when planted near garlic or onions.

Growing guidelines: Providing peas with just the right amount of water is a little tricky. They should never be so waterlogged that the seeds and plants rot, and too much water before the plants flower will reduce yields. On the other hand, don't let the soil dry out when peas are germinating or blooming or when the pods are swelling. Once the plants are up, they only need about ½ inch of water every week until they start to bloom; at that time, increase their water supply to 1 inch a week until the pods fill out.

Peas growing in good soil need no additional fertilizer. If your soil is not very fertile, you may want to side-dress with compost when the seedlings are about 6 inches tall.

The vines are delicate, so handle them as little as possible. Gently hand-pull any weeds near the plants to keep from damaging the pea roots. To reduce weeds and conserve moisture, lay 2 inches of organic mulch once the weather and soil warms. This also helps keep the roots cool. Soil that becomes too warm can result in peas not setting fruit or can prevent already-formed pods from filling out. Mulch fall crops as soon as they are planted, and add another layer of mulch when the seedlings are 1 to 2 inches tall.

Once a vine quits producing, cut it off at ground level, leaving the nitrogen-rich root nodules in the ground to aid the growth of a following crop, such as brassicas, carrots, beets, or beans. Add the vines to your compost pile, unless they show obvious signs of disease or pest problems.

Problems: Aphids often attack developing vines. For information on controlling these pests, see page 454.

Pea weevils can chew on foliage, especially along the edges of young leaves. They are serious only when they attack young seedlings. Apply *Beauveria bassiana* as soon as damage is spotted to head off problems.

Thrips—very tiny black or dark brown insects—often hide on the undersides of leaves in dry weather. They cause distorted leaves that eventually die; thrips also spread disease. Control them with an insecticidal soap spray.

See the Animal Pests entry for information on protecting seeds and seedlings from birds.

Crop rotation is one of the best ways to prevent diseases. To avoid persistent problems, don't grow peas in the same spot more than once every 5 years.

Plant resistant cultivars to avoid fusarium wilt, which turns plants yellow, then brown, and causes them to shrivel and die.

Root-rot fungi cause water-soaked areas or brown lesions to appear on lower stems and roots of pea plants. Cool, wet, poorly drained soil favors development of rots. To avoid root rot, start seeds indoors in peat pots and wait until the soil is frostless before setting out the plants. Provide good fertility and drainage for strong, rapid growth.

Warm weather brings on powdery mildew, which covers a plant with a downy, white fungal coating that sucks nutrients out of the leaves. Bicarbonate sprays can help to prevent mildew. Destroy seriously affected vines, or place them in sealed containers for disposal with household trash. Avoid powdery mildew by planting resistant cultivars.

Control mosaic virus, which yellows and stunts plants, by getting rid of the aphids that spread it. Choose resistant cultivars.

Harvesting: Pods are ready to pick about 3 weeks after a plant blossoms, but check frequently to avoid harvesting too late. You should harvest the peas daily to catch them at their prime and to encourage vines to keep producing. If allowed to become ripe and hard, peas lose much of their flavor. Also, their flavor and texture are much better if you prepare and eat them immediately after harvesting; the sugar in peas turns to starch within a few hours after picking.

Pick shell and snap peas when they are plump and bright green. Snow-pea pods should be almost flat and barely showing their developing seeds. Cut the pods from the vines with scissors; pulling them off can uproot the vine or shock it into nonproduction.

Preserve any surplus as soon as possible by canning or, preferably, by freezing, which retains that fresh-from-the-garden flavor. To freeze peas, just shell and blanch for 1½ minutes, then cool, drain, pack, and freeze. Snow peas, which are frozen whole, are treated the same way, but don't forget to string them first if necessary. Peas have a freezer life of about 1 year.

If peas become overripe, shell them and spread

them on a flat surface for 3 weeks or until completely dry. Store in airtight containers and use as you would any dried bean.

PEACH

Prunus persica
Rosaceae

There may be no greater pleasure than biting into a peach fresh from the tree. Growing peaches organically can be a challenge, and your harvest may not look picture-perfect. However, the flavor will more than make up for any surface imperfection!

These wonderful fuzzy fruits are the same species as nectarines. Only a single gene controls whether a cultivar bears smooth- or fuzzy-skinned fruit.

The Fruit Trees entry covers many important aspects of growing peaches and other tree fruits; refer to it for more information on planting, pruning, and care.

Selecting trees: Most peach trees are self-fertile. One tree will set a good crop, although yields typically are better when two or more cultivars are planted for cross-pollination.

Select cultivars to match your climate, or see the explanation of chill hours on page 414 for a more exact way to determine which cultivars to plant. Choose disease-resistant peaches when available.

Base your choice of cultivar on what you plan to do with your harvest. Freestone fruit are easy to separate from the pit and great for fresh eating, but the melting flesh often turns soft when canned. Clingstone fruit hang onto the pit for dear life, but their firm, aromatic flesh is great for cooking and preserving.

Yellow flesh is standard, but white-fleshed peaches are quite tender and equally tasty.

If you have the space for several trees, pick cultivars that will give you a succession of harvests. Just be sure your growing season is long enough for the fruit to mature.

Rootstocks: Peach trees are sold as grafted trees; common rootstocks in the United States include 'Lovell', 'Halford', and 'Guardian'. Where nematodes are severe, try 'Nemared' or 'Nemaguard' rootstock. If you have late winter warm spells, seedling rootstocks may be less likely to break dormancy prematurely. If you're planting peach trees for the first time, ask your local extension office for recommendations of the best rootstocks for your region.

Planting: Peaches prefer soil that is well drained and sandy-light on the surface with heavier texture in the subsoil. This keeps the crown and roots dry, helping to prevent disease problems, but still provides a deep reservoir of moisture and nutrients. For best results in any soil, add organic matter and correct any drainage problems before planting. Peaches need a pH of 6.0 to 6.5. Don't add lime if the pH is 6.2 or higher, since a high level of calcium in the soil reduces absorption of potassium and magnesium by tree roots. Fertilize with compost. Space standard peaches 15 to 20 feet apart, and space dwarfs 12 feet apart.

Peach blossoms are easily damaged by frost. In areas where late-spring frosts are common, avoid planting in frost pockets (see page 223). Instead, choose a site on the upper half of a north-facing slope. A north-facing slope warms slowly, which may delay flowering by as much as 1 to 2 weeks. Planting about 15 feet away from the north side of a building may have the same effect. A thick mulch under the trees will help

Chill Hours

Like other tree fruits, peach trees need a period of cold-weather rest or dormancy. The number of hours of cold between 32° and 45°F needed before a tree breaks dormancy is referred to as chill hours. (Cold below 32°F doesn't count toward meeting the dormancy requirement.) Once the number is reached, the tree assumes winter is over, and it starts growing the next warm day. Peaches bloom rapidly once their requirement has been met, which makes them more prone to frost damage than other tree fruits that are slower to burst into bloom.

Call your local extension office to find out how many chill hours your area receives and what cultivars match that requirement. If you choose a cultivar that needs fewer chill hours than you normally receive, it may flower too early and be prone to bud damage. But if you choose one that needs more chill hours, it won't get enough chilling to stimulate normal bloom.

delay flowering by keeping the soil cool.

Peaches ripen best when the sun shines and temperatures hover at about 75°F. If temperatures are consistently cooler, the fruit can develop an astringent flavor or be almost tasteless. Plant your tree in a sheltered location that conserves heat to help the fruit ripen.

Since most peach trees have a maximum productive life of about 12 years, plant replacements periodically. If you plan ahead, you will always have mature trees and fresh fruit. Don't replant in the same location, though. Viruses and nematodes, which will shorten the life of new trees, may have built up in the soil.

Care: Healthy peaches should grow 1 to 1½ feet a year. If growth is slower or the foliage is a light yellow-green or reddish purple, have the leaves and soil tested for nutrient content, and correct deficiencies. The Soil entry gives specifics on soil testing. In cold climates, fertilize only in early spring so wood can be fully hardened before winter. Mulch with compost or other low-nitrogen organic materials to maximize water and nutrient availability.

Peach trees need even moisture around their roots to produce juicy, succulent fruit. If the weather is dry or the soil is sandy, install drip irrigation over the entire root system out to the drip line. Keep the soil moist, not wet. Mulch to reduce evaporation. See the Drip Irrigation entry for more information.

Sometimes peaches flower when the weather is still too cool for much insect activity. To ensure fruit set, you must take the place of insects and spread pollen from flower to flower. Use a soft brush to dab pollen from one flower onto its neighbor. Hand-pollinate newly opened flowers every day, and you'll have a decent crop.

Frost protection: Winter temperatures of −10°F or lower will kill some or all of the flower buds of most peach cultivars. Some may even suffer cold damage to the wood, branch crotches, or trunk. The closer the cold snap comes to spring flowering time, the more severe the damage will be. Plant cold-tolerant cultivars to minimize losses. Or try letting the tree grow taller than you normally would; the upper boughs may escape frost damage.

If frost is predicted, spray an antitranspirant the

day before for 2° to 3°F of extra protection. Or get up and hose down trees with water just before sunrise.

Pruning: Train peaches to the open center system. This makes an attractive, productive tree that is low and spreading and easy to reach. For instructions, see page 226.

Start training your tree when you plant it. The first few years, prune as needed to shape the tree. After that, prune only to keep the tree fruiting and reasonably small. Prune each year just before the tree breaks dormancy. If canker is a problem or spring frosts are common, prune after flowering to minimize disease problems and ensure that you will have a good crop. Dry weather at pruning discourages canker invasion, and you will be able to prune more or less depending on how many buds survived winter. Heading back new growth now reduces the fruit load and your later thinning chores.

Try central leader training if your trees suffer sunscald, or protect trees by painting the larger branches with diluted white latex paint. In very cool climates, try training your peach tree against a stone or brick wall that reflects sun and radiates heat. For training instructions, see page 225.

No matter what training method you choose, try to minimize the amount of wood you remove the first few years. Rub off unwanted shoots and suckers as soon as they appear during the growing season. Your tree will bear earlier and more heavily if you do.

As the tree gets older, continue to prune each spring for maintenance and renewal. Peaches fruit only on 1-year-old wood. Encourage new growth by cutting off old branches that are no longer productive. Head back new growth by a third to half of its length to keep the tree compact. Cut back to just above an outward-facing branch or bud.

Heading back also encourages more small side branches, which are the best fruit producers, and keeps the tree from overbearing.

Thinning: Once your tree starts bearing, it may set more fruit than it can handle. Remove some of the green fruit before the pits harden, so the remaining fruit will grow large and sweet and the tree won't break under the weight of the ripe fruit. Leave one peach every 4 to 6 inches. If you don't remove enough, prop up heavily laden branches with a forked stick until harvest. Prune and thin harder the next year.

Harvesting: Peach trees bear within 3 years. As peaches ripen, the skin color changes from green to yellow; the flesh slightly gives to the touch when ripe. Hold the fruit gently in your palm and twist it off the branch. Avoid bruising it. You can store ripe peaches for about a week in a refrigerator.

Problems: Peach trees can be plagued by various pests and diseases; the most serious are canker and peach tree borers. Nectarine fruits are even more likely to be attacked by fruit pests than peaches are, perhaps because pests dislike the fuzzy skin on peaches.

Common peach pests include green fruitworms, two types of peach tree borers, mites, and plum curculios. For descriptions and control methods, see page 231. Aphids, Japanese beetles, scale, and tarnished plant bugs can also cause problems; see page 454 for descriptions and controls.

Oriental fruit moths lay eggs on shoots and the larvae bore into the tissue early in the season. Later generations of larvae burrow to the center of fruits to feed. Young fruits exude a gummy substance and often drop prematurely. Control this pest by removing infested shoots and fruit and destroying them. Encourage native parasitic wasps that attack the eggs and larvae.

Fall webworms and tent caterpillars spin webs and munch on leaves. Gypsy moth caterpillars also eat leaves. Destroy webs and caterpillars as soon as you see them. Spray Bt (*Bacillus thuringiensis*) where they are feeding.

Trees infected by root knot nematodes may have weak growth and yellow leaves. Affected trees won't bear fruit and will eventually die. If you suspect a nematode problem, ask your local extension office about having your soil tested for nematodes. To avoid nematode problems, don't replant where peaches have grown previously, solarize soil before planting, and enrich soil with organic matter to encourage natural fungi or apply parasitic nematodes to soil before planting. 'Nemaguard' rootstock is resistant to root knot nematode.

Some common diseases of peaches are bacterial leaf spot, brown rot, and perennial canker (also known as valsa and cytospora). See page 231 for descriptions and controls.

Peach leaf curl is a fungal disease that causes leaves to become thick, puckered, and reddish. It's a common problem in cool, humid areas. Symptoms appear about a month after bloom. Leaves drop soon after. Fruit will look distorted and off color. To prevent peach leaf curl, remove infected leaves and destroy them. Increase air circulation by pruning trees every year when they are dormant. It's rare for peach leaf curl to become a serious problem, but if it's threatening to kill off your trees, spray with Bordeaux mix (a blend of copper sulfate and hydrated lime) in fall after leaves drop or in early spring while the trees are still dormant.

Peach scab causes small, olive green spots, usually clustered near the stem end of half-grown fruit about a month after infection. Later the spots turn brown and velvety, and the skin cracks. Twigs and leaves also get peach scab. Remove and destroy infected fruit and clean up fallen leaves and fruit. Weather that is warm and either wet or humid encourages scab. Control as you do brown rot. If you've had problems with scab in previous seasons, spray sulfur weekly from the time the first green shows in the buds until the weather becomes dry.

Certain cankers cause wilting or yellowing of new shoots or leaves and can also girdle limbs. Delay routine pruning until after bud break to reduce the chance of infection by canker organisms. Prune out and destroy any gummy cankers on trees whenever you spot them.

Crown gall and crown rot sometimes attack peach trees; providing good drainage helps to avoid these problems. Use a sharp knife to remove galls that form near the soil line.

Virus diseases such as yellows and mosaic may cause leaf distortion, discoloration, and mottling. Buy only certified disease-free stock. Destroy infected trees immediately.

PEANUT

Arachis hypogaea
Fabaceae

Contrary to popular belief, the peanut is not a nut; it is actually a vegetable belonging to the legume family, which includes peas and beans. These tropical natives of South America require about 120 days to mature, but fortunately they can withstand light spring and fall frosts. 'Jumbo Virginia' is a productive variety for home gardens. Although peanuts are generally considered a southern crop, northern gardeners can also grow them successfully if they choose early cultivars such as 'Early Spanish' and start plants indoors.

Planting: Peanuts need full sun. If you have heavy soil, ensure good drainage by working in enough organic matter to make it loose and friable.

Peanut seeds come in their shells and can be planted hulled or unhulled. If you do shell them, don't remove the thin, pinkish brown seed coverings, or the seed won't germinate.

Northern growers should start plants indoors in large peat pots a month before the last frost. Sow seeds 1 inch deep, place in the sunniest spot possible, and water weekly. Transplant seedlings to the garden when the soil warms to between 60° and 70°F. Space transplants 10 inches apart, being careful not to damage or bury the crown.

In the South, plant outdoors around the date of the last expected frost. Space seeds 2 inches deep and 5 inches apart in rows 2 to 3 feet apart. Firm the soil and water well. Thin plants to 10 inches apart.

Growing guidelines: When the plants are about 1 foot tall, hill the earth around the base of each plant. Long, pointed pegs (also called peduncles) grow from faded flowers and then push 1 to 3 inches down into the soil beside the plant. A peanut will form on the end of each peg. Lay down a light mulch, such as straw or grass clippings, to prevent the soil surface from crusting so that the pegs will have no difficulty penetrating the soil.

One inch of water a week is plenty for peanuts. Being legumes, peanuts supply their own nitrogen, so avoid nitrogen-rich fertilizers, which encourage foliage rather than fruits. Well-prepared soil will provide all the nutrients the plants need.

Problems: Peanuts are usually problem-free. For aphid controls, see page 454.

Harvesting: The crop is ready to harvest when leaves turn yellow and the peanuts' inner shells have gold-marked veins, which you can check periodically by pulling out a few nuts from the soil and shelling them. If you wait too long, the pegs will become brittle, and the pods will break off in the ground, making harvesting more difficult. Pull or dig the plants and roots when the soil is moist. Shake off the excess soil, and let plants dry in an airy place until the leaves become crumbly; then remove the pods. Unshelled peanuts, stored in airtight containers, can keep for up to a year.

PEAR

Pyrus communis, P. serotina, **and hybrids**
Rosaceae

With their glossy leaves and white blossoms, pear trees are a beautiful accent in a home landscape. Plus, they produce bushels of delicious fruit, are long lived, and suffer fewer insect and disease problems than many tree fruits.

Most gardeners are familiar with European pears, including the familiar 'Bartlett' and 'Bosc' pears. However, Asian pears, which have crisp, juicy, almost round fruits, will also grow well in most parts of the United States and Canada. The Fruit Trees entry covers many important aspects of growing pears and other tree fruits; refer to it for additional information on planting, pruning, and care.

Selecting trees: Pears need cross-pollination to set a good crop. Most European and Asian cultivars pollinate each other. A few cultivars don't product viable pollen; if you select one, you'll need to plant three different cultivars to ensure good fruit set. Certain cultivars will not pollinate other specific cultivars. Check pollination requirements before you buy.

European pears are hardy to −20°F, but Asian pears generally are hardy only in Zones 5 and warmer. European and Asian pear varieties have a range of chilling requirements, so check on this when deciding what to grow. (For more information on fruit tree chilling requirements, see page 220.)

Fire blight can be a devastating disease problem in some regions, especially areas with warm, wet spring seasons. 'Magness' and 'Warren' are resistant to fire blight. 'Magness' doesn't produce viable pollen, so be sure to plant it with two other cultivars. Asian pears seem to be less appealing to pear psylla, another common problem.

Rootstocks: Standard pear trees are grafted onto seedling rootstocks, but they can grow 30 feet tall. Semidwarf and dwarf varieties are easier to care for and harvest. Many dwarf and semidwarf pear trees are grafted onto quince rootstock. 'Old Home ×Farmingdale' rootstock is resistant to fire blight and pear decline and makes a semidwarf tree.

Planting and care: Pear trees are quite winter hardy. They bloom early but tend to be more resistant to frost damage than other fruits. (Opened pear blossoms can be damaged at 26°F.)

Pears will tolerate less-than-perfect drainage but need deep soil. They are vulnerable to water stress, which causes foliage to turn brown and prevents fruits from enlarging. To prevent this, mulch with a thick layer of organic matter out to the drip line, and irrigate deeply if the soil dries out.

Pears prefer a pH of 6.4 to 6.8. If pH is too low, the tree may be more susceptible to fire blight. A healthy pear tree grows 1 to 1½ feet a year. If growth is less, have the foliage tested and correct any deficiencies. The Soil entry gives details on how to get foliage tested. Go easy when fertilizing with nitrogen; it encourages soft new growth that is susceptible to fire blight. If there is too much new growth on the tree, let weeds or grass grow up beneath the tree to consume excess nutrients in the soil.

Pruning: Pear trees grow tall. However, you can keep all the limbs within an arm's reach of a ladder by training your young tree. How you choose to prune and train your tree will greatly affect its lifespan as well as its ability to produce large crops. Start training as soon as you plant your tree. Be sure to spread the branches, because pears tend to grow up, not out, if left on their own. Minimize pruning, because too much pruning can also stimulate more growth than you want.

If you develop a strong, spreading framework, it will be easier to prune, and the tree will bear earlier. When you do start to prune, prune just before the tree breaks dormancy in spring. Or in locations where pears suffer winter bud damage, prune just after flowering.

Train European pears to a central leader system and Asian pears to an open center system (see the Fruit Trees entry for pruning details). In areas where fire blight is severe, you may want to leave two main trunks as crop insurance.

To minimize fire blight attack on susceptible trees, discourage soft young growth and make as few cuts as possible. Thin out whole branches rather than heading them back. This will reduce the total number of cuts made and won't stimulate the growth of soft, highly susceptible side shoots. Snip off any flowers that appear in late spring or summer. They are easy targets for fire blight.

Remove unproductive and disease-susceptible suckers that sprout from the trunk and branches. As the tree gets older, you may want to leave a renewal sucker to replace a limb with 4- or 5-year-old spurs, or one damaged by fire blight. During summer, select a sucker near the base of the branch to be replaced. Spread the crotch so it will develop a good outward angle. Carefully remove the old branch the next spring so the sucker will have room to develop.

Thinning: Pears are likely to set more fruit than they can handle. Fruits will be small, and the heavy fruit load may break branches or prevent flowering the following year if not thinned. A few weeks after the petals fall, remove all but one fruit per cluster. Prop up heavily laden limbs with a forked stick.

Harvesting: Pears bear in 3 to 5 years after planting. Pick European pears before the flesh is fully ripe; the fruit will finish ripening off the vine. To test ripeness, cut a fruit open; dark seeds indicate ripe fruit. Also, if you can pull the fruit stem away from the branch with a slight effort but without tearing the wood, the fruit is prime for harvesting. Store pears at just above 32°F. Many European cultivars store well; hard, late-bearing cultivars store better than earlier cultivars. When you're ready to eat them, place them in a 60° to 70°F room to soften and sweeten (putting them in a bowl with some bananas will speed their ripening). Pears that won't ripen may have been in cold storage too long, or the ripening temperature may be too high. If a pear is brown and watery inside, it was harvested too late.

Asian pears are sweetest when allowed to ripen on the tree. Watch for a color change, and taste to decide when they are ripe.

Problems: Apple maggots, codling moths, green fruit worms, mites, and plum curculio can attack pears. For descriptions and control methods, see page 231. Pears also attract aphids, scale, and tarnished plant bugs; see page 454 for descriptions and controls. See the Apple entry for description and control of leaf rollers and other leaf-eating caterpillars.

Pear psylla is a major pest in many areas. These tiny sucking insects are nearly invisible to the naked eye. They are often noticed only when the foliage and twigs at the top of pear trees turn black in late summer. The black color is actually a sooty mold that grows in the honeydew produced by the psylla. Left uncontrolled, psylla and sooty mold can reduce fruit production or even kill the tree. Psylla also can infect trees with viruslike diseases, such as pear decline. Native beneficial insects can help keep psylla in check. To prevent psylla problems, spray trees with kaolin clay beginning in spring, and if possible, keep the trees coated by repeat spraying all through the growing season. The psylla don't like to lay their eggs on sprayed trees, and the clayey coating also irritates psylla nymphs.

Thrips are tiny insects too small to see, but you can see their small dark droppings on leaves. Leaves will appear bleached and wilted, fruit may show scabs or russeting. Predatory mites will control thrips, but if populations are high, spray with insecticidal soap.

Pear slugs are the small sluglike larvae of sawflies. They eat leaf tissue but leave a skeleton of veins behind. Handpick, wash them off leaves with a strong water spray, or spray with insecticidal soap.

Fire blight, a bacterial disease that affects many fruit trees, is especially severe on pears. It can rapidly kill a susceptible tree or orchard in humid conditions. The sooty mold that goes with psylla can also look like fire blight. Sooty mold wipes off; fire blight doesn't. For control measures, see page 231. Pear trees also suffer from cedar-apple rust; see the Apple entry for description and controls.

Pseudomonas blight symptoms resemble fire blight, but it thrives in cool fall conditions when fire blight is less common. Control as for fire blight.

Pear scab looks much like apple scab. See the Apple entry for description and controls.

Fabraea leaf spot causes small, round, dark spots with purple margins. Leaves turn yellow and drop. Fruits develop dark, sunken spots and may be misshapen. If many leaves drop, trees are weakened, and future crops are reduced. Clean up fallen leaves each winter. If leaf spot has been a problem in the past, spray copper just before the blossoms open and again after the petals fall off.

Many viral diseases affect pears, causing leaf or fruit distortion and discoloration. Buy certified virus-free stock, and control insects such as aphids, which may transmit viruses.

PELARGONIUM

Pelargonium ×hortorum, zonal geranium, garden geranium, scented geranium. Tender perennials grown as annuals or houseplants.

Description: Flower colors include white, pink, rose, red, scarlet, purple, and orange shades, plus starred, edged, banded, and dotted patterns of two or more colors. Pick from single (five-petaled) or double forms resembling rosebuds, tulips, cactus flowers, or carnations. The rounded flower clusters may be very dense or quite open and airy, measuring 1 to 6 inches across. Geraniums normally grow 1 to 2 feet in a single season. Smaller sizes include miniature (3 to 5 inches), dwarf (6 to 8 inches), and semidwarf (8 to 10 inches). Upright, mounded, and cascading habits are available. The soft and fuzzy, rounded, scalloped, or fingered leaves can grow from $\frac{1}{2}$ to 5 inches wide. Leaves may be all green, chartreuse and maroon, banded in dark green, or green combined with one or more shades of white, red, yellow, chartreuse, or brown. *Pelargonium peltatum*, ivy geranium, brings color to window boxes and baskets throughout summer and fall. Clusters of white, red, pink, salmon, lavender, and purple flowers bloom profusely on trailing stems above shiny, scalloped, ivy-shaped leaves.

Some of the many cultivars have variegated leaves, including 'Crocodile', with unusual yellow-netted leaves. Plants can grow 2 to 5 feet in a season. There are also more-compact hybrids between the ivy and garden (zonal) geranium.

Ivy geraniums are excellent hanging-basket plants. You can also grow them in the traditional window box, in a raised planter, or as a flowering groundcover.

P. ×domesticum, Martha Washington or regal geraniums, are the glamour queens of the genus. They take the spotlight in cooler regions, where their 6-inch clusters of azalea-like flowers bloom profusely in white, pink, red, lavender, burgundy, salmon, violet, and bicolors. Rounded leaves up to 8 inches wide grow thickly on mounded 1- to 2-foot plants.

Spectacular in beds, regal geraniums also make great houseplants and dazzling standards. If you live where summers are hot, you can still enjoy these beauties as spring pot plants, discarding them after bloom.

How to grow: Buy blooming plants of cutting-grown cultivars from a nursery; try to buy locally grown cultivars that are suitable for your region, especially in the humid South. Or sow seeds in February for plants that will bloom by summer. Plant out after all danger of frost is past. Most prefer full sun, but shade variegated cultivars from the hottest afternoon sun to prevent leaf browning. Geraniums adapt to most well-drained soils with average moisture, although they prefer sandy loam. Avoid high-nitrogen fertilizers, which encourage leaf growth at the expense of flowers, unless you're growing cultivars such as 'Vancouver Centennial' or 'Crystal Palace Gem' for their fabulous foliage. Pinch the tips of plants that are reluctant to branch on their own to avoid tall, leggy plants with leaves and flowers only toward

Scented Geraniums

Although not as colorful as zonal geraniums, scented geraniums (*Pelargonium* spp.) also deserve a place in your garden. A few of them have attractive blooms, producing small clusters of pink, white, or lavender flowers, but they're really grown for their fragrant foliage. Leaf form varies from tiny ½-inch rounded leaves to 6-inch oaklike giants, but all release their powerful aromas with a gentle rub. Habit ranges from loose, spreading plants to strong bushes reaching 4 feet or more.

Scented geraniums require much the same care as zonal geraniums, but don't overfeed them or the fragrance won't be as strong. They grow well in pots of loose, well-drained soil, and their scented foliage makes them ideal houseplants. Grow them in your flower borders for a green accent, or show them off in an herb or kitchen garden. Both flowers and foliage are edible and can be used fresh or dried in herb teas.

There are many, many scented geraniums available. The list here is a small sample.

NAME	FRAGRANCE
Pelargonium crispum	Lemon
P. denticulatum	Pine
P. ×fragrans	Nutmeg
P. graveolens	Rose
P. ×nervosum	Lime
P. odoratissimum	Apple
P. scabrum	Apricot
P. tomentosum	Peppermint

Hybrids between these and other species have given rise to many cultivars, among them 'Grey Lady Plymouth', with rose-scented, gray-green leaves edged in white; 'Mabel Gray', with an intense lemon fragrance and sharply lobed leaves; and 'Prince Rupert Variegated', bearing small, cream- and white-variegated lemony foliage.

the top. In late summer, root 4- to 5-inch cuttings in clean sand, or dig up your favorites and pot them before frost.

Buy ivy geraniums in bloom to set in sunny spots but provide afternoon shade in summer. Water container plants frequently, but don't let them stand in water. Use a rich, well-drained potting mix and feed monthly with liquid organic fertilizer. Pinch back for more flowers.

Set purchased regal geranium plants in a sunny,

cool spot with good, slightly alkaline soil. They require plenty of water while in bloom. Treat them as true annuals and discard at season's end, or take cuttings or pot up plants to bring indoors for winter.

Landscape uses: Mass geraniums in beds of their own, or use them to brighten a mixed border. Geraniums in containers will light up a deck, patio, or sunny porch; if you use them in a sitting area, choose plants with attractively colored foliage as well as showy flowers for double the viewing pleasure. Use ivy geraniums in hanging baskets. Plants may live for years in pots and look especially handsome if trained into standards. (For more information on creating standards, see page 302.) Fill a window box with a single color or a mixture, and add splashes of color to slightly shaded corners or areas under tall trees with variegated types.

PENSTEMON

Penstemon, beardtongue. Late-spring- to summer-blooming perennials; wildflowers.

Description: Penstemons produce clusters of tubular flowers with scalloped tips and a fuzzy area (beard) inside the throat. Flowers range from white to pink, red, scarlet, orange, wine, and indigo. They bloom at the ends of creeping or 1- to 3-foot upright stems bearing pointed, often evergreen leaves. Zones 3–9, depending on the species. Many penstemons are common wildflowers in the West; only a few species are native to the eastern United States. The best bet for eastern gardens is the white-flowered *Penstemon digitalis*, foxglove penstemon, and its cultivars, such as 'Husker Red', which has deep red foliage and pink flowers. Unlike other penstemons, it thrives in moist soil. Zones 4–8.

How to grow: Plant or divide in spring in sunny, average, very well-drained soil. Provide partial shade in warmer areas. Mulch with gravel or other inorganic material; organic matter holds too much moisture and will rot the crowns. Divide clumps every 4 to 6 years to maintain vigor.

Landscape uses: Use penstemons as a filler in borders and beds and in rock gardens.

PEONY

See *Paeonia*

PEPPER

Capsicum annuum, C. chinense
Solanaceae

Pepper choices—ranging from crispy sweet to fiery hot, from big and blocky to long and skinny—increase each year. This native American vegetable is second only to tomatoes as a garden favorite, and it needs much the same care. Peppers are also ideal for spot planting around the garden. The brilliant colors of the mature fruit are especially attractive in flowerbeds and in container plantings.

New varieties of bell peppers are released every year, in mature colors ranging from bright red to orange to white, purple, and nearly black. If you've had past problems with diseases such as tobacco mosaic virus or bacterial spot, choose disease-resistant varieties.

Planting: Choose a site with full sun for your pepper plot. Don't plant peppers where tomatoes or eggplants grew previously, because all three are members of the nightshade family and are subject to similar diseases. Make sure the soil drains well; standing water encourages root rot.

Garden centers offer a good variety of transplants, but the choices are greater when you grow peppers from seed. Pepper roots don't like to be disturbed, so plant them indoors in peat pots 2 months before the last frost date, sowing three seeds to a pot. Maintain the soil temperature at 75°F, and keep the seedlings moist, but not wet. Provide at least 5 hours of strong sunlight a day, or ideally, keep the plants under lights for 12 or more hours daily. Once the seedlings are 2 to 3 inches tall, thin them by leaving the strongest plant in each pot and cutting the others off at soil level.

Seedlings are ready for the garden when they are 4 to 6 inches tall. Before moving the young plants to the garden, harden them off for about a week. Peppers are very susceptible to transplant shock, which can interrupt growth for weeks. To avoid shocking the plants, make sure the soil temperature is at least 60°F before transplanting; this usually occurs 2 to 3 weeks after the last frost. Transplant on a cloudy day or in the evening to reduce the danger of sun scorch; if this is not possible, provide temporary shade for the transplanted seedlings.

When buying transplants, look for ones with strong stems and dark green leaves. Pass up those that already have tiny fruits on them, because such plants won't produce well. Peppers take at least 2 months from the time the plants are set out to the time they produce fruit, so short-season growers should select early-maturing cultivars.

Space transplants about 1½ feet apart in rows at least 2 feet apart, keeping in mind that most hot-pepper cultivars need less room than sweet ones. If the plot is exposed to winds, stake the plants, but put these supports in place before transplanting the seedlings to keep from damaging roots. To deter cutworms, place a cardboard collar around each stem, pushing it at least an inch into the ground. If the weather turns chilly and rainy, protect young plants with hot caps.

Growing guidelines: Evenly moist soil is essential to good growth, so spread a thick but light mulch, such as straw or grass clippings, around the plants. Water deeply during dry spells to encourage deep root development. Lack of water can produce bitter-tasting peppers. To avoid damaging the roots, gently pull any invading weeds by hand.

Although peppers are tropical plants, temperatures over 90°F often cause blossoms to drop and plants to wilt. To avoid this problem, plan your garden so taller plants will shade the peppers during the hottest part of the day. If you plant peppers in properly prepared soil, fertilizing usually isn't necessary. Pale leaves and slow growth, however, are a sign that the plants need a feeding of liquid fertilizer, such as fish emulsion or compost tea. See the Compost entry for instructions for making compost tea.

Problems: Since sprays of ground-up hot peppers can deter insects, it's logical that pests don't usually bother pepper plants. There are, however, a few exceptions. The pepper weevil, a ⅛-inch-long, brass-colored beetle with a brown or black snout, and its ¼-inch-long larva, a white worm with a beige head, chew holes in blossoms and buds, causing misshapen and discolored fruits. It's a common pest across the southern United States. Prevent damage by keeping the garden free of crop debris. Handpick any weevils you spot on the plants.

Other occasional pests include aphids, Colorado potato beetles, flea beetles, hornworms, and cutworms. See page 454 for information on these insect pests and how to control them.

Crop rotation and resistant cultivars are your

best defense against most pepper diseases. Here are some common diseases to watch for.

- 🌿 Anthracnose infection causes dark, sunken, soft, and watery spots on fruits.
- 🌿 Bacterial spot appears as small, yellow-green raised spots on young leaves and dark spots with light-colored centers on older leaves.
- 🌿 Early blight appears as dark spots on leaves and stems; infected leaves eventually die.
- 🌿 Verticillium wilt appears first on lower leaves, which turn yellow and wilt.
- 🌿 Mosaic—the most serious disease—is a viral infection that mottles the leaves of young plants with dark and light splotches and eventually causes them to curl and wrinkle. Later on, mosaic can cause fruits to become bumpy and bitter.

See the Plant Diseases and Disorders entry for more information on some of these diseases and control measures.

Harvesting: Most sweet peppers become even sweeter when mature as they turn from green to bright red, yellow, or orange—or even brown or purple. Mature hot peppers offer an even greater variety of rainbow colors, often on the same plant, and achieve their best flavor when fully grown. Early in the season, however, it's best to harvest peppers before they ripen to encourage the plant to keep bearing; a mature fruit can signal a plant to stop production.

Always cut (don't pull) peppers from the plant. Pick all the fruit when a frost is predicted, or pull plants up by the roots and hang them in a dry, cool place indoors for the fruit to ripen more fully. To preserve, freeze peppers (without blanching), or dry hot types.

PERENNIALS

Perennials are part of our lives, even if we're not flower gardeners. Most of us grew up with daylilies, irises, and peonies in our yards or neighborhoods, and perennials like astilbes and hostas are familiar faces, too. But many less-well-known perennials have an exotic mystique: We may admire them, but we're not sure we'd know what to do with them in our own gardens.

Technically speaking, most plants grown in the garden are perennial, if you count every plant that lives more than a year, including trees and shrubs. But to most gardeners, a perennial is a plant that lives and flowers for more than one season but dies to the ground each winter. These are referred to as herbaceous perennials to differentiate them from woody perennials (shrubs and trees).

Many perennials—including peonies (*Paeonia* spp.), Oriental poppies (*Papaver orientale*), and daylilies (*Hemerocallis* spp.)—are long lived. Others, like coreopsis and columbines (*Aquilegia* spp.), may bloom just a few years before disappearing, but they are prolific seeders, and new seedlings keep coming back just like their longer-lived cousins. Most popular perennials fall somewhere between the two extremes and will reappear year after year with reassuring regularity.

Landscaping with Perennials

Perennials are all-purpose plants—you can grow them wherever you garden and in any part of your garden. There's a perennial to fit almost any spot in the landscape, and with a little planning, it's possible to have them in bloom throughout the frost-free months. In addition to the endless variety of sizes, shapes, colors, and plant habits, there are perennials for nearly any cultural condition your garden has to offer.

Most perennials prefer loamy soil with even moisture and full sun. Gardeners who have these conditions to offer have the widest selection of plants from which to choose. However, if you have a shaded site, there are dozens of perennials for you, too, such as those listed on page 427. For ideas for other types of sites, see the lists on pages 432 and 433 as well.

Perennials add beauty, permanence, and seasonal rhythm to any landscape. Their yearly growth and flowering cycles are fun to follow—it's always exciting to see the first peonies pushing out of the ground in April or the asters braving another November day. Look at your property and think about where you could add perennials. There are a number of ways to use perennials effectively in your yard.

Shade gardens: Turn problem shady sites where lawn grass won't grow, such as under trees or between buildings, into an asset by creating a shade garden. Many perennials tolerate shade, but remember that shade plants often have brief periods of bloom. For the most successful shade garden, you should count on the plants' foliage to carry the garden through the seasons. The most engaging shade gardens rely on combinations of large-, medium-, and small-leaved plants with different leaf textures. For example, try mixing ferns with variegated hostas, astilbes, Virginia bluebells (*Mertensia virginica*), and shade-tolerant groundcovers like Allegheny foamflower (*Tiarella cordifolia*) and creeping phlox (*Phlox stolonifera*) to create a diverse mix of size, foliage, and texture.

Bog and water gardens: If you have a low area that's always wet, you know that fighting to grow grass there is a losing battle. Instead, turn that boggy patch into a perennial bog or water garden. Some perennials will even grow with their roots submerged in the shallows. For more on making a bog or water garden, see the Water Gardens entry.

Rock gardens: If you have a rock wall that edges a bank or a dry, stony slope in full sun, you have a perfect site for a rock garden. A host of plants thrive in poor soil and relentless sunshine, including yarrows, sedums, stonecrops, and hens and chicks. For more on rock gardening, see the Rock Gardens entry. (For a design featuring a rock garden, see page 635.)

Containers: To add color and excitement to a deck, patio, balcony, or entryway, try perennials in containers. Mix several perennials together, combine them with annuals, or plant just a single perennial per container. Try a daylily in a half barrel in a sunny spot or hostas with variegated foliage in a shady one. Remember, containers dry out quickly, so choose plants that tolerate some dryness for best results. For more ideas, see the Container Gardening entry.

Perennial Plant of the Year: Every year, the Perennial Plant Association (PPA), the professional organization for the promotion of perennial plants, announces the winner of its Perennial Plant of the Year competition. The PPA is composed of nurserymen and -women, perennial plant breeders, educators, landscape and garden designers, and others with a serious interest in perennial plants. Each year, the members nominate the plants they feel deserve the honor of being named Perennial Plant of the Year, based on such criteria as consistency, low maintenance, ornamental value in multiple seasons, pest and disease resistance, wide adaptability to a range of climatic conditions, easy propagation, and wide availability. What this means is that gardeners can count on the winning perennials to perform well in their gardens, wherever they live, with minimal care.

KEY WORDS *Perennials*

Perennial plant. A plant that flowers and sets seed for two or more seasons. Short-lived perennials like coreopsis and columbines may live 3 to 5 years. Long-lived perennials like peonies may live 100 years or more.

Tender perennial. A perennial plant from tropical or subtropical regions that can't be overwintered outside, except in subtropical regions such as Florida and Southern California. Often grown as annuals, tender perennials include zonal geraniums, wax begonias, cannas, and coleus.

Hardy perennial. A perennial plant that tolerates frost. Hardy perennials vary in the degree of cold that they can tolerate, however, so make sure a plant is hardy in your zone before you buy it.

Herbaceous perennial. A perennial plant that dies back to the ground at the end of each growing season. Most garden perennials fall into this category.

Semiwoody perennial. A perennial plant that forms woody stems but is much less substantial than a shrub. Examples include lavender, Russian sage, and some of the thymes.

Woody perennial. A perennial plant such as a shrub or tree that does not die down to the ground each year. Gardeners generally refer to these as woody plants.

You can't go wrong by adding these great perennials to your garden. You'll find more information on the Perennial Plant of the Year program on the Internet; see Resources on page 673 for the address.

Designing Beds and Borders

Designing with perennials may seem overwhelming, since there are so many to choose from. Just take your design one step at a time. Chances are, your growing conditions are right for only a fraction of what's available. Let your moisture, soil, and light conditions guide you in choosing plants. For example, if you have a garden bed in full sun that tends toward dry soil, cross off shade- and moisture-loving perennials like hostas and ferns from your list. Instead, put in plants that like full sun and don't like wet feet, like daylilies and ornamental grasses. And don't forget to choose only plants that are hardy in your area. For information on combining perennials to create a lush bed or border, see the Garden Design entry.

Planting Perennials

Because perennials live a long time, it's important to get them off to a good start. Proper soil preparation and care at planting time will be well rewarded.

Soil preparation: The majority of perennials commonly grown in beds or borders require evenly moist, humus-rich soil of pH 5.5 to 6.5. A complete soil analysis from your local extension office or a soil-testing lab will give you a starting point. For more on soils and do-it-yourself soil tests, see the Soil entry.

Dig deeply when you prepare your perennial bed. Plants' roots will be able to penetrate the friable soil easily, creating a strong, vigorous root system. Water and nutrients will also move easily through the soil, and the bed won't dry out as quickly. As a result, your plants will thrive. Have any necessary soil amendments and organic fertilizers on hand before you start, and add them to the bed once you've worked it.

Turn the soil evenly to a shovel's depth at planting time. Thoroughly incorporate appropriate soil amendments and fertilizer as required. Break up all clods and smooth out the bed before planting. For soil preparation techniques see the Soil entry. If your soil is particularly bad or you'd like to avoid the effort involved in digging a garden, try techniques outlined in the Raised Bed Gardening entry.

Best Perennials for Shade

There are dozens of choice perennials to brighten a shady site. Most prefer woodland conditions: rich, moist, well-drained soil and cool temperatures. Many plants in this list grow well in partial shade. Plants that tolerate deep shade include species of *Actaea*, *Brunnera*, *Epimedium*, *Heuchera*, *Hosta*, *Mertensia*, *Polygonatum*, and *Pulmonaria*. Plant name is followed by bloom time and color.

Aconitum spp. (monkshoods): Summer to early fall; blue

Actaea spp., formerly Cimicifuga spp. (bugbanes): Summer to fall; white

Aquilegia spp. (columbines): Spring to early summer; all colors, bicolors

Astilbe spp. (astilbes): Late spring to summer; red, pink, white, purple

Bergenia spp. (bergenias): Early spring; rose, pink, purple, white

Brunnera macrophylla (largeleaf brunnera, largeleaf brunnera): Spring; light blue

Dicentra spp. (bleeding hearts): Spring; rose pink, white

Epimedium spp. (epimediums): Spring; pink, red, yellow, white

Helleborus spp. (hellebores): Early spring; white, rose, green, purple

Heuchera spp. (heucheras, coralbells): Spring to summer; pink, red, white, green

×Heucherella selections (foamy bells): Spring and summer; pink, white, cream

Hosta spp. (hostas): Early to late summer; violet, lilac, white

Mertensia virginica (Virginia bluebells): Spring; blue, white

Polemonium spp. (Jacob's ladders): Spring to summer; blue, pink, white, yellow

Polygonatum spp. (Solomon's seals): Spring; white, greenish white

Pulmonaria spp. (lungworts): Spring; purple-blue, blue, red

Tiarella cordifolia (Allegheny foamflower): Spring; white, pink

Perennials with Striking Foliage

Most perennials bloom for only a few weeks, so it makes sense to think about what they'll look like the rest of the season. These dual-purpose perennials have especially interesting foliage when not in flower. Try species of *Ajuga*, *Asarum*, *Bergenia*, *Epimedium*, *Hosta*, *Hylotelephium*, *Lamium*, *Liriope*, *Saxifraga*, *Sedum*, *Sempervivum*, *Stachys*, and *Tiarella* for three-season interest, and don't forget ferns and ornamental grasses. Plant name is followed by foliage interest.

Acanthus spp. (bear's-breeches): Shiny; lobed or heart-shaped; spiny

Ajuga reptans (ajuga): Striking variegations and colors, including gray, green, pink, and purple

Alchemilla mollis (lady's mantle): Maple-like; chartreuse

Artemisia spp. (artemisias): Ferny; silver or gray; aromatic

Asarum spp. (wild ginger): Leathery; glossy or matte; dark green

Bergenia spp. (bergenias): Glossy; evergreen; burgundy fall color

Heuchera spp. (alumroots): Maplelike; dark purple, silver, reddish, green, often with contrasting veins

Hosta spp. (hostas): Smooth; puckered; variegated; green, blue-gray, chartreuse, yellow, cream, white

Hylotelephium spp., formerly Sedum (stonecrops): Rounded, fleshy, often glaucous, many colors

Lamium spp. (lamiums, dead nettles): Green-, yellow-, white-variegated

Polygonatum odoratum (Solomon's seal): Long, graceful shoots; variegated forms

Pulmonaria spp. (lungworts): Dark green; gray- or silver-spotted

Rodgersia spp. (rodgersias): Huge; maplelike or buckeyelike; bronze

Saxifraga stolonifera (strawberry geranium, creeping saxifrage): Silver-veined; reddish undersides

Sedum spp. (sedums): Fleshy; many colors; variegated forms

Sempervivum spp. (hens and chicks): Fleshy rosettes; some red-or purple-tinged

Stachys byzantina (lamb's ears): White, gray green, yellow; velvety

Tiarella cordifolia (Allegheny foamflower): Maplelike; green with red or purple veining; evergreen

Yucca spp. (yuccas): Sharply pointed; large; evergreen; variegated forms

Planting: Plant perennials any time the soil is workable. Spring and fall are best for most plants. If plants arrive before you are ready to plant them, be sure to care for them properly until you can get them in the ground.

Planting is easy in freshly turned soil. Choose

an overcast day whenever possible. Avoid planting during the heat of the day. Place container-grown plants out on the soil according to your design. To remove the plants, invert containers and knock the bottom of the pot with your trowel while keeping one hand spread over the soil on top so the plant doesn't fall to the ground and snap off. The plant should fall out easily. The roots will be tightly intertwined. It's vital to loosen the roots—by pulling them apart or even cutting four slashes, one down each side of the root mass—so they'll spread strongly through the soil when planted out. Clip any roots that are bent, broken, or circling. Make sure you place the crown of the plant at the same

Perennials for the North

These perennials flourish in the cooler summers of northern zones and withstand cold winters to Zone 3. Species of *Campanula*, *Delphinium*, *Hemerocallis*, *Papaver*, *Penstemon*, *Phlox*, *Primula*, and *Veronica* are hardy to Zone 2. Many of these same plants will grow as far south as Zone 9, but only a few prosper under hot, humid conditions. Plant name is followed by bloom time and color.

Achillea **spp. (yarrows):** Spring to summer; yellow, white, red, terra cotta, pink, purple, cream

Actaea racemosa, **formerly** *Cimicifuga racemosa* **(black snakeroot):** Late summer; white

Aquilegia **spp. (columbines):** Spring to early summer; all colors, bicolors

Campanula **spp. (bellflowers):** Spring to summer; blue, white, purple

Delphinium **spp. (delphiniums):** Summer; blue, red, violet, white

Dianthus **spp. (pinks):** Spring; pink, red, white, yellow

Dicentra **spp. (bleeding hearts):** Spring; rose pink, white

Echinacea **spp. (coneflowers, echinacea):** Summer; purple, white, pink, orange, yellow

Gypsophila **spp. (baby's breath):** Summer; white, pink

Hemerocallis **spp. (daylilies):** Spring to summer; all colors except blue

Hosta **spp. (hostas):** Early to late summer; violet, lilac, white

Iris **spp. (irises):** Spring to summer; all colors, bicolors

Papaver orientale **(Oriental poppy):** Early summer; scarlet, pink, white, purple

Penstemon barbatus **(common beard-tongue):** Spring; pink, white

Phlox **spp. (phlox):** Early spring to summer; pink, white, blue

Primula **spp. (primroses):** Spring; all colors

Rudbeckia **spp. (black-eyed Susans, coneflowers, rudbeckia):** Summer; yellow

Sedum **spp. (sedums):** Spring to fall; yellow, pink, white

Thermopsis **spp. (Carolina lupine, false lupines):** Spring; yellow

Veronica **spp. (veronicas, speedwells):** Spring to summer; blue, white, pink

Perennials for the South

These perennials stand up to the heat and humidity of southern summers, although most benefit from partial shade in the hottest months. Species of *Achillea, Baptisia, Boltonia, Coreopsis, Echinacea, Helianthus, Hemerocallis, Hibiscus, Iris, Rudbeckia,* and *Verbena* will tolerate full southern sun. Plant name is followed by bloom time and color.

***Achillea* spp. (yarrows):** Spring to summer; yellow, white, red, terra cotta, pink, cream, purple

***Asclepias tuberosa* (butterfly weed):** Summer; orange, yellow, red

***Baptisia* spp. (false indigo, baptisias):** Spring to summer; blue, white, yellow, purple

***Boltonia asteroides* (boltonia):** Late summer; white, purple, pink

***Coreopsis* spp. (coreopsis):** Spring to summer; yellow, red, pink, bicolors

***Echinacea* spp. (purple coneflowers, echinacea):** Summer; mauve, white, yellow, orange, pink

***Helianthus* spp. (perennial sunflowers):** Late summer to fall; yellow

***Hemerocallis* spp. (daylilies):** Spring to summer; all colors except blue

***Hibiscus moscheutos* (common rose mallow):** Summer; white, pink, red

***Hosta* spp. (hostas):** Early to late summer; violet, lilac, white

***Iris* spp. (irises):** Early spring to summer; all colors, bicolors

***Liatris* spp. (blazing stars):** Summer; mauve

***Liriope muscari* (liriope, blue lilyturf):** Late summer; lilac, white

***Platycodon grandiflorus* (balloon flower):** Summer; blue, white

***Rudbeckia* spp. (black-eyed Susans, coneflowers):** Summer; yellow

***Salvia* spp. (sages):** Summer to fall; all colors

***Sedum* spp. (sedums):** Spring to fall; yellow, pink, white

***Verbena* spp. (verbenas):** Spring to summer; red, pink, purple

***Veronica* spp. (veronicas, speedwells):** Spring to summer; blue, white, pink

depth at which it grew in the pot.

Planting bareroot perennials and transplants requires more care. Inspect the roots carefully and prune off any irregularities. Dig a hole large enough to accommodate the full spread of the roots. Build a mound with tapering sides in the center of the hole. Spread the roots of fibrous-rooted plants evenly over the mound and rest the crown of the plant at its apex. Check to be sure that the crown will end up just below the soil surface. Build up the mound to raise the crown if necessary. Do not plant too deeply!

Position rhizomes such as those of iris at or just below the soil surface, depending on the species. Spread the roots evenly over a mound of soil as described above. Spread tuberous roots like those of daylilies evenly in a similar fashion. Fill in the planting hole with soil, then firm it down and add more soil if necessary before you water the new plant.

Water plants thoroughly after planting so the soil is completely settled around the roots. Give your newly planted perennials a layer of organic mulch to conserve soil moisture. Provide extra water for the first month or so while plants are becoming established.

Maintaining Your Perennials

Perennials benefit from some regular care throughout the growing season. In return, they'll reward you with strong growth and vigorous flowering year after year.

Weeding: Weeds compete for water, nutrients, and light, so weeding is a necessary evil. Catch them while they're small and the task will seem easier. A light mulch of bark or shredded leaves allows water to infiltrate and keeps weeds down. Mulch also helps soil retain water.

Watering: Regular watering is essential. Most plants need 1 inch per week for best growth. Bog and pond plants require a continual supply of water. Dry-soil plants are more tolerant of a low water supply, but during the hottest summer months, even they may need watering. Water all your perennials with a soaker hose where possible. If using aboveground irrigation, avoid watering during the heat of the day when the water evaporates quickly, and mulch to conserve soil moisture and cut down on watering.

Staking: Staking may be necessary for thin-stemmed plants such as coreopsis, yarrow, and garden phlox. Extremely tall plants such as delphiniums require sturdy stakes to keep flower spikes from snapping off. Heavy, mounding flowers like peonies may need hoop supports (circular wire supports set up on legs) to keep their faces out of the mud. You can also stake up a clump of perennials by inserting three or four stakes around the outside of the clump and then winding twine around the stakes. Or circle clumps with twine, then tie the twine to a sturdy stake.

Pinching: Pinching keeps plants bushy. Plants like chrysanthemums and asters have a tendency to grow tall and flop. Pinch them once or twice in spring to encourage production of side shoots. Early pinching promotes compact growth without sacrificing bloom.

Thinning: Plants like delphiniums and phlox produce so many stems that the growth becomes crowded and vigor is reduced. Cut out excess stems to increase air circulation and promote larger flowers on the remaining stems.

Disbudding: Disbudding is another technique used to increase flower size. Peonies and chrysanthemums produce many buds around each main bud. Simply pinch off all but the largest bud to improve your floral display.

Deadheading: Removing spent flowers will help promote production of new buds in many plants. Just pinch or cut off faded flowers, or shear bushy plants just below the flower heads if the plant blooms all at once. Some perennials like baptisias and 'Autumn Joy' sedum will not rebloom, and their seed heads are decorative. Leave these for winter interest in the garden.

Winterizing: In autumn, begin preparing the perennial garden for winter. Remove dead foliage and old flowers. After the first frost, cut down dead stems and remove other growth that will die to the ground. (Leave ornamental grasses and other plants that add winter interest.) After the ground freezes, protect plants from root damage due to frost heaving with a thick mulch of oak leaves or marsh hay. Evergreen boughs are also good for this purpose. Snow is the best insulator of all, but most of us can't count on continuous snow cover. Mulching helps keep the ground

Best Perennials for Dry Soil

These tough plants tolerate heat and dry soil, making them useful for spots that the hose can't reach and nice for sunny meadow gardens. Some actually become invasive and weedy in rich, moist soils, while others survive drought but suffer in humid conditions. All prefer well-drained soil. Plant name is followed by bloom time and color.

Achillea spp. (yarrows): Spring to summer; yellow, white, red, terra cotta, pink, purple, cream

Anthemis tinctoria (golden marguerite): Summer; yellow, orange

Armeria maritima (common thrift): Summer; pink, white

Artemisia spp. (artemisias): Summer; gray, white, yellow

Baptisia spp. (false indigo, baptisias): Spring to summer; blue, white, yellow, purple

Coreopsis spp. (coreopsis): Spring to summer; yellow, red, pink, bicolors

Dianthus spp. (pinks): Spring; pink, red, white, yellow

Echinops ritro (globe thistle): Summer; dark blue

Eryngium spp. (sea hollies): Summer; blue, silver-blue

Euphorbia spp. (spurges): Spring to summer; yellow, red

Gaillardia ×grandiflora (perennial blanketflower): Summer; red, yellow, bicolors

Hemerocallis spp. (daylilies): Spring to summer; all colors except blue

Kniphofia spp. (torch lilies, red-hot pokers): Late spring; red, orange

Liatris scariosa (spike blazing star): Summer; purple, white

Limonium spp. (sea lavender, statice): Summer; blue, red, white, lavender

Linum perenne (blue flax): Spring; blue

Rudbeckia spp. (black-eyed Susans, coneflowers): Summer; yellow

Salvia spp. (salvias): Summer to fall; all colors

Scabiosa spp. (pincushion flowers, scabious): Summer; blue, pink, yellow, white

Sedum spp. (sedums): Spring to fall; yellow, pink, white

Solidago spp. (goldenrods): Late summer to fall; yellow

Stachys spp. (lamb's ears): Spring; purple

Yucca spp. (yuccas): Summer; white

Best Perennials for Moist Soil

Grow these perennials if you have a poorly drained or boggy spot in your yard. True to their streamside origins, most prefer at least partial shade and cool nights. Species of *Caltha*, *Chelone*, *Filipendula*, *Iris*, *Lobelia*, *Lysimachia*, *Rodgersia*, and *Thalictrum* tolerate full sun, while *Hibiscus* and *Tradescantia* demand it. Plant name is followed by bloom time and color.

Actaea spp., formerly Cimicifuga spp. (bugbanes): Late summer to fall; white

Aruncus spp. (goatsbeards): Late spring; creamy white

Astilbe spp. (astilbes): Late spring to summer; red, pink, white, purple

Caltha palustris (marsh marigold): Spring; yellow

Chelone glabra (white turtlehead): Summer; white with red tinge

Eupatorium spp. (bonesets): Late summer to fall; purple, blue, white

Filipendula spp. (meadowsweets): Summer; pink, white

Iris ensata (Japanese iris): Summer; pink, blue, purple, white

Iris pseudacorus (yellow flag): Early summer; yellow

Iris sibirica (Siberian iris): Spring; blue, white, purple, wine red, bicolors

Ligularia spp. (ligularias): Summer; yellow, orange

Lobelia siphilitica (great blue lobelia): Late summer; blue

Mertensia virginica (Virginia bluebells): Spring; blue, white

Monarda didyma (bee balm): Summer; red, white, pink, purple

Primula japonica (Japanese primrose): Late spring; pink, red, white, purple

Rodgersia spp. (rodgersias): Late spring to summer; creamy white, red

Thalictrum spp. (meadow rues): Summer; lilac, pink, yellow, white

Tradescantia spp. (spiderworts): Summer; blue, pink, white, red

Trollius spp. (globeflowers): Spring; orange, yellow

frozen during periods of warm weather.

Dividing: Sooner or later, even the slow-growing perennials become crowded and need dividing. Divide plants in spring or fall in the North and in fall in the South. (Some plants such as peonies should only be dug in fall.) Some fast growers like bee balms, chrysanthemums, and asters should be lifted every 2 or 3 years. They have a tendency to die out in the middle, while new growth forms a circle of growth around the old center of the clump. Lift the plants in spring or fall to cut away any old or dead growth. Take

Staking perennials. For clumping perennials such as peonies, pound in four or more stakes around the clump, ideally just after planting or as shoots emerge in spring. Then wrap strings around the stakes; add tiers of string as the plant continues to grow taller and bushier.

advantage of the bare spot to work the soil, adding compost and fertilizer. Replant the rejuvenated clump in the center of the freshly worked planting hole.

Lift and pull or cut apart overgrown clumps of irises, daylilies, and hostas. You'll know a clump is overgrown because it looks crowded, doesn't have as large or as many blooms as it used to, and may have died out in the center. You may need to separate large clumps with a shovel; see the Division entry for more on this technique. Replant a reasonably sized clump or group of clumps into freshly prepared soil.

Controlling pests and diseases: On the whole, perennials are tough, durable plants, but they're not completely problem-free. The best way to avoid problems is to give plants the condi-

tions they need to thrive. If you plant a moisture-loving bog plant in a dry, windy site, you're asking for trouble. Poor or inappropriate growing conditions stress plants, and a stressed perennial is more likely to lose the struggle against an invading pest or ailment.

If you know that a perennial is prone to a certain problem, either choose another species or look for a resistant cultivar. Garden phlox (*Phlox paniculata*), for instance, is mildew prone, and there's nothing like powdery mildew to ruin the appearance of a plant. The best way to avoid this is to plant cultivars of a similar but mildew-resistant species, meadow phlox or wild sweet William (*Phlox maculata*). If you must have garden phlox or other mildew-prone perennials, choose a mildew-resistant cultivar like 'David',

A Sunny Perennial Border

This beautiful flower border is a blaze of color from early summer to frost. If you don't have room to plant an 8- by 20-foot border, you can narrow down this plant list to create your own design that fits the space you have available.

1. New England aster (*Symphyotrichum novae-angliae*)

2. 'Autumn Joy' sedum (*Hylotelephium* 'Herbstfreude')

3. 'Moonshine' yarrow (*Achillea* 'Moonshine')

4. Missouri evening primrose (*Oenothera macrocarpa*)

5. Spike blazing star cultivar (*Liatris spicata*), mauve-flowered

6. Garden phlox cultivar (*Phlox paniculata*)
(a) purple-flowered
(b) white-flowered

7. Balloon flower (*Platycodon grandiflorus*)

8. Daylily cultivar (*Hemerocallis* hybrid), yellow-flowered

9. Purple coneflower (*Echinacea purpurea*)

10. Peony cultivar (*Paeonia lactiflora*), white-flowered

11. Siberian iris cultivar (*Iris sibirica*)
(a) blue-flowered
(b) purple-flowered

12. Columbine cultivar (*Aquilegia ×hybrida*), yellow-flowered

13. Bloody cranesbill cultivar (*Geranium sanguineum*)
(a) white-flowered
(b) pink-flowered

14. Obedient plant cultivar (*Physostegia virginiana*), white-flowered

15. Baby's breath (*Gypsophila paniculata*)

16. Catmint (*Nepeta racemosa*)

17. Switchgrass (*Panicum virgatum*)

SMART SHOPPING

Perennials

Smart shopping begins at home. Make a list of the plants you intend to buy, then stick to it. Buying at a garden center has an advantage: You can see what you're getting. Many have display gardens where you can see the mature sizes of the plants. The plants will be larger than those available by mail, and they will become established more quickly. But your selection may be limited. Here are some tips to keep in mind when buying plants at garden centers:

- The best selection is available in spring.
- If you want a specific color, buy a named cultivar.
- Avoid plants that are visibly rootbound. Check the root systems of plants that are leggy or disproportionately large in relation to the size of the pot.
- Choose plants with lush, nicely colored foliage and multiple stems. Avoid plants with dry, pale, or shriveled leaves.
- Check for insects on the tops and undersides of leaves and along stems.
- When buying in fall, plants will look rough. Check the root system first. If it is in good shape, the plant is likely to be healthy.
- If you can't plant immediately, keep containers in the shade and well watered. Check them daily!

Mail-Order Nurseries

Ordering plants from a catalog or Internet supplier requires trust, since you can't examine the plants until you have purchased them. Start small. Order from a few nurseries at a time until you get the quality you want.

Some nurseries ship in containers; others ship bareroot. If a nursery sells bareroot

'Bright Eyes', or 'Tracy's Treasure', but understand that even resistant selections may fall prey to mildew when conditions favor the disease. Plant in a sunny site with good air circulation, thin plants to the strongest four or five shoots so air can circulate in the clump, water from the bottom to keep the foliage dry, and never water at night.

Similarly, when confronted by a pest, start at the low end of the control spectrum rather than rushing for the sprayer. Handpicking insects may not be pleasant, but it's often effective. A simple soap spray will control most pests. If a pest is a major problem on the same perennial every year, it's better to replace it with one of the many pest-free perennials rather than waging a discouraging, time-consuming battle again each season. For more on organic pest and disease control techniques, see the Pests entry and the Plant Diseases and Disorders entry.

plants, order them in fall. Some plants such as irises, peonies, and poppies are only available in fall. To get the most from mail ordering:

- Order early for the best selection.
- Specify desired shipping time when ordering.
- Once they arrive, evaluate plants in the same way you would evaluate plants at the garden center.
- Examine bareroot plants for pests and diseases. Check the roots, crowns, and stems for hidden pests.
- If roots on bareroot plants are not plentiful and in good condition, return the plants.
- Rewrap bareroot plants after examination and store in a cool place until you are ready to plant them.

- Before planting, soak roots of bareroot plants in a bucket of water for a minimum of 1 hour.
- Make all claims of substandard or damaged plants to the supplier immediately.

Perennials from Seed

If you have more time and patience than money to spend on your perennials, buying seed is smart shopping. A packet of seed is much cheaper than the equivalent number of purchased plants (or even one plant!). In exchange for a good buy, though, you must be willing to forgo instant gratification. You'll need to set up a cold frame or nursery bed and care for your seedlings for 2 to 3 years before they reach blooming size. For more on growing from seed, see the Seed Starting and Seed Saving entry.

Propagating Perennials

Time and patience are the only requirements for growing your own perennials. Seeds take longer to produce flowering plants than cuttings, but not all perennials can be grown from cuttings. Of course, you can also propagate by dividing—cutting apart established clumps of perennials.

Seeds: Perennial seeds are available from most major seed companies, although some offer a wider variety than others. Plant societies often have seed exchanges. You can also save seeds of your own plants and trade with friends. *Note:* Most cultivars cannot be produced from seed. They must be propagated by cuttings or division.

If you leave seed heads of your perennials to mature in the garden, you'll get self-sown seedlings. Transplant these to appropriate spots or trade them with friends. For more on growing plants from seed, see the Seed Starting and Seed Saving entry.

Cuttings: Cuttings are a quick and easy way to increase perennials. Unlike seed, which produces seedlings genetically different from the parent plants, all cuttings taken from a single plant will be identical to the parent plant.

Take cuttings in late spring or early summer for best results. Cut a 3- to 6-inch section from the stem and strip the leaves off the lower half of the cutting. If the leaves are large, cut them in half. Stick the cuttings in a 1:1 mixture of peat and perlite. Keep them in a high-humidity environment for 1 to 2 weeks, or until they are well rooted.

Transplant them to pots or directly into the garden. To learn how to grow cuttings in a nursery bed, see the Nursery Bed entry.

PERMACULTURE

Combining the best of natural landscaping and edible landscaping, permaculture aims for a site that sustains itself and the gardener. The ultimate purpose of permaculture is to develop a site until it meets all the needs of its inhabitants, including food, shelter, fuel, and entertainment. (The word *permaculture* was coined in the mid-1970s by two Australians, Bill Mollison and David Holmgren.) While it's the rare home gardener who can follow permaculture principles to the ultimate degree, most can borrow ideas from permaculture to create a new way of landscaping based on production and usefulness.

Gardening and Permaculture

Permaculture emphasizes the use of plants that are native or well adapted to your local area. Plant things you like, but make sure they have a purpose and somehow benefit the landscape. Plants such as fruit trees provide food as well as shade; a patch of bamboo could provide stakes for supporting pole beans and other vining plants. Along with a standard vegetable garden, permaculture gardeners would grow many types of perennial food plants, too, such as arrowhead, sorrel, chicory, and asparagus.

Like all gardeners, permaculture enthusiasts love plants for their beauty and fragrance, but they seek out plants that offer practical benefits along with aesthetic satisfaction. Instead of a border of flowering shrubs, for instance, a permaculture site would have a raspberry or blackberry border.

Disease-prone plants such as hybrid tea roses and plants that need lots of watering or other pampering are not good permaculture candidates. Choose a native persimmon tree that doesn't need spraying and pruning, for example, instead of a high-upkeep peach tree. Consider the natural inclinations of your site along with the needs of its inhabitants, and put as much of your site as possible to use. Work with the materials already on your site, rather than trucking in topsoil or stone. Remember that a permaculture design is never finished, because the plants within a site are always changing.

There is no set formula for developing a permaculture design, but there are practical guidelines. Here are some of them.

🌿 Copy nature's blueprint and enhance it with useful plants and animals. Think of the structure of a forest and try to mimic it with your plantings. A canopy of tall trees will give way to smaller ones, flanked by large and small shrubs and, finally, by the smallest plants. Edge habitats, where trees border open areas, are perfect for fruiting shrubs, such as currants, and for a variety of useful native plants, such as beargrass (*Xerophyllum tenax*), which is used for weaving baskets. Mimicking these natural patterns provides for the greatest diversity of plants.

🌿 Stack plants into guilds. A guild includes plants with compatible roots and canopies that might be stacked in layers to form an edge. As you learn more about your site, you'll discover groups of plants that work well together. For example, pines, dogwoods, and wild blueberries form a guild for acid soil.

🌿 Make use of native plants and others adapted to the site. Plan for diversity.

🌿 Divide your yard into zones based on use. Place heavily used features, such as an herb garden, in the most accessible zones.

🌿 Identify microclimates in your yard and use them appropriately. Cold, shady corners, windswept places in full sun, and other microclimates present unique opportunities. For instance, try sun-loving herbs like creeping thyme on rocky outcroppings; plant elderberries in poorly drained spots.

Permaculture designers are now working to conceptualize and create whole communities that embody permaculture concepts. If permaculture intrigues you, there's a wealth of opportunities to learn more about it through books, Web sites, and hands-on courses; see Resources on page 673 for examples.

PERSIMMON

Diospyros kaki, D. virginiana
Ebenaceae

Persimmons are attractive trees with large, leathery leaves that turn bright colors in fall. The bright orange fruit often hangs on the branches long after the leaves drop. Persimmon fruit can be very astringent before the fruit is mushy ripe, but some cultivars can be enjoyed while firm.

Selecting trees: American persimmons (*Diospyros virginiana*) are hardy to −25°F, bear small fruit, and grow to 40 feet. Most bear better crops if you have two trees. Buy named cultivars for reliable fruit. 'Meader' has only female flowers and bears seedless fruit if not cross-pollinated. Asian or Japanese persimmons (*D. kaki*) are hardy to 0°F, bear large fruit, and grow to 30 feet, and most are self-pollinating. Buy young persimmon trees, because older trees have long taproots and don't transplant well. Also check whether you are buying an astringent or nonastringent cultivar.

Planting and care: Persimmons bloom late and usually avoid frost damage. They tolerate a wide range of soils but perform best in fertile, well-drained soil. Give Asian persimmons a sheltered location. Space trees 20 feet apart to avoid crowding. Persimmons need little fertilizer. A thick organic mulch will conserve water and supply plenty of nitrogen for new growth. Refer to the Fruit Trees entry for additional information on planting and care.

Pruning: Persimmons require only light pruning, but if you want to keep them small, prune each spring before bud break. Train your tree to a central leader as shown on page 225. Cut back long shoots to an outward-facing bud or branch. Spread new scaffolds when they are young to make them strong and to reduce upward growth. Persimmons flower on the current season's wood. Encourage new growth by cutting out old branches periodically and allowing new ones to replace them. Head back long branches to encourage side branches.

Persimmons produce a lot of root suckers. If not removed, they will form a dark, crowded thicket.

Discourage suckers by spreading a thick layer of organic mulch such as compost over the root zone. Avoid cultivating or tramping over the roots, and remove suckers whenever you see them.

Thinning: Young trees may drop immature fruit. However, if an older tree continues to drop fruit, the tree is probably suffering from some kind of stress. Check nutrient levels, winter temperatures, and the severity of your pruning. On Asian cultivars, you may need to hand thin to encourage larger fruits; American cultivars bear only small fruit.

Problems: Persimmons are reasonably pest-free in the home garden. They can be troubled by scale and borers, and by persimmon psylla and citrus mealybug in the South. See the Pear entry for information on psylla; see pages 454 and 456 for controls for other pests. In areas where persimmon wilt is a problem, plant Asian cultivars, which are resistant. Paint the trunk and main branches with diluted white latex paint to prevent sunscald. If your tree often fruits every other year, you need to thin the fruit more heavily so the tree is not over-stressed.

Harvesting: Persimmons mature in mid-fall. Use pruning shears to clip off the ripe fruits when they are still slightly firm. Let astringent cultivars get very soft before eating. Nonastringent cultivars can be eaten while firm. Ripening often coincides with frost, but chilling is not essential for softening and sweetening. Freezing or drying can remove astringency. Or ripen fruit by putting it in a bag with an apple for a few days.

PESTS

From aphids to slugs, pests are an occasional problem in almost every garden. On rare occasions, a pest problem escalates from a mild annoyance to an onslaught that can ruin the looks of a flower garden or the harvest from the kitchen garden. The good news is that there are plenty of ingenious and safe methods that organic gardeners can use to outwit insect pests and prevent major problems.

Insects and insectlike creatures aren't the only pests that can interfere with our gardening efforts, though. Hungry animals and plant diseases are lumped into the pest category as well. You'll find information about combating animal pests in the Animal Pests entry and advice for dealing with disease problems in the Plant Diseases and Disorders entry.

The Organic Outlook on Pests

In conventional gardens and landscapes, gardeners often set perfection as the goal, and they use chemical insecticides, fungicides, and herbicides as their tools for ensuring that no leaves ever have holes in them, no weeds appear among the flowers, and no spots or rots ever invade the beds. Organic gardeners have a different outlook. They understand that pests are part of nature's plan and that, in a well-tended garden, plants will rarely suffer from serious pest problems.

Basic organic gardening practices bring your yard and garden into natural balance. You create a stable system where there are no huge population explosions of pests, but rather a diverse ecosystem where pest populations are regulated naturally. If you take good care of your soil and plants, your garden will be healthier and have fewer problems with insect pests, diseases, and weeds.

Garden Patrol

One of the best ways to minimize pest woes is to keep a watchful eye out for problems. Make it a habit to walk through your garden at least three times a week—daily is best—looking carefully at your plants. The list on page 442 offers suggestions of what to look for on your patrols.

Preventing Pest Problems

As you plant and care for your garden, there are plenty of useful practices you can employ to make it less hospitable to pests, including choosing pest-tolerant plants, keeping plants healthy at all times, minimizing residues that can harbor pests, timing plantings to avoid pests, and planting special plants that attract and shelter beneficial insects (which help control pest insects).

Pest-Tolerant Plants

Plant breeders have made great strides in developing disease-resistant cultivars of food crops, roses, trees, and many other plants, but developing plants that are resistant to insect pests is a bigger challenge. However, some varieties have physical characteristics that make them more or less attractive to pests. For example, corn cultivars with good husk cover are least damaged by corn earworms, and imported cabbageworms rarely trouble purple cabbage and broccoli varieties.

Healthy Plants

Plants grown on fertile soils with adequate water tolerate insect attack better than plants suffering from nutrient deficiency, water stress, crowding, or low light levels. Healthy plants also mount their own chemical defenses against insect pests and diseases faster.

Healthy soil: Healthy soils contain a complex community of soil organisms that are vital to plant health. Mycorrhizal fungi protect fine roots from infections and aid plants in taking up nutrients. Nitrogen-fixing bacteria live symbiotically with roots of legumes, beneficial fungi trap harmful nematodes, and many fungi and bacteria produce antibiotics that suppress pathogens. Nutrient deficiencies and imbalances make plants more attractive to pests. Conversely, overfertilizing with nitrogen can cause soft, lush growth, which is very attractive to sucking pests such as aphids.

Proper moisture: Water-stressed plants are more attractive to pests and more susceptible to diseases. For example, aphids and thrips are more likely to attack wilted plants, while wet, waterlogged soil encourages soilborne diseases. Plants usually grow best when moisture is maintained at a constant level. Most plants need about 1 inch of water per week from rain and/or irrigation while they are actively growing. Learn your plant's specific likes and dislikes. Some plants have critical times during their development when sufficient water is crucial.

Be sure to water effectively. Apply water to the soil, below mulch if possible. Avoid routinely wetting leaves, because water helps spread many leaf diseases and may burn leaves in full sun. Water thoroughly: A long, slow soak every few days is much better than a short sprinkle every day. For more information on effective watering, see the Watering and Drip Irrigation entries.

Mulches: Mulching saves water, controls weeds, and may add organic matter. It provides pest control by acting as a barrier, preventing soilborne problems from reaching plants, and/or providing a home for beneficial insects. You can mulch with a variety of organic or inorganic materials. A deep straw mulch in the potato patch can help prevent damage caused by Colorado potato beetles. Reflective aluminum mulch confuses

The Garden Detective

Plant problems fall into three general categories: insects and animals, disease, and cultural problems (water stress, heat or cold, nutrient imbalances). Symptoms caused by different problems may look remarkably similar. In order to diagnose a problem correctly, you need to investigate a number of possibilities and do some detective work.

1. Look at the entire plant and those around it. Is just one plant, or is an entire row affected? Is the whole plant affected or just part of it? Does it seem to be random, or is there a distinct pattern, such as only new growth that's affected?

2. Check the undersides of leaves and the stems, flowers, and roots for insects, eggs, webs, or damage such as borer holes. Examine the affected areas with a hand lens, looking for tiny insects or fungal growth.

3. Collect sample insects and samples of damaged leaves for later identification. Put samples in pill bottles or plastic bags.

4. Do some research to identify the pests. The Diagnosing Plant Problems chart on page 664 can help you decide what type of problem you may have. Pest guides and problem-solving garden books can help, too. Some are arranged by plant type and list the common problems for each; see Resources on page 673. Ask knowledgeable gardeners, garden center employees, or extension agents for help, too.

5. Once you have identified the problem, find out as much as you can about it. Then develop a plan to control it.

6. Some problems are hard to diagnose. Don't despair; give the plants the best care you can. Plants often recover when conditions improve. But if more plants develop the same symptoms, put your detective hat back on.

---

aphids and prevents them from landing on your plants. For more information on what materials to use and how and when to apply them, see the Mulch entry.

Spacing and training: Proper spacing, staking, and pruning can reduce pest problems. Crowded plants are weak and spindly and are more prone to disease and insect problems. Staking keeps plants from coming in contact with soilborne diseases, prevents them from being stepped on or damaged, and increases air movement. Pruning plants increases air movement and makes it easier to spot insects before they become a major problem. Leafy crops can be their own living mulch and suppress weeds if spaced so that the plants just touch at maturity.

Clean Gardening

Keeping the garden clean is a basic principle of preventing pest problems. Don't bring diseased or infested plants into your garden, and remove pest-ridden plant material from the garden promptly.

Don't bring in problems: Check all new plants for signs of insects, disease, or hitchhiking weeds. Thoroughly inspect leaves, buds, bark, and if possible, roots. Discard, reject, or treat infested plants. Choose certified disease-free plants and seed when possible. Avoid buying grass or cover-crop seeds that are contaminated with weed seeds, and avoid hay or other mulches that contain weed seeds.

Clean up pest-damaged plants: Pull up diseased plants or prune off damage. Burn them, put them in sealed containers for disposal with household trash, put them in the center of a hot compost pile, or feed them to animals. Picking up and destroying dropped fruit weekly is an effective way to reduce infestations of apple maggots, currant fruit flies, codling moths, and plum curculios.

Clean up crop residues: Good sanitation includes cleaning up all crop residues promptly. Compost them well or turn them under. Cultivating to incorporate crop residues into the soil after harvest kills pests, including corn earworms, European corn borers, and corn rootworms.

Solarizing soil: Another approach to "cleaning" the soil of pest insect eggs and pupae involves using heat from the sun to kill them. This technique of covering soil with clear plastic to raise soil temperature is called soil solarization. It also works for killing some types of nematodes, disease organisms, and weed seeds. To learn more about this technique, turn to the Plant Diseases and Disorders entry.

Timed Planting

Getting the timing right can help your plants fight pests and diseases. Here are some examples.

- Seeds planted before the soil has warmed up in spring are more susceptible to disease. Learn the soil temperature each crop requires to germinate, and use a soil thermometer to determine proper planting time.

- Some pests have only one or two generations a year. You can reduce damage by scheduling planting or harvesting times to avoid peak pest populations. For example, to avoid damage from cabbage root maggots, plant radishes so they'll mature before the first generation of these pests appear, and delay setting out cabbage-family plants until after the first generation has passed.

- Rotating the position of crops from year to year in your garden may also help control certain insect pests, especially if you have a very large garden. See the Crop Rotation entry for more details.

Companion Planting

Neat rows or patches of a single crop make ideal places for pests to thrive. Many organic growers interplant two or more crops or combine certain companion plants with a crop to help reduce pest damage.

A few successful plant combinations work by directly repelling or confusing pests, or by changing the microclimate around the crop. Planting cabbage seedlings among taller plants that provide

Animal Helpers

We tend to think of animals and other critters as pests first, but many animals really are a gardener's friend because they eat insects, rodents, and other garden pests. In summer, a toad can put away 3,000 grubs, slugs, beetles, and other insects every month. A bat can catch 1,000 bugs in one night. You'll find information on the more lovable beneficial animals in the Bats, Birds, Earthworms, Toads, and Beneficial Insects entries. Read on to learn about an unlikely trio of garden helpers: spiders, snakes, and skunks.

All-Star Spiders

Cars, cigarettes, and unhealthy diets kill far more people every year in the United States than spiders have in a whole century. Yet more people panic at the sight of a spider than at more legitimate threats.

Actually, spiders are a lot of fun to watch. The gold-and-black garden spider spins a new web each day, gluing 1,000 to 1,500 connections among strands to form the pattern it has made perfectly since its first try. The spinner eats the old web before making a new one, recycling the silk proteins. As you brush by leaves in the garden, jumping spiders will leap aside in fast, basketball-style arcs.

Most spiders have a trace of venom, but only two spiders in the United States—the black widow and the brown recluse—have enough to injure a human. The female black widow has a glossy black body a little smaller than a garbanzo bean, marked on the underside with a red hourglass. It weaves a small matted web that it rarely leaves. These spiders are placid and bite only if extremely provoked. The bites are painful but can be treated.

The brown recluse or violin spider lives only in the southern half of the United States (south of Kansas). Its distinguishing feature is a dark violin-shaped patch on the top of the orangish yellow body segment behind its head. Its bites form deep sores that can linger for months.

To avoid mishaps with either of these spiders, don't reach with bare hands into dark crevices of woodpiles, tool sheds, and the like. Shake out clothing and towels, especially in rustic cabins or garages, before putting them on or holding them against your body. Avoiding those two unpleasant spiders leaves almost 3,000 species in the United States to enjoy without alarm. Some of these also bite if teased or startled, but they don't do more damage than a mosquito bite.

shade helps protect them from flea beetles, which prefer to feed in full sun. Other companion plants attract adult beneficial insects. After eating, the beneficials lay their eggs among the pests on nearby plants. When the predatory offspring hatch, they attack the pests.

The Scoop on Snakes

Of the 115 species of snakes in North America, only four kinds are poisonous: rattlesnakes, copperheads, coral snakes, and cottonmouths, also called water moccasins. Most of the snakes that find their way to a backyard will only bite if handled or stepped on, and even then the bite is harmless. In fact, garden pests, especially insects and rodents, are the real prey of snakes.

Beneficial backyard snakes include the common garter snake, eastern ribbon snake, western terrestrial garter snake, green or grass snake, and brown snake, all of which eat slugs, snails, and insects. The corn snake, black rat snake, and milk snake eat mice and rats. Most of these beneficial snakes are beautiful, too.

How can you tell if a snake is poisonous? Rattlers, copperheads, and cottonmouths are all thick-bodied snakes with large, triangular heads. A rattlesnake will rattle a warning if threatened. The position of the bands on the red, black, and yellow coral snake tells its story: "Red next to yellow kills a fellow."

If you don't like the idea of snakes patrolling your garden, take a few simple precautions. First, don't mulch your plots. Mulch provides shelter and attracts mice, a favored food. Keep your yard cleaned up and stack wood away from the house: Cordwood, junk, brush piles, and other debris will attract snakes to your yard. So will dog or cat food set outdoors and left unattended.

Skunks Earn Their Stripes

At the turn of the century, hops growers in New York State pushed for regulations protecting, of all things, the skunk. The growers claimed that skunks were controlling the dreaded hop grub. Modern gardeners have been less enthusiastic, since in addition to their offensive odor, skunks dig holes in lawns. Actually, the skunks are digging for grubs of Japanese beetles and other pests.

Skunks are known to react to menaces within 25 feet and can spray accurately at distances of 12 to 15 feet. Yet skunks seem inclined to mind their own business and ignore all but loud, blatant menaces like cars and charging dogs.

The bigger concern with skunks is rabies. They're the number one carrier of the disease, followed by raccoons. Stay away from skunks that seem disoriented or too bold, and have pets vaccinated.

Interplanting crops with different harvest dates also makes good use of garden space. One crop is harvested as the second needs more room to spread out and mature. When interplanted with other plants, legumes may help provide them with nitrogen. For more information on what combinations work, see the Companion Planting and Herbs entries.

Biological Controls for Insect Pests

Biological controls are living organisms—insects, animals, parasitic nematodes, and microbes that are predators or parasites of pest insects. Encouraging these naturally occurring helpers in your yard and garden is a nontoxic, nonharmful way to help minimize pest problems. Some biological controls are available as commercial products you can apply in your garden. Specialty companies also raise some types of beneficial insects, such as lady beetles and aphid midges, for farmers and gardeners to release in their greenhouses, fields, and gardens.

Beneficial Insects and Animals

Conserving and attracting native beneficial insects, birds, and animals is one of the best and most economical ways for gardeners to control pests. In a well-balanced garden, thousands of beneficial species do most of the work of suppressing pests for you. Learn to identify your helpers and find out what they like. Attract and encourage them to stay by providing food and nesting sites. For more information on beneficials, see the Beneficial Insects, Birds, Bats, and Toads entries.

Releasing commercially raised beneficial insects can be highly effective in greenhouses and large-scale plantings but usually isn't very effective for bringing a specific pest problem in a home garden under control. You'll be more successful if you create habitats that attract the native beneficial in your area, and let them wrap up your pest problems for you. For more on this, see the Beneficial Insects entry.

Microbial Products

Microbial controls are strains of disease organisms that kill garden pests.

Bt: Some of the most widely sold biological controls in the world are strains of *Bacillus thuringiensis* (Bt). Bt kills many species of caterpillars, beetles, flies, and mosquitoes. *Bacillus thuringiensis* bacteria produce crystals and spores that paralyze the digestive tract of certain insect larvae. Bt products are nontoxic to mammals, are specific to the target pest, do not harm beneficial insects, and may be used right up to harvest. There are several Bt varieties. Btk (*B.t.* var. *kurstaki*) controls cabbage looper, cabbage worm, tomato horn-worm, fruitworms, European corn borer, and similar larvae. Bti (*B.t.* var. *israelensis*) controls mosquitoes, blackflies, and fungus gnats. Btsd (*B.t.* var. *san diego*) controls small larvae of the Colorado potato beetle. Unfortunately, many Btsd products are manufactured using genetic engineering processes, so they're not allowable for use by certified organic farmers. Concerned home gardeners may want to avoid these products, too. To learn more about genetic engineering and its impact on home gardens, see the Biotechnology entry.

Milky disease: Milky disease infects the grubs of the Japanese beetle and its close relatives. The disease is caused by bacteria (*Bacillus popilliae* and *B. lentimorbus*) commonly called milky spore bacteria. Once established, milky disease will persist in the soil for many years (not as long in areas with harsh winters).

Spinosad: Spinosad is a microbial product that contains toxins produced by an actinomycete (*Saccaropolyspora spinosa*), which is a type of bacterium. It controls fire ants, leaf-eating caterpillars, and some other types of pests. It's a relatively new type of microbial control, and scientists are still studying its effectiveness in controlling different types of pests as well as its possible effects on beneficial insects.

Beauveria bassiana: This is a fungus that can kill aphids, Colorado potato beetles, whiteflies, and other pests. It can also harm beneficial insects. *Beauveria bassiana* products work best in cool and moist conditions.

Beneficial nematodes: Some nematodes parasitize insect larvae and grubs. They attack an insect and release bacteria that paralyze and kill the insect within 2 to 4 days. The nematode then feeds on the dead insect and reproduces rapidly. About 10 to 20 days later, huge numbers of nematodes leave the dead insect in search of new victims. Their larvae can survive for long periods in the soil, but for the greatest effect, you need to release more each year. Because nematodes perish in sunlight or dry places, they are most useful against pests in soil or hidden locations. *Steinernema carpocapsae* and *Heterorhabditis bacteriophora* nematodes are two of the most widely used species. It's critical to follow package directions precisely when applying nematodes.

Barriers and Traps

Barriers such as floating row covers are among the most effective ways to prevent pest damage because they stop the pests from reaching the crop in the first place, or deter pests from feeding if they do reach the plant.

Traps generally consist of one or more attractive components or lures (usually a color, odor, or shape) and a trapping component (usually sticky glue, a liquid, or a cage). Traps are used in one of two ways: to catch enough individual insects to prevent significant plant damage, or to monitor the emergence or arrival of a pest.

When using traps to control pests directly,

Homemade Traps

Here are a few simple traps you can make yourself.

Sticky traps: You can make sticky traps from wood, cardboard, or stiff plastic. Paint the base with a coat of primer and two coats of bright yellow or medium blue paint. Coat with a sticky compound using a paintbrush, or spread it on with a knife. Use stiff adhesives like Tanglefoot for large insects and thinner glues such as petroleum jelly or STP oil treatment for small insects. Scrape off insects and recoat as needed. To make apple maggot traps, paint plastic apple-size balls red and coat them with a sticky substance. Plastic soda bottles make good cherry fruit fly traps—paint the shoulders of the bottle yellow and fill the bottle with lure.

Traps to use with pheromone lures: You can make a simple trap from a 1-quart, plastic ice-cream or yogurt container. Cut three large holes in the upper half of the sides. Paint the lid, or line it with cardboard to shade the lure. Tape a commercial lure to the inside of the lid. Fasten the trap to a sturdy stake. Fill the bottom half of the container with soapy water and snap on the lid, securing the lure inside the trap.

judge their effectiveness by the reduction in plant damage, not just by the number of dead insects in the trap. If damage does not decrease, try other controls. Monitoring traps are useful for timing

Some Handy Hints

When you're looking through catalogs or Web sites at all the products available to help prevent and control garden insect pests, don't forget that one of the best tools for controlling insects is your own hands.

Handpicking insects is an effective, though rather tedious, way to control light or moderate infestations of large, easy-to-see caterpillars, such as tomato hornworms or cabbage loopers. Here are examples of some other pests you can handpick.

- Dig cutworms out of their daytime hiding place at the base of plants.
- Pick and destroy spinach or beet leaves with leaf miner mines.
- Scrape gypsy moths' egg masses off tree trunks.
- Pry newly hatched corn earworms out of the tips of corn ears before they can get very far into the cob.

Shaking pests from plants is a variation of handpicking and works especially well for heavy beetles, such as Japanese or Colorado potato beetles and plum curculios. Shake or beat them off the foliage onto a sheet of plastic, then pour them into a pail of soapy water. This is especially effective in the early morning when the pests are still sluggish.

Vacuuming is a high-tech version of handpicking that works well for removing adult whiteflies from tomato plants in a greenhouse. Some commercial growers pull giant bug vacuums behind their tractors to suck up pests. You can achieve similar results by using a handheld portable vacuum cleaner to suck up those pesky whiteflies, and try it for leafhoppers, Japanese beetles, and tarnished plant bugs, too. Be sure to dump the insects into soapy water afterward to kill them.

---

application of a control product to stop a pest problem quickly.

Floating row covers: Floating row covers of spunbonded polypropylene material improve plant growth and extend the growing season. They are also excellent barriers to such insect pests as carrot rust flies, cabbage maggots, flea beetles, and Mexican bean beetles. They also stop aphids and other insects whose feeding transmits plant diseases. In addition, row covers deter some small animals and birds that might feed on crops. For more informa-

tion on types of row covers and how to work with them, see the Row Covers entry.

Fences and netting: Deny larger animal pests access to your garden riches with fences, barriers, repellents, and scare tactics. See the Animal Pests entry for specific ways to frustrate hungry moochers.

Cutworm collars: These collars fit around transplant stems to protect them from nocturnal cutworm raids. To make collars, cut strips of lightweight cardboard about 8 by 2½ inches, overlap the ends to make a tube, and fasten with tape. Or cut sections of cardboard tube such as the inner tube from a paper-towel or toilet-paper roll to similar dimensions. When transplanting, slip a collar over each plant and press it into the soil around the stem so about half of the collar is below the soil line.

Rootfly barriers: Tar-paper squares are an old-fashioned and effective barrier to cabbage root flies (adult form of the cabbage root maggot), preventing them from laying their eggs around the roots of cabbage-family plants. Cut tar paper into 6- to 8-inch squares and make a small X-shaped cut in the center of each. Slide the square over the plant and flat against the soil, press the center flaps firmly around the stem, and anchor it with pebbles.

You can also make root-fly barriers out of heavy cloth, pieces of old carpeting, or foam rubber.

Tree bands: Tree bands are effective against pests that can't fly, such as snails, slugs, ants, and gypsy moth caterpillars. Some prevent pests from crossing; others actually trap pests.

Make cloth tree bands from strips of heavy cotton cloth or burlap about 15 inches wide and long enough to form a generous overlap when wrapped around the trunk. Tie the band to the trunk with a string around the middle of the lower half to make a dead end for creatures climbing up the tree. Check daily and destroy any pests trapped in the material.

Make corrugated cardboard tree bands by wrapping long strips around the trunk several times, with the exposed ridges facing in, and tying snugly with string. These bands attract codling-moth caterpillars looking for a sheltered place to spin their cocoons. Check for and destroy cocoons weekly.

Sticky tree bands: Pests get caught on sticky bands when they try to cross them and eventually die. Paint a 3-inch band of sticky compound all the way around the trunk of mature trees, reapplying as needed. Younger trees may be damaged by the compound. Instead, wrap a strip of fabric tightly around the trunk and cover that with a strip of plastic wrap. Apply the sticky compound to the plastic wrap. When the barrier loses effectiveness, replace the plastic.

Copper barriers: Strips of copper sheet metal make an excellent and permanent barrier against slugs and snails. Fasten them around the trunks of trees and shrubs, wrap them around legs or edges of greenhouse benches, or use them to edge garden beds. Be sure that there are no alternate routes over the strips for slugs to get to the plants. Pull or cut back leaning or overhanging weeds and plants.

To install a copper barrier around a garden bed, press the edge of a 3- to 4-inch-wide strip about 1 inch into the soil around the entire perimeter of the bed. Bend the top edge outward at a right angle to form a ½-inch lip. Eliminate slugs from inside the barrier by using slug traps and by leaving the soil bare as long as possible.

Kaolin clay: This very fine clay is sprayed on plants to repel insects. It may also prevent some types of disease organisms from penetrating plant surfaces. It is mixed with water and applied as a spray. It can deter many kinds of leaf-feeding beetles, including flea beetles, cucumber beetles, and Japanese beetles, as well as leafhoppers and thrips.

Dusty barriers: Dusts that have sharp particles, such as a layer of cinders or diatomaceous earth (DE), scratch the protective outer coating of insects and slugs, causing them to die from dehydration. Dusts work best during dry conditions; renew them after a rain.

Keep in mind that these dusts, particularly

diatomaceous earth, may kill as many or more beneficial insects than they do pests. DE is a good control for pests like ants in indoor situations, but be very cautious about using it in the garden.

To deter cabbage root maggots from laying eggs, sprinkle wood ashes, DE, or lime in a 6-inch-wide ring on the soil surface around cabbage-family transplant stems. Be sure to buy garden-quality DE; don't use DE intended for swimming pools in your garden.

Colored sticky traps: Colored sticky traps are useful to control or monitor a variety of species. Bright blue traps are suitable for monitoring flower thrips numbers; white traps attract tarnished plant bugs, but they also attract beneficial flies, so should be used only early in the season. Yellowish orange traps lure carrot rust flies.

Yellow sticky traps are effective controls for whiteflies, fungus gnats, and imported cabbageworms. However, they work only as monitors for thrips and aphids.

Apple maggot traps: Red spheres covered with sticky glue attract female apple maggot flies and are often the only control necessary in a home orchard. Starting in mid-June, hang one trap in a dwarf tree and up to six traps in a full-size tree, renewing the glue every 2 weeks. Some research shows that attaching an apple-scented lure to the trap increases its attractiveness, but not necessarily to the target pest—other related species may gum up the trap instead.

Cherry fruit fly traps: Yellow sticky traps catch cherry fruit flies if a small bottle of equal parts water and household ammonia or a commercial apple maggot lure is hung up with the trap. Hang one trap in each tree or four traps in a small orchard, and renew the sticky glue and the ammonia bait as necessary.

Yellow water traps: Fill a bright yellow pan or tray with water, to which a small amount of liquid soap has been added, to attract and drown aphids. These traps are effective monitors but not controls. They also attract tiny beneficials; remove the traps if this happens.

Traps with pheromone lures: Pheromones are chemical cues that insects use to communicate with others of their species. Sex pheromones are wafted onto the air by females to attract males, who follow the direction of the odor until they find a mate. Synthetic pheromones are available in

Pheromones

Pheromones are hormonelike chemicals produced and emitted by insects and other animals to communicate with other members of their species. They are highly specific and can attract insects from great distances. Pheromone products are available for many pests, including peach tree borers, codling moths, corn earworms, cabbage loopers, apple maggots, and Japanese beetles.

Traps baited with pheromones are used to keep track of specific pest populations. Small capsules containing pheromones are placed inside cardboard traps coated with a sticky material. The species attracted to the pheromone flies into the trap and gets caught in the glue. Gardeners and orchardists may also be able to control certain pests by hanging large numbers of traps. Pheromone lures without traps confuse pests and keep them from finding food or mates.

Home-Brewed Pest Controls

Organic gardeners have long relied on homemade sprays that are safe to use and easy to prepare. Results aren't guaranteed, so monitor the plants after treating them.

Garlic oil: Finely chop 10 to 15 garlic cloves and soak in 1 pint of mineral oil for 24 hours. Strain and spray as is, or dilute with water and add a few drops of soap.

Hot-pepper spray: In a blender, blend ½ cup of hot peppers with 2 cups of water. Strain and spray. *Caution:* Hot peppers burn skin and eyes.

You can also use a combination spray by blending up to 6 cloves of garlic with 1 or 2 peppers in 1 quart of water. Strain the mixture before spraying, and use caution to keep the spray off your skin and well away from your face and eyes.

long-lasting lures and are widely used in sticky traps to monitor pest populations, especially the various species of moths that attack fruit trees. When enough pheromone traps are used, they can control the population by trapping so many males that a significant portion of the females go unmated and don't lay eggs.

Commercial lures are long lasting, and many are available in small quantities for home use and can be incorporated into homemade traps. Set out traps about 2 to 3 weeks before the target pest is expected to emerge; one trap is usually enough for a home orchard or garden. Check the traps daily or weekly; follow package directions.

Pheromones can also be used without traps to control pests. When large numbers of pheromone lures are put out, the air becomes saturated with aroma and males can't locate females to mate. Twist ties impregnated with pheromones are available for controlling oriental fruit moth and other pests.

Food lures: Slugs and snails are attracted to stale beer, spoiled yogurt, or a mixture of yeast and water. Set out the bait in saucers or tuna cans, buried with the lip of the container level with the soil surface, so the pests fall in and drown. Put a cover with holes in it on the trap to keep rain from diluting the beer and to keep large animals from drinking it.

Food traps: Control onion maggots by planting sprouted or shriveled onions between rows of onion seeds in early spring. The onion maggot flies lay their eggs in the soil nearby, and the maggots burrow into the trap onions. About 2 weeks after the trap onions sprout, pull and destroy them to prevent the next generation of flies from developing.

If wireworms are a problem for you, you can use a trap to reduce their numbers before you plant. Cut potatoes in half and poke a stick into each to serve as a handle. Bury the pieces of potato in the soil in early spring. Wireworms will be attracted to the trap potatoes; check the traps every few days, and destroy the wireworms or replace the potatoes.

Trap crops: Plants that are more attractive to certain pests than the crop you want to protect are useful as trap crops. For example, dill or lovage lures tomato hornworms away from tomatoes, and early squash is useful to trap pickleworms before late melons are set out. Pull and destroy trap plants as soon as they are infested, or the pests may reproduce on the crop and thus provide a larger pest population.

The Safest Way to Spray

Sometimes the most effective control is also the simplest. A strong spray of plain old water from your garden hose can physically injure aphids, leafhoppers, and other delicate pests, and knock them off plants. Spray plants in early morning or late afternoon. If you have problems with diseases that thrive in wet conditions, you may want to choose another control method.

Sprays and Dusts

In the rare instances when an insect pest could cause serious injury to plants, you may need to use an organic insect-killing product such as insecticidal soap or neem. In some cases, one or two well-timed applications of a product like spinosad while the first generation of a pest is just emerging can knock back the pest and head off the crisis.

Botanical sprays (sprays that contain plant-derived substances that can kill pests) such as neem break down into more-harmless compounds in a relatively short time. Some sprays and dusts are less toxic than others to beneficial insects and other living things. Note that a number of botanical sprays widely used by organic gardeners decades ago—rotenone, nicotine, ryania, and sabadilla—are no longer recommended because of their toxic effects on people or the environment. Pyrethrin is a botanical spray that's still in use, although it should be used with caution (see the opposite page).

Always choose the least toxic but most effective method available. When using commercial products, follow the directions on the label. *Caution:* Do not mix products together or add activators or boosters unless the label directs you to do so. To be safe when you apply these products, follow these precautions.

- Keep all garden sprays and dusts in their original container with product name and instructions.
- Store these products tightly closed and away from food and out of reach of children.
- Don't store pest-control solutions in recycled beverage/food containers.
- Mix and apply exactly according to directions.
- Wear protective clothing when mixing, applying, and cleaning up. This may include a long-sleeved shirt and pants, rubber boots, rubber or other waterproof gloves, goggles, and a dust mask or respirator. Read the product label for requirements.
- Wash clothing, skin, containers, and sprayers thoroughly when cleaning up.
- Stay out of treated areas until spray is dry or dust has settled.

Iron phosphate baits: These are commercial products that kill slugs and snails. Iron phosphate is a mined mineral mixed into a bait such as wheat gluten. While it is very effective at killing slugs and snails, it is not toxic to people or wildlife.

Insecticidal oils: Petroleum and plant oils have long been used to kill eggs and immature stages of insects. Oils block the insect's supply of oxygen and are especially effective because they spread well over surfaces. Oils may also poison or repel some insects. They break down quickly and are more toxic to pests than to beneficial insects.

Dormant oils are heavy petroleum oils that can be sprayed on dormant orchard trees and ornamental plants to control overwintering stages of mites, scales, aphids, and other insects. Spray a 1 to 3 percent mixture of oil in water when the air temperature is above 40°F. Certain plants such as Japanese maple are very sensitive and can be severely damaged by dormant oil. It also removes the blue "bloom" from blue spruce, turning it green. Before spraying a whole plant, spray a small area and see if yellowing occurs.

Summer oils, also called superior or supreme oils, are lighter petroleum oils that contain fewer of the impurities that make dormant oils toxic to plants. Spray up to a 2 percent mixture of summer oil and water even on fully leafed-out plants as long as the air temperature is below 85°F and the plants are not drought or heat stressed. Summer oil controls aphids, spider mites, scales, psylla, mealybugs, and some caterpillars. It is slightly toxic to mammals and registered for ornamental and greenhouse use. Oils may cause leaf damage to some plants under certain conditions. Spray a small area and wait a few days. If the plants are unharmed, spray thoroughly.

Vegetable oils provide similar control. Mix 1 cup of cooking oil with 1 tablespoon of liquid soap. Use 2½ teaspoons per cup of water to spray.

Insecticidal soaps: Insecticidal soaps are specially formulated solutions of fatty acids that kill insect pests like aphids, mites, and whiteflies. Insecticidal soap is a contact insecticide that paralyses insects, which then die of starvation. Spray plants every 2 to 3 days for 2 weeks for bad infestations. Mix with soft water. Soaps may damage plants if applied too strongly or if plants are drought or heat stressed. Soaps break down within 1 to 2 weeks.

Many organic gardeners use 1 to 3 teaspoons of household soap (not detergent) per gallon of water as a garden insecticide.

Neem oil: Neem oil is extracted from the neem tree, *Azadirachta indica*, native to India. The oil is extracted from seed kernels, leaves, bark, flowers, and wood. Neem oil is a broad-spectrum insect poison, repellent, and feeding deterrent. It also stops or disrupts insect growth and sterilizes some species. Research is ongoing, but neem oil appears to be easy on beneficials and of very low toxicity to mammals.

Neem oil solution can be used as a spray to control many insects and as a soil drench to control soil stages of pests. Spray when the leaves will remain wet for as long as possible.

Sulfur: You can use sulfur to control mites and chiggers. Sulfur is gentle on large predaceous insects but will kill tiny parasitic wasps. See the Plant Diseases and Disorders entry for more details about sulfur.

Pyrethrins: Pyrethrins are derived from the flowers of pyrethrum daisies (*Chrysanthemum cinerariifolium* and *C. coccineum*). The dried flowers are finely ground to make an insecticidal dust. Pyrethrins are extracted from the dust and used in sprayable solutions. Pyrethrins attack an insect's central nervous system, providing the rapid knockdown that gives many gardeners a satisfying feeling of revenge. At low doses, however, insects may detoxify the chemical and recover. Read labels carefully before buying a pyrethrin product. Many of them are synthetic versions of pyrethrins (pyrethroids) or contain synthetic synergists, like piperonyl butoxide (PBO), which may be toxic themselves. Avoid these products. Check labels to be sure you're getting a plant-derived, organically acceptable product.

Pyrethrins are effective against a broad spectrum of pest insects, including flies, mosquitoes, and chewing and sucking insect pests. You can apply them up to 1 day before harvest because they break down rapidly in heat and light. Pyrethrins are moderately toxic to mammals and highly toxic to fish and bees. Don't apply them around ponds, waterways, or plants where bees are active. Apply pyrethrins only as a last resort.

The Top 10 Garden Insect Pests

The following list of pest descriptions and control measures provides a good starting point for tackling pest control in gardens throughout the United States and Canada. Control solutions are listed in order of environmental friendliness. Botanical sprays, which can have detrimental effects on beneficial insects and other animals, should be used only as a last resort.

PEST	HOST/RANGE	DAMAGE	CONTROL
Aphids (many species). Tiny, pear-shaped; long antennae; 2 tubes projecting rearward from abdomen.	Most fruits and vegetables, flowers, ornamentals, shade trees. Found throughout North America.	Aphids suck plant sap, causing foliage to distort and leaves to drop; honeydew excreted on leaves supports sooty mold growth; feeding spreads viral diseases.	Wash plants with strong spray of water; encourage native predators and parasites such as aphid midges, lacewings, and lady beetles; when feasible, cover plants with floating row cover; apply hot-pepper or garlic repellent sprays; for severe problems, apply horticultural oil, insecticidal soap, or neem.
Cabbage maggot (*Delia radicum*). Adults: ¼-inch gray flies. Larvae: white, tapering maggots.	Cabbage-family crops. Found throughout North America.	Maggots tunnel in roots, killing plants directly or by creating entryways for disease organisms.	Apply floating row covers; set out transplants through slits in tarpaper squares; avoid first generation by delaying planting; apply parasitic nematodes around roots; burn roots from harvested plants; mound wood ashes or red pepper dust around stems.
Caterpillars (many species). Soft, segmented larvae with distinct, harder head capsule; 6 legs in front, fleshy false legs on rear segments.	Many fruits and vegetables, ornamentals, shade trees. Range varies with species.	Caterpillars chew on leaves or along margins; droppings soil the produce; some tunnel into fruits.	Encourage native predators, parasites; handpick; apply floating row covers; spray with Bt (*Bacillus thuringiensis*) or spinosad.

PEST	HOST/RANGE	DAMAGE	CONTROL
Colorado potato beetle (*Leptinotarsa decemlineata*). Adults: yellow-orange beetles with 10 black stripes on wing covers. Larvae: orange, hump-backed grubs with black spots along sides. Eggs: yellow ovals, laid in upright clusters.	Potatoes, tomatoes, eggplant, petunias. Found throughout North America.	Beetles defoliate plants, reducing yields or killing young plants.	Apply floating row covers; use deep straw mulches; handpick; attract native parasites and predators; spray with *Beauveria bassiana* or spinosad; spray with neem.
Cutworms (several species). Fat, 1-inch-long, gray or black segmented larvae; active at night.	Most early vegetable and flower seedlings, transplants. Found throughout North America.	Cutworms chew through stems at ground level; they may completely devour small plants; most damaging in May and June.	Use cutworm collars on transplants; delay planting; handpick cutworms curled below soil surface; scatter bran baits mixed with Btk (*B.t.* var. *kurstaki*) and molasses before planting.
Flea beetles (several species). Small, dark beetles that jump like fleas when disturbed.	Most vegetable crops. Found throughout North America.	Adults chew numerous small, round holes in leaves; most damaging to young plants; larvae feed on plant roots.	Apply floating row covers; repel the pests by spraying plants with garlic spray or kaolin clay; for a serious infestation, try repeated sprays of *Beauveria bassiana* or spinosad.
Japanese beetle (*Popillia japonica*). Adults: metallic blue-green, ½-inch beetles with bronze wing covers. Larvae: fat, white grubs with brown heads.	Many vegetables and flowers, small fruit. Found in all states east of the Mississippi River.	Adults skeletonize leaves, chew flowers, may completely defoliate plants; larvae feed on lawn and garden plant roots.	Shake beetles from plants in early morning; apply floating row covers; set out baited traps upwind of your garden on two sides and at least 30 feet away; apply milky disease spores or *Heterorhabditis* nematodes to soil; spray beetles with insecticidal soap.

(continued)

The Top 10 Garden Insect Pests *(cont.)*

PEST	HOST/RANGE	DAMAGE	CONTROL
Mexican bean beetle (*Epilachna varivestis*). Adults: oval, yellow-brown, ¼-inch beetles with 16 black spots on wing covers. Larvae: fat, dark yellow grubs with long, branched spines.	Cowpeas, lima beans, snap beans, soybeans. Found in most states east of the Mississippi River; also parts of Arizona, Colorado, Nebraska, Texas, Utah.	Adults and larvae chew on leaves from beneath, leaving characteristic lacy appearance; plants defoliated and killed.	Apply floating row covers; plant bush beans early; handpick; plant soybean trap crop; put out lures to draw spined soldier bugs (predators) to your yard. Spray *Beauveria bassiana*, insecticidal soap, or neem.
Scales (more than 200 species). Adults: females look like hard or soft bumps on stems, leaves, fruit; males are minute flying insects. Larvae: tiny, soft, crawling larvae with thread-like mouthparts.	Many fruits, indoor plants, ornamental shrubs, and trees. Found throughout North America.	All stages suck plant sap, weakening plants. Plants become yellow, drop leaves, and may die. Honeydew is excreted onto foliage and fruit.	Prune out infested plant parts; encourage native predators; scrub scales gently from twigs with soft brush and soapy water, rinse well; apply dormant or summer oil sprays; spray with neem oil.
Tarnished plant bug (*Lygus lineolaris*). Fast-moving, mottled, green or brown bugs, forewings with black-tipped yellow triangles. Nymphs: similar to adults, but wingless.	Many flowers, fruits, vegetables. Found throughout North America.	Adults and nymphs suck plant juices, causing leaf and fruit distortion, wilting, stunting, and tip dieback.	Keep garden weed-free in spring. Apply floating row covers; encourage native predatory insects; spray young nymphs with *Beauveria bassiana* or neem.

PETUNIA

Garden petunia. Summer- and fall-blooming annuals.

Description: Petunias bear abundant 2- to 4-inch, often-fragrant trumpets in white, pink, rose, red, yellow, blue, and purple. Single- or double-flowered cultivars may have lacy or starred shapes and ruffled or smooth margins. Most grow upright or mounded to 1 foot tall. Smallish, sticky leaves are unremarkable.

How to grow: Indoors, sow the minute seeds in late winter or early spring for planting out after frost, or choose from the wide selection of bedding plants at garden centers. At 3 to 4 inches, pinch out the centers to promote bushiness, even if the plants are in bloom. Grow petunias in full sun or with some afternoon shade in average soil and moisture.

They tolerate drought very well, and pests rarely bother them. Cut the plants back hard in midsummer if they grow tall and straggly, and give them a little extra water and fertilizer. They will bloom again in fall. Take cuttings of favorites and overwinter them indoors in a warm, bright spot.

Landscape uses: Grow petunias in beds, borders, pots, hanging baskets, and window boxes. Let them tumble over rocks or space them out and use them as a groundcover. Small-flowered petunias add a lovely soft touch to the front of the perennial border; they'll self-sow if flowers are allowed to mature in fall. Petunias will look tired by late summer, so grow them where other plants can take over while they recover.

PH

You'll often read the recommendation to check soil pH, but what does that really mean? pH is simply a measure of how acid or alkaline a substance is, and soil acidity or alkalinity (soil pH) is important because it influences how easily plants can take up nutrients from the soil. Many gardening books and catalogs list the preferred pH for specific plants. The good news for gardeners is that, with a few exceptions, most plants will tolerate a fairly wide range of soil pH. The diagram below shows how pH values relate to soils.

Nutrient uptake and pH: Plant roots absorb mineral nutrients such as nitrogen and iron when they are dissolved in water. If the soil solution (the mixture of water and nutrients in the soil) is too acid or alkaline, some nutrients won't dissolve easily, so they won't be available for uptake by roots.

Most nutrients that plants need can dissolve easily when the pH of the soil solution ranges from 6.0 to 7.5. Below pH 6.0, some nutrients, such as

nitrogen, phosphorus, and potassium, are less available. When pH exceeds 7.5, iron, manganese, and phosphorus are less available.

Regional differences: Many environmental factors, including amount of rainfall, vegetation type, and temperature, can affect soil pH. In general, areas with heavy rainfall and forest cover such as the eastern states and the Pacific Northwest have moderately acid soils. Soils in regions with light rainfall and prairie cover such as the Midwest tend to be near neutral. Droughty areas of the western United States tend to have alkaline soils. However, the pH of cultivated and developed soils often differs from that of native soil, because during construction of homes and other buildings, topsoil is frequently removed and may be replaced by a different type of soil. So your garden soil pH could be different from that of a friend's garden across town.

Changing pH: Most garden plants grow well in slightly acid to neutral soil (pH 6.0–7.0). Some common exceptions include blueberries, potatoes, azaleas, and rhododendrons, which prefer moderately acid soil. You can make small changes to soil pH by applying soil amendments. However, you'll have best success if you select plants that are adapted to your soil pH and other soil characteristics. Adding organic matter such as compost to the soil buffers the pH, which means that it tends to bring both acid and alkaline soils closer to neutral.

If you have your soil analyzed by a lab, the lab report will include soil pH. See the Soil entry for information on how to sample your soil and have it tested. You can also test soil pH yourself with a home soil test kit or a portable pH meter. Home kits and portable meters vary in accuracy but can be helpful in assessing the general pH range of your soil.

The quantity of liming or acidifying material needed to change soil pH depends on many factors, including current pH, soil texture, and the type of material. A soil lab report will contain recommendations on types and quantities of amendments to use.

You can spread liming or acidifying materials with a garden spreader or by hand for small areas. If hand-spreading, be sure to wear heavy gloves to protect your skin.

Correcting acid soil: If your soil is too acid, you must add alkaline material, a process commonly called liming. The most common liming material is ground limestone. There are two types: calcitic limestone (calcium carbonate) and dolomitic limestone (calcium-magnesium carbonate). In most instances, you'll use calcitic lime. Apply dolomitic lime only if your soil also has a magnesium deficiency.

Ground limestone breaks down slowly in the soil. Apply it to the garden and lawn in fall to allow time for it to act on soil pH before the next growing season. A rule of thumb for slightly acidic soils is to apply 5 pounds of lime per 100 square feet to raise pH by one point. In general, sandy soils will need less limestone to change pH; clay soils will need more.

The amount of lime you must add to correct pH depends not only on your soil type but also on its initial pH. For example, applying 5 pounds of limestone per 100 square feet will raise the pH of a sandy loam soil from 6.0 to 6.5. It would take 10 pounds per 100 square feet to make the same change in silty loam soil. However, if 5.6 was the initial pH of the soil, 8 pounds per 100 square feet would be required for the sandy loam soil, and 16 pounds per 100 square feet for the silty loam soil. There is no simple rule of thumb that applies to all soils. The safest approach to take if you plan to apply limestone is to have your soil tested and follow the lab recommendations.

Applying wood ashes also will raise soil pH. Wood ashes contain up to 70 percent calcium carbonate, as well as potassium, phosphorus, and many trace minerals. Because it has a very fine particle size, wood ash is a fast-acting liming material. Use it with caution, because overapplying it can create serious soil imbalances. Limit applica-

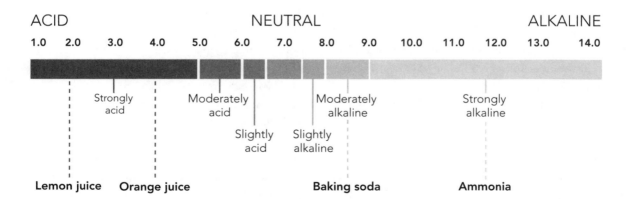

The pH scale. The overall pH scale ranges from 1.0 to 14.0, but soils are rarely more acidic than 4.5 or more alkaline than 8.0. Thus, most soils are less acidic than orange juice and less alkaline than baking soda. Some gardeners refer to alkaline soils as "sweet" and acidic soils as "sour."

Why Is It Called pH?

What does pH stand for, and why is it spelled in that odd way? Thank chemistry for this incomprehensible abbreviation. It stands for "potenz Hydrogen" (*potenz* means "the potential to be"). In chemistry, the elements of the periodic table—remember that from school?—such as Oxygen and Hydrogen, are capitalized; that's why it's pH rather than ph, Ph, or PH. But what does hydrogen—much less the potential of hydrogen—have to do with soil acidity or alkalinity? Well, the activity of hydrogen ions in solution—and soil is actually a solution at the microscopic level—determines the acidity or alkalinity of the solution. Acidic solutions have a high concentration of hydrogen ions; alkaline solutions have a low concentration. This may all seem arcane, but here's a fun fact: The inventor of the pH scale developed it to determine the acid content of his beer!

tions to 25 pounds per 1,000 square feet, and apply ashes only once every 2 to 3 years in any particular area. At this rate, your soil will get the benefits of the trace minerals without adverse effects on pH.

Correcting alkaline soil: If your soil is too alkaline, add a source of acidity. The most common material to add is powdered elemental sulfur. As a rule of thumb, add 1 pound of sulfur per 100 square feet to lower pH 1 point. But as with lime, the correct amount will depend on your soil type and its initial pH. Testing your soil and following lab recommendations is the best approach if

you want to lower the pH of an entire bed or area of your yard.

Mixing peat moss with the soil will also lower pH. Peat moss can be expensive, so it's generally only a feasible choice for small areas such as flowerbeds, when planting one or two acid-loving shrubs (such as blueberries), and in container gardens. Peat moss has also been overharvested in many areas; incorporating ample organic matter (such as shredded leaves) is a more environmentally friendly option.

PHENOLOGY

See Weather and Weather Lore

PHLOX

Phlox. Summer-blooming perennials.

Description: *Phlox paniculata*, garden phlox, enjoys star billing in many summer gardens. Hundreds of 1-inch rounded blooms crowd into massive, roughly pyramidal clusters of white, pink, rose, red, orange, and purple, many with a contrasting "eye" in the center of each bloom. Most have a sweet, light, musty scent, especially during dusk and early evening. Plants form 3- to 4-foot-tall upright mounds with pairs of 3- to 6-inch pointed leaves set at a 90-degree angle to the pair below. To make it easier to combat mildew, the bane of garden phlox, choose mildew-resistant cultivars such as white-flowered 'David' or 'Bright Eyes', which has pink flowers with crimson eyes. Zones 3–8.

How to grow: Plant or divide phlox in spring or fall in a sunny, well-drained spot with fertile, humus-rich soil. Partial shade may prolong bloom

More Fine Phlox

Not all phlox are as imposing as garden phlox, but several are just as useful and attractive in the garden. Native wild blue phlox (*Phlox divaricata*, also called wild sweet William) and creeping phlox (*P. stolonifera*) both bear a profusion of delicate 1-inch blooms in shades of white, blue, and lavender on thin stems to 1 foot in spring. These gently spreading plants give a misty quality to lightly shaded moist woodlands and provide a cheerful contrast to bulbs and perennials in a border. Wild blue phlox is hardy in Zones 3–9, creeping phlox in Zones 2–8. Lowest growing of all is moss pink (*P. subulata*), which is hardy in Zones 2–9. Myriad ½-inch blooms in white, pink, magenta, and lilac shades hide its spreading 1- to 3-inch mats of dense, needlelike evergreen leaves in spring. They thrive in sun and lean to rich, well-drained soil. Allow them to fill spaces in rock gardens and walls, or let them carpet a steep bank. All of these phlox have many fine cultivars.

in the South. Phlox are heavy feeders and benefit from a scattering of organic fertilizer in early spring. Water frequently in summer. For best growth and reasonable powdery mildew control, divide every other year into renewed soil, and thin to about 6 shoots per plant. Never grow in airless spots or allow the clumps to become dense. If you do, the result will be a mildewed mess of ratty leaves and small flower heads. Remove flower heads before they drop their seeds to prevent vig-

orous seedlings (usually in vivid magenta shades) from crowding out their more desirable parents.

Landscape uses: Feature a variety of colors in a border, or tie a planting together with shades of a single color. Phlox look good in a bed or cutting garden. Allow reverted seedlings to naturalize in thin woods or a field.

PICEA

Spruce. Evergreen trees or shrubs.

Description: Large trees that reach heights of 30 to 60 feet in the landscape, spruces are pyramidal to conical in habit, with short stiff needles and drooping cones.

Picea abies, Norway spruce, has horizontal limbs and branchlets that dangle with age. Cones grow 4 to 6 inches long. Norway spruce grows 40 to 60 feet. Zones 2–6.

P. glauca, white spruce, is a native species that becomes spirelike with age and reaches heights of 40 to 60 feet. White spruce has drooping branchlets, four-sided needles, and 2-inch cones. Zones 2–6.

P. mariana, black spruce, another native, is also spirelike with age. It grows 30 to 40 feet tall. Zones 1–6.

P. omorika, Serbian spruce, is a slim-trunked tree of 50 to 60 feet with branches that droop but point upward at the tips. The flattened needles are deep green on top and whitish underneath; cones are 2½ inches long. Zones 4–6.

P. orientalis, Oriental spruce, is a graceful tree that grows 50 to 60 feet tall. Four-sided needles are waxy, deep green, and crowded on branches. Cones are about 3 inches long. Zones 5–7.

P. pungens, Colorado spruce, is a stiffly pyramidal native tree that grows 30 to 60 feet tall in the landscape. The four-sided needles are stiff and prickly; branchlets are yellowish brown and smooth. *P. pungens* 'Glauca' and other cultivars with blue- or silver-green needles are commonly called Colorado blue spruce. Zones 2–6.

How to grow: Spruces need a cool climate and plenty of room. They grow quickly (as much as 1 to 2 feet per year), astounding homeowners with their ability to take up space, especially when they looked so small at planting time. Spruces transplant easily because of their shallow spreading root systems, and even large specimens can be relocated. In addition to space, spruces require evenly moist, well-drained, acid soil and full sun, although they can be grown successfully in clay soils. Most species will tolerate light shade but grow open and untidy looking in heavy shade. To encourage dense growth, prune in spring when new growth is nearly half developed, removing half to two-thirds of the candle of new growth. Spruces generally require little pruning; some species tolerate heavy pruning and can be used to form hedges.

Pests that attack spruces include spider mites, sawflies, spruce gall adelgids, and bagworms. Spider mites often afflict trees that are under drought stress, and infestations tend to appear in very hot, dry weather. Avoid spider mite problems with proper culture—plant trees in cool areas and water deeply in dry weather. Use a strong spray of water to knock spider mites from trees, or spray with an insecticidal soap. Sawfly larvae feed on needles and disfigure trees. See the Pinus entry for sawfly control information.

Spruce gall adelgids are small, aphidlike insects that suck sap from needles, causing a pinecone- or pineapple-shaped gall to form around them at the ends of branches. The galls turn brown and crack open in summer, releasing mature adelgids that lay powdery egg masses near the base of the tree's buds. Remove and burn spruce galls from the twig tips before the new generation of adelgids emerges. If you can't take off all the galls, spray with dormant oil before growth begins or with summer oil during the growing season. Don't use oil sprays on blue spruces—they discolor the foliage. Sprays of insecticidal soap also give control if applied prior to bud break in early spring or timed to coincide with adelgid emergence from galls in July and August.

Bagworms are moth larvae that chew the needles of spruces and many other kinds of evergreens. The bagworms take their name from their ability to spin silken bags, which they stud with bits of needles so that the bags resemble pinecones. Uncontrolled feeding can defoliate evergreens and eventually kill the plants. The larvae use the bag as a shelter. They also pupate in the bags, and adult females lay eggs inside the bags as well. Handpick and destroy the bags in winter. Spray Btk (*Bacillus thuringiensis* var. *kurstaki*) for larvae in spring. Catch adult males in pheromone traps in summer.

Landscape uses: Use spruces as screens, hedges, and windbreaks. Many are attractive trees that work well as focal points in large-scale situations. Use blue spruces with discretion if color harmony is important to you—their strong blues are often hard to combine with other colors in the landscape.

PIERIS

Pieris. Spring-blooming, broad-leaved evergreen shrubs.

Description: *Pieris floribunda*, mountain pieris or fetterbush, is a rounded, spreading shrub that grows to 6 feet tall. This plant bears upright clusters of creamy white flower spikes in spring. Zones 5–7.

P. japonica, Japanese pieris or lily-of-the-valley bush, can reach 10 feet at maturity. Glossy green foliage forms a background for the creamy white, cascading flower clusters. Zones 6–7.

How to grow: Pieris need partial shade and humus-rich, well-drained, evenly moist, well-mulched soil. Prune after flowering to remove dead wood. Remove spent flowers for good bloom next year. If lace bugs are a problem, control with soap sprays.

Landscape uses: Japanese pieris makes a fine specimen; plant where you can enjoy it at close range. Mountain pieris is a good choice for massed plantings and woodland gardens.

PINUS

Pine. Evergreen trees or shrubs.

Description: *Pinus bungeana*, lacebark pine, is a multitrunked tree that reaches 30 to 50 feet in the landscape, becoming flattopped with age. The bark flakes off, revealing attractive olive, gray, and tan patches. The 4-inch needles grow in bundles of three; the cones are about 3 inches long. Zones 5–7.

P. densiflora, Japanese red pine, has crooked trunks and horizontal branches. This picturesque pine becomes flattopped with age and attains a mature height of 40 to 60 feet. The 5-inch, blue-green needles grow in bundles of two. The bark is orangish and the cones are about 2 inches long. Zones 5–6.

P. flexilis, limber pine, is pyramidal in youth and flattopped with age, growing to a height of 30 to 50 feet. The twisted, blue-green, 3-inch needles grow in bundles of five; the cones can be 3 to 10 inches long. This North American native devel-

ops deep fissures in its old bark, but its most interesting feature is its rubbery, fun-to-play-with, flexible branches. Zones 5–6.

P. mugo, Swiss mountain pine, is a shrub or small tree that grows 15 to 20 feet tall. Valued for its dwarf cultivars, it has a low, round, bushy habit and 2-inch needles in bundles of two. Zones 3–7.

P. nigra, Austrian pine, becomes massive and picturesque with age. In youth, it's pyramidal, but it develops a flat top and gray—almost white—bark with deep fissures forming blocky patterns. It grows 50 to 60 feet tall in the landscape, bearing 6½-inch needles in bundles of two and cones about 3 inches long. Austrian pine is one of the few pines that tolerate urban conditions. Zones 4–6.

P. strobus, eastern white pine, is soft and graceful in texture, pyramidal in youth, and stout with age. The branches appear in whorls on the trunk, with bluish green 5-inch-long needles in bundles of five. The cones are 4 to 6 inches long. This native evergreen grows 50 to 80 feet tall; it has little tolerance for road deicing salts. Zones 3–6.

P. sylvestris, Scots pine, aka Scotch pine, is pyramidal in youth and gnarled with age, reaching a mature height of 30 to 60 feet. The bark of the upper trunk flakes off to reveal a colorful orange inner bark that shows through the stiff, twisted, blue-green needles. The 3-inch-long needles are borne in bundles of two. Scotch pine tolerates poor, dry soils and is grown as a Christmas tree in northern states. Zones 2–6.

P. taeda, loblolly pine, is a fast-growing southern native that can reach 60 to 90 feet. Its 6- to 10-inch needles are in bundles of three. Older trees have few lower branches; the exposed trunk's furrowed bark makes a nice background for small trees like dogwoods (*Cornus florida*). Zones 7–9.

P. thunbergii, Japanese black pine, is pyramidal in youth, growing irregular, open, and picturesque with age. Its usual mature height in North America is 20 to 30 feet, although in its seaside habitat in its native Japan it grows to 130 feet. The 3- to 4½-inch needles are borne in bundles of two; the bright green, sharply pointed cones are 2½ inches long. Japanese black pine is good for coastal areas because it is resistant to salt spray. Zones 6–7.

P. virginiana, Virginia pine, is a scrubby pine of 15 to 40 feet with paired needles and an irregular branching habit. Virginia pine is not particularly desirable as a landscape plant, but it is a native species and tolerates poor, dry soils and can be used in difficult sites. Zones 5–9.

P. wallichiana, Himalayan white pine, is a pyramidal tree that becomes massive with age. Soft, gray-green needles are 8 inches long and borne in bundles of five; they droop gracefully from the branches. The cones are 6 to 12 inches long; the tree reaches a height of 50 to 80 feet. Zones 5–6.

How to grow: Somewhat more adaptable to poor soil, exposed sites, and urban conditions than firs and spruces, pines prefer full sun, well-drained soil, and plenty of room. Several pest and disease problems trouble pines, but serious damage is usually limited to stressed trees or those found in large plantings such as Christmas tree farms.

Pine needle scales appear as small yellowish white bumps on the needles. A heavy infestation gives branches a snowy look. The scales feed while attached to the needles; eggs mature beneath the scales, and one or two generations of tiny reddish crawlers emerge during the growing season. Infested needles may turn yellow and drop from the tree. Apply dormant oil and lime sulfur spray in late winter before growth begins; spray insecticidal soap or summer oil when crawlers appear in spring and again in early summer.

Sawfly is a name given to several species of nonstinging wasps that insert their eggs into the needles of pines and other evergreens. The larvae emerge to feed on the needles; one generation occurs per year in the North, but as many as three may attack southern pines. These pests usually eat old foliage first, but severe infestations can defoliate entire trees. Pick off any caterpillars that you can reach, or spray with summer oil or neem.

Pine tip and pine shoot borers are the caterpillars of several species of small moths. Pine tip moth larvae bore into needle and bud bases, killing the shoots. Damaged trees have brown, slightly curled shoot tips. Remove and destroy infested branch tips; apply sprays of Btk (*Bacillus thuringiensis* var. *kurstaki*) when caterpillars are visible.

Landscape uses: Grow pines as specimen plants, screens, windbreaks, and hedges. They can make glorious focal points in large-scale situations.

PLANT DISEASES AND DISORDERS

When plants are well nourished and well taken care of, they have a natural ability to resist disease. And since keeping plants healthy is at the heart of organic gardening, disease problems tend to be minor in organic gardens. Organic gardeners feed the soil regularly with compost and organic matter, which keeps disease organisms in check both by producing stronger plants and by encouraging beneficial soil organisms that actually fight against pathogens.

Factors other than diseases can produce disease-like symptoms, and these problems are called plant disorders. Extreme weather conditions or soil imbalances may be the cause, and, in fact, people are often indirectly the cause of common plant disorders such as salt damage or ozone damage. Choosing plants that are well suited to the site is

KEY WORDS *Disease*

Pathogen. An organism that causes disease.

Host. A plant or animal that a parasite or pathogen depends on for sustenance.

Spore. A one- or many-celled reproductive unit.

Nematode. A microscopic, unsegmented, threadlike worm; also called an eelworm.

Parasite. An animal or plant that lives in or on and draws nourishment from another

organism (the host) without contributing anything toward the host organism's survival.

Infection. Entry or growth of a disease-causing organism into a host.

Interveinal chlorosis. A condition in which leaf veins remain green while the tissue between veins turns yellow.

---

the best way to prevent many frustrating, costly, and sometimes fatal plant disorders.

Figuring Out What's Wrong

If a plant in your garden has, say, leaves that are turning yellow or black spots on its fruit, how can you tell what's causing the problem—an insect, a disease, a nutrient imbalance, or something else?

Start by ruling out insect damage and cultural problems. Inspect the plant carefully, using a magnifying lens. If it's an insect problem, you can usually find some evidence of the insects on the plants. Review the symptoms of nutrient deficiencies (page 476), and consider recent unusual weather patterns and nearby sources of pollution. See Diagnosing Plant Problems starting on page 664 for more tips on how to detect the cause of garden problems.

If you can rule out insects and cultural problems, then you'll need to consider diseases or other kinds of disorders. Become familiar with the general types of plant diseases and the common disease problems in your area. Or you can consult books

on plant diseases and garden problem solving, which often are organized by plant and list the diseases that each can get (see Resources on page 673). The chart on page 664 may also help you determine whether the symptoms on your plants are due to insects, disease, a plant disorder, or a nutrient imbalance.

A Who's Who of Plant Pathogens

Microorganisms that can cause diseases include fungi, bacteria, viruses, and pathogenic nematodes.

Fungi: Fungi are primitive plants. They don't have chlorophyll, the pigment that allows green plants to convert sunlight and air into food. Instead, fungi obtain nutrients by inserting special rootlike structures (called haustoria) into host plants or dead organic matter. Many fungi live on and decompose dead organic materials. These beneficial fungi are an important ally in the garden. Parasitic fungi, on the other hand, are a leading cause of plant disease. Some attack only one species of plants, while others attack a wide array of plants.

Fungi produce tiny spores that are spread by wind, water, insects, and gardeners. Spores germinate to form mycelia—the body of the fungus. Mycelia rarely survive winter, but spores easily survive from season to season.

It's often easy to spot signs of fungi; mushrooms are the most common example. Often the structures that produce fungal spores look like dots or discolored areas on leaves, stems, or fruit. These structures are one of the best ways to distinguish fungal diseases from other plant problems.

Bacteria: Most bacteria are beneficial—they help to break down dead organic matter. Some, however, cause plant diseases. Bacteria usually reproduce asexually—the cells simply split in half. Bacteria spread via wind, water, insects, garden tools, and gardeners' hands. Bacterial diseases are usually more difficult to control than fungal diseases, and they spread more quickly than other types of diseases. You need a microscope to see actual bacterial cells, but some of the disease symptoms they cause, such as dark streaks on leaves or stems and bacterial slime, are easy to see with the naked eye. (The slime often smells bad, too.)

Nematodes: Nematodes swim freely in the film of moisture surrounding soil particles and plant roots. A few types are barely visible to the naked eye. Many nematodes do not cause plant diseases and are important members of the soil community. In fact, beneficial nematodes often prey on the nematodes that attack plants.

Parasitic nematodes can be very destructive. They lay eggs that hatch into tiny larvae. Larvae molt several times before maturing to adults. Nematodes puncture plant cell walls, inject saliva, and suck out the cell's contents. Some species move from plant to plant to feed; others attach themselves permanently to one root. They can travel short distances on their own but are spread through the garden by water and on tools or gardeners' hands.

Viruses: Viruses are so small, they're difficult to see even with a microscope. Viruses are not complete cells and must be inside living cells of a host in order to reproduce. The symptoms they cause vary widely from distorted growth to mottling of leaves to stunting. Viruses are transmitted by vegetative propagation, in seeds and pollen, and on tools and gardeners' hands. Viruses are also transmitted by aphids and other insects, mites, nematodes, and parasitic plants.

Natural Defenses against Disease

There may be hundreds of species of disease organisms in your garden soil or living in weeds in and around your yard. However, even though disease-causing organisms are nearly always present, that doesn't mean that your garden crops and ornamentals will develop a disease. Untold millions of potential diseases never amount to anything, because conditions aren't favorable for their development.

Plants have intriguing defenses that help protect them from infection. Leaves have a waxy coating called the cuticle that prevents them from staying wet, making it hard for disease-causing organisms to survive. The leaf cuticle may also prevent spore germination and slow the penetration of disease-causing organisms. Leaf hairs trap spores and hold them away from the surface of the leaf. Some leaf hairs actually secrete chemicals that prevent spores from germinating or sticky substances that help catch pathogens and/or the insects that transmit them. Leaves exude substances that promote the growth of beneficial microorganisms that compete for space with, or are antagonistic to, pathogens.

Plants can spring to their own defense when pathogens try to invade. For example, some plants can form a corky layer of tissue around the site of attack. Other plants may seal off the diseased part, which then dies along with the disease organisms.

Plants also have natural chemical defenses that repel or damage the pathogens themselves. Some of these defenses are present all the time and some are "turned on" when disease-causing organisms are present.

The discovery of these natural defense mechanisms (and more new discoveries are still being made) has been of great benefit to organic farmers and gardeners, because plant breeders can select for these mechanisms when they're working to develop disease-resistant cultivars. It also appears that products containing harpin and other plant growth promoters help to prevent disease by triggering plants to turn on their natural chemical defenses.

Preventing Diseases

Most of the time, simple preventive controls will stop disease problems from developing or limit their severity. In a few instances, you may have to resort to spraying substances such as neem or sulfur to prevent a disease from ruining a plant or crop. These substances are considered organic because they derive from natural sources—however, they are not innocuous. For example, sulfur can burn plant leaves, and spraying sulfur too often can cause soil imbalances that harm beneficial soil organisms.

Smart Gardening Helps

The smartest way to help prevent disease problems in your garden is simply to take good care of your plants. It also pays to take simple steps that avoid the risk of infection. Some of the most important smart gardening practices to prevent diseases are listed here; see page 470 for more.

- Build up soil organic matter content, and correct nutrient imbalances.

- In the vegetable garden, interplant crops and use crop rotation if you can (see the Crop Rotation entry).

- Some disease problems can be avoided by planting earlier or later than usual.

- Prune your plants at the proper time of year and thin out growth as needed throughout the growing season to promote good air circulation around plants.

- Put up a barrier against insects such as leafhoppers and cucumber beetles that spread disease by covering crops with row covers from seeding until harvest when possible.

Clean Gardening Helps

Fungi, bacteria, and other pathogens have evolved many ways of surviving cold temperatures or other unfavorable conditions. They may spend winter inside the bodies of insects or in the soil—even in bits of soil clinging to tools stored in a garden shed. Some can survive winter in infected plant debris, seeds, or plant tissue. A few widespread diseases can produce "resting spores" that stay dormant in the soil for years until conditions are right or a host plant is planted in the area.

Many good gardening practices help prevent disease because they prevent disease organisms from overwintering and spreading from place to place during the gardening season. You probably already take some of these steps routinely in your garden.

- Choose disease-resistant or tolerant cultivars, and make sure all transplants and seeds you plant are free of disease.

🌿 Stay out of your garden when the leaves are wet because disease organisms spread easily in wet conditions.

🌿 Avoid damaging plants, as every wound is an opening for disease to enter.

🌿 Clean and disinfect tools, hands, and feet regularly, whether you are working with diseased material or not.

🌿 Do an annual fall garden cleanup.

🌿 Dispose of diseased material throughout the season. Pull up plants or prune off infected portions, and get rid of them by burning, putting them in sealed containers for disposal with household trash, burying them deeply, or putting them in the center of a hot compost pile.

Growth Promoters Help

Going beyond the basics of maintaining healthy plants and a clean garden, you can apply homemade and commercially produced sprays that will make your plants even more resistant to disease problems. These products are different from fungicides, which work by killing fungal spores via toxic or caustic chemicals. Instead, these growth-promoting sprays work by stimulating beneficial microorganisms, and seemingly by triggering plants to turn on their own natural defense systems.

Homemade sprays: Compost tea is one of the homemade sprays that help boost plant defenses. Applying sprays of seaweed extract or comfrey tea may have similar beneficial effects. See the Compost entry for instructions for making compost tea. Make comfrey tea using a similar method, but dilute comfrey tea half-and-half with water before applying. A homemade garlic spray may work by killing spores on plant surfaces. Mix 5 to 10 cloves with 1 pint of water in a blender, strain, and spray on plants.

Harpin: Harpin is a protein that reportedly stimulates plant defense systems, and some commercial products are available with harpin as the active ingredient. It has no reported adverse side effects on plants or the environment, but it has not been listed for use by certified organic growers.

Fighting Disease

For organic gardeners, the two primary ways to fight disease are to take steps to kill spores in the soil or on plant surfaces—before the spores infect roots or leaves. Soil solarization kills many types of disease spores, along with some pests and weed seeds. Applying biocontrol agents to soil or plants can kill or outcompete pathogens. And as a last resort, sulfur and copper sprays will kill spores and in some cases even prevent a disease organism from spreading within a plant.

The more you learn about the common disease problems in your area, the less often you'll need to resort to using dusts and sprays. Keep records of the disease problems that occur in your garden, or ask fellow gardeners what diseases to expect in your area and when to expect them. This way, you can limit spraying or dusting to those seasons and weather conditions when your plants are most vulnerable to becoming infected.

It's also important to make sure you know what disease you're trying to control by applying a spray or dust. If you run into a problem that you can't identify, submit a fresh plant sample to a diagnostic laboratory or your local extension office for identification.

Always take appropriate safety precautions when applying sprays and dusts; see the Pests entry for guidelines. The following descriptions of disease-control methods and products are arranged from least to most toxic.

Soil Solarization

If an area of your vegetable garden has been troubled by disease, or if you plan to start a new planting of any kind and are concerned about soilborne diseases, consider solarizing the soil before you plant. You'll need to plan ahead, because it's important to solarize soil during the hottest period of the year if you live in the North.

Solarizing is a simple procedure: You tightly cover the soil with clear plastic for 1 to 2 months. This can generate high enough temperatures in the top 6 to 12 inches of soil to kill many disease organisms, nematodes, pest insects, and weed seeds. The beneficial effects seem to last for several seasons. The illustration at right shows how to prepare a bed for solarizing. For even better results, support a second layer of plastic on wire hoops over the covered bed to provide added insulation.

Midsummer is the best time to solarize soil, especially in the North. Cultivate and remove crop residues from the soil, rake it smooth, and water if it is dry. Dig a trench several inches deep around the bed, and spread thin clear plastic film (1 to 4 mils) over the bed. Press the plastic into close contact with the soil, and seal the edges by filling the trench with soil. Leave in place for 1 to 2 months, then remove the plastic.

Bear in mind that solarization will wipe out many beneficial microorganisms along with the pathogens, and it will drive out soil-dwelling beneficials such as earthworms and ground beetles. After solarization, amend the bed with compost to replenish the beneficial organisms that also contribute to soil and plant health.

Biological Controls

One of the most exciting areas of plant disease research focuses on using naturally occurring bac-

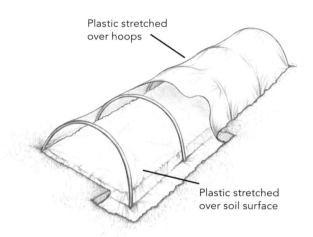

Plastic stretched over hoops

Plastic stretched over soil surface

Solarization. Covering a bed of moist soil that's a minimum of 6 feet by 9 feet with clear plastic during sunny, hot weather helps to kill disease spores. A second layer of plastic supported by wire hoops increases effectiveness.

teria and fungi to fight against plant pathogens. The bacterium *Bacillus subtilis* kills or outcompetes the fungus that causes powdery mildew as well as some other plant pathogens. The fungus *Trichoderma harzianum* (sold as RootShield) kills the pathogen *Rhizoctonia* (one of the many fungi that cause damping-off). *Trichoderma* locates *Rhizoctonia* by a chemical the pathogen releases, then it attacks the damaging fungi and destroys it. In a study testing biological fungicides on vinca plants, researchers at Clemson University found that greenhouse plants treated with SoilGard (*Trichoderma virens*, formerly *Gliocladium virens*) had excellent shoot and root growth and were the equal of those treated with chemical fungicides.

Among the most beneficial root-inhabiting organisms, antibiotic-producing mycorrhizal fungi (sold as BioVam) cover plant roots to protect against pathogens, forming a "fungal mat," which also increases nutrient-uptake ability.

Barriers

A thorough spray of vegetable or light horticultural oil coats plant surfaces, acting as a barrier to infection. Oils seem to help prevent fungal rusts and mildews. For application rates, see page 452.

Garlic appears to be a fungicide as well as an insecticide. Horsetail (*Equisetum arvense*) infusion sprayed on plants may help prevent fungal diseases. For more information on making homemade sprays, see "Home-Brewed Pest Controls" on page 451.

Bicarbonate Sprays

Commercial products containing potassium bicarbonate (such as GreenCure and other products) and homemade baking soda (sodium bicarbonate) sprays prevent fungal spores from establishing themselves on plants and may even prevent established fungi from continuing to develop. Dissolve 1 teaspoon of baking soda and 1 drop of liquid soap in 2 quarts of water, mix well, and spray on plants. A higher concentration isn't better: If these sprays are too concentrated, they may burn plant foliage.

Neem

An oil extracted from the seeds of the neem tree is an ingredient in many products formulated to kill a wide variety of pest insects. Neem oil also is effective at killing some types of fungal disease spores. For more information on neem, turn to page 453.

Sulfur

Direct contact with sulfur prevents the development of disease organisms. However, it also damages important soil microorganisms and beneficial insects and is moderately toxic to mammals, including humans. Apply sulfur sparingly, and always take appropriate safety precautions.

Both a plain spray mix of elemental sulfur and mixtures of sulfur and other substances are effective preventive fungicides. Powdered sulfur is almost insoluble in water. Wettable sulfur has been finely ground with a wetting agent and is easier to use. Liquid sulfur is the easiest to dissolve. Sulfur also can be applied as a dust or as a fumigant.

Adding lime to sulfur increases its effectiveness as a fungicide. Lime allows the sulfur to penetrate leaves and kill recently germinated disease spores. However, lime sulfur sprays are more likely to damage plant tissue than are plain sulfur sprays. Certified organic growers must follow strict guidelines when using sulfur for disease control.

At temperatures above 85°F, sulfur can injure plant tissues. Combining sulfur and oil also causes damage to growing plants. A combination of oil and lime sulfur can be applied to dormant trees; see the Pests entry for details on oils.

Copper

Copper is a powerful, nonspecific fungicide that kills disease organisms. It damages beneficial soil microorganisms and beneficial insects and is more toxic than sulfur to plants. Repeated applications of any copper product will stunt plants. Copper sulfate is classified as very toxic to humans. Organic gardeners often choose to avoid copper fungicides when possible because of their negative effects on nonpest species.

Copper is available as a powder or liquid. Fixed-copper fungicides are available as dusts or sprayable solutions.

Common Plant Diseases and Disorders

The common names of plant diseases often reflect the type of symptom they cause. If you can identify

Stress-Free Plants Don't Get Sick

Plants are more prone to disease problems when conditions are not optimum for the plant, such as when they're not getting enough water or nutrients. Be on the lookout for factors such as these that may leave your plants open to disease.

Moisture stress: Plants need a steady supply of moisture in the soil for proper growth. Too little and plants wilt. Too much and the roots become stunted from lack of oxygen. Either way, the plants are less able to resist disease-causing organisms.

Nutrient imbalance: It's easy to understand that a nutrient deficiency can lead to disease, but too much fertilizer can also increase disease problems. For example, too much nitrogen can stimulate young succulent growth that is susceptible to powdery mildew, rusts, and fire blight. Such growth is also susceptible to cold injury, which in turn can lead to other diseases. Nutrient imbalances also cause symptoms that can be mistaken for disease symptoms (see "Common Nutrient Deficiency Symptoms in Plants" on page 476).

Lack of beneficial microorganisms: In a healthy garden environment, the multitude of good microorganisms in the soil and on plant surfaces tends to keep disease organisms in check. The balance, however, can be upset by overtilling, failing to add organic matter, or the improper use of pest- and disease-killing products (even organic ones). When the balance is upset, the disease-causing organisms often bounce back faster than the beneficial organisms that normally keep them in control.

Weather: The climate, weather conditions, and exposure also have major effects on plant growth. Cold injury, sunscald, hail, and wind can injure plant tissues, leaving openings for infection. Too much shade can result in weak growth. High humidity and lack of air movement encourage many plant diseases.

Mechanical damage: Lawn mower damage to bark and other types of injuries weaken plants and, more important, provide openings in a plant's protective layers. Many diseases gain access to plants through wounds.

Chemical damage: Air pollutants, road salt, and herbicide drift are added insults that can weaken plants and leave them open to disease.

---

the symptoms as a blight or wilt, for example, you may be able to successfully take steps to limit the disease, even if you don't know the specific pathogen causing the infection. The most common garden plant diseases and disorders are described below.

Remember: If you're considering applying a spray or dust, take time to identify the specific disease problem first so that you apply the appropriate product at the correct time to be effective.

Blights

When plants suffer from blight, leaves or branches suddenly wither, stop growing, and die. Later, plant parts may rot.

Fire blight: This bacterial disease affects apples, pears, fruit trees, roses, and small fruits. Infected shoots wilt and look blackened. For further description and controls, see the Pear entry.

Alternaria blight (early blight): This fungal blight infects ornamental plants, vegetables, fruit trees, and shade trees worldwide. On tomatoes, potatoes, and peppers, it is called early blight. On leaves, brown to black spots form and enlarge, developing concentric rings. Heavily blighted leaves dry up and die as spots grow together. Lower leaves usually show symptoms first. Targetlike, sunken spots will develop on tomato branches and stems. Fruits and potato tubers also develop dark, sunken spots. Alternaria spores are carried by air currents and are common in dust and air everywhere. They are a common cause of hay fever allergies. Alternaria fungi overwinter on infected plant parts and debris, or in or on seeds. Control this disease by planting resistant cultivars and growing your own transplants from disease-free seed. Apply *Trichoderma harzianum* to the soil just before planting. Promote good air circulation. For early blight, apply potassium bicarbonate or sodium bicarbonate (baking soda) sprays starting 2 weeks before the time of year when symptoms would normally first appear. Dispose of infected plants and, when possible, use a 3-year rotation.

Phytophthora blight (late blight): Lilacs, rhododendrons, azaleas, and holly infected by phytophthora fungi suffer dieback of shoots and develop stem cankers. Prune to remove infected branches and to increase air movement.

On peppers, potatoes, and tomatoes, phytophthora infection is known as late blight. The first symptom is water-soaked spots on the lower leaves. The spots enlarge and are mirrored on the undersurface of the leaf with a white downy growth. Dark-colored blotches penetrate the flesh of tubers.

These spots may dry and appear as sunken lesions. During a wet season, plants will rot and die. The pathogen overwinters on infected tubers and in plant debris. Avoid problems by planting only in well-drained soil, and use resistant varieties if possible. For late blight, keep foliage dry as much as possible, and check frequently for symptoms whenever the weather is wet. Preventive sprays of compost tea or *Bacillus subtilis* may help prevent the disease. Immediately remove and destroy plants infected with late blight; prune off cankered shoots of shrubs. After harvest, remove and destroy all plant debris that may be infected.

Bacterial blight: This bacterial disease is particularly severe on legumes in eastern and southern North America. Foliage and pods display water-soaked spots that dry and drop out. On stems, lesions are long and dark colored. Some spots may ooze a bacterial slime. To control, plant resistant cultivars, remove infected plants, and dispose of plant debris. Use a 3-year rotation and don't touch plants while they are wet, as you may spread the disease.

Cankers

Cankers usually form on woody stems and may be cracks, sunken areas, or raised areas of dead or abnormal tissue. Sometimes cankers ooze conspicuously. Cankers can girdle shoots or trunks, causing everything above the canker to wilt and die. Blights and diebacks due to cankers look quite similar. Cold-injury symptoms may look like, or lead to the development of, cankers and diebacks.

Cytospora canker: This fungal disease attacks poplars, spruces, and stone fruits, such as peaches and cherries. The cankers are circular, discolored areas on the bark. To control, plant resistant trees and cut out branches or trees with cankers.

Nectria canker: This fungus attacks most hardwoods and some vines and shrubs. It is most damaging on maples. Small sunken areas appear on the bark near wounds, and small pink spore-producing structures are formed. It kills twigs and branches and may girdle young trees. Control by limiting pruning cuts and removing diseased branches.

Rots

Rots are diseases that decay roots, stems, wood, flowers, and fruit. Some diseases cause leaves to rot, but those symptoms tend to be described as leaf spots and blights. Rots can be soft and squishy or hard and dry. They are caused by various bacteria and fungi. Many are very active in stored fruits, roots, bulbs, or tubers.

Fruit rots: Grapes infected with black rot turn brown, then harden into small, black, mummified berries. Brown rot of stone fruits causes whole fruit to turn brown and soft. Control fruit rots by planting resistant cultivars, removing and destroying infected fruit, and pruning to increase air movement. Applying compost tea or *Bacillus subtilis* may help prevent the disease from developing. Sulfur sprays throughout the season can be effective, too, as a last resort.

Root and stem rots: Control these troublesome rots by providing good drainage and good air circulation. Try drenching the soil with beneficial fungi or bacteria. Start cuttings in sterilized mix, and plant only healthy plants. Dispose of all infected plant material. Winter injury may invite problems on woody plants.

Mushroom and wood rots: These rots can damage or kill trees. Some of them form obvious mushrooms or other fungal growths. Cutting out infected areas can provide control. Keep soil well drained, and plant resistant species and cultivars where problems are severe.

Rusts

Rusts are a specific type of fungal disease. Many of them require two different plant species as hosts to complete their life cycle. Typical rust symptoms include a powdery tan to rust-colored coating. Applying neem oil can help prevent rust by killing spores on the leaves.

Asparagus rust: This disease appears as a browning or reddening of the small twigs and needles, and a release of rusty, powdery spores. It overwinters on stalks and infects new shoots as they emerge the following spring. Rust is also carried to other plants by wind. To control, space plants to allow air circulation. Plant resistant cultivars. Remove infected plants and burn them in fall.

Other rusts: Wheat rust, cedar-apple rust, and white pine blister rust require alternate hosts. Wheat rust needs barberry to survive, cedar-apple rust needs both juniper and an apple relative, and white pine blister rust needs a susceptible member of the currant family. Removing the alternate hosts in the area can control outbreaks.

Wilts

Plants wilt when they don't get enough water. When fungi or bacteria attack or clog a plant's water-conducting system, they can cause permanent wilting, often followed by the death of all or part of the plant. Wilt symptoms may resemble those of blights.

Stewart's wilt: This bacterial disease is widespread on sweet corn in eastern North America. It overwinters in flea beetles and infects corn when they begin feeding on its leaves. Infected leaves wilt and may have long streaks with wavy margins. Bacterial slime will ooze out if the stalks or leaves are cut. Plants eventually die or are sufficiently stunted that no ears are produced. To control, plant resistant cultivars and eliminate flea beetles. Destroy infected plants.

Fusarium and verticillium wilt: These fungal wilts attack a wide range of flowers, vegetables, fruits, and ornamentals. Plants wilt and may turn yellow. To control, plant resistant cultivars. Rotate crops, or do not replant in areas where problems have occurred. If wilt only affects a branch, it may help to cut it out well below the wilt symptoms. Destroy infected branches or plants.

Other Diseases

Anthracnose: Anthracnose, or bird's-eye spot, is a fungal disease. It causes small dead spots that often have a raised border and a sunken center, and that may have concentric rings of pink and brown.

Bean anthracnose infects beans and other legumes. The symptoms are most obvious on the pods as circular, black, sunken spots that may ooze pink slime and develop red borders as they age. To control, buy disease-free seed, rotate crops, turn under or hot-compost infected plants, and avoid touching plants when they are wet so you won't spread the disease.

Clubroot: Clubroot affects vegetables and flowers in the cabbage family. Plants infected by the fungus wilt during the heat of the day, and older leaves yellow and drop. Roots are distorted and swollen. Avoid clubroot by choosing resistant cultivars and raising your own seedlings. The fungus has spores that can persist in soil for many years. If you've had past clubroot problems, adjust

the soil pH to at least 6.8 before planting susceptible crops.

Damping-off: Damping-off is caused by a variety of soilborne fungi. Seeds rot before they germinate, or seedlings rot at the soil line and fall over. It can be a problem with indoor seedlings and also in garden beds. Prevent damping-off by keeping soil moist, but not waterlogged. Provide good air movement in seed-starting areas. Wait until soil is warm enough for the specific plant before seeding. Sterile seed-starting mix or a mix that includes compost can help prevent problems, too. If you've had past problems with this disease, add compost to your soil, and use a product containing *Trichoderma harzianum* to drench the soil before planting.

Downy mildew: Downy mildews are fungal diseases that attack many fruits, vegetables, flowers, and grasses. The primary symptom is a white to purple, downy growth, usually on the undersides of leaves and along stems, which turns black with age. Upper leaf surfaces have a pale color. Lima bean pods may be covered completely, while leaves are distorted. The disease overwinters on infected plant parts and remains viable in the soil for several years. It is spread by wind, by rain, and in seeds. To control it, buy disease-free seeds and plants, follow a 3-year rotation, and remove and dispose of infected plants. Preventive sprays of potassium or sodium bicarbonate may be effective.

Galls: Galls are swollen masses of abnormal tissue. They can be caused by fungi and bacteria as well as by certain insects. If you cut open a gall and there is no sign of an insect, suspect disease.

Crown gall is a serious bacterial disease that infects and kills grapes, roses, fruit trees, brambles, shade trees, flowers, and vegetables. Galls are rounded with rough surfaces and are made up of corky tissue. They often occur on the stem near the soil line or graft union but can also form on roots or branches. To control it, buy healthy plants, and reject any suspicious ones. Don't replant in an area where you have had crown gall. Avoid wounding stems, and disinfect tools between plants when pruning. Remove and destroy infected plants, or cut out galls.

Leaf blisters and curls: Leaf blister and leaf curl are fungal diseases that cause distorted, curled leaves on many trees. Oak leaf blister can defoliate and even kill oak trees. Blisters are yellow bumps on the upper surface of the leaves, with gray depressions on the lower surface. Peach leaf curl attacks peaches and almonds. New leaves are pale or reddish and the midrib doesn't grow along with the leaves, so the leaves become puckered and curled as they expand. Fruit is damaged, and bad cases can kill the tree. Both diseases are controlled with a single dormant oil spray just before buds begin to swell.

Leaf spots: A vast number of fungi can cause spots on the leaves of plants. Most of them are of little consequence. A typical spot has a definite edge and often has a darker border. When lots of spots are present, they can grow together and become a blight or a blotch.

Blackspot is a common disease on roses. The spots appear on the leaves and are up to ½ inch across with yellow margins. Severe cases cause leaves to drop. To control blackspot, plant resistant cultivars, and destroy all dropped leaves and prunings. Mulch to prevent dirt and spores from being splashed up onto plants. Bicarbonate sprays can be very helpful in preventing leaf spot diseases.

Molds: Molds are characterized by a powdery or woolly appearance on the surface of the infected part.

Gray mold, or botrytis, is a common problem on many fruits and flowers. It thrives in moist con-

ditions and is often seen on dropped flower petals or overripe fruit. It appears as a thick, gray mold or as water-soaked, blighted regions of petals, leaves, or stems. In most cases, it first infects dead or dying tissue, so removing faded flowers and blighted buds or shoots will control the problem. Peonies, tulips, and lilies can be severely damaged in wet seasons. Destroy infected material, and space, prune, and support plants to encourage good air movement.

Nematodes: Nematodes themselves are described earlier in this entry. Symptoms of nematode invasion include reduced growth, wilting, and lack of vigor.

Some nematodes cause excessive branching of roots, rotted roots, and enlarged lumps on roots. Other nematodes attack leaves, causing triangular wedges of dead tissue.

Root knot nematodes attack a variety of plant root systems, including most vegetable and ornamental crops. Carrot plants will be stunted, with yellowed leaves, and roots may be distorted. Roots of other plants will have swollen areas. Remember that legumes are supposed to have swellings on their roots that are caused by nitrogen-fixing bacteria.

Prevent nematodes from invading your plants by maintaining your soil organic matter. Plant resistant varieties when possible. Take care not to spread soil from nematode-infested areas to other parts of your garden or yard. Reduce nematode populations by solarizing soil. Use a marigold (*Tagetes patula* or *T. erecta*) cover crop to reduce nematodes. Rotate susceptible crops. Adding products containing chitin to the soil can help reduce problems.

Hot-water dips can eradicate nematodes from within roots, bulbs, and the soil on them.

Powdery mildew: Mildews are one of the

most widespread and easily recognized fungi. They are common on phlox, lilac, melons, cucumbers, and many other plants. Mildew forms a white to grayish powdery growth, usually on the upper surfaces of leaves. Small black dots appear and produce spores that are blown by wind to infect new plants. Leaves will become brown and shrivel when mildew is extensive. Fruits ripen prematurely and have poor texture and flavor. To control mildews, prune or stake plants to improve air circulation and dispose of infected plants before spores form. Apply bicarbonate sprays to prevent the spread of infection.

Scabs: Scabs are fungal diseases that cause fruits, leaves, and tubers to develop areas of hardened, overgrown, and sometimes cracked tissue. Fruit scab can be a major problem on apples and peaches. Control by disposing of fallen leaves and pruning to increase air movement. If you've had past serious problems with scab, ask your local extension office about the best spray schedule for sulfur to control the disease.

Smuts: Smuts are fungal diseases. They are most commonly seen on grasses, grains, and corn. Enlarged galls are soft and spongy when young but change to a dark, powdery mass as they age.

Corn smut can form on kernels, tassels, stalks, and leaves. Smut galls ripen and rupture, releasing spores that travel through the air to infect new plants and overwinter in the soil, awaiting future crops. To control corn smut, select resistant cultivars. Remove and burn galls before they break open, and follow a 4-year rotation.

Viruses: Infected plants often grow slowly and yield poorly. Leaves may cup or twist, and develop mottling, streaking, or ring-shaped spots. Identification is often the elimination of all other possible causes. Professional growers use heat treatments and tissue culture to control viral disease. Purchase certified plants to avoid problems. Control insects that spread viruses. Remove and burn all plants with viral disease to prevent the disease from spreading.

Common Cultural Disorders

Cold injury: Freezing injury can cause death or dieback. Symptoms of cold stress are stunting, yellowing, bud or leaf drop, and stem cracking. Fruit may form a layer of corky tissue or be russeted if exposed to cold when young.

Heat injury: Temperatures that are too high cause sunscald of fruits, leaves, or trunks on the sunny side of the plant. Discoloration, blistering, or a water-soaked and sunken appearance are other symptoms of heat stress.

Moisture imbalance: Plants need a relatively constant supply of water. If they don't have enough, they will wilt. Long periods of wilting, or repeated wilting, can cause stunting, pale color, and reduced flowering and fruit production. Plant roots also need oxygen. Too much water in the soil damages roots and will cause symptoms like frequent wilting, pale color, root decay, leaf dropping, and lack of vigor. Irregular moisture contributes to fruit cracking and problems such as blossom-end rot.

Wind damage: High winds also take their toll on plant appearance. Silvery discoloration and tattered leaves are symptoms of wind damage.

Salt damage: Ocean spray and road salt, as well as animal urine, can injure plants. Salts can accumulate on leaves, stems, and buds or build to toxic levels around the roots. Over time, salt burn weakens the entire plant and causes droughtlike symptoms.

Ozone damage: Ozone is a common air pollutant that can cause a wide range of symptoms in susceptible plants, including withered leaves on citrus and grapes and tipburn on conifers. If you

Common Nutrient Deficiency Symptoms in Plants

The plant nutrition problems gardeners most often face are the result of nutrient deficiencies. Some deficiency symptoms are easy to identify, but others can be difficult to distinguish from disease or general stress symptoms. Unfortunately, plants can't tell us what nutrients they may be lacking, and visual diagnosis of deficiencies is an imprecise art. One helpful tip is to remember that some nutrient deficiencies are likely to appear on new growth first, while others appear first on older plant parts. This table groups deficiency symptoms according to where symptoms are likely to show up first.

NUTRIENT	DEFICIENCY SYMPTOMS
SYMPTOMS APPEAR FIRST ON OLDER OR LOWER LEAVES	
Nitrogen	Lower leaves yellow, overall plant light green, growth stunted
Phosphorus	Foliage red, purple, or very dark green; growth stunted
Potassium	Tips and edges of leaves yellow, then brown; stems weak
Magnesium	Interveinal chlorosis, growth stunted
Zinc	Interveinal chlorosis, leaves thickened, growth stunted
SYMPTOMS APPEAR FIRST ON YOUNGER OR UPPER LEAVES	
Calcium	Buds and young leaves die back at tips
Iron	Interveinal chlorosis, growth stunted
Sulfur	Young leaves light green overall, growth stunted
Boron	Young leaves pale green at base and twisted, buds die
Copper	Young leaves pale and wilted with brown tips
Manganese	Interveinal chlorosis on young leaves with brown spots scattered through leaf
Molybdenum	Interveinal chlorosis, growth stunted

confirm that ozone is a common pollutant where you live, your only recourse is to avoid planting sensitive species.

PLANTING

One of the best ways to ensure that plants will thrive is to do a good job planting them. Preparing planting areas thoroughly is time well spent, because it ensures that roots can quickly extend through the soil.

Matching Plant with Site

Before you dig that planting hole or plant those seeds, try to make a good match between the plant and its environment. Learning to know your soil and growing conditions—and using that knowledge to pick the right plants—is just as important as knowing the best planting techniques. So before you plant:

- Take a close look at your soil. Is it red clay or deep loam? Waterlogged or sandy or dry? Is it acid or alkaline?

- Check the amount of sunlight your site gets. Is it full sun all day or just afternoon sun? Is the shade dappled through the small, shifting leaves of a birch, or deep and heavy, as beneath an evergreen? A tomato plant must have at least 6 hours of direct sunlight daily for good fruit set, but the same amount of sun fades and burns tender fern fronds.

- Know your hardiness zone. Your local nurseries and garden centers generally stock only plants that are hardy in your area, but big box stores are often less careful in their selections and may sell plants that are not winter hardy in your area. If you shop at these types of outlets or if you do any Internet shopping or mail-order buying, knowing your zone will save you money and disappointment. If you're not familiar with the concept of hardiness zone, see the Weather and Weather Lore entry for an explanation.

- Be aware of seasonal conditions. Is the spot you picked sheltered by a wall or windbreak, or is it exposed to chilling winter wind? Is it low lying and prone to late-spring frost?

- Learn the growth rate and size of your plants. Choose a site where they won't cause problems or overgrow your garden. This is especially important for permanent plants such as trees and shrubs.

Getting Soil in Shape

If you set plants into poorly drained soil, the roots are likely to rot and die. If you plant seeds into poorly drained soil, they may never even germinate. Before you plant a pumpkin seed or a pine tree, be sure that your soil drains well. If drainage is poor, see page 555 for ways to improve it. Or consider growing plants in raised beds. The Raised Bed Gardening entry explains how to make and plant raised beds. For very wet areas, your best bet may be to grow plants that can tolerate wet conditions. See the Water Gardens entry for ideas.

If you till the soil for a vegetable garden or dig a hole for a tree when the soil is too wet, you'll destroy the soil's structure. Your soil will compact, causing water to run off or sit in puddles rather than penetrate. Without air, root growth suffers. If your soil is too wet, let it dry before planting. Pick up a handful of soil and squeeze it. If it crumbles, it's perfect for planting. But if it forms a muddy

Planting by the Moon

Since our ancestors first poked a seed into the ground, astrology has played a role in gardening and farming. Today it's easy to scoff at people who plant by moon signs and phases, but in truth, we don't know whether the idea is valid or not. The moon's position in the sky does appear to influence plant and animal behavior. People who plant and garden by zodiac signs claim they mark the cyclical movement of the planets and are, therefore, good indicators of natural rhythms in the universe.

Even those who don't believe that planting by signs of the zodiac makes any difference can understand why the sun, moon, and stars were so important to ancient peoples. They were constants in our ancestors' daily lives. Men and women used the pattern made by the stars' regular cycles in the heavens as a calendar. Then they saw that crops fared better when planted at certain times than at others. The moon was believed to be the mistress of growth. During a certain period of time (29½ days on average), the moon passed through 12 constellations. This was the zodiac, or circle of animals, also thought to influence plants and planting.

As centuries passed, ancient civilizations learned that some of the celestial objects they had called stars were actually planets. The planets also were given characteristics, and all living things were placed under both the sign of a planet and a zodiac sign. These beliefs gave rise to elaborate systems of gardening, where every task was linked to a certain planet and constellation, ideally when the moon was in a complementary phase.

Enough first-rate farmers and gardeners follow the signs to make us take notice. Maybe they would do just as well if they didn't garden by the signs. We don't know. We do know that planting by the moon signs and moon phases does no harm. Why not try an experiment? Plant half your garden by the signs; the other half as you normally would. See for yourself which plot does best. Be fair and let common sense be the overriding factor. Even the most devout "sign planters" take weather and temperature into account before undertaking a gardening project.

For more information about planting by the moon, see Resources on page 673.

ball, the soil is too wet for planting.

Most plants pay less attention to pH than gardeners do. If your soil is fertile and well drained and neither extremely acid nor extremely alkaline, most plants will do just fine. But a few popular garden plants are more demanding. Acid-loving azaleas and blueberries, for instance, will do poorly in soil that's on the alkaline side. If you don't know the soil pH in an area you plan to plant, it's a good idea to test it.

Enrich flower and vegetable beds with lots of compost or leaf mold before planting. For more about soil testing and enriching your soil, see the Compost, Cover Crops, Fertilizers, and Soil entries.

Seeds

Plant flowers and vegetables in fertile, well-drained soil that is rich in organic matter. If you're starting a new garden, prepare the soil by working in plenty of organic matter. Double-digging loosens the top 2 feet of the soil, increasing pore space to hold soil and water. For more information on soil preparation techniques, see the Soil entry.

If you must, you can prepare seedbeds with a rotary tiller, but it's preferable to turn the soil gently with a spade or garden fork instead. If you can dig or till in fall, you'll be one step ahead come spring. Rake the soil to a fine tilth, breaking up clods and removing stones and weeds.

Check seed packages to find out when to sow and if the plants have any special germination requirements. Some plants, such as peas, prefer cool weather; others, such as corn, will rot if planted before soil warms up. Many will produce flowers or fruit earlier if given a head start indoors or in a cold frame. If you're interested in starting seeds early, see the Cold Frames and Seed Starting and Seed Saving entries.

Sow seeds thinly to avoid thinning chores later. Sprinkle flower seeds in long single rows for cutting, or broadcast with a flinging motion over a wider area for a free-form display. Plant small vegetable seeds such as lettuce and spinach in rows, or scatter them in a wide band. Plant large flower and vegetable seeds individually, spaced according to package instructions. Vining plants such as melons and cucumbers can be planted in slightly raised mounds called hills, with three to five seeds per hill.

Cover the seeds with fine soil to a depth two to three times the diameter—not the length—of the seed. Firm the soil (use the palm of your hand or the back of your hoe) to establish good contact between seed and soil. Some seeds, such as lettuce, petunias, and begonias, must have light to germinate. Lightly press seeds like these onto the surface of moistened soil. (Always read seed packet directions for special germination requirements.)

Always water gently after you plant seeds, taking care not to wash the seeds away. A fine, misty spray is best; you can buy a hose attachment at garden centers and hardware stores. Keep the soil evenly moist until you see stems and leaves popping above the ground.

Bulbs and Herbaceous Perennials

Plant bulbs and perennials in prepared beds that have been enriched with organic matter and have excellent drainage. Bulbs are especially quick to rot in soggy conditions. If you are making a naturalistic bulb planting in a lawn area, add a handful of bonemeal to each planting hole.

Bulbs

Plant bulbs individually, or dig a hole big enough for several bulbs at a time. Even an entire bed can be dug out, then refilled after the bulbs are placed. Dig the planting hole to the depth recommended for each type of bulb, generally three to four times their widest diameter. When planting bulbs individually, dig holes just slightly wider than the widest diameter of the bulb. Place bulbs pointed end up in their holes and cover with soil. If you can't tell which end is up, plant the bulb sideways, and the roots and stems will grow in the proper direction. Firm the soil, and water. If you're planting in a lawn area for naturalizing, carefully replace plugs of grass atop the holes.

Perennials

Perennials generally are available either bareroot or growing in containers. There's no time to waste with bareroot perennials—if you can't plant right away, remove packaging and store roots in moist peat, or heel in the plants in a trench with one vertical and one slanted side, as shown below. For best results with heeling in, uncover the plants and move them to a permanent position while they're still dormant.

When planting, dig a hole wide enough to allow you to fully spread out the roots and deep enough so the plant is set at the same depth at which it grew previously. Fill soil in around the plant, but avoid burying the crown, from which new shoots will spring. Water thoroughly and mulch. Punch holes in four sides of a cardboard box for ventilation, then upend the box over the newly planted perennial and leave it there for a few days. This blocks light but allows for some ventilation, and encourages the plant to direct its energies into root growth instead of leaves and stems.

Container-grown perennials are gratifyingly easy to add to the garden. Dig a hole just a bit

Heeling in. If you can't plant bareroot perennials, shrubs, or trees right away, keep the roots moist by heeling them in in a spot sheltered from direct sun and wind. Lay the plants against the slanted side of the trench, and cover the roots with soil.

wider than and the same depth as the pot. To prevent wilting, make a mud puddle of your planting hole by filling it with water. Wait till the water drains away, then fill again. When the water drains the second time, you're ready to plant.

To remove the plant from the container, hold one hand firmly across the soil surface, with the plant stems between your fingers. Then flip the pot over. With a bit of wiggling and gentle tugging, the pot should slide free. If not, give it some encouragement by smacking the bottom with your trowel. Untangle pot-bound roots, and set the rootball in the hole. Fill, firm the soil, water once more, and mulch.

Trees and Shrubs

Trees and shrubs represent a sizable investment, and time spent digging and preparing a suitable hole will yield long-term benefits in terms of faster and healthier growth. Keep in mind that although some trees' roots may go deep, the small but all-important feeder roots grow mainly in the top 6 to 8 inches of soil. For this reason, it's important to shape the hole to accommodate the feeder roots, sculpting the sides to be widest near the surface.

Plant trees and shrubs at the same depth at which they were previously planted. Look for the dark mark on the plant stem that indicates how deep the plant was grown at the nursery. Checking depth by hauling the tree or shrub in and out of the hole is a lot of wear and tear on you and the plant. Here's an easier way: Measure from the stem mark to the bottom of the roots or rootball to find out how deep the hole should be. As you dig, check depth now and then by laying a board cross the hole and measuring from the board's center to the bottom of the hole.

To encourage feeder roots to spread out, pre-

Planting Pointers

Take the time for small details when you plant any new tree or shrub. Preparing the rootball, settling the plant properly, mulching, and pruning dead and diseased branches all will contribute to your new plant's health, beauty, and longevity.

- Dig a planting hole at least twice as wide as the rootball's diameter.

- Cut or remove ropes around the rootball or top of wire basket.

- Peel burlap back from the top of the rootball.

- Sculpt planting hole sides to be widest near the surface.

- If using support stakes, drive them into soil outside the rootball.

- Set the tree so that the flare of the rootball is just above soil level.

- Sit the rootball on a small cone of undisturbed soil.

- Spread a 2-inch layer of mulch, keeping mulch away from the crown.

- Prune away diseased, dead, and crossing branches.

- Wrap the tree trunk from soil level to lowest branches if damage by animal pests is a concern.

- Cover guy wires with protective material where they encircle the tree.

- Leave guy wires slightly slack.

pare a planting site that is shallow and wide, as shown on the opposite page. To loosen ground surrounding the hole, plunge a garden fork in as deep as the tines allow, and wiggle it slightly to break up compacted soil. Repeat every 1 to 1½ feet to a distance of 5 feet or more on all sides.

Settling Them In

Your new trees and shrubs may be bareroot, balled-and-burlapped (B&B), or planted in a container. Many deciduous trees and shrubs, such as apples, maples, lilacs, and roses, are sold as dormant, bareroot plants. Evergreens are usually sold B&B because even when they're dormant, they have leaves that draw water from the roots. Container-grown plants have roots established in the container (sometimes a little too well established!); these plants are easy to add to your garden, even in full growth.

When planting any tree or shrub, fill the hole with native soil that has not been amended with fertilizer or compost. Otherwise, the roots tend to stay in the cushy, rich, improved soil rather than spreading out into the surrounding soil. For best results, follow these guidelines when planting.

Bareroot plants: As long as you plant bareroot trees or shrubs while the stock is still dormant, your chances of success are good with these generally low-cost plants.

Leave a small cone of undisturbed soil in the center of the hole. Remove any circling, broken, or diseased roots. Spread out the roots over the cone of soil. After settling the plant in the hole, observe it from all angles to be sure it is positioned straight up and down. There's nothing more frustrating than filling your planting hole and then discovering that the plant is set crookedly. Once you're sure the plant is positioned properly, add soil gradually. Give the tree or shrub an occasional shake as you refill the hole to sift soil among the roots. Water well and mulch.

Balled-and-burlapped plants: It's best to get balled-and-burlapped (B&B) plants in the ground while they're dormant, so the roots can get a good start before they have to supply food and water to burgeoning top growth. But the B&B method gives you more leeway; even actively growing trees and shrubs can be held until the weekend for planting.

Remove binding ropes or twine and all nails. Leave natural burlap in place: It will eventually rot. Slit synthetic wrapping material in several places so roots can penetrate it. Try to keep the rootball intact. If the rootball is in a wire basket, cut off the loops on top to keep them from sticking up through the soil, and snip and remove the top few wires. As with bareroot plants, make sure the plant is set vertically before filling the hole. If the tree is large, have a helper hold it in place as you fill the hole. After every few shovelfuls of dirt, add water to help settle air pockets.

Container-grown plants: Remove any labeling tags to keep the tags or wires from cutting into the stems. Support the plant while you turn it upside down and remove the pot. Even fiber pots of compressed peat or paper are best removed; exposed edges wick away moisture, and the walls slow down root growth.

Snip off dead or sickly roots and use your fingers to comb out any pot-bound roots. Cut through circling roots. Set plant as deep as it grew before, make sure it's straight, then fill the hole.

Finishing Touches

Level the soil around the base of the plant. Don't stomp all the air out of your newly filled hole: Instead of using your feet, tamp the soil with your hands or the back of a hoe to settle it and eliminate air pockets.

Water and mulch: Soak the soil thoroughly after planting. Apply a 2- to 3-inch layer of mulch to retain moisture, keeping it a couple of inches away from the trunk. Make it a habit to water new plants once a week during their first year, especially if rainfall is less than 1 inch per week. By the time you notice wilting or other signs of stress, the roots may already be damaged and it may be too late.

Pruning: You don't need to prune newly planted trees and shrubs, except to remove branches that are broken, diseased, narrow angled, or overlapping. If you cut back all the branches, you may actually slow your tree's or shrub's establishment, because buds produce chemicals that aid root growth. The exception is young fruit trees, which you must prune promptly if you plan to train them for easier harvesting and care. See the Fruit Trees and Pruning and Training entries for more information.

Wrapping the trunk: A tree wrap protects the trunk from sunscald, nibbling rodents, and lawn mower nicks. Wrap the trunk from the base to the lowest branch, and tie in place. Remove wrapping after no more than a year.

Staking: Stake trees only if they're located in a windy area or if they're top-heavy. One or two stakes will hold a small tree, while three stakes may be needed for a large tree. Allow a few inches of slack in the wire or other material that you use to attach the tree to the stake so that the tree can sway a bit in the wind. Remove stakes and attaching materials after 1 year to prevent damage to enlarging stems.

Don't Coddle the Roots

Standard tree-planting instructions used to include a recommendation to enrich the soil in planting holes with organic amendments and fertilizers. But recent studies show this can hinder, not help, new trees and shrubs as they adjust to your native soil.

A hole filled with peat moss and rotted manure encourages roots to grow only in the hole instead of branching out into the surrounding soil. These pockets of overly amended soil stay too wet during rainy periods and too dry during drought. This means tree roots can suffocate from too much moisture or can be more prone to wilting during drought. Also, since the roots don't spread and anchor the plant strongly, it will be more susceptible to windthrow—being toppled during high winds.

PLATYCODON

Balloon flower. Summer-blooming perennials.

Description: *Platycodon grandiflorus*, balloon flower, bears inflated, balloonlike buds that open into 2-inch starry bowls of violet-blue, white, or pink, on 1½- to 3-foot plants with attractive 3-inch oval leaves. Dwarf cultivars are available that form tidy mounds only 9 inches tall. Zones 3–8.

How to grow: Set out small or container-grown plants in spring, or divide by carefully separating the fleshy roots before shoots emerge. Plant in a sunny or lightly shaded spot with average to rich, well-drained soil. Balloon flowers come up late in spring; mark their location so you won't damage them while digging. Stake taller cultivars. Deadhead spent blooms to prolong the bloom season. Plants will self-sow.

Landscape uses: Balloon flowers are beautiful with *Rudbeckia* 'Goldsturm', daylilies (*Hemerocallis* spp.), and other summer-flowering perennials in beds and borders. Dwarf cultivars make attractive container plants.

PLECTRANTHUS

Coleus, flame nettle. Tender perennials grown as foliage annuals.

Description: *Plectranthus scutellarioides* (formerly *Solenostemon scutellarioides*) is the familiar coleus whose foliage brightens semishady spots with its many hues of green, white, pink, red, yellow, and almost black. Choose from 8-inch mounded midgets to bushy 3-foot giants with pointed, scalloped, lacy, or oaklike leaves.

How to grow: Sow seeds as early as February; plant outdoors after frost. Coleus grow best in semishade in average, fairly moist soil. Pinch taller types at 6 inches to encourage branching; remove flower buds as they appear. Cuttings root easily in water.

Landscape uses: Mass one color pattern or many in beds, borders, and pots. Match the colors of the coleus leaves with nearby flowers.

PLUM

Prunus **spp.**
Rosaceae

Plum trees bear greenish, yellow, red, purple, and blue fruit in a wide range of shapes, sizes, and flavors to suit every taste. The Fruit Trees entry covers many important aspects of growing plums; refer to it for more information on planting, pruning, and care.

Selecting trees: Most European plums (*Prunus domestica*) and damson plums (*P. insititia*) are partly self-fruitful. They are more hardy (Zones 4–9) and tend to bloom and ripen later than Japanese cultivars. They have a high sugar content and can be dried to make prunes. 'Castleton' and 'Victoria' are self-fruitful and highly productive.

Most Japanese plums (*P. salicina*) require cross-pollination. In fact, you may need three compatible cultivars for good crop set because some cultivars don't produce much pollen. Early-blooming European cultivars may pollinate Japanese cultivars. Japanese plums are less hardy (Zones 6–10) and tend to have larger fruit than European cultivars. Fruits are quite juicy, with a blend of sweet and tart flavor. 'Beauty' is self-fruitful; 'Crimson' resists black knot and bacterial canker diseases. European/Japanese hybrids, which combine the characters of both types, are available. Choose disease-resistant trees to prevent many common problems.

Many native *Prunus* species are sold as bush plums. They tend to have small fruit but tolerate drought and hot summers well. Hybrids of plum and cherry or apricot can be fun to try.

Plumcots are a cross between plum and apricot; they require a Japanese plum planted nearby for pollination.

Rootstocks: Trees grafted on 'Myrobalan' rootstocks will reach about 20 feet tall. They tend to be hardy and long lived, resistant to canker and nematodes, and tolerant of clay. Good dwarf and semidwarf rootstocks are available and produce trees as small as 8 feet; 'Pumiselect' is a cold- and drought-tolerant dwarfing rootstock.

Planting and care: Space plum trees 20 to 25 feet apart. Plums don't compete well with grass in lawns. Spread a thick layer of organic mulch out to the drip line to conserve moisture.

Pruning: Generally, European plums grow upright and Japanese plums spread. Train European types to a central leader as shown on page 225 and Japanese types to an open center as shown on page 226. European plums bear fruit on long-lived spurs in the tree's interior. Thin suckers and overly thick outer growth to let in sunlight and encourage ripening. Japanese types fruit on older spurs as well as year-old wood. Encourage new growth by pruning off old wood, but leave the still-fruitful inner spurs.

Thinning: Shake limbs to thin or pinch off small, odd-shaped, or overcrowded fruits before the pits harden. Leave 1 to 3 inches between small fruits, 4 to 5 inches between larger ones.

Problems: Plums have many of the same problems as other stone fruits. Expect birds to take their share as well. See the Cherry and Peach entries for common problems. Select resistant trees and prune for good air circulation.

Harvesting: Most plum trees bear in 3 to 4 years from planting. Harvest plums for cooking when they are slightly immature. For fresh eating, let European types grow sweet and soft on the tree. Pick Japanese plums a little early and let ripen indoors. Leave the stems on the fruit and handle as little as possible, and the plums will store better.

POISONOUS PLANTS

Most of us know that some houseplants, such as dieffenbachia, and holiday plant decorations, like mistletoe, are quite toxic. But common backyard plants can also pose a hazard. By learning which plants are poisonous, you can avoid growing them while you have small children, or you can make the garden childproof.

Common plants that are poisonous to touch may be found in wooded or suburban areas. In the eastern United States and Canada, look out for poison ivy (*Toxicodendron radicans*) and its cousin, poison sumac (*T. vernix*). In the western regions of these countries, watch out for poison oak (*T. diversilobum*) and western poison ivy (*T. rydbergii*). In some areas, you may find stinging nettles (*Urtica dioica*) in fields, ditches, or open areas. All these plants cause a burning rash, which, in the case of poison ivy, oak, and sumac, can linger and itch for weeks.

Common vegetables with poisonous leaves are potatoes, tomatoes, and rhubarb.

It's wise to learn which ornamental plants are mildly to fatally poisonous when eaten, too. All parts of autumn crocus (*Colchicum autumnale*), bittersweet (*Celastrus scandens*), bleeding hearts (*Dicentra* spp.), boxwood (*Buxus sempervirens*), daffodils (*Narcissus* spp.), English ivy (*Hedera helix*), flowering tobacco (*Nicotiana alata*), red horse chestnut (*Aesculus ×carnea*), hydrangeas (*Hydrangea* spp.), mountain laurel (*Kalmia latifolia*), rhododendrons and azaleas (*Rhododendron* spp.), and Virginia creeper (*Parthenocissus quinquefolia*) are poisonous.

Leaves of foxglove (*Digitalis purpurea*), larkspurs and delphiniums (*Delphinium* spp.), monkshoods (*Aconitum* spp.), and oleander (*Nerium oleander*) are poisonous. Berries of lily of the valley (*Convallaria majalis*) and hollies (*Ilex* spp.), hyacinth bulbs (*Hyacinthus orientalis*), and lupine seeds (*Lupinus* spp.) are also poisonous.

An excellent resource for identifying poisonous plants is the *Handbook of Poisonous and Injurious Plants* by Lewis S. Nelson, Richard D. Shih, and Michael J. Balick.

POLLINATORS

Pollinators are the creatures that carry out the important act of pollination. Pollination takes place when pollen from a male flower—or a male flower part, i.e., a stamen—is transferred to a female flower or flower part, known as the pistil. This process of sexual reproduction is carried out countless times and in countless ways by every kind of flowering plant around the world.

While wind and water account for a significant percentage of the pollination that takes place, a great many of the plants that we depend upon for food rely upon creatures—typically insects—to carry out the transfer of pollen from male flower to female. Honeybees come first to mind when we think about those essential pollen carriers, but there are hundreds of native bee species, as well as flies, moths, beetles, and some wasps, that also serve as pollinators. Hummingbirds and even some kinds of bats also carry pollen from flower to flower as they go about their business.

As gardeners and as humans who eat food, it's important to do all we can to support the pollinators that make that food happen. The crisis of colony collapse disorder (CCD) that continues to affect honeybees throughout North America underscores our dependence on pollinators. Farmers who grow crops from apples and strawberries to squash and almonds rely on hives of traveling honeybees to pollinate their fields. No bees means no food.

Gardening organically is fundamental to supporting pollinators of all types. Although pesticides are thought to be only part of the cause of CCD, bees are especially vulnerable to broad-spectrum insecticides. By eschewing the use of nonspecific pesticides and by limiting the use of even organically approved products, organic gardeners create safe zones where pollinators can live and reproduce.

In addition to gardening organically, here are other steps to take to give pollinators the support they need and deserve:

🐝 Commit to eating organic as much as possible. Eating organic is a great way to help all types of pollinators, since it's been proven that the neonicotinoid pesticides permitted in nonorganic farming contribute to colony collapse disorder, and even harm social bumblebees by affecting their ability to collect food and find their way home.

🐝 Buy honey from a trusted local apiary. (If you're not managing your own bee hives, that is.) Thanks to CCD, it's a rough time to be a beekeeper, and apiaries need your support in order to replace lost colonies and keep surviving colonies healthy. Plus, buying local honey means you're supporting local farmers who rely on those local bees to pollinate their crops. Yes, honey at the farmers' market may be more expensive than the generic brands in the supermarket, but you're paying for a quality product and investing in a vital industry in your community.

🐝 Create a pollinator-friendly garden (and landscape). Plant flowers, especially those that have clustered flower heads with lots of small, nectar-rich blossoms. Think sunflowers (actually composite flowers made up of hundreds of small disk flowers), dill, mints, yarrows (*Achillea* spp.), and many more. See the Beneficial Insects entry for more tips on gardening for pollinators.

🐝 Make sure something is blooming in your landscape as much of the year as possible in your climate. Consider shrubs and trees that bloom in late winter, early spring-blooming bulbs, and asters and goldenrods that hang on into the fall. Honeybees can travel up to 6 miles searching for food. You can help hungrybees by creating a bee-friendly habitat on your property (native pollinators will benefit, too!). Focus on native plants to provide the foods most sought by native pollinators. See the Native Plants entry and find a list of native plants for your region at PlantNative.org. Bees prefer varieties with single flower tops, like marigolds, because they have an easier time accessing the pollen. They also love clover, so consider spreading clover seeds over all or a portion of your yard

🐝 Do what you can to fight climate change. According to the Natural Resources Defense Council, a warming planet means that there could be a timing issue between bees and bloom: Bees can't survive if they come out of their winter hibernation before flowers begin blooming. A changing climate could also cause a disconnect between flowers' and bees' ranges, meaning critical food sources may no longer grow in areas where bees live. You can help by pressing your legislators to take action on climate change and pollinator conservation, voting for lawmakers who have these values, and taking steps to reduce your personal impact on climate change.

POPPY

See *Papaver*

PORTULACA

Portulaca, moss rose. All-season annuals.

Description: *Portulaca grandiflora*, moss rose, produces 1-inch single or double roselike flowers, in white, pink, red, yellow, orange, or magenta bloom freely on sprawling, 4- to 6-inch mats of succulent, needlelike leaves.

How to grow: Sow seeds directly after the soil warms up, or set out transplants no more than 6 inches apart. Plants thrive in sunny, hot, dry areas with poor soil. Plants self-sow readily, but the flower color may revert to bright magenta.

Landscape uses: Use portulaca as a filler between paving stones and cracks. It also adds color to pots and baskets.

POTATO

Solanum tuberosum

Solanaceae

Growing potatoes is fun as well as practical, thanks to the development of disease-resistant varieties and varieties in a range of colors, shapes, and sizes. Native to the Andes mountains of South America, potatoes thrive in the cool northern half of the United States and the southern half of Canada. Growers in other areas, however, can have successful crops by planting potatoes in very early spring or, in warm regions, in fall or winter for a spring harvest.

Planting: Although you can grow some potato varieties from seed, it's easier to plant certified, disease-free "seed potatoes" purchased from garden centers or Internet and catalog suppliers. (Potatoes you buy at the grocery store often are chemically treated to prevent the eyes from sprouting.) You'll need 5 to 8 pounds of potatoes to plant a 100-foot row. Along with standards such as 'Kennebec', try some fingerlings, such as 'Russian Banana' or 'French Fingerling', and those with colorful tubers like 'Rose Gold', 'Adirondack Red', 'Adirondack Blue', 'Purple Peruvian', or 'Cranberry Red'.

Potatoes need space, sunshine, and fertile, well-drained soil. Acid soil provides good growing conditions and reduces the chance of a common disease called scab.

Plant seed potatoes whole, or cut them into good-sized pieces, each of which should contain two or three eyes. Cure the cut pieces by spreading them out in a bright, airy place for 24 hours, or until they are slightly dry and the cut areas have hardened. In wet climates, some gardeners take the precaution of dusting seed potatoes with sulfur to help prevent rot.

Plant early cultivars 2 to 3 weeks before the last spring frost, or as soon as you can work the soil. Folklore advises planting potatoes on St. Patrick's Day; however, that recommendation only works if your garden is snow-free by March 17! Time the planting of late cultivars so they will mature before the first fall frost.

Plant potatoes in rows spaced 3 feet apart. Place the seed pieces 6 inches apart, and cover them with 4 to 5 inches of soil. As the vines grow, hill soil, leaves, straw, or compost over them to keep the developing tubers covered. (When exposed to sunlight, tubers turn green and develop a mildly toxic substance called solanine.) Leaving only a small portion of the growing vines exposed encourages additional root development.

Many growers prefer to plant potatoes in hills. The illustration on page 488 shows potatoes planted in soil hills and mulch mounds. The mulch-planting method is especially good for growing potatoes in containers, such as large barrels. This "dirtless" method makes harvesting extremely clean and easy but can produce a smaller crop of small tubers.

Growing guidelines: Once the plants blossom, stop hilling up the soil, and apply a thick mulch to conserve moisture and keep down weeds. Water deeply during dry spells.

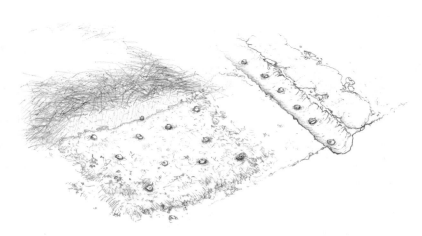

Planting potatoes. Dig furrows about 6 inches deep, space the seed pieces 6 inches apart, and hill up the soil around the stems as they grow. Or spread compost or shredded leaves over the surface of your potato bed, space your seed potatoes evenly over the mulch, and top with about a foot of straw or hay.

Problems: Climate and growing conditions can create a number of problems. Speckle leaf, a disorder that appears as dark splotches on leaves with sunken areas on the leaf undersides, is apparently caused by too much ozone in the atmosphere. Breeders are developing resistant cultivars. Keeping plants healthy and well cultivated is the best prevention.

Hollow areas in tuber centers are caused by rapid and uneven growth. To prevent this, plant seed potatoes closer together, cut down on watering and fertilizer, and avoid susceptible cultivars.

Potatoes are attractive to several kinds of pests, including aphids, Colorado potato beetles, cutworms, and flea beetles. For control measures, see page 454.

Other possible pests include blister beetles, leafhoppers, and wireworms. Blister beetles are ¾ inch long, slender, dark-colored insects that feed on leaves; reduce damage by handpicking (be sure to wear gloves to avoid blisters). Thin, wedge-shaped, ¼-inch-long leafhoppers cause leaves to curl and yellow; apply soap spray for control. Wireworms are ½- to ¾-inch-long larvae of the click beetle; these orange "worms" feed on and damage developing tubers. They are more prevalent in newly cultivated areas, so wait a few years after converting a lawn area into garden to plant potatoes there; crop rotation and frequent cultivation can also help, as can wireworm traps like those described on page 450.

An intriguing development in pest control is varieties such as 'Prince Hairy' and 'King Harry'. These varieties discourage leafhopper and Colorado potato beetles from feeding by virtue of their hairy leaves. The hairs contain sticky fluid that leaks out when hairs are touched, coating the insects with goo.

Avoid most potato diseases by rotating crops, providing good air circulation, keeping the garden clean, selecting resistant cultivars, and planting disease-free seed potatoes. If disease does strike, remove and destroy affected plants. Here are some diseases that might occur.

🌿 Black leg, a bacterial infection, begins as yellowing of top foliage and progresses to a black, slimy rot that destroys stems and tubers.

🌿 Early blight, also called leaf spot, is a fungus that shows up on leaves as enlarging brown spots that develop concentric rings. The blight eventually spreads to the tubers, reducing yields and creating puckered skins with discolored spots.

🌿 Late blight hits crops after they've blossomed. It begins with dark, watery spots on leaves and spreads to stems and tubers.

🌿 Ring rot is a highly infectious bacterial disease that is not generally obvious aboveground. Underground, it starts with a ⅛-inch ring of decay under a tuber's skin; eventually the whole interior decays, leaving a shell of firm tissue.

🌿 Scab causes rough, corky spots on tubers. It is most commonly a problem in soils that have a near-neutral or alkaline pH or in those that are on the dry side. Keep the pH low and maintain an even moisture level in the soil to avoid scab.

🌿 Verticillium wilt turns older leaves yellow and eventually causes the whole plant to wilt and die.

Harvesting: Blossoming plants are a sign that the first "new" potatoes are ready to harvest. Pull aside the earth around the base of plants and gently pick off cooking-size tubers, which are delicious boiled with the skins on.

Once the foliage starts to wither and die back, the tubers will be fully grown. If the weather is not too warm or wet, they will keep in the ground for several weeks. Dig them up with a spading fork before the first frost. Potatoes that are nicked or bruised during harvesting won't store well, so eat them as soon as you can. Clean and dry the crop as quickly as possible, but never expose it to sunlight. Store tubers in a dark place at around 40°F.

Note that potatoes with colored flesh often lose that color when cooked in water. To keep red and purple potatoes colorful, try roasting them instead of boiling.

PRIMULA

Primrose. Spring-blooming perennials.

Description: Primroses bear rounded, five-petaled flowers in clusters above dense rosettes of paddle-shaped, wrinkled leaves.

Primula ×polyantha, polyanthus primrose, practically hides its 6-inch paddlelike leaves in early spring under 8- to 12-inch-tall, dense clusters of 1½-inch blooms in rich shades of white, yellow, red, and blue, many with a distinct yellow eye. Best in Zones 5–7; widely grown as annuals elsewhere.

P. sieboldii, Siebold's primrose, carries its 1½-inch blooms in white, lilac, pink, and magenta-purple shades 8 to 10 inches above spreading masses of scalloped 4-inch leaves that die down in summer. Zones 4–8.

P. vulgaris, English or common primrose, bears yellow, 1-inch, slightly fragrant blooms just above dense rosettes of 3-inch leaves. Zones 4–8.

How to grow: Plant in spring or divide after bloom every 2 to 3 years. Grow in partially shaded, average to fertile, well-drained but moisture-retentive soil enriched with organic matter. They tolerate full sun if the soil remains moist, although common primroses tolerate drier soils than most. Individual plants are usually short-lived, but they self-sow or produce offsets generously. Mulch in summer to retain moisture and in winter to prevent the shallow-rooted plants from being heaved out of the ground by the freezing and thawing of the soil. Handpick or trap slugs and snails; wash spider mites off plants with a strong spray of water.

Landscape uses: Group primroses along paths, at the edge of borders, and in cottage gardens. Combine with bulbs, ferns, and other spring flowers in a wooded area. Make a late sowing of sweet alyssum to fill bare spots left by dormant Siebold's primroses.

PRIVET

See *Ligustrum*

PROPAGATION

Learning to propagate plants—to make new plants from existing ones in your home and garden—is one of the most exciting and rewarding aspects of gardening. Many of the methods are easy, and you don't need fancy or expensive tools. Propagation is cheaper than buying large numbers of plants, so with a little time and effort you can fill your garden quickly at minimal cost. Propagating new plants will keep your house and garden full of vigorous specimens, and you'll probably have plenty to give away, too!

You can reproduce most plants by several methods. There are two major types of propagation: sexual and asexual. Sexual propagation involves seeds, which are produced by the fusion of male and female reproductive cells. Asexual propagation methods use the vegetative parts of a plant: roots, stems, buds, and leaves. Division, cuttings, layering, budding, and grafting are all asexual methods. Spores (produced by ferns and mosses) may look like seeds, but they are technically asexual structures, because they have a specialized way of forming new plants.

Select a technique by considering the plant you are working with, the materials you have, the season, and the amount of time you are willing to wait for a new plant.

Seeds: Growing from seed is an inexpensive way to produce large numbers of plants. Annuals, biennials, and vegetables are almost always reproduced by seed. You can also grow perennials, shrubs, and trees from seed, although the seedlings they produce may not resemble the parent plants. Raising seeds requires few materials: a container, a growing medium, and seeds. The time to sow seeds depends on the type of plant. For most garden plants, you can sow seeds indoors in late winter or outdoors in spring. Tree, shrub, and many perennial seeds may need a cold period or other treatment before they will germinate. Depending on the type of plant, it could take anywhere from weeks to years to get a garden-size specimen. For complete information on growing plants from seeds, see the Seed Starting and Seed Saving entry.

Spores: Spores are the reproductive structures of ferns and mosses. To produce new plants, sow these dustlike "seeds" on a sterile medium and cover them to maintain humidity and prevent contamination. Clear plastic shoe boxes or cups are ideal containers for propagation. You can collect spores from your own ferns or buy them from specialty catalogs. You can sow spores whenever they are available. The new plants will be ready for the garden after a period of months or years, depending on the species.

Division: Division is an easy way to produce more plants with almost 100 percent success. This method involves digging up an established plant and separating it into several pieces. Division is used for bulbs and mat-, clump-, or crown-forming plants, including ferns, bamboos, bugleweed, daylilies, and hostas. Single-stemmed plants like trees cannot be divided.

All you'll need for division is a tool to dig up the plant and your hands or a sharp implement to separate the pieces. You can divide most plants in either spring or fall. Division produces full-size plants that can be placed directly in the garden. For more information, see the Division entry.

Cuttings: Cuttings are pieces of leaves, stems, and/or roots that are separated from a parent plant. When placed in the proper conditions, these pieces form new roots and shoots. Stem cuttings are used for a wide range of plants, including geraniums, pachysandra, and coleus. Use root cuttings for perennials such as Oriental poppies (*Papaver orientale*) or globe thistles (*Echinops* spp.) and some trees, including golden rain tree (*Koelreuteria paniculata*). You can also try leaf petiole cuttings, used for African violets and peperomias, and leaf pieces, used for such plants as gloxinias and snake plant (*Sansevieria* spp.).

The materials you'll need depend on the plant and the method you are using. Leaf petiole cuttings of African violets will root in a simple glass of water. You can stick stem and root cuttings in a pot or flat of regular potting soil. A plastic bag or other clear cover will help to maintain high humidity around the cuttings. More complicated structures, such as cold frames and mist boxes, are good for hard-to-root shrub and tree cuttings. Plants reproduced by cuttings can be ready for the garden in a matter of weeks or months. See the Cuttings entry for more details on this method.

Layering: Layering is a way to get stems to root while they are still attached to the parent plant. Some plants produce layers naturally. Strawberries form rooted plantlets on runners; raspberries produce new plants where the stem tips touch the ground. The technique of simple layering involves bending a low-growing stem to ground level and burying a few inches of the stem behind the tip. Simple layering is an easy way to reproduce such plants as camellias, forsythias, and magnolias. To air-layer, you shallowly wound a stem a few inches below the tip to stimulate root production, and then wrap moist sphagnum moss around the stem. Covering the moss with a thin sheet of plastic holds in moisture and secures the moss to the stem. Weeping fig trees (*Ficus benjamina*), corn plants (*Dracaena fragrans*), and witch hazels (*Hamamelis* spp.) are all good candidates for air layering.

You don't need much equipment to try these techniques. A trowel (for digging the trench) is sufficient for simple layering. For air layering, you'll need sphagnum moss, waterproof tape, a piece of thin plastic, and a knife. Early spring is the best time for simple layering. For outdoor plants, you can set up air layers in spring or late summer. Indoor air layers can be started anytime. It will probably take several months to a year to get a new well-rooted plant. For more information, see the Layering entry.

Grafting: Grafting is a more advanced propagation technique. It involves joining a stem piece of one plant (the scion) to the root system of another plant (the rootstock) in such a way that the parts unite and continue to grow. You can reproduce many types of trees by grafting, including pines (*Pinus* spp.) and rhododendrons, and even some herbaceous plants, such as cacti. Grafting has several advantages over other propagation methods. It allows you to propagate plants that are difficult to raise from seeds or cuttings. Through grafting, you can produce a plant adapted to your particular needs. Some rootstocks have a dwarfing effect, while others encourage vigorous topgrowth. They can also provide tolerance to soilborne insects and diseases, or to less-than-perfect soil conditions.

The most important grafting tool is a sharp knife. You may also need string or tape (to keep the graft pieces together) and grafting wax (to prevent water loss and avoid contamination). You'll have to have suitable rootstocks, too. You can raise your own from seeds or cuttings, or buy them from a specialty catalog or nursery. Spring is the most common time for grafting. Herbaceous plants will join successfully in a few weeks; woody plant grafts usually take a month or two to unite firmly and begin growing. See the Grafting entry for more details on this technique.

Budding: Budding is a particular type of grafting. In this method, you use only a single bud from the desired plant. Budding is commonly used to propagate fruit trees as well as ornamentals, such as hybrid tea roses. For the home gardener, the advantages of budding are similar to those of grafting. In some cases, budding is more successful than grafting because it is easier to get close contact between the bud and the rootstock. Budding also allows you to propagate more plants if you have a limited amount of scion material.

For this technique, you'll need a sharp knife and some string or tape to secure the bud to the stem. As with grafting, compatible rootstock plants are necessary. Budding is best done in late summer or early fall. Buds inserted at this time will produce new growth the following spring. See the Budding entry for a more complete discussion of this technique.

PRUNING AND TRAINING

Pruning and training are both a science and an art—and probably the least-understood gardening practices. Proper pruning and training bring out the best in each plant. Not only do well-pruned plants produce more and better fruit and flowers, they also are healthier and more vigorous. Pruning and training can improve the health of an ailing plant, make trees stronger and safer, channel growth away from buildings or traffic, and restore a sense of order to an overplanted or overgrown yard.

While pruning and training are most often thought of as techniques used on woody trees, shrubs, and vines, they're also used to direct the growth of herbaceous plants. Roots can be pruned as well to prepare a plant for transplanting or to encourage the roots of a new plant to branch out into the surrounding soil. The roots of bonsai trees are pruned to restrict growth.

Pruning can be used to:

- Remove diseased and dead wood.
- Encourage branching and bushy growth.
- Direct a plant to grow in a particular direction.
- Eliminate unattractive, crowded, and congested growth.
- Increase the structural strength of a tree or shrub.
- Reduce the overall size of a tree or shrub without causing rampant regrowth.
- Improve air circulation and reduce disease problems.
- Increase flowering and vigor by removing old, nonblooming wood.
- Help a newly planted plant become established.
- Eliminate reverted growth (such as all-green shoots on an otherwise variegated plant).

Pruning Cuts

Most pruning comes down to making one of two kinds of pruning cuts: thinning cuts and heading cuts.

Thinning cuts: Thinning cuts remove branches totally. They open up a plant but don't make it shorter. Thinning directs growth into alternate patterns. Use thinning cuts to establish good structure of young trees and shrubs and to allow sunlight and air to reach the interior of a plant. Also use thinning cuts to remove unattractive or unruly branches, branches that block a view, and any stems that rub or cross. Thinning cuts can eliminate sharp crotches and make a plant less likely to break under a heavy snow load.

Heading cuts: Heading cuts shorten plant stems and stimulate latent buds behind the cut to grow, making the plant more dense. Selective heading reduces overall size or height of a plant without changing its natural shape. The plant suffers less stress, and selective heading doesn't cause vigorous, out-of-control growth the way that nonselective heading does. To make a selective heading cut that will direct plant growth, cut just above a bud or branch that's pointed in the direction you want the growth to go.

Nonselective heading is the technique used to shape formal hedges and topiary. Pruning encourages growth, and nonselective heading cuts cause a burst of growth from all of the cut stems. Branches are cut back partway along the stem, resulting in rapid, bushy regrowth just below the cut. Nonselective heading is often misapplied, resulting in forlorn lollipop-shaped

KEY WORDS *Pruning and Training*

Branch collar. The part of the trunk that helps hold the branch to the trunk, often recognizable as a bulge at the base of the branch.

Branch crotch. The angle where a tree branch meets the trunk or parent stem.

Cane. A long, slender branch that usually originates directly from the roots.

Leader. The main, primary, or tallest shoot of a tree trunk. Trees can be single-leadered or multiple-leadered.

Pinching. Nipping out the end bud of a twig or stem with your fingertips to make the plant more compact and bushy.

Thinning cut. Cutting a limb off at the base, either at ground level or at a branch collar.

Heading cut. Cutting a branch back to a side bud or shoot.

Skirting or limbing up. Pruning off the lower limbs of trees.

Sucker. An upright shoot growing from a root or graft union; also, in common usage, straight, rapid-growing shoots or watersprouts that grow in response to wounding or poor pruning.

Espalier (pronounced is-PAL-yuhr). A fruit tree or an ornamental shrub that is pruned to grow in a flat plane. Although sometimes freestanding, an espaliered plant is generally attached to a framework against a wall and is usually trained in a well-defined pattern.

Topiary. Plants sculpted into sheared geometric shapes or likenesses of animals or people.

shrubs or trees that would look more attractive, and would likely be healthier, if pruned to follow their natural form. Selective heading combines the best of thinning and heading, but it can't be applied to all plants. The older, larger, and woodier the plant, the fewer selective heading cuts should be used.

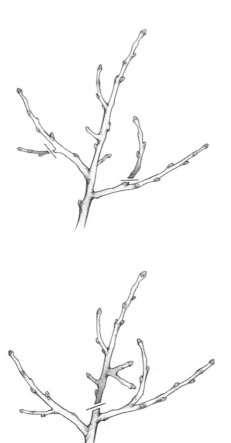

Making thinning and heading cuts. Make thinning cuts at the branch collar where the branch originates. Avoid a flush cut; leave the branch collar intact, but don't leave a stub. To make selective heading cuts, cut directly above a bud or side branch that's pointing in the direction you want the new growth to take.

Pruning Do's and Don'ts

Proper technique: Prune from the bottom up and, in the case of large plants, from the inside out. Prune out all dead wood first—an important step for health and good looks. Dead wood is easiest to spot in summer because the branches have no green leaves. Also remove diseased and damaged wood.

Next look for a few of the worst rubbing, crossing branches. Leave the best-placed one of any pair. Try to keep branches that head up and out from the center or that fill an otherwise empty space. Step back from the plant you're working on frequently and look at it from all angles.

Prune to open up center areas and to clean up the base of shrubs. This improves plant health by admitting light and increasing air circulation. It also has a large impact on the beauty of a plant. Depending on what shrub you are pruning, you may want to concentrate on removing excess twiggy growth or removing a few of the older stems that no longer bloom well.

Selectively thin or head back misplaced branches: those that touch the ground, lay upon or crowd other plants, or come too close to the house, windows, and walkways.

Save any heading cuts until the end of a pruning job. Locate the longest, most unruly branch first, follow it down inside the shrub, and cut it off to a side branch or a bud. Remember: Next year's new growth will be channeled into the bud or side branch you cut above, so choose which way you want growth to go.

Pruning large limbs: A large branch that is sawed from above will tear bark from the trunk as it falls. Use the three-cut method shown on the opposite page to prevent damage when removing large limbs.

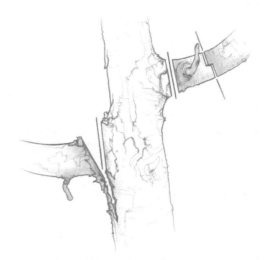

Pruning large limbs. Make three cuts in the order shown to safely remove a large limb without causing bark tears.

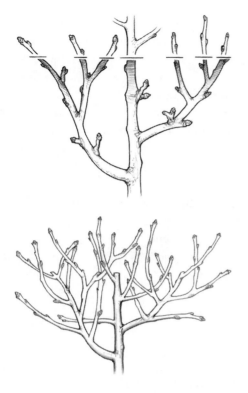

Nonselective heading cuts. To trim a hedge or shear branches to a uniform surface, make nonselective heading cuts anywhere on the stem.

1. About 1 foot out from the trunk, cut halfway through the branch from underneath.

2. A few inches in from the first cut, saw off the branch from the top.

3. Remove the stub by cutting along, but never into, the branch collar. On tight crotches, saw from the bottom up.

Pruning mistakes: The most common pruning mistake is to cut back everything in the yard in an ill-fated attempt to make it all smaller again. This actually stimulates an upsurge of messy regrowth, making the final solution more difficult. Tree topping, indiscriminate shearing, and overthinning are the three major forms of "malpruning." Instead, plan to correct the sizes and shapes of your landscape plants by pruning them properly over the course of several years. If a tree or shrub is simply too large for its site, remember that removing it is one option. You can also hire professionals to transplant even fairly large shrubs or trees that are in the wrong place, so don't be afraid to ask at your local nursery.

The cure for badly pruned plants is time. Most will reestablish their natural habits given a few years to recover. Rehabilitative pruning can hasten the process and make plants look better. Meticulously prune all dead wood, removing all stubs. Use thinning cuts to simplify tangled branch ends. Take out entire canes. If treelike shrubs have rampantly produced suckers because of heading cuts, slowly remove the worst of them over a period of years. Let the strongest and best-placed suckers grow back into branches. Some plants, including cane growers like weigela, mock oranges (*Philadelphus* spp.), and forsythia, can be radically renovated by cutting them entirely to the ground. In about 3 years they'll regrow to mature size and bloom again. Many lovely but rampant vines are treated this way to good effect.

Most needled evergreens will not regrow once they are cut back to wood that does not have needles on it. This makes their size difficult to control and radical renovation impossible.

Pruning Timetable

Plan your pruning schedule depending on what you want to accomplish. Removing dead and diseased wood, as well as general thinning can be done in any season. Follow these seasonal guidelines.

🌿 Spring pruning stimulates the most rapid regrowth, so it's a good time for heavy pruning. Prune evergreens in spring, but avoid pruning deciduous trees as they leaf out. Prune spring- and early-summer-flowering shrubs such as azaleas and rhododendrons as soon as they finish blooming, so they'll have time to grow and set new buds during summer.

🌿 Cut shrubs that flower in summer or fall on the current season's growth back in spring as buds begin to swell. This includes Russian sage (*Perovskia atriplicifolia*) and bluebeard (*Caryopteris ×clandonensis*).

Elegant Espalier

An espalier is a fruit tree or shrub trained to grow flat, usually against a wall, supported on a strong lattice, trellis, or wire fence. Wire is easiest and usually the most practical support for fruit trees.

Classic espalier patterns include fan training and a Belgian fence, which has a geometric pattern of crossing branches. In addition to the usual ones, you can also establish an informal pattern to suit a more naturalistic garden and plants that don't form spurs. Train the branches (or at least the tips) of informal, fruit-bearing espaliers at an angle of at least 30 degrees above the horizontal to encourage branch vigor and flower production.

Plant your young tree about 1 foot away from the framework to allow room for the trunk to expand as it grows. Space it midway between two posts.

Start careful pruning early in the life of the tree, and continue it at regular intervals during the whole life of the espalier. As an espalier gets older, less and less pruning is needed. It may take several years of training to "finish" a pattern.

Balancing the pattern: In general, strive for a balanced pattern by encouraging weaker branches and discouraging branches that are too vigorous. Do this by pruning the strong branches shorter and allowing weaker ones to grow longer. Rub off side buds on the stronger branches right away, but leave the buds on weaker branches. Tie the more vigorous branches frequently and closely to the supports. Leave weaker

❧ Summer pruning has a less stimulating effect on growth. Hot or dry weather is extremely stressful for plants, so avoid heavy pruning. This is a good time to tidy up plants and to remove suckers and watersprouts.

❧ In mid- to late fall, make only thinning cuts. Heading cuts made late in the season can stimulate soft new growth that is easily damaged in fall freezes. Don't prune plants during the period when their leaves are falling.

❧ Late winter is the traditional time to prune dormant plants; leaves have dropped, and it's easy to see plant form. Winter pruning stimulates growth, but the results are delayed until spring. This is a good time to prune landscape trees as well as apples and other fruit trees, brambles, grapes, roses, and shrubs that form flowers on the current year's wood.

Good Tools for Good Cuts

Choose pruning tools that cut cleanly and easily. Keep the cutting edges sharp. You'll probably need only three pruning tools: pruning shears for stems and twigs, lopping shears for branches that are finger-size and larger, and a pruning saw for larger branches and crowded areas.

Pruning shears are available in two types. Anvil

branches growing freely a little while longer. Remove some leaves from the stronger ones, and remove all fruit from the weaker ones.

Maintenance training: Early in summer, pinch back each lateral branch as soon as it has made three or four leaves. Also pinch back terminal shoots when they have made a few inches of growth. If a lot of leafy growth occurs as summer progresses, nip out a few shoots entirely.

Throughout the growing season, remove branches that are not growing in the right direction or that are growing out from the framework. Don't let fruiting spurs develop more closely than 5 to 7 inches apart. When very old spurs bear repeatedly, either prune the spur or thin out the fruit in early summer.

During the dormant season (late winter is better in the North), cut back every lateral branch to two or three buds. If laterals are close together, remove some to prevent a bunchy look. At the same time, shorten every vertical shoot. If there has been moderate growth (from 4 to 8 inches), just cut back each tip to a healthy-looking side bud. If growth has been vigorous (more than 9 inches), remove up to two-thirds of the shoot. Also cut back the leader if it is growing above the desired height.

Prune evergreen espaliers throughout the growing season. Start early in spring just before growth begins. Remove crowding branches entirely. Cut back terminal shoots to within a few inches of the previous year's wood.

pruners cut with a sharp blade that closes against a metal plate, or anvil; bypass pruners work like scissors. A leather holster for your shears is a wise investment.

Lopping shears have long handles that extend your reach and give you leverage for more cutting strength. A small rubber shock absorber is a welcome addition on some models. Folding pruning saws fit nicely into a back pocket, but you'll have more blade choices if you buy a nonfolding saw. One feature to look for is a blade that cuts on both the push and the pull strokes, making it easier to cut in close quarters. Pole pruners can be used for overhead work. The pruning head can consist of either a saw or a cord-operated hook-type shear, or a combination of the two. You may find hedge shears useful for keeping formal hedges neat.

PRUNUS

Ornamental cherry, plum, almond. Deciduous or evergreen spring-flowering trees or shrubs.

Description: Many members of this genus produce edible fruit; you'll find more information in the Cherry, Peach, and Plum entries.

Prunus cerasifera, myrobalan plum, is a deciduous shrub or small tree with a rounded, spreading habit and a mature height of 15 to 25 feet. Pale to deep pink flowers precede the leaves, which are purple on most cultivars. Zones 4–8.

P. glandulosa, dwarf flowering almond, is a diminutive shrub of 3 to 5 feet with slender twigs and a delicate, open branching habit. Single or double, pink or white flowers appear before the leaves in early to mid-spring. Zones 4–8.

P. laurocerasus, cherry laurel, is an evergreen shrub that bears white flowers in early to mid-spring. Leaves are shiny and leathery; fruits are black. Zones 6–8.

P. serrulata, Japanese flowering cherry, grows 20 to 25 feet tall and is vase-shaped; single or double blooms are white to pink. Zones 5–7.

P. subhirtella, Higan cherry, grows 25 feet tall and bears pale to deep pink single or double flowers before leaves appear. Zones 5–9.

How to grow: Except for the cherry-laurels (which prefer shade), most species need full sun and well-drained soil. Protect the thin bark from lawn mower injuries. Prune after flowering. *P. cerasifera* and *P. laurocerasus* have been identified as invasive in some states.

Landscape uses: Most tree cherries make fine focal points or groupings in a sunny area. Cherry-laurels work well in shade individually or grouped. Most *Prunus* attract birds.

PUMPKIN

See Squash

PURPLE CONEFLOWER

See *Echinacea*

PYRACANTHA

Pyracantha, firethorn. Spring-blooming evergreen or semievergreen shrubs.

Description: *Pyracantha coccinea*, scarlet firethorn, is an upright, irregular, spiny shrub reaching 15 feet tall. It has oval, 1- to 1½-inch, dark to medium green leaves, clusters of small white flowers in spring, and showy orange-red berries that persist through fall. Zones 6–8.

How to grow: Provide full sun and good drainage. In southern climates, site firethorns where air circulation will be good; in the North, site them out of the winter wind. Once established, they need little supplemental water. Prune diligently to remove watersprouts and suckers and to maintain shape. A neglected pyracantha is soon out of control. Once overgrown, it is difficult to coax back to size without some awkward pruning cuts.

Pyracantha is susceptible to many of the same diseases that trouble apples and pears, including scab and fire blight. Avoid planting near fruit trees to prevent shared problems.

Landscape uses: Scarlet firethorn makes an attractive espalier—its flowers and berries are set off by a wall or trellis. You can also use firethorn as a hedge; it makes a nearly impenetrable barrier. Plant it to attract berry-eating birds in winter. In the Pacific Northwest, plants may become invasive because birds eat and spread the seeds. Although pyracantha is an attractive landscape plant, its disease susceptibility and tendency to spread aggressively via seedlings can make it a poor choice for adding to a landscape. If you're installing new plants, consider native alternatives such as viburnums or hollies (*Ilex* spp.) instead.

PYRUS

Pear. Spring-flowering deciduous trees.

Description: Members of this genus produce edible fruit; you'll find more information in the Pear entry.

Pyrus calleryana, Callery pear, is familiar in city landscapes because its cultivar 'Bradford' has been widely planted as a street tree. This popular cultivar, which has escaped cultivation and is considered invasive in some states because birds eat and spread the seeds, is pyramidal when young and rounded with maturity, with a dense crown. It attains a mature height in the range of 25 to 40 feet. Its winter buds are a woolly buff color, and its white, malodorous flowers appear in early to mid-spring before the leaves, which are glossy dark green. Spectacular fall leaf colors of reds, russets, oranges, and yellow are reliable most years, especially in the North. Small (½-inch), round pears appear in fall. Zones 5–8.

How to grow: Provide full sun and good drainage. Pears can have serious problems with fire blight, a bacterial disease, during wet summers. Watch for branches forming fire blight's distinctive "shepherd's crooks" at their tips following warm, wet weather during periods of rapid growth. 'Bradford' shows good resistance to fire blight, but like many other Callery pears, it has naturally narrow (and therefore weak) crotch angles that often break under the weight of mature (perhaps snow-laden) branches. Instead of planting 'Bradford', choose other flowering trees such as serviceberry (*Amelanchier* spp.), white redbud (*Cercis* cvs.), and Carolina silverbell (*Halesia carolina*).

Landscape uses: Callery pears look nice when massed or as a focal point, especially for an early splash of white flowers. Their tolerance of urban conditions, combined with abundant flowers, attractive foliage, and availability of small to midsize cultivars, makes them a common sight (some would say too common) along the sidewalks of many American cities.

Q-R

QUERCUS

Oak. Large deciduous or evergreen trees.

Description: Large shade trees with toothed or lobed leaves, oaks are pyramidal trees when young, developing a rounded to spreading habit with age. With the exception of *Quercus acutissima*, and *Q. robur*, all the species listed here are native in some part of North America.

Q. acutissima, sawtooth oak, grows 35 to 45 feet in the landscape. Its oblong leaves with bristlelike teeth usually turn brown and persist through winter. Zones 6–8.

Q. alba, white oak, grows 60 to 80 feet in the landscape; its most outstanding feature is the ash gray bark layered on its trunk. The leaves have rounded lobes and turn to shades of red and russet late in fall. Zones 3–8.

Q. imbricaria, shingle oak, has oblong, leathery, deep green leaves that turn brown in autumn and often persist on the tree well into winter, rattling in the wind. This native tree tolerates limestone (alkaline) soils well. Zones 5–7.

Q. macrocarpa, bur oak, is a massive native of the North American prairie. Growing 70 to 80 feet tall, it has imposing limbs, a wide trunk, and deeply furrowed bark. The leaves have rounded lobes and can grow up to 10 feet long. The cup on the acorn is fringed. Bur oak also performs well in limestone soils. Zones 2–7.

Q. palustris, pin oak, is a popular lawn tree with a strongly pyramidal form and a mature height of 60 to 70 feet. The leaves are sharply lobed with a fine spine, or pin, at the tip of each lobe, and may develop chlorosis (yellowing) when the tree is grown in limestone soils. Zones 5–8.

Q. phellos, willow oak, is similar in form, size, and popularity to pin oak, but has smooth narrow leaves about 4 inches long. Some consider its leaf size and shape to make for easier cleanup in fall because the leaves don't mat and tend to disappear amid groundcovers. Zones 6–9.

Q. robur, English oak, is a sturdy tree with a short trunk, deeply furrowed, dark gray bark, and a broadly spreading to rounded crown. Dark green, alternate leaves are 2 to 5 inches long with rounded lobes; like other oaks native to Europe, fall color is not significant. English oak reaches heights of 40 to 60 feet. Zones 5–8.

Q. rubra, red oak, is a vigorous tree that matures to 60 to 75 feet in the landscape. Lobes are sharply pointed to rounded on shiny dark green leaves; red fall color is not always strong. Red oak tolerates air pollution but may show leaf chlorosis in limestone soils. Zones 4–8.

Q. virginiana, live oak, is an evergreen native of the southeastern coastal forest. Massive and sprawling, live oak grows 40 to 80 feet in the landscape and often larger in the wild. Its elongated oval leaves are shiny dark green above and felted beneath. The huge boughs often host other plants such as Spanish moss and mistletoe. Coastal areas of Zones 7–10.

How to grow: Choose a site with full sun, well-drained, humusy soil, and plenty of room. Although adaptable to a variety of soil conditions, oaks generally perform better in acidic soils. Prune oaks only during dormancy to avoid spreading oak wilt, a fungal disease that causes leaves to curl, brown, and droop. Oak wilt moves rapidly through a tree, often killing it within a year. Susceptibility varies among species; white, bur, English, and live oaks show resistance. The disease is more likely to be fatal to red, pin, sawtooth, shingle, and willow oaks. The fungus travels via root grafts; dig a trench between infected and healthy trees to destroy root connections. There is no cure for oak wilt.

The foliage of oaks is a favored food of gypsy moth larvae. Identified by the rows of blue and red stripes along their backs, these 2½-inch hairy gray caterpillars often occur in sufficient numbers to defoliate a tree, and repeated leaf loss causes severe decline and death. Egg masses appear as tan or buff fluffy patches on tree trunks and branches, build-ings, and fences; scrape these off into a bucket of soapy water. Tie bands of burlap around tree trunks to capture climbing larvae; crush or hand-pick trapped caterpillars. Spray Btk (*Bacillus thuringiensis* var. *kurstaki*) to control young caterpillars.

Homeowners are often alarmed by unusual swellings of their oak's leaves, floral parts, or twigs; such galls are caused by various insects and mites. Not all galls injure their hosts, but some kill twigs and branches. Remove and destroy galls to limit further infestation. Spray young trees with dormant oil in late winter to kill overwintering gall-forming pests.

Landscape uses: Use any of these oaks as long-lasting shade trees; in a large-scale situation, they make fine focal points as well. Most bear acorns that attract wildlife. Good street-tree choices are sawtooth and willow oaks. Look to native oaks if your landscape needs include colorful autumn leaves.

QUINOA

Chenopodium quinoa
Chenopodiaceae

While it's not actually a grain, quinoa's tiny seeds make a fine substitute for grains like rice and barley in all kinds of cuisines. A staple food in the South American Andes where it is native, quinoa may be grown in North American gardens but performs best in mountain highlands and is unlikely to produce its tasty seeds in places where temperatures reach 95°F.

Planting: Plant after the soil warms to 60° to 65°F, sowing seeds 1 inch deep in rows 4 inches apart in well-prepared soil. A few ounces of seed will plant a 200-square-foot plot.

Growing guidelines: If the weather is dry,

water during germination, then gradually cut back on watering. When seedlings are 2 to 3 inches tall, thin them to 8 inches apart.

Problems: Quinoa has few pest problems. Fungal diseases may appear in wet conditions late in the season.

Harvesting: Quinoa ripens in 70 to 80 days. Harvest when the seed heads are dry, but before they begin to shatter and scatter their tiny, tasty contents. A 200-square-foot plot may yield 15 to 20 pounds of seeds where growing conditions are favorable. Store dry seed in glass jars or other sealed containers.

Quinoa seeds are naturally covered with bitter saponin, which must be removed with thorough rinsing before using the seeds in cooking. Wash/rinse quinoa in several changes of water right before you use it.

RADISH

Raphanus sativus
Brassicaceae

Colorful and crisp, radishes are a popular addition to salads and vegetable trays. Radishes mature very quickly—some in as little as 3 weeks. They're a useful marker crop when sown lightly along rows of slow germinators such as carrots and parsnips.

Planting: Dig the soil to a depth of 6 inches for quick-growing radishes and up to 2 feet for large, sharper-tasting, slower-growing winter types. Space seeds ½ inch deep and 1 inch apart; firm the soil and water gently. Make weekly spring sowings as soon as you can work the soil (4 to 6 weeks before the last expected frost) until early summer; start again in late summer. Sow winter radishes in midsummer for a fall harvest.

Growing guidelines: Thin seedlings to 2 inches apart, 3 to 6 inches for the larger winter types. Mulch to keep down weeds. For quick growth and the best flavor, water regularly.

Problems: Cabbage maggots are attracted to radishes but seldom ruin a whole crop; for controls, see page 454.

Harvesting: Pull as soon as the roots mature. Oversize radishes often crack and are tough or woody.

RAIN BARRELS

Collecting rainwater for garden use can be fun—all it takes is a little ingenuity and effort. And if you do rely on tap water or well water for watering your garden, collecting rainwater is an energy saver, too, since it often requires fossil fuel energy to pump municipal or well water. With a rainwater collection setup in place, you can then start the longer-term process of converting your yard to a water-wise landscape.

A rain barrel is simply a large container connected to a downspout from your roof. When it rains, water that runs off the roof collects in the barrel. You can collect an impressive amount of water this way. For instance, a 1,000-square-foot roof will yield 625 gallons of water from 1 inch of rain. You can buy a barrel specifically designed for this purpose, with a tap already installed for decanting the collected water, but it could easily cost $150 (models designed to look like decorative planters may cost even more). This type of barrel holds about 50 gallons of water and will last for many years. You may decide it's worth the cost if you're setting up your barrel in a prominent spot or where it will be visible to your neighbors or from the street.

Set Up a Rain Barrel

Making your own rain barrel from a plastic storage barrel is less expensive, and not difficult. Heavy-duty plastic barrels are used to ship and store everything from pickles to pesticides; be sure you find a barrel with a benign history. Try asking local food distributors or bottling companies for a barrel (they may charge $5 or so per barrel), or ask your local extension office for possible sources.

Once you've procured your barrel, here's how to prepare and install it.

1. Use a jigsaw to cut a hole in the top of the barrel large enough for a 1-gallon bucket or plastic pot to fit in.

2. Drill several holes in the bottom of the bucket or pot, and cut a piece of old window screening to size and tuck it into the bucket or pot (the screening will keep debris and insects out of the barrel).

3. Drill a ¾-inch hole in the side of the barrel near the bottom. Insert a faucet or hose bib into the hole, using Teflon tape on the threads and silicone sealant to ensure a watertight seal.

4. Prepare the site by removing the downspout and setting two concrete blocks in place (use a level to make sure the blocks are seated level with one another, but sloping a bit downward and away from the wall).

5. Put the barrel in place, measure, and then use a hacksaw to cut the downspout to fit. Flexible attachments are available that make it easy to connect the downspout to the opening in the barrel.

6. Remove the bucket from the hole temporarily so that you can drill a small hole near the top of the barrel as an overflow. Install a male hose adapter using Teflon tape and silicone sealant as you did for the hose bib. Screw on a length of garden hose and direct it to a mulched area that will be able to absorb overflow.

7. Set the bucket in place and reconnect the downspout.

If you live in an area with wet winters and dry summers, you may want to stockpile water in several barrels, each one connected to the next. If you use this approach, keep in mind that each barrel will need a faucet for draining water, but only the last barrel in the sequence will need an overflow valve.

Depending upon where you live, the rainwater that washes off your roof may carry pollutants, chemical residues, ash, and soot, as well as bird and animal droppings. Ideally, apply water from your rain barrel to the soil of your garden and not to the edible parts of plants, especially leafy greens. Make sure that anyone who has access to the rain barrel understands that its contents are *not* safe for drinking or handwashing.

RAIN GARDENS

If you rarely need to apply supplemental water to your garden, you may not need to set up a rain barrel. But it's still worthwhile to analyze where rainwater that falls on your property ends up. If you have an acre or more, most of it unpaved, then perhaps all the rainwater is absorbed onsite. But if you have a smaller suburban or urban lot, chances are that rainwater ends up running off your property into the stormwater drainage system. If so, you can contribute to protecting water quality by

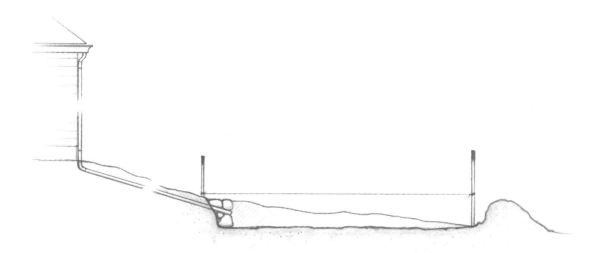

Digging a rain garden. On a slope, use soil removed from the center of the garden to fashion a berm on the downhill side. The floor of the garden will be level, and it will have sloping sides.

diverting rainwater into a rain garden.

A rain garden is a depression built into the landscape to catch water and allow it to slowly seep into the soil, where natural microbial processes help to clean it of impurities and pathogens. The water then will follow natural pathways to rejoin the groundwater reservoirs in your area. The area will drain and dry out between rainfalls, so the plants will not be waterlogged. A rain garden can include perennials, ornamental grasses, wildflowers, ferns, shrubs, and small trees.

Here's how to plan and install a rain garden.

Pick a location. This could be a spot where you can direct a downspout from your roof, an area in the center of a driveway, or on a slope. The garden should be at least 10 feet away from your foundation if you have a basement (or you may end up with a damp basement). Avoid siting a rain garden in a septic leach field area or close to a well.

Check the drainage. Dig a hole 18 inches deep and fill it with water; the hole should be empty within 24 hours. If not, the site is too slow draining to serve the function, and you may need to amend the soil with stone to improve drainage.

Determine the size and layout. Your garden needs to be large enough to handle the volume of water generated during a rainstorm. A rule of thumb is that the garden should be 30 to 50 percent of the size of the impervious surface area it will serve. Here's an example: Say you want to capture water that runs off a roof surface that's approximately 20 by 50 feet (1,000 square feet). Your garden will need to be 300 to 500 square feet. As you determine the boundaries of your garden, remember that it needs to function as a bowl that can fill up with water. Thus, even if it's on a slope, the garden needs to have a level surface. You may need to design it with a berm along the lower side (use some of the soil you dig out of the "bowl" to make the berm), as shown in the illustration.

Strip and dig. If the area is lawn, it's best to strip off the sod before you dig, otherwise the lawn grass will end up coming back as weedy growth in the garden. Use the sod to repair other lawn areas, or stack it upside down on the compost pile. Then dig the garden, loosening the soil at least 12 inches deep. The outside rim of the garden should have sloped walls.

Channel the water. You may need to extend gutter pipe across the surface of the ground to reach the garden. Or you can install underground piping or make a swale to direct water. Whatever technique you use, make a stone catchment area where the water first enters the garden to prevent erosion.

Add an overflow pipe. Like a rain barrel, a rain garden needs to include an escape route for excess water when the garden fills up. Use 1- to 3-inch-diameter pipe, positioned a few inches below the soil, 12 inches away from the high end of the garden.

Choose plants. Select plants that can thrive in alternating conditions of wet and dry. Native species often have deeper, stronger roots that can help them get through dry periods.

Plant the garden. Start at the center and work your way out to the edges. Put the plants that are the most moisture-loving at the low point of the garden and more drought-tolerant plants higher up the sloping sides.

Fill 'er up. For the initial filling, unless a downpour is imminent, you'll need to use your garden hose. Turn it on at low pressure and direct it to the catchment area of the garden.

Maintaining a Rain Garden

Taking care of a rain garden is similar to other gardens. It will need to be mulched and weeded; at

A new rain garden. Once a rain garden is planted and growing, it will look very similar to a typical island bed of flowering and foliage ornamentals.

first, hardwood mulch is best for a rain garden, because shredded leaf mulch and other light mulches tend to float away when the rain garden fills up. If there's a prolonged dry spell, you may even need to water the garden (filling it with the hose, not sprinkling). One extra job is to check the overflow pipe periodically to ensure that it's not clogged with debris.

RAISED BED GARDENING

For space efficiency and high yields, it's hard to beat a vegetable garden grown in raised beds. Raised beds can improve production as well as save space, time, and money. They are the perfect solution for dealing with difficult soils such as heavy clay. In addition, raised beds improve your garden's appearance and accessibility.

Raised gardening beds are higher than ground level, and consist of soil that's mounded or surrounded by a frame to keep it in place. The beds are separated by paths. Plants cover the entire surface of the bed areas, while gardeners work from the paths. The beds are usually 3 to 5 feet across to permit easy access from the paths, and they may be any length. You can grow any vegetable in raised beds, as well as herbs, annual or perennial flowers, berry bushes, or even roses and other shrubs.

One reason raised beds are so effective for increasing efficiency and yields is that crops produce better because the soil in the beds is deep, loose, and fertile. Plants benefit from the improved soil drainage and aeration, and plant roots penetrate readily. Weeds are easy to pull up, too. Since gardeners stay in the pathways, the soil is never walked upon or compacted. Soil amendments and improvement efforts are concentrated in the beds

and not wasted on the pathways, which are simply covered with mulch or planted with grass or a low-growing cover crop. Also, the raised bed's rounded contour provides more actual growing area than does the same amount of flat ground.

Raised beds also save time and money because you need only dig, fertilize, and water the beds, not the paths. You don't need to weed as much when crops grow close together, because weeds can't compete as well. Gardeners with limited mobility find raised beds the perfect solution—a wide sill on a framed raised bed makes a good spot to sit while working. A high frame puts plants in reach of a gardener using a wheelchair. For best access, make beds 28 to 30 inches high, and also keep the beds narrow—no more than 4 feet wide—so it's easy to reach to the center of the bed.

Many gardeners have written entire books about their method of using raised beds to produce great gardening results. For titles, see Recommended Reading on page 675.

Building Raised Beds

The traditional way to make a raised bed is to double-dig. This process involves removing the topsoil layer from a bed, loosening the subsoil, and replacing the topsoil, mixing in plenty of organic matter in the process. Double-digging has many benefits but can be time consuming and laborious. See the Soil entry for details.

The quickest and easiest way to make a raised bed is simply to add lots of organic matter, such as well-rotted manure, compost, or shredded leaves to your garden soil. In the process, mound up the planting beds as the organic content of the soil increases. Shape the soil in an unframed bed so that it is flattopped, with sloping sides (this shape helps conserve water), or forms a long, rounded mound.

The soil in an unframed bed will gradually spread out, and you'll need to periodically hill it up with a hoe. A frame around the outside edge of the bed prevents soil from washing away and allows you to add a greater depth of improved soil. Wood, brick, rocks, or cement blocks are popular materials for framing. Choose naturally rot-resistant woods such as cedar, cypress, or locust. If you choose some other type of wood (don't use chemically treated wood), keep in mind that you'll need to replace it when the wood eventually wears and rots away.

If your garden soil is difficult—heavy clay, very alkaline, or full of rocks—you may want to mix your own soil from trucked-in topsoil, organic matter, and mineral amendments. Then you can build beds up from ground level, without disturbing or incorporating the native soil. You may also need to add extra materials to raised beds if you want them to be tall enough for a gardener in a wheelchair to reach easily.

Lasagna Gardening

This is a no-till option for building raised beds and great soil. It is similar to sheet composting, and allows you to build raised beds without stripping grass or weeds off the site. You can also build a lasagna garden on top of an existing vegetable garden site.

If you are starting on a new site, first cut the grass as short as possible and/or scalp the weeds at ground level. Next cover the bed with a thick layer of newspaper (6 to 10 sheets) to smother existing vegetation. Use sheets of cardboard or flattened cardboard boxes if there are vigorous perennial weeds on the site. Either wet down the newspa-

pers as you spread them or have a supply of soil or mulch at hand and weigh them down with handfuls as you spread. Be sure to overlap the edges of the newspaper or cardboard as you work.

After that, begin layering organic matter on top of the site. Combine materials as you would in a compost pile, by mixing "browns" and "greens." (See the Compost entry for more information.) Add layers of organic materials such as grass clippings, finished compost, chopped leaves, kitchen scraps, coffee grounds, seaweed, shredded mail or newspaper, garden trimmings, used potting soil, sawdust, and weeds (don't add ones that have gone to seed or perennials with vigorous rhizomes, which will spread and grow in the bed). You can also add topsoil, which will help speed things along. Make a pile that is 1 foot or more deep, and top it off with a layer of mulch to keep weeds from getting a foothold. Then wait several months for materials to decompose.

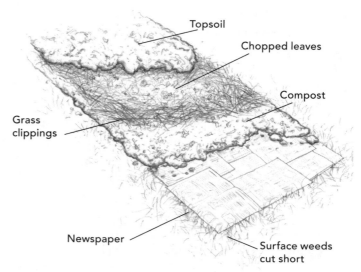

Gardening in layers. To make a lasagna garden, spread newspapers or cardboard to smother existing vegetation, then pile layers of grass clippings, chopped leaves, kitchen scraps, finished compost, and topsoil.

You can build a lasagna garden any time of year. Building one in fall to plant in spring is a good idea, and there are plenty of leaves available for chopping and adding to the mix. If you're building in spring or summer, you can speed up the time when it will be ready to plant by adding extra compost and topsoil in the mix. Top the bed with 2 to 3 inches of topsoil and/or compost for annual crops (more for perennial plants) and then plant seedlings directly into the topsoil/compost mix.

Intensive Gardening

Rich soil coupled with intensive gardening practices are what make raised bed gardening so successful. Intensive horticulture has been practiced for centuries in many parts of the world. In America, one of the best-known methods is French intensive gardening. Intensive gardening methods all have their own disciplines, but all use raised growing beds, close spacing between plants, careful attention to building and maintaining soil fertility, and succession planting to make the best use of available growing space.

Applied skillfully, intensive growing methods can (and consistently do) produce harvests 4 to 10 times greater than might be expected from a conventional garden. But intensive gardening also demands more initial work, planning, and scheduling than row gardens. If you wish to convert to intensive methods, it's best to start gradually. For example, you could try building one or two raised beds each gardening season for a few years.

Plantings managed using intensive planting systems require fertile, well-balanced soil rich in organic content. Without plentiful additions of compost along with soil amendments, intensively gardened soil soon loses its vitality. Cover crops or green manures also help keep the soil fertile. See the Fertilizers, Compost, Cover Crops, and Soil entries for more information on soil management.

Close Plant Spacing

One reason that raised beds are so productive is that they are planted intensively, putting as much as 80 percent of a garden's surface area into crop production. Pathways and spaces between crop rows make up the remainder. Plants are placed close together over the entire bed, usually in a triangular or staggered pattern, so that their leaves overlap slightly at maturity. This allows for more plants per square foot, and produces a continuous leafy canopy that shades the bed, moderates soil temperature, conserves moisture, and discourages weeds. Close spacing also means plantings must be carefully planned according to each crop's growing habits, including root spread, mature size, and water and nutrient needs.

Succession Planting

Another technique used to maximize harvests in raised bed gardens is succession planting, which is the practice of rapidly filling the space vacated by a harvested crop by planting a new crop. This can be as simple as following harvested cool-season spring vegetables, such as peas or spinach, with a planting of warm-season summer crops, such as beans or squash. Once harvested, those crops could be followed by a cold-tolerant fall crop such as spinach. Another technique is to stagger plantings at 1- or 2-week intervals to prolong the harvest. Advanced intensive gardeners also interplant compatible short-, mid-, and full-season vegetables in the same bed at the same time. They then harvest and replant the faster-growing plants two, three, or even four times during the season.

RASPBERRY

See Brambles

RHODODENDRON

Rhododendron, azalea. Spring- or summer-blooming broad-leaved evergreen or deciduous shrubs.

Description: *Rhododendron arborescens*, sweet azalea, is an upright, horizontally layered native deciduous shrub growing to 10 feet. Fragrant, trumpet-shaped white flowers appear in late spring. The leaves usually turn red before they fall. Zones 5–8.

R. calendulaceum, flame azalea, is an upright, layered native species growing 5 to 10 feet tall. Its orange-yellow to red flowers appear in spring either before or with the deciduous medium green leaves. Zones 5–8.

R. catawbiense, Catawba rhododendron, is a spreading native evergreen species with thick, leathery leaves, sometimes growing 15 feet or more, though usually closer to 6 feet. This native bears large trusses of lilac-colored blooms in late spring. Zones 4–7.

R. mucronulatum, Korean rhododendron, is a deciduous shrub growing to 8 feet. The purple flowers appear in late winter or early spring before the leaves. Zones 5–7.

R. schlippenbachii, royal azalea, is a deciduous species that blooms in late spring. Flowers are fragrant, pale to rose pink, and spotted in the throat with light red-brown. Grows to 15 feet; turns yellow to orange-red in fall. Zones 5–8.

R. yakushimanum, Yakushima rhododendron, is an evergreen with a mounded, compact habit,

growing 3 feet tall and wide. Pink or white flowers appear in late spring. Zones 6–7.

Hybrid rhododendrons and azaleas are extremely popular landscape plants and have been developed for flower form and color as well as other characteristics. There are groundcover azaleas that reach only 12 inches tall but spread to several feet wide, as well as rhododendrons and azaleas selected for their hardiness or tolerance of heat and humidity. For best results, look for hybrids recommended for your area and climate conditions.

How to grow: Provide azaleas and rhododendrons with partial to full shade, good drainage, even moisture, and humus-rich soil. Site evergreen rhododendrons out of direct wind and deadhead them when the blooms are spent, pruning only to remove dead wood or to correct stray branches. Deciduous azaleas rarely need pruning (except to remove dead wood), but evergreen azaleas usually need postbloom pruning to keep their size in scale. Azalea lace bugs are tiny insects that damage foliage by sucking sap from the undersides of leaves (use a hand lens to look for these bugs with lacy-looking wings or their spiny black nymphs). Leaves become splotched and grayish above, rusty below. Lace bugs can be especially troublesome on plants growing in sunny sites. Try washing them off plants with a strong spray of water or apply insecticidal soap. Fungi can attack rhododendron and azalea flowers and foliage, especially when conditions are wet or humid. Minimize these with good sanitation (fungal diseases often overwinter in ground litter) and by removing infected parts with pruners sanitized between cuts.

Landscape uses: Azaleas and rhododendrons are great in a woodland garden setting, either as specimens or in massed plantings.

RHUBARB

Rheum ×hybridum, R. rhabarbarum

Polygonaceae

Rhubarb is one of the kitchen garden's early spring treats. Weeks before the first strawberry ripens, you can enjoy the tart yet sweet flavor of rhubarb's celerylike red or green leaf stalks in pies, jams, and jellies. 'Victoria', 'Canada Red', and 'Valentine' are three popular varieties that produce red stalks. Don't eat the foliage, though: It's poisonous.

Rhubarb needs at least 2 months of cold weather and does best in areas with 2- to 3-inch-deep ground freezes and moist, cool springs.

Planting: Grow rhubarb from root divisions, called crowns, rather than from seed, which can produce plants that are not true to type. Three to six plants are plenty for most households.

Choose a sunny, well-drained, out-of-the-way spot for this long-lived perennial. Dig planting holes 3 feet wide and up to 3 feet deep to accommodate the mature roots. Mix the removed soil with generous amounts of aged manure and compost. Refill each hole to within 2 inches of the top, and set one crown in the center of each hole. Top off with the soil mix, tamp down well, and water thoroughly.

Growing guidelines: Once plants sprout, apply mulch to retain soil moisture and smother weeds. Renew mulch when the foliage dies down in fall to protect roots from extremely hard freezes. Provide enough water to keep roots from drying out, even when they're dormant. Side-dress with compost in midsummer and again in fall. Remove flowerstalks before they bloom to encourage leaf-stalk production. After several years, when plants become crowded and the leaf stalks are thin, dig up the roots in spring just as they sprout. Divide so that each crown has one to three eyes (buds); replant.

Problems: Rhubarb is usually pest-free. Occasionally it's attacked by European corn borers and cabbage worms; see page 454 for control ideas. A more likely pest is rhubarb curculio, a ¾-inch-long, rust-colored beetle that you can easily control by handpicking. To destroy its eggs, remove and destroy any nearby wild dock in July.

Diseases are also rare, but rhubarb can succumb to verticillium wilt, which yellows leaves early in the season and can wilt whole plants in late attacks. Crown rot occurs in shady, soggy soil. For either disease, remove and destroy infected plants; keep stalks thinned to promote good air circulation, and clean up thoroughly around crowns in fall. If stands become seriously diseased, destroy the entire stand. Replant disease-free stock in a new location. 'MacDonald' is a rot-resistant variety that grows well in heavy soils.

Harvesting: In spring when the leaves are fully developed, twist and pull stalks from the crowns. Don't harvest any the first year, though, and take only those that are at least 1 inch thick the second year. By the third year, you can harvest for 1 to 2 months. After the third year, pick all you can eat.

ROCK GARDENS

A rock garden can add natural beauty to a landscape in a way few other gardens can. The best rock gardens start with a natural-looking construction of rocks that is planted with a wide variety of tiny, low-growing plants with colorful flowers.

There are many ways to incorporate a rock garden into your landscape.

🌿 Build one on a natural slope, like a steep bank that's awkward to mow.

🌿 Use rocks to build a slope and add interest to a flat yard.

🌿 Design one near a pond.

🌿 Use dwarf evergreens or a clump of birches as a background for a rock garden.

🌿 Plant a rock garden on a rock outcrop or in a woodland area.

🌿 Make a raised bed for rock plants edged with stone or landscape ties.

Design and Construction

A site with full sun or morning sun and dappled afternoon shade is best. If your property is mostly shaded, you still can have a lovely rock garden—choose dwarf, shade-loving perennials, wildflowers, and ferns. Good drainage is an important concern. Most rock garden plants grow best in very well-drained soil high in organic matter—a mixture of equal parts topsoil, humus, and gravel, for example. Plants like moisture about their deep roots but can't tolerate constantly wet soil.

Stone that is native to your area will look most natural and will be easiest and cheapest to obtain. Stick to one type of rock, repeating the same color and texture throughout to unify the design. Weathered, neutral gray, or tan rocks are ideal. Limestone and sandstone are popular.

If you don't have enough rocks in your own yard, other good sources are nearby landowners, rock yards, and quarries. Try to pick out the rocks yourself. Choose mostly large, irregular shapes. Be sure to get some large and some midsize rocks, but keep in mind you'll need smaller sizes, too.

Plan your garden before you start moving rocks, although you'll modify the design as you build. A good way to visualize your plan is to make a 3-D scale model with small stones and sand on a large tray. Mound the sand and arrange your rocks in the model. You might start with a photograph of a favorite mountain scene. Decide how many rocks—and what sizes—you'll need, and plan for a path or large rock stepping-stones for working in the garden and viewing the plants. Keep working until you find a design you like. The key to a successful rock garden—one that is harmonious and natural looking—is studied irregularity.

To begin construction, mark out the area you've selected, remove any weeds or sod, and excavate to a depth of a foot or so. Save the soil for fill. You'll need extra topsoil for filling in between rocks and building up level areas. If you need to improve drainage, lay in about 8 inches of rubble or small rocks, and cover it with coarse gravel. You may have to remove more soil to accommodate this layer.

You'll need a garden cart or small dolly to move good-sized rocks, or use iron pipes about 4 inches in diameter as rollers. Use a crowbar for a lever and a block of wood for a fulcrum to position rocks. For massive rocks, a professional with a backhoe might be the answer.

On a flat site, first place large stones on the perimeter to form the garden's foundation. On a sloping site, place the largest, most attractive rock, the keystone, first. As you work, be sure each rock is stable. Place the wider, heavier part down, and angle rocks to channel water back into the garden. When placing rocks, dig a hole larger than the rock to allow room for moving it into the best position. For the most natural look, lay the rocks so lines in them run horizontally and are parallel throughout the garden.

After positioning each rock, shovel soil around it, ramming it in with a pole so each rock is firmly anchored. Bury a good portion of each rock—two-thirds is traditional—for a natural effect.

Plants for Rock Gardens

There are literally hundreds of easy-to-grow rock garden plants. The following are good choices for a garden in full sun.

Dwarf shrubs: Consider dwarf and low-growing forms of evergreens such as false cypresses (*Chamaecyparis* spp.), junipers (*Juniperus* spp.), spruces (*Picea* spp.), pines (*Pinus* spp.), and hemlocks (*Tsuga* spp.). Or look for dwarf or creeping natives such as bearberry (*Arctostaphylos uva-ursi*), winterberries and inkberries (*Ilex* spp.), and azaleas (*Rhododendron* spp.).

Perennials: Perennials with evergreen foliage also add winter interest. Consider sedums (*Sedum* spp.), stonecrops (*Hylotelephium* spp.), hens and chickens (*Sempervivum* spp.), and candytuft (*Iberis sempervirens*). Spring- and summer-blooming perennials include basket-of-gold (*Aurinia saxatilis*), creeping phlox (*Phlox subulata*), dwarf bellflowers (*Campanula* spp.),

pinks (*Dianthus* spp.), catmints (*Nepeta* spp.), and thymes (*Thymus* spp.). Windflowers (*Anemone* spp.), primroses (*Primula* spp.), and columbines (*Aquilegia* spp.), are fine choices, too. Consider ferns, hostas, shade-loving wildflowers, and hardy bulbs for a garden in a shady spot. There are many diminutive hardy bulbs for rock gardens in sun or shade, including dwarf daffodils (*Narcissus* spp.), squills (*Scilla* spp.), and snowdrops (*Galanthus* spp.).

Visit local rock gardens—especially in spring—to get ideas about what will grow in your area. The Internet, garden catalogs, books, and magazines are good sources, too. The North American Rock Garden Society has an excellent publication, a seed exchange, regional meetings, and also local chapters, many of which hold annual plant sales; see Resources on page 673 for contact information.

Continue adding tiers of rocks in the same manner until you've reached the top of the garden. As you work, try to create miniature ridges and valleys and intersperse small, level areas to make an interesting design and provide space for plants. End with a series of flat ledges at different levels rather than a peak.

After you've placed all the rocks, shovel soil mix under and around them, making deep planting pockets. A good basic mix is one-third topsoil, one-third humuslike screened leaf mold, and one-third gravel. Tamp it in, wait a week for the soil to settle, and add more to fill to the desired level.

Planting and Care

Plan your planting scheme with tracing paper over a scale drawing of your rock garden, or use labeled sheets of paper and lay out your "plants" right where they'll grow in the garden. Adjust your design as you visualize it for each season. Record your decisions on paper or with a garden-design app or software. Allow low, creeping plants like small bellflowers (*Campanula* spp.) and thymes (*Thymus* spp.) to cascade over rocks. Wedge rosette-forming plants such as hens-and-chickens (*Sempervivum* spp.) into vertical crevices. Fill open spaces with mats of ajuga (*Ajuga reptans*), pussy-toes (*Antennaria* spp.), or sedums (*Sedum* spp.). Use upright stonecrops (*Hylotelephium* spp.) or dwarf shrubs to soften the harshness of rocks.

Once planted, all the garden requires in return is faithful weeding, watering during extended droughts, and light pruning. A 1-inch layer of very small pea gravel or granite chips helps conserve moisture, keeps the soil cool, reduces weeds, keeps soil off foliage, and prevents crown rot. Spread the gravel up to, but not over, the crown of each plant. Use chopped leaves to mulch woodland rock gardens.

ROSA

Rose. Summer-blooming deciduous shrubs.

The rose is the best-loved flower of all time, a symbol of beauty and love. Roses have it all—color, fragrance, and great shape. Many roses produce flowers from early summer until frost, often beginning in the year they're planted. Some also produce showy scarlet or orange fruits called rose hips that are high in vitamin C and are used in teas and jams. Some roses also have ornamental foliage that is reddish, blue-gray, or purple, and some also turn red, orange, or gold in fall.

Over the years, roses have gained a reputation for being difficult to grow. But many of the "old roses," plus a great number of the newer cultivars, especially the "landscape roses," are disease-resistant, widely adaptable plants able to withstand cold winters and hot summers.

Selecting Roses

Members of the genus *Rosa* are prickly stemmed (thorny) shrubs with a wide range of heights and growth habits. There are as many as 200 species and thousands of cultivars. With so many roses available, deciding on the ones you want can be a challenge. This large, diverse genus can be divided into four major types: bush, climbing, shrub, and groundcover roses.

Bush roses: Bush roses form the largest category, which has been divided into seven subgroups: hybrid tea, polyantha, floribunda, grandiflora, miniature, heritage (old), and tree (standard) roses.

🌿 Hybrid tea roses usually have narrow buds, borne singly on a long stem, with large, many-petaled flowers on plants 3 to 5 feet tall. They bloom repeatedly over the entire growing season.

🌿 Polyantha roses are short, compact plants with small flowers produced abundantly in large clusters throughout the growing season. Plants are very hardy and easy to grow.

🌿 Floribunda roses were derived from crosses between hybrid teas and polyanthas. They are hardy, compact, easily grown plants with medium-size flowers borne profusely in short-stemmed clusters all summer long.

🌿 Grandiflora roses are usually tall (5 to 6 feet), narrow plants bearing large flowers in long-stemmed clusters from summer through fall.

🌿 Miniature roses are diminutive, with both flowers and foliage proportionately smaller. Most are quite hardy and bloom freely and repeatedly.

🌿 Heritage (old) roses are a widely diverse group of cultivars developed prior to 1867, the date of the introduction of the hybrid tea rose. Plant and flower forms, hardiness, and ease of growth vary considerably; some bloom only once, while others flower repeatedly. Among the most popular are the albas, bourbons, centifolias, damasks, gallicas, mosses, and Portlands. Some species roses are also included in this category.

🌿 Tree (standard) roses are created when any rose is bud-grafted onto a specially grown trunk 1 to 6 feet tall to form a "tree" shape.

Climbing roses: Roses don't truly climb, but the long, flexible canes of certain roses make it possible to attach them to supports such as fences, posts, arbors, and trellises. The two main types are large-flowered climbers, with thick, sturdy canes growing to 10 feet long and blooms produced throughout summer, and ramblers, with thin canes growing 20 feet or more and clusters of small flowers borne in early summer.

Shrub roses: Shrub roses grow broadly upright with numerous arching canes reaching 4 to 12 feet tall. Most are very hardy and easily grown. Some only bloom once in early summer, while others bloom repeatedly. Many produce showy red or scarlet fruits called hips. Some species roses are considered shrub roses.

Groundcover roses: Groundcover roses have prostrate, creeping canes producing low mounds; there are once-blooming and repeat-blooming cultivars.

Landscape roses: Groundcover roses are sometimes included with easy-care shrub roses in a category called landscape roses that are renowned for toughness and low maintenance. Roses like the Knock Out, Carefree, and Simplicity series of shrub roses and the Flower Carpet and Baby Blanket series of groundcovers, as well as individual cultivars like Bonica ('Meidomonac') and the award-winning floribunda rose Livin' Easy ('HARwelcome'), are disease resistant, long

blooming, and require minimal pruning. They're a great choice if you'd like the beauty of roses in your landscape without the fussiness of many hybrid teas.

Using Roses in the Landscape

To grow well, roses need a site that gets full sun at least 6 hours a day, humus-rich soil, and good drainage. If these conditions are met, you can use roses just about anywhere in the landscape. Try roses in foundation plantings, shrub borders, along walks and driveways, surrounding patios, decks, and terraces, or in flowerbeds and borders. Combine roses with other plants, especially other shrubs, perennials, and ornamental herbs, and try planting them in containers, too.

Use climbing roses to cover walls, screen or frame views, or decorate fences, arbors, trellises, and gazebos. Grow groundcover roses on banks or trailing over walls. Plant hedges of shrub, grandiflora, and floribunda roses.

Growing Good Roses

The key to growing roses is to remember they need plenty of water, humus, and nutrients.

Soil: Prepare a new site in fall for planting the following spring, or in summer for fall planting. If you plan to grow roses in an existing planting, then no special preparation is needed. For a new site, dig or till the soil to a depth of at least 1 foot. Evenly distribute a 4-inch layer of organic material such as compost, leaf mold, or dehydrated cow manure over the soil surface. Also spread on organic fertilizer. A general recommendation is to add 5 pounds of bonemeal and 10 pounds of greensand or granite dust per 100 square feet. Dig or till the fertilizer and soil amendments into the soil.

SMART SHOPPING

Roses

Whether they're sold locally or by mail order, roses are sold by grade, which is based on the size and number of canes. Top-grade #1 plants grow fastest and produce the most blooms when young. The #11/2-grade plants are also healthy and vigorous. Avoid #2-grade plants, which require extra care. Rose grades are usually listed only for bareroot roses, while container-grown roses are typically listed by the size of the container (for example, 3 gallons).

You can buy either dormant, bareroot roses or container-grown plants. Both mail-order companies and local outlets sell dormant plants, offering the widest range of cultivars. Healthy dormant plants have smooth, plump, green or red canes. Avoid plants with dried out, shriveled, wrinkled, or sprouted canes.

One excellent resource for information about roses is the American Rose Society, which publishes the *Handbook for Selecting Roses*, updated every year, with a listing of rose cultivars rated for quality. Another is the *Combined Rose List*, which lists all roses available, with their sources; it is also updated annually.

Roses that have been awarded the All-America Rose Selections (AARS) seal of approval or those that have been honored by American Garden Rose Selections (AGRS) have been recognized for their desirable qualities. To learn more, see Resources on page 673.

Planting: For much of the West Coast, South, and Southwest, or wherever winter temperatures remain above 10°F, plant bareroot roses in January and February. In slightly colder areas, fall planting gives roses a chance to establish a sturdy root system before growth starts. In areas with very cold winters, plant bareroot roses in spring, several weeks before the last frost. For all but miniature and shrub roses, space roses 2 to 3 feet apart in colder areas, 3 to 4 feet apart in warmer regions, where they'll grow larger. Space miniatures 1 to 2 feet apart, shrub roses 4 to 6 feet apart.

To plant bareroot roses, dig each hole 15 to 18 inches wide and deep, or large enough for roots to spread out. Form a soil cone in the planting hole. Removing any broken or damaged roots or canes, position the rose on the cone, spreading out the roots. If you are planting a grafted rose, place the bud union (the point where the cultivar is grafted onto its rootstock) even with the soil surface in mild climates and 1 to 2 inches below the soil surface in areas where temperatures fall below freezing.

Add soil around the roots, making sure there are no air pockets, until the hole is three-quarters full. Fill the hole with water, allow it to soak in, and refill. Make sure the bud union is at the correct level. Finish filling the hole with soil and

Rose Pests and Diseases

Your best defense against rose problems is to buy healthy, disease-resistant roses and to plant them where there's good air circulation. Be diligent about preventive maintenance, such as destroying diseased foliage and flowers immediately and cleaning up around roses in fall. Control pests as soon as you see them. If a rose suffers from repeated pest or disease problems, your best course of action is to get rid of that rose and try another—preferably a disease-resistant variety.

These are the rose pests and diseases you're most likely to encounter.

Aphids: These tiny insects cluster on new growth, causing deformed or stunted leaves and covering buds with sticky residue. Control with a strong blast of water or spray with insecticidal soap.

Borers: Larvae of rose stem girdler, rose stem sawfly, or carpenter bees bore holes in rose canes; new growth wilts. Prune off damaged canes and seal ends with putty, paraffin, or nail polish.

Japanese beetles: Handpick beetles every day while they're in the area and drop them in a bucket of soapy water. Spray roses with neem oil to deter beetle feeding.

For more control tips, see page 454.

Spider mites: These tiny spiderlike creatures cause yellowed, curled leaves with fine webs on the undersides. Spray in early morning with a strong jet of water for 3 days, or use insecticidal soap. Be sure to spray the undersides of the leaves.

Blackspot: This fungal disease causes black spots and yellowed leaves; defoliation is worst during wet weather. Prune off all damaged plant parts, don't splash foliage when watering, water in the morning, and spray every 10 to 14 days with neem oil, with fungicidal soap, or a bicarbonate fungicide. Avoid problems by choosing blackspot-resistant roses.

Powdery mildew: This coating of white powder on leaves, stems, and buds is worst in hot, humid (but not wet) weather with cool nights. Provide good air circulation; prune off infected plant parts; and treat with fungicidal soap or neem oil.

Rust: This disease causes red-orange spots on the undersides of leaves and yellow blotches on top surfaces. Prune off infected plant parts; spray with fungicidal soap or neem oil.

lightly tamp it down. Trim canes back to 8 inches, making cuts ¼ inch above an outward-facing bud and at a 45-degree angle. To prevent the canes from drying out, lightly mound moist soil over the rosebush. Gently remove the soil when growth starts in 1 to 2 weeks.

Plant container-grown roses as you would any container plant. For more on this technique, see the Planting entry.

Water: Ample water, combined with good drainage, is fundamental to rose growth. The key is to water slowly and deeply, soaking the ground at least 16 inches deep with each watering. Water in the early morning, so if foliage gets wet, it can dry quickly. Use a soaker hose, drip irrigation system, or a hose with a bubbler attachment on the end. Water roses grown in containers much more frequently. Check containers daily during summer.

Mulch: An organic mulch conserves moisture, improves the garden's appearance, inhibits weed growth, keeps the soil cool, and slowly adds nutrients to the soil. Spread 2 to 4 inches of mulch evenly around the plants, leaving several inches unmulched around the stem of each rose.

Fertilizing: Feed newly planted roses 4 to 6 weeks after planting. After that, for roses that bloom once a year, fertilize in early spring. Feed established, repeat-blooming roses three times a year: in early spring just as the growth starts, in early summer when flower buds have formed, and about 6 weeks before the first fall frost. The last feeding should not contain nitrogen.

For all but the last feeding in fall, use a commercial, balanced organic plant food containing nitrogen, phosphorus, and potassium, or mix your own, combining two parts bloodmeal, one part rock phosphate, and four parts wood ashes for a 4-5-4 fertilizer. This mix, minus the bloodmeal, also works well as a fall fertilizer. Use about ½ cup for each plant, scratching it into the soil around the plant and watering well. As an alternative, apply dehydrated cow manure and bonemeal in spring and use fish emulsion for the other feedings.

Pruning: Prune in early spring to keep hybrid tea, grandiflora, and floribunda roses vigorous and blooming. Many of the newer, shrub-type ("landscape") roses need very little pruning; simply remove dead canes and any canes that are growing where you don't want them. Heritage, species, and climbing roses that bloom once a year bear flowers on the previous year's growth. Prune these as soon as blooming is over, cutting the main shoots back a third and removing any small, twiggy growth.

Remove suckers coming up from the rootstock of any grafted rose whenever you see them.

In the first pruning of the season, just as growth starts, remove any dead or damaged wood back to healthy, white-centered wood. Make each pruning cut at an angle ¼ inch above an outward-facing bud eye, which is a dormant growing point at the base of a leaf stalk. This stimulates outward-facing new growth. Also remove any weak or crossing canes. Later in the season, remove any diseased growth and faded flowers on repeat-blooming roses, cutting the stem just above the first five-leaflet leaf below the flower.

Winter protection: Most landscape roses and many shrub roses as well as some of the polyanthas, floribundas, and miniatures need only minimal winter protection. Hybrid teas, grandifloras, and some floribundas and heritage roses usually require more. If you're growing these cold-sensitive plants in your garden, protect them according to the following recommendations.

In areas with winter temperatures no lower than 20°F, no winter protection is necessary. Elsewhere, apply winter protection after the first frost and just before the first hard freeze. Remove all leaves from the plants and from the ground around them and destroy them. Apply ¼ cup of greensand around each plant and water well. Prune plants to half their height and tie canes together with twine.

Where winter temperatures drop to 0°F, make an 8-inch mound of coarse compost, shredded bark, leaves, or soil around the base of each plant. In colder areas, make the mound 1 foot deep. Provide extra protection with another layer of pine needles or branches, straw, or leaves. Where temperatures reach −5°F or colder, remove the canes of large-flowered, repeat-blooming climbers from supports, lay them on the ground, and cover both the base and the canes.

ROW COVERS

It is the rare gardener who finds the growing season long enough. Fortunately, gardeners can satisfy the itch to plant early and to keep crops producing through fall by using row covers. Made of light, permeable material, usually polypropylene or polyester, row covers can be laid loosely on top of plants or supported with wire hoops. They're available in different weights that provide varying degrees of frost protection.

Floating row cover: The lightest-weight row covers, also called floating row covers, allow air, water, and up to 85 percent of ambient light to pass through. They provide only a few degrees of frost protection, but they are an excellent barrier against damage by a wide range of pests.

You can cover newly seeded beds or pest-free transplants with floating row covers, leaving plenty of slack in the material to allow for growth. Be sure to bury the edges in the soil or seal them in some other way. Otherwise, pests will sneak in and thrive in the protected environment.

You can leave row covers over some crops, such as carrots or onions, all season. Uncover other crops, such as beans or cabbage, once the plants are well grown or the generation of pests is past. Plants such as squash that require pollination by insects must be either uncovered when they start to flower or hand-pollinated. In a hot climate, you may have to remove covers to prevent excessive heat buildup.

Heavier covers: Gardeners can also use heavier row covers to protect plants from freezing and extend the gardening season. These row covers can provide as much as 8 degrees of frost protection. They also block more light, so plants underneath them may not grow as quickly. Or you can get a similar effect to heavy covers by using two layers of a lighter-weight cover.

Plastic row covers: Row covers made of plastic or slitted plastic require careful management because temperatures under plastic row covers can be as much as 30°F higher than the surrounding air. You will need to vent them on warm days and close them back up at night. Slitted plastic row covers don't require venting. Colored or shaded plastic covers are available for southern gardeners. The coloring blocks out some of the sunlight, reducing the heat inside the tunnel. Suspend plastic row covers over the row with metal, plastic, wire, or wooden hoops to prevent injuring plants. Anchor row cover edges securely in place with soil, boards, pipes, or similar material.

Handling Row Covers

Working with fabric row covers may seem awkward at first, because the lightweight fabric tends to blow around while you're putting it in place if there's even a small breeze. The fabric also tears easily on sharp edges. But with a little experience, you'll learn how to work with the material. Here are some tips for getting the best from row covers:

Row covers are available in small pieces that are easy to manage, but it's more economical to buy a larger roll and cut pieces to fit as you need them.

The quick and easy way to anchor row cover is with rocks or soil, but this also tends to tear the fabric quickly. Instead, try using plastic soda bottles partially filled with water as weights, or make "sandbags" by filling plastic shopping bags partway with soil.

Wire hoops, which you can buy from garden suppliers or make yourself from 9-gauge wire, are perfect for supporting row covers over garden beds. Use hoops both under and over the fabric to hold it in place.

At the end of the season, shake the covers to

Supporting row covers. If you don't want to fuss with wire hoops to support row covers, use plastic soda bottles as "tent poles" instead. Put some water in each bottle, cap it tightly, and upend the bottles between rows of plants to support the cover above the foliage.

loosen dirt and debris, and make sure they're dry. Fold or roll them and store them in a plastic storage bin for winter, either in a garden shed or outdoors. Weight the cover of the tub with rocks or bricks to keep it tightly closed.

If a piece of row cover is torn in several places, cut it up into small pieces for patching larger sections of cover that have small holes. Waxed dental floss works well for "sewing" the patches.

To protect upright plants with row cover, put a small tomato cage in place around the plant and wrap row cover fabric around the cage, pinning it in place with clothespins.

RUDBECKIA

Coneflower, black-eyed Susan. Summer-blooming annuals and perennials.

Description: Summer-blooming annual *Rudbeckia hirta*, black-eyed Susan, bears single yellow, dark-centered daisies on 3-foot stems. The beloved cottage and cutting garden staples, Gloriosa daisies, with their marvelous blends of gold, orange, reddish, and mahogany petals on daisies up to 6 inches across, are a strain of this species; like black-eyed Susans, they bloom the first year from seed and are usually treated as annuals, though they may live a second or even third year if left in place.

Perennial *R. fulgida*, orange coneflower, bears 3- to 4-inch single, dark-centered gold daisies on 1½- to 3-foot plants in late summer and autumn. *R. fulgida* var. *sullivantii* 'Goldsturm' is a widely grown, very floriferous cultivar, often grown from seed. Zones 3–9.

How to grow: Coneflowers need a sunny spot with average to rich, well-drained soil. Sow annuals indoors in spring to set out after frost. Plant perennials in spring or fall. Divide every 3 to 4 years; deadhead to avoid self-seeding unless you want them to spread in a meadow or prairie garden. Mildew can be an issue on the foliage, so avoid overhead watering and don't crowd the plants.

Landscape uses: Mass in borders with other summer bloomers, in informal plantings, and cutting gardens. Coneflowers are naturals for the meadow or prairie garden, where their showy blooms add welcome color. Leave them standing in the meadow or prairie until spring—birds (including goldfinches) love the seeds, and the cones will remain showy through winter.

RUTABAGA

See Turnip

S

SAGE

Salvia officinalis
Lamiaceae

Description: Culinary sage is a small, 2- to 3-foot shrub with woody stems. It has pebbly, grayish green leaves, spikes of lavender flowers, and a warm, spicy, earthy flavor that characterizes sausage and turkey stuffing. Ordinary sage is best for culinary purposes, but there are several ornamental cultivars worth the space in your herb or kitchen garden, among them 'Berggarten', with broad oval leaves and showy, blue-violet flowers; 'Icterina' (aka 'Aurea'), with green-and-yellow variegated leaves; 'Purpurascens' (aka 'Purpurea'), with purple-tinged green foliage; and 'Tricolor', with variegated pink, purple, white, and green leaves. Zones 3–9, although variegated cultivars may be less hardy than the species. For information on ornamental sages, see the Salvia entry.

How to grow: Culinary sage craves sun, good drainage, and average, not overly rich soil. Grow it from seed, or divide plants that are at least 2 years old. Prune in spring to keep plants shapely and strong.

Harvesting: Clip off leaves and stems throughout the growing season for culinary use. Dry individual leaves on trays in a food dehydrator or hang stems in a warm, dark, dry place like an attic to dry, then strip off leaves and store for future use. Avoid cutting back drastically in fall.

Uses: Try sage with poultry, in sausage and stuffing, with veal, fish, and liver, and in cheese and egg dishes. Perk up cooked vegetables like carrots, asparagus, tomatoes, and cabbage with a crumbling of dried leaves. If you drink tea made with dried sage leaves, according to the herbalists, you will never grow old. The dried leaves, if left on their branchlets, are wonderful in herb wreaths.

SALAD GREENS

Growing salad greens other than lettuce is no harder than growing lettuce, and in many cases, a lot easier. (See the Lettuce entry for lettuce-growing tips and types.) Creating a salad that's bursting with flavor and color is an art, but since most salad greens and enhancements go well together, it's hard to go wrong. And fortunately, most seed companies now carry a wide range of mixes and individual species and cultivars that take the guesswork out of growing salad greens.

Salad Essentials

If you want to go beyond lettuce, try these delicious greens in your salads. You can eat some of them—spinach, arugula, and bok choy, for example—on their own, or mix them with lettuces and other greens like radicchio and mustard greens to give your salads spice and depth. Mesclun can also be the base of a salad or be mixed in with other greens. And don't forget red, green, and savoy cabbages, which are excellent as accents in tossed salads or in starring roles in coleslaw. (See the Cabbage entry for more on growing and using cabbage.)

Arugula (*Eruca vesicaria* ssp. *sativa*): Also called rocket and roquette. Rich, peppery flavor. Sow seed in early spring or fall, thinning seedlings to space plants 4 to 6 inches apart with 10 inches between rows. Use thinnings in salads, and start harvesting mature greens in 6 to 8 weeks. Tends to bolt quickly in hot, dry weather.

Bok choy (*Brassica rapa* var. *chinensis*): Also called bok choi and pak choi. Attractive cabbage relatives with long, thick white stems and dark green leaves. Young bok choy is delicious in salads and makes a succulent coleslaw. Sow seed in early spring or fall; grow like cabbage. (See the Cabbage entry.) Plants prefer cool growing conditions. 'Joi Choi' is a more heat-tolerant cultivar. Space plants 8 to 12 inches apart in the row and 12 inches between rows. Harvest entire small heads or larger individual leaves.

Chicory (*Cichorium intybus*): A relative of endive and escarole, chicory (also called witloof chicory or Belgian endive) is delicious as a winter salad green when forced indoors. See the Endive entry for details on growing and forcing chicory.

Endive and escarole (*Cichorium endivia*): The lacy, cream green, frilly leaves of endive are often called frisée, while the broad-leaved forms are often sold as escarole. Start these bitter greens indoors for an early summer harvest or in the garden in summer for an autumn crop, thinning plants to stand a foot apart. (*Note:* That touch of bitterness is prized in Europe, adding sophistication to a potentially bland salad.) Blanch plants for a buttery color and milder flavor. For more on growing and harvesting endive and escarole, see the Endive entry.

Kale (*Brassica oleracea*, Acephala Group): Kale adds substance, color, and nutrition to a salad—the thick, blue-green, purple-green, green-black, or white-green leaves are packed with vitamins and minerals. Some cultivars are deeply frilled while others are deeply puckered; all add texture and variety to a mixed salad. Sow in early spring or late summer, thinning plants to 2 feet apart. Harvest the young leaves individually for salads. See the Kale entry for more on growing and harvesting kale.

Mizuna (*Brassica juncea* var. *japonica*): Attractive, compact green plant matures in 35 days, tolerates heat, and is easy to grow. Serrated leaves add a cabbagy, mustardy flavor to salads. Sow seed in early spring; grow like spinach (see the Spinach entry).

Mustard greens (*Brassica juncea*): Attractive red or green loose-leaf or heading mustards. Loose-leaf types mature in 45 days; heading mustards need 60 to 75 days to head up. Plants tolerate heat and light frost, and they're easy to grow. Leaves of

Mesclun Mixes

Mesclun isn't the name of a plant—it's a term for a mix of salad greens that are harvested and eaten together. The greens are sown close together and picked young, like spring mix. Because of mesclun's popularity, most seed companies sell their own custom mesclun mixes. The composition of mixes varies: Some lean toward spicy, with lots of arugula and mustard greens; others are slightly bitter, going heavy on the radicchio and endive. Still other mixes focus on creating the most colorful combination.

It pays to read the packet or catalog descriptions and see what's in a given mix before deciding which one to choose. It should also tell you the percentage of each type of seed, so you can see the actual composition of a mix before you make your selection. Here are three representative mesclun mixes to give you an idea of what's available—or in case you want to mix up your own. There are many more!

Mesclun Salad Mix

'Ruby' lettuce

'Royal Oak Leaf' lettuce

'Red Salad Bowl' lettuce

Curled chervil

'Green Ice' lettuce

'Paris White Cos' lettuce

Mesclun Spicy Mix

'Red Salad Bowl' lettuce

'Rossa di Treviso' radicchio

Mizuna

'Rocket' arugula

'Green Curled' endive

European Mesclun Mix

Mix of colorful lettuce cultivars

Mizuna

Radicchio

Kale

Arugula

Mustard greens

Endive

Corn salad (mâche)

Orach

Oriental mustard cultivars tend not to be as hot or biting as southern mustard greens. Direct-seed in early spring or fall, barely covering with soil. Space plants 6 inches apart in the row, thinning to 10 inches; leave 10 to 12 inches between rows.

Radicchio (*Cichorium intybus*): This bitter Italian heading chicory has become a favorite of salad lovers everywhere. Its gorgeous deep garnet, white-based leaves add rich color and texture to salads, and the flavor adds sophistication. Start indoors as with endive and escarole for spring planting; space 6 inches apart when you transplant them outdoors. Plants form tight, 4-inch heads. See the Endive entry for more on planting and growing.

Spinach (*Spinacia oleracea*): This salad staple can be harvested when the leaves are small ("baby spinach") to use whole in salads or when they're mature. Sow seed in early spring and late summer for spring and fall crops, thinning to 4 to 6 inches apart. (Use thinnings in salads or stir-fries.) Spinach is rich in vitamins and minerals, so it's one of the healthiest salad choices. See the Spinach entry for more on growing and harvesting spinach.

Growing Guidelines

Salad greens enjoy the same growing conditions as lettuce: humus-rich, evenly moist but well-drained soil. Greens typically grow best in cool weather; hot weather makes them bolt to seed or, with plants like mustard greens, develop a more fiery flavor than plants grown in cooler spring or fall weather. Broadcast the seeds of salad greens and rake lightly to cover them, or sow seeds ¼ inch apart and as thinly as possible in rows 1½ feet apart. Sow in spring once the soil has reached at least 35°F, and again in late summer for a fall crop.

For the most beautiful salad greens you can imagine, cover seeded areas with floating row cover and leave the cover in place throughout the duration of the crop. The greens will retain their color and tenderness better under the protection of the cover. Check underneath occasionally to remove weeds (which will also enjoy the sheltered environment) and to handpick any slugs that might have found the crop.

When the seedlings have four leaves, thin plants to 6 inches apart. Make sure the crop gets at least 1 inch of water a week from rain or irrigation. To help prevent disease, try to water on sunny mornings, so the leaves can dry by evening. If you aren't using row

---

Salad Enhancements

There's no reason to limit your salad-growing exploits to the main crops. Add additional excitement to your salads with fresh leaves of the plants in this list. All add distinctive, delicious bites of flavor that will give your salads depth and take them from good to great. Nasturtium and chive flowers also are edible and will give your salads added beauty. See the Onion entry for tips on growing scallions; for the herbs, see the Herbs entry.

Basil	Parsley
Chives	Pepper cress
Cilantro	Scallions
Garlic chives	Sorrel
Mint	Thyme
Nasturtium	Watercress

---

cover, apply a thick layer of mulch to conserve moisture, suffocate weeds around the easily damaged roots, and keep leaves free of dirt. To promote quick growth, side-dress with compost tea or fish emulsion once or twice during the growing season. See the Lettuce entry for more growing guidelines.

SALIX

Willow. Deciduous single- or multistemmed trees or shrubs.

Description: This genus is best known for "weeping willows," a term applied to several species and cultivars with pendulous branches.

Salix alba, white willow, is an upright tree growing to 75 feet. Its slender, pliant branches turn an intense yellow as sap rises in spring. Leaves and catkins follow. Zones 2–8.

S. caprea, goat willow, is often confused with *S. discolor*, pussy willow. Both species bear the fuzzy male catkins for which pussy willow is named; both are shrubby small trees that can grow to 25 feet tall and 15 feet wide. Zones 4–8.

S. matsudana, Peking willow, grows to 40 feet. It is best known for the cultivar 'Tortuosa', corkscrew willow, which has contorted branches and a gnarled appearance. Zones 5–8.

How to grow: Willows grow naturally at streamside and perform best in sunny, moist locations. Willow wood is brittle, and branches often break under ice or snow. Because willows have invasive roots, plant them far away from septic systems, underground water pipes, and drains.

Landscape uses: Willows make fine accent plants and mood setters for watery or low-lying areas.

SALVIA

Salvia, ornamental sage. Summer- and fall-blooming annuals and perennials.

Description: Annual *Salvia splendens*, scarlet sage, flaunts brilliant red two-lipped blooms in spikes 8 to 30 inches over dark green leaves. Many cultivars are available in all shades of red as well as scarlet, pink, white, burgundy, salmon, and lilac.

Many other annual and tender perennial salvias are now available to add panache to the garden, including *S. greggii*, autumn sage (Gregg's sage), and *S. leucantha*, velvet sage (Mexican bush sage). Both are shrubby plants that will survive winters in Zones 8–10; autumn sage may survive in Zone 7, though it's often killed back to the ground in winter. And

for the herb garden or a container, *S. elegans*, pineapple sage, is indispensable with its fruit-scented leaves and spikes of brilliant scarlet flowers. Zones 8–11.

Perennial salvias are staples of the summer flower border. *S. nemorosa*, woodland sage, bears numerous upright spikes of violet-blue flowers in early to midsummer over bushy plants that reach 1½ to 3 feet tall, depending on the cultivar. 'East Friesland' (aka 'Ostfriesland', deep purple) and 'Caradonna' (blue-violet) are two of the best cultivars of this species. Zones 4–8. The similar *S. ×sylvestris*, wood sage, bears blue-purple flowers in plumy spikes to 2 feet above mounded leaves; some cultivars have white flowers. Purple-flowered May Night ('Mainacht') is a beloved cultivar. Zones 4–7.

See the Sage entry for information on the culinary species.

How to grow: Salvias grow best in full sun to very light shade and average, well-drained soil. Sow scarlet sage in early spring to plant out after the last frost, or buy bedding plants. Plant or divide perennial sage every third year in spring or fall. Deadhead for rebloom. Mulch tender perennial sage in fall to improve its chances of survival, removing mulch when growth resumes. Cut salvias back in early spring to rejuvenate them.

Landscape uses: Plant a solid bed of scarlet sage or group with other bright colors in a border. Use perennials in a border or cottage garden. All salvias are hummingbird magnets, so be sure to include some in your hummingbird garden, or grow some in containers on the deck or patio to lure hummingbirds closer to the house.

SEASON EXTENSION

Thanks to the ingenuity of market gardeners, plant breeders, and garden product designers, any gardener can enjoy growing plants well beyond the start and end of the traditional gardening season. Season extension materials can be as simple as a modified plastic milk jug or as grand as a greenhouse, and you can extend the season by growing everything from houseplants and bulbs to herbs and vegetables.

Extending the Season Outdoors

Season extenders are materials or structures used to keep the air and soil around plants warmer. Backyard gardeners have used cold frames, cloches, and hot caps as season extenders for generations.

Organic market gardeners have raised season extension to an art form with the use of large plastic-covered structures called high tunnels, using a second layer of coverings inside the plastic tunnels to keep hardy crops such as spinach and kale producing nearly year-round in areas as chilly as Zone 5.

One simple way to extend the growing season outdoors is to start seedlings indoors ahead of the traditional schedule, and then plant the seedlings outdoors with individual cloches for protection. On a larger scale, you can use heavyweight row covers supported by wire hoops, switching to lighter-weight covers as the weather warms up. You can also reverse this process in fall, planting crops in late summer and covering them once the weather turns cool.

Keep in mind that season extenders such as cloches and row covers are most effective if you prewarm the garden soil before planting. Seeds will not germinate and transplants will suffer in cold soil, even if the air temperature is high enough. To warm the soil, put the season extender in place 1 to 2 weeks prior to planting, or cover the soil with clear or black plastic several weeks before planting.

Cloches: Cloches are small plant coverings that trap the sun's warmth, raising the air temperature around an individual or small group of plants. Once made of glass, cloches are now made of paper or plastic, and you can easily make your own, too. Short ultraviolet rays from the sun pass through the cloche and warm the soil and air inside. The soil collects and stores the heat, then releases it slowly, creating a greenhouselike atmosphere and protecting plants from frost. The warmer conditions under a cloche also encourage growth. Commercial cloches include the popular Wall O' Water and similar plastic tubular structures that are filled with water and set around plants. To make a simple cloche, cut off the bottom section of a gallon plastic jug and set the jug over an individual plant. Some gardeners mimic the Wall O' Water concept by using duct tape to fashion a ring of clear plastic soda bottles to set around a tender plant (fill the bottles with water for extra heat-storage capacity). Or you can wrap clear plastic around a tomato cage to create a miniature greenhouse.

Cold frames: The best-known season extender is a cold frame. Homemade cold frames are usually made of wood with a transparent glass or plastic top; garden suppliers sell cold frames made of various types of plastic or polycarbonate with aluminum or plastic frames and bases. Use cold frames to trap the sun's energy and keep transplants and seedlings warm at night. Hotbeds are cold frames with an auxiliary heat source. Manure, compost, a heating cable, or some other heating source maintains warm temperatures inside the frame. See the Cold Frames entry for details on using cold frames and hotbeds.

Row covers: A row cover is a versatile season

extender that you can use to protect rows, small garden areas, or the whole garden from frost or cold temperatures. Row covers are sheets of transparent plastic or fabric. They're available in different weights and sizes. By using row covers you can extend the season by a month or more. See the Row Covers entry for more details.

Doubling up: If extending your growing season captures your imagination, you may want to try building your own garden-scale plastic tunnel and raising crops inside it throughout winter. This requires covering the interior beds with cold frames or heavyweight row covers. Excellent books are available with detailed information on how to raise hardy food crops through winter with this type of system; see Recommended Reading on page 675 for titles.

Extending the Season Indoors

Indoor gardening is a great way to extend the season well into winter, especially if you're not a person

---

Marvelous Microgreens

Growing microgreens is a fun and easy way to enjoy crispy, fresh garnishes for salads, sandwiches, and stir-fries throughout the year. Microgreens are simply vegetable and herb crops harvested very young—usually within a few weeks of germination. All you need to grow microgreens are an organic potting mix, some plastic or foam clamshell containers (take-out food containers), and seeds. In fact, growing microgreens is a great way to use up your leftover seed from the past couple of gardening seasons— seed that may no longer be germinating at its full potential but that you just hate to throw away.

To grow microgreens in a clamshell container, first cut off the lid. Use a pointed object (a shish kebab skewer works well) to poke several holes in the bottom of the container. Fill it with 1 to 11/2 inches of dampened potting mix, and spread the seed thickly over the surface (about 1/2 inch apart). Cover the seed with about 1/4 inch

of mix (less for seeds like lettuce that need light to germinate). Mist the surface thoroughly and put the container in a warm place to germinate. Check it daily; when seedlings pop through, move the container to a sunny windowsill. Use plastic flats, old trays, or aluminum pie plates as drip catchers under the containers, and bottom-water the containers as needed to keep the mix constantly moist. When your seedlings have developed one or two true leaves, use scissors to cut off the greens close to the soil surface. Or, if you'd like to try for a second cutting, cut them off about 1 inch above the soil, so the growing tip can resprout.

What crops can you use for microgreens? All traditional salad crops, plus any radishes, broccoli, and any other crop in the cabbage family (Brassicaceae). Young pea shoots are a delicious choice, as are many herbs, including dill and basil. Avoid nightshade-family crops such as tomatoes and peppers.

who enjoys working outdoors in cold weather or if you just want a break from outdoor gardening. Gardening indoors can be just as exciting as outdoor gardening—there's a fabulous array of houseplants for various conditions, and a simple indoor light setup makes it possible to grow a wide variety, even if your house doesn't have many sunny windowsills to offer; see the Houseplants entry for details. If you want to pursue gardening on a large scale in a protected environment, see the Greenhouse Gardening entry.

Another delightful indoor gardening activity is to force flowering bulbs such as narcissus and amaryllis. You can enjoy bright fresh flowers indoors beginning in late winter using this technique; see the Bulbs entry for details.

Starting seeds indoors in pots or flats is a type of season extension that any gardener with a sunny window or a simple grow-light setup can try. Whether you're a vegetable gardener or flower enthusiast (or both), you'll love the new world of unusual and new varieties of veggies and annuals you can grow when you start your own plants from seed beginning in late winter. And at any time of year, you can start seeds for a nutritious and tasty crop of microgreens, as described at left. For full information on indoor seed starting, see the Seed Starting and Seed Saving entry.

SEDUM

Sedum, stonecrop. Perennial flowers or groundcovers.

Description: Sedums have succulent green leaves on fleshy stems that form somewhat sprawling, trailing rosettes. Leaves of many species turn red in late fall; some cultivars have brilliantly colored or variegated foliage. Most sedums bloom from May through August with white or yellow flowers.

Several upright perennials, including the popular hybrid 'Autumn Joy'/'Herbstfreude', formerly included in the genus *Sedum* have been reclassified as *Hylotelephium*. See that entry for information about the upright stonecrop species. Other species formerly included in *Sedum* are reclassified as *Phedimus* or *Rhodiola*. If you are seeking these versatile plants for a rock garden or dry, sunny site, bear in mind that they may appear under new names.

Creeping or low-growing species sedums make good groundcovers for dry, sunny or lightly shaded sites. *S. kamtschaticum* (also called *Phedimus kamtschaticus*), orange or Kamschatka stonecrop, is a 2- to 4-inch trailer with yellow starlike flowers that appear in May, complementing its light green leaves. *Sedum album*, white stonecrop, is trailing, with short leaves that turn a reddish color in winter. The flowers open white to pink in late summer.

S. spurium (*Phedimus spurius*), two-row stonecrop, grows 2 to 6 inches tall and forms mats of foliage that turns bronze in fall; it produces open clusters of pink flowers in summer. Zones 3–8.

S. ternatum, woodland stonecrop, tolerates partial shade and moist soil better than many sedums and grows to 3 to 6 inches tall. Creeping stems root at the nodes; clusters of small, starry, white flowers bloom in spring. Zones 4–8.

How to grow: Sedums are easy to grow in any well-drained, average soil in sun or light shade. They are tolerant of poor soil and hot, dry weather. Propagate them in spring or summer by division or cuttings.

Landscape uses: Use the smaller species as groundcovers for banks, or plant in pots, rock gardens, and the front of borders. They also look wonderful trailing over a stone wall.

SEED STARTING AND SEED SAVING

Seeds come in an amazing variety of forms and sizes, from the dustlike seeds of begonias to the hefty coconut. But all seeds have one quality in common: They are living links between generations of plants, carrying the vital genetic information that directs the growth and development of the next plant generation. Seeds are alive. They even carry on respiration—absorbing oxygen and giving off carbon dioxide.

As long as a seed is kept cool and dry, its life processes hum along on low. Most seeds remain viable for 1 to 3 years after they ripen on a plant. Some, such as parsnip seed, can't be counted on to sprout after more than 1 year, but others, like muskmelon seeds, can germinate after 5 years or more if storage conditions are favorable. In fact, certain seeds recovered from archaeological digs have proven viable even though they are hundreds of years old.

Growing your own plants from seed can be one of the most satisfying and intriguing aspects of gardening. Almost all gardeners have grown vegetables from seed. But if you're interested in a challenge, you can start your own annuals, perennials, herbs, and even trees from seed. For tips on buying seeds, see page 530.

Seed Germination

Moisture and warmth encourage seeds to germinate. When a seed absorbs water, its internal pressure rises, rupturing the seed coat. Growth hormones within the seed go into action, directing

KEY WORDS *Seeds and Seedlings*

Seed. A plant embryo and its supply of nutrients, often surrounded by a protective seed coat.

Germination. The beginning of the growth of a seed.

Viable. Capable of germinating; alive.

Seed dormancy. A state of reduced biochemical activity that persists until certain conditions occur that trigger germination.

Seedling. A young plant grown from seed. Commonly, plants grown from seed are termed seedlings until they are first transplanted.

Cotyledon. The leaf (or leaves), present in the dormant seed, that is the first to unfold as a seed germinates. Cotyledons often look different from the leaves that follow them. In seeds such as beans, they contain stored nutrients. Also called seed leaves.

Endosperm. Specialized layer of tissue that surrounds the embryo.

Scarification. Nicking or wearing down hard seed coats to encourage germination.

Stratification. Exposing seeds to a period of cool/moist (35° to 40°F) or warm/moist (68° to 86°F) conditions that break dormancy.

Damping-off. A disease caused by various fungi that results in seedling stems that shrivel and collapse at soil level.

vital compounds to where they are needed and encouraging the growth of new tissue.

All of these changes depend on temperature as well. Most garden seeds started indoors germinate best at a soil temperature of 75° to 90°F. Sprouting seeds also need air. A porous soil kept evenly moist (but not swampy) will provide enough air to support the germination process. Seeds often rot if they are submerged in water for days or if they are planted in completely waterlogged soil.

After the germination process has been in action for several days (or, in some cases, for a week or more), a seed will change in visible ways. The root emerges and starts to grow, the stem grows longer, and then the cotyledons unfold. Once germination has begun, you can't reverse the process. If the sprouted seed continues to receive moisture, warmth, air, and light, it keeps growing. If not, it dies.

Most seeds have no specific light requirement for germination. However, some kinds of seeds need light to break dormancy and germinate, including many tiny seeds, such as begonia, columbines (*Aquilegia* spp.), snapdragon (*Antirrhinum*), and petunia seeds. Some larger seeds such as impatiens, dill, spider flower (*Cleome hassleriana*), and sweet alyssum (*Lobularia maritima*) are also best left uncovered. Sow light-sensitive seeds on the surface of fine, moist soil or seed-starting mix. Just press them onto the surface of the medium. Then cover them loosely with clear plastic to retain moisture, or mist them frequently.

A few seeds require darkness to germinate. For example, Madagascar periwinkle (*Catharanthus roseus*) seed germinates far better if the flat is covered with black plastic or kept in a dark closet until seeds sprout.

Other seeds will germinate readily only if planted soon after they ripen. Angelica, hawthorns (*Crataegus* spp.) and Solomon's seals (*Polygonatum* spp.) are three types of seed best sown soon after they are collected.

Check seed packet information to find out whether the seeds you want to raise have special germination requirements.

Pretreating Seeds

Some kinds of seeds require certain treatments before they'll start to germinate. No matter how ideal conditions are for germination, the seeds will remain dormant if the pregermination requirements have not been met. This characteristic, called innate dormancy, helps ensure survival in nature, because the seeds wait out winter or the dry season before sprouting.

Certain seeds require a period of moist cold. This mechanism is common in plants native to climates with cold winters, especially perennials, trees, and shrubs. Other seeds have chemicals in their seed coats that must be soaked away before the seeds will germinate. Some seeds are slow to absorb enough water to start germination because of thick or impermeable seed coats. Plants native to areas with seasonal dry spells often have this type of dormancy. If you understand these dormancy mechanisms, you can work around them and coax the seeds to germinate.

Even seeds that don't have dormancy requirements may be slow to germinate. Appropriate pretreatment can significantly increase germination rate and reduce germination time.

Stratification: Some seeds must be exposed to cold, moist conditions for a certain period before they will break dormancy and germinate. Stratification simulates natural conditions when a seed overwinters in cold, moist ground. To stratify seeds, layer them in pots or plastic bags filled with

SMART SHOPPING
Buying the Best Seeds

Here are some tips to help you to get the most from your seed order.

- Send for several seed catalogs or visit several Web sites so you can compare offerings and prices.

- Seed catalogs can be handy for reference; keep them on a shelf in your seed-starting area.

- Some companies offer small seed packets at reasonable prices. Seed mixtures give you a wide variety of plants from a single packet.

- Days to maturity (the number of days from seed sowing or transplanting to harvest) is an average—the actual days in your area may be different.

- Hybrids may offer advantages such as early harvest or high yields but hybrid seed is usually more expensive. Open-pollinated cultivars may taste better and produce over a longer season, and they tend to be cheaper.

- Some seed is routinely treated with synthetic chemical fungicide. Specify untreated seed if you prefer it, or buy from companies that sell only untreated seed.

- Read descriptions and choose cultivars with qualities that are important to you.

- Certain suppliers specialize in plants suited to specific regions of the country.

- All-America Selections seeds grow and produce well over a wide range of conditions.

---

damp sphagnum moss, peat moss, or vermiculite and keep them in a cold place (34° to 40°F) for 1 to 4 months. Or plant seeds in fall or late winter, mulch the tops of the pots with tiny gravel, and set them outside in a cold, protected spot where they will germinate in spring.

Seeds of various perennials, including wild bleeding heart (*Dicentra eximia*), gas plant (*Dictamnus albus*), and cardinal flower (*Lobelia cardinalis*), need a cold period. You can plant them outdoors in fall, or spring plant after giving them a cold treatment. The illustration on the opposite page shows how to prepare seeds for cold treatment.

Many woody plant seeds also require stratification, including birches (*Betula* spp.), dogwoods (*Cornus* spp.), false cypresses (*Chamaecyparis* spp.), and spruces (*Picea* spp.). Some tree and shrub seeds, including arborvitaes (*Thuja* spp.), cotoneasters, and lilacs (*Syringa* spp.), are double dormant, which means they require a warm, moist stratification period followed by a cold period to germinate. If planted outdoors in fall, these seeds may not germinate for 2 years.

Scarification: Some seeds, such as morning glory, sweet pea, okra, and others, have hard seed coats that inhibit water absorption. To make a

Preparing seeds for stratification. Layer large seeds with damp sphagnum moss in a labeled plastic container with a tight-fitting lid for cold storage. Mix small seeds into a seed-starting medium in a plastic bag. Close with a twist tie and label.

hard-coated seed absorb water more readily, nick the seed coat. Be careful not to damage the embryo inside the seed. On large seeds, use a knife to cut a notch in the seed coat, or make several strokes with a sharp-edged file. Scarify medium-size or small seeds by rubbing them between two sheets of sandpaper. After scarifying, soak seeds in lukewarm water for several hours before planting.

Presoaking: Even seeds that have thin seed coats can benefit from a soak in lukewarm water for several hours before planting. Large seeds such as peas and okra will germinate faster if soaked overnight first. Before planting, drain the seeds and dry them briefly on paper towels to make them easier to handle.

Presprouting: Presprouting takes seeds one step further than presoaking. It's a good way to handle such seeds as melons, squash, and their relatives, which need plenty of warmth for germination. Because sprouted seeds can tolerate cooler temperatures, you can concentrate your population of germinating seeds in one warm place and farm out the sprouted seedlings to cooler spots, where they will receive plenty of light. See page 532 for step-by-step instructions for this technique.

Sprouted seeds are fragile; handle them with great care. Be sure to plant them before their roots grow together and tangle. Plant sprouted seeds in individual containers of premoistened potting mix. Cover them gently but firmly with potting mix and treat them as you would any container-raised seedling. Sprouted seeds may be planted directly in the garden, but it is better to keep them in containers until the roots become established.

Starting Seeds Indoors

Starting seeds indoors will give you earlier vegetables and flowers, and your cultivar choices will be endless. The process of germination may seem complex, but the act of seed planting is reassuringly simple. Just take it step-by-step, and you'll soon be presiding over a healthy crop of seedlings.

Select your work area—a surface at a comfortable height and close to a water supply where you'll have room to spread things out. Assemble your equipment: seed-starting containers, starting medium or soil mix, watering can, labels, marking pen, and seed packets.

Choosing Containers

You can start seeds in almost any kind of container that will hold 1 to 2 inches of starting medium and won't become easily waterlogged. Once seedlings form more roots and develop their true leaves, though, they grow best in containers that provide more space for root growth and have holes for drainage.

Presprouting Seeds

Sprouting seeds before you plant them can boost germination rates and give you more control when working with expensive or scarce seeds. Here's how to presprout seeds.

1. Spread a double layer of damp paper towels on a flat surface.

2. Evenly space seeds 1 inch or so apart on the moist towels.

3. Roll up the towels, being careful to keep the seeds from bunching up.

4. Label the seed roll and enclose it in a plastic bag. Close the bag loosely—germinating seeds need some air. You can put several rolls in one plastic bag.

5. Put the seeds in a warm place—near a water heater or on top of a refrigerator. Make a note on your calendar to check them in 2 or 3 days.

6. After the first inspection, check the seeds daily for signs of sprouting.

Plant the sprouted seeds in individual containers using a fine, loose potting soil mix, or plant them directly in the garden. Handle them gently. The fleshy roots and stems are easily broken. Then treat as you would other newly germinated seedlings.

You can start seedlings in open flats, in individual sections of a market pack, or in pots. Individual containers are preferable, because the less you disturb tender roots, the better. Some containers, such as peat pots, paper pots, and soil blocks, go right into the garden with the plant during transplanting. Other pots must be slipped off the rootball before planting.

Square or rectangular containers make better use of space and provide more root area than round ones do. However, individual containers dry out faster than open flats. Many gardeners start seeds in open flats and transplant seedlings to individual containers after the first true leaves unfold. Choose flats and containers to match the number and types of plants you wish to grow and the space you have available.

Excellent seed-starting systems are available from garden centers and mail-order suppliers. You can also build your own wooden flats. If you raise large numbers of seedlings, it's useful to have interchangeable, standard-size flats and inserts.

You can reuse your seedling containers for many years. To prevent problems with damping-off disease, you may want to sanitize flats at the end of the season by dipping them in a 10 percent solution of household bleach (1 cup of bleach plus 9 cups of water).

Homemade containers: You can recycle milk cartons and many types of plastic containers as seed-starting pots. Just be sure to poke a drainage hole in the bottom of each. Cut lengths of clothes hanger as a frame for your flats so you can wrap them in plastic to encourage germination. You can bend the wire to fit into a plastic flat filled with pots or six-packs, or staple the wire to the sides of a wooden flat as shown at right. Use clear plastic wrap or plastic bags (like the ones from the dry cleaner) to enclose the flat.

Two make-at-home seed-starting containers are newspaper pots and soil blocks. To make pots from newspaper, begin by cutting bands of newspaper about twice as wide as the desired height of a pot (about 4 inches wide for a 2-inch-high pot). Wrap a band around the lower half of a jar a few times, and secure it with masking tape. Then form the bottom of the pot by creasing and folding the paper in around the bottom of the jar. You can also put a piece of tape across the pot bottom to hold it more securely in place. Slip the newspaper pot off the jar. Set your pots in high-sided trays with their sides touching. When you fill them with potting mix, they will support one another. There are also commercial molds for making newspaper pots.

Soil blocks encourage well-branched roots and produce good seedlings. You can buy molds to make soil blocks, but making them is a messy, labor-intensive process.

Begin by mixing a wheelbarrow-load of potting soil. Use plenty of peat moss or coir and lots of water to make a thick, wet, gummy mass with the texture of peanut butter. Jam the soil-block mold into the block mix. Press the mold hard against the bottom of the wheelbarrow, and then lift and eject

Homemade greenhouses. A homemade greenhouse fashioned from a flat, some clothes-hanger wire, and a large plastic bag is a simple, inexpensive setup that provides the high-humidity environment germinating seeds require.

the blocks from the mold onto a tray. Then arrange the blocks in flats and plant directly into them. Don't let soil blocks dry out: Because of their high peat content, they don't absorb moisture well once they have become dry. Water from the bottom or mist gently until roots grow. Once roots fill the blocks, they become solid and easy to handle.

Seed-Starting and Potting Mixes

Seeds contain enough nutrients to nourish themselves through sprouting, so a seed-starting mix does not have to contain nutrients. It should be free of weed seeds and toxic substances, hold moisture well, and provide plenty of air spaces. Don't use plain garden soil to start seedlings; it hardens into a dense mass that delicate young roots can't penetrate.

Make your own seed-starting mix by combining one part vermiculite or perlite with one part peat moss, milled sphagnum moss, coir, or well-screened compost. Or buy bagged seed-starting mix. Let your seedlings grow in such a mixture until they develop their first true leaves, and then transplant into a nutrient-rich potting mix (be sure the mix you choose is labeled organic, or check the list of ingredients, and avoid mixes that contain added synthetic fertilizer). To make your own potting mix, combine equal parts compost and vermiculite. For more recipes for mixes, see the Houseplants entry. For safe handling instructions for seed-starting and potting mixes, see the Container Gardening entry.

Some gardeners prefer to plant seeds directly in potting mix and eliminate transplanting. Planting in large individual pots is ideal for plants such as squash and melons that won't grow well if their roots are disturbed.

Moisten the planting mix before you fill your containers, especially if it contains peat moss or milled sphagnum moss. Use warm water, and allow the mix time to absorb it. When you squeeze a handful of mix it should hold together and feel moist, but it shouldn't drip.

If you're sowing directly in flats, first line the bottom with a sheet of newspaper to keep soil from washing out. Scoop premoistened planting medium into the containers or flats, and spread it out. Tap the filled container on your work surface to settle the medium, and smooth the surface with your hand. Don't pack it down tightly.

Sowing Seeds

Space large seeds at least 1 inch apart, planting two or three seeds in each pot (snip off the weaker seedlings later). Plant medium-size seeds ½ to 1 inch apart, and tiny ones about ½ inch apart. If you're sowing only a few seeds, use your fingertips or tweezers to place them precisely. To sprinkle seeds evenly, try one of these methods.

🌱 Take a pinch of seeds between your thumb and forefinger and slowly rotate thumb against finger—try to release the seeds gradually while moving your hand over the container.

🌱 Scatter seeds from a spoon.

🌱 Sow seeds directly from the corner of the packet by tapping the packet gently to make the seeds drop out one by one.

🌱 Mix fine seeds with dry sand, and scatter the mixture from a saltshaker.

To sow seeds in tiny furrows or rows, just make shallow ¼- to ½-inch-deep depressions in the soil with a plant label or an old pencil. Space the seeds along the bottom of the furrow.

Cover the seeds to a depth of three times their thickness by carefully sprinkling them with light, dry potting soil or seed-starting medium. Don't cover seeds that need light to germinate (check the

Sowing Timetable

To plan the best time to start seedlings indoors in spring, you need to know the approximate date of the average last spring frost in your area. Count back from that date the number of weeks indicated below to determine the appropriate starting date for various crops. An asterisk (*) indicates a cold-hardy plant that can be set out 4 to 6 weeks before the last frost.

- 12 to 14 weeks: Onions,* leeks,* chives,* pansies,* impatiens, and coleus

- 8 to 12 weeks: Peppers, lettuce,* cabbage-family crops,* petunias, snapdragons,* alyssum,* and other hardy annual flowers

- 6 to 8 weeks: Eggplants, tomatoes

- 5 to 6 weeks: Zinnias, cockscombs (*Celosia* spp.), marigolds, other tender annuals

- 2 to 4 weeks: Cucumbers, melons, okra, pumpkins, squash

seed packet for special germination requirements). Instead, gently pat the surface of the mix so the seeds and mix have good contact.

Write a label for each kind of seed you plant and put it in the flat or pot as soon as the seeds are planted, before any mix-ups occur.

Set the flats or pots in shallow containers of water and let them soak until the surface of the planting medium looks moist. Or you can gently mist the mix. If you water from the top, use a watering can with a rose nozzle to get a gentle stream that won't wash the seeds out of place.

Cover the container, using clear plastic or a floating row cover for seeds that need light, or black plastic, damp newspaper, or burlap for those that prefer the dark.

Finally, put the containers of planted seeds in a warm place where you can check them daily. Unless the seeds need light to germinate, you can save space the first few days by stacking flats. Just be sure the bottom of a flat doesn't actually rest on the planting mix of the flat below. Check the flats daily; unstack as soon as the seeds start to sprout. Keep the soil moist but not waterlogged. As soon as you notice sprouts nudging above the soil surface, expose the flat to light.

Raising Healthy Seedlings

Seedlings need regular attention. Provide the right amount of light, heat, and humidity to grow robust, healthy seedlings.

Light: Seedlings need more intense light than full-grown plants. If they don't get enough light, or if the light isn't strong enough, they will become spindly and leggy. Sixteen hours of light a day is ideal, 14 hours is acceptable, and plants can get along with 12 hours in a cool location. Up to 18 hours will do no harm, but most plants won't thrive in continuous light.

Windowsills are a popular spot for starting seedlings. Wide windowsills are suitable as is, but you can also widen narrow windowsills by installing shelf brackets and boards. Keep in mind that the air close to the window glass can be too cold for some tender seedlings, especially at night. Pull curtains or prop up cardboard next to the glass at night for protection. Short winter days provide inadequate light for many plants. Turn plants regularly to prevent them from developing a one-sided leaning, or rig up a mirror or a reflector made of aluminum foil and cardboard. A sunporch offers more room and often longer exposure to the sun than do windowsills, and the cooler temperatures in a sunporch can be great for cold-loving plants.

If you have a greenhouse, you can easily raise high-quality seedlings in quantity. Cold frames can shelter small batches of cold-hardy seedlings like pansies and broccoli early in the season, followed by tomatoes and annual flowers as the season progresses. The addition of heating can transform a cold frame into a hotbed. For more information on greenhouses, cold frames, and hotbeds, see the Greenhouse Gardening and Cold Frames entries.

Fluorescent lights use energy and will raise your electric bill, but they do help in raising good seedlings. Special plant-growth lights, often called grow lights, are expensive. The light from less-expensive cool-white tubes produces comparable plants. For best results, mount your lights using chains and "S" hooks, so you can easily raise the height of the lights as the seedlings grow. Keep tubes close to the seedlings; no more than 3 inches away for the first few weeks. Then raise the lights to 4 or 6 inches above the top of the seedlings.

Water: Seedlings need a steady supply of moisture. Dry air in a heated house can suck moisture rapidly from the shallow soil in seedling flats. Check for dryness by poking your finger into the soil and by lifting the flats. A flat with dry soil weighs less than one that's well watered. For delicate seedlings, bottom watering is best, since it does not disturb roots and helps prevent disease problems such as damping-off. Use tepid water rather than cold water to water seedlings, especially warmth-loving plants like okra, eggplant, and melons. In a warm, dry, house, seedlings may need to be watered every 2 to 3 days or even more frequently.

Temperature: Young plants require less warmth than germinating seedlings. Average room temperatures of about 60° to 70°F, dropping by about 10°F at night, will keep most seedlings growing steadily. Slightly lower temperatures will make seedlings stocky but slower growing. Cool-weather plants such as cabbage and lettuce prefer cooler temperatures.

Temperatures of 30° to 45°F can cause chilling injury in some warmth-loving flowers and vegetables. Temperatures higher than about 75°F tend to produce weak, spindly plants that are vulnerable to harsh outdoor conditions.

Ventilation: Remove any plastic or other coverings as soon as seeds sprout. Lack of air circulation can lead to the development of damping-off.

Fertilizer: Seedlings growing in a soilless or lean mix will need small doses of plant food, starting at the time the first true leaves develop. Use a half-strength fertilizer solution once a week for the first 3 weeks. Fish emulsion and compost teas are good choices. After that, use a full-strength solution every 10 to 14 days. Seedlings grown in a potting mix that contains compost or other nutrients may not need supplementary feeding for several weeks. If the seedlings start looking pale, feed as above. See the Compost entry for instructions for making compost tea.

Transplanting: Most gardeners tend to sow seeds thickly, but seedlings grow faster, develop better, and are less prone to disease if they have plenty of space and good soil. Transplanting gives you a chance to select the best seedlings and to move them into a larger container of richer soil. You can transplant seedlings from their nursery flat to another flat with wider spacing, or you can move them to individual pots. Seedlings are ready for transplanting when they have developed their first set of true leaves. For details on how to handle seedlings see the Transplanting entry.

Planting Out

Before you can plant your seedlings in the garden, you must prepare them for life outdoors. Sheltered plants are unaccustomed to wind, strong sun, cold air, and varying temperatures. They will do better if you help them develop tougher tissues gradually, before you plant them outside.

When it's time to plant the hardened-off seedlings in the outdoor garden, wait for an overcast or drizzly day, or plant them in the late afternoon. Seedlings will suffer less stress if they are not set out during a hot, sunny day. If you plant transplants out just before a rain, they'll get off to a good start, and you'll have less watering to do.

After planting out, you may want to put wooden bushel baskets or cut-open plastic jugs over seedlings or drape the row with a floating row cover to protect them from sun, wind, or frost. If the sun is strong or the plants are in an exposed location, water the soil around them several times during their first week in the ground, until their roots take hold. If plants wilt, water the soil promptly and shade the plants from the sun for a day or two.

For more information on hardening off and planting out seedlings, see the Transplanting entry.

Starting Seeds Outdoors

You can plant seeds of many flowers, herbs, and vegetables directly in the garden. If you live where winters are mild, you can sow seeds outside pretty much year-round. In cold-winter areas, the outdoor seed-sowing season begins in spring when the ground thaws and continues until early autumn.

When the soil is soft enough to dig and dry enough to crumble readily in your hand, you can make your first outdoor plantings. Don't try to work the soil while it is wet (see the Soil entry for information on determining when the soil is ready to dig and suitable preparation techniques.) Start with the hardiest seeds, such as peas and radishes, and gradually work up to more tender crops as the season progresses and frost danger diminishes and finally disappears.

Avoid stepping on the seedbed; compacted soil lacks the air spaces so necessary for good root growth. Sprinkle seed thinly over the entire bed, or plant in straight rows, using a string stretched between two sticks to help you mark out the rows. Follow seed packet directions for seed spacing: Thick stands of seedlings compete with each other just like weeds and are more prone to disease problems such as damping-off. After you have sown the seeds, mark the spot with a label, and record the planting on your garden calendar or plan. For more detailed instructions on outdoor seed sowing, see the Planting entry.

To figure the latest possible planting date for late-summer seed sowing, subtract the average days to maturity for the crop from the average date of your first hard frost. Subtract 5 to 10 extra days to compensate for cooler fall nights and slower growth. If frost comes in mid-October, for instance, make a final planting of 50-day lettuce in early to mid-August. If you use season extenders like floating row covers, delay the final planting date a few weeks.

Saving Seeds

Saving seeds is fun, and you can save a bit of money by doing it. You can save seeds from individual plants with traits you desire, such as earliness, dis-

ease resistance, high yield, or flower color. By carefully selecting individual plants each year and saving their seed, you can develop strains that are uniquely suited to your growing conditions.

Seed saving is also an important way to perpetuate heirloom varieties that are in danger of becoming extinct. For further information, see the Heirloom Plants entry.

Selecting seed to save: Only save seed from

Troubleshooting

If your seeds fail to germinate or if only a few sprout, it is probably due to one or more of these factors.

- Old seed that is no longer viable
- Seed produced under poor growing conditions that is not viable
- Seed that is damaged
- Too much or not enough moisture
- Temperature too high or too low
- Germination-inhibiting substances in the soil (herbicide residues, for example) or high salt content in soil
- Top watering or heavy rain washed seeds out of soil mix or covered them too deeply, or seed was planted too deeply to start with
- Damping-off disease
- Seeds not in good contact with soil
- Lack of light or lack of darkness for seeds that need these for germination
- Dormancy requirement not met

plants grown from open-pollinated seed. Open-pollinated cultivars produce seed that comes true—the seedlings are very like the parents. They also are somewhat variable by nature, and repeated selection for a particular character will yield a strain that is slightly different from the original one. Seed harvested from hybrid plants produces seedlings unlike the parents and in most cases inferior to them.

When selecting plants to save seed from, choose those that are vigorous, disease-free, and outstanding in whatever qualities you wish to encourage. Mark chosen plants with a stake or colored string so you won't forget and harvest them for other purposes by mistake.

Some garden plants, such as tomatoes, peas, and lettuce, are self-pollinated. Each flower pollinates itself. You don't have to take any precautions to prevent one cultivar from crossing with another—just let the seed mature, and harvest it.

Others, such as corn and plants of the pumpkin, squash, and cabbage families, are cross-pollinated and can cross with other cultivars of the same plant. To keep a strain pure, keep plants from which you want to save seed separate from other blooming cultivars of the same species by at least 200 feet. Or use bags to cover the blooms you plan to harvest seed from before they open, and pollinate them by hand with flowers of the same cultivar.

Certain garden plants normally grown as annuals, such as carrots and cabbage, are biennials—these crops will not produce seed the first year. Select superior plants and allow them to overwinter in place if possible. If you can't work around them, transplant them carefully to a new location.

Harvesting: Pick seedpods when they have turned dry and brittle but before they break open and scatter the seed. Some plants have very fragile seedpods or ripen unevenly. Cover the pods of these plants with a bag before the seeds ripen completely, and tie it snugly to the stem so seeds can't escape. Remove the seeds from the pods after harvesting. You can split the pods by hand or thresh the seeds out by beating them with a stick on a large piece of plastic.

Allow fleshy fruits like tomatoes, squash, and cucumbers to get a little overripe on the plant before harvesting them, but don't allow them to start to rot. Separate the seeds from the flesh and wash them clean in water. Some seeds are covered with a thick, jellylike coating. Clean the seeds by removing as much flesh as possible by letting them sit in water in a jar for a few days. The seeds will sink to the bottom of the jar and the pulp will float. Pour off the pulp and dry the seeds.

Drying and storing: After gathering seeds, spread them on newspaper and let them air-dry for about a week. Write seed names on the newspaper so you don't get them confused. Then pack them away in airtight jars and keep them in a cool, dry place. Label packaged seeds with cultivar, date, and any other pertinent information. Remember that heat and dampness will shorten the seed's period of viability.

SHADE GARDENING

Gardening in the shade challenges the talents of many gardeners because they fight the shady conditions rather than adapting to them. You can't grow a lovely lawn or prairie-style wildflower meadow under trees. But you can grow a diverse, beautiful garden. Instead of struggling to grow sun-loving flowers and lawn grass on a shady site, why not design a garden that will actually thrive in shade? By carefully choosing flowering shrubs, perennials, annuals, groundcovers, and ferns adapted to shady conditions, your garden will be not only colorful and interesting but also easy to care for!

The Challenges of Shade Gardening

Study your shady site to decide if you have dense, light, or partial shade. In partial shade, where some direct sun shines for a few hours a day, you'll be able to grow a wider selection of plants. Light or dappled shade also allows a wider selection than dense all-day shade cast from a thick-foliaged tree. If tree shade is very dense, you might want to thin out a few tree branches (cutting them off at the trunk) so that more light reaches the ground, creating a light or filtered shade. You may have to thin out branches every few years to maintain the effect.

In a shady area, it's often the case that poor, dry soil limits plant growth more than lack of light. Shade spots under trees can often be remarkably dry, because the trees' surface roots suck up all the available moisture and nutrients. The lack of moisture often limits your endeavors more than the shade. You'll know if dry, root-clogged soil poses a problem because the ground will feel hard and compacted, and you'll have trouble digging a hole with a trowel.

If the soil in your shady spot is compacted, you can layer chopped-up leaves and twigs over the area. In a year or so, they will decompose into a rich humus. Chop the dry leaves to the size of 50-cent pieces with a bagging lawn mower, and spread them several inches deep beneath the tree boughs. Sprinkle the leaves with a compost activator and keep them moist. Repeat this procedure annually until the leaves have rotted into a deep humus. By then, earthworms will have moved in

and begun to loosen up the subsoil. Only when you have a loose, friable soil can you begin installing a diverse shade garden, though tough groundcovers such as epimediums (*Epimedium* spp.) will grow in dense tree shade and poor soil.

Sometimes tree roots interfere with digging a planting hole for a shade-loving shrub. When this happens, dig an extra-large planting hole and sever all interfering tree roots smaller than 1 inch in diameter. Mulch the soil with compost to nourish the young shrub. The large planting hole should give the shrub enough growing room to get established before tree roots return.

Creating a Shade Garden

For the most pleasing effect, arrange plants beginning with the tallest at the back of the garden, or in the center if it is to be viewed from all sides, and filling in with the shortest. You might start by planting a shade-loving understory tree, then arranging groups of broad-leaved evergreen shrubs. After these woody plants are in place, add large groups of flowering perennials and underplant them with groundcovers to keep the soil cool and moist. Spring-flowering bulbs often flourish beneath deciduous trees, soaking up all the sun they need in spring before the tree leaves emerge. Plant them in large drifts together with the perennials.

Choose white and pastel-colored flowers as well as white-, cream-, or yellow-variegated and gold- and chartreuse-leaved foliage plants, such as hostas and golden hakone grass, for your shady site. These light colors pop out of the shadows rather than receding into the gloom like red or purple flowers tend to do. For more on designing a garden, see the Garden Design entry; for more on landscaping your shady areas, see the Landscaping entry.

With a careful selection and placement of plants,

Plants for Shady Gardens

The wide selection of plants listed here will brighten up any shady corner. Most prefer partial or filtered shade, but some can do well even in full shade. Check plant hardiness of perennials, groundcovers, and shrubs and choose plants that are hardy in your area. If you have room, consider flowering understory trees like dogwoods and redbuds that do well in woodland conditions. For more plants that tolerate shady conditions, see the Ferns entry, and the plant lists on pages 17, 59, 276, and 427.

Annuals

Begonia ×*semperflorens-cultorum* hybrids (wax begonias)

Browallia speciosa (browallia)

Plectranthus scutellarioides (coleus)

Impatiens walleriana (impatiens)

Myosotis sylvatica (woodland forget-me-not)

Torenia fournieri (wishbone flower)

Viola ×*wittrockiana* (pansy)

Perennials

Astilbe spp. and cultivars (astilbes)

Dicentra eximia (fringed bleeding heart)

Dicentra spectabilis (common bleeding heart)

Digitalis grandiflora (yellow foxglove)

Digitalis purpurea (common foxglove; reseeding biennial)

Filipendula ulmaria (queen-of-the-meadow)

Helleborus spp. (hellebores)

Hemerocallis spp. and cultivars (daylilies)

Heuchera spp. and cultivars (heucheras, alumroots)

Hosta spp. and cultivars (hostas)

Mertensia virginica (Virginia bluebells)

Osmunda cinnamomea (cinnamon fern)

Phlox divaricata (wild blue phlox)

Phlox stolonifera (creeping phlox)

Polygonatum spp. (Solomon's seals)

Primula spp. (primroses)

---

you can transform your dim spot into a cool, flowery retreat. It just might become the best-looking part of your yard.

SHRUBS

Some of the most familiar and beautiful plants around our homes are shrubs. Arching mounds of forsythia, the formal evergreen shape of a false cypress (*Chamaecyparis* spp.), and the layered, flower-laden branches of a viburnum (*Viburnum* spp.) show the diversity of these woody perennials. Shrubs have multiple stems and range in height from a few inches to approximately 15 feet at maturity, although individual shrubs may grow as high as 30 feet. A shrub trained to a single stem, called a standard, resembles a miniature tree.

It's hard to imagine a home landscape without shrubs. Their combined features of easy care,

Pulmonaria spp. (lungworts)

Tiarella cordifolia (Allegheny foamflower)

Groundcovers

Ajuga reptans (ajuga)

Asarum spp. (wild gingers)

Bergenia crassifolia (heartleaf bergenia)

Carex spp. (sedges)

Convallaria majalis (lily of the valley)

Fragaria vesca (alpine strawberry)

Galium odoratum (sweet woodruff)

Epimedium spp. (epimediums)

Hakonechloa macra (hakone grass)

Lamium maculatum (spotted dead nettle)

Liriope spp. (lilyturfs)

Mitchella repens (partridgeberry)

Pachysandra procumbens (Allegheny spurge)

Pachysandra terminalis (Japanese pachysandra)

Shrubs

Calycanthus floridus (Carolina allspice)

Daphne cneorum (rose daphne)

Ilex crenata (Japanese holly)

Kalmia latifolia (mountain laurel)

Kerria japonica 'Variegata' (variegated Japanese kerria)

Leucothoe spp. (leucothoes)

Mahonia spp. (mahonias and Oregon grapes)

Nandina domestica (heavenly bamboo)

Prunus laurocerasus (cherry laurel)

Rhododendron spp. and cultivars (rhododendrons and azaleas)

Ribes alpinum (alpine currant)

Sarcococca hookeriana (sweet box)

Skimmia japonica (Japanese skimmia)

interesting forms, and attractive flowers, foliage, and fruit make them a great asset to all gardens.

Types of Shrubs

Deciduous shrubs drop their leaves at the end of each growing season and grow new leaves the following spring. Leaves may first change color—redvein enkianthus (*Enkianthus campanulatus*) and fothergillas (*Fothergilla* spp.) feature leaves with spectacular autumn color—but after leaf fall, the shrub enters winter dormancy.

Evergreen shrubs have leaves year-round. They do drop some or all of their old leaves each year, but they always have new leaves to keep them looking green. Narrow-leaved or needle evergreens, such as junipers (*Juniperus* spp.) and bird's-nest spruce (*Picea abies* 'Nidiformis') have needles or scalelike leaves. Broad-leaved evergreens such as boxwoods (*Buxus* spp.) and mountain laurels

Showy Shrubs

Shrubs are a highlight during their blossom time, but they may have other features that can add color and diversity throughout the year. Many have attractive foliage in summer and/or fall, some have colorful berries, and others have unusual bark. To add four-season interest to your home landscape, try planting a few of the plants from this list. Plant name is followed by special features and seasons of interest.

Cornus sericea (red-osier dogwood): Flowers, bark; spring, winter

Corylus avellana 'Contorta' (Harry Lauder's walking stick): Leaves, flowers, twisted stems; all seasons

Cotoneaster horizontalis (rockspray cotoneaster): Flowers, fruit, growth habit; all seasons

Hamamelis spp. (witch hazels): Flowers, leaves; winter, spring, fall

Hydrangea quercifolia (oakleaf hydrangea): Leaves, flowers; all seasons

Ilex spp. (hollies): Flowers, foliage, fruit; all seasons

Itea virginica (Virginia sweetspire): Flowers, fall foliage; summer, fall

Lagerstroemia indica (crape myrtle): Flowers, fruits, bark; all seasons

Mahonia spp. (mahonias, Oregon grape hollies): Evergreen leaves, flowers, fruits; all seasons

Pieris spp. (pieris): Flowers, evergreen foliage; all seasons

Rhododendron spp. (rhododendrons and azaleas): Flowers, evergreen leaves; all seasons

Rosa spp. (shrub roses): Flowers, fruits; spring, summer, fall

Vaccinium spp. (blueberries): Flowers, fruits, autumn color; summer, fall

Viburnum spp. (viburnums): Flowers, fruits; spring, fall

(*Kalmia latifolia*) have wide, generally thick leaves.

Semievergreen shrubs such as glossy abelia (*Abelia ×grandiflora*) keep at least part of their leaves well into winter. These are often evergreen in the South and semievergreen farther north.

A few genera of shrubs contain both deciduous and evergreen species. For example, the handsome evergreen leaves of American holly (*Ilex opaca*) hide many of its berries. But when the leaves drop from the deciduous winterberry (*I. verticillata*), clusters of bright red berries are revealed. There also are both deciduous and evergreen species of rhododendrons and azaleas (*Rhododendron* spp.).

Landscaping with Shrubs

There are shrubs for every possible situation in your landscape. For single-specimen accent plants, look to individual shrubs that feature colorful or variegated leaves, large flowers or fruits, and unusual stems or bark. The list at right suggests several excellent accent shrubs. Use specimen or accent plants to mark the entrance to your garden, anchor the end of a perennial border, or add a decorative touch to a deck or patio.

Shrubs are also ideal for creating hedges and screens, and shrub borders make a very effective backdrop for smaller plants in your yard. While conventional hedges generally consist of one species that has been mass planted—privet (*Ligustrum* spp.) or a compact cultivar of false cypress (*Chamaecyparis* spp.), for example—plan on using a mix of different shrubs for a screen planting or shrub border. See the Hedges entry for suggestions of shrubs that make effective hedges.

To create an attractive, unified design for a screen or shrub border, select a few different shrubs (both different species and different cultivars of those species), then repeat them along the length of the border to create a rhythm. (See the Garden Design entry for more on selecting and arranging plants.) For year-round interest, select shrubs that have an interesting mix of characteristics—different foliage shapes and colors as well as flowers or fruit that appear at various times of the year. Also mix evergreen and deciduous shrubs. Add vines if you need a tall screen but space is at a premium.

Large shrubs such as witch hazels (*Hamamelis* spp.) and evergreen viburnums (*Viburnum* ×*rhytidophylloides*) are good choices for screens and also can be used singly or in groups to frame outdoor spaces, provide privacy, hide unsightly views, and act as a buffer against wind and noise.

A low-growing hedge, such as common boxwood (*Buxus sempervirens*), can direct traffic around walkways and define borders of flower- and herb beds.

Low-growing shrubs such as rockspray cotoneaster (*Cotoneaster horizontalis*), shore juniper (*Juniperus conferta*), or dwarf forms of forsythia are effective groundcovers. Use them to control erosion and ease maintenance on steep banks.

Low-growing Japanese holly (*Ilex crenata*) and compact abelias (*Abelia* spp.) make good foreground plants for foundation plantings. Medium and tall shrubs, such as yews (*Taxus* spp.), are effective background plants for foundation plantings, as well as for perennial beds.

Many medium- and tall-growing shrubs, as well as trees, have compact or dwarf forms, and these often make better landscape plants than their full-size cousins. For example, Chinese juniper (*Juniperus chinensis*) reaches 70 feet at maturity, but there are many cultivated forms that mature at 3 or 6 feet. When your planting site is small or if you need low-growing plants for a particular spot, look for dwarf and miniature forms of popular shrubs, including many junipers and false cypresses as well as heavenly bamboo (*Nandina domestica* 'Nana') and dwarf mugo pine (*Pinus mugo* var. *mugo*). Planting compact and dwarf cultivars ensures you'll have attractively shaped plants and also greatly reduces pruning maintenance.

Try shrubs with edible fruits, such as blueberries and bush cherries. Plant hollies and viburnums for berries that attract birds and other wildlife.

There are many outstanding native shrubs to choose from that are ideal for both native and conventional landscapes, including sweetspires (*Itea* spp.), summersweet (*Clethra alnifolia*), bottlebrush buckeye (*Aesculus parviflora*), fetterbush (*Pieris floribunda*), hypericum (*Hypericum frondosum*), and fothergillas (*Fothergilla* spp.)

For more ideas on using shrubs in the landscape, see the Hedges, Landscaping, Native Plants, and Rock Gardens entries.

Selecting Shrubs

The best shrubs for your garden will depend on where you live. Before you head to the nursery or

Unusual Flowering Shrubs

The gorgeous flowers of shrubs like forsythia, azaleas, rhododendrons, and shrub roses are a common sight in gardens, but there are many more outstanding flowering shrubs. Try some of the following.

Abeliophyllum distichum (white forsythia)

Caryopteris ×clandonensis (bluebeard)

Corylopsis pauciflora (buttercup winter hazel)

Hydrangea arborescens (smooth hydrangea) 'Annabelle'

Hypericum spp. (hypericums, St. John's worts)

Itea virginica (sweetspire) 'Henry's Garnet', 'Little Henry'

Jasminum nudiflorum (winter jasmine)

Philadelphus spp. (mock orange) 'Avalanche', 'Enchantment', 'Mont Blanc'

Pieris japonica (lily-of-the-valley bush, Japanese pieris)

Syringa pubescens ssp. *patula* (lilac) 'Miss Kim'

Viburnum plicatum f. *tomentosum* (doublefile viburnum) 'Mariesii', 'Shasta', 'Shoshoni'

Weigela spp. (old-fashioned weigela) 'Wine and Roses', 'Spilled Wine'

serve as a specimen? How big can the shrub get, how often will you have time to prune it, and what showy features do you want? You may also want to visit botanical gardens or private gardens in your area to look for outstanding shrubs.

Make a second list of the conditions of your site—soil, water, and exposure. For healthy, vigorous shrubs, match the plant to the site. Since they are important landscape features, select shrubs that are completely hardy in your area. Many gardeners stick to shrubs that are hardy one zone north of where they live to make sure plantings won't suffer damage during an unusually cold winter. Stick to shrubs hardy in Zone 4, for example, if you live in the northern part of Zone 5.

Combine your two lists to discover what you need to look for when selecting shrubs at the nursery. With your list in hand, you're ready to buy. Remember that shrubs are a long-term feature of the home landscape. It's well worth your time and money to seek out and buy good-quality shrubs. Don't base your selection on price alone. Follow these guidelines when you shop.

- Choose healthy plants. Look for plump, firm buds and leaves that are the correct size and color.

- Reject shrubs with broken branches or scratched bark, dry or brown leaf margins, or dry rootballs.

- Read tags and labels, and don't buy unlabeled plants. Be sure the flowers, fruit, and form of the plant are what you want. Check if the plant will grow well in the site you have chosen.

- Buy bareroot shrubs only when they're dormant and only if the roots have been kept moist.

- Inspect container-grown shrubs, and don't buy rootbound plants. Many large roots on the outside of the rootball or protruding from drainage

garden center to buy shrubs, make a list of desired features. What should the shrubs do—form a windscreen, complete your foundation planting, or holes mean the plant may be stunted by growing in a too-small container.

🌿 Select balled-and-burlapped shrubs with firm, well-wrapped rootballs.

Planting and Care

Plant bareroot shrubs while dormant, from late fall until early spring. Plant container- and field-grown shrubs all year, except when the ground is frozen. If you transplant shrubs from one location to another in your yard, move them while they are dormant. Slide the rootball onto a piece of burlap so it stays intact during the move. For complete instructions on how to plant shrubs, see the Planting entry.

In general, follow the spacing recommendations on plant tags, but to create an effective hedge or screen, plant shrubs slightly closer together than recommended so they will grow together more quickly and will form an unbroken line or group.

Newly planted shrubs require more care than shrubs with well-established roots. Water your shrubs well when you plant or transplant them. Continue to water them each week when less than 1 inch of rain falls, especially in summer and fall. A layer of mulch helps retain water. Keep mulch a couple of inches away from the stems to discourage mice and prevent extra moisture that may cause rot.

Pruning: As your shrubs grow, you'll need to prune them to control their size, rejuvenate old plants, repair damage and remove pests, and control flowering and fruiting.

Maintain the natural form of your shrubs either by pruning back to outward-facing buds or by removing whole branches. While shearing is faster than naturalistic pruning, it destroys the natural beauty of the plant—and you'll need to do it often. Learn the natural shape and type of a plant, prune accordingly, and you'll have to prune far less often. Many plants combine characteristics and may need more than one pruning technique.

Cane growers such as forsythia, heavenly bamboo, and roses are often fountain-shaped. They renew themselves by sending up new canes from the base. Make heading cuts to stimulate lower growth where desired. Thin some branches to maintain an open, uncluttered form. Renew and control cane-growing shrubs by removing older canes at ground level.

Mounding shrubs such as abelias and cotoneasters are generally rounded and have fine or supple branches and small leaves. Mounding shrubs are the easiest type to reduce in size and keep at a given height. You'll use mostly selective heading cuts to remove unruly and overly long branches, hiding cuts in the shrub interior. Remove up to one-third of the foliage in a year.

Treelike shrubs such as rhododendrons, witch hazels, and viburnums, which have stiff, woody branches, are the most difficult to control in size. Use thinning cuts to remove dead wood, rubbing and crossing branches, and watersprouts to reduce clutter and create definition. Don't remove more than one-quarter of the greenery in a year.

Prune spring-flowering shrubs soon after they finish blooming in spring and summer-flowering shrubs from late fall until spring bud break. Flower buds form on old wood on spring-flowering shrubs but on new wood for summer-flowering shrubs.

Prune evergreens year-round, except in late summer and early fall. Pruning late in the growing season encourages new growth that may be killed by frosts.

Refer to the illustrations on page 546 for examples

of these pruning strategies. Consult the Pruning and Training entry for basic information on making proper pruning cuts.

Growing tips: Inspect your shrubs often to minimize problems with insects and diseases. Aphids feed on the new growth and flower buds of almost any shrub. Various caterpillars and beetles chew holes in the leaves, while whiteflies feed on leaf undersides. Scales feed on leaves and stems. Shrub diseases range from leaf spots and blights to stem cankers and root rots.

Avoid problems by selecting insect-tolerant or resistant shrubs. Be sure your plants have well-drained soil, sufficient light, and good air circulation to help prevent pest and disease problems before they start. Handpicking, putting out pheromone traps, and spraying insecticidal soap or Bt (*Bacillus thuringiensis*) are all useful insect controls. For more on pest and disease control, see the Pests and Plant Diseases and Disorders entries.

Heavy ice or snow can sometimes injure dense shrubs, and winter winds can dry out evergreen leaves. For special winter protection, build a temporary structure of boards and burlap. Spray the leaves of evergreen shrubs with an antidesiccant or antitranspirant, a protective coating that keeps the leaves from drying.

Small, yellow leaves or too few flowers or fruits may indicate a nutrient deficiency. A dose of organic fertilizer should help matters, unless it's a case of the right plant in the wrong place. See the Plant Diseases and Disorders entry for more information.

Propagating: Starting shrubs from seed is an iffy proposition—plant form and flower and leaf color and size can be quite unlike the parent shrub. Making stem or root cuttings or layering are more reliable methods that exactly duplicate the parent plant. Almost any shrub can be propagated using stem cuttings. Forsythia, winter jasmine, and others are easy to propagate by layering. See the Cuttings and Layering entries for particulars.

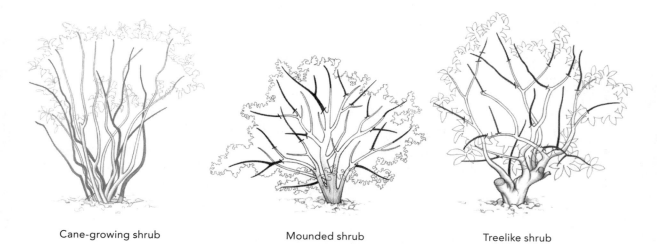

Cane-growing shrub   Mounded shrub   Treelike shrub

Pruning strategies. Remove older canes at ground level to renew cane-growing shrubs. Selective heading cuts are best for keeping mounding shrubs looking neat. Thinning cuts are important for removing dead wood and maintaining form of treelike shrubs.

SLUGS AND SNAILS

Slugs and garden snails have an appetite for so many fruits, vegetables, and ornamentals that they top many gardeners' lists of most-hated pests. Slugs and snails are mollusks, not insects, and their soft, muscular bodies secrete slime. Several species, ranging in size from less than 1 inch to more than 4 inches, feed on garden plants.

Slugs and snails need moist surroundings and will hibernate during dry periods. They hide under rocks, garden debris, and mulches during the day. At night, they emerge and chew large ragged holes in leaves. You may find shiny slime trails and damaged plants without ever spotting a slug. For every slug you find, there may be 20 more you don't see. Damage usually is worst in spring, when soil is moist and plants are young. Follow these guidelines to control slugs and snails.

- Create a diverse garden ecosystem to encourage biological controls. Ants, beetle grubs, earwigs, flies, birds, snakes, toads, and turtles prey on slugs.

- Don't plant dense groundcovers or lay mulch near plants you want to protect.

- Armed with a flashlight, handpick slugs and snails from plants at night and drop them in a bucket of soapy water.

- Set out boards or inverted flowerpots as traps. Check the undersides of traps daily and kill the slugs or snails hidden there.

- Sink shallow containers of beer in soil near your plants. Snails and slugs are attracted to beer and will drown after they climb in to drink it.

- For serious slug infestations, sprinkle iron phosphate baits (sold at garden centers) around your garden, following label directions. Be sure the bait you buy is an iron phosphate product and not metaldehyde, which is a toxic chemical. Iron phosphate is a natural mineral that eventually breaks down in the soil; it is not toxic to people or pets.

- Sprinkle dry soil around the stem bases of your plants.

- Make a slug-proof barrier around garden beds by edging them with copper-based strips. Be sure to remove any slugs that are already in the bed when you put up the barrier.

- Traditional organic controls include repelling the pests with an oak-leaf mulch and drenching the soil with wormwood tea.

SNAPDRAGON

See *Antirrhinum*

SOIL

Organic gardeners live by a basic principle: Feed the soil, and let the soil feed the plants. Feeding soil with organic matter, from compost to grass clippings, is the key to successful organic gardening. Of course, it's not the soil itself that consumes the organic matter, it's the living organisms in the soil—animals, insects, bacteria, fungi, and other organisms—that do. In the process, they break down the organic material into nutrients that can be taken up by plant roots.

Few gardeners start out with balanced soil—that is, well-aerated soil that is rich in organic matter—that's ideal for gardening. There are many reasons why the soil in your yard and garden could be out of balance. Surface soil is often disturbed—or even

KEY WORDS *Soil*

Sand, silt, and clay. Tiny fragments of rock or minerals that make up nearly half the material in the soil. They are distinguished from one another by size. Sand particles are from 0.05 to 2.0 millimeters in diameter, silt particles are from 0.002 to 0.05 millimeter, and clay particles are less than 0.002 millimeter in diameter.

Soil texture. The relative proportions of sand, silt, and clay in the soil.

Soil structure. The arrangement of soil particles in the soil.

Loam. Soil that has moderate amounts of sand, silt, and clay. Loam soils are generally considered the best garden soils.

Soil pH. A measurement of the acidity or alkalinity of the soil.

Organic matter. Various forms of living or dead plant and animal material.

Microorganisms. Animals and plants that are too small to be seen clearly without the use of a microscope.

Decay cycle. The changes that occur as plants grow, die, and break down in the soil. The action of soil animals and microorganisms break down plant tissues to release nutrients that new plants then take up to fuel their growth and development.

Humus. A dark-colored, stable form of organic matter that remains after most of the plant and animal residues in it have decomposed. When soil animals and microbes digest organic matter, such as chopped leaves or weeds, humus is the end product.

Erosion. The wearing away of soil by running water, wind, ice, or other geological forces. Erosion can be accelerated by the activity of people or animals.

---

removed—during construction, and nothing is done to restore the soil afterward. Your soil may be compacted, which means it has too little space for air and water, because of repeated walking or driving on it with equipment such as lawn tractors. Here are some other reasons your soil may need some TLC before it is ready for planting.

🌿 Your soil's natural characteristics may not be favorable for gardening. For example, you may have such sandy soil that it can't hold sufficient water and nutrients to support vigorous plant growth. Or your soil's pH may be so acidic that many kinds of plants won't thrive.

🌿 Unless you're a longtime organic gardener, the soil may be depleted of nutrients because no one has fed it with organic matter for many years.

🌿 If you've used chemical fertilizers, the soil microorganisms that play an important role in maintaining natural fertility may have died off.

A good first step in the process of improving your soil is to make some tests that will help you learn about its characteristics. After testing, you'll know what problems your soil has, and you can take steps to remedy them. Your soil improvement process will include adding organic matter and possibly other soil amendments. While you work on improving your soil, you may want to use organic fertilizers to boost plant performance.

How Soil Works

Soil is much more than just dirt. It's an intricate, fascinating mix of fine rock particles, water, air, organic matter, microorganisms, and other animals. Surprisingly, in ideal garden soil only about 45 percent of it consists of minerals, which we classify by size as sand, silt, and clay. Half the volume of good garden soil is pore space filled with either water or air—large pores hold air, while smaller pores hold water and dissolved nutrients. Ideally, the remaining 5 percent is organic matter.

Texture and Structure

The size differences between the three types of soil particles—sand, silt, or clay—are very small yet highly important. The relative proportion of these tiny rock fragments—referred to as soil texture—influences how well soil holds water and air, and also how fertile it is.

Texture differences: The spaces between sand particles are comparatively large, so they do not tend to granulate, or stick together. Thus, sandy soils have few small pores and often do not hold enough water and/or dissolved nutrients to support the growth of many kinds of plants.

Clay soils are rich in very tiny particles that are attracted to each other when wet. While these clay particles can be interspersed with tiny pore spaces that can hold large reserves of water and dissolved nutrients, too much clay also can create problems. When clay particles dry, they stick together and form a hard layer with no pore spaces. When a hard layer forms at the soil surface (this is called crusting), water cannot penetrate easily. A clay layer deeper in the soil can form a hardpan that impedes water drainage.

Soil with a good balance of sand, silt, and clay particles is called loam, and it is often ideal for gardening, because it forms lots of large and small pore spaces and does not tend to crust over like clay soil does.

It takes a huge effort to change soil texture. For example, to have a beneficial effort on clayey soil in a 20- by 50-foot garden bed, you'd have to add about 3 to 5 tons of sand to the top 6 inches of soil.

Soil structure: Fortunately, there are steps you can take to improve another important characteristic, soil structure—the way in which soil particles clump together. A soil's structure determines how well it retains water and how quickly water drains through the soil, how much air is available in the soil, and how easily nutrients are released for uptake by plant roots.

Ideal garden soil is friable—the soil particles are held together in clumps called aggregates that can easily break apart. Such loose clumping allows water to drain through, and oxygen and carbon dioxide can easily move from the air above into the spaces below. Pore space can vary from 30 to 50 percent of soil volume.

Many factors contribute to the creation of soil structure. Soil water freezes and thaws, plant roots grow and die, earthworms move through the soil, and bacteria and other microorganisms secrete substances that help aggregates form. Soil structure is also affected by soil pH, the amount of humus in the soil, and the combination of minerals in the soil. The best way to improve soil structure, and thus the water-holding capacity and aeration of your soil, is to add organic matter—lots of it. (You'll learn more about how to add organic matter to your soil later in this entry.)

It's important to remember that soil structure is

very easy to destroy. Tilling excessively, walking on soil, or working soils that are too wet or too dry (see page 556 for tips on determining when your soil is ready to work) can break apart soil aggregates, thus destroying soil structure, and the damage is not easily undone.

Air and Water

Why is there air in the soil? One reason is that many beneficial soil organisms cannot live without oxygen. Gaseous nitrogen, another component of soil air, is a raw material for nitrogen-fixing bacteria that manufacture protein materials. These are later broken down to yield nitrogen compounds that can be absorbed by plant roots. Plant roots also "breathe" and need good air exchange between soil air and the atmosphere for proper develop-

ment. If soil doesn't drain well (meaning it has too few large pores), water occupies all the soil pore space. This suffocates the plants because their roots cannot get the air they need.

Plant roots absorb water from the small soil pores where it's stored, and that water then travels through the plant's conduction system (like a system of pipes) to leaves and stems, where it serves as a nutrient, a coolant, and as an essential part of all plant cells. Water is also the carrier for mineral nutrients, such as nitrogen and potassium, that plants need for growth and development.

Soil pore spaces should vary in size and be evenly distributed. Soil with sufficient organic matter will have this quality. Walking on the soil or driving yard and garden equipment over it can cause pore spaces to collapse.

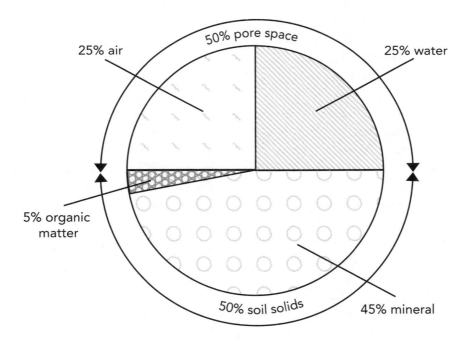

A soil summary. Soil that has good structure is about half solids and half open space (pores). Surprisingly, the all-important organic matter component of soil is its smallest component by volume.

Life in the Soil

Although they are only a minute portion of the soil by weight and volume, the living organisms in soil play a vital role. Soil microorganisms power the decay cycle—nature's perfect system for recycling organic matter and maintaining healthy soils. Soil microorganisms include nematodes, protozoa, fungi, bacteria, and actinomycetes (threadlike bacteria). These microorganisms, along with mites, insects, millipedes, and earthworms, break down dead and dying plant tissues into simpler components. Their waste products, in addition to the bodies of the organisms themselves, become part of the soil's organic matter content. As the cycle progresses, complex proteins are converted to simple nitrogen compounds that plant roots can absorb, and minerals such as potassium and phosphorus are changed into soluble compounds.

Plant roots secrete substances that encourage a variety of beneficial microorganisms, and they also benefit from a symbiotic relationship with mycorrhizal fungi: These special fungi obtain carbohydrates and sugars from the plant's roots, and the plant uses the mycelium (masses of threadlike cells) produced by the fungi to absorb soil water and dissolved nutrients.

Earthworms serve as natural "tillers" and soil conditioners, moving organic matter around in the soil. Many soil-dwelling insects are parasites and predators of insects that harm crop plants. And soil animals, including the much-maligned mole, also help improve soil aeration and eat some harmful insects.

Ultimately, soil microorganisms convert plant material to humus. Humus is important because it has a complicated (microscopic) structure with lots of tiny openings where soil microbes can thrive and that help store water in the soil. Humus also has a chemical makeup that allows it to "hang on" to many important nutrients such as calcium, potassium, magnesium, and iron so they won't be lost by leaching (water moving quickly through the soil).

Investigating Your Soil

One question home gardeners frequently ask is, "Should I add anything to my soil this spring?" While adding organic matter is always the best answer to that question, you can get a more detailed answer by investigating your soil to learn about its structure and content.

There are several simple tests you can do yourself to learn about your soil's structure, drainage, and earthworm activity (earthworms are a key indicator of soil health). You can also submit soil samples from your yard for soil analysis—see below for more on collecting and using soil test results.

Do-It-Yourself Tests

An easy way to learn about your soil's condition is to try simple tests that rely not on precise chemical analysis but rather on your observations of the soil. With these tests, there is little or no cost and no waiting for results.

The squeeze test: This test helps you determine soil texture. Do this test 2 or 3 days after a rainy spell. Take a loose ball of soil about the size of a Ping-Pong ball in the palm of your hand. Gently squeeze it between the ball of your thumb and the lower outside edge of your index finger and think about what it feels like. Sand feels gritty, silt feels like moist talcum powder, and clay feels slippery.

Squeeze the ball in your hand, and release. If it crumbles, it has a reasonably balanced texture. If the soil ball can hold its shape, it has a substantial percentage of clay. If you can roll it into a sausage shape or press it into a thick ribbon, it has even more clay.

Run the palm of your other hand firmly over the handful of soil. If you see scratch marks on the surface of the soil, there is a sizable proportion of sand present. If the soil feels greasy, this indicates silt.

The perc test: This test is an easy way to assess water drainage through your soil. Dig a hole about 1 foot across and 1 foot deep. Fill the hole with water and let it drain. As soon as the water has drained completely, fill it again. This time, keep track of how long it takes for the hole to drain. If it takes more than 8 hours, you have a drainage problem that needs attention.

The watering test: A variation on the perc test will tell you if your soil drains too rapidly. Start by watering a small area of your lawn or garden bed very thoroughly. Two days later, dig a small hole 6 inches deep where you watered. If the soil already is dry to the bottom of the hole, your soil likely doesn't retain enough water for good plant growth.

Another way to monitor soil moisture is to use a manual or automatic moisture sensor. These are small, electronic devices that measure available water in the soil, letting you know how long water levels are adequate for your plants' needs. If a meter indicates that the soil needs rewatering only a few days after you've watered thoroughly or after a soaking rain, then you need to improve the soil's water-retention capacity.

The undercover test: The best way to learn about some aspects of your soil is to get right down into it. If you plan to plant a new tree or shrub, check out your soil as you prepare the hole. Your new plant will benefit from the extra-large planting hole, and you'll get valuable information about what's happening beneath the soil surface.

Dig a hole at least 2 feet across so you can get a view down into it and, ideally, dig down 2 feet deep as well. Pile soil on a tarp as you dig, so you can neatly refill the hole when you're done. Then observe your soil closely. Abundant earthworms and other soil organisms, as well as healthy plant roots and a dark topsoil layer indicate healthy soil. If you can't find many earthworms or other organisms, if roots are stunted or malformed, and if the topsoil layer is thin or nonexistent, your soil strongly needs improving.

Other Tests

If you have your soil tested by a soil-testing laboratory, the test results will include a nutrient analysis and also a measurement of your soil's pH. However, at times you may want to test pH only. For example, if you plan to plant blueberries, which require acid soil, you may want to quickly check pH at several sites to see if the soil pH needs adjusting. For more information about pH testing and changing soil pH, see the pH entry.

An indirect way to find out about nutrient levels in your soil is to analyze the content of the plants growing in it. Plant analysis is not a do-it-yourself test. Many extension offices and some private labs will analyze samples of leaf tissue for nutrient content. This type of testing may provide more accurate results for certain nutrients, including nitrogen, than soil analysis does. The labs analyze the nutrient content in the samples and compare the readings with compiled research data that show the normal range of nutrients required for optimal growth of that species. Based on that comparison, they make recommendations for treatment.

Preparing a Soil Sample

If you decide to use the extension office or a privately run soil-testing laboratory to test your soil, you'll need to collect a soil sample. Contact your local extension office for a soil test kit or see Resources on page 673 for a Web site that lists soil-testing firms. Both will offer recommendations on soil improvement based on the results of their tests.

You may want to collect many samples from around your yard and combine them to submit for a single test and report. Or you may want to prepare separate samples from your vegetable garden soil, your lawn, and an area where you hope to create a flower border, for example. However, you'll have to pay three times as much to get the three separate sets of recommendations.

Follow these steps to prepare a sample that will accurately reflect the content of your soil.

1. Scrape away any surface litter or plant growth from a small area of soil. Use a soil probe to cut a core of soil, or dig a hole with a stainless steel trowel or other tool (if you don't have stainless steel tools, use a large stainless steel spoon) and collect a slice of soil from the side of the hole. For cultivated areas, collect a core or slice to a depth of 6 inches. For lawns, collect your samples only from the top 4 inches of soil.

2. Repeat the sampling procedures at 10 to 15 different locations around your yard or the particular area you are sampling.

3. Mix the soil cores or slices in a clean plastic or stainless steel container.

4. Place some of the mixed sample in a plastic container or bag, and put it in the bag supplied by the soil-testing laboratory for shipment.

Don't touch the sample with soft steel, galvanized, or brass tools or with your bare skin. The content of some minerals in soil is so small that minerals picked up from these metals or your skin could throw off test results.

You'll send your sample, along with an information sheet concerning your soil's history and your future gardening plans, to the testing laboratory by mail. Be sure to write on the information form that you want recommendations for organic soil amendments.

Interpreting Recommendations

After analyzing your soil, the test lab will send you a report on the results of their analysis and recommendations for improving your soil.

Test results may include soil pH, organic matter content, and content of calcium, magnesium, nitrogen, phosphorus, potassium, sodium, sulfur, and trace minerals.

Soil labs make recommendations based on results of their research programs on plant responses to additions of mineral amendments. When you send in your sample, be sure to ask clearly for recommendations for organic amendments.

Keep in mind that making the recommendations is an imprecise science because the researchers must try to relate the data from the research soils they study to your individual soil. However, all soils are different. They do not all respond equally to applications of minerals or organic materials. (Typically, soil fertility studies are performed on soils that have low organic matter content. Analysis of such low-organic-matter soils may be more accurate because organic matter makes the soil more biologically diverse and complex.)

Improving Your Soil

There are no overnight or even single-season organic solutions for an imbalanced soil. Unlike gardeners who rely on soluble synthetic chemical fertilizers to keep their plants green and growing, organic gardeners boost the soil's natural fertility through a 2-, 3-, or 4-year program that results in a fertile, rich soil. Fortunately, your plants don't have to suffer during the soil-building years: You can provide organic fertilizers as a supplement to meet your plants' needs for nutrients.

Adding Organic Matter

Organic matter is almost like a miracle cure for soil problems (but remember, it's a slow-acting one). The benefits of organic matter include:

🌿 Improving soil structure and biological activity

🌿 Stimulating the growth and reproductive capacity of the bacteria and other microorganisms that help create a vital and productive soil

🌿 Increasing the water- and nutrient-holding capacity of the soil

🌿 Alleviating mineral deficiencies and buffering soil pH

There is a wide range of organic materials available to gardeners. The best of these is compost—a mixture of decayed organic materials. To learn how to make and use compost, read the Compost entry. Other good organic materials include chopped leaves, straw, grass clippings, and aged manure.

How to add organic matter: You can add organic matter by digging or tilling it into the surface of the soil, by planting cover or green manure crops, or simply by adding mulches and allowing them to break down over time. See the Cover Crops and Mulch entries for more information on these methods.

It's relatively easy to increase the humus content of vegetable gardens because they are usually cleared of plants every year. But how do you increase the organic material in a perennial garden or under an existing lawn? Or around trees and shrubs? Wherever you have existing plants, including lawn grass, shrubs, or perennials, you can spread compost or other decayed organic material on the surface. In a few months, the earthworms and other soil organisms will have begun to work that organic material down into the soil. The other method for flower gardens and around trees and shrubs is to use some kind of organic mulch— chopped leaves, for example, or a thin layer of compost under conventional mulch—and let it break down naturally, giving the soil an organic material boost as it does. You can do this at any convenient time of year.

How much to add: Five percent organic matter is a good goal to strive for in your soil. One inch of compost or other fine-textured organic material spread over the soil surface equals about 5 percent of the volume of the first foot of soil. Thus, as a rule of thumb, if you add about 1 inch of fine organic matter to a garden every year, you will gradually increase that soil's organic matter content to a desirable level. If you use a bulkier material such as chopped leaves or straw, you will have to apply a thicker layer, because there is less actual matter per volume. A 4-inch layer of bulky organic material is equivalent to a 1-inch layer of fine material.

In the South, it's more difficult to maintain organic matter content in soil. Microbial populations grow faster (and so "eat" more organic matter) in warmer temperatures. Organic material can break down twice as fast in hot southern soils as it does in cooler northern soils. Organic matter also breaks down more quickly in sandy soil than it does in loam or clay.

Fresh versus dry: On the average, fresh organic matter—such as grass clippings, kitchen waste, and green weeds—worked into the soil will be 50 percent decayed in just 2 months. The material will be 75 percent decayed after 4 months, and about 87 percent decayed after 6 months.

Dry materials decompose more slowly than moist materials. For example, if you dig chopped dried leaves into your garden, it may take 4 or 5 months for them to be halfway along the path of transformation to humus.

The decay process works best if there is a constant supply of food for the soil microorganisms that act as the decay "machine." In areas where you've incorporated partially decayed material, it's a good idea to spread some dry organic matter as a

Problem Soils

Two of the most common problems gardeners face are soils that are high in clay and soils that don't drain well.

Clay soils: If you have heavy clay soil that is low in organic matter, you will have to add considerable amounts of organic material and energy to make that soil as loose and friable as you can. Digging it deeply into the soil—to a spade's depth, or by double-digging—is your best option. Some gardeners will add sand along with the organic material to heavy clay soils in beds where they want to grow root crops or flower bulbs. A lot of sand is required to make a significant difference, though. Adding small amounts of sand may actually cause your soil to harden, worsening its condition (think concrete). To boost the sand component of the top 6 to 8 inches of the soil by 5 to 10 percent, you will need about 3 to 5 tons per 1,000 square feet of garden. If you have a close and convenient source of sand, it may be worth the effort to spread and till in the sand. However, adding sand alone will not remedy problems with heavy clay. Using cover or green manure crops and incorporating organic matter are the best long-term solutions.

Poorly drained soils: If your soil tests and observations have alerted you to a drainage problem in your yard, you have three options. Your first option could be to accept the wet spot and create a small bog garden. If you have other plans for the site, you'll have to find a way to improve drainage.

The drainage problem may be due to a hardpan somewhere in the top 2 feet of soil. You may be able to break up the compaction layer by double-digging. If the layer is deeper than you can reach by double-digging, try planting deep-rooted sweet clover in spring and allow it to grow for two full growing seasons. The roots may penetrate the deep hardpan and naturally create better drainage.

Another way to sidestep a drainage problem is to create a raised bed in the wet area. You'll have to bring in extra topsoil and build up the bed, essentially creating a layer of soil with good drainage for plants to grow in above the poorly drained area.

Lastly, you can install a drainage system, but this is a project for which you'll probably need to hire a professional landscaper.

Is It Ready to Work?

Tilling or digging the soil when it is either too wet or too dry is disastrous for soil structure. Wet soils will form large clumps when tilled. The clumps will dry hard and solid, without the many tiny pores that hold water and air in the soil. Without air, root growth suffers. Cultivating soil that's too wet can also cause water to run off or sit in puddles on the surface rather than percolate down into the root zone. If your soil is too wet, let it dry before planting. Pick up a handful of soil and squeeze it. If it crumbles into smaller, light-textured pieces, it's perfect for planting. But if it forms a muddy ball, the soil is too wet to be worked. Wait a few days, and test again to see if it has dried out. Dry soils can turn to fine dust when tilled, which also destroys the structure you've worked so hard to build. If a handful of soil crumbles immediately to dust, water the site thoroughly and wait a day before testing it again.

surface mulch. The mulch serves two functions. It protects the decomposing organic matter from excessive heat, which can cause some organic compounds to volatilize (turn from a solid state into a gas) and be lost. It also provides a longer-term food source for the soil microorganisms that are stimulated by the dug-in organic matter.

The rule of mulch: There is one cardinal rule in your efforts to increase the organic content of your soil. Once you've added whatever material your soil needs, there should not be 1 square inch of bare soil left anywhere on your property. It should be covered with grass, a groundcover, plants, or mulch. Bare soil loses humus much faster than covered soil because the nutrients created by the decomposition of the organic matter are leached away more readily. In addition, the impact of raindrops on bare soil can destroy the loose soil structure you have worked to obtain. Covered soil is also much less prone to surface erosion by wind or water.

Adding Microbes

Some garden suppliers sell products purported to enrich and/or boost populations of soil microbes. Some of these products list vitamins and enzymes as their active ingredients, while others contain mycorrhizal fungi and other microorganisms. Soil that has been amended with compost and other organic matter probably already contains a diverse population of microorganisms. However, if you're a gardener who's switching to organic methods from chemical methods, or if you've inherited a garden that's been treated with pesticides, you may have soils with very low biological activity. You may want to experiment by adding a microbial booster product to your soil and/or compost pile. Some of these cultures are in a dry, dormant, powdered form. After you spread this material over your soil or into a compost pile, the microbes become activated and biological activity accelerates. Keep in mind that you must keep adding sufficient organic matter to feed the increased populations of soil microbes, or you won't get any lasting benefit from your investment

Encouraging earthworms: If your earthworm count is low, don't despair. Once you provide more organic material to feed them, they will usually return. Earthworm egg casings may lay dormant as deep as 20 feet in the soil for as long as 20 years.

Dry or granular, fast-acting chemical fertilizers can repel earthworms when they dissolve in soil water and leach down into the soil. Earthworms are highly sensitive to changes in the physical and chemical environment and will avoid the salty conditions created by the chemical fertilizers. If you are making the transition from chemical fertilizers to organic soil amendments and fertilizers, have patience. As your soil reaches a healthy balance, you will see more earthworm activity.

Adding Minerals

Several organic soil amendments are available to help correct specific pH and mineral imbalances. In most cases, it's wisest to add these amendments only according to recommendations from soil tests or plant analyses. If you add too much of a natural mineral supplement such as rock phosphate, you can create an excess of a particular nutrient. The excess may damage plants or may interfere with uptake of some other nutrients. For more information on soil amendments, see the Fertilizers entry.

Working the Soil

To many gardeners, starting a new garden bed means using a rotary tiller. While a tiller is a powerful and helpful tool, tilling is not the best way to work the soil. One good alternative is to start new garden beds by building them from the ground up, a method known as lasagna gardening. To learn more about this, turn to the Raised Bed Gardening entry.

Some vegetable gardeners use their rotary tillers several times during the season. They may till in a green manure crop in early spring, and then till again a few weeks later to make a fine seedbed for planting. During the season, they may get out a smaller tiller for weed control, then till the garden under again in fall. While tillers seem convenient, their use gets costlier all the time as fuel prices increase, plus there's the environmental cost for the carbon dioxide they produce and the damage they do to the living organisms in your soil.

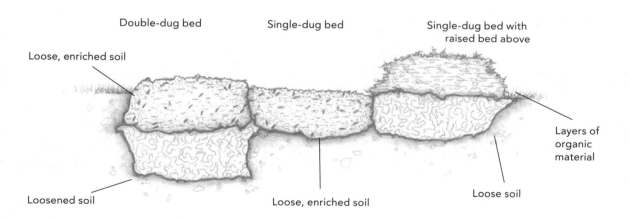

Double-dug bed   Single-dug bed   Single-dug bed with raised bed above

Loose, enriched soil

Layers of organic material

Loosened soil   Loose, enriched soil   Loose soil

Double-digging. Double-digging creates a deep, loose bed that's excellent for deep-rooted crops such as carrots and parsnips and for long-term plantings such as a perennial garden. Single digging is more than adequate for many veggies, herbs, and annual flowers. Building a raised bed on top of a single-dug area offers the same benefits as double-digging.

Erosion on the Home Front

The loss of topsoil through erosion isn't just a problem on farms and at construction sites. Erosion can happen in our own front and back yards. Take these steps to minimize soil erosion around your home.

- On slopes, build terraced garden beds, or at the very least, be sure your garden rows run across the slope, not up and down.

- Don't leave sloping areas unplanted. Plant groundcovers, vines, or other plants with spreading roots and top growth that will hold soil in place.

- Mulch permanent pathways with stone or a thick layer of organic mulch, or plant a durable groundcover or lawn grass.

- In fall and winter, mulch bare vegetable or flowerbeds, or plant a cover crop to prevent wind or water erosion.

- Keep areas cleared for construction well mulched with straw. Try to minimize the use of heavy equipment. Soil compacted by machinery cannot absorb water well; the runoff will carry valuable soil with it.

Digging and Double-Digging

Digging a garden bed takes considerable time and effort, but it's work well rewarded by more-vigorous, higher-yielding plants. Plants growing in deeply prepared soil also have deeper roots and are thus more drought tolerant.

The traditional technique for preparing a perennial garden or improving drainage on a poorly drained site is to double-dig. This process improves the structure and fertility of the top 2 feet of the soil.

To double-dig a new bed, start by marking off the edges of the bed and watering deeply several days before you plan to dig. Then follow the steps below.

1. Strip off weeds or sod. Discard roots of perennial weeds in the trash. Turn sod strips upside down on the compost pile, or use them to patch existing lawn.

2. Dig a 1-foot-wide, 1-foot-deep trench along one edge of your site. Put the soil into a wheelbarrow or onto a tarp.

3. Loosen the soil at the bottom of your trench by inserting a garden fork and wiggling or twisting it around. Top it with a 1- to 2-inch layer of organic matter.

4. Dig a second 1- by 1-foot trench next to the first, placing the soil on top of the layer of organic matter in the first trench. Then loosen the soil beneath it and add another layer of organic matter.

5. Continue systematically down the bed, digging trenches and loosening subsoil. When you get to the end, use the reserved soil from the first trench to fill the final one.

6. Spread compost or other organic material over the entire bed, then use a spading fork to work it into the top 4 to 6 inches of soil. The amount of organic material you add can vary, but 2 to 3 inches is adequate.

When you double-dig, lavish most of the organic material on the topsoil. Add only small amounts of compost or chopped leaves to the lower soil layer because the rate of decay is much slower in the second 6 inches of soil than it is in the top 6 inches. Double-digging your beds will raise them about 3 to 4 inches because it thoroughly loosens and aerates the soil.

Double-digging is hard work. If you have back problems, it's probably best not to double-dig your garden. And if you've never tried double-digging a bed before, start small. Try working a 3- by 3-foot bed, and build up from there. And remember, you don't have to dig an entire bed in one stint—you can spread out the work over several days or a few weekends.

Another method for improving soil, that's less work than double-digging, is single-digging. In this case, you loosen the soil to a shovel's depth—about 6 inches—and incorporate organic matter in that portion of the soil. Yet another option is to single-dig, then create a raised bed on top of the prepared soil.

Tilling or hand-digging, no matter how carefully done, has a major impact on soil microorganisms. When you turn the soil, you add an enormous amount of oxygen to it. This creates an environment primed for an explosion of microbial activity. In most soils, more than 80 percent of the aerobic bacteria are present in the top 6 inches; more than 60 percent are in the top 3 to 4 inches. If you add organic matter as you till, you supply fuel for the population explosion, and your soil will remain in balance. On the other hand, if you till repeatedly, thus increasing the microbial population, you'll speed the decomposition of your soil's organic reserves and soil organic matter levels will decrease.

So for your soil's and plants' sakes, don't use a tiller unless you really need it. Instead, hire a neighbor's teenage daughter or son to dig a new garden bed if you can't do it yourself. Once a bed is dug, keep the soil loose and healthy by relying on mulch to reduce weed problems and conserve soil moisture, by avoiding walking on beds, and by cultivating shallowly when weeds are small.

SOLIDAGO

Goldenrod. Summer- and fall-blooming perennials.

Description: There are many species of our native goldenrod that are fine for naturalizing, and some of their cultivars have become stars of the late-summer garden.

Solidago canadensis, Canada goldenrod, is the wide-ranging North American wildflower that turns fields and roadsides golden-yellow in late summer. *S. rugosa* 'Fireworks' ('Fireworks' rough goldenrod) bears a profusion of arching sprays of bright yellow blooms over 2½- to 3½-foot upright, leafy stems. *S. sphacelata* 'Golden Fleece' ('Golden Fleece' autumn goldenrod) is just 1 foot tall, perfect for the front of the border. It bears abundant sprays of golden yellow blooms over deep green, paddle-shaped leaves. Zones 4–9.

Hybrid goldenrods are also excellent garden plants. Hybrid goldenrods bear tiny yellow and gold flowers in showy 4- to 12-inch clusters over upright to vase-shaped clumps. Elongated leaves spiral up the stiff, 1- to 3-foot stems. One of the best is 'Crown of Rays'. Zones 3–8.

Several species once included in the genus *Solidago* have been reclassified as *Euthamia* and dubbed "goldentops" rather than goldenrods. Whatever the name, these attractive summer and fall bloomers make handsome companions for late-blooming asters in naturalistic plantings and wildflower meadows where their bright flower sprays welcome all manner of pollinators.

How to grow: Plant or divide in spring or fall in a sunny or lightly shaded spot. Goldenrods do best in average, moist, well-drained soil, though most tolerate fairly dry soil. Divide every 3 years to keep in bounds. Goldenrods can self-sow; keep an eye out for seedlings and remove them where they're not wanted.

Landscape uses: Grow goldenrods in small clumps in borders; mass in fields and meadow gardens. Combine with asters, other fall-blooming perennials, and ornamental grasses. Remember, it's ragweed that causes hay fever, not goldenrod.

SPINACH

Spinacia oleracea
Chenopodiaceae

Spinach is one of the most satisfying cool-weather crops to grow, producing large yields of vitamin-rich, dark green leaves that are excellent for salads and for cooking. Since both hot weather and long days trigger spinach to bolt (send up a seedstalk) quickly, the secret to success with this crop is to start sowing seeds as soon as possible in spring, to make small, frequent plantings during late spring and summer, and to concentrate on fall as the season for the main crop.

Planting: Spinach does best when growing in moist, nitrogen-rich soil. Spinach plants form a deep taproot; for best growth, loosen the soil at least 1 foot deep before planting.

Sow spinach seed as early as 6 weeks before the last frost or as soon as you can work the soil. Prepare the soil the previous autumn, and you can drop the seeds in barely thawed ground. In areas with a long, cool spring, make successive plantings every 10 days until mid-May.

In warm climates, plant spinach in the shade of tall crops such as corn or beans. The young plants will be spared the hottest sun and be ready for harvest in fall or winter. Using cold frames or heavyweight row covers, you can grow spinach all winter in many parts of the country. In colder regions, try planting in fall (October) and protecting the young plants through winter for a spring harvest. In regions where the soil doesn't freeze, try planting spinach in February for a March harvest.

Spinach seed doesn't store well, so buy fresh seeds every year. Sow them ½ inch deep and 2 inches apart in beds or rows. If the weather isn't extremely cold, seeds will germinate in 5 to 9 days. Spinach produces beautifully in cool fall conditions, but it's tricky to persuade the seed to germinate in the hot conditions of late summer. Sow seed heavily, because the germination rate drops to about 50 percent in warm weather, and water the seedbeds frequently—even twice a day—because watering helps to cool the soil.

Growing guidelines: Overcrowding stunts growth and encourages plants to go to seed. To avoid crowding, thin seedlings to 4 to 6 inches apart once they have at least two true leaves. Fertilize with compost tea or fish emulsion when the plants have four true leaves. (See the Compost entry for instructions for making compost tea.)

Since cultivating or hand-pulling weeds can harm spinach roots, it's best to spread a light mulch of hay, straw, or grass clippings along the rows to suppress weeds instead. Water stress will encourage plants to bolt, so provide enough water to keep the soil moist but not soggy. Cover the crop with shade cloth if the temperature goes above 80°F.

Problems: Since most spinach grows in very cool weather, pests are usually not a problem. Leaf

Spinach Stand-Ins

Where high temperatures make spinach growing difficult, consider these heat-tolerant alternatives to add spinach-like flavor to your salads.

Vegetable amaranth (*Amaranthus tricolor*)

Orach (*Atriplex hortensis*)

Tatsoi (*Brassica rapa* var. *narinosa*)

New Zealand spinach (*Tetragonia tetragonioides*)

Malabar spinach (*Basella rubra*)

miner larvae can burrow inside leaves and produce tan patches. Prevent leaf miner problems by keeping your crop covered with floating row cover. For unprotected plants, remove and destroy affected leaves to prevent adult flies from multiplying and further affecting the crop. For information on controlling aphids, cutworms, and cabbage loopers, see page 454. Slugs also feed on spinach; see the Slugs and Snails entry for controls.

Spinach blight, a virus spread by aphids, causes yellow leaves and stunted plants. Downy mildew, which appears as yellow spots on leaf surfaces and mold on the undersides, occurs during very wet weather. Reduce the spread of disease spores by not working around wet plants. Avoid both of these diseases by planting resistant cultivars.

Harvesting: In 6 to 8 weeks, you can start harvesting from any plant that has at least six leaves 3 to 4 inches long. Carefully cutting the outside leaves will extend the plants' productivity, particularly with fall crops. Harvest the entire crop at the first sign of bolting by using a sharp knife to cut through the main stem just below the soil surface.

SPIRAEA

Spirea, bridal wreath. Deciduous, spring-blooming shrubs.

Description: *Spiraea japonica*, Japanese spirea, is a 6-foot shrub that spreads to 5 feet. Plants bear toothed leaves and flat 4- to 6-inch-wide clusters of lacy pink or white flowers in summer. Cultivars of this species are much more common in gardens than the species. 'Goldflame', to 3 feet tall and wide, features chartreuse leaves. 'Little Princess' is just under 2 feet and spreads 3 feet. The variety *S. japonica* var. *bullata* is a 12- to 15-inch-tall dwarf shrub with blue-green, crinkled leaves and 1½- to 3-inch rosy red flower clusters in summer; its size makes it excellent in rock gardens or as a groundcover. The hybrid *S. ×bumalda* grows to 2 feet tall and spreads to 3 feet. Zones 4–9.

S. prunifolia, bridal wreath spirea, has an upright, rounded form, growing to about 10 feet. Its slender, oval, shiny dark green leaves are 1 to 2 inches long. The flowers are pure white and double, blooming in profusion along each branch in spring. For fall color, bridal wreath is one of the most reliable spireas, usually turning a soft orange-red. Zones 5–8.

S. ×vanhouttei, Vanhoutte spirea, has an arching form that's narrow and bare at the base, reaching 6 to 8 feet tall and 10 to 12 feet wide. It bears white flowers in flat clusters along the branches in late spring, and blue-green, ¾- to 1¾-inch, fine-textured foliage. Zones 3–8.

How to grow: All spireas need full sun and

good drainage. Promote vigorous growth by removing a third of the oldest branches to a few inches above ground level after bloom time. If drastic renewal is needed, cut the entire shrub in this way.

Landscape uses: Because of their compact form, cultivars of Japanese spirea make fine foundation plants. All spireas are useful for massed plantings, specimens, and borders.

SPRUCE

See *Picea*

SQUASH

Cucurbita spp.
Cucurbitaceae

From acorn squash to zucchini, this group of vegetables has a delightful range of shapes, sizes, colors, and flavors. These frost-tender plants need warm weather, lots of sun, and plenty of room.

Types: Squash come in two main types: summer squash and winter squash. While there's not much difference among the flavors and textures of summer squashes, winter squashes offer a wide array of flavors.

Summer squash (*Cucurbita pepo*) produces prolifically from early summer until the first frost. This group includes both green and yellow zucchini, most yellow crookneck and straightneck squash, and scallop (or pattypan) squash. Most summer squash are ready to pick 60 to 70 days after planting, but some reach harvestable size in 50 days. You can use them raw for salads and dips or cook them in a wide variety of ways, including squash "french fries" and such classics as zucchini bread.

Summer squash blossoms, picked just before they open, are delicious in soups and stews, or try them sautéed, stuffed, or dipped in batter and fried. (You'll want to use mostly male flowers for this purpose, though, and leave the female flowers to produce fruit. See the illustration on page 565 to distinguish male from female flowers.) Summer squash keep for only a week or so in the refrigerator, so you'll probably want to freeze most of the crop.

Winter squash (*C. maxima*, *C. mixta*, *C. moschata*, and *C. pepo*) is a broad category that includes butternut, acorn, delicata, Hubbard, banana, buttercup (or turban), and spaghetti squash. Pumpkins are also in this group, but their flesh is often less sweet than other winter squash. Most winter squash take 75 to 120 days to mature.

Steam the young fruits, or harvest and bake the squash when they're fully mature. Dry and roast the seeds. Winter squash are even more nutritious than their summer kin, but the sprawling vines, which can grow 10 to 20 feet long, require more space. If you have only a small garden, try one of the bush or semibush cultivars.

Butternuts produce fruits up to 1 foot long with tan skins and orange flesh. Acorn squash have dark green to yellow fruits that are round and usually furrowed; they generally weigh 1 to 2 pounds. Acorns don't store as well as most winter squash, but they are very productive.

Delicata squash can take more than 100 days to mature, but the wait is worth it; the wide-spreading vines produce wonderfully sweet fruit. Hubbards are best for storing, but standard cultivars can weigh up to 30 pounds, which is a lot of squash to eat. Pink-skinned banana squash can grow up to 75 pounds. Buttercup, or turban, squash have a sumptuous flavor that makes them a winter squash favorite.

Planting: These sun lovers are sensitive to cold, though winter squash tolerate light shade and cooler nighttime temperatures better than summer squash.

Both types of squash are heavy feeders and need a light and well-drained but moisture-retentive soil. You can give them exactly what they need by planting them in specially prepared hills. See the Melon entry for details on creating supercharged planting hills. Space the hills 3 feet apart for summer squash; vining winter squash need 6 to 8 feet between hills.

Summer squash can cross-pollinate with various cultivars of both summer and winter squash, as well as with several types of pumpkins. This won't affect the current season's fruit, but if you want to save seed, be careful not to let crops cross-pollinate. Otherwise, the seed won't be true to type, and the following season's crop will potentially be strange-looking or -tasting hybrids.

A week after the last frost date, or when the soil temperature is at least 60°F and the weather has settled, sow six seeds ½ inch deep in a circle on the top of each hill. Thin to the two strongest seedlings per hill.

If planting in rows instead of hills, space vining cultivars 3 to 4 feet apart in rows 8 to 12 feet apart; space bush types 2 to 3 feet apart in rows 4 to 6 feet apart. To conserve space in small gardens, train squash vines on a tripod. Tie three long poles together at one end, stand them upright, and spread them out to form the tripod; plant a squash seed at the base of each pole. You can also grow vining types on fences and well-supported growing nets.

In areas with short growing seasons, sow the seeds indoors a month before the last frost date. Plant two seeds per 3- or 4-inch pot, using potting soil enriched with extra compost. Clip off the weaker seedling after seedlings emerge. Water well just before transplanting, and disturb the roots as little as possible. Full-grown plants can tolerate cold weather, but seedlings are very cold sensitive. Use hot caps or cloches to protect them until the weather turns hot.

Summer squash will produce more heavily than winter squash. In either case, unless you plan to preserve or store a great deal of your crop, two vines of either summer or winter squash are probably adequate to feed four people. Unused seeds are viable for 4 to 5 years as long as you store them properly (as described in the Seed Starting and Seed Saving entry). To spread out the harvest, start a second crop about 6 weeks after the first planting; it will begin to produce fruit about the time your first planting has peaked and the plants are declining.

Growing guidelines: Give seedlings lots of water and keep the planting area moist throughout the growing season. To avoid such diseases as mildew, water the soil, not the foliage, and don't handle plants when they are wet. Dig weeds by hand until the squash vines begin to lengthen, then spread a thin layer of compost and top it with a thick mulch of hay, straw, or chopped leaves.

About 6 weeks after germination, male blossoms will appear, followed by the first of the female flowers. Squash depend on bees and other insects for pollination; female blooms that drop off without producing fruit probably weren't fertilized. You can transfer pollen from the male stamen to the female pistil by hand, using a soft paintbrush. Or simply pluck a male flower, remove the petals, and whirl it around inside a female flower.

If your garden soil is less than ideal, side-dress plants with compost or a balanced organic fertilizer or drench them with compost tea when the first fruits set. For instructions on making compost tea, see the Compost entry.

When vines grow to about 5 feet, pinch off the growing tips to encourage fruit-bearing side shoots. By midsummer, winter squash will have set all the fruit they will have time to mature; remove all remaining flowers so the plant can put its energy into ripening the crop. To avoid rot, keep maturing fruit off the soil by setting them on a board or flat rock or by spreading a thick mulch. This is particularly important with winter squash, which take a long time to ripen.

Problems: Well-cultivated squash will be trouble-free as long as you protect young plants with a floating row cover to keep out insect pests. Remove the cover when the plants start to flower to allow for pollination. The two pests most likely to attack are squash vine borers and squash bugs.

Squash vine borers, which are most damaging to winter squash, look like 1-inch-long white caterpillars. They tunnel into stems and can go undetected until a vine wilts. Keep a constant lookout for entry holes at the base of the plants, surrounded by yellow, sawdustlike droppings. Cut a slit along afflicted stems and remove and destroy the larvae inside, or inject the stems with Btk (*Bacillus thuringiensis* var. *kurstaki*). Hill up moist soil over the stem wounds to encourage the plant to sprout new roots there.

To prevent borer damage, keep an eye out for the adult borer, a wasplike orange-and-black moth; it lays eggs at the base of the stem in late June or early July in the North, or in April to early summer in the South. During these times, check the base of the stems and just below the surface of the soil regularly for very tiny red-and-orange eggs. Rub the eggs with your finger to destroy them.

Squash bugs are grayish brown bugs up to ¾ inch long; nymphs are similar, but do not have wings. Feeding by adults and nymphs causes leaves

to wilt and blacken. Handpick them and drop them in a container of soapy water. Also destroy their red-brown egg clusters on the undersides of leaves. To trap adults, lay boards on the soil at night; the squash bugs will tend to congregate beneath them, and you can destroy the pests the next morning. Planting radishes, nasturtiums, or marigolds among your squash plants may help repel squash bugs. If plants are heavily infested with young squash bugs, try spraying insecticidal soap or neem as a last resort to save your crop.

Striped and spotted cucumber beetles may also attack squash plants. These 1-inch-long black-headed beetles with green or yellow wings can transmit bacterial wilt as they feed. Since these are spring pests, you can avoid them by planting squash later in the season, when cucumber beetles are less prevalent. Handpick daily first thing in the morning when the beetles are sluggish. To make the vines less appealing to the beetles, spray them with kaolin clay as often as twice a week.

In most cases, you can avoid squash diseases by choosing resistant cultivars, rotating crops, and choosing planting sites with good air circulation. Here are some diseases to watch for.

- Anthracnose, a soilborne fungus, causes leaves to develop hollow, water-soaked spots that eventually grow large and brown.

- Bacterial wilt is a disease that causes plants to wilt suddenly; infected plants usually die quickly.

- Downy mildew produces yellow-brown spots on leaf surfaces and downy purple spots on the undersides. These spots eventually spread, and the leaves die.

- Mosaic, a viral disease that results in rough, mottled leaves, stunted growth, and whitish fruit, is spread by cucumber beetles and aphids. Reduce the chance of disease by controlling problem insects. (For aphid control measures, see page 454.)

🌿 Powdery mildew causes fuzzy white spots on leaves. Affected leaves are distorted, and the plant may appear stunted.

Immediately remove and destroy vines afflicted with any of these diseases, or place them in sealed containers and dispose of them with household trash.

Harvesting: Pick zucchini and crookneck cultivars at a tender 6 to 8 inches long; round types are best when they're 4 to 8 inches in diameter. Summer squash will continue setting buds until the first frost, but only if you pick the fruit before it matures—that is, just as its blossom drops off the tip. If you allow even one fruit to mature, the plant's overall productivity may decline. Enjoy summer squash fresh, or preserve them by canning or freezing; they can also be dried, pickled, or turned into relish.

Winter squash will taste bland and watery and won't store well unless you allow them to fully ripen on the vine. Wait until the plants die back and the shells are hard. A light frost can improve the flavor by changing some of their starch to sugar, but it will also shorten their storage life. It's better to pick all ripe fruits before an expected frost and cover any unripe ones with a heavy mulch. You can even carefully gather the vines and fruit close together and protect them with tarps or blankets.

Harvest during dry weather. Use a sharp knife or pruners to cut the fruit from the vine, leaving 2 to 3 inches of stem on the fruit. Pulling the fruit off may damage the stem, and the whole fruit may soon rot from that damaged end. (For that same reason, never carry squash by their stems. If a stem breaks

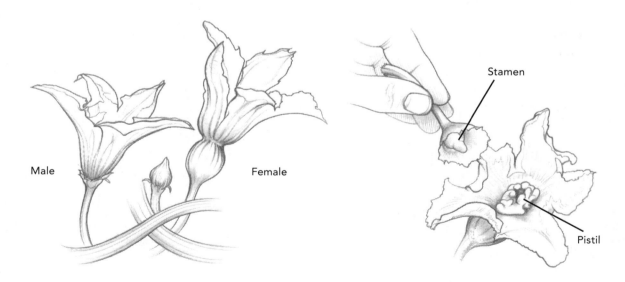

Hand-pollinating squash. Male squash blossoms appear first, followed about a week later by female flowers, which have a large swelling (the ovary) just beneath the blossom and a pistil at the flower's center. Strip petals off a male blossom to expose the stamen; rub the stamen on a pistil to transfer pollen and pollinate the female flower.

off accidentally, use that fruit as soon as possible.) Clean your harvesting knife between cuts to avoid spreading diseases. Handle squash carefully because bruised fruit won't keep.

Never wash any winter squash that you intend to store. Dry all types in the sununtil the stems shrivel and turn gray; the exception is acorn squash, which doesn't need curing. If placed in a cool, dry area with temperatures of 45° to 50°F and with 65 to 70 percent humidity, winter squash will keep for up to 5 months. Acorn squash needs a slightly cooler and moister storage area.

STAKING

Staking plants in the flower and vegetable garden is a task that busy gardeners sometimes skip. In most cases, however, the time you spend staking will be amply rewarded by the improved health and appearance of your garden.

Vining plants virtually require stakes or other support. Top-heavy, single-stemmed flowers like delphiniums, lilies, and dahlias benefit from support. Left unstaked, they are apt to bend unattractively and may snap off during heavy storms. Staking also improves the appearance of plants with thin floppy stems that flatten easily.

Choose stakes and supports that match the needs of the plant and of you as a gardener. They must be tall enough and strong enough to support the entire mature plant when wet or windblown, and they must be firmly inserted in the soil. A stake that breaks or tips over can cause more damage than using none at all. Take care not to damage roots when inserting a stake, and avoid tying the shoots too tightly to the stake. Install the supports as early in the growing season as possible so that the plants can be trained to them as they

grow, not forced to fit them later on. When growing plants from seed, install the support before planting.

In the flower garden, choose supports that are as inconspicuous as possible. Thin, slightly flexible stakes that bend with the plant are less conspicuous and may be better than heavier, rigid ones. In general, select stakes that stand about three-quarters of the height of the mature plant. Insert them close to or among the stems so that as

Individual plant stakes. Sink stakes firmly in the soil at planting time to avoid damage to plant roots or bulbs. Add ties in a loose figure eight as the plant grows.

Pea brush. The traditional staking technique for pea vines, pea brush (also called pea sticks) also works well for annuals and perennials such as coreopsis and baby's breath. Cut lengths of twiggy brush or branches to the final height of the plants, and push them 6 inches into the ground between the young plants.

the plant grows, the foliage will hide the supports. Choose colors and materials that blend with the plants. Bamboo stakes tinted green are available in a variety of sizes and are a reliable, inexpensive choice for many plants. You can also buy wood, metal, and plastic stakes and trellises and a wide assortment of metal rings and support systems. Soft string, strips of T-shirts, or panty hose work well as ties, and green-tinted twine or plastic-covered wire are inconspicuous ways to fasten plants to their supports.

In the vegetable garden, sturdiness is more important than appearance. Staking vegetables like tomatoes, peppers, and beans makes them easier to cultivate and harvest. It increases yields by preventing contamination with soilborne diseases and allowing for more plants in a given area. Choose

tall, sturdy stakes or cages that can support the plant even when it is heavy with fruit, and insert stakes firmly into the ground. Use narrow strips torn from rags or bands cut from stockings to gently fasten plants to supports. See individual entries for more detailed information on staking specific vegetable crops.

Perennial vines such as roses and grapes are commonly grown on trellises or on wires between sturdy posts. For more information on trellises, see the Trellising entry. Raspberries and other brambles are also trellised; see the Brambles entry for support ideas.

Trees and tall shrubs are sometimes staked temporarily at planting to help hold them upright until their roots become established. Fruit trees on dwarfing rootstocks may need to be permanently staked. For more information on staking trees, see the Trees entry.

STONESCAPING

Retaining walls, walkways, stepping-stone paths, and terraces are just some of the features you can add to your landscape with stone. Stonework features can fit into any type of landscape and can be formal or informal in design. While designing and building stone features properly is expensive and hard work, once installed, stonescaping is very low maintenance.

Choose a type of stone and a design that fits the style of your garden. For formal gardens, plan on using pavers and stone cut into regular shapes, which conform to the geometric shapes used in this style of landscape. Informal designs can use cut pavers and stone, but they also can incorporate irregularly shaped pavers and stone to create features that are more free-form.

Stonework Options

There are many ways to incorporate stone features in your garden. Books on stonescaping are a great place to look for more ideas about what types of stone features would enhance your landscape and how to construct them. See Recommended Reading on page 675 for some titles. Consider some of the following options.

Stone patios and terraces: These can be built of flagstone cut into squares or rectangles, or from random-shaped pavers. Flagstones may be made of slate, limestone, bluestone, or other types of rock, and the most economical material varies by region. Brick or precast cement pavers are other options for creating flat surfaces in the garden, as are precast landscape pavers, which come in many different colors and styles. Tile and terra-cotta pavers are suitable for gardens in frost-free areas. If your site is under trees, consider a ground-level deck instead of a stone patio or terrace, since a deck can be designed and built to minimize damage to tree roots, and since it's raised, it can't be heaved up by root growth.

Patios and terraces can be dry-laid, without mortar between the pavers, or the pavers can be mortared in place. Another option is to install a gravel patio surrounded by a stonework edging to keep the gravel in place.

Walls, walkways, and steps: There are nearly as many ways to plan and construct these elements as there are gardens. All can be dry-laid or mortared, and they can be designed for a formal garden or an informal one. For a steep slope, a low wall, or a series of low walls, is the best option for creating level gardening space. (Stick to walls 3 feet tall or less if you're planning on building garden walls yourself. Otherwise, consult an expert.) Freestanding walls can be used to separate different parts of

the landscape—a formal terrace and a less formal lawn area, for example. Build walls from naturally shaped fieldstone, cut stone, brick, or blocks precast for building. Raised beds with stone walls are another handsome option.

Hardscape walkways and steps are constructed from the same materials as patios and terraces. Keep in mind that materials can be combined to add interest and appeal to walkways and other structures. Edge a pathway with different-size pavers, for example, or work a pattern into a design by combining large flagstones with a network of smaller ones. It's also a good idea to use a contrasting size or color of paver to mark the edge of a step.

Rock gardens: It comes as no surprise that rocks are essential to a garden designed to grow alpines and other rock-garden plants. Rock gardens can make use of existing rock outcrops on a site, or they can be built over rocks arranged to re-create a natural-looking outcrop. A sloping site is the best choice for a rock garden. Start with a 6-inch layer of coarse gravel, rocks, or broken bricks to provide excellent drainage, then top it with landscape fabric and a 1-foot-deep layer of topsoil. (The landscape fabric keeps the soil from washing down into the drainage layer.) Then arrange the rocks on top of the topsoil. Be sure to position them securely (wedge small stones under large ones to keep them in position) and fill in around them with topsoil. See the Rock Gardens entry for more information on planting and care.

Edgings and ornaments: You can use stonescaping to create permanent edgings for beds and borders that keep lawn and flowers apart without the need to trim. Stone can be used to create a base for garden sculpture, too, and stones can be used as garden ornaments in their own right. Finally, use stonescaping to surround a water garden and hide the edge of the liner.

Construction Guidelines

Stonescaping is hard work. Before you start a project, make sure that you are physically able to move and place stone or that you can bring in equipment to help you. (A backhoe is invaluable for digging foundations, and a small front-end loader equally so for moving stone, gravel, and other materials, provided your site will accommodate them.) Don't hesitate to seek professional help, both for design and for construction.

Whether you are building a wall or creating a patio, it's important to realize that water in the soil is the biggest enemy of any stone feature, especially in northern zones where it freezes, because freezing and thawing cycles will crack stone. If you are building a retaining wall, it's important to incorporate drainage so that water in the soil behind the wall can drain away. This isn't a problem for a dry-laid wall, since water can flow through it. In this case, plan on two courses of stone below the soil line and pile the wall so the front edge leans slightly (1 or 2 inches per foot of height) back into the slope of the hill to make the wall more stable. You can build a dry-laid wall right on packed ground or on 6 inches of packed sand. For a mortared wall, use a poured concrete foundation that is below the frost line. You'll also need drain tile behind the wall along with ditches and/or gutters as well as weep holes through the wall to direct water away from it. Consult your local extension office or building code office for requirements in your area.

Water in the soil is a problem with patios and walkways, since cycles of freezing and thawing will heave them up to create an uneven surface. Set dry-laid paving stones on top of packed sand—use 2 inches in mild climates, 6 inches in very cold regions. Sweep sand over the top of the terrace once the stones are in place to fill the cracks. If you are planning a mortared patio or walkway, you'll need a poured concrete foundation. Again, consult your local extension office or building code office for requirements in your area.

For steps and walkways, width is another consideration. If you are building a path to the front door or a major walkway into the garden, keep in mind that a width of 5 or 6 feet is necessary for two people to walk side by side. For single-file paths, such as those that may wind through your garden, 4 feet is fine, and for little-used areas, paths as narrow as 2 feet can be perfectly serviceable. If you are building steps, keep in mind that the width of the tread should not be less than 12 inches, and riser height should not be more than 6 inches.

STRAWBERRY

Fragaria ×ananassa, F. vesca
Rosaceae

Strawberries are justly celebrated each spring in festivals from coast to coast. Fresh strawberry shortcake, strawberry ice cream, strawberry pie, and chocolate-covered strawberries—or plain berries right from the bush—are hard to beat. The plants are inexpensive, bear a full crop within a year of planting, and are relatively simple to grow.

Selecting Plants

Garden strawberry cultivars (*Fragaria ×ananassa*) are divided into three types: June-bearers, ever-bearers, and day-neutrals, which flower at different times in response to day length.

June-bearers: These bear fruit in June or July, or as early as April in Florida and California. They produce a single large crop over 3 to 4 weeks. If you want to freeze lots of fruit at one time, plant June-bearers. There are early-, mid-, and late-season cultivars. June-bearers produce many runners and spread rapidly.

Everbearers: These produce a moderate crop in June, scattered berries in summer, and a small crop in late August. They are especially productive in northern areas with long summer days. The total harvest for everbearers, though, is generally less than the total harvest for June-bearers. Plant everbearers if you want berries for fresh eating all season. They produce fewer runners than June-bearers and so are easier to control.

Day-neutrals: These are unaffected by day length. They are extremely productive and bear fruit from June through frost in northern areas, or January through August in milder climates. Unfortunately, day-neutrals can be sensitive to heat, drought, and weed competition. If you are willing to give them the care they need, they'll reward you with a generous supply of berries throughout the season from relatively few plants. They produce few runners, so they rarely get out of control.

Alpine strawberries: Alpine strawberries (*F. vesca*) produce small, aromatic berries from early summer through frost. Alpines are grown from seed or divisions and produce no runners. They are carefree and make good ornamental edgings and container plantings.

Whichever type of strawberries you decide to grow, choose disease-resistant cultivars adapted to your climate and daylength; check with suppliers or your local extension office for recommendations. Certified virus-indexed plants are worth the extra cost because the plants are more vigorous and productive.

Planting

Strawberries do best in full sun, sandy loam, and a pH of 6.0 to 6.5, although they'll tolerate less than ideal conditions, provided they have good drainage. Prepare a planting bed by tilling in 3 to 4 inches of compost.

Plant strawberries in spring, as soon as the ground has warmed. In the South, you can plant them in fall as well.

If you buy plants, or receive them through the mail, and can't plant them immediately, you can store them in the refrigerator for a few days. Be sure the packing material is moist but not soggy. When planting, place the plants in a bucket of water and carry it to the garden with you. This lets plants rehydrate and keeps them from drying out while you're planting.

Dig a hole deep enough so the roots will not be bent, and make a cone-shaped pile of soil in the bottom. Arrange the roots over the soil cone and gently fill the hole with loose soil. Hold the crown while you work to make sure it remains level with the soil line. Double-check to make sure the crown is neither protruding above the soil nor buried too deeply, and firm the soil with your hand. The illustration on the opposite page shows you how.

Bed Layout

Most strawberries spread by producing runners—long, slender shoots with a cluster of leaves at the top. The tips root when they touch the ground, forming daughter plants. Each daughter plant sends out its own runners, often in the same season it was formed.

There are three traditional methods for managing strawberries: matted rows, hills, and spaced runners. The methods differ in how runners are managed and how the plants are renewed.

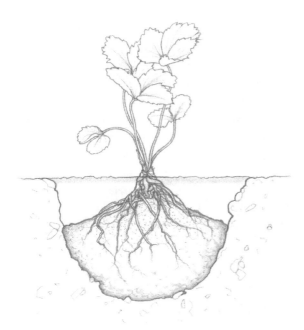

Proper planting level. Set the middle of a strawberry plant's crown level with the soil surface, and spread out the roots before refilling the planting hole and firming the plant in place.

Matted row system: Space plants 1½ to 2 feet apart in rows, with 4 feet between rows. Allow the runners to grow in all directions, so the daughter plants fill in between the mother plants to form a wide, solid row. Remove all flowers that appear in the first 3 to 4 months after planting to give the plants a good start.

The second and subsequent years, rejuvenate the bed immediately after the harvest is finished. Set your lawn mower blade at 2½ inches, mow the entire bed, and rake up all the debris. Then till or turn under the edges of the rows to leave a 1-foot strip down the center with the original mother plants in it. Spread several inches of compost over the bed and work it in on either side of the remaining plants. Water the bed well and renew the mulch between the rows. The undamaged crowns

of the strawberry plants will vigorously send out runners throughout the rest of the summer and produce a great crop the following year.

In most cases, even strawberries given the best of care will decline and produce low yields after as few as three seasons. It pays to start a fresh patch in a new location with new plants every few years, so as one declines, the next one is ready to produce.

The matted row system is well suited to June-bearers. For everbearers and day-neutrals, reduce the initial spacing within the row.

Hill system: Space plants 1 foot apart in rows, with 2 to 3 feet between rows. Remove all flowers the first 3 to 4 months after planting to give the plants a good start. Ruthlessly remove every runner so each plant remains a separate hill, channeling all of its energy into producing fruit. You'll get luscious, large berries and fewer disease problems because the crop will get good air circulation.

Renew the bed the third year by allowing enough runners to root in the row to replace the mother plants, which will be less productive because they have formed multiple crowns. Remove the mother plants in the fall after harvest.

The hill system is well suited to everbearers, since they produce fewer runners than June-bearers. It's a lot of work to keep up with runner removal with June-bearers.

Modified hill system for day-neutrals: Space plants 7 inches apart each way in double, staggered rows. Allow 3½- to 4-foot aisles between rows. Remove all flowers for the first 6 weeks after planting and all runners during the first growing season. Side-dress with compost or well-rotted manure once a month during the growing season. Mulch around plants to conserve moisture and smother weeds. Renew as for the hill system.

Spaced runner system: The spaced runner system is intermediate between the matted row and the hill systems. Space plants as for the matted row, and allow only a few runners to remain. Pin down the tips so the new plants will be spaced about 8 inches apart each way. Renew and care for as for matted row.

An interesting variation of renewing matted or spaced runners is to preserve a 1-foot strip of plants next to, but not including, the mother plants each year. This may add a few years to the productivity of your patch.

Care

Vigilant weed control is essential to prevent aggressive perennial weeds from outcompeting shallow-rooted strawberry plants. It helps to lay down a thick mulch of straw around the plants during summer.

Strawberries need 1 inch of water per week throughout the growing season. Drip irrigation works best; for information on installing a drip irrigation system, see the Drip Irrigation entry.

After the ground has frozen, cover the plants with fresh straw, pine boughs, or row cover to protect them from alternate freezing and thawing, which can heave plants from the soil. (In climates where a snow cover remains through the winter, strawberries need no special winter mulch.) Pull the mulch away from the plants in early spring so the ground can warm up. Reapply fresh mulch around the plants to smother early weeds. Leave row covers on over winter and into spring for slightly earlier harvests. Remove it when flowers open so bees can pollinate the blossoms.

Harvesting

Spring-planted June-bearers won't provide a harvest until a year after planting. Everbearers will produce a sizable late-summer crop, and day-neutrals will produce from midsummer through fall the year they're planted. Fall-planted berries will bear a full harvest the next growing season.

Harvest berries by pinching through the stem rather than pulling on the berry. Pick ripe berries every other day; always remove all ripe berries and any infected or malformed ones from the patch to prevent disease problems. During wet or humid weather, pick out diseased berries every day. Cull the moldy berries, wash your hands, and then pick the ripe berries. At the least, carry a second basket or a plastic bag to put moldy or damaged berries in while you pick.

Problems

Verticillium wilt and red stele infect the roots. They are often carried in on new plants and made worse by heavy, wet soil. Remove and destroy infected plants. Replace new plants in a new location or choose resistant cultivars. Vegetables like tomatoes and potatoes are also infected by verticillium wilt, so grow only resistant cultivars where these vegetables have grown in the last 3 years, and vice versa.

Gray mold rots the berries. Wet, humid weather and overcrowded beds with poor air circulation invite it. Keep rows narrow, thin out crowded plants, and remove moldy berries from the plants immediately to control gray mold.

Berries injured by the tarnished plant bug don't grow or ripen properly but remain small and woody or form hard, seedy tips. See page 454 for controls. Birds love strawberries; cover plants with netting, and see the Animal Pests entry for other suggestions. Slugs can take a bite out of your ripe berries; the Slugs and Snails entry lists controls.

SUNCHOKE

Helianthus tuberosus
Asteraceae

This hardy perennial, also called Jerusalem artichoke and sunroot, is a type of sunflower grown for its vitamin- and mineral-rich roots. Cook them as you would potatoes, or enjoy their sweet nutty flavor by adding raw slices to a salad or a stir-fry.

Planting: Plant whole tubers or large pieces in spring or fall in loose, fertile soil. Allow them plenty of room because the root systems can spread widely. If you have the space, plant this crop in an out-of-the-way place, separate from your regular vegetable garden. Place the tubers 1 foot apart in 4-inch-deep furrows spaced 3 feet apart. The plants will grow into 6- to 10-foot single stalks topped with 3-inch, rough-looking sunflowers.

Growing guidelines: Apply a layer of mulch in late spring to keep weeds down and retain soil moisture. This crop spreads rapidly if not controlled. Each year, dig up all the tubers beginning in late summer and continuing until the soil freezes. Chances are you'll miss a few, which will resprout the following spring to provide next year's crop.

Problems: Sunchokes are usually free of insect and disease problems. The only problem you may have with this crop is keeping it under control. The invasive root and topgrowth can overwhelm neighboring crops.

Harvesting: Once the foliage has died down (after the first frost), dig roots with a spading fork as needed. The tubers are thin skinned, so keep them moist until you're ready to eat them, otherwise they will shrivel. Roots keep best in the ground, even over winter.

SUNFLOWER

Helianthus annuus
Asteraceae

While often admired as ornamentals, sunflowers have an amazing variety of uses. They make a good fodder for poultry and livestock, dyes come from the petals, and paper can be made from the stalk pith. Its seeds and seed meal feed countless people, animals, and birds; sunflower-seed oil is used in cooking and in soaps and cosmetics. In the garden, you can grow sunflowers as windbreaks, privacy screens, or living supports for pole beans. Of course, they're also the stars of any bird garden.

Sunflowers come in a wide assortment of sizes and colors. Some cultivars grow as tall as 15 feet, and the flower heads can be as big as 1 foot across; dwarf types, however, are only 1½ to 2 feet tall. There are also early, medium-height sunflowers that stand 5 to 6 feet tall but have heads that are 8 to 10 inches across. Some cultivars produce a single large flower; others form several heads. A renaissance in sunflower breeding has produced a host of ornamental cultivars for bouquets, including smaller flowers in shades of cream, yellow, mahogany, burgundy, cinnamon, lemon, and bronze, often with bicolored petals and contrasting dark centers. If you're planning to grow sunflowers for seed, good choices are 'Snack Seed', 'Sunzilla', 'Kong', 'American Giants', and 'Titan'. There are many others. If you fall in love with sunflowers, be sure to visit the Web site of the National Sunflower Association; see Resources on page 673.

Planting: If possible, choose a site in full sun on the north side of the garden, so the tall sunflower plants won't shade your other vegetables. Sunflowers aren't fussy about soil.

Seedlings are cold resistant, so short-season growers may want to get a head start by planting several weeks before the last frost. In most areas, though, it's best to wait until the soil is warmer, around the last frost date. Sow seeds 1 inch deep and 6 inches apart. Thin large types to 1½ feet apart and dwarf or medium-size cultivars to 1 foot apart. Water well after planting.

Growing guidelines: Apply a 3- to 4-inch layer of mulch to conserve moisture and keep down weeds. Sunflowers are drought resistant, but they'll grow better if you water regularly from the time the flowers begin to develop until they're mature.

Problems: Sunflowers are remarkably trouble-free, but for details on controlling aphids, see page 454. Rotate the crop if leaf mottle, a soil fungus that produces dead areas along leaf veins, becomes a problem. An early autumn may interfere with pollination and cause the plant to form empty seeds; plant earlier the next year. To protect seeds from birds, cover the flowers with mesh bags, cheesecloth, old panty hose, or perforated plastic bags.

Harvesting: Harvest as soon as seeds start to turn brown or the backs of the seed heads turn yellow. The heads usually droop at this time. Cut them along with 2 feet of stem and hang upside down in a dry, well-ventilated place, such as a garage or attic, until fully dry. Rub two seed heads together to extract the seeds, or use a wire brush or similar tool. Spread out damp seeds on a rack until fully dry; store in plastic bags for birds and animal food. To eat, soak overnight in water (or in strong salt water, if a salty flavor is desired), drain, spread on a shallow baking sheet, and roast for 3 hours at 200°F, or until crisp. You can also set out an entire dried head for the wild birds, who prefer black oil sunflower seeds but will eat any, even from dwarf flower heads; or shell the seeds and set them out in a feeder.

SWEET PEA

See *Lathyrus*

SWEET POTATO

Ipomoea batatas
Convolvulaceae

Sweet potatoes grow well in a sunny vegetable garden, but you can also grow them in other parts of your home landscape. Try them as a temporary groundcover or a trailing houseplant. In a patio planter, a sweet potato vine will form a beautiful foliage plant that you can harvest roots from in fall.

Sweet potato flesh is classified as moist or dry. Moist, deep orange types are sometimes called yams; the most popular varieties for home gardens are moist types, including 'Centennial' and 'Georgia Jet'. Sweet potatoes are grown worldwide, from tropical regions to temperate climates. This warm-weather crop is remarkably nutritious and versatile. Each fleshy root is rich in vitamins A and C, along with many important minerals. Use them raw, boiled, or baked, in soups, casseroles, desserts, breads, or stir-fries—and don't forget to try some homemade sweet potato fries!

Planting: Sweet potatoes will grow in poor soil, but roots may be deformed in heavy clay or long and stringy in sandy soil. To create the perfect environment, build long, wide, 10-inch-high ridges spaced 3½ feet apart. (A 10-foot row will produce 8 to 10 pounds of potatoes.) Work in plenty of compost, avoiding nitrogen-rich fertilizers that produce lush vines and stunted tubes. In the North, cover the raised rows with black plastic to keep the soil warm and promote strong growth.

It's best to plant root sprouts, called slips, which are available from nurseries and mail-order suppliers. Or you can grow your own by saving a few roots from your previous crop or by buying untreated roots (store-bought sweet potatoes often are waxed to prevent sprouting). About 6 weeks before it's time to plant sweet potatoes outdoors in your area, place the roots in a box of moist sand, sawdust, or chopped leaves in a warm spot (75° to 80°F). Shoots will sprout, and when they reach 6 to 9 inches long, cut them off the root. Remove and dispose of the bottom inch from each slip, as that portion sometimes harbors disease organisms.

Sweet potatoes mature in 90 to 170 days and are extremely frost sensitive. Plant in full sun 3 to 4 weeks after the last frost when the soil has warmed. Make holes 6 inches deep and 12 inches apart. Bury slips up to the top leaves, press the soil down gently but firmly, and water well.

Growing guidelines: If you're not using black plastic, mulch the vines 2 weeks after planting to smother weeds, conserve moisture, and keep the soil loose for root development. Occasionally lift longer vines to keep them from rooting at the joints, or they will put their energy into forming many undersized tubers at each rooted area rather than ripening the main crop at the base of the plant. Otherwise, handle plants as little as possible to prevent wounds that might be invaded by disease spores.

If the weather is dry, provide 1 inch of water a week until 2 weeks before harvesting, then let the soil dry out a bit. Don't overwater, or the plants—which can withstand dry spells better than rainy ones—may rot.

Problems: Southern gardeners are more likely to encounter pest problems than gardeners in northern areas.

Sweet potato weevils—¼-inch-long insects with dark blue heads and wings and red-orange bodies—puncture stems and tubers to lay their eggs. Developing larvae tunnel and feed on the fleshy roots, while adults generally attack vines and leaves. They also spread foot rot, which creates enlarging brown to black areas on stems near the soil and at stem ends. Since weevils multiply quickly and are hard to eliminate, use certified disease-resistant slips and practice a 4-year crop rotation. Destroy infected plants and their roots, or place in sealed containers and dispose of them with household trash.

Fungal diseases include black rot, which results in circular, dark depressions on tubers. Discard infected potatoes, and cure the undamaged roots from the same crop carefully. Don't confuse this disease with less-serious scurf, which creates small, round, dark spots on tuber surfaces but doesn't affect eating quality. Stem rot, or wilt, is a fungus that enters plants injured by insects, careless cultivation, or wind. Even if this disease doesn't kill the plants, the harvest will be poor. Minimize the chances of disease by planting only healthy slips; avoid black and stem rot by planting resistant cultivars. Reduce the incidence of dry rot, which mummifies stored potatoes, by keeping the fleshy roots at 55° to 60°F.

Harvesting: You can harvest as soon as leaves start to yellow, but the longer a crop is left in the ground, the higher the yield and vitamin content. Once frost blackens the vines, however, tubers can quickly rot.

Use a spading fork to dig tubers on a sunny day when the soil is dry. Remember that tubers can grow a foot or more from the plant, and that any nicks on their tender skins will encourage spoilage. Dry tubers in the sun for several hours, then move them to a well-ventilated spot and keep at 85° to 90°F for 10 to 15 days. After they are cured, store at around 55°F, with a humidity of 75 to 80 percent. Properly cured and stored sweet potatoes will keep for several months.

SYMPHYOTRICHUM

See *Aster*

SYRINGA

Lilac. Deciduous, spring-blooming shrubs or trees.

Description: *Syringa laciniata* (aka *S.* ×*laciniata*), cutleaf lilac, has a rounded, arching form and grows to a mature height of about 6 feet. Its leaves are opposite, often deeply lobed. Fragrant, lavender flowers are borne in 3-inch-long, loose clusters along the branches in spring. Cutleaf lilac is one of the few lilacs to flower reliably in the South. Zones 4–8.

S. meyeri, Meyer lilac, is a broad shrub, 4 to 8 feet tall. It bears ¾- to 1¾-inch, dark green, oval leaves. Violet-purple, fragrant flowers are borne in 4-inch clusters in spring, covering the plants. Zones 4–7.

S. reticulata, Japanese tree lilac, is a large shrub or small tree with a rounded crown, growing to a mature height of 30 feet. The 5-inch, dark green leaves are broad and nearly heart-shaped. Plants bloom in summer, bearing fragrant yellowish white flowers in loose, lacy, 6- to 12-inch clusters at the branch tips. Zones 3–7.

S. vulgaris, common lilac, is an upright, vase-shaped shrub that can grow to a mature height of 20 feet. Dark green, 2- to 5-inch leaves are basically heart-shaped. The flowers are purplish or white, fragrant, and borne in 4- to 8-inch terminal clusters in spring. Zones 3–7.

How to grow: Provide lilacs with full sun and good drainage. Once established, they need minimal watering. Remove spent blooms, or flower bud formation for the following year may be inhibited by seed development. Prune immediately after bloom by removing a few of the oldest stems a few inches above ground level each year. This will keep the plant growing vigorously. Powdery mildew can be a problem. Choose cultivars that are resistant to this fungal disease, and don't plant them in shade. Meyer lilac is mildew resistant.

Landscape uses: Japanese tree lilac makes a fine street tree. The other lilacs are useful as hedges, specimens, or in shrub borders.

T

TAGETES

Marigold. Summer- and fall-blooming annuals.

Description: French marigolds, derived from *Tagetes patula*, include most of the dwarf cultivars, while the generally taller African cultivars arose from *T. erecta* (aka Aztec marigold). Hybridizing has also produced many cultivars with intermediate characteristics. As a group, marigolds grow 8 to 42 inches tall, as low mounds or erect bushes. The 1- to 4-inch flowers may be rounded, tufted, or shaggy puffs in shades of white, yellow, orange, mahogany, maroon, and rust. Dark green leaves are dense, ferny, and often strongly scented. Other worthy marigolds include the signet group from *T. tenuifolia*, which has 8-inch mounds of lacy, lemon-scented leaves and edible, ½-inch red, orange, or yellow single flowers. *T. filifolia*, Irish lace marigold, is grown for its dense 1-foot mounds of delicate foliage.

How to grow: Marigolds are so easy to grow that they're often a child's first garden success. Given warmth, they grow quickly. Sow seed indoors a few weeks before the last frost (especially recommended for the taller cultivars) or direct-seed when the soil is warm. Give them full sun in average soil and moisture for best results, but don't worry if the soil is poor or dry. Excess fertility may promote lush growth, few flowers, and soft stems, especially in the tall cultivars, which then need to be staked. Wash spider mites off with regular, strong hosings or control with soap spray. Remove spent flowers regularly to encourage more blooms.

Landscape uses: Marigolds are the backbone of many plantings due to their diversity and adaptability. Use them in beds, borders, edges, pots, and boxes. Disguise dying bulb foliage with marigolds, or fill gaps left by discarded spring-blooming annuals and biennials. They also make long-lasting cut flowers, excellent for informal arrangements.

TAXUS

Yew. Needle-leaved evergreen shrubs or trees.

Description: *Taxus baccata*, English yew, is a tree or shrub with deep green foliage. The shrubby cultivars usually mature under 4 feet tall, while the trees grow 15 to 25 feet. Weeping forms are available. The bark is cinnamon brown and sinewy. Zones 6–7.

T. cuspidata, Japanese yew, is a shrub or tree ranging from 4 to 40 feet when mature, depending on the cultivar. As with the other yews, the needles are flattened and green, having two white lines on the (usually) lighter green undersides. Zones 4–7.

T. ×*media*, hybrid yew, has cultivars in numerous shapes and sizes, from 2 to 20 feet tall; like the other yews, it has dark green needles and bears seeds with fleshy red coats in fall. Zones 4–7.

How to grow: Provide good drainage, as yews cannot tolerate standing water for any length of time. In the North, site yews out of direct wind; in the South, plant out of direct sun. Provide even moisture and mulch. Yews don't need much supplemental water once they're established. Black vine weevil occasionally feeds on yew, leaving C-shaped notches on the needles. Note that all parts of the yew, including its tempting red fruits, are poisonous when eaten.

Landscape uses: An exceptional specimen can make a striking focal point, but yews are useful mostly for hedges, massed planting, and foundation plantings.

Try combining the rounded shapes of yews with tall, narrow cedars, or make a low planting of yews and creeping junipers.

THUJA

Arborvitae. Scaly-leaved evergreen trees or shrubs.

Description: *Thuja occidentalis*, American arborvitae or eastern white cedar, is a native pyramidal tree that can grow 40 to 60 feet tall. Its medium to light green foliage is fanlike, rather vertical, and aromatic when crushed. Zones 3–7.

T. plicata, giant arborvitae or western red cedar, also has a pyramidal form and can reach a mature height of 50 to 70 feet. Native to the West Coast, it has darker green, glossier foliage than American arborvitae and is more aromatic when crushed. Zones 4–6.

How to grow: Provide arborvitaes with full sun, good drainage, and even moisture. Pruning is rarely necessary except where these plants are used as a formal hedge. Watch for damage from bagworms; remove these pests before they become a problem. If you attempt to tear the bag away, you'll almost certainly leave a coil of tightly wound silk that will girdle the twig. To avoid this hazard, use a knife to cut the silk from the branch or twig. Mites may be a problem in hot weather; control by hosing the plant with water or using a soap spray.

Landscape uses: Use arborvitaes as a hedge, specimen, windbreak, or screen.

THYME

Thymus spp.
Lamiaceae

Description: Versatile and beautiful, thymes should have a place in every herb garden. All thymes are perennial herbs with very small leaves and tiny flowers ranging in color from white through pink to deep rose-magenta. The creeping types, such as mother-of-thyme (*Thymus praecox*, formerly *T. serpyllum*), will cover bricks and stones or low walls and can tolerate a certain amount of foot traffic. *T.* 'Coccineus' is a mat-forming cultivar with showy reddish purple flowers and bronze fall foliage. The bush forms are 6 to 8 inches high and have woody, wiry stems and branches. Zones 4–8.

Common thyme (*T. vulgaris*) is the type of thyme most frequently used for cooking. Most cultivars are very fragrant, with aromas reminiscent of coconut, orange, balsam, oregano, lime, or nutmeg. Golden lemon thyme (*T. ×citriodorus* 'Aureus', aka *T. pulegioides*) has yellow-edged leaves and a strong lemon odor. Zones 4–9 and 5–9, depending on the species and cultivar.

How to grow: Thymes need full sun and a dry, gritty soil. Buy named cultivars as plants, or plant thyme seed outdoors in a prepared bed in fall or spring, or start your seeds in flats indoors. Bush thymes (except for variegated cultivars) often seed themselves freely, so there should be no shortage of new plants if the old ones don't come through a hard winter. To propagate cultivars, separate rooted pieces or take cuttings. In the North, protect plants from winter damage with a covering of evergreen boughs.

Harvesting: When plants are beginning to flower, cut off the top half and hang to dry in a shady place or dry on trays in a food dehydrator. Once the leaves are thoroughly dry, strip them from the stems and store in a dark place until ready to use. You may harvest pieces from thyme plants all summer, but don't cut them back severely in fall.

Uses: One of the essential oils in thyme is thymol, still used by pharmacists, especially in cough remedies. Thyme is antiseptic, as well as an aid to digestion. In the kitchen, thyme is a wonderful addition to pasta and pizza sauces, salad dressings, stews, stuffings, meat loaf, and soups, and it is especially good with poultry, fish, and eggs.

TOADS

Like ladybugs and earthworms, toads are humble heroes in the garden. One toad will eat 10,000 to 20,000 insects a year (that's 50 to 100 every night from spring until fall hibernation). Toads will clean up slugs, flies, grubs, wood lice, cutworms, grasshoppers, and anything else that's smaller (and slower) than they are. And unlike many part-time garden allies, toads won't do an about-face and head for your vegetables and flowers as dessert.

To encourage toads to make your garden their home, provide shelter and water and, above all, use only the least-toxic organic pesticides. Toads like to live in places that are fairly light, humid, and out of the wind; you might find them in a rock garden or an old stone wall. Make your own toad shelters by digging shallow depressions in the garden (just a few inches deep) and loosely covering them with boards. (Leave the toad room to get in!) A plant saucer or ground-level birdbath will provide water for your toads. Of course, you can also buy a cute ready-made "toad house" from a garden catalog or your local garden center. Set it near rocks or plants where the toads can take shelter from predators.

Once a toad has found your garden, it may live there for decades. Remember, too, that toads, like frogs, lay their eggs in ponds. Adding a water garden to your yard may provide a breeding ground for future generations of toads.

The toads most likely to find a home in your garden in the East are the American toad, a brown, rusty, or tan amphibian that's 2 to 4½ inches long, and the eastern spadefoot toad, which is 1¾ to 4 inches long with pale lines running down its back. In the South, the southern toad, which may be brown, gray, or brick red and is 1½ to 4 inches long is the common species. Gardeners in the West will find the western spadefoot toad, which is 1½ to 2½ inches long. There's also a midwestern species, the Plains spadefoot, a plump toad that is 1½ to 2½ inches long. Spadefoot toads are burrowers that dig their homes in dry soil. They are brown and comparatively smooth skinned.

Don't forget: Toads are not poisonous, and they don't cause warts. They are your garden allies, so encourage them to make themselves at home in your landscape!

TOMATO

Solanum lycopersicum
Solanaceae

Since tomatoes are America's favorite garden vegetable, it's no surprise that there are hundreds of varieties to choose from. Home garden tomatoes range from bite-size currant, cherry, and grape tomatoes to huge beefsteak fruits, in nearly every color except blue. You can grow varieties that produce fruit extra early, and there are varieties for every type of climate, including many that are resistant to one or more common tomato diseases. Don't forget tomatoes especially developed for slicing, canning, juicing, or stuffing, too.

Types: Discovering which tomato varieties are best for your garden will involve some experimenting, and your climate; personal taste will play a role, too. Some early types such as 'New Girl' and 'First Lady II' will be ready to pick about 2 months after you set plants in your garden, while main-season hybrid and heirloom varieties can take up to 80 days. To extend your harvesting season, be sure to plant some of each type.

Many standard cultivars are adapted for a variety of uses, including slicing, canning, and salads. The large, meaty fruits of beefsteak tomatoes are especially popular for slicing. Italian or paste tomatoes are favorites for cooking, canning, and juicing. Sweet bite-size tomatoes in a range of colors are very popular for salads or as snacks.

Tomato plants are vines, and they have two basic ways of growing, called determinate and indeterminate. The vines of determinate varieties (sometimes called bush tomatoes) grow only 1 to 3 feet long, and the main stem and side stems produce about three flower clusters each. Once flowers form at the vine tips, the plant stops growing. This means determinate types set fruit over about a 2-week period and then stop, which makes them excellent choices for canning. Indeterminate tomatoes have sprawling vines that grow 6 to 20 feet long. Most produce about three flower clusters at every second leaf. They keep growing and producing unless stopped by frost, disease, or lack of nutrients, which means you can keep picking fresh tomatoes the whole season. Pruning is necessary, however, or they will put too much energy into vine production.

Planting: Nurseries and garden centers offer a wide range of dependable, disease-resistant varieties such as 'Jet Star', 'Celebrity', and 'Sweet 100', and many sell transplants of popular heirloom tomatoes such as 'Brandywine', 'Green Zebra', and 'Cherokee Purple' as well. But if you want to take advantage of the full range of available cultivars, you'll have to grow tomatoes from seed. Unless you plan to preserve a lot of your crop, three to five plants per person is usually adequate. Unused seeds are good for 3 years. Specialty mail-order suppliers also offer individual tomato plants for sale, which could be a good option if you don't have space for growing your own from seed.

At 6 to 8 weeks before the average last frost, sow seeds ¼ inch deep and 1 inch apart in well-drained flats. Seeds will germinate in about 1 week when the soil temperature is 75° to 85°F; at 60°F the germination process can take 2 weeks.

In most places, a sunny spot indoors, such as a south-facing window, provides the warm, humid environment young seedlings need. If you don't have sunny windows, use a heating coil for bottom heat and a fluorescent or grow light overhead. Lack of adequate light will make seedlings leggy and weak.

Once the seedlings emerge, keep the temperature no higher than 70°F, and water regularly. Once a week, feed with compost tea or fish emulsion, and discard any weak or sick-looking seedlings. When the second set of leaves—the first true leaves—appear, transplant to individual pots or deep containers (such as plastic cups), burying the stems deeper than they stood previously. Whatever container you use, make sure it has drainage holes in the bottom. After this initial transplanting, give the seedlings less water and more sun. As the weather warms, harden off the plants before planting them in the garden. Again, discard any weaklings that might harbor disease.

If you buy a four-pack or six-pack of transplants from a garden center, it's a good idea to transplant them to individual pots and harden them off for a week or two before setting them out in the garden. They'll have a more vigorous root system, and you can make sure that the soil is warm and the weather settled before planting day.

Except in extremely hot climates, plant tomatoes where they will get full sun. To lessen shock, though, transplant seedlings on a cloudy day. Make the planting holes larger than normal for each seedling; cover the bottom of the hole with several inches of sifted compost mixed with a handful of bonemeal. For magnesium, which promotes plant vitality and productivity, sprinkle 1 teaspoon of Epsom salts into each hole. Disturb the soil around

seedling roots as little as possible when you set them in contact with the compost.

Set the transplant so the lowest set of leaves is at soil level; fill the hole with a mixture of compost and soil. Or you can bury the stem horizontally in a shallow trench so that only the top leaves show; make sure you strip off the leaves along the part of the stem that will be buried. Many growers claim this planting method produces higher yields. Press down the soil gently but firmly to remove air pockets, and water well.

If you're planting a bit early, or in general want to speed the growth of your tomatoes, you can shelter them with a commercial device such as a Wall O' Water or simply wrap tomato cages with clear plastic. For more on such techniques, see the Season Extension entry.

Spacing between planting holes depends on how you grow your tomatoes. If you're going to stake and prune the plants or train them on trellises, space the seedlings 2 feet apart. If you plan to let them sprawl, space them 3 to 4 feet apart.

Letting plants sprawl involves less work, but it requires more garden space. And unless protected by a very thick mulch, the plants and fruits are also more subject to insects and diseases due to contact with the soil—not to mention being more accessible to four-legged predators, such as voles.

If you plan to train your tomato plants on stakes or in cages, install the supports before planting. Pound 5-to 7-foot-long stakes 6 to 8 inches in the ground or insert the cages (it's a good idea to secure cages with stakes, too). As the vines grow on staked tomatoes, tie them loosely to the stake at 6-inch intervals with soft twine or strips of cloth or nylon stockings.

There are also ready-made tomato cages, but they are expensive to buy and usually aren't tall enough. For details on making your own tomato

Long-Lasting Tomato Cages

Tomato cages made from concrete reinforcing wire will last many years. You can buy the wire at just about any building-supply center. Figure on buying at least 16 feet—enough for two cages.

The only tool you need is a small pair of bolt cutters to cut the heavy wire. Be sure to wear work gloves to avoid cuts and blisters.

Building a cage is easy. Lay the mesh strip flat on the ground, and use bricks or concrete blocks to weigh down the edges; otherwise it can spring up suddenly as you cut the mesh. Measure an 8-foot piece by counting off 16 sections of the mesh (each section of mesh is 5¼ by 6 inches). At that point, cut through the cross wires flush with one of the vertical wires. Then also cut away the pointed wire pieces that result on the other section of wire. Now gently bend the prepared mesh section into a circle, and use flexible wire to fasten the edges together.

You'll need to set two stakes in place to hold the cage in place. Do that before planting. Once you have planted your young tomato plants, set a cage upright around each plant, and fasten the cages securely to the stakes. At the end of the season, clear off old vines and store the cages for winter, or leave the cages standing and have them double as compost bins. Fill them with organic material, and you'll have plenty of good organic fertilizer ready for next summer's tomato crop.

---

cages, see "Long-Lasting Tomato Cages" above.

Any slight frost will harm young tomato plants, and nighttime temperatures below 55°F will prevent fruit from setting. In case of a late frost, protect transplants with cloches or hot caps, because cold damage early in a tomato's life can reduce fruit production for the entire season.

Growing guidelines: Cultivate lightly to keep down any weeds until the soil is warm, then lay down a deep mulch to smother the weeds and conserve moisture. Give the plants at least 1 inch of water a week, keeping in mind that a deep soaking is better than several light waterings. Avoid wetting the foliage, since wet leaves are more prone to diseases.

A weekly dose of liquid seaweed will increase fruit production and plant health, as will side-dressing with compost two or three times during the growing season.

If you stake your plants, you may want to prune them to encourage higher yields. Pruned tomatoes take up less space and are likely to produce fruit 2 weeks earlier than unpruned ones; they do, however, take more work. Pruning tomatoes is different from pruning trees and shrubs—the only tools you should need are your fingers. You'll be removing suckers, which are small shoots that emerge from the main stem or side stem at the base of each leaf, as shown on the opposite page.

Leave a few suckers on the middle and top of the plant to protect the fruit from sunscald, especially if you live in a hot, sunny area, such as in the South. Sunscald produces light gray patches of skin that are subject to disease. When the vine reaches the top of the stakes or cage, pinch back the tips to encourage more flowering and fruit.

Problems: Although tomatoes are potentially subject to a range of pests and diseases, plants that are growing in rich soil with adequate spacing and support to keep them off the soil usually have few problems. Here are some of the common potential tomato problems.

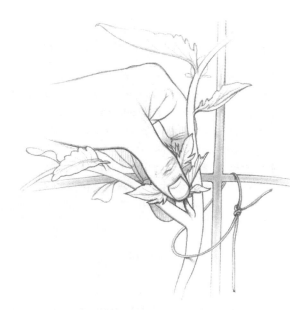

Pinching tomato suckers. Use your thumb and forefinger to snap off the small, tender shoots that sprout at the base of tomato leaf stems. If you need to use scissors or pruning shears, you've waited too long.

- The tomato hornworm—a large, white-striped, green caterpillar—is an easy-to-spot pest. Just handpick and destroy, or spray plants with Bt (*Bacillus thuringiensis*). If you're handpicking, check to see whether hornworms have been attacked by parasitic wasps first—if they have, the wasp larvae will have pupated, forming structures that look like small white grains of rice on the back of the hornworm. Leave these hornworms be so the wasps can spread. Also, plant dill near your tomatoes. It attracts hornworms, and they're easier to spot on dill than they are on tomato plants.

- Aphids, flea beetles, and cutworms may also attack your tomato plants. See page 454 for details on controlling these pests.

- Hard-to-spot spider mites look like tiny red dots on the undersides of leaves. Their feeding causes yellow speckling on leaves, which eventually turn brown and die. Knock these pests off the plant by spraying with water, or control with insecticidal soap.

- If you are new to growing tomatoes, check with your county extension agent to find out what diseases are prevalent in your area. If you can, choose varieties that are resistant to those diseases. Such resistance is generally indicated by one or more letters after the cultivar name. The code "VFNT," for example, indicates that the cultivar is resistant to verticillium (V) and fusarium (F) wilts, as well as nematodes (N) and tobacco mosaic (T).

- Nematodes, microscopic wormlike creatures, attack a plant's root system, stunting growth and lowering disease resistance. The best defenses against nematodes are rotating crops and planting resistant cultivars.

- Verticillium wilt and fusarium wilt are two common tomato diseases. Should these wilts strike and cause leaves to curl up, turn yellow, and drop off, pull up and destroy infected plants, or put them in sealed containers and dispose of them with household trash.

- Another disease, early blight, makes dark, sunken areas on leaves just as the first fruits start to mature. Late blight appears as black, irregular,

Tomatoes in Small Spaces

Even if you don't have much room to grow vegetables, you can still enjoy the taste of a fresh-picked tomato. Tomatoes are easy to grow in containers, making them perfect for decks, patios, or balconies. If you have the space, try growing full-size tomatoes in large fiberglass tubs or wooden barrels. For people with less room, there are dwarf cherry tomato cultivars, such as 'Tiny Tim' and 'Pixie Hybrid II', that can grow in 6-inch-deep pots.

All container tomatoes need lots of sun, plenty of water, and a rich, well-drained potting mixture. Compensate for the restricted root zone by applying liquid fertilizer, such as compost tea, lightly but frequently, increasing both water and nutrients as the plants grow. See the Compost entry for instructions for making compost tea.

water-soaked patches on leaves and dark-colored spots on fruits. Both blights tend to occur during cool, rainy weather. To avoid losing your whole crop, quickly destroy or dispose of affected plants. The best defense is to plant resistant cultivars. Bicarbonate sprays can also help prevent the disease from infecting your plants.

- Blossom drop, where mature flowers fall off the plant, is most prevalent in cool rainy weather or where soil moisture is low and winds are hot and dry. It can also be from a magnesium deficiency or from infection by parasitic bacteria or fungi. Large-fruited tomatoes are particularly vulnerable. Fruit set can sometimes be encouraged by gently shaking the plant in the middle of a warm, sunny day or by tapping the stake to which the plant is tied.

- Blossom-end rot appears as a water-soaked spot near the blossom end when the fruit is about one-third developed. The spot enlarges and turns dark brown and leathery until it covers half the tomato. This problem is due to a calcium deficiency, often brought on by an uneven water supply. Blossom-end rot can also be caused by damaged feeder roots from careless transplanting, so always handle seedlings gently. Try to keep the soil evenly moist by using a mulch and watering when needed.

- Prolonged periods of heavy rainfall that keep the soil constantly moist can cause leaf roll, which can affect more than half the foliage and cut fruit production significantly. At first, the edges of leaves curl up to form cups; then the edges overlap and the leaves become firm and leathery to the touch. Keeping soil well drained and well aerated is about the only method of preventing this problem.

- Fruit cracks that radiate from the stems or run around the shoulders are often caused by hot, rainy weather or by fluctuating moisture levels in the soil. Such cracks, aside from being unsightly, attract infections. To avoid them, make sure you don't overwater.

- Tomatoes—like eggplants, potatoes, and peppers—are related to tobacco and subject to the same diseases, including tobacco mosaic. Therefore, don't smoke around such plants, and wash your hands after smoking before handling them. Plan your garden so that nightshade-family crops, such as peppers and tomatoes, are separated by plants from other families.

Harvesting: Once tomatoes start ripening, check the vines almost daily in order to harvest fruits at their peak. Cut or gently twist off the fruits, supporting the vine at the same time to keep from damaging it.

Most plants can survive a light frost if adequately mulched, but at the first sign of a heavy frost, harvest all the fruits, even the green ones. To continue enjoying fresh tomatoes, cut a few suckers from a healthy and preferably determinate plant and root them. Plant in good potting soil in 3-gallon or larger containers. Keep in a warm, sunny spot, and with a little luck and care, you can enjoy fresh tomatoes right through winter.

Ripe tomatoes will keep refrigerated for several weeks, and green ones will eventually ripen if kept in a warm place out of direct sunlight. To slowly ripen green tomatoes, and thereby extend your harvest, wrap them in newspaper and place in a dark, cool area, checking frequently to make sure that none rot. Sliced green tomatoes are delicious when lightly dipped in egg, then in flour or cornmeal and black pepper, and fried.

TOOLS AND EQUIPMENT

The wise gardener starts with a small collection of basic tools and builds from there. Stores and catalogs are packed with both familiar and outlandish-looking hand tools. And if that weren't enough, there are gas- or electric-powered versions of many tools. Deciding which tools you need takes time, and the ideal collection depends on your gardening style and scope.

Your starter collection will include a fork or spade for digging, a garden rake for smoothing the soil and preparing beds, a hoe for cultivating and weeding, and a trowel for working closely around plants. Pruning tools and a lawn mower round out a basic tool collection.

Whenever it's practical, use hand tools rather than power tools. Power tools are expensive and contribute to air and noise pollution as well as global warming. Designing your yard to be low maintenance will reduce your tool needs and increase your enjoyment of the garden. For more details on low-care landscapes, see the Landscaping entry.

Hand Tools

Hand tools form the basis for a garden tool collection. If you keep them sharp, good-quality hand tools will make your garden work go quickly and easily.

Hoes: You can use hoes to lay out rows, dig furrows, cultivate around plants to loosen the soil and kill weeds, create hills and raised beds, break up clods, and prepare bare spots in lawns for reseeding.

The standard American pattern hoe is a long-handled tool that allows you to work without too much bending. It has a broad, straight blade, a little larger than 6 inches wide and 4 inches deep. However, many gardeners prefer a nursery hoe, which is lighter and has a 2- to 3-inch-deep blade.

Use an oscillating hoe, also called a hula or action hoe, with a moving blade that cuts on both the push and pull stroke to slice weeds just below the soil surface.

Narrow hoe blades use your arm power more efficiently than wider blades. The hoe handle should be at least 4½ feet long so you can work without bending over and straining your lower-back muscles. In general, when working with hoes, try to remain standing upright and run the hoe blade below and parallel to the soil surface. Keep your hoe sharp so it will cut through weeds rather than yank them out.

Shovels: A standard American long-handled shovel is good for mixing cement and for scooping up soil, gravel, and sand. You can use it to pry rocks and root clumps from the soil, although a heavy-duty prybar is more effective and efficient for these tasks. You also can use a shovel to dig planting holes, but a garden fork or a spade generally works better for most digging.

The standard shovel handle is about 4 feet. The shovel handle should come to shoulder height or higher. Shovels should also have a turned edge or footrest on the top of the blade to protect your feet when you step on the tool.

Spades: Spades have a flat, rather than scooped, blade with squared edges. With a spade, you can cut easily through sod and create straight edges in soil. Use a spade for digging planting holes, prying up rocks, dividing and moving perennials, cutting unwanted tree and shrub roots, tamping sod, and digging trenches.

A spade handle is generally shorter than a shovel handle, usually ranging from 28 to 32 inches. Like shovels, spades should also have a turned edge or footrest on the top of the blade.

Forks: Spading forks cut into soil, usually more easily than solid-bladed tools can. A spading fork is handy for loosening and mixing materials into the soil, dividing perennials, and for harvesting potatoes, carrots, and other root crops. The tines of a standard spading fork are broad and flat; those of the English cultivating fork are thinner and square. The English version is better for cultivating and aerating soil. Use a pitchfork (three tines) or a straw fork (five or six tines) for picking up, turning, and scattering hay mulch, leaf mold, and light compost materials.

The standard handle length for a spading fork is 28 inches. Very tall gardeners may prefer a 32-inch handle. Short gardeners, including children, should use a border fork, which has shorter tines and handle.

Trowels: Use a trowel to dig planting holes for small plants and bulbs, for transplanting seedlings, or for weeding beds and borders.

Some trowels are made from forged steel and fitted with hardwood handles; good ones are also available in unbreakable one-piece cast aluminum. Trowels come with a variety of blade widths and lengths. Choose one that feels comfortable in your hand.

Rakes: Rakes generally fall into one of two categories: garden rakes and leaf rakes. Garden rakes are essential for leveling ground, creating raised beds, killing emerging weeds, gathering debris from rows, covering furrows, thinning seedlings, working materials shallowly into the soil, erasing footprints, and spreading mulch. Garden rakes come in many widths, with long or short teeth that are widely or closely spaced. The handle should be long (4½ to 5 feet), and the head should be heavy enough to bite into the soil easily. If you have rocky soil, choose a rake with widely spaced teeth.

Lawn or leaf rakes, also called fan rakes, are good for gathering up leaves, grass clippings, weeds, and other debris and for dislodging thatch from the lawn. Metal lawn rakes last longest and are the springiest, although many gardeners prefer the action and feel of bamboo tines, and some prefer plastic or rubber.

Pruning tools: There are two types of pruning shears: the anvil type, with a straight blade that closes down onto an anvil or plate, and the bypass type, which cuts like scissors. Anvil pruners are often easier to use, requiring less hand pressure to

SMART SHOPPING
Tools

The first rule of tool buying is to avoid cheap tools at all costs. They are poorly designed and constructed, they don't do the job well, and they break easily. Also, don't buy cheap tools for children; they won't learn to love gardening if the first tools they use don't work well. Here are some other tips to keep in mind when shopping for tools.

- The best wood for the handle of a shovel and all long-handled garden tools is North American white ash, which is strong, light, and resilient. Hickory is stronger but heavier and is ideal for hammers and other short-handled tools.

- Examine the lines (rings) in a wooden handle; they should run straight down the entire length of the handle, with no knots. Avoid tools with painted handles; the paint often hides cheap wood. Good-quality tools with fiberglass, metal, and even high-grade plastic handles are also available.

- The attachment of the metal part of the tool to its handle affects durability. Buy tools with solid-socket or solid-strapped construction, forged from a single bar of steel that completely envelops the handle, thus protecting it and adding strength.

- If you have arthritis, back problems, or in general want to avoid excess strain, look for ergonomic garden tools that are designed to require less bending and "elbow grease" to get the job done. Examples are loppers with a ratchet mechanism for easier cutting, trowels and other hand tools with gel-impregnated handles for less stress while gripping, and garden forks made of polypropylene that weigh much less than a standard wood-and-metal fork.

- If you plan on buying a rotary tiller, borrow or rent various models as a test before buying one. Wheeled tillers are always easier to operate than those without wheels, and large wheels provide more maneuverability than small ones. Look for heavy, heat-treated carbon steel blades.

make a cut. Bypass shears make a cleaner cut, can work in tighter space, and can cut flush against a tree trunk or branch (anvil pruners leave a short stump). Most models of either type will cut hardwood branches up to ½ inch in diameter.

Lopping shears, also called loppers, are heavy-duty pruners with long handles. Both anvil and bypass loppers can cut branches up to 2 inches in diameter. Hedge shears have long blades and relatively short handles. They can cut branches up to

½ inch thick. Pruning saws cut through most branches that are too thick for shears.

Push mowers: Push mowers have several revolving blades that move against a single fixed blade, producing a neat trim. They do a fine job, cutting evenly and quietly. For those with small, level lawns, the push mower is the ideal lawn-cutting instrument. It is inexpensive, not difficult to push, nonpolluting, quiet, and produces a neat-looking lawn.

Power Tools

In some cases, you may need the extra power of engine-driven equipment. Keep in mind, though, that handwork can be part of the pleasure and relaxation of gardening. If you routinely use power tools to speed through garden chores, you'll miss the opportunity to observe the growth of your plants and to keep an eye out for problems.

Power mowers: The best choice is a mulching mower, which blows finely cut grass pieces back into the lawn, building up soil organic matter while removing the need to rake or bag clippings. If you don't have a large lawn, investigate a battery-powered electric mower rather than a gas mower.

Tillers: Rotary tillers are useful for breaking new ground. Some gardeners also use them for cultivating, aerating, weeding, and mixing materials into the soil, but this convenience comes with a high cost to the critical beneficial organisms that help build a healthy soil. See the Soil entry for more on using tillers.

Chipper/shredders: This machine, powered with gasoline or electricity, reduces leaves, pruned branches, and plant debris to beautiful mulch or compost material. Shredders are better for chopping up weeds and other soft plant material; chippers can handle heavier, woody materials. Since a good quality, heavy-duty chipper/shredder is a major purchase, consider renting this tool if you'll only need it occasionally, or go in on a shared machine with neighbors to make the cost more reasonable.

Keeping Tools in Shape

After making the considerable investment in good-quality tools, it is wise to spend some time to keep them in good shape.

Routine care: Clean, dry, and put away all hand tools after each use. Keep a large plastic kitchen spoon handy to knock dirt off metal blades. Don't use a trowel or other metal tool, as you could damage the blades of both tools. A 5-gallon bucket of sharp builder's sand in the toolshed or garage is useful for cleaning tools. Dip the metal blade of each tool into the sand and plunge it up and down a few times to work off any clinging soil. Use a wire brush to remove any rust that may have formed. Keep power equipment in good repair and properly adjusted.

Handles: Regularly sand and varnish wooden handles to maintain their resilience and good looks. You can repair split handles temporarily with tape and glue, but replace broken handles as soon as possible.

Sharpening: To keep your tools working efficiently and with ease, keep blades of spades, pruners, and other tools sharp. Take the time to study the angle of the bevels on all your tools, then sharpen each, as needed, to keep the proper bevel. If you have tools that are especially difficult to sharpen, take them to a professional for sharpening.

Winter care: At the end of the season, polish all metal parts of hand tools with steel wool, oil them to prevent rust, and store them in a dry place. Lubricate all tools that have moving parts. This is also a good time to take hard-to-sharpen tools to the sharpening shop.

TRADESCANTIA

Spiderwort. Late-spring- to summer-blooming perennials.

Description: *Tradescantia* ×*andersoniana*, common spiderwort, produces triangular 1½-inch blooms in shades of white, red, blue, pink, lavender, and violet. Clustered buds open one by one at the tops of angular 2-foot stems with 1-foot straplike leaves. Foliage declines after bloom and plants go dormant but may reemerge in fall. Plants form loose mounds. 'Sweet Kate' bears electric blue flowers over bright yellow foliage. *T. virginiana*, Virginia spiderwort, is an eastern native perennial that grows to 3 feet tall and bears blue-violet three-petaled flowers in late spring and early summer. Zones 4–9.

How to grow: Plant or divide in spring or fall in sun to shade with average, moist to wet soil. Cut back 6 to 8 inches from the ground after flowering to promote new growth and rebloom. Plants will form dense clumps; divide every 3 years. Plants may also self-sow.

Landscape uses: Grow spiderworts in borders among other plants, such as geraniums, ferns, and hostas, to disguise their declining foliage. Naturalize in wet spots. Spiderworts tolerate partial to full shade and heavy soil, making them useful for bringing flowers to sites that are difficult for many perennials.

TRANSPLANTING

Transplanting simply means moving a rooted plant from one place to another. If you prick out tiny parsley seedlings from a flat into individual pots, you're transplanting. If you move tomato plants from your windowsill into the garden, you're transplanting. And if you decide to move the big forsythia to the backyard, you're transplanting, too.

For information on planting seeds, see the Seed Starting and Seed Saving entry. Instructions for planting perennials, shrubs, and trees are in the Planting entry.

Transplanting to containers: If you start seeds in flats, transplant when seedlings are still very young. Watch for the emergence of the first pair of true leaves and transplant soon after. The choice of planting containers ranges from homemade newspaper cylinders to plastic cell packs and clay pots. Peat pots and similar containers made of coir or compressed manure are favored by many gardeners, because the pots can be transplanted with the plant. Plastic and clay containers are reusable.

Before you start, collect your transplanting supplies and put down a layer of newspaper to catch spills. Follow these steps:

🌿 Fill the containers with soil mix. Either buy bags of mix (be aware that these may contain synthetic chemical fertilizer) or mix your own using the recipes in the Seed Starting and Seed Saving as well as the Houseplants entries. The depth of the soil depends on seedling size: Fill nearly to the top for small seedlings; start with only 1 inch of soil for large ones, since you fill the pots as you transplant.

🌿 Pour warm water onto the soil mix and let it sit for an hour to soak in. Moist potting soil prevents seedling roots from drying out.

🌿 Carefully dig out either individual seedlings or small groups of seedlings. A wooden plant marker makes a good all-purpose tool for digging, lifting, and moving tiny plants. A tablespoon or narrow trowel works well for larger transplants.

🌿 Hold each seedling by one of the leaves, as shown, not by (or around) the stem: You could crush the tender stem, or if you grasp the stem tip, you could kill the growing point and ruin the seedling's further growth.

🌿 For very young seedlings, poke small holes into the soil mix with a pencil. For larger seedlings, hold the plant in the pot while you fill in around the roots with soil. Firm the soil gently with your fingertips.

🌿 Return the seedlings to the window, light rack, or cold frame. If seedlings wilt from the stress of transplanting, mist lightly with water and cover loosely with a sheet of plastic wrap. Keep them cool and out of direct sun for a day or two, then remove the wrap and return to the light.

🌿 Keep soil lightly moist but not soggy by pouring water into the tray holding the containers. Feed regularly with a weak solution of water-soluble organic fertilizer.

🌿 As the plants grow, pinch or snip off any extra seedlings, leaving only the strongest one.

🌿 If you miscalculated the seed-starting date or if the weather turns nasty, you may need to transplant your plants again to larger containers so they won't stop growing and become stunted. Roots pushing through drainage holes are a clue that it's time to transplant.

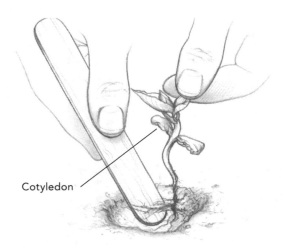

Cotyledon

Handling seedlings. Hold and move seedlings by grasping a leaf between thumb and forefinger and lifting up from beneath the roots with a plant label or similar tool. Yanking up seedlings by their stems will damage roots.

Transplanting to the garden: Toughen your plants for outdoor growing conditions by hardening off. Two weeks before outdoor transplanting time, stop feeding and slow down on watering. About a week before you plan to plant out the seedlings, put them outdoors in a protected area, out of direct sun and wind. Leave them outdoors for only 1 hour at first, then 2 hours, then a morning, until they are used to a full day. Water frequently.

Transplant on a cloudy or drizzly day or in early evening to spare transplants from the sun's heat. Water the plants before you start. Dig a hole slightly wider than and of the same depth as the container. (Plant tomatoes deeper, so that roots form along the stem. See the Tomato entry for details.)

If your transplants are in plastic or clay pots, turn the pots upside down and slide out the plants. Whack the pot with your trowel to dislodge stubborn ones. Plants in peat or paper pots can be planted pot and all.

Gently place the plant in the hole, and spread out roots of plants that aren't in pots. The illustration below shows how to open up peat pots (and other biodegradable containers) for better root penetration after planting. Stripping away the top rim of the pot above the soil line is also important, because if even a small piece of peat pot is exposed after transplanting, it will draw water from the soil surrounding the transplant's roots, leaving the plant in danger of water stress.

Fill the hole and tamp with your hands, forming a shallow basin to collect water.

Slowly pour plenty of water—at least a quart—at the base of the transplant. Keep transplants well watered until they become estab-

Transplanting plants from peat pots. Before transplanting a seedling grown in a peat pot, slit the sides of the pot and remove the bottom, unless many roots have already penetrated it. Tear off the top rim of the pot.

lished and start showing new growth.

Transplanting large plants: Sometimes a favorite tree or shrub gets too big for its place or is threatened by construction. Or maybe you just want to move a certain plant to a different spot in the landscape. If hard work doesn't scare you off, consider transplanting. See the Trees entry for the particulars.

TREES

The biggest, longest-lived plants in the landscape, trees bring beauty and a wealth of other benefits to our gardens. While a landscape without trees looks bare and uninviting, the presence of a few trees softens the look of house and surroundings. Well-placed trees will cool your house and yard with shade in summer and buffer it from winter winds. They'll create shady areas for you to sit underneath their branches. Trees also intercept glare off buildings and paved surfaces and soak up noise. Their leaves soften the impact of rain, reducing soil erosion, and act as purifiers by absorbing pollutants and releasing oxygen. Their wood and roots are carbon sinks that collectively help to buffer the impact of the release of carbon dioxide into the atmosphere.

Trees enhance your home, but not only in terms of monetary value or ecological good sense. You also benefit psychologically when trees are present, with an improved sense of well being that's very important in our stressful world.

Types of Trees

Trees are woody perennials, usually with a single trunk, ranging in height at maturity from 15 feet to giants exceeding 100 feet. A plant thought of as a tree in some parts of the country may be considered a shrub in others. For example, crape myrtle (*Lagerstroemia indica*) is grown as a small flowering tree that reaches about 15 feet tall in the South, but in the Mid-Atlantic area, it may die back to the ground after cold winters and only reach shrub heights.

Deciduous trees drop all of their leaves at the end of the growing season and grow new leaves the following spring. They are good choices for fall color. Once trees drop their leaves, they generally have gone dormant for winter, with the exception of some limited root growth.

Evergreen trees hold most of their leaves year-round. Needled evergreens like pines (*Pinus* spp.) and spruces (*Picea* spp.) are also known as conifers because they bear cones. But not all coniferous trees are evergreen: Larches (*Larix* spp.) and bald cypress (*Taxodium distichum*) are deciduous conifers. See the Evergreens entry for more about evergreen conifers. Evergreens with wide, generally thick leaves, such as southern magnolia (*Magnolia grandiflora*) and live oak (*Quercus virginiana*), are called broad-leaved evergreens.

If you live in warmer areas, you may be able to select a third type of "evergreen" tree. Palms are categorized as evergreens, although they are monocots, not dicots like other trees. A dicot forms annual growth rings that increase the trunk's diameter, and their crown is formed of branches. Palms don't form annual growth rings, and they generally don't branch—their crowns are made up entirely of their large leaves.

Broad-leaved evergreens like southern magnolia and live oak may lose their leaves in the winter in the northern parts of their hardiness range. These trees are called semievergreen, although they may be fully evergreen in the South.

KEY WORDS *Tree Shapes*

Clump. A tree grown with several closely growing trunks. Birches (*Betula* spp.) are often sold as clumps.

Vase-shaped. A tree with upswept branches, narrower in silhouette near the base than at the top, such as American elm (*Ulmus americana*).

Globe-shaped. A tree with a rounded, usually low-growing silhouette, such as crabapples (*Malus* spp.).

Oval. A tree with branches that form an oval silhouette, such as 'Bradford' flowering pear (*Pyrus calleryana* 'Bradford').

Columnar. A column-shaped form with extremely upright branches, also called fastigiate, such as Lombardy poplar (*Populus nigra* 'Italica').

Pyramidal. A cone-shaped tree, wide at the bottom and narrowing to a tip at the apex, such as most spruces (*Picea* spp.).

Conical. Cone-shaped, but with a narrower profile than a pyramidal tree, such as American arborvitae (*Thuja occidentalis*).

Weeping. A tree with branches that droop toward the ground, such as a weeping willow (*Salix babylonica*). Also called pendulous.

SMART SHOPPING
Mail-Order Trees

It's often difficult to find a new or unusual tree you read about because your local garden center doesn't stock it. Although they may be more expensive than commonly sold species, you can buy many new or unusual trees from specialty mail-order nurseries. They're often well worth the extra effort it takes to search them out.

Most trees from mail-order nurseries are less than 6 feet tall and are sold bareroot to reduce shipping costs. Here are some tips to help you use mail-order shopping with success.

- Buy from reputable firms. Check with friends, ask a local nursery owner or your extension agent, or order from sources recommended by gardening magazines. Check online customer reviews to see if others have been satisfied with their purchases.

- Read the catalog descriptions carefully. Be sure the tree will have the features you want and will grow in the conditions of your landscape. If the prices or the claims about the trees sound too good to be true, they probably are: Avoid them.

- Be sure a guarantee is offered and know what to save should the tree grow poorly or die. Some nurseries will take your word; others insist you ship them the tree (at your expense). Find out if a refund or only a replacement is offered.

- Have the tree shipped during the best time of year to plant in your area (especially if the tree will be shipped bareroot). If you work outside the home, consider delivery to your workplace to avoid having it left on your doorstep, where it could be damaged by exposure to cold, wind, and sun.

- For new species or cultivars, order early to avoid receiving a "sold out" notice or an inferior substitute. Specify "no substitution" if you won't accept one.

- When your tree arrives, unpack it immediately. Read the label to be sure the correct tree was shipped. Check the plant's condition: If roots are totally dry, or the plant is broken, repackage and return it.

Selecting Trees

Trees are an investment that will be a part of your life for a long time, so it pays to choose them with care. To start the selection process, first think about what you want from a tree. Do you need a large tree that will shade your house or a small decorative one that will serve as an accent for a flower garden? If you enjoy feeding birds, perhaps a native tree that provides food for wildlife would be a good choice. If a flowering tree is important to you, are flowers in spring most important, or would you rather have flowers later in the season? What about brightly colored leaves in fall, showy bark, or colorful fruit that clings to the branches even in winter?

If privacy is important, plan on using groups of trees to enclose a patio, block unwanted views, or accent desirable ones, both on and off your property. Evergreens provide year-round concealment, but deciduous trees provide shade in summer yet let in the winter sun. A unified group of trees in a single bed—perhaps underplanted with shrubs and/or groundcovers—looks better than a widely scattered planting, and the arrangement helps protect the trees from lawn mower nicks and gouges.

Use specimen or accent trees alone to call attention to an attractive feature such as the finely cut leaves of full-moon maple (*Acer japonicum*), or the showy flowers of saucer magnolia (*Magnolia* ×*soulangiana*). Unusually textured bark, bright fall color, or an interesting shape are other good reasons to showcase a tree as a specimen plant.

Trees supply food, shelter, and nesting sites for birds and other wildlife. Native species that produce berries or other fruits are especially welcome. See the Birds entry for a list of wildlife-friendly trees and shrubs.

You may want to add trees to your landscape that will provide food for you, not just for wildlife and birds. Many common fruit trees, such as apples, pears, peaches, and plums, are available in dwarf sizes that fit neatly into a small corner or even a large container. See the entries for specific fruits and the Fruit Trees entry to guide your selection. Many lesser-known trees also produce good food.

For fleshy fruit to be eaten fresh or cooked, try pawpaw (*Asimina triloba*), American persimmon (*Diospyros virginiana*), and Japanese persimmon (*D. kaki*).

For small, fleshy fruits for jams and jellies, try cornelian cherry (*Cornus mas*), crabapples (*Malus* spp.), hawthorns (*Crataegus* spp.), and wild cherries (*Prunus* spp.).

For nuts, try hickories (*Carya* spp.), walnuts and butternuts (*Juglans* spp.), pecan (*Carya illinoinensis*), filberts (*Corylus* spp.), and chestnuts (*Castanea* spp.). See the Nut Trees entry for advice on selecting and growing nut trees.

For beekeepers interested in a new taste to their honey, try sourwood (*Oxydendrum arboreum*), lindens (*Tilia* spp.), and water tupelo (*Nyssa aquatica*).

Be realistic about the amount of maintenance you're willing to do. Do you want to plant trees and forget them, as you can do with many evergreens? Or do you enjoy pruning and raking up baskets of leaves on a brisk fall day? For some gardeners, the beauty of the tree or the bounty of the crop outweighs the extra work.

Match the Tree to the Site

Before you head to the nursery to buy a tree, learn all you can about the characteristics of your planting site. Selecting a tree that will thrive in the conditions your site has to offer is one of the most important things you can do to ensure success. Determine your hardiness zone, and make sure the tree you want is compatible. While most nurseries stock plants that are hardy in their area, borderline-hardy plants are sometimes offered with no warnings. It's always a good idea to ask. Remember to check catalogs for hardiness information, too.

Know your soil—its pH, fertility, and consistency. Take a close look at drainage; if you see standing water at any season, stick to trees that

Small Flowering Trees

Trees can add the beauty of flowers to your landscape. Those that bloom early in the spring help support pollinators by providing a source of nectar when few other plants are flowering. The list that follows is arranged by time of bloom, beginning with the trees that flower in early spring and progressing through trees that bloom in summer. Plant name is followed by flower color.

Spring

Aesculus pavia (red buckeye): Red

Amelanchier spp. (serviceberries): White

Cercis canadensis (eastern redbud): Pink

Chionanthus virginicus (white fringe tree): White

Cornus florida (flowering dogwood): White, pink

Cornus mas (cornelian cherry): Yellow

Halesia carolina (Carolina silverbell): White

Laburnum ×watereri (golden chain tree): Yellow

Magnolia ×soulangiana (saucer magnolia): White to wine

Magnolia stellata (star magnolia): White to pale pink

Malus spp. (crabapples): White, pink, red

Prunus spp. (cherries): White, red, pink

Pyrus calleryana (Callery pear): White

Late Spring, Early Summer

Cornus kousa (Kousa dogwood): White

Koelreuteria paniculata (golden rain tree): Yellow

Styrax japonicus (Japanese snowbell): White

Syringa reticulata (Japanese tree lilac): White

Summer

Franklinia alatamaha (franklinia): White

Lagerstroemia indica (crape myrtle): White, pink, lavender

Oxydendrum arboreum (sourwood): White

Stewartia pseudocamellia (Japanese stewartia): White

Styphnolobium japonicum (Japanese pagoda tree): Creamy white

will tolerate wet feet or choose another planting site. Check the amount of light the tree will receive. Be sure to scout out overhead wires, nearby walkways, or other limiting factors. Think about the size of your tree in 5, 10, or 20 years. You can save loads of pruning headaches down the road if you select a tree that won't grow too large for the site at maturity.

If a tree's branches extend 25 feet from the trunk, its supporting roots reach out that far into the surrounding soil. Other plants within its radius will compete for nutrients and water. More

Trees for Fall Color

Enhance your landscape with bright fall colors from these deciduous trees.

Yellows and Oranges

Acer saccharum (sugar maple)

Betula spp. (birches)

Carya spp. (hickories)

Cercis canadensis (eastern redbud)

Cladrastis kentukea (Kentucky yellowwood)

Fraxinus spp. (ashes)

Ginkgo biloba (ginkgo)

Gleditsia triacanthos var. *inermis* (thornless honey locust)

Larix spp. (larches)

Liriodendron tulipifera (tulip tree)

Taxodium distichum (bald cypress)

Red

Acer rubrum (red maple)

Cornus florida (flowering dogwood)

Nyssa sylvatica (black gum)

Oxydendrum arboreum (sourwood)

Pistacia chinensis (Chinese pistache)

Quercus coccinea (scarlet oak)

Q. rubra (northern red oak)

Stewartia spp. (stewartias)

Mixed Colors

Cotinus coggygria (smoke tree)

Lagerstroemia indica (crape myrtle)

Liquidambar styraciflua (sweet gum)

Pyrus calleryana (Callery pear)

Sassafras albidum (sassafras)

---

aggressive plants often win this battle, while losers grow slowly, have poor appearance, and produce few fruits. Trees with surface roots will destroy sidewalks or invade sewer and water lines within that radius, too.

Some trees, such as thornless honey locust (*Gleditsia triacanthos* var. *inermis*) produce only light or filtered shade; grass and other plants generally have enough light to grow under or in the shade of these trees. Other trees, like the sugar and Norway maples (*Acer saccharum* and *A. platanoides*), produce very dense shade coupled with shallow, surface-level roots that make growing even shade-tolerant grasses and popular shade plants nearly impossible. Under established maples, a thick layer of mulch is the best way to cover the ground. Oaks (*Quercus* spp.), on the other hand, cast full shade, but their roots penetrate the soil much more deeply than maples, leaving room to grow a shade garden with hostas (*Hosta* spp.), ferns, and other shade lovers. Even shade-tolerant plants may have difficulty growing under or near a tree, particularly a large one. If the crown of the tree is dense, as with maples, most rain is shed off the canopy of the tree. The ground immediately below may be dry even after a rain. Tree roots absorb much of the available water from surrounding soil. See page 276 for a list of plants that will tolerate these conditions.

City-Smart Trees

City trees must be able to survive despite constricted root space, compacted soil, wind tunnels between buildings, limited moisture and nutrients, high temperatures, and pollutants.

Trees used along streets, in raised planters, in median strips, or in parking lots endure the harshest and most stressful of any landscape environment. These often-neglected trees face all the hazards of city trees and must put up with drought, paving heat, and human vandalism. Despite relentless pruning to make them fit under overhead utility lines or within narrow corridors, and even when main branches are whacked off to permit people and cars to pass by, street trees manage to survive. But all these stresses take their toll: On average, street trees live only 10 to 15 years.

In addition to resisting insects and diseases, good street trees also share other characteristics. They should be "clean" trees with no litter problems, such as dropping large leaves or fruit, although sometimes, as with sycamores (*Platanus* spp.) and oaks, the litter is overlooked because of other good qualities. Avoid trees with dangerous thorns or spines, such as hawthorns (*Crataegus* spp.); shallow-rooted trees, such as silver maples (*Acer saccharinum*), that buckle paving; and thirsty trees, like weeping willows (*Salix babylonica*), whose roots seek water and sewer lines. Trees with branches that angle downward, such as pin oaks, also don't make the best street trees, unless they are limbed up high enough for pedestrians and traffic to pass easily. See page 605 for a list of city-smart trees to consider.

Buying Trees

Trees are sold bareroot, balled-and-burlapped (B&B), or in containers. The heeling-in technique, described in the Planting entry, is a good way to hold bareroot or B&B stock until you're able to plant.

For do-it-yourself planters, small- and medium-size trees are probably the best choice, since rootballs can be very heavy and difficult to handle. If you want to plant a larger specimen, plan on having the tree delivered and dig the planting hole before it arrives. That way, the tree can be moved off the truck directly into the hole. Position the plant while you still have help from the delivery crew. Yet another option for a big tree is one that has been dug with a commercial tree spade, which is a mechanical digger mounted on a truck. While big trees take longer to get established than smaller trees because more of their roots were lost when they were dug, they may be worth the extra care and expense.

Know how to spot a good buy when you go tree shopping, because sometimes a low-priced tree is no bargain, and sometimes higher-priced trees aren't worth their price tag.

- Buy only trees that are clearly tagged or labeled with the botanical and common names to make sure you get the flowers, fruits, and crown shape you want.
- Look for a relatively straight trunk with a slight natural flare at its base—if no flare exists, the tree has had too much soil placed atop its roots.
- Buy trees with widely spaced, even branches, not trees with branches that are tightly spaced and mostly at the top of the trunk.
- Buy trees from retailers who offer guarantees, and find out the terms of the guarantee.
- Shop reputable local nurseries whenever possible, and buy trees that are native to your area.
- Look for healthy trees, with plump buds.

- Watch out for broken branches or scratched bark. Also look for dry or brown leaf margins, or dry root balls.

- B&B or container-grown trees may be putting out new leaves; check for healthy growth. Examine leaves and bark for pests and diseases.

- Buy bareroot trees only when they're dormant, and only if the roots have been kept moist.

- Roots that are evenly spaced around the base of the stem make a secure anchor.

- On B&B trees, look for a well-wrapped, secure rootball.

- Container-grown trees may be rootbound, with crowded roots wrapped around the rootball. Avoid trees that pull easily from the container, leaving the potting soil behind. Also avoid those whose roots have left the container and anchored themselves firmly in the soil beneath.

Planting Trees

Plant a bareroot tree while it is dormant, either in fall or early spring. A few trees have roots so sensitive to disturbance that you should not buy or transplant them bareroot. Your chances of success are best when these trees are container grown: Kentucky coffee tree (*Gymnocladus dioicus*), crape myrtle (*Lagerstroemia indica*), sweet gum (*Liquidambar styraciflua*), black gum (*Nyssa sylvatica*), white oak (*Quercus alba*), and sassafras (*Sassafras albidum*).

Trees with Attractive Bark

For adding interest and color to the landscape in winter—or any season of the year—there's nothing like trees with ornamental bark. For many homeowners, the white flaking bark of birches—especially canoe birch (*Betula papyrifera*) and European white birch (*B. pendula*)—represents the epitome of ornamental bark. But white-barked birches are prone to insect problems and are not good choices for dry sites. Heritage river birch (*B. nigra* 'Cully') is a good substitute: It has tan, flaking bark and resists common birch pests.

The smooth, gray bark of trees such as beeches (*Fagus* spp.) and Kentucky yellowwood (*Cladrastis kentukea*) is ornamental, too, as is the blocky gray bark of flowering dogwood (*Cornus florida*), which resembles alligator's hide. The following trees have exfoliating or flaking bark in a variety of colors, including red, brown, or combinations of cream, gray, and brown.

Acer griseum (paperbark maple)

Betula nigra (river birch)

Cornus kousa (Kousa dogwood)

Lagerstroemia indica (crape myrtle)

Pinus bungeana (lacebark pine)

Pinus densiflora (Japanese red pine)

Platanus spp. (sycamores or plane trees)

Prunus spp. (flowering cherries)

Stewartia spp. (stewartia)

Ulmus parvifolia (Chinese or lacebark elm)

You can plant most B&B or container-grown trees any time of the year except when the ground is frozen. There are a few exceptions, however. A few trees, especially those with thick and fleshy roots, seem to suffer less of a transplant shock if planted in spring in areas where the soil freezes deeply during winter. Though tree roots will continue to grow until the soil temperature drops below 40°F, these trees are slow to get established and are best reserved for spring planting: dogwoods (*Cornus* spp.), golden rain tree (*Koelreuteria paniculata*), tulip tree (*Liriodendron tulipifera*), magnolias (*Magnolia* spp.), black gum (*Nyssa sylvatica*), ornamental cherries and plums (*Prunus* spp.), most oaks (*Quercus* spp.), and Japanese zelkova (*Zelkova serrata*).

A close examination of the roots of your new tree will prevent problems that can limit growth. Trim any mushy, dead, or damaged roots. Comb out pot-bound roots and straighten or slice through roots that circle the rootball before you set the plant in its hole. Look carefully for girdling roots, which can strangle the tree by wrapping tightly around the base of its trunk. This stops the upward movement of water and nutrients absorbed by the roots and needed by the leaves and branches.

See the Planting entry for details on planting trees and helping them settle into your home landscape.

Staking

Staking is done to straighten or strengthen the trunk, or to prevent root movement and breakage before the tree anchors itself in the soil. Trees under 8 feet with small crowns, which aren't located in windy sites, usually don't need staking.

Although it would seem that rigidly staking a newly planted tree so it doesn't move even slightly in the wind is the best approach, it's actually best to allow the trunk to flex or move slightly when the

Lollipop Tree Syndrome

If you need to reduce the size of a tree, use thinning cuts to remove branches back to the main branches from which they originated, or back to the tree trunk. Topping your tree by chopping branches off in the middle leaves large branch stubs and destroys the natural crown shape of your tree, making it look like a unappealing lollipop. It also stimulates the growth of watersprouts, which are upright-growing, unbranched stems that develop very quickly and never return to the normal branch pattern of your tree. Topping also weakens your tree, turning it into a liability or a potential hazard in your landscape.

When large branches are topped, the branch stub that is left begins to die. As the wood dies, decay fungi and insects can get into the wood, further weakening the tree. During wind, ice, and snow storms, these weakened branch stubs break from the tree more easily than healthy branches that have been properly pruned.

wind hits it. This movement encourages the tree to produce special wood that will naturally bend when the wind hits it. A tree that is rigidly staked will often bend over or break after it is unstaked. Given a choice, avoid buying staked, container-grown trees—you will generally be buying a weak stem.

Unstake all trees 1 year after planting. Any tree that had an adequate root system and was properly planted will by then be able to stand on its own. If you want to leave the stakes in place to keep lawn mowers and other equipment from hitting the trunk, remove the guy wires or ropes but leave the stakes as a barrier.

Care and Maintenance

Carefully selected and planted trees need only occasional attention, especially once they become well established.

During the first year after planting, water each week when less than 1 inch of rain falls, especially in summer and fall. Water to thaw the ground, and provide water for the leaves of evergreen trees during warm winter weather.

The mulch you applied at planting time will gradually decompose. Replenish it as needed, but only use a few inches. To avoid rodent problems and to encourage good air circulation, keep the mulch away from the trunk. To find out more about using mulch to conserve moisture and reduce maintenance, see the Mulch entry.

Small, yellow leaves, premature fall coloration, stunted twig growth, or too few flowers or fruits often indicate a nutrient deficiency. Your trees will generally receive enough fertilizer if they are located in a lawn that you regularly fertilize. If your trees are located in isolated beds, in areas surrounded by paving, or in containers, you may need to apply compost or a balanced organic fertilizer. Simply broadcast the needed fertilizer on the soil surface. See the Fertilizers entry for more information about blended organic fertilizers.

Most trees are too large for you to provide them with special winter protection such as a burlap enclosure. If snow or ice loads bend the trees' branches, avoid vigorously shaking the branches to remove the ice or snow. Frozen, brittle branches can easily break. Either allow the ice or snow to melt away naturally or very gently sweep it off.

Pruning and Training

Prune young trees at planting time and as they grow, to correct structural problems and improve their form. Training a young tree with several years of judicious pruning leads to a structurally sound, well-shaped mature tree. Remove crossing and rubbing branches and suckers or watersprouts. Also remove branches with narrow crotch angles. Repair storm and vandalism damage immediately after it occurs to reduce wound injury and subsequent decay. See the Pruning and Training entry for information on how to make pruning cuts.

After a few years, begin the limbing-up process if the tree is planted where passersby will walk below it. Remove the lowest branch or two by sawing through the limb just outside of the branch collar. Repeat every year until the lowest branches are high enough to permit easy passage. About 5 to 6 years after planting, thin to open up the canopy, reducing wind resistance and allowing light to reach the interior. If your tree is intended to block an undesirable view, use heading cuts to encourage denser branching.

If you've inherited a mature tree, some judicious pruning can make it better looking and healthier. If you're not an experienced tree climber, hire an arborist to rejuvenate your tree. Correct the following types of problems.

- Remove diseased or dead wood. Also removed damaged and broken branches.
- Correct rubbing and crossing branches by removing the weaker branch or cutting off branches that grow into and across the center of the canopy.
- Cut out watersprouts.
- Reduce the number of branches to open up the canopy to light and air.

🌿 Eliminate branches that have narrow, weak crotch angles.

Trees can generally be pruned at any time of year, but avoid spring pruning of beeches (*Fagus* spp.), birches (*Betula* spp.), elms (*Ulmus* spp.), and maples (*Acer* spp.), which tend to bleed (exude sap) if pruned in spring. Spring-pruning these trees can increase certain disease and insect problems. Prune oaks only during the winter months to reduce the risk of oak wilt disease, which is spread by insects. If you grow trees for their flowers or fruits, prune them before the next year's flower buds develop. A good time to prune broad-leaved evergreen trees or thin needle evergreens is during winter, especially if you can use the leaves, such as those on hollies (*Ilex* spp.) and southern magnolia (*Magnolia grandiflora*), for Christmas greenery.

Transplanting Trees

It's a little harder to move a tree than it is to shove the sofa around in the living room. But if you redo your landscape, or if a tree gets in the way of a planned addition or pool or driveway, it may be worth a try.

Be realistic about the size of tree you can move yourself. Very young deciduous trees may sometimes be successfully moved bareroot. But the bigger the rootball you can dig and move, the more successful your transplanting operation will be. Earth is heavy—very heavy. Figure on a rootball at least 1½ feet across and 1 foot deep for every inch of trunk. If you want to move a tree with a 2-inch trunk, that's a ball of earth roughly 3 feet across and 2 feet deep—and that will weigh a few hundred pounds! If your back aches just thinking about it, consider hiring a nursery owner or arborist to dig and transplant the tree, either by hand or using a mechanical tree spade.

When you transplant a tree, you cut many of its roots, leaving them behind in their old location.

Transplanting while the tree is dormant lessens the chance of leaves drying out while new roots are growing. Root pruning in advance of the move encourages the remaining roots to branch and makes it easier for the tree to become reestablished. If possible, 6 months to a year before transplanting, slice through the soil around the tree to a depth of 8 to 12 inches, outlining the rootball. Make a narrow trench and fill it with chopped leaves, so that any roots that regrow will be easy to lift. Prune the tree, thinning out about a third of the branches, so there is less topgrowth for the roots to support.

When you're ready to move the tree, widen the trench, digging outward until it is at least 1½ feet wide around the full diameter of the rootball. Slice through any small roots that have grown beyond

---

Where Are the Roots?

Contrary to old beliefs, tree roots don't stop where the tree canopy stops—the "drip line"—nor do they penetrate to great soil depths. The roots of almost all trees, both in wooded and in open areas, spread out one to three times beyond the canopy. For this reason, if possible, apply fertilizer over this entire area, and protect it from soil compaction and other stresses that damage roots.

Most of the roots of your trees are located in the top few inches of soil. Only a limited number of trees in native stands have deep roots called taproots. Most other trees have no taproots—they stopped growing either due to limited soil oxygen or because they were cut off when the nursery dug the trees.

Nuisance Trees

Some trees have less-than-ideal features—weak wood, disease or insect problems, and prolific self-sowing abilities, to name three—and as a result aren't the best choices for landscapes. All of the trees listed here have some negative characteristics and aren't good choices in most areas. Trees like box elder and black locust are tough and adaptable and may be a sensible choice for sites with poor soil or other extreme conditions. Plant name is followed by the nuisance features of the tree.

Acer negundo (box elder): Weak wood, pest problems.

Acer saccharinum (silver maple): Shallow roots, weak wood, seeds prolifically.

Aesculus hippocastanum (common horse chestnut): Poisonous fruit, disease problems.

Ailanthus altissima (tree of heaven): Invasive grower, seeds prolifically; leaves and male flowers are foul smelling.

Albizia julibrissin (mimosa, silk tree): Insect and disease problems, seeds prolifically.

Ginkgo biloba (ginkgo): Female trees have foul-smelling fruit; plant only males.

Gleditsia triacanthos (honey locust): Dangerous thorns; plant only thornless cultivars (which are cultivars of *G. triacanthos* var. *inermis*).

Morus spp. (mulberries): Messy fruit.

Populus deltoides (eastern cottonwood): Messy fruit, weak wood.

Populus nigra 'Italica' (Lombardy poplar): Incurable canker disease kills top.

Robinia pseudoacacia (black locust): Seeds prolifically, insect problems.

Salix bablyonica (weeping willow): Weak wood, roots invade water lines.

the original cut. Deepen the trench until you get to a depth where the soil contains few roots. Then begin digging under to shape the ball.

If your soil has enough clay to hold the ball together well, completely undercut the ball. If you can lift the tree and ball—lifting from under the ball—put it into a large container to move it. If the tree is too heavy to lift, gently tip the ball, then position a piece of burlap or other covering material under the ball. Gently work the material under and around the ball, and secure it with rope or nails.

If your soil is sandy, prior to undercutting the ball, wrap the top of the ball with burlap or other strong material, and secure it with heavy cord or twine as close to the base as possible. Then undercut the ball, gently tip it over, and secure the rest of the covering material across the bottom of the ball.

Get help lifting the tree out of its hole, levering it out from below. Then transport it to its new location and replant. Water well and mulch.

Trees and Construction

Many home buyers ask that large trees on a lot be saved during construction. However, few trees will withstand the rigors of construction—changing grades and drainage, topsoil removal, and soil compaction around roots.

To preserve trees on a new homesite, consult a tree specialist and walk the site with all contractors to identify the trees needing protection. Professional pruning may be necessary to compensate for root loss.

Direct tree damage occurs when you cut roots; damage or tear away trunk bark; break, tear away, or incorrectly prune off branches; or tie or nail items to the tree. Indirect tree damage occurs when you strip away topsoil and leaf litter, compact the soil, dump additional fill soil atop the roots, and burn or bury waste materials near the trees. You also indirectly damage trees by paving over open areas that absorbed rainfall, removing neighboring plants that provided wind and sun protection, and creating new drainage patterns for rainwater and runoff.

Your top priority is to preserve the natural root environment. If you keep people and equipment away from the tree, you will minimize the chances of damage being done to the tree's trunk and branches. If possible, erect fences outside the drip line of trees before construction begins to keep vehicles and piles of building materials away from the sensitive root zone and trunk. Once construction is completed, apply mulch to replace leaf litter that was removed, prune structurally weak branches, and provide water and fertilizer to help stimulate new roots.

Pests and Problems

Frequent inspection of your trees will help minimize problems. Your best defenses are to buy good-quality, pest-free trees to avoid introducing pests or disease; to plant your trees in proper envi-

ronments to encourage vigorous growth; to use good maintenance practices; and to minimize environmental stresses.

Biotic or pathological problems are caused by living organisms—insects, mites, fungi, bacteria, viruses, nematodes, and rodents. Abiotic or physiological problems are caused by nonliving things—improper planting and maintenance, poor soil conditions, air pollution, injury, compacted soil, construction damage, and lightning.

Far more tree problems are caused by abiotic problems, which weaken trees, allowing boring insects and decay fungi to attack. If your tree shows signs of ill health, check for poor conditions that may have allowed the pest or disease to get a foothold.

The plant family bothered by the greatest number of insect and disease problems is the rose family, Rosaceae. This large family includes such trees as crabapples, flowering pears (*Pyrus* spp.), hawthorns (*Crataegus* spp.), serviceberries (*Amelanchier* spp.), and mountain ashes (*Sorbus* spp.), along with cherries, peaches, almonds, and plums (all *Prunus* spp.). Crabapples are particularly susceptible to problems; buy only those cultivars that are resistant to these diseases: rust, scab, powdery mildew, and fire blight. (See the *Malus* entry for a list of disease-resistant crabapples.) Other trees, such as flowering dogwood (*Cornus florida*), maples (*Acer* spp.), sycamores (*Platanus* spp.), birches (*Betula* spp.), elms (*Ulmus* spp.), locusts (*Robinia* spp.), honey locusts (*Gleditsia* spp.), and oaks (*Quercus* spp.), may also have numerous pest or disease problems. Ask your nursery owner for advice before making the purchase.

Whenever a disease or insect problem is seen, try to control it by removing the pest or the affected plant part. Don't compost or burn infected plants. Remember to sanitize tools after pruning infested or infected wood by cleaning them with a 10 percent bleach solution.

Insects

Most insect problems of trees are caused by a relatively small number of insects and mites (technically classed as arachnids). These pests have their preferences: Some primarily damage leaves, and others primarily damage branches and trunk.

Insects eat leaves and suck plant sap from them. The larvae of moths and butterflies, such as bagworms, cankerworms, webworms, tent caterpillars, and gypsy moths, are especially voracious leaf eaters. Highly noticeable webs of eastern tent caterpillars and fall webworms protect the larvae from predators while they munch your leaves. Although the nests are unsightly, otherwise healthy trees usually recover from infestation. Remove and destroy any webs you can reach.

Gypsy moth populations rise to a peak in cycles of several years, causing almost complete defoliation in areas of heavy infestation. Handpicking and spraying Bt (*Bacillus thuringiensis*) are the best defenses against severe attacks of gypsy moths. In winter, check your trees for the light brown egg masses and scrape them off into a container of soapy water.

Other major insect pests that damage leaves are aphids and adelgids, various beetles and bugs, miners, scales, and spider mites.

Insects are always present on trees. Populations must be extreme before the tree suffers any real damage. Don't rush to the sprayer as soon as you spot a caterpillar or two. Remember, the goal is a healthy tree, not complete insect annihilation. Learn to recognize harmful pests and the signs of infestation: curled leaves, stunted growth, deformed flowers.

Try handpicking and pruning off affected branches before you reach for other controls. Even

Bt is not innocuous. It does kill gypsy moth larvae, tent caterpillars, and other undesirables—but it will also kill any other caterpillar that happens to eat a tainted leaf, including the beautiful luna moth, giant silk moths, and the caterpillars of your favorite butterflies. Leaf-eating caterpillars actually are a benefit of native tree species, since those caterpillars are an important food source for many species of songbirds, particularly when they are feeding their nestlings.

Stems are damaged when insects such as borers and scales either bore into them or feed on them. Cicadas cause stem damage when they lay their eggs into slits in twigs. Microscopic, wormlike nematodes also cause problems on the roots of many trees.

Turn to the Insects and Pests entries to find out more about controlling insect problems.

Diseases

Tree diseases occur on leaves, stems, and roots. Many pathological diseases are difficult to distinguish from physiological problems. For instance, while fungi and bacteria can cause leaf spot diseases, spots on tree leaves can also be caused by nutrient deficiencies, improperly applied pesticides, road salts, and even drought. Be careful to properly identify a tree problem before you look for a control or corrective measure.

Most tree diseases are caused by fungi, although a few major diseases, such as fire blight on pears and other members of the rose family, are caused by bacteria. Flowering peaches and plums are also bothered by viral diseases.

Diseases of tree leaves are generally spots, anthracnoses, scorches, blights, rusts, and mildews. You will see them on your trees most frequently during moist weather and when plants are under environmental stress. Diseases of tree stems are generally cankers, blights, and decays. You

Street Trees

These trees are tough enough to tolerate the difficult growing conditions of city streets. All will tolerate poor soil, pollution, and droughty conditions.

Small Trees

Acer buergerianum (trident maple)

A. campestre (hedge maple)

A. ginnala (amur maple)

A. tataricum (Tatarian maple)

Crataegus crus-galli var. *inermis* (thornless cockspur hawthorn)

Koelreuteria paniculata (golden rain tree)

Prunus sargentii (Sargent cherry)

Pyrus calleryana (Callery pear) 'Aristocrat', 'Redspire'

Syringa reticulata (Japanese tree lilac) 'Ivory Silk', 'Summer Snow'

Medium to Large Trees

Acer pseudoplatanus (sycamore maple)

Carpinus betulus 'Fastigiata' (upright European hornbeam)

Celtis occidentalis (hackberry) 'Prairie Pride'

Ginkgo biloba 'Fastigiata' (upright ginkgo)

Gleditsia triacanthos var. *inermis* (thornless honey locust) 'Skyline', 'Shademaster'

Platanus ×acerifolia (aka Platanus ×hispanica, London plane tree)

Quercus acutissima (sawtooth oak)

Q. phellos (willow oak)

Q. robur 'Fastigiata' (upright English oak)

Styphnolobium japonicum (Japanese pagoda tree)

Taxodium distichum (bald cypress)

Tilia tomentosa (silver linden)

Ulmus parvifolia (Chinese or lacebark elm)

Zelkova serrata (Japanese zelkova) 'Green Vase' and 'Village Green'

---

will see these diseases when trees have been damaged by improper pruning, mechanical injury, and other maintenance and environmental factors. The major diseases of tree roots are root rots. Root rots occur when soils are poorly drained and may be intensified if roots have been injured by such things as construction damage and trenching. Refer to the Plant Diseases and Disorders entry for more information on disease prevention and control.

Physical Damage

You can damage a tree by nailing items to it or ramming into its trunk with a lawn mower. String trimmer injury is more insidious than that caused by lawn mowers—the injury may be completely invisible, but the multiple small cuts in bark caused by a string trimmer create entry points for insects and disease organisms. Animals also damage trees. Birds may occasionally break branches or drill holes in them, looking for sap or insects. Moles may cause root injury by disturbing the roots of newly planted trees or creating air pockets that let the roots dry out as they tunnel, and voles actually feed on the roots. Mice and rabbits damage trees by feeding on the bark. Deer damage trees by browsing on young branch tips and by rubbing their antlers on the trunks and branches.

Handle your trees gently. Avoid lawn mower damage by using mulch or beds of groundcovers to surround the trunk. Pull any weeds close to the trunk by hand. A cat that patrols outdoors now and then is one way to control rodents. Fence to keep out deer. For more on controlling animals, see the Animal Pests entry.

Propagating Trees

Tree seeds are often notoriously slow to germinate, and many need special treatment to break dormancy. Variations in plant form, or in flower and leaf color or size, may occur with seed propagation. A good example is the range of needle colors, from pale blues to grayish and greenish blues, that develop on seed-propagated Colorado spruce (*Picea pungens*). But if you have the space for a small nursery bed, and plenty of time and patience, you might enjoy the challenge of growing from seed. The Seed Starting and Seed Saving entry will help you start seeds successfully.

When you take cuttings or use the layering method, you preserve the exact characteristics of the parent tree. Some trees can be propagated from stem cuttings, and some from cuttings from the roots. Timing and technique are important. The Cuttings, Layering, and Propagation entries will give you a start.

More complicated techniques such as grafting and tissue culture also produce an exact duplicate of the parent tree. Try your hand at grafting with a flowering dogwood (*Cornus florida*) or a crabapple (*Malus* spp.). See the Grafting entry for more details.

TRELLISING

Designed to support climbing plants, trellises run the gamut from lightweight lattice to wrought-iron arches. They can be permanent structures, with posts set in concrete in the soil, or temporary moveable structures designed for a single growing season. While garden twine is strong enough for annual vines like beans and morning glories to climb, larger, heavier plants like tomatoes, climbing roses, and wisteria need trellises constructed of sterner stuff. Trellises used in vegetable gardens or to support fruit crops tend to be structural first and ornamental second, while the reverse is true when trellising roses or climbers like clematis.

Beyond their role as supports for vines or plants with long canes, trellises can function as a windbreak or a privacy screen. They also work well for displaying vines at the back of a flower garden; this adds height and color without taking up space. Install a small trellis in a large container for a summertime patio display, or use trellises to encourage vines to grow across and decorate an otherwise plain fence.

When designing a trellis, it's important to decide first what kinds of vines you will be growing on it. Vines like clematis need lightweight lattice, mesh, or wire to cling to, because their twining leafstalks can't grip large-diameter supports. (Or install mesh or other lightweight material on top of a larger trellis so they can.) Similarly, twining annual vines need relatively small-diameter supports at least until they've started growing vigorously. Roses need sturdy, well-built supports because the plants are heavy; tie them to trellises with soft string or strips of panty hose or T-shirt material, since their sprawling canes don't attach themselves to supports. Finally, twining woody vines like wisterias (*Wisteria* spp.) need heavyweight, permanent trellises made of wood or metal, since the vines will simply crush smaller supports.

When planning a trellis that will be located against a wall or fence, determine what kind of maintenance that surface will require. If the wall or fence will require painting or other maintenance, build the trellis at least 4 or 5 inches out from the wall so you'll be able to slide a long-handled paint roller in behind it.

Preconstructed trellises are available at garden centers and on the Internet. To build your own, look for designs in gardening books or on how-to Internet sites. Here are some general trellis types to get you started.

A-frame trellis: Create an A-frame structure with wood, bamboo stakes, PVC pipe, or galvanized pipe. Build two, three, or more A-shaped section supports, then connect them with crosspieces made of a similar material to create a freestanding structure that can be erected over a row of melons, beans, or other plants.

Cattle panel supports: Wire panels used to confine cattle and other livestock can be made into super-sturdy utilitarian trellises for tomatoes and other vegetables. The panels are 16 feet long and 4 feet wide; some suppliers will cut them in half. Set them along the row and use 6-foot-tall T-posts driven 2 feet into the ground at each end and at 2-foot intervals along the panel. Wire the panels to the posts.

Ornamental trellises: To build a lath trellis, create a frame strong enough to suit the vines you are going to grow: 1- by 4-inch or 2- by 4-inch wood frame pieces connected by smaller 1- by 1-inch or 1- by 2-inch slats will work well for smaller vines. You can also use strings or wire mesh inside the frame for vines to climb. For large vines, build the framework out of 4- by 4-inch posts and 2- by 4-inch crosspieces. Or build heavyweight trellises out of galvanized pipe, using pipe fittings to connect the pieces. The design can be simple, with slats running at right angles across the frame, or the slats can run diagonally or be fitted together in a pattern. Look at books on garden ornament or on the Internet for design options.

See the Brambles and the Grape entries for information on supports that will help maximize yields on these popular crops. See the Bean entry for a simple upright trellis suitable for the vegetable garden. See the Annuals entry for some quick-and-easy trellising methods for encouraging vines to climb lampposts, tepees, and other structures.

TROPAEOLUM

Nasturtium. Summer- and fall-blooming annuals; edible flowers.

Description: Long-spurred, cup-shaped, 2-inch flowers in yellow, orange, and red bloom among round, yellowish green leaves on short vines or 1-foot mounds.

How to grow: Because they transplant poorly, sow seeds directly where they are to bloom after the soil has warmed up. Nasturtiums thrive in sunny, cool areas in average soil, but they adapt fairly well to heat. Provide support for the climbers. Control aphids with soap spray.

Landscape uses: Nasturtiums look pretty in beds, borders, edges, pots, and hanging baskets as well as on short trellises. The leaves and flowers are edible and add a pleasant, peppery flavor to salads; the buds may be pickled and used in place of capers.

TSUGA

Hemlock. Needle-leaved evergreen trees.

Description: *Tsuga canadensis*, Canada or eastern hemlock, has soft, fine-textured foliage and a loosely pyramidal form. It grows 40 to 75 feet tall. Zones 3–8.

T. caroliniana, Carolina hemlock, has needles that are somewhat darker green and blunter. Plants can reach 70 feet. Zones 5–7.

Both species are native and produce decorative, tiny (1-inch) cones.

How to grow: Hemlocks grow naturally in cooler mountain climates in rocky, shallow soil. In the landscape, they do best with shaded roots, even moisture, and a deep mulch. Hemlocks can grow in full sun in the North, but are best for shade or partial shade elsewhere. They rarely need pruning. Hemlock woolly adelgid is a serious pest of both species. Thoroughly spraying the needles of infested trees with a horticultural oil and soap spray will control them, but it's difficult to adequately cover tall hemlocks. Spray both in spring, when adelgids hatch, and in fall, before the nymphs produce their woolly protective coverings. Ask your extension office for the recommended spray schedule for your area.

Landscape uses: Hemlocks make charming specimens or effective informal screens or hedges. Canada hemlock can also be sheared to make a formal hedge.

TULIPA

Tulip. Spring-blooming bulbs.

Description: The most familiar tulips are hybrids that bear oval to cuplike blooms on long stems, but within the genus are flowers from barely 1 inch to over 8 inches wide, resembling stars, bowls, or eggs; some are double and resemble peonies, while others look like lilies and water lilies. The most exotic bear fanciful fringes on the petal tips, or their petals are deeply cut and feathered like tropical parrots' plumage. Colors cover virtually the entire range except blue. Some have subtly blended colors, while others offer strikingly striped or edged patterns.

Although generally not fragrant, a few, especially the parrots, have a sweet, fruity perfume. Tulips bloom singly or (rarely) in clusters on gracefully curving to strictly upright stems, reaching from 3 to 36 inches above broad, fleshy, green to blue-green leaves. Some (mostly the Greigii cultivars) have foliage that is beautifully lined with dark purple. The species typically produce much smaller leaves and blooms than their hybrid relatives.

Species worth trying include *Tulipa acuminata*, horned or fire flame tulip, with red-and-yellow blooms; *T. clusiana*, lady or peppermint stick tulip, with red-and-white blooms, and *T. clusiana* var. *chrysantha*, with red-and-yellow blooms; and *T. praestans*, especially its cultivar 'Fusilier', with clustered blooms in bright red-orange. Most tulips are hardy to Zones 4–5; they do poorly in Zones 8 and warmer.

How to grow: Virtually all tulips are easy to grow. Plant in fall before the ground freezes, in a sunny to partly shady spot with average, well-drained soil. Space tulip bulbs 2 to 6 inches apart, depending on the ultimate size of the plant. Bury bulbs at a depth 2 to 3 times their width, measuring the depth from the top of the bulb. You should plant many of the cultivars even deeper to help encourage the bulbs to remain blooming size. Shallow planting usually results in good bloom the first year, followed by progressively disappointing displays in succeeding years. Fertilize like daffodils (see the Narcissus entry) to prolong the useful life of your tulips.

If you are bedding tulips out and plan to remove them after they fade, or if you are growing them as annual cut flowers, don't fertilize—the bulb contains everything the flower needs to bloom its first year. Water if spring rains amount to less than 1 inch or so per week. Deadhead tulips after bloom if you want them to remain for another display the next year, but expect the flowers to be smaller and on shorter stems. Don't remove the foliage until it has turned quite yellow and starts to die down. If you need to divide a clump, do so as you would for daffodils.

Control tulip fire (a fungal disease that will spread rapidly through an infected planting) by deep planting and immediate destruction of plants that wilt suddenly. Botrytis sometimes attacks the flowers, turning them into a twisted or collapsed mess; remove and destroy the flowers as soon as you notice it. Mice, squirrels, and chipmunks eat the bulbs with gusto. Planting a small group of

Choosing Terrific Tulips

For longest life in the garden, choose Triumph, Darwin Hybrid, and/or Single Late tulips, as well as the reliably perennial species tulips, or make sure you choose tulips labeled as "perennial tulips" when you place an order or buy bulbs at a nursery or garden center.

Here are some popular tulip types listed according to bloom season. Species tulips bloom early or during midseason.

Early-Blooming Tulips

Single Early: 2- to 4-inch flowers; 12- to 14-inch stems; often fragrant. The much-loved cultivar 'Apricot Beauty' is in this group.

Double Early: 3- to 4-inch many-petaled flowers; 12- to 14-inch stems.

Greigii: 3-inch-long starry flowers; 8- to 12-inch stems; purple-striped foliage.

Kaufmanniana: 3-inch-long flowers; 4 to 8 inches tall; also called waterlily tulips; foliage sometimes mottled.

Fosteriana: 4-inch-long flowers; 10 to 20 inches tall; includes 'Emperor' strain tulips.

Midseason Tulips

Darwin Hybrid: 3- to 4-inch flowers; 2- to 2½-foot stems.

Triumph: 2- to 4-inch flowers; 18- to 24-inch stems.

Late-Season Tulips

Lily Flowered: 2- to 4-inch flowers with curved, spreading petals; 2-foot stems.

Single Late: 3- to 4-inch-long, egg-shaped flowers; 1½- to 3-foot stems. 'Queen of the Night' is in this group.

Parrot: 6-inch-wide feather-edged flowers; 14- to 20-inch stems.

Double Late: 6-inch-wide, peonylike flowers; 12- to 16-inch stems; the last tulips to bloom.

bulbs in baskets made of ⅓-to ½-inch wire mesh should discourage them; so will a large piece of wire mesh laid 1 inch over the bulbs in a larger planting. See the Animal Pests entry for techniques to repel rabbits and deer.

Landscape uses: Grow small to large masses of tulips throughout a border in between perennials and annuals, which will disguise the yellowing foliage. Plant them in formal beds and in sweeps in lawns, removing them after bloom and replacing with annuals. They look marvelous against an evergreen hedge and in groups at the edges of patios. Smaller species are perfect for rock gardens, and many are wonderful forced in pots, particularly the early bloomers. All combine nicely with phlox (*Phlox* spp.), pansies (*Viola* ×*wittrockiana*), bleeding hearts (*Dicentra* spp.), rock cress (*Arabis* spp.), candytuft (*Iberis* spp.), irises, azaleas (*Rhododendron* spp.), and lilacs.

TURNIP

Brassica rapa, Rapifera Group
Brassicaceae

Fast-growing turnips thrive in cool temperatures; hot weather makes the leaves tough and the roots woody and bitter. Ample moisture and temperatures of 50° to 70°F encourage rapid growth and a high-quality crop. Enjoy the roots and tops either raw or cooked.

Rutabagas are related to turnips, but they take a month longer to grow. Bake rutabaga roots whole; or chop, boil, and mash them.

Planting: Turnips thrive in well-drained, deeply worked soil on a sunny site.

Plant seeds outdoors 3 weeks before the last frost in spring. The soil must be at least 40°F for germination, which takes from 7 to 14 days. Fall crops of turnips are often sweeter and provide a longer harvest period than spring plantings. For a fall harvest, plant in midsummer about 2 months before the first frost. Plant rutabagas for fall harvest only.

Sow spring crops ¼ inch deep and fall crops ½ inch deep. Broadcast the seeds, and later thin them to 3 to 4 inches apart, or plant seeds in rows spaced 12 to 18 inches apart.

Growing guidelines: Keep the soil evenly moist to promote fast growth and the best flavor. When plants are 5 inches tall, apply a mulch at least 2 inches thick. No extra fertilizer is necessary in well-prepared soil.

Problems: See Cabbage entry for details on pest and disease control.

Harvesting: Harvest greens when they're large enough to pick. If you plan to harvest both leaves and roots from a single planting, remove only two or three leaves per plant. Small roots are the most tender, so pull when they are 1 to 3 inches in diameter. It's easy to harvest small turnips growing in light garden soil simply by hand-pulling them. For large storage roots, though, try loosening the soil by inserting a spading fork beside the row first. To store the roots, twist off the tops, leaving ½ inch of stem. Place undamaged roots in a cool, dark place, such as a basement or root cellar. Don't wash off soil that clings to roots; it helps protect roots in storage. They will keep for several months. You can also leave your fall crop in the ground until early winter (or throughout winter in mild climates) by covering the roots with a thick mulch.

TWINSPUR

See *Diascia*

U-V

ULMUS

Elm. Deciduous trees.

Description: *Ulmus alata*, winged elm, has a pyramidal form and is 30 to 40 feet tall. It flowers inconspicuously in spring and bears small, fuzzy, waferlike fruits. The small (2½-inch) leaves turn soft reds and oranges in fall most years. Thin twigs sport corky wings. This Southeastern native elm can be weedy and is considered undesirable by some, but it grows beautifully in poor, compacted soils. Zones 6–8.

U. americana, American elm, is the stately 60- to 80-foot, vase-shaped tree that for many years shaded North American campuses and avenues. Much publicized in the wake of the Dutch elm disease (DED) epidemic that decimated huge numbers of this species, American elm is a beautiful, but no longer recommended, shade tree. Zones 2–8.

U. parvifolia, Chinese or lacebark elm, is a handsome tree with flaking bark that exposes patches of tan, green, and cream. Growing 40 to 50 feet, Chinese elm has inconspicuous, late-summer flowers and small (1- to 3-inch) leaves that turn yellow or purple shades when conditions favor good autumn color development. Zones 5–8.

U. pumila, Siberian elm, is a fast-growing, weak-wooded tree with few assets beyond its hardiness and ability to grow on very poor sites. It has an irregular, open form and a landscape height of 50 to 70 feet. During dormancy, Siberian elm's round black buds distinguish it from the highly desirable Chinese elm, which has relatively flat buds. Zones 2–8.

How to grow: Elms are adapted to a variety of soil types but require good drainage and full sun. While many American elms still stand, far more have fallen to DED. Control programs are somewhat effective, but until DED is controlled, admire American elms but don't plant them. Breeding programs continue to search for DED-resistant American elm cultivars, often crossing it with Asian elm species. No reliably resistant trees have yet been selected that have American elm's desirable features.

Elm leaf beetles will feed on all elms but seem to prefer Siberian elm. The ½-inch-long adults are drab yellow-green, black-striped beetles that eat round holes in young elm leaves in spring, then lay eggs that hatch into leaf-skeletonizing larvae. The result is an unhealthy-looking tree with brown foliage. Elms often respond with another flush of growth just in time for the next generation of beetles. Adults also overwinter in nearby buildings. Spray Btsd (*Bacillus thuringiensis* var. *san diego*) after eggs hatch (late May through June) to control larvae.

Landscape uses: Naturalize winged elm among other trees. Use Chinese elm for shade and as a focal point, much as you would American elm. Plant Siberian elm hybrids on difficult sites.

URBAN GARDENING

Urban gardeners face different challenges than their rural and suburban counterparts. It can take ingenuity and determination to garden in small city lots where neighboring buildings block the sunlight, the soil quality may be dreadful, and water sources unreliable. Soil and air pollutants, theft, vandalism, and politics further complicate city gardening.

There are some benefits to city gardening, too—no pesky deer or other wildlife to eat the flowers and fruits is one. Another benefit is a frost-free season as much as 1 month longer than that in surrounding areas, due to the warming effects of buildings and pavement. Easily managed smaller gardens demand less time but inspire creativity in the quest for productive beauty. City farmers turn yards, rooftops, fire escapes, and a variety of containers into fields of plants.

In 1976, Congress established urban gardening programs through the Cooperative Extension Service. The not-for-profit American Community Gardening Association (ACGA) also promotes gar-

dening nationwide. See the Community Gardens entry for more information on ACGA programs.

Urban Concerns

The key to city gardening success is adapting traditional gardening methods to suit the limits imposed by an urban environment.

Space: Design your garden to maximize growing area while preserving living space. Make the most of your garden space by growing compact (bush-type) cultivars. Use containers to maximize your gardening potential. To utilize vertical space, build trellises or fences for vines. See the Container Gardening and Trellising entries for more information on these techniques.

Light: Select plants and a design to suit each location, based on the total light it receives. Most edible plants need at least 6 hours of daily sunlight to produce flowers and fruits.

Soil: In general, urban soils are compacted and clayey, and they may be contaminated with lead and other heavy metals. Improve such soils by adding compost, aged sawdust, or other types of organic matter. Many cities make compost or mulch from tree trimmings and leaf pickups. Contact local parks or street departments about these often-free soil amendments.

Some urban lots have no soil, or soil that's so poor it can't easily be improved. An alternative to amending existing soil is to bring in soil for raised beds or containers.

Theft and vandalism: Most urban gardening takes place in densely populated or publicly accessible places. Theft and vandalism can be a frustrating reality. Fences keep honest people honest, but involving area youth and adults in gardening is a more effective tactic. Share garden space and/or knowledge with your neighbors.

To reduce vandalism and theft, keep your garden well maintained, repair damage immediately, harvest ripened vegetables daily, and plant more vegetables than you need. Grow ornamentals in the garden to hide ripening vegetables.

Soil contaminants: Excessive lead, cadmium, and mercury levels are common in urban soils. Sources of such pollution include leaded paint, motor vehicle exhaust, and industrial waste. Poisoning from eating contaminated produce can affect all gardeners, especially young children whose bodies are actively growing and who tend to put their hands in their mouths.

You can reduce the amount of lead that plants absorb from soil and also keep down dust that may carry lead by adding organic matter to soil and mulching heavily. Planting food crops away from streets and keeping soil pH levels at 6.7 or higher will also help prevent plants from taking up lead. If contaminant levels are too high, garden in containers filled with clean soil and wash crops thoroughly before eating them.

Testing to monitor soil contaminants is strongly urged for city gardens, particularly those used by children. Contact your local extension office to find out what soil tests are available.

VEGETABLE GARDENING

Fresh-picked sweet corn and snap peas are a taste treat you can get only from your backyard vegetable garden. The quality and flavor of fresh vegetables will reward you from early in the growing season until late fall. And when you garden organically, your harvest will be free of potentially harmful chemical residues. Plus, vegetables you grow yourself are free of the "food mile" cost to the environ-

ment of growing produce in one region of the country (or the world) and shipping it to another.

Although the plants we grow in our vegetable gardens are a diverse group from many different plant families, they share broad general requirements. Most will thrive in a garden that has well-drained soil with a pH of 6.5 to 7.0 and plenty of direct sun. Some crops can tolerate frost; others tolerate some shade. If you pick an appropriate site, prepare the soil well, and keep your growing crops weeded and watered, you should have little trouble growing vegetables successfully.

This entry will serve as your guide to planning, preparing, and tending your vegetable plot through the seasons. Throughout, you'll find references to the many other entries that provide detailed information on topics such as soil improvement and pest control that you'll find helpful.

Planning Your Garden

Planning your garden can be as much fun as planting it. When you plan a garden, you'll balance all your hopes and wishes for the crops you'd like to harvest against your local growing conditions, as well as the space you have available. Planning involves choosing a site (unless you already have an established garden), deciding on a garden style, selecting crops and cultivars, and mapping your garden.

Site Selection

Somewhere in your yard, there is a good place for a vegetable garden. The ideal site has these characteristics.

1. **Full or almost full sun.** In warm climates, some vegetables can get by on 6 hours of direct sunshine each day, while a full day of sun is needed in cool climates. The best sites

for vegetable gardens usually are on the south or west side of a house.

2. **Good drainage.** A slight slope is good for vegetable gardens. The soil will get well soaked by rain or irrigation water, and excess will run off. Avoid low places where water accumulates; these are ideal breeding places for diseases.

3. **Limited competition.** Tree roots take up huge amounts of water. Leave as much space as possible between large trees and your garden. Plant shade-tolerant shrubs or small fruits between trees and your garden.

4. **Easy access to water.** If you can't run a hose or irrigation line to a prospective garden site, don't plant vegetables there. No matter what your local climate is, you'll most likely have to provide supplemental water at some point in the growing season.

5. **Accessibility.** Organic gardens need large amounts of mulch, plus periodic infusions of other bulky materials such as compost or rock fertilizers. If you have a large garden, try to leave access for a truck to drive up to its edge for easy unloading. In narrow city lots, the garden access path should be wide enough for a cart or wheelbarrow.

Once you find a site that has these characteristics, double-check for hidden problems. For example, don't locate your garden over septic-tank field lines, buried utility cables, or water lines.

Garden Layout

Once you've decided on a site, think about the type of vegetable garden you want. Raised beds offer lots of advantages, and old-fashioned rows work well for some crops. Containers are a great choice for small or shady yards.

Raised beds: Productivity, efficient use of space, less weeding, and shading the soil are all benefits of intensively planted beds. Beds are raised planting areas, generally with carefully enriched soil, so they can be planted intensively, with crops spaced close together. While they require more initial time to prepare, beds save time on weeding or mulching later in the season. Because they're more space efficient, you'll also get higher yields per area than from a traditional row garden.

Beds for vegetables should be no more than 4 feet wide so you can easily reach the center of the bed to plant, weed, and harvest. See the Raised Bed Gardening entry for directions on making raised beds.

Row planting: A row garden, in which vegetables are planted in parallel lines, is easy to organize and plant. However, it's not as space efficient as a raised bed garden, so you'll reap less of a yield per square foot. You also may spend more time weeding unless you mulch heavily and early between rows.

Row planting is quick and efficient for large plantings of crops such as beans or corn. You may decide to plant some crops in rows and others in beds. "Sod Strips Save Work" describes an easy way to start a row garden.

Spot gardens: If your yard is small, having no suitable space for a separate vegetable garden, look for sunny spots where you can fit small plantings of your favorite crops. Plant a small bed of salad greens and herbs near your kitchen door for easy access when preparing meals. Tuck vegetables into flowerbeds. You can dress up crops that aren't ornamental, such as tomatoes, by underplanting them with annuals such as nasturtiums and marigolds. For ideas on incorporating

Sod Strips Save Work

When transforming a plot of lawn into a vegetable garden, try cultivating strips or beds in the sod. You'll only have to contend with weeds in the beds. Plus, you'll have excellent erosion control and no mud between the rows, which makes picking easier and more enjoyable.

Tilling the bed: Overlap your tilling so that the finished bed is 1½ to 2 times the cutting width of your tiller. Start out with a slow wheel speed and shallow tilling depth. Gradually increase speed and depth as the sod becomes more and more workable. Make the beds as long or as short as you want, but space the beds about 3 feet apart and leave sod between them. Depending on how tough the sod and your tiller are, you may have to retill the beds in a week or two or hand-dig stubborn grass clumps to make a proper seedbed. On your final pass, first spread 1 to 2 inches of rich compost over the soil surface. This will help your soil to recover from the detrimental impact of tilling and will also provide nutrients for your crops.

Weed control: You can control weeds easily in the rows with a wheel-hoe cultivator or hand hoe or by hand-weeding. What about weeds along the outside edges of the beds? Just mow them down with your lawn mower when you mow the grassy areas between the beds. You'll be rewarded with a ready supply of grass clippings for compost or mulch.

Caution: Before mowing, be sure to pick up all of the larger rocks that your tiller brought to the surface. Rocks will quickly dull and chip your mower blade, and they're downright dangerous to people, pets, and property when your mower kicks them up and hurls them through the air.

Once your garden is finished for the season, sow a cover or green manure crop such as buckwheat, clover, or ryegrass in the beds. The following spring, just till the strips that were in sod. They'll become your planting beds, and the previous year's beds will be pathways. It's crop rotation made easy!

You can also let your sod strips be permanent pathways. Either way, after the initial tilling, you should never need to use your tiller to prepare the soil again. Simply add more organic matter yearly through cover cropping and mulching and work it in lightly with hand tools, or plant directly through the surface cover.

---

vegetables into your landscape, see the Edible Landscaping entry.

Containers: You may not be able to grow all your favorite vegetables in containers, but many dwarf cultivars of vegetables will grow well in pots or planters. Garden catalogs include dwarf tomato, cucumber, pea, pepper, and even squash cultivars suitable for container growing. Vegetables that are naturally small, such as leaf lettuce, scallions, and many herbs, also grow nicely in containers. See the Container Gardening entry for details on choices of containers and soil mixes.

Small-Garden Strategies

If your appetite for fresh vegetables is bigger than the space you have to grow them in, try these ways to coax the most produce from the least space:

- Emphasize vertical crops that grow up rather than out: trellis snow peas, shell peas, pole beans, and cucumbers.

- Interplant fast-maturing salad crops (lettuce, radishes, spinach, and beets) together in 2-foot-square blocks. Succession plant every 2 weeks in early spring and early fall.

- Avoid overplanting any single vegetable. Summer squash is the number one offender when it comes to rampant overproduction. Two plants each of zucchini, yellow-neck, and a novelty summer squash will yield plenty.

- Choose medium- and small-fruited cultivars of tomatoes and peppers. The smaller the fruits, the more the plants tend to produce. Beefsteak tomatoes and big bell peppers produce comparatively few fruits per plant.

- Experiment with unusual vegetables that are naturally compact—such as kohlrabi, bok choy, and Oriental eggplant—and with dwarf varieties of larger vegetables.

- Maintain permanent clumps of perennial vegetables such as hardy scallions, and perennial herbs such as chives. Even a small garden should always have something to offer.

Crop Choices

Generally, vegetables can be divided into cool-weather, warm-weather, and hot-weather crops, as shown on the opposite page.

Consider the length of your growing season (the period of time between the last frost in spring and the first one in fall), seasonal rainfall patterns, and other environmental factors when choosing vegetables. Fast-maturing and heat- or cold-tolerant cultivars make it easier for northern gardeners to grow hot-weather crops such as melons and okra and for southern gardeners to be able to enjoy cool-loving crops such as spinach and lettuce.

Make some of your selections for beauty as well as flavor. Beans with purple or variegated pods are easy to spot for picking and lovely to behold. Swiss chard with red ribs makes a dramatic statement, and purple kohlrabi is oddly eye-catching. Small-fruited Japanese eggplants look elegant in an attractive container. Try some historical heirlooms or little-known imports. Cultivars endorsed by All-America Selections (AAS) also are good bets. For more details, refer to the Heirloom Plants and All-America Selections entries.

Garden Mapping

As you fill in seed order forms, it's wise to map planned locations for your crops. Otherwise, you may end up with far too little or too much seed. Depending on the size of your garden, you may need to make a formal plan drawn to scale.

Consider these points as you figure out your planting needs and fill in your map.

- Are you growing just enough of a crop for fresh eating, or will you be preserving some of your harvest? For some crops, it takes surprisingly

Some Like It Hot

Because vegetables differ so much in their preferred growing temperatures, planting the vegetable garden isn't a one-day job. Be prepared to spend several days over the course of early spring to early summer planting vegetable seeds and plants. You'll start planting cool-weather crops a few weeks before the last spring frost, and continue making small seedings every couple of weeks. Set out warm-weather crops just after the last spring frost. Hot-weather crops cannot tolerate frost or cold soil. Unless you can protect them with a portable cold frame or row covers, plant them at least 3 weeks after the last spring frost. In warm climates, plant cool-weather crops again in early fall so that they grow during fall and winter. Here is a guide to the temperature preferences of 30 common garden vegetables.

Cool Weather

Beets	Garden peas
Broccoli	Onions
Cabbage	Radishes
Cauliflower	Spinach
Celery Lettuce	Turnips

Warm Weather

Cantaloupes	Potatoes
Carrots	Pumpkins
Chard, Swiss	Snap beans
Corn	Squash
Cucumbers	Tomatoes
Peppers	

Hot Weather

Eggplant	Peanuts
Field peas	Shell beans
Lima beans	Sweet potatoes
Okra	Watermelons

little seed to produce enough to feed a family. You can refer to seed catalogs or check individual vegetable entries for information on how much to plant.

🌿 Are you planning to rotate crops? Changing the position of plants in different crop families from year to year can help reduce pest problems.

🌿 Are you going to plant crops in spring and again later in the season for a fall harvest? Order seed for both plantings at the same time.

Preparing the Soil

Since most vegetables are fast-growing annuals, they need garden soil that provides a wide range of plant nutrients and loose soil that plant roots can penetrate easily. Every year when you harvest vegetables, you're carting off part of the reservoir of nutrients that was in your vegetable garden soil. To keep the soil in balance, you need to replace those nutrients. Fortunately, since you're working the soil each year, you'll have lots of opportunities to add organic matter and soil amendments that keep your soil naturally balanced.

If you're starting a new vegetable garden or switching from conventional to organic methods (or if you've just been disappointed with past yields or crop quality), start by testing your soil. Soil acidity or alkalinity, which is measured as soil pH, can affect plant performance and yield, especially for heavy-feeding crops such as broccoli and tomatoes. A soil test will reveal soil pH as well as any nutrient imbalances. See the Soil entry for details on soil testing, and the pH and Fertilizers entries for more on providing ideal conditions for your plants.

SMART SHOPPING
Making the Right Choices

Seed catalogs and seed racks present a dazzling array of choices for the vegetable gardener. They all look tasty and beautiful in the pictures, but here's how to choose.

- If you're a beginning gardener, talk with other gardeners and your local extension agent. Ask what vegetables grow best in your area, and start with those crops. Most extension offices also provide lists of recommended cultivars.

- Seek out catalogs and plant lists offered by seed companies that specialize in regionally adapted selections.

- Match cultivars to your garden's characteristics and problems. Look for cultivars that are resistant to disease organisms that may be widespread in your area, such as VF tomato cultivars—which are resistant to verticillium and fusarium fungi.

- If you buy seeds by the packet, take note of how many seeds you're getting. Seed quantity per packet varies widely. Some packets of new or special cultivars may contain fewer than 20 seeds. Consider buying a half ounce or ounce of seeds and then dividing them up with gardening friends.

- When buying transplants at local garden centers, always check plants for disease and insect problems. Don't forget to check roots as well as leaves.

- Ask whether the transplants you're buying have been hardened off yet. If the salesperson doesn't know what you're talking about, take the hint and buy your transplants from a more knowledgeable supplier.

- Remember, with transplants, larger size doesn't always mean better quality. Look for stocky transplants with uniform green leaves. Avoid buying transplants that are already flowering—they won't survive the shock of transplanting as well as younger plants will.

New Gardens

If you're just starting out, using a rotary tiller may be the only practical way to work up the soil in a large garden. But whether you're working with a machine or digging by hand, don't turn the soil when it's too wet or too dry. It will have serious detrimental effects on soil structure and quality. You'll find more information on preparing new garden beds in the Soil entry, including how to tell whether soil is ready to work. See "Sod Strips Save Work" on page 615 for a simple method for creating a new garden in a lawn area and the Raised Beds entry for another excellent approach to creating rich, fertile soil for a vegetable garden.

Depending on the results of your soil tests, you may need to work in lime to correct pH or rock fertilizers to correct deficiencies as you dig your garden. In any case, it's always wise to incorporate organic matter as you work.

Soil Enrichment

If you're an experienced gardener with an established garden site, you can take steps to replenish soil nutrients and organic matter as soon as you harvest and clear out your garden in fall. Sow seed of a cover crop in your garden, or cover the soil with a thick layer of organic mulch to protect your soil and replenish organic matter content. See the Cover Crops and Mulch entries for details on using both of these to improve your soil. In spring, you'll be ready to push back or incorporate the mulch or green manure and start planting.

If you don't plant a cover crop, spread compost over your garden in spring and work it into the soil. The best time to do this is a few weeks before planting, if your soil is dry enough to be worked.

Baby Vegetables

Baby carrots have become a staple in grocery stores, but there are other easy-to-grow baby vegetables. Some, like leeks, cauliflower, onions, lettuce, and other greens, are produced by a combination of close spacing and early harvest. Sow seed close together and harvest as soon as the plants are large enough. To produce baby summer squash, give plants normal spacing, but harvest when the fruit is still quite small and tender. Full-size cherry tomato plants naturally produce small fruit, although you can also find dwarf plants. Fingerling potatoes also are naturally small.

To produce other baby vegetables, start with cultivars specially designed for that purpose. Look at vegetable seed catalogs or specialty Internet sites for seed for baby carrots, beets, petits pois peas, filet beans, and eggplant.

Be conservative when you work the soil. While some cultivation is necessary to prepare seedbeds and to open up the soil for root growth, excess cultivation is harmful. It introduces large amounts of oxygen into the soil, which can speed the breakdown of soil organic matter. Never cultivate extremely wet soil, because that will compact it instead of aerating it.

Other opportunities for improving your soil will crop up at planting time, when you add compost or other growth boosters in planting rows or holes, and during the growing season, as you mulch your developing plants.

Planting

Spring can be the busiest time of year for the vegetable gardener. Some careful planning is in order. To help you remember what you have planted and how well cultivars perform in your garden, keep written records. Fill in planting dates on your garden map as the season progresses. Later, make notes of harvest dates. If you would like to keep more detailed records, try keeping a garden journal, or set up a vegetable garden data file on index cards or your computer or smartphone. With good records, you can discover many details about the unique climate in your garden, such as when soil warms up in spring, when problem insects emerge, and when space becomes available for replanting.

Getting Set to Plant

Once the soil is prepared, lay out your garden paths. Then rake loose soil from the pathways into the raised rows or beds. As soon as possible, mulch the pathways with leaves, straw, or another biodegradable mulch. Lay mulch thickly to keep down weeds. If you live in a region that has frequent heavy rain, place boards down the pathways so you'll have a dry place to walk.

You can prepare planting beds and rows as much as several weeks before planting. However, if you plan to leave more than 3 weeks between preparation and planting, mulch the soil so it won't crust over or compact.

Plant arrangement: There are practically no limits to the ways you can arrange plants in a vegetable garden. In a traditional row garden, you'll probably plant your crops in single rows of single species. If you have raised rows or raised beds, you can interplant—mix different types of crops in one area—and use a variety of spacing patterns to maximize the number of plants in a given area.

Single rows are good for upright, bushy plants and those that need good air circulation such as tomatoes and summer squash. Use double rows for trellised crops such as cucumbers and for compact bushes such as snap beans and potatoes. Matrix planting is good for interplanting slow- and fast-growing crops. Plant slow growers such as Brussels sprouts, leeks, peppers, or tomatoes, then fill in between them with fast-growing crops like leaf lettuce, radishes, or bush beans. The fast growers will be ready to harvest by the time the slower-growing plants need the space. See the illustration on the opposite page for ideas on planning the layout of your garden crops.

Planting combinations: Succession cropping is growing two vegetable crops in the same space in the same growing season. You'll plant one early crop, harvest it, and then plant a warm- or hot-season crop afterward. To avoid depleting the soil, make sure one crop is a nitrogen-fixing legume and the other a lighter feeder, or add plenty of compost to the soil after harvesting the first crop. All vegetables used for succession cropping should mature quickly. For example, in a cool climate, plant garden peas in spring, and follow them with cucumber or summer squash. Or after harvesting your early crop of spinach, plant bush beans. In warm climates, try lettuce followed by field peas, or plant pole beans and then a late crop of turnips after the bean harvest. In southern zones where the season is long and summers are sweltering, consider growing a spring to early-summer garden, then let the garden lie dormant during the hottest summer weather. Replant the garden in late summer or early fall for a harvest that lasts through early winter.

Planting for extended harvest: If you'd like to expand your vegetable gardening horizons, one of the most exciting challenges is extending the

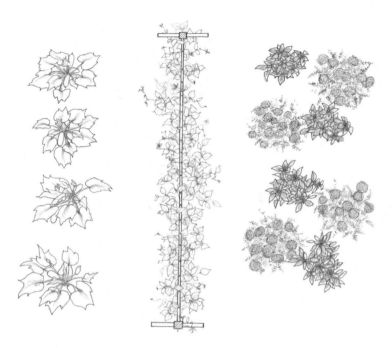

Spacing and interplanting. Use single rows for bushy crops like zucchini and double rows with a trellis down the middle for beans and other vining crops. With slow growers like peppers, try filling spaces between with low-growing annual flowers that attract beneficial insects.

harvest into fall and winter. It takes some advance planning to accomplish this, especially if you have cold, snowy winters, but some gardeners find the rewards well worth the effort. To learn more about this, see the Season Extension entry.

Seeds and Transplants

Some vegetable crops grow best when seeded directly in place. Other crops will benefit from being coddled indoors during the seedling stage and will grow robustly after transplanting. See the Seed Starting and Seed Saving entry for complete information on starting vegetables from seed.

Direct seeding: You can plant many kinds of vegetable seeds directly into prepared soil. How-

ever, even when you follow seed-spacing directions given on the seed packet, direct-seeded crops often germinate too well or not well enough. When germination is excellent, thin plants ruthlessly, because crowded vegetable plants will not mature properly. When direct seeding any vegetable, set some seeds aside so you can go back in 2 weeks and replant vacant spaces in the row or bed.

Soil temperature and moisture play important roles in the germination of vegetable seeds. Very few vegetable seeds will sprout in cold soil. High soil temperatures also inhibit germination. Also, be sure to plant seeds at the recommended planting depth, and firm the soil with your fingers or a hand tool after planting to ensure good contact of seed and soil.

Starting seeds indoors: Starting seeds indoors offers several advantages: You can get a head start on the growing season, keep on planting when outdoor conditions are too hot and dry for good seed germination, and try rare and unusual cultivars. Tomatoes, peppers, eggplant, cabbage, broccoli, cauliflower, Brussels sprouts, onions, and celery are almost always started from seed indoors, and cold-climate gardeners might add lettuce and members of the squash family to this list.

Keep in mind that most vegetable seedlings need strong light to grow well. A sunny windowsill is adequate for vegetable seedlings, but natural sun and supplemental artificial light are best. Also remember that vegetables started indoors are protected from stress factors such as wind, fluctuating temperatures, and intense sunlight. One week before you plan to transplant, begin hardening off vegetable plants by exposing them to these natural elements. Move them to a protected place outdoors, or put them in a cold frame.

If temperatures are erratic and windy weather is expected, use cloches to protect tender seedlings from injury for 2 to 3 weeks after transplanting. Remove cloches when the plants begin to grow vigorously—a sign that soil temperature has reached a favorable range and roots have become established. See the Transplanting and Season Extension entries for more details.

In late summer, sun and heat can sap moisture from the new transplants of your fall crops faster than the roots can replenish it. Protect seedlings and transplants with shade covers instead of cloches. You can cover plants with cardboard boxes (prop them up to let air circulate under them) or bushel baskets on sunny days for 1 week after transplanting, or you can cover them with a tent made of muslin or some other light-colored cloth.

Care during the Season

After the rush of planting, there's a lull while most of your crops are growing, flowering, and setting fruit. But regular plant care is important if you want to reap a good harvest later in the season. Get in the habit of taking regular garden walks to thin crops, pull weeds, and check for signs of insect and disease problems.

Weeding

Start weed control early and keep at it throughout the season. Remove all weeds within 1 foot of your plants, or they will compete with the vegetables for water and nutrients. If you use a hoe or

Weed Control: Long-Term Strategies

Over a period of years, you can reduce the number of weed seeds present in your vegetable garden. Here's how:

- Mulch heavily and continuously to deprive weed seeds of sunlight.
- Remove all weeds before they produce seeds.
- Plant windbreaks along any side of the garden that borders on woods or wild meadows. Shrubs and trees can help filter out weed seeds carried by the wind.
- Grow rye as a winter cover crop. Rye residue suppresses weed germination and growth.
- Solarize soil to kill weed seeds in the top 3 inches of prepared beds.

hand cultivator, be careful not to injure crop roots.

Some vegetables benefit from extra soil hilled up around the base of the plant. When hoeing around young corn, potatoes, tomatoes, and squash, scatter loose soil from between rows over the root zones of the plants. Once the garden soil has warmed (in late spring or early summer), mulch around your plants to suppress weeds and cut down on moisture loss. If you have areas where weeds have been a problem in the past, use a double mulch of newspapers covered with organic material such as leaves, straw, grass clippings, or shredded bark.

Another solution to weed problems is to cover beds with a sheet of black plastic. The plastic can help warm up cold soil, and it is a very effective barrier to weeds. See the Mulch entry for more information about using black plastic.

Watering

Almost all vegetable gardens need occasional watering, especially from midsummer to early fall. Most vegetables need ½ to 1 inch of water each week, and nature rarely provides water in such regular amounts. Dry weather can strengthen some vegetable plants by forcing them to develop deep roots that can seek out moisture. However, the quality of other crops suffers when plants get too little water. Tomatoes and melons need plenty of water early in the season when they're initiating foliage and fruit. However, as the fruit ripens, its quality often improves if dry conditions prevail. The opposite is true of lettuce, cabbage, and other leafy greens, which need more water as they approach maturity.

When to water: How can you tell when your crops really need supplemental water? Leaves that droop at midday are a warning sign. If leaves wilt in midday and still look wilted the following morning, the plants are suffering. Provide water before soil becomes this dry.

If you don't water in time and the soil dries out completely, replenish soil moisture gradually, over a period of 3 days. If you soak dry soil quickly, your drought-stressed crops will suddenly take up large amounts of water. The abrupt change may cause tomatoes, melons, carrots, cabbage, and other vegetables to literally split their sides, ruining your crop.

Watering methods: Watering by hand using a spray nozzle on the end of a hose is practical in a small garden but can be too time consuming in a large one. Sprinklers are easier to use but aren't water efficient because some of the water falls on

areas that don't need watering. And on a sunny day, some water evaporates and never reaches your plants' roots. Using sprinklers can saturate foliage, leading to conditions that favor some diseases, especially in humid climates. The one situation in which watering with a sprinkler may be the best option is when you have newly seeded beds, which need to be kept moist gently and evenly. See the Watering entry for efficient hand-watering strategies.

In terms of both water usage and economy of labor, the best way to water a vegetable garden is to use a drip irrigation system. See the Drip Irrigation entry for more information.

Irrigation pipes do not take the place of a handy garden hose—you need both. Buy a two-headed splitter at the hardware store, and screw it onto the faucet you use for the vegetable garden. Keep the irrigation system connected to one side, leaving the other available for hand watering or other uses.

Staking

Many vegetables need stakes or trellises to keep them off the ground. Without support, the leaves and fruits of garden peas, tomatoes, pole beans, and some cucumbers and peppers easily become diseased. Also, many of these crops are easier to harvest when they're supported because the fruits are more accessible. You'll find many handy tips for staking and supporting crops in the individual vegetable entries as well as in the Trellising entry.

Fertilizing

Keeping the soil naturally balanced with organic matter will go a long way toward meeting the nutrient needs of your crops. Crops that mature quickly (in less than 50 days), like lettuce and radishes, seldom need supplemental fertilizer when growing in a healthy soil, especially if they're mulched. But vegetables that mature slowly (over an extended period), such as tomatoes, often benefit from a booster feeding in midsummer.

Plan to fertilize tomatoes, peppers, and corn just as they reach their reproductive stage of growth. Sprinkle fish meal, alfalfa meal, or a blended organic fertilizer beneath the plants just before a rain. Or rake back the mulch, spread a ½-inch layer of compost or rotted manure over the soil, and then put the mulch back in place. When growing plants in containers, feed them a liquid fertilizer such as fish emulsion or compost tea every 2 to 3 weeks throughout the season. See the Compost entry for instructions for making compost tea.

Foliar fertilizing—spraying liquid fertilizer on plant leaves—is another option for midseason fertilization. Kelp-based foliar fertilizers contain nutrients, enzymes, and acids that tend to enhance vegetables' efforts at reproduction. They're most effective when plants are already getting a good supply of nutrients through their roots. Use foliar fertilizers as a midseason tonic for tomatoes, pole beans, and other vegetables that produce over a long period.

Pollination

You'll harvest leafy greens, carrots, and members of the cabbage family long before they flower. But with most other vegetables, the harvest is a fruit— the end result of pollinated blossoms. A spell of unusually hot weather can cause flowers or pollen grains to develop improperly. Conversely, a long, wet, cloudy spell can stop insects from pollinating. Either condition can leave you with few tomatoes, melons, or peppers, or with ears of corn with sparse, widely spaced kernels. The blossom ends of cucumbers and summer squash become wrinkled and misshapen when pollination is inadequate.

To prevent such problems, place like vegetables together so the plants can share the pollen they produce. One exception is supersweet and regular hybrid corn: Separate these by at least 25 feet to limit the amount of cross-pollination that takes place, or your harvest may not be true to type.

Tomatoes, corn, and beans are pollinated primarily by wind, although honeybees and other insects provide a little help transporting pollen about the plants. The presence of pollinating insects is crucial for squash, cucumbers, and melons. Plant flowers near these crops to lure bees in the right direction. You'll find more suggestions for helping with pollination in individual vegetable entries.

Coping with Pests

Pests and diseases of vegetable crops include insects, fungi, bacteria, and viruses, as well as larger animals such as raccoons and deer. Fortunately for organic gardeners, there are ever-increasing numbers of varieties that are genetically resistant to insects and diseases. If you know a pest or disease has been a problem in your garden, seek out and plant a resistant cultivar whenever possible.

Prevention goes a long way toward solving insect and disease problems in the vegetable garden. Also, remember that a weed-free or insect-free environment is not a natural one. If your garden is a diverse miniature world, with vigorous plants nourished by a well-balanced soil and an active population of native beneficial insects and microorganisms, you'll likely experience few serious pest problems.

Sometimes pests do get out of hand. In most cases, once you've identified the pest that's damaging your crop, you'll be able to control it by implementing one of the following four treatments:

✎ Handpick or gather the insects with a net or handheld vacuum. As you gather them, put the bugs in a container filled with soapy water. Set the container in the sun until the bugs die.

🌿 Use floating row covers as a barrier to problem insects. Row covers are particularly useful in protecting young squash, cucumber, and melon plants from insects. Remember to remove the cover when the plants begin to flower. You can also wrap row covers around the outside of tomato cages to discourage disease-carrying aphids and leafhoppers.

🌿 Bt (*Bacillus thuringiensis*) gives excellent control for leaf-eating caterpillars. It is often indispensable when you're growing members of the cabbage family, which have many such pests, and when hornworms are numerous enough to seriously damage tomatoes.

🌿 Spraying insecticidal soap is effective against aphids on leafy greens, thrips on tomatoes, and several other small, soft-bodied pests.

There are other types of barriers, traps, and sprays that help keep vegetable pests under control. For more recommendations, see the Pests entry and individual crop entries.

Diseases: Vegetable crop diseases are less threatening in home gardens than they are in farm fields, where crops are grown in monoculture. When many different plants are present, diseases that require specific host plants have a hard time gaining a firm foothold. Plus, a healthy, naturally balanced soil contains many beneficial microorganisms capable of controlling those that are likely to cause trouble.

If you have a large garden, you can help avoid some disease problems by planting crops in different places in the garden from one year to the next. See the Crop Rotation entry for more information.

Where diseases, weeds, soil-dwelling insects, or root knot nematodes seriously interfere with plant health, you can often get good control by subjecting the soil to extreme temperatures. Leave the soil openly exposed for a few weeks in the middle of winter. In the hottest part of summer, a procedure known as solarization can kill most weed seeds, insects, and disease organisms present in the top 6 to 12 inches of soil. See the Plant Diseases and Disorders entry for instructions for solarizing soil.

Animal pests: Rabbits, woodchucks, deer, and other animals can wreak havoc in a vegetable garden. A sturdy fence is often the best solution. For tips on controlling animal pests, see the Animal Pests and Fencing entries.

Harvesting and Storage

As a general rule, harvest your vegetables early and often. Many common vegetables, such as broccoli, garden peas, lettuce, and corn, are harvested when they are at a specific and short-lived state of immaturity. Also be prompt when harvesting crops that mature fully on the plant, as do tomatoes, peppers, melons, and shell beans. Vegetable plants tend to decline after they have produced viable seeds. Prompt harvesting prolongs the productive lifespan of many vegetables. See individual vegetable entries for tips on when to harvest specific crops.

Use "Days to Maturity" listed on seed packets as a general guide to estimate when vegetables will be ready to pick. Bear in mind that climatic factors such as temperature and daylength can radically alter how long it takes for vegetables to mature. Vegetables planted in spring, when days are becoming progressively longer and warmer, may mature faster than expected. Those grown in the waning days of autumn may mature 2 to 3 weeks behind schedule.

In summer, harvest vegetables in midmorning, after the dew has dried but before the heat of

Crops That Wait for You

Few things are more frustrating than planting a beautiful garden and then not being able to keep up with the harvest. Leave your sugar snap peas on the vine for a few too many days, and you might just as well till them under as a green manure crop.

Fortunately, there are many forgiving crops that will more or less wait for you. They include onions, leeks, potatoes, garlic, many herbs, kale, beets, popcorn, sunflowers, hot peppers (for drying), horseradish, pumpkins, winter squash, and carrots. You can measure the harvest period for these crops in weeks or even in months.

To keep your harvest from hitting all at once, stagger plantings. Make a new sowing every 10 days to 2 weeks. Mix early, midseason, and late cultivars. Bok choy and other Asian greens can be harvested through Thanksgiving.

Never have time to pick all of your fresh snap or shell beans at their prime? Relax. Plant cultivars meant for drying, and enjoy hearty, homegrown bean dishes throughout winter.

You can pick leeks young and small or wait the full 90 to 120 days until they mature. Leeks have excellent freeze tolerance. When protected by mulch, they can be harvested well into winter. In mild winter areas where hard freezes are few, winter is the best time to grow collards, spinach, turnips, carrots, and onions.

In all climates, be prepared to protect overwintering vegetables from cosmetic damage by covering them with an old blanket during periods of harsh weather. Or you can try growing cold-hardy vegetables such as spinach and kale under plastic tunnels during winter months.

---

midday. Wait for a mild, cloudy day to dig potatoes, carrots, and other root crops so they won't be exposed to the sun. To make sure your homegrown greens are as nutritious as they can be, harvest and eat them on the same day whenever possible.

Refrigerate vegetables that have a high water content as soon as you pick them. These include leafy greens, all members of the cabbage family, cucumbers, celery, beets, carrots, snap beans, and corn. An exception is tomatoes—they ripen best at room temperature.

Some vegetables, notably potatoes, bulb onions, winter squash, peanuts, and sweet potatoes, require a curing period to enhance their keeping qualities. See individual entries on these vegetables for information on the best curing and storage conditions.

Bumper crops of all vegetables may be canned, dried, or frozen for future use. Use only your best vegetables for long-term storage, and choose a storage method appropriate for your climate. For example, you can pull cherry tomato plants and hang them upside down until the fruits dry in arid climates, but not in humid climates. In cold climates, you can mulch carrots heavily to prevent them from freezing and dig them during winter. In warm climates, carrots left in the ground will be subject to prolonged insect damage.

Off-Season Maintenance

After you harvest a crop in your vegetable garden, either turn under or pull up the remaining plant debris. Many garden pests overwinter in the skeletons of vegetable plants. If you suspect that plant remains harbor insect pests or disease organisms, put them in sealed containers for disposal with your trash, or compost them in a hot (at least 160°F) compost pile.

As garden space becomes vacant in late summer and fall, cultivate empty spaces and allow birds to gather grubs and other larvae hidden in the soil. If several weeks will pass before the first hard freeze is expected, consider planting a green manure crop such as crimson clover, rye, or annual ryegrass. See the Cover Crops entry for instructions on seeding these crops.

Another rite of fall is collecting leaves, which can be used as a winter mulch over garden soil or as the basis for a large winter compost heap. If possible, shred the leaves and wet them thoroughly to promote leaching and rapid decomposition. You can also till shredded leaves directly into your garden soil.

VERBENA

Verbena, vervain. Summer-blooming perennial flowers.

Description: Verbenas bear clusters of small, 5-petaled flowers on wiry stems. Rose verbena (*Glandularia canadensis*, formerly *Verbena canadensis*) is a native perennial with trailing stems with flat flower clusters in rose, white, or purple. Plants are 8 to 18 inches tall. Zones 4–10.

Blue vervain (*V. hastata*) bears branched spikes of blue flowers on 3- to 5-foot plants. Zones 3–8.

Moss verbena (*Glandularia pulchella*, aka *V. tenui-*secta) is a trailing plant, 4 to 8 inches tall, with plentiful clusters of pink, lavender, purple, or white flowers. Zones 7–10.

How to grow: Plant verbenas in well-drained sandy or loamy soil. Give them full sun to part shade. Blue vervain also grows in moist to wet soil. Plants are tough and tolerate both heat and drought. Remove flowers as they fade or prune plants back after flowering to keep them blooming. Propagate by stem cuttings or seed.

Landscape uses: Use rose verbena to weave in and around other perennials such as purple coneflowers (*Echinacea purpurea*) and ornamental grasses. Use blue vervain as a vertical accent in perennial plantings.

VERONICA

Veronica, speedwell. Spring- and summer-blooming perennials.

Description: Speedwells bear small flowers in spikes above lance-shaped leaves. *Veronica incana*, woolly speedwell, bears pink or blue-violet flowers on 1- to 1½-foot spikes above spreading 6-inch gray-green mats of leaves in summer. Zones 3–8.

V. longifolia (aka *Pseudolysimachion longifolium*), longleaf speedwell, produces white, pink, blue, or violet spikes on 2- to 4-foot upright plants in summer. Zones 3–8.

V. prostrata, prostrate or creeping speedwell, grows just 3 to 8 inches tall. 'Aztec Gold' bears violet-blue flowers above bright yellow foliage. Zones 3–8. *V. spicata*, spike speedwell, bears spikes of pink, rose, blue, or white flowers on 1- to 3-foot plants in summer. Zones 4–8.

How to grow: Plant or divide in spring or fall in sun or very light shade and average, well-drained soil. Support tall plants with thin stakes.

Cut back to encourage continued bloom. Divide every 3 to 4 years.

Landscape uses: Group in borders and cottage gardens. Prostrate speedwell makes an attractive groundcover or path edging. Try woolly speedwell in a rock garden. Spike and longleaf speedwells make good cut flowers.

VIBURNUM

Viburnum, arrowwood. Deciduous or evergreen spring-blooming shrubs or small trees.

Description: Viburnums are excellent shrubs for the landscape. These are just a few of the dozens of outstanding species and cultivars available.

Viburnum dentatum, arrowwood viburnum, is a native species with an upright habit, arching with age, and growing to a mature height of 6 to 8 feet. Its oval or round, 2- to 3-inch leaves are coarsely toothed and turn red in fall. Flowers appear in spring, borne in flat, creamy white, 3-inch clusters followed by berries turning from blue to black. Zones 4–8.

V. plicatum f. *tomentosum*, doublefile viburnum, is a deciduous, rounded shrub with a horizontally layered habit, growing 8 to 10 feet tall. Dark green, deeply veined, 2- to 4-inch, toothed leaves turn reddish purple in fall. Flowers are borne in spring in flat, 3-inch clusters with larger, sterile flowers ringing a center of smaller, fertile flowers. These white clusters appear in pairs along the horizontal branches, inspiring the common name. Fruit follows bloom on the fertile flowers, changing from red to black as autumn progresses, and the foliage turns dull red. Zones 5–7.

V. prunifolium, black haw, is a small (12- to 15-foot) native tree with a single trunk and a round-headed habit. Broadly oval, finely toothed, 2- to 3-inch leaves turn shades of purple and crimson in fall. White flowers are borne in 4-inch clusters in spring, followed by blue-black fruits. Zones 3–8.

How to grow: Site viburnums in partial shade, with good drainage and even moisture. Prune black haw for form. Doublefile viburnum produces vertical watersprouts that ruin the graceful lines of this shrub; remove them annually. Prune the other viburnums for vigorous growth, removing some of the oldest branches a few inches above ground level each year after bloom.

Landscape uses: Plant viburnums in woodland gardens, where their berries are great wildlife food. Viburnums also do well as specimens, hedges, and massed plantings.

VINCA

Periwinkle, vinca, myrtle. Evergreen perennial groundcover.

Description: Periwinkles are hardy, trailing vines that root along the stems. While pretty, both of the commonly grown species are very vigorous spreaders that are difficult to eradicate, and they have been declared invasive in many states. *Vinca major*, big periwinkle, has glossy oval 1- to 3-inch leaves on 2-foot-long stems. Leaves may be dark green or variegated with cream, and plants bear blue or white 1- to 2-inch flowers in late spring. Zones 7–9.

V. minor, common periwinkle or creeping myrtle, is similar to big periwinkle but bears 1½-inch leaves that are more oblong. Plants produce 1-inch-wide blue, blue-purple, red-purple, or white flowers in spring. Zones 4–9.

How to grow: Periwinkles grow in shade or full sun and quickly outcompete nearby perennials that are less vigorous. Keep them away from sites where they can escape the garden. They are especially invasive in woodlands, where they easily smother native wildflowers. Periwinkles don't spread as quickly on dry sites as they do on ones with rich, moist soil, and they cannot tolerate hot, dry locations.

Landscape uses: While periwinkles are popular groundcovers, it's usually best to avoid using them because of their invasive characteristics. If you do decide to grow periwinkles, or already have them in your garden, keep them on sites that will naturally contain them, such as in an island bed under a tree surrounded by lawn or in a planting edged with a concrete walkway, for example. In such situations, they'll stay put and are pretty underplanted with drifts of white or yellow daffodils. Variegated big periwinkle is often planted in window boxes in the South; in the North, it is commonly treated as an annual.

VINES

Vines are versatile plants with long, flexible stems that climb or scramble. They range from tough, woody plants like grapes, to beloved perennial favorites like climbing roses and clematis, to popular annuals like morning glories (*Ipomoea* spp.) and sweet peas (*Lathyrus odoratus*). Several popular vegetables are vines as well, including peas and scarlet runner beans (*Phaseolus coccineus*). Other popular vines include Boston ivy (*Parthenocissus tricuspidata*), Virginia creeper (*P. quinquefolia*), climbing hydrangea (*Hydrangea anomala* ssp. *petiolaris*), and passionflowers (*Passiflora* spp.). Beware: Some of the most notorious and problematic invasive plants are vines as well, including English ivy (*Hedera helix*), Oriental bittersweet (*Celastris orbiculatus*), Japanese honeysuckle (*Lonicera japonica*), wintercreeper (*Euonymus fortunei*), and wisterias (*Wisteria* spp.).

There are vines for almost any kind of site, sun or shade, as well as rich or poor soil that is loamy, sandy, boggy, or dry. You're better off matching the vine to the situation than trying to alter the environment to suit the plant. In general, most vines are tolerant of a wide range of cultural conditions. It is the exceptions, such as clematis (which requires cool soil around its roots) or roses (most of which require full sun), that have specialized requirements. Be sure to check the specific needs of any plant before adding it to your garden. For basics on planting, propagating, and pest control, see the Planting, Propagation, Pests, and Plant Diseases and Disorders entries.

How Vines Climb

Vines attach themselves to trellises and other supports in several different ways, and it's important to understand how each species climbs so you can choose an appropriate support. Some vines wrap tendrils around a support—garden peas and sweet peas climb by tendrils and need strings or poles that are slender enough for the tendrils to wrap around. Clematis also need slender supports because they attach by twining leafstalks. Other vines wrap the entire stem around the support. Annuals like morning glories climb this way. Wisterias wrap their stems around supports, and as a result can climb heavy trellises, arbors, and even trees. The weight of the woody vines is considerable, and wisterias also can pull gutters off a house and crush smaller trellises. Grapes use two methods to climb: trailing stems aided by woody tendrils.

Boston ivy and Virginia creeper use adhesive discs at the end of tendrils to attach directly to walls or other supports, while English ivy, wintercreeper, and trumpet vine (*Campsis radicans*) attach themselves with adhesive rootlets. While vines that can attach with discs or rootlets are useful for covering masonry or brick walls, with time the discs or rootlets can work their way into cracks in the mortar and damage it.

Some vines, such as climbing roses, don't have any way to attach directly to supports. Instead, they weave up through a trellis (or the branches of a shrub) or can be tied to supports.

Landscaping with Vines

There are countless creative ways to use vines. They're perfect for adding height and color in a small garden, since they essentially grow in two dimensions. Train them up against a wall or trellis to create a tree-size plant without taking up precious horizontal space. Use vines on fences, gates, and other structures to quickly give a new garden an established look. Or use them to soften the hard edge of your house (or another structure) and link it to the garden by covering it with climbing roses, clematis, or other vines. Vines also can be used to scramble over and hide eyesores such as tree stumps or even falling-down sheds or other structures.

While hedges are traditionally used to create garden rooms, vines also can be used to create green walls around an outdoor room, and they will take up less room than hedges, an important consideration where space is limited. Simply give them something to climb and they will happily create green walls around a sitting area. Or use them to cover an arbor that marks the entrance to a garden. Large woody vines are useful for providing shade when trained over a pergola.

Use vines that attach with discs or rootlets to screen unsightly walls or affix wires to an otherwise flat wall so tendril climbers can scale them. A planting of Boston ivy or climbing hydrangea will transform an ugly concrete wall into a feature and add seasonal interest. Plus, if they are planted on the south- or west-facing wall, vines help cool the house or the space behind the wall.

Use vines to transform an unattractive chain-link fence and create a soft, hedgelike barrier instead. For example, cover the fence with trumpet vine, which will produce showers of brilliant red-orange blooms in midsummer that attract hummingbirds. Also use vines like roses, clematis, or scarlet runner beans to decorate lampposts or pillars, and train vines such as morning glories up into shrubs to add a spot of unexpected color to your garden. Clematis vines can be trained up into shrubs like roses as well, to create a two-season flower display.

Vines also are effective when used to cover deck railings or when they're grown up and along windows and door frames. They quickly transform a small garden or terrace into a magical hideaway. Annual vines can be grown in window boxes and are useful on terraces. Morning glories, ornamental sweet potato vines, and black-eyed Susan vines (*Thunbergia alata*) are good window-box choices. And don't forget attractive vines with edible parts such as scarlet runner beans, cucumbers, pole beans, and peas.

Pruning and Training Vines

While annual vines don't require much pruning, they do need gentle training to grow up and onto supports. If you're starting your own vines from seeds, be sure to provide each seedling with a small stake to climb soon after it germinates. Otherwise, the seedlings will quickly tangle together, making them difficult to separate and transplant or train. In the garden, use small stakes or pieces of twiggy brush to give vines the support they need to grow up onto a larger trellis. After they've begun to twine around a trellis or other support, check them every few days and redirect stems to keep them climbing in the right direction.

Woody vines do need regular pruning to train and control them. Before cutting anything, though, look hard at the plant to determine what growth isn't healthy and what needs to be removed to increase flowering, direct growth, or keep the vine in bounds. The first step in any pruning operation is removal of dead, damaged, and diseased wood. Whether you're pruning dead or live wood, always use a sharp tool—a hand pruner, lopper, or saw—and make cuts just above a live bud or nearly flush with the stem.

Remove dead, damaged, or diseased wood any time, but only prune live wood after the vine has finished blooming for the season. This means you'll prune spring bloomers in early summer, summer bloomers in early fall, and fall bloomers in winter or early spring. Pruning depends on the growth habit of the plant. Clinging vines like Boston ivy and Virginia creeper merely need trimming to keep them in bounds. Other vines like wisteria, clematis, and grapes need annual pruning to maximize flowering or fruiting. For more on pruning techniques, see the Pruning and Training and Grapes entries.

VIOLA

Pansy, violet. Mostly spring- and fall-blooming biennials and perennials.

Description: Cheerful biennial *Viola ×wittrockiana*, pansy, bears long-stemmed, five-petaled 1½- to 3-inch-wide, flat blooms in a range of solid colors and combinations, many marked with a dark central "face" or blotch. They begin to bloom in early spring on tight clumps of spatula-like leaves; most types reach less than 1 foot tall. If plants bear numerous small flowers, they are usually sold as violas; these come in the same color range as the larger-flowered pansies. Zones 5–9.

Perennial *V. cornuta*, horned violet, produces smaller flowers to 1½ inch with a little curved spur (the "horn") at the back of the flower. Blooms come in many colors, including blue, white, yellow, orange, and purple, often marked with a black or yellow blotch in the center. 'Rebecca' is fragrant, with white and yellow petals and purple picotee edges. Spreading evergreen plants grow 6 to 12 inches tall. Zones 6–9.

How to grow: For pansies, buy plants or sow seeds indoors (in late winter in the North for spring planting, or in midsummer to fall in the South for late-fall planting). Plant in full sun to light shade (plants fare better in light shade in the South). Give them average, moist but well-drained soil loosened with organic matter. Plant no more than 6 inches apart for a good show. Deadhead regularly and water if dry. Older types die out when hot weather approaches, but many newer cultivars will live on to bloom again in fall.

Plant horned violets in spring or fall; divide every 3 to 4 years. They like the same conditions as pansies but tolerate heat better. They bloom for several weeks each spring and usually bloom again when cool weather returns.

Landscape uses: Grow pansies in beds, borders, and containers for a splash of early color. They combine well with other early-spring flowers, like forget-me-nots and primroses. Use horned violets in the same way or as a colorful groundcover for smaller areas. These late-blooming flowers also add color to rock gardens.

W-Z

WALNUT

See *Juglans*

WATER CONSERVATION

At one time or another, most of us have experienced a water shortage. We couldn't wash our cars, water our lawns and gardens, or let the children play in the sprinkler. The restrictions lasted maybe a few weeks; then it rained and life returned to normal. But demand for water continues to outpace supply, and running on empty is becoming a way of life in regions across the United States and in countries around the world.

Lack of Quantity, Loss of Quality

The world has lots of water, but only 3 percent of it is fresh; the rest is salt water. Although fresh water is a renewable resource, human demand is exceeding the capacity of both natural systems and water-treatment systems to supply it.

In the 1980s, many cities adopted water conservation standards for the first time in response to prolonged droughts. By the 1990s, some regions reported that their water table was dropping significantly—as much as 4 feet a year.

This problem isn't limited to the United States. Population growth has led to increased water consumption worldwide as well. Between 1900 and 1995, global water consumption increased at more than double the rate of the world population and it continues to rise, creating water demands that cannot be met with existing supplies and delivery systems. Even if new reservoirs and pipelines are built, there is no guarantee of enough water to fill them, especially if climate change leads to significant disruptions of rainfall. According to a United Nations study of the world's supply of fresh water, as many as seven billion people in 60 countries could be out of water by 2050.

Water quality is also an increasing concern. In

the past decade, stormwater runoff has emerged as the number one water quality problem in the United States. Water that runs off roofs, parking lots, roads, driveways, and landscapes into stormwater collection systems often ends up contaminated with sediment, pesticides and other toxic substances, invasive organisms (such as seeds and aquatic creatures), excess nutrients (from lawn fertilizers), road deicing salts, and even pathogens when municipal sewage facilities overflow during heavy rains.

The good news is that stormwater runoff is a

Simple Water-Protection Ideas

There are lots of small things you can do to protect water quality.

Read labels. This includes labels on organic fertilizers and pest-control products, paint, and cleaning products. Choose least-toxic options and apply according to label directions. Follow the guidelines for use and disposal. Never pour these products down the sink or toilet or into storm drains or sewers.

Separate hazardous waste from your trash. Find out where and when there are hazardous waste collections, and spread the word in your community to dispose of hazardous products properly.

Prevent runoff and soil erosion. Keep your yard planted and bare areas mulched. Use lots of organic matter (typically in the form of compost) in your soil. Organic matter increases the soil's capacity to hold water and keep it where the plants can use it. (See the Soil entry for more on this.)

Try mulch or gravel. Instead of concrete or blacktop, consider a mulch, brick, flagstone, or gravel surface that lets water percolate through. For a casual outdoor living area, pavers and gravel can get very hot, so consider shredded bark mulch, which is much cooler underfoot.

Use permeable paving. Ask your contractor or look in hardware stores for permeable paver systems that have a honeycomb-type structure that gives you space to grow plants, allows water to flow through, and also provides a framework that lets you drive or walk on pavers without damaging plants.

Stockpile manure carefully. Gardens love compost made with manure, but rainwater that runs through a pile of fresh manure and then into drainage systems can carry pathogens and excess nitrogen. Keep manure covered, on a level site, and out of the path of surface runoff. Ideally, don't stockpile manure at all—mix it into compost as soon as you procure it.

Plant the banks of your pond or stream. Ask the staff at your local soil and water conservation organization for recommendations for waterside planting in your region. A lawn is the worst thing to plant near water; willows (*Salix* spp.), dogwoods (*Cornus* spp.), or buttonbush (*Cephalanthus occidentalis*) might be the best. (Even if your lawn is organic, grass clippings add undesirable nutrients to the water.)

problem that nearly every home gardener can help to solve in some small way. That's because soil and plants are great filters; they absorb lots of water and capture pollutants. When rain falls on (or is channeled into) planted surfaces, less of the bad stuff goes down the storm drains and into lakes or groundwater.

To learn more about water-conservation techniques and wise water use for home gardens, see the entries for Graywater, Rain Gardens, Rain Barrels, Watering, Water-Wise Landscaping, and Xeriscaping.

WATER GARDENS

Water is calming and refreshing—the most magical garden feature. It's possible to have a water garden in even the smallest yard, especially now that almost all garden and home centers sell water garden and pond supplies. You can choose a wall fountain, barrel or other container, pool, or pond. Water gardens can be formal or informal. Formal pools have geometric shapes like squares, rectangles, or circles, and can be made of precast fiberglass liners or concrete. Concrete pools require a professional for proper construction, so most gardeners use fiberglass for formal pools.

But for most backyard gardeners, an informal, do-it-yourself water garden is more practical and better suited to today's yards and lifestyles. Informal water gardens can be kidney-shaped or really any shape that pleases you. You can even shape the water garden to suit your site. Most container gardens are considered informal as well, even if they're round like a half barrel.

If you are starting a water garden from scratch, your first task is to choose a site. Select a level spot that receives at least 6 hours of sun daily. (You can create a water garden in a shaded spot, but you won't be able to grow water lilies.) Water gardens under trees are beautiful, but clearing out dropped leaves can be a maintenance nightmare.

An informal pool looks best set against a background. Site a large pool where plantings of shrubs and flowers will serve as a backdrop. You can site smaller pools against a wall or fence. If you want a waterfall, blend it into the landscape with background plantings. Avoid vigorous fountains; most water plants prefer still water.

Installing a Water Garden

When planning your water garden, you can choose a flexible liner made of PVC (polyvinyl chloride) plastic or butyl rubber, or a rigid fiberglass liner for the pool. All three types are available from water-garden supply companies. A PVC or butyl rubber liner will adapt to any shape pool you want to dig; fiberglass pools are preshaped, so you have to dig a hole that's the same shape as your liner. Both flexible liners and rigid liners are easy to install.

If you opt for a flexible liner, consider its lifespan when ordering, and choose the best liner you can afford. Butyl rubber liners are stretchy and last longest—up to 30 years—but are also the most expensive. The thicker a PVC liner, the better it is. PVC liner thickness is measured in mils. A 32-mil PVC liner will last 15 to 20 years and is the next best choice, followed by 20-mil PVC, which must be replaced every 7 to 10 years. Imagine emptying your whole pond to replace the liner, and choose accordingly!

Plastic and rubber liners: First, draw the shape and dimensions of your garden pool on graph paper. Make the pool as large as you can to set off the water plants—3 by 5 feet is a nice minimum

A Water, Bog, and Rock Garden

In the design shown here, a bog garden forms a natural transition between a lovely water garden and the surrounding landscape. Rocks go beautifully with water, and this rock garden frames the pool and bog garden.

Water Garden

1. Lotus (*Nelumbo nucifera* or *N. lutea*)
2. Water lily (*Nymphaea* hybrid)
3. Yellow flag (*Iris pseudacorus*)

Bog Garden

4. Pickerelweed (*Pontederia cordata*)
5. Pink turtlehead (*Chelone lyonii*)
6. Japanese primrose (*Primula japonica*)
7. Marsh marigold (*Caltha palustris*)
8. Marsh fern (*Thelypteris palustris*)

Rock Garden

9. Harry Lauder's walking stick (*Corylus avellana* 'Contorta')

10. Creeping juniper (*Juniperus horizontalis*)
11. Common beardtongue (*Penstemon barbatus*)
12. 'Vera Jameson' stonecrop (*Hylotelephium* 'Vera Jameson')
13. Heartleaf bergenia (*Bergenia crassifolia*)
14. Yellow-flowered dwarf daylily (*Hemerocallis* 'Happy Returns' or 'Bitsy')
15. Golden hakone grass (*Hakonechloa macra* 'Aureola')
16. Lady's mantle (*Alchemilla mollis*)
17. Candytuft (*Iberis sempervirens*)
18. Cinnamon fern (*Osmunda cinnamomea*)
19. Lavender (*Lavandula* spp.)
20. Thyme (*Thymus* spp.)
21. Carpathian harebell (*Campanula carpatica*)
22. Maiden pinks (*Dianthus deltoides*)
23. Hens and chickens (*Sempervivum* spp.)
24. 'Autumn Joy' sedum (*Hylotelephium* 'Herbstfreude')
25. Purple moor grass (*Molinia caerulea*)
26. Dwarf goldenrod (*Solidago* 'Peter Pan' or 'Goldenmosa')

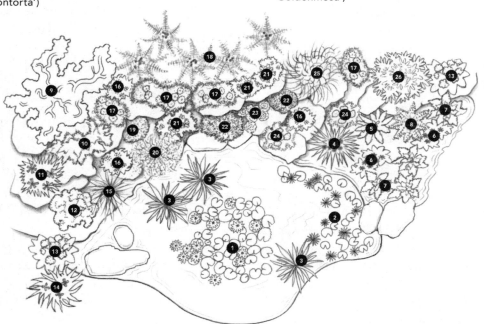

size. Give the pool a natural shape, with smooth, flowing curves; avoid tight angles. Keep it simple, like a kidney or amoeba shape. Make your pool 1½ to 2 feet deep if you want to grow water lilies and lotuses.

To determine the size liner to buy, add the width of the pool to two times the depth, and then add 2 more feet for the edges. (So, if your pool is 3 feet wide and 2 feet deep, multiply 2 by 2 feet = 4 feet, add 3 feet = 7 feet, plus 2 feet = 9 feet for the liner width.) Do the same, substituting length for width, to get the overall dimensions.

Use a tape measure and a garden hose to re-create your chosen shape on the garden site. Strip the sod inside the marked area with a flat-bottomed shovel. Excavate the hole 20 to 24 inches deep, sloping the side gradually and keeping the bottom as flat as possible. Pile the excavated soil on a tarp. Make shelves about 9 inches wide along the pool sides to accommodate shallow-water plants. A good shelf depth is 9 to 12 inches, depending on the plant and pot size. Check to make sure the pool sides are level by placing a two-by-four over the opening. Use a builder's level on the board to check for high spots. Remove or add soil as necessary to make the rim even.

Remove rocks, sticks, and other sharp objects, then line the entire hole with 1 to 2 inches of builder's sand, packed down firmly. Cover the sand layer with a piece of old carpet pad or, better yet, purchase underlayment from a water garden supplier. (Underlayment prevents sharp objects from piercing the liner.) Then gently place the pool liner over the hole, with the center at the deepest point. Let the liner sink into the hole and check to make sure it will reach the edges on all sides, then slowly add water to the new pool. The liner will be pushed snug against the sand or carpet-pad lining as the pool fills. The liner is very difficult to move

and readjust once you've started to add water, but watch as the pool fills and adjust the liner to remove wrinkles and reshape the sides.

Give the filled pool a day to settle, then cut off the excess liner, leaving at least a 6-inch lip along the level edge. Disguise the rim with flagstones, bricks, rocks, or plants. Bury any edges that aren't covered by the border stones.

Fiberglass liners: Follow a similar procedure for a rigid fiberglass pool. Many shapes and sizes of these comparatively inexpensive, preshaped, portable pools are available. The best have two or three levels—a deep center and at least one or possibly two shallower ledges for marginal (shallow-water) plants. Dig a hole larger than the pool, shaping it to fit the pool's levels, and line it with 1 to 2 inches of sand. Place the liner into the hole, leaving the rim just above ground level. Place a builder's level across the top and make any necessary adjustments so the pool edge is absolutely level. Fill the pool slowly, backfilling with sand as the liner settles into the hole. Disguise the rim the same way you would for a flexible liner.

Growing Aquatic Plants

The amount of water a plant requires or tolerates determines where you can grow it. Moisture-loving plants such as cardinal flower (*Lobelia cardinalis*) and Siberian iris (*Iris sibirica*) prefer to grow on the land around a pond, with their roots penetrating into the wet soil. See the information on page 638 for more plants to grow in or around your water garden.

You can create an exciting landscape around your water garden, but use restraint when choosing plants for the pool itself. One of the chief pleasures of water gardening is enjoying reflections in the water, so you don't want to completely cover the surface with water plants. Strive for a balance of one-third open water to two-thirds plant cover. Consider the mature spread of the plants you plan to order. Plant water lilies 3 to 5 feet apart to give them room to spread out in their typical bicycle-spoke pattern, and make sure you position them in full sun (they need at least 6 hours of sunlight daily).

Wait at least a week after filling your pool before adding plants or fish, so the chlorine can evaporate and the water can warm up. If your community uses chloramines (a chlorine-ammonia compound) to treat its water, it won't evaporate. Use a product such as DeChlor or AquaSafe to neutralize the chloramines before adding plants or fish.

Plant water plants in containers before placing them in the water garden. Use black or brown plastic tubs or pails. You can find special containers designed for water garden plants at water garden and pond specialty stores and Web sites and at many garden centers that carry water garden supplies. Plants like water lilies need sizeable containers; plant them in a 5- to 30-quart (1 to 4 feet wide and about half that deep) bucket, tub, or basket-type container.

The best soil is heavy garden loam, with some clay mixed in for stability, and well-rotted (not dried) cow manure added for fertility. (Mix one part cow manure for five parts soil.) Do not use commercial potting mixes with lightweight peat and perlite that will float to the water's surface. There are many types of fertilizer pellets for water garden plants as well, but most of these contain synthetic chemical fertilizers. Ask specifically for pellets that contain only organic ingredients if you want to try this approach instead of using manure.

Fill containers one-half to two-thirds of the way with soil, depending on the size of the root-

Skip This Plant

Water hyacinth (*Eichhornia crassipes*) is a lovely water garden plant that floats serenely on the surface of the water, forming large clumps and sending up beautiful lavender flowers. But unfortunately, it has escaped in Florida and other mild-winter areas and become a major invasive in canals, lagoons, and other bodies of fresh water, covering the surface of the water and choking out native plants. Unless you live in the North and your water garden is isolated from natural bodies of water, including streams and ponds, choose from the many other attractive water garden plants instead.

stock. Position the roots around a cone of soil with the crown 2 inches below the rim of the pot. Fill the remainder of the container with soil up to the crown of the plant. Cover the top of the soil with 1 inch of pea gravel. Do not bury the growing points. Fill the container with water and allow it to settle. Refill and allow a gentle stream of water to run over the rim of the container until it runs clear. Sink the pots to the proper depth in the pool. (For water lilies, depending on the cultivar, the pots should be sunk so there are 6 to 18 inches of water above the crown.) In 2 to 4 weeks, your plants will have adjusted and be growing vigorously.

Water Garden Maintenance

Water gardens need routine maintenance. To avoid the buildup of decaying plant material, remove

Plants for Water Gardens

There are plants for the shallow edges of a water garden as well as the deeper water in the center. Here are some of the best hardy plants for your water garden along with information on water depth preferences.

You can choose from many plants for growing along the water's edge or in up to 6 inches of water. Blue flag (*Iris versicolor*) and copper iris (*I. fulva*) have clumps of sword-shaped leaves and showy flowers. Sweet flag (*Acorus calamus*), arrowhead (*Sagittaria latifolia*), golden club (*Orontium aquaticum*), and pickerel weed (*Pontederia cordata*) are other fine plants for the pool's edge.

Other aquatics need deeper water—3 to 12 inches—and will float their foliage on the water surface. These include plants such as water clover (*Marsilea* spp.), parrot's-feather (*Myriophyllum aquaticum*), and water snowflake (*Nymphoides indica*). Grow them along the pond edges or with pots set on bricks in the center of the pool.

Lotuses (*Nelumbo* spp.) are hardy perennials that grow in about 4 inches of water. They bloom in summer and hold their leaves above the water's surface. Prop the tubs in which they are growing on bricks to provide them with the proper depth.

Water lilies (*Nymphaea* spp.) grow in up to 2 feet of water and float their rounded or heart-shaped leaves on the water's surface. Flowers rest on or above the water and come in a wide variety of colors, including white, pink, yellow, and purple. They may be hardy or tropical. Hardy water lilies can overwinter in your water garden, but tropicals must be overwintered indoors or replaced annually. Give water lilies plenty of room; their floating, rounded leaves (lily pads), often beautifully splashed with red or purple, can spread out in a 6-foot circle, covering the water surface. Divide plants every 2 to 3 years for renewed vigor and abundant bloom.

Specialty water garden catalogs, Web sites, and nurseries carry many lovely water lily cultivars. Usually the less expensive cultivars and those with Latin-sounding names are older tried-and-true plants, such as yellow 'Chromatella' (a good choice for small pools and barrels), pink 'Fabiola', and white 'Virginalis'. Make sure to choose miniature water lily plants for smaller water gardens (remember that 6-foot spread for standard sizes!).

Every pond should also contain submerged plants that help trap debris in the leaves and compete with algae for dissolved nutrients in the water, thus helping to keep the water clear. These include anacharis (*Egeria densa*), Carolina fanwort (*Cabomba caroliniana*), elodea (*Elodea canadensis*), and American eelgrass (*Vallisneria americana*).

Hardy water garden plants—plus many tropical water plants—are available from companies specializing in water gardening.

yellowing leaves and spent flowers of water garden plants. Weed the banks and edges regularly, too. Divide plants every 2 to 3 years; pot-bound plants will quickly lose vigor.

Winter protection is important. If you live in a moderate climate, you can leave hardy plants in the pool over winter. (In severe climates, where the water may freeze to the bottom of the pool, store hardy plants indoors as you would tropical ones.) Make sure the pots are below the ice at all times. You can use a stock tank deicer (available from water garden specialists or farm stores), which floats directly in the pool, to keep the water from freezing if you like. Lift tropical water lilies each fall and store them in a frost-free place. Place the containers in a cool spot and keep the soil evenly moist throughout the storage period. A cellar or cool greenhouse is ideal.

Maintaining a balanced environment is essential to prevent algae from covering the pond with green scum. Algae need nitrogen and sunlight to grow. Grooming water plants will reduce the buildup of excess nitrogen in winter, while shade from their foliage will reduce sunlight.

You should treat water plants like any garden plant during the season as well, removing yellow and damaged leaves and dead flowers. If aphids infest the leaves, submerge the plants, leaves and all, to dislodge the pests, or hose them off with a jet of water. Keep an eye on the plants; you may need to repeat this procedure several times before the plants are aphid-free.

Plants that grow entirely underwater are good natural filters. They absorb excess nitrogen and are important for maintaining a balanced pool. Fresh-water clams, which are filter feeders, and black Japanese or trapdoor snails, which are scavengers, are available from water garden suppliers and will

Barley Balls

Barley straw has been shown in numerous tests to prevent algae growth. For a small or container water garden, you can buy a plastic "barley ball" via garden centers, home stores, or water garden specialty suppliers and catalogs. Float this barley-straw-filled ball in your water garden to keep algae at bay. For a large in-ground water garden or pond, bales of barley straw will keep your water garden sparkling clean and algae-free.

also help keep your water clear. So will the tadpoles that may appear in spring.

Goldfish and koi add color and movement to the water garden. Though they may stir up the pond bottom in search of food, they'll keep the water free of mosquito larvae. Fish are also great biological controls for plant pests—if your water plants are bothered by aphids or caterpillars, hose the pests into the water and the fish or frogs will finish them off.

If the water becomes cloudy despite your best efforts, or if you have fish in your pool, you may need to install a recirculating pump and filtering system to aerate the water. A recirculating pump will enable you to lift water to a height from which it can fall, adding oxygen (which the fish need) to the water while also adding the lovely sound of moving water. Pumps and filters are available from garden centers, home stores, and Web sites, catalogs, and companies specializing in water gardening. You can find many models of pumps and waterfalls that are solar powered, a

Introducing Fish

When you bring your new fish home, don't just dump them into your water garden. Being cold-blooded, they need time to adjust to the difference in water temperature. Float their plastic, water-filled bag on the surface of the water to give their air bladders a chance to adjust, then release them into their new homes. You'll be glad you took this extra step—your new fish will thrive.

great convenience if your water garden is located far from power sources or if you're trying to reduce dependence on nonrenewable energy sources.

Making a Bog Garden

Another enjoyable garden project that can turn a low, wet spot into a landscape asset is a bog garden. With a little effort, you can turn an unused area into a garden feature. A bog garden is also a natural companion for a water garden, as shown in the design on page 635.

Building a Bog Garden

Even if you don't have a low wet spot, you can still have a bog garden. All you need to do is to excavate a hole and line it with a plastic pool liner. The larger you make your bog garden, the better, since small excavations dry out quickly. Choose a level spot in sun or shade, depending on the plants you wish to grow. Excavate a bowl-shaped hole 1½ to 2 feet deep at the center. Line the hole with a commercial pool liner or a sheet of 6-mil plastic.

Unless you have sandy soil, don't use the soil you dig out for your future bog garden. The best mix for a bog is 50 percent sand and 50 percent compost or peat. Fill the excavation with soil mix until it mounds in the center, packing it down as you go. Fill your new bog garden with water. Wait at least a month before planting to let the soil settle. Keep the soil wet at all times.

Choosing Bog Plants

Natural bogs contain plants that are adapted to wet, acid soils. Perennial bog plants you can grow include water arum (*Calla palustris*), creeping snowberry (*Gaultheria hispidula*), twinflower (*Linnaea borealis*), and bogbean (*Menyanthes trifoliata*). Woody plants for backyard bogs include winterberry (*Ilex verticillata*), sheep laurel (*Kalmia angustifolia*), rhodora (*Rhododendron canadense*), and blueberries and cranberries (*Vaccinium* spp.). Many bog plants, such as pitcher plants (*Sarracenia* spp.) and sundews (*Drosera* spp.), are becoming rare in the wild. If you choose to plant them, buy only from reputable dealers who propagate their plants.

If your soil is neutral rather than acid or if you'd like to grow a more colorful collection of plants, your choices are wider than if you're duplicating true bog conditions. There are quite a few plants that enjoy wet feet. Perennials that grow well in wet garden soils in full sun include swamp milkweed (*Asclepias incarnata*), spotted joe-pye weed (*Eutrochium maculatum*), rose mallow (*Hibiscus moscheutos*), Siberian iris (*Iris sibirica*), blue flag (*I. versicolor*), rodgersias (*Rodgersia* spp.), and globeflowers (*Trollius* spp.). Perennials for a partially shaded bog site include jack-in-the-pulpit (*Arisaema triphyllum*), marsh marigold (*Caltha palustris*), turtleheads (*Chelone* spp.), ligularias (*Ligularia* spp.), cardinal flower (*Lobelia cardinalis*), water forget-me-not (*Myosotis scorpioides*), and Japanese primrose (*Primula japonica*). Woody plants for soggy soils include red-osier dogwood (*Cornus sericea*), willows (*Salix* spp.), swamp azalea (*Rhododendron viscosum*), and blueberries.

Bog Garden Maintenance

The most important maintenance job for a bog garden is watering, especially if it is an artificial bog. Never allow the soil to dry out. Dry soil is sure death for water-loving plants. If you're re-creating an acid-soil bog, grow a living mulch of sphagnum moss (available from biological supply houses). Mulch your bog garden with pine straw or oak leaves in winter to protect delicate plants. Remove the mulch in spring to allow the sphagnum to grow. If you don't have sphagnum, leave the mulch in place to rot into the soil. Remove weed seedlings before they become a problem. Since bogs are naturally low in nutrients, bog plants don't need fertilizing.

WATERING

It sounds strange, but water is the best fertilizer you can give your plants. Adequate water is simply essential for plant growth, because plant cells are made up largely of water. Without sufficient water, plant cells can't enlarge, and that results in weak, stunted plants. You can have the best soil, seed, and intentions in the world, but without water, nothing will grow.

The need to supply water is an ever-increasing concern for gardeners because the world's supply of clean water is ever more threatened. Your goal in planning and planting your garden is to minimize the need for supplemental watering. Fortunately, there are many ways to reduce water use in the garden. To learn more about the threats to the world's water supply and about water-wise landscaping techniques that help conserve water and minimize water use, see the entries on Water Conservation and Water-Wise Landscaping.

Roots, Soil, and Water

Plants use—and lose—water continuously. Roots absorb water, which is drawn upward to the leaves. Leaves have microscopic pores in their surfaces called stomates, which can be open or closed. Much of the time, stomates are open, which allows carbon dioxide to enter the leaves. That's a good thing, because through the process called photosynthesis, plants use carbon dioxide and energy from the sun to make food (sugars) that fuel their growth. Unfortunately, when stomates are open, water escapes out of the leaves. (This process, called transpiration, has a purpose: It cools the leaves and prevents them from overheating in the sun.)

Since plants are continuously losing moisture, roots need to keep drawing water from the soil. Thus, our goal as gardeners is to make sure the soil can hold plenty of water. How much water the soil can hold depends on its texture and organic matter content. The best way to increase your soil's water-holding capacity is to add organic matter. You can learn how to do this by consulting the Soil entry.

As you continually build your soil with organic matter, you can use other gardening practices that help protect soil water and encourage plants to make the best use of it. For example, in deep, rich soil protected by mulch, plants find it much easier to develop the strong, deep root systems necessary to find water during dry periods. This won't "drought-proof" your plants, but research has shown that crops grown in organically managed soils withstand drought much better than those in unimproved soil. Lightly cultivating the soil between row crops also helps water filter into the soil.

Deciding When to Water

One important skill to develop is assessing when it's necessary to water. If you're waiting until you see your plants wilt, then you're waiting too long (although it is natural for many kinds of plants to wilt briefly during the hottest part of a summer day).

Instead of relying on wilting as a cue to water, learn how to check your garden's soil moisture instead. An easy way to do this is to stick your index finger into the soil of your garden beds. The top 2 to 3 inches of the soil may feel dry, so be sure you push down at least 3 inches. You should be able to feel the difference when you hit moist soil. If the soil is dry at the 3-inch level, it's time to water, unless rain is in the forecast that day.

An exception to this rule is for seeds and seedlings. Since they are just starting to grow, they need moisture right in the top inch of soil. Keep them constantly moist.

In warm weather, water in the morning to avoid hot sun or strong winds that cause water to evaporate faster. If that's not feasible, then wait until late afternoon, but not too late, as you want foliage to dry off before nighttime to reduce the chance of diseases developing.

Wise Watering Techniques

For those situations where you have to water, always strive for the most efficient method. When you water with the hose or an overhead sprinkler, some of the water is immediately lost to evaporation from plant surfaces, through surface runoff, or by falling in areas that don't need water, such as a street or walkway.

Drip irrigation is the most efficient watering method. You can design a system for nearly any part of your landscape, including trees and shrubs, container gardens, and flower gardens. Also called "trickle" or "weep" irrigation, drip systems are as beneficial for dryland gardeners in the arid Southwest as for those in the northern, eastern, and southern parts of the country. They more than make up for the cost and effort involved in design and installation in water savings and increased plant growth. For details on drip irrigation, see the Drip Irrigation entry.

Sometimes drip irrigation isn't practical or convenient, such as when you sow a small patch of seeds in your vegetable or flower garden or add a single new perennial or shrub to an island bed. In those cases, old-fashioned hand watering is the way to go. A soaker hose represents a compromise between watering by hand and installing drip irrigation. A soaker hose has pores that let the water seep out of its sides, letting it leak gradually into the soil where the hose lays. Think of a soaker hose as a temporary drip irrigation system that you can place next to newly planted seeds or seedlings and use to water them slowly and gently. You can also position a soaker hose in a perennial border or landscape planting and leave it in place all season. Of course, a soaker hose lacks the precision of drip irrigation, but it is much more efficient in terms of both your time and water use than a sprinkler. You can even put a timer on a soaker hose at the tap to turn it on and off when you're away.

Be gentle with seeds: For watering newly seeded areas, always use a watering can with a rose-type nozzle, or a hose nozzle that has a mist setting. You want to water the soil surface as gently as possible, with small droplets of water, to avoid washing out the newly planted seeds.

A reservoir at the ready. An upturned soda bottle buried partway in the soil serves as a handy watering reservoir that wicks water directly to plant roots and encourages plants to develop a deeper root system.

Add a cover-up: Newly sown vegetable and flower seeds will germinate fastest and best if the soil is constantly moist. Some seeds, such as carrots, are very sensitive to moisture, and if the soil dries out at all during the germination process, it will reduce the germination percentage significantly. One way to ensure the soil stays moist is to cover the seeds with compost instead of soil, because compost is better at retaining water. Or you can sprinkle a light layer of grass clippings over the well-watered seedbed, or cover it with a small piece of row cover or burlap. For slow-to-germinate seeds, try an even heavier cover, such as a piece of scrap plywood, suspended just above the soil surface (use stones at the corners to prop up the wood).

Try using a wand: A spray wand is a watering nozzle with a long handle that attaches to a garden hose. With a wand, it's easy to direct water right to the base of a plant. They're also handy for watering containers and hanging baskets.

Make a reservoir: Gallon-size plastic juice jugs work well for this purpose. They're made of tougher plastic than milk or water jugs, so they last longer. Fill the jug with water, screw on the lid, and take it to the newly planted tree or shrub. Use a large safety pin to poke one or two holes in the bottom of the jug and then nestle the jug beside the plant. Then loosen the lid slightly to allow water to drip slowly through the holes and into the soil. Just remember to remove the jug when it's empty so it doesn't blow away. You can also "install" watering reservoirs more permanently in the vegetable garden, as shown in the illustration at left.

WATERMELON

See Melon

WATER-WISE LANDSCAPING

With some ingenuity and retooling, nearly every gardener and homeowner can have a beautiful yard and garden while watering less often and more efficiently. This is especially important for gardeners in arid areas, where they may adopt a system of landscaping called xeriscaping. Xeriscaping reduces water use by improving the soil's water-holding capacity, relying on plants (often native) that thrive in a region's natural climate conditions, grouping plants together according to their water needs, and using efficient watering systems. You can read more about this approach in the Xeriscaping entry.

Even if you don't live in a dry climate, it's important to cut down on water use in the garden. You can start right away with small changes and over time make the bigger landscape conversions that help to save water. Here's a list of water-wise techniques you can start using today.

- Mulch trees, shrubs, and other plants with up to 3 inches of mulch. See the Mulch entry for suggestions of materials to use.

- Water less frequently, but water deeply, until you saturate the soil to the depth of the plant's roots. In the case of a lawn, that might be 4 inches, but it's 14 inches for a shrub or a tomato plant. Daily watering encourages lazy, shallow root systems.

- Avoid using a sprinkler as much as possible. Water small plants (vegetables, perennials, annuals, small shrubs) at their base with a watering wand to supply water directly to the root zone. If the root area is small or extremely dry, you may have to go back to the same plant more than once in a watering cycle.

- If your time or water supply are limited, and you have to choose what to water, choose whatever you've planted most recently. Trees and shrubs that were planted in the last 2 or 3 years are at risk of dying if they do not get adequate water. If you're choosing among thirsty plants, keep in mind that the trees are a big investment; annuals like petunias last one summer.

- Recycle household wastewater from the kitchen sink, bath, or dishwasher. See the Graywater entry for more on this.

Sunken Beds and Sheltered Beds

If you garden in an arid climate, there may be little to no rainwater to catch for weeks at a time. You'll have to provide supplemental water for food crops and some other plants. To make the most of that water, take extra steps to conserve moisture. For example, you can create recessed beds that are several inches deeper than the surrounding soil by digging down several inches and using the removed soil to create raised sides around the garden bed (as you do this, set aside the first few inches of topsoil to return to the recessed area). This shelters the soil surface from drying winds and slows moisture loss from the soil. If you've already planted a garden with level beds, then put up mulch berms made of hay bales or layers of soil and mulch alongside the beds to block the wind.

Water-Wise Planting Projects

Once you've adopted water-wise maintenance techniques, think about planting projects that can ultimately help you reduce the amount of water you use. The single most important one for most situations is to start converting your lawn to other uses. That doesn't mean you have to cover your yard with cement, asphalt, or stones. You can add a new measure of beauty and enjoyment to your yard with groundcovers, mulches, and shade trees to help you and your yard keep cool. The Lawns and Groundcovers entries include many suggestions for lawn alternatives.

Here are other water-wise planting practices to keep in mind.

- Whenever you plant, add some compost or other organic matter to the soil.

🐝 Select native plants that require less water. The Native Plants entry offers many tips on using natives in your yard.

🐝 Plant more perennials (especially those labeled drought tolerant) and fewer annuals.

🐝 Cut back on container plantings during water shortages. If you love those constantly blooming annuals in hanging baskets, try planting them in the soil instead. Trailing petunias, for example, will drape their flowers lavishly over the soil and need only occasional watering compared to the same plant in a little plastic pot.

🐝 Garden more in the shade. Create more shade by putting up pergolas, awnings, and trellises. Water evaporates less there, and plants don't dry out so quickly. Most garden centers now offer a full range of shade-tolerant plants.

🐝 Add a walkway, deck, or patio to help reduce water consumption by expanses of turfgrass while adding more enjoyment to your yard.

WEATHER AND WEATHER LORE

Gardeners have always been interested in the weather, and with the advent of major media coverage of climate change, weather is an almost daily concern for people everywhere. Weather is especially critical to those of us who grow plants because the weather affects not only the health and growth rates of our crops but also determines to a large extent which plants we can grow well in the first place.

When you're choosing plants and designing gardens, keep in mind that there are climatic variations within a geographic region and even within each garden. Your garden's immediate climate may be different from that of your region overall. Factors such as altitude, wind exposure, proximity to bodies of water, terrain, and shade can cause variations in growing conditions by as much as two hardiness zones in either direction. It is also important to realize that your area's climate can change over time.

Cold Hardiness and Heat Tolerance

Hardiness is the ability of a plant to survive in a given climate. In the strictest sense, this includes not only a plant's capacity to survive through winter but also its tolerance of all the climatic conditions characteristic of the area in which it grows. Still, most gardeners refer to a hardy plant as one capable of withstanding cold and to a tender plant as one that's susceptible to low temperatures and frost.

To help growers determine which plants are best for their regions, in 2006 the National Arbor Day Foundation, using data from 5,000 National Climatic Data Center stations, released an updated version of the 1990 USDA Plant Hardiness Zone Map (the USDA map is shown on page 682). The USDA released an updated map in 2012. Hardiness zone maps divide the United States into 12 climatic zones, based on the average annual minimum temperature for each zone. Zone 1 is the coldest, most northerly region (in Alaska), and Zone 12 is the warmest, most southerly (in Hawaii). If you live somewhere in Zone 6 and a plant is described as "suitable for Zones 5–9" or "hardy to Zone 4," you can expect the plant to do well in your area. If you live in Zone 3, on the other hand, you should select a more cold-tolerant plant. You can find out which zone you live in by referring to the map. If you access the map online,

Using a Rain Gauge

Natural rainfall is an important factor in which crops you can grow and how to take care of those you do grow. Keep track of the rainfall in your garden with a rain gauge. You can buy a gauge, or simply use an empty tin can—or any straight-sided container—and a ruler. An inch of rain in the can equals an inch of rain on the garden.

you can make use of its interactive capabilities to zoom in very specifically on the area in which you live to precisely identify the hardiness zone.

In addition, recognizing that hot weather can also limit plant growth, the American Horticultural Society (AHS) released its AHS Plant Heat-Zone Map, based on 12 years of climatic data ending in 1995. On this map, the United States is divided into 12 zones based on the number of days the region experiences temperatures above 86°F ("heat days"). Zone 1 experiences less than one heat day; Zone 12, over 210 heat days. Use this map the same way you would the Hardiness Zone Map.

You can view the Arbor Day Foundation map and the Heat Zone map at the Web sites of the respective organizations; see Resources on page 673.

Frost

Many food and ornamental plants are native to warm climates and can't withstand freezing temperatures. Others go dormant for winter. Thus, the primary growing season for most North American gardeners is between the last frost in spring and the first killing frost of fall.

Air temperature is only one of the factors that determine whether or not plants will be damaged by a frost. Sometimes when the temperature dips a little below freezing, the air is sufficiently moist for water vapor to condense (in the form of ice crystals) on the ground and on plants. When water condenses, it gives off heat and warms the air around plants, protecting them from extensive damage. On clear, windless, star-filled nights when the forecast calls for near- or below-freezing temperatures, it's wise to protect plants. Heat is lost rapidly under these conditions, and frost damage often occurs. When temperatures fall more than a few degrees below freezing, frost damage to growing leaves and shoots is likely no matter how humid conditions are.

Frost damages plants when the water in the plant's cells freezes and ruptures the cell walls. Different plants and parts of plants have different freezing points. Plants that are native to northern regions have many ways of protecting themselves from the cold. Many perennials die down each fall. The roots buried in the insulating soil remain alive to sprout again the next season. Some plants such as kale have cold-tolerant leaves that will survive unharmed under a blanket of snow, but not when exposed to drying winds. Deciduous shrubs and trees drop their leaves each fall and form leaf and flower buds that stay tightly wrapped in many layers and go dormant until spring comes again. Or, like cold-hardy evergreens, they may have a natural antifreeze in their sap that helps prevent them from cold injury.

Frost heaving of soil can also cause problems for gardeners. Soil moves as it freezes, thaws, and refreezes. This action can push newly planted perennials, shrubs, or other plants that don't have established root systems out of the soil. Mulch heavily around these plants after (not before) the soil freezes to prevent thawing during sudden warm spells in winter or early spring.

Weather Lore

Our ancestors understood the role weather played in growing food. They saw that nature gave ample warning of approaching rain, storms, and frost. The sky is filled with weather indicators, especially cloud formations. For example, "When ye see a cloud rise out of the west, straightway cometh the rain" (Luke 12:54) refers to the fact that weather fronts usually move from west to east.

"Rainbow at night, shepherd's delight. Rainbow in morning, shepherd's warning" refers to the same phenomenon. A rainbow seen in the evening to the east is caused by the setting sun shining from the west, indicating fair weather in that direction. A morning rainbow, caused by the rising sun from the east, indicates rain to the west, heading your way.

"If the sun goes pale to bed, 'twill rain tomorrow, it is said" is another saying that involves cloud patterns. High cirrus clouds in the west give the setting sun a veiled look. When appearing as bands or mares' tails, they signal an approaching storm.

Finally, who among us will argue with "Clear moon, frost soon"? Cloud cover acts like a blanket over the earth, keeping temperatures from dipping as low as they would on a clear night.

The skies are not the only aspect of nature filled with weather signs. Animal and plant behavior also indicates changes. Here belong all the sayings about the thickness and color of an animal's coat, the bark on a tree, or the skin of a vegetable, such as "When the corn wears a heavy coat, so must you." A related saying is "The darker the color of a caterpillar in fall, the harder the winter."

Certain animals and plants do respond in a consistent way to a change from a high- to a low-pressure system, which often brings rain. This is why a saying such as "When the sheep collect and huddle, tomorrow will become a puddle" is reliable. "The higher the geese, the fairer the weather," a saying that applies to all migratory birds, also refers to this phenomenon.

Many plants are sensitive to drops in temperature and to high humidity. "When the wild azalea shuts its doors, that's when winter temperature roars" refers to the fact that azaleas and rhododendrons draw their leaves in when the temperature drops.

Cold weather lore often merges weather phenomena with common sense. Snow, for example, is known as "the poor man's fertilizer," which may be because it acts as mulch, protecting plants and keeping nutrients in the soil that rain would otherwise wash away. Frost is "God's plough" because it breaks up the ground and kills pests.

Phenology

Going beyond folk wisdom is phenology, the study of the timing of biological events and their relationships to climate and to one another. Such events include bird migration, animal hibernation, and emergence of insects, and the germination and flowering of plants.

Phenologists have found that many plants and insects within the same region or climate pass through the stages of their development in a consistent, unified sequence. The budding of a given plant, for example, may correlate with the hatching of a particular pest insect. Variations in weather from one year to the next affect the timing of such events, but the order in which they occur tends to remain the same.

As a result, it's possible to foretell when conditions are right for a crop to germinate or an insect to appear by learning to read the various growth stages of indicator plants. You may want to experiment with phenology in your own yard. For example, you could plant a variety of perennials as indicators that will provide a steady succession of blooms throughout a season. Then observe and record the indicators' growth phases, along with weather data, the appearance of insects or diseases in your garden, and the progress of food crops.

Sooner or later, patterns will emerge. You may notice that daffodils always begin to bloom when the soil becomes warm enough to sow peas, or that Mexican bean beetle larvae appear at about the same time foxgloves open. You can then use that information in subsequent years to help you decide when to plant peas or when to start handpicking beetle larvae. Your observations may also help you discern if and how the local climate in your area is changing over time.

Climate Change and Your Garden

Melting glaciers and rising sea levels are large-scale outcomes of a changing climate, but what about climate change on a smaller scale? Does climate change affect how plants grow in home gardens?

The answer is yes. Some of the shifts are subtle, but others could be dramatic, depending on where you live. For example, you may find that you can plant zinnias and other tender annuals a week or two earlier in spring than you used to. In many areas, gardeners are enjoying a longer season of garden-ripe tomatoes and delaying the time when they move houseplants back indoors in fall. Perhaps you've noticed that local garden centers are now selling trees and shrubs that once were considered too tender to survive through the winter in your area.

These are changes we can celebrate, but the slow-and-steady rise in temperatures has its downside, too. For example, insect pests such as armyworms may become more frequent problems because they can survive winters farther north than in the past, allowing them an earlier start at feeding on your crops in the spring or summer. Climate change may mean that new types of weeds and insect pests will appear in your garden, and new invasive species will infiltrate the woodlands, wetlands, and other natural areas in your community. One example is kudzu, a nonnative vine that has overrun many areas in the South and is now predicted to take hold as far north as southern Canada within the next 10 years.

Shifting Seasons

One form of climate change that many of us can notice in our own gardens and neighborhoods is a shift in seasonal and temperature patterns. This change is verified in data collected nationally including average annual minimum temperature, the basis for determining plant hardiness zones. This climatic data show that most of North America has become significantly warmer in the past 30 years—so much so that portions of many states could now be rated as a warmer zone. Updated hardiness zone maps from the Arbor Day Foundation and the USDA reflect recent data (see Resources, page 673, and the USDA Plant Hardiness Zone Map on page 682).

A phenological study that compared the date of first bloom of plants in Washington, DC, showed that, over a 30-year period, 89 out of 100 species of plants—including common garden plants such as lilacs and honeysuckle—bloomed earlier in spring (by 4.5 days on average). Other studies indicate that apples and grapes are blooming earlier in the Northeast than they did 50 years ago.

If the area where you garden has a change in hardiness zone or other temperature patterns, is that a good thing or a problem? The answer depends on the region and on what you're trying to grow. For example, an earlier spring is a boon to northeast veggie gardeners eager to sow their peas and spinach, but for California gardeners and farmers, it means the hot, dry summer will start even sooner—forcing them to irrigate more than ever. And warming can be bad news for anyone who grows perennials such as hostas that require a few weeks of winter cooling (below 40°F) as a rest period in their annual cycle.

Some areas may benefit from warming because they won't have any frost periods at all, or fewer incidents of unexpected freezes—in Florida, for instance, where the orange crop is sometimes devastated. (Of course, global climate change also means extreme fluctuations, so this benefit could also backfire.) And in the grand scale of things, if seasonal plants live a week or two longer each year, they will do an even better job of consuming carbon dioxide, which could help counteract global warming.

In broad terms, for agriculture worldwide, the warming trend will probably increase yields in colder climates for a while and damage those in warmer regions. It's a mixed bag of good and bad news.

Back in the home garden, what if you can now grow a crape myrtle, formerly considered a southern beauty, in Pennsylvania or Connecticut? A previously unavailable plant may be a horticultural delight, but responsible gardeners should look carefully at whatever we introduce, whether exotic (from another country) or native, to other areas of this country. When you bring in a new plant, watch that it doesn't pop up in a nearby field or spread into the woods. Look for insects you may

not have seen before that came with it and may now affect other plants. One gardener's intriguing new groundcover could turn out to be the next Japanese knotweed, kudzu, or giant hogweed.

Severe Weather

Windstorms, snowstorms, floods, and other kinds of bad weather have always been with us, but never as fully tracked, recorded, and reported as in the past 100 years. And all of that data shows that weather patterns are tending toward more rapid and extreme changes, including more frequent tornadoes and severe thunderstorms, and also record-breaking cold temperatures at unusual times. While freeze damage to plants may not seem logically connected to global warming, it's all related. For example, consider what happened in the spring of 2007, when the East Coast hit some record warm spring temperatures much earlier than normal. The plants broke dormancy, began to leaf out, and buds swelled. Then in April an abnormally deep freeze killed plants over a wide area. In preceding decades, a late freeze like that one wouldn't have done much harm, but in 2007, the plants were way ahead of themselves. Many plants died, became stunted, or produced fewer leaves, flowers, or fruit. For some gardeners, that meant no flowers on the rhododendron or magnolia. For others—and for many commercial orchardists—it meant no apple crop.

What Gardeners Can Do

As we experience global climate change, or even simple weather extremes from one season to the next, smart gardeners observe and adapt. Use these three basic guidelines to help guide your gardening and landscaping decisions.

Project BudBurst

In 2007, the US Geological Survey (USGS) and the University of Arizona initiated a nationwide program to begin collecting data that will help federal and university scientists analyze how climate change is affecting the timing of key stages of plant development, such as the date when dandelions or Virginia bluebells start to bloom, or when the native trees in a region start to leaf out. "Citizen scientists" (home gardeners, schoolchildren, and others) across the country are the key to this project, collecting phenological data on nearly 4,000 species of plants. Participation is free and easy to do: Simply register at the Project Bud-Burst Web site and begin submitting periodic reports. The data collected will help USGS scientists track climate variation at the local, regional, and national level, and analyze the impact of climate change by comparing the Project Bud-Burst data to historical records.

Don't discount the potential for a cold year. Be cautious about plant choices. A trend to milder winters is not necessarily the signal to start planting marginally hardy species in your windy front yard, because occasional harsh winters may still occur. Perhaps it's a good time to start a log of weather patterns in your own yard, a record that will be more meaningful as years go by. Meanwhile, if you are going to bet on a warming trend, prepare to protect that "iffy" plant with a winter shelter. Or, for your first experiments with tender specimens, choose sheltered spots on the protected side of your house.

Count on extremes, and prepare. Most scientists predict more droughts, harder rains when they come (leading to flooding), and windstorms—if not hurricanes. For a gardener, that means planning water-wise gardens (see the Water-Wise Landscaping entry), designing for drainage and stormwater runoff, keeping the soil covered, and figuring out how to stake or cover large plants before storms occur.

Stick with good gardening principles. They're even more important in harder times. Take care of the soil first, recycle yard waste and use organic matter, match the plants to the site, and provide the care they need. Since climate change may also bring new pests and diseases to your area, avoid putting all your bets on any one food crop or a long hedge of a single species of tree or shrub. Instead, diversify. Plant a mixed hedge, and sow small plots of many different crops in your vegetable garden. That way, when a new pest or disease strikes, it won't cause a crisis in your garden.

WEEDS

Fast, tough, and common—that's all it takes to earn a plant the name *weed*. But any plant growing in the wrong place—especially if it's growing there in abundance—is a weed. Maple tree seedlings that sprout between your rows of lettuce and radishes are weeds. So is the Bermuda grass that keeps invading your perennial beds from your lawn.

Some weeds can be useful as well as a nuisance. For example, purslane is a weed that often sprouts in vegetable gardens, yet you can eat the leaves of this weed in salads. The cultivated species of purslane—known as rose moss (*Portulaca grandiflora*)—has large, colorful flowers and is prized as a bedding plant for warm, sunny places. And while honeysuckle vines can cause considerable damage as they twine around tree trunks and branches, they might serve well as a groundcover for a bank that's too steep to mow.

Weeds make a lawn, garden, or landscape look untidy and neglected. But aesthetics aside, there are other important reasons for keeping your weeds in check. Weeds compete for water, nutrients, light, and space. The competition can weaken your plants and reduce your harvest. They grow fast, shading out less vigorous plants. Weeds serve as alternate hosts or habitats for insects and diseases. For example, aphids and Japanese beetles on smartweed can move from the weeds onto your food and landscape plants.

Some weeds have poisonous parts, such as pokeweed berries or poison ivy leaves, stems, and roots. A few weeds secrete chemicals from their roots that are toxic to other plants. Garlic mustard falls in this category, which contributes to its ability to outcompete wildflowers and other native plants in eastern and midwestern woodland habitats.

The Life of a Weed

Just like flowers, weeds may be annuals, biennials, or perennials. Annual weeds, the easiest to control, complete their life cycles in a year or less. Summer annuals sprout in spring and go to seed in fall; winter annuals sprout in fall, live over winter, and go to seed by spring or summer. Summer annuals such as crabgrass, giant foxtail, pigweed, and lamb's quarters will be your biggest weed problem in the vegetable garden. Winter annual weeds, such as chickweed and henbit, will sprout along with fall plantings of crops like lettuce and radishes. It's easy to hand-pull or cultivate these weeds in late fall or even on a warm winter day so they won't have a chance to go to seed the following season.

Biennial weeds, such as Queen Anne's lace, form only roots and a rosette of leaves the first year, then flower and set seed the second year. Perennial weeds, which live for more than 2 years, reproduce not only by seed but also by roots, stems, and stolons. Gardeners dread perennial weeds such as quackgrass or ground ivy, which spring into new life from an overlooked fragment of stem or root.

A Waiting Horde

A single weed can produce as many as 250,000 seeds. Though some seeds are viable for only a year, others can lie dormant for decades, just waiting for their chance to grow. Buried several inches deep, the lack of light keeps them from germinating. But bring weed seeds to the surface, and they'll germinate right along with your flower and vegetable seeds.

Even if you're diligent at hoeing and pulling weeds, more seeds arrive—by air, by water runoff, and in bird droppings. You may accidentally introduce weeds by bringing seeds in on your shoes, clothing, or equipment or in the soil surrounding the roots of container-grown stock. Even mulches spread on garden beds or straw that's spread to protect a newly seeded lawn area may be contaminated with weed seed. Grass seed itself, unless certified as weed-free, may contain seeds of undesirables.

An Ounce of Prevention

Keeping weeds from getting started is easier than getting rid of them. Here's how.

- After preparing garden soil for planting, let it sit for 7 to 10 days. Then slice off newly emerged weeds with a hoe, cutting them just below the soil surface and disturbing the soil as little as possible. If you have time, wait another week or so and weed again. This tactic puts a considerable dent in the reservoir of surface weed seed that could germinate and cause problems later in the season.

- Cover the soil with black plastic to kill existing weeds and stop seeds from germinating. (Don't leave plastic in place for more than a few months; soil needs air and water to remain healthy.)

- Use weed-free mulches like pine bark or shredded leaves. See the Mulch entry for more information on mulches.

- Use vertical barriers, such as wood or metal edgings, between lawn and garden areas to prevent grass from infiltrating.

- Be a good housekeeper in your garden by pulling weeds before they set seed. Police nearby areas, too, or weed seeds from those spots may blow onto your freshly prepared seedbeds.

- Switch to drip irrigation. By directing water right to plant roots and leaving the areas between rows or plants unwatered, this type of watering discourages weed seed germination and weed growth.

- Let the sun's heat weed your vegetable garden by solarizing the soil. Covering bare soil tightly with clear plastic for several weeks can kill weed seeds in the top few inches of the soil. For details on this technique, which also helps reduce soilborne diseases and pests, see page 468.

Getting Rid of Weeds

The bigger your weeds get, the more difficult they are to control. Get into the habit of a once-a-week weed patrol to cut your weed problem down to size. Using the right tools and techniques also will help to make weeding a manageable—maybe even enjoyable—task.

Weeding by Hand

Hand-pulling weeds is simple and effective. It's good for small areas and young or annual weeds such as purslane and lamb's quarters. Using your hands allows you to weed with precision, an important skill when sorting the weeds from the seedlings. For notorious spreaders like ground ivy, the only choice for control is to patiently hand-pull the tops and sift through the soil to remove as many roots as you can find.

Short-handled tools such as dandelion forks (sometimes known as asparagus knives), pronged cultivators, and mattocks are good for large, stubborn weeds, especially in close quarters such as among perennials. Use these tools to pry up tough perennial weeds. Hand weeders come in all shapes, and everybody has a favorite. If one type feels awkward, try another.

If the weeds you pull haven't yet set seed, recycle them: Leave the weeds upside down on the soil to dry, then cover with soil or mulch. If they have gone to seed, add them to the compost pile only if you keep the pile temperature high (at least 160°F).

Otherwise the weed seeds will survive the composting process, and you'll spread weed problems along with your finished compost. See the Compost entry for instructions on keeping a compost pile hot.

Hoeing

A hoe is the best tool for weeding larger areas quickly and cleanly. Use it to rid the vegetable garden of weeds that spring up between rows. When you hoe, slice or scrape just below the soil surface to sever weed tops from roots. Don't chop into the soil—you'll just bring up more weed seeds to germinate. There are hoes designed for many purposes other than weeding. Use an oscillating hoe, circle hoe, or other hoe that's especially designed for weeding, and keep the hoe blade sharp. Hoeing kills most annual weeds, but many perennial weeds will grow back from their roots. Dig out these roots with a garden fork or spade. See the Tools and Equipment entry for help in choosing the right tools.

A rotary tiller is not helpful for weeding, because tilling has detrimental effects on soil structure and will bring up more weed seeds in the process. Also, tilling perennial weeds chops their rhizomes into small pieces, each of which will then sprout into life as a new weed.

Mulching

One of the best low-effort ways to beat weeds is to block their access to light and air by covering the soil surface with mulch. A 3- to 4-inch layer of mulch smothers most weeds, and weeds that manage to poke through are easy to pull.

Black plastic mulch can practically eliminate weeding in the vegetable garden. Spread the plastic tightly over the soil surface and bury the edges. Cut small slits through the plastic so you can slip transplant roots through into the soil below.

Not All Bad

When weeds overwhelm you, and your aching back says it never wants to see another wheelbarrow of mulch, think of the good side of weeds.

- Weeds produce quick cover for land that's been laid bare by fire, flood, or construction.
- Weedy areas provide a haven and an alternate food source for many of the beneficial insects that prey on garden insect pests.
- Songbirds and other wildlife depend on weed seeds as a food source.
- Weeds are sources of drugs and dyes. Ragweed produces a green color; dock and smartweed, yellow. Coltsfoot is used for cough syrup, castor bean for castor oil. Oil from jewelweed soothes poison ivy rash.
- Dried flowers, seedpods, and stems of many weeds, especially weedy grasses, make attractive fall and winter bouquets.

Remove the plastic at the end of the growing season to let the soil breathe. You can use biodegradable materials such as newspaper or corrugated cardboard to temporarily suppress weeds, tilling them into the soil at the end of the season. See the Mulch entry for more information on organic and black plastic mulches.

A living mulch of a low-growing grass or legume crop seeded between rows of plants in your vegetable garden can keep down weeds and improve the soil's organic matter content at the same time. See the Cover Crops entry for suggestions on planting living mulches in your garden.

Even stubborn perennial weeds such as poison ivy or field bindweed will succumb to being smothered by a multilayered mulch treatment, as shown in the illustration below. Start by using a mower or string trimmer to cut the weeds as close as possible to the soil surface (but skip this step for poison ivy). Leave the cut material in place and cover it with 2 to 3 inches of compost or manure. Next, spread a thick layer of dry organic mulch such as hay, wood chips, or shredded leaves. Top the mulch with an opaque, impenetrable cover: Black plastic, old carpeting, or a 2-inch-thick layer of newspaper work well. Leave the mulch and heavy cover in place for the season. The following spring, pull back one corner of the cover and dig down to the soil to check for weed roots. If the roots aren't dead yet, recover the area. Two years

under this kind of cover will kill virtually any weed.

Some gardeners attempt to avoid weed problems around trees and shrubs by spreading landscape fabric over the soil surface under the plants, but this can create as many problems as it solves. The usual practice is to cover landscape fabric with an attractive organic mulch, but weed seedlings can take root in the mulch. Also, roots of desirable plants may grow up into the fabric, reaching for the loose mulch on top; then, in times of drought, these plants suffer. Ultimately, these materials do degrade and need to be replaced, so if tree or shrub roots have grown through the fabric, it can be very difficult to dislodge. Before you decide to use landscape fabric for weed control and prevention, experiment with it in one small area—where it won't be too hard to remove if it doesn't work out.

Smother Crops

One way to reclaim an area that is covered with tough weeds like quackgrass is to smother them out over the course of a year with dense plantings of buckwheat. This cover crop grows so quickly and thickly that it can outcompete almost any weed when it's carefully managed.

Here's one case where you may want to till a weed-covered site to prepare an even seedbed for the buckwheat seed. Starting in spring, sow buckwheat at a rate of 3 to 5 ounces per 100 square feet. Several weeks later, once you see flowers on the buckwheat plants, cut them down close to the soil surface. Let them dry out for a day or two, then till or dig them in and replant in the

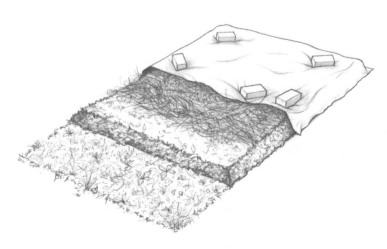

Mulching perennial weeds. Covering a weedy area with organic matter, mulch, and a heavy opaque cover weighted with bricks or rocks will eventually solve even the toughest weed problems.

same way. Continue growing, cutting, and replanting buckwheat until frost kills off a crop. At that point you can plant the area with your desired plants, such as wildflowers or perennials. Or if it's a vegetable garden, sow a winter cover crop that you can turn under in early spring, and plant your vegetables after that.

Shading Out Weeds

Just as weeds compete with your garden and landscape plants for water, food, and growing space, you can encourage your desirable plants to crowd out weeds. For example, spacing vegetable and flower plants closely in beds decreases the time until the leaves form an effective light-blocking canopy, and that means fewer bouts of weeding for you.

Reduce weed growth in your lawn by setting your lawn mower blade a notch or two higher. Taller grass is generally healthier and lets less light reach the soil.

Using Weed-Killing Products

One important development in organic weed control is corn gluten meal. Corn gluten meal, a by-product of corn processing that's often used to feed livestock, inhibits the germination of seeds—bear in mind, once the weeds have gone beyond the sprout stage, corn gluten will not affect them. Also, corn gluten doesn't discriminate between seeds you want to sprout and those you don't want, so avoid using corn gluten meal where and when you've sown seeds. It works best in established lawns and perennial beds. You can find corn gluten meal for sale at almost any garden center. Follow package instructions when applying.

There are a few types of weed-killing sprays that are acceptable for use in organic gardens. The active ingredients in these products are fatty acids

Bring the Heat

Two heat-based methods also offer organic gardeners ways to deal with weeds. For those cracks in the sidewalk or driveway, pouring boiling water on weeds can be enough to scald them out of existence—just be careful not to scald yourself while applying this technique.

Flame weeders use a propane torch with a long nozzle to scorch weeds and can be an effective way to stop young weeds before they get out of control. The key to flame weeding is to simply scorch weeds until they wilt—there's no need to burn them completely. Flame weeding should only be done on a calm (not windy) day and with water close at hand to douse any stray flames that pop up. Never use a flame weeder in dry conditions or where there is lots of dry tinder. And don't use flames on poison ivy or its kin—smoke can carry the volatile oils to skin, eyes, and lungs!

or vinegar; you can find these products at some garden centers or through mail-order companies that specialize in organic gardening supplies. These herbicides provide effective spot control for annual weeds and grasses but probably won't work well for controlling tough perennial weeds. Always follow label safety precautions and application instructions when you use these herbicides. Some vinegar-based herbicides contain a higher percentage of acetic acid than household vinegar, and contact with these products can burn eyes and skin.

Some organic gardeners have traditionally relied

on salt to kill weeds. However, salt will affect soil balance and can harm your garden plants as well. Only use salt in areas where you don't want any plants to grow, such as between cracks in a patio.

WILDFLOWERS

Wildflowers bring casual good looks and sturdy dispositions to the garden, linking the cultivated landscape to the natural environment around it. Wildflowers are at home in informal shade gardens, sunny meadows, and formal borders, and many stars of the perennial garden are tamed and cultured versions of their wilder kin. Some native wildflowers, such as garden phlox (*Phlox paniculata*), bee balm (*Monarda didyma*), and purple coneflower (*Echinacea purpurea*), have grown in gardens for years. But others weren't commonly cultivated in this country until recently, although they were widely grown and hybridized in Europe. Ironically, today we grow European-produced cultivars of many American wildflowers, such as goldenrods and asters.

When You Buy Wildflowers

Wildflowers are available as containerized or bareroot plants from nurseries across the country. While reputable nurseries propagate the plants they sell, a few less-scrupulous dealers offer plants collected from the wild. If you buy collected wildflowers, you could be depleting the population of these plants in the wild.

Fortunately, the growing popularity of wildflowers and their cultivars as garden plants has brought these plants into mainstream nursery production, and the outcry among gardeners against wild-collected plants means that this problem is not

as common as it once was. Use this checklist to make sure you're buying nursery-propagated plants.

- Cultivars, such as *Echinacea purpurea* 'Leuchtstern' (sold as Bright Star), are always nursery-propagated. To be safe, buy the cultivar (rather than the species) if one is offered.

- Don't buy plants that look like they were just dug out of the ground and stuffed into nursery pots. Battered or wilted leaves, leaves growing in unlikely directions, and plants that are too big for their pots but are not pot bound are a few telltale signs. Before you buy such a plant, verify its source.

- Beware of the phrase "nursery-grown." It doesn't necessarily mean that the plants are nursery-propagated; they may have been collected, then grown on in the nursery for a couple of years.

- Wildflowers that take a long time to propagate are the most likely victims of collection from the wild. Be especially careful to determine the source of trilliums, trout lilies, and other spring woodland wildflowers.

- Don't buy native orchids such as ladyslipper unless they're from a reputable nursery that guarantees they're nursery propagated. One clue is that they'll be quite pricey, since it's challenging to propagate native orchids in commercial quantities.

- Be wary of inexpensive wildflowers or quantity discounts offered by mail-order nurseries.

Growing Wildflowers

Success with wildflowers depends on replicating the plants' native environment. Prairie plants will pine

KEY WORDS *Wildflowers*

Wildflower. An herbaceous (nonwoody) flowering plant capable of reproducing and becoming established without cultivation.

Native wildflower. An herbaceous flowering plant indigenous to a particular region, state, or country.

Indigenous plant. A plant that originated in a given area and grows there naturally.

Spring ephemeral. A woodland wildflower that grows, blooms, sets seed, and dies back in spring before the forest trees leaf out and create summer shade.

away in a shaded garden, and plants from cool mountains are unsuitable for hot southern gardens. The right light, moisture, and soil type are essential.

If you can match conditions of light and moisture, you can amend the soil to support a wide variety of species. Woodland plants like moist, humus-rich soils. Canada wild ginger (*Asarum canadense*), Jacob's ladder (*Polemonium caeruleum*), bloodroot (*Sanguinaria canadensis*), and Virginia bluebells (*Mertensia virginica*) are a few examples of these beautiful plants. They are perfect for growing in a shade garden with hostas, ferns, astilbes, and woodland phlox.

Prairie plants such as blazing stars (*Liatris* spp.) and queen of the prairie (*Filipendula rubra*) need deep, loamy soils. Meadow and old-field species like butterfly weed (*Asclepias tuberosa*) and goldenrods (*Solidago* spp.) can survive in thin, poor soil. Mountain soils are often thin on slopes of scree (loose rock) and humus-rich under trees. Most mountain wildflowers, including some phlox (*Phlox* spp.), gentians (*Gentiana* spp.), and lupines (*Lupinus* spp.), grow best in rock gardens.

Propagate wildflowers as you would other garden flowers. Collect seed from the garden or buy from a reputable seed company. If sowing outside, plant the seeds as soon as you collect them. It's espe-

cially important to sow seeds of spring ephemerals such as spring beauties (*Claytonia virginica*), trout lilies (*Erythronium* spp.), and bloodroot right away—if these seeds are allowed to dry out, they enter a dormancy that is very difficult to overcome. If you plan to raise seedlings under lights or in a greenhouse, clean the seeds and store them in moist sphagnum or peat moss in the refrigerator for early spring sowing. For more on growing plants from seed, see the Seed Starting and Seed Saving entry.

You can grow many perennial wildflowers easily from cuttings. Or divide clumps of established perennial wildflowers in your garden. For more on taking cuttings and making divisions, see the Cuttings and Division entries.

Wildflowers growing in their native habitats have evolved to cope with local pests and diseases. If yours are struck by an occasional outbreak, see the Pests and Plant Diseases and Disorders entries for help.

Most wildflower cultivars have been developed for use in perennial beds and borders. Check their sun and moisture requirements, then plant them in a sunny bed or border, shade garden, rock garden, or cottage garden with other perennials. Shade-loving species thrive in woodland gardens, and sun lovers are perfect for meadow or prairie gardens.

Avoid Inferior Mixes

Wildflower seeds need the same growing conditions as any other plants—a well-prepared bed, careful sowing, regular watering until they're well established, and a light mulch to reduce competition from weeds and grass.

We're not saying you should avoid wildflower seed mixes. If you're planting a prairie garden, wildflower meadow, or even a colorful wildflower bed, a carefully composed seed mix may be the easiest and most economical way to go. Just make sure you're buying a mix from a reputable company that specializes in wildflowers and/or native plants. Choose seeds or seed mixes that are selected for your area and conditions, plant and tend them with care, and you'll be rewarded with beautiful flowers.

Check for local wildflower centers, wildflower or nature preserves, and native plant nurseries near you. They often have experts on staff as well as informative Web sites and educational programs, fascinating wildflower display gardens, and native plant libraries. Many have seed exchanges and plant swaps, and offer wildflowers both onsite and through mail order. See Resources on page 673 for the names of some specific organizations and Web site listings.

WILD GINGER

See *Asarum*

WILDLIFE GARDENING

While wild birds are welcome visitors in nearly any yard, many gardeners have mixed feelings about other forms of wildlife in their backyards. Fortunately, growing numbers of gardeners are taking a new look at wildlife and adapting their gardens to attract all kinds of creatures, including squirrels, rabbits, mice, toads, salamanders, crickets, and all the rest the neighborhood ark might hold.

The key to transforming your landscape into a haven for local wildlife starts by examining it from a new perspective—one of wildlife in search of food, water, cover, and a safe place for their young. When viewed in this light, tangled brush, tall weeds, and dead trees take on a much more essential role than manicured lawns and rows of flowers. With careful planning, even a tiny yard can attract a surprising array of wildlife. Of course, the bigger the space you have to work with, the better the potential of your backyard. Smaller occupants, such as rabbits, squirrels, and birds, can become near-permanent breeding residents. Animals with larger territories, such as deer, raccoons, and foxes, may appear for a visit as their travels through their feeding ranges come to include your backyard as a regular stop.

Food

To make your sanctuary into a habitat that attracts a number of species, you'll need to include a variety of plants. Native plants are often the best choice; see the Native Plants and Wildflowers entries for more on selecting species for your garden. Tall and midsize trees, shrubs, tall herbaceous plants, grasses, and groundcovers all provide for varying needs of different species. Weeds and wildflowers also play their part where local ordinances and neighbors will allow. The cottontail rabbit, for example, eats green plants such as grasses and clovers for much of the year and in winter adds the twigs and bark of young trees and shrubs. The eastern gray squirrel is most decidedly a nut eater (primarily acorns, hickory nuts, and beechnuts), but corn is also a great attraction. Birds depend on insects as their mainstay but also eat seeds, berries, and fruits. The browsing diet of the white-tailed deer consists largely of twigs from trees and shrubs but is supplemented in spring and summer by many of the same leafy plants cottontail rabbits eat.

Raccoons relish crayfish, grasshoppers, frogs, and birds' eggs, but almost any living creature that is smaller and slower than a raccoon will find its way into its diet. Acorns, corn, and fleshy fruits also are favorite raccoon foods. Most of the diet of the red fox is small rodents, such as mice, voles, and rabbits. In summer and fall, fox diets include as much as 25 percent fleshy fruits.

Be sure to consider seasonal diversity when selecting plants to include in your wildlife habitat. Different plants produce their buds, fruits, and seeds at different times of the year, and ideally you want a steady supply of food throughout the year.

Cover and Safe Haven

When selecting plants that supply food for wildlife, think too about areas where creatures can hide and build homes to raise young. Some plants, such as evergreens, supply shelter year-round. The brambly interior of a blackberry patch makes a good escape route for rabbits, even in winter.

You'll attract the most wildlife by mimicking the plantings of nature. Wild animals stay safe from predators by moving from place to place through protective cover. A berry-covered bush surrounded by a sea of lawn grass may attract a migrating group of cedar waxwings, but a grouse who tries to reach it could soon become hawk food. If you add another few bushes, and perhaps a hemlock (*Tsuga* spp.), then plant meadow grasses and wildflowers in front of the shrubs, you'll make the planting attractive to a variety of wild creatures.

To this living landscape, add snags, logs, brush piles, and rock piles to provide places for smaller creatures to hide and to rear their young. You can camouflage these elements by planting vines like wild grapes or Virginia creeper (*Parthenocissus quinquefolia*) to trail over them. In the process, you'll provide additional food sources.

Water

Water is the most overlooked aspect of backyard wildlife habitats. Food and cover preferences vary widely, but nearly all creatures need water. A birdbath will serve many birds, many insects, and some mammals. A ground-level fountain will provide for even more drinkers and might attract some amphibians. Or consider adding a small pond to your landscape. To make it most accessible and appealing to wildlife, include a pebble-covered beach area with a gradual incline so small animals can creep to the water's edge without falling in. Or place a large log in the pond that serves as a platform from which to drink. A pond that features varying depths will be used by nearly every creature that you can expect to draw into the backyard and can even provide a permanent home for frogs and turtles. See the Water Gardens entry for more details.

Native Landscapes

The creatures attracted to a wildlife garden will vary depending on where you live. For information on what you can expect to see, contact your local extension office, Department of Natural Resources, or fish and wildlife office. Or talk to the staff at a local natural area or nature center. For more on attracting birds, butterflies, and other beneficial wildlife, see the Birds, Butterfly Gardening, Bats, and Toads entries. Since some wildlife species are less welcome than others, see the Animal Pests entry for help in discouraging animals that may be destructive.

The National Wildlife Federation is another good source of information for creating wildlife-friendly landscapes. The Web site of its Backyard Wildlife Habitat Program provides plant lists and other information on a state-by-state basis. See Resources on page 673 for contact information.

WILLOW

See *Salix*

WISTERIA

Wisteria. Spring-blooming woody vines.

Description: Wisterias are vigorous woody twining vines that can grow more than 10 feet a year, ultimately reaching over 30 feet long. The deciduous, dark green, compound leaves drop in late fall, revealing gray trunks that become twisted with age. Showy, drooping, violet-blue flower clusters (12 to 20 inches long) appear in April or May. Cultivars have reddish violet, pink, and white blooms. Clusters of velvety brown pods follow the blooms and remain after leaf drop, adding winter interest. The two most common species in cultivation both match this description. *Wisteria sinensis*, Chinese wisteria, blooms in May and is the most commonly grown. Zones 5–9. The earlier-blooming *W. floribunda*, Japanese wisteria, has larger flower clusters and is slightly hardier (to Zone 4). *W. frutescens*, American wisteria, is a similar southeastern native species that blooms in summer. Zones 6–9.

How to grow: Wisterias prefer full sun. Transplant container-grown plants to well-drained, fertile soil. Make sure you buy cutting-grown plants from wisterias known to flower. Wisterias require strong support—metal is best because the heavy vines can crush wood supports. The most frequent problem of wisteria is failure to bloom, usually due to an abundance of nitrogen (which promotes vegetative growth rather than bloom) and a phosphorus deficiency. To avoid this situation, amend the soil in fall with ½ pound of colloidal phosphate or bonemeal per 1 inch of main trunk diameter. Be aware that it may be several years after planting before the vine blooms. Root pruning of established plants may encourage shy bloomers to perform. Prune wisteria severely after blooming to encourage bloom and control rampant growth; cut all new growth back to three buds.

Landscape uses: Wisteria is dramatic growing up the side of a building or on an arbor shading a patio or walkway. It may also be trained to grow in a tree form called a standard.

WITCH HAZEL

See *Hamamelis*

XERISCAPING

In areas of the country where drought is measured in years—years in which winter rain did not replenish the reservoirs—xeriscaping is becoming a way of life in the garden. This method depends on basic water-saving principles, such as increasing soil organic matter content and mulching, as well as on using native plants and reducing areas of water-guzzling lawn grass.

A xeriscape (from the Greek *xeros*, meaning dry) is a water-saving garden designed for a dry region. Xeriscaping is especially useful in the western half of North America, where little rain falls in summer and gardeners depend heavily on irrigation. Savvy gardeners have been incorporating some of these principles in their own gardens for years. The idea gained more widespread notice, and an official name, in 1981, when the Denver Water Department developed the concept and the policy of xeriscaping as a way to deal with the West's chronic water shortages. Even eastern gardeners in areas of relatively dependable rainfall can benefit through an offshoot called mesiscaping, or planning a garden that is only moderate in water use. To learn more about water use and gardening, see the Water Conservation and Water-Wise Gardening entries.

Water-Saving Principles

Xeriscapes do not have to be desert gardens. Xeriscapers emphasize that these gardens can be lush and colorful. Gardeners in any region can use the seven principles of xeriscaping in designing or rejuvenating a garden.

1. **Incorporate water savings into your planning and design.** Map your yard's microclimates and soil types, paying special attention to the places that stay moist longest and those that dry out fastest or are most difficult to irrigate. In your design, plan zones of high, moderate, and low water use, based on your map. Group plants with similar water needs in these zones. Put your high-water-use plants where you'll appreciate them most—for example, near an entryway or patio.

2. **Improve your soil or select adapted plants.** For plants with high or moderate water needs, dig the soil deeply and add plenty of organic matter. Many drought-tolerant plants prefer unimproved soil. Group these and leave their soil unamended. See the Soil entry for more information on improving your soil organically.

3. **Limit the area in lawn.** Lawns are high-water-use areas. Although some grasses tolerate drought better than others, all lawn grasses need similar amounts of water to look good and stay healthy.

   Design your lawn to be a small oasis of green. Xeriscape experts calculate that the average single-family garden needs no more than 800 square feet of lawn. Site your lawn next to a patio or driveway, so activities can spill over from one into the other.

   Keep edges rounded, and avoid irregularly shaped areas or narrow strips of lawn. Irregular shapes and peninsulas have more edge area that will abut pathways or areas of bare soil that heat up quickly, and the heat will promote faster moisture loss from the lawn. Plant lawns only on level ground to reduce runoff. Select grasses that are drought tolerant and adapted to your region and soil type.

4. **Use mulches.** Mulch any unplanted soil areas with 2 to 3 inches of organic mulch or a thick mulch of gravel or stone. Either can be laid over weed-resistant landscape fabric. The little rain that does fall will be able to soak through these porous mulches. Keep overall design in mind: You don't want such a large area of mulch that your garden is no longer a green landscape. See the Mulch entry for details on using mulch.

5. **Irrigate efficiently.** If you water by hand, test your soil before you water. Water established plants only if the soil is dry several inches below the surface. Better yet, construct a water-efficient irrigation system. Plan it to allow different watering schedules for areas of high, moderate, and low water use. Lawns require sprinklers, but water other plants with soaker hoses or drip irrigation. See the Watering and Drip Irrigation entries for more information.

6. **Use plants that don't demand as much water.** There is no one best list of plants for a xeriscape. Plant lists for Denver, for instance, include native Colorado maples (*Acer* spp.), but California is so dry that no maples are recommended. Another plant, Catalina lilac (*Ceanothus arboreus*), is an excellent choice for California gardens but would be killed by Denver's higher summer rainfall and colder winters. Xeriscapers often turn to plants native to a particular region or to regions with similar climates and soils. Many familiar landscape plants are also adaptable. Water even drought-tolerant plants until well established.

7. **Maintain the garden in ways that save water.** Tend your garden well, fertilizing and pruning when needed, and checking for pests.

Inspect your irrigation system frequently for leaks or other malfunctions. Adjust the timing so that the system releases more or less water as needed during drier and wetter seasons of the year.

Planning a Xeriscape

Learn more about xeriscaping by visiting a demonstration garden in your area. Denver built the first of such gardens. To find out the location of the one nearest you, call your local water department or botanical garden.

When you're ready to select plants, learn as much as you can about the ones you're considering. Watching a plant grow for a year is the best way to judge, but you can also get recommendations from nurseries. Plant lists in books and water department publications can help you decide if a plant is suited to your region. Books and other publications will provide details such as height, bloom season, and any potential problems. Another easy way to choose is to observe your neighborhood and note plants that thrive without irrigation.

YARROW

See *Achillea*

YEW

See *Taxus*

YUCCA

Yucca, Adam's needle. Summer-blooming woody perennials.

Description: Massive, dramatic *Yucca filamentosa*, Adam's needle, bears creamy white 2-inch hanging bells in giant spikes up to 10 feet. Plants have mounded, evergreen, 2½-foot dark green sword-like leaves with sharp tips and curly-haired edges. Several cultivars are available with yellow- or white-variegated foliage. Zones 4–10.

Other species, including beaked yucca (*Y. rostrata*) and dwarf pale-leaf *Y. pallida*, are less hardy but make excellent choices for arid landscapes in the West and Southwest.

How to grow: Plant in spring or fall from containers in a sunny spot with average to poor, very well-drained soil. Heavier soils may cause rotting during wet winters. Sandy soil, drought, heat, high humidity, and pests don't bother these rugged plants.

Landscape uses: Yuccas are unequaled as specimens or in small groups among rocks or around buildings and pools. Grow in irregular groups on grassy slopes or in hot corners. Avoid placing these spiky plants in high-traffic areas; conversely, yuccas can make an effective informal hedge for a droughty site.

pointed petals in single, semidouble, and double forms. Bloom colors include white, cream, yellow, orange, red, green, and bronze, plus combinations. Cultivars may be 6 to 36 inches tall, forming low mounds or upright bushes. All zinnias have dull green leaves.

How to grow: Start seed indoors no more than 3 weeks before the last frost, or direct-sow outdoors when the ground is warm. Give plants full sun in average soil and water only when very dry. Keep the flowers cut to encourage more bloom.

Powdery mildew is a fungal disease that causes dusty white spots on leaves and flowers. The disease is most prevalent in hot, humid weather and when plants are grown close together. Good air circulation and antidesiccant sprays help control mildew. Mexican zinnias (*Zinnia angustifolia*, aka *Z. haageana*) and some cultivars of common zinnia (*Z. violacea*, widely known as *Z. elegans*) are mildew resistant.

Landscape uses: Use zinnias in masses in beds, borders, and edges, as cut flowers, or to screen dying bulb foliage.

ZINNIA

Zinnia. Summer- and fall-blooming annuals.

Description: Zinnia flowers range from less than 1 inch to over 6 inches wide with rounded or

ZUCCHINI

See Squash

Diagnosing Plant Problems

Some plant problems are a cinch to diagnose. When you see a fat green caterpillar feasting on your broccoli, you know immediately who the culprit is. But if your roses have yellowish foliage and just don't seem to be doing well, you may be dealing with an insect problem, a disease problem, or a nutrient deficiency. Use the following table to help pinpoint the cause. While not comprehensive, it does include many of the common plant problems you may encounter. Using this table will help you learn how to examine plants carefully and distinguish among problems that look similar at first glance.

The key has five sections: Whole Plant Symptoms, Leaf Symptoms, Stem Symptoms, Fruit/Flower Symptoms, and Root Symptoms.

In each section, you'll see categories of symptoms. Each category is broken down into more specific distinguishing symptoms. In most cases, these specific symptoms are followed by a cause. In a few cases, the table will direct you to another section, where you'll find more symptom information.

Begin by finding the section of the table that relates to your plant problem. Then skim the symptom categories and find the one that best matches the problem. Read through the specific symptoms in that category, studying your plant again, if need be, to narrow down the possible causes. Once you've decided what the cause of your problem may be, refer to the page number given in parentheses after the cause for more information and solutions.

WHOLE PLANT SYMPTOMS	CAUSE
WHOLE PLANT OR PLANT PART WILTS	
Plant not stunted	
• whole plant or tips wilt; recovers when watered	Water stress (p. 441)
• whole plant or branch wilts; stays wilted	Borers (p. 564), wilts (p. 472), blights (p. 470), or viruses (p. 465)
Plant stunted	*See* Root Symptoms

WHOLE PLANT SYMPTOMS	CAUSE
ALL FOLIAGE AND STEMS DISTORTED	
Leaves, stems, long and narrow; plant stunted	Viruses (p. 465)
LEAF SYMPTOMS	**CAUSE**
DISCOLORED LEAVES	
New leaves yellow or light green	
• veins paler; growth rigid	Yellow virus (p. 465)
• yellow patches on older leaves; stem center brown	Wilts (p. 472)
New leaves dark green	
Leaves blotchy, light green, yellowish, or white	
• between veins	Nutrient deficiency (p. 476)
• patterns crossing veins, may be ring-shaped	Mosaic virus (p. 465)
Leaves black or scorched	
• wipes off	Sooty mold (from insect feeding) (p. 454)
• won't wipe off	Fire blight (p. 233)
Leaves gray or whitish	Mildew (pp. 473–74)
Leaves yellow or pale, stippled	
• fine webbing on underside	Spider mites (p. 231)
• silvery sheen to damage	Thrips (pp. 120, 394)
• blotchy patterns, spots of excrement present	Lace bugs (p. 509)
HOLES IN LEAVES	
Small holes	
• with cleanly cut edges	Flea beetles (p. 455)
• with dry, dark edges; leaves also have spots	Bacterial leaf spot (pp. 114, 232)
Medium to large holes, including veins	
• greenish droppings on leaves	Caterpillars (p. 454)

LEAF SYMPTOMS (continued)	CAUSE
• shiny trails	Slugs or snails (p. 547)
• no clues	Beetles (p. 455), animals (pp. 7–13)
Leaves skeletonized, only veins remain	Mexican bean beetles (p. 456), Japanese beetles (p. 455)
DISTORTED LEAVES	
Puckered, twisted leaves or growing tips	
• honeydew present	Aphids (p. 454)
• no honeydew	Plant bugs (p. 456)
Leaves rolled up	
• webbing inside rolled leaves	Leafrollers (p. 27)
• no webbing	Nutrient deficiency (p. 476), diseases (pp. 463–77, 583–84)
OTHER SYMPTOMS	
Small dark spots on leaves	Scab (p. 27), blackspot (p. 516), other diseases (pp. 463–77, 583–84)
Curving whitish trails in leaves	Leafminers (p. 561)
Galls on leaves	Gall insects (p. 461), diseases (pp. 463–77, 583–84)
Sticky coating on leaves	Scale (p. 456), aphids (p. 454)
ROOT SYMPTOMS	**CAUSE**
ROOTS DISTORTED, ABNORMALLY THICKENED	
Small swollen areas on roots	
• white or gray, hard knots	Root knot nematodes (pp. 416, 474)
• round nodules, on legumes	Nitrogen-fixing bacteria (pp. 441, 474)
Whole root thickened (on cabbage-family plants)	Club root (p. 473)
Corky lumps on roots and stem near soil line	Crown gall (p. 473)
SHORT OR SPARSE ROOTS, TOPS OFTEN WILTED	
Roots brownish or dark-colored	Diseases (pp. 463–77, 583–84), salt buildup (p. 475)
Roots have soft, water-soaked appearance	Root rots (p. 472)
Roots chewed	Rootworms (p. 148), grubs (p. 350)

ROOT SYMPTOMS (continued)	CAUSE
OTHER SYMPTOMS	
Numerous woody secondary roots (on carrot-family plants)	Yellow virus (p. 465)
Tunnels and rot in roots (cabbage, carrot, onion)	Root maggots (p. 454)
Tree blows over; roots never left planting hole	Windthrow (pp. 599–600)
FRUIT/FLOWER SYMPTOMS	**CAUSE**
FLOWERS DISTORTED	
Petals have silvery patches, or streaks	Aphids (p. 454), viruses (p. 465)
Petals have water-soaked patches	Botrytis rot (p. 472)
FLOWERS APPEAR, BUT NO FRUIT	
Flowers open normally	Lack of pollination (p. 229), cold damage (p. 646), excess nitrogen (p. 476)
Flowers drop before opening	Plant bugs (p. 456)
FRUIT DROPS BEFORE RIPENING, MAY COLOR EARLY	
Fruits with normal exterior	
• interior tunneled and mined	Insect damage (p. 317)
• interior normal	Normal self-thinning (pp. 229–30)
Shriveled fruits, early-ripening cultivars most affected	Fruit maggots (p. 231)
Scarred, distorted fruits	Disease (pp. 232–233), plant bugs (p. 456)
FRUIT DAMAGED, STAYS ON TREE	
Fruits with large, chewed holes	Caterpillars (p. 454), animals (pp. 7–13)
Fruits have discolored areas	
• always at tip end	Blossom-end rot (p. 584)
• also soft areas	Fungal or bacterial rots (p. 472)
Fruits have small, dark scabs or spots	Bacterial or fungal disease (pp. 464–65)
Fruit distorted, puckered	Inadequate pollination (p. 229), plant bugs (p. 456), leaf curl (p. 474)

FRUIT/FLOWER SYMPTOMS (continued)	CAUSE
OTHER SYMPTOMS	
Buds shrivel or rot before opening	Bud blast (p. 406), insects (p. 317)
Chewed flowers	Japanese beetles (p. 455), other insects (p. 317)
STEM SYMPTOMS	**CAUSE**
BRANCH OR WHOLE PLANT WILTS	
Holes in stem or trunk; gummy sap or sawdust	Boring insects (p. 232)
Collapsed areas on stem with soft, watery, brown discoloration	Botrytis (p. 474), soft rots (p. 472)
Raised areas on stems	
• cracks	Temperature injury (p. 475), mechanical injury (pp. 602, 605), cankers (p. 471)
• hard growths	Galls (p. 461), cankers (p. 471), graft incompatibility (p. 253)
Stems brown or reddish when cut open	Wilts (p. 472)
SEEDLING OR TRANSPLANT STEMS COLLAPSED OR CUT OFF	
Cut stem crisp, appears healthy	
• trail of silvery mucus on soil	Slugs or snails (pp. 547)
• no mucus trail present	Cutworms (p. 455), animals (pp. 7–13)
Stem soft, watery	Damping-off (p. 473), collar rot (p. 28)
TIPS OF BRANCHES, TWIGS DIE BACK	
Growth blackened	Insects (p. 317), frost (p. 646), blights (p. 470)
• also distorted and wilted	Plant bugs (p. 456)
Don't leaf out in spring	Cold injury (p. 475)
OTHER SYMPTOMS	
Small bumps on stems and leaf veins; honeydew present	Scale (p. 456), mealybugs (p. 312)
Stems and crowns hollow, corky (on cabbage-family plants)	Boron deficiency (p. 476)

Glossary

Alternate. Having one leaf or bud at each node along a stem.

Annual. A plant that germinates, grows, flowers, sets seed, and dies in one growing season.

Anther. A pollen-bearing capsule borne on a slender stalk; part of the stamen.

Arthropod. A cold-blooded animal that has an armored skeleton, called an exoskeleton, on the outside of its body. Crustaceans, insects, mites, spiders, millipedes, and centipedes are arthropods.

Biennial. A plant that completes its life cycle in 2 years, growing vegetatively in the first year and producing flowers and seeds in the second year.

Blade. The flattened leafy portion of a frond.

Branch collar. The part of the trunk that helps hold the branch to the trunk, often recognizable as a bulge at the base of the branch.

Broadcast. To spread seed or fertilizer evenly across an area, by hand or with a spreading tool.

Bulb. A plant storage structure, usually underground, that consists of layers of fleshy scales (modified leaves). The term *bulbs* is also used to describe a diverse group of perennial plants including those that grow from true bulbs, corms, rhizomes, and tuberous roots.

Callus. A mass of plant cells that have not yet developed a specific function; produced in a wounded area.

Cambium. A thin layer of actively growing tissue between the bark and wood of a woody plant.

Candles. New shoots that grow from the branch tips of needle-leaved evergreens in a flush of spring growth.

Cane. A long, slender branch that usually originates directly from the roots.

Caterpillar. The larva of a moth or butterfly.

Cellulose. A fibrous material that is the primary component of plant cell walls.

Chlorosis. A condition characterized by pale green, yellowish, or nearly white leaves; often due to a nutrient deficiency.

Chrysalis. The pupa of a butterfly.

Clay. Tiny fragments of rock or minerals in the soil. Clay particles are less than 0.002 millimeter in diameter. *See also* sand *and* silt.

Cocoon. A protective cover for a pupa.

Coir. Fibers from the husk of a coconut, used as an ingredient in potting mixes.

Compound leaf. A leaf whose blade is divided into distinct leaflets.

Conifer. A cone-bearing plant, often an evergreen.

Corm. A rounded, swollen stem covered with a papery tunic. Unlike true bulbs, corms are solid, with a bud on top that produces leaves and flowers.

Cotyledon. The leaf (or leaves), present in a dormant seed, that is the first to unfold as the seed germinates. Also called seed leaf.

Cover crop. A crop grown to protect and enrich the soil or to control weeds.

Crotch. The angle of emergence of a branch from the trunk.

Crown. The base of a plant where stems and roots meet. Also, a general term for the top part (branches and leaves) of a tree or shrub. Also used as a term (mainly in regard to propagation) for a piece of rhizome and attached roots.

Damping-off. A disease caused by various fungi that results in seedling stems that shrivel and collapse at soil level.

Decay cycle. The changes that occur as plants grow, die, and break down in the soil. Animals and microorganisms in the soil break down dead plant tissues to release nutrients that new plants then take up to fuel their growth and development.

Deciduous. A plant that drops all of its leaves in autumn.

Dioecious. Producing male and female flowers on separate plants.

Dormancy. A state of reduced biochemical activity that persists until certain conditions occur that trigger germination of a seed or resumption of growth of a plant.

Dwarf. The term used to describe certain fruit trees grafted on size-controlling rootstocks. Dwarf trees often mature to 8 to 10 feet in height. *See also* semidwarf.

Endosperm. Specialized layer of tissue that surrounds the embryo.

Erosion. The wearing away of soil by running water, wind, ice, or other geological forces. Erosion can be accelerated by the activity of people or animals.

Espalier. A fruit tree or an ornamental shrub that is pruned to grow in a flat plane.

Evergreen. A plant that retains its leaves year-round.

Fiddlehead. The young, unfurling frond of a fern.

Floret. A very small flower, such as one of the individual flowers in a Shasta daisy.

Floricane. A second-year shoot of a bramble plant, such as a raspberry, that bears flowers and fruit.

Foliar feed. To supply nutrients by spraying liquid fertilizer directly on plant foliage.

Frond. The leaf of a fern, including the blade and the stipe.

Germination. The beginning of growth of a seed.

Grafting. The process of joining a stem piece to another plant in such a way that the parts are united by living tissue and continue to grow.

Green manure. A crop that is grown and then incorporated into the soil to increase soil fertility or organic matter content.

Grub. The larva of a beetle.

Hardscape. Elements of a landscape other than plants and soil, such as paved pathways, walls, and woodwork.

Hardy annual. An annual plant that tolerates frost and self-sows. Seeds winter over outside and germinate the following year.

Hardy perennial. A perennial plant that tolerates frost.

Heading cut. Cutting a branch back to a side bud or shoot.

Herbaceous perennial. A perennial plant that dies back to the ground at the end of each growing season.

High chill. Requiring more hours of cool temperatures to break dormancy.

Host. A plant or animal that a parasite or pathogen depends on for sustenance.

Humus. A dark-colored, stable form of organic matter that remains after most of the plant and animal residues in it have decomposed.

Indigenous plant. A plant that originated in a given area and grows there naturally.

Infection. Entry or growth of a disease-causing organism into a host.

Inoculant. A seed treatment medium that contains the symbiotic bacteria that captures nitrogen when in contact with legume roots.

Interstem. A section of stem between the rootstock and scion of a grafted plant. Also called an interstock.

Larva. An immature stage of an insect.

Leaching. The removal of nutrients from soil by water moving downward through the soil.

Leader. The main, primary, or tallest shoot of a tree trunk. Trees can be single-leadered or multiple-leadered.

Legume. A plant whose roots form an association with soilborne bacteria that can capture atmospheric nitrogen.

Loam. Soil that has moderate amounts of sand, silt, and clay. Loam soils are generally considered the best garden soils.

Low chill. Requiring fewer hours of cool temperatures to break dormancy.

Maggot. The larva of a fly.

Microorganisms. Animals and plants that are too small to be seen clearly without the use of a microscope.

Monoecious. Producing male and female flowers on the same plant.

Mycorrhiza. A symbiotic association of plant roots and fungi in which the roots supply a protected environment and secrete sugars as an energy source for the fungi and the fungi help extract nutrients and water from the soil to nourish the plants.

Naturalize. To spread naturally in the landscape like a wildflower.

Nematode. A microscopic, unsegmented, threadlike roundworm; also called an eelworm.

Nitrogen fixation. The capture and conversion of atmospheric nitrogen gas into nitrogen compounds that are stored in soil and can be used by plants.

node. A point along a plant stem where a leaf, side branch, or flower originates.

NPK ratio. A ratio of three numbers such as 10-10-10 that identifies the percentage of three major nutrients—nitrogen (N), phosphorus (P), and potassium (K)—in fertilizers.

Nymph. An immature stage of an insect that does not form a pupa.

Opposite. Having two leaves or two buds at each node along a stem.

Organic matter. Various forms of living or dead plant and animal material.

Ovary. The seed-bearing base of a pistil.

Overseed. To seed an area that is already planted (such as a lawn) with another type of plant.

Palmate. Resembling a hand with the fingers spread; having lobes that radiate from a common point.

Parasite. An animal or plant that lives in or on, and draws nourishment from, another organism (the host) without contributing anything toward the host organism's survival.

Parasitoid. An insect that parasitizes another insect.

Pathogen. An organism that causes disease.

Perennialize. To come up year after year.

Perennial plant. A plant that flowers and sets seed for two or more seasons.

pH. A measure of acidity or alkalinity, expressed as a number between 0 and 14, with 7 being neutral. High numbers are alkaline, lower values are acidic.

Pinching. Nipping out the end bud of a twig or stem with your fingertips to make the plant more compact and bushy. Pinching entire side shoots prevents bushiness.

Pinnate. Having similar parts arranged along the opposite sides of an axis.

Pistil. The female reproductive part of a flower.

Pore (or leaf pore). A small opening, as in the surface of a leaf or in the matrix of the soil.

Predator. An animal that attacks and feeds on other animals. Many insects are predators of other insects.

Primocane. A first-year shoot of a bramble plant.

Pupa. A resting stage in the life cycle of many insects between the larval and adult phases.

Raceme. A type of flower cluster, with individual blossoms borne along an upright stem.

Reverted growth. New growth that is different from the growth for which the plant was originally grown, such as a branch with all-green leaves on an otherwise variegated plant.

Rhizome. An underground plant stem, usually thick and horizontal, that may grow slowly or rapidly. Many kinds of plants and ferns produce rhizomes. Leaves (or fronds) and flowers sprout from the upper side; roots from the underside.

Rootstock. A cultivar onto which another cultivar (the scion) is grafted. Rootstocks are selected for strong, healthy roots or for dwarfing effect. The grafted cultivar is selected for fruit or ornamental qualities.

Sand. Tiny fragments of rock or minerals in the soil. Sand particles are from 0.05 to 2.0 millimeters in diameter. *See also* clay silt.

Scaffolds. The main structural branches on a fruit tree.

Scarification. Nicking or wearing down hard seed coats to encourage germination.

Scion. The stem piece joined to a rootstock in a graft.

Seed. A plant embryo and its supply of nutrients, often surrounded by a protective coat.

Seedling. A young plant grown from seed. Commonly, plants grown from seeds are termed *seedlings* until they are first transplanted.

Self-fruitful. A tree that produces pollen that can pollinate its own flowers.

Semidwarf. The term used to describe certain fruit trees grafted on size-controlling rootstocks.

Semidwarfs mature to 12 to 18 feet. *See also* dwarf.

Semievergreen. A plant that keeps some of its leaves year-round. Many semievergreen plants, such as cotoneasters and many perennials, are evergreen in mild climates and semievergreen to deciduous in colder regions.

Semiwoody perennial. A perennial plant that forms woody stems but is much less substantial than a shrub.

Sepals. Leaflike flaps, often green, at the base of a flower.

Side-dress. To apply fertilizer alongside plants growing in rows.

Silt. Tiny fragments of rock or minerals in the soil. Silt particles are from 0.002 to 0.05 millimeter in diameter. *See also* sand *and* clay.

Simple leaf. A leaf with an undivided blade.

Soil pH. A measurement of the acidity or alkalinity of the soil.

Soil structure. The arrangement of soil particles in the soil.

Soil texture. The relative proportions of sand, silt, and clay in the soil.

Spore. An asexual reproductive unit, usually single-celled.

Spur. Short branches produced on trees, especially fruit trees.

Stamen. The male reproductive part of a flower.

Standard. A full-size fruit tree, usually maturing to at least 20 feet in height. Also, a plant trained to a single stem with a rounded top; often grown in containers.

Stomate. A microscopic pore on the surface of a leaf (usually the underside) through which air and nutrients (dissolved in water) enter and water vapor escapes.

Stratification. Exposing seeds to cool/moist (35° to 40°F) or warm/moist (68° to 86°F) conditions to break dormancy.

Suckers. Shoots that sprout out of or near the base of a tree or shrub or from a stem node on an herbaceous plant; also, in common usage, straight, rapid-growing shoots or watersprouts that grow in response to wounding or poor pruning.

Tender perennial. A plant that survives more than one season in tropical or subtropical regions but that is easily killed by frost.

Thinning cut. Cutting a limb off at the base, either at ground level or at a branch collar.

Top-dress. To apply fertilizer evenly over a field or bed of growing plants.

Topiary. Plants sculpted into lightly sheared geometric shapes or likenesses of animals or people.

Transpiration. The process by which water is lost from leaves through the stomates.

Trifoliate. Having three leaflets.

Tuber. Fleshy underground stem that has eyes or buds on all sides; leaves and flowers sprout from the eyes.

Tuberous roots. Swollen, fleshy roots that have a pointed bud on top. Dahlias have tuberous roots.

Undersow. Sowing seed under the canopy of a growing crop.

Viable. Capable of germinating; alive.

Watersprouts. Upright shoots that sprout from the trunk and main limbs of a tree.

Whip. A young tree, often the first-year growth from a graft or bud.

Whorl. A group of three or more buds, leaves, petals, or flowers arranged in a circle around a stem.

Wildflower. An herbaceous (nonwoody) flowering plant capable of reproducing and becoming established without cultivation.

Woody perennial. A perennial plant such as a shrub or tree that does not die down to the ground each year. Gardeners generally refer to these as woody plants.

Resources

All-American Daylilies: www.allamericandaylilies.com

All-America Selections:
www.all-americaselections.org

American Bonsai Society: www.absbonsai.org

American Community Gardening Association:
www.communitygarden.org

American Garden Rose Selections:
www.americangardenroseselections.com

American Gourd Society:
www.americangourdsociety.org

American Horticultural Society: www.ahsgardening.org

AHS Plant Heat Zone Map: ahsgardening.org
/gardening-resources/gardening-maps/heat-zone-map

American Horticultural Therapy Association:
www.ahta.org

American Rose Society: www.rose.org

Arbor Day Foundation: www.arborday.org

Bat Conservation International: www.batcon.org

Biodynamic Association: www.biodynamics.com

Bonsai Clubs International: www.bonsai-bci.com

Bowdoin College Web Site on Japanese Gardens:
http://learn.bowdoin.edu/japanesegardens/

Butterflies and Moths of North America:
www.butterfliesandmoths.org
    Online database of information on butterflies and
    moths

College of Natural Resources, University of California, Berkeley: www.helpabee.org
    Urban bee garden information and plant list

Combined Rose List: www.combinedroselist.com
    Information on more than 14,000 rose varieties
    and hundreds of rose sources

Cornell University Vegetable MD Online:
http://vegetablemdonline.ppath.cornell.edu
    Detailed information on management of vegetable
    diseases

Edible Forest Gardens: www.edibleforestgardens.com
    Information and workshop listings about
    permaculture

Falling Fruit: www.fallingfruit.org
    Maps identifying unpicked local fruit trees
    available for foraging

Garden Writers Association's Plant a Row for the
Hungry (PAR): www.gardenwriters.org/par
    A program that coordinates collection of locally
    grown produce for donation to soup kitchens and
    food banks

Garlic Seed Foundation:
www.garlicseedfoundation.info
    Planting stock and information on growing garlic

The Helpful Gardener: www.helpfulgardener.com
    Useful gardening tips, including Japanese garden
    design principles

The Honeybee Conservancy:
http://thehoneybeeconservancy.org

International Palm Society: www.palms.org

The Japanese Garden Database: www.jgarden.org

Jungle Music Palms and Cycads:
www.junglemusic.net/palms
　　Photographs and growing information on palm
　　trees

Lady Bird Johnson Wildflower Center:
www.wildflower.org

Living Lots NYC: https://livinglotsnyc.org

Local Harvest: www.localharvest.org
　　Lists of local farms, CSAs, and crops growing near
　　you

National Center for Home Food Preservation:
www.nchfp.uga.edu
　　Research-based recommendations for home food
　　preservation

National Christmas Tree Association:
www.realchristmastrees.org

National Organic Program:
www.organic.ams.usda.gov

National Sunflower Association:
www.sunflowernsa.com

National Wildlife Federation Backyard Wildlife Habitat Program:
www.nwf.org/garden-for-wildlife

Natural Resources Conservation Service:
www.nrcs.usda.gov

New England Wildflower Society: www.newfs.org

North American Butterfly Association: www.naba.org

North American Fruit Explorers: www.nafex.org
　　Information on growing fruits and nuts, including
　　many types of unusual fruit

North American Raspberry & Blackberry Association:
www.raspberryblackberry.com

North American Rock Garden Society:
www.nargs.org

Perennial Plant Association: www.perennialplant.org
　　Bestows the Perennial Plant of the Year award

Permaculture Institute: www.permaculture.org

Pick Your Own: www.pickyourown.org
　　Directory of U-pick farms

PlantNative: www.plantnative.org
　　Native plant nursery finder and regional lists of
　　native plants

Project BudBurst: http://budburst.org
　　Citizen science phenology project

Rodale's Organic Life: www.rodalesorganiclife.com

Seed Savers Exchange: www.seedsavers.org
　　Members of this seed exchange preserve and
　　disseminate hundreds of heirloom and rare
　　varieties of vegetables, herbs, and flowers

Sustainable Agriculture Research and Education:
www.sare.org

Tropicopia: www.tropicopia.com
　　Houseplant, tropical plant, and indoor plant care

Veseys Information for Gardeners:
www.veseys.com/ca/en/learn/guide/wildflower
　　Information on planting wildflower meadows

The Xerces Society: www.xerces.org
　　Dedicated to protecting biological diversity
　　through conservation of bees and other
　　invertebrates

Recommended Reading

Appelhof, Mary. Worms *Eat My Garbage: How to Set Up and Maintain a Worm Composting System*, 2nd Edition. Fayetteville, AR: Worm Woman, Inc., 2016.

Armitage, Allan M. *Armitage's Garden Annuals: A Color Encyclopedia*. Portland, OR: Timber Press, 2004.

————. *Armitage's Garden Perennials*, Second Edition. Portland, OR: Timber Press, 2011.

————. *Armitage's Manual of Annuals, Biennials, and Half-Hardy Perennials*. Portland, OR: Timber Press, 2001.

————. *Armitage's Vines and Climbers: A Gardener's Guide to the Best Vertical Plants*. Portland, OR: Timber Press, 2010.

Ashworth, Susan. *Seed to Seed: Seed Saving and Growing Techniques for Vegetable Gardeners*, Second Edition. Decorah, IA: Seed Savers Exchange. 2002.

Bubel, Nancy and Jean M.A. Nick. *The New Seed-Starters Handbook*. Emmaus, PA: Rodale, 2017.

Byczynski, Lynn. *The Hoophouse Handbook, Second Edition*. Lawrence, KS: Fairplain Publications Inc. 2014.

Bradley, Fern Marshall, Barbara Ellis, and Deborah L. Martin, eds. *The Organic Gardener's Handbook of Natural Insect and Disease Control*. Emmaus, PA: Rodale, 2010.

Bradley, Fern Marshall. *Rodale's Vegetable Garden Problem Solver*. Emmaus, PA: Rodale, 2007.

Brill, Steve with Evelyn Dean. *Identifying and Harvesting Edible and Medicinal Plants*. New York: William Morrow/Harper Collins, 1994.

Cebenko, Jill Jesiolowski, and Deborah L. Martin, eds. *Insect, Disease & Weed I.D. Guide*. Emmaus, PA: Rodale, 2001.

Cranshaw, Whitney and David Shetlar. *Garden Insects of North America*, Second Edition. Princeton, NJ: Princeton University Press, 2017.

Drzewucki, Vincent. *Gardening in Deer Country*. New York: Brick Tower Press, 2003.

Ellis, Barbara. *Covering Ground*. North Adams, MA: Storey, 2007.

Halpin, Anne. *Homescaping*. Emmaus, PA: Rodale, 2005.

Hart, Rhonda Massingham. *Deerproofing Your Yard & Garden*. North Adams, MA: Storey, 2005.

Hemenway, Toby. *Gaia's Garden: A Guide to Home-Scale Permaculture*, Second Edition. White River Junction, VT: Chelsea Green Publishing, 2009.

Jabbour, Niki. *The Year-Round Vegetable Gardener*. North Adams, MA: Storey, 2011.

Jacke, Dave, and Eric Toensmeier. *Edible Forest Gardens*. White River Junction, VT: Chelsea Green Publishing, 2005.

Jeavons, John. *How to Grow More Vegetables . . .* Ninth Edition. Berkeley, CA: Ten Speed Press, 2017.

Lanza, Patricia. *Lasagna Gardening*. Emmaus, PA: Rodale, 1998.

Lewis, Colin. *Bonsai Survival Manual*. North Adams, MA: Storey, 1996.

Marshall, Roger. *How to Build Your Own Greenhouse*. North Adams, MA: Storey, 2006.

Martin, Deborah L. *Rodale's Basic Organic Gardening: A Beginner's Guide*. Emmaus, PA: Rodale, 2014.

Pleasant, Barbara and Deborah L. Martin. *The Complete Compost Gardening Guide*. North Adams, MA: Storey, 2008.

Pleasant, Barbara. *Homegrown Pantry: A Gardener's Guide to Selecting the Best Varieties & Planting the Perfect Amounts for What You Want to Eat Year-Round* Paperback. North Adams, MA: Storey, 2017.

Pleasant, Barbara. *The Complete Houseplant Survival Manual*. North Adams, MA: Storey, 2005.

Roth, Sally. *Attracting Butterflies and Hummingbirds to Your Backyard*. Emmaus, PA: Rodale, 2002.

———. *The Backyard Bird Feeder's Bible*. Emmaus, PA: Rodale, 2000.

Sagui, Pat. *Landscaping with Stone*, Second Edition. Upper Saddle River, NJ: Creative Homeowner Press, 2009.

Schiller, Lindsey and Marc Plinke, *The Year-Round Solar Greenhouse: How to Design and Build a Net-Zero Energy Greenhouse*. Gabriola Island, BC: New Society Publishers. 2016.

Smith, Edward C. *The Vegetable Gardener's Bible*, Second Edition. North Adams, MA: Storey, 2009.

———. *The Vegetable Gardener's Container Bible*. North Adams, MA: Storey, 2011.

Smith, Shane. *Greenhouse Gardener's Companion*. Golden, CO: Fulcrum Publishing, 2000.

Young, James A., and Cheryl G. Young. *Collecting, Processing and Germinating Seed of Wildland Plants*. Portland, OR: Timber Press, 1986.

Contributors

Contributors to *Rodale's Ultimate Encyclopedia of Organic Gardening*, revised edition:

Bonnie Lee Appleton

Helen Atthowe

Cathy Barash

Fern Marshall Bradley

Nancy Bubel

Rita Buchanan

C. Colston Burrell

Pat Corpora

Peggy Walsh Craig

Sally Jean Cunningham

George DeVault

Barbara W. Ellis

Alexander Eppler

Peggy Fisher

Stephen Flickinger

Grace Gershuny

Linda Gilkeson

John Greenlee

Sari Harrar

Brent Heath

Lewis Hill

Beth Huxta

L. Patricia Kite

Terry Krautwurst

Hiram Larew

B. Rosie Lerner

Cheryl Long

Deborah L. Martin

Bill MacKentley

Diana MacKentley

Leslie May

Sally McCabe

Susan McClure

Scott Meyer

Pat Michalak

Susan C. Milius

Carol Munson

Melinda Myers

Ellen Ogden

Nancy J. Ondra

Maggie Oster

Paul Otten

Sara Pacher

Pam Peirce

Cass Peterson

C. Robert Phillips III

Ellen Phillips

Barbara Pleasant

Frank Pollock

Joanna Poncavage

Sarah F. Price

Lee Reich

Raymond J. Rogers

Susan A. Roth

Marcus Schneck

E. H. Sheldon

Miranda Smith

Nancy Tappan

Kris Medic Thomas

Cass Turnbull

Eileen Weinsteiger

Bill Wolf

Quick Reference Guide

Use this summary to find all the related entries offering information on a topic of interest, such as annual flowers, herbs, or landscaping.

ANNUALS

Ageratum	3
Antirrhinum	24
Begonia	50
Calendula	103
Calibrachoa	103
Celosia	110
Centaurea	111
Coleus	483
Consolida	141
Coreopsis	146
Cosmos	150
Diascia	177
Fuchsia	233
Gaillardia	234
Gypsophila	279
Helianthus	288
Iberis	315
Impatiens	316
Lathyrus	343
Lobelia	357
Lupinus	362
Papaver	408
Pelargonium	420
Petunia	456
Portulaca	486
Rudbeckia	519
Salvia	524
Tagetes	577
Tropaeolum	607
Verbena	627
Zinnia	663

BULBS

Allium	5
Anemone	6
Begonia	50
Caladium	102
Canna	104
Crocus	158
Dahlia	174
Gladiolus	247
Hippeastrum	303
Hyacinthus	313
Lilium	356
Narcissus	380
Tulipa	608

EDIBLE LANDSCAPING

Brambles	75
Fruit (see entry opposite)	
Fruit Trees	220
Herbs	289
Kitchen Gardens	329
Nut Trees	386
Vegetable Gardening	613

EVERGREENS

Christmas Trees	114
Groundcovers	274
Hedges	284
Rock Gardens	510
Shrubs	540
Trees	591

USDA Plant Hardiness Zone Map

The 2012 USDA Plant Hardiness Zone Map is the standard by which gardeners and growers can determine which plants are most likely to thrive at a location. The map is based on the average annual minimum winter temperature, divided into 10-degree F zones.

For the first time, the map is available as an interactive GIS-based map, for which a broadband Internet connection is recommended, and as static images for those with slower Internet access. Users may also simply type in a ZIP Code and find the hardiness zone for that area. www.planthardiness.ars.usda.gov

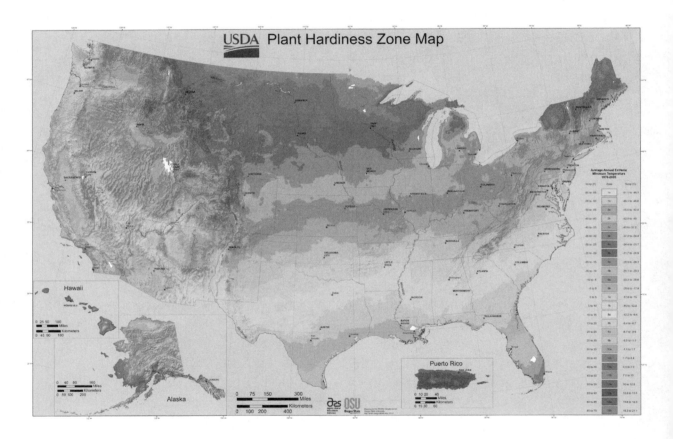

Index

A

AADSC (All-American Daylily Selections Council), 5

AARS (All-America Rose Selections), <u>515</u>

AAS (All-America Selections), 4–5

Abies spp. (firs), <u>204</u>, **204**

Acca sellowiana (pineapple guava, feijoa), <u>191</u>

Acer (maple), 1–2

Acer buergerianum (trident maple), 1, 2

Acer floridanum (Florida maple), 1, 2

Acer ginnala (Amur maple), 1, 2

Acer japonicum (full-moon maple), 1, 2

Acer negundo (box elder), 1, 2

Acer palmatum (Japanese maple), 1–2

Acer pensylvanicum (moosewood maple, striped maple), 2

Acer platanoides (Norway maple), 2

Acer rubrum (red maple, swamp maple), 2

Acer saccharinum (silver maple), 2

Acer saccharum (sugar maple, hard maple, rock maple), 2

Achillea (yarrow), 3

Achillea 'Coronation Gold' (yarrow), 3

Achillea millefolium (common yarrow), 3

Achillea 'Moonshine' (yarrow), 3

Aconites, winter (*Eranthis hyemalis*), 87

Actinidia spp. (kiwi), 331–32

Adam's needle (*Yucca*), 662–63

Ageratum (ageratum, flossflower), 3

AHS (American Horticultural Society), 646

Ajuga (ajuga, common bugleweed), 3

Alcea (hollyhock), 4

Alfalfa (*Medicago sativa*), <u>156</u>

All-American Daylily Selections Council (AADSC), 5

All-America Rose Selections (AARS), <u>515</u>

All-America Selections (AAS), 4–5

Alliaria petiolata (garlic mustard), <u>321</u>

Allium (ornamental onion), 5–6

Allium aflatunense (Persian onion), 5, 6

Allium caeruleum (blue globe onion, azure-flowered garlic), 5, 6

Allium christophii (star of Persia), 5, 6

Allium giganteum (giant onion), 5, 6, 87

Allium moly (lily leek, golden garlic), 5, 6, 87

Allium oreophilum (pink lily leek), 5, 6

Allium sphaerocephalon (drumstick chives), 6

Almond (*Prunus* spp.)
dwarf flowering (*P. glandulosa*), 498
edible (*P. dulcis*), <u>388</u>

Alumroot (*Heuchera*), 303

Alyssum, sweet (*Lobularia*), 358

Amaranth (*Amaranthus* spp.), <u>258</u>

Amaryllis (*Hippeastrum* hybrids), 303–4

Amelanchier spp. (serviceberry, Juneberry, saskatoon), <u>195–96</u>

American Horticultural Society Plant Heat-Zone Map, 646

American Rose Society (ARS), 5, <u>515</u>

Anemone (anemone, windflower, pasqueflower), 6–7

Anemone blanda (Grecian windflower), 6–7, 87, 90

Anemone x *hybrida* (*A. hupehensis* var. *japonica*) (Japanese anemone), 6–7

Anemone tomentosa 'Robustissima' (Japanese anemone) (*A. vitifolia*, grapeleaf anemone), 6–7

Animal and wildlife pests, 7–12
accessing damage, 7
armadillos, 11
birds as pests, 12–13, 67